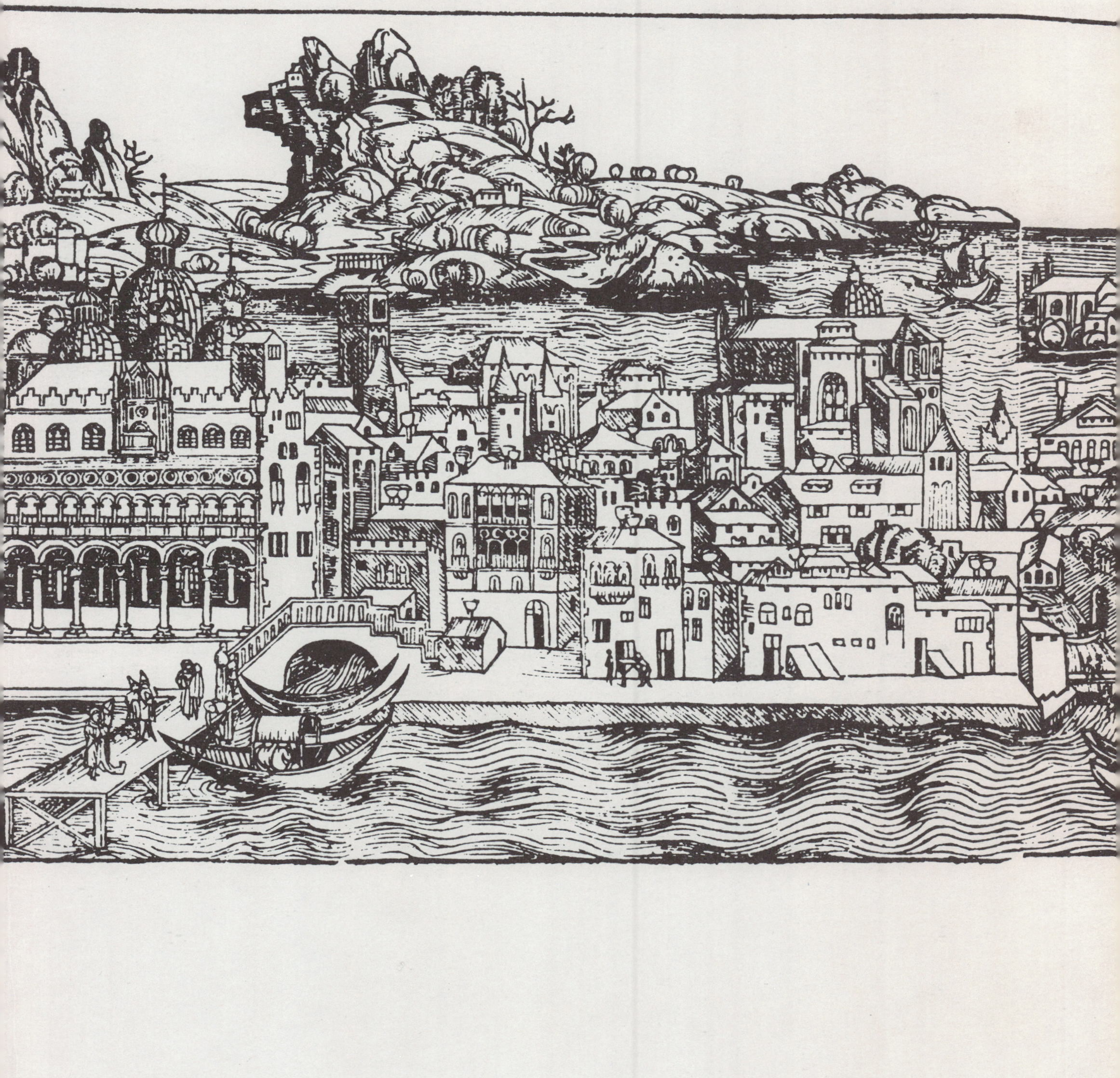

THE PAPACY AND THE LEVANT
(1204–1571)

MEMOIRS OF THE

AMERICAN PHILOSOPHICAL SOCIETY

Held at Philadelphia

For Promoting Useful Knowledge

Volume II

THE PAPACY AND THE LEVANT

(1204–1571)

Volume II

The Fifteenth Century

KENNETH M. SETTON

THE AMERICAN PHILOSOPHICAL SOCIETY
Independence Square · Philadelphia
1978

Library of Congress Catalog Card Number 75-25476
International Standard Book Number 0-87169-127-2
US ISSN 0065-9738

PREFACE

This volume, like its predecessor, is largely concerned with the relationship of the papacy to Orthodox Christianity and to Islam. The subject is alive with difficulties, and carries one in several directions. Amid the complexities of the fifteenth century, however, I have tried to maintain a clear perspective by viewing the scene from the Italian standpoint, that of Venice as well as that of the Holy See. They were both much concerned, though in different ways, with the gradual rise of the Ottoman Turks, as we have seen in the first volume. During the Quattrocento, the great Italian century, Christendom suffered at Ottoman hands a series of military and political defeats, which left an ineffaceable mark upon the mentality and the fortunes of those who dwelt in eastern and southern Europe. The effects of those events are still apparent to this day. The first half of the Quattrocento provided the sad setting for Graeco-Latin strife in the Morea and for the Christian defeat at Varna, after which nothing could prevent the fall of Constantinople to the young sultan Mehmed II.

The half-century before Mehmed's triumph on the Bosporus had been a time of tribulation for the papacy. The debilitation caused by the Great Schism was prolonged by the advocates of Conciliarism. Division within the Church was a reflection of that which prevailed in secular society. The Spains and Germany were rent by political discord. Serious problems required settlement in the Netherlands and in Burgundy. England and France were caught up in the Hundred Years' War until 1453, at which time a boy was king of Hungary and Bohemia. In the latter kingdom the Hussites were as strong as ever, and years of warfare lay ahead. For generations the Italian states had been in ruinous conflict with one another. There was in fact war in Italy when Constantinople fell, and four months after the fall Aeneas Sylvius wrote his friend Leonardo de' Benvoglienti, then the Sienese envoy to Venice, that the Europeans were themselves preparing the way for Turkish conquest. The era of Italian dominance in the Mediterranean was drawing to a close. The Turkish empire was beginning[1].

Mehmed II's new capital ceased to be the city of Constantine, although Europeans continued to call it Constantinople. In its Ottoman context I have called it Istanbul. Mehmed's seizure of the city began his remarkable career of conquest, extending over thirty years in time and thousands of square miles of territory. He did not always win. He was put to flight at Belgrade in 1456, and his reign ended with the temporary failure of the Turks at Rhodes in 1480 and with their short-lived success at Otranto in 1480–1481. Fortunately for Italy, Mehmed's reign fell within the period of the so-called peace of Lodi (1454–1494), when the Italians managed somewhat to mitigate their predilection for warfare and self-destruction. A new era, and a tragic one, began with the expedition of Charles VIII into Italy (1494–1495), the consequences of which will loom large in the next volume.

Major events in Europe had their impact on the Levant, and the reverse was equally true. The fifteenth century found Venice the leading power in Italy and still possessed of a so-called empire which dated back to the Fourth Crusade. It soon became clear, however, that she was no match for the Turks. Her inability to hold Thessalonica in 1430 portended her loss of Negroponte in 1470, which came at the midpoint in a terrible sixteen years' war with the Porte (1463–1479). The close of the century found her again at war with the Porte, in 1499–1502, when she lost Lepanto, Modon, Navarino, and Coron. The decline of Venice was beginning. She did hold Crete into the seventeenth century—and when she lost it, it was to the Turks.

---

[1] Rudolf Wolkan, ed., *Der Briefwechsel des Eneas Silvius Piccolomini*, in the Fontes rerum austriacarum, II. Abt., vol. 68 (Vienna, 1918), *Ep.* 153, pp. 279, 281, dated 25 September, 1453: "Omnes Turchi procuratores sumus, Maumetho viam omnes preparamus. . . . Fuerunt Itali rerum domini, nunc Turchorum inchoatur imperium."

Throughout the fifteenth century some remarkable figures trod the crowded stage of history. In the annals of the Osmanlis Mehmed II has no rival. The Byzantine emperors Manuel II, John VIII, and Constantine XI played notable if disheartening roles. Of the western emperors Sigismund was given the most important part to play, and Frederick III the longest and the most wretched. Popes Martin V, Eugenius IV, Calixtus III, Pius II, Sixtus IV, and (alas) Alexander VI stand out in the papal procession, as they do in the following pages, bearing in this century larger mundane than spiritual burdens. Some of the most interesting and stalwart characters in the complex drama that lies before us wore neither a crown nor a tiara—Bessarion and Isidore of Kiev, Ciriaco of Ancona and Lodovico Trevisan, John Hunyadi, Giovanni da Capistrano, and Scanderbeg, Vettore Capello and Pierre d'Aubusson, and finally Hunyadi's son Matthias Corvinus, who did ascend a throne, to be sure, and Mehmed's son Jem Sultan, who did not. In the Italian background, too, there come before us the Medici in Florence, the Sforzeschi in Milan, the Estensi in Ferrara, the Malatesti in Rimini, and the Gonzagas in Mantua, some of which families will be as conspicuous in the third volume as in this one.

However inadequately, I have tried *en passant* to assess the more immediate effects of Ottoman rule in the Balkans as well as to deal with the perennial preachment of the crusade and the almost perennial mismanagement of crusading funds. What contemporaries called a crusade, a *sancta expeditio*, I have also called a crusade. The canonists' definitions of a crusade, like the legists' disquisitions on an embassy, seem often to have little to do with the world of *Realpolitik*, the world as it was, which is the world I have tried to depict. Year after year the peoples of Europe had the crusade dinned in their ears, as preachers never tired of dilating on the Turkish peril. Some of the humanists served as publicists of the crusade, and the printing press was employed in anti-Turkish propaganda.

When in 1460 Thomas Palaeologus, despot of the Morea, fled before the Turks, he brought the head of S. Andrew with him to Italy. Pius II regarded the reception of the sacred relic at the Vatican in 1462 as almost the chief event in his reign, just as thirty years later Innocent VIII looked upon his receipt of the iron head of the Holy Lance, a gift of Sultan Bayazid II, as perhaps the chief event in his reign. The inscription below Pius's tomb in S. Andrea della Valle in Rome still recalls his dedication to the crusade and his joy in the *caput S. Andreae . . . ex Peloponeso advectum*, just as the epitaph on Pollaiuolo's monument to Innocent in S. Peter's still recalls the *lancea quae Christi hausit latus a Baiazete Turcarum tyranno dono missa.* The entry of each relic into Rome was accompanied by excited crowds and various manifestations of perfervid devotion.

Such was the mentality of the age, but what did Cardinal Rodrigo Borgia, later Pope Alexander VI, think of such religiosity? This volume ends with the history of the Borgias and the machinations of Alexander's pontificate. Oddly enough, when it is all said and done, he was more of a crusader than Nicholas V. I have tried to let the sources speak for themselves, often by paraphrase when not by direct quotation, for those who lived and wrote in the past are best able to describe the political events, the military encounters, the intellectual struggles, the social problems, and the economic conditions of their time. Like us, they led their lives in day-to-day detail. If I seem not to have eschewed detail, I have sought to be selective. Indeed, when I consider the mountains of notes and of transcripts of archival documents I have made during these last twenty years, I almost marvel at my moderation. If I have dealt at length with events and personalities, it is because I regard them as important. If Mohammed had been killed in a fall from his camel on the eve of the Hegira, I have no doubt that the whole history of eastern Europe and the Mediterranean would have been different from the seventh century to the twentieth.

It has not been possible to equip this volume and its two companions with the detailed maps which some readers may wish or require. I can only refer them to the standard atlases which are easy of access in most libraries. I have also had to abandon the hope I once entertained of providing these volumes with illustrations—portraits of persons of note as well as prints of churches, palaces, fortresses, and certain sites that figure prominently in the text—but the wide scope of the work made selection baffling, and the cost of suitable reproductions was the final deterrent.

In the Preface to the first volume I have expressed my indebtedness to my old friend and colleague Dr. Harry W. Hazard. I am glad again to acknowledge the assistance I have derived through the years from his criticism and concern. Once more he has most generously made an index for me, thus lightening immeasurably the task of getting this volume through the press. My secretary Mrs. Jean T. Carver prepared the typescript, read the proofs, and helped me in ways too numerous to mention. My assistant Dr. Susan Babbitt has checked the typescript and the proofs, and located books and journals that I could never have found. I wish there were some way to repay my predecessors, some long dead, whose distant footsteps echo through the notes in the following pages. I wish, too, there were some way to render the full extent of my thanks to the archivists and their assistants at the Vatican and in Venice, Mantua and Malta, Modena and Milan, Siena and Florence. To the Vatican and Venice I have made almost annual archival pilgrimages for more than twenty years.

My wife has read the typescript and the galleys with painstaking attention. I shall not seek to contrive an adequate expression of my indebtedness to her. I must, however, once more record my deep sense of obligation to the American Philosophical Society and to The Institute for Advanced Study.

K. M. S.

The Institute for Advanced Study
Princeton, N. J.
1 March, 1978

CONTENTS

1. VENICE AND THE LATIN FAILURE TO HALT THE OTTOMAN ADVANCE IN GREECE (1402–1431)

By the beginning of the fifteenth century the popes had been preaching crusades for about three hundred years. The crusade was in a sense an armed pilgrimage, the original purpose of which was not merely to visit the scenes of Christ's earthly existence but to wrest them from the Moslems and to hold them forever. In the earlier middle ages the hazardous journey to the Holy Land, the "pilgrimage" (*peregrinatio*), had become almost a social ritual for those of such piety and knowledge, courage and money as to undertake it. When from the end of the eleventh century the pilgrims (*peregrini*) carried arms, and were organized into armies, they began to take the cross in ecclesiastical ceremonies, binding themselves by a solemn oath to make their way to the Holy Sepulcher and to fight the holy war against the infidels beyond the sea. They gradually became known as "crusaders" (*cruce signati*). The popes and church councils declared their privileges, which were similar to but exceeded those of pilgrims. The canon lawyers and the councils defined their obligations.

Princes, nobles, and the high clergy always took the cross when their own desires or public pressure caused them to join or promise to join a crusading expedition. They were too conspicuous to do otherwise. On the other hand large numbers of "crusaders" were hardened mercenaries and lowly adventurers. It is doubtful whether many of them ever formally took the cross. Year after year crusades were preached. Expeditions were often organized, as we have seen in the first volume, without Jerusalem in mind. Despite the papal indulgences, with the full remission of the participants' sins, these expeditions were well named *passagia generalia*, containing as they did a motley crowd of pious "pilgrims" and fugitives from justice. Under the aegis of the Holy See, however, the Crusade had quickly become a sacred concept, useful long after Jerusalem was irrecoverably lost to Christendom. It provided the canonical and institutional means (one hoped) of saving Byzantium and the Balkans, Hungary, Rhodes, the Morea, and the Greek islands from the onward surge of Turkish conquest.

The general term "crusade"—*cruciata* with such rare variants as *crosata* and *croseria*—occurs in the sources, but less frequently than one might think. A crusade was a *sancta expeditio* or, as we have just said, a *passagium generale*. Indeed in papal documents after 1462 the word *cruciata* often denotes the papal revenues from the alum mines at Tolfa which, as we shall see, were supposed to be reserved for the crusade against the Turks. In the Spains, Portugal, and the later kingdom of Naples the word *cruzada* came to mean not only a crusade but also a financial levy for use against the Moors, or the money raised by the sale of indulgences, or finally even the right to eat meat, eggs, and dairy products during Lent, the last indult being still granted for a proper consideration by papal *bulas de cruzada* in the present century.

From the early thirteenth century "crusaders" who had changed their minds about the "Jerusalem journey" (the *iter Hierosolymitanum*) could commute or redeem their vows by paying in cash or otherwise an appropriate sum which could be used for the hire of mercenaries to assist in the Lord's doing. Tithes and twentieths had long been levied for the crusade, and the funds had sometimes been expended against the western opponents of the Holy See—the Albigensians in southern France, the Hohenstaufen in Germany and Italy, the Catalans in Spain and Sicily, and various others who readily come to mind. Boniface VIII had even launched a crusade against the Colonna family and their supporters.

The popes alone could declare a military enterprise a crusade. They alone, or those they authorized, could commission preachers of the crusade and collectors of crusading imposts. Although with the passage of time the princes looked upon the crusade with less and less enthusiasm, especially after the disaster at Nicopolis (in 1396), the popes remained dedicated to the idea of the just war against the infidel menace to the Christian commonwealth. As some princes and certain intellectuals came to regard the crusade as a military and religious anachronism, the legendary Godfrey of Bouillon became an ever greater hero in the popular imagination.

When the earthly Jerusalem seemed unattainable by force of arms, popular preachers saw the victory of the Antichrist at hand. Prophets with the apocalyptic gift foretold the assembly of the world's peoples at Jerusalem, which would truly become the heavenly city, the scene of the ultimate triumph of the godly in the second coming of Christ. The Church began at Jerusalem. It would return to Jerusalem, the beginning of the end (the *eschaton*) of history. The crusading ideal would thus live on for centuries in the dark recesses of the mind, become a powerful element in Christian eschatology, and emerge in strange prophecies from the later middle ages to the nineteenth century. The last chapter of our third volume will deal with prophecies of Turkish doom.

Crusade has meant different things to different people at different times. In this volume, as in its predecessor, it means (concretely) an authorized expedition against the Moslems or (abstractly) one of the major foreign policies of the Holy See, i.e., the papal effort to find an answer to the so-called eastern question. Until the papacy of Eugenius IV little could be done at the Curia Romana to advance the Christian cause against the Turks, whose power increased rapidly from 1421, when Murad II ascended the Ottoman throne. The popes had no money.

The years of the Great Schism (1378–1417), the reform measures of the conciliarists at Constance (1414–1418), the renewal of the Hundred Years' War, and the religious disaffection in England and Bohemia had apparently reduced the income of the Holy See by the year 1430 to less than one-third of its former level (see below, Chapter 2, note 21). Pope Martin V (1417–1431) could play little part in the history of the anti-Turkish movements of his time. Timur the Lame had crushed the Ottoman sultan Bayazid I at Ankara in July, 1402, while the papacy was still caught in the Schism. The Turks recovered from their defeat, however, before the popes could regain their power and prestige, if indeed they ever did, for after the Schism they were hamstrung by the Councils. The Greeks and the Venetians were the sole western beneficiaries of Ankara, and their benefits were shortlived.

There can be little doubt that the victory of Timur the Lame over Sultan Bayazid at Ankara prolonged the life of the Greek empire for a half century. Almost every historian of Byzantium emphasizes the obvious fact. During the year after Ankara, Timur withdrew his hordes from Asia Minor to Samarkand, after which he died at Otrar in February, 1405, planning an expedition to China. The defeated Bayazid, who had been taken prisoner at Ankara, had already passed from the scene, having succumbed to the hardships of captivity in March, 1403. His sons Suleiman, Musa, and Mehmed fought among themselves for the coveted succession, until the elimination of Suleiman (1411) and Musa (1413) finally left Mehmed I undisputed ruler of the Ottoman empire, with many problems to solve both in Europe and in Asia Minor.[1] During the eight years of

[1] In January or February, 1403, Suleiman made peace with the Byzantine empire, the Hospitallers of Rhodes, Venice, Genoa, and Chios, and the duchy of Naxos, members of a *liga Christiana*. For the treaty see G. M. Thomas and R. Predelli, eds., *Diplomatarium veneto-levantinum (1300–1454)*, II (Venice, 1899), no. 159, pp. 290–93; N. Iorga, in the *Bulletin historique de l'Académie roumaine*, II (Bucharest, 1914), 26–29; *idem, Geschichte des osmanischen Reiches*, I (Gotha, 1908), 328–30; and especially George T. Dennis, "The Byzantine-Turkish Treaty of 1403," *Orientalia Christiana periodica*, XXXIII (1967), 72–88. On 12 August, 1411, the Venetians negotiated a treaty of peace with Musa (Thomas and Predelli, *Dipl.*, II, no. 164, pp. 302–4; Predelli, *Regesti dei Commemoriali*, III [1883], bk. x, no. 137, p. 354).

For a survey of Ottoman history in the first half of the fifteenth century, see Paul Wittek, "De la Défaite d'Ankara à la prise de Constantinople," *Revue des études islamiques*, XII (1938), 1–34; on the titles and legal relationships of Bayazid's three sons after the battle of Ankara, *cf.* Wittek, "Zu einigen frühosmanischen Urkunden," *Wiener Zeitschrift für die Kunde des Morgenlandes*, LIV (1957), 244 ff.; LV (1959), 126–38; and LVI (1960), 276–84; and in general, *idem, Das Fürstentum Mentesche: Studie zur Geschichte Westkleinasiens im 13. -15. Jh.*, Istanbul, 1934, pp. 88 ff. (Istanbuler Mitteilungen, no. 2). Bayazid had had five sons, all of whom were present at Ankara (*cf.* Marie-Mathilde Alexandrescu-Dersca, *La Campagne de Timur en Anatolie [1402]*, Bucharest, 1942, pp. 74–77), Mustafa disappeared in the battle although an impostor later appeared claiming to be he (1415–1422), and Isa was soon eliminated in the fratricidal strife which followed Bayazid's defeat, captivity, and death.

Turkish attacks upon the Albanians and the South Slavs during these years may be followed in the rich collection of Sime Ljubić, *Listine* [*Documents*] *o odnošajih izmedju južnoga slavenstva i mletačke republike*, vols. V, VII, in the *Monumenta spectantia historiam slavorum meridionalium*, vols. V, XII, Zagreb, 1875, 1882, although we shall notice such attacks only in later and more decisive periods. Note also J. Gelcich and L. Thallóczy, eds., *Diplomatarium relationum reipublicae ragusanae cum regno Hungariae* [abbr. *Diplomatarium ragusanum*], Budapest, 1887, nos. 148–49, pp. 225, 226, and *cf.* nos. 163–70, 173, 175, 180, *et alibi*. The chief collection of Venetian archival documents relating to the Albanians (and ranging more widely than its title would suggest) is to be found in Giuseppe Valentini, ed., *Acta Albaniae veneta saeculorum XIV et XV*, 20 vols. (thus far), Palermo, Milan,

Mehmed's sultanate (1413–1421), peaceful relations were maintained between the Ottoman and Byzantine empires, one severely shaken by the disaster of Ankara and the civil wars that followed it, the other worn away by generations of failure, internal decay, and the harsh attrition of poverty.

Nevertheless, the Emperor Manuel II Palaeologus could hardly leave the Bosporus without fear of the Turks, and only in March, 1415, did he appear in the Morea to place his second son, Theodore [II], on the throne of the "despotate" vacated by the death of Theodore I, Manuel's brother, eight years before (1407). Some time after his brother's death Manuel had composed a lengthy oration in his honor, embellishing Theodore's undistinguished career with a wealth of classical allusions,[2] and even attempting to represent as acts of the sagest statesmanship Theodore's pusillanimous efforts to sell the great castles of Acrocorinth, Kalavryta, and Mistra to the Knights Hospitaller of Rhodes (1397–1400).[3] Theodore in fact tried to sell the entire despotate to the Knights. The emperor did not himself appear in Mistra to deliver his tedious oration (which is of some historical value), but had the monk Isidore do so, probably in the fall of 1409. Isidore read half of it, and a certain Gaza (Γαζῆς) the other half, to a gathering that must have had remarkable stamina.[4] The passing years were to provide the monk Isidore with an extraordinary career. He will figure prominently in later chapters of this volume, and a footnote concerning him seems appropriate before we meet him again.[5]

Rome, and Munich, 1967–74 (and still in progress). Fifteenth-century documents begin in Valentini's third volume; the latest volume I have seen is the twentieth, which ends with documents dated in December, 1450. Along with this work goes the slender volume of Ignatius Parrino, *Acta Albaniae Vaticana res Albaniae saeculorum XIV et XV atque cruciatam spectantia*, I (Città del Vaticano, 1971; Studi e testi, no. 266), with *regesta* and texts of documents ranging from 1328/30 to 1482, but largely from the reign of Calixtus III in the mid-fifteenth century.

[2] Sp. P. Lampros, *Palaiológeia kaì Peloponnesiaká*, III (Athens, 1926), 11–119. Geo. Sphrantzes, *Chronicon minus* (*PG* 156, 1025C), makes brief mention of an earlier visit which Manuel had made to the Morea, apparently toward the end of 1407 or in 1408. A better text of Sphrantzes has become available in Vasile Grecu, ed., *Georgios Sphrantzes: Memorii (1401–1477), în anexă Pseudo-Phrantzes: Macarie Melissenos, Cronica (1258–1481)*, Bucharest, 1966, p. 4. Grecu provides a Rumanian translation for his editions of both the genuine *Chronicon minus* and the "forged" *Chronicon maius* (of 1575–1577) by Macarius Melissenus, whose true name was actually Melissurgus, on which see below, note 99, and Volume I of this work, Chapter 13, note 206. On the present occasion Manuel arrived at Cenchreae, near Corinth on the Gulf of Aegina, on 29–30 March, 1415; for the date see R. J. Loenertz, "Pour l'Histoire du Péloponnèse au XIVe siècle," *Revue des études byzantines*, I (1943), 156–57, and J. W. Barker, "On the Chronology of the Activities of Manuel II Palaeologus in the Peloponnesus in 1415," *Byz. Zeitschr.*, LV (1962), 42–43, 47. *Cf.* Giuseppe Schirò, "Manuele II Paleologo incorona Carlo Tocco despota di Gianina," *Byzantion*, XXIX–XXX (1959–60), 210–11, 217 ff., with some of whose assertions Barker correctly takes issue. Manuel wrote the Venetian Signoria from the Hexamilion on 26 June (1415), as shown by the reply of the Senate, dated 23 July (Arch. di Stato di Venezia, Misti, Reg. 52, fol. 48^{v} [50^{v}]); the text of the letter has been published by Lampros, *Pal. kaì Pel.*, III, 127–28, and "registered" in Freddy Thiriet, ed., *Régestes des délibérations du Sénat de Venise concernant la Romanie*, II (Paris and The Hague, 1959), no. 1583, p. 136, and in Franz Dölger and Peter Wirth, eds., *Regesten der Kaiserurkunden des oströmischen Reiches*, pt. 5 (Munich and Berlin, 1965), no. 3351, p. 102.

[3] Laonicus Chalcocondylas, bk. II (Bonn, pp. 97–98; ed. E. Darkó, I [Budapest, 1922], 90–92), and bk. IV (Bonn, p. 206). The people of Mistra refused to accept the rule of the Knights, who did, however, secure both Corinth and Kalavryta, which they held until June, 1404, when they receded these places to Theodore I (*cf. Chronicon breve*, ad ann. 6912 [1404], appended to Ducas, *Hist. byzantina* [Bonn, p. 517], and especially R. J. Loenertz, in *Revue des études byzantines*, I, 186–96, and "La Chronique brève moréote de 1423," *Mélanges Eugène Tisserant*, II [Città del Vaticano, 1964], 426–27 [Studi e testi, no. 232]).

The account in the Pseudo-Sphrantzes, *Chronicon maius*, I, 16 (Bonn, pp. 63–64; ed. J. B. Papadopoulos, I [Leipzig, 1935], 68–69; ed. Grecu [1966], pp. 202, 204), as to the efforts of the Greek bishop of Mistra to make peace between the irate inhabitants of Mistra and the Knights when the latter sought to take over the city (although accepted by D. A. Zakythinos, *Le Despotat grec de Morée*, I [Paris, 1932], 159–60) should be rejected as a perversion of the facts, as shown by R. J. Loenertz, "Autour du Chronicon maius attribué à Georges Phrantzes," *Miscellanea G. Mercati*, III (Città del Vaticano, 1946), pp. 290–93 (Studi e testi, no. 123).

[4] Wm. Miller, *Latins in the Levant*, London, 1908, p. 377, incorrectly assumes that Manuel read the oration himself on the occasion of his visit to the Morea in 1415. See Lampros, *Pal. kaì Pel.*, III, introd., pp. 1–2, and esp. D. A. Zakythinos, "Manuel II Palaeologus and Cardinal Isidore in the Peloponnesus" [in Greek], *Mélanges offerts à Octave et Melpo Merlier*, III (Athens, 1957), 45–69, with refs. Although according to its descriptive title the oration was *ῥηθεὶς ἐπιδημήσαντος εἰς Πελοπόννησον τοῦ βασιλέως*, this was not the case. It should also be noted that the Gaza in question could not have been Theodore Gaza (who was born about 1400), as assumed by Lampros.

[5] Isidore first emerges in the light of history as a very young man in the year 1403. His career until the Council of Basel has been the subject of much doubt and some controversy. Zakythinos has maintained (against Cardinal Giovanni Mercati and Fr. Vitalien Laurent) that Isidore was himself the metropolitan of Monemvasia from 1412–1413 until about 1430, when he was apparently obliged to give up the see, possibly as a result of his violent contest with the metropolitan of Corinth and because of the antipathy of the Patriarch Joseph II (Zakythinos, *Mélanges Merlier*, III [1957], 64–69). There are too many

For some reason, presumably the tense Turkish situation, Manuel had been unable to come to the Morea himself to do honor to his brother's memory at the time the funeral oration was read. But now in 1415, when he did come, the emperor immediately began work on the "six-mile" wall, the Hexamilion, across the Isthmus of Corinth. He threw up the rampart,

---

arguments from silence and rationalizations of the slender facts on both sides for either one to present a case with absolute certainty, but Zakythinos has clearly not demolished Mercati's views concerning Isidore's early career: Mercati, *Scritti d'Isidoro il Cardinale Ruteno e codici a lui appartenuti che si conservano nella Biblioteca Apostolica Vaticana*, Rome, 1926 (Studi e testi, no. 46), corrected his own earlier, erroneous views expressed in "Lettere di un Isidoro, arcivescovo di Monembasia e non di Kiew," *Bessarione*, XXXII (1916), 200–7, on which note V. Laurent, "Isidore de Kiev et la métropole de Monembasie," *Revue des études byzantines*, XVII (1959), 150–57.

Isidore served as advocate of the metropolitical see of Monemvasia in 1429, in a jurisdictional dispute with the metropolitan of Corinth (*cf.* K. M. Setton, in *Speculum*, XXV [1950], 525–26, note). As the "venerabilis Isidorus, abbas monasterii S. Demetrii," he was a member of the Byzantine embassy to the Council of Basel in 1434–1435, seeking to arrange an oecumenical assembly to discuss church union, preferably in Constantinople (J. D. Mansi, ed., *Sacrorum conciliorum nova et amplissima collectio*, XXIX [Venice, 1788, repr. Paris, 1904], cols. 93C, 97D, 125C, 127A, and 446C). In 1436–1437 he became the Orthodox metropolitan of Kiev, and was very active on behalf of church union at the Council of Ferrara-Florence in 1438–1439, on which see Georg Hofmann and M. Candal, eds., *Isidorus Arch. Kioviensis et totius Russiae: Sermones inter Concilium Florentinum conscripti*, in the *Concilium Florentinum, Documenta et scriptores*, ser. A, vol. X, fasc. 1 (Rome, 1971).

Already employed by Pope Eugenius IV as *legatus de latere* "in the provinces of Lithuania, Livonia, and all Russia" before being raised to the cardinalate (Arch. Segr. Vaticano, Arm. XXXIX, tom. 6, fol. 46^r, by modern stamped enumeration), Isidore stood seventh in the list of seventeen new cardinals created by Eugenius on 18 December, 1439 (according to the first entry in the Acta Consistorialia [1439–1486], in the Arch. Segr. Vaticano, Arm. XXXI, tom. 52, fol. 48^r, and *cf.* Conrad Eubel, ed., *Hierarchia catholica medii aevi*, II [1914, repr. 1960], 7–8). His relations with the Venetian Senate became very close, and on 15 June, 1443, he was granted honorary citizenship by the Republic, being admitted on the twentieth of the month to the Grand Council by a vote of 637 to 19, with eight neutral ballots cast (Iorga, "Notes et extraits," in *Revue de l'Orient latin* [abbr. *ROL*], VII [1899–1900, repr. 1964], 104, 105, 106).

Isidore's influence in the Curia Romana increased steadily, and he was appointed successor to the deceased Latin Patriarch of Constantinople, Giovanni Contarini, on 24 January, 1452, but with his rights and revenues limited to Crete, Negroponte, and other Venetian possessions (Arch. Segr. Vaticano, Reg. Vat. 398, fol. 56; N. Iorga, *Notes et extraits pour servir à l'histoire des croisades*, II [Paris, 1899], 461–62). Full appointment to the Latin patriarchate was not made, because Gregory III (improperly called "Mammas"?), then Catholic patriarch of the Greek rite, was still living, on which see Georg Hofmann, "Papst Kalixt III und die Frage der Kircheneinheit im Osten," in the *Miscellanea Giovanni Mercati*, III (Città del Vaticano, 1946), 218–21 (Studi e testi, no. 123), and *cf.* V. Laurent, "Le Vrai Surnom du patriarche de Constantinople, Grégoire III (d. 1459)," *Revue des études byzantines*, XIV (1956), 201–5. On 26 July (1452) the doge of Venice informed the duke of Crete of Isidore's new charge (Iorga, *ROL*, VIII [1900–1, repr. 1964], 85–86).

Isidore was in Constantinople when the city fell to the Turks, and barely escaped with his life, as we shall see later on. He was untiringly active under four pontificates, and there are dozens of documents relating to him in the Vatican Archives. In an undated document of 1455, for example, Isidore, cardinal bishop of Sabina, was granted by Calixtus III "quedam domus sita iuxta ecclesiam beate Marie in Via lata de Urbe" (Reg. Vat. 439, fols. 140^r–141^r). On 1 May, 1456, he received canonries in the churches of Nicosia and Paphos (*Nicosien. et Paphen.*) as well as the archdeaconry of Nicosia (Reg. Vat. 444, fols. 262^r–263^r, by mod. stamped enumeration), and on 17 September of the following year (1457) he was assigned full rights to the Euboeote village of Prino, which was under the jurisdiction of the patriarchal church of Negroponte (Reg. Vat. 449, fols. 216^v–217^v, by mod. stamped enumeration, an interesting document). On 5 September, 1458, he was appointed archbishop of Corfu (Reg. Vat. 468, fol. 25), and shortly thereafter, on 9 November, he was granted the church of S. Agatha in Rome (*ibid.*, fol. 320, by mod. stamped enumeration).

In 1461 Isidore suffered a stroke of apoplexy, but could still participate in the elaborate ceremonies attending the reception into Rome of the head of the Apostle S. Andrew in April, 1462 (Pius II, *Commentarii*, bk. VIII, trans. Florence A. Gragg, *Smith College Studies in History*, XXXV [1951], 536–37; ed. Frankfurt, 1614, p. 200, lines 27 ff.; and *cf.* O. Raynaldus, *Annales ecclesiastici*, ad ann. 1462, nos. 1–5, vol. XIX [1693], pp. 111–12). Isidore died in Rome on Wednesday, 27 April, 1463, according to the Acta Consistorialia (1439–1486), in Arch. Segr. Vaticano, Arm. XXXI, tom. 52, fol. 64^r: "Obitus d. Cardinalis Ruteni: Anno a nativitate Domini MCCCCLXIII, die vero Mercurii XXVII mensis Aprilis, reverendissimus in Christo pater dominus Cardinalis Rutenus appellatus Ysidorus Rome diem suum clausit extremum. Eius anima in pace requiescat." The year of his death is given incorrectly as 1462 in Eubel, *Hierarchia catholica*, II, 8. On Isidore, see in general Mercati's monograph, cited above, *Scritti d' Isidoro il Cardinale Ruteno* (1926); Adolf W. Ziegler, *Die Union des Konzils von Florenz in der russischen Kirche*, Würzburg, 1938, pp. 56 ff.; "Vier bisher nicht veröffentlichte griechische Briefe Isidors von Kijev," *Byz. Zeitschr.*, XLIV (1951), 570–77; and "Die restlichen vier unveröffentlichten Briefe Isidors von Kijev," *Orientalia Christiana periodica*, XVIII (1952), 135–42; G. Hofmann, "Quellen zu Isidor von Kiew als Kardinal und Patriarch," *ibid.*, pp. 143–57; and the sketch of his career in Joseph Gill, *Personalities of the Council of Florence*, Oxford, 1964, pp. 65–78, as well as the notices concerning him in Gill's book on *The Council of Florence*, Cambridge, 1959. On the fifth centenary of Isidore's death the Basilian Fathers in Rome brought out a volume of essays dedicated to his memory, *Miscellanea in honorem Cardinalis Isidori (1463–1963)*, in the *Analecta Ordinis S. Basilii Magni*, IV [X], fascs. 1–4 (1963), which contains, however, little or nothing pertinent to the present work.

said to have had 153 defense towers, along the line, still discernible today, which the Peloponnesians had fortified against Xerxes, the Emperor Valerian against the Goths, and Justinian against the Bulgars, the Huns, and the Slavs. Manuel's builders in fact discovered an inscription commemorating Justinian's construction of the Isthmian wall some eight and a half centuries before.[6]

Although the Byzantines might be thus induced to ponder the long continuity of their history, the find was no augury of better times. Behind the wall they built against the Turks they soon alienated their only possible ally, the Venetians, although it must be admitted that the statesmen of the Serenissima would rarely fight for or defend any cause but their own. The Turks were, however, as constant a worry to the Venetians as they were to the Byzantines. Venetian documents mention them again and again. An interesting letter in one of the files of the Senate (*Deliberazioni miste*) warns Antonio Acciajuoli, the duke of Athens, "that he should preserve and keep well his fortifications, and not place his trust in the promises of the Turks, to whom good faith cannot be ascribed. . . . But considering the fact that the Turk himself is very wise and well informed concerning our places over there, it seems to us most important for the security of our places and even of our dominion not to disregard him. . . ."[7] The Venetians knew better than anyone else the value of the advice they sent to Athens, for Turkish raids were already depopulating the nearby island of Negroponte, one of the chief centers of Venetian enterprise in the Levant.[8]

On the whole the merchants of the lagoon were probably good neighbors. After the fall of Boudonitza the Florentine duchy of Athens and Thebes was especially vulnerable to Turkish attack, and the Venetian Signoria agreed to assist Duke Antonio Acciajuoli against the common enemy, to allow him to buy "munitions" (*le cosse de la munition*) from Negroponte, and to let the Athenians and Thebans send animals and property there for safekeeping in an emergency.[9] Antonio was also allowed to

---

[6] N. A. Bees, *Die griechisch-christlichen Inschriften des Peloponnes*, Athens, 1941, no. 1, pp. 1, 4 (in the Corpus der griechisch-christlichen Inschriften von Hellas, I, 1: Isthmos-Korinthos). The Hexamilion made a great impression: Chalcocondylas, bk. IV (Bonn, pp. 183–84, 215; ed. Darkó, I, 172–73); *Chronicon breve*, ad ann. 1415 (Bonn. p. 517); Sphrantzes, *Chron. minus* (*PG* 156, 1026BC; ed. Grecu, p. 6); and *cf.* Pseudo-Sphrantzes, I, 24 [33], 26 [35] (Bonn, pp. 96, 107–8; ed. Papadopoulos, I, 99–100, 111–12, with corrected date in second passage; ed. Grecu [1966], pp. 234, 236, 246), on which see Loenertz, in the *Miscellanea G. Mercati*, III (1946), 288–89, with refs.; Mazaris, in Fr. Boissonade, *Anecdota graeca*, III (Paris, 1831), 177–79; Loenertz, "Chronicon breve . . . e codice Vaticano graeco 162," in *Ἐπετηρὶς τῆς Ἑταιρείας Βυζαντινῶν Σπουδῶν*, XXVIII (1958), 209, and *idem,* "Epître de Manuel II Paléologue aux moines David et Damien (1416)," in *Silloge bizantina in onore di S. G. Mercati*, Rome, 1957, pp. 297–304 (Manuel's letter discusses the importance of the wall for the defense of the peninsula, the opposition of certain Greek *archontes* to the building of it, etc.). *Cf.* Edw. W. Bodnar, "The Isthmian Fortifications in Oracular Prophecy," *American Journal of Archaeology*, LX (1960), 165–71, and see esp. Loenertz, "La Chronique brève moréote de 1423," *Mélanges Eugène Tisserant*, II, 429–32.

The Hexamilion is the chief subject of a work written in 1430 by Cardinal Isidore to a despoina of Mistra, evidently Cleopa Malatesta. This work, which relates to a prophecy concerning the Hexamilion, is contained in Vatican MS. gr. 1852, fols. 105–6, on which see Mercati, *Scritti d' Isidoro il Cardinale*, pp. 34–36, and for the text see Zakythinos, *Mélanges Merlier*, III (1957), 60–63. Sp. P. Lampros, "The Walls of the Isthmus of Corinth" [in Greek], Νέος Ἑλληνομνήμων, II (1905), esp. pp. 444–69, deals at length with the sources for Manuel II's building of the Hexamilion (according to Mazaris in twenty-five days, apparently from 8 April to 2 May), and also publishes, *ibid.*, pp. 475–76, the prophecy which Isidore interpreted for Cleopa Malatesta. (Lampros mistakenly dates this prophecy between 1446 and 1449, after Constantine [XI] Dragases' rebuilding of the wall in 1443 and its destruction by the Turks in 1446, on which see below.) On Manuel's journey to the Morea in 1415 and the building of the Hexamilion, see also John W. Barker, *Manuel II Palaeologus (1391–1425): A Study in Late Byzantine Statesmanship*, New Brunswick, N.J., 1969, pp. 301–18.

[7] Arch. di Stato di Venezia, Misti, Reg. 51, fol. 4^{r}, publ. in C. N. Sathas, *Documents inédits relatifs à l' histoire de la Grèce*, 9 vols., Paris, 1880–90, repr. Athens, 1972, III, no. 649, p. 101, dated 7 March, 1415. On Venetian precautions taken against the "prave machinationes et voluntates ipsorum Turchorum" in the Adriatic and the Aegean, *cf.* the resolutions of the Senate of 26 March, 1415, from the Misti, Reg. 51, fols. 15^{v}–16^{r}, published in Sime Ljubić, ed., *Listine* [*Documents*] *o odnošajih izmedju južnoga slavenstva i mletačke republike*, VII (1882), 196–200 (in the Monumenta spectantia historiam slavorum meridionalium, vol. XII). A document dated 30 August, 1415, in Sen. Secreta, Reg. 6, fol. 67^{r} [68^{r}], in Ljubić, *op. cit.*, pp. 209–11, shows how dangerous had become the raids of a Turkish army, "qui, vagans in partibus occidentis, fines Hungarie et Illirie sevis incursionibus populatur," making clear the extent of Ottoman recovery from the defeat of Ankara and the subsequent strife among the sons of Sultan Bayazid.

[8] Misti, Reg. 51, fols. 94^{r}–95^{r} [97^{r}–98^{r}]; Sathas, III, no. 679, pp. 125–27, dated 4 February, 1416 (Ven. style 1415); *cf.* in general Marino Sanudo, *Vite de' duchi di Venezia*, in L. A. Muratori, ed., *RISS*, XXII (Milan, 1733), cols. 895C, 896, 898E.

[9] Doc. of 7 March, 1415, cited in note 7 (Sathas, III, no. 649, pp. 100–2), and republished, like many other such Venetian texts, in Valentini, *Acta Albaniae veneta*, VII, no. 1948, pp. 185–88.

transport grain from Negroponte, provided it was not required locally.[10] There was certainly need for such co-operation, of which there was never enough among the Latin states in the Levant. To participants in the events of the time it was doubtless not as clear as it is to the historian, with his retrospective knowledge, that the very survival of these states was to depend on their being willing and able to make common cause with one another against the Turks.

After his accession Sultan Mehmed I had received a Byzantine embassy with exceptional courtesy, probably in late July, 1413, confirming a treaty he had already made with the Emperor Manuel, to whom he surrendered various fortresses on the Black Sea, as well as certain towns and castles in Thessaly and the Propontis, acknowledging that he had secured his paternal inheritance with Byzantine aid and acclaiming Manuel as a father, to whom he would always show a filial obedience. Mehmed had also received at his table envoys from Serbia, Vlachia, Bulgaria, and Ianina, and those sent by the Despot Theodore II of Mistra and Prince Centurione Zaccaria of Achaea, informing all of his desire to live at peace with them.[11] Mehmed, however, apparently entertained no such desire for peace with the Venetians, whose island of Negroponte the Turks pillaged in June, 1414. Although the Turks failed in an effort to seize the city and castle of Carystus, they did effect the surrender of Boudonitza, near Thermopylae, thus terminating the Latin history of the famous margraviate over which the Pallavicini and the Zorzi had ruled for more than two centuries.[12]

For years the Venetians and Sigismund, king of Hungary and *electus rex Romanorum*, had been at odds over their conflicting interests in Dalmatia. Their enmity was generally regarded as an obstacle to organizing a crusade against the Turks. The Emperor Manuel II offered on several occasions to act as mediator in their disputes. On 30 August, 1415, the Senate addressed an encyclical "with anger and indignation" (*iram et indignationem concepimus*) to the kings of France, England, and Aragon, the duke of Austria, the count of Savoy, the duke of Bavaria, count palatine of the Rhine, and the apostolic vicar in Avignon, protesting Sigismund's hideous "calumny" that Venice had acted in collusion with a Turkish army, *qui vagans in partibus Occidentis fines Hungarie et Illirie sevis incursionibus populatur*. Sigismund had written to various kings and princes, making this entirely unwarranted accusation against Venice, and acting as though the Turk were some wholly new and unforeseen enemy who was attacking Hungary for the first time!

[10] Misti, Reg. 51, fol. 8ᵛ; Sathas, III, no. 650, p. 103, doc. dated 9 March, 1415.

[11] Ducas, *Hist. byzant.*, chap. 20 (Bonn, pp. 97–98); Dölger and Wirth, *Regesten der Kaiserurkunden*, pt. 5 (1965), no. 3334, p. 98. It would be wrong, however, to regard Mehmed I as friendly to Byzantium, as Manuel makes clear in his letter to the monks David and Damian in 1416 (ed. Loenertz, in the *Silloge bizantina in onore di S. G. Mercati*, pp. 303–4). Since the text of Ducas in the Bonn corpus is very good, and is furnished with the valuable notes of Ismael Bullialdus, I have usually not added references to the edition of Vasile Grecu, *Ducas: Istoria turco-bizantină (1341–1462)*, Bucharest, 1958, who gives page references to the Bonn edition.

[12] Misti, Reg. 51, fol. 44ʳ [46ʳ]; Sanudo, *Vite de' duchi di Venezia*, in *RISS*, XXII, col. 890DE, and *cf.* cols. 911–12; Andrea Navagero, *Storia veneziana*, in *RISS*, XXIII (Milan, 1733), cols. 1080DE–1081AB. See also Amadio Valier, *Cronica di Venezia*, 2 vols., Codd. Cicogna, nos. 3630–31 (MS. of later sixteenth-century, formerly nos. 296–97, in the Bibl. Correr, Venice), vol. I, fol. 259: "A di 20 zugno li Turchi prexeno lixola de Negroponte et mesela a sachomano: Esendo signor de Turchi uno nominato Charaman, el fece una grandissima armada per mare et per terra, el qual armò 6 galie conpide et 18 fuste et molte palandarie, el qual andò a uno castello per terra dito la Boginniza [Boudonitza], el qual lui l'hebe per tratado. Da poi la note andò a lasalto alixola de Negroponte et prexela et menò via cum lui 800 anime, et quelli che el non puote menare via, el li feceno amazare, et da poi el fece meter il fuogo in molti luogi de lixola. Et questo fu uno grandisimo danno a Venetiani et a tuta la Crestianità." Although Valier was well informed on some topics, including the present one, this MS. is quite as noteworthy for its droll and macabre miniatures as for its historical content.

Note also Sathas, III, nos. 1022–23, pp. 429–31, docs. dated September, 1436, the first confirming Marchesotto Zorzi (or Giorgi) in the barony of Carystus, after the death of his father Niccolò II, lord of Carystus (1406–1436) and apparently titular margrave of Boudonitza from some time after 1416, and the second confirming Niccolò III Zorzi in the castellany of Pteleum.

The father of the last-named was Jacopo I, the margrave ousted by the Turks in 1414, who seems to have ceded to his uncle (Niccolò II) the title to Boudonitza some time after 1416 in return for the less exalted but attainable castellany of Pteleum. (Both Carystus and Pteleum were held as fiefs from the Venetian state.) The Zorzi had acquired Boudonitza through the marriage of Guglielma de' Pallavicini with Niccolò I Zorzi about 1335. After the fall of the castle to the Turks the branch of the family in Carystus held the title (*cf.* Predelli, *Regesti dei Commemoriali*, IV [1896], bk. XIII, no. 17, p. 210), until the Turkish occupation of the whole island of Negroponte in 1470 (*cf.* Sanudo, *op. cit.*, col. 1043A; Iorga, *ROL*, IV [1896, repr. 1964], 561, and V [1897, repr. 1964], 173, 195–96, *et alibi*; Ch. Hopf, *Chroniques gréco-romanes inédites ou peu connues*, Berlin, 1873, geneal. tables, p. 478, with errors; Miller, *Latins in the Levant*, pp. 374–75).

The Senate called Sigismund to witness that after the Christian defeat at Nicopolis (in 1396) the Venetians had rescued him, *victus fugatusque . . . errabundus et pavens*, from the very jaws of the enemy, and their galleys had landed him safely in Dalmatia. The duke of Burgundy and many another French lord could attest to the fact. The king of Poland, who had tried to adjust the differences between Sigismund and Venice, was well aware of the generous offers the Senate had made to render assistance against the Turks, *ad subversionem status et exterminium Teucrorum*. Every year Venice expended large sums to prevent the audacity of the Turks from achieving a mastery of the seas. The Venetian-held island of Negroponte was subject to daily attack by the Turks, who had slaughtered an "incredible multitude" of Venetian citizens and subjects, *nam inter illos et nos eternum bellum maxima inequalitate crudescit*. The Turks were a terrible menace to all Christians who dwelt between the Black Sea and the Adriatic. The Venetians knew it well and, *incedentes per vestigia progenitorum nostrorum*, they stood ready always to join the Christian princes in an expedition which would destroy the Ottoman state and the very name of Turk.[13]

The Venetians had, it is true, negotiated with the Ottoman government general treaties (in 1403, 1406, and 1411) which had included an understanding with respect to both Negroponte and Boudonitza,[14] but it had become abundantly clear that only by force could the Turks be restrained from depredation. When on 2 April, 1416, Pietro Loredan received his commission as "captain-general of the Gulf," he was instructed to assemble a fleet of some dozen galleys, and proceed straightway to Gallipoli. With rare unanimity the Senate ordered him to attack the Turks if the usual efforts to make peace with Sultan Mehmed had failed. Although Antonio Acciajuoli, the Florentine duke of Athens, was said to be "with the Turk," the duchy was to be spared if Antonio was abiding by the terms of his peace with the officials of Negroponte.[15]

Galleys had been armed in Candia, Nauplia, Negroponte, and the Archipelago, as well as in Venice and elsewhere. On 29 May (1416) Loredan won a resounding victory over a large Turkish armada off the Gallipoli peninsula. We have a long account of the battle in a letter written to the Signoria by Loredan, who was wounded in action, describing how the encounter began when the Venetians tried to put ashore at "la punta di Gallipoli" to get water which they needed badly, how many Turkish ships were captured and who took them, and so on. A number of Genoese, Catalans, Sicilians, Provençaux, and Cretans had fought on the Turkish side; most of them were killed in the battle, according to Loredan, and those who fell into his hands were promptly put to death. The captain-general emphasizes at great length that the battle began with a Turkish attack upon his vessels, and according to him the Venetian fleet had won the great victory with almost pacific intentions. One sees

---

[13] Sen. Secreta, Reg. 6, fol. 67^r [68^r]; Ljubić, *Listine*, VII, 209–11; Iorga, *ROL*, IV, 550, and *Notes et extraits*, I, 235. On 10 September (1415) the Senate informed a delegation from the Council of Constance "quod sumus certissimi toti mundo notorium fore et etiam suis paternitatibus et sapientiis [i.e., the envoys of the Council] clarissimum esse quod inter alios Christicolas semper fuimus et sumus omnium infidelium et potissime Teucrorum persecutores assidui, et debeat . . . serenissimus dominus dux [the Doge Tommaso Mocenigo] cum illis verbis que sue Serenitati videbuntur sustinere honorem nostri dominii et declarare antiquam guerram et inimiciciam que continue fuit inter nos et dictos Turchos. . . ." (Sen. Secreta, Reg. 6, fol. 68^v [69^v], with further reference to Sigismund and the deplorable fact "quod etiam scripserat per orbem disfamando nostrum dominium"). *Cf.*, above, note 7.

There had been Turkish raids into Bosnia, Hungary, and Croatia in 1398, into Carniola in 1408 and 1411, and into Carniola, Styria, and lower Austria in 1415, after which the Friulani never felt safe (Pio Paschini, "Primi Timori d'un'invasione turca in Friuli," *Memorie storiche forogiuliesi*, VIII [1912], 65–73).

[14] *Cf.* Thomas and Predelli, *Diplomatarium veneto-levantinum*, II, nos. 159, 162, 164, pp. 290 ff. From 1413 to 1416 Manuel II addressed several appeals and admonitions to Venice against the Turks (Dölger and Wirth, *Regesten*, pt. 5, nos. 3335, 3338, 3348, 3352, 3354–55, pp. 99–103).

[15] Sen. Secreta, Reg. 6, fols. 93^v–94^r [94^v–95^r]; Iorga, *ROL*, V, 562–63; *Notes et extraits*, I, 247–48; Thiriet, *Regéstes*, II, no. 1610, p. 143, the commission to Loredan, who was to patrol the northern Aegean from Negroponte to Gallipoli: "Et ubicumque poteris offendere et damnificare Turchos tam in terra quam in mari debeas illud audacter facere tam veniendo de Galipoli versus Nigropontem quam stando in partibus illis et aliter quocumque poteris, non ponendo tamen galeas nec homines earum ad periculum, excepto quod nolumus quod inferas damnum aliquod super ducamine [the duchy of Athens] in casu quo loca ducaminis que sunt cum Turcho stent in pace et benivolentia cum nostra insula Nigropontis" (*doc. cit.*, fol. 94^r [95^r]). The vote in the Senate was: *De parte* 113, *de non* 0, *non sinceri* 2. At the same time as Loredan received these instructions the Senate undertook to send an envoy to the Turks to make peace if satisfactory terms could be arranged (see the documents [including parts of Loredan's commission] dated 2 April, 1416, in Valentini, *Acta Albaniae veneta*, VIII [1970], nos. 2,013–16, pp. 13–25). The truncation of many of Valentini's texts, as that of Loredan's commission (*ibid.*, no. 2016), makes them awkward to use and sometimes even misleading.

clearly from this letter the restraint which the everlasting caution of the Serenissima imposed upon her commanders. Despite Loredan's orders to attack, he must not suffer loss through defeat. Even in victory it must be clear that he had not risked the honor and resources of the Republic in a doubtful engagement. One must be sure of winning before making an attack. Withdrawing to Tenedos, whence he had sailed a few days before, Loredan found that only 340 of his men had been wounded, "of whom the greater part will be well again," and only a dozen had lost their lives, "of whom part were drowned, and may God grant them pardon."[16]

The uncertain relations, whether of war or peace, which led Loredan to send such a careful explanation to the home government lasted for another three years. In November, 1419, however, Sultan Mehmed I swore to a treaty with the Venetians by Allah, the maker of heaven and earth; the Prophet Mohammed; the seven copies of the Koran (*li sette Mussaffi*); the 124,000 prophets, of whom the first was Adam and the last Mohammed; and finally by the souls of his grandfather and his father. A settlement was declared of problems relating to the captives taken by the Turks from Negroponte and by the Venetians at Gallipoli, to the independent position of the Venetian duchy of Naxos, and to the mutual rights of each of the contracting parties to trade in the other's territories. The sultan recognized Venetian suzerainty over thirty-eight castles and places identified by name, including (among others) Candia, Santorin, Astypalaea, Amorgos, Tenos, Mykonos, Andros, Negroponte, Pteleum, Nauplia, Argos, Modon, Coron, Corfu, Lepanto, Durazzo, Scutari, and Zara, together with "all those which raise the banner of S. Mark."[17]

The Turk would of course still bear watching, and he was well watched, as was everything else that related to the well-being of the Venetian commercial empire in the Levant. Many hundreds of documents in the rich series of Senato Misti and Secreti,[18] preserved today in the Venetian Archives on the Campo dei Frari, vouch for the unremitting vigilance exercised over eastern affairs by the "most serene ducal Signoria of Venice." The Senate passed resolutions relating to taxes, excises, duties, and fines, external relations and foreign exchange, the use of state galleys, protection of fisheries, the purchase of sugar, the sale of wine and meat, the export of grain, and dozens of other matters relating to the economic life of Venetian colonies in the Morea and the various islands. Members of noble families, docile by necessity at home, could not escape the discipline of the Signoria by going abroad, for when they put their own

---

[16] Sen. Secreta, Reg. 6, fol. 107ʳ [108ʳ]; Iorga, *ROL*, IV, 566–67; *Notes et extraits*, I, 251–52; Thiriet, *Régestes*, II, no. 1622, p. 145, a letter of the Senate to Loredan, dated 5 July, 1416: "Cum maxima animi iocunditate literas vestras datas Tenedi die secundo mensis Junii elapsi recepimus continentes felicem victoriam per vos obtentam contra exercitum maritimum perfidorum Teucrorum. . . ." Loredan's letter of 2 June is given by Sanudo, *Vite de' duchi di Venezia*, in *RISS*, XXII, cols. 901–9, on which note Iorga, *locc. citt.* Amadio Valier, *Cron.*, in Cod. Cicogna, no. 3631, fols. 261–62, incorrectly dates the battle of Gallipoli on 30 June.

On the general background, note Sathas, III, nos. 671–72, pp. 118–20, docs. dated 30–31 August, 1415, and no. 679, pp. 125–27, dated 4 February, 1416 (Ven. style 1415), in which it is stated that the Turks had taken 1,500 captives from the island of Negroponte, and that the inhabitants had just petitioned the Signoria for the right to become tributaries of the Turks, which the Senate categorically rejected, *quia hoc numquam consentiremus*! (Misti, Reg. 51, fol. 94 [97], doc. cited above in note 8). On the Venetian victory at Gallipoli, *cf.* Jos. von Hammer-Purgstall, *Geschichte des osmanischen Reiches*, I ([Buda]pest, 1827, repr. Graz, 1963), 368–70; N. Iorga (Jorga), *Gesch. d. osman. Reiches*, I (Gotha, 1908), 371–72; Wm. Heyd, *Histoire du commerce du Levant*, trans. Furcy Raynaud, II (repr. 1967), 277.

[17] Thomas and Predelli, *Diplomatarium*, II, no. 172, pp. 318–19; *cf.* Predelli, *Regesti dei Commemoriali*, IV, bk. XI, no. 25, p. 16, and Valier, *Cron.*, Cod. Cicogna, no. 3631, fol. 263, who dates the peace on 26 September. Venice agreed to pay the sultan an annual tribute of one hundred ducats for Lepanto and two hundred for Alessio, Drivasto, and Scutari. The picturesque words of the sultan's oath are from the preamble common to such treaties, the same formula occurring in the famous treaty of 25 January, 1479, which ended almost seventeen years of war between Venice and the Porte (on which see, below, p. 328, and *cf.* Franz Babinger, *Maometto il Conquistatore e il suo tempo*, Turin, 1957, p. 550); the formula also occurs in the Turco-Venetian treaties of September, 1430 (Thomas and Predelli, *Dipl.*, II, no. 182, p. 343), February, 1446 (see, below, Chapter 3, note 51), September, 1451 (*Dipl.*, II, no. 209, p. 382), and April, 1454 (Sanudo, *Vite de' duchi*, in *RISS*, XXII, col. 1154AB). The sultan cautioned Duke Antonio Acciajuoli of Athens, who had become a Turkish tributary, to keep the peace which he had solemnly sworn with Venice or suffer the consequences (Thomas and Predelli, *Dipl.*, II, no. 173, p. 320; Predelli, *Regesti*, IV, bk. XI, no. 26, p. 16): Although the Signoria had instructed its government in Negroponte to assist Antonio, the latter appears to have given offense to the Venetian colony, possibly at the direction of the Turks, who now commanded him to desist (*cf.* Sathas, III, no. 743, p. 90, dated 5 January, 1419 [Ven. style 1418], from the Misti, Reg. 52, fols. 141ᵛ–142).

[18] In referring to these two series, I have commonly preferred the Italian form Misti to Mixta and the Latin form Secreta to Secreti.

self-interest ahead of the common good, reprimand was swift and the penalty might be heavy. This was certainly the case when ambition or avarice manifested itself in the Levant. Thus in 1412–1413 Giovanni (Zanachi) Querini, soon after his appointment as rector of Tenos and Mykonos (in 1411), purchased the island of "Stampalia," the ancient Astypalaea, between Naxos and Rhodes. He assumed the title Count of Stampalia, and proceeded to populate his new fief, which had been deserted for more than seventy years, by removing families from Tenos and Mykonos to his own island in vessels belonging to the Republic, "quod esset causa destructionis et depopulationis ipsarum nostrarum insularum." The Senate would not allow a citizen, however, to provide for the security and enrichment of his own possessions at the expense of the state, and imposed on Querini a fine of two hundred ducats for each person thus removed and not immediately returned to the twin islands with all his property.[19]

Leaving aside in the present context the handsome, wooden-bound volumes of the Senatus Secreta, we may note in the Misti (also handsome volumes and wooden-bound) the replacement of one colonial physician by another, the recruitment of bowmen and the purchase of arms for defense, the salaries of officials in the islands, the terms and restrictions of their tenures, and hundreds of other details. We can follow the construction of walls, a well, and a windmill at Corfu, and the reconstruction of the mole in the harbor of Modon; the assignment of the revenues of the Latin archbishopric of Corfu to the repair of the cathedral church, *que minatur ruinam*, and to the purchase of various ecclesiastical necessities; the limitation on the number of Greek priests to be allowed in Negroponte as well as the imposts laid on the Jews of Negroponte, Corfu, and elsewhere, and the services required of them; and, for a last example, the authorization to the bailie and councillors of Negroponte to spend 125 hyperperi (already spent) for the entertainment of the Emperor Manuel II Palaeologus when he landed at Negroponte early in the year 1415.[20] Upon the emperor's arrival in the Morea, however, the Signoria was careful to replace its Greek mercenaries at Coron and Modon with Latin soldiers for whom the imperial presence and personality would have no natural appeal,[21] and after the construction of the Hexamilion the Venetians declined to contribute to the expense of maintaining watch and ward on the long wall. They stated quite truly that, as Manuel knew, they were constantly under "multe et intollerabiles expense . . . in diversis partibus et locis," owing to the treacherous attacks of the Turks upon their possessions and the costly necessity of maintaining armed galleys for the defense of Negroponte.[22]

Negroponte inevitably looms large in these documents, and Negropontine documents were themselves important. On 26 January, 1417, the Venetian Senate passed a resolution to the effect that,

---

[19] Misti, Reg. 49 [March, 1411–June, 1413], fol. 180^v; Sathas, III, no. 552, pp. 4–5, dated 18 May, 1413. On the complicated history of the Querini of Stampalia (and Amorgos, which a later Giovanni Querini purchased in 1446), see R. J. Loenertz, "Les Querini, comtes d' Astypalée, 1413–1537," *Orientalia Christiana periodica*, XXX (1964), 385–97, and esp. "Les Querini, comtes d' Astypalée et seigneurs d' Amorgos, 1413–1446–1537," *ibid.*, XXXII (1966), 372–93, with corrections of the genealogical tables in Hopf, *Chron. gréco-romanes*, p. 489, and of various notices concerning the Querini in Hopf's other works. Note also Giuseppe Gerola, *I Monumenti medioevali delle tredici Sporadi*, Bergamo, 1914–15, pp. 258–64, who gives an inscription dated 30 March, 1413, commemorating the recolonization of Stampalia by "Count" Giovanni: "Johannes Quirinus comes Astineai qui eo primus duxit accolas anno MCCCCXIII die XXX marcii translationis Sancti Quirini." Astinea (new town) is apparently a play on the name Astipalia (*Astypálaia*, old town).

The island of Stampalia had been sacked and depopulated before 1341 by the Turks of the emirate of Aydin under the well-known Umur Pasha (on which see Cristoforo de' Buondelmonti, *Liber insularum Archipelagi* [written in 1420], ed. G. R. L. von Sinner, Leipzig and Berlin, 1824, p. 78, and *cf.* Paul Lemerle, *L' Émirat d' Aydin*, Paris, 1957, pp. 123–25). Stampalia was still uninhabited when the Capuan pilgrim Niccolò da Martoni landed there in July, 1394 (*ROL*, III [1895, repr. 1964], 581–82): ". . . applicuimus prope insulam que dicitur Stampalea, que girat milearia XXX et alias fuit habitata, sed destructa a Turchis est inhabitabilis, vero apparet ibi castrum cum m[o]eniis, et sunt in dicta insula animalia silvestria. . . ."

[20] Misti, Reg. 51, fol. 18^v [20^v]; Sathas, III, no. 660, p. 110, dated 24 April, 1415.

[21] Misti, Reg. 51, fol. 33^r [35^r]; Sathas, III, no. 664, p. 113, dated 11 June, 1415 (misdated, *loc. cit.*, by a typographical error).

[22] Sen. Secreta, Reg. 6, fols. 84^v–85^r [85^v–86^r], dated 8 February, 1416 (Ven. style 1415), esp. fol. 85^r [86^r]; Valentini, *Acta Albaniae veneta*, VIII (1970), no. 2,007, pp. 8–10, where the text is incomplete; Lampros, *Palaiológeia kaì Peloponnesiaká*, III, 129–31, esp. p. 131; and *cf.* Iorga, *ROL*, IV, 558, and *Notes et extraits*, I, 243; Thiriet, *Régestes*, II, no. 1599, p. 140; Dölger and Wirth, *Regesten*, pt. 5, no. 3354, pp. 102–3; Zakythinos, *Despotat grec de Morée*, I, 169; Barker, *Manuel II Palaeologus*, pp. 315–16.

> since the chancellors of our bailie at Negroponte . . . prepare many notarial acts for which they are asked, such as wills, notices of possessions, sales, and other public instruments, and have formularies [*protocolli*] of these wills, charters, and instruments, as notaries do, in which they keep copies which are considered in proper form—but [since] many of the chancellors keep their formularies on paper [*in bombinico*], so that in the process of time, at the chancery of Negroponte, registers are found torn and worn out because of the fragility of the paper document, which results many times in the greatest loss and damage to citizens there,

the motion was made and carried "that henceforth all chancellors should keep on parchment the formularies in which they will record [copies of] wills, notices, conditions of possession, and other such acts in the Venetian style, just as all the notaries do here at Venice."[23]

The records were carefully kept almost everywhere in the far-flung Venetian domain. Those relating to the Morea show that troubled land to have been a constant concern to the sage councillors who were daily to be seen entering and leaving the palace on the Bacino di S. Marco. In March, 1416, the Emperor Manuel II left the Morea, whither his eldest son and co-emperor John VIII came some months later to join young Theodore II and assist him to rule the so-called despotate. The two brothers were soon engaged in vigorous warfare against Centurione Zaccaria, the Latin prince of Achaea. They also invaded Venetian territories, and answered a protest of the Signoria with the promise to spare her Moreote possessions, "et tamquam propria conservarent," which disarmed the Venetian castellans of Coron and Modon into making no provision for the defense of Venetian subjects in those areas (in 1417): "but the men-at-arms of the aforesaid lords, the emperor and despot, caring no whit for their promise, have been responsible for many wrongs and losses, robberies and acts of incendiarism in the regions of Coron and Modon against our subjects and followers, treating them as if they were public and manifest enemies. . . ."[24]

Throughout this period the Venetian bailie in Constantinople, Fantino Viaro, had been kept so busy running back and forth between his house in the Venetian compound and the imperial palace (and dealing also with the unpleasant problems which the citizens and subjects of the Republic were then facing on the Bosporus) that he had not been able to look to the badly needed repairs in the *domus baiulatus*, which was going to wrack and ruin for want of attention. The Senate had authorized Fantino to spend one hundred ducats on the bailie's house, and now on 25 July, 1417, made the same sum available to his successor Giovanni Diedo to put the house in order.[25]

It was well for the bailies to make sure of a roof over their heads. They were going to be in Constantinople for a long time. Although John VIII, *imperator iuvenis*, and Theodore II, *despotus*, had taken peasants and other persons

---

[23] Misti, Reg. 51, fol. 184^v [187^v]; Sathas, III, no. 709, pp. 153–54, dated 1417 (Ven. style 1416).

[24] Sen. Secreta, Reg. 6, fol. 154^r; Sathas, I, no. 48, pp. 65–66, resolution of the Venetian Senate, dated 25 July, 1417, instructing the bailie in Constantinople to seek indemnity for the damage done. *Cf.* Sanudo, *Vite de' duchi*, in *RISS*, XXII, col. 916. Venice now made provision for the defense of Modon and Coron (Misti, Reg. 52, fol. 35^v, in Iorga, *Notes et extraits*, I [Paris, 1899], 267, resolution dated 19 July, and Sen. Secreta, Reg. 6, fol. 154^v, also in Sathas, I, no. 49, p. 67, dated 25 July), and tried at the same time to stop the war (Sathas, I, nos. 50 and ff.).

Owing to his fear of the Palaeologi, Centurione Zaccaria had appealed to Genoa (his family was of Genoese origin), which had been very disquieting to the Venetians, who warned the Palaeologi of the possible introduction of the Genoese into the affairs of the Morea and prescribed peace with Centurione as the best means of preventing it—although if Centurione was disposed, as was reported, "to place control of the principality in the hands of the Genoese," the Venetians wished to occupy Navarino (Zonklon) and two other places for the protection of Modon and Coron, and would favor acquisition by the Palaeologi of as much of the rest of the principality as they could take (Sathas, I, no. 44, pp. 52–60, dated 31 March, 1416, and *cf.* no. 45, pp. 60–62).

[25] Misti, Reg. 52, fol. 37^r, dated 25 July, 1417: "Cum alias concessum fuerit nobili viro Ser Fantino Viaro, baiulo nostro Constantinopolis, posse expendere in aptatione et reparatione domus baiulatus Constantinopolis que erat usque tunc in pessimo termino usque ad summam ducatorum C de pecunia nostri communis, et ipse Ser Fantinus per alias multas diversas occupationes quas habuerit non potuerit facere fieri dictam reparationem itaque dicta domus adhuc stat in valde peiori termino per modum quod nisi reparetur et presto esset penitus ruitura, vadit pars quod concedatur viro nobili Ser Iohanni Diedo, baiulo nostro Constantinopolis, possendi facere dictam reparationem et expensas ducatorum C. . . ."

That the Venetians were encountering serious difficulties in Constantinople, where they were always unpopular, appears from a letter of the Senate to the Emperor Manuel II, dated 11 March, 1418 (*ibid.*, fol. 80^v): "Quod scribatur domino Imperatori Constantinopolis in hac forma: Per literas baiuli nostri Constantinopolis quas nuperime suscepimus, fuimus informati quod cives, subditi, et fideles nostri in civitate Constantinopolis existentes male videntur et peius tractantur et eisdem multe iniurie et novitates inferuntur non solum reales sed personales . . . ," and *cf.*, *ibid.*, fol. 111.

captive in Venetian territory, and seized their goods and animals, such was life in the Morea.[26] There is no need to cite a dozen texts to illustrate the fact. Byzantine policy may have been short-sighted, but the desire to expel alien intruders from the ancient homeland must have been very strong. The Albanians in the Greek "despotate" were hard to control, and the Venetian protests against their depredations were largely in vain. Nevertheless, the Byzantines were anxious to maintain peace with the Republic. Two years before this, in July, 1415, the Signoria had given a very cautious answer to the Emperor Manuel's request that the Venetian governors of Coron, Modon, and Nauplia should help defend the recently built Hexamilion against the Turks in times of emergency.[27] As time went on, however, the Hexamilion, expensive to build, proved expensive also to keep up, and Greek serfs were found to be fleeing from the despotate to Venetian territory to escape the general levy for its maintenance, to which the Signoria declined to make any contribution in June, 1418, because every year, winter and summer alike, the Venetians bore exceptional costs in their ceaseless opposition to the Turks "for the universal good and well-being of all Christendom, without the assistance of any other ruler or government."[28]

In August, 1417, John VIII's wife, the Russian princess Anna, died, and he withdrew from the Morea the following summer.[29] Before leaving, however, he concluded a truce with Prince Centurione Zaccaria. John was now replaced by a younger brother, Thomas, who was accompanied to the Morea by the future diplomat and historian George Sphrantzes, who was then sixteen years of age.[30] Thomas was only a boy at the time, but he soon proved to be restless. For some forty years the history of the Byzantine despotate was to be marked by Thomas's efforts, often inept, to expel the weaker Latin lords from the Morea and to ward off the Turks. Despite the truce arranged by John VIII before his departure, Venice continued to have trouble. Although the peace was pretty well maintained in 1420, the Despot Theodore II renewed his attacks upon Centurione Zaccaria early in the following year, and his ill-disciplined forces were soon guilty again of violent trespass on Venetian territory. On 8 May, 1421, the Venetian Senate decided to send Benedetto Emo (Aymo) as envoy and bailie to Constantinople.

Emo's first instructions were to stop off in the Morea and make a formal (but courteous) protest to the Despot Theodore:

> You are to explain to his Excellency that again and again we have written letters, and likewise our castellans of Coron and Modon have sent messengers and written letters to his Excellency, demanding that, since many losses have been inflicted by his people upon our subjects of Coron and Modon, he be prepared to make restitution for these losses to our aforesaid subjects.

The despot's troops had sacked four villages in the district of Modon, looting everything to such an extent that the poor inhabitants had lost "even their shirts" (*usque ad camisiam*). The Republic viewed this attack with grave concern, "because we hold the territories of Modon and Coron no less dear than Venice." The envoy was to make it clear to Theodore that the Venetians would not tolerate such conditions and would carry the expression of their indignation and their insistence upon restitution to the most serene lord emperor of Constantinople—for whatever good that would do, because envoys from both the despot and the emperor had already complained in Venice that the castellans of Coron and Modon had supplied the despot's enemies with arms, artillery, and even a galiot, *quod non est verum*, for it was the Republic's intention to maintain a strict neutrality in these

---

[26] *Cf.*, *ibid.*, fols. 95^{v}–97^{r}, doc. dated 11 June, 1418, and fol. 108^{v}.

[27] Sathas, III, no. 668, p. 116, dated 23 July, 1415; Dölger and Wirth, *Regesten*, pt. 5, no. 3351, p. 102. Actually, the Venetians had no intention of defending the faraway Hexamilion against the Turks (D. A. Zakythinos, *Despotat grec de Morée*, I [1932], 168–69), and refused directly on 8 February, 1416, to contribute to the defense of the Hexamilion because of the "many and intolerable expenses" with which the Republic was constantly faced in warding off Turkish attacks, especially in Negroponte (Lampros, *Palaiológeia kaì Peloponnesiaká*, III [1926], 130–31, and *cf.* Lampros, in *Neos Hellenomn.*, II [1905], 461–67).

[28] Sathas, III, no. 731, pp. 174–80, dated 11 June, 1418; the text appears also in Valentini, *Acta Albaniae veneta*, X (1971), no. 2,251, pp. 26–32, where it is incomplete.

[29] Sphrantzes, *Chron. minus* (*PG* 156, 1027C; ed. Grecu, p. 8).

[30] Sphrantzes, *Chron. minus* (*PG* 156, 1027; ed. Grecu, p. 8); Pseudo-Sphrantzes, I, 26–27 [35–36] (Bonn, p. 110; ed. Grecu [1966], p. 248); *cf.* Ducas, chap. 20 (Bonn, p. 98), and Karl Hopf, "Griechenland im Mittelalter," in J. S. Ersch and J. G. Gruber, eds., *Allgemeine Encyklopädie der Wissenschaften und Künste*, vol. 86 (Leipzig, 1868, repr. New York, 1960, vol. II), p. 79a.

wars in the Morea. For whatever reason Emo's instructions were canceled, but the original form of his commission is still preserved in the register, and bears witness to the Senate's utter lack of confidence in Palaeologian rule in the Morea.[31]

Unfortunately for both Greeks and Latins in the Morea a military alliance, not internecine strife, was the only possible defense against the growing power of the Turks in the north. At Adrianople, toward the end of May, 1421, Murad II succeeded his father Mehmed I, and began the new era of Ottoman strength and expansion that was to continue, almost without abatement, into the later sixteenth century. During the last years of the Emperor Manuel II's reign, the conduct of state affairs fell almost entirely upon the shoulders of his son and co-ruler John VIII, who was officially crowned as emperor in January, 1421. Dabbling unwisely in Turkish politics, John supported the pretender Mustafa, who claimed to be the son of Bayazid, in opposition to Murad's accession to the Ottoman throne. It was a bad mistake. In retaliation the angry young sultan, having dispatched Mustafa, laid siege to Constantinople with a large, well-equipped army (from 10 June to 6 September, 1422); it was said that the ancient seers and astrologers had forecast that the city would fall in this very year on the day and at the hour of the final attack (which came on 24 August). At the critical moment, however, there appeared the figure of a woman clad in purple, walking along the battlements of the outer wall. The Turks saw her. Darkness and a storm descended upon them. Fear and trembling entered their hearts. They fled awe-struck in breathless haste, and the siege was over. Once again the Virgin had saved her city.[32] Be this as it may, it was apparent to all Europe that a new day had dawned in Graeco-Turkish relations, and the significance to the Greek world of Mehmed I's death had already been well understood in the Morea.

The Despot Theodore was now willing to make peace, for a time at least, with Prince Centurione of Achaea. In late February, 1423, the Venetian government authorized the castellans of Coron and Modon to arrange the details of a one-year truce between Theodore and Centurione, in which Carlo I Tocco, duke of Leucadia (Santa Maura), count palatine of Cephalonia and Zante, and despot of Ianina

---

[31] Sen. Secreta, Reg. 8, fols. 11^{v}–12^{v} [12^{v}–13^{v}]; Sathas, I, no. 75, pp. 109–12; Valentini, *Acta Albaniae veneta*, X, no. 2,479, pp. 285–90. Although Sathas gives no indication of the fact, the notation "Revocata" is written in the margin of folio 11^{v} of Emo's first commission. The Senate apparently believed it useless for another envoy to wait upon the Despot Theodore II. On 23 May (1421) Emo was directed merely to gather information from the castellans of Coron and Modon, and (without going to see the despot) to seek satisfaction directly from the emperor in Constantinople (*ibid.*, Reg. 8, fol. 13^{v} [14^{v}]):

"Cum castellani Coroni et Mothoni multotiens et modo noviter per suas literas scripserint nostro dominio de multis novitatibus et damnis factis et datis fidelibus et subditis nostris dictorum locorum per subditos domini Despoti Misistre et bonum sit pro honore nostri dominii providere superinde, vadit pars quod committatur viro nobili Ser Benedicto Aymo ituro baiulo nostro Constantinopolis quod quando erit in partibus locorum nostrorum predictorum debeat se informare a castellanis predictis de omnibus et singulis damnis et novitatibus factis et datis ipsis nostris fidelibus novis et veteribus, et quando erit in Constantinopoli debeat cum nostris literis credulitatis, quas sibi fecimus exhiberi, comparere ad presentiam domini Imperatoris et exponere querellam de omnibus et singulis damnis predictis et procurare satisfationem omnium ipsorum damnorum cum illis verbis et modis que et qui continentur in commissione pridie sibi facta, capta in hoc consilio. De parte 93. De non 3. Non sinceri 1."

[32] John Cananus, *De Constantinopoli oppugnata* (in the Bonn corpus, following the Pseudo-Sphrantzes, pp. 457–79), who dates the siege from 10 June to 24 August. *Cf.* Ljubić, *Listine*, VIII (1886), 188. The pagan historian Zosimus in the fifth century tells a similar story to the effect that a vision of Athena Promachos, ranging the walls of the Acropolis, frightened the Visigoth Alaric into sparing Athens although he ravaged the rest of Greece (bk. v, 6, ed. Mendelssohn, pp. 222–23, and *cf.* K. M. Setton, *Athens in the Middle Ages*, London, 1975, III, p. 179). The Venetians and Genoese were caught in the cross-fire between Murad II and the pretender Mustafa, who called himself a son of Bayazid and so Murad's uncle (*cf.* Iorga, *ROL*, V, 117–18, doc. dated 2 February, 1422, *et alibi*, and on the several Mustafas who appear in the documents and the chroniclers, see *ibid.*, p. 193, note 1). As of 26 August, 1422, the Venetian Senate was still uncertain whether Murad had made peace with the Byzantines or was still engaged in the siege (Sen. Secreta, Reg. 8, fols. 67 ff. [68 ff.]; Sathas, I, 120–21; Thiriet, *Régestes*, II, no. 1854, p. 197).

As we might expect, the Byzantine historians describe the Turkish siege of Constantinople in 1422: Sphrantzes, *Chron. minus* (*PG* 156, 1029C–1030A; ed. Grecu, p. 14), who supplies dates (8 June–6 September) at variance with those given by Cananus, and *cf.* Pseudo-Sphrantzes, I, 30 [39] (Bonn, pp. 116–17; ed. Papadopoulos, I, 120; ed. Grecu, pp. 254, 256); Chalcocondylas, bk. v (Bonn, pp. 231–34); Ducas, chap. 28 (Bonn, pp. 183–88); *cf.* Iorga, *ROL*, V, 124–26, 137–38; *Notes et extraits*, I, 323–25, 336–37; *Gesch. d. osman. Reiches*, I (1908), 379–81; Dölger and Wirth, *Regesten*, pt. 5, nos. 3390–93, pp. 108–9; Hopf, in Ersch and Gruber, eds., *Allgemeine Encyklopädie*, vol. 86 (repr. II), p. 81b; and esp. Barker, *Manuel II Palaeologus* (1969), pp. 354–66, on the background and duration of the siege.

(Arta), was also to be included.[33] The Venetians had been trying hard for some time to introduce order into the Morea. Almost a year before, on 2 April, 1422, the Doge Tommaso Mocenigo had issued a commission, with the usual senatorial authorization, to Delfino Venier as Venetian ambassador and provveditore to Modon, Coron, and the Morea, whereby he was to investigate fully the damages and disturbances caused to Venetian subjects and possessions by the Despot Theodore's people. Armed with the information thus obtained, Venier was to go to the despot's court and remonstrate with his Excellency—with the courtesy and firmness appropriate to an envoy of the Republic—requesting full restitution for the losses thus far sustained and the assurance of their cessation for the future. Venier was to perform various other duties and, if possible, to exert his best efforts with the despot and his rivals, to effect a badly needed truce in the Morea.[34]

On 22 July, 1422, further instructions were prepared for Venier as envoy to the three Moreote princes. A number of senators were now willing to extend Venetian authority in the Morea, although the government had previously refused certain offers of territory from the Despot Theodore, who might well express surprise at this apparent change in Venetian policy: ". . . You are to reply that his Excellency need not wonder about this, because our Signoria is not ambitious nor eager to extend our dominion, but is content with the boundaries which the Almighty has given us. . . ." The concessions which Venice would be seeking from all three princes were motivated solely by fear lest the continuance of the conditions which then existed in the peninsula should lead to its acquisition by the Turks. Despite marked differences of opinion in the Senate, Venetian policy was now as always to pick and choose among possible landed possessions. The government looked askance at accepting the Hexamilion, which Theodore had offered to give up to the Republic, for of course he wished to retain Corinth. Even the more adventurous members of the Senate would accept the Hexamilion only if Venice might also receive, as necessary to its defense, a strip of territory one or two miles wide, along its inner (south) side, and they would undertake to keep up the wall and its fortifications only if the costs might be borne locally,

> and to remove all cause for altercation, it may be stated that our Signoria will pay one half the aforesaid expense for that part of the country which belongs to our Signoria, and the lord despot should pay the other half for his part of the said country, notwithstanding the fact that the lord despot's territory is much better and more populous [than ours].

According to the proposal of 22 July, the envoy Venier was to try to persuade Prince Centurione Zaccaria to surrender the title, lands, and castles of the principality of Achaea to Venice for their preservation against the Turks. Centurione would retain his baronial rights over the lands he held by inheritance from his parents, for which he should do homage and swear fealty to the Republic. Venier was to go next to the court of Carlo Tocco, and try to induce him to give up Glarentza and his other possessions in the Moreote principality, for which the Signoria would pay 3,000 to 4,000 ducats. Carlo Tocco had purchased Glarentza in 1421 from an Italian freebooter named Oliverio Franco, who had seized it from Centurione in 1418, when he had also forced the prince to give him a daughter in marriage. But if Carlo Tocco would not sell these places, the envoy was to seek an oath of fealty from him.[35] Illuminating as this document may be, it

---

[33] Sen. Secreta, Reg. 8, fols. 91ʳ–92ᵛ [92ʳ–93ᵛ], resolutions dated 24 and 28 February, 1423 (Ven. style 1422); Sathas, I, nos. 83–84, pp. 127–29; Valentini, *Acta Albaniae veneta*, XI (1971), nos. 2685, 2690, pp. 195, 200–2; and *cf.* Thiriet, *Régestes*, II, nos. 1871, 1873, pp. 200–1; Miller, *Latins in the Levant*, pp. 384–86; Zakythinos, *Despotat grec de Morée*, I, 180–86, 188, 191–92.

[34] Sen. Secreta, Reg. 8, fol. 47 [48]; Thiriet, *Régestes*, II, no. 1840, p. 194. When submitted to the Senate, the terms of Venier's commission excited much discussion and provoked some fifteen different votes.

[35] Sen. Secreta, Reg. 8, fols. 63ʳ–64ʳ [64ʳ–65ʳ], doc. dated 22 July, 1422; Valentini, *Acta Albaniae veneta*, XI, no. 2,610, pp. 112–18, where the date on p. 118, line 15, should be "die XXII [*not* XXI] Julii" (fol. 64ʳ [65ʳ]). There is a brief summary in Thiriet, *Régestes*, II, no. 1849, p. 196. This resolution was submitted to the Senate for four successive votes, as follow (fol. 64ʳ [65ʳ]):

De parte	63	66	64	67
De non	47	48	52	47
Non sinceri	24	20	17	20

Since a majority of affirmative votes was not secured, and the successive items of the resolution lack the characteristic crosses (+) commonly placed in the left-hand margin to was never officially sent to Venier, because enough votes could not be secured by the militant party in the Senate to win its approval.

Another and much briefer set of instructions, however, was also prepared on the same day (22 July), and these comprise the mandate which was sent to Venier, directing him to examine the Hexamilion and try to assess the cost of its maintenance both in time of peace and in that of war. He was also to investigate the resources of the country and the probable cost of its defense.[36] This was all that Venier was authorized to do in the Morea, and doubtless all he did—except for advocating peace wherever he went.

It is clear that the more daring members of the Venetian Senate were now ready to divide the strife-torn Morea with the Greeks, willing to assume the obvious risks for the likely advantages, but they could not persuade quite enough of their fellows to support their proposals. They had also wanted to get control of the important city of Patras, which they had already administered for some years (1408–1413), by leasing it from Archbishop Stefano Zaccaria under an arrangement whereby they had paid him an annual rent of 1,000 ducats.[37]

Stefano, brother of Prince Centurione, had preferred the happy prospect of three years at the University of Padua to the worrisome responsibilities of Patras, which was always subject to Turkish attack. Patras had been restored to Stefano in 1413, when he had found himself hard pressed by his brother Centurione as well as by the Turks and the Greek despot of the Morea, and so in 1417 he had renewed the previous agreement with the Venetians. In the Curia Romana, however, Stefano's attempt to solve his problems looked too much like the alienation of ecclesiastical property. The pope had exercised a special surveillance over the see of Patras since the first years of the Latin conquest, and in the summer of 1419 the archbishop was required to take back his onerous charge.[38] Three years later he was apparently trying to interest the Hospitallers of Rhodes in the Morea, but on 10 May, 1422, the master of the Hospital sent an envoy to the archbishop (and also to the Despot Theodore and Prince Centurione) to explain that Turkish activity in the eastern Aegean rendered impossible the Order's involvement in Moreote affairs. Rhodes was in constant danger, and so were Chios and Mytilene.[39] If the Zaccaria brothers could not get along with each other, they managed still less well with the despot, who attacked the archiepiscopal see of Patras with the same alacrity that he employed against the Latin principality. There were good reasons then for the Venetian anxiety to secure Patras, which we find clearly expressed in the long mandate prepared on 22 July for the envoy Delfino Venier.[40]

Venetian plans were usually far-reaching. Instructions to envoys of the Republic commonly reflected an effort to anticipate every eventuality and to extract from a given situation every advantage. Venier's inquiries and cautious

---

denote items in a given resolution approved by a majority vote, it is more than doubtful whether this long mandate was ever sent to Venier. Indeed, a subsequent resolution sent as instructions to Venier, dated 22 October, 1422 (Sen. Secreta, Reg. 8, fols. 79^v–80^r [80^v–81^r]; Valentini, *Acta Albaniae veneta*, XI, no. 2,639, pp. 152–53), suggests that this mandate was in fact not sent to him, although all historians have apparently assumed that it was, following the incomplete and improper publication of the document by Sathas, I, no. 78, pp. 115–19, inc. "Cum nobilis vir ser Delphinus Venerio. . . ." Unfortunately the materials published in C. N. Sathas, *Documents inédits relatifs à l'histoire de la Grèce au moyen-âge*, are sometimes misleading. Where several documents relating to a particular problem or episode exist in the Venetian registers, Sathas may omit some quite as important as those he supplies. Sometimes a given text is incompletely published. He did not transcribe these documents himself (and obviously did not supervise their selection very closely), but relied on paid copyists, who could hardly be expected to serve his readers as well as Sathas might have done himself.

According to Amadio Valier, *Cron.*, Cod. Cicogna, no. 3631, fol. 275: "Anchora in questo tempo el dispoti de la Morea volse donare la Morea ala Signoria de Venetia, et la Signoria non la volse acetare." On the marriage of Oliverio Franco to Centurione's daughter, note Hopf, *Chron. gréco-romanes*, geneal. tables, p. 502, and on his occupation of Glarentza, *cf.* Sathas, III, no. 731, p. 177, lines 32–33, dated 11 June, 1418. See also Hopf, in Ersch and Gruber, eds., *Allgemeine Encyklopädie*, vol. 86 (repr. II), p. 79; Zakythinos, *Despotat grec*, I, 193–95; Ant. Rubió i Lluch, *Los Navarros en Grecia y el ducado catalán de Atenas*, Barcelona, 1887, pp. 420–21 (in the Memorias de la Real Academia de Buenas Letras, vol. IV).

[36] Sen. Secreta, Reg. 8, fol. 62^v [63^v], resolution dated 22 July, 1422 (but a separate action from the preceding), publ. by Sathas, I, 115, inc. "Per literas vestras. . . ." *Cf.* Sanudo, *Vite de' duchi*, in *RISS*, XXII, cols. 942D, 943, 962C, with reference to the wealth of the Morea, on which see also, below, p. 209.

[37] Ernst Gerland, *Lateinisches Erzbistum Patras*, Leipzig, 1903, pp. 162–71, doc. dated 20 August, 1408, and *cf. ibid.*, pp. 55 ff., with a full indication of the sources and historical background.

[38] Gerland, pp. 9 ff., 62–63; Miller, *Latins in the Levant*, pp. 363–64. In March, 1421, Archbishop Stefano was trying to negotiate the sale of Zonklon (Navarino) to the Venetian Signoria (Sen. Secreta, Reg. 8, fol. 3^r [4^r]).

[39] Gerland, pp. 63, 171–73.

[40] See Sen. Secreta, Reg. 8, fol. 63^v [64^v]; Sathas, I, no. 78, p. 117.

efforts to make peace at first found no favor with the Despot Theodore. When the news of the Turkish threat to Constantinople reached the Morea, however, the despot became frightened, and quickly negotiated a six months' truce with both Prince Centurione and Archbishop Stefano Zaccaria.[41] Pope Martin V, having learned of this development, wrote immediately to the Emperor Manuel, on 5 July, 1422, expressing the hope that the latter would add his imperial authority to the papal exhortation to Theodore to preserve the peace "which he has recently made with our venerable brother Stefano, archbishop of Patras," whose see had been suffering severely from attacks, not by the neighboring Turks but by Theodore. The pope hoped that this peace might be lasting. He stated further that he had cautioned the archbishop against any infringement of its terms, and forbidden him recourse to arms without the special permission of the Holy See, "lest by this means his church, which is our particular care, should suffer some injury." The pope had also requested Theodore to maintain the peace and asked him not immediately to wage war in retaliation for any grievance, real or fancied, which he might have against the archbishop, but to send envoys and letters to Rome, where prompt justice would be done and punishment meted out to any person guilty of offense against him.[42]

The pope's other letters in this connection are also extant, all dated 5 July, 1422—to the Despot Theodore, Archbishop Stefano, Carlo Tocco, Centurione Zaccaria, and Tommaso Mocenigo, the doge of Venice.[43] Mocenigo was given credit for arranging the truce which, the pope had been informed, was to last for a year and two months.[44]

Truces were rarely adhered to at this period in the Morea, and some confusion attends their history. In December, 1422, the envoys of the Moreote princes assembled in Venice, accompanied by Riccardo de Glemona, the chancellor of Modon. The militant members of the Senate saw no prospect of realizing their desires, the feasibility of which they had wanted Venier to investigate. They had to be satisfied therefore with a one-year truce which the envoys generally agreed to in late February, 1423,[45] but they found neither their conferences with the representatives of the contracting parties nor subsequent events in the Morea very reassuring. The following September we find the Senate urging maintenance of the truce upon Carlo Tocco, the Despot Theodore, and Centurione Zaccaria.[46]

---

[41] Sen. Secreta, Reg. 8, fols. 79^{v}–80^{r} [80^{v}–81^{r}], doc. dated 22 October, 1422, published by Sathas, I, no. 80, pp. 123–24 (with the date 27 October); Valentini, *Acta Albaniae veneta*, XI, no. 2,639, pp. 152–53, in answer to a letter dated 10 September from Venier in the Morea. *Cf.* Hopf, in Ersch and Gruber, *Encykl.*, vol. 86 (repr. II), p. 81a.

[42] Martin V's letter of 5 July, 1422, to Manuel II may be found in Arch. Segr. Vaticano, Arm. XXXIX, tom. 5 [*Martini V brevia, tom. II*], fols. 167^{v}–168^{v} (fols. 173^{v}–174^{v} by mod. stamped enumeration), "datum Rome apud S. Marcum, III non. Iulii, anno quinto." This letter is published with a somewhat different text by Raynaldus, *Ann. eccl.*, ad ann. 1422, no. 3, vol. XVIII (1694), p. 41, who does not, however, give the date, which was lacking in the register he employed (Arm. XXXIX, tom. 6, fol. 17, later fol. 31, now fol. 51 by mod. stamped enumeration, the fly-leaf to which register bears the interesting annotation: "Codex hic laudatur a Raynaldo, Annal. Eccl., ad A. 1422, n. 3 et alibi," written in what appears to be an eighteenth-century hand). Although tom. 5 in Arm. XXXIX is a seventeenth-century register (and so considerably later than the copies of Martin's briefs contained in tom. 6), it is especially valuable as preserving the dates of his letters (*cf.*, below, p. 42, note 9). See the following note, and *cf.* Parrino, *Acta Albaniae Vaticana*, I (1971), nos. 6–9, pp. 6–8, who does not date Martin's letter of 5 July to Manuel more closely than "1422."

[43] Arch. Segr. Vaticano, Arm. XXXIX, tom. 5: to Theodore, fols. 170^{v}–172^{r} (also in Arm. XXXIX, tom. 6, fol. 84); to Stefano, fols. 172^{r}–173^{v} (also *ibid.*, tom. 6, fols. 106^{v}–107^{r}); to Carlo Tocco, "dispoto de la Camna" [i.e., Ianina!], fol. 174^{v} (*ibid.*, tom. 6, fol. 86^{r}); to Centurione, fols. 175^{r}–176^{r} (*ibid.*, tom. 6, fol. 88^{r}); and to Tommaso Mocenigo, fol. 176 (*ibid.*, tom. 6, fols. 84^{v}–85^{r}), all refs. being to the foliation by mod. stamped enumeration. (Undated copies of two or three of these letters may be found in Arm. XXXIX, tom. 4, also a seventeenth-century volume of Martin V's briefs.)

[44] Arch. Segr. Vaticano, Arm. XXXIX, tom. 5, fol. 176^{r}: ". . . Placuit valde nobis quod nuper audivimus tua opera atque interventu inducias factas esse usque ad annum unum et menses duos inter dilectos filios nobiles viros despotum Achaie ex parte una et principem Achaie, despotum de la Ianna, ac venerabilem fratrem nostrum archiepiscopum Patracensem ex parte altera, quarum beneficio induciarum Patracensis ecclesia hoc tempore poterit ab assiduis laboribus et belli cladibus respirare."

[45] Arch. di Stato di Venezia, Sen. Secreta, Reg. 8, fols. 90^{v}–92^{v} [91^{v}–93^{v}], published in Sathas, I, nos. 82–84, pp. 125–29; Thiriet, *Régestes*, II, nos. 1868, 1870–71, 1873, pp. 199–201, docs. dated 4, 18, 24, and 28 February, 1423 (Ven. style 1422). *Cf.* Sanudo, *Vite de' duchi*, in *RISS*, XXII, col. 973D; Hopf, in Ersch and Gruber, *Allgemeine Encyklopädie*, vol. 86 (repr. II), p. 81a; Iorga, *Gesch. d. osman. Reiches*, I, 399. The "forma treugue" is given in the Sen. Secreta, Reg. 8, fol. 92^{v} [93^{v}], publ. by Sathas, I, no. 84, pp. 128–29.

[46] Sen. Secreta, Reg. 8, fol. 123^{r} [124^{r}]; Sathas, I, no. 91, pp. 151–52; Thiriet, *Régestes*, II, no. 1904, p. 209 (and note no. 1901), doc. dated 1 September, 1423. The Despot Theodore's envoy had come to Venice with an insufficient mandate. At the end of the month (30 September, 1423) John VIII Palaeologus confirmed a five years' peace between Byzantium and Venice which had been negotiated in the doge's palace on 25 July (Sathas, I, no. 92, p. 153, and Thomas and Predelli, *Dipl. veneto-levantinum*, II, no. 178, p. 341).

Even the invasion of the Morea by the formidable Turkish commander Turakhan Beg could not draw these self-seeking opportunists together.[47] The Venetians tried to be just and reasonable, as shown for example by the fairness of their position in a jurisdictional dispute with Centurione.[48] The latter, who was the least secure among the greater personages in the Morea, was also the least wise. On 30 December, 1423, the Venetian Senate notified the castellans of Coron and Modon that Theodore was accusing Centurione of having broken the truce, thus incurring an alleged penalty of 5,000 ducats according to the terms of the agreement.[49] There was always trouble in the Morea. On 8 January, 1424, Archbishop Stefano Zaccaria died, and the Senate wrote Pope Martin V, requesting the appointment of a Venetian to the see of Patras, which lay in the territory of the schismatic Greeks and was always exposed to the attacks of the infidel Turks.[50] The Curia Romana turned down the request, however, and the pope appointed Pandolfo Malatesta, Theodore's brother-in-law, the new archbishop. It was meant to be a gracious gesture toward the Palaeologi, although they paid little or no attention to their relationship to the Malatesti.[51] Pandolfo went into the Morea immediately, but proved no more able than his predecessor to cope with the problems of Patras.

Although there was no end to the bickering and battling in the Morea, there must soon be an end to the space which we can allot to the subject. In June, 1424, Theodore II suddenly descended on Centurione, took him captive, and again plundered Venetian territory.[52] Carlo Tocco was, quite understandably, concerned by this flagrant violation of the truce, which should not have been broken without at least two months' advance notification to the Venetian castellans of Coron and Modon. Tocco therefore promptly sent envoys to the Venetian Senate, whose spokesmen wearily replied that the Signoria had of course been distressed to learn that the truce (arranged by Delfino Venier) had been taken so lightly, but now there seemed nothing more to be said. If Tocco could make profitable provision for his own state (presumably by attacking the Greeks), Venice would have no objection, and would be quite content to watch the augmentation of his power and well-being.[53]

The Venetians were having their own difficulties with the obstreperous Theodore, whose attacks upon Coron and Modon had been continuous for some months. On 17 April, 1424, the new doge, Francesco Foscari, and the Senate resolved to present their complaint directly to the "old emperor," Manuel, as well as to his lieutenant (*locum tenens*) in Constantinople, where there had also been attacks upon Venetians. (The "young emperor," John VIII, was at this time in Italy, and Constantine was the imperial lieutenant.) The Venetian bailie was directed to request the punishment of the offenders, especially one "Johannes Turchus," as an example to others. The Byzantine government should see to it that such acts of violence to subjects of the Republic ceased both in Constantinople and in the Morea. There must be no repetitions. Otherwise the Venetians would take such firm measures as to make their displeasure unmistakably clear to the Greeks. Their captain-general of the sea was ordered

---

[47] Turakhan Beg had entered the Morea on 21–22 May, 1423, on a terrifying razzia, laying waste the countryside and attacking Mistra, Leondari, Gardiki, and Tabia, on which see below, p. 38, and for the sources, note 118.

[48] Sathas, I, no. 93, pp. 154–55; Thiriet, *Régestes*, II, no. 1906, p. 210, dated 11 October, 1423.

[49] Sathas, I, no. 98, pp. 159–60; *cf.* Thiriet, II, no. 1916, p. 212.

[50] Sathas, I, no. 99, pp. 160–61; Thiriet, *Régestes*, II, no. 1921, p. 213, dated 10 February, 1424 (Ven. style 1423), and *cf.* no. 100; Iorga *ROL*, V (1897, repr. 1964), 167, docs. dated 26 April, 1424.

[51] *Cf.* Hopf, in Ersch and Gruber, *Encykl.*, vol. 86 (repr. II), p. 82b; Gerland, *Lateinisches Erzbistum Patras*, pp. 64–65.

[52] Hopf, II, 82–83.

[53] Misti, Reg. 55, fol. 41r [42r]; Sathas, III, no. 844, pp. 267–68; Valentini, *Acta Albaniae veneta*, XII (1971), no. 2,936, pp. 107–9; Thiriet, *Régestes*, II, no. 1946, p. 219, dated 7 July, 1424, Venetian statement to envoys of Carlo Tocco, *magnificus dominus despotus Arte*: "Quod cum dominus despotus Grecorum convenerit treuguis factis inter eum et dictum dominum suum per medium nostri ambassiatoris et etiam aliis treuguis postea inter eos factis, placeat nostro dominio committere nostris castellanis Coroni et Mothoni quod ponant concordium inter eos, etc., respondemus quod certe nostro dominio displicet audire quod treugue facte primo per nostrum ambasiatorem nobilem virum Ser Delfinum Venerio et similiter alie postea facte prout dicunt nullam habuerint firmitatem. Et considerantes illud quod de novo secutum est, quod dominus despotus Grecorum ceperit principem, non videtur nostro dominio aliud dicere super hoc quia non esset cum honore nostri dominii ulterius aliquid querere super hac causa. Sed si domino suo videtur aliquam provisionem facere pro bono et utile et augmento sui status potest facere prout eidem placet, quia de omni re que redundabit ad bonum et utile et ad augmentum sui status nostrum dominium remanebit contentum."

into the area of Constantinople, and reparations were demanded of the Byzantine government for the damages thus far sustained.[54]

The threatening stance of the Venetians apparently made little impression in either Constantinople or Mistra, although the Greeks knew the Venetians too well to mistake for weakness the civility with which their protests were always made. Three months later, on 16 July (1424), the Senate instructed the Venetian bailie in Constantinople to appear before the "old emperor," if he was in condition to receive him (Manuel had suffered a stroke on 1 October, 1422), or before his lieutenant, to make clear that Theodore's unending depredations in the Morea were absolutely insupportable. He dealt with Venetian subjects as though there were war between the Republic and the Greeks. Now the bailie was to state that he was making Venice's last remonstrance to the Byzantine government before retaliating with an armed offensive.[55]

The times were troublous, and lesser barons in the Morea had to take cover. The campaign of Turakhan Beg in the spring and summer of 1423 had frightened every petty dynast in the peninsula. In late February and early March, 1425, some 25,000 Turks invaded the Morea again, taking more than 1,260 prisoners from Venetian territory and about 6,000 Greeks and Albanians, who were to be sold into slavery.[56] The Catalan family of the Caupenas turned for protection to Venice, the chief Latin power in Greece. On 6 March, 1425, the Senate acted favorably on a petition from Alioto II, lord of Aegina, and his brother Arnau, "at present governor of Piada," who with their Catalan and other adherents "have been of service in the preservation of Argos and Nauplia in emergencies against the Greeks and Albanians as well as against the Turks both by

[54] Misti, Reg. 55, fol. 17ᵛ [18ᵛ]. The Byzantines were to take care: ". . . quod ille Johannes Turchus et alii qui inferunt novitates, iniurias, et violentias nostratibus substineant penam et supplicium suorum delictorum ut aliis transeat in exemplum et quod eis placeat tam utilibus et efficacissimis provisionibus mandare et ordinare quod tales novitates, violentie, et iniurie omnino cessent et damna data per dominum despotum Misistre reficiantur et emendentur et quod de cetero non fiant nec inferantur: que si facient, nobis summe placebunt. Si autem non facient, nostra diuturna tolerancia nos docet et inducit ut ad provisionem debitam et amplissimam transeamus sic quod sine dubio ipsi sencient nos maximam et inextimabilem displicentiam habuisse et animos nostros multum esse turbatos. Et cum his et aliis verbis que tibi videbuntur debeas solicitare quod suprascripta nostra intentio habeat effectum, stando ibi per quatuor dies, quibus transactis postmodum habita vel non habita sua responsione debeas ascendere in galeam et ire ad reperiendum capitaneum nostrum generalem maris. . . ." Iorga has published a French summary of this document (*ROL*, V [1897, repr. 1964], 166–67; *Notes et extraits*, I, 365–66), as has Thiriet, *Régestes*, II, no. 1930, p. 215.

[55] Sen. Secreta, Reg. 8, fol. 162ʳ [163ʳ]; Valentini, *Acta Albaniae veneta*, XII, no. 2,940, pp. 115–17, summarized by Iorga, *ROL*, V, 171–72; *Notes et extraits*, I (1899), 370–71, and *cf.* Thiriet, *Régestes*, II, no. 1948, p. 219. The imperial *locum tenens* was at this time the young Constantine [XI], whose brother John VIII was in Italy, seeking aid against the Turks. John is said to have arrived in Venice on 15 December, 1423 (Raynaldus, *Ann. eccl.*, ad ann. 1423, no. 26, vol. XVIII [1694], p. 62a), and so had been there for some time when on 8 January, 1424, the Venetian Senate agreed to make him a loan of 1,500 ducats "ante recessum suum ab hinc" (Sen. Secreta, Reg. 8, fol. 138ᵛ [139ᵛ]). This loan was, incidentally, made on the *eighth*, not the thirteenth as stated by both Iorga, *ROL*, V, 152–53; *Notes et extraits*, I, 351–52, and Thiriet, *Régestes*, II, no. 1919, p. 212. (No entries were made in this register on 13 January.) On the ninth the Senate limited John's living allowance to eight ducats a day since too many people were apparently passing themselves off as members of the imperial entourage (Misti, Reg. 54, fol. 169ʳ, and *cf. ROL*, V, 152): ". . . Vadit pars . . . quod melius parabitur tempore debito et modo suo si providebitur sibi de peccunia neccessaria et habili pro expensis, quod ducale dominium habeat libertatem limitandi et dari faciendi pro expensis dicti domini Imperatoris et familie sue id quod sibi videbitur non transeundo summam ducatorum octo in die donec stabit Venetiis" (by a vote of 142 to 3, with one neutral ballot).

John was still in Venice on 17–27 January (see below, note 81). The Venetians lodged him at the Benedictine abbey of S. Giorgio Maggiore (Predelli, *Regesti dei Commemoriali*, IV, bk. XI, no. 136, p. 52; Iorga, *ROL*, V, 155; *Notes et extraits*, I, 354). From Venice John went to Milan; he left there on 9 February, and was at Lodi on 17 March (*ROL*, V, 162–63; *Notes et extraits*, I, 361–62). He was back in Milan on 3 May (Dölger and Wirth, *Regesten*, pt. 5, no. 3417, p. 112; Lampros, *Pal. kaì Pel.*, III, 353), and left some time thereafter for Hungary, where he conferred with the Emperor Sigismund (on his itinerary see Gill, *Council of Florence*, pp. 38–39, and Barker, *Manuel II Palaeologus*, pp. 377–79). John arrived back on the Bosporus on or about 1 November, 1424, where he presumably received Filippo Maria Visconti's letter of the sixteenth (*ROL*, V, 178–79; *Notes et extraits*, I, 377–78).

Contrary to the impression of Barker, *Manuel II Palaeologus*, pp. 381–82, that the Venetians reserved the title of Emperor for Manuel (*cf.* Sen. Secreta, Reg. 8, fol. 136ᵛ [137ᵛ], *serenissimus dominus Imperator Constantinopolis senior*), and withheld the title from his son and co-ruler John VIII, the Senate regularly called John emperor: *serenissimus dominus Imperator . . . iunior* (*ibid.*, fol. 138ᵛ [139ᵛ]) and *serenissimus dominus Imperator Constantinopolis* (*ibid.*, fols. 136ʳ [137ʳ], 138ᵛ [139ᵛ], and 139ʳ [140ʳ], letter of the Senate to their resident notary in Milan, Francesco della Siega, dated 17 January, 1424 [Ven. style 1423]).

[56] Sanudo, *Vite de' duchi*, in *RISS*, XXII, col. 978E; *cf.* Iorga, *ROL*, V, 190, 192; *Notes et extraits*, I, 389, 391.

land and by sea. . . ." Being uncommitted to any other suzerain power or person, and being moved (they said) by affection for and loyalty to Venice, Alioto and his son Antonello together with his brother Arnau humbly asked the Serene Signoria to accept them and their heirs "as good and true friends of the friends, and as enemies of the enemies, of the aforesaid illustrious ducal Signoria. . . ." The Caupenas also proposed that, if their house should die out (*manchando i dicti signori e suo heriedi*), Aegina, Piada, and their other possessions should pass into Venetian hands.[57]

At this time Duke Antonio Acciajuoli was worrying about his stud farm, and on 6 November, 1425, the Venetian Senate voted to allow him to transfer his horses and other animals to Negroponte "in the event of sudden danger" (*pro casibus novitatum*). The Senate declined his request for a license to build two galiots, however, and rejected a protest Antonio had made with respect to the terms under which Venice had taken the Caupenas under her wing:

Concerning the affair of the lord of Aegina, in whose island the said lord Antonio [Acciajuoli] says that the wife of the lord of Aegina has her rights, etc., we reply that should the situation arise that the said lady has reason to press for her rights in the island, the lord Antonio must be certain that our Signoria will always do what is in accord with law and justice.[58]

The "said lady" was Antonio Acciajuoli's adopted daughter, who had married Antonello, the bastard son and successor of Alioto II in the little seigniory. Although they sought the shelter of Venetian power and prestige, the Caupenas (like almost everyone else in the Morea) were given to fighting among themselves. Owing to their contentiousness, Venice was to acquire the island of Aegina a generation later.

Nothing could keep peace in the Morea, neither Venetian diplomacy nor the Turkish menace. In 1426–1427 Theodore II of Mistra found himself embroiled with Carlo Tocco. The latter's purchase of Glarentza from Oliverio Franco a half-dozen years before had given him a center for military operations in the peninsula, from which he had extended his sway southward over much of ancient Elis to the river Alpheus and Mount Pholoe. At first Theodore, having all he could handle in his troubles with the Venetians and Centurione's Navarrese (the remnants of Pedro Bordo de San Superano's old "Company"), was inclined to recognize for the time being Tocco's dominion of the territory he had overrun, seeing in him primarily an enemy of Centurione. During the late fall and early winter of 1426, however, Tocco watched the Albanians bringing their flocks and herds down from the highlands to the Elian plain, where they were accustomed to pasture their animals during the cold season. By mid-winter, his forces probably being short of food, Tocco began rounding up a great many of the Albanians' horses, cattle, sheep, and pigs. The Albanians were subjects of the Byzantine despotate, and so Theodore perforce went to war with Tocco. The situation was sufficiently grave to cause the return of the Emperor John VIII to the Morea to take command of an offensive against Tocco, whose city of Glarentza he promptly placed under siege.[59] Byzantine ships patrolled the coast, trying to cut off the promontory of Glarentza from Tocco's island domain of Cephalonia and Zante. Tocco, however, put together a fleet from the islands and from Epirus; he was also joined by some ships,

---

[57] Sathas, III, no. 858, pp. 281–82; Iorga, *ROL*, V, 191; Thiriet, *Régestes*, II, no. 1973, p. 224; and *cf.* K. M. Setton, *Los Catalanes en Grecia*, Barcelona, 1975, pp. 175 ff.

[58] Sen. Secreta, Reg. 9, fol. 48^{v} [49^{v}]; Sathas, I, no. 116, pp. 178–79; Thiriet, *Régestes*, II, no. 2007, p. 232. According to Hopf, in Ersch and Gruber's *Encyklopädie*, vol. 86 (repr. II), pp. 141b–142a, an adopted daughter of Antonio Acciajuoli married Antonello, the bastard son of Alioto II, which seems to be the case (*cf.* Chalcocondylas, bk. IV [Bonn, p. 215; ed. Darkó, I (1922), 202]). A later text refers to Antonello as "filius naturalis domini Aleoti, qui natus fuit ex una villana" (Arch. di Stato di Venezia, Senato Mar, Reg. 1, fol. 12^{r}, doc. dated 17 January, 1441). The senatorial resolution of 6 November, 1425, however, suggests that the "said lady" was married to Alioto himself: ". . . dicit dictus dominus Antonius [de Azaiolis] *uxorem dicti domini* Legene ius habere. . . ." The genealogical table of the Caupenas in Hopf's *Chron. gréco-romanes*, p. 475, requires some rectification for the first members of the family who became lords of Aegina, and the Venetian Senate itself was not always fully informed concerning the family relationships of the island dynasts as when on 12 June, 1461, we find Antonello's uncle Arnau being identified as his brother! (Mar, Reg. 7, fol. 21^{r}).

[59] John VIII had expected a break with Carlo Tocco for some time, and had been arming ships and galleys against him from the early spring of 1426, as Tocco's ambassador informed the Venetian Senate on 3 June (Iorga, *ROL*, V, 322; *Notes et extraits*, I, 422). There is a brief sketch of Venetian difficulties with and the Senate's policy toward the Albanians, especially in the Morea in the first half of the fifteenth century, in Alain Ducellier, "Les Albanais dans les colonies vénitiennes au XVe siècle," *Studi veneziani*, X (1968), 47–64.

presumably merchantmen, from Marseille; and over this motley armada he placed his bastard son Turno. John VIII gave the command of his naval forces to one Leontarius. The battle took place among the "prickly isles" of Echinades (the Curzolari, where the famous battle of Lepanto was later fought), and Tocco's fleet was badly defeated, many of his ships being captured. The Greeks took more than one hundred and fifty prisoners, including one of Tocco's nephews; many of the Latins were killed, and Turno barely escaped from the fray with his life.[60] It was the last victory to be won by the Byzantine navy.

The Turks were on all the roads and passes in the Balkan peninsula as well as on all the seaways of the Aegean. The Venetians were constantly worried about their command posts and trading centers in Albania, at Durazzo (Durrës), Scutari (Shkodër), Alessio (Lezhë), Drivasto (Drisht), Budua (Budva), Dulcigno (Ulcinj), and Antivari (Bar). There is an abundance of documents concerning the defense of these places against the Turks and pro-Turkish Albanian chieftains.[61] To these long-standing concerns the Venetians now added a short-lived but most important episode in their history. Sultan Murad II, having failed in his summer-time siege of Constantinople in 1422, transferred his army and his ambition to Thessalonica, the second city of the Byzantine empire, which was in great danger of falling to a serious assault. The walls of the city had not been kept up, and its ruler, the Despot Andronicus Palaeologus, an ailing younger son of the aged Manuel II, lacked both the means to hire soldiers and the ships to bring provisions into the city. He saw only one way to save Thessalonica from the barbarians. He would give it to Venice.

The Venetian Senate was in a more adventurous mood than it had been for some years. The cautious and conservative doge, Tommaso Mocenigo, had died on 4 April, 1423, and on the evening of the fifteenth Francesco Foscari was elected his successor. Foscari was leader of the war party (still a minority in the Senate), which feared the advance of the Turk more than a temporary suspension of trade in the Levant.[62] It was under a new doge, then, that the Senate considered the Despot Andronicus's remarkable offer on 7 July, 1423. Andronicus had first informed the colonial government of Negroponte of his willingness to turn the city over to the Republic to secure its salvation from the Turks. On 2 June the officials of Negroponte had forwarded copies of the despot's letters by armed brigantine to Venice. Andronicus was gravely concerned about "la extrema condition della terra de Salonichi per la assedion de Turchi," and in his own name and that of the people of Thessalonica he offered the city to the Venetian Signoria, asking only that it should be governed "according to its usages and statutes;" that the Orthodox metropolitan of Thessalonica be confirmed in his ecclesiastical charge;[63]

---

[60] The battle and the events which led up to it are described in an anonymous Greek panegyric on Manuel II and John VIII (in a fifteenth-century MS. in the Bibl. Apost. Vaticana, Cod. pal. gr. 226, fols. 110^r–111^r, published by Lampros, *Pal. kaì Pel.*, III [1926], introd., pp. 26–31, 195–97, on which *cf.* Zakythinos, *Despotat grec de Morée*, I, 200–201). The admiral Leontarius of this encounter is presumably Demetrius Lascaris Leontarius (Leontaris), well-known Byzantine soldier and diplomat, who died on 6 September, 1431, on whom see Ducas, chaps. 22–24 (Bonn, pp. 118–21, 133–34, 139 ff.); Sphrantzes, *Chron. minus* (*PG* 156, 1028; ed. Grecu, p. 10); Pseudo-Sphrantzes, I, 28–29 [37–38] (Bonn, pp. 111 ff.; ed. Papadopoulos, I, 115 ff.; ed Grecu, pp. 250 ff.); F. Miklosich and J. Müller, eds., *Acta et diplomata graeca medii aevi*, III (Vienna, 1865, repr. 1968), 162, 172, 185; Iorga, *Notes et extraits*, I, 44, 49, 66, cited by Lampros, *Pal. kaì Pel.*, I (1912), introd., pp. 47, 213–14; Hopf, in Ersch and Gruber, *Encykl.*, vol. 86 (repr. II), p. 54b; Iorga, *Gesch. d. osman. Reiches*, I, 374, 376. On the Echinades, *cf.* John Murray's *Handbook for Travellers in Greece*, London, 1854, pp. 89–90, 120b.

[61] For the period 1421–1428 alone, *cf.* Iorga, *ROL*, V, 111–13, 120–21, 126, 130–31, 135, 139–41, etc.; *ibid.*, pp. 330–31, 335, 374–76, 382, 385. The Venetians were, however, quite capable of purchasing Turkish assistance against their own enemies in Albania (*cf.* Ljubić, *Listine*, VIII [1886], 3, 5–6, docs. of the year 1419). Various relevant documents of this period may be found in Gelcich and Thallóczy, *Diplomatarium ragusanum* (1887), esp. pp. 300 ff., 319, and see Sen. Secreta, Reg. 8, fols. 28^v ff. [29^v ff.], 35^r [36^r], 50 [51], 51^v ff. [52^v ff.], *et alibi* in this register (1421–1424), as well as Valentini, *Acta Albaniae veneta*, vols. X ff., *passim*.

[62] *Cf.* Heinrich Kretschmayr, *Geschichte von Venedig*, II (Gotha, 1920, repr. Aalen, 1964), 277–78, 331 ff., 354–56, 634, on Venice and the occupation of Thessalonica. The Venetian political background, as well as the naval operations of Venetian commanders in the Aegean throughout this period, is explored in the old but excellent article of Camillo Manfroni, "La Marina veneziana alla difesa di Salonicco (1423–1430)," *Nuovo Archivio veneto*, XX (new ser., X, 1910), 5–68.

[63] The Greek archbishop of Thessalonica proved a good friend to the Venetians, who appropriated fifty ducats on 16 July, 1424, to send gifts to him (Misti, Reg. 55, fol. 42^r [43^r]): "Quia per provisores nostros Salonichi multum fuit persuasum dominio nostro quod mittantur et presen-

that the Greek inhabitants should retain their local rights of jurisdiction, be able to come and go as they chose, and have full disposition of their goods and properties; and, finally, that Venice should guarantee the proper defense of the city against all aggressors, including the Turks. The Senate promptly instructed the bailie in Constantinople to wait upon the Emperor Manuel, if he was well enough to receive him. The bailie was to inform the imperial government of the despot's offer, which Venice was prepared to accept if it was agreeable to Manuel. The Venetian officials in Negroponte, the duke of Naxos, the podestà and captain of Nauplia, and the commissioner of Tenos and Mykonos were to arm galleys and hold them in readiness to execute the Signoria's command, when it should come, to occupy Thessalonica in the name of the Serenissima.[64]

Three weeks after the Senate voted to accept Thessalonica if the Emperor Manuel would give his consent thereto, the Doge Francesco Foscari issued to Santo Venier and Niccolò Giorgi (Zorzi), who had been appointed provveditori to receive Thessalonica, detailed instructions as to their procedure. Their commission is dated 27 July, 1423. Venier and Giorgi were to go to Negroponte, where they should receive some further word from the Despot Andronicus, to whom the Senate had written of Venetian willingness to accept Thessalonica on the terms he had outlined. In the event of a still favorable reply from the despot, the provveditori were to continue with their projected journey to Thessalonica, where they would give the despot the most solemn assurance that the Venetians would abide by the conditions under which he had stated he would relinquish the threatened city to the superior power of Venice, "et quod estis parati dictam civitatem accipere. . . ."

Having taken over the city from the despot, with all due formality, Venier and Giorgi were to provide for its defense and set the hilltop garrison in order, taking the necessary funds from the city's revenues. They were also immediately to send letters to the colonial government at Negroponte which would straightway forward them by brigantine to Venice. Thereafter one of the two provveditori (it was to be Giorgi) was to go, when the time seemed opportune, as an envoy to the Turks,

---

tentur aliqua dona reverendo domino Archiepiscopo Salonichi, qui est fidelissimus nostri dominii, vadit pars quod possint expendi usque ducati quinquaginta pro mittendo presentatum dicto Archiepiscopo in illis rebus que dominio nostro videbuntur." *Cf.* Thiriet, *Régestes*, II, no. 1947, p. 219, who mistakenly says five hundred ducats.

[64] Sen. Secreta, Reg. 8, fols. 110^v ff. [111^v ff.], dated 7 July, 1423, published in Sathas, *Docs. inédits*, I (1880, repr. 1972), no. 86, pp. 133–39; Valentini, *Acta Albaniae veneta*, XI, no. 2,765, pp. 265–75; and *cf.* in general Amadio Valier, *Cron.*, Cod. Cicogna, no. 3631, fol. 277; Hopf, in Ersch and Gruber, *Encykl.*, vol. 86 (repr. II), pp. 82a, 87–88; Wm. Miller, *Latins in the Levant* (1908), pp. 394–95; Iorga, *Gesch. d. osman. Reiches*, I (1908), 399 ff.; Const. D. Mertzios, Μνημεῖα Μακεδονικῆς Ἱστορίας, Thessaloniki, 1947, pp. 34–36 (Μακεδονικὴ Βιβλιοθήκη, vol. 7); and Paul Lemerle, "La Domination vénitienne à Thessalonique," in the *Miscellanea Giovanni Galbiati*, III (Milan, 1951), 219–25 (Fontes Ambrosiani, vol. XXVII).

Most of the chroniclers notice the Venetian acquisition of Thessalonica: Ducas, chap. 29 (Bonn, pp. 197–98); Chalcocondylas, bk. IV (Bonn, pp. 205–6); and, of course, from the Pseudo-Sphrantzes, I, 17 (Bonn, p. 64; ed. Papadopoulos, I, 69), and I, 31 [40] (Bonn, p. 122; ed. Papadopoulos, I, 125; ed. Grecu, p. 260), comes the famous statement that Andronicus sold the city to Venice for 50,000 ducats: *ἔδοξεν [τῷ δεσπότῃ κὺρ Ἀνδρονίκῳ] πωλῆσαι τὴν Θεσσαλονίκην τῇ τῶν Ἑνετῶν γερουσίᾳ διὰ χρυσίνους χιλιάδας πεντήκοντα*. On the Venetian chroniclers, *cf.* Iorga, *ROL*, V, 141, note 2, and Hopf, II, 87a, note 1. While it has often been assumed that Andronicus did sell the city to the Venetians, Mertzios, *Mnemeia*, pp. 30–34, and Lemerle, *Miscell. Galbiati*, III, 222, quite rightly dispute the assumption on the grounds that "il n'est nulle part question de vente dans les documents jusqu'ici connus." *Cf.* Barker, *Manuel II Palaeologus*, pp. 373–74, note. Although Iorga, *ROL*, V, 165, and *Notes et extraits*, I, 364, summarizes the instructions given by the Senate to the Venetian captain-general of the sea on 17 April, 1424 (Sen. Secreta, Reg. 8, fols. 150–151^r [151–152^r]), to the effect that ". . . Venise a acheté la ville à son vrai seigneur," the document actually reads ". . . quia dictam civitatem *accepimus* ab illo qui erat verus dominus civitatis predicte quam intromissionem non fecimus in vilipendium domini . . . [Turchi]" (*ibid.*, fol. 150^v [151^v]), which is quite a different matter. This document makes no reference to any purchase of Thessalonica, for there was none. The text may also be found in Valentini, *Acta Albaniae veneta*, XII, no. 2,887, p. 55.

Actually the statement of the Pseudo-Sphrantzes, I, 31, that Andronicus sold Thessalonica to the Venetians for 50,000 ducats was apparently copied from the sixteenth-century chronicle attributed to "Dorotheus of Monemvasia," *διὰ φλωρία χιλιάδες πενῆντα* (*Biblion historikon*, repr. 1743, p. 406, cited by R. J. Loenertz, *Miscellanea Giovanni Mercati*, III [1946], 304, 306–7, in Studi e testi, no. 123, on which, however, see below, note 99), merely an indication of the fact that the Pseudo-Sphrantzes' *Chron. maius* is a late sixteenth-century compilation (from the 1570's). Here is also the evidence which Mertzios, *Mnemeia*, p. 34, needed to explain away the embarrassing text of the *Chron. maius*, which he believed to be the authentic work of Sphrantzes. One is astonished to find Jean Tsaras, "La Fin d'Andronic Paléologue, dernier despote de Thessalonique," *Revue des études sud-est européennes*, III (1965), 419–32, referring on almost every page to Andronicus's sale of Thessalonica to the Venetians.

"to state and explain that the illustrious lord despot of Saloniki has given to our Signoria the city of Saloniki, which for the love of God we have accepted. . . ." The envoy was to emphasize the friendship which had commonly existed between Venice and the Porte, express the hope of its uninterrupted continuance, and seek the safety of the roads for merchants. The Senate had instructed the bailie in Constantinople, some time before this, to enter into a formal peace with the Turk, but no one knew yet in Venice whether this had been done. If the envoy in question, however, knew that the bailie had not been able to conclude such a peace with the Turk, he was to try to do so when he waited on him to explain the Venetian occupation of Thessalonica. This was an unenviable assignment, as Giorgi was to find it.

The envoy was also to try to arrange peace between the Turk and the Byzantine emperor, because the Signoria loved them both as brothers and friends. Reverting now to the despot, the doge's commission to Venier and Giorgi provided detailed instructions as to what to do in the event of the despot's having changed his mind. If the despot required an income to live on, the provveditori might promise him an annual pension of from 20,000 to 40,000 aspers, to be paid from the revenues of Thessalonica. If everything went well with their mission, Venier and Giorgi might direct the colonial government of Crete to send them fifty *ballistarii*, if necessary for the defense of Thessalonica, and they might hire a hundred mounted *stradioti*, Vlachs, or any other mercenaries at the rate of two ducats a month per man, for four or six months, as should seem advisable. The provveditori were supplied with the necessary funds for their mission and with presents for the sultan, among which were various bolts of cloth of Venetian, Florentine, and Veronese manufacture. The important enterprise on which they now embarked was approved in the Senate by a vote of eighty-six to eight, with ten uncommitted ballots returned.[65]

The Emperor Manuel II did give his consent, with whatever searchings of heart, to the Venetian occupation of Thessalonica, where Venier and Giorgi arrived in September, 1423. A Turkish army of 5,000 men was laying siege to the city, which is said to have had at this time a population of from 25,000 to 40,000 persons, beset by famine and terrified at the prospect of capture by the barbarians. The Venetian fleet brought them both food and freedom. Soon the lion banner of the Evangelist was flying from the acropolis.[66] Later, presumably in February, 1424, Giorgi went to the Turkish capital at Adrianople to try to fulfill the difficult mission with which the home government had entrusted him and his colleague Venier. He failed, of course, and as he was on his way back to Thessalonica, Murad placed him under arrest. What is surprising is that there should have been surprise in Venice when the news of Giorgi's arrest arrived in early April in letters

---

[65] Sen. Secreta, Reg. 8, fols. 114^{v}–118^{r} [115^{v}–119^{r}]; Sathas, I, no. 89, pp. 141–50; Thiriet, *Régestes*, II, no. 1898, pp. 207–8; and *cf.* Mertzios, *Mnemeia*, pp. 36–39, who also gives a poor facsimile reproduction of the document with no indication of its previous publication by Sathas. The facsimile (pl. DD') shows Mertzios, p. 38, to be wrong in stating that Venier and Giorgi might ask the government of Crete to send them 500 *ballistarii*, and shows that the copyist employed by Sathas, I, 146, has quite correctly transcribed the Venetian authorization "ut ad omnem vestram requisitionem vobis mittere debeant ballistarios quinquaginta" (fol. 116^{r} [117^{r}]).

The *stradioti* were usually recruited from the Morea, Albania, and Dalmatia. The term comes from the ancient Greek *stratiotes*, meaning "soldier" (in modern Greek "wanderer, passer-by, itinerant peddler"); it may have suggested the word *strata*, "street," the mounted mercenary being a frequent sight on the highways in the fifteenth century (see H. and R. Kahane and A. Pietrangeli, "Cultural Criteria for Western Borrowings from Byzantine Greek," in the *Homenaje a Antonio Tovar*, Madrid, 1972, p. 212).

[66] Sanudo, *Vite de' duchi*, in *RISS*, XXII (1733), cols. 970CD, 974BC, who says much the same thing as the *Cron. Zancaruola*, cited by Iorga, *ROL*, V, 141–42, note, and *cf. Gesch. d. osman. Reiches*, I, 400; Lemerle, *Miscellanea G. Galbiati*, III, 222. Mertzios, *Mnemeia*, pp. 39–44. Manuel II's consent to the Venetian occupation of Thessalonica is directly stated in the commission given by the Doge Francesco Foscari to Fantino Michiel, when the latter succeeded Pietro Loredan as captain-general of the sea. Michiel was instructed, if he found himself in contact with the sultan, "quod dicto Turcho sive illis qui ad dictam praticam mitterentur dicere et exponere debeas quod per nobilem virum Nicolaum Georgio militem, ambassiatorem nostrum quem ad presentiam sue Excellentie misimus, dici et exponi fecimus quod illustris dominus despotus Salonichi dedit nostro dominio civitatem Salonichi, quam nostra dominatio ob reverentiam Dei *etiam de assensu serenissimi domini Imperatoris* accepit et acceptavit, et quia sentiebamus quod dictus dominus despotus, si dictam civitatem non accepissemus, illam volebat in manibus aliorum Christianorum non amicorum sue Excellentie ponere, ob hanc causam fuimus contenti illam potius habere quam ad manus aliorum perveniret, quia sumus dispositi cum sua Excellentia amicabiliter vivere et vicinare . . ." (Sen. Secreta, Reg. 9, fol. 6^{v} [7^{v}]). This text also makes clear that the Venetians did not purchase Thessalonica "for 50,000 ducats."

from the colonial government of Corfu (dated 31 March).[67]

The Senate hastened to replace the imprisoned Giorgi by naming another provveditore as a colleague for the harassed Venier, and soon decided to replace the latter also. Jacopo Trevisan and Fantino Michiel were appointed, but declined the charge, and presumably paid the fine customarily involved in such refusals; thereupon in May (1424) Bernardo Loredan was appointed with the title of duke (of Thessalonica), and Jacopo Dandolo with that of captain, showing the importance which the Signoria attached to its new possession. In the meantime the Senate had instructed Venier that Giorgi's release must be sought; Sultan Murad might be promised an annual tribute of 1,000 to 2,000 ducats, to be paid from the revenues of Thessalonica; and some 5,000 ducats might be distributed among the sultan's chief pashas to enlist their aid in securing the desired peace with the Porte. At the same time Venice wished to receive the villages (*casalia*) around Thessalonica and the castle on the nearby height of Kortiach (modern Khortiatis).[68]

The Senate had already provided for the armament of two more galleys and the election of a captain of the Gulf, who should have command of five or six galleys for the protection (*custodia*) of the Adriatic. He would serve under Pietro Loredan, then captain-general of the sea. Loredan himself was to proceed to Thessalonica with all other available galleys. If he found Murad II in the area, he was to do his best to secure Giorgi's release (as Venier was also being instructed to do), trying to purchase peace by the offer of an annual tribute of 1,000 to 2,000 ducats, to be paid *de introitibus Salonichi*. If Loredan found, however, that the sultan had put Thessalonica under siege or that the sultan was not in the area, he was to sail for Gallipoli and attack the Turks. He must try to prevent the passage of Turkish forces back and forth across the Dardanelles. He might also find it worthwhile to stir up trouble for Murad in Europe and especially in Asia Minor among the Turkish princes who were fearful of and hostile to the spectacular rise of Ottoman power.[69]

---

[67] Misti, Reg. 55, fol. 15^r [16^r], "MCCCCXXIIII, die XII Aprilis:" "Cum pridie per litteras specialium personarum habitas de Corphoy habuerimus nobilem virum Ser Nicolaum Georgio militem ambassiatorem nostrum, qui ivit ad presentiam Turchi, a dicto Turcho discordem recessisse et modo nuper per litteras regiminis nostri Corphoy datas ultimo mensis Martii habuerimus dictum regimen persensisse per viam Ianine quod dum dictus Ser Nicolaus Georgio miles recessisset a dicto Turcho et reverteretur Salonicum, dictus Turchus eundem in itinere retineri fecit, et pro honore et fama nostri dominii neccessarium sit providere. . . ." *Cf.* Sen. Secreta, Reg. 8, fols. 150^v–151^r [151^v–152^r], doc. dated 17 April, 1424; Valentini, *Acta Albaniae veneta*, XII, nos. 2,885 and 2,887, pp. 49–50, 51 ff; Iorga, *ROL*, V, 164, and *Notes et extraits*, I, 362–63; Mertzios, *Mnemeia*, p. 45; Thiriet, *Régestes*, II, no. 1929, p. 214.

[68] Sen. Secreta, Reg. 8, fols. 156^r [157^r], 158^v–160^r [159^v–161^r]; Sathas, I, nos. 101–8, pp. 163–70, dated 21 May and 28 June, 1424; Iorga, *ROL*, V, 168, docs. dated 19–25 May, 1424, on the election of Bernardo Loredan and Jacopo Dandolo, and *cf.* pp. 169, 170, and *Notes et extraits*, I, 367, and *cf.* pp. 368, 369; Thiriet, *Régestes*, II, nos. 1933–35 ff., pp. 216 ff.

The record of the meeting of the Senate on 19 May (1424) illustrates how the duke and captain of Thessalonica were chosen (Misti, Reg. 55, fol. 24^r [25^r]): "Volunt [Sapientes Consilii, etc.] quod eligi debeant per scruptinium in isto Consilio [Rogatorum, i.e., the Senate] duo solemnes nobiles quorum alter, scilicet ille qui plures ballotas habuerit transeundo medietatem Consilii, habeat titulum duche et secundus habeat titulum capitanei. . . ." They were to serve for two years and as much longer as it took their successors to reach Thessalonica. The posts paid 1,000 gold ducats in salary, but were obviously perilous. Before Bernardo Loredan's election as duke, Jacopo Trevisan, Sr., had declined the charge, and before Jacopo Dandolo's acceptance of the captaincy of Thessalonica, it had been refused by Fantino Michiel, Sr., Francesco Bembo, Marco Dandolo, Bartolommeo Morosini, and Andrea Contarini!

[69] Misti, Reg. 55, fol. 15^r [16^r], and Sen. Secreta, Reg. 8, fols. 150^r–151^r [151^r–152^r], with summaries in Iorga, *ROL*, V, 163–66, and *Notes et extraits*, I, 362–65, docs. dated 12 and 17 April, 1424: ". . . Facta autem provisione necessaria ad bonam custodiam et conservationem civitatis Salonichi si Turchus vel gentes sue essent contra dictam civitatem, in dimittendo ad custodiam dicte civitatis unam vel duas galeas sicut vobis melius videbitur, volumus quod cum residuo dictarum galearum ire debeatis quam celerius poteritis intra strictum Romanie. Et si Turchus vel gentes sue non essent contra Salonichum, si ibi non foret necesse dimittere galeam aliquam, volumus quod cum omnibus nostris galeis intra dictum strictum ire debeatis ad damna, ruinam, et destructionem gentium et locorum dicti Turchi a marina, ubi illos damnificare poteritis per omnes modos et vias vobis possibiles et ad obviandum quod per passus Gallipolis et alios passus dicti strictus nemo transire possit de Gretia in Turchiam et de Turchia in Gretiam . . . (Sen. Secreta, Reg. 8, fol. 150^v [151^v]). Ceterum relinquimus in libertate vestra tenendi praticam tam cum domino Theologi [Ephesus] et Palatie [Miletus] quam cum Caramano et aliis dominis de inde pro inducendo eos ad damna et novitates contra dominum Turchorum predictum . . ." (*ibid.*, fol. 151^r [152^r]).

Pietro Loredan arrived at Gallipoli on 14 June (*ROL*, V, 175); dated a letter there on 1 July (*ibid.*, p. 171); and was still there, Niccolò Giorgi (Zorzi) being still in danger, on the nineteenth (*ibid.*, pp. 172–73). Loredan described his operations against the Turks at Gallipoli in a letter which reached Venice on 12 September (given

Venice thus began her costly seven years' occupation of Thessalonica (1423–1430), but her sons got little for their money and their trouble. Recent scholarship has even robbed them of the credit for having built the famous White Tower, which still stands on the shore as a sentinel of the past.[70] Sathas, Iorga, Mertzios, Thiriet, Valentini, and others have published numerous documents relating to the Venetian regime in Thessalonica. The Senate made it abundantly clear "to the Turk and to all the world . . . that we hold dear the city of Saloniki, and we do not intend to give it up. . . ."[71] On 30 October, 1424, the Senate passed a motion to send provisions, money, and one hundred and fifty to two hundred foot soldiers to Thessalonica in answer to an appeal from the city, then said to be in an "extreme condition and necessity."[72] It had become only too clear that there was not the slightest hope of reaching an agreement with the Turks. Venice was at war. On 13 January, 1425, the Senate voted to elect another captain-general of the sea and to equip a fleet of twenty-five galleys.[73]

A few months later (on 2–4 April, 1425), when Fantino Michiel replaced Loredan as captain-general, he was instructed to go to Thessalonica, after attending to certain matters at Coron, Modon, and Negroponte, and assure the archbishop and notables of Thessalonica of Venetian determination to hold on to the city. Michiel was to try to secure Turkish recognition of his government's occupation on the same terms as the Despot Andronicus had held the city. The sultan might retain his former rights to the salt flats of Thessalonica, provided the trade routes were allowed to remain open; he would also receive the annual tribute of 100,000 aspers which Andronicus had paid the Porte. Turks in Thessalonica, however, would have no right to be judged only by a Moslem *qāḍī* or *kadi* (as under the despot). The old customs-offices were to be re-established at the city gates. Michiel might promise the grand vizir, Ibrahim Pasha, 15,000 to 20,000 aspers a year, to be sure of a powerful friend at the Turkish court, and distribute another 150,000 in gifts to Ibrahim and other officials of the Porte. He was also to secure the release, if he could, of some 1,500 Venetian subjects taken prisoner in the Turkish invasion of the Morea the preceding March. An effort was to be made to negotiate the renewal of the last treaty between Venice and the Porte (1419), with certain modifications, and even to get back for the Margrave Niccolò Zorzi the fortress of Boudonitza (which the Turks had held since 1414).[74]

---

in the *Cron. Zancaruola*, fol. 360^v, Venetian MS., quoted by Iorga, *ROL*, V, 175–76). Sanudo, *Vite de' duchi*, in *RISS*, XXII, cols. 975E–976, summarizes Loredan's letter also, but mistakenly says that he arrived at Nauplia in the Morea on 14 June, whereas (according to the *Cron. Zancaruola*) Loredan wrote, "Nuy zomzesimo ha Garipoli adi XIIII zugno. . . ." (The material found in Iorga's article in the *Revue de l'Orient latin* [*ROL*], V, 163–76, may also be found without change in his *Notes et extraits*, I [1899], 362–75, and summaries of various relevant documents are given in Thiriet, *Régestes*, II, nos. 1929 ff., pp. 214 ff.).

[70] M. Kiel, "A Note on the Exact Date of Construction of the White Tower of Thessaloniki," *Balkan Studies*, XIV (1973), 352–57. The tower was built in 1535–1536, during the reign of Sultan Suleiman the Magnificent.

[71] Misti, Reg. 55, fol. 15^r [16^r], doc. cited above, dated 12 April, 1424, and rather incorrectly quoted by Iorga, *ROL*, V, 164: ". . . Et ut appareat dicto Turcho et toti mundo quod retentio dicti ambassiatoris [Nicolai Georgio] fuerit et sit nostro dominio gravis et molesta et quod habeamus caram civitatem Salonichi et non intendimus illam derelinquere et etiam, si possibile erit, devenire possimus ad pacem cum dicto Turcho. . . ." Iorga's faulty transcription of the latter part of this text is preserved in the *Notes et extraits*, I, 363. In the tedium of copying documents I fear that we all make errors, large or small. I note that Valentini, whose later volumes appeared as the present work was being finished, omits the "etiam" in this passage (*Acta Albaniae veneta*, XII [1971], no. 2,885, p. 50).

[72] Iorga, *ROL*, V, 178, and *cf.* pp. 180, 182, 183, 190, and *Notes et extraits*, I, 377, and *cf.* pp. 379, 381, 382, and 389.

[73] Misti, Reg. 55, fol. 80^r [81^r], doc. dated 13 January, 1425 (Ven. style 1424): "Cum propter guerram quam habemus cum Turcho et pro securitate et defensione civitatis nostre Salonichi et aliarum terrarum et locorum nostrorum Levantis et pro aliis agendis nostris necessarium sit providere de potenti armata pro honore nostri dominii et pro bona executione agendorum nostrorum, vadit pars quod in nomine Jesu Christi et in bona gratia eligi debeat unus capitaneus generalis maris galearum vigintiquinque. . . ." Putting twenty-five galleys to sea involved a huge expense. There is a summary of the document in Thiriet, *Régestes*, II, no. 1965, p. 223.

[74] Sen. Secreta, Reg. 9, fols. 5^r–8^v [6^r–9^v]; Valentini, *Acta Albaniae veneta*, XII, no. 2,958, pp. 135–47 (incomplete), Michiel's commission as captain-general of the sea, dated 2 April, 1425, with summaries in Iorga, *ROL*, V, 192–96; *Notes et extraits*, I, 391–95; Mertzios, *Mnemeia*, pp. 66–67; and Thiriet, *Régestes*, II, no. 1980, pp. 225–26: ". . . Et sumpta plena informatione volumus quod esse debeas cum domino Archiepiscopo et cum illis nobilibus et fidelibus nostris de inde de quibus bonum numerum facias convocari et eis declarari quod dominatio nostra diligens bonum et comodum dicte civitatis et disposita eos tenere et conservare sub nostro dominio te misit ad dictas partes cum potenti armata nostra pro deffensione dicte civitatis et ad inpugnationem et ruinam volentium illam opprimere, hortando eos ad bonam fidelitatem erga nostrum dominium cum illis pertinentibus verbis que tue sapientie videbuntur . . ." (fol. 5^v [6^v]). If Michiel found, upon arriving at Thessalonica, that the Turkish pretender Mustafa

Although the Greeks in Thessalonica were not ungrateful to the Venetians, they could not regard their new masters with unalloyed happiness. The Despot Andronicus, after turning the city over to the Venetians, is said to have gone to Mantineia with his son John, "because of the mildness of the air." According to Sphrantzes, however, Andronicus became a monk under the name Acacius, taking up residence in the monastery of the Pantokrator in Constantinople, where he died and was buried near his father (in March, 1429).[75] In June, 1425, the Greek inhabitants sent an embassy to Venice with a lengthy petition, urging that the peninsula of Cassandra be fortified and the walls of the city itself strengthened against the Turks (subjects of rather frequent occurrence in the documents), and containing some interesting information about local conditions in Thessalonica. We learn the names of some sixty Greek stipendiaries of the Republic, most of whom are ranked as nobles, as well as the fact that gentlemen, presumably Latins (*cavalieri*), in the suites of the duke and captain had been making themselves obnoxious to the citizens by their disregard of the rights and customs of the city. The Doge Francesco Foscari and the Senate tried to satisfy the Greek envoys' requests (on 7–23 July),[76] and Michiel's reports soon reached the Senate that he had taken the "turris Cassandrie" as well as the seaport of Platamona across the bay, and was negotiating with the Turks: 20,000 aspers a year had been promised to the redoubtable Turakhan Beg in addition to the 20,000 which Michiel had been authorized to offer the grand vizir, Ibrahim Pasha.[77]

The Turkish siege of Thessalonica had been well maintained by land. The Venetians used the sea lanes, but were always hard pressed to import sufficient quantities of food. A number of severe attacks upon the city were successfully repulsed. The gates were locked, and few merchants ventured out upon the dangerous roads. At last, in April, 1426, it appeared that Michiel had negotiated a truce with Khalil Beg, the governor (*subashi*) of Gallipoli, whereby Venetian dominion was recognized over Thessalonica, which was to pay the Porte an annual tribute of 100,000 aspers. The Turks were also to have the salt works. Financial disputes among Turks might be settled by a *kadi*, who would have no other jurisdiction. Both sides were to restore fugitives. The city gates were to remain open, and merchants might go to and fro as they had done "in the time

---

and other dissident Turks were "prospering" and likely to be successful in their opposition to Murad, he was to reach an understanding with them. Otherwise he was to try to make peace with Murad: "In isto casu apparet nobis quod debeas sequi modum pacis cum Turcho et permittimus in libertate tua querendi dictam pacem . . ." (fol. 6^v [7^v]). "Ceterum mandamus tibi quatenus perveniendo ad pacem ut prefertur debeas solicitare et procurare, reducere et includere nobilem virum Nicolaum Georgio militem cum loco Bondinicie in pace predicta . . ." (fol. 8^v [9^v]).

[75] Sphrantzes, *Chron. minus* (*PG* 156, 1034D; ed. Grecu, p. 26); Pseudo-Sphrantzes, I, 31 [40]; II, 3 (Bonn, pp. 122, 134; ed. Papadopoulos, I, 125, 137; ed. Grecu, pp. 260, 272, 274). Chalcocondylas, bk. IV (Bonn, pp. 205–6), suggests that Andronicus died in the Morea, and for other stories concerning Andronicus's life and death after the Venetian occupation of Thessalonica, see Mertzios, *Mnemeia*, pp. 95–97. In an unconvincing article (*cf.*, above, note 64) J. Tsaras, "La Fin d' Andronic Paléologue," *Revue des études sud-est européennes*, III, 432, comes to the conclusion that "après la vente de la ville de Thessalonique aux Vénitiens" Andronicus went to Mantineia, where he remained until his death.

[76] Misti, Reg. 55, fols. 139^r–142^v [140^r–143^v], "MCCCCXXV, die septimo Iulii:" "Cum ad presentiam nostri dominii accesserint tres spectabiles ambassiatores civitatis nostre Salonichi . . . et pro parte universitatis civitatis predicte [i.e., the "municipal corporation"] porrexerint quedam capitula ad que cum maxima reverentia et humili supplicatione petant responsionem nostram, vadit pars quod ipsis capitulis respondeatur. . . ." The three ambassadors were Calojanni Radino, Thomas Chrysoloras (Crussulora, Chrussolora, Grusulora), and George Jalca (Γιάλκας). They presented twenty-one separate requests (recorded in the Venetian dialect), to which the Senate returned answers (in Latin); the record of concessions made was then incorporated in a ducal privilege, which was duly sealed and dated 23 July ("datum in nostro ducali palatio die XXIII mensis Iulii, MCCCCXXV, indictione tertia"). *Cf.* Hopf, II, 88b; Iorga, *ROL*, V, 199–200; Lemerle, *Miscellanea G. Galbiati*, III, 222–23; Thiriet, *Régestes*, II, no. 1995, p. 229; and esp. Mertzios, *Mnemeia*, pp. 46–61, who gives a facsimile reproduction of the document as well as a detailed analysis of its contents.

[77] Sen. Secreta, Reg. 9, fol. 36^v[37^v], letter of the Senate to Michiel, dated 3 September, 1425, summarized in Iorga, *ROL*, V, 208, and *Notes et extraits*, I, 408, and *cf. ROL*, V, 202, an excerpt from the *Cron. Zancaruola*, describing Michiel's capture of Cassandra and Platamona ("Platanea"), which also appears in Sanudo, *Vite de' duchi*, in *RISS*, XXII, cols. 979D–980. *Cf.* the summaries of documents in Mertzios, *Mnemeia*, pp. 62–63, from the Sen. Secreta, Reg. 9, fols. 24^v, 36^v, 39^v [25^v, 37^v, 40^v], dated 23 July and (as just noted) 3 September, 1425: ". . . Continent etiam litere vestre predicte [Michiel's letters to the Signoria dated at Cassandrea, the ancient Potidaea, on 12 and 22 June and 2 July] praticam pacis quam habuistis cum Turichambey et Bazarino [the latter being unknown] pro quibus omnibus vestram sapientiam, diligentiam, et solicitudinem merito commendantes fidelitati vestre . . . respondemus quod multum etiam nobis placuit audire tractatum dicte pacis quam libenter videremus ad perfectionem [Valentini, *Acta Albaniae veneta*, XII, no. 3,002, p. 188, incorrectly

of the lord despot."[78] Since the Porte would not give up the peninsula of Cassandra and the castle on Mount Kortiach, obviously not relaxing its intention ultimately to seize Thessalonica, Michiel's negotiations had little immediate effect, and hostilities continued between the two rival powers, the presage of a vast struggle which was to entrain the full strength of both later on in the century.

In the meantime, on 4 December, 1425, Venice had finally joined Florence in a ten-year alliance to halt the aggressions of Filippo Maria Visconti, the duke of Milan. Filippo Maria's conquests in the Romagna and Tuscany were to go to Florence, those in Lombardy to Venice. On 11 July, 1426, the new allies were joined by Amadeo VIII of Savoy, who had also found the Milanese dangerous neighbors.[79] Like Gian Galeazzo before him, Filippo Maria now seems to have thought of making contact with the Turks. Iorga has published the first draft of a letter to one Federigo de Petiis, whom Filippo Maria was planning to send to Sultan Murad; in this letter, dated at Milan on 24 July, 1426, Filippo Maria refers to the "desired destruction of the trembling Venetian sheep" (*optata destructio tremularum ovium venetarum*).[80] It is not clear that the Milanese envoy was ever sent to the Porte, but the Venetians were bent on ending hostilities with the Turks if they could find some way to do so and still keep Thessalonica.

In July (1426) a new Venetian admiral, Andrea Mocenigo, "captain-general of the Gulf," was directed by the Senate to resume negotiations with the sultan's emissaries, not insisting this time upon retention of Cassandra and the "castrum vocatum Cortiati," "which castle the said [Sultan] Murad Beg has been unwilling to allow to remain to us." Giovanni II Crispo, duke of the Archipelago (1418–1437), and his brothers, lords of various islands in the Aegean, were to be included in the peace with the Turks. If such a peace still proved unobtainable, Mocenigo was to attack the Turkish ships at Gallipoli, even within the straits, but there seemed to be some hope of peace, because Jacopo Gattilusio, lord of Lesbos (1409–1428), "who is a friend of the said Turk," was interested in helping to remove the causes of friction.[81] In August, 1426, the old despot of

reads 'prosecutionem'] deductam et speramus quod illam duxeritis ad complementum. . . . Et ultra promissionem factam Turichambey de aspris vigintimilibus annuatim de introitibus Salonichi, que nobis placuit et placet, solicitetis etiam cum Bassa [Ibrahim Pasha, the grand vizir] quod ad conclusionem dicte pacis pervenire possitis, cui Basse etiam promittere possitis annuatim illud quod in vestra commissione continetur . . ." (fol. 36^v [37^v]).

[78] Sen. Secreta, Reg. 9, fol. 109^v [107^v], doc. dated 20 April, 1426, published in Iorga, *ROL*, V, 317–18; *Notes et extraits*, I, 416–18; Valentini, *Acta Albaniae veneta*, XII, no. 3,034, pp. 225–26; Thiriet, *Régestes*, II, no. 2018, pp. 234–35; and *cf.* Mertzios, *Mnemeia*, pp. 67–68.

[79] *Cf.* Kretschmayr, *Gesch. v. Venedig*, II, 336–37.

[80] Iorga, *ROL*, V, 326–27; *Notes et extraits*, I, 426–27, on which see Manfroni, "La Marina veneziana alla difesa di Salonicco," *Nuovo Archivio veneto*, XX, 37–38.

[81] Sen. Secreta, Reg. 9, fols. 141^r–142^v [139^r–140^v], Mocenigo's commission dated 7 July, 1426, published in Valentini, *Acta Albaniae veneta*, XII, no. 3,058, pp. 254–60, and summarized in Iorga, *ROL*, V, 324–25, and *Notes et extraits*, I, 424–25. By a slip of the pen Iorga wrongly identifies the "lord of Mytilene" (Lesbos) as Francesco Gattilusio, an error which he repeats in *Gesch. d. osman. Reiches*, I, 403. *Cf.* Hopf, II, 150–51; Wm. Miller, *Essays on the Latin Orient*, Cambridge, 1921, pp. 324–26; and esp. Geo. T. Dennis, "The Short Chronicle of Lesbos," in *Lesbiaka*, V (1965), 19–21 (pagination of offprint). In September, 1426, Mocenigo received further orders with reference to the hoped-for peace (*ROL*, V, 328–29, 330; *Notes et extraits*, I, 428–29, 430).

In October, 1426, the Senate was still contemplating a Hungarian alliance for a joint expedition against the Turks (Sen. Secreta, Reg. 9, fols. 176^v–177^v [174^v–175^v], and *cf.* fol. 178^r [176^r]; Iorga, *ROL*, V, 334–35; *Notes et extraits*, I, 434–35). Venice and the Emperor Sigismund, who was also king of Hungary, had long been at odds, as we have seen; now, however, Amadeo VIII of Savoy, whom Sigismund had created duke in 1416, was trying to effect a reconciliation between them, at Sigismund's request. Elaborate plans for a Hungarian-Venetian alliance had already been formulated a year before, in October, 1425, but nothing had come of them (Sen. Secreta, Reg. 9, fols. 45^v–46^v [46^v–47^v]; Iorga, *ROL*, V, 210–11; *Notes et extraits*, I, 409–10). The hostility of Hungary and Venice toward each other during these years continued to hamper the efforts of both powers against the Turks.

At the time of his mission to Venice, in December, 1423, and January, 1424 (*cf.* above, note 55), the young Emperor John VIII had offered his services as mediator between Sigismund and the Signoria to help effect a formal peace. The Senate assured him "quod dominatio nostra semper fuit inclinata et prompta ad pacem et bonam concordiam cum omnibus et precipue cum ipso serenissimo domino Rege Romanorum et Hungarie." Venice had tried constantly, through numerous envoys and embassies, to make peace with Sigismund, according to the Senate, "sed ipso domino Rege semper se retrahente ad illam [pacem] nunquam potuimus pervenire, propter quam causam nos vigilantes ad conservationem et bonum status nostri devenimus ad confederationem et ligam cum illustri domino duce Milani . . ., et in uno capitulo dicte lige continetur quod aliqua partium non possit ad tractatum concordii et pacis devenire cum dicto domino Rege Romanorum et Hungarie sine consensu et voluntate alterius partis. . . ." Thus they would have to wait for Filippo Maria Visconti's assent before Venice could authorize John to try to negotiate a peace with Sigismund (Sen. Secreta, Reg. 8, fol. 136^r [137^r], doc. dated 30

Serbia, Stephen Lazarević, offered through his adopted son and nephew George Branković to mediate with the Turks, to which the Venetians replied gratefully and courteously, acknowledging that possession of Thessalonica had cost them much in money and effort, but asserting that they could not abandon the city.[82] In September and October the Turks of another pretender named Mustafa, who also claimed to be a son of Bayazid, and was stationed in Thessalonica as an ally of the Venetians, made large-scale and rather ill-advised sorties from the city. A report of 8 December, describing these events, shows that the picturesque countryside around Thessalonica was swarming with the sultan's troops.[83]

Venetian efforts to make peace were as unceasing as they proved unavailing. War might be an exciting and profitable game to the Turks, but it was a grim, costly business as far as the merchants of Venice were concerned. In November, 1426, Andrea Mocenigo succeeded, through the efforts of the Venetian notary John de Bonisio, in securing Sultan Murad's general acceptance (on the twenty-eighth of the month) of the terms of the projected treaty of the preceding April, which Mocenigo's predecessor Fantino Michiel had negotiated. Venice promised now an annual tribute of 150,000 aspers; she still claimed the peninsula of Cassandra, but was willing to drop the matter of Mount Kortiach. The other terms remained the same except that Venice would distribute rather greater largesse at the Porte and provide more in annual incomes for the sultan's chief functionaries. On 24 July, 1427, the Doge Francesco Foscari issued an ambassadorial commission to Benedetto Emo, hopeful that he might secure the Porte's official ratification of the agreement.[84]

December, 1423; Iorga, *ROL*, V, 151–52; *Notes et extraits*, I, 350–51; Thiriet, *Régestes*, II, no. 1915, pp. 211–12).

On 15 January, 1424, John VIII had renewed his inquiries as to the Senate's intentions. In the meantime Filippo Maria's response had come but, as the Senate wrote their notary Francesco della Siega in Milan on the seventeenth, "dicta responsio videtur nobis ambigua" (Sen. Secreta, Reg. 8, fol. 139ʳ [140ʳ]). Pending further clarification of the Milanese position, however, which della Siega was asked to obtain, the Senate was willing to proceed. On the same day the Senate voted (*de parte* 127, *de non* 0, *non sinceri* 0) "quod hortamur multum suam Serenitatem [dominum Imperatorem Constantinopolis iuniorem, as John VIII is called in these texts] quod perseveret et sequatur suum bonum propositum in eundo in Hungariam ad presentiam serenissimi domini Romanorum Regis pro bona et votiva executione eorum que sua Serenitas . . . die Sabati [15 January] nobis exposuit . . ." (Reg. cited, fol. 138ᵛ [139ᵛ], resolution of the Senate dated 17 January, 1424 [Ven. style 1423]; Iorga, *ROL*, V, 153–54; *Notes et extraits*, I, 352–53; Thiriet, *Régestes*, II, no. 1920, p. 213).

At this session (on the seventeenth) the Senate also passed the following resolution: "Ad id autem quod requirit [imperator iunior] quod mittamus galeas nostras ad partes Constantinopolis pro conforto civium et subditorum suorum et conservatione sui imperii, respondeatur quod, sicut sue Excellentie notum est, nos sumus missuri de brevi nostrum generalem capitaneum [Pietro Loredan] cum armata potenti, et si dicta armata non erit nobis necessaria in aliis partibus, nos mittemus illam versus partes Romanie et eundo dictam nostram armatam versus dictas partes, nos faciemus dictam armatam ascendere usque Constantinopolim pro conforto illarum partium et subditorum suorum et pro bono et conservatione pacifici status imperii sui predicti" (*ibid.*). There is a careless transcription of this passage in Valentini, *Acta Albaniae veneta*, XII, no. 2,840, p. 4.

On John VIII's venture into Italy and Hungary (he returned to Constantinople on 1 November, 1424), see Barker, *Manuel II Palaeologus*, pp. 375–79. I have excluded from the text an account of the various efforts to reconcile Sigismund with the Venetians, because they ended in failure, and Sigismund finally made a separate peace with the Turks, blaming the Venetians for the alleged necessity of his doing so (see below, p. 28a and note 90).

[82] Sen. Secreta, Reg. 9, fol. 165ᵛ [163ᵛ], doc. dated 2 September, 1426, summarized in Iorga, *ROL*, V, 329–30, and *Notes et extraits*, I, 429–30. Branković succeeded Stephen as despot of Serbia in July, 1427 (Iorga, *Gesch. d. osman. Reiches*, I, 394).

---

[83] Iorga, *ROL*, V, 337–39; *Notes et extraits*, I, 437–39, doc. dated 8 December, 1426. On Mustafa, *cf.* Mertzios, *Mnemeia*, pp. 48, note, and 63–64. Fantino Michiel's commission as captain-general of the sea, dated 2 April, 1425, had contained the following instructions (Sen. Secreta, Reg. 9, fol. 5ᵛ [6ᵛ]): "Et quia rectores nostri Salonichi . . . nostro dominio scripserunt applicuisse in Salonicho quendam Mustafa Turchum qui dicitur fuisse filius quondam Baysit [Bayazid]: Si ita invenies esse veritatem propter informationem quam habebis a rectoribus nostris predictis et videres eundem habere sequellam aliorum Turchorum dictarum partium, debeatis tu et rectores nostri predicti cum illis modis et viis qui et que vobis utiles videbuntur, mediante favore dicti Mustafe, providere ad damna et ruinam dicti Turchi in illis partibus, sicut vobis melius videbitur," etc. *Cf.* Valentini, *Acta Albaniae veneta*, XII, no. 2,958, p. 136.

[84] Sen. Secreta, Reg. 10 [1426–1428], fol. 65ᵛ [69ᵛ]; Sathas, I, no. 117, pp. 182–86; Thiriet, *Régestes*, II, no. 2066, p. 245. Apparently a Byzantine envoy to the Porte, objecting to the Turkish peace with Venice, gave Murad the idea—after he had virtually accepted all the terms—that the Porte should not make peace as long as Venetian ships rode at anchor off Gallipoli (Iorga, *ROL*, V, 341). On 28 February, 1427 (Ven. style 1426), the Senate decided to send an ambassador to the Porte, "quoniam, sicut refert prudens vir Johannes de Bonisio notarius noster rediens a presentia Morati Bey domini Teucrorum et sicut scribit capitaneus generalis Culphi [Andrea Mocenigo], videtur quod idem Moratus inter cetera destiterit ratificare pacem, quia vellet quod mitteremus nostrum solemnem ambaxi-

Conditions in beleaguered Thessalonica constantly worsened. The inhabitants were gradually losing confidence in the Venetians' ability to handle the Turkish problem. The shortage of food had made the winter of 1426–1427 a long nightmare for the Republic's administrators in the city.[85] Months dragged on, and no treaty was made. The mounting Greek offensive in the Morea worried the Senate. Emo was replaced in August, 1428, by Jacopo Dandolo, who was also unable to secure Murad's final and formal ratification of the illusory peace.[86] Dandolo had been empowered, nevertheless, to increase the tribute to 300,000 aspers as well as to distribute 10,000 to 15,000 ducats in gifts and to promise annual pensions amounting to another 2,000 to the chief officials of the Porte. For the peaceable possession of Thessalonica, Cassandra, the saltworks, and the neighboring lands and villages Venice would pay even more, making an especial pecuniary allowance for the saltworks, but peace must be confirmed also with respect to Venetian possessions in Albania. Unless Murad showed, however, a sincere disposition to yield to all the Venetian requests, Dandolo was not to mention these larger sums, for obvious reasons.[87] Dandolo had no opportunity to speak of the larger sums. In fact the news finally reached Venice that when poor Dandolo was ushered into the sultan's presence, explained his mission, and presented his gifts, Murad asked him: "Have you authority to give me the land of Saloniki?" Dandolo acknowledged that he had no such authority; he was dismissed, presently arrested, and on the sultan's orders confined to prison, never to be released.[88]

This was too much even for Venetian patience, and on 29 March, 1429, the Senate approved a public declaration of war against the Porte, and decreed that three more light galleys should be armed in Venice and one in Zara. Of the three Cretan galleys in his fleet the captain-general Mocenigo was to be instructed to choose the two strongest and add to their armaments by stripping the third; this last galley was to be replaced by a new one which the colonial government of Crete was to arm.[89]

---

atorem ad presentiam suam ad confirmandum dictam pacem, et consideratis conditionibus temporis presentis ac novitatibus in quibus sumus cum duce Milani [Filippo Maria Visconti, with whom the Venetians were also trying to settle their differences] et aliis multis negotiis occurrentibus multum faciat pro factis nostris habere pacem cum dicto Morato" (Sen. Secreta, Reg. 10, fol. 26ᵛ [30ᵛ]). After Giovanni Giorgio and Tommaso Michiel declined to accept the appointment as ambassador (on 6 March), Benedetto Emo (Aymo) was chosen on 2 April, and agreed to go to the Ottoman court (*ibid.*, and *cf.* Iorga, *ROL*, V, 349, 351, 362, and Valentini, *Acta Albaniae veneta*, XIII [1972], no. 3,097, p. 14). Emo was an old hand at Levantine affairs, having been the Republic's bailie in Constantinople a half dozen years before (*cf.* Ljubić, *Listine*, VIII [1886], 116–17, doc. dated 10 October, 1421). I assume this is the same Benedetto Emo who in 1429 was the captain of Zara (*ibid.*, IX [1890], 37, 43).

[85] *Cf.* Iorga, *ROL*, V, 336, 343, 346, 350, 353; Mertzios, *Mnemeia*, pp. 64–65. The shortage of food in Thessalonica persisted until the Turkish occupation of the city.

[86] Misti, Reg. 57, fol. 29ʳ [31ʳ]; Valentini, *Acta Albaniae veneta*, XIII, no. 3,168, pp. 81–82, resolution of the Senate to send an ambassador to Murad, dated 17 August, 1428, with the note that "electus ambaxiator Ser Jacobus Dandulo maior et acceptavit," and *cf.* Iorga, *ROL*, V, 379, doc. dated 31 August. The Greeks then held Patras under siege (Sen. Secreta, Reg. 10, fols. 172ᵛ–173ᵛ [176ᵛ–177ᵛ], docs. dated 31 August). According to Sanudo, *Vite de' duchi*, in *RISS*, XXII, col. 1002E, Dandolo was elected ambassador to the Porte on 7 August, an obvious scribal or typographical error. His commission is dated the thirty-first (Sen. Secreta, Reg. 10, fols. 173ᵛ–175ʳ [177ᵛ–179ʳ]; Valentini, *Acta Albaniae veneta*, XIII, no. 3,173, pp. 94–100).

[87] Sen. Secreta, Reg. 10, fols. 173ᵛ–175ʳ, "die ultimo Augusti," Dandolo's commission alluded to in the preceding note; summaries of the document may be found in Iorga, *ROL*, V, 380–81, and *Notes et extraits*, I, 480–81; Mertzios, *Mnemeia*, pp. 70–71; and Thiriet, *Régestes*, II, no. 2111, pp. 253–54.

[88] Sanudo, *Vite de' duchi*, in *RISS*, XXII, cols. 1004E–1005A. Dandolo died in his Turkish prison (*ibid.*, col. 1006B). On 13 August, 1429, his son Gerardo informed the Senate that Dandolo (still alive and still in prison) had been condemned by the sultan to pay 4,000 ducats because of the losses inflicted on the Turks by "our people" at Thessalonica: ". . . quod per dictos Teucros condemnatus est ad solvendum pro damnis per nostros de Salonicho ipsis Teucris illatis ducatorum quatuor milia et ob hoc carceribus miserabiliter est inclusus" (Misti, Reg. 57, fol. 144ᵛ [148ᵛ], and *cf.* Iorga, *ROL*, VI [1898, repr. 1964], 63).

[89] Misti, Reg. 57, fols. 86ᵛ–87ʳ [90ᵛ–91ʳ], "MCCCCXXVIIII, die XXVIIII Martii:" "Cum propter nova que senciuntur de partibus Romanie de mala intentione Turchorum et propter retentionem viri nobilis Ser Jacobi Dandulo, qui fuerat noster orator ad dominum Teucrorum, non sit amplius de pace sperandum, et proinde oporteat facere bonam provisionem tam pro honore nostri dominii quam pro salute, custodia et defensione terrarum et locorum nostrorum partium aliarum quibus iminet magnum periculum nisi cito provideatur, vadit pars quod in nomine Dei de presenti armari debeant in Venetiis galee tres subtiles quanto celerius sit possibile per illum modum qui deliberabitur per Collegium . . ., et insuper etiam armari debeat una alia galea in Iadra. . . . *Et ex nunc declaretur quod simus in guerra cum Turchis*. . . .

"Insuper scribatur et mandetur viro nobili Ser Andree Mocenigo, capitaneo generali maris, quod ex tribus galeis Crete secum existentibus debeat eligere et apud se tenere illas duas que sibi meliores videbuntur . . . , et de alia tercia accipiat illos homines, arma, et res que sibi videbuntur oportune ad ponendum illas duas bene in ordine ita quod

While the sounds of saws and hammers and the shouts of workmen and sailors were heard along the docks at the arsenal in Venice, members of the Senate continued to debate the many aspects of the Turkish problem from Durazzo and Alessio to Modon and Coron, Negroponte and Thessalonica. The Emperor Sigismund had made a three years' peace with the Turks (in 1428), alleging that the Venetians had virtually forced him into it by their hostility toward Hungary, a charge which the Doge Francesco Foscari indignantly denied in a letter of 29 June, 1429, to Pope Martin V, recalling the Republic's services to eastern Christendom and their current war with the Turks.[90] They had in truth been at war with the Turks for six years, ever since their acceptance of Thessalonica from the Despot Andronicus, which had proved a most unsatisfactory business.

On 14 July, 1429, the Senate gave formal replies to a detailed petition presented by an embassy representing the Greek population of Thessalonica, showing that the inhabitants had become disenchanted with Venetian rule as the years had passed. The Greek envoys protested against the infringement of their rights to leave the city and sell their goods as they chose, since the Senate refused to relax the wartime restrictions which had been imposed, lest the movement of people and property from the city result in its fall to the Turks: ". . . eadem [civitas] subito veniret ad manus perfidorum Teuchrorum." The Greeks wanted some positive action taken with respect to the always critical state of the city's grain supply, the still unfortified condition of Cassandra, and the miserable plight of those refugees who wanted to return to the city, but whose houses had been or were being ruined in their absence. To all these requests the Senate gave reassuring answers. The envoys complained that the walls of Thessalonica itself were almost ready to fall down, especially on the sea side, and the Senate promised to have them repaired every year. The Senate was informed that some of their soldiers were unreliable (even communicating with the Turks), and that certain officials, especially the rectors' chancellors, were guilty of constant extortion. The envoys requested the renewed confirmation of the privileges of the Orthodox archbishop, the right of asylum in the ancient church of S. Sophia, and a greater respect for their churches and monasteries on the part of the soldiers, who apparently employed them as barracks, and introduced prostitutes into the historic and holy buildings. The envoys wanted also a general recognition of ecclesiastical courts. To these and to three or four other requests relating to ecclesiastical affairs the Senate gave affirmative or sympathetic replies, but declined to recognize the archbishop's jurisdiction over laymen.[91]

---

sint bene armate et in puncto, et quod illam terciam cum hominibus et rebus restantibus mittat in Candidam ad disarmandum. Scribatur quoque regimini nostro Crete quod de presenti provideat armare et armet unam aliam galeam loco illius que venire debet ad disarmandum. . . ." This document is summarized in Iorga, *ROL*, V, 388, and *Notes et extraits*, I, 488, and in Thiriet, *Régestes*, II, no. 2127, p. 258; it is partially (and somewhat carelessly) given in Valentini, *Acta Albaniae veneta*, XIII, no. 3,204, pp. 124–27.

[90] Sen. Secreta, Reg. 11, fols. 16^r–17^r [17^r–18^r], with a summary in Iorga, *ROL*, VI (1898, repr. 1964), 54–55: "Quod summo pontifici scribatur in forma infrascripta [the Senate had to approve the text of the doge's letter]: Sensimus, beatissime pater, ego meaque communitas, vestre Sanctitatis filii devotissimi, serenissimum dominum Sigismundum Romanorum et Hungarie regem in detractionem honoris nostri et ad conflandum contra nos odium nonnulla scripsisse Beatitudini vestre ac quibusdam principibus Christianis, presertim quod cum sua Serenitate concordiam habere recusaverimus quodque ob eam causam treuguas triennales cum Teucris conclusit. . . ." *Cf.* Iorga, *Gesch. d. osman. Reiches*, I, 395–96. In September and October, 1429, Gaspar Schlick, the chancellor of Bohemia, was trying to arrange an anti-Turkish entente between Sigismund and Venice (*ROL*, VI, 66–67; *Notes et extraits*, I, 504–5), with small chance of success. On Sigismund's embassies to the Tatars, Greeks of Constantinople and Trebizond, the Genoese at Caffa, and other possible anti-Turkish allies in the East, as well as his relations with the Turks (and his attempts to form an eastern alliance against them), see Wolfgang Freiherr Stromer von Reichenbach, "König Siegmunds Gesandte in den Orient," in the *Festschrift für Hermann Heimpel*, II (Göttingen, 1972), 591–609.

[91] Misti, Reg. 57, fols. 129^r–132^v [133^r–136^v], "MCCCCXXVIIII, die XIIII Iulii:" "Quod respondeatur ad capitula porrecta pro parte communitatis nostre Salonichi in hac forma," etc.; there are thirty-one articles in the petition, on which *cf.* Iorga, *ROL*, VI, 58–59; *Notes et extraits*, I, 495–97; Lemerle, *Miscellanea G. Galbiati*, III, 224–25; and Thiriet, *Régestes*, II, no. 2149, p. 263. From this long petition, of which the requests are given in Venetian and the Senate's answers in Latin, it may be well to print the answers to the twelfth and thirteenth articles relating to ecclesiastical affairs (fol. 130^v [134^v]):

"Respondemus quod non videtur nobis conveniens neque iustum quod seculares subiaceant foro ecclesiastico, et propterea volumus quod clerici subiaceant foro et iudicio domini archiepiscopi Salonicensis et seculares subiaceant foro et iudicio seculari. Sed ad factum ecclesie Sancte Sophie respondemus quod sumus contenti quod franchisia dicte ecclesie observetur, et ita mandabimus quod observabitur. Et volumus etiam quod ecclesie et monasteria debeant gaudere omnibus introitibus et redditibus tam a mari quam a terra et etiam illis quos habent in Cas-

The Venetians never made adequate provision for the defense of Thessalonica against the Turks. They had certainly expended large sums, as they constantly reminded the Greek envoys, but they were always apprehensive of the sultan's refusal to recognize their title to the city, and they had some reason to doubt their ability to hold so important a place so close to the Turkish capital of Adrianople. They always found it difficult, therefore, to know whether they were spending too much or too little.

The Venetians naturally looked around for allies whom they might oppose to the Gran Turco, finding the most likely in the prince of Caramania, Ibrahim Beg (1423–1464), who was, it so happened, a brother-in-law of Sultan Murad. He was known as the "Gran Caramano," but he feared his brother-in-law no less than the Venetians did. In August, 1429, we find Venice trying to arrange an alliance with Ibrahim Beg, to help achieve which they enlisted the good offices of King Janus of Cyprus, who was reputed to maintain a "bona amicicia cum magno Caramano."[92] If the Venetians spent too little on the defense of Thessalonica, they had still spent a good deal, and it was only too obvious that the future did not hold the slightest prospect of diminished expenditure. Andrea Suriano, a member of the war party, stated in a most interesting speech in the Senate on 3 January, 1430, that Venice must prepare a really powerful armada to force Murad into an acceptance of peace. For years money had been spent, and the Republic had achieved little or nothing. It was necessary to strike one great blow against the Turk, a decisive blow to reduce the vast costs of holding Thessalonica, "so that the Turk may either be reduced to peace with our Signoria or be so damaged that he fears our power, and we are not forever caught in these continuous expenses." Suriano stated that Venice had spent on an average more than 60,000 ducats every year to maintain the city against the Turks. He introduced the resolution to arm a dozen galleys and two large ships; of the galleys, seven were to be armed in Venice, three in Crete, and one each in Zara and Sebenico.[93] Such an armada

---

sandra, et ita mandabimus quod dicti rectores debeant observare. Ad factum aptandi monasteria que ruine tradita sunt, respondemus quod pro presenti propter novitates guerre non est modus ad aptandum dicta monasteria, sed cessatis istis novitatibus poterit postea provideri aptationi eorum prout videbitur fore opportunum. Ad factum autem stipendiariorum qui habitant ecclesias et monasteria et destruunt ea, et in eis ducunt meretrices et ibidem committunt multas inhonestates, respondemus quod nobis summe displicet audire tales novitates et inhonestates, sed mandabimus rectoribus nostris Salonichi quod debeant providere sub illis gravibus penis que sibi videbuntur quod dicte novitates et inhonestates cessent." Mertzios, *Mnemeia*, pp. 72–86, has analyzed the whole document in detail and given a facsimile reproduction of the text.

[92] Sen. Secreta, Reg. 11, fols. 29^v–31^r [30^v–32^r]; Valentini, *Acta Albaniae veneta*, XIII, nos. 3,257–60, pp. 179–85; Iorga, *ROL*, VI, 64–66; *Notes et extraits*, I, 502–4; Thiriet, *Régestes*, II, no. 2160, p. 266, docs. dated 30–31 August, 1429. The Senate's purpose was "ut refrenari valeat ipsius Teucri rabies pro universali bono et sue Serenitatis [the king of Cyprus] et nostro ac totius Christianitatis," and the Venetians hoped that an alliance with Ibrahim Beg might lead "ad ipsius Teucri damna et exterminium" (Reg. cit., fol. 30^r [31^r]).

King Janus had recently been captured by Egyptian forces in the Mamluk invasion of Cyprus (during the summer of 1426); after eight months' imprisonment in Cairo he was ransomed, and returned to Cyprus in May, 1427. Depressed in spirit, weakened in health, and at the end of his resources, Janus could give Venice nothing but information concerning his "friend" the Gran Caramano (*cf.* below, p. 45b, and Sir Geo. Hill, *History of Cyprus*, II [Cambridge, 1948], 493–94).

[93] Misti, Reg. 57, fol. 179 [183], "MCCCCXXVIIII, die tertio Januarii:" "Cum per reditum viri nobilis Ser Andree Mocenigo, capitanei nostri generalis maris, videatur non potuisse sequi pacem inter nostrum dominium et dominum Teucrorum nec sperandum sit de pace ob nequiciam et perfidiam ipsius Turchi, et neccessarium ac honor nostri dominii sit providere hostiliter contra Teucros et ad conservationem navigiorum fidelium et subditorum nostrorum navigantium ad partes Romanie: . . . [in margin: Ser Andreas Suriano:] Cum propter guerram quam habemus cum Turcho et pro securitate nostrorum civium et mercatorum navigantium per strictum neccessarium sit providere de potenti armata que sit causa reducendi hunc dominum Turchorum, inimicum nostrum, ad bonam pacem cum nostro dominio attento maxime quod postquam dominium civitatis Salonichi habuimus computato uno anno cum alio expendite fuerunt ultra ducatorum sexaginta milia in anno, que expensa continua corrodit nostrum dominium, et non videtur quod aliquid fiat, nec aliquid magnificum demonstratur per quod detur causa huic Turcho timendi nostrum dominium [Valentini, *Acta Albaniae veneta*, XIV (1972), no. 3,305, p. 9, reads 'nomen dominii'] aut veniendi nobiscum ad bonam pacem, ideoque neccessarium sit uno ictu facere quod fiendum est ut ipse Turchus aut reducatur ad pacem cum nostro dominio aut ita damnizetur quod expavescat potentiam nostram et nos continue non stemus in istis continuis expensis, vadit pars quod in nomine Jesu Christi ad executionem predictorum armari debeant galee XII et due naves magne nostri communis, quarum galearum septem armentur hic Venetiis, tres in Creta, una in Jadra, et una in Sibinico . . ." [de parte 32, de non 5, non sincerus 1, but Suriano's proposals all lack the cross in the left-hand margin of the register, which indicates they were not accepted by the Senate, and were not put into effect]. The text is summarized in Iorga, *ROL*, VI, 70, and *Notes et extraits*, I, 508, and in Thiriet, *Régestes*, II, no. 2175, p. 269, incorrectly dated 1429. *Cf.* Manfroni, "La Marina veneziana," *Nuovo Archivio veneto*, XX, 59–61.

was hardly large enough to serve the purpose Suriano had in mind. Nevertheless, he could not secure the passage of his motion in the Senate.

A great blow was soon struck. It relieved Venice of the heavy expense of which Suriano complained, but it was the Turk who struck the blow. Thessalonica was stormed on 29 March, 1430, after a three-day assault, under the watchful eyes of Sultan Murad himself. Most of the Venetians escaped in three galleys they had in the harbor, but some important personages were captured. Sanudo says that the Republic had expended more than 700,000 ducats on the city, which would be almost twice the sum named by Suriano in the Senate.[94] In any event the issue of Thessalonica was now definitely resolved, and the sage statesmen of the Republic gave no thought to the reconquest of the city. Indeed, a month after they had lost Thessalonica they informed their captain-general of the sea, now Silvestro Morosini, that they were willing to cede their rights to the city for an honorable peace with the Porte.[95]

Venice had other important possessions in the Levant and other problems to worry about. Durazzo, Scutari, and Antivari, Lepanto and Nauplia, Modon, Coron, and above all Negroponte must not fall into Turkish hands. Still mistress of the Aegean, Venice nurtured less anxiety about Crete and the Archipelago. As for Thessalonica, few cities in the Levant have a more interesting history. Although subjected to a cruel sack upon its occupation by the Turks, Thessalonica remained an important place. The surviving inhabitants were allowed to rebuild

---

[94] Sanudo, *Vite de' duchi*, in *RISS*, XXII, cols. 1007E–1008; Amadio Valier, *Cron.*, Cod. Cicogna, no. 3631, fols. 302–3, 304; Ducas, chap. 29 (Bonn, pp. 198–201). John Anagnostes, *De Thessalonicensi excidio narratio*, 13 (Bonn, with the Pseudo-Sphrantzes and Cananus, p. 507), dates the Turkish occupation of Thessalonica on 29 March, 1430, as does the *Cron. Morosini* (on which *cf.* Lemerle, *Miscellanea G. Galbiati*, III, 225). Some of the Venetian chronicles give the date inaccurately as 13 March (*cf.* Iorga, *ROL*, VI, 73, note 1; *Notes et extraits*, I, 511, note 1; and, *ibid.*, II, 266, 272).

Chief among the Venetian captives were Leonardo Gradenigo and Lorenzo Contarini (Sanudo, *loc. cit.*, and Iorga, *ROL*, VI, 78, 79, and *Notes et extraits*, I, 516–17, docs. dated 29 April, 1430). As late as 3 March the Senate was still instructing their new captain-general of the sea, Silvestro Morosini, to try to arrange peace through Byzantine mediation on the same general terms as the unfortunate Jacopo Dandolo had been directed to present to Murad (Sen. Secreta, Reg. 11, esp. fols. 86^v–87^v [87^v–88^v]; Iorga, *ROL*, VI, 76–77, Morosini's commission from the doge upon election to the captaincy-general). On the Turkish capture of Thessalonica, see Mertzios, *Mnemeia*, pp. 88–93, with a (Greek) translation and text of the pertinent passage in the *Cron. Morosini*. The chroniclers give different figures for the costs of the seven-year Venetian occupation of Thessalonica—the *Cron. Morosini* putting the cost at 740,000 ducats, "and I, Antonio Morosini, witnessed this and have written with my own hand, and this is the truth," while the *Cron. Zancaruola* gives the figure as 502,000, and other chronicles put it at 300,000 and 200,000, for all of which see Mertzios, *op. cit.*, pp. 98–99, who seems to have missed Suriano's speech in the Senate (see preceding note), the most important evidence of all.

[95] Sen. Secreta, Reg. 11, fols. 101^r–102^r [102^r–103^r]; Valentini, *Acta Albaniae veneta*, XIV, no. 3,355, pp. 64–68; Iorga, *ROL*, VI, 79–80, doc. dated 29 April, 1430: "Quod viro nobili Ser Silvestro Mauroceno, capitaneo generali maris, scribatur in hac forma: Propter casum amissionis civitatis Salonichi, sicut considerare potestis, commissio quam vobis dedimus circa factum pacis tractande cum Turcho non habet nec potest habere locum in illa forma quam vobis fecimus. Nichilominus quia omnibus consideratis vellemus devenire ad pacem cum Turcho, si possibile foret, cum modis congruis et honestis, mandamus vobis cum nostris consiliis Rogatorum et Additionis [the Senate and the Giunta] quod si videbitis aliquem modum et viam per quam cum honore nostro veniri posset ad aliquam praticam pacis, ad illam veniatis per illa meliora et convenientiora media que vestre sapientie videbuntur. Et ut informatus sitis de nostra intentione et de conditionibus cum quibus habere vellemus pacem cum dicto Turcho, vobis dicimus et declaramus quod veniatis ad pacem predictam cum his modis et conditionibus, videlicet:

"Primo quod si idem Turchus volet quod renuntiemus omni juri et actioni quod et quam aliquo modo haberemus in dominio civitatis Salonichi et quod numquam nos impediamus de recuperando et habendo ipsam civitatem, sumus contenti in casu quo aliter fieri non posset quod hoc capitulum sibi promittatis in eo solum quod eidem Turcho spectare posset. Verum debeatis procurare in pratica dicti capituli, si possibile est, quod viri nobiles Ser Leonardus Gradonico et Laurentius Contareno, filius viri nobilis Ser Pauli Contareno, olim duche Salonichi, et alii cives et fideles nostri qui fuerunt capti a Teucris pristine libertati restituantur. Quando autem hoc obtinere non possetis, concludatis ipsum capitulum, ut superius continetur."

The Venetians were then held to pay the Porte an annual tribute of one hundred ducats for the castle of Lepanto (*pro castro Nepanti*) and two hundred ducats for Scutari, Alessio, and Drivasto. Now, however, they wanted the tribute reduced, "quia locus Drivasti non est amplius sub nostro dominio." (Drivasto had been lost in 1419, on which see Iorga, *ROL*, IV, 609, note, and *Notes et extraits*, I, 294, note.) But if the sultan was prepared to guarantee the security of Venetian possessions in Albania, the captain-general Morosini might promise the Porte a tribute of up to five hundred ducats a year (*doc. cit.*, fol. 101^r [102^r]). And, as usual in treaties with the Turks, the Senate wanted freedom of trade and passage throughout the Ottoman empire. *Cf.* the summaries of Morosini's instructions in Iorga, *ROL*, VI, 79–80; *Notes et extraits*, I, 517–18; Thiriet, *Régestes*, II, no. 2192, p. 273.

The fall of Thessalonica was known in Venice by 27 April (1430), and caused the Senate promptly to take steps for the safety of Zara, Sebenico, and Corfu (Misti, Reg. 57, fol. 209^v [213^v]).

their lives as best they could, and the Greek fugitives were allowed to return to their homes. Turkish rule lasted in Thessalonica for almost five centuries, until October, 1912, when the Greeks recovered the city and added it to the growing dominion of the new Hellenic kingdom.[96]

Shortly after the withdrawal of Murad II's troops from the siege of Constantinople in early September, 1422, the old Emperor Manuel had suffered a stroke (on 1 October), and all affairs of state had to be left in the hands of his son and co-ruler, John VIII, although the Venetian documents suggest that from time to time, as his health permitted, Manuel still received foreign envoys and made decisions. In July, 1425, Manuel died, and was buried in the capital in the monastery of the Pantokrator. Six sons survived him, the last tragic actors in the Greek theaters of Byzantium and the Morea. Besides the Emperor John VIII and the Despot Theodore II, there were Thomas, then in the Morea; Constantine [XI] "Dragases," ruler of Anchialus, Mesembria, and some other places on the Black Sea; Andronicus, onetime despot of Thessalonica; and Demetrius, who was still without an assigned share in the imperial heritage.[97] Of these Constantine, who was born in February, 1405, was destined to catch the world's attention as the last emperor and the last defender of Constantinople against barbarian attackers, a true martyr to the cause of Greek independence. It is at this time that Constantine made his first conspicuous appearance on the stage.

The Despot Theodore, having thought for a while of becoming a monk and relinquishing the rule of the Morea to Constantine, changed his mind when the latter arrived in the peninsula in December, 1427, with their imperial brother John VIII, who had approved the proposed transfer of power.[98] It was now that the diplomat and historian George Sphrantzes returned to the Morea in the service of the Palaeologi,[99]

[96] On Thessalonica, see in general A. E. Vacalopoulos [Bakalopoulos], *A History of Thessaloniki*, Thessaloniki, 1963, and on Venetian-held Crete (historical sources and bibliography), about which I shall have little occasion to speak in this volume, see M. I. Manussacas, "L'Isola di Creta sotto il dominio veneziano: Problemi e ricerche," in Agostino Pertusi, ed., *Venezia e il Levante fino al secolo XV*, 2 vols., Florence, 1973–74, I-2, 473–514.

[97] Ducas, chap. 23 (Bonn, p. 134); Chalcocondylas, bk. IV (Bonn, p. 205; ed. E. Darkó, I, 192); Pseudo-Sphrantzes, I, 31 [40] (Bonn, pp. 121–22; ed. Papadopoulos, I, 124–25; ed. Grecu, p. 260), on which note R. J. Loenertz, in the *Miscellanea Giovanni Mercati*, III (1946), 287–88 (Studi e testi, no. 123), and the chronicle attributed to Dorotheus of Monemvasia in Loenertz, *ibid.*, p. 304. Sphrantzes, *Chron. minus* (*PG* 156, 1031CD; ed. Grecu, p. 18), notes the death of Manuel II without giving the customary catalogue of his sons. *Cf.* Hopf, II, 81–82; Iorga, *Gesch. d. osman. Reiches*, I, 383–84; Barker, *Manuel II Palaeologus*, pp. 383–85.

[98] Sphrantzes, *Chron. minus* (*PG* 156, 1032A; ed. Grecu, p. 20), who says that John VIII married Maria of Trebizond in September, 1427, left Constantinople in November, and arrived in the Morea with Constantine on 26 December (the year 6936 of the Byzantine era ran from 1 September, 1427 through 31 August, 1428); and *cf.* Pseudo-Sphrantzes, II, 1 (Bonn, pp. 123–24; ed. Papadopoulos, I, 126–27; ed. Grecu, p. 262); Chalcocondylas, bk. IV (Bonn, p. 206). There is a sympathetic sketch of John VIII's career in Gill, *Personalities of the Council of Florence* (1964), pp. 104–24.

[99] Sphrantzes, *loc. cit.*, and *cf.* Pseudo-Sphrantzes, II, 1 (Bonn, p. 124, lines 3–4; ed. Papadopoulos, I, 127, line 1; ed. Grecu, p. 262, lines 18–20). Sphrantzes is an important source for the Byzantine world in the fifteenth century. Quite understandably, therefore, his "memoirs" have received much attention in recent years. Formerly called "Phrantzes," his name is now known to be Sphrantzes (see Volume I, Chapter 13, note 206, of the present work). The form Sphrantzes appears in the oldest (sixteenth-century) MS. of the *Chronicon minus* (Bibl. Apost. Vaticana, Cod. Ottobon. gr. 260) and also in the title of the printed text in *PG* 156, 1025–26, 1025A, although the name is given thereafter as "Phrantzes" (*ibid.*, 1031B, 1058D). For the MSS. and various editions of the *Chron. minus*, see Vasile Grecu, *Georgios Sphrantzes: Memorii (1401–1477), în anexă Pseudo-Phrantzes* (cited above, note 2), pp. XIV–XVII.

While there now appears to be no doubt that Sphrantzes wrote the memoir called *Chronicon minus* (ed. Jan Franz, in Card. Angelo Mai's *Classici auctores*, IX [Rome, 1837], 594 ff., repr. in *PG* 156, cols. 1025–80), no one any longer believes him to be the author of the *Chronicon maius* (ed. Imm. Bekker in the Bonn Corpus, 1838, repr. in *PG* 156, cols. 637–1022, the first two books being also available in the better edition of J. B. Papadopoulos, I, Leipzig: Teubner, 1935, and all four books in the [best] edition of V. Grecu, Bucharest, 1966). MSS. of the *Chron. maius* range from the late sixteenth to the eighteenth and nineteenth centuries (Papadopoulos, I, pp. X–XV). Working with the constant errors and peculiarities in the text, Papadopoulos doubted whether Sphrantzes could have been the author of the *Chron. maius*, to which one refers as the work of the "Pseudo-Sphrantzes" (or less accurately the "Pseudo-Phrantzes").

Fr. R. J. Loenertz, "Autour du Chronicon maius attribué à Georges Phrantzès," *Miscellanea G. Mercati*, III (Città del Vaticano, 1946), 273–311 (in Studi e testi, no. 123), first proved decisively that Sphrantzes could not have written the *Chronicon maius*, and makes it clear that the *Chron. maius* is the work of Macarius Melissenus, late sixteenth-century metropolitan of Monemvasia, who has become well known as a forger. Papadopoulos had already perceived the fact (*cf.* St. Binon, "L'Histoire et la légende de deux chrysobulles d'Andronic II en faveur de Monembasie: Macaire ou Phrantzès?" *Échos d'Orient*, XXXVII [1938], 274–304). The form "Phrantzes" occurs in all especially attached to Constantine. Although John Eugenicus had addressed a long and wearisome oration to Theodore in commendation of his noble decision to enter a monastery,[100] the despot yielded to the alleged entreaties of the local aristocracy, and continued his rule in Mistra. Having hitherto got on badly with his Italian wife, Cleopa Malatesta, Theodore now became reconciled with her, "and henceforth lived happily with her," according to Chalcocondylas. If the disappointed Constantine was to have lands in the Morea, they would have to be conquered for him. Theodore had already annexed most of Centurione's so-called principality to the despotate of Mistra, but Carlo Tocco still held Glarentza, the "capital of Elis," to which John VIII now laid siege again. Carlo, badly defeated in the battle of the Echinades the preceding year, decided to give up Glarentza and his other possessions in the area. A marriage was arranged between his niece, Maddalena de' Tocchi, daughter of Leonardo II of Zante, and Constantine, to whom Carlo now ceded as a dowry both Glarentza and the rest of his fortified places in the Morea (ὅσα δὴ καὶ εἶχεν εἰς τὸν Μορέαν). On 1 May, 1428, Sphrantzes occupied the castle of Glarentza in Constantine's name, and other officers were dispatched to take over the other places.[101]

At the beginning of July the three brothers encamped before Patras, whither Maddalena was brought. She married Constantine in the Greek camp amid preparations for a siege of the city, changing her name in Byzantine fashion to Theodora. (A pawn in the harsh game of politics, she died some seventeen months later.) By this time the brothers were quarreling among themselves, and Theodore was quite sure he did not want to become a monk. Working at cross purposes, they could not take Patras, a papal fief then held (as we have seen) by Archbishop Pandolfo Malatesta, Theodore's brother-in-law, but they did succeed in capturing three fortified villages (καστελλόπουλα) and exacting from the inhabitants of Patras the promise of an annual tribute of five hundred gold pieces for Constantine. The campaign was over. John VIII departed for Mistra. Constantine took his bride to Glarentza; they occupied the old Villehardouin castle of Chloumoutsi. When a little later John VIII decided to return home, Constantine joined him for some days at Mistra. Now four of the brothers were together, for Thomas was also in the Morea, and in October (1428) they all went to Corinth, where John took ship for Constantinople. Theodore then returned to Mistra; Thomas accompanied him as far as Kalavryta. Constantine went to

---

MSS. of the *Chron. maius* (more than a score are known), an error which shed some doubt on its genuineness.

The compiler of the *Chron. maius* follows Nicephorus Gregoras up to 1360 and Chalcocondylas to 1402, but sometimes repeats the latter's mistakes and even fails to understand him; according to Loenertz, the compiler also employs the sixteenth-century chronicle attributed to "Dorotheus of Monemvasia." Since Sphrantzes died about 1477–1478, he obviously did not use Dorotheus in the expansion of his memoir (*Chron. minus*) into the general Turco-Byzantine history which has passed under his name in the *Chron. maius*. In an interesting article, however, Elizabeth A. Zachariadou, "An Italian Source of the Pseudo-Dorotheus for the History of the Ottomans" [in Greek], Πελοποννησιακά, V (1962), 46–59, esp. pp. 47–48, has noted that the half-dozen passages which Loenertz, *op. cit.*, pp. 296–309, thought originated in the Pseudo-Dorotheus were actually drawn from the *Ecthesis chronica* of about 1517. Obviously Sphrantzes could not have used a work produced in or about 1517, and Miss Zachariadou's discovery only reinforces Loenertz's argument. *Cf.* also her study of *The Chronicle of the Turkish Sultans* [*Cod. Barberini graecus 111*] *and its Italian Original* [πρότυπο] [in Greek], Thessaloniki, 1960, pp. 61 ff.

Although the Pseudo-Sphrantzes or rather Macarius Melissenus, *Chronicon maius*, IV, 23 (Bonn, p. 453; ed. Grecu, p. 590), ends with the statement that old age and extreme infirmity have prevented the author from covering every aspect of his subject properly, and dates his conclusion 29 March, 1478 (A.M. 6986), he has evidently forgotten his references to the Turkish occupation of Zante and Cephalonia (in 1479), the siege of Rhodes (1480), the taking of Otranto (1480), and the death of Mehmed II in May, 1481, all this in book I, chap. 23 (Bonn, pp. 94–95; ed. Papadopoulos, I, 98; ed. Grecu, p. 234).

Melissenus was a gifted stylist, but most of his sources (when imagination did not provide them) have yet to be identified, and his work must be used with the utmost caution. Finally, as we have observed above (vol. I, chap. 13, note 206), his name was not Melissenus, but Melissurgus. He sought to glorify his family by assuming one of the more distinguished names in Byzantine history (*cf. Chron. maius*, II, 2 [Bonn, p. 132, lines 6–7, and p. 134, lines 3–4; ed. Papadopoulos, I, 134, line 11, and p. 137, lines 1–2; ed. Grecu, p. 270, lines 8–9, and p. 272, line 6, and note 1, lines 25–26]). On Macarius's family, see J. K. Casiotes, *Makarios, Theodoros and Nikephoros, the Melissenoi (Melissourgoi), 16th and 17th Centuries* [in Greek], Thessaloniki, 1966.

[100] John Eugenicus's oration πρὸς τὸν δεσπότην κῦρ Θεόδωρον τὸν Πορφυρογέννητον was published by Lampros, *Pal. kai Pel.*, I (1912), 67–111, from Eugenicus's autograph MS. in the Bibliothèque Nationale, Cod. gr. 2075, fols. 199r–226.

[101] Sphrantzes, *Chron. minus* (*PG* 156, 1033D–1034A; ed. Grecu, p. 24); Pseudo-Sphrantzes, II, 1–2 (Bonn, p. 128; ed. Papadopoulos, I, 130–31; ed. Grecu, p. 266); Chalcocondylas, bk. IV (Bonn, pp. 239–40).

Vostitza, which Theodore had ceded to him together with a number of other castles in the western part of the Morea extending all the way down south to Androusa, Nesi, and Kalamata. The faithful Sphrantzes took over the various castles in the name of his master Constantine, whose vigorous presence was soon felt everywhere in the Morea and seemed to betoken the beginning of a new era in Greek affairs.[102]

In the meantime, during June and July, 1428, Archbishop Pandolfo Malatesta had been in Venice, seeking aid for the threatened see and city of Patras. The Senate, however, which had warned the pope of the likelihood of the city's falling into the hands of either the Greeks or the Turks, was little disposed to intervene at this late and critical juncture of affairs. The Venetians declared their affection for the great house of Malatesta, for Pandolfo's father and sister. They granted him permission to purchase munitions in Venice for export to Patras, but they saw no point in sending an envoy to the Greek government in the Morea, although they held themselves ready to treat with the Greeks if the latter took the initiative.[103]

Early in March, 1429, Constantine Dragases resumed the siege of Patras, and on Palm Sunday his forces took their positions before the city gates. Some days later, after the celebration of Holy Saturday (26 March, 1429) a sudden sortie of the Patrenses from the "Jews' gate" caught the Greek commanders in idle conversation in Constantine's tent. In the skirmish which followed, Constantine had his horse shot from under him by an arrow. The attackers pressed on to kill or capture him, but Sphrantzes stood by in defense of his master until the latter could extricate himself from the fallen horse and escape on foot. Sphrantzes was himself wounded, however, and taken prisoner, losing his favorite horse in the fray. Chained and tossed into a dark dungeon in an abandoned granary, poor Sphrantzes spent a month contending with ants, weevils, and mice. At length on S. George's day (23 April), having prayed to his patron, the deliverer of captives, Sphrantzes had his chains struck off, and his jailers explained that the miserable food they had been giving him was all they had. A day or two later they asked him to communicate with Constantine about his release, and said he might make preliminary arrangements for the surrender of Patras, provided Constantine would withdraw to Glarentza and wait until the end of May. If Archbishop Pandolfo, who was seeking aid in Italy, had not returned by that time, Constantine would receive the surrender of the city. The terms were agreed upon, and Sphrantzes, more dead than alive, according to his own account, was greeted with joy and relief by Constantine, who loaded him with gifts of handsome clothes and other things. They returned to Glarentza, waiting for May to pass.[104]

---

[102] Sphrantzes, *Chron. minus* (*PG* 156, 1034; ed. Grecu, pp. 24, 26); Pseudo-Sphrantzes, II, 2 (Bonn, pp. 129–33; ed. Papadopoulos, I, 131–36; Grecu, pp. 266–270, with improvements in the text). Before his departure from the Morea John VIII confirmed the Platonic philosopher Geo. Gemistus Pletho in his possession of the manorial villages of Brysis and Phanarion by a chrysobull dated October, 1428 [A.M. 6937, of the seventh indiction] (Lampros, *Pal. kaì Pel.*, III [1926], 331–33). Pletho had been granted Phanarion by Theodore the preceding November (*ibid.*, IV [1930], 104–5), and in September, 1433, Theodore was to guarantee the succession of Pletho's sons to these properties, Demetrius Gemistus to Phanarion and Andronicus Gemistus to Brysis, at the request of their father, who is highly praised in the preamble to the document (an argyrobull, *ibid.*, IV, 106–9). For the general history of these grants, see Lampros, in the *Neos Hellenomn.*, II (1905), 457–60.

Maddalena de' Tocchi was the sister of Carlo II Tocco, despot of Arta, etc. (1429–1448), on which *cf.* the genealogical tables in Hopf, *Chron. gréco-romanes*, pp. 530, 536. Maddalena-Theodora was buried, like Cleopa Malatesta four years later, in the *Katholikon* of the monastery of the Zoodotes at Mistra, identified as the church of Hagia Sophia, which apparently served as the palace chapel. Many graves have been excavated here, but none has yielded any evidence relating either to Theodora or to Cleopa. In the narthex of the Pantanassa at Mistra there is another grave sometimes identified as that of Theodora, but again without convincing evidence.

[103] Sathas, I, nos. 119–22, pp. 188–90, from Sen. Secreta, Reg. 10, fols. 152^v–153^r, 156^v, 157^v [156^v–157^r, 160^v, 161^v], docs. dated 14 June and 9–10 July, 1428. The Venetian Senate, nevertheless, did try for a while by means of diplomacy to prevent the Greeks from taking Patras, which was of course unavailing (Iorga, *ROL*, V, 379–80, 385, 387; *cf.*, *ibid.*, VI, 67, 73). Knowing that Constantine was not to be dissuaded from his designs upon Patras, the Venetians spent little time and money on the effort.

[104] Sphrantzes, *Chron. minus* (*PG* 156, 1036, 1039; ed. Grecu, pp. 30, 32, 36 ff.); Pseudo-Sphrantzes, II, 3–4, 6 (Bonn, pp. 137–39, 144–46; ed. Papadopoulos, I, 140–42, 147–49; ed. Grecu, pp. 280 ff., 288, 290), who adds to the fine clothes which Sphrantzes received from Constantine the further gift of 3,000 gold pieces.

During this period the Palaeologi were clearly paying more attention to the conquest of territory than to the governance of their possessions in the Morea, and even a Greek magnate thought that conditions in the so-called "despotate" bodied ill for the safety of his property. By a safe-conduct issued in the name of the Doge Francesco Foscari, and dated 18 July, 1429, the Senate allowed one Manoli Magaducha to deposit all or part of his

Within a few days a messenger reached Glarentza from Sultan Murad II, forbidding Constantine to molest Patras since the city paid tribute to the Porte. Nevertheless, on 1 June (1429), since Pandolfo Malatesta had still not returned from Italy, Constantine moved against the city. At the same time his brother Thomas was besieging nearby Chalandritza, the chief stronghold left to Centurione Zaccaria. The brothers joined forces for a show of strength which helped them both to achieve their objectives, although Sphrantzes feared they might come to blows. On Sunday, 5 June, Constantine was given the keys to the city of Patras in the ancient church of S. Andrew amid the rejoicing of the populace. The streets were strewn with flowers, and there was a holiday mood as the Patrenses passed again under Greek rule for the first time since the Latin conquest in 1205. But the troops of Pandolfo Malatesta still held the citadel and the archiepiscopal palace near it, refusing to surrender. Although they shot at the merrymakers from the high battlements of the citadel, they did little damage, and on 6 June Constantine received the homage of the citizenry in the church of S. Nicholas. Sphrantzes was appointed governor of Patras.[105]

Sphrantzes had a mission to perform, however, before he could take up his new office. On 8 June he departed for Naupactus (Lepanto) on his way to Constantinople to report to the emperor on the occupation of Patras, and thence to Adrianople to explain and justify the situation to the sultan. At Naupactus he fell in with two Turkish envoys, one sent by the sultan and the other by Turakhan Beg, to warn Constantine not to take over the city of Patras. Soon Pandolfo Malatesta himself put into Naupactus on a Catalan ship, having already heard of the Greek occupation of his city. He asked Sphrantzes to delay his northward journey for a day or so in order that they might confer with each other. The Greek diplomat and the Latin archbishop sat down together, *Arcades ambo*, each trying to learn the other's intentions, with no success. Pandolfo, however, gave the Turkish envoys letters for the sultan and Turakhan Beg, as Sphrantzes knew, and the latter would not rest until he could learn their contents. He engaged the Turks in a drinking bout, and got almost as drunk as they did, but he managed to extract their letters, which he read, copied, and resealed. Thereafter Sphrantzes went on to the Byzantine capital, where he was assigned Marcus Palaeologus Iagrus as a fellow envoy to the Porte. Marcus proved less a help than a hindrance, and the two were told when they first arrived at the Ottoman court that Patras must be restored to the Latins. But the wily Sphrantzes told Ibrahim Pasha, the grand vizir, that he dared not take back such a reply to the despot; he asked that a Turkish envoy might return with him to the Morea to inform the despot of the sultan's decision. There was nothing like prolonging the matter by an exchange of embassies. In the following September (1429) Sphrantzes was on the road again, going this time to Trikkala or Larissa to see Turakhan Beg, with whom, he informs us, he "finally straightened out the business about Patras."[106]

Sphrantzes had done very well indeed, and Pandolfo Malatesta had already despaired of regaining the city. On 18 October, 1429, the Venetian Senate passed the following resolution, a brief but graphic chapter in the history of Patras:

Since the reverend father, the lord [arch]bishop of Patras, has recently proposed to our government that, if we wish, he is ready to put in our hands the castle of Patras, which is still held in his name, and to

---

movable goods in Coron because of the insecurity of conditions in the despotate (Misti, Reg. 57, fol. 107ʳ [111ʳ], apparently dated 31 May, 1429), "cum per literas viri nobilis Ser Zanoti Calbo, castellani Coroni et Mothoni, informati simus quod quidam Manoli Magaducha dictus Protostratora, subditus domini dispoti Musistre, videns malum dominium quod fit per Grecos, deliberaverit depositare in loco nostro Coroni totum aut partem sui haveris requisiveritque quod sibi fiat salvusconductus ut possit mittere ad ipsum locum nostrum vel ponere in eo suum havere vel partem ipsius. . . ."

[105] Sphrantzes, *Chron. minus* (*PG* 156, 1039D–1041B), where in col. 1040D the dates 4–5 January are an absurd error, which is corrected to 4–5 June in the better text of V. Grecu, ed., *Georgios Sphrantzes, Memorii* (1966), p. 42; Pseudo-Sphrantzes, II, 7–8 (Bonn, pp. 146–48; ed. Papadopoulos, I, 149–52; ed. Grecu, pp. 290, 292). The church of S. Nicholas, near the citadel, was destroyed in 1811 by the explosion of a powder magazine. Famous as one of the Franciscan centers in Greece, it appears often in documents relating to the Latin dominion (see Gerland, *Lateinisches Erzbistum Patras* [1903], p. 117, note 1). Sphrantzes says that he became governor of Patras in September, 1430 (*Chron. minus*, ed. Grecu, p. 50, lines 1–2).

[106] Sphrantzes, *Chron. minus* (*PG* 156, 1041B–1042C; ed. Grecu, pp. 44, 46): ". . . *καὶ τὴν περὶ τῆς* Πάτρας *δουλειὰν τελείως διώρθωσα*" (*opp. citt.*, col. 1042C; p. 46, line 32, reading *δουλειάν* for *δουλείαν*, which appears in both editions, but makes less sense); Pseudo-Sphrantzes, II, 8–9 (Bonn, pp. 150–54; ed. Papadopoulos, I, 152–56; ed. Grecu, pp. 292 ff.).

secure from the supreme pontiff [Martin V] permission to recover the city from the hands of the Greeks and to hold it under our dominion, the motion is carried that he be answered in appropriate words that it does not seem best to us, for good and proper reasons, to become involved in this affair.

There were no dissenting votes.[107]

Pandolfo's garrison was still holding the castle of Patras, which was not surrendered to Constantine until May, 1430, when its defenders had been weakened by famine and the plague.[108] Chalcocondylas says that Martin V sent ten galleys (τριήρεις) to try to regain the city. However many galleys there may have been, they were manned by Catalans, who made no attempt to retake Patras, but on 17 July (1430) seized Glarentza, which they held for a while and then sold back to Constantine, according to Chalcocondylas for 5,000 gold pieces and according to the Pseudo-Sphrantzes for 12,000. Fearing that Glarentza might again fall into Latin hands from which he should not so easily recover it, Constantine is said to have destroyed the walls of the city, famous in the annals of Frankish Greece for some historic meetings of the old high court of Achaea.[109]

In the meantime Thomas Palaeologus had besieged Chalandritza all through the summer of 1429. In September he had finally forced Prince Centurione into a settlement which assured the Palaeologi eventual possession of the sparse remains of the old Franco-Navarrese principality of Achaea. The prince had been obliged to agree to the marriage of his elder daughter Caterina to Thomas, who thus became his heir, and after the wedding was celebrated at Mistra in January, 1430,[110] nothing remained to Centurione but the empty title of prince and the barony of Arcadia (Kyparissia), the latter being an inheritance from his father. Centurione was a direct descendant of Benedetto I Zaccaria, who had married a sister of the Byzantine Emperor Michael VIII, as well as of the famous Martino Zaccaria, onetime lord of Chios, who was killed before Smyrna in January, 1345. He was the last important member of his house, but in after years his bastard son, Giovanni Asan, who was passed over in the settlement with Thomas, was briefly to reclaim the title of prince and plunge the Morea into turmoil (in 1454), as we shall have occasion in due time to note. In August, 1430, Thomas received the title of despot from his brother John VIII. Two years later Centurione died, and Thomas took over the barony of Arcadia. In March, 1432, Constantine accepted Thomas's castle town of Kalavryta in exchange for Glarentza, where Thomas now took up his residence with Caterina. If Constantine had destroyed the city walls, as the Pseudo-Sphrantzes says, Thomas may now have restored them. It was about this time also that the Teutonic Knights lost their important fief of Mostenitza and its dependent lands to the Greeks.[111] The Venetians still held Modon and Coron, Argos and Nauplia. The rest of the Morea belonged to the Palaeologi. Theodore II, Constantine, and Thomas shared somewhat uneasily the broad lands and bright honors of the despotate. They had won out in the long struggle with the Latins, but what would be the issue of their struggle with the Turks? Here their natural ally might have been the Venetians, with whom they did not get along very well, as we have observed, despite the fact there was little real conflict of interest between the Venetians and the Greek despots. Their failure to co-operate had proved costly to them both, and the worst was yet to come.

The stately registers of the Senato Secreti,

---

[107] Sathas, I, no. 124, p. 191; Valentini, *Acta Albaniae veneta*, XIII, no. 3,277, pp. 198–99, from Sen. Secreta, Reg. 11, fol. 40ᵛ [41ᵛ].

[108] Sphrantzes, *Chron. minus* (*PG* 156, 1043A; ed. Grecu, p. 48); Pseudo-Sphrantzes, II, 9 (Bonn, p. 156; ed. Papadopoulos, I, 157–58; ed. Grecu, p. 298); Chalcocondylas, bk. v (Bonn, pp. 240–41). The mid-fifteenth century Byzantine rhetorician John Docianus (Δοκειανός) lauds the acquisition of Patras in an encomium of Constantine (Hopf, *Chron. gréco-romanes*, p. 251; Lampros, *Pal. kaì Pel.*, I, 228).

[109] Chalcocondylas, bk. v (Bonn, p. 241); Sphrantzes, *Chron. minus* (*PG* 156, 1043A; ed. Grecu, p. 48); Pseudo-Sphrantzes, II, 9 (Bonn, p. 156; ed. Papadopoulos, I, 158; ed. Grecu, p. 298). *Cf.* Hopf, in Ersch and Gruber, *Encykl.*, vol. 86 (repr. II), p. 85; Gerland, *Latein. Erzbistum Patras*, pp. 66–67; Miller, *Latins in the Levant*, pp. 388–91; Zakythinos, *Despotat grec de Morée*, I, 207–9. In December, 1430, an ambassador of Constantine was in Venice to effect some kind of rapprochement with the Signoria, but the brief entry in the Misti, Reg. 58, fol. 18ᵛ, sheds little light on his mission. Archbishop Pandolfo Malatesta died on 17 April, 1441, in his native Pesaro, where he was buried (*Cronaca riminese*, in L. A. Muratori, ed., *RISS*, XV [Milan, 1729], col. 939C).

[110] Sphrantzes, *Chron. minus* (*PG* 156, 1042C; ed. Grecu, p. 48, lines 5–7).

[111] Sphrantzes, *Chron. minus* (*PG* 156, 1043B; ed. Grecu, p. 48, lines 34–35); Pseudo-Sphrantzes, II, 9 (Bonn, pp. 154, 156; ed. Papadopoulos, I, 156, 158; ed. Grecu, pp. 296, 298, 300); Chalcocondylas, bk. v (Bonn, p. 242); Hopf, II, 86, and on the family relationships of Centurione Zaccaria, *Chron. gréco-romanes*, geneal. tables, pp. 471, 502, 536; Zakythinos, *Despotat grec de Morée*, I, 210.

Misti (to 1440), and Mar in the Venetian State Archives are full of letters to the harassed castellans of Modon and Coron throughout the fifteenth century. The distance between the two stations was only about fifteen miles, some five hours' ride for a mounted troop. Although undoubtedly more heavily wooded in those days than today, the road ran over barren hills. It was a lonely route, and danger kept pace with every step of those who took it. The Greeks attacked Venetian territory quite often; Turkish raids were less frequent but, when they came, were more severe. Expensive gifts to Turakhan Beg seemed about the only means of preventing such raids. The Venetians were themselves doubtless not without some responsibility for their troubles with the Greeks. On one occasion an envoy of the Despot Theodore complained to the Senate that the castellans of Modon and Coron confiscated the money and goods of his subjects for the pettiest thefts. If a Moreote Albanian or Greek subject of the despot stole an ass, a pack animal, or a horse, the castellans should seek proper redress of the grievance. In such a case there was no reason to confiscate the property of other subjects of the despot. The complaint probably sounds more reasonable to us than it did to the Venetians. The machinery of justice moved very slowly then (especially Theodore's justice), and reprisal was almost universally employed as the only effective means of recovering the value of stolen goods and discouraging the repetition of such assaults upon the property (and the persons) of one's own citizens and subjects. In the present instance, however, the Venetian Senate agreed with the despot's remonstrance, and directed the castellans to cease such retaliation and request satisfaction of the despot's government, at least so long as he maintained a neighborly attitude in more important respects.[112]

Past policy had doubtless been based upon the difficulty of recovering either stolen property or its value by any due process of law at the despot's court. The castellans of Modon and Coron obviously believed that only reprisals would encourage the officials at Mistra to exercise sufficient surveillance over their unruly subjects to see that such infractions of the peace did not occur in the first place, and yet justice would have obliged every informed Venetian to agree that such surveillance was almost impossible along lonely roads, in secluded valleys, and on mountain passes in various parts of the Morea. There is a self-righteous tone to many Venetian documents (common to the style of every chancery whose registers might be opened for inspection), but the Venetians unquestionably did make better neighbors than the despot's Greeks and Albanians. By and large the Venetians had a good record throughout the Levant. On 18–20 June, 1427, for example, the Senate finally rejected on the second ballot, by a vote of forty-seven to forty, the petition of one Alvise Michiel to embark upon a career of semi-privateering against the Turks and other enemies of the Republic.[113] Under the circumstances one might well have expected an affirmative vote on Michiel's proposal.

---

[112] Misti, Reg. 57, fol. 133^r [137^r], "MCCCCXXVIIII, die XIIII Iulii:" ". . . Vadit pars quod ipsis nostris castellanis [Mothoni et Coroni] scribatur in hac forma: . . . quia . . . orator [domini dispoti Amoree] nobis exposuit quod pro omni levi re, viz., si occurrit quod per suos surripiatur de territorio nostro unus asinus sive sommerius aut unus equus et similia, vos ad requisitionem damnificati sequestrari facitis denarios subditorum ipsius domini qui reperiuntur esse in manibus subditorum nostrorum locorum vobis commissorum cum magno interesse et damno eorum quorum sunt denarii taliter sequestrati super quo amicabiliter et instanter per nos provideri requisivit cum dispositio domini sui sit quod novitates predicte cessent omnino. Volumus vobisque mandamus quod faciente ipso domino bonam vicinantiam et bonum tractamentum locis et subditis nostris, ut dictum est, vos abstineatis pro huiusmodi causis levibus surreptionis unius asini vel unius equi et similium ipsos sequestros de cetero facere, sed debeatis amicabiliter requirere satisfactionem damni, quam si obtinere non poteritis, tunc damna passo provideatis et subveniatis per viam iuris uti noveritis iustum esse. . . ." The despot's envoy appeared before the Senate 14–16 July, 1429. There is a misleading French summary of this document in Iorga, *ROL*, VI, 59–60, and *Notes et extraits*, I, 497–98: "Les volés devraient tout d' abord demander satisfaction. Le sénat décide de délibérer sur ce point, qu' il approuve en principe (*volvatur*)." The document makes it clear that it was the castellans who were to request satisfaction of the Greek government in the Morea, not "les volés;" the Senate reached a definite decision; and *volvatur* means to turn the page, the resolution being continued on fol. 133^v [137^v]! There are some hasty summaries of documents in Iorga's articles in the *ROL* and in the *Notes et extraits*, but on the whole one can only admire both his industry and his accuracy.

[113] Misti, Reg. 56, fols. 103^v–104^r [105^v–106^r], and *cf.* Iorga, *ROL*, V, 360; *Notes et extraits*, I, 460; Thiriet, *Régestes*, II, no. 2058, p. 243. Michiel proposed to arm a government galley at his own expense: ". . . mi offerisso de armar una galia a tute mie spexe a danno e destruxion de Moratbei [Murad II], turcho inimigo de la vostra Signoria e de chi altri la vostra Signoria mi commitexe. . . ." The vote on the second ballot was: *De parte* 40, *de non* 47, *non sinceri* 4.

It was the Turks who created the major problem which Venice faced in the Levant. As long as the Porte remained a great military force, neither Venice, the papacy, nor any other western power ever found an answer to the "eastern question." The chief historical irony of Levantine history in more modern times is of course that the eastern question remained to harass the chancelleries of Europe (and Russia) when Turkish military might declined so markedly in the eighteenth century, and the Christian statesmen who had been so exercised for centuries to destroy the Ottoman empire now schemed to keep it alive, lest their competitors move into the important areas which the Turks could easily have been made to vacate. But this is a subject which lies quite beyond the scope of this work; we deal with a period of ever-increasing Turkish strength when not only the Balkan but even the Italian peninsula itself was in danger of invasion. Turkish attacks upon Venetian territories are too numerous to mention, especially upon the Republic's outposts in Albania. No Venetian stronghold in the Levant was secure from such attacks. On 22 April, 1428, for example, an armed brigantine arrived in Venice from Modon with news of a great Turkish naval assault upon Negroponte. The Turkish fleet was large, variously reported as containing from forty to sixty-five galleys and *fuste*. Some seven hundred Venetian subjects were said to have been captured and carried off into slavery. The torch had been set to vineyards and olive groves, causing severe losses. The Turks disembarked next at Coron and Modon, where they repeated the horrors of their earlier visitation at Negroponte. Now they were said to be offshore at Glarentza, preparing to do even worse on their return voyage. This was all part of Sultan Murad's repayment to Venice for the attempted occupation of Thessalonica. According to Sanudo, fifteen galleys were armed in the arsenal at Venice, and immediately dispatched "to go and find the said Turkish armada."[114]

In the treaties which Venice had made at Adrianople with Mehmed I in November, 1419, and thereafter with Murad II in September, 1430, she had included Giovanni II Crispo, duke of Naxos, and his brothers, who held certain fiefs in the "Archipelago" (*Egeopelagus*).[115] Although in these treaties the sultans had recognized the independence of the Crispi as subjects of Venice (*in la obediencia de Veniexia*), and exempted them from "tribute and servitude," fear of the Turk was vastly increased after the fall of Thessalonica. Already in July, 1426, when the Venetians were hard pressed in the Thermaic Gulf, the Senate had voted to allow Giovanni (and his brother Niccolò) to effect a "concord with the Turks as best he can for the preservation of his state, provided he does not bind himself to give them shelter, neither to their ships nor to their forces. . . ." Pietro Zeno, lord of Andros, was granted the same consideration with the same proviso.[116]

Giovanni hastened to make peace with Murad, after which he abandoned the practice he had hitherto pursued of lighting beacons (*quedam signalia cum igne*) to warn the Venetian authorities on Negroponte every time Turkish galleys or fuste were sighted off the shores of his island duchy. Presently he was assisting the Turks in one way or another (what else could he do?) "to the loss of our subjects on the aforesaid island." On 3 March, 1430, six months before the Venetian peace with Murad, the Senate voted to write Giovanni, demanding that he stop thus aiding and abetting the Turks in their attacks upon Negroponte. Indeed, if he wished to preserve his "neighborliness and fraternity" with Venice, he must resume the

---

[114] Sanudo, *Vite de' duchi*, in *RISS*, XXII (1733), col. 999DE, whose account differs slightly from the contemporary reports noted in Iorga, *ROL*, V, 371, note 1. The Turkish attack left its impress upon the Venetian documents also (Misti, Reg. 56, fol. 182^r [184^r], "MCCCCXXVIII, die XXII Aprilis in consilio C."): "Cum propter nova que nuper habentur de potenti armata Turchi, que nuper descendit ad partes insule Nigropontis, pro defensione et conservatione dicte insule et civitatis nostre Salonichi et aliarum terrarum et locorum nostrorum Levantis et pro aliis agendis nostris neccessarium sit prestissime providere de sufficienti armata pro honore nostri dominii et pro bona executione agendorum nostrorum, vadit pars . . ." [etc.], provision being made for the election of a captain-general of the sea and two *supracomiti ad Culphum*, while the colonial government of Crete was to be directed to elect two more *supracomiti* and send them with two galleys to Negroponte. The date of this document and Sanudo's date for the arrival of the brigantine from Modon with the news of the Turkish attack are the same (22 April, 1428). *Cf.* Iorga, *ROL*, V, 371; *Notes et extraits*, I, 471; Thiriet, *Régestes*, II, no. 2084, p. 248.

[115] Thomas and Predelli, *Dipl. veneto-levantinum*, II, nos. 172, 182, pp. 319, 345; Predelli, *Regesti dei Commemoriali*, IV, bk. XI, no. 25, p. 16, and bk. XII, no. 140, p. 164.

[116] Sathas, I, no. 116, p. 179; Thiriet, *Régestes*, II, no. 2026, p. 236. When Giovanni Crispo's only galley burned, the Senate replaced it with another, requiring him to pay for it over a period of five years (Sathas, III, no. 890, p. 304).

wholesome practice of lighting the beacons to warn of the approach of the Turks.[117] But he doubtless did not dare to do so, and as no more warning fires were lighted along his shores, the lights burned longer into the night in the ducal palace in Venice, where the Senate gathered almost daily to decide upon their next move against the Turks.

In the meantime the Moreote Greeks had been faring less well than the Venetians in Negroponte. The ambitions of the Palaeologi in the distant peninsula had excited, for some years, the hostile attention of the pashas who gathered at the sultan's palace set amid the poplar trees at Adrianople. Eight years after the erection of the Hexamilion, the Turkish warrior Turakhan Beg, son of the well-known pasha Yigit Beg, had destroyed it on 21–22 May, 1423, after which he made the terrible raid into the Morea to which we have already alluded. He ravaged the land, and attacked the cities of Mistra, Leondari, Gardiki, and Tabia.[118] This was Turakhan Beg's first appearance in history.[119] The Hexamilion was partially rebuilt, but he came back in 1431, demolishing it again.[120] Thenceforth, for almost four centuries the presence of the Turk was to be the dominant political fact in the Morea. For another thirty years the Greeks were to exercise some effort, to be sure, to maintain the semblance if not the substance of independence, and indeed under Constantine Dragases Palaeologus they were to make more than one effort to throw off fear of the Turk and even seek to extend their dominion northward into continental Greece. The advantage lay increasingly with the Turks, however, as their pace of conquest quickened, and success was in almost constant attendance upon their arms.

---

[117] Misti, Reg. 57, fol. 200ᵛ [204ᵛ]; Sathas, III, no. 960, p. 372; Valentini, *Acta Albaniae veneta*, XIV, no. 3,330, p. 43; Thiriet, *Régestes*, II, no. 2184, p. 271.

[118] An undated Venetian report of late May or early June, 1423, fixes the date of Turakhan Beg's assault upon the Hexamilion (Iorga, *ROL*, V, 136; *Notes et extraits*, I, 335): ". . . videlicet quod die XXI mensis Maii exercitus Teucrorum, cuius est capitaneus quidam Turacham-bey, cum decem M. equitibus, se presentavit ad muros Eximilii et repertis illis destitutis omni custodia et defensione . . . dicti Teucri sine aliquo strepitu intraverunt, incipientes statim ruinare et destruere dictos muros . . . ," etc. Tabia (or Dabia) had already been sacked five years before by the Navarrese under Prince Centurione Zaccaria in the war with the Palaeologi (*Chron. breve*, ad ann. 6926 [1418], appended to Ducas, *Hist. byzantina* [Bonn, p. 517]). On the history of Tabia, note Sp. P. Lampros, in the *Byz. Zeitschr.*, VII (1898), 311–15, and in Greek in Lampros' Μικταὶ Σελίδες, Athens, 1905, pp. 448–56.

Although Sphrantzes, *Chron. minus* (*PG* 156, 1030BC; ed. Grecu, p. 16), gives only a brief notice of the destruction of the Hexamilion, he says that "Turakhan . . . killed many of the Albanitae;" Chalcocondylas, bk. v (Bonn, pp. 238–39; ed. Darkó, II-1, 16–17), also describes Turakhan's defeat of the Albanians who attacked him as he was withdrawing from the Morea. *Cf.* Pseudo-Sphrantzes, I, 31 [40] (Bonn, pp. 117–18; ed. Papadopoulos, I, 121; ed. Grecu, p. 256) and *Chron. breve*, ad ann. 6931 [1423] (Bonn, p. 518), which dates the defeat of the Albanians on 5 June. Sanudo, *Vite de' duchi*, in *RISS*, XXII, cols. 970B, 975B, 978E, says that from the year 1424 the Byzantine government paid the Porte an annual tribute of 100,000 hyperpyri for the Morea. There seems to be a reference to Turakhan's razzia in J. A. C. Buchon, *Nouvelles Recherches historiques*, II (Paris, 1845), *Florence*: doc. LIV, p. 272, and see R. J. Loenertz, "La Chronique brève moréote de 1423," *Mélanges Eugène Tisserant*, II (Città del Vaticano, 1964), 434–35 (Studi e testi, no. 232).

[119] *Cf.* Franz Babinger, "Turakhān-Beg," in the *Encyclopaedia of Islām*, IV (1924–34), 876–78. Turakhan Beg is now known to have been the son of the pasha Yigit Beg, who captured Üsküb (Skoplje) in January, 1392, apparently while he was governor of part of Bosnia; the grand vizir Ishak Beg was also a son of Yigit Beg, and so the brother of Turakhan. *Cf.* Gliša Elezović, *Turski spomenici u Skoplju* [*Turkish Remains in Skoplje*], Skoplje, 1927 (cited by Babinger), and N. Iorga, *Gesch. d. osman. Reiches*, I (1908), 382–83.

[120] Chalcocondylas, bk. VI (Bonn, p. 283), and *cf.* Iorga, *Gesch. d. osman. Reiches*, I, 409; Pseudo-Sphrantzes, II, 9 (Bonn, p. 157, lines 18–20; ed. Papadopoulos, I, 159, lines 9–12; ed. Grecu, p. 300, lines 25–27), who refers to the plague in Patras, which the *Chron. breve*, ad ann. 6939 [1431] (Bonn, p. 518), identifies as the ninth pestilence since the Black Death in 1348, there having been visitations of the plague in 1348, 1361–2, 1373–4, 1381–2, 1391–2, 1398–9, 1409–10, 1417–8, 1422–3, and 1431, all in the Morea (*cf.* Sp. P. Lampros and K. I. Amantos, eds., Βραχέα Χρονικά, Athens, 1932–33, pp. 36, 46–47, and esp. Loenertz, "La Chronique brève moréote," *Mélanges Eugène Tisserant*, II, 415–36).

2. MARTIN V AND EUGENIUS IV, CONSTANCE AND FERRARA-FLORENCE, OPPOSITION TO MURAD II

ON MONDAY, 5 NOVEMBER, 1414, the Council of Constance opened with a procession and a solemn high mass in the cathedral overlooking the western shores of the Bodensee. Its purpose was to end forty years of schismatic strife, effect the suppression of heresy, and bring about reform of the Church "in head and members." Quite as notable as the Fourth Lateran Council of 1215, it was an assembly of momentous importance. After three years of work and wrangling, setting aside the three competing popes (John XXIII, Gregory XII, and Benedict XIII) and suppressing some of the hostilities which divided them, twenty-three cardinals and the thirty "co-electors" representing the five "nations" at Constance entered the conclave in the Kaufhaus or Merchants' Hall during the evening of 8 November, 1417. In the early morning hours of the eleventh (it was S. Martin's day) Oddone Colonna, cardinal deacon of S. Giorgio in Velabro, emerged as pope. He took the name Martin V.[1]

Leaving Constance in May, 1418, Martin spent some time in Geneva, Milan, Mantua, Ferrara, and finally in Florence, where the hostility of Braccio da Montone, a soldier of fortune who was all-powerful in Umbria, obliged him to remain for almost two years. Until he made a short-lived peace with Braccio, and the Neapolitan troops of Joanna II had been cleared out of Rome, Martin had to delay his return to the city. He finally made a memorable entrance into Rome at the end of September, 1420. As he began the decade of his rule and residence in and about Rome (he died on 20 February, 1431), Martin had too many Italian and European problems to worry about, to allow him much time or money for the affairs of the East. Few popes have begun their reigns with so much to do and with so many obstacles in the way. The years at Avignon and the Great Schism had wrought havoc both in the Church and in Rome. Martin had to begin rebuilding a city from the lawless shambles into which Rome had declined, restoring the dilapidated and impoverished churches, reforming the College of Cardinals and attending to the local clergy, regaining the recognition of papal suzerainty in the states of

---

[1] Martin V described his election, which took place "hora quasi decima" (between three and four A.M. in November), in a letter to the officials and citizens of Viterbo and Corneto (Augustin Theiner, ed., *Codex diplomaticus dominii temporalis Sanctae Sedis*, 3 vols., Rome, 1861–62, repr. Frankfurt am Main, 1964, III, doc. no. CLII, pp. 219–20, dated 11 November, and *cf.* Ludwig von Pastor, *Geschichte der Päpste*, I [repr. Freiburg im Breisgau, 1955], 219, note). The chief collections of sources for the Council of Constance are those of Hermann von der Hardt, ed., *Magnum oecumenicum Constantiense concilium* [with alterations of title in successive volumes], 6 vols., Frankfurt and Leipzig, 1697–1700, with a seventh (index) volume by Georg C. Bohnstedt, Berlin, 1742; J. D. Mansi, ed., *Sacrorum conciliorum nova et amplissima collectio*, vols. XXVII–XXVIII (Venice, 1784–85, repr. Paris, 1903); and Heinrich Finke, ed., *Acta concilii Constanciensis*, 4 vols., Münster in W., 1896–1928.

On the history and background of the Council, see especially H. Finke, *Forschungen und Quellen zur Geschichte des Konstanzer Konzils*, Paderborn, 1889; Chas.-Jos. Hefele, Jos. Hergenroether, H. Leclercq, *et al.*, *Histoire des conciles d'après les documents originaux*, 11 vols. in 21 parts, Paris, 1907–1952, VII, pt. 1 (1916), whose treatment of Constance is largely concerned with the condemnation of the heretical doctrines of John Wyclif and the executions of John Hus and Jerome of Prague, with almost no attention to the Greek missions to Constance (*op. cit.*, pp. 215, 504–5); Noël Valois, *La France et le Grand Schisme d'Occident*, 4 vols., Paris, 1896–1902, repr. Hildesheim, 1967, IV, 262–436, who also has little interest in the Greeks at Constance; August Franzen and Wolfgang Müller, eds., *Das Konzil von Konstanz: Beiträge zu seiner Geschichte und Theologie*, Freiburg im Breisgau, 1964; and Theodor Mayer, ed., *Die Welt zur Zeit des Konstanzer Konzils*, Constance and Stuttgart, 1965 (in the Vorträge und Forschungen des Konstanzer Arbeitskreises für mittelalterliche Geschichte, vol. IX). On Martin V's election, note K. A. Fink in Franzen and Müller, *Konzil v. Konstanz*, pp. 138–51; on the expenses incurred at his election and coronation and during the first months of his pontificate, see Fink, "Zum Finanzwesen des Konstanzer Konzils," in the *Festschrift für Hermann Heimpel*, II (Göttingen, 1972), 727–51. Selections from three important literary sources relating to the Council have been translated into English by the late Louise Ropes Loomis, *The Council of Constance*, eds. J. H. Mundy and K. M. Woody, New York and London, 1961 (Records of Civilization, Columbia University, no. LXIII)—i.e., selections from the *Chronicle* of Ulrich von Richental, a burgher of Constance, the diary of Cardinal Guillaume Fillastre, and the "journal" of Jacopo Cerretano. A summary of Cerretano's journal is now available in P. Glorieux, *Le Concile de Constance au jour le jour*, Tournai, 1964. The texts of the most important decrees and canons of the Council [and in fact of all twenty-one oecumenical councils from Nicaea in 325 to the Second Vatican Council in 1962–1965] may be found in the *Conciliorum oecumenicorum decreta*, eds. Jos. Alberigo *et al.*, 3rd ed., Bologna, 1973, pp. 403–51.

the Church, and frustrating the conciliarists at the Council of Pavia-Siena (1423–1424).[2] It was necessary to combat the anti-papal sentiment and legislation in Aragon-Catalonia, France, England, Germany, and elsewhere, the pope's severest struggles being with King Alfonso V of Aragon and Count Jean d'Armagnac. Even if the pope had not had so much to do in Italy, Europe was in no position and no mood to support an anti-Turkish crusade. The English were fighting the French, the Spaniards were fighting the Moors, and the Germans were fighting the Hussites.

A Byzantine mission to the Council of Constance, headed by the influential diplomat Nicholas Eudaimonoïoannes, had been present at Constance since March, 1416.[3] The Greeks had declined, however, to discuss church union until schism had been eliminated from the Latin Church. It has indeed been suggested that to some extent Martin V owed his election to the Greeks, who did not conceal their impatience with the slow pace of the conciliar proceedings. Martin was especially taken with the unionist assurances of Eudaimonoïoannes, and on 6 April, 1418, before the dissolution of the Council, he had written the six sons of the Emperor Manuel II, expressing the bitterness of heart which the devastation of the Greek world had caused him, and granting each of the princes the right of marrying (should any choose to do so) women of the Latin faith, provided the latter were allowed to remain in full possession of their faith and in obedience to the "sancta Romana et universalis Ecclesia."[4]

---

[2] Theiner, *Codex diplomaticus*, III, nos. CLIII–CCXLVI, pp. 220–301, publishes more than ninety documents relating to the pope's problems in Italy. On the struggle to reassert papal control over the cities of Rome and Bologna, the March of Ancona, Umbria and the Romagna, the Patrimonium S. Petri in Tuscia, and the duchy of Spoleto, especially against the enterprising condottiere Braccio da Montone, see Peter Partner, *The Papal State under Martin V: The Administration and Government of the Temporal Power in the Early Fifteenth Century*, London, 1958, esp. pp. 42–94, and on the background of events in the first two decades of the century, note Karl Dieterle, "Die Stellung Neapels und der grossen italienischen Kommunen zum Konstanzer Konzil," *Römische Quartalschrift*, XXIX (1915), 3–21, 45–72 (with some attention to the Turkish peril, pp. 56–58), whose study seems to be unfinished. For Martin's correspondence from 1418 (or rather almost entirely from 1421) to 1430, see K. A. Fink, "Die politische Korrespondenz Martins V. nach den Brevenregistern," *Quellen und Forschungen aus italienischen Archiven und Bibliotheken*, XXVI (1935–36), 172–244. On the Council of Pavia-Siena, see Hefele and Leclercq, *Hist. des conciles*, VII-1 (1916), 610–45; Noël Valois, *Le Pape et le concile*, 2 vols., Paris, 1909, I, 1–93; and especially Walter Brandmüller, *Das Konzil von Pavia-Siena, 1423–1424*, 2 vols., Münster, 1968–74, of which the second volume contains the (Latin) texts of conciliar decrees, papal letters, sermons, and the "protocol" or proceedings of the Council by Guillermo Agramunt.

After another break with Martin V, Braccio da Montone lost the bloody battle of L'Aquila (on 2 June, 1424), was severely wounded, and died on 5 June (see the detailed study of Roberto Valentini, "Lo Stato di Braccio e la guerra aquilana nella politica di Martino V [1421–1424]," *Archivio della R. Società romana di storia patria*, LII [1929], 223–379, with thirty-four documents from the Vatican Archives, and *cf.* Partner, *op. cit.*, pp. 74–79). Martin was thus rid of his most obstreperous enemy in Italy. The defense of L'Aquila against Braccio was celebrated in a vernacular epic, written shortly after his death (ed. R. Valentini, *Cantari sulla guerra aquilana di Braccio, di anonimo contemporaneo*, Fonti per la Storia d'Italia, Rome, 1935), in which he and his followers were assailed as "worse than the Saracens," *myno che Sarracyny* (*ibid.*, Cant. VII, 15, p. 136). Martin V is very sympathetically presented as fighting for the liberty of the Aquilani as well as for the freedom of the Church (e.g., *ibid.*, Cant. V, 35 ff., pp. 105 ff.). Florence, under the Albizzi, generally resisted Martin's efforts.

[3] Before the opening of the Council, John XXIII was said to be eager to see every effort expended to effect the union of the churches. He also hoped to see a crusade organized when the Council had done its work, in which connection King Sigismund wrote Henry IV of England some time after 12 March, 1412, "[speravimus] quod ecclesia Greca reconsiliaretur et reuniretur Romane ecclesie sacrosancte, quoniam et sanctissimus dominus noster dominus Johannes papa vicesimus tertius libenter videret quod passagium fieret ad terram sanctam post concilii celebrationem" (Finke, *Acta concilii Constanciensis*, I [1896], 91).

The University of Paris wanted the Greeks to send "solempnes ambasiatores" to the Council, to which John XXIII readily agreed (*Acta*, I, 156), and for which Sigismund constantly pressed, because ecclesiastical union was going to be the prelude to a great crusade (*ibid.*, I, 233–37, 391–401)—"eo ferventiores etiam ceteri principes catholici redderentur," as Sigismund wrote the Emperor Manuel II in May or June, 1411, "ad succurrendum vobis eoque libentius et cum maiori sinceritatis zelo contra Turcos vos utique adiuvarent" (I, 394). Although a crusade would be almost impossible without the co-operation of Venice, Sigismund's hatred of the Republic was such that in the spring of 1412 he offered Manuel his assistance to enable the Greeks to recover Modon and Coron (I, 398). Quite clearly, whatever result the *negotium unionis* might achieve, it was not going to be a crusade. If the enmity between Venice and Sigismund was not enough to prevent the launching of an anti-Turkish expedition, the renewal of warfare between France and England (in 1415) certainly was.

[4] Georg Hofmann, ed., *Epistolae pontificiae ad Concilium Florentinum spectantes*, 3 pts., Rome, 1940–46, I, doc. no. 2, pp. 4–5 (Concilium Florentinum, Documenta et scriptores, ser. A, vol. I); Raynaldus, *Ann. eccl.*, ad ann. 1418, no. 17, vol. XVIII (Cologne, 1694), pp. 10–11: "Martinus, etc., dilectis filiis nobilibus viris, Ioanni, Theodoro, Andronico, Constantino, Demetrio, et Thomae, filiis carissimi in Christo filii Manuelis imperatoris Constantinopolitani illustris, salutem," etc.

And thus the way was prepared for the unhappy marriages of Sophia of Montferrat to John VIII and of Cleopa Malatesta to Theodore II, the despot of Mistra.

The Greek envoys to Constance may have received insufficiently precise instructions. Very likely, however, they went beyond the terms of their commission. They clearly created the impression that, when the western schism had ended, the larger division of Christendom would also cease. When the integrity of the Holy See had been restored, the Byzantine Church would submit to the papacy. The delegates of the University of Cologne wrote home from Constance in late March, 1416, that

> the ambassadors of Manuel, the emperor of Constantinople, have just arrived here, dilating on the distress which [the Greeks] are suffering at the hands of the Turks and seeking the assistance of Christ's faithful, giving [us all] the assurance that with the mediation of our king [Sigismund] it may well come about that the Greeks themselves will conform to the Roman Church in their rites and articles of faith.[5]

Although the Greeks had always insisted upon the acceptance of church union by an oecumenical council, officials at the Curia remained hopeful of progress, as negotiations with Constantinople continued during 1419 and 1420. According to Sylvester Syropoulos, Martin V granted the crusading indulgence to Latin Catholics who would go into the Morea and by force of arms defend the Hexamilion against the Turks. He also says that no Latins chose to do so.[6]

At the same time, perhaps, Pope Martin addressed an encyclical to all grades of the Catholic clergy (from Florence on 12 July, 1420), extolling the crusade against the Turks and depicting its spiritual rewards, for the especial benefit of Sigismund, king of the Romans and of Hungary, Bohemia, Dalmatia, and Croatia.[7] The following month, on 21 August, he notified the archbishops and clergy of the three German electoral provinces of Cologne, Mainz, and Trier that he had appointed Pedro Fonseca, the Portuguese cardinal deacon of S. Angelo, as papal legate to Byzantium. The Emperor Manuel and the Patriarch Joseph II had requested the legation. Declaring that the papal treasury was empty, Martin assessed each of the three provinces 6,000 gold florins for the expenses of Fonseca's mission, "pro reductione Grecorum . . . ad unitatem et obedientiam . . . Romane Ecclesie."[8]

(Martin's letter names the six imperial brothers in the order of their birth.) Martin was also attentive to Polish, Russian, and Lithuanian affairs (*ibid.*, nos. 18–20, pp. 11–12, and *cf.* O. Halecki, "La Pologne et l'empire byzantin," *Byzantion*, VII [1932], 52–54). On the Byzantine missions to the Council of Constance, note also Franz Dölger and Peter Wirth, eds., *Regesten der Kaiserurkunden des oströmischen Reiches*, pt. 5 (Munich and Berlin, 1965), esp. nos. 3345, 3354–55, 3369, 3372, 3374, pp. 100 ff.

[5] Edm. Martène and Urs. Durand, eds., *Thesaurus novus anecdotorum*, II (Paris, 1717, repr. New York, 1968), col. 1661. The letter is dated "on the morrow of the Annunciation of the Blessed Mary" [25 March, 1416].

[6] Vitalien Laurent, ed. and trans., *Les "Mémoires" du Grand Ecclésiarque de l'Église de Constantinople Sylvestre Syropoulos sur le concile de Florence (1438–1439)*, Rome, 1971, sect. II, chaps. 5–6, pp. 104, 106, 108 (Conc. Florentinum, Documenta et scriptores, ser. B, vol. IX). Laurent's long-awaited edition of Syropoulus, needless to say, renders obsolete the work of Robert Creyghton, ed. and trans., *Vera historia unionis non verae inter graecos et latinos sive Concilii Florentini exactissima narratio, graecè scripta per Sylvestrum Sguropulum* . . . , The Hague, 1660.

[7] Raynaldus, *Ann. eccl.*, ad ann. 1420, no. 26, vol. XVIII, pp. 30–31, "datum Florentie, IV Idus Iulii, [pontificatus nostri] anno III." On 6 March, 1418, the Venetians had sent an embassy to the newly elected pope at Constance to encourage his efforts to make peace between them and the Emperor Sigismund and to inform his Holiness in some detail of the Republic's needs and expectations in Greece, Dalmatia, and elsewhere (Ljubić, *Listine*, VII [1882], 243–55, 257, 258–59, 265–66, 268 ff.).

[8] Arch. Segr. Vaticano, Reg. Vat. 353 [*Martinus V de Curia, anno III–IV, liber III*], fols. 19^r, 21^r, and *cf.* fols. 21^r–22^r, partially given in Raynaldus, *Ann. eccl.*, ad ann. 1420, nos. 27–29, vol. XVIII (1694), pp. 31–32, "datum Florentie XII Kal. Septembris, pontificatus nostri anno III," and now published in full by Hofmann, *Epistolae pontificiae ad Concilium Florentinum spectantes* [hereafter cited as *Epistolae pontificiae*], pt. 1, nos. 11–13, pp. 7–10. The diocese of Liége was also assessed 4,000 florins to help pay for Fonseca's proposed mission to Constantinople (*ibid.*, pt. 1, no. 14, p. 11). An interesting register in the Vatican Archives (Reg. Vat. 347), containing selections from the correspondence of several popes (especially of Urban VI) gives a list of all the cardinals as of late November, 1420 (fol. 1^r, unnumbered), the name of "Petrus Sancti Angeli" being scratched out with the notation "mortuus" when he died at Vicovaro on 21 August, 1422. Pedro Fonseca had been made a cardinal by Benedict XIII on 14 December, 1412 (Conrad Eubel, *Hierarchia catholica medii aevi*, I [1913, repr. 1960], 30, and II, 5).

Fonseca's appointment to the Byzantine legation is dated 27 March, 1420 (Eubel, II, 5, note 11). Relevant letters of Martin V are to be found in Reg. Vat. 353, fols. 9^r–11^v, 23^r–24^r, addressed: "Dilecto filio Petro Sancti Angeli diacono Sancte Romane Ecclesie cardinali in Constantinopolitano imperio et nonnullis aliis partibus apostolice sedis legato." The first is dated at Florence on 10 April, 1420 ("datum Florentie IIII Idus Aprilis, pontificatus nostri anno tertio"), and the second on 26 August, 1420 ("datum Florentie VII Kal. Septembris, pont. nostri anno tertio"). Martin was much more concerned, however, about the affairs of Pedro de Luna "contra prefatum perdicionis

During the great Turkish peril in the summer of 1422, when Sultan Murad II laid siege to Constantinople, the Curia Romana bestirred itself on the Greeks' behalf. Pope Martin V wrote the Emperor Manuel from Rome on 8 October (1422) that he had addressed appeals to the Hospitallers, Venetians, Genoese, and Duke Filippo Maria Visconti of Milan to send aid to the beleaguered city, indicating also that the surest road to safety from the Turks as well as from the dangers of schism lay through reunion with the Roman Church. Martin had already nominated the Minorite friar Antonio da Massa as apostolic nuncio to Constantinople (on 15 June, 1422) to lay the groundwork for the general council which (Martin apparently believed) was going to declare the union of the churches.[9]

Fra Antonio da Massa arrived at Galata with a half-dozen fellow Franciscans on 10 September, a mere four days after the conclusion of the Turkish siege. Conducted by the Venetian bailie to the palace of Blachernae on the sixteenth, Antonio was received by Manuel, to whom he presented his letters of credence. He was scheduled to set forth in detail the purpose of his mission on 3 October, but by that time Manuel had suffered a paralytic stroke, which caused him to lose both the power of speech and the use of his limbs.[10] Two weeks later (on the fifteenth) Antonio was granted a private audience with the "young emperor" John VIII, to whom he presented nine arguments, observations, or "conclusions" relating to the hoped-for union of the churches. John said that Antonio might expect his answer within a few days. On 19 October the Patriarch Joseph II received Antonio into the presence of the Holy Synod, probably in Hagia Sophia, and received him again the following day in the Church of S. Stephen, where Antonio once more advanced his nine "conclusions" before a public gathering of bishops, monks, priests, and laymen both Greek and Latin. Like the emperor, the patriarch promised his response "within a few days."[11]

As befitted an apostolic nuncio, Fra Antonio made his *prima conclusio* a statement of Pope Martin's overwhelming desire for union, "to celebrate this paschal feast of union, communion, and peace . . . together with you Greeks." His second "conclusion" was that evils without number had come about as a result of the schism. The Greeks had suffered grievous losses of dominion, wealth, and population. They were even then being crushed by the enemies of the cross. Unless the schism was brought to an end, the Tatars and Turks would lord it over them all; they would have to renounce the gospel of Christ and become the slaves of Mohammed. As his third point Antonio insisted upon the clear and categorical assurances made to Martin V by the Dominican friar Theodore Chrysoberges, a Greek convert to Catholicism and bishop of Olena in the Morea,[12] and by the lord Nicholas

filium Petrum de Luna, Benedictum XIII in eius dudum obediencia nuncupatum, hereticum et scismaticum" (fol. 9v), than about conditions in the Levant. Consequently, although Fonseca's primary mission was supposed to be "pro reductione Grecorum et Orientalium" (*ibid.*, fols. 203r, 204v), by the letter of 10 April Martin sent him to Spain "ad prosternendam audaciam temerariam ac damnatam perfidiam ipsorum Petri de Luna ac fautorum . . . et sequacium ipsius hereticorum ac schismaticorum. . . ." It was well for Fonseca to try to deal with Benedict; after all, it was Benedict who had given him the red hat. *Cf.* Raynaldus, ad ann. 1420, no. 2, where the date "pontificatus nostri anno II" is a typographical error for "anno III."

Upon his return from Spain, Fonseca found that conditions in Constantinople made a formal legation no longer appropriate. The Greeks wanted a council, and someone of less exalted rank than a cardinal would have to try to arrange the hundred preliminary details with them. By September, 1421, Fonseca's eastern mission had once more been postponed, and a papal letter now identifies him as legate in Naples, the "kingdom of Sicily" (Reg. Vat. 353, fols. 249v–251v, "datum Rome apud Sanctam Mariam Maiorem undecimo Kal. Octobris, pontificatus nostri anno quarto"). *Cf. ibid.*, fols. 268r–274v, 275v–276r, docs. also dated 21 September, 1421. On the whole the extant letters of Martin are of only secondary importance for the history of eastern affairs.

[9] Hofmann, ed., *Epistolae pontificiae*, I, nos. 15–17, pp. 11–14. Martin V's letter of 8 October, 1422 (inc. "Iam pridem audiebamus"), is published by Hofmann, *ibid.*, no. 17, pp. 12–14, from the text of Raynaldus, *Ann. eccl.*, ad ann. 1422, no. 2. The letter may be found in the Arch. Segr. Vaticano, Arm. XXXIX, tom. 5, fols. 168v–170v, by mod. stamped enumeration. It bears the date "datum Rome apud S. Marcum XVIII Idus [*sic!*] Octobris, anno quinto," which is lacking in Arm. XXXIX, tom. 6, fols. 50v–51r, the text transcribed by Raynaldus (see above, Chapter 1, note 42). Another undated copy of this brief may be found in Arm. XXXIX, tom. 4, fols. 120r–122v, by mod. stamped enumeration.

[10] According to Sphrantzes, *Chron. minus*, IX, 2, in *PG* 156, 1030A, and ed. Grecu (1966), p. 14, "on the sixth day of the month of September in the year 6931 [i.e., 1422, Murad] left the City . . . without having accomplished anything." He also dates Manuel's stroke to 1 October (1422).

[11] *Relatio de ambaxiata facta ad Graecos*, in J. D. Mansi, ed., *Sacrorum conciliorum nova et amplissima collectio*, XXVIII (Venice, 1785, repr. Paris, 1903), cols. 1063–64.

[12] According to Jacopo Cerretano, *Liber gestorum*, ed. Finke, *Acta*, II (1923), 266, 268, Andreas Lascary Goslawicki, bishop of Poznań (*cf.* C. Eubel, *Hierarchia catholica*, I [1913, repr. 1960], 408), spoke approvingly of "Frater Theodorus ordinis Predicatorum in greco et sacris scripturis eruditus" in a sermon given in the cathedral of Constance "on

Eudaimonoïoannes, the Byzantine envoy to the Curia Romana, "that it was the wish of the most reverend patriarch of Constantinople and of the most serene emperor of the Greeks [*Romani*] to effect and secure without deceit or guile the most sacred union of the Greek with the Latin Church in that faith which the Holy Roman Church holds and in obedience to the said Church of Rome."

In his fourth observation Antonio dwelt on Martin's prompt appointment of Cardinal Pedro Fonseca as papal legate to Constantinople because of Chrysoberges' and Eudaimonoïoannes' "promissa tam mirifica." Fonseca's arrival on the Bosporus had, to be sure, been delayed by certain needs of the Church in Spain, whither he had gone, however, with the knowledge and approval of Eudaimonoïoannes. Fonseca's appointment had not come at a good time for a voyage to Greece (*τότε γὰρ οὐκ ἦν καιρὸς ἐπιτήδειος τοῦ πλέειν πρὸς τὴν Ἑλλάδα*). Furthermore, the necessary arrangements had not yet been made for holding the proposed council in Constantinople, and the Greeks had made it clear that there could be no union without the council. Unfortunately a grave illness had also detained Fonseca in Spain. But when he was getting ready for the voyage to Greece (says Antonio in his *quinta conclusio*) Theodore Chrysoberges and many other persons had written that no assembly of Greek prelates was possible at the time "because of the savage war of the Turks and because of their passage from Asia to Greece." And in Constantinople there was still no sign of preparation for the council. Obviously the legate could not come under these circumstances.

Antonio's sixth point concerned himself. The pope had sent him as *nuntius apostolicus* to help pave the way for a council with full Greek representation, for the sad experience of Lyon must not be repeated. In his so-called eighth "conclusion" Antonio promised the assistance of the kings of Aragon, Castile, and Portugal if the Greeks embraced the union with sincerity of word and deed. Glib and self-assured, Antonio did not make a very favorable impression upon the Greeks. His nine points possess no little historical interest for us, but they are repetitious and poorly developed. It is most unlikely that they were prepared in the papal chancery or the Camera. The Greek version was presumably hammered out in the Catholic convents of Galata.

With rigid courtesy the Patriarch Joseph II answered Antonio da Massa's nine contentions, one by one and at some length. He denied absolutely that Eudaimonoïoannes' commission had ever included any assurance that the Greek Church would submit to the disciplinary or theological dictates of the Church of Rome. If Eudaimonoïoannes ever gave the pope the assurances which Antonio had just recounted, it was plain and simple calumny (*συκοφαντία σαφής*) of the Greek patriarchate and the Church. Indeed, every communication of the Church of Constantinople to that of Rome, the patriarch declared, had always insisted upon the necessity of a truly oecumenical council to deal with the thorny problem of church union. Such a council would not be an assembly *pro forma* to confirm the objectives of the Latin Church. Disappointed by the patriarch's response, Antonio was certainly taken aback by that of the emperor.[13]

Wednesday, 13 December, in the year 1415" [which date fell on a Friday, but no matter]. A letter of King Ladislas of Poland, dated 29 August, 1415, recommends to the Council in the highest terms "dominus frater Theodorus Constantinopolitanus vicarius generalis societatis ordinis . . . Predicatorum, vir catholicus et devotus, prout sua opera manifeste ostendunt, peritus in greco, tartarico ydeomatibus et latino, ex litteris multorum principum christiane fidei nobis multipliciter commendatus . . ." (Finke, *Acta*, III [1926], 281).

There were three brothers Chrysoberges, all converts to Catholicism and all Dominicans, Maximus, Theodore, and Andreas. The first was not active in the unionist negotiations of their time; Theodore and Andreas were, on which see especially R. J. Loenertz, "Les Dominicains byzantins Théodore et André Chrysobergès et les négociations pour l'union des Églises grecque et latine de 1415 à 1430," *Archivum Fratrum Praedicatorum*, IX (1939), 5–61. Theodore died in or shortly before 1429 (*ibid.*, p. 47), and Andreas about 1451, at which time he had been archbishop of Nicosia in Cyprus for about four years (*ibid.*, p. 8, and C. Eubel, *Hierarchia catholica*, II [1914, repr. 1960], 202). Note also M. H. Laurent, "L'Activité d'André Chrysobergès, O. P., sous le pontificat de Martin V (1418–1431)," *Échos d'Orient*, XXXIV (1935), 414–38, and esp. Jean Darrouzès, in the *Arch. FF. Praed.*, XXI (1951), 301–5.

[13] On Antonio da Massa's mission to Constantinople, with the Greek and Latin texts of the pope's "nine articles," see Vitalien Laurent, "Les Préliminaires du concile de Florence: Les Neuf Articles du pape Martin V et la réponse inédite du patriarche de Constantinople Joseph II (Octobre 1422)," in the *Revue des études byzantines*, XX (1962), 5–60, with refs. Note also Syropoulos, *Mémoires*, II, 10–11, ed. Laurent (1971), p. 112; Joseph Gill, *The Council of Florence*, Cambridge, 1959, pp. 31–36, and *Personalities of the Council of Florence*, Oxford, 1964, pp. 233–35; and J. W. Barker, *Manuel II Palaeologus*, New Brunswick, N. J., 1969, pp. 327–29. Antonio da Massa presented a report of his mission to the Council of Siena on 8 November, 1423.

On Saturday, 14 November (1422), after further discussion with his advisers, John VIII replied to Pope Martin's proposals. Although he had been informed, as John wrote the pope, that Nicholas Eudaimonoïoannes and Bishop Theodore of Olena had declared (at the Curia Romana) that the Byzantine government wanted to see ecclesiastical union achieved *secundum Ecclesiam Romanam*, John denied that he or his father had ever given Nicholas and Theodore authority to make any such statement. He had always intended that the question of church union should be dealt with by a general council to be held in the hallowed tradition of the *sancta septem universalia concilia*. The council must be held at Constantinople, for John could not leave his capital in the then foreseeable future. All the Greek patriarchs and bishops must be in attendance at the council, for which the papacy must pay the expenses. The imperial treasury was exhausted. John wished that the council might meet immediately (*hodie*), but it was unfortunately not possible, *propter guerras infidelium*, to bring together the bishops either from Asia Minor or from Europe. When peace had been re-established, and some stability introduced into imperial affairs, John would notify the pope promptly, and then the first steps might be taken toward assembling the council. In the meantime he asked Martin for an armed force to help defend his territories, and requested the promulgation of a bull of *excommunicatio generalis, terribilis et insolubilis* against Latins who collaborated with the Turks or who failed to help the Greeks defend themselves. Martin should send to Constantinople a cardinal with full authority to act, at the same time presumably as he sent the men-at-arms, and the *unionis opus* might begin from the very day of the cardinal's arrival on the Bosporus.[14]

Although Martin V seems not to have been offended at the emperor's rather brusque reply, he was impeded in his desire to assist the Greeks by lack of funds. But the Curia Romana regarded the Greeks as schismatics, and the schism had political and social as well as religious implications. Some seven months or more after the conclusion of the Council of Constance, which was dissolved on 22 April, 1418, a Venetian ambassador was directed to remind Martin that granting bishoprics and prelacies *in commendam* was a pernicious practice which should be halted. The Republic had long observed the results in its possessions in Greece and the islands. If bishops did not reside in their sees and make clear the error of schism and provide instruction in the Latin faith, the schism would soon embrace everyone in the Latin Levant (and the Venetian hold upon Coron, Modon, Negroponte, and the islands would become more difficult to maintain). It often happened that, owing to the absence of bishops and other prelates, Catholics died and were buried with Greek rites. Others were baptized by Greek priests. His Holiness must not allow the continuance of this tragic neglect, but must strive to see that Christianity increased rather than decreased in the lands overseas.[15]

The Venetians were more worried about the expansion of the Turks, however, than about the extension of schismatic rites in their territories. As usual, the Italian states were lacking in enthusiasm for a crusade, but in March, 1423, Martin V sent the ever-ready Antonio da Massa to Venice, appealing for aid to be sent to the Bosporus "to rescue and defend the city of Constantinople, lest it should fall into the hands of the infidel Turks." Fra Antonio could inform the Senate in detail concerning conditions in the Byzantine capital, and he evoked a good response from the Venetians. They expressed high praise for Martin's concern with Byzantine affairs, which they urged him not to relax, so that the Christian world might

[14] Georg Hofmann, ed., *Orientalium documenta minora*, Rome, 1953, doc. no. 1, pp. 3–4 (Concilium Florentinum, Documenta et scriptores, ser. A, vol. III, fasc. 3); Dölger, *Regesten der Kaiserurkunden*, pt. 5, no. 3406, pp. 110–11, with refs.; Raynaldus, *Ann. eccl.*, ad ann. 1422, nos. 1–15, vol. XVIII (1694), pp. 40–45a. (Raynaldus is, as usual, well informed, but he makes the error here [no. 5] of assuming that Manuel II died of his stroke, as certain other older writers have done.)

[15] Arch. di Stato di Venezia, Sen. Secreta, Reg. 7, fol. 50^r, dated 29 November, 1418, from the commission issued in the name of the Doge Tommaso Mocenigo to Lorenzo Bragadin, who was being sent as the Venetian ambassador to Martin V: "In facto autem commendarum que fiunt et dantur et specialiter de episcopatibus existentibus in locis et insulis nostris partium Grecie similiter debeas iustificare rationes et causam nostri dominii et precipue quia si episcopi earum ibi non residebunt, qui convincant sci[s]ma Grecorum et instruant in recta fide catolica, illud sci[s]ma in tantum multiplicabitur quod omnes deinde fient Greci. Nam multociens occursum est quod propter absentiam episcoporum et aliorum non facientium residentiam in prelaturis suis multi catolici mortui sunt qui habueurunt sacramenta greca et sepulti more Grecorum et multi pueri orti defectu prelatorum more greco fuerunt batizati quod sua Beatitudo non debet velle consentire per aliquam viam mundi cuius debet esse maxima et precipua cura ut Christianitas augeatur et non minuatur per tales modos."

know the supreme pontiff was ever on guard. They believed that the Turkish menace might be removed, for some time at least, by a flotilla of ten well-armed galleys which should act in unison with those of John VIII. Speedy action was essential. A legate could be put in command of the ten galleys, of which the Venetians would supply three at their own expense, provided that other Christian states would supply the remainder. There can be no question either of papal or of Venetian sincerity in these expressed desires to assist the Greeks in Constantinople, but it was no easy matter to recruit galleys from other western powers.[16]

Actually Martin already had his hands full. It was the era of the Hussite crusades; Bohemia was ablaze with religious revolt; Czech valor crowned with victory every Hussite campaign against the Catholics.[17] And now unexpected disaster fell upon the Latin kingdom of Cyprus. Having ravaged parts of the island in August, 1425, the Mamluks of Egypt returned the following July, defeated and captured King Janus, killed his brother Prince Henry of Galilee, took the capital city of Nicosia, and looted the island far and wide. For eight months Janus was kept in captivity in Cairo (until April, 1427), and during this period the woeful affairs of Cyprus distressed both the Curia and the Italian states.[18] But there were other distractions in Italy, the

---

[16] Sen. Secreta, Reg. 8, fol. 98ᵛ [99ᵛ], dated 31 March, 1423; Giuseppe Valentini, ed., *Acta Albaniae veneta saeculorum XIV et XV*, XI (1971), no. 2,708, pp. 218–19, summarized in N. Iorga, *Notes et extraits pour servir à l'histoire des croisades au XVᵉ siècle*, 6 vols., Paris and Bucharest, 1899–1916, I, 332–33, and *cf.* pp. 336–37, 352–53, reprinted from *Revue de l'Orient latin* (abbr. *ROL*), V (1897, repr. 1964), 133–34, 137–38, 153–54; F. Thiriet, *Régestes des délibérations du Sénat de Venise concernant la Romanie*, II (1959), no. 1876, p. 201. Documents relating to Antonio da Massa may be found in the Arch. Segr. Vaticano, Reg. Vat. 354 [*Martini V de Curia, anno IV–VI, liber IV*], fols. 90ᵛ–91ʳ, 190ᵛ.

[17] For a succinct account, see F. G. Heymann, "The Crusades against the Hussites," in K. M. Setton and H. W. Hazard, eds., *A History of the Crusades*, III (1975), 586–646; and at longer length, Heymann, *John Žižka and the Hussite Revolution*, Princeton, 1955. The Czechs and the Greeks, in their common antipathy to Rome, were inevitably drawn together in consultation. Although John Hus had declared in 1404 that "Greci sunt extra ecclesiam Romanam, extra quam nemo salvatur, quia non recipiunt papam cum cardinalibus" (*Opuscula*, II, 113), his break with the Curia Romana led him and the later Hussites to take a more conciliatory attitude toward the Greeks. The evasiveness and intransigence of the Curia in dealing with the Hussites, especially after the apparent union of the Roman and Byzantine Churches (as declared at Florence in July, 1439), led to a Czech mission to Constantinople at the turn of the years 1451–1452, when the envoy, one "Constantine Platris Anglicus," was received into the Greek Church by Gennadius (George Scholarius) and the anti-unionists.

Anglicus assailed the pope in a public discourse, and received a letter signed by seven anti-unionist dignitaries (including Gennadius and Sylvester Syropoulos, the historian of the Council of Ferrara-Florence), addressed to the Czechs, inviting their adhesion to the Orthodox Church. Anglicus and certain of the Utraquists in Prague presumably looked upon his mission as the beginning of another "union," this time an unlikely alignment of the anti-Roman Hussites and the anti-Roman Greeks (see the knowledgeable but discursive study of M. Paulová, "L'Empire byzantin et les Tshèques avant la chute de Constantinople," *Byzantinoslavica*, XIV [1953], 158–225, and Antonín Salač, "Constantinople et Prague en 1452: Pourparlers en vue d'une union des Églises," *Rozpravy Československé Akademie Věd*, LXVIII [1958], 1–111, with texts [and facsimiles] of the important documents).

F. M. Bartoš, "A Delegate of the Hussite Church to Constantinople in 1451–1452," *Byzantinoslavica*, XXIV (1963), 287–92, and XXV (1964), 69–74, has tried to show that the mysterious Constantine Anglicus was the Czech Hussite diplomat Matthew of Hnátnice, who became known as Matthew English, owing to his connection with the Wycliffites. Bartoš believes that he received the name Constantine, "unknown in Bohemia," when he was received into the Greek church. A number of Czech scholars have tried to identify Constantine Anglicus. Their efforts have been more ingenious than convincing.

[18] Sir Geo. Hill, *A History of Cyprus*, II (Cambridge, 1948), 471–95. Nevertheless, on 9 December, 1425, Martin V granted the Venetians a license to trade with the Egyptians. The customary prohibition of dealing in such articles of contraband as arms, metals, timber, etc., was imposed, of course, but was often evaded (*cf.* R. Predelli, *Regesti dei Commemoriali*, IV [1896], bk. XI, no. 199, pp. 66–67). The archival copy of the pope's *licentia* to trade with Egypt may be found in Arch. Segr. Vaticano, Reg. Vat. 356 [*Martini V Bullar. secret. tom. VI*], fols. 11ᵛ–12ʳ, "datum Rome apud Sanctos Apostolos, V Idus Decembris, pontificatus nostri anno nono." On the Cypriote disaster of July, 1426, see the contemporary report in Gelcich and Thallóczy, *Diplomatarium ragusanum* (1887), no. 203, p. 321, dated 12 December, 1426, and *cf.* pp. 323–24, 325.

In a letter, the preamble to which obviously rehearses King Janus's own account of the Egyptian invasion of Cyprus, Martin V's successor Eugenius IV granted Janus an assessment on all ecclesiastical benefices in the Spanish kingdoms, France, England, and Viennois, to help relieve his distress and that of his subjects, observing "quod soldanus Babilonie cum magna infidelium comitiva regnum tuum Cypri manu armata violenter invasit, necnon terras dicti regni spoliavit et devastavit nonnullosque utriusque sexus fideles eiusdem regni incolas gladio crudeliter interemit: necnon te eorum nequitie fortiter resistentem cum magna fidelium multitudine captivavit captumque abduxit et tandem pro tua liberatione a te maximas pecuniarum quantitates exegit pro qua partim exsolvenda magnam partem introituum regni tui diversis creditoribus pignori obligare ac quosdam ex tuis subditis pro parte restante obsides in captivitate dimittere miserabiliter coactus fuisti . . ." (Arch. Segr. Vaticano, Arm. XXXIX, tom. 6, fol. 199). Eugenius also had to protect Janus from the usurers who sought to profit from his misfortune (*ibid.*, fols. 199ᵛ–201ʳ).

northern and central states being much disturbed by the war which Duke Filippo Maria was fighting with the Florentines (1422–1428) and finally with the Venetians (1426–1428). The latter carried off the palm of victory, and much increased their strength on land by pushing their westward frontier beyond Brescia and Bergamo. Well might the pope rejoice when peace was made on 19 April, 1428.[19] Despite the troubles of these years, the pope had pursued plans for a council which might re-unite the Greek and Latin Churches. The Greek Dominican Andreas Chrysoberges, Theodore's brother, had been active as an envoy between Rome and Constantinople from June, 1426,[20] and in 1430 Martin V reached an agreement with the Byzantine court whereby the Emperor John VIII, the Patriarch Joseph II, and the other three patriarchs of Jerusalem, Antioch, and Alexandria with their attendant high clergy should come "to some coastal city of Calabria as far [north] as Ancona, which the emperor of the Greeks shall choose." The Holy See would pay the expenses for the four heavy galleys required to bring to Italy a Greek delegation of up to 700 members. It would also pay for the maintenance of two light galleys and 300 crossbowmen for the defense of Constantinople during the emperor's absence. If by some mischance, *quod absit*, union should not be achieved, the Greeks were nevertheless to be conveyed back to the Bosporus "at the expense of the Latin Church."[21] This was the agreement, and from 1430 the Greeks always insisted upon the fulfillment of its terms. Martin was certainly willing to do so, and more, but during the last years of his reign he could do little or nothing to promote the crusade or to relieve the Turkish pressure on Constantinople. He was as likely to ponder the broken fortunes of King Janus and the humiliation of the Latin Christians in Cyprus as to worry about the well-being of the Greeks and the future of the Palaeologi.

In the middle ages as in modern times the lure of the East drew many Europeans as travelers and even residents into the Levant. Often piety or curiosity attracted them to religious or historical sites, and natural beauty captivated the merchant as well as the poet. But there were dark sides to life in the Levant. The modern historian, who dwells on the inconstancy and self-seeking of the Greeks in the fifteenth century, must also take account of the undoubted cruelty of the Turks and the cynical greed of Latin Christians who made what they could of immoral opportunities in distant lands, anxious to profit in ways they would never have tolerated at home, where such practices would have entailed obloquy and penalties. There was no Turk so lecherous that the Christian slave trader would not sell him a beautiful girl or a handsome boy. As the captives of many eastern nations were assembled in the Genoese marts at Caffa and elsewhere, healthy youngsters and strong men brought a good price. The aged and infirm were not salable; physicians' services and medicines were expensive; and thousands of persons were left to die (and encouraged thereto) by traders who regarded them merely as undesirable items on the debit side of the ledger. The papacy was the conscience of Europe. More than one conclave was marred by simony in the fifteenth century, and the Curia was not without its sly politicians. The papacy was still the conscience of Europe, however, and it spoke out against those aspects of the slave trade which were offensive to the fifteenth century. Slavery as such was part of the social fabric of the age, accepted by almost everyone. There were few propagandists for abolition. On 3 June, 1425, Martin V declared anathema those miscreants who sold their fellow Christians to the Moslems, who often made them abjure their faith, treated them harshly, and employed them for immoral purposes.[22]

Christian captives already in Turkish and Egyptian hands were naturally a problem

---

[19] Arch. Segr. Vaticano, Arm. XXXIX, tom. 5, fols. 331^v–334^r, by mod. stamped enumeration; Raynaldus, *Ann. eccl.*, ad ann. 1428, nos. 2–4, vol. XVIII (1694), pp. 65–66a; Predelli, *Regesti dei Commemoriali*, IV, bk. XII, no. 15, pp. 125–27.

[20] Hofmann, *Epistolae pontificiae*, I, nos. 23–25, pp. 17–19; Loenertz, "Les Dominicains byzantins Théodore et André Chrysobergès," *Arch. FF. Praedicatorum*, IX (1939), 49 ff.

[21] *Epistolae pontificiae*, I, no. 26, p. 20, and *cf.* nos. 66, 75, pp. 67, 75–76. The offer Martin V made to the Greeks was generous, for at this very time (1429–1430) a commission of cardinals asked him to reduce the overgrown staff of clerks in the Camera Apostolica to its erstwhile number of four, "which was sufficient when the Camera had more than three times [its present income!]," . . . *qui sufficiebat cum camera in triplo plus habundabat* . . . (Johannes Haller, ed., *Concilium Basiliense*, I [1896, repr. 1971], 168, on which work see below, note 37). I owe this reference to Dr. Peter Partner. Allusion has already been made to this text at the beginning of Chapter 1.

[22] Raynaldus, *Ann. eccl.*, ad ann. 1425, no. 19, vol. XVIII (1694), pp. 79b–80a, "datum Rome apud SS. Apostolos, tertio non. Iun., [pontif. nostri] anno VIII."

which concerned the Holy See, for they often exchanged the worst miseries of their lot for conversion to Islam (and the assumed loss of salvation). Many such converts to Islam were to be found among Serbian and Balkan slaves and captives in the Ottoman empire. There were Cypriote and other former Christians in Egypt. On 19 February, 1429, Martin V proclaimed an indulgence with full remission of sins for those who, contrite in heart and by confession, should have made themselves worthy by ransoming or otherwise redeeming such captives from the torment to body and peril to soul which captivity had brought them.[23]

One wonders of course what effect papal pronouncements had upon slave traders. Although ransoming Christian captives from the infidels had long been recognized as a good work, we must not fail to mention at this point the unusual efforts of one Pietro da Vernazza, a Genoese, who almost came to grief in the self-sacrificing pursuit of a noble enterprise. On 12 March, 1428, the Genoese government wrote Martin V of the singular example of Christian charity provided by Vernazza, who had long before abandoned the petty pomp and circumstantial comforts of life to aid the poor to the fullest extent of his own slender resources. Learning that there were many Christians held captive in the kingdom of Tunis, Vernazza had made his way into the Libyan desert where the king of Tunis was then encamped, ransomed as many captives as he could, and repaired to the Holy See, where he had obtained bulls of indulgence. Collecting more money, he sailed back to Africa, where again he ransomed many Genoese captives. Moved by the sufferings of the enslaved of every nation, he returned to Rome and obtained a new set of indulgences. Soon he undertook a voyage to England, "that is, to the far corner of the North, . . . in order that he might collect in that most wealthy island as much money as would suffice for the redemption of so many unfortunate captives." Poor Vernazza, who had impoverished himself to help others, had been charged in England with employing forged bulls, had been imprisoned, and might have lost his life but for the intervention of Humphrey, duke of Gloucester, who had had confidence in his innocence. Vernazza had found, like many a man before and after him, "in medio Christianitatis barbaros ipsis barbaris crudeliores," but the Genoese government could supply the proofs of his innocence, and asked the pope to send him the necessary bulls. The government also wrote the young King Henry VI on Vernazza's behalf, declaring that his calumniators had taken advantage of his vulnerability as a foreigner to level false charges against him, and asking the king's intervention "for God, for justice, and for truth."[24] It is pleasant to note that Vernazza was rescued from his predicament, and was subsequently employed (in March, 1431) by the Genoese on another mission of mercy and diplomacy to Tunis, where he was again to secure the release of captives, and to introduce some order into the Genoese colony there, pending the arrival of a new consul who was being sent from Genoa.[25]

Popes might come and go, but the problems faced by the Curia tended to remain the same. Consistent policies were easily pursued from one reign to the next. After Martin V we find his successor, Eugenius IV, in communication with the Genoese government on the question of slavery in the Levant. On 13 February, 1434, the Genoese wrote Eugenius, acknowledging the reverent receipt of a papal letter, informing them that they were being held up to opprobrium for shipping Christian slaves from their Black Sea port of Caffa to Egypt and other infidel states. The government strenuously denied the charge, claiming that Caffa had in fact become a "pillar of the Christian faith." Colonial officials in Caffa were bound by treaties with neighboring lords not to export slaves outside the Black Sea region except on Genoese vessels which put into the port of Caffa itself. Here before their embarkation the slaves were counted, and a special tax (*vectigal*) levied on them. Then the bishop, accompanied both by religious and by laymen, came aboard the vessel on which they were to be exported. He called to each slave in turn, asking to what nation he belonged, whether he was a Christian, and (if not) whether

[23] Raynaldus, ad ann. 1429, no. 21, vol. XVIII, pp. 75b–76a (*sic*, by error in pagination), "datum Rome apud SS. Apostolos, XI Kal. Martii, [pontif. nostri] anno XII."

[24] Arch. di Stato di Genova, Litterae comunis Janue, Reg. 3/1779 (1427–1431), nos. 184, 191, fols. 73, 76, summarized in Iorga, *ROL*, V, 369–70, and *Notes et extraits*, I, 469–70. On 26 October (1428), the Genoese government wrote again to the pope and to the cardinals of S. Marcello and S. Clemente on Vernazza's behalf (Litterae, *ibid.*, nos. 307–8, fols. 124–25; *ROL*, V, 382–83), and on 23 November thanked Humphrey of Gloucester for the protection he afforded Genoese citizens (Litterae, *ibid.*, no. 324, fol. 131; *ROL*, V, 383).

[25] Iorga, *ROL*, VI (1898, repr. 1964), 100, and *Notes et extraits*, I, 538.

he did not wish to adopt the Christian faith. Any slave thus converted was removed from the vessel and sold on land to a Christian purchaser. This procedure, the Genoese government piously informed the pope, resulted in conversions. But for such treaties as those which controlled the slave trade in Caffa, it was said, one would have seen ships loading slaves from Trebizond, Tana, Vosporo, Phasis, and other ports on the Euxine for transport to Egypt. The Genoese therefore deserved praise rather than censure, and the government reminded the pope that these statements could easily be verified, because Caffa was a frequent port of call.[26]

By March, 1431, when Gabriele Condulmer, cardinal-priest of S. Clemente, succeeded Martin V as Pope Eugenius IV, the Turks had extended their sway throughout much of the Balkans. During the fifteenth century, however, they probably did not bear as heavily upon the native Christian peoples as has commonly been assumed (except, as we shall see, for the brutality manifested by Mehmed II the Conqueror in his constant campaigns). Christians were allowed to continue in their faith and preserve most of their local customs and practices with little hindrance or oppression so long as they paid the poll-tax or *kharaj* levied on non-Moslems (the *raya*). In addition every landholder paid a tax, according to the number of his sheep, goats, cattle, and oxen, and a tithe was levied upon every harvest. The animus with which modern Balkan peoples recall the long period of Ottoman hegemony is partly the consequence of the corruption of Turkish officialdom in the seventeenth and eighteenth centuries. In the age of the conquest there was a good deal of integrity at the sultan's court although in the chapters which follow we shall note some appalling examples of cruelty, especially on the part of Mehmed II and his chief officers.[27] In many areas, nevertheless, the native populations subjected by the Turks may not have found them much worse than their previous masters.

As Bulgarian, Serbian, and Byzantine resistance was beaten down, the Turks are alleged to have taken over (or imitated) various Byzantine institutions, retaining especially the military fiefs. From the end of the fourteenth century the Ottoman government had been establishing great fiefs which were conferred upon the beys or begs of the border, margraves of proven faith, in whose families they became hereditary, and in Bosnia, southern Serbia, Macedonia, and Thessaly such feudal families were to remain in possession of large estates almost until our own day.[28] Although the Turks destroyed a large pro-

---

[26] Iorga, *ROL*, VI, 128, and *Notes et extraits*, I, 566. The Genoese assertions are borne out by the provisions composed in Genoa for a treaty between the Republic and the soldan of Egypt (*ibid.*, I, 533–36, doc. dated 1–3 February, 1431). On the slave trade, see in general Charles Verlinden, "Esclaves du Sud-Est et de l'Est européen en Espagne orientale à la fin du moyen âge," *Revue historique du Sud-Est européen*, XIX (1942), 371–406. As Caffa on the Black Sea was a center of the Genoese slave trade, so Tana on the Sea of Azov supplied quantities of slaves to Venetian merchants (*cf.* Verlinden, "La Colonie vénitienne de Tana, centre de la traite des esclaves au XIVe et au début du XVe siècle," *Studi in onore di Gino Luzzatto*, II [Milan, 1950], 1–25). See also the excellent article by Verlinden, "La Crète, débouché et plaque tournante de la traite des esclaves aux XIVe et XVe siècles," *Studi in onore di Amintore Fanfani*, III (Milan, 1962), 591–669, and note Helga Köpstein, *Zur Sklaverei im ausgehenden Byzanz*, Berlin, 1966, esp. pp. 87 ff. (Berliner byzantinistische Arbeiten, no. 34).

The Genoese were among the most conspicuous slave dealers of the fifteenth century, handling for the trade Tatars, Russians, and Circassians from the Caucasus; Greeks, Bulgarians, Serbs, and Albanians from the Balkans; and Arabs, Moors, and a few blacks from North Africa. See Domenico Gioffré, *Il Mercato degli schiavi a Genova nel secolo XV*, Genoa, 1971, whose work makes clear (esp. pp. 39 ff., 126) that Christians were indeed held as slaves, especially if their conversion occurred after their captivity. Slaves were employed in commerce, industry, and agriculture as well as in domestic service, concubinage, and prostitution. In Genoa females brought a much better price than males; they usually cost from about 70–80 *lire* to about 250 or so. On the whole 150–160 *lire* was a high price, but the cost of slaves rose in the last two decades of the century. The Genoese sold slaves for export, the Catalans being among their best customers.

[27] D. Angelov, "Certains Aspects de la conquête des peuples balkaniques par les Turcs," *Byzantinoslavica*, XVII (1956), 220–75, has described the undeniable destructiveness of the Turkish invasions of the fourteenth and fifteenth centuries with a sense of almost personal outrage.

[28] *Cf.* Franz Babinger, *Maometto il Conquistatore e il suo tempo*, Turin, 1957, pp. 56–57 and 29: ". . . but the history of these fiefs can be placed in a clearer light only when the oldest Ottoman tax records are accessible, and studies are made of the fiefs in Rumelian territory." It is easily possible to exaggerate the extent to which the Porte borrowed from Byzantium at the time of the capture of Constantinople and to draw specious parallels between the Byzantine and the Ottoman empires (*cf.*, *ibid.*, pp. 171–72), but on the Turkish *timar* (fief), in some respects like the Byzantine *pronoia*, *cf.* the suggestive but rather diffuse article of J. Deny, *Encyclopaedia of Islām*, IV (1924–34), 767–76. In the Turkish National Archives are registers which go back to the time of Mehmed the Conqueror, and at least one important register of the fiefs going back to his father's time (1431–1432), on which see the interesting article of Halil Inalcik, "Timariotes chrétiens en Albanie au XVe siècle d'après un

registre de timars ottoman," *Mitteilungen des Österreichischen Staatsarchivs*, IV (Vienna, 1951), 118–38. As indicated by the title, the register dating from 1431–1432 relates to Albania: After the Turkish victory on the river Viyosa (Vijosë) in the fall of 1385 (*cf.* N. Iorga, *Geschichte des osmanischen Reiches*, I [Gotha, 1908], 255, 261), the Christian lords of Albania apparently recognized the suzerainty of the sultan, and some of them were enrolled as fief-holding vassals (*timariotes*), becoming *sipahis* (cavalrymen) in the Ottoman service. In some cases their sons were educated (as hostages) at the Ottoman court, and their families tended gradually to be islamized. Although fiefs (*timars*) might be granted to a Christian, the latter's involvement in the Ottoman feudal nexus often resulted in conversion to Islam. Inalcik later published this document in Turkish, *Hicrî 835 tarihli sûret-i defter-i Sancak-i Arvanid* [*Copy of the Register for A.H. 835 for the Sanjak of Albania*], Ankara, 1954, with a number of plates of pages of the MS., full indices, and a detailed map of Albania in 1431 (=A.H. 835).

The further publication of Ottoman documentary records will elucidate many doubtful points in the institutional history of the Turkish empire. Ottoman "feudalism" appears by and large to have been a continuation of the Anatolian Seljuk ("Selchükid") system, itself allegedly preserving older Turkish traditions as well as borrowing from Byzantine, Arab, and Persian practices. The question, however, of Byzantine influence upon Ottoman institutions remains nebulous and controversial; modern Turkish scholars usually deprecate or try to minimize it, insisting upon the antediluvian character of Turkish traditions. Considering that Anatolia and Rumelia, former Byzantine territories, became in a sense the "homelands" of the Osmanlis, it would seem *a priori* difficult to escape the conclusion that there must have been a good deal of such influence, but up to now the problem of the Byzantine impact upon Ottoman ideas and institutions has usually been discussed with more subjective rationalization than objective documentation. On the question of feudalism, see the illuminating study of Mehmed Fuad Köprülü, *Alcune Osservazioni intorno all' influenza delle istituzioni bizantine sulle istituzioni ottomane*, Rome: Istituto per l'Oriente, 1953, pp. 6–12, 64–89, who denies altogether "la pretesa influenza bizantina" (p. 86), believing that "possiamo affermare decisamente che il sistema ottomano dei *tīmār* non fu preso da Bisanzio, né anteriormente, né posteriormente alla conquista di Costantinopoli, ma rientrava nell'eredità tramandata dai Selgiuchidi d'Anatolia" (p. 89). The common Turkish word for fief (*timar*) is apparently of Persian origin; the Greek work *τιμάριον* is said not to occur before the sixteenth century; the Turkish word for feudatory or cavalryman (*sipahi*) is also of Persian origin (Köprülü, *op. cit.*, pp. 86–87, note, and *cf.* Şerif Baştav, *Ordo Portae*, Budapest, 1947, pp. 29–35). There were three general grades of Ottoman fiefs (*ḫāṣṣ*, *zi'āmet*, and *tīmār*, ranging from highest to lowest); for these and various other kinds of Ottoman fiefs, see H. A. R. Gibb and Harold Bowen, *Islamic Society and the West*, I-1 (London, 1950, repr. 1963), pp. 39–56, 69–70, 144–60, 235–58, and *cf.* pt. 2 (1957, repr. 1965), pp. 1 ff., the whole forming an instructive presentation of Ottoman feudalism.

It may not be amiss to take notice of the thesis which underlies the *Geschichte des osmanischen Reiches*, 5 vols., Gotha, 1908–1913, of the great Rumanian historian, Nicolas (Neculaï) Iorga (1871–1940), who was sometimes intoxicated by the grandeur of his own historical concepts, but whose work is always illuminating. Iorga saw the Ottoman conquest of Constantinople less as the destruction of a Greek state than as the establishment of a Byzantine-Turkish empire, which alone could meet the needs of an epoch which had seen the dissolution of the Greek, Latin, and Slavic states throughout the Balkan peninsula. Under the Ottomans a new Pax Romana was eventually to extend from the Danube to the Nile and from the Adriatic to the Euphrates (*cf.*, *ibid.*, II, 196–97, *et passim*). Iorga was less interested in the history of the Turkish people than in what he conceived to be the historic mission of the Ottoman empire, which fulfilled (in collective fashion) for the peoples of the Balkans and the whole Levant the same functions as the absolute monarchies were discharging in western Europe. *Cf.* in general Maria M. Alexandrescu-Dersca, "N. Iorga, historien de l'empire ottoman," *Balcania*, VI (Bucharest, 1943), 101–22, and D. M. Pippidi [Iorga's son-in-law], ed., *Nicolas Iorga, l'homme et l'œuvre*, Bucharest, 1972, esp. pp. 175–86.

Iorga emphasized that the catastrophe of 1453 merely destroyed in the Greek areas the dynasty of the Palaeologi and the pre-eminence of the archontic class, but that Byzantine civilization as such survived in the Ottoman state, which means the whole social fabric of Orthodox Christianity, Graeco-Roman law, Greek literature, and various fundamental political and economic institutions. He denied that the Ottoman Turks introduced basic changes into the life of the Balkans and most of the Levant, "ainsi que le prétend un nationalisme turc d'origine très récente," as he states in the preface to his book on *Byzance après Byzance*, Bucharest, 1935, in which he explored the survival of Byzantine civilization and especially Byzantine political ideals in the Balkans, from the mid-fifteenth to about the close of the eighteenth century when he would date the "passage du byzantinisme au nationalisme" (*ibid.*, p. 243).

Although the bibliography is far too extensive for serious consideration here, we may note that the Anatolian and Rumelian backgrounds are explored in Speros Vryonis, Jr., *The Decline of Medieval Hellenism in Asia Minor and the Process of Islamization from the Eleventh through the Fifteenth Century*, Berkeley, Los Angeles, and London, 1971, and Franz Babinger, *Beiträge zur Frühgeschichte der Türkenherrschaft in Rumelien (14.–15. Jahrhundert)*, Munich, 1944 (Südosteuropäische Arbeiten, no. 34). The instructive article by Halil Inalcik, "Ottoman Methods of Conquest," *Studia Islamica*, II (1954), 103–29, deals chiefly with the fifteenth century. Various aspects of Ottoman domination in the Balkans and elsewhere are illustrated by P. Karlin-Hayter, "La Politique religieuse des conquérants ottomans dans un texte hagiographique (a. 1437)," *Byzantion*, XXXV (1965), 353–58; J. Kabrda, "Les Problèmes de l'étude de l'histoire de la Bulgarie à l'époque de la domination turque," *Byzantinoslavica*, XV (1954), 173–208, and "Les Sources turques relatives à l'histoire de la domination ottomane en Slovaquie," *Archiv orientální*, XXIV (1956), 568–80, who ranges over several centuries; Ömer Lütfi Barkan, "Les Déportations comme méthode de peuplement et de colonisation dans l'empire ottoman," *Revue de la Faculté des Sciences Économiques de l'Université d'Istanbul*, XI (1949–50), 67–131, apparently unfinished; Barkan, "Essai sur les données statistiques des registres de recensement dans l'empire ottoman aux XVe et XVIe siècles," *Journal of Economic and Social History of the Orient*, I, pt. 1 (1957), 9–36, and *cf.*, *ibid.*, pt. 3 (1958), 329–33; Bernard Lewis, "Studies in the Ottoman Archives" [on Palestine in the sixteenth century], *Bulletin of the School of Oriental and African Studies*, XVI (1954), 469–501; H.-J. Kissling, "Militärisch-Politische Problematiken zur portion of the ruling families in the territories which they conquered, and left the Serbs, Bulgars, Greeks, and others without leadership at the highest level, they usually respected the urban dwellers' and small landholders' rights to private property. The near obliteration of the ruling families in most areas caused a cultural but not an economic stagnation. Indeed, the wide extent of Ottoman rule in the Balkans and Asia Minor, the *pax Ottomanica*, eventually brought political stability in a new order of social stratification, with the pashas, begs, and members of the military class (*'askeri*), administrators and intellectuals, merchants and artisans all resting on the firm foundation of a peasantry (*köylü takimi*) protected from external invasion. Troublesome groups were removed from one part of the empire to another by deportation (*sürgün*). Peace made possible the agricultural surplus which bound the village to the town, where in the fifteenth century at least goods were freely exchanged, although as in the Byzantine empire there might be embargoes on the export of foodstuffs. Merchants accumulated capital in an open market. Conditions were far from ideal, and Turkish rule might be oppressive, but food was grown, cloth was woven, houses were built, money was made, and life went on.

The accession of Eugenius IV had little effect on the Levant. The same risks and fears and dangers continued year after year. Through much of 1431–1432, however, the Venetians were distracted from both Turkish and Greek advances on the continent and in the Morea by the threatening attitude of the Genoese, who were preparing for a full-scale war against their old rivals.[29] The Venetians could find no allies, but at last on 4 June, 1433, they finally concluded a five years' truce with Sigismund,[30] who had been crowned Emperor in Rome by Eugenius a few days before (on 31 May).[31] Venice also appropriated 10,000 ducats as a subsidy for Sigismund, taking measures on 1 July to raise the money for him.[32] Despite the various expenses accruing because of Sigismund's coronation journey, the Senate sent 2,000 ducats to the pope to help him meet the heavy costs of maintaining the imperial guest, who had arrived at Viterbo and gone on to Rome with four hundred horse. The Senate then paid another 2,000 to those who had arranged the truce and general agreements with the impecunious Sigismund,[33] whose need for money (as Europe had observed for almost fifty years) was exceeded only by his love of it.

While the Venetians were thus preoccupied, life in Greece was being disrupted by the petty lordlings within as well as by the Turks from without. In the early summer of 1435, after the death of the half-Florentine Duke Antonio I Acciajuoli of Athens, his Greek wife (whom

---

Türkenfrage im 15. Jahrhundert," in *Bohemia: Jahrbuch des Collegium Carolinum*, V (Munich, 1964), 108–36, and "Die türkische geographische Nomenklatur auf dem Balkan als Erkenntnismittel für die Südosteuropaforschung," *Zeitschrift für Balkanologie*, III (Wiesbaden, 1965), 126–42; and Kemal Karpat, *An Inquiry into the Social Foundations of Nationalism in the Ottoman State: From Social Estates to Classes, From Millets to Nations*, Princeton, N.J., 1973 (Center of International Studies, no. 39), with extensive citation of the recent bibliography.

[29] Iorga, *ROL*, VI, 108–15, and *Notes et extraits*, I, 546–53; F. Thiriet, *Régestes des délibérations du Sénat de Venise concernant la Romanie*, III (Paris and The Hague, 1961), nos. 2227, 2229, 2232, 2237, 2241–42, 2249–50, etc., 2405, pp. 10 ff., 50, on the Venetians' difficulties with the Genoese, who then lay under Milanese domination.

[30] R. Predelli, *Regesti dei Commemoriali*, IV (1896), bk. XII, nos. 189–90, p. 177; the truce was arranged "with the personal mediation of Pope Eugenius IV." *Cf.*, *ibid.*, nos. 192, 195. Two years later, on 31 August, 1435, Sigismund and Venice negotiated a ten years' alliance against Filippo Maria Visconti of Milan (*ibid.*, bk. XIII, no. 1, pp. 201–2, and *cf.* nos. 25–26).

Despite Timur the Lame's defeat of Sultan Bayazid I at Ankara in 1402 and the subsequent strife among the latter's sons, by 1415 the Turks were carrying their raids into Carniola and Styria, threatening the patriarchate of Aquileia. In 1420 the Venetians took over Friuli, and the Turkish peril had come close to home (see Pio Paschini, "Primi timori d'un' invasione turca in Friuli," *Memorie storiche forogiuliesi*, VIII [Udine, 1912], 65–73).

[31] Raynaldus, *Ann. eccl.*, ad ann. 1433, no. 14, vol. XVIII (1694), pp. 113–14; Joseph [von] Aschbach, *Geschichte Kaiser Sigmund's*, 4 vols., Hamburg: Perthes, 1838–45, repr. Aalen, 1964, IV, 114 ff.

[32] Arch. di Stato di Venezia, Misti, Reg. 58, fol. 216^v ("MCCCCXXXIII, die primo Iulii"): "Cum captum et deliberatum sit per istud consilium dandi ducatorum decem M. serenissimo domino Imperatori, et sit providendum de recuperando illos cum quam minori gravedine fieri possit . . . ," etc., details following for a duty on all merchandise imported into Venice.

[33] Misti, Reg. 58, fol. 224^v ("MCCCCXXXIII, die tercio Augusti"): "Cum iam diu stipendiariis nostris solutum non fuerit, et hoc quia imposita non fuit impositio aliqua, et sit neccessarium ad hoc providere quia quotidie congruuntur, sit insuper etiam providendum habendi denarios pro ambaxiata mittenda Bononiam ad serenissimum dominum Imperatorem pro associando suam Maiestatem per territoria domini Marchionis et nostra et faciendo ei expensas ac etiam dare summo Pontifici ducatorum duos mille pro parte nos tangente pro expensis factis predicto domino Imperatori de mense Iulii et alios ducatorum duos mille pro dando illis qui procurarunt conclusionem treuguarum prout captum est per hoc consilium, nam summus Pontifex accepit illos quos miseramus. . . ."

the Pseudo-Sphrantzes identifies as "Maria Melissena") tried to secure the duchy of Athens and Thebes for herself and her kinsman, the Athenian George Chalcocondylas. The latter is described by his son, the historian Laonicus, as one of the chief figures in the ancient city. The widowed duchess sent Chalcocondylas to the Ottoman court well equipped with funds to persuade Sultan Murad II to recognize their authority over the hitherto Latin duchy. After Chalcocondylas's departure from Athens, however, the Florentine party lured the duchess from the security of the Acropolis, where they installed as duke the late Antonio's young cousin and adopted heir, Nerio II, driving the Chalcocondylae and their supporters from the citadel. The Florentine party then arranged Nerio's marriage with the enterprising widow, installed themselves on the Acropolis, expelled the Chalcocondylae from the city, and drew in the reins of government. In the meantime George Chalcocondylas himself had arrived at the sultan's court, where he was imprisoned, and despite his offer to the Porte of 30,000 gold pieces for the duchy, he was ordered to give up all claim to Attica and Boeotia. He had already heard, moreover, that the sultan had sent an army to occupy Boeotia and take over the city of Thebes. He now managed to escape from the Turkish court to Byzantium, where he took ship for the Morea, but the crews of vessels belonging to the Florentine party in Athens boarded the one on which he was traveling. Chalcocondylas was seized, put in fetters, and sent back to Sultan Murad, who merely pardoned and released him, bearing him no ill will for his unceremonious and unauthorized departure. Chalcocondylas, however, was asked for the 30,000 gold pieces, which he said he could no longer pay, and the land he had aspired to was ravaged by the Ottoman forces in Thessaly.[34] The Greeks in this region as in others might have preferred Greek to Latin rule, but actually it could have made little difference in their way of life, for by now the Turks were everywhere and disposed of all things.

The diplomat George Sphrantzes, who was a participant in the events which followed the death of Antonio I of Athens, gives a different account from that of Chalcocondylas, who had doubtless received his information from his father. Sphrantzes does not mention the joint effort of the widowed duchess and the Chalcocondylae to seize control of the duchy although he was probably well acquainted with conditions in Athens, having been sent there by his master, Constantine Dragases, then one of the despots of the Morea, on an embassy to Antonio the year before the latter's death. In Sphrantzes' account of what now transpired we find one more effort of Constantine Dragases to build up the Moreote domain and to extend the political cause of Hellenism.[35] Here is the fuller version of this account, given in the so-called Pseudo-Sphrantzes' *Chronicon maius* (the much-expanded version of Sphrantzes' *Chronicon minus*, prepared by the "forger" Macarius Melissurgus alias Melissenus in the 1570's), which as usual contains apparently irresponsible changes as well as some interesting information not to be found in the shorter text, although of course the question arises as to Melissurgus's sources:

> At the beginning of the summer of the year (of Creation) 6943 [1435] there died the ruler of Athens and Thebes, the aforesaid lord Antonio de'Acciajuoli Comnenus, and by request of his widow Maria Melissena, daughter of Leo Melissenus, first cousin of Nicephorus Melissenus, . . . I was sent with a sworn argyrobull and many soldiers to take over Athens and Thebes, for which I should give her another place in the Peloponnesus, in the region of

[34] Laonicus Chalcocondylas, bk. VI (Bonn, pp. 320–22); ed. E. Darkó, II-1 (1923), 93–94. The Venetian government instructed its officials in Negroponte not to interfere whether Athens was occupied by the Turks or by the heirs of the late Duke Antonio Acciajuoli (*cf.* C. N. Sathas, ed., *Documents inédits relatifs à l'histoire de la Grèce au moyen âge*, 9 vols., Paris, 1880–90, repr. Athens, 1972, I, no. 131, p. 199, dated October, 1435). That Antonio's widow [was she really a "Maria Melissena"?] actually married Nerio II appears from Sathas, III, no. 1020, pp. 427–28, dated 5 September, 1435, to the bailie and captain of Negroponte (*cf.* Thiriet, *Régestes*, III, no. 2396, p. 48): "Scripsistis nobis quod post mortem magnifici domini Antonii de Azaiolis eius uxor introivit castrum [the Acropolis], et eius nepos civitatem Athenarum, et denique ex matrimonio secuto in pace et concordia remanserunt." The Signoria's officials in Negroponte were to try to secure recognition by Nerio II and his newly acquired wife of Venetian suzerainty over the Athenian duchy, which the Duke Antonio had acknowledged in his lifetime. (The document here referred to, of October, 1435, exists only in the rubric, the scribe lamenting that it had not been copied in the folio and might be lost, "ut multe alie que [*sic*] scribere non potui," but it seems to have been merely repetitious of the second document cited, that of 5 September, 1435.)

[35] Sphrantzes, *Chronicon minus* (*PG* 156, 1044A–1045A, and ed. Vasile Grecu, *Georgios Sphrantzes, Memorii* [*1401–1477*], *în anexă Pseudo-Phrantzes: Macarie Melissenos, Cronica* [*1258–1481*], Bucharest, 1966, pp. 50, 52, 54).

Laconia, near which she had properties from her paternal inheritance and dowry, which were the lands, cities, and villages herewith listed—Astron, S. Peter, S. John, Platamonas, Meligon, Proasteion, Leonidas, Kyparissia, Reontas, and Sitanas. And so I should give her a place near these of such size and sort as should seem best to me and accord with her wish and preference. But Turakhan got the start of me and invested Thebes, which he captured after some days. I returned from the Isthmus with nothing accomplished, for such were my instructions, and arrived at Stylaria, where my lord the despot [Constantine Dragases] then was, waiting for the Venetian merchantmen in order to go to the city [of Constantinople]. Alas for my failure!

We got on board the Venetian ships, and when we had reached Euboea [Euripos, Negroponte], my lord decided to send me to Turakhan, who was still at Thebes, in order to explain to him the negotiations with respect to Athens. When I was ushered into his presence, he received me with expressed delight, and assured me with an oath:

"If I had known about this before leaving home to come here, I could have gladly done what you ask because of my love for the despot and my knowledge of you, for I have done this without any command from the great lord [the sultan]; therefore if I were only at home, I could find many excuses [for the Greek occupation of Athens], but now I have no excuse."

Having shown me much kindness and honor, he brought his sons to greet me, and recommended them to me and to my lord. One of them is now a famous and powerful commander [ἀμήρης, obviously Omar Beg]. And so I took my leave of them, returning unsuccessful. Since the people in Euboea, anticipating trouble, had reluctantly raised the bridge on 29 August, we spent that night among the rocks outside by the bridge. We suffered many hardships that night both from cold and hunger and the harshness of the rocks, as well as from fear of robbers and Turakhan's troops. The horses we had borrowed from the city [of Thebes?] were strange to us, which became a by-word for trouble at a later time among those who were then with me. In any event we got on board ship the next morning, and on 23 September of the year (of Creation) 6944 [still 1435] we arrived at Constantinople.[36]

Before his elevation to the papacy Eugenius IV had become well known in Italy as the "cardinal of Siena." Able and austere, he was elected on 3 March, 1431, and crowned on the eleventh of the month. A Venetian, a nephew of Gregory XII, and a good friend of the Florentines, Eugenius found a ready-made enemy in Filippo Maria Visconti, the duke of Milan, who was always an opponent of Venice and was again at war with Florence. Filippo Maria invaded the states of the Church, and was soon supporting every anti-papal activity at the Council of Basel, where statesmen, scholars, and schemers, men of vision, orators, and short-sighted opportunists were gathering to reform the Church or make their fortunes. Eugenius's early years as pope were as difficult as Martin's. The world fell to pieces around him. Expelled from Rome by a popular revolution (on 29 May, 1434), he fled to Florence, where like Martin he resided in the Dominican convent of S. Maria Novella. The conciliarists at Basel were approaching the height of their influence. From 1434 to 1437 they prepared long and detailed documents on plans for a western subvention of the Greek embassy of 700 members, which should include both the emperor and the patriarch of Constantinople, to come westward and discuss church union in an oecumenical council. To the ambitious fathers assembled at Basel this meant of course their own council.[37]

---

[36] Pseudo-Sphrantzes, *Chron. maius*, II, 10–11 (Bonn, pp. 159–61; ed. J. B. Papadopoulos, I [Leipzig, 1935], 160–62; ed. Grecu [1966], pp. 302, 304). Since the new *annus mundi* began in September, the parts of both the years 6943 and 6944 to which reference is made fell in the year A.D. 1435. An argyrobull is a document with a silver seal. On the historical background, *cf.* Wm. Miller, *Latins in the Levant*, London, 1908, pp. 404–6; D. G. Kampouroglous, *The Chalkokondylai* [in Greek], Athens, 1926, pp. 32–34, 94 ff.; D. A. Zakythinos, *Le Despotat grec de Morée*, 2 vols., Paris and Athens, 1932–53, repr. London, 1975, I, 204–13; Gyula Moravcsik, *Byzantinoturcica*, 2 vols., 2nd ed., Berlin, 1958, I, 391; K. M. Setton, *Catalan Domination of Athens, 1311–1388*, Cambridge, Mass., 1948, and 2nd ed., London, 1975, pp. 202–6. The passages referring to the Melisseni and their properties are lacking in Sphrantzes, being added by Macarius Melissurgus-Melissenus, who as usual glorifies the family of the Melisseni (see above, Chapter 1, note 99).

[37] *Cf.* J. D. Mansi, *Sacrorum conciliorum nova et amplissima collectio*, XXIX (Venice, 1788, repr. Paris, 1904), cols. 92–98, 121–37. As was to be expected, the conciliarists quickly met papal opposition to their plans for dealing with the Greeks (*ibid.*, cols. 171D ff., 285–313, 322C ff., 445D ff., *et alibi*, and note cols. 617E–618, 627–29, 649–50, 651–65; also vol. XXX [1792, repr. 1904], cols. 848D–849, 871 ff., 890, 922–23, 934 ff., 965D–966, 1033 ff., 1094D ff., 1121–22, 1136C ff.; and vol. XXXI [1798, repr. 1906], cols. 197 ff., 248–72). Martin V had died on 20 February, 1431, and Eugenius IV was elected at Rome on 3 March (*cf.* Eugenius's announcement of Martin's death and his own election in Arch. Segr. Vaticano, Reg. Vat. 359, fols. 59^v–60^r, letter dated at Rome on 12 March, 1431).

Besides the materials assembled for the history of the Council of Basel in Mansi's collection, reference should be made to the *Monumenta conciliorum generalium seculi decimi quinti. . . . Concilium Basileense . . .*, 3 [actually 4] vols., Vienna and Basel, 1857–1932, which contains the histories

To have drawn the Greeks to Basel and got credit for an act of union would have enhanced the conciliarists' prestige immensely. But the Greeks found the Council more difficult to deal with and less reliable than the pope, who was unreliable only when he dealt with the conciliarists. Until the year 1436 the conciliarists had made few mistakes, and Eugenius had made many, but their success made many of them reckless, and the pope had learned caution from his setbacks. The Council finally became divided into two fiercely inimical factions over the question whether union must be discussed at Basel, at Avignon, or in Savoy, or whether the members might remove to an Italian city to meet with the Greeks, who steadfastly refused in any event to go to Basel, Avignon, or Savoy, the places upon which the majority finally and foolishly insisted.[38] Several embassies were exchanged between Constantinople and Basel. In the end the Greeks were dismayed by the conciliarists' apparent drift toward schism. If the majority in the Council would not work with the pope except on their own impossible terms, and the Latin Church was itself divided, how could they ever achieve union with the Greek Church? In the past, Byzantine emperors and patriarchs had always dealt with the popes on unionist issues. John VIII and the Patriarch Joseph II could not conceive of an oecumenical success without the presence of the Roman pontiff.

When a minority in the Council at Basel, who regarded themselves as the *sanior pars*, were driven by the intransigence and hostility of their more numerous colleagues to make peace with the Curia Romana, and were also joined by the Greek envoys to Basel, they all found Eugenius in a conciliatory mood, as he had been for the past two years. In May, 1437, the envoys and the representatives of the conciliar minority waited upon him at Bologna, whither he had moved with the Curia the preceding year. He agreed fully to abide by the agreement which the Greeks had negotiated with Martin V in 1430 (and this the conciliarists at Basel had consistently declined to do). Much encouraged, Eugenius acted with great dispatch. He arranged for the lease of four Venetian galleys, of which he appointed his nephew Antonio Condulmer the captain-general on 6 July (1437), to convey the Greek delegation of 700 members from Constantinople to Italy. Florence had been discussed as a possible site for the unionist sessions of the Council, which was to be "transferred" from Basel, and the Florentines were willing to provide the Greeks with both money and transport. Filippo Maria Visconti was forever opposed to the Florentines, however, and both the Emperor Sigismund and Charles VII of France objected to the removal of the Council to Italy (for it would clearly lead to "schism," as it did). It was therefore decided that the new location of the Council would be designated only upon the arrival of the Greeks "ad partes Italie."[39] Eugenius soon announced,

---

of the Council by the conciliarists John of Ragusa and John of Segovia, and also to the work of the late Johannes Haller (1865–1947) *et al.*, eds., *Concilium Basiliense: Studien und Quellen zur Geschichte des Concils von Basel*, 8 vols., Basel, 1896–1936, which contains letters, tracts, memorials, expense accounts, day-to-day records (*protocolli*) of events and proceedings, diplomatic correspondence, and the sources relating to the Basler embassy to Constantinople in 1437 to fix the site of the unionist council at Avignon or Basel (vol. III [1904], pp. 175–362).

At the eighteenth general session of the Council of Basel, held on 26 June, 1434, the assembled fathers renewed the decree of the fifth session of the Council of Constance (of 6 April, 1415, for which see von der Hardt, *Magnum oecumenicum Constantiense concilium*, IV [1698–99], 98a; Mansi, *op. cit.*, XXVII, col. 590DE; and *cf.* Fillastre, *Gesta*, in Finke, *Acta*, II, 28), declaring that a general council derived its authority directly from Christ, and was superior to all persons of whatsoever rank or dignity, including the pope, in matters concerning the faith, the extirpation of heresy, and the reform of the Church, on which note Hefele and Leclercq, *Hist. des conciles*, VII, pt. 2 (Paris, 1916), 849 ff., and Mansi, XXIX, col. 91CD. In the fall of 1439 the Dominican Juan de Torquemada assailed the Basler allegation of conciliar supremacy over the pope, in his *Oratio synodalis de primatu*, ed. Emmanuel Candal, Rome, 1954 (Concilium Florentinum, Documenta et scriptores, ser. B, vol. IV, fasc. 2).

[38] During the years that the Council of Basel was at its height, its members were in close and amicable contact with the Emperor John VIII and the Patriarch Joseph II (Hofmann, *Orientalium documenta minora* [1953], nos. 3–5, 8–19, pp. 6–10, 12–25, dated from October, 1433, to March, 1436). The conciliarists refused to hold the unionist council in a *locus maritimus* easy of access to the Greeks, as Martin V had agreed to do (and the hard-pressed Eugenius said that he was even willing for it to be held in Constantinople, on which see, *ibid.*, no. 8, pp. 12–13). Some place on or near the Adriatic was necessary for Joseph II, *qui est senex et continua infirmitate gravatus* (no. 14, p. 20). The emperor and the patriarch categorically refused to go as far as Basel (nos. 22–23, pp. 26–28, dated 11 February, 1437). They also rejected Avignon as a site for the council (no. 26, p. 30). *Cf.* Dölger, *Regesten*, pt. 5, nos. 3437–40, 3443–52, 3454, 3466, pp. 116 ff., and Thiriet, *Régestes*, III, nos. 2418 (an appeal of the conciliarists at Basel for Venetian co-operation to convey John VIII westward, dated 28 June, 1436), 2435, 2445, 2461–62, 2472–73, pp. 53 ff.

[39] *Epistolae pontificiae*, I, nos. 66–86, pp. 64–88, esp. pp. 67, 69, 71–72, 75–77, 83; Hefele and Leclercq,

however, that Ferrara was to be the site of the Council, for which he issued a *salvus conductus generalis* on 17 September (1437),[40] with the intention conceivably of seeking the occasion of transferring it to Florence, where he felt at home among the Medici, whose money and banking facilities he doubtless assumed he was going eventually to need.

While the contending orators at Basel disputed the location of the forthcoming council of union, Eugenius could see a steady improvement in his affairs in Italy. After his arrival in Florence in June, 1434, the pope had remained there for some time, on good terms with the Albizzeschi at first and then with the Medici. He showed little inclination to leave, although meanwhile his doughty legate Giovanni Vitelleschi restored order in Rome and the states of the Church. Vitelleschi was titular patriarch of Alexandria, archbishop of Florence, and a cardinal from August, 1437; more condottiere than cleric, he fell from power in the early spring of 1440, and was rather mysteriously put to death. He was replaced as legate in command of the papal troops by Lodovico Trevisan, the patriarch of Aquileia, and here was indeed a remarkable man, whose wealth and influence grew with each passing year of Eugenius's pontificate. For four centuries Trevisan has been wrongly known as Lodovico Scarampo, and is so called by Pastor and other modern historians. Some word concerning Lodovico's career up to the year 1440 seems in order, because we shall find him very active in the affairs of the Curia for many years. Under Calixtus III he will be a conspicuous figure in the Levant (in 1456–1458) as commander of a papal fleet sent on a crusade against the Turks.

Lodovico was born in Venice in November, 1401, the son of a physician named Biagio Trevisan. Having himself studied medicine as well as the liberal arts at Padua, Lodovico became physician to Cardinal Gabriele Condulmer shortly before the latter's election as pope. Lodovico was made a papal chamberlain (*cubicularius*), and appears to have abandoned the practice of medicine, from which clerics were debarred by canon law. He was now embarked on a distinguished ecclesiastical career, becoming a canon of Padua before April, 1435. Although his advancement was not particularly rapid at first, it was certainly steady. He was appointed bishop of Traù (modern Trogir) on 24 October, 1435, but remained papal chamberlain and administered his see through a local vicar. On 6 August, 1437, he became the archbishop of Florence,[41] being by this time one of the most influential figures at the papal court. Interested in classical antiquities, Lodovico was the friend of Niccolò Niccoli, Francesco Barbaro, and Ciriaco of Ancona. An adept politician, he was also close to Cosimo de' Medici. Through these years the Curia Romana was, for the most part, established in Florence where, as we have noted, Eugenius IV lived at the convent of S. Maria Novella. In September, 1437, Lodovico went on a papal mission to his native Venice,[42] to deal (among other matters) with the location of the forthcoming unionist council. The Venetians had preferred Bologna or some other place in the papal states as a site for the council or indeed some city in the Veneto for the honor and advantages which would have accrued to the Republic. But they were content to accept Lodovico's explanation of the reasons for the pope's preference for Ferrara, and they would

Hist. des conciles, VII-2 (1916), 939–40. On the tangled relations of Eugenius IV, the Greeks, and the conciliarists at Basel, see, *ibid.*, VII-2, 673–74, 684, 688–89, 697, 699, 705, 743–45, 746–47, and esp. pp. 875 ff., 916–49; and in less detail, Joseph Gill, *The Council of Florence*, Cambridge, 1959, pp. 46–84. Although the conciliarists at Basel also sent galleys to Constantinople to convey the Greeks westward, John VIII refused to embark in them, and accepted the papal galleys, because Basel had not kept faith with him as to the site of the unionist council, "et in aliis quamplurimis non observatum ex parte vestra" (*Orientalium documenta minora*, no. 25, pp. 29–30, dated 25 October, 1437).

[40] *Epistolae pontificiae*, I, no. 87, pp. 89–90, in which the pope expresses the hope "quod per operam Altissimi, cuius causa agitur, concilium Basiliense transferetur de proximo ad civitatem Ferrariensem pro tractanda in eo et occidentalis et orientalis ecclesiarum unitate, pro reformatione universalis ecclesie, Christiane fidei augmento et pace fidelium. . . ." The Council of Basel was finally and formally "translated" to Ferrara by the bull *Pridem ex iustis* promulgated from Bologna on 30 December, 1437, its work to be resumed, according to the bull, on the following 8 January (*ibid.*, I, no. 108, pp. 110–12), when in fact the first Ferrarese session was held (Gill, *Council of Florence*, pp. 94–95). Eugenius arrived in the city toward the end of the month, at which time (on 24 January) the recalcitrant conciliarists at Basel declared him suspended from office and deprived of all spiritual and temporal authority (John of Segovia, *Historia gestorum generalis synodi Basiliensis*, XIII, 7, in the *Monumenta conciliorum generalium seculi decimi quinti*, III [1886], 25–30).

[41] On 11 August (1437) the Venetian Senate wrote Lodovico to congratulate him upon his promotion from the see of Traù to that of Florence (Arch. di Stato di Venezia, Sen. Secreta, Reg. 14 [1436–1439], fol. 50^{v}).

[42] Marino Sanudo, *Vite de' duchi di Venezia*, in L. A. Muratori, ed., *RISS*, XXII (Milan, 1733), col. 1043B.

show their acquiescence in the pope's decision by themselves requesting safe-conduct for those attending the council from their neighbor, the Marquis Niccolò III d'Este. As they reminded Lodovico, they had willingly allowed his Holiness to arm his galleys in Venice as well as recruit crossbowmen in Venetian territories to reinforce the defenses of Constantinople during John VIII's absence from the Bosporus.[43]

When Eugenius IV appointed "monsignor Lodovico Trevisano" to the patriarchate of Aquileia (on 19 December, 1439),[44] the latter gave up the archbishopric of Florence. By a bull of 11 January, 1440, the Patriarch Lodovico was next appointed papal treasurer, *camerarius*.[45] He distinguished himself as a commander of the papal troops in the battle of Anghiari on the upper Arno (on 29 June, 1440), when the pope's Florentine allies defeated a Milanese army of invasion under the condottiere Niccolò Piccinino and that of the anti-Medicean Florentine exiles under Rinaldo degli Albizzi. The Venetians were of course delighted by "this happy news of the victory obtained against Niccolò Piccinino."[46] In recognition of his signal services to the Holy See, Lodovico was made a cardinal on 1 July, 1440, with the title of S. Lorenzo in Damaso. Not yet forty years of age, he had achieved a great reputation in Italy. Thereafter he was known as the cardinal of Aquileia,[47] as he is usually called

---

[43] Sen. Secreta, Reg. 14, fol. 55^r, dated 10 September, 1437: ". . . Respondeatur [reverendo patri domino archiepiscopo Florentino] . . . quod, ut novit Beatitudo sua, nos ut veri et devotissimi filii Sanctitatis sue et dispositi ad ea que grata forent Beatitudini sue fuimus contenti ei complacere quod armaret hic eas galeas quas armari fecit ac quod de terris nostris ballistarios haberet ad eius stipendia mittendos ad custodiam civitatis Constantinopolitane. . . . Et fuit nostra intentio, quemadmodum Sanctitati sue declarari fecimus, quod concilium celebraretur in Bononia vel aliis terris Sancte Ecclesie aut in terris nostris, nam si in terris nostris celebraretur, Beatitudo sua ample cognoscit honores et commoda que nostre reipublice pervenissent. Sed nunc intellectis causis que Beatitudinem suam moverunt ad celebrandum concilium suprascriptum in civitate Ferrarie dispositi ob filialem reverentiam et sinceritatem nostram ad omnia commoda sue Beatitudini contenti remanemus quod in dicta civitate Ferrarie celebretur predictum concilium ac si celebraretur in terris nostris, et parati sumus pro Beatitudine sua a . . . domino marchione petere salvumconductum, ut requirit Sanctitas sua." On Lodovico's mission, *cf.* also, *ibid.*, fols. 57^v–58^r and ff., 79, 83^v, 84^r, 93^v, 94^v–95, *et alibi*, and Sanudo, *Vite de'duchi*, in *RISS*, XXII, col. 1043B.

[44] Andrea Navagero, *Storia veneziana*, in *RISS*, XXIII (1733), col. 1105, another indication that Lodovico was a Trevisan and not a member of the family of Scarampo-Mezzarota (on which see below, in this note). Eugenius had already sent an envoy to Venice to sound out the Senate on their acceptance of a certain Venetian, obviously Lodovico, for papal nomination to the lucrative patriarchate of Aquileia. Motions to assure Lodovico an annual income of 4,000 ducats, however, and to assign him Aquileia, S. Vito, and S. Daniele *in temporalibus et spiritualibus* were defeated in the Senate on 14 December, 1439 (Sen. Secreta, Reg. 15, fols. 2^v–3^r), but after Lodovico's victory at Anghiari over the condottiere Niccolò Piccinino (which we shall note in a moment) and his elevation to the cardinalate, the Senate was ready to add somewhat to his territorial jurisdictions and to offer him 5,000 ducats a year (*ibid.*, fol. 77, docs. dated 10 and 29 April, 1441). But by this time Lodovico's emissary to the Senate proved so demanding that "vadit pars quod in futurum non possit poni per aliquem in isto consilio de dando pecunias, loca, aut aliquid aliud ultra ea que capta sunt et oblata nisi istud consilium congregatum fuerit numero C . . ." (fol. 79^r, and *cf.* fol. 86^v), and on 21 September, 1441, the Senate informed Lodovico directly of the limits of their offer when he was himself in Venice (fol. 97^v, and *cf.* fols. 112^v, 113^r, 115).

Known incorrectly as a Scarampo from about the mid-sixteenth century, Lodovico has been restored to the family of Trevisan by Pio Paschini, "La Famiglia di Lodovico cardinal camerlengo," in *L'Arcadia*, V (1926), 91 ff.; "Da Medico a patriarca d'Aquileia, camerlengo e cardinale di S. Romana Chiesa," *Memorie storiche forogiuliesi*, XXIII (1927), 1–56; "Lodovico cardinale camerlengo e i suoi maneggi sino alla morte di Eugenio IV (1447)," *ibid.*, XXIV (1928), 39–72, and XXVI (1930), 27–74; and "Prelati e curiali di Casa Scarampi," *Rivista di Alessandria*, XLV (1936), 362–66. For Lodovico's career in general I have depended on Paschini's biography of *Lodovico Cardinal Camerlengo (+1465)*, Rome, 1939, in *Lateranum*, new ser., V-1, Facultas Theologica Pontificii Athenaei Lateranensis. Ernesto Pontieri, *Alfonso il Magnanimo, re di Napoli (1435–1458)*, Naples, 1975, pp. 94, 269–70, 323, 362, still calls Trevisan "Scarampo."

Whatever lies behind the erroneous assignment of the surname Scarampo to Lodovico, he had close relations with various members of this family; *cf.* the letter of Pius II to Lodovico, dated 9 August, 1460 (Arch. Segr. Vaticano, Arm. XXXIX, tom. 9, fol. 136^v): "Audivimus que nomine tuo retulit nobis dilectus filius Nicolaus Scarampo, scutifer tuus, super negotiis terrarum abbatie Montiscasini. . . ." *Cf.*, *ibid.*, fol. 137^r. Lodovico Trevisan in fact made this Niccolò and Lodovico Scarampo his heirs, having brought them up almost from boyhood, although Paul II did not recognize Trevisan's *facultas testamenti*, and claimed most of his vast possessions for the crusade (after his death on 22 March, 1465), thus depriving the Scarampi of their legacy but leaving them nonetheless considerable property, on which see Paschini, *Lodovico Card. Camerlengo*, pp. 208–10. Since it was well known that Lodovico had left most of his estate to the Scarampi, a fact widely publicized by Paul II's intervention, it was natural for later writers to assume that he must have belonged to this family.

[45] Arch. Segr. Vaticano, Reg. Vat. 382 [*Eugenii IV Officior. tom. II*], fol. 111^r, paying especial tribute to Lodovico's *experiencia in agendis rebus*. *Cf.*, *ibid.*, fols. 144^v–145^r.

[46] Sen. Secreta, Reg. 15, fol. 28^v, doc. dated 3 July, 1440. On the political importance of Anghiari to Eugenius IV, see Gill, *The Council of Florence*, pp. 320–21.

[47] *Cf.* Arch. di Stato di Venezia, Sen. Secreta, Reg. 15, fol. 33^r, doc. dated 8 August, 1440, and, *ibid.*, fols. 42, 43^r, 77, 79^r, 86^v, 97^v, *et alibi*.

in the Vatican registers. If Cardinal Vitelleschi fell from power with the suddenness of Sejanus, Lodovico had all the pride and love of luxury of Lucullus, becoming known in fact as the "cardinale Lucullo."[48]

When Prince Centurione Zaccaria died in 1432, the last remnants of the old Frankish principality of Achaea disappeared, and the protection of the Morea against the Turks devolved upon the Palaeologian despots. Through the remaining years of Greek independence these were, as is well known, Theodore II and Constantine, Thomas and Demetrius, brothers of the reigning emperor John VIII. The only one of them who showed much ability was Constantine, known as Dragases after his mother Helena, a daughter of Constantine Dejanović (of the Serbian house of Dragaš, which ruled in eastern Macedonia).[49] Despite the signal successes achieved by the Turks in the fourth decade of the century, Constantine was to try to bring together both the Morea and continental Greece under the unified rule of the Moreote despotate. Before John VIII had departed for Italy on 27 November, 1437, to attend the Council of Ferrara-Florence (he arrived in Venice on 8 February, 1438), Constantine had left the Morea for Constantinople to serve as regent during his imperial brother's absence,[50] and from the shores

---

[48] *Cf.* Paschini, *Lodovico Cardinal Camerlengo*, pp. 7–51, 103, 115–16, 136, 208 ff.; on Lodovico's command of the papal troops, see Predelli, *Regesti dei Commemoriali*, IV (1896), bk. XIII, no. 66, p. 226, dated 21 March, 1440, and nos. 147–48, 156, and *cf.* Arch. Segr. Vaticano, Reg. Vat. 382, fols. 162^{v}–163^{v}, dated 1 September, 1442, and fols. 204^{v}–206^{r}.

Various chronological data relating to Cardinal Lodovico's career may be found in a slender but most important register in the Vatican Archives (Arm. XXXI, tom. 52), to which Ludwig von Pastor called attention many years ago (*Hist. Popes*, I, 392–93, and *Gesch. d. Päpste*, I [repr. 1955], 815–16). Since in fact numerous chronological data will be found to depend on this volume for almost half a century, I think that some description of it at this point will be worthwhile.

The original lettering on the spine of the volume has been preserved (the back of the original binding being glued into the present inner cover), identifying it as *Littere Sacri Collegii Federico 3. Imperatore: Quietantie varia: Bulla Eugenii pro Camerae clericis: 2611: De officio et potestate Camerarii S. Collegii: Computa et res spectantes ad Sacrum Collegium*. Despite the various titles, the volume actually contains detailed notes relating to the Consistory from 1439 to 1486 (fols. 48^{r}–104^{v}, by mod. stamped enumeration; fols. 15^{r}–71^{v} by an earlier numbering), and may be regarded as one of the earliest in the valuable series of Acta Consistorialia. The (first) writer identifies himself as Jacobus Radulphi, ". . . et sic michi Jacobo Radulphi, clerico dicti collegii, retullit idem dominus . . ." (fol. 53^{r}, and *cf.* 57^{r}). This Jacobus wrote also some *Ephemerides sacri consistorii*, which were used by Domin. Georgius in his *Vita Nicolai V*, Rome, 1742, but Arm. XXXI, tom. 52, is not the work to which Georgius alludes (*cf.* Pastor, *Hist. Popes*, I, 393). Pastor believed the Acta "to have been extracted from a larger register," which is possible. They form, however, a week-to-week report of both secret and public consistories (note the partly marginal addition of 13 October, 1469, to an entry dated 13 November, 1467, on fol. 69^{v}), especially the cardinals' participation in the *communia et minuta servitia*, of which the *camerarius* or treasurer of the Sacred College kept record, commonly passing the information on to the clerks of the College, who kept the "*acta*" preserved in this register.

At the beginning of the year 1468 appears the note (Arm. XXXI, tom. 52, fol. 70^{r}): "Mutatur annus MCCCCLXVIII^{s}, pontificatus S. D. N. domini Pauli anno quarto, inceptus per me Ieronimum Iunium die XXVI. Aprilis—ex libro domini Gabrielis Rovira clerici collegii" (the first entry for this year is dated 10 January). Junius was elected one of the two clerks of the Sacred College on Saturday, 23 April, as he records himself in the register (fol. 70^{v}): "Creatio mei Ieronimi Iunii in clericum Collegii reverendorum dominorum cardinalium: Die sabati XXIII. Aprilis, anno et pontificatu quibus supra [1468], reverendissimus in Christo pater et dominus, dominus Gulielmus, episcopus Ostiensis cardinalis Rothomagensis [Guillaume d'Estouteville], Sacri Collegii reverendissimorum in Christo patrum dominorum S.S.R.E. cardinalium camerarius de ipsorum omnium voluntate et consensu admisit et constituit me Ieronimum Iunium decretorum doctorem, canonicum Florentinum, in clericum ipsius Sacri Collegii, et iuravi in manibus ipsius reverendissimi domini Gulielmi secundum constitutiones ipsius Sacri Collegii in presentia domini Gabrielis Rovira, alterius clerici, de quibus rogatus fuit dominus Johannes Fortini, notarius camere apostolice." *Cf.*, *ibid.*, fol. 71. Such glimpses behind scenes in the Curia are always interesting.

The first entry in this register of Acta Consistorialia is also important as marking the first appearance of the Greeks Isidore "of Kiev" and Bessarion of Nicaea as cardinals, both of whom were long to serve the Latin cause in the East (fol. 48^{r}): "Anno incarnationis dominice MCCCCXXXIX, die Sabbati XVIII mensis Decembris, pontificatus domini Eugenii anno nono: Sanctissimus dominus noster divina providentia [Eugenius] papa quartus Florentie assumpsit [MS. assupmsit!] ad cardinalatum XVII dominos cardinales, videlicet:" [seventh in the list stands "dominum Isidorum, archiepiscopum Russensem," and eighth "dominum Bissarionem, archiepiscopum Nicenum."] It was a historic consistory at which these elevations to the cardinalate were announced, but the notice in the Acta is at least deficient to the extent that in 1439 the eighteenth of December fell on Friday, not Saturday. Selections from the register (Arm. XXXI, tom. 52), beginning with 22 January, 1440, are given in Conrad Eubel, *Hierarchia catholica medii aevi*, II (1914, repr. 1960), 26 ff.

[49] Constantine Dejanović was killed in the battle of Rovine in May, 1395, when Mircea the Elder of Wallachia, assisted by the Hungarians, tried in vain to halt the Turkish advance into the Dobruja and over the Danube (*cf.* G. Ostrogorsky, *History of the Byzantine State*, Oxford, 1956, pp. 489–90, and Iorga, *Gesch. d. osman. Reiches*, I, 275 ff.).

[50] According to Sphrantzes, *Chron. minus* (*PG* 156, 1045D–1046A; ed. Grecu, p. 56), Constantine left Patras on 5 Sep-

of the Bosporus he could see from month to month the northward extension of Turkish arms.

This was a very depressing period for Balkan Christendom. Before the Council of Ferrara-Florence had assembled, the Emperor Sigismund died in December, 1437. He was succeeded by the Hapsburg Albert [II] of Austria, his daughter Elizabeth's husband, who now became king of Hungary and Bohemia. In March, 1438, Albert was also elected to the imperial throne (or, to be more precise, was elected king of the Romans), beginning that almost continuous succession of Hapsburg rulers which was to last as long as the Holy Roman Empire. Sultan Murad II took advantage of Sigismund's death to launch attacks upon Transylvania and Hungary. We are well informed concerning the events of 1438.[51] Gustav Beckmann's careful edition of the *Deutsche Reichstagsakten* of this year contains the most detailed reports of a wide range of imperial problems and affairs. Here documents are given in abundance depicting the rival claims of Eugenius IV and the conciliarists at Basel, details relating to church union and the forthcoming Council of Ferrara, the views of German princes and cities, ambassadors' instructions and their speeches replete with biblical and classical allusions, notarial instruments, proposed reforms and taxes, military preparations, and even an exchange of letters between the Byzantine Emperor John VIII and the German electors.[52] Actually there are surprisingly few references to the Turks in this material although in late November, 1438, Albert II in a letter to the pope (denouncing King Ladislas III of Poland) does dwell on the fearful depredations of the Turks in Hungary during the preceding summer.[53] The king of Poland was accused of giving aid and counsel to the Turks. An extremely important letter, however, of one Jodocus de Helpruna written from Vienna on 11 September, 1438, to an official of the Council of Basel describes the recent Turkish attacks upon Siebenbürgen (Transylvania) and the "Wurzland:" the sultan himself had led the expedition, and carried off 80,000 persons into slavery, not counting the many priests and others who were killed. The city of Mühlenbach (modern Sebeş) in Transylvania was entirely destroyed, and the territory roundabout thoroughly pillaged. The Turks had had about a thousand camels bearing their tents and other equipment. The sultan was said to have employed as his guide none other than Vlad II Dracul, the voivode of Wallachia, an imperial vassal, upon whom Albert had in fact depended for the defense of the eastern marches.[54]

Among those carried off by the Turks at this time was George of Siebenbürgen, whose captivity lasted about twenty years (1438–1458), but who returned to write the valuable record of his long residence among the Turks. His account was to have a wide circulation in both Latin and German.[55] In the following year (1439) the sultan

---

tember (1437), went to Negroponte, and thence to Constantinople, where he arrived on the twenty-fourth (*cf.* Pseudo-Sphrantzes, II, 12, ed. Bonn, pp. 162–63; ed. J. B. Papadopoulos, I [Leipzig, 1935], 164; ed. Grecu, p. 306), which is in general accord with the information supplied by the Venetian government to the pope (Iorga, *ROL*, VI, 389, doc. dated 22 October, 1437). On the circumstances and chronology of John VIII's voyage to Venice, see Iorga, *ROL*, VI, 391–92, note; 398–99, note; and Gill, *Council of Florence*, pp. 88–90, 98.

[51] *Cf.* in general the Venetian Sen. Secreta, Reg. 14, fols. 109 ff., 149v ff., and von Aschbach, *Gesch. Kaiser Sigmund's*, IV, 396 ff.

[52] G. Beckmann, ed., *Deutsche Reichstagsakten unter König Albrecht II.*, pt. 1, Göttingen, 1957, nos. 121, 128, pp. 184, 195 (Deutsche Reichstagsakten, XIII), dated at Venice on 25 February, 1438, and at Frankfurt between 11 and 19 March of the same year.

[53] Beckmann, *op. cit.*, no. 370, p. 729; *cf.* Ladislas's rejoinder to the pope, dated in February, 1439 (*ibid.*, no. 375, p. 747); and note A. Sokołowski and J. Szujski, eds., *Codex epistolaris saeculi decimi quinti*, I, pt. 1 (Cracow, 1876, repr. New York and London, 1965), nos. XCIV–XCVI, XCIX, CII, pp. 88 ff. (Monumenta medii aevi historica res gestas Poloniae illustrantia, tom. II).

[54] Beckmann, *op. cit.*, no. 283, p. 525; note also, *ibid.*, no. 399, p. 839; *cf.* Iorga, *Gesch. d. osman. Reiches*, I, 419–20, and Aurel Decei, "Deux Documents turcs concernant les expéditions des sultans Bayazid Ier et Murad II dans les pays roumains," *Revue roumaine d'histoire*, XIII-3 (1974), 395–413, esp. pp. 403 ff. Mühlenbach (Sebeş) was not "entirely destroyed," as Jodocus says (*Mulenbach civitas totaliter est destructa*), on which note Radu Florescu and R. T. McNally, *Dracula: A Biography of Vlad the Impaler (1431–1476)*, New York, 1973, pp. 34 and 188, note 13. The Turks invaded Siebenbürgen in 1395–1396, 1420–1421, 1432, 1434, 1438, 1440, 1442, and frequently thereafter (Gustav Gündisch, "Die Türkeneinfälle in Siebenbürgen bis zur Mitte des 15. Jahrhunderts," *Jahrbücher für Geschichte Osteuropas*, II [1937], 393–412, and Gündisch, "Siebenbürgen in der Türkenabwehr, 1395–1526," *Revue roumaine d'histoire*, XIII-3, 415–43).

[55] After his escape from the Turks, George of Siebenbürgen (or Georgius de Hungaria) joined the Dominican Order. He wrote a well-known work entitled *Tractatus de moribus, condicionibus et nequicia Turcorum*, which first appeared in Rome in 1480, although the authorship of the work long remained rather foggy. George died in Rome at the age of eighty on 3 July, 1502. He was buried near

led another great offensive, this time into Serbia; captured Semendria (Smederevo), the capital of the Balkan despotate, in August after a three months' siege; and reduced to servitude all but the province of Novo Brdo in southern Serbia, which held out for two more years. Novo Brdo was rich in gold and silver mines, and one of the largest cities in the Balkans. At the end of October (1439) Albert II died unexpectedly; competitors struggled for his dangerous crowns, and the Turks availed themselves of the ensuing anarchy. The roads of the northern Balkans were full of refugees, harried and looted by Turkish soldiers. From April, 1440, Murad's forces laid siege to Alba Greca (Belgrade), at the confluence of the Sava with the Danube, and devastated the country over a wide area. The stalwart garrison at Belgrade held out, however, and in September Murad was obliged to raise the siege. By now Albert had been succeeded as king of the Romans by his distant cousin Frederick III [IV] of Hapsburg, who was to be the last emperor crowned in Rome (in 1452). During his long and dreary reign of more than half a century Frederick built up the fortunes of his house, but never distinguished himself by his efforts against the Turks.[56]

In the meantime the Council of Ferrara-Florence had met, with remarkable results. According to George Sphrantzes, Manuel II had once told his son John VIII that the Turks lived in constant fear of a Graeco-Latin alliance, which they knew could only bode ill for them. Whenever John had need, therefore, of putting fear in the infidels' hearts (*ὅταν ἔχῃς χρείαν τινα φοβῆσαι τοὺς ἀσεβεῖς*), he should entertain the proposal for a council to effect the union of the churches. But since Manuel could see no hope of the Greeks' ever finding spiritual peace and understanding with the Latins, John should never risk the parlous venture into actual union, for it would prove impossible, and "I fear lest an even worse schism may result—and then look! we have left ourselves uncovered to the infidels' [attacks]."[57] Whether or not this was good advice, we need not try to say. At all events it was not the spirit in which John and the Greek delegation had come to Italy,[58] and (as many a schoolboy knows or used to know) the union of the churches was in fact proclaimed, and with rare unanimity.[59]

Fra Angelico in the church of S. Maria sopra Minerva "cum maxima populi frequentia per triduum," although the site of his interment is no longer identifiable. See J. A. B. Palmer, "Fr. Georgius de Hungaria, O. P. . . . ," *Bulletin of the John Rylands Library*, XXXIV (Manchester, 1951), 44–68.

[56] Iorga, *Gesch. d. osman. Reiches*, I, 417–20, 422–25; Babinger, *Maometto il Conquistatore* (1957), pp. 40–44, 618. Novo Brdo was occupied by the Turks in 1441, recovered by the Serbs, and reoccupied by the forces of Mehmed II on 1 June, 1455. On the Turkish exploitation of the mines, see Nicoară Beldiceanu, *Les Actes des premiers sultans . . .* , I: *Actes de Mehmed II et de Bayezid II . . .* , Paris, 1960, docs. 3–6, pp. 68–73, with refs., and vol. II: *Règlements miniers, 1390–1512*, Paris, 1964, pp. 53–55, 85–87, 103, 148 ff., 161 ff., and docs. 9, 10, 16, 19, esp. 20, 22, 25, and 26–28.

Many of Frederick III's activities both as king of the Romans and as emperor may be followed, almost from day to day, in Joseph Chmel, *Regesta chronologico-diplomatica Friderici IV. Romanorum regis (imperatoris III.)*, Vienna, 1838, repr. Hildesheim, 1962. Among the almost 9,000 documents summarized by Chmel (largely dealing, to be sure, with the internal affairs of the empire) there are surprisingly few concerned with the Turkish peril, the most important being nos. 2232, 3009, 3175, 3356, 3369, 3535, 3689, 3699, 3781, 3857, 4490, 4739, 5031, 6177, 6336, 6431, 7468, 8001, and *cf.* nos. 3706, 3711, 3721, 4542. Frederick was always far less concerned with the *Türkenfrage* than with the aggrandizement of his family. On his reign, see the various essays and bibliographies by Alphons Lhotsky, Hermann Wiesflecker, Hanna Dornik-Eger, *et al.*, *Friedrich III., Kaiserresidenz Wiener Neustadt*, Vienna, 1966, and Lhotsky, "Kaiser Friedrich III.: Sein Leben und seine Persönlichkeit" [reprinted from the *Kaiserresidenz Wiener Neustadt*], in his *Aufsätze und Vorträge*, 5 vols., Munich, 1970–76, II, 119–63.

[57] Sphrantzes, *Chronicon minus*, in the *Patrologia graeca* [*PG*], vol. 156, cols. 1046D–1047A; Vasile Grecu, ed., *Georgios Sphrantzes, Memorii (1401–1477), în anexă Pseudo-Phrantzes: Macarie Melissenos, Cronica (1258–1481)*, Bucharest, 1966, *Mem.*, XXIII, 5–6, p. 58; and *cf.* Pseudo-Sphrantzes ("Phrantzes"), *Chron. maius*, II, 13 (Bonn, pp. 178–79; ed. Papadopoulos, I, 177–78; ed. Grecu, p. 320). This text is often referred to (*cf.* Gill, *Council of Florence*, p. 30; Barker, *Manuel II Palaeologus*, pp. 329–30; V. Laurent, in *Revue des études byzantines*, XX, 14).

[58] In actual fact Syropoulos, *Mémoires*, IX, 15, ed. Laurent (1971), p. 448, represents John VIII as telling the Greek delegation at Florence that his father Manuel had favored church union, and worked toward it. Since Manuel was not able to bring it about, however, he had bequeathed the task to John for fulfilment: "*Οὐκ ἔφθασε δὲ ἰδεῖν ταύτην [τὴν ἕνωσιν] τετελεσμένην, διὸ καὶ ἐπαφῆκέ μοι ἵνα τελειώσω αὐτήν, καὶ ἔστι τὸ ἔργον ἐκείνου καὶ ὡς ἀπ'ἐκείνου πράττω τοῦτο καὶ αὐτός.*"

[59] The major sources for the Council of Ferrara-Florence have become fully available only during the last generation, in excellent editions prepared by Frs. Georg Hofmann, Emmanuel Candal, Joseph Gill, Bernard Schultze, Vitalien Laurent, and others, in the *Concilium Florentinum, Documenta et scriptores*, published by the Pontifical Institute of Oriental Studies, Piazza S. Maria Maggiore, Rome. Reference is made to the individual volumes where the need to do so occurs. The old work, however, of Eugenio Cecconi, *Studi storici sul concilio di Firenze*, I, Florence, 1869, with some 200 documents, still remains very useful.

Of the abundant secondary literature relating to the Council, mention should be made of the following: Georg

After being sumptuously entertained in Venice, which he had reached with the Greek delegation on 8 February, 1438, the Emperor John VIII went on to Ferrara, where the Council had been in session since 8 January.[60] He arrived on 4 March in a driving rain. The Patriarch Joseph II, aged and ailing, entered the city four days later. According to a papal letter of 9 April (when the Council became "oecumenical" with the advent of the Greeks),[61] the Holy See had already expended 80,000 ducats on the Greeks' behalf besides the then current cost of 5,000 ducats a month for their support and for the maintenance of the 300 crossbowmen and the two light galleys which the pope had added to the defense of Constantinople.[62]

Although he was paying the piper, Eugenius IV found it hard to call the tune. The Latins reluctantly agreed to a four months' postponement of any serious discussion of the chief differences which divided the two Churches (the procession of the Holy Spirit, the use of leavened or of unleavened bread [τὰ ἄζυμα] in communion, the Latin doctrine of purgatory, and the perennial question of papal supremacy), to give the kings and princes of Europe an opportunity to send their delegates to the Council. The condottiere Niccolò Piccinino, in Milanese employ, seized Bologna in late May (1438), and July and August brought the plague to Ferrara. There were rumors that a massive Turkish attack upon Constantinople was impending. A few states sent representatives to Ferrara, but in the Pragmatic Sanction of Bourges (in July) Charles VII, while leaning toward Basel, made France neutral in the continuing conflict between the pope and the conciliarists. The German electors persisted in the expression of a favorable attitude toward Basel, but they too adopted a neutral stance. The doctrine of purgatory was debated in private meetings in June and July (1438) without reaching a satisfactory settlement of opposing views.[63] The Ferrarese fathers began the formal discussions of their dogmatic differences as late as 8 October with the thorny question of the Latin addition of the *filioque* clause to the Nicene creed. The controversy dragged on, with displays of ingenuity and learning, through fourteen or fifteen sessions (until 13–14 December), by which time the colossal financial burden of supporting the Council had already turned Eugenius's eyes toward Florence, where the Medici were waiting to receive the pope and the Curia, the emperor and the patriarch, the contending divines, their notaries and attendants, and the hangers-on who flocked to councils.[64]

Hofmann, "Die Konzilsarbeit in Ferrara," *Orientalia Christiana periodica*, III (1937), 110–40, 403–55; "Die Konzilsarbeit in Florenz," *ibid.*, IV (1938), 157–88, 372–422; and *Papato, conciliarismo, patriarcato (1438–1439): Teologi e deliberazioni del concilio di Firenze*, Rome, 1940; also V. Chiaroni, *Lo Scisma greco e il concilio di Firenze*, Florence, 1938; Jean Décarreaux, *Les Grecs au concile de l'union Ferrare-Florence (1438–1439)*, Paris, 1970, which brings together articles published in the *Revue des études italiennes*, 1961–67; Ivan N. Ostroumoff, *The History of the Council of Florence*, trans. Basil Popoff, Boston, 1971; and Stephan Mösl, *Das theologische Problem des 17. ökumenischen Konzils von Ferrara-Florenz-Rom (1438–1445)*, Innsbruck, 1974 (Studien und Arbeiten der Theologischen Facultät, Universität Innsbruck), which is concerned, so to speak, with the *aggiornamento* of the work of the Council. A good deal of relevant bibliography is collected in Angelo Mercati, "Il Decreto d'unione del 6 luglio 1439 nell'Archivio Segreto Vaticano," *Orient. Christ. periodica*, XI (1945), 5–44. For general accounts of the proceedings and conflicts at Ferrara-Florence, see especially Joseph Gill, *The Council of Florence*, Cambridge, 1959, with a French translation by M. Jossua, Tournai, 1964; *Personalities of the Council of Florence*, Oxford, 1964; and *Constance et Bâle-Florence*, Paris, 1965, pp. 119 ff. (Histoire des conciles oecuméniques, vol. 9).

[60] Georg Hofmann, ed., *Fragmenta protocolli, diaria privata, sermones*, Rome, 1951, no. 1, pp. 3–6 (Conc. Florent., Docc. et scripp., ser. A, vol. III, fasc. 2).

[61] Ten sessions of the Council had been held before the enrollment of the Greeks (*cf.* the *Fragmenta protocolli*, no. 10, p. 24, dated 3 April, 1438, and *cf.* pp. 29–30).

[62] Iorga, *Notes et extraits*, II, 351–52, citing the Arch. Segr. Vaticano, Reg. Vat. 370, fols. 211–12; *Epistolae pontificiae*, II (1944), no. 150, p. 48; *cf.* Gill, *Council of Florence*, pp. 108–9, 174–75, 299–300.

[63] Louis Petit and Georg Hofmann, eds., with an introduction by Jos. Gill, *De purgatorio disputationes in concilio Florentino habitae*, Rome, 1969 (Conc. Florent., Docc. et scripp., ser. A, vol. VIII, fasc. 2). The title of this work can be misleading; the debates on purgatory were held in Ferrara. On the doctrinal differences between the Greek and Latin Churches, note Fantino Vallaresso, Venetian bishop of Crete (d. 18 May, 1443), *Libellus de ordine generalium conciliorum et unione Florentina*, ed. Bernard Schultze, Rome, 1944, pp. 20 ff. (Conc. Florent., Docc. et scripp., ser. B, vol. II, fasc. 2).

[64] Hefele and Leclercq, *Hist. des conciles*, VII-2, 967–87; Gill, *Council of Florence*, pp. 117–25, 145–69. On the proposed transfer of the Council to Florence for financial reasons, see Gill, *ibid.*, pp. 174–76. An unknown member of the Council of Basel, when it still seemed possible to attract the Greeks to a site of the conciliarists' choice, had estimated that the costs of their transport, maintenance, and various miscellanea, plus the necessary reinforcements to the defense of Constantinople would amount to about 186,000 to 200,000 ducats if their participation in the Council lasted for about a year. The known expenditures which Eugenius had to meet and the known sources and assumed amounts of his income, all the data being quite incomplete, are explored in an article by Gill, "The Cost of the Council of Florence," *Orientalia Christiana periodica*, XXII (1956), 299–318.

After the Council was transferred from Ferrara to Florence by papal decree (dated 10 January, 1439),[65] its members met from February, 1439, to April, 1442, although John VIII and the Greek delegation left the banks of the Arno in late August, 1439, and returned to Constantinople by way of Venice. The Council brought profit as well as prestige to the Florentines, and so quite appropriately the Signoria met some of the costs of transporting the Greeks from Ferrara to Florence and maintaining them after their arrival.[66] Despite the reluctance of the Greeks to participate in formal theological debates with the Latins, eight public sessions were devoted to discussions concerning the procession of the Holy Spirit (from 2 to 24 March, 1439). Giovanni di Montenero, the provincial of the Dominicans in Lombardy, certainly seemed in the opinion of all the Latins and most of the Greeks, including Bessarion, Isidore of Kiev, and George Scholarius (until after his return home), to have swamped by his learning and the acuity of his reasoning the stubborn repetitiveness of Marcus Eugenicus, the Greek metropolitan of Ephesus and the κορυφαῖος of the Greek theological chorus.[67]

Many of the Greeks had a ready command of the theological clichés formulated in more than three centuries of unionist disputation, but this was not enough. They feared the Latin employment of the syllogism, and distrusted the scholastic solution of theological problems. The debates at Florence made manifest once more the superiority of the western university training over the rather haphazard study of Scripture and patristic literature in the monastic schools of Constantinople. After more than two months of confusion and altercation among themselves, although most of the uninformed Greek clergy were probably not entirely sure of what they were doing, they did in effect accept the long-controverted *filioque* clause.[68] Bessarion had already urged them to do so, in all sincerity, in a long *Oratio dogmatica* which he delivered on 13 and 14 April, 1439.[69] In a tense and eloquent

---

[65] *Epistolae pontificiae*, II, no. 160, pp. 60–61, the reason given for the *translatio concilii* being the pollution of the air in Ferrara (and of course the plague might return with the spring) and the greater convenience and healthfulness of Florence (for Eugenius could not acknowledge that without the financial backing of the Medici the Council could hardly go on).

[66] *Cf.* Iorga, *Notes et extraits*, II, 33, a text interesting enough to cite (from the Florentine series of "Uscita," Reg. 268, fol. 35, and very similar to numerous entries in the accounts of the Camera Apostolica for this period): "Adi XVIII di maggio [1439]. A Chosimo di Giovanni de'Medici e Llorenzo e ciaschuno di loro, in tutto. Per ispese per loro fatte del mese di febraio prossimo passato, per chamino e per vivere de' Greci, della venuta loro della città di Ferrara alla città di Firenze, fiorini mille dugiento di Chamera, e per le spese fatte a detti Greci nella città di Firenze, per primo e sechondo mese, chomincato adi XV del mese di febraio prossimo passato, a ratione di fiorini 1,700 di Chamera per ciaschun mese; in tutto fiorini quatromile secento di Chamera, a fiorini sette, soldi dieci auro pro cento, 4,945 di sconto,—fiorini 4,600 di Camera [the last words are erased].

"Alloro detti e a ciaschuno, in tutto fiorini per le spese per loro facte nella città di Firenze a detti Greci, per lo vivere per terzo mese, inchomincato adi XV d'aprile prossimo passato, a ratione chome di sopra, fiorini mille seicento [*sic*] di Chamera, e fiorini sette, soldi dieci auro pro cento, di sconto, 1,827, grossi [?] due, soldi due, denari quattro,—1,700 di Camera [last words erased]. Confessati per detto Chosimo. Pagha netti fiorini 6,300 di Chamera."

The papal, Florentine, and other financial accounts would seem to belie, to some extent at least, the charge often repeated by Syropoulos, George Scholarius (Gennadius), John Eugenicus, Amiroutzes, and others that the Latins sought, more or less, to starve the Greeks into acceptance of a decree of union (*cf.* Jos. Gill, "The 'Acts' and the Memoirs of Syropoulos as History," *Orientalia Christiana periodica*, XIV [1948], 331–340).

Some idea of the financial importance of the Medici to Eugenius IV, the Greeks, and the Council of Florence may be got from the *Epistolae pontificiae*, I (1940), no. 68, pp. 70–71; II (1944), nos. 138, 194, 221, pp. 32–33, 86, 120–21; III (1946), no. 246, p. 23, and from the *Acta camerae apostolicae* (1950), nos. 59, 60, 69, 71, 72, etc., pp. 48–49, 50 ff., 59, 61, 63, 67–68, 69, 76–77, 78–80, 83–84, 90–91, 99, 101, 102–3, 106, 109. The Medici continued as papal bankers throughout Eugenius's reign (*cf.* B. Krekić, *Dubrovnik [Raguse] et le Levant au moyen âge*, Paris and The Hague, 1961, no. 1097, pp. 346–47).

[67] The Latin doctrine of the twofold procession of the Holy Spirit was the chief stumbling block to the Greeks' reunion with the Latin Church. Hefele and Leclercq, *Hist. des conciles*, VII-2, 988–95, have most unaccountably confused Giovanni di Montenero with the Basel conciliarist John of Ragusa, as noted by Gill, *Council of Florence*, pp. 194–226, who has given us an excellent summary of the debate and of its immediate aftermath. On Montenero and his confrères, see G. Meersseman, "Les Dominicains présents au concile de Ferrare-Florence jusqu'au décret d'union pour les Grecs (6 juillet 1439)," *Archivum Fratrum Praedicatorum*, IX (1939), 62–75. Until the Latins dropped the *filioque* clause from the creed and gave up the use of unleavened bread (the *azyma*) in the mass (let alone the different Latin views and practices as to baptism, the eucharist, and purgatory), Marcus Eugenicus could not consider ecclesiastical reunion as doctrinally tenable. He is the subject of two recent monographs (N. P. Basileiades, *Marcus Eugenicus and the Union of the Churches* [in Greek], Athens, 1972, and C. N. Tsirpanlis, *Mark Eugenicus and the Council of Florence*, Thessaloniki, 1974). Marcus Eugenicus was withal a valiant as well as a learned man.

[68] *Cf.* Syropoulos, *Mémoires*, X, 28–29, ed. Laurent (1971), pp. 516–20.

[69] Emmanuel Candal, ed., [*Bessarionis Nicaeni*] *Oratio dogmatica de unione*, Rome, 1958, pp. 10–15 and ff. (Conc. Florent., Docc. et scripp., ser. B, vol. VII, fasc. 1).

discourse George Scholarius, then a judge and a layman, implored his fellow Greeks to accept union with the Latin Church. Indeed, he said that Latin learning had demonstrated they could do so in all conscience. The Latins would help them defend Constantinople against the Turks, who (it was said) had already laid siege to the city or would soon be doing so.[70] Isidore of Kiev was no less strong an advocate of union, urging the reverend fathers at the Council to have done with their contentiousness, for they could find nothing more that might assist them in the vast theological heritage which their forebears had left.[71]

The last obstacles to union or at least to the declaration of union were removed during the month of June, 1439. The differences relating to the eucharist, purgatory, and papal supremacy were resolved by the Greeks' giving way to compromise, fatigue, and ignorance, and by the Latins' contenting themselves with some measure of ambiguity and by not making too rigid issues of them.[72] On 5 July the higher clergy of both Churches signed the Greek and Latin texts of the decree of union (written in parallel columns). The Greeks, however, were not unanimous in their subscription. As Gregory the Protosyncellus, who represented Philotheus, the patriarch of Alexandria, wrote the latter shortly afterwards, all the Greek prelates had accepted the union except two, "[Marcus Eugenicus,] the metropolitan of Ephesus, who is certainly a learned man, and the completely ignorant Bishop [Isaias] of Stauropolis, for whom nothing makes sense" (*metropolita Effesinus, homo certe eruditus, et Stauropolitanus, vir omnino literarum nescius, cui nihil constat*).[73] Although ignorant, Isaias was presumably not stupid; he had quietly slipped away, and doubtless saved himself much embarrassment later on. The union of the churches was announced on the forenoon of 6 July, 1439, in a long session over which Eugenius himself presided in the cathedral of S. Reparata, now S. Maria del Fiore, where a huge crowd had gathered to witness the colorful ceremony. Cardinal Giuliano Cesarini read the Latin text of the decree; Bessarion, the Greek; and both Eugenius and John VIII with their respective clergies made public acknowledgment of their assent. It was a memorable day, a Monday. All the shops in Florence were closed, just as though it were Sunday. It was a proud day indeed for the Florentines, who knew that history was being made in their city.[74]

The church councils of the fifteenth century all required extensive advance planning. They caused the descent upon Pisa or Pavia, Siena or Florence, Constance or Basel, of hundreds and (in some cases) even of thousands of persons, many of whom required appropriate housing and all of whom required food. Inevitably lodgings became scarce, and the costs rose despite the imposition of ceilings on rents. Foodstuffs became more expensive. Exchange rates fluctuated to the usual advantage of the bankers. Merchants and artisans prospered from the concentration of customers, but they were also impeded by the financial stringency which resulted from the fact that ecclesiastical revenues were rarely equal to current expenses or at any

[70] Geo. Scholarius, "De pace deque adiuvanda patria adhortatio," in Jos. Gill, ed., *Orationes Georgii Scholarii in concilio Florentino habitae*, Rome, 1964, esp. pp. 12–18 (Conc. Florent., Docc. et scripp., ser. B, vol. VIII, fasc. 1). *Cf.*, *ibid.*, pp. 40 ff., 62 ff.

[71] G. Hofmann and Em. Candal, eds., *Isidorus arch. Kioviensis et totius Russiae, Sermones inter concilium Florentinum conscripti*, Rome, 1971, pp. 54–80, esp. p. 70, Isidore's "Exhortatoria oratio ad concilium" (Conc. Florent., Docc. et scripp., ser. A, vol. X, fasc. 1).

[72] *Cf.* Hofmann's essay on *Papato, conciliarismo, patriarcato*, Rome, 1940.

[73] G. Hofmann, ed., *Orientalium documenta minora*, Rome, 1953, no. 34, p. 44 (Conc. Florentinum, Docc. et scripp., ser. A, vol. III, fasc. 3). The original Greek text of this letter breaks off in the middle; the Latin version, which seems to be contemporary, is complete.

[74] The decree or bull of union of 6 July, 1439, may be found in A. Theiner and F. Miklosich, eds., *Monumenta spectantia ad unionem ecclesiarum graecae et romanae*, Vienna, 1872, pp. 46–56, and in G. Hofmann, ed., *Documenta concilii Florentini de unione orientalium*, I: *De unione Graecorum* . . . , Rome, 1935 (Pontificia Universitas Gregoriana, Textus et documenta, ser. theologica, no. 18). Hofmann's text is better. The original still exists in the Biblioteca Medicea-Laurenziana, in the Cassetta Cesarini, no. 1, which is now "on exhibition under glass," as Hofmann notes in the *Epistolae pontificiae*, II (1944), pp. VII–VIII. *Cf.* Dölger, *Regesten*, pt. 5, no. 3486, p. 126. According to the *Acta graeca*, ed. Gill, II, 471–72, the Greeks (and Latins) signed five more copies of the decree on 20 and 21 July (1439); Syropoulos, *Mémoires*, X, 25, ed. Laurent (1971), pp. 510, 512, says that the pope wanted five copies, but the Curia settled for four. Actually hundreds of copies were prepared and distributed unsigned or with signatures added for the record. On 2 August, 1439, Francesco Condulmer, the *cardinalis camerarius*, ordered the payment of nineteen florins to the notary Arnoldo "pro trecentis decem copiis decreti sanctissime unionis Grecorum factis pro mittendo ad nonnullas mundi partes" (*Acta camerae apostolicae* [1950], no. 82, p. 71). Hofmann, *Epp. pontificiae*, II, pp. VIII–IX, has identified eighteen copies with subscriptions, autograph or otherwise.

rate they were rarely available when needed to pay bills. As one stood on a street corner, a social panorama of the times passed before his eyes. The councils attracted pimps and prostitutes as well as those who sought benefices, privileges, or the resolution of legal or administrative problems at the Curia.

Most of the texts relating to the Council of Ferrara-Florence are of a formal nature, showing the participants in full dress, more rarely *en déshabillé*. The minor records, however, are often as interesting, if not so important, as the theological and other arguments which finally led to the solemn decree embodying the best efforts of the assembled intelligence of Christendom.

Sylvester Syropoulos, for example, relates in his account of the Council how, in April, 1438, Cardinal Giuliano Cesarini invited Bessarion, George Gemistus Pletho, and George Amiroutzes to dine with him for the discussion of philosophical problems.[75] If this is an attractive picture, we may contrast with it Syropoulos's description of Amiroutzes during the eleventh session at Ferrara (on 18 November, 1438), when he stood with a companion in a far corner, facing the intractable Marcus Eugenicus, but out of sight of the conciliar fathers, surreptitiously jeering and making funny faces at the Ephesian to distract him from the defense of Orthodoxy.[76]

Almost eighty years ago Iorga published in the second series of his *Notes et extraits* dozens of financial accounts relating to Greek affairs from the early 1430's, paid by the Camera Apostolica for the expenses of Greek ambassadors and of other officials and agents "going into Greece on the business of our lord, the pope, and of the Church." Drafts were drawn in favor of shipowners and landlords, copyists and couriers. The benches necessary for public disputation in the church of S. Francesco in Ferrara cost three florins. One day paper cost the treasury ten florins, and on another more than 80 florins were spent on Malmsey, confections, spices, and wax for the Russian ambassadors, who were headed by the Metropolitan Isidore (19 September, 1438). We may imagine that more was spent on Malmsey than on confections. In any event Isidore, soon to become the "Ruthenian cardinal," rode into Ferrara in an entourage (it is said) of 400 horsemen, whom he is stated to have maintained largely at his own expense, a fact which, if true (and it was not), would have endeared him to Pope Eugenius IV, who was constantly pressed for money. Papal income had declined markedly since the period of the Great Schism, and now the conciliarists at Basel were impeding the flow of funds to the Curia Romana. Many of the larger accounts settled by the papal treasurers during the years 1437–1439 represent the repayment of funds disbursed for the Holy See by the Florentine bankers Cosimo and Lorenzo de' Medici.[77]

Among the Florentine expenditures on behalf of the Greeks are two items published by Iorga on which he makes no comment, but to which we must call attention here:

> [31 July, 1439:] A Francescho di Ghuccio, maziere de Singnori, grossi quaranta, per ispese per lui fatte e che arà affare di mandare a Prato e a Pistoia e innantri luoghi chollo 'nperadore de Greci e cho messere Agnolo Acciaiuoli.[78]
>
> [30 September, 1439:] A Francescho di Ghuccio, maziere, per resto di spese per lui fatte innandare a Prato e a Pistoia, chome ser Angnolo Acciaiuoli, quamdo achonpangnò lo 'nperadore de' Greci, grossi quattordici p̄.[79]

---

[75] Syropoulos, *Mémoires*, V, 3, ed. Laurent (1971), p. 258.

[76] *Ibid.*, VI, 42, p. 338.

[77] Iorga, *Notes et extraits*, II (Paris, 1900), 1–20 (to the year 1440). Iorga has published here many orders (*mandata*) on the papal treasury (preserved in the Arch. di Stato di Roma, Mandata, Regs. 828–30). Fr. Hofmann has followed the payment of these orders in the accounts of papal income and expenditure (Arch. Segr. Vaticano, Introitus et exitus, Regs. 402, 404, 406, 408, 410) in his *Acta camerae apostolicae* (*cf.* note 66), where some documents already available in Iorga have been republished together with a number which the latter had missed.

The Metropolitan Isidore had left Moscow with more than a hundred persons in his suite on 8 September, 1437. On his journey to Riga and thence through a dozen German cities, Trent, and Padua to Ferrara, which he entered on 18 August, 1438, see Jan Krajcar, "Metropolitan Isidore's Journey [*Khoženie*] to the Council of Florence . . . ," *Orientalia Christiana periodica*, XXXVIII (1972), 367–87. Isidore arrived back in Moscow on 19 September, 1440. In this connection see also Krajcar's study of "Simeon of Suzdal's Account of the Council of Florence," *ibid.*, XXXIX (1973), 103–30. Simeon's account, which survives in three recensions, is historically worthless, but became politically influential in Russia as an anti-Latin tract.

[78] Iorga, *Notes et extraits*, II, 34, from the "Uscita," Reg. 269, fol. 49ᵛ, not in Hofmann. The Greek Acts of the Council of Florence, which give some information on the activities of the Emperor John, mention no events between 21 July and 13 August, and so contain no reference to this trip to Prato and Pistoia (Jos. Gill, ed., *Quae supersunt actorum graecorum Concilii Florentini*, Conc. Florent., Docc. et scripp., ser. B, vol. V, fascs. I–II [Rome, 1953], II, 471–72).

[79] Iorga, *Notes et extraits*, II, 34, from the "Uscita," Reg. 270, fol. 38, not in Hofmann. The sign p̄. I take to mean *di piccioli*.

These entries are clear enough: 1) On 31 July, 1439, forty groats were paid one Francesco di Guccio, mace-bearer of the Signoria, for expenses incurred by him in going to Prato and Pistoia and other places with the emperor of the Greeks and with Angelo Acciajuoli. 2) On the following 30 September, Francesco received 14 groats, the balance owed him for the expenses he had incurred in going to Prato and Pistoia with Angelo Acciajuoli when he accompanied the emperor of the Greeks. Having taken such an active and fatiguing part in the Council both at Ferrara and at Florence, John VIII, with all that now behind him (his last day of conciliar business being 22 July), had gone on an excursion to Prato and Pistoia. But why did he go? Who went with him? In what condition was he? These are questions which, as a matter of fact, we can answer. Our information comes from a text contained in an intriguing manuscript from the old Biblioteca Magliabecchiana in Florence, now part of the Biblioteca Nazionale Centrale (II, IV, 128, fols. 108^{v}–110^{r}=Magl., Cl. VI, num. 132). The manuscript is a miscellany of letters, notes, orations, and various items, including even a recipe for making white wine. Written on paper and bound in vellum, it contains 125 small folios, and is written in the hand of one Giovanni de' Pigli, who kept it for many years in the mid-fifteenth century as a beehive of items of literary and historical interest.[80]

The text with which we are concerned is a memorandum prepared by Giovanni as a record of what was probably the most exciting event of his career. How many later generations of Pigli read and discussed Giovanni's great experience one cannot say, but this memorandum gives a wonderfully intimate (and rather quaint) description of a day in the life of the Emperor John VIII, spent at Peretola, about three and one-half miles northwest of Florence:[81]

On the twenty-seventh day of July, 1439, I, Giovanni di Jacopo di Latino de' Pigli, finding myself, at the hour of terce or a little before, in the public square of Peretola, saw coming along the road from Prato Messer Angelo di Jacopo Acciajuoli with some servants.[82] He went up to the door of the church of Peretola, and knocked several times. Seeing that it was not opened, I went up to him and asked what he was doing, and what he wanted of the prior, if he did not mind my inquiring. He answered me:

"I come from Pistoia and Prato in the suite of the emperor of Constantinople, who wanted to go see Pistoia and the Girdle of Our Lady at Prato,[83] and I was assigned to his suite by the Signoria. And because the hour is late for us to get to Florence to eat,[84] and he is tired and sick, as you know, I wanted to put him up in the church until this evening."

I replied to him: "Messer, I am at home alone. If our house should be adequate to receive so great a lord, it would give the utmost pleasure, but I must warn you that there is nothing at home except beds and the four walls of the house."

He answered me, saying: "I did have the intention of taking him either to the house of Antonio, son of Messer Ricciardo, or to your house, but considering that such burdens should not be imposed upon friends, I was going here to this priest."

---

[80] *Cf.* the *Inventari dei manoscritti delle biblioteche d'Italia*, X (Forlì, 1900), 134–35, where the contents of the MS. are analyzed. I am grateful to Dr. Cesare Olschki for assisting me to get a complete microfilm of the MS.

[81] This document was first published by Pietro Ferrato, *Relazione di Giovanni de'Pigli da Peretola intorno a un viaggio dell'imperadore di Costantinopoli fatto nel 1439* (Bologna, 1867), from which it was republished with a Greek translation by Sp. P. Lampros, "*Μία ἡμέρα Ἰωάννου τοῦ Παλαιολόγου ἐν Περετόλῃ τῆς Τοσκάνης*," *Δελτίον τῆς Ἱστορικῆς καὶ Ἐθνολογικῆς Ἑταιρίας τῆς Ἑλλάδος*, VI (Athens, 1901), 351–57. Being subsequently furnished with an improved but still faulty Italian text, Lampros, who apparently never saw the manuscript, reprinted it in his *Παλαιολόγεια καὶ Πελοποννησιακά*, III (Athens, 1926), 327–29, where he gives the wrong date (1438 for 1439) both in his title and the incipit of the text. Lampros notes that Ferrato's brief commentary is inaccurate, but his own is also very slight, and does not include the references given above to the entries which Iorga published from the Florentine "Uscita," recording the Signoria's payments for the emperor's expenses on the journey to Pistoia and Prato. The text was re-edited by Setton, in *Speculum*, XXXIII, 225–26. Following the account of the emperor's day in Peretola, Giovanni de' Pigli gives some notes on members of his family and their places of burial (fols. 110 ff.).

[82] Angelo di Jacopo di Donato Acciajuoli was a second cousin of Antonio I Acciajuoli, Florentine duke of Athens (d. 1435), and a first cousin of Dukes Nerio II and Antonio II. Angelo was a follower of the Medici, and had been exiled to Cephalonia in 1433 when Rinaldo degli Albizzi and Palla Strozzi had forced Cosimo de' Medici out of Florence (Chas. Hopf, *Chroniques gréco-romanes inédites ou peu connues*, Berlin, 1873, p. 476; Wm. Miller, *The Latins in the Levant*, London, 1908, p. 400; K. M. Setton, *Catalan Domination of Athens, 1311–1388*, rev. ed., London, 1975, pp. 205, 208). *Cf.* Vespasiano da Bisticci, *Commentario della vita di Messer Agnolo Acciaiuoli*, in the *Archivio storico italiano*, vol. IV, pt. 1 (1843), pp. 339–61 (where much is made of Angelo's diplomatic activities, but Vespasiano knew nothing of this episode), and Niccolò Machiavelli, *Istorie fiorentine*, bk. IV, chap. XXX, ed. Plinio Carli, I (Florence, 1927), 227–29.

[83] At the Duomo in Prato may still be seen the Pulpit of the Holy Girdle by Donatello and Michelozzo (1439), and opening off the left aisle is the Chapel of the Holy Girdle with frescoes by Angelo Gaddi (1367).

[84] References to the Emperor John's poor health appear in the Greek Acts (*Praktika*) of the Council of Florence under the dates 29 April and 10–13 May, 1439 (Jos. Gill, ed., *Acta graeca*, II, 414, 417, and *cf.* Gill, in *Orient. Christ. periodica*, XIV, 314, 315, 345).

He thanked me profusely, and agreed to bring him to our house, saying: "I do not want you to go to any expense beyond the use of your house. The Commune is paying his way."

He went back toward Prato, where he met the emperor on the road, and brought him straight to our house. He appeared with forty to fifty knights, in good order, and with his many barons, lords, and gentlemen. And because he had lost the use of his legs, he came right into our hall on horseback, without anyone's seeing him dismount except his own gentlemen and servants. I had had prepared for him the bed of the chamber to the left of the entrance into the hall with the bedding which was there, a green coverlet and a pair of white sheets. But the emperor, as I understood, did not want to go into the bedroom; instead he had a sort of couch made on two benches with a little mattress and with a rug, by the door of the hall to the left of the passageway in, under the arbor, and there he slept until his people produced something for him to eat. When food was provided, he had a small table placed before his couch. I found him some white table cloths, and then he ate alone; the others, his barons and lords, [ate] under the arbor both outside and inside, like a soldiers' mess. And the rest, the servants, after the lords had eaten, had their own dinner in the same place. And note, the first food the emperor ate was a salad of purslain and parsley, with some onions, which he himself wished to clean. After that there were chickens and pigeons, boiled, and then chickens and pigeons quartered and fried in the frying pan with lard. As the dishes came, they were all placed before him, and he took what he wanted, and sent them along to the others. His last dish was eggs thrown on hot bricks where the other things were cooked. And they set them before him in a bowl with many spices; I cannot imagine how they were done, but such is the fact.

Messer Angelo and I, with his servants, went to dine at the house of Antonio, son of Messer Ricciardo, where the latter's wife had cooked for us the chickens and pigeons which had been sent there at the expense of the aforesaid gentleman, the mace-bearer of the Signoria. Next, when we felt he had dined and rested enough, we left for my house, and we found the emperor playing backgammon [*giuchare a tavole*] with one of his barons. Some of his people stood watching; others were going for a walk in the garden; and others were sleeping throughout the bed chambers, very much at home. Messer Angelo and Ciriaco of Ancona, a man most learned in Greek and Latin, and I stood there all day in the hall, the emperor always playing backgammon and joking with his people.[85]

In the evening, at the twenty-third hour [about 8:00 P.M. in July], or perhaps later, Messer Angelo asked me to go into the garden with the gentlemen, and had me kneel at the feet of the emperor. He expressed thanks through his interpreter for the honor which I had done him in receiving him into my house, and having made me the offer that, if I should ever get to his country, he would do me the honor, etc., he took my name, how it was said, where he had stayed, and had note made of these things. I answered his Majesty something that occurred to me, and having kissed his foot, I withdrew from his presence. The horsemen were already in the saddle, and most of the barons mounted, in the meadow, when everybody left the hall, except for a few. The emperor's horse was led into the hall, the door was shut, he mounted his horse, and they took the road to Florence along the Arno. Afterwards in commemoration of these events, we had his arms painted over the door of the hall, as may still be seen.

The Patriarch Joseph II had departed this life in an odor of Latin sanctity on 10 June, 1439; he was buried in Florence, in S. Maria Novella, where his tomb may still be seen. John VIII left Florence on 26 August and, with a brief stop at Bologna, returned to Venice on 6 September. Here he encountered numerous delays, including a fire in the Arsenal, and so he took the opportunity to indulge his passion for hunting by a two days' jaunt into the region of Padua. He seems, therefore, to have recovered "the use of his legs." The imperial party set sail for home on 19 October, and by way of Pola, Corfu, Modon, Coron, Negroponte, and Lemnos they made their way to the Dardanelles, where the Turkish governor of Gallipoli sent John a courteous greeting. In the early morning hours of 1 February, 1440, the Despot Constantine Dragases, accompanied by Genoese and Venetians as well as by many *archontes*, boarded a galley and went out to meet him.[86] John had been absent from the capital for twenty-six months. His effort seemed to have been worthwhile. On 7 October, 1439, Eugenius IV had addressed a bull to all Christians, soliciting financial aid "pro tuitione et custodia ipsius civitatis Constantinopolitane." Two days later, practicing what he preached, Eugenius arranged through the Medici bank in Florence to send 12,000 florins to the imperial court for the defense of Constantinople.[87]

---

[85] This charming picture of the Emperor John VIII is at variance with the rather harsh and prejudiced account we have of him in Syropoulos's *Memoirs*.

[86] Syropoulos, *Mémoires*, XI, 4, 12–23, ed. Laurent, pp. 524–44, and *cf*. Thiriet, *Régestes*, III, nos. 2507, 2510–13, pp. 76–78.

[87] *Epistolae pontificiae*, II, nos. 220–21, esp. pp. 119–21. The 12,000 florins were "pro solutione ibidem [in Constantinopoli] fienda certis balistariis ad custodiam dicte civitatis pro certo tempore deputandis." *Cf*. in general Raymond de Roover, *The Rise and Decline of the Medici Bank, 1397–1494*, New York, 1966, pp. 124, 194, 212–13, 217.

The Greek acceptance of the *filioque* clause meant a good deal to Eugenius and the Curia. The conciliarists at Basel had lost prestige in the pope's success. Union with Rome was now affirmed by Armenian envoys (on 22 November, 1439)[88] and thereafter by the Copts in Egypt (on 4 February, 1442).[89] Despite the astonishing outcome of his unionist efforts, however, Eugenius still faced disquieting uncertainties. France and Germany continued their "neutrality," and seemed still to lean toward the conciliarists at Basel, who elected Amadeo VIII of Savoy as Pope Felix V (on 5 November, 1439).[90] Eugenius also had to face for some time the unabated hostility of Filippo Maria Visconti of Milan and Alfonso V of Aragon-Naples, although he finally managed a *modus vivendi* with both of them, the latter's price being his recognition as king of Naples (on 14 June, 1443).[91]

Although Eugenius IV's position in Italy gradually improved, his expectations of union with the Greeks proved disappointing. He had been informed that, as the imperial party made its way back to the Bosporus through "Modon, Coron, Negroponte, and the Peloponnesus," the Greeks had accepted news of the union "with great alacrity." Cristoforo Garatone, his nuncio to Constantinople, whom he had made bishop of Coron, had apparently written him to this effect. Now, however, as Eugenius wrote Garatone from Florence on 25 August, 1440, Marcus Eugenicus, "ille Ephesinus," was spewing forth his poison, "and yet if the emperor had agreed that he should be punished as befitted his offense, . . . you would have had far fewer adversaries." The emperor had so far neglected to publish the decree of union, as he should have done, if he had been properly mindful of his duty. This had caused doubt and confusion in Constantinople.[92] John was in favor of union; it was militarily advisable. The pope's crossbowmen were still walking the walls of his capital. When in early May, 1440, Metrophanes, the metropolitan of Cyzicus, became patriarch of Constantinople, he wrote the Greek community at Modon (on 10 June) that "what the Latins now say about the procession of the Holy Spirit was and is the word and doctrine of our own blessed saints and teachers." Furthermore, he assured them, their rites and the "symbol" of their faith remained absolutely unchanged, ὡς καὶ πρότερον, οὐδὲν τὸ σύνολον ἐναλλάξαντες.[93]

The Patriarch Metrophanes [II] persisted in his unionist activities, as did his successor Gregory the Protosyncellus, but the monks, most of the clergy, and the masses of people would have none of it. The historian Ducas relates that when the Greek delegation to Florence had disembarked from the galleys (on 1 February, 1440), the inhabitants of the capital went down to the docks to welcome them: "How did your efforts fare? How did the synod go? Did we win our cause?" The clergy answered, "We have sold our faith overseas, we have exchanged piety for impiety, we have forsaken the purity of the 'sacrifice,' and become *azymitai*!"[94] If Ducas's account is not to be taken literally, it is *ben trovato*. Bessarion and Isidore of Kiev were made cardinals in December, 1439, which rendered them suspect in Greek eyes. Besides, Bessarion

---

[88] *Epistolae pontificiae*, II, no. 224, pp. 123–38; Gill, *Council of Florence*, pp. 306–8; note also G. Hofmann, *et al.*, eds., *Orientalium documenta minora*, Rome, 1953, nos. 29–31, 35, pp. 32–36, 45.

[89] *Epistolae pontificiae*, III, no. 258, pp. 45–65; Gill, *Council of Florence*, pp. 325–26; and on the background, see Hofmann, *Orientalium documenta minora*, nos. 39, 41, 43, pp. 53 ff.

[90] If he did not repent (and he did not), Felix V, who is called "Amadeus antichristus," was to be condemned and punished with all his adherents as a schismatic, blasphemer, heretic, and traitor (*Epistolae pontificiae*, III, nos. 238–39, pp. 4–13, dated 23 March and 27 May, 1440).

[91] Raynaldus, *Ann. eccl.*, ad ann. 1443, nos. 1–5 and ff., vol. XVIII (Cologne, 1694), pp. 273–75 and ff.; Pio Paschini, "Lodovico cardinale camerlengo e i suoi maneggi sino alla morte di Eugenio IV (1447)," *Memorie storiche forogiuliesi*, XXIV (1928), 62–63.

[92] *Epistolae pontificiae*, III, no. 243, pp. 17–21. On Garatone, who had served as chancellor of the bailie in the "curia Venetorum in Constantinopoli" (G. M. Thomas and R. Predelli, *Diplomatarium veneto-levantinum*, II [1899, repr. 1965], no. 178, p. 341, doc. dated 30 September, 1423), see the excellent study of Luigi Pesce, "Cristoforo Garatone trevigiano, nunzio di Eugenio IV," *Rivista di storia della Chiesa in Italia*, XXVIII (1974), 23–93. As a consequence of at least a half dozen years' residence on the Bosporus (1423–1428/29), Garatone had acquired an excellent knowledge of Greek and an important collection of Greek MSS., especially of classical authors. He served the Holy See long and well. Eugenius employed him on six missions to Constantinople—in 1433, 1434, 1435, 1436, and 1437, after which he returned to Italy with the Greek conciliar delegation early in 1438, and then went back with the Greeks (as papal nuncio) on their homeward voyage in 1439–1440. Garatone was also sent on a mission to Basel in 1435, and was assigned the task of papal collector in Crete in 1444. He went on four crusading missions to Hungary—in 1442, 1443, 1446, and 1448, when he was present at the battle of Kossovo (17–19 October, 1448), where he was killed. On the pope's letter of 25 August, 1440, *cf.* Pesce, *op. cit.*, pp. 78–79.

[93] *Orientalium documenta minora*, no. 36, pp. 45–47; Gill, *Council of Florence*, pp. 350–51.

[94] Ducas, *Hist. byzantina*, chap. 31 (Bonn, pp. 215–16), and ed. Grecu (1958), pp. 269, 271.

went to live in Italy, and Isidore traveled interminably and ubiquitously.[95] George Scholarius, the most learned Greek layman of his time, had subscribed to the union at Florence, but a few years after his return home, he became an anti-unionist, following in the hallowed footsteps of his old friend and teacher Marcus Eugenicus. Indeed, Scholarius, under his monastic name Gennadius, became the first patriarch of Constantinople after the fall of the city to the Turks, at which point (as far as the Greeks were concerned) the union had ceased to exist.[96]

Every day through the last years of his life John VIII had to raise his tired eyes above the theological strife and ecclesiastical slander that filled his capital, and watch the movement of Turkish troops beneath his very walls as well as on the more distant horizons. From 1440 on, the intrepid John Hunyadi, voivode or ruler of Transylvania, won a number of much-heralded victories over the Turks, and inspired both central Europeans and Greeks with the resolve to try to halt the Ottoman advance. The Venetian Senate observed his success with silent approval. For the time being, however, they intended to keep out of the fray, as they told Niccolò da S. Severino, who had come to the lagoon as envoy of King Ladislas of Poland and Hungary.[97] The Republic had already paid a heavy price, they informed the disappointed Niccolò (on 17 December, 1440), in blood and gold, defending the Christian faith against the Turks. Unfortunately Venice had been obliged to carry on the unequal struggle by herself, and had been forced into making peace with the Turk. That peace had been—and was being—scrupulously observed by both sides. Venice could not break it without incurring dishonor and courting disaster. "But in the process of time matters might be so arranged that we could do what we want, and have done in the past, for the well-being of Christendom."[98]

---

[95] On Isidore of Kiev, see above, Chapter 1, note 5; on Bessarion, who is the subject of a large literature, see Ludwig Mohler, *Kardinal Bessarion als Theologe, Humanist und Staatsmann*, 3 vols., Paderborn, 1923–42, repr. Aalen and Paderborn, 1967. Mohler, I, 56–191 and ff., has dealt at length with the Council of Ferrara-Florence and its aftermath.

[96] C. J. G. Turner, "George-Gennadius Scholarius and the Union of Florence," *The Journal of Theological Studies*, new ser., XVIII (1967), 83–103. Gennadius was born about 1403. He had learned Latin well at a fairly early age, and was quite at home in Thomist theology before the Council of Ferrara-Florence. He defended Aristotle against the Platonist George Gemistus Pletho. Scholarius is a proper name, not a title. See Turner, "The Career of George-Gennadius Scholarius," *Byzantion*, XXXIX (1969–70), 420–55. The events of 1438–1439 at Ferrara and Florence have had an impact upon pro- and anti-unionist activities into the present century (*cf.* Ihor Ševčenko, "Intellectual Repercussions of the Council of Florence," *Church History*, XXIV [1955], 291–323). The religious fortunes of the Greeks in Italy from Venice to the Terra d'Otranto, Sicily, and Malta over a period of some eight centuries are explored in more than fifty articles in *La Chiesa greca in Italia dall'VIII al XVI secolo: Atti del convegno storico interecclesiale* [held at Bari from 30 April to 4 May, 1969], 3 vols., Padua, 1972–73 (Italia sacra: Studi e documenti di storia ecclesiastica, vols. 20–22).

When the Orthodox clergy returned home, they had a good deal of explaining to do, and public repentance was presumably in order for a score or more of Greek ecclesiastics who had signed the Florentine decree of union. *Cf.* N. G. Polites, "The Repentance of Sylvester Syropoulos" [in Greek], Ἐπετηρὶς Ἑταιρείας Βυζαντινῶν Σπουδῶν, XXXIX–XL (1972–73), 386–402, who identifies the text of one "repentance" (*metanoia*) as that of the memorialist Sylvester Syropoulos, who had signed the decree "unwillingly with his hand and not his heart" (*ἀλλὰ καὶ ἄκων ὑπέγραψα ἐν τῷ ἐκεῖσε συντεθέντι ὅρῳ χειρὶ καὶ οὐ γνώμῃ*).

In after years John Joseph Plousiadenus (1429?–1500), Greek bishop of Modon (from 1492), defended the union of Florence both among the Greeks on his native island of Crete and among the Greek refugees in Italy. On his career, see especially M. Manoussakas, "Recherches sur la vie de Jean Plousiadénos (Joseph de Méthone) . . . ," *Revue des études byzantines*, XVII (1959), 28–51; Manuel Candal, "La 'Apologia' del Plusiadeno a favor del Concilio de Florencia," *Orientalia Christiana periodica*, XXI (1955), 36–57; and Fane Mavroeidi-Ploumidi, "Documents Relating to the Controversies among the Greeks at Venice toward the End of the Fifteenth Century" [in Greek], *Thesaurismata*, VIII (Venice, 1971), 115–87, with several (Venetian) documents concerning Plousiadenus.

[97] After the death of Albert II, king of the Romans and of Hungary, Ladislas III of Poland was elected king of Hungary on 6 March, 1440, as he informed Eugenius IV on the following day (*Codex epistolaris*, I-1 [1876, repr. 1965], no. CXI, pp. 119–21). The Turco-Hungarian wars during Ladislas's brief reign (1440–1444), especially the Turkish siege of Belgrade in 1440 and the Hungarian "long campaign" in 1443 (*cf.* above, note 54, and below, note 134), are the subject of an old but still very useful article by Alfons Huber, "Die Kriege zwischen Ungarn und den Türken, 1440–1443," *Archiv für österreichische Geschichte*, LXVIII (1886), 159–207. Venetian documents relating to the plans and activities of the European powers *contra Teucros hostes crucis* during the years 1443–1444 are now conveniently available in Valentini, *Acta Albaniae veneta*, XVIII (1974), who covers a much wider area than the title of his work would seem to indicate.

[98] Sen. Secreta, Reg. 15 [1439–1442], fols. 56^v–57^r [57^v–58^r]; Valentini, *Acta Albaniae veneta*, XVI (1972), no. 3,945, pp. 130–31: ". . . Ad factum Teucrorum dicimus, . . . ut notorium est toti orbi, quod pro Christiana fide longissimo tempore cum multa nostra gravedine et expensa ac nostrorum civium et subditorum clade et effusione sanguinis guerram Teucro fecimus sine alicuius

The coming months, as the Senate soon learned, increased the danger to which Hungary was exposed. Conditions were no less desperate elsewhere. Bosnian and Byzantine envoys appeared in Venice (in February, 1442) to warn the Senate of the despair which existed in these quarters. The king of Bosnia requested permission to transfer his movable property into Venetian territory if the situation worsened, and to come himself with his family into the domain of the Republic, "and he offers us that kingdom to rule in our own name, openly or secretly as we choose, and [in the meantime] he would have arms and other materials of war from our towns." The Senate declared that the Bosnian envoy could return home and state that

> we are entirely willing that his serene Highness should feel free to send his property and also personally to seek refuge with his family in this our city [of Venice] or in any other of our cities which he may prefer, . . . and we shall be prepared, as often as his Highness may wish, to furnish him with our safe-conducts, letters patent, and all those guarantees [*cautiones*] which his Highness may find desirable. . . .

As for the offer of the kingdom of Bosnia, the Senate solemnly expressed heartfelt thanks, realizing (they said) that it proceeded from his Highness's esteem for Venice and from his faith in the Republic, but the Senate thought it better that he retain the kingdom. They fervently hoped that he could do so, "and from now on we are willing that he should be entirely free to export from this our city [of Venice] the munitions he needs, and have them taken into his kingdom, in order that he may be able to defend his aforesaid kingdom and maintain his dominion."

At the same time the envoy from Constantinople, of whom we shall see more presently, described to the doge the "mala conditio regni Hungarie et Christianitatis ac mala dispositio Teucri." The envoy, one Zanachio or John Torcello, explained the measures which John VIII believed must be taken to safeguard Hungary. Torcello said that he was going from Venice to Hungary and thereafter to the Curia Romana in Florence. The Senate seemed taken aback to learn of the extent of the danger in Hungary, and took note of the provisions which the emperor considered essential "for repressing the madness and evil disposition of the Turk." The whole matter was certainly of the highest importance; the Senate must take counsel; Torcello should go on to Hungary, thereafter to Eugenius; "and afterwards let him come back to us." The Senate would then be better able to decide what Venice could do, for Torcello himself would be in a better position to report at first hand on conditions in Hungary and on the pope's intentions. In the meantime, the Senate piously concluded, "we shall always be of that sincere disposition, which we have ever maintained, of doing everything that seems appropriate [*nobis convenientia*] for the good of the Christian religion and the increase of our sacred faith."[99]

Eugenius IV now appointed Giuliano Cesarini, cardinal-priest of S. Sabina, called the cardinal of S. Angelo, as papal legate to the kingdoms of Bohemia, Hungary, and Poland (on 22 February, 1442). He was to receive his share of the *servitia* from the day of his departure from the Curia, which was still at Florence, to the day of his return. Cesarini left Florence on 14 March.[100] A week later he was in Venice, where he explained his mission to the Doge Francesco Foscari, who transmitted the information to the Senate. Cesarini spoke of the pope's desire for

---

subsidio vel favore, et tandem videntes nos solos esse quasi coacte devenimus cum ipso Teucro ad pacem que per utramque partem peroptime extitit observata, cui cum honore et sine nostro multo preiudicio et damno contravenire ad presens non possemus. Sed in processu temporis res taliter dirigi possent quod possemus pro salute Christianitatis facere de his que optamus et per elapsum fecimus."

[99] Sen. Secreta, Reg. 15, fol. 112^v [113^v], docs. dated 21 February, 1442 (Ven. style 1441). *Cf.* Dölger, *Regesten*, pt. 5, no. 3494, p. 128; Thiriet, *Régestes*, III, no. 2568, p. 92. The Doge Francesco Foscari had received the two envoys separately on 20 February, presumably in the Collegio, and reported on their missions to the Senate on the following day. Giuseppe Valentini, "La Crociata da Eugenio IV a Callisto III (dai documenti d'archivio di Venezia)," *Archivum historiae pontificiae*, XII (1974), 91–123, esp. pp. 95–110, has prepared a most useful *regesto* of Venetian documents relating to the crusade from February, 1442, to August, 1458. He has also published the two documents in question (of 21 February, 1442) in his *Acta Albaniae veneta*, XVII (1973), nos. 4,002–3, pp. 174–77.

In August, 1442, Fra Jacopo de Primaditiis, a Franciscan, was in Venice as an envoy of John VIII, seeking three armed galleys, *que ad custodiam ipsius civitatis* [*Constantinopolis*] *stent pro hac hyeme*. Since Fra Jacopo was also going to Florence to appeal to Eugenius for aid, the Senate postponed any decision until they could learn "what he shall have received from his Holiness" (Sen. Secreta, Reg. 15, fol. 135^v [136^v]). *Cf.* Dölger, *Regesten*, pt. 5, no. 3495, p. 128; Thiriet, *Régestes*, III, no. 2588, p. 96.

[100] Hofmann, *Fragmenta protocolli, diaria privata, sermones*, pp. 44–45; Arch. Segr. Vaticano, Arm. XXXI, tom. 52, fol. 16, ed. Eubel, *Hierarchia*, II (1914, repr. 1960), 27, no. 29.

political stability in Italy, and said that he was going as legate to Hungary to try to make peace "inter regem Polonie [Ladislas] et reginam Hungarie [Elizabeth]," and to take such steps as he could for the safety of their fellow Christians and for the obstruction of the Turks. The Senate bade him Godspeed, and hoped that he could allay the discords which beset the turbulent lords and barons of the realm.[101] Shortly thereafter another Bosnian delegation arrived on the lagoon to ask the Senate to send an ambassador to Sultan Murad II, but despite the *singularis benivolentia* which the Venetians entertained for the king of Bosnia, whom they would assist in all possible ways, such an embassy seemed impracticable, "considering that the emperor of the Turks has now gone with his army toward Hungary, and that our ambassador could not reach him without the greatest danger because of the upheavals of war, the perils of the journey, and the suspicion of the Hungarians. . . ." Seeking a more secure base for operations, the king of Bosnia had proposed the exchange of a Venetian fortress town in Dalmatia for one of his own cities in Bosnia. To this proposal, however, the Senate replied that Venice was bound by the most solemn undertakings not to alienate her Dalmatian possessions, *non dare nec alienare unquam illas [civitates] alicui ullo modo*, but the king could rest assured that if he sought refuge in any Venetian stronghold in Dalmatia or elsewhere, he would be as safe and secure as in any place of his own.[102] Since it was doubt on the latter score which had led the king to make his request, he presumably found small assurance to rest upon in this response.

The imperial envoy John Torcello was as well known at the Curia Romana as in Constantinople. About three or four years before this (on 20 August, 1439) Eugenius had made him a member of the papal household (*famiglia*) with all the honors and privileges thereto appertaining. He also granted Torcello an "annual provision" of 400 gold florins "from our revenues and those of the Church," in order to keep him available for the papal service at all times.[103] Now Eugenius was going to need Torcello. On 8 May, 1443, he appointed Francesco Condulmer, cardinal-priest of S. Clemente, as apostolic legate in Greece. In the bull of nomination Eugenius stated that, since his chief desire (to see the Greeks and "orientales populi" united with Rome) had been so happily fulfilled, he now wanted most of all to see the East freed from the foul tyranny of the Turks. God was showing the clearest signs of his clemency, "for last year in Hungary, Poland, and Wallachia a small army of the [Christian] faithful defeated a huge multitude of infidels in repeated engagements, [and] not without a vast slaughter of the infidels. . . . We are also striving, to the extent of our resources,

---

[101] Sen. Secreta, Reg. 15, fol. 116ʳ [117ʳ], doc. dated 26 March, 1442. The text may be found in Aug. Cieszkowski, ed., *Fontes rerum polonicarum e tabulario reipublicae venetae*, ser. I, fasc. 2 (Poznań, 1890), no. xxvii, pp. 61–62. On the purposes of Cesarini's mission, see Domenico Caccamo, "Eugenio IV e la crociata di Varna," *Archivio della Società romana di storia patria*, LXXIX (3rd ser., X, Rome, 1956), 45–46.

[102] Sen. Secreta, Reg. 15, fol. 117ʳ [118ʳ]; Valentini, *Acta Albaniae veneta*, XVII (1973), no. 4,015, pp. 186–88, doc. dated 5 April, 1442.

[103] *Epistolae pontificiae*, II, no. 206, pp. 97–98, and note Iorga, *Notes et extraits*, II, 365–66. Torcello is referred to in this document as a "young lord from Crete" (*domicellus Cretensis*). He was probably not very young, because in 1433 he had served as consul for the Catalans and Sicilians in Constantinople (Const. Marinescu, "Contribution à l'histoire des relations économiques entre l'empire byzantin, la Sicile et le royaume de Naples de 1419 à 1453," *Studi bizantini e neoellenici*, V [1939], 211–12, 217). Some thirty years later Torcello was quite old (*in hac sua senecta*), and had lost everything in the fall of Constantinople to the Turks. He had served Venice as faithfully as he had the pope and the Byzantine emperor. By a special "grace" passed by the Venetian Senate on 27 August, 1467, Torcello, his sons, and legitimate descendants were granted the right to hold office and fiefs on the island of Crete (Arch. di Stato di Venezia, Senato Mar, Reg. 8, fol. 138ᵛ):

"Constat peramplo testimonio complurium notabilium nobilium nostrorum egregium militem dominum Johannem Torcellum, fidelem civem nostrum Cretensem, continue ab ineunte etate fideliter et honorifice se gessisse in rebus dominii nostri studiosissime in vigilando amplitudini et dignitati status nostri ubique et presertim tempore quo erat in serviciis quondam serenissimi Imperatoris Constantinopolis, et imprimis quando classis nostra bello genuensi prefecto quondam nobile viro Ser Silvestro Mauroceno ivit contra civitatem Pere, cuius opera dicta classis in summa necessitate sua habuit subventionem panis, armigerorum et pecuniarum, et ipsemet ducebat quoddam tractatum dande ipsius civitatis dominio nostro, quod fuit detectum cum maximo damno, viz., ultra ducatorum duo milia et periculo vite ipsius dicti Johannis, et ut senciat aliquod premium fidei et laboris suorum in hac sua senecta, amissis presertim omnibus facultatibus suis in casu Constantinopolis, et vivere possit cum filiis suis sub umbra nostri dominii, vadit pars quod auctoritate huius consilii ipse dictus Johannes cum suis filiis et legitime descendentibus participare possit de officiis et beneficiis Crete, sicuti plerisque aliis concessum fuit per gratiam, consulentibus et suadentibus sic dictis omnibus nobilibus nostris. De parte 89, de non 9, non sinceri 8." The motion was passed, and a scribal note adds: "[Pars] facta in litteris die ultimo Augusti."

to build a fleet so that this sacred task may be brought to a successful conclusion, in accord with our heart's desire, by Catholic power both on land and at sea."[104] Francesco Condulmer was the pope's nephew, vice-chancellor of the Church; he was put in command of the fleet, which was to correlate its movements with those of the army, to which Cesarini would be attached as the crusading legate in central Europe.[105]

On 6 July (1443) Eugenius wrote John VIII that he had been glad to see John Torcello, "nuntius tuus," who had presented him with an imperial letter. Upon his return to Constantinople, Torcello would inform the emperor what was being accomplished "in materia expeditionis et apparatus classis adversus Teucros." Although acting as John VIII's envoy, Torcello was apparently still serving as a papal agent, and three days later (on 9 July) Eugenius, recalling his loyalty and devotion at the time of the negotiations for union at Ferrara-Florence, made him a "papal knight" (*miles apostolicus*). He directed Torcello, who is described as a "citizen of Constantinople," to swear an oath of fealty to Condulmer in the usual fashion.[106] And, to be sure, Condulmer might well find him useful in the East. Torcello had attracted some attention at the Council in Florence by his plans for a crusade.[107]

While John Hunyadi stood out as the anti-Turkish champion in the north, Constantine Dragases began to play a similar role among the Greeks. On 1 March, 1443, Constantine received from his brother John VIII the city of Selymbria on the Sea of Marmara. Sphrantzes informs us that he was himself sent there as governor. Early in the following summer, however, an emissary arrived in Constantinople, sent from the Morea by the Despot Theodore II, offering to exchange the Moreote despotate for Selymbria. Regarding himself as the heir apparent to the

---

[104] *Epistolae pontificiae*, III, no. 264, esp. pp. 78–79, and note the *Codex epistolaris*, I-1, nos. CXVI, CXX, and CXXIII, pp. 127 ff. The last text is a letter dated 27 April, 1443, in which Ladislas states that the pope had promised him thirty-eight galleys for service against the Turks, and he expected twelve galleys from the Venetians, ten from the king of Aragon, six from the duke of Burgundy, eight from the duke of Milan, and two from the master of Rhodes (*ibid.*, p. 137). Rhetoric was replacing reality.

[105] *Epistolae pontificiae*, III, nos. 265–66, pp. 80–84, esp. p. 81, dated 28 May and 13 June, 1443. The Curia was then at Siena. *Cf.* Thiriet, *Régestes*, III, nos. 2607–8, p. 102.

[106] *Epistolae pontificiae*, III, nos. 267–68, pp. 84–85. For "Ebrcellus," read "Torcellus" (*cf.* Iorga, *Notes et extraits*, II, 397–98, and Dölger, *Regesten*, pt. 5, no. 3504, p. 129). At the same time Torcello, *orator serenissimi d. imperatoris Grecorum*, received 100 gold florins from the Camera "pro sua subventione" (Iorga, II, 22, and Hofmann, *Acta camerae apostolicae*, no. 143, p. 110, dated 9 July, 1443). On 27 November, 1444, the Camera reimbursed the Medici bank thirty gold florins for payment made to Torcello, now described as *orator apostolicus pro factis sanctissimi domini nostri pape* (*Notes et extraits*, II, 23).

[107] On Monday, 16 March, 1439, between the sixth and seventh sessions of the Council at Florence, Torcello, "chevallier, serviteur et chambellan, comme il dit, de l'empereur de Constantinoble," had advanced plans for a crusade which were later assessed by the traveler Bertrandon de la Broquière for the guidance of Philip the Good of Burgundy. According to Torcello, the Grand Turk could put into the field about 100,000 *hommes de cheval*. Some 20,000 of them were mercenaries, apparently always on call to arms, of whom 10,000 were well armed, the rest being without arms except for shields, swords, and bows and arrows. The Turk also had 10,000 *gens de pié*, who lacked arms except for swords and bows and arrows; some of these had shields also, but others did not. Such was the total force which the Turk could muster—"c'est cy toute la puissance du Grant Turc"—break it, subdue it, and in less than a month Christendom could conquer "la saincte Terre de promission."

To defeat the Turk, according to Torcello, one would need 80,000 combatants, and the best approach to Ottoman territory would be through Hungary by way of the Danube. The Christian forces should be assembled in three armies, of which the largest (of 50,000 men) would cross the river at Vidin, and a second army (of 20,000 men) should cross at Belgrade. The Christians had more than ample manpower: [Not counting Hungarians, Poles, and others,] the ruler of Serbia, "qui est tributaire au Turc," could provide 40,000 *combatans à cheval*; the Albanians, 20,000 horse; the Greeks in the Morea, another 15,000; and 50,000 Christian subjects of the Turk would rise in revolt once the crusaders appeared on the scene to assist them. The army which crossed the Danube at Vidin would head for Adrianople, "le principal siège du Turc," a distance of fifteen days for mounted men, etc., etc. And Torcello could cap his exposition with the assurance to the conciliar fathers at Florence that "en tenant ceste manière, le Turc seroit perdu et tres-brief." For Torcello's text and de la Broquière's comment on it, see Chas. Schefer, ed., *Le Voyage d'Outremer de Bertrandon de la Broquière*, Paris, 1892, pp. 263–74. De la Broquière is not uncritical of Torcello's views, concluding with the observation "quant à la conqueste de la Terre Saincte de quoy Messire Jehan Torzelo met en son advis qui se feroit ung mois par apprez, il me samble que la chose n'est pas si legière à faire, au moins par terre comme le dit Messire Jehan . . ." (*ibid.*, pp. 273–74). In fact, any talk about recovering the Holy Land was nonsense.

For further notices concerning Torcello, see Franz Babinger, "'Bajezid Osman' (Calixtus Ottomanus), ein Vorläufer und Gegenspieler Dschem-Sultans," in *Aufsätze und Abhandlungen zur Geschichte Südosteuropas und der Levante*, I (Munich, 1962), 305–8 [reprinted from *La Nouvelle Clio*, III Brussels, 1951], and "Veneto-kretische Geistesstrebungen um die Mitte des XV. Jahrhunderts," *Byzantinische Zeitschrift*, LVII (1964), 73–75.

imperial throne, for he was older than Constantine, Theodore thus undertook to secure his right to the succession. The exchange was effected. Constantine, who was in the capital at the time, returned to the Morea in October. Theodore withdrew from Mistra to take up his residence in Selymbria in December.[108] The two brothers had got along very badly in the Morea, but now Constantine held chief sway in the peninsula, and the internal strife which had been dissipating Greek strength was largely terminated. The third brother Thomas occupied an inferior position. The unstable Demetrius had been rendered *hors de combat* as a result of an ill-advised revolt against John VIII during the summer of 1442.

Encouraged by Hunyadi's successes, Constantine Dragases soon made his presence felt in continental Greece as well as in the Morea. In February, 1444, he launched an attack which brought him wide recognition north of the Isthmus of Corinth. A letter written to John VIII by the famous antiquarian and scholar Ciriaco de' Pizzicolli of Ancona informs us of the situation as it existed early in this year when Constantine was embarking on his ambitious program of expansion. Ciriaco wrote his interesting letter on shipboard at Oreos in northern Euboea about the beginning of March, 1444:

> . . . When I had got to the Achaean or Peloponnesian city of Patras, I immediately wrote to your most illustrious brother Constantine, and on this very subject [of an expedition against the Turks] I set forth what seemed important. And when I had gone from there to Corinth, we learned from Demetrius Asanes, his lieutenant, that he had recently gathered large forces from everywhere in the Peloponnesus, and was coming with his worthy brother Thomas from Lacedaemonian or Spartan Mistra with the army to the Isthmus. When the long bulwark of the walls has been restored, and the fatal Isthmus again fortified with turreted ramparts, he will then lead his forces through the Megarid and all Achaea. He has recently received the city of Thebes in surrender, and will attack with separate detachments of troops Livadia, sacred Daulia at the foot of Mount Parnassus, and the city of Delphi, and with the aid of God will free them honorably from the barbarians. But in the meantime after I had arrived at Euripean Chalcis,[109] the renowned city of Euboea, to sail the more safely to your royal city, on 26 February I boarded a Euripean trireme under the command of Maffio Molin, a Venetian noble, and we have begun to sail—his purpose being to free the Aegean of the troublesome Catalans and pirates, mine to explore sacred Delos along the way and the other Cyclades scattered through the sea, and then from Chios to take care to come to Constantinople more safely on a royal ship of your own. . . .[110]

[108] Sphrantzes, *Chron. minus* (*PG* 156, 1049CD; ed. Grecu, p. 66); Pseudo-Sphrantzes, II, 18–19 (Bonn, pp. 195–96; ed. Papadopoulos, I, 193–94; ed. Grecu, pp. 336, 338); *cf.* Zakythinos, *Despotat grec de Morée*, I, 216–17. Whether in Selymbria or the Morea, Constantine Dragases' ultimate goal was Constantinople and the imperial throne, which he finally attained (*cf.* H. G. Beck, "Reichsidee und nationale Politik im spätbyzantinischen Staat," *Byzantinische Zeitschrift*, LIII [1960], 86–94, esp. pp. 89–90). On Constantine's aggressive policy after his return to the Morea, note Wm. Miller, *The Latins in the Levant*, London, 1908, pp. 409 ff. He seized Veteranitza (on the north shore of the Gulf of Corinth) from the Venetians, to whom the Turks had given the town. His action produced a protest from the doge and Senate *locum nostrum predictum . . . rectori nostro Nepanti restituere* (Valentini, *Acta Albaniae veneta*, XIX [1973], no. 5,090, pp. 54–55, dated 20 April, 1445).

[109] Ciriaco writes, ". . . cum Euripeam Chalcidiam insignem Euboeae civitatem advenissem. . . ." *Euripea* is a Latin adjective derived from the Greek Εὔριπος (*Evripos*), meaning strait or channel, and denoting especially the channel between Boeotia and Euboea. From *Evripos* come the modern names Egripo and, by prefixing the final "n" of the Greek article in popular pronunciation to the proper name, Negroponte (εἰς τὸν Εὔριπον, *eis ton Evripon*).

[110] Francesco Pall, "Ciriaco d'Ancona e la crociata contro i Turchi," *Bulletin historique de l'Académie roumaine*, XX (Bucharest, 1938), 60–61 (Latin text), and *cf.* pp. 24–25; Oskar Halecki, *The Crusade of Varna*, New York, 1943, p. 84 (with the same text). This letter, written by Ciriaco from Oreos in Euboea some time after 26 February, 1444, has been regarded by most scholars as the first installment of a long letter finally sent to John VIII on 24 June after Ciriaco had reached Pera.

Actually, however, the letter from Oreos is apparently the first in a series of six texts, and appears to be the only one of the group addressed to John VIII. It seems best to identify these six texts, long cited as a single letter to the emperor, in connection with the present reference to the first of them (the others are employed below in their chronological order). The second (Pall, *op. cit.*, pp. 61–62) was probably written to Ciriaco's friend, Andreolo Giustiniani-Banca, from Adrianople about 12 June, 1444 (the addressee being unidentified and the letter undated); with this letter there went as enclosures (the third and fourth texts of the series) copies of King Ladislas of Hungary's letter of 24 April, 1444, to Sultan Murad II (*ibid.*, pp. 62–63) and Murad's reply thereto dated 12 June (*ibid.*, pp. 63–64). The fifth and sixth texts of the series are two letters, dated 12 June and 24 June, 1444 (*ibid.*, pp. 64–65, 65–66), which Ciriaco sent, possibly together on the latter date, to John Hunyadi, with whose exploits against the Turks we shall soon be concerned.

This division into six parts of the so-called letter of "24 June" to John VIII, I take from Halecki, *Crusade of Varna*, pp. 79–82, who has thus, in my opinion rightly, corrected some aspects of Pall's valuable account (*Bull. hist. Acad. roum.*, XX, esp. pp. 34–36) of the Hungarian-Turkish peace negotiations of 1444, to which we shall also come shortly.

We shall have occasion more than once in the following pages to speak of Ciriaco of Ancona, traveler and diplomat, archaeologist and linguist. He was born about 1391; made his first visit to Constantinople in 1418; his second in 1425, and a number of other visits in later years. Ciriaco was a good friend of Pope Eugenius IV, who as papal legate in the March of Ancona had known him in 1420–1422. During the fourth decade of the century Ciriaco's travels took him into Dalmatia and Epirus, continental Greece and the Morea, Chios, Rhodes, and Cyprus, Asia Minor and Egypt; he visited the courts of Carlo II Tocco at Arta, the Palaeologi at Mistra, Nerio II Acciajuoli at Athens, and Murad II at Adrianople and elsewhere.[111] Always dedicated to the ideas of church union and the crusade against the Turks, Ciriaco had been in Florence during the months of the Council in 1439 when, as we have seen, in late July he had accompanied John VIII on the excursion to Prato and Pistoia. His knowledge and opinions of Levantine affairs were much valued by Greek, Latin, and even Turkish rulers. Some scholars have claimed that Ciriaco was in close contact with Murad's son Mehmed II the Conqueror after the latter's (second) accession to the Ottoman throne in February, 1451. It has even been asserted, quite erroneously, that he was in the Turkish camp before Constantinople fifteen months later, entering the city with the Turks. It seems most unlikely, however, that he ever had any change of heart concerning the "barbarians." Emil Jacobs believed Jacopo de' Languschi's statement, which Zorzo Dolfin incorporated in his chronicle, that Ciriaco was reading certain Greek and Roman historians (and western chroniclers) to Mehmed II shortly before the siege of Constantinople. It has also been alleged, quite improperly, that Ciriaco served as the sultan's secretary, for which, to be sure, his easy command of Greek and Latin would have made him well suited. Ciriaco may indeed have been constrained on various occasions to furnish information to the Porte concerning Italian affairs, but he obviously never deserted the Christian cause for that of the Turks. Undoubtedly he employed his knowledge of Turkish affairs to gather information which he made available to the western powers. After his final sojourn in the East he appears to have returned to spend his last days in Cremona.[112] Ciriaco may have died as early as 1452.[113] His

[111] *Cf.* Roberto Weiss, "Ciriaco d'Ancona in Oriente," in Agostino Pertusi, ed., *Venezia e l'Oriente fra tardo medioevo e Rinascimento*, Venice, 1966, pp. 323–37. Bernard Ashmole, "Cyriac of Ancona," *Proceedings of the British Academy*, XLV (1959), 25–41, with sixteen plates, has shown that the sketches of antiquities in the Hamilton Codex in Berlin, attributed to Ciriaco, can hardly be drawings from his own hand. Note the references to his travels in a letter which Ciriaco wrote on 13 April, 1442, to the Veronese scholar Martino Rizzoni and the laudatory appraisal of Ciriaco's antiquarian studies in a letter of Martino's brother Giacomo, dated on 6 May of the same year—for the texts see Gian Paolo Marchi, "Due Corrispondenti veronesi di Ciriaco d'Ancona," *Italia medioevale e umanistica*, XI (1968), 317–23.

[112] *Cf.* Franz Babinger, *Maometto il Conquistatore e il suo tempo*, trans. Evelina Polacco, 1957, pp. 729–32; E. Jacobs, "Cyriacus von Ancona und Mehemmed II," *Byz. Zeitschr.*, XXX (1929), 197–202, on which however see Babinger, "Notes on Cyriac of Ancona and Some of his Friends," *Journal of the Warburg and Courtauld Institutes*, XXV (1962), 321–23.

[113] On the date of Ciriaco's death, see Chr. G. Patrinelis, "Cyriacus of Ancona: His Alleged Service at the Court of the Sultan Mehmed the Conqueror and the Time of his Death" [in Greek], *Ἐπετηρὶς τῆς Ἑταιρείας Βυζαντινῶν Σπουδῶν*, XXXVI (Athens, 1968), 152–60. Ciriaco's last years are shrouded in obscurity, and the date of his death remains uncertain. Babinger, "Mehmed II., der Eroberer, und Italien," *Aufsätze und Abhandlungen*, I (1962), 175–78, thinks he may have lived until 1455 (this article was first printed in *Byzantion*, XXI [1951]). According to Jacopo de'Languschi, as quoted by the Venetian chronicler Zorzo Dolfin, *Assedio e presa di Costantinopoli nell' anno 1453*, inserted in the latter's *Cronaca delle famiglie nobili di Venezia*, ed. G. M. Thomas, in the *Sitzungsberichte d. k. bayer. Akad. d. Wissenschaften zu München*, philos.-hist. Kl., II (1868), 5–6, in the year 1452 Mehmed II, "aspiring to a glory like that of Alexander of Macedon, every day has the histories of the Romans and of others read to him by a companion, Ciriaco of Ancona and another Italian—he has them read Laertius, Herodotus, Livy, Quintus Curtius, as well as chronicles of the popes, the emperors, the kings of France, and the Lombards." Languschi's reliability has been questioned, and the source of his information is unknown. In 1452 Languschi (or de Langusco) was in the papal service (see Walther von Hofmann, *Forschungen zur Geschichte der kurialen Behörden vom Schisma bis zur Reformation*, 2 vols., Rome, 1914, II, 111).

It has, however, been further alleged that Ciriaco was still alive early in 1454 on the basis of a letter which Francesco Filelfo addressed to Mehmed II, presumably from Milan, on 11 March of that year. Filelfo sought the release of his mother-in-law Manfredina Chrysolorina and her daughters, for whom he offered to pay a ransom if the sum required was not beyond his means, in which connection Mehmed's secretary, *grammateùs Kyrízis*, could provide whatever further information might be necessary. Babinger accepted P. A. Dethier's conjecture "dass sich hinter *Kyrizes* der Name des *Kyriakos* von Ancona verbirgt" (*Aufsätze u. Abhandlungen*, I, 177–78, with refs., and *cf. Maometto*, p. 731), which seemed very unlikely, and has now been disproved. Patrinelis, *art. cit.*, pp. 159–60, has shown that, while Kyrízis was indeed Mehmed's secretary, he was in fact Demetrius Apocaucus Kyritzes, and not at all un-career requires further investigation; the chronology of his travels still contains many uncertainties. Despite numerous studies concerning him, no scholar has yet written a satisfactory biography.[114]

As Ciriaco has informed us, Constantine Dragases secured possession of Thebes early in the year 1444. He also gained suzerainty over the Athenian duchy of Nerio II Acciajuoli, who was thus forced from his Turkish allegiance, now paying his tribute to Constantine rather than to Sultan Murad. Encouraged by his success, Constantine pushed northward to the Pindus range; was recognized by the Vlachs of the region as their ruler; and succeeded in occupying Zeitounion, Loidoriki, and some other towns.[115] The Turks were having their troubles, and being assailed on all fronts. A new and formidable opponent had suddenly appeared against them in Albania, George Castriota, known by the Turkish name of Scanderbeg.

On 28 November, 1443, Scanderbeg had gained from the Turks by a ruse the important fortress of Croia (modern Krujë), once the possession of his father.[116] With this episode began a truly remarkable career of twenty-five years' persistent and successful opposition to the Porte, making Scanderbeg a legend even in his own day.[117] His name figures prominently in many contemporary documents, and his career has often been dealt with by modern historians,[118] to whose works the reader must turn for detailed accounts of his rule in Albania. A few months after his occupation of Croia, an Albanian league was formed at a congress of the chieftains in the Venetian-held city of Alessio (Lezhë). Scanderbeg was now elected captain-general of Albania, and his annual income from Epirote sources is set at the unlikely sum of more than 200,000 gold ducats by his biographer Barletius,[119] who elsewhere notes, however, that

known (*cf.* G. M. Thomas and R. Predelli, eds., *Diplomatarium veneto-levantinum*, II [1899, repr. 1965], nos. 199, 202, pp. 369, 371; Iorga, *Notes et extraits*, III [1902], 212–13, on which note Patrinelis, *loc. cit.*). It still remains to be shown that Ciriaco lived beyond the year 1452, which is the date given for his death by a MS. in the Bibl. Ambrosiana in Milan, Trotti 373, fol. 41^r: "Kyriacus Anconitanus Cremone moritur anno domini MCCCCL secundo . . ." (Fr. Edw. W. Bodnar, who examined the MS., informs me that the word *secundo* is written over an erasure).

[114] The late James Morton Paton left behind at his death an unfinished edition of Ciriaco's letters (the typescript is now in the Houghton Library, Harvard University).

[115] Eugen (Jeno) Darkó, *Laonici Chalcocandylae historiarum demonstrationes*, 2 vols., 1922–23, II-1, 91–92; ed. Bonn, pp. 318–19. In his edition of Chalcocondylas, Darkó gives marginal references to the Paris edition (1650, reprinted in that of Venice, 1729) as well as to the Bonn edition (1843, reprinted in Migne, *PG* 159). *Cf. Chronicon breve* (following Ducas in the Bonn Corpus, pp. 518–19); Sphrantzes, *Chron. minus* (*PG* 156, 1049D–1050A; ed. Grecu, pp. 66, 68); Pseudo-Sphrantzes, II, 19 (Bonn, pp. 196–97; ed. Papadopoulos, I, 195; ed. Grecu, p. 338); Sp. P. Lampros, "The Walls of the Isthmus of Corinth" [in Greek], Νέος Ἑλληνομνήμων, II (1905), 477–79, a letter of congratulation from Bessarion to Constantine, containing both encouragement and advice; and E. W. Bodnar, "The Isthmian Fortifications in Oracular Prophecy," *American Journal of Archaeology*, LXIV (1960), 165–71.

[116] Marinus Barletius, *Historia de vita et gestis Scanderbegi, Epirotarum principis*, 1st ed., "impressum Romae per B. V." [Bernardinus Venetus de Vitalibus], ca. 1509, bk. I, fols. VIII^r–IX^v; bk. XIII, fol. CLIX; ed. Zagreb, "typis Ioannis Baptistae Weitz," 1743, pp. 14–17, 372.

[117] On the occasion of the fifth centenary of Scanderbeg's death (on 17 January, 1468), the Albanians themselves paid tribute to their national hero by devoting both issues of *Studia Albanica* to his memory. On the Scanderbeg legend, note Androkli Kostallari, "La Figure de Skanderbeg dans la littérature mondiale," and Johannes Irmscher, "Skanderbeg und Deutschland," *ibid.*, V-1 (1968), 191–215, 217–33, as well as Nicolas Ciachir, Gelcu Maksutovici, and Dumitru Polena, "La Personnalité du héros albanais Georges Kastriote-Skanderbeg dans quelques ouvrages roumains," *ibid.*, V-2 (1968), 121–30.

[118] Scanderbeg is the subject of a large literature, many important titles having been added in the last few decades, on which *cf.* George Chr. Soulis, "More Recent Researches on George Castriotes Scanderbeg" [in Greek], Ἐπετηρὶς τῆς Ἑταιρείας Βυζαντινῶν Σπουδῶν, XXVIII (1958), 446–57. Jovan Radonić has collected the major documentary and literary sources concerning Scanderbeg in his very convenient work *Djuradj Kastriot Skenderbeg i Arbanija u XV veku* [George Castriota Scanderbeg and Albania in the Fifteenth Century], Belgrade, 1942. On conditions in Albania from the late fall of 1441, see Arch. di Stato di Venezia, Sen. Secreta, Reg. 15, fols. 102^r, 116^v, 129, 131^v–133^r, 134, 154^v, and *ibid.*, Reg. 16, fols. 9^r, 10, 15^r, 24^r, *et alibi*.

[119] Barletius, *Vita*, 1st ed., Rome, 1509, bk. II, fols. XVII, XIX; ed. Zagreb, 1743, pp. 35, 40; Giovanni Musachi, *Breve Memoria de li discendenti de nostra casa Musachi*, in Ch. Hopf, *Chroniques gréco-romanes*, Berlin, 1873, p. 274; *cf.* Giammaria Biemmi (but see below), *Istoria di Giorgio Castrioto detto Scander-Begh*, 2nd ed., Brescia, 1756, bk. I, pp. 30–38, who supplies the date of the congress of Alessio, "ch'era pei due di Marzo" (p. 30); Hopf, "Griechenland im Mittelalter und in der Neuzeit," in J. S. Ersch and J. G. Gruber, eds., *Allgemeine Encyklopädie*, vol. 86 (repr. New York, 1960, vol. II), p. 123b, who places it in the summer of 1444, being followed by Babinger in the first edition of his life of Mehmed II (*Mehmed der Eroberer und seine Zeit,* Munich, 1953, p. 56), on which note Soulis, *op. cit.*, pp. 454–55, but the general criticism which Soulis directs at Babinger is actually applicable to Hopf. Of the older sources relating to Scanderbeg, the "Anonymous of Antivari" is a fraud, and therefore Biemmi (who "discovered" this source) is to be used with extreme caution or rather not to be used at all.

For the career of Scanderbeg, Barletius is a valuable source, but he also should be used with extreme caution. Quite apart from his constant exaggerations and chronological errors, Barletius (being a good humanist who liked the chieftains used to say in jest that enemy territory was Scanderbeg's treasury.[120]

Francisc Pall has shown that most accounts of Scanderbeg's career during the years 1443–1444 owe far more to fancy than to fact.[121] Of the best-known biographers of Scanderbeg, Barletius wrote fiction in the early sixteenth century, and Biemmi perpetrated an entertaining fraud in the eighteenth. In June, 1444, Scanderbeg is alleged to have scored his first important victory over a large Turkish army, which he caught in the narrow valley of Torviolli in the lower Dibra (Deber) region, and the astonished Hungarians are said to have sung his praises and immediately to have urged him to join the alliance of Hungary, the papacy, and Burgundy against the Turks.[122]

During the preceding winter, as we shall see, the Hungarians and Serbs had concluded a victorious campaign against the northern outposts of the Ottoman empire. Sultan Murad II found it advisable to enter into negotiations for peace with them at Adrianople in June, 1444. Although the sultan could not yet know how serious Scanderbeg's revolt was, Constantine Dragases' daring enterprise was undoubtedly an important factor in disposing Murad to peace with the northern powers, for little could be done about Constantine's pretensions in the Morea and his bold incursion into continental Greece until Murad had settled his long-standing differences with the Hungarians and Serbs either by making peace with them or by defeating them decisively enough to keep them from unsettling his northern frontiers by annual invasions.

Constantine's attempts to reconstruct Byzantine authority in Greece were merely part of a much larger Christian effort to dismantle the Turkish regime in Europe. In this connection attention tends to be concentrated, quite understandably, upon the papacy and Venice, Hungary and Serbia, and even Byzantium, but there were other states involved. Ragusa (modern Dubrovnik), for example, had been anxiously following for generations the westward march of Turkish conquest. Never so prominent or powerful as Venice, the city has a proud and rather neglected past.

Ragusa has been aptly called the step-daughter of the Adriatic. But as the historian makes his way, however idly, through the documents relat-

---

literary speeches and letters) invented the correspondence between Scanderbeg and Ladislas the Jagiellonian in 1443 (Francisc Pall, "Les Relations entre la Hongrie et Scanderbeg," in *Revue historique du Sud-Est européen*, X [Bucharest, 1933], 121–26). He also invented a correspondence between Scanderbeg and Sultan Mehmed II to fit his interpretation of events in 1461–1463 (*Vita*, 1st ed., Rome, 1509, bk. XI, fols. CXXXIV^r–CXL^v; ed. Zagreb, 1743, pp. 312–26).

Marinus Barletius (1450?–1512?) was a native of Scutari (Shkodër) in Albania, perhaps of Italian origin, and served as a Catholic priest at Scutari until the Turkish occupation in 1479 (*cf.* Gazmend Shpuza, "La Lutte pour la défense de Shkodër dans les années 1474 et 1478–1479," in *Studia Albanica*, V-1 [1968], 181–90). Thereafter Barletius resided in Venice and Rome. He wrote an account of the siege of Scutari (*De obsidione Scodrensi*, first printed at Venice in 1504) and the famous life of Scanderbeg (first printed at Rome about 1509–1510). For his life, of which very little is known, his works, etc., see Pall, "Marino Barlezio: Uno storico umanista," in *Mélanges d'histoire générale*, ed. Const. Marinescu, II (Bucharest, 1938), 135–315; for the sources employed by Barletius in his account of Scanderbeg, note esp. pp. 177–86, and for the general reliability of the work, pp. 199–202, 223–28.

Giammaria Biemmi, a priest of Brescia, pretended to have discovered a Latin incunable written by an unknown author from Antivari (*Historia Scanderbegi edita per quendam Albanensem*, allegedly printed by Erhard Ratdolt at Venice on 2 April, 1480), which he claims to have used in his *Istoria di Giorgio Castrioto detto Scander-Begh*, Brescia, 1742 (2nd ed., 1756). Of course no such incunable was known to G. R. Redgrave, *Erhard Ratdolt and his Work at Venice*, London: Bibliographical Society, 1894, repr. 1899; *cf.* Kurt Ohly, in the *Gutenberg Jahrbuch*, Mainz, 1933, pp. 53–61; R. Janin, in the *Échos d'Orient*, XXXVII (1938), 210–11; and Willy Steltner, "Zum Geschichtsbild des albanischen Nationalhelden Georg Kastriota genannt Skanderbeg," *Zeitschrift für Geschichtswissenschaft*, IV-5 (1956), 1035–38. Biemmi also forged two "early" chronicles of Brescia, and was at work on a third when death overtook him in 1778 (Pall, *op. cit.*, pp. 201–2, note, who properly observes that Biemmi had a talent for scholarship worthy of more honest application). Biemmi worked very hard to ensure that modern scholarship should find his work worthless. Alessandro Serra, "Relazioni del Castriota con il Papato nella lotta contro i Turchi (1444–1468)," *Archivio storico italiano*, CXIV (1956), 713–33, and vol. CXV (1957), pp. 33–63, had not yet discovered that Biemmi's life of Scanderbeg was based upon a fraudulent source. Serra has done somewhat better in his essay *L'Albania e la Santa Sede ai tempi di G*[*iorgio*] *C*[*astriota*] *Scanderbeg*, Cosenza, 1960.

[120] Barletius, *Vita*, 1st ed., Rome, 1509, bk. IV, fol. XLV^r; ed. Zagreb, 1743, p. 97b: ". . . iocylariter saepe vicini principes aerarium Scanderbegi agrum hostilem appellabant."

[121] Pall, "Les Relations entre la Hongrie et Scanderbeg," *Revue historique du Sud-Est européen*, X (1933), 119–27; "Skanderbeg et Janco de Hunedoara (Jean Hunyadi)," *Studia Albanica*, V-1 (1968), 103–7; and "Skanderbeg et Ianco de Hunedoara," *Revue des études sud-est européennes*, VI (1968), 6–9.

[122] Pall's articles should be read before Barletius, *Vita*, 1st ed., Rome, 1509, bk. II, fols. XXII–XXVII; ed. Zagreb, 1743, pp. 47–57, who was followed by Raynaldus, *Ann. eccl.*, ad ann. 1443 [*sic*], no. 21, vol. XVIII (1694), pp. 285–86; Biemmi, bk. I, pp. 42–55, 59–60, who supplies 29 June, 1444, as the date of Scanderbeg's first victory over the Turks (p. 54). The spurious correspondence of July and August, 1443, between Ladislas and Scanderbeg (made up by Barletius, who should have assigned it to the year 1444) is reprinted in Radonić, *Djuradj Kastriot Skenderbeg*, pp. 5–7.

ing to the Mediterranean in the fourteenth and fifteenth centuries, he is constantly struck by the importance of this city in the affairs of the Balkans. In 1358 the Ragusei had accepted the mild hegemony of King Louis the Great of Hungary when the Venetians were forced by the treaty of Zara (18 February) to yield all claim to Dalmatia, including the important ecclesiastical, military, and commercial centers of Nona (Nin) and Zara (Zadar), Scardona (Skradin) and Sebenico (Šibenik), Traù (Trogir) and Spalato (Split), as well as Ragusa itself. The peace of Zara had brought to an end some years of warfare and negotiation between the Venetians and the king of Hungary. Oddly enough in March (1358) the Ragusei had ordered from Venice a standard and banners for their galleys and other ships "with the arms of our lord, the lord king of Hungary." A little later, on 27 June, the final agreement was reached at Visegrad between King Louis and Archbishop Giovanni Saraca of Ragusa whereby Hungarian sovereignty was recognized in the city instead of that of Venice, but the Ragusei were left largely to their own devices. The local nobility continued to rule with little interference from the royal court at Buda, where schemes were constantly entertained for a crusade against schismatic Serbia, less strongly defended after the death of the great Stephen Dushan. For Ragusa the peace of Zara had meant an escape from the domination of Venice, a superior rival. The Ragusei had been happy to acknowledge the suzerainty of Louis of Hungary, whose kingdom was not a naval power, and with whom they could have little conflict of interest. A depot in transit for the exchange of goods between Italy and the Balkans, a center of banking and diplomatic intrigue, Ragusa maintained her virtual independence and reared her stone buildings all through the Quattrocento.[123]

In 1440–1441, to be sure, Ragusa was obliged to conclude a "good peace" (*bona paxe*) with the Ottoman government, agreeing to pay the sultan, the pasha of Romania, and the vizirs 1,000 ducats a year, and providing in addition gratuities (*certae simoniae*) to the extent of 400 ducats a year to make certain that officials of the Porte were sufficiently attentive to the commercial and other interests of the republic.[124] The future of Ragusa obviously had its precarious aspects, but her enterprising merchants acquired freedom of trade throughout the wide territories of the Ottoman empire and its various satellite states. The Ragusei continued to recognize the suzerainty of Hungary, to which they looked for protection from time to time against the Bosnians and the Turks. A letter to John Hunyadi, the regent of Hungary, a decade later describes the situation of Ragusa amid the movements of the greater powers as "like a ship tossed by fortune in the midst of the sea."[125]

Important events were in the meantime taking place in Hungary. Young King Ladislas the Jagiellonian of Poland had been called to the Hungarian throne (1440–1444) by a dominant faction of the Magyar nobility anxious to escape the rule of a woman and an infant king, Ladislas "Postumus." The latter was the son of Albert II of Hapsburg and Elizabeth of Hungary, daughter of Sigismund, whose lands and titles Albert had acquired in 1438, as we have seen. Ladislas

---

[123] The text of the famous treaty of Zara (18 February, 1358) may be found in Sime Ljubić, *Listine*, in the *Monumenta spectantia historiam slavorum meridionalium*, III (Zagreb, 1872), 368–71, with accompanying instruments, and *cf.* J. Gelcich and L. Thallóczy, *Diplomatarium ragusanum*, Budapest, 1887, nos. 1 ff., pp. 3 ff. On the treaty and its consequences, *cf.* Sam. Romanin, *Storia documentata di Venezia*, III, 200–6; Giuseppe Gelcich, *Dello Sviluppo civile di Ragusa*, Ragusa, 1884, p. 44; Luigi Villari, *Republic of Ragusa*, London, 1904, pp. 103–6; H. Kretschmayr, *Geschichte von Venedig*, II (Gotha, 1920, repr. 1964), 217–18; Louis de Voinovitch, *Histoire de Dalmatie*, I (Paris, 1934), 451–54; and Bálint Hóman, *Gli Angioini di Napoli in Ungheria, 1290–1403*, trans. from the Hungarian by Luigi Zambra and Rudolfo Mosca (Reale Accademia d'Italia, Studi e documenti, VIII, Rome, 1938), pp. 367–71. Also see, above, Volume I, p. 228. On the appearance of walled Ragusa, *cf.* Lukša Beritić, *Utvrdenja grada Dubrovnika* [The Fortifications of Dubrovnik], Zagreb, 1955, and see in general the rambling but interesting lectures of N. Iorga, "Raguse," in the *Bulletin historique de l'Académie roumaine*, XVIII (Bucharest, 1931), 32–100. Present-day Ragusa (Dubrovnik) dates largely from the period after the earthquake of 1667.

[124] Iorga, *Notes et extraits*, II, 371–74, 376–78, and esp. pp. 381–84, 386. The difficult negotiations with the Porte were finally concluded by the Ragusan ambassador Nicholas de Simon de Goze, but the Ragusei continued to have trouble with Turkish officials (*ibid.*, pp. 395, 412). On their economic relations with the Turks in Serbia, Albania, Bosnia, Greece, Bulgaria, Wallachia, and Anatolia at this time, see B. Krekić, *Dubrovnik (Raguse) et le Levant au moyen âge*, Paris and The Hague, 1961, nos. 958, 962, 964–66, 969, 972, pp. 323 ff. The Ragusei had extensive consular privileges and legal exemptions in the kingdom of Sicily (Naples), for which see Ljubić, *Listine*, IX (Zagreb, 1890), 36–37.

[125] Jovan Radonić, ed., *Acta et diplomata ragusina*, I, pt. 2 (Belgrade, 1934), no. 231, p. 518, doc. dated 28 January, 1451 (Fontes rerum slavorum meridionalium, ser. I); Gelcich and Thallóczy, *Dipl. ragusanum*, no. 285, p. 477: ". . . come la nave agitata da fortuna in mezzo pelago. . . ."

Postumus, born after his father's death, could only assert the Hapsburg claim to Hungary from the safety of Vienna, where he lived as a ward of his father's relative and successor Frederick III, duke of Styria, Carinthia, and Carniola (and crowned king of the Romans in February, 1440). The small Ladislas's cause was supported in Hungary by his mother Elizabeth and by Ulrich, count of Cilli. For good reasons the Magyar barons wanted none of a "king in his cradle." They needed a leader against the Turks, who were able, however, to profit from the anarchy caused in Hungary by the three years' war of succession which was now waged against the Jagiellonian by the legitimist party.[126] Nevertheless, John Hunyadi's victories seemed to show that it might be possible to drive the Turks back into Asia Minor.[127]

Hunyadi served as general of Ladislas the Jagiellonian, who became leader of the crusade in eastern Europe when he became king of Hungary. Ladislas and Hunyadi planned a great expedition for the summer of 1443. They could of course depend upon Pope Eugenius IV, who was winning his prolonged struggle with the embattled fathers at Basel. Eugenius had been planning for some time to send a fleet into eastern waters against the Turks, but its organization was proceeding slowly. Already on 8 August, 1442, the Venetian Senate had complained in a letter to Cardinal Giuliano Cesarini that the pope was making inadequate financial provision for arming the fleet which the Senate was ready to provide. Eugenius had so far imposed the crusading tithe only in Florence and Venice, "and other funds he employs elsewhere;" the tithe did not yield much, and would prove hard to collect under the circumstances.[128] But Eugenius soon did much better. Still rejoicing publicly in the union of the Churches, *beneficium et usque ad nostra tempora inauditum*, Eugenius issued a universal appeal from Rome on 1 January, 1443, for the defense of the Christian East against the Turks, whose atrocities he rehearsed with an angry rhetoric. He imposed a special tithe on "all the world," and declared his intention of spending a fifth of the chief revenues of the apostolic treasury to equip a fleet and an army.[129] Eugenius made a special alliance with Ragusa, whose statesmen foresaw an easier future in Turkish defeat,[130] despite the "good peace" they had concluded with the Porte. The pope's correspondence reveals an anxious desire to launch a crusade, but except for Hungary, Poland, Wallachia, and Burgundy, Christendom gave a poor response to his appeals for war against the enemies of the faith.[131]

---

[126] *Cf.* Iorga, *Gesch. d. osman. Reiches*, I, 423–25, and D. Caccamo, "Eugenio IV e la crociata di Varna," *Archivio della Società romana di storia patria*, LXXIX, 43–45. Albert died on 27 October, 1439; Elizabeth on 19 December, 1442.

[127] The Hungarians had been particularly successful against the Turks during the latter half of the year 1442 (*cf.* Iorga, *ROL*, VII [1899, repr. 1964], 78–79, and *Notes et extraits*, III [Paris, 1902], 105–6, doc. dated 30 October, 1442, and Iorga's note on the document). For this period, see Francisc Pall, "Le Condizioni e gli echi internazionali della lotta antiottomana del 1442–1443, condotta da Giovanni di Hunedoara," *Revue des études sud-est européennes*, III (Bucharest, 1965), 433–63.

[128] Iorga, *ROL*, VII, 73, and *cf.* pp. 98, 100, 377, and *Notes et extraits*, III, 100, and *cf.* pp. 125, 127, 136.

[129] Hofmann, *Epistolae pontificiae*, III, no. 261, pp. 69–75: ". . . incipientes a nobis ipsis, omnium reddituum et proventuum ex communibus servitiis et annatis ad cameram apostolicam spectantibus partem quintam ad eundem usum classis et exercitus fidelium deputamus . . ." (p. 75). *Cf.*, *ibid.*, nos. 264–65, etc., also the notices in Sanudo, *Vite de'duchi*, in *RISS*, XXII (1733), cols. 1106, 1109B, 1110AB, 1114C. Eugenius IV's crusading encyclical is misdated 1442 in Pastor, *Hist. Popes*, I, 325, but given correctly as "zu Anfang des Jahres 1443" in the last edition of his *Gesch. d. Päpste*, I (repr. 1955), 333. Note also Iorga, *ROL*, VII, 94–95, 95–96, 98–100, etc., and *Notes et extraits*, III, 121–22, 122–23, 125–27, etc. Eugenius and the Venetians generally did not see eye to eye, and the latter continued to complain about the financing of the fleet and the unsettled conditions in Italy (Sen. Secreta, Reg. 16 [1443–1445], fols. 9^v, 11^v, 12^v–13^r, 13^v, 14^v, 26^v, 30^v–31^r, 37, 61, 87^v, 95^v–96^r, and 116^v).

[130] *Cf.* Iorga, *Notes et extraits*, II, 403, 417; *cf.* Krekić, *Dubrovnik* (1961), nos. 1054, 1097, pp. 339, 346.

[131] In a letter to Eugenius, dated 13 April, 1443, the Doge Francesco Foscari expressed the pleasure of the Venetian Senate in the receipt of a letter from Giuliano Cesarini, cardinal of S. Angelo, explaining "quam bene preparantur res Christiane religionis quamque omnes populi illarum partium ad repprimendam infidelium rabiem ferventissime disponuntur" (Sen. Secreta, Reg. 16, fol. 5^v; Iorga, *Notes et extraits*, III [Paris, 1902], 121). In central Europe at least there was still a willingness to proceed against the Turks. *Cf.* Valentini, *Acta Albaniae veneta*, XVIII (1974), no. 4,805, p. 20, whose reading of the doge's letter differs from mine.

On 3 May, 1443, the doge reported to the Senate on the mission of a Byzantine envoy, one "Theodorus Carastinus" (ὁ ἐκ Καρύστου ?), who had just stated [in the Collegio] that the Turks were not observing the peace they had made with the Emperor John VIII, "et tandem dicit condictionem Teucrorum et quam facile expellerentur de Gretia, sed neccessarie essent galee et ob hoc videt penitus necessarium esse ut per nos fiat provisio galearum et habet in mandatis eundi aut scribendi summo pontifici et illustrissimo domino duci Burgundie ut pecunias nobis contribuant pro armamento galearum predictarum et petit consilium et parere nostrum, asserens in mandatis habere in

Plans for the Hungarian expedition were carried through, nonetheless, and by July, 1443, the news of the Christians' southeastward advance had reached Sultan Murad II's court at Adrianople. Murad had just returned from Anatolia, where he had diminished for a while the ambition of his brother-in-law, Ibrahim Beg, the ruler of Caramania (*il Gran Caramano*), who had been flirting for some time with King Ladislas the Jagiellonian, Pope Eugenius, and the Venetians. For more than twenty years (until his death in early August, 1464), Ibrahim Beg was to be the chief eastern enemy of the Ottoman sultans. More than once he entertained the idea of an alliance with the western powers. The Venetians were to send several embassies to him through the years, but no effective results ever came of them, and the Ottoman armies were never caught in a pincers' movement of simultaneous attacks from Caramania and the West. Now, however, having held his eastern enemy in check, Murad prepared to deal with the Hungarians. His young son, Mehmed Chelebi ("the Gentleman"), the future conqueror of Constantinople, had just joined him at Adrianople. Mehmed was beginning to play some part in the affairs of state, and the events of the next few years undoubtedly made a deep impression on him.[132]

The crusaders pressed onward under Ladislas and Hunyadi, accompanied by Cardinal Cesarini. The Serbian despot George Branković was with them too, now a landless fugitive, who (like John VI Cantacuzenus a century before) had derived no profit from marrying his daughter to an Ottoman ruler. The Christian army, containing some 25,000 mounted men and archers (according to Ducas), including about 8,000 Serbs, both horse and foot, met up with Turkish troops between the castle of Bolvani and the city of Niš (Nish) in early November, 1443. The crusaders defeated them easily and went on to take Sofia, whence on 4 December Cesarini wrote the Venetian government of the *excellens et gloriosa victoria* which God had granted them.[133] Branković, old campaigner in the Balkans, knew every path and pass through the Haemus range. The crusaders dragged along a heavy (and yet insufficient) baggage train for provisions, and as they got into the region of the Maritsa, they found the enemy's resistance much increased.

---

hoc sequendi parere nostrum." The Senate voted to inform the envoy "quod summus pontifex fecit apud nos fieri instantiam ut decem hic posset armare galeas et nos, qui sequentes vestigia predecessorum nostrorum semper comodum et utile Christianitatis quesivimus, fuimus contenti ei corpora ipsarum galearum accomodare et sue requisitioni de armando hic eas consentire. . . ." Cardinal Cesarini had been urging Pope Eugenius to provide the funds necessary to arm the ten galleys which Venice was prepared to make available to the crusading fleet. There must be no delay (*res hec in longum non est ducenda*). Theodore should go to the Curia Romana (*ad pedes apostolicos*) to request dispatch of the money to Venice, but he should write Eugenius before going. The Senate also advised Theodore to write the duke of Burgundy before leaving Venice, but to say nothing of his willingness to wait upon the duke in person unless he found support at the Curia and had the time and means to undertake such a distant journey. ". . . Verum cum, ut intelligere potuit, res Italie in non parva sint confusione, hortamur ut suadere debeat prefato summo pontifici et supplicare cum instantia ut pro eius officio, quia caput Christianorum est, taliter operari et providere dignetur quod ipse res Italie taliter cum securitate componantur quod ad hoc sanctum et utilissimum opus vacare possimus ut optamus. De parte omnes alii, de non 2, non sinceri 1" (*ibid.*, Reg. 16, fol. 7^r; Valentini, *Acta Albaniae veneta*, XVIII [1974], no. 4,807, pp. 22–23; Iorga, *Notes et extraits*, III, 122–23; and note the summaries of documents, *ibid.*, pp. 125 ff.).

Theodore "Carastinus" did in fact venture into the duchy of Burgundy, where Philip the Good received him at Chalon-sur-Saône: ". . . vint illec ung ambaxadeur de par lempereur de Constantinoble devers ycellui duc, nomme Theodore Crystins, lequel ledit duc recheupt moult honnourablement . . ." (Jehan de Waurin, *Recueil des croniques d'Engleterre*, VI, I, 6, ed. Hardy, vol. V [1891, repr. 1967], p. 20; for the full citation of this edition, see, below, note 134). Philip assured him of Burgundian help against the Turks (*ibid.*, p. 22, and *cf.*, below, note 135).

[132] On the background, see Bistra Cvetkova, "Analyse des principales sources ottomanes du XVe siècle sur les campagnes de Vladislav le Varnénien et Jean Hunyadi en 1443–1444," *Studia Albanica*, V-1 (1968), 137–58. Ibrahim Beg, the ally of the Byzantine Emperor John VIII, was under the protection of the Timurid ruler Shah Rukh, who was especially feared by the Ottomans (see Halil Inalcik, "Byzantium and the Origins of the Crisis of 1444 under the Light of Turkish Sources," *Actes du XIIe Congrès international d'études byzantines* [Ohrid, 1961], II [Belgrade, 1964], 159–63). *Cf.* also Gyula Rázsó, "Una Strana Alleanza: Alcuni pensieri sulla storia militare e politica dell'alleanza contro i Turchi (1440–1464)," in Vittore Branca, ed., *Venezia e Ungheria nel Rinascimento*, Florence, 1973, pp. 79–100, whose article begins with a wrong reference, misquotes a line from Pius II (which he attributes to Calixtus III), and thereafter perpetrates in his notes a series of mangled Latin texts.

[133] *Cf.* Sen. Secreta, Reg. 16, fols. 73^r–74^r; Valentini, *Acta Albaniae veneta*, XVIII (1974), no. 4,925, pp. 129–34, doc. dated 6 March, 1444, by which time the Senate knew that Cesarini and Ladislas had returned to Hungary, "[illos] cum exercitu Christianorum retrocessisse et in Hungariam remeasse bonis necessariisque causis," and see Ducas, chap. 32 (Bonn, pp. 217–18), and the account given by Aeneas Sylvius Piccolomini, later Pope Pius II, in a letter apparently dated 13 January, 1444, to Giovanni Campisio (Rudolf Wolkan, ed., *Der Briefwechsel des Eneas Silvius Piccolomini*, in the Fontes rerum austriacarum, II. Abteilung, *Diplomataria et acta*, vol. 61 [Vienna, 1909, on which edition see, below, note 149], *Ep.* 117, pp. 281–83, dated 15 January in Wolkan, p. 278).

The Turks had blocked the approaches to Adrianople and Constantinople, felling trees to build barriers all along the ancient military road from Belgrade to the Bosporus. To the enterprise of the Turks was now added the severity of the winter. Meeting determined opposition, suffering from the cold, and lacking sources of supply, the crusaders began their return in late December, hard pressed by the Turks, whom they repulsed toward the end of the month in a battle near Sofia. Although the crusaders had to continue their withdrawal, they defeated the Turks again, in early January, 1444, between Pirot and Niš, taking a number of important captives. They were little disposed, however, to follow Branković's bold advice to entrench themselves in winter quarters in Serbia in order to resume their march in the spring. They wanted to go home and they did so, the army arriving in Buda on 2 February, worn by cold and hunger: "Clutching in emaciated hands," says Babinger, "the banners of the infidel, which they had taken as the spoils of war, they returned to their own country amid the jubilation of the population of the Hungarian capital, singing hymns of triumph."[134]

If the expedition had not entirely merited hymns of triumph, it had been successful, and had impressed Murad II, who was also impressed by the unrest in the Balkans and in Greece, as well as by the renewed hostility of Ibrahim Beg of Caramania. To prepare for another war with the Gran Caramano the sultan wanted peace with King Ladislas, and directed his efforts toward this end during the spring of 1444. The Sultana Mara, daughter of George Branković, assisted in the negotiations which seemed to promise her father some restoration of his lost power. Branković's two sons, Gregory and Stephen, whom their brother-in-law Murad II had seized and blinded a few years before, were also to be restored to their father.

Pope Eugenius IV had constructed one of those perennial anti-Turkish alliances, this time comprising Hungary, Venice, Burgundy, and Ragusa; the Burgundian adherence proved to be more than a mere gesture of good will. Philip the Good wrote encouraging letters to the Venetians, promising subsidies for the proposed maritime expedition against the Turks. He was willing to outfit and arm four galleys in the Venetian Arsenal. The Senate (having made the offer) was prepared to do so without compensation for the hulls of the galleys in the event of loss or damage, which was more than generous.[135] One could not be sure to what extent Philip would exert himself

---

[134] Babinger, *Maometto* (1957), p. 56, and *cf.* Babinger's article "Von Amurath zu Amurath: Vor- und Nachspiel der Schlacht bei Varna (1444)," *Oriens*, III (1950), 229–31, reprinted in his *Aufsätze und Abhandlungen zur Geschichte Südosteuropas und der Levante*, 2 vols., Munich, 1962–66, I, 128–29. See Ladislas's own account of the expedition of 1443 in his letter of 2 July, 1444, to the Florentine priors and gonfalonier of justice in Iorga, *Notes et extraits*, II, 404, and Aeneas Sylvius's letter to Leonhard Laiming, the bishop of Passau, dated 28 October, 1445, in Wolkan, *Briefwechsel*, *op. cit.*, vol. 61, *Ep.* 192, pp. 565–66; Raynaldus, *Ann. eccl.*, ad ann. 1443, nos. 15–19, vol. XVIII (1694), pp. 282–84; Iorga, *Gesch. d. osman. Reiches*, I, 433–36; and *cf.*, in general, *ROL*, VII, 80 ff., 387–88, 398–401, and *Notes et extraits*, III, 107 ff., 146–47, 157–60. The campaign of 1443 is described in detail and with some confusion by Jehan de Waurin, *Recueil des croniques et anchiennes istories de la Grant Bretaigne, a present nomme Engleterre*, VI, I, 5, 7–8, eds. Wm. Hardy and E. L. C. P. Hardy, 5 vols., London, 1864–91, repr. Nendeln, Liechtenstein, 1965–72, vol. V, pp. 15–19, 25–30 (Rolls Series). There is an account of the "langer Feldzug" of 1443 in L. Kupelwieser, *Die Kämpfe Ungarns mit den Osmanen bis zur Schlacht bei Mohács (1526)*, Vienna and Leipzig, 1895, pp. 68–79, with sketch maps of the Turco-Hungarian engagements near Niš (up to 3 November, 1443) and at the foot of Mount Kunoviza in early January, 1444. Although he was a professional soldier, Kupelwieser, p. 69, believed that Murad had 150,000 men under his command during the campaign. Halil Inalcik has devoted much attention to the decade preceding the fall of Constantinople in his volume of *Fatih devri üzerinde tetkikler ve vesikalar* [*Studies and Documents on the Period of the Conqueror*], I, Ankara, 1954.

A resolution of the Venetian Senate, passed on 15 January, 1444 (Ven. Style 1443), provided that ". . . quia honor nostri dominii est congratulari cum reverendissimo domino Cardinale Sancti Angeli ac serenissimo domino rege Polonie, qui nobis scripserunt de victoriis obtentis, ex nunc captum sit quod mittatur unus noster secretarius ad presentiam prefati reverendissimi domini cardinalis et serenissimi domini regis ac etiam magnifici domini Iohannis, vayvode transsilvani, ad congaudendum de victoriis suprascriptis et persentiendum de novis et progressibus Christianorum . . ." (Sen. Secreta, Reg. 16, fol. 57^v, and see fol. 58^v). But if Ladislas and Cesarini were not going to follow up their victory by another campaign in the late spring and summer of 1444, other plans would have to be made for the galleys which the Venetians were preparing for themselves and for the pope "ut infidelibus Teucris impediretur omnino transitus de Asia in Europam et econverso . . . quoniam si aliter esset, frustra esset accessus galearum predictarum." The Senate therefore sent Giovanni de' Reguardati as an envoy to Ladislas and Cesarini for information on this score (*ibid.*, fols. 73^r–74^r, doc. dated 6 March, 1444; *cf.* Iorga, *Notes et extraits*, III, 155; Cieszkowski, *Fontes rerum polonicarum*, I-2 [1890], no. XXXIX, pp. 79–85; and Valentini, *Acta Albaniae veneta*, XVIII, no. 4,904, pp. 93–94, and no. 4,925, pp. 129–34).

[135] Sen. Secreta, Reg. 16, fol. 81, dated 23 March, 1444, the Senate to Philip of Burgundy, and note fol. 91^r; *cf.* Jehan de Waurin, *Recueil des croniques d'Engleterre*, VI, I, 6, ed. Hardy, vol. V (1891, repr. 1967), pp. 19–23, and Thiriet, *Régestes*, III, nos. 2597, 2603, 2639, 2645, pp. 98 ff.

for the Christian cause, but in fact his galleys were to see effective service under Geoffroy de Thoisy and Waleran de Wavrin at Rhodes, in the Bosporus, and along the Danube (in 1442–1445).[136] The Ottoman emissaries, sent to the court at Buda, had their difficulties, although Branković himself urged peace upon the Hungarian diet in April, 1444. Now that he was supposed to recover most of Serbia, Branković was anxious to halt plans for the continuance of the crusade.[137]

Ladislas and Cesarini would hear nothing of peace, however, and in letters of 25 and 28 April, 1444, the latter answered inquiries from the Venetian Senate with the unequivocal assurance "that, yes, the most serene lord king has firmly decided and sworn in my hands—together with the barons and other lords and primates of this realm—to march with a powerful army against the perfidious Turks this very summer!"[138] Ladislas had made this oath on the fifteenth at the diet in Buda. The Senate received Cesarini's letters with transports of joy. They could continue with their plans for the fleet, which would very shortly be ready to sail for the strait of Gallipoli.[139] As a matter of fact the fleet was ready. It would soon sail, and in the following chapter we shall follow its course. As for Cesarini, he was a militarist at heart. His determination to suppress the Hussite heresy by "crusades" had provided clear evidence of the fact. He had, however, no choice but to march against the Turks. Eugenius IV had promised the Greeks that, when they returned to the bosom of the Church, they would receive aid from the West, and (after some wavering) he was now determined to keep that promise.[140]

Letters of Ciriaco of Ancona, who was at the sultan's court during the critical weeks of May and June, 1444, inform us of the events which now took place at Adrianople. On or shortly before 12 June, Ciriaco wrote to a friend, probably his patron, the rich Genoese Andreolo Giustiniani-Banca of Chios:

> . . . moreover, when I had made preparations for my removal from Adrianople and departure for Byzantium, we learned that the envoys from Hungary would get here very soon to see the sultan himself. And as I had decided to wait for them, we witnessed the arrival a few days later of the four envoys, accompanied by some sixty horsemen—the first being Stojka Gisdanić, from the illustrious King Ladislas of Poland and Hungary; the second Vitislao, from the eminent commander John Hunyadi; and the remaining two from George [Branković], despot of silver-rich Moesia and the Serbian province, one of whom was the venerable Metropolitan A[thanasius Frašak of Semendria], and the other indeed the chancellor [of Branković, whose name was Bogdan]. And when after two days they betook themselves to the august presence of the sultan—the royal envoy going first, then the representative of the despot, and finally the one from the doughty John [Hunyadi]—they gave the great prince their letters of credence, written in Latin, Greek, and Serbian, and each one presented his own modest gifts. . . .

After some days of discussion as to the return of towns which had been occupied by the Turks, who wanted especially to retain Golubac on the Danube, the sultan gave way on all points, and arranged to send Suleiman Beg and a Greek named Vranas to Buda as his envoys to conclude a ten years' peace with King Ladislas and his followers.[141]

---

136 Waurin, *Croniques*, VI, i, 9, 11, 14–19, vol. V, pp. 30–41, 44–51, 58–119, and note Richard Vaughan, *Philip the Good: The Apogee of Burgundy*, London, 1970, pp. 270–72. Waleran de Wavrin was the nephew of the chronicler Jehan de Waurin (Wavrin). There is a miscellany of notes and a half-dozen texts relating to the Burgundian "emprises" against the Turks from 1443 to 1466 in N. Iorga, *Les Aventures "sarrazines" des français de Bourgogne au XVe siècle*, Cluj, 1926.

137 Iorga, *Gesch. d. osman. Reiches*, I, 438–39.

138 Sen. Secreta, Reg. 16, fol. 91; Valentini, *Acta Albaniae veneta*, XVIII, no. 4,962, p. 174, doc. dated 12 May, 1444, the Senate to Cesarini, repeating and adapting the latter's own words, ". . . videlicet, serenissimum illum dominum regem omnino firmiter statuisse ac iurasse in manibus vestris una cum baronibus et aliis dominis ac primatibus regni illius adversus perfidos Teucros hac presenti estate potenti exercitu se transferre. . . ."

139 *Ibid.*, Reg. 16, fol. cit., from the letter referred to in the preceding note: "Intelligit itaque reverenda vestra paternitas [i.e., Cesarini] quale ad rem hanc sit ardens desiderium nostrum et quam potens maritima classis in brevissimo spacio strictum Galipolis petitura sit," and note fols. 95–96^r^, doc. dated 25 May, 1444.

140 D. Caccamo, "Eugenio IV e la crociata di Varna," *Archivio della Società romana di storia patria*, LXXIX, 35–87, esp. pp. 77–78.

141 J. A. Fabricius, *Bibliotheca latina mediae et infimae aetatis*, VI (Padua, 1754), *Addenda*, p. 13; Francesco [Francisc] Pall, "Ciriaco d'Ancona e la crociata contro i Turchi," *Bulletin historique de l'Académie roumaine*, XX (1938), 61–62, and *cf.* pp. 32 ff., with refs.; Halecki, *Crusade of Varna* (1943), pp. 86–87. Some five months after the disaster at Varna, Andreas de Palatio wrote Cardinal Lodovico Trevisan from Poznań on 16 May, 1445, that Branković and Hunyadi had carried on the negotiations with Murad without consulting Ladislas, which seems to be Polish propaganda: "Sed non potuit [i.e., rex Wladislaus] in termino constituto delectas ad hoc copias aggregare neque cum ipsis omnibus transfretare Danubium propter tractatum pacis, quem illustris Georgius despotus Rascie eiusdem regis subditus ac magnificus Iohannes de Huniad wagewoda Transsilvanus eciam *inconsulto rege* habuerunt

We have the text of Murad II's letter, dated 12 June, to Ladislas, ending with the Turkish understanding "that we should have a good and solid peace with your Excellency without any reservation or fraud for ten years, and for this we send our noble and distinguished subject, Suleiman Beg, that your Excellency should be willing to swear in person, truthfully and faithfully without any reservation, that you will keep a good and solid peace with us through ten years."[142]

There has long been some dispute whether the Christian disaster at Varna in November, 1444, was the consequence of a broken pledge to Murad II. On the whole it seems reasonable to assume that neither Murad nor the Christians intended to keep the peace "sine aliquo dolo vel fraude usque ad annos decem." On the very day of Murad's letter to Ladislas (12 June, 1444), Ciriaco of Ancona wrote an admiring letter, undoubtedly addressed to John Hunyadi, to the effect that the latter would soon know what had been done at Adrianople both from his own legation and from the sultan's letter, and he, King Ladislas, and Branković would know what to do: "For you, therefore, and for the honored and noble religious expedition of the Christians we hope that all things will turn out ever better and more favorable."[143] Ciriaco was well informed. He had met the Hungarian and Serbian envoys, but was obviously still thinking in terms of a crusade against the Turks. Three weeks before (on 21 or 22 May) the sultan had admitted him to an audience with Francesco Drapperio, Genoese envoy and proprietor of rich alum mines at New Phocaea on the Anatolian coast.[144] About a week later (on 18 June) Ciriaco sent his friend Giustiniani his own pompous version of the form in which the Latin translator should have cast Murad's letter to Ladislas, of which, as we have seen, he had secured a copy.[145]

That Ciriaco did not expect the peace to be observed is clear from the important letter he wrote, certainly to Hunyadi, from Pera in Constantinople on 24 June: He had already written as much as he had dared from Adrianople [on 12 June]—but for fear of the Turks he would have discussed conditions at greater length, and especially the peace which the envoys had forced on the sultan (*coacta pax*), which Ciriaco believed the latter had accepted merely to protect Thrace against attack while he was absent in Asia Minor. The Turks were not relying very heavily on this peace, however, for thoroughly frightened, as Hunyadi's people would bear witness, they were hastily repairing the walls and fortifying the towers of Adrianople, while at the same time equipping their soldiery "for flight rather than for fight." The war against the Caramano would be pressed, but when Ibrahim Beg had been subdued, pacified, or driven out of Konya, the sultan would come back over the Hellespont, bringing with him a still greater army, and invade Moesia and Hungary again: "He will strive with all his might to avenge the past and recent harm that you have done him!" To Ciriaco the ten years' peace was a monstrous device of the sultan to gain time (*pax haec improba et penitus execranda . . . pax maligna*). Hunyadi and the members of the Christian alliance should move against Thrace and the Hellespont: "Come, great princes, declare a war worthy of the Christian religion, and may you never cease to carry on the sacred and glorious expedition, already begun under happy auspices, to the conclusion we long for!"[146] In this life-and-death struggle which was to settle the fate of the Balkans for four centuries, neither side was to be bound by scraps of paper, for

cum eodem magno Theucrorum principe Omorathbegha . . ." (A. Lewicki, ed., *Codex epistolaris saeculi decimi quinti*, II [Cracow, 1891, repr. New York and London, 1965], no. 308, p. 460). On the importance of this text for Ant. Prochaska, who claimed that Ladislas did not ratify the peace, see Jan Dąbrowski, *L'Année 1444*, Cracow: Académie polonaise des sciences et des lettres, 1952, p. 3, and *cf.* pp. 6 ff., 17–18, 20.

142 Murad II's letter to Ladislas is given in Pall, *Bull. hist. Acad. roum.*, XX, 63–64, as well as Ciriaco's own "stylized" version of the same text (*ibid.*, pp. 57–58); *cf.* Giov. Targioni Tozzetti, *Relazioni d'alcuni viaggi fatti in diverse parti della Toscana*, V (Florence, 1773, repr. Bologna, 1971), 422; Halecki, *Crusade of Varna*, pp. 88–90; Babinger, *Maometto*, pp. 62–63.

143 Pall, *Bull. hist. Acad. roum.*, XX, 64–65; Halecki, *Crusade of Varna*, pp. 90–91.

144 Ciriaco, *Ep.* XVII, in Cod. Palat. Florent. 49 (Serie Targioni), fol. 19r (earlier enumeration, 71r), letter dated 22 May, 1444, to Andreolo Giustiniani-Banca; Targioni Tozzetti, *Relazioni d'alcuni viaggi*, V, 422; Pall, *Bull. hist. Acad. roum.*, XX, 25, 56–57; Halecki, *Crusade of Varna*, p. 86. There are numerous references to the commercial activities of "Ser Franzesco di Drapieri dal bancho" in Umberto Dorini and Tommaso Bertelè, eds., *Il Libro dei conti di Giacomo Badoer* (*Costantinopoli 1436–1440*), Rome, 1956, pp. 34, 45, 70, 73, 90, 91, 94, 99, 102, *et passim* (Il Nuovo Ramusio, vol. III).

145 Targioni Tozzetti, *Relazioni*, V, 422; Pall, *Bull. hist. Acad. roum.*, XX, 58; Halecki, *Crusade of Varna*, p. 91.

146 Pall, *Bull. hist. Acad. roum.*, XX, 65–66; Halecki, *Crusade of Varna*, pp. 91–92. This letter could not have been written, as commonly supposed, to the Byzantine Emperor John VIII (see above, note 110).

each adversary knew well what the other thought, and knew that in this game there were no rules.

Some animus has been engendered among historians, nevertheless, by the highly controverted problem of whether Ladislas did or did not ratify the treaty of Adrianople (of 12 June) by an oath taken at Szeged toward the end of July, 1444. We have already alluded to this dispute. The Polish historians Antoni Prochaska and Oskar Halecki have tried to exonerate the young crusader of Varna from the charge of perjury. In defense of their position it may be asked (even though an oath given to the infidel would lack canonical sanction anyway), why should Ladislas bother to swear to a treaty that he knew he would denounce a week later? He could not have ratified the treaty before 26 July; he swore to continue with the crusade on 4 August. However baffling such inconsistency may now appear, Pall has advanced strong arguments to show that Ladislas was nevertheless guilty of it.[147] There had been of course no need of Ladislas's taking the oath. The device of pretending to make peace in June in order to mislead Sultan Murad II had already served its purpose (insofar as it had in fact misled him). If Ladislas did, however, fail to ratify the treaty which his plenipotentiary Stojka Gisdanić had negotiated with Murad at Adrianople in June, he broke the promise explicitly given in the letter of credence (dated the preceding 24 April) with which he had furnished Gisdanić as the latter got ready to go on his mission.[148]

In any event, as we know, the charge of perjury against Ladislas appears as early as 1445 in two letters of the youthful Mehmed [II] and, more significantly, in some letters of the humanist Aeneas Sylvius (also written shortly after Varna), receiving further currency in the works of Filippo Buonaccorsi (Callimachus) and the Polish historian Jan Długosz.[149] Although the nations of western

[147] Pall, "Autour de la Croisade de Varna: La Question de la paix de Szeged et de sa rupture," *Bull. hist. Acad. roum.*, XXII (1941), 144–58, and "Un Moment décisif de l'histoire du Sud-Est européen: la croisade de Varna (1444)," *Balcania*, VII (Bucharest, 1944), 102–20; *cf.* also Babinger, "Von Amurath zu Amurath," *Oriens*, III (1950), 239–42, reprinted in his *Aufsätze und Abhandlungen*, I (1962), 136–38. D. Caccamo, "Eugenio IV e la crociata di Varna," *Archivio della Società romana di storia patria*, LXXIX (1956), 78–79, simply says that "giunto a Szeged non dopo il primo agosto, il re ratificava il trattato. . . ." Caccamo rehearses briefly the bibliography of the controversy, which has been explored at some length by Dąbrowski, *L'Année 1444* (1952).

[148] Pall, *Bull. hist. Acad. roum.*, XX, 62–63; Halecki, *Crusade of Varna*, p. 85: "Et quidquid ipse Stoyka, noster fidelis, cum vestra magnitudine disposuerit et concluserit, fidem et vinculum quodcunque volueritis, promittimus . . . vestris nuntiis dare et conferre" (from the letter presenting Gisdanić to Murad II).

[149] See Halecki, *Crusade of Varna*, pp. 67–75, and Jan Dąbrowski, *Władysław Jagiellańczyk na Węgrzech (1440–1444)*, Warsaw, 1922, pp. 154–55 (cited by Pall and Halecki). Filippo Buonaccorsi (1437–1496), called "Callimachus," was a native of San Gimignano near Florence. As a young man he joined Pomponio Leto's Roman Academy, and got caught up in the "conspiracy" against Paul II. When the Academy was suppressed in 1468, Buonaccorsi fled to Naples, and thereafter to Crete, Cyprus, Chios, and Constantinople, and found refuge in Poland, where from the mid-1470's he embarked on an influential diplomatic and political career, which took him to Venice, Constantinople, and other centers of power. He is well known, in the present context, for his *Historia de rege Vladislao seu clade Varnensi*. Upon his death in 1496, he was buried at Cracow (*cf.*, J. A. Fabricius, *Bibl. latina med. et infim. aetatis*, I [Florence, 1858], 300, and see the brief account of his life, with an excellent bibliography, by Domenico Caccamo, in the *Dizionario biografico degli italiani*, XV [1972], 78–83).

Not enamored of either the Poles or the Hungarians in 1445, Aeneas Sylvius discusses their affairs in numerous letters (Rudolf Wolkan, ed., *Der Briefwechsel des Eneas Silvius Piccolomini* [1431–1454], 4 vols., Vienna, 1909–18, in the Fontes rerum austriacarum, II. Abteilung, *Diplomataria et acta*, vols. 61–62, 67–68, *Epp.* 170, 172–74, 186–89, etc.). In a very abusive letter to the chancellor of Queen Sophia (Sonka) of Poland, the mother of Ladislas III the Jagiellonian, written in the summer of 1445, Aeneas explicitly accuses Ladislas of having broken his pact with the Turks (*ibid.*, I [1909], *Ep.* 175, p. 519): "Nec enim federa tenentur cum infidelibus concussa, nisi consensus apostolice sedis interveniat, qui hic non fuit, sed legatus apostolicus [Cesarini] ea omnino scindi mandavit." A staunch defender of the Hapsburg claims to Hungary, Aeneas was nevertheless not wholly unsympathetic to the catastrophe which had engulfed the Jagiellonian "quamvis federa essent indutiarum juramento firmata" (*Ep.* 179, p. 530, dated 13 September, 1445). Alluding again to the broken peace in a letter of 28 October, 1445, to the bishop of Passau, Aeneas blames Cesarini, "qui treugas nullius momenti fore dicebat," etc. (*Ep.* 192, p. 566). Although at this time inclined to spare the pope in his letters (for good reasons perhaps), in 1458 when he wrote his work *De Europa*, 5, in *Opera quae extant omnia*, Basel, 1551, repr. Frankfurt a. M., 1967, p. 397C, Aeneas holds both Eugenius IV and Cesarini responsible for forcing the Jagiellonian to break the ten years' peace he had solemnly sworn with the Turks: "Induciae belli in decem annos dictae iusiurandum per sua sacra ambae partes praestitere, Despoto Serviae quae bello amiserat reddita. . . . Iuramenta remisit . . ." [at the pope's command]. There are other pertinent references in Aeneas's works, but these should suffice to illustrate his point of view, held over a long period of years, concerning the broken treaty which preceded Varna.

The chronicler Jehan de Waurin, writing probably in 1446, "while the facts and impressions were fresh in the memory" (according to his editor Wm. Hardy, *Croniques*, I [1864, repr. 1972], introd., pp. xli–xlii), also believed "que le roy et les seigneurs furent contentz de rompre la paix quilz avoient faite avec le Turcq, et ledit cardinal [Cesarini] leur donna absollution de leurs sermens et

Europe were protected in their political and cultural development, from the later fifteenth century to the seventeenth, by the Poles and Hungarians, Serbs and Wallachians, modern historians have subjected to much adverse criticism some of those (including Ladislas the Jagiellonian) who in their time defended European culture and Christianity against the Turks. The victim of Varna, however, was widely believed in the generations which followed his death to have suffered divine judgment for his broken pledge. Whether the lie was spoken at Adrianople in mid-June or at Szeged in late July seems unimportant. The lie was clearly spoken by a much harassed, confused, and overwrought young man who took hard the grave responsibility which destiny had placed upon his shoulders. As great events in the north moved toward their final resolution, the fate of both Greek and Latin states in the Levant hung in the balance. As Ladislas and Hunyadi disputed the future of the Balkans with Murad, they were determining also the future of the enfeebled empire of Byzantium and the "despotate" of the Morea, the Venetian colonies in Greece and the Aegean, and the Florentine duchy of Athens.

---

promesses" (*ibid.*, VI, I, 10, in vol. V, pp. 41–43). Waurin, however, revised the last part of his work between 1471 and 1474 (*ibid.*, I, xlviii, note).

Later on, Erasmus, who had a fair knowledge of eastern affairs, blames the pope for the violation of the ten years' truce, which he says that Murad had sought and obtained (*Utilissima consultatio de bello Turcis inferendo*, Freiburg-im-Breisgau, 1530, unnumbered fols. 8^{r}, 10^{v} = signatures A-8, B-2). He seems to have got his information from Aeneas Sylvius.

3. THE CRUSADE OF VARNA AND ITS AFTERMATH (1444–1453)

THE EVIDENCE of Ciriaco of Ancona's letters is particularly valuable in helping us to assess the events which led to Varna. The Anconitan moved among the Greeks, Genoese, Venetians, and even the Turks with surprising ease. Interested in diplomacy as well as in archaeology, he copied documents with the same avidity as Greek inscriptions. On Wednesday, 15 July, 1444, Ciriaco was a member of a large hunting party which left Constantinople for Thrace. The party was joined by Boruele Grimaldi, Genoese podestà of Pera, and a group of his countrymen; from Constantinople many Venetians came also, headed by the young Niccolò Soranzo, son of the bailie Marino. The masters of the hunt were the Emperor John VIII and his brother Theodore, formerly despot of Mistra and now lord of Selymbria. They pitched their camp first at the ancient Thracian city of Aphamnia, "rising like a beautiful fountain," and later went on to Myliadema (*undique collapsa vetustate*), where they saw long, crumbling lines of walls and the remains of great temples. Although there were many Venetian and Genoese nobles in the company, the emperor paid especial attention to Ciriaco, whom he had known for some years, and who undoubtedly informed him in complete detail of the peace negotiations at Adrianople and the agreement reached on 12 June.[1] Obviously they had much to talk about, and the coming months were to supply all Europe and the Levant with a topic for conversation, the Christian defeat at Varna.

It is well known that the young Ladislas of Poland and Hungary is accused of having signed a peace treaty with Murad II as a prelude to making war upon him. We cannot be much concerned here with the justice of this charge of perjury. The historian need not be accused of undue cynicism who would take a generous view of tactics in both love and war in the fifteenth century. The opinions of the canon lawyers are quite clear concerning the inadmissibility of oaths given to the infidel to the disadvantage of Christendom. The crusade was the last hope of saving Constantinople from the Turks. The fall of the Byzantine capital would inevitably inspire the Turks with the ambition completely to occupy continental Greece and the Morea. We must acknowledge, however, that Ladislas had a flair for dramatic confusion. At the diet of Buda on 15 April, 1444, he had sworn in the presence of Cardinal Cesarini to renew the war against the Turks during the coming summer, and yet on the twenty-fourth he dispatched his agent Gisdanić with full and binding powers to treat with the Ottoman government. He assured the Venetian ambassador Giovanni de' Reguardati that he was going to war.[2] On 2 July he informed the Florentine priorate that the object of his strug-

[1] Ciriaco, *Ep.* XXIX, in Cod. Palat. Florent. 49 (Serie Targioni), fol. 26 (earlier enumeration 79), dated "Ex Bizantio XIIII Kl. Sextilis. Euggenii pp^{e}. A. XIIII" [19 July, 1444]; Giov. Targioni Tozzetti, *Relazioni d'alcuni viaggi*, V (Florence, 1773, repr. Bologna, 1971), 66–69; L. T. Belgrano, "Seconda Serie di documenti riguardanti la colonia di Pera," in *Atti della Società ligure di storia patria*, XIII (1877–84), 977–79, incorrectly dated 18 July. The hunting party began on 15 July, a Wednesday (*ad Iduum Quintilium serenum et genii nostri iocundissimum diem*). *Cf.* Francisc Pall, "Ciriaco d'Ancona e la crociata contro i Turchi," *Bull. hist. Acad. roum.*, XX (1938), 42–43. According to Oskar Halecki, *The Crusade of Varna*, New York, 1943, pp. 26–31, the information which Ciriaco gave the Emperor John VIII on this occasion caused the latter to hasten directly to the Morea (reaching Mistra in about two weeks) in order to confer with his brother, the Despot Constantine.

Halecki thinks that the Latin letter addressed to Ladislas of Hungary, and ascribed to John VIII (given in Jan Długosz, *Historia polonica*, bk. XII, Leipzig edition, 2 vols., 1711–12, II, cols. 790–93, and ed. I. Z. Pauli, vol. IV, in Alex. Przezdziecki, ed., *Joannis Długosz Senioris, canonici Cracoviensis, opera omnia*, 14 vols., Cracow, 1863–87, vol. XIII, pp. 704–7), dated at Mistra on 30 July, is a poor Latin translation of an authentic Greek text. In this letter John urges Ladislas not to make peace with Sultan Murad II, although "it has come to our attention that the Despot George [Branković] and your Serenity have begun and actually carried through certain treaties of peace with the said Murad, and that the latter is sending his envoys to your Excellency to conclude and confirm the agreements." This is obviously a reference to the pact of Adrianople of 12 June, although Pall (*op. cit.*, p. 43, note 3) may be correct in rejecting Mistra as the place from which John sent the letter.

[2] Reguardati's commission, dated 6 March, 1444, is published in Aug. Cieszkowski, ed., *Fontes rerum polonicarum e tabulario reipublicae venetae*, ser. I, fasc. 2 (Poznań, 1890), no. XXXIX, pp. 79–84. He was given further instructions on 23 March (*ibid.*, pp. 84–85). *Cf.*, above, Chapter 2, note 134. The documents of 6 and 23 March have been republished by Giuseppe Valentini, ed., *Acta Albaniae veneta saeculorum XIV et XV*, XVIII (1974), nos. 4,925, 4,933, pp. 129 ff.

gle for peace in Hungary had been to embark in person upon the holy war.[3] Again, on the twenty-fourth, he wrote the king of Bosnia that he was setting out to encompass the destruction of the accursed Turks.[4] Only the next day, however, he left Buda for Szeged to meet Suleiman Beg and Vranas and apparently to sign the treaty of peace (on 1 August?) which they had brought from Sultan Murad. But on 4 August, at Szeged, Ladislas finally took the most solemn vow with his chief nobles to drive the Turks from Europe within the year, "notwithstanding any treaties or negotiations whatsoever . . ." (*non obstantibus quibuscumque tractatibus aut praticis seu conclusionibus aut capitulis treuguarum factis vel fiendis cum imperatore Turchorum*).[5] The die was cast. It rolled to Varna.

A contemporary Serbian annalist says that George Branković made a separate peace with the Porte on 15 August, 1444,[6] which obviously means that he ratified for himself the treaty of Adrianople of 12 June after Ladislas's declaration of war on 4 August. The Serbian defection was serious. Branković, landless in '43, had still supplied 8,000 fighting men, one-third of the army which had campaigned successfully in that

[3] N. Iorga [Jorga], *Notes et extraits pour servir à l'histoire des croisades*, II (Paris, 1899), 404–5, letter of 2 July to the Florentines, and see Pall, in *Bull. hist. Acad. roum.*, XX, 27–31, with refs. A dispatch from the Venetian Senate dated 9 September, 1444, to Alvise Loredan, captain of the papal fleet in eastern waters (Arch. di Stato di Venezia, Senatus Secreta, Reg. 16, fols. 119ᵛ–120ʳ, published by Cieszkowski, *Fontes rerum polonicarum*, I–2, no. LVII, pp. 129–31, and by Sime Ljubić, ed., *Listine*, IX [Zagreb, 1890], 212 [in the Monumenta spectantia historiam slavorum meridionalium, vol. XXI]), states that letters of 12 and 14 August just received in Venice from Cardinal Cesarini and Reguardati contained the assurance that they had kept Loredan fully informed "de nonnullis praticis habitis per imperatorem Teucrorum tam cum serenissimo domino rege Hungarie et Polonie quam etiam cum illustrissimo domino despoto quas tamen nescimus si locum habiture sint cum idem reverendissimus dominus legatus Sancti Angeli [Cesarini] ac secretarius noster [Reguardati] nobis scribant serenissimum dominum regem predictum ac barones Hungarie, predictis non obstantibus, promisisse velle procedere exercitualiter anno isto ad exterminium Teucrorum . . ." (fol. 119ᵛ). Loredan was directed to proceed with his commission if King Ladislas and the Christian army took the offensive against the Turks, "ut ex Grecia expellantur," but if they abandoned the enterprise, the Venetians should not try to fight the Turks alone, and Loredan should refrain from attacking territories belonging to the sultan.

[4] Ragusan ambassadors at the court of Bosnia reported to the home government, in a letter which reached Ragusa on 15 August, 1444, "haver vista una lettera del serenissimo rè de Ungaria, fata in Ungaria alle XXIIII del passato, la qual scrive al deto rè de Bosina, digando chome de presente se mette in ordene per andar alla destrution delli maledeti Turchi . . ." (Iorga, *Notes et extraits*, II, 407). *Cf.* Pall, *Bull. hist. Acad. roum.*, XX, 37–39.

[5] Iorga, in *ROL*, VII (1900, repr. 1964), 423–24, and *Notes et extraits*, III (Paris, 1902), 182–83, publishes an extract from the "manifesto of Szeged;" the text may be found in Cieszkowski, *Fontes rerum polonicarum*, I–2, no. LV, pp. 119–25; and note its citation by the contemporary Polish historian Jan Długosz (well-known canon of Cracow), *Historia polonica*, bk. XII, ed. I. Z. Pauli, vol. IV [=*Opera omnia*, ed. Alex. Przezdziecki, XIII], Cracow, 1877, pp. 708–11, and ed. Leipzig, 1711–12, II, cols. 794–96, to whom we owe our fullest and earliest literary account of the meeting at Szeged. The documentary source for the proceedings of 4 August, 1444, is the Venetian Commemoriali, Reg. 13, fols. 161ᵛ–162, also given in Predelli, *Regesti dei Commem.*, IV (1896), bk. XIII, no. 264, pp. 286–87. *Cf.* Halecki, *Crusade of Varna*, pp. 35–50, but see also Pall, *Bull. hist. Acad. roum.*, XX, 28–41, 44, and Franz Babinger, *Maometto il Conquistatore e il suo tempo*, Turin, 1957, pp. 66–67.

Halecki, *op. cit.*, has attempted to show that Ladislas did not ratify the treaty of Szeged, a view which the Polish historian Prochaska had previously advanced. Halecki's book is very interesting (and has stimulated discussion) although the apparent inaccuracy of this particular contention has aroused considerable opposition, on which note Fr. Pall, "Autour de la Croisade de Varna: La Question de la paix de Szeged et de sa rupture," *Bull. hist. Acad. roum.*, XXII (1941), 144–58, and "Un Moment décisif de l'histoire du Sud-Est européen: la croisade de Varna (1444)," *Balcania*, VII (1944), esp. pp. 108–18; see also in general Fr. Babinger, "Von Amurath zu Amurath: Vor- und Nachspiel der Schlacht bei Varna," *Oriens*, III (1950), esp. pp. 239–42, and *Maometto*, pp. 65–67. Both Pall and Babinger believe that Ladislas did in fact sign the peace treaty of Szeged, and (as noted in the preceding chapter) so does Domenico Caccamo, "Eugenio IV e la crociata di Varna," *Archivio della Società romana di storia patria*, LXXIX (3rd ser., X, 1956), 35–87, esp. pp. 78–79. For details of the fatal campaign of 1444 and for the bibliography in general, see Caccamo's article and Dąbrowski's monograph on *L'Année 1444* (1952). The latter also has no doubt that Ladislas broke the pledge of Adrianople and Szeged.

Works published before Pall employed the letters of Ciriaco of Ancona to depict the background to the peace of Szeged are inevitably limited in their scope (ee. g., David Angyal, "Le Traité de paix de Szeged avec les Turcs [1444]," *Revue de Hongrie*, VII [1911], 255–68, 374–92; Angyal, "Die diplomatische Vorbereitung der Schlacht von Varna [1444]," *Ungarische Rundschau*, II [1913], 518–24; and Rudolf Urbánek, *Vladislav Varnenčík: Skutečnost i legenda* [in Czech, with a French summary], Prague, 1937, pp. 43–94). T. V. Tuleja, "Eugenius IV and the Crusade of Varna," *Catholic Historical Review*, XXXV (1950), 257–75, believes that Halecki's *Crusade of Varna* "completely destroys the traditional interpretation of the Varna crusade," which is hardly the case.

[6] *Cf.* Franz Babinger, "Von Amurath zu Amurath: Vor- und Nachspiel der Schlacht bei Varna (1444)," *Oriens*, III (1950), 240, 242–43, reprinted in his *Aufsätze und Abhandlungen zur Geschichte Südosteuropas und der Levante*, 2 vols., Munich, 1962–66, I, 137, 138–39.

year. Hope of a victorious crusade must have depended largely upon the continuance of the unusual Hungarian-Serbian alliance. The Serbs were to be sorely missed on the battlefield of Varna. It is not strange that the Turks almost hastened to restore to Branković the territories they had seized from him,[7] including his capital city of Semendria (Smederevo), Novo Brdo, and even the fortress town of Golubac on the Hungarian-Serbian frontier.[8] The old despot had good reason to confirm the peace. The negotiations at Adrianople appeared to have been for his benefit, which has made it easy for the Polish historians Cieszkowski, Prochaska, and Halecki to insist that Ladislas never did ratify the treaty of Adrianople, which provided chiefly for his erstwhile enemy Branković.[9] Hunyadi's interest in the negotiations had been twofold, to encourage Murad to proceed against the Gran Caramano in Asia Minor, which would much increase the Christian chances of success against the Turks in Europe, and to gain time enough to be sure that the allied fleet was really going to set out for the Bosporus, for without the Christian naval armament the land army was not likely to achieve a victory.

Soon there was little doubt that the fleet would sail eastward, and that the crusade would actually begin on the sea. Some two dozen galleys under the command of the cardinal legate Francesco Condulmer, Eugenius IV's nephew, with Alvise (Luigi) Loredan serving as captain, sailed from Venice to the Dardanelles in two or three different squadrons. The pope had armed ten galleys in the Venetian arsenal, and Duke Philip of Burgundy, four; Philip had sent letters of exchange to Venice amounting to 3,500 ducats to arm these four galleys, over which Waleran de Wavrin was set.[10] Other ships may also have joined the armada. Venice had contributed eight galleys, and Ragusa very cautiously, two. Two Byzantine vessels were also to be added when the fleet had finally reached its eastern destination. It was a sizable fleet, probably large enough for its purpose of holding the Dardanelles and the Bosporus against the Turks.

A year earlier than this, before the first expedition of Ladislas and Hunyadi, the Venetian government had advised the pope (in May, 1443) that a fleet of sixteen to twenty galleys would be required to patrol the straits against the Turks when a plan was envisaged very like that now to be attempted. Twenty galleys would be preferable, of course, the pope had been told, "ut cum securitate res fieri valeat," and in addition there might well be a transport to carry food and munitions. The Senate had indicated at the same time that it would cost Venice more than 20,000 ducats to prepare the ten galleys as such (*corpora galearum*), which the pope was supposed to arm at his own expense. These ten galleys were to fly the standard of the Church. Since the duke of Burgundy was also asking for four galleys, Venice was being put to further expense, it was said, and while the Senate was willing to supply these galleys with the necessary rigging and cordage (*corredi*), the pope and the duke would have to arm them.[11]

---

[7] Later on, the Venetians congratulated Branković upon receiving the news "vestram inclitam magnificentiam terras et loca sua recuperasse et in dominio suo restitutam esse," and sought to settle some differences with him (Sen. Secreta, Reg. 16, fols. 139ᵛ–140ʳ, doc. dated 17 January, 1444 [Ven. style 1443]; Cieszkowski, *Fontes rerum polonicarum*, I-2, no. LXI, p. 140).

[8] On the strategic importance of Golubac, see Dąbrowski, *L'Année 1444*, pp. 22–24.

[9] *Cf.* Halecki, *Crusade of Varna*, pp. 54–57.

[10] Marino Sanudo, *Vite de' duchi*, in L. A. Muratori, ed., *RISS*, XXII (Milan, 1733), col. 1114D. On 12 February, 1444, Pope Eugenius wrote Cesarini that the Christian successes in central Europe betokened the coming liberation of those parts of Greece and Europe which were occupied by the Turks, so that the Greeks and other easterners would soon enjoy the fruits of the union of the Churches proclaimed at Florence. The pope also sent Cesarini assurance that plans were going forward for sending into the Levant a papal fleet to be commanded by his nephew, Cardinal Francesco Condulmer, *tituli Sancti Clementis presbyterem Cardinalem Sancte Romane Ecclesie vicecancellarium*, for service against the Turks (Arch. Segr. Vaticano, Reg. Vat. 382, fols. 206ᵛ–208ᵛ, "datum Rome apud Sanctum Petrum, anno etc., MCCCCXLIII, pridie Id. Februarii, pontificatus nostri anno XIII"). *Cf.* J. Gelcich and L. Thallóczy, *Diplomatarium ragusanum*, Budapest, 1887, nos. 268, 270, pp. 448 ff., and no. 273, pp. 457–59, which last document, dated at Ragusa on 31 July, 1444, credits the pope with eight galleys; Venice with five; and the duke of Burgundy, four; and acknowledges the Ragusan contribution as two (*cf.* B. Krekić, *Dubrovnik [Raguse] et le Levant au moyen âge*, Paris and The Hague, 1961, no. 1060, p. 340).

[11] Sen. Secreta, Reg. 16, fols. 9ᵛ–10ʳ; Iorga, *ROL*, VII, 98–99; *Notes et extraits*, III, 125–26, letter of the Senate to Leonardo Venier, Venetian ambassador to the papacy, dated 10 May, 1443. A year later, on 23 March, 1444, the Venetians informed the duke of Burgundy that fourteen galleys would suffice to guard the straits (Sen. Secreta, Reg. 16, fol. 81, dated by a scribal error "MCCCCLXIIII[!], die XXIII Martii;" *ROL*, VII, 403). The following May, however, it was reported in Venice that the duke was arming at Nice three more galleys and a galiot, as well as another vessel which was being prepared elsewhere for naval combat (Sen. Secreta,

In March, 1444, Cardinal Cesarini had been informed that the fourteen galleys which the Republic was supplying at the request of the pope and the duke comprised almost a quarter of the total number of which the Venetians could dispose.[12]

By early June, 1444, Cardinal Francesco's fleet had at length been got ready. Some galleys had already set sail. It had taken months of diplomatic effort, to be sure, to get the pope to meet the costs of the galleys which had been prepared for him.[13] Now, however, after the settlement of a score of problems, the Senate issued its instructions on 17 June, 1444, to Alvise Loredan, who, besides being captain of the pontifical fleet, had eight Venetian galleys under his direct command. Loredan was to serve under Cardinal Francesco. He was to avoid any encounter with the Egyptian fleet and also to steer clear of Rhodes. His mission lay on the Dardanelles and the Bosporus.[14] On 4 July (1444) the Senate wrote Cesarini of Francesco's departure on 22 June "with his last galley:" now the pope's ten galleys and the eight supplied by Venice were on the sea. The duke of Burgundy's four galleys were expected to leave in two or three days. The Venetians were urging Cardinal Francesco to send, upon his arrival at Gallipoli, eight or more galleys into the Black Sea and even up the Danube as far as Nicopolis to establish contact with the Hungarian army when it should reach that area. Francesco could thus assist the army to cross the Danube, and victory in this glorious enterprise would lie in the army's getting across the river successfully.[15]

Reg. 16, fol. 91^{r}; *ROL*, VII, 408, "MCCCCXLIIII, die XII Maii, reverendissimo domino cardinali sancti Angeli legato apostolico"). For the two galleys supplied by Ragusa, see Iorga, *Notes et extraits*, II, 403, 407, 412, and *cf.* p. 417, and Gelcich and Thallóczy, *Diplomatarium ragusanum*, nos. 268, 270, pp. 448 ff., letters dated 17 December, 1443, and 10 February, 1444; and Bariša Krekić, "Dubrovnik's Participation in the War against the Turks" [in Serbocroatian, with English summary], *Zbornik Radova Vizantološkog Instituta*, II (1953), 145–58.

[12] Iorga, *ROL*, VII, 400, and *Notes et extraits*, III, 159, letter of Cristoforo Cocco to the cardinal of S. Angelo (Cesarini), dated 15 March, 1444: ". . . quamvis . . . aerarium . . . nostrum non parum exhaustum sit continuis bellis, tamen triremes XIIII scite factas ex LX eligi iussimus. . . ." The Genoese petitioned the pope that their clergy be exempted from the ecclesiastical tithe which was being levied to support the fleet (*ROL*, VII, 382, 388; *Notes et extraits*, III, 141, 147).

[13] *Cf.* Iorga, *ROL*, VII, 99–100, 101–2, 107, 376, 377, 379–80, 386–88, 389–90, 391, 393, 397–98, 400–1, 403–4, 408–11, 413–17, and *Notes et extraits*, III, 126–27, 128–29, 134, 135, 136, 137–38, 145–47, 148–49, 150, 152, 156–57, 159–60, 162–63, 167–70, 172–76. The overall problem was that the hulls and basic equipment of the galleys were costing the Venetian government 2,000 ducats apiece, and while Venice had done its part, the pope was (owing to other commitments) unable to meet the costs of arming his ten galleys for some months. The financing was finally arranged, however, largely from Venetian sources.

[14] Sen. Secreta, Reg. 16, fols. 100^{r}–101^{r}; Valentini, *Acta Albaniae veneta*, XVIII, no. 4,983, pp. 195–99; Iorga, *ROL*, VII, 414–15, and *Notes et extraits*, III, 173–74, doc. dated 17 June, 1444: "Quod fiat commissio viro nobili Alvisio Lauredano procuratori ecclesie S. Marci, capitaneo galearum nomine summi pontificis hic armatarum: . . . In bona gratia et victoria vadas capitaneus presentium galearum que iuxta promissiones nostras nomine Romani pontificis hic armate sunt ut in strictum Galipolis in tam divino opere contra perfidos Teucros exerceantur. . . . Verum quia galee predicte hic armate nomine summi pontificis solummodo pro agendo contra nequissimos Teucros parate et expedite sunt, sicut diximus reverendissimo domino cardinali legato et sicut ipse nobis amplissime promisit se facturum, declaramus tibi quod si forte alique galee sive fuste aut alia navigia sive armata sultani [the "soldan"] se repperirent in mari seu exirent de terris et locis sultani pro tempore quo stabis extra, nostre intentionis est et volumus quod nullo modo aliqua novitas eis inferratur, immo volumus quod ab ipsa armata, fustis, aut aliis navigiis sultani galee hic armate se allonginquare debeant et ab omni molestia et novitate penitus abstinere. Volumus quoque quod Rhodum nullo modo cum galeis predictis te conferas nec etiam pacto aliquo permittere quod aliqua de predictis galeis Rhodum se conferrat . . ." (fol. 100). The Senate wanted no disruption of the still profitable commercial runs to Alexandria and Beirut and no embroilment with the Hospitallers, with whom for generations the Venetians did not get along very well.

[15] Sen. Secreta, Reg. 16, fol. 103^{r}; Valentini, *Acta Albaniae veneta*, XVIII, no. 4,996, pp. 213–15; Iorga, *ROL*, VII, 417, and *Notes et extraits*, III, 176, letter of the Senate to Cesarini, dated 4 July, 1444: ". . . Commemoramusque et hortamur suam reverendissimam paternitatem [Cardinal Francesco Condulmer] ut cum erit in strictu Galipolis, communicata re ista cum capitaneo galearum summi pontificis cui etiam nos scripsimus opportune, mittat pro meliori executione facti utque potentius fiant quecunque fienda sunt, octo vel plures galeas cum illo ordine qui videbitur opportunus que per Danubium usque Nicopolim seu quo opus erit vadant ad omnem favorem possibilem impendendum ut exercitus Christianorum Danubium transire possit, in quo transitu consistere videmus victoriam illius gloriose impresie. . . ."

Note also Sanudo, *Vite de'duchi*, in *RISS*, XXII, cols. 1106C, 1109B, 1114, who is not far wrong in placing the departure of the fleet on 21 June (1444). *Cf.* Marcantonio Coccio Sabellico, *Historiae rerum venetarum* (ed. Venice, 1718), decad. III, bk. VI, pp. 654–55; Raynaldus, *Ann. eccl.*, ad ann. 1444, nos. 1–4, vol. XVIII (Cologne, 1694), pp. 289–91; Alberto Guglielmotti, *Storia della marina pontificia*, II (Rome, 1886), 158 ff.; N. Iorga, *Gesch. d. osman. Reiches*, I (Gotha, 1908), 436 ff.

On 4 August (1444) the government of Ragusa wrote their envoys at the Bosnian court "chome le quattro galee del ducha de Bergogna zonsino qui alle 22 del passato bene

The extent of Venice's investment in the crusade of 1444 has probably not been sufficiently appreciated, perhaps because the fleet achieved so little in the end. In view of the constant rumors of a Turco-Hungarian peace Loredan was inclined to be cautious, and it must not be forgotten that Cardinal Francesco was also a Venetian. In the meantime, however, on 4 July (1444) the Senate wrote their envoy in Hungary, the secretary Giovanni de' Reguardati, directing him not to conceal the fact that Venice had spent some 30,000 ducats on the Christian fleet. She had provided the pope with eight [or ten?] galleys and the duke of Burgundy with four. Moreover, the papal galleys had been armed largely by the tithe imposed on the Venetian clergy and (to a much lesser extent) on the Florentine clergy. These "twelve" papal and Burgundian galleys were all manned by Venetian crews, and Venice had decided to send another six to eight galleys into the east "sub nostro nomine et cum nostris propriis banderiis."[16] By mid-July the fleet was at Modon,[17] and soon sailed on to the straits of Gallipoli. Sultan Murad II had already crossed over into Asia Minor on the campaign against Ibrahim Beg of Caramania, and Cardinal Francesco and Loredan were supposed to prevent his re-entry into Europe by holding the straits against him.

Many of the Hungarian magnates had opposed the plans for another expedition against the Turks. For the time being they were content with the success achieved by Christian arms in the five months' campaign from September, 1443, to the following January. As we have seen, however, the Holy See was committed to a crusade against the Turks. The future of church union as well as the safety of Constantinople seemed to depend upon an early victory. There was also a war party at the Hungarian court. Eugenius IV and the Venetians had financed a fleet. On 15 March, 1444, Eugenius had also instructed Andreas de Palatio, *cubicularius ac in Polonie et Bohemie regnis nuntius noster*, to turn over to Ladislas (to assist his preparations for the crusade) all the funds to be collected in Poland and the Polish dependencies under the name of "Peter's pence" for two years from the date of the papal letter.[18] Philip the Good of Burgundy had made a sizable contribution to the crusade. Cesarini was unrelenting in his insistence, and he was a powerful personality.

Doubt as to the advisability of the expedition was not confined to the Hungarians. On 26 August, 1444, a Polish diet meeting at Piotrków, southwest of Warsaw, set forth the dangers besetting Ladislas's northern realm, and urged him to accept the incredible terms of peace which Murad II was said to have proposed. *Conquievitque et cessavit furor ille barbaricus, quo gloriati sunt Teucri.* Murad had offered (the Poles believed) to give up the realm of Serbia, surrender the Turkish dominion in Albania, restore the occupied parts of Hungary, and release the captives he was holding. He was also ready, *offerens conditiones pacis nunquam credibiles*, to pay an indemnity of 100,000 ducats and to provide Ladislas with 25,000 armed men "for any war of your Highness's choice." The Poles' understanding of these terms was derived "from your Highness's own letters and statements" (*prout haec omnia ex litteris et intimatione vestrae Serenitatis accepimus*). The Turkish peace (they wrote) would enable Ladislas

---

et triumfevelmente armate, et alle 23 del detto se partirno per seguir l'armata che era passata avanti. . . ." Three galleys of the king of Aragon had arrived at Trani, and four others were expected, but "a che intentione, per ora non savemo" (Iorga, *Notes et extraits*, II [Paris, 1899], 405–6). On 20 August the Ragusei informed the envoys "che per tuto lo mexe de luyo debiano esser arivate et zonte nel streto de Galipoli . . . a numero più che XXV [galee]" (*ibid.*, II, 406, and *cf.* Krekić, *Dubrovnik [Raguse] et le Levant*, nos. 1060–61, 1066, pp. 340–41).

[16] Cieszkowski, *Fontes rerum polonicarum*, I–2 (1890), no. LI, pp. 110–14, esp. p. 112; Iorga, *ROL*, VII, 418, and *Notes et extraits*, III, 177; Sen. Secreta, Reg. 16, fol. 104. On 28 August (1444) the Venetians informed the pope that they had spent more than 40,000 ducats on the fleet (*ROL*, VII, 425–26; Cieszkowski, *op. cit.*, no. LVI, p. 127; Sen. Secreta, Reg. 16, fol. 116^{v}). Less than two weeks later, however, on 9 September, when the possibility was considered in Venice that Ladislas might make peace with the Turks, whom the Venetians did not wish to fight alone, Loredan was instructed to inform the sultan (in the event of peace) that the galleys belonged to the pope, who had armed them at his own expense, and "whom it was necessary for us to obey since he is the supreme lord in our faith, and we could not do otherwise" (*ROL*, VII, 427–28; Cieszkowski, *op. cit.*, no. LVII, pp. 129–31; Sen. Secreta, Reg. 16, fols. 119^{v}–120^{r}).

[17] Iorga, *ROL*, VII, 421, 425, and *Notes et extraits*, III, 180, 184. The latter reference is to a letter of the Venetian Senate to the pope, dated 28 August, 1444 (Sen. Secreta, Reg. 16, fol. 116^{v}): ". . . Significamus . . . reverendissimum dominum cardinalem vicecancellarium legatum apostolicum cum triremibus sue rev. dominationi commissis ac cum aliqua parte galearum et fustarum nostrarum ad hoc opus sanctissimum dessignatarum die XVII Julii preteriti Mothonum incolumen [*sic*] attigisse indeque ipse die XX discessit ut accessum suum Deo auspice persequeretur in strictum. . . ."

[18] Raynaldus, *Ann. eccl.*, ad ann. 1444, no. 1, vol. XVIII (1694), pp. 289–90.

to return to Poland, where the raids of the Tatars (and the negotiations for peace with them) were only one of the problems being faced by his people, and to re-establish peace and security in the kingdom.[19] But neither Hungarian doubt nor Polish remonstrance could slow the gathering momentum which would lead the Christian forces to the field of Varna.

There were disquieting reports of a Hungarian-Turkish treaty, a copy of which Turkish officers were said to have shown Waleran de Wavrin, when the Christian fleet reached Gallipoli. Cardinal Condulmer soon received assurance, however, from his fellow legate Cesarini in Hungary that no such peace was in the offing.[20] Another letter from Cesarini brought the same news to Constantinople on 5 September when Ciriaco of Ancona, after an excursion on the Sea of Marmara, happened to be at the imperial court. In a letter to Cesarini, dated 12 September, Ciriaco states that he had read the cardinal's letter to the Emperor John VIII, as well as letters from Ladislas, Hunyadi, and other leaders of the crusade. He had in fact translated them from Latin into Greek for the benefit of the Byzantines, who were overjoyed by the news, as were the Genoese at Pera. Anxious to share the good news with western Christendom, Ciriaco sent copies of the letters to Alfonso V and the Neapolitan nobility, whom he hoped to see join the expedition. "And to say no more," Ciriaco concludes,

> be assured that this great emperor and his illustrious brothers are employing every effort and resource to promote this undertaking and to increase the fleet of triremes they have already prepared. They have also seen to it that not only the imperial city but all the Aegean islands, Lemnos, Imbros, Skyros, Skiathos, and Skopelos should be enlisted in the enterprise.[21]

Ciriaco ended his letter with a postscript, dated 19 September, informing Cesarini of the notable victory of the Hospitallers of Rhodes over the Egyptian fleet. The Knights had repulsed a strong assault upon their walls (on 10 September), taking six emirs (*admirati*) and killing or capturing some 9,000 Moslems. On the following day, the twentieth, Ciriaco left Constantinople with the Byzantine admiral Alexius Dishypatos on another antiquarian tour of the Sea of Marmara. On the twenty-fourth they landed on the island of Marmara (the ancient Proconnesus), and on the twenty-seventh reached Lampsacus. On the opposite shore, at Gallipoli, the crusaders' fleet rode at anchor. Ciriaco crossed the strait and discussed the war with the commander Loredan. He soon departed, however, going on with Dishypatos the same day to the island of Imbros, whence the latter left for Lemnos while Ciriaco went sightseeing on Imbros on the twenty-eighth, having as his guide Michael Critobulus, who later wrote the life of Mehmed the Conqueror:

> On 28 September from the eastern shore of Imbros we traveled by land on horses with Hermodorus Michael Critobulus, a learned Imbriote noble, to the western part of the island, to ancient Imbros, once an important city and of great antiquity, and through high hills we reached the plain by the city where we found at the height of the citadel Manuel Acanius, a noble from Byzantium, and worthy governor of the island for the Emperor John Palaeologus, and we learned that he had recently built the citadel from two earlier parts. Here indeed we saw the remains of a very ancient wall which had collapsed from age. . . .[22]

---

[19] A. Sokołowski and J. Szujski, eds., *Codex epistolaris saeculi decimi quinti*, I–1 (Cracow, 1876, repr. 1965), no. cxxv, pp. 140–44; *cf.* Dąbrowski, *L'Année 1444*, p. 21, and on the Tatars, note O. Halecki, "La Pologne et l'empire byzantin," *Byzantion*, VII (1932), 62–63.

[20] Jehan de Waurin (Wavrin), *Recueil des croniques et anchiennes istories de la Grant Bretaigne* [see above, Chapter 2, note 134], VI, I, 11, eds. Wm. Hardy and E. L. C. P. Hardy, vol. V (1891, repr. 1967), pp. 45–46, and *cf.* N. Iorga, *La Campagne des croisés sur le Danube*, Paris, 1927, pp. 30–31. The reference is presumably to the preliminary peace of Adrianople (12 June, 1444). The sultan was said to have a "bonne paix au roy de Hongrye," as the Turks could show by "les lettres du traitie," on which *cf.* Halecki, *Crusade of Varna*, p. 68. The chronicler Jehan, as we have already observed, was the uncle of the Burgundian commander Waleran de Wavrin.

[21] Halecki, *Crusade of Varna*, pp. 68, 92–93 (Ciriaco's letter to Cesarini, 12 September, 1444).

[22] From the small volume (a copy) of Ciriaco's *Commentarii odeporici*, in the Bibl. Apost. Vaticana, Cod. lat. 5,250, fols. 11^r–11^v: "Ad IIII Kal. Octob. ex orientali Imbre littore una viro cum docto et Imbriote nobili Hermodoro Michaeli Critobulo ad occidentalem eiusdem insulae partem, ad Imbron antiquam insignemque olim et vetustissimam civitatem terrestri itinere equis devecti, et arduos per colles et prope civitatem planiciem venimus, ubi ad summam civitatis arcem Manuelem Acanium, virum ex Byzantio nobilem, et eius insulae pro Johanne Palaeologo Imperatore benemerentem praesidem, quem et arcem ipsam duabus iam ex partibus noviter condisse comperimus. Ibidem vero longe antiqui et vetustate collapsi muri vestigia vidimus, et hic nonnullam e moenibus partem extare pulcherrimae suae architecturae ordine conspicuam vidimus, et ingentes ad portum antiqua ex mole lapides, et nonnulla marmorum statuarumque fragmenta, bases, et vetustissimis

Ciriaco's letters show that he entertained much hope of a Christian victory over Islam. It was not an entirely vain hope. There was religious dissension in Adrianople, where a member of the Shiite Persian sect of the Ḥurūfīs, who allegedly sought the reconciliation of Islam with Christianity, caused havoc among the Turks.[23] Shortly afterwards the janissaries embarked on a riotous demand for more pay, and burned a good part of Adrianople. And now, on 20 September (1444), the army of Ladislas and Hunyadi crossed the Danube,[24] beginning its march to the Black Sea to make contact with the Christian fleet. Throughout the weeks of the Varna campaign Eugenius IV continued his efforts to assist Ladislas, Hunyadi, and Cesarini, imposing another tithe "pro apparatu et expeditione maritima adversus Teucros."[25] On 4 October (1444) Eugenius released the Albanian chieftain George Arianiti Topia "Comnenus," lord of Cerminitza and Catafigo, from the peace he had made with and the oath he had sworn to the Turks, "since it is absurd that the religious observance of good faith and an oath, which should be reserved for the honor of God, should redound to the detriment of the faith and result in offense to God."[26] The Ottoman establishment in Europe was clearly in some danger.

In Adrianople Mehmed Chelebi, later the

---

characteribus epigrammata. . . ." A different text was transcribed by G. B. de Rossi in the *Schede De Rossi* in the Cod. Vat. lat. 10,518, fol. 2^v, left column (from the "Schede epigrafiche relative a Ciriaco d'Ancona e notizie intorno ad esso"). The same text, in less good form, appears also in Cod. Napol. lat. V. E. 64, fol. 2^r.

Much the same account is also to be found in a letter which Ciriaco addressed on 29 September to George Scholarius, who later took the monastic name Gennadius, and became patriarch of Constantinople under the Turks (publ. by Erich Ziebarth, "Cyriacus von Ancona in Samothrake," in the *Mitteilungen des k. deutschen archäol. Instituts*, Athen. Abteilung, XXX [1906], 405–6, and *cf.* Pall, *Bull. hist. Acad. roum.*, XX, 46–47). Critobulus's famous work on Sultan Mehmed II was first discovered by Constantin Tischendorf on 19 September, 1859, in Istanbul in the Library (Kütüphane) of Ahmed III; it survives in a unique copy, apparently the most important of an alleged 5,000 MSS. in the collection (*cf.* Adolf Deissmann, *Forschungen und Funde im Serai*, Berlin and Leipzig, 1933, pp. 28, 43–44).

The siege of Rhodes by the Mamluks, referred to in the text, lasted forty days. Their fleet of seventy-five vessels appeared offshore on Monday, 10 August, 1444. The Mamluk forces broke camp on 13 September, and the fleet departed on the eighteenth. The main assault took place on Thursday, 10 September. The chief contemporary account is a poem in Catalan, in 240 rhymed verses, by one Francesc Ferrer, *Romanç dels actes e coses que l'armada del gran soldà féu en Rodes*, which has been published by L. Nicolau d'Olwer, "Un Témoinage catalan du siège de Rhodes en 1444," *Estudis universitaris catalans*, XII (1927), 376–87. Ferrer was present throughout the siege, and gives us a chronology of events.

[23] Babinger, *Maometto*, pp. 69–71. The episode of the Persian preacher must have become widely known in Europe (*cf.* Sanudo, *Vite de'duchi*, in *RISS*, XXII [1733], col. 1116); see also the extract from the *Cronaca Zancaruola*, ed. Babinger, in *Oriens*, III (1950), 244–45, and on the doctrine of the Ḥurūfīs, *ibid.*, pp. 245–48; reprinted in Babinger's *Aufsätze und Abhandlungen*, I, 139–43. Earlier in the century a dervish named Mustafa, who is said to have come from Samos, had also preached the spiritual amity of Moslems and Christians (Ducas, chap. 21 [Bonn, pp. 111–15], on which see H. I. Cotsonis [Kotsonis], "Aus der Endzeit von Byzanz: Bürklüdsche Mustafa," *Byzantinische Zeitschrift*, L [1957], 397–404).

[24] On 19 October, 1444, the Venetians wrote the pope, ". . . Ecce mittimus Sanctitati vestre copiam unius capituli literarum nobis scriptarum per unum ex secretariis nostris [Reguardati] ex Buda, datarum VI presentis, per quas nobis scribit, Christianorum exercitum in felici omine Danubium traiecisse die XX Septembris nuper decursi ut ad exterminium perfidorum Teucrorum procederet" (Sen. Secreta, Reg. 16, fol. 126^v, with a faulty transcription in Cieszkowski, *Fontes rerum polonicarum*, I–2 [1890], no. LVIII, p. 132, and *cf.* no. LIX, p. 134, and Valentini, *Acta Albaniae veneta*, XVIII, no. 5,036, pp. 266–67).

[25] *Cf.* Raynaldus, *Ann. eccl.*, ad ann. 1444, nos. 6–10, vol. XVIII (1694), pp. 292–97. On 4 October, 1444, Eugenius sent a brief of condolence to Lodovico II [III] Gonzaga, consoling him for the death of his father Gian Francesco, first marquis of Mantua (Arch. di Stato di Mantova, Arch. Gonzaga, Busta 834), and six weeks later, on 16 November, informed him that he was sending one Jacopo de Cortonio to Mantua to see to the collection of the crusading tithe (*ibid.*):

"Dilecto filio nobili viro Carolo de Gonragha [!], marchioni Mantuano: Dilecte fili, salutem et apostolicam benedictionem. Pro executione litterarum nostrarum dudum promulgatarum cum istic tum in quampluribus partibus orbis super solutione unius integre decime pro apparatu et expeditione maritima adversus Teucros et alios barbaros Christiane fidei hostes indicte, prout in nostris litteris inde confectis plenius continentur, mittimus dilectum filium Magistrum Jacobum de Cortonio utriusque iuris doctorem in nostro registro supplicationum presidentem. Quocirca nobilitatem tuam pro nostra et Apostolice Sedis reverentia in domino requirimus et hortamur quatenus pro efficatiori et magis celeri executione huiusmodi mandatorum nostrorum eidem Jacobo faveas et assistas consiliis, auxiliis et favoribus oportunis prout de tua prudentia et devotione erga nos et sedem predictam specialem in domino fiduciam obtinemus. Datum Rome apud Sanctum Petrum sub anulo nostro secreto die sextadecima mensis Novembris pontificatus nostri anno quartodecimo. A. de Florentia."

[26] Raynaldus, *Ann. eccl.*, ad ann. 1444, no. 6, vol. XVIII (1694), pp. 292–93, and on Arianiti, one of whose daughters married Scanderbeg, see Franz Babinger, *Das Ende der Arianiten*, Munich, 1960, pp. 9–27 (in the Sitzungsberichte d. bayer. Akad. der Wissen., Philos. -Hist. Kl., 1960, Heft 4), and *cf.* Francisc Pall, "Skanderbeg et Ianco de Hunedoara," *Revue des études sud-est européennes*, VI (1968), 7, 9.

Conqueror, ruled for his father, but he was a boy, at odds with his chief counsellors, and Sultan Murad II was still in Asia Minor. Fortune was not on the Christian side, however, for after two months of waiting for the army of Ladislas and Hunyadi the crusaders' fleet had become short of food and water. Murad had been able to bring the Caramanian war to a successful conclusion. Ibrahim Beg, the Gran Caramano, who is believed to have been allied with Ladislas,[27] had reached an agreement with the sultan more quickly than public opinion had thought likely. With some 30,000 to 40,000 men Murad crossed the Bosporus above Constantinople in late October, under the shadow of Bayazid I's castle of Anadolu Hisar, where Europe and Asia come closest together. The Christian fleet was stalled by adverse winds and by the cautious policy of the Venetians; having prevented Murad's return to Europe across the Dardanelles, its commanders made no effort to impede his crossing of the Bosporus. Attributing this failure to incompetence (*negligentia*), the humanist Poggio Bracciolini was to claim later that it ruined all the crusading plans of 1444.[28] There was also a widespread rumor at the time that Genoese merchants and sailors had accepted Murad's money to assist his westward passage.[29]

After crossing the Bosporus, Murad hastened to Adrianople, where he found much to depress but nothing to detain him. Soon he was leading thousands of soldiers along the roads to the Black Sea. The crusaders under Ladislas and Hunyadi, delayed on their eastward march, had not crossed the Danube until 20 September,[30] as we have just noted. According to the eyewitness account of Andreas de Palatio, the papal collector, there were hardly 16,000 men-at-arms

---

[27] *Cf.* in general Halil Inalcik, "Byzantium and the Origins of the Crisis of 1444 . . .," *Actes du XIIe Congrès international d'études byzantines*, II (1964), 159–63 (referred to above, Chapter 2, note 132).

[28] In his funeral oration on Cardinal Cesarini, killed at Varna, Poggio writes: ". . . Neque eventus consiliis defuisset si classis, que summa cura a summo pontifice Helesponto ad id parata erat, Teucros aditu Europe [MS. *Euripi*] prohibuisset. . . . At vero Teucrorum imperator, qui id temporis erat in Asia, contractis plurimis copiis et auxiliis undique a finitimis accitis, cum XXX milibus hominum in Europa [transivit] per negligentiam classis, que aditum illum prohibere debebat . . ." (Iorga, "Notes et extraits," *ROL*, VIII [1900–1, repr. 1964], 271). *Cf.* Mehmed II's account, at least as reported by Ducas, *Hist. byzantina*, chap. 34 (Bonn, pp. 239–40), of his father Murad's crossing the Bosporus, and on the Turks' subsequent moves, see the Ragusan documents of 10 and 20 October (1444), in V. V. Makušev, *Monumenta historica slavorum meridionalium vicinorumque populorum deprompta e tabulariis et bibliothecis italicis*, II (Belgrade, 1882), 81–84.

[29] Already on 7 October, 1444, Eugenius IV had condemned those Christians who were supplying "arms, iron, food, and other kinds of assistance to the Turks" (letter given in Raynaldus, *Ann. eccl.*, ad ann. 1444, no. 8, vol. XVIII [1694], p. 294). The Genoese were especially indicted for such dealings with the Turks (*cf.* Guglielmotti, *Storia della marina pontificia*, II, 160). Aeneas Sylvius Piccolomini wrote the bishop of Passau on 28 October, 1445, that ". . . magnus Teucer . . . non sine magna Januensium infamia in Europam venit, nam et quedam Januensium naves prebuisse transitum illis [centum milibus virorum, si vera est fama] referebantur" (Rudolf Wolkan, ed., *Der Briefwechsel des Eneas Silvius Piccolomini*, in the Fontes rerum austriacarum, II. Abt., vol. 61 [Vienna, 1909], *Ep.* 192, p. 566). Thirteen years later Aeneas noted in his tract *De Europa*, 5, in *Opera quae extant omnia*, Basel, 1551, repr. Frankfurt a. M., 1967, p. 398A, that *si vera est fama*, 100,000 Turks were transported across the Bosporus by "Genuenses quidam" at a ducat a head. Lorenzo Buonincontri, *Ann.*, ad ann. 1444, in *RISS*, XXI (Milan, 1732), col. 152D, says that Murad hired Genoese to assist in the transport of 70,000 Turks "from Asia into Greece;" Paolo Petrone, *Miscellanea*, in *RISS*, XXIV (Milan, 1738), col. 1128A, states, "Avvisandovi che non . . . traditori Cristiani, i quali furono Veneziani e Genovesi . . . [the text is corrupt] segretamente LXXX mila Turchi, che ne guadagnarono un ducato per testa d'uomo." (Petrone wrote in the mid-fifteenth century.) From this text it would appear that members of the Venetian colony in Constantinople as well as the Genoese of Pera took Turks across the straits for a ducat each, the same price as Aeneas gives. The latter was well informed, being close to the Emperor Frederick III, who had made him "poet laureate" on 27 July, 1442 (Jos. Chmel, *Regesta chronologico-diplomatica Friderici IV. Romanorum regis [imperatoris III.]*, Vienna, 1838, repr. Hildesheim, 1962, no. 801, p. 93, and no. 17, p. XXIX).

See also Jehan de Waurin (Wavrin), *Recueil des croniques d'Engleterre*, VI, I, 11–12, ed. Hardy, vol. V (1891, repr. 1967), pp. 46–47, 49–50; Wavrin, ed. Iorga, *La Campagne des croisés*, Paris, 1927, pp. 32–36; Babinger, "Von Amurath zu Amurath," *Oriens*, III (1950), 251–52, reprinted in *Aufsätze und Abhandlungen*, I, 145–46. Laonicus Chalcocondylas, bk. VII (Bonn, pp. 330–38; ed. Darkó, II-1 [1923], 102–9), gives a rather detailed account of the battle of Varna, to which George Sphrantzes, *Chron. minus* (*PG* 156, 1050AB; ed. V. Grecu, *Georgios Sphrantzes: Memorii [1401–1477], în anexă Pseudo-Phrantzes: Macarie Melissenos: Cronica [1258–1481]*, Bucharest, 1966, pp. 66, 68), merely alludes in passing. The "Pseudo-Sphrantzes" (Macarius Melissenus-Melissurgus), *Chron. maius*, II, 19 (Bonn, pp. 197–200; ed. Grecu, pp. 338, 340), had read Chalcocondylas and other sources.

[30] So the Venetians had informed Eugenius IV on 19 October, 1444 (see above, note 24, and *cf.* Iorga, *ROL*, VIII, 1, and *Notes et extraits*, III, 188), and Loredan on 9 November (C. N. Sathas, *Documents inédits*, I [Paris, 1880, repr. Athens, 1972], no. 140, p. 209). *Cf.* Ljubić, *Listine*, IX (1890), 212, and Sen. Secreta, Reg. 16, fol. 129^v. Ladislas sent an urgent appeal to the Venetians "ut provideamus quod galee tam nostre quam armate per summum pontificem perseverent in strictu [Gallipolis] contra Teucros" (*ibid.*, fol. 131^r).

or "knights" (*equites*) in the army of the crusaders, whose baggage train consisted of more than 2,000 wagons (*currus*), "not only loaded with supplies, but with gold and furniture and other things which are part of the accoutrement and make for the dignity of knights."[31]

In the area of Nicopolis they were joined by Vlad, the voivode of Wallachia, *qui et Dracula dicitur*, or by his sons, with some 4,000 Vlachs. Vlad wanted to make amends for his erstwhile pact with the Turks. Ladislas, Hunyadi, and the crusaders had hardly reached Varna when Murad overtook them. By this time the Turkish army may have contained 60,000 men (probably Murad himself did not know how many he had), almost outnumbering the Christians by three to one. The crusaders' fleet, largely manned by Venetians, did not venture into the Black Sea. The battle of Varna took place on 10 November, 1444. If a miracle was required for a Christian victory, a miracle almost happened. Had Branković and his 8,000 Serbs been present, victory would probably have attended the tattered Christian banners, rent by the terrible windstorm that swept the battlefield. As it was, the crusaders beat off the first assaults of the Turks, who sustained severe losses. Christian strength and heroism almost made up for lack of men. The struggle was a desperate one, and its issue undecided for hours.

Murad is said to have contemplated flight at one point, but the janissaries restrained him. Hunyadi displayed those qualities of courage, caution, and leadership which had made him one of the foremost soldiers in Europe, but the young Ladislas lost his life, apparently seeking glory in a reckless charge. His head was mounted on a pole (it was said), a grim sight which helped to destroy the crusaders' morale. When night fell, both sides moved off to their camps, but the Christian army had suffered beyond recovery, and its frightened members now began to flee in all directions. Turkish casualties were so heavy that it took Murad three days to be sure that he had won.[32] As the battle of Hattin had prepared the way for the fall of Jerusalem to Saladin two and one-half centuries before, so Varna was the prelude to the Moslem occupation of Constantinople in 1453.

For weeks, even months, after the battle the fate of both King Ladislas and Cardinal Cesarini remained uncertain. From Cracow as late as May or early June, 1445, Queen Sophia of Poland wrote a diet of Hungarian prelates and barons that she had reliable evidence that her son Ladislas had not fallen at Varna. In fact a merchant from the domain of her other son Casimir, grand duke of Lithuania, had assured the latter of his brother's continued existence and safety. Sophia was confident "quod vivit quodque sanus est cum multis suis fidelibus," and begged the Hungarian estates not to proceed to the election of a new king with undue haste, unmindful of the great services her son had rendered their realm "contra barbaricam rabiem:"

> And although he had regarded it as a salutary [move] to preserve the peace and agreement made with the Turks, in accordance with the advice and pleas he had heard from the prelates and barons of the kingdom of Poland, nevertheless he then preferred to hearken to your wishes, and for your safety and peace of mind to set at naught his own reputation and his life [*famam et vitam negligere*].[33]

---

[31] Andreas de Palatio, in a letter dated at Poznań on 16 May, 1445, to Lodovico Trevisan, the Cardinal Camerlengo (A. Lewicki, ed., *Codex epistolaris saeculi decimi quinti*, II [Cracow, 1891, repr. New York and London, 1965], no. 308, p. 461, in the Monumenta medii aevi historica res gestas Poloniae illustrantia, XII).

[32] The battle of Varna was apparently reported in Venice as a Christian victory (Sanudo, *Vite de'duchi*, in *RISS*, XXII, col. 1113B): "Ancora Ladislao Re di Polonia ebbe vittoria contro i Turchi, de'quali furono morti 80,000 [!]. Fu morto il Re, e Giuliano cardinale legato, et molti vescovi." *Cf.*, *ibid.*, col. 1117AB. A Greek poem on the battle of Varna (ed. Gyula Moravcsik, Budapest, 1935), of more linguistic than historical importance, records that a janissary "tried and true" threatened to kill Murad if he attempted to flee from the field of Varna (*ibid.*, pp. 36, 37, from Bibl. Nat., MS. Coisl. gr. 316, verses 299–307, on which *cf.* Robert Devreesse, *Catalogue des manuscrits grecs de la Bibliothèque Nationale*, II: *Le Fonds Coislin*, Paris, 1945, pp. 305–6, attributing the poem to Paraspondylos Zotikos; and from the Library of the Topkapi Seraglio, Istanbul, MS. Ser. gr. 35, verses 302–10, on which *cf.* Deissmann, *Forschungen u. Funde im Serai* [1933], pp. 71–72, attributing the poem to George Argyropoulus, this MS. being dated 1461).

A detailed account of the campaign of 1444 may be found in L. Kupelwieser, *Die Kämpfe Ungarns mit den Osmanen bis zur Schlacht bei Mohács (1526)*, Vienna and Leipzig, 1895, pp. 83–103, who provides a good map, with the stages dated of Ladislas's march from Orsova (near the "Iron Gate"), where he crossed the Danube on 20 September, to his arrival on the field of Varna (9–10 November) as well as a map of the battlefield to the northwest of the walled city. Kupelwieser's account is readable, and rich in topographical detail, although he seems to believe that the Christian fleet consisted of 120 galleys (p. 91), and that Murad's army contained about 100,000 men (p. 96).

[33] *Codex epistolaris*, I–2, no. III, pp. 4–5. In Cracow, as of 24 August, 1445, one still knew nothing of Ladislas's fate, "et dolemus quod de vita et sanitate ipsius domini nostri

The uncertainty attending Ladislas's death quickly produced the legend of a penitent king, who having expiated the sin of perjury, would some day return to the throne and do justice to the oppressed peasantry.[34]

As for Cesarini, the humanist Aeneas Sylvius Piccolomini wrote Filippo Maria Visconti, duke of Milan, from Wiener Neustadt on 13 December, 1444, that although Cesarini's death had been reported, there was also a rumor of his escape, "which I could readily wish, but his death seems more probable to me, because he was not fortunate in his wars."[35] Nineteen years later, Aeneas in alluding to Varna states that Cesarini "was wounded by three arrows and in his retreat fell from his horse in a marsh where he breathed out his noble spirit."[36] Poggio Bracciolini celebrated Cesarini's "martyrdom" in a jejune oration unworthy of its subject. Hunyadi escaped to Wallachia, where the treacherous voivode Vlad Dracul, never his friend, held him captive for a while but later released him.[37]

In retrospect it seemed to good Christians that the disaster at Varna was divine retribution for breaking the pledge of Szeged. The Polish historian Jan Długosz (1415–1480) says clearly and categorically—*temerato iuramento, rupto foedere Turcis promisso*—that Cesarini had declared null and void the oath which Ladislas had sworn and the peace he had made with the Turks.[38] There can be little doubt that the agreement made at Adrianople was confirmed at Szeged. It is not enough to say, as Halecki does, that Długosz's explicit references to the "violated oath, the broken peace" merely reflect the conciliarists' hostility to Cesarini, whose abandonment of the extremists at Basel had helped diminish the prestige of the council. Długosz was, to be sure, the devoted friend, secretary, and servitor of Bishop Zbigniew Oleśnicki of Cracow, who was a strong conciliarist and an opponent of the Prussian policy of Ladislas's brother and successor, Casimir IV. Długosz began his history in 1455, the year of Oleśnicki's death; he had known everyone of importance at the Polish court for years, and had direct access to those who had witnessed the events at Szeged as well as to the diplomatic correspondence of his time. While he may be accused of prejudice, he was not given to calumny, not in any event to blacken the memory of the young king who had died fighting the archenemy of the faith—whose own mother stated that he had set at naught his reputation as well as his life.[39]

The news of the Christian defeat had hardly reached the West when the Venetians and the pope began wrangling over who should assume the responsibility for the sailors' unpaid wages. Eugenius was unwilling to do so because of the dismal failure of the fleet to do its part against the Turks. He held the Venetian high command to have been at fault, and charged that Loredan had wasted twenty-five entire days searching for provisions between Tenedos and Constantinople.[40] The pope finally agreed,

---

regis non potuimus ad hanc diem aliquem audire certitudinem" (*ibid.*, II-2, no. v, p. 10, from a letter of Zbigniew Oleśnicki, bishop of Cracow [Kraków], to Matthias, bishop of Vilna [Vilnius] in Lithuania). Ladislas was succeeded a year later by his brother Casimir IV (*cf.*, *ibid.*, no. vi, p. 12).

[34] R. Urbánek, *Vladislav Varnenčík* (1937), pp. 167 ff., 223–24.

[35] Rudolf Wolkan, ed., *Der Briefwechsel des Eneas Silvius Piccolomini*, in the Fontes rerum austriacarum, ii. Abteilung, vol. 61, *Ep.* 167, p. 490: ". . . quod magis optaverim, sed mors sua mihi probabilior est, quia non fuit in bellis fortunatus." He alludes of course to Cesarini's unsuccessful role in the Hussite wars; four of the five anti-Hussite "crusades" (1420–1422, 1427, and 1431) had ended in disaster. Aeneas reports also that Murad II had crossed the Bosporus with 40,000 men (p. 489), and gives a vivid description of the battle of Varna, "the bloodiest encounter within the memory of our fathers." *Cf.* N. Iorga, *Notes et extraits*, IV (Bucharest, 1915), pt. 1, no. xvi, pp. 36–37, letter of Cardinal Archbishop Dionysius Széchy of Gran to Frederick III, dated "in campo" 30 November, 1444, and Jehan de Waurin, *Recueil des croniques d'Engleterre*, VI, i, 14, ed. Hardy, vol. V (1891, repr. 1967), pp. 54–57, and Iorga, *La Campagne des croisés*, Paris, 1927, pp. 38–41. We do not lack for contemporary accounts of the battle, among the most notable being that contained in Andreas de Palatio's letter of 16 May, 1445, to Cardinal Lodovico Trevisan (see above, note 31), in the *Codex epistolaris*, II, no. 308, pp. 459–69.

[36] Pius II, *Commentarii*, Frankfurt, 1614, bk. xii, p. 326, lines 5–6, and Engl. trans. F. A. Gragg and L. C. Gabel, in *Smith College Studies in History*, XLIII (1957), 797–98. On Cesarini's career see Roger Mols, in the *Dictionnaire d'histoire et de géographie ecclésiastiques*, XII (1953), cols. 220–49.

[37] On Varna, *cf.* also Iorga, in *ROL*, VIII (1901, repr. 1964), 4–6, note; *Notes et extraits*, III (1902), 191–93, note; *Gesch. d. osman. Reiches*, I, 440–43, with refs. to the sources; Babinger, *Maometto*, pp. 74–77.

[38] Długosz, *Hist. polonica*, bk. xii, ed. Pauli, IV, 708, and *cf.*, *ibid.*, p. 704; ed. Leipzig, 1711–12, II, cols. 793–94, and *cf.* col. 790.

[39] *Cf.* Dąbrowski, *L'Année 1444*, pp. 35, 38–40, against Halecki, *Crusade of Varna*, pp. 71 ff.

[40] Iorga, *ROL*, VIII, 8 ff., and *Notes et extraits*, III, 195 ff., docs. dated 29 January to 15 February, 1445, from the Sen. Secreta, Reg. 16, fols. 142^r ff., 146^v. The Venetians expressed disappointment in the pope's attitude, claiming that their sailors were sometimes reduced to the consumption of bread with salt water; that the cold had been unbelievable in

however, to pay 10–12,000 ducats by Genoese letters of exchange to be drawn on Pera, which brought the prompt response from the Senate that payment should be made directly to Venice or the letters of exchange be negotiable at Negroponte or Constantinople. The Venetian ambassador in Rome, Andrea Donato, informed his government that the pope had had letters read in consistory relating to the defeat at Varna and the death of Cesarini. Blame for the disaster was being put upon the fleet (*et imponebatur defectus galeis*). And so it went. Affairs had been in a bad way in Hungary since the young king's death. On 12 March, 1445, the Venetian Senate claimed to have received no news from the East for two months.[41] Shortly before, upon the appointment of a new Venetian ambassador to the Holy See, Orsato Giustinian,[42] the Senate had instructed him to inform the pope, if the latter complained of the Turks' crossing over from Asia into Europe because of the failure of the Venetian galleys to intervene, that Loredan was in no way culpable, and that the Republic had not only made great sacrifices for the expedition, but had thereby provoked Turkish attacks upon the island of Negroponte, Albania, and other Venetian possessions, attacks which were still continuing. The sailors had suffered severely; some commanders (*supracomiti*) had been killed as well as many citizens "of good condition." Venice was, however, willing to continue the struggle against the Turks (at least so the pope was to be informed), although the island of Rhodes was now believed to be in especial danger, for the soldan of Egypt had prepared a fleet to send against the Hospitallers.[43] In urging the pope to pay the "subvention" which he still owed on his galleys, the Senate wrote Giustinian (on 26 April, 1445), instructing him to tell his Holiness

> that we see the weight of war with the Turk has been left entirely upon our shoulders since the most serene lord emperor of Constantinople, the Genoese, and other peoples [*nationes*] neighboring upon the Turks are at peace with them, but for the longest stretch of territory in Dalmatia, Albania, and Greece we have borders contiguous with those of the Turks, who have already invaded some of our lands in Albania and Greece, and carried off a considerable number of people from the island of Negroponte.[44]

The fleet remained in the East,[45] until Cardinal Francesco and Alvise Loredan finally returned to Venice on 10 January, 1446, the cardinal departing for Rome four days later, allegedly full of plans for another expedition in the spring "to drive the Turks out of Greece."[46]

No Latin resident in the Levant was more saddened by the Christian defeat at Varna than Ciriaco of Ancona, who continued his scholarly journeys through wide areas of both Greek and Turkish territory. He visited Thrace, Mount Athos, and Aenos, the Cyclades and Crete, Asia Minor and Lesbos. No man of his time traveled so indefatigably in the interests of archaeology. On one occasion, in late December, he revisited "snowy Paros," which he felt he had to see again, "for it is not enough to have seen once the famous and noble monuments of its precious antiquity, but one must linger there." The lord of Paros, Crusino I Sommaripa, himself obviously an antiquarian, accompanied Ciriaco as he sought out various

---

the straits during the winter, men having their limbs frozen; that many Venetians had been killed, etc. The letter of 15 February, from the Senate to Andrea Donato, the Venetian ambassador to the Curia Romana, is given in Cieszkowski, *Fontes rerum polonicarum*, I–2 (1890), no. LXII, pp. 141–45, and in Valentini, *Acta Albaniae veneta*, XIX (1973), no. 5,063, pp. 17–19, who also gives the text of the Senate's deliberations on 29 January (*ibid.*, no. 5,057).

[41] Sen. Secreta, Reg. 16, fols. 148v and 153; Iorga, *ROL*, VIII, 9–10, and *Notes et extraits*, III, 196–97, docs. dated 22 February and 12 March, 1445. Through Andrea Donato, Eugenius IV asked the Venetian Senate for advice: Should the crusade be continued, another appeal sent to the *principes mundi*, a cardinal legate sent to Hungary? To this the Senate replied, "Sed ei [i.e., summo pontifici] denotamus quod iam duobus mensibus preteritis novum de partibus Romanie non habuimus ita quod ei sufficienter consulere non possemus, sed in dies nova habere expectamus, quibus habitis fidelissime iuxta requisitionem sue Beatitudinis ei dicemus id quod honori suo cedere sentiemus, et sua Sanctitas eius infinita sapienta determinare poterit ut ei placebit" (fol. 153v). Eugenius finally sent 12,000 ducats for the sailors' wages in August, 1455 (*ROL*, VIII, 15–16, and *Notes et extraits*, III, 202–3).

[42] Sen. Secreta, Reg. 16, fols. 146r, 150v, docs. dated 11 and 26 February, 1445 (Ven. style 1444).

[43] Sen. Secreta, Reg. 16, fols. 158v–159r; Iorga, *ROL*, VIII, 10–11, and *Notes et extraits*, III, 197–98, from the addenda to Orsato Giustinian's commission, which was hammered out in the Senate on 16 and 18 March, 1445 (Sen. Secreta, Reg. 16, fols. 156–59). *Cf.* also, *ibid.*, fol. 162v, a letter to Giustinian, dated 3 April, which was never sent, and note Babinger, *Oriens*, III, 257, reprinted in his *Aufsätze u. Abhandlungen*, I, 150.

[44] Sen. Secreta, Reg. 16, fol. 171v.

[45] *Cf.*, *ibid.*, fols. 168r, 174, 179, 180v–181r and ff., 211r–212v.

[46] Iorga, *ROL*, VIII, 19, note; *Notes et extraits*, III, 206, note; and *cf. Gesch. d. osman. Reiches*, I, 446–47.

marble treasures that he knew from an earlier stay on Paros, but, better still, this time Crusino showed him ancient marble busts and bodies which had recently been excavated. Crusino was a generous archaeologist, and apparently gave some of his finds to Ciriaco, who concludes a letter to his friend Andreolo Giustiniani-Banca with the words: "Receive from the bearer, A. Galafato, one marble head, and one leg, etc." Ciriaco was so impressed by his gracious host that he composed a sonnet, described by Targioni as a "miserabile sonetto pedantesco," in praise of Paros and Crusino Sommaripa, beginning:[47]

Snowy Paros, of white marble gleaming . . .

The wanderings of Ciriaco furnish us with pleasant reminders that life went on in the Levant despite Christian defeats and Turkish victories. Boats ran from island to island, and Greeks, Latins, and Turks extended their hospitality to weary travelers. Archaeologists like Crusino Sommaripa were already making the rocky soil of Greece give up its classic treasures, and antiquarians like Ciriaco and his friend Andreolo Giustiniani copied inscriptions, read the ancient authors, wrote poetry, and (these two at least) enjoyed the friendship of Pope Eugenius IV. Andreolo, however, was no better a poet than Ciriaco, as shown by some fourteen pages of verse he composed on the Venetian attack upon Chios in 1431.[48] Andreolo was a member of one of those one hundred and twenty families of Chios which had taken the name Giustiniani. While the world around Chios seemed to be going up in smoke, Andreolo was collecting a large library and corresponding with literati both in Italy and the East. Latins resident in the East had undoubtedly become quite accustomed to living in an atmosphere of political and military tension, and they could take in their stride even the bad news of Varna.

The defeat at Varna gave a hollow sound to the ecclesiastical union of Florence. Papal efforts to defend the Greeks against the Turks had failed. More and more it seemed as though only divine intervention could save Constantinople. Scanderbeg was still to enact the great Albanian epic of resistance to the Turks, but the Bulgarians and Wallachians had already succumbed. The Serbs, overcome in 1389, would lose the last vestige of their independence in 1459. The Turks were to take over Bosnia in 1463, as we shall see, and the Herzegovina in 1482. The Greek "despotate" of the Morea, with its small but brilliant capital at Mistra, could not long survive the effects of Varna, and the Venetian fortresses at Negroponte, Nauplia, Argos, Coron, and Modon, as well as

---

[47] Targioni Tozzetti, *Relazioni*, V (1773, repr. 1971), 423–24; Cod. Vat. lat. 10,518 ("Schede epigrafiche relative a Ciriaco d'Ancona e notizie intorno ad esso" [from the *Schede De Rossi*]), fol. 98, where the entire poem is transcribed):

Nivea Paros di marmor candente
Cycladum decus aequoris Egei
honor delli heroi magni et delli dei
Sicchè 'l mondo di te si fa splendente. . . .

Cf. Wm. Miller, *Latins in the Levant*, London, 1908, pp. 422–23, 605.

After the death of Andrea Zeno, lord of Andros, in 1437, possession of the island had been disputed (*cf.* Miller, *Latins in the Levant*, pp. 604–5). The case was brought before the Venetian Senate, which by a decision of 22 December, 1439 (published as a ducal privilege on 5 January, 1440, Ven. style 1439), awarded Andros to Crusino I Sommaripa, son and heir of the late Maria Sanudo, rightful possessor of the island by reason of the feudal grant made to her by her brother, the late Niccolò dalle Carceri, who was at the time "true duke of the Archipelago" (Sen. Secreta, Reg. 15, fols. 3, 4ᵛ–5ʳ, 7). Crusino was supposed, however, to give up the islands of Paros and Antiparos, which the Senate had granted to his mother in 1423 in compensation for her having been unlawfully deprived of Andros, to which the Senate had recognized her right, but could not give her the island, "quia non erat in manibus nostris" (*ibid.*, fol. 4ᵛ). Obviously Crusino had not given up Paros, where he was still pursuing his archaeological interests. The background of Maria Sanudo's litigation (with Pietro Zeno [d. 1427], father of Andrea) may be studied at length in the Sen. Secreta, Reg. 8, fols. 51ʳ [52ʳ], 80ᵛ [81ᵛ], 86ʳ [87ʳ], 102ʳ–104ᵛ [103ʳ–105ᵛ], 106ʳ ff. [107ʳ ff.], docs. dated 1422–1423.

Crusino's rights to Andros were contested by Petronilla, daughter of the late Andrea (*cf.* Sen. Mar, Reg. 4, fol. 198ᵛ [199ᵛ], doc. dated 2 July, 1453; *ibid.*, Reg. 6, fol. 80ʳ [81ʳ], dated 28 July, 1458, and fol. 120ʳ [121ʳ], dated 28 April, 1459). The case dragged on until 1462 when Crusino paid 5,000 ducats to settle the claims of Petronilla, who was then living in the convent of Santa Croce on the Giudecca in Venice (F. Thiriet, *Délibérations des assemblées vénitiennes concernant la Romanie*, II [Paris and The Hague, 1971], nos. 1478, 1609, and 1613, pp. 195, 232, 234, docs. dated 14 March, 1453, and 22 February and 1 June, 1462, and *cf.* D. Jacoby, *La Féodalité en Grèce médiévale*, Paris and The Hague, 1971, pp. 282–83, 304–5). Incidentally, Crusino was in Venice defending himself when the news arrived of Mehmed II's seizure of Constantinople. The Senate granted him leave to return to Andros to look to his island possessions (Sen. Mar, Reg. 4, fol. 197ᵛ [198ᵛ], doc. dated 30 June, 1453).

[48] Andreolo's poem was published by Giulio Porro-Lambertenghi, "Relazione dell'attacco e difesa di Scio nel 1431 di Andreolo Giustiniani," *Miscellanea di storia italiana*, VI (Turin, 1865), 543–58; and on the event itself, see Philip P. Argenti, *The Occupation of Chios by the Genoese*, I (Cambridge, 1958), 176–87.

those in the islands, were obviously imperiled. Turkish control in the Balkans was not yet absolute, however, and according to the Venetian annalist Stefano Magno (d. 1572), Constantine Dragases received 300 men-at-arms from Philip the Good of Burgundy to continue the struggle against the Turks.[49] *Dum vivitur, speratur*. Despite past failures, the papacy remained the cynosure of Christian hopes in the Levant, especially Latin hopes, and the papacy and Venice were drawn more closely together. Now more than ever Hungary had become the chief Catholic bulwark against the Turks. The popes and even the Venetians would try to help the Hungarians, who were to find stalwart leadership for a while in Matthias Corvinus, the son of John Hunyadi. Varna had been primarily a Hungarian defeat, however, and the future looked grim.

Shortly after his victory at Varna, Sultan Murad II, a fat voluptuary, renounced the Ottoman throne (in December, 1444, or the following January). He withdrew to Asia Minor, spending a short while in his favorite city of Brusa (Bursa) before going on to more distant Magnesia (Manisa), where he built himself a palace. The thirteen-year-old Mehmed Chelebi, Mehmed II, succeeded him; coins were issued in the new sultan's name, which was also included in the Friday prayer.[50] The Venetians thought it wise to make peace with the Turks, both the young sultan in Europe and his father, the "sultano d'Asia." Despite papal hostility to the idea, the Venetians negotiated a treaty of peace with Mehmed II at Adrianople on Wednesday, 23 February, 1446. An original text of this treaty, in a rather ignorant form of demotic Greek but written in a practiced hand, is still preserved in the Venetian State Archives (among the Pacta secreta, Ser. 2, no. 230), probably the only such state document surviving from the first reign of Mehmed II.[51] The latter's father Murad pursued a life of ease and pleasure for about a year and a half at Magnesia, where he received Ciriaco of Ancona and his friend Francesco Drapperio in his private quarters on Easter Sunday of 1446 (17 April), as Ciriaco has recorded in a letter sent to his friend Andreolo Giustiniani-Banca three days later.[52]

In Adrianople, however, the ambitious and willful young Mehmed, who may not yet have added to his ample resources the art of deception which he was afterwards to cultivate with consistent success, worried his older and wiser ministers, especially Khalil Pasha, the grand vizir, who appealed to Murad to return to Adrianople and resume the government of the Ottoman state.[53] A half-century or so later the historian Giovanni Maria degli Angiolelli of Vicenza, who lived for years as a "slave" at the court of Mehmed (and knew him well), wrote that he was planning an attack in 1445–1446 upon Constantinople, which would have been no inconsiderable undertaking for a boy of fourteen.[54] Whatever the reasons, Murad set out

[49] Stefano Magno, *Estratti degli Annali veneti*, ed. Chas. [Karl] Hopf, *Chroniques gréco-romanes*, Berlin, 1873, repr. Brussels, 1966, p. 195: "1444: Constantino Peloponnesi despotae trecenti milites e Burgundia auxilio missi sunt, qui martio vel aprili anni 1445 in Peloponnesum venere."

[50] See in general Babinger, *Oriens*, III, 254–56, and *Aufsätze u. Abhandlungen*, I, 147–49.

[51] The Greek version of the Turco-Venetian treaty has been edited with a full commentary by F. Babinger and F. Dölger, "Mehmeds II. frühester Staatsvertrag," *Orientalia Christiana periodica*, XV (1949), 225–58, reprinted in Dölger's *Byzantinische Diplomatik*, Ettal, 1956, pp. 262–91, and *cf.* Babinger, *Oriens*, III, 258–59, and *Aufsätze u. Abhandlungen*, I, 151–52. Sanudo, *Vite de'duchi*, in *RISS*, XXII, col. 1120, records the treaty; the preamble is much the same as that employed in Mehmed I's peace with Venice in 1419 (see above, Chapter 1, note 17): in Sanudo's text, however, Mehmed II is represented as swearing by the 124 prophets of Islam instead of 124,000, the copyist having overlooked a superscript M (=*milia*) in the Latin version (on the oath see J. Pedersen, quoted by Babinger in *Or. Christ. period.*, XV, 286–87, note 51). The treaty is given in its entirety, in the Venetian dialect, by G. M. Thomas and R. Predelli, *Diplomatarium veneto-levantinum (1300–1454)*, II (Venice, 1899, repr. New York, 1965), no. 198, pp. 366–68; Iorga, *ROL*, VIII, 23–28; *Notes et extraits*, III (1902), 210 ff.; and Predelli, *Regesti dei Commemoriali*, IV (1896), no. 289, p. 296 (from Comm., Reg. 13, fol. 190, and *cf.* fol. 198). Although the Venetian text is dated Wednesday, 25 February, the twenty-fifth fell on a Friday in 1446 (the calendar is given correctly in Louis de Mas Latrie, *Trésor de chronologie*, Paris, 1889, repr. Turin, 1962, col. 448, but incorrectly in A. Cappelli's popular *Cronologia*, etc., 2nd and 3rd edd., Milan, 1952, 1969, p. 88, where both 20 and 21 February are given as Sunday!). In his Venetian version of the Turco-Venetian treaty of April, 1454, Sanudo (*op. cit.*, col. 1154AB) also does violence to the Islamic oath, reporting Mehmed II as swearing "ne'ventiquattro Profeti d'Iddio o più o meno."

[52] Targioni Tozzetti, *Relazioni*, V, 450, and *cf.* Cod. Vat. lat. 10,518, fols. 97^r–98^r (from the *Schede De Rossi*), for the portions of the letter omitted from Targioni's transcription, but not relevant to our present interest. On Drapperio, *cf.* Babinger, *Oriens*, III, 233–34, 259, and *Aufsätze u. Abhandlungen*, I, 131–32, 152, and see above, Chapter 2, note 144.

[53] Ducas, chap. 32 (Bonn, pp. 220, 222); Chalcocondylas, bk. VII (Bonn, pp. 352–53).

[54] Giovanni Maria degli Angiolelli (Anzolelli), *Historia turchesca, 1300–1514*, ed. Ion Ursu [who has erroneously attributed the work to Giovanni Maria's friend, the Venetian

from Magnesia on 5 May, 1446, with some 4,000 men. Ciriaco and Drapperio went with the great Turkish entourage to a point beyond Pergamum, after which Murad and his followers turned northeast toward Brusa while Ciriaco and his friend continued on to New Phocaea, whence the antiquarian addressed another letter dated Wednesday, 11 May, to his friend Andreolo Giustiniani.[55] Ciriaco thought that Murad was returning to Europe at the request of his son Mehmed, but it is clear that Ciriaco was not acquainted with the facts, which were obviously kept from public knowledge.

Murad made a most leisurely advance to Adrianople, apparently stopping for some months at Brusa where on 1 August, 1446, he made his will, providing detailed instructions for his burial when death should come to him. It is difficult to say whether or not Murad expected his return to the court at Adrianople to be opposed by Mehmed, who descended from the throne peacefully, however, and withdrew in his turn to Magnesia, always harboring thereafter a strong resentment of Khalil Pasha, who had thus contrived his loss of sovereignty. Murad resumed control over the Ottoman empire in late August after some twenty months of semi-retirement.[56]

Always on the move, Ciriaco of Ancona spent part of the summer of 1446 in Constantinople, and at the beginning of the next year embarked on a new *voyage archéologique* in the Aegean. From New Phocaea he wrote his friend Andreolo on 13 February, 1447, of a three days' visit to Gallipoli where he sought, as always, the remains of antiquity. Here he had an anguished sight of the Turks driving a long, pitiable column of Greek and other Christian prisoners in chains to the slave marts of Gallipoli, long a center for the trade, and across the Dardanelles into Asia. From the prisoners Ciriaco learned that on the preceding 13 December (1446) Murad's forces had destroyed with heavy artillery most of the Hexamilion, which the Despot Constantine Dragases had so carefully restored about three years before. The Turks had then devastated the Peloponnesus. Ciriaco could hardly bear to hear the weeping voices tell the dismal tale of Turkish

Donado da Lezze (1479–1526), under whose name he has published it], Bucharest, 1909, p. 15. Ursu has derived his text of the *Historia* from an Italian MS. in the Bibliothèque Nationale in Paris (no. 1238, fols. 1–120), dating from about the year 1600. See the rather too imaginative book of J. Reinhard, *Essai sur G. M. Angiolello noble vicentin (1452–1525), premier historien des Ottomans (1300–1517) et des Persans (1453–1524): Sa vie, son œuvre*, Angers, 1913, and the valuable study of N. Di Lenna, "Ricerche intorno allo storico G. Maria Angiolello (degli Anzolelli), patrizio vicentino (1451–1525)," in the *Archivio veneto-tridentino*, V (Venice, 1924), 1–56.

Considering the historical importance of Giovanni Maria's *Historia turchesca*, some facts concerning him will not be out of place. He was born of patrician parents in Vicenza in 1451 or '52. Leaving Venice in 1468 with his elder brother Francesco, a captain of infantry in the service of the Republic, he was present at the siege of Negroponte, of which he has left us a valuable account (*cf.* Ursu, introd., p. x, and Di Lenna, *op. cit.*, pp. 10–11), and where his brother was killed. Being assigned to Sultan Mehmed II as a slave on 13 July, 1470, when he was eighteen years old (hence our conjecture as to the date of his birth), Gianmaria is found two years later (1472) in the service of Mehmed's second son Mustafa, then in command of part of the Ottoman troops later to march against Uzun Ḥasan, the ruler of Persia. Gianmaria was to write Uzun Ḥasan's life in after years (*Breve Narratione della vita et fatti d'Ussuncassan Rè di Persia*, ed. G. B. Ramusio, *Navigationi et viaggi*, II [Venice, 1559, and later editions], fols. 66–78, trans. Chas. Grey, *Italian Travels in Persia in the Fifteenth and Sixteenth Centuries*, Hakluyt Society, London, 1873, and on the first printing of the *Breve Narratione*, see Gotthold Weil, "Ein verschollener Wiegendruck von Gio. Maria Angiolello," in Fritz Meier, ed., *Westöstliche Abhandlungen: Rudolf Tschudi zum siebzigsten Geburtstag überreicht . . .*, Wiesbaden, 1954, pp. 304–14). Gianmaria was in the Ottoman army during Mehmed II's campaigns against Uzun Ḥasan in 1472–1473 (see, below, p. 316). After the young prince Mustafa's death (in 1474) he passed into the sultan's own service, and participated in the Turkish campaigns against Stephen the Great of Moldavia (1476), against Matthias Corvinus in Bosnia (1476–1477), and against the Venetians in Albania (1478), being in the sultan's retinue in fact at the time of the latter's death (on 3 May, 1481).

Finding the Porte less congenial under Sultan Bayazid II, Gianmaria made his escape in 1483 or 1488–9, returning to Vicenza, where he must have supervised in 1490 the printing of the first edition of his *Breve Narratione . . . di Ussuncassan* ("impressum Vincentiae per magistrum Leonardum de Basilea MCCCCLXXXX die primo mensis Septembris"). Going back to the East later on, Gianmaria seems to have spent the years from 1507 to 1514 in Persia. The facts of his career are far from certain, but he apparently resided in Vicenza from 1514; in 1517 he was appointed president of the Vicentine College of Notaries, which office he held until his death about the end of the year 1524 (Ursu, introd., p. xv, and Di Lenna, *op. cit.*, pp. 25–26, 36–39). Some scholars have believed that Gianmaria translated the Koran (from Turkish!), a distinction which can hardly be claimed for him. He did, however, follow his biography of Uzun Ḥasan with one of Ismā'īl, shah of Persia (1502–1524). Gianmaria's chief work, and a most important one, is the *Historia turchesca*, the content and sources of which Di Lenna has analyzed (pp. 44 ff.). On Donado da Lezze, see Ursu, introd., pp. xviii ff., and *cf.* Franz Babinger's notice of Gianmaria in the *Dizionario biografico degli italiani*, III (Rome, 1961), 275–78.

[55] Targioni Tozzetti, *Relazioni*, V, 453; and *cf.* Cod. Vat. lat. 10,518, fols. 102^r–102^v, for omitted portions of the text, which are not relevant to our present subject.

[56] Babinger and Dölger, in *Orientalia Christiana periodica*, XV, 227, and Babinger, *Maometto* (1957), pp. 85–86; *Oriens*, III, 259–62; *Aufsätze u. Abhandlungen*, I, 151–54.

success, and he reflected grimly on how, but a short time before, the Turks had been almost cleared out of Thrace, Macedonia, and all Greece, and driven into Asia and Lydia. But now, with the withdrawal of the western and Hungarian forces, fortune had lifted Murad up, made him daring, and, aided indeed by the slothful inattention of the princes of Europe, allowed him to invade the noble and once powerful Greek state in the Peloponnesus. Alas, the enormity of it all! "For I believe that such a lamentable blow to Christendom—this miserable slaughter which the Turks have perpetrated upon this people, even though they are Greeks and deserving of some measure of punishment—cannot be thought of except as a grievous loss to our own religion and as a vast dishonor to the Latin name."[57]

The expedition which the Turks sent into the Morea in 1446 had been provoked by Constantine Dragases' attacks upon the Turkish commandery in Thessaly and upon the Latin duchy of Athens, which latter Duke Nerio II had restored to Turkish suzerainty after the battle of Varna. Constantine had been riding high; he was well served both in continental Greece and in the Morea. In 1445 he had appointed John Cantacuzenus the governor of Corinth;[58] John was an old friend of Ciriaco of Ancona, whom he entertained at Acrocorinth in April, 1448.[59] On 22 June, 1446, in order to recognize and repay "our beloved son, the noble Constantine Cantacuzenus Palaeologus," the son of John Cantacuzenus, Pope Eugenius IV had appointed him count palatine of the Lateran, one of those Roman honors accorded the Greek nobility which were to prove so valuable to them after the fall of the "despotate" of the Morea to the Turks. Constantine Cantacuzenus was to take the oath of fealty to the pope at the hands of Niccolò Protimo, the Latin archbishop of Athens.[60]

Counts palatine of the Lateran were of no avail, however, when Sultan Murad himself descended from Macedonia into Greece with a great army which Constantine Dragases and his brother dared not meet on the continent, believing it wiser to withdraw behind the Hexamilion. It was an imposing line of defense, and Murad was discouraged by the sight of it, chiding Turakhan Beg for urging him to attack such a bulwark so close to the winter season. But the old warrior, who had already destroyed the Hexamilion twice before (in 1423 and 1431), was certain the Greeks would flee before they would fight. The historian George Sphrantzes informs us that Murad was halted by the wall from 27 November to 10 December

---

[57] Ciriaco, *Ep.* IV, in Cod. Palat. Florent. 49 (Serie Targioni), fols. 7–9v (earlier enumeration, 59–61v); *cf.* Targioni Tozzetti, *Relazioni*, V, 441–45, *ex eodem novo Phocarum emporio, eo quo ad ipsum venimus die Id. Febr.* [1447]: ". . . Nunc equidem contra vidimus barbaros longo ordine preda nostre quoque religionis homines et potissimum Graia ex natione captivos miserandum in modum ferreis sub catenis ad eiusdem civitatis emporium [Gallipoli] atque litora per Hellespontum in Asiam transvecturos, quorum et a miseris nonnullos pientissimo ab ore certius intelligimus Murath Begh, superbum Theucrorum principem, Peloponensiacum Isthmon ingentibus admotis copiis hostiliter Idibus Decembribus [1446] invasisse, turritis ibidem paulo ante menibus a Constantino Spartano rege curiosissime restitutis, arto tandem milite superatis et magna ex parte machinarum vi disiectis et solo convulsis, ac inde sparto milite regionem late populatum esse.

"Quibus flebilibus auditis vocibus scis, vir clarissime, quantum non egre molesteve ferre non potui audire trucem et pernitiosum illum Christiane religionis hostem, quem hac tempestate vel vix anno peracto nostratum armis religioso vel milite superatum fugatumque et penitus e Thracum Macedonumque regnis simul et tota vel e Grecia pulsum et tergiversatum in Asyam atque Lidiam putabamus. Nunc vero ignava quadam nostratum incuria principum, nostris et Pannonum paulisper abmotis et retractis viribus, tantum eum fortunam elatum atque audentem fecisse ac sibi Peloponensiacum tam nobile et olim potentissimum Grecie regnum invadere licuisse. Proh scelus! et heu prisca nostrorum generosissime gentis nobilitas! Nam et illatam huic genti miserabilem a barbaris cladem, tametsi Grecos in homines et penas quodamodo dare merentes, non sine gravi tamen nostre religionis iactura et magna Latini nominis indignitate, tam lachrymabilem Christicolum calamitatem existimandam puto . . ." (*MS. cit.*, fol. 8 [60]).

[58] Sphrantzes, *Chron. minus* (*PG* 156, 1050D; ed. Grecu, p. 68); Pseudo-Sphrantzes, II, 19 (Bonn, p. 200; ed. J. B. Papadopoulos, I [Leipzig, 1935], 198; ed. Grecu, p. 342); *cf.* Hopf, *Chron. gréco-romanes*, geneal. tables, p. 536, and D. Zakythinos, *Le Despotat grec de Morée*, I (1932, repr. 1975), 228, 231.

[59] Remigio Sabbadini, *Miscellanea [Antonio] Ceriani*, Milan, 1910, pp. 230–31 (see below, note 64).

[60] Georg Hofmann, ed., *Epistolae pontificiae ad concilium Florentinum spectantes*, III (1946), no. 285, p. 109, and N. Iorga, *Notes et extraits*, II, 418. This Constantine does not appear in Hopf's genealogical table of the Cantacuzeni in the *Chron. gréco-romanes*, p. 536; Francesco Cerone, "La Politica orientale di Alfonso di Aragona," *Archivio storico per le province napoletane*, XXVII (1902), 597, assumes him to be a relative of the Manuel Cantacuzenus, lord of Maina, who was proclaimed despot by the Albanians in the Morea in 1453 (see, below, pp. 147–48), which was close to the mark. Fr. Hofmann seems to have missed the text of Ciriaco of Ancona which identifies him as the son of John Cantacuzenus, governor of Corinth (1445–1453), for which see Sabbadini, *Miscellanea Ceriani* (1910), pp. 230–31. On Nerio II's return of the Athenian duchy to the status of a Turkish satellite state and the resumption of his tribute to Sultan Murad, see Chalcocondylas, bk. VI (Bonn, p. 320).

(1446).[61] In any event several days' cannonading prepared the Hexamilion for the assault in which a young Serbian janissary distinguished himself by being the first to go over the top. Turakhan Beg had been right. The Greeks abandoned their positions under the twin pressures of fear and force despite the best efforts of Constantine and Thomas to hold them on the endangered rampart. Finding the impetus of battle running against them, and distrusting their Albanian contingents, the imperial brothers also fled, making their way to the southern extremity of the Morea, whence further flight would be possible if it should prove to be necessary. Turakhan Beg followed them for a while in a destructive razzia while Murad moved along the northern coast of the Morea, capturing and burning Basilicata (the ancient Sicyon), Vostitza, and the lower town of Patras, extending his devastation as far as the promontory of Glarentza. When Murad withdrew from the Morea at the onset of winter, he left Constantine the vassal ruler of a ruined country, his continental conquests all lost, and 60,000 of his Peloponnesian subjects reduced to that slavery which Ciriaco could not bear to contemplate.[62] Now there was nothing for the Greeks to do but seek to cultivate good will at the Ottoman court, and so (apparently in April, 1447) we find the ailing Emperor John VIII inquiring with feigned solicitude about "the health of my brother, the most illustrious Great Emir [Murad]."[63]

A little later, in July, 1447, Ciriaco himself went into the Morea, where he appears to have remained until April, 1448. In an account of 30 July (1447) he tells of going from Leondari to the court of Constantine Dragases at Mistra, which he had already visited ten years before, apparently to see the Platonic philosopher George Gemistus Pletho, whom he had probably known at the Council of Florence. At Mistra Ciriaco also met the youthful Nicholas (Laonicus) Chalcocondylas, who later became the chief historian of his generation. Laonicus was the son of Ciriaco's friend George Chalcocondylas, an important member of one of the few medieval Athenian families known to us. With Laonicus as his guide, Ciriaco went, on 2 August, the few miles from Mistra to Sparta to see the sparse remains of celebrated Lacedaemon.[64] The following year (1448) he went to Epirus, arriving in the capital city of Arta in October. The ruling family of the Tocchi was interested in literature and antiquarian pursuits; Ciriaco had found various members of the family very congenial on earlier visits a dozen years before. But on 30 September,

---

[61] Sphrantzes, *Chron. minus* (*PG* 156, 1051B; ed. Grecu, p. 70); Pseudo-Sphrantzes, II, 19 (Bonn, pp. 202–3; ed. Papadopoulos, I, 200; ed. Grecu, p. 344).

[62] Chalcocondylas, bk. VII (Bonn, pp. 341–50; ed. Darkó, II-1, 112–19), indicates that upon Murad's arrival in Thebes, Duke Nerio II Acciajuoli of Athens joined him with an armed force (στρατὸν ἀγόμενος ἀπὸ Ἀθηνῶν). Ducas, chap. 32 (Bonn, pp. 222–23), informs us that Murad carried off 60,000 Christians into slavery (thus giving the same figure as Ciriaco of Ancona), but places Murad's expedition and destruction of the Hexamilion (which he says Constantine had rebuilt "four years before," πρὸ τεσσάρων χρόνων) after Hunyadi's defeat at Kossovo in October, 1448, an obvious error. The *Chronicon breve*, ad ann. 1446 (Bonn, following Ducas, pp. 519–20), says that Murad arrived at the Hexamilion on Saturday, 3 December. *Cf.* Stefano Magno, *Estratti degli Annali veneti*, ed. Hopf, *Chron. gréco-romanes*, p. 194, and Ioann. Cartanus, *Anthos*, *ibid.*, p. 267; also Wm. Miller, *Latins in the Levant* (1908), pp. 411–14; Pall, *Bull. hist. Acad. roum.*, XX (1938), 50–51; Babinger, *Maometto*, pp. 90–92; and esp. Sp. P. Lampros, *Neos Hellenomn.*, II (1905), 479–84, who collects the sources, and shows that the (Bonn) editors of the *Chron. breve* have misread the text: the chronicle actually states that Murad took the Hexamilion on Friday, 9 December, 1446. Note also Edward W. Bodnar, "The Isthmian Fortifications in Oracular Prophecy," *American Journal of Archaeology*, LXIV (1960), 165–71, to whose work we shall return in the last chapter of our third volume.

[63] The letter is dated "in the month of April of the tenth indiction" (i.e., 1432 or 1447), the latter date being preferred by F. Babinger and F. Dölger, "Ein Auslandsbrief des Kaisers Johannes VIII. vom Jahre 1447," *Byzantinische Zeitschrift*, XLV (1952), 20–28, reprinted in Babinger's *Aufsätze u. Abhandlungen*, II (Munich, 1966), 162–69. N. A. Oikonomides, "On the Date of John VIII's Letter to Sarîdja Beğ," *Byzantion*, XXXIV (1964), 105–9, believes the letter was written in April, 1432.

[64] The text has been published by Remigio Sabbadini, "Ciriaco d'Ancona e la sua descrizione autografa del Peloponneso trasmessa da Leonardo Botta," in the *Miscellanea* [*Antonio*]*Ceriani*, Milan, 1910, pp. 203–4: ". . . Ad antiqua et celeberrima illa spartanae civitatis monumenta revisenda venimus: cum nec equidem vidisse semel satis fuerat, iuvabat sed usque morari . . ." [*cf.* Vergil, *Aen.*, VI, 487]. The historian Laonicus Chalcocondylas, who later lived and wrote in Athens, and the humanist Demetrius Chalcocondylas, who later lived in Italy, were not brothers, as Lampros, Sabbadini, and others have assumed (with Antonius Calosynas, whose biographical notices on Laonicus and Demetrius represent them as brothers, for which see Hopf, *Chron. gréco-romanes*, p. 244, and *cf.* p. xxx). Actually they were cousins, Laonicus's father being named George, and Demetrius's father Basil (George and Basil were brothers); see Dem. Gr. Kampouroglous, *The Chalkokondylai* [in Greek], Athens, 1926, pp. 104 ff., 123, 171 ff., and Giuseppe Cammelli, *I Dotti bizantini e le origini dell'umanesimo*, III: *Demetrio Calcondila*, Florence, 1954, pp. 4–5.

1448, the Despot Carlo II Tocco had died at Arta,[65] being succeeded by his son Leonardo III, and there were doubtless other topics for discussion than the latest finds of antiquities. What was to be Leonardo's future as the Turks scored victories everywhere on the long front from Varna to the Morea? Very likely some Byzantine priest at Arta had already read the future in the past, perceiving in the wisdom of Ecclesiastes (2:14) "that one event happeneth to them all." Leonardo was to wait thirty years for the final event as the Turks occupied, first, his mainland possessions and finally his island dominions of Leucadia (S. Maura), Cephalonia, and Zante (in 1479), after which he was to seek refuge in the kingdom of Naples.[66] We shall return to Leonardo Tocco in a later chapter. Actually he was to be more fortunate than most of the many refugees of his generation; he was to receive the lordship of Calimera, in the Greek-speaking area south of Mileto in the region of Calabria. But even the assurance of this haven, could they have known this much of the future, would have brought small solace to the Tocchi and their learned guest during their conversations in the autumn of 1448. There was a sense of impending doom in the East, prelude to an even greater disaster than any that had yet happened.

The Byzantine Emperor John VIII died on 31 October (1448), and was buried the next day in the monastery of the Pantokrator. Like Michael VIII before him, he had remained true to the union he had negotiated with Rome, and like Michael he was buried without the last rites of the Greek Church.[67] He was succeeded by his ablest and his favorite brother, Constantine XI.[68]

About 10 o'clock in the morning of 6 March, 1447, on the third scrutiny, eighteen cardinals in conclave at the Dominican convent of S. Maria sopra Minerva elected Tommaso Parentucelli, the cardinal of Bologna, as Pope Nicholas V, and his coronation took place on the nineteenth of the month.[69] With surprising skill and swiftness Nicholas V restored order in the states of the Church, which had been harassed by mercenary troops and freebooters for a full decade. He reasserted the papal authority in Bologna, where for five years the eminent Cardinal Bessarion fulfilled a difficult legatine mission to the general satisfaction of the Bolognesi. Urbane and usually genial, the new pope was harsh in his punishment of dissension or rebellion in his temporal domain. He did encourage unrest elsewhere in Italy, however, doing little to forestall the hostile moves of King Alfonso of Naples against the Florentines, but (quite reasonably) opposing Alfonso's assumed desire to take over the duchy of Milan after the death of Filippo Maria Visconti in mid-August of 1447.[70] Although Nicholas took some satisfaction in the Italian wars, so long as they left him at peace to establish his control over the states of the Church, he had no intention of allowing Alfonso

[65] The date, furnished by Ciriaco, corrects the genealogical table in Hopf, *Chron. gréco-romanes*, p. 530, as noted by Pall, *Bull. hist. Acad. roum.*, XX, 52.

[66] Sen. Secreta, Reg. 29, fols. 34ᵛ–35ʳ [44ᵛ–45ʳ], a Venetian document of 7 September, 1479 (and see below, Chapter 10, p. 341, and Chapter 17, pp. 514–15), and *cf.* Stefano Magno, *Estratti degli Annali veneti*, ed. Hopf, *Chron. gréco-romanes*, pp. 201, 208.

[67] *Cf.* Joseph Gill, *The Council of Florence*, Cambridge, 1959, pp. 370–71, and "John VIII," in *Personalities of the Council of Florence*, Oxford, 1964, esp. pp. 123–24.

[68] On the reasons for designating Constantine the XIth and not the XIIth, note Franz Dölger, *Byzantinische Zeitschrift*, LII (1959), 445, in his notice of Joan M. Hussey, *The Byzantine World*, London, 1957.

[69] *Cf.* Aeneas Sylvius, *Oratio Fred. III*, in *RISS*, III–2 (Milan, 1734), cols. 893–97; Raynaldus, *Ann. eccl.*, ad ann. 1447, nos. 15 ff., vol. XVIII (1694), pp. 336 ff.; Mandell Creighton, *History of the Papacy*, II (London, 1882), 274 ff.; Ludwig von Pastor, *History of the Popes*, II (7th ed., London, 1949), 5–31, and *Geschichte der Päpste*, I (12th ed., Freiburg im Breisgau, 1955), 372–94. On 27 November, 1444, Eugenius IV had appointed Parentucelli, called Thomas de Sarzana, to the bishopric of Bologna, but since the city was then in revolt against the Holy See, his occupation of the cathedra was long delayed (*cf.* Pastor's *Gesch. d. Päpste*, I, 383, and his *Acta inedita*, I [Freiburg, 1904], no. 16, pp. 28–29). The Acta consistorialia (1439–1486), ad ann. 1447, in Arch. Segr. Vaticano, Arm. XXXI, tom. 52, fol. 52ᵛ, places the election of Nicholas V on 6 March "hora nona vel quasi," which is reckoning the first hour from midnight or 1:00 A.M., although the customary Italian practice of the time was to reckon the first hour from sundown, about 7 to 8:00 P.M. in March, on which see B. M. Lersch, *Einleitung in die Chronologie*, 2nd ed., 2 pts., Freiburg, 1899, I, 9. Contemporary reports place the election at the sixteenth or seventeenth hour, which would be between 10 and 11:00 A.M. (*cf.* Lersch, *loc. cit.*, and note Pastor, I, 378, note 2).

[70] Gian. Manetti, *Vita Nich. V*, II, in *RISS*, III–2 (Milan, 1734), cols. 943–46. Nicholas did, to be sure, formally urge peace upon the Florentines and Alfonso (*cf.* Raynaldus, *Ann. eccl.*, ad ann. 1448, no. 8, vol. XVIII [1694], p. 351). See in general Luigi Rossi, "Niccolò V e le potenze d'Italia dal maggio del 1447 al dicembre del 1451," *Rivista di scienze storiche*, III–1 (Pavia, 1906), 241–62, 392–429, and *ibid.*, III–2 (1906), 22–37, 177–94, 225–32, 329–55, 385–406, with a series of appendices containing forty-four documents, of which the last is dated 17 November, 1451.

to put into effect the designs of a Hohenstaufen. And Alfonso lacked the power to do so anyhow. The early years of Nicholas's pontificate were most successful, witnessing the final defeat of the conciliarists at Basel and Lausanne, and winning the recognition of France, Germany, and indeed most of Europe except Bohemia. But the major problem of this period was the advance of the Gran Turco, and it can hardly be claimed for Nicholas that he appreciated the full extent of its gravity.

The advance of the Turk in the Balkans might be slowed, but apparently it could not be stopped. Whatever hope of liberation the Greek and Latin inhabitants of former Byzantine territories had, lay in the north. John Hunyadi, who served as regent of Hungary from 1446 through 1452, watched with anxious eyes the constant deployment of Turkish troops on his borders. The defeat at Varna, which had tarnished his hard-earned fame in Europe, could be redeemed only by victory. The despot of Serbia, George Branković, however, had learned much from Varna by not being there, and obviously believed that his country could better withstand the hostility of Hungary than that of the Turk.[71] Venice had renewed her commercial relations with the Porte (on 23 February, 1446),[72] and was unwilling to jeopardize them by joining forces with Hunyadi, whose bellicose intentions were well understood at the Ottoman court in Adrianople. Alfonso V, king of Aragon, Naples, and Sicily, would not risk an expedition against the Turks, even though he entertained the irresponsible dream of re-establishing the Latin empire of Constantinople, with himself as emperor. Nicholas V responded to Hunyadi's appeals with little more than spiritual support and the sonorous preachment of another crusade (on 8 April, 1448).[73]

Hunyadi had been able, however, to reach an understanding with Scanderbeg, whose reputation was already challenging his own, and who was to keep the Turks at bay in the rugged highlands of Albania for a quarter of a century (1443–1468). In September and October, 1448, the impatient Hunyadi marched through Serbia, burning and pillaging as though Branković and the Serbs were his enemies instead of the Turks. On 17 October he reached the historic "Field of the Blackbirds" at Kossovo, where in June, 1389, Sultan Murad I had lost his life, and his son Bayazid I had secured both the Ottoman throne and one of the more resounding victories ever gained by the Turks over Christendom. Hunyadi had not been able to wait for Scanderbeg and the Albanians, for the advance of Murad II to meet him had been too rapid. His army, the last hope of Hungarian ascendancy in the struggle, was reinforced by a large Vlach contingent together with some Germans and Czechs. It was considerably smaller, however, than the army which Murad II had assembled at Sofia, and which had reached Kossovo shortly before the Christian host. The young Mehmed II had accom-

---

[71] In fact Chalcocondylas, bk. VII (Bonn, p. 355, lines 10–13), states that George Branković warned Murad II of Hunyadi's forthcoming expedition (*cf.*, *ibid.*, p. 356, lines 17–22).

[72] Thomas and Predelli, *Diplomatarium veneto-levantinum*, II (1899, repr. 1965), no. 198, pp. 366–68, where the date 25 February is wrong; Babinger and Dölger, "Mehmeds II. frühester Staatsvertrag," *Orientalia Christiana periodica*, XV, 225–28, on which see above, note 51.

[73] Raynaldus, *Ann. eccl.*, ad ann. 1448, nos. 6–7, vol. XVIII (1694), pp. 350–51. As for Alfonso V, he enjoyed posing as a Christian champion against the Moslems, and since Albania was Naples's first line of defense against the Ottoman threat to the Adriatic, he was generous (as we shall note) in his support of Scanderbeg. Although contemporaries expected more of Alfonso than he ever delivered, he did declare himself the protector of both the Hospital of Rhodes and the kingdom of Cyprus. He sent two or three fleets into the Levant (in 1450 and 1451–1453) against the Mamluks, who had destroyed the Hospitaller castle on the island of Castellorizzo (*Castrum Rubeum*, Castelrosso, the modern Kastellórizon) at the time of their attack upon Rhodes (in 1444). Alfonso's admiral Bernard of Villamarina (Vilamarí) rebuilt the castle, renaming it "Castel Alfonsi," to the annoyance of Jean de Lastic, grand master of the Hospitallers, on whose behalf Bernard had been sent eastward.

Alfonso had sought and obtained authorization from Nicholas V to occupy the island, "cuius edificia . . . per Theucros et Sarracenos . . . dirruta et solo equata sunt," which was granted on 6 October, 1450, lest the Mamluks take over the island and use it as a base against Rhodes (Arch. Segr. Vaticano, Reg. Vat. 392 [*Nich. V Secret. tom. VIII*], fols. 102^r–103^r; Sebastiano Paoli [Pauli], *Codice diplomatico del sacro militare ordine Gerosolimitano*, II [Lucca, 1737], no. CX, p. 130). While in eastern waters Bernard of Villamarina raided the coasts of Egypt and Syria, disrupted commerce, and brought Jean de Lastic almost as much trouble as assistance, on which see Const. Marinescu, "L'Île de Rhodes au XVe siècle et l'Ordre de Saint-Jean de Jérusalem d'après des documents inédits," *Miscellanea Giovanni Mercati*, V (1946), esp. pp. 388–95 (Studi e testi, no. 125).

The Spanish traveler Pero Tafur sailed past Castellorizzo on his way to the Holy Land in 1436, and stopped there during the course of his return journey the following year. He has left us a brief description of the place seven years before its destruction by the Mamluks (Malcolm Letts, trans., *Pero Tafur: Travels and Adventures, 1435–1439*, New York and London, 1926, pp. 53, 106).

panied his father to Kossovo, and now witnessed his first major encounter, stationed with the Anatolian troops on the right wing of the Turkish army (where he was also to place them in the assault upon the landward walls of Constantinople almost five years later). The second battle of Kossovo was hard fought for almost three days. On 19 October, while the issue was still undecided, the Vlachs deserted the Hungarians, fearful of the outcome, and Hunyadi had to retreat under the cover of German and Czech gunners. He made his way back through Serbia, but just before he could reach the Danube, he was captured by Serbian peasants and taken to Branković. Hunyadi got back to Szeged at the end of the year only by accepting a harsh treaty dictated by Branković to govern the future relations of Hungary and Serbia.[74] While Hunyadi signed the pact to gain his freedom, he had no intention of adhering to it, and the pope soon released him from a promise made under duress.[75]

In the spring and summer of 1448 Murad II had led a large expedition into Albania and captured the fortress of Sfetigrad on the lower Dibra after a siege of some three months.[76] Two years later Murad II returned to Albania with his son Mehmed, who seems to have divided his time between his retreat at Magnesia and the court at Adrianople. Their objective was the most important fortress in Scanderbeg's possession, Croia, whose defense the Albanian leader had placed in charge of loyal comrades, who had a garrison of 1,500 men.[77] In mid-

[74] The second battle of Kossovo and its aftermath are described in great detail, some of it obviously imaginary, by Chalcocondylas, bk. VII (Bonn, pp. 355–77); *cf.* Iorga, *Notes et extraits*, IV, pt. 1, no. 20, pp. 41–42; *Gesch. d. osman. Reiches*, II (Gotha, 1909), 450–52; and esp. "Du Nouveau sur la campagne turque de Jean Hunyadi en 1448," *Revue historique du Sud-Est européen*, III (1926), 13–27; Fr. Pall, "Les Relations entre la Hongrie et Scanderbeg," *ibid.*, X (1933), 127–31; Gelcich and Thallóczy, *Diplomatarium ragusanum* (1887), nos. 279–82, pp. 466–70; and Babinger, *Maometto*, pp. 93–100. Iorga discounts the presence of the Germans and Czechs (mentioned by Aeneas Sylvius) in Hunyadi's army.

Scanderbeg intended to go "personalmente" with an army to assist Hunyadi (S. Ljubić, *Listine*, IX [1890], p. 283, doc. from Commemoriali, Reg. 14, fol. 79, dated 4 October, 1448; Giunio Resti, *Chronica ragusina*, in *Monumenta spectantia historiam slavorum meridionalium*, vol. XXV: *SS.*, II [Zagreb, 1893], pp. 295, 298; and Antonio Bonfini, *Historia pannonica*, Cologne, 1690, decad. III, bk. VII. p. 339AB), but was prevented from doing so by Branković, whose lands he ravaged as punishment for the Serbian desertion of the Christian cause (Marinus Barletius, *Historia de vita et gestis Scanderbegi*, 1st ed., Rome, 1509, bk. II, fols. XXVII^v–XXVIII^r; ed. Zagreb, 1743, pp. 58–59, who puts these events under the year 1444!), on which note Francisc Pall, "Skanderbeg et Ianco de Hunedoara," *Revue des études sud-est européennes*, VI (1968), 10–14. Murad II had cut short his Albanian campaign of 1448 and a siege of Croia in August in order to march against Hunyadi, as shown by Ljubić, *op. cit.*, IX (1890), 283–84, from the Venetian Sen. Secreta, Reg. 18, fol. 52 [54], doc. dated 10 October, 1448. The documents of 4 and 10 October, 1448, are reprinted in Jovan Radonić, *Djuradj Kastriot Skenderbeg i Arbanija u XV veku*, Belgrade, 1942, p. 16, and *cf.* Riccardo Predelli, *Regesti dei Commemoriali*, V (Venice, 1909), bk. XIV, no. 31, p. 16. There is a spurious exchange of undated letters between George Branković and John Hunyadi (clearly of seventeenth-century origin), on which see Fr. Pall, "Preteso Scambio di lettere tra Giorgio Brankovich, principe di Serbia, e Iancu de Hunedoara (Hunyadi) a proposito del pericolo ottomano intorno al 1450," *Revue des études sud-est européennes*, XII (1974), 79–86.

Reports reached Venice from Durazzo at this time that Scanderbeg's preparations were really intended for an attack upon the Venetian-held coast of Albania, and so the Senate took appropriate action (Sen. Mar, Reg. 3, fol. 82^r [83^r], doc. dated 6 October, 1448): "Quoniam per ea que habentur per litteras noviter habitas ex Durachio Scanderbegus solicite parat potentem exercitum suum pro veniendo ad illas partes contra terras et statum nostrum . . . , vadit pars quod au[c]toritate istius consilii scribatur et mandetur vicecapitaneo Culphi quod cum duabus galeis sibi commissis remaneat in illis aquis Durachii pro hortamine locorum et subditorum nostrorum. . . ." *Cf.* Valentini, *Acta Albaniae veneta*, XX (1974), no. 5,397, p. 58.

[75] Raynaldus, *Ann. eccl.*, ad ann. 1450, no. 7, vol. XVIII (1694), pp. 366–67, doc. dated 12 April, 1450, in which the pope summarizes the terms of the pact. In June, 1450, the city of Ragusa congratulated Hunyadi upon his making peace with Branković (Gelcich and Thallóczy, *Diplomatarium ragusanum*, no. 283, pp. 471–72; Jovan Radonić, *Acta et diplomata ragusina*, I, pt. 2 [Belgrade, 1934], no. 222, pp. 499–501, and *cf.* nos. 231–33 [in the Fontes rerum slavorum meridionalium, ser. I]).

[76] Chalcocondylas, bk. VII (Bonn, pp. 350–51), who calls Sfetigrad Σφετία, passage reprinted (with several mistakes in the Greek accents) by Radonić, *Djuradj Kastriot Skenderbeg* (1942), p. 220, from E. Darkó's edition, vol. II (1923), pp. 119–21. *Cf.* Raynaldus, *Ann. eccl.*, ad ann. 1449, no. 10, vol. XVIII (1694), pp. 359–60, after Barletius, *Vita*, 1st ed., Rome, 1509, bk. V, fols. LII^v–LXIV; ed. Zagreb, 1743, pp. 115–42. The Venetians had been encouraging the Turks to overrun Albania "ad ruinam illius Scandarbeghi perfidi" (from the commission, issued on 27 June, 1448, to Andrea Venier, who was being sent on a mission "ad partes Albanie," of which the text may be found in the Sen. Secreta, Reg. 18, fols. 14^r–15^r [16^r–17^r], published by Ljubić, *Listine*, IX, 269 ff., and reprinted by Radonić, *op. cit.*, pp. 10–13). *Cf.* Ljubić, *op. cit.*, IX, 274–76, 282–85, 289–90. There is a brief sketch of events in Giuseppe Capra, "Skanderbeg nel quadro della politica pontificia," *Bollettino della Badia greca di Grottaferrata*, XXII (1968), 71–84.

[77] Gelcich and Thallóczy, *Diplomatarium*, no. 284, p. 473, dated 13 August, 1450, reprinted in Radonić, *Djuradj Kastriot Skenderbeg*, pp. 19–20. If the garrison maintained its courage and kept faith, it was believed that Croia could hold out against the Turks. *Cf.* Gelcich and Thallóczy, *Dipl.*, no. 286, p. 485, and Radonić, *Acta et diplomata*, I, no. 234, p. 525 (see, below, note 81). *Cf.* Chalcocondylas, bk. VII

May (1450) Murad II arrived with his army under the walls of Croia. He had cannon cast of metal he had brought in his baggage train; at least two cannon were employed against the fortress walls, the larger of which could shoot stone balls weighing 400 pounds.[78] The cannon did their work well, but the Turks could not penetrate the battered walls. Scanderbeg and a determined force of some 8,000 men, among whom were Slavs, Italians, Germans, and others, kept descending from the nearby heights he knew so well, making day-and-night attacks upon the Turks. While the Venetians of Scutari sold food to the Turks, those of Durazzo aided the Albanians.[79]

In early October Scanderbeg, who had grown discouraged, offered Croia to the Venetians, threatening to cede it to the Turks if they did not accept it. Toward the end of the month, however, Sultan Murad raised the five months' siege, doubtless fearing the advent of winter, and began his eastward march toward Adrianople. The Senate finally decided upon a reply to Scanderbeg. Affirming their affection for him and their desire for the independence of his state, the Venetians proposed to send an envoy to Murad to try to arrange a "concord" between Scanderbeg and the Turks. The Senate had been overjoyed to hear that the sultan had raised the siege *re infecta*; as for the offer of Croia, however, they thanked Scanderbeg, but they preferred that he keep the fortress. Venice had more than enough territory already.[80]

(Bonn, p. 354); Angiolello, *Hist. turchesca*, ed. Ursu (1909), p. 16. Having made his peace with the Venetians, Scanderbeg was seeking their assistance against the Turk in the spring of 1449, offering to pay the Republic the annual *census* of 6,000 ducats which he had to pay the Porte, but the cautious Senate declined "to separate him from the adherence and recommendation of the Turk" (Ljubić, *Listine*, IX, 302, and Radonić, *Djuradj Kastriot Skenderbeg*, pp. 18–19, doc. of 21 April, 1449, from Senato Mar, Reg. 3, fol. 111^r [112^r]).

[78] Gelcich and Thallóczy, *Dipl.*, no. 284, pp. 473–74, dated 15 August, 1450; Radonić, *Djuradj Kastriot Skenderbeg*, pp. 19–20. Barletius says that the sultan had ten cannon cast, of which four were capable of hurling stones of more than 600 pounds (*Vita*, 1st ed., Rome, 1509, bk. VI, fol. LXXII; ed. Zagreb, 1743, pp. 161–62).

[79] On the Turks' receiving flour and fresh bread from the "count" of Scutari, a Venetian official, see Sime Ljubić, *Commissiones et relationes venetae*, I (Zagreb, 1876), no. I, p. 4 (in the Monumenta spectantia historiam slavorum meridionalium, vol. VI), reprinted in Radonić, *Djuradj Kastriot Skenderbeg*, no. 35, p. 20; Iorga, *Notes et extraits*, III, 260–61, note, extracts from Stefano Magno's *Annali veneti*. There was always a fair amount of trade with Moslems, especially the Egyptians. Trade with the Turks also was probably inevitable in military contraband as well as in foodstuffs and luxuries. Although Scanderbeg had until lately been hostile to Venice as a result of a war he had waged with the Republic over the territory of Dagna (Danja), peace was now supposed to obtain between him and the Venetians, who had promised him an annual pension of 1,400 ducats in return for his cession of Dagna to them (Ljubić, *Listine*, IX, 282–83; Radonić, *op. cit.*, pp. 15–16, *Pax cum magnifico Scanderbego et aliis dominis Albanie*, dated 4 October, 1448). With Croia under siege, it would seem to have been very poor policy for the Venetians in Scutari to supply food to the Turks. They were doubtless well paid for it. According to Barletius, *Vita*, 1st ed., Rome, 1509, bk. VI, fol. LXXVII^v; ed. Zagreb, 1743, p. 175, ". . . multitudo ingens mercatorum ex proximis Venetorum oppidis cum annona, vino, oleo, et omnis generis cibariis in castra [i.e., Turcica] quotidie confluebat."

Occasionally papal licenses were granted to trade with the infidels (especially for foodstuffs) as when on 8 May, 1451, Pope Nicholas V granted two merchants of Barcelona the right to trade in Saracen ports, but excluded arms, iron, wood, and similar materials from the permitted objects of trade (Arch. Segr. Vaticano, Reg. Vat. 396, fol. 248). Supplying flour and fresh bread to the Turks while they held Croia under siege in 1450 was of course a very different affair, but we may nevertheless note here that a few years later, on 26 February, 1455, King Alfonso V of Portugal received papal permission to trade in foodstuffs and other wares with the Saracens, subject to the customary prohibition on "ferramenta, lignamina, funes, naves seu aliquarum armaturarum genera" (Reg. Vat. 440, fols. 22^r–23^r). Numerous grants of such permission have been published (e.g., Iorga, *Notes et extraits*, IV, pt. 1, no. 19, pp. 38–40, confirmation by Nicholas V on 10 May, 1447, of such a concession made by Martin V to the Genoese "usque ad centum annos").

[80] Sen. Mar, Reg. 4, fol. 22^r; Iorga, *Notes et extraits*, III, 260, doc. dated 23 November, 1450; "Ser Augustino de Renerio, provisori Dagni: Recepimus literas vestras datas die XIIII Octobris et per eas intelleximus quid vobis dici fecit Scandarbegus per illum abbatem de volendo dare nobis civitatem Croye quodque nisi eam acceptemus, necesse erit quod ipsam det in manibus Turchi, etc., volumus igitur et vobis cum nostro consilio Rogatorum [i.e., the Senate] respondentes mandamus quatenus si ad vos redierit vel suprascriptus abbas vel alius nomine predicti Scandarbegi pro tali materia sibi dicere debeatis quod quecunque vobis dici fecit intelleximus et sicut per experientiam potuit intellexisse sincere amavimus ipsum Scandarbegum et status sui conservationem caram habuimus paratique eramus mittere ad presentiam Imperatoris Turchorum pro concordando eum cum sua Excellentia et omnia facere pro paterna nostra affectione que statui suo et conservationi eius expedientia esse credebamus quodque quando sensimus Turchum ab obsidione Croye re infecta se levasse plurimum letati sumus, quia non dubitabamus ipsum Scandarbegum dominium suum recuperaturum esse, debere et per consequens sibi non debere deficere aliquam bonam concordiam et compositionem cum predicto domino Turchorum.

"Ad oblationem vero quam nobis facit de loco Croye, ei plurimum regratiamur et dicimus quod re vera ad huiusmodi rem nunquam ullam inclinationem sive intentionem habuimus nobisque gratius est quod ipse eam teneat et possideat quam nos qui nunquam res alienas desideravimus, sed nobis nostra satis superque sunt. Et eum hortamur ad viriliter agendum et manutenendum civitatem illam sicut hucusque

Croia had been saved. The Turk had left none too soon. Scanderbeg was absolutely at the end of his resources. The independent Albanian highlanders, who resented Scanderbeg's efforts to achieve some measure of centralization in the country (at their expense, to be sure), had made accords with Murad as though he were their deliverer from oppression. After the Turkish withdrawal the highland chiefs continued their opposition to Scanderbeg's resumption of authority over Albania. Their chances of success looked good. He had lost all the country except Croia, and now lacked even the means to maintain the loyal garrison which had kept the fortress from the invader. While the highland chiefs looked forward to his ruin, Scanderbeg went to Ragusa, armed with papal letters urging the rector and the council of the city to help him, and the following February (1451) the Ragusei informed Nicholas V that by their financial assistance Scanderbeg had been enabled both to hold Croia and even to regain a good part of his territory.[81]

Scanderbeg had fought bravely and emerged from it all brilliantly. His heroism caught the imagination of Europe. Ambassadors and assistance were sent to him from Rome and Naples, Hungary and Burgundy. Croia was rebuilt, Christians everywhere looked upon its lord as their champion against the Turks. Scanderbeg now entered into especially close relations with King Alfonso of Naples, who still talked of a crusade; he recognized the king's suzerainty over Albania in a treaty dated at Gaeta on 26 March, 1451.[82] They got along very well to-

fecit, quoniam nos omnes eius statum et bonum rerum suarum successum iocundissime et leto animo audiemus.

"Vos vero, provisor noster, in omnem eventum non impediatis de occurentibus inter dominum Turchum et predictum Scandarbegum, sed neutralis stetis sicut hucusque fecistis: De parte 90, de non 7, non sinceri 5." There is a careless transcription of this text in Valentini, *Acta Albaniae veneta*, XX (1974), no. 5,634, pp. 272–73.

As early as 12 September (1450), when it appeared likely that "concord" would be re-established between Scanderbeg and the Turks, "quia dictus Imperator [Turchorum] non posset habere Croyam," the Venetians had become anxious that peace should be made rather "by the intervention of our Signoria than otherwise" (Sen. Mar, Reg. 4, fol. 8^v).

[81] Gelcich and Thallóczy, *Dipl.*, no. 286, p. 485, and Radonić, *Acta et diplomata*, I, no. 234, p. 525: The Ragusan ambassador, sent to Pope Nicholas V on 27 February, 1451, was to inform his Holiness that ". . . a questo anno proxime passato [1450], siando venuto el dicto Turcho et el suo fiolo sopra el dicto Schanderbegh et soi colligati cum potentissimi exerciti et aparati de guerra, et siando accordati col detto Turcho li detti colligati de Schandarbegh, habiando esso Schandarbegh perso tutto lo suo paese, salvo che la città de Cruya, la qual esso Turcho non potè vincere per l'asperità de monti et fortezza del dicto luogo et per la fidelità delle persone che erano in essa, che se portono virilmente, se deliberò el dicto Turcho levarse dalla dicta citade de Cruya. E così, siando levato et partito dalle parte d'Albania, dubitandose esso Schandarbegh, si per la rebellion delli soi subditi, si per l'accordio delli soi colligati fatto col detto Turcho, non poter tegnir et conservar la dicta citade de Cruya et rehaver el suo paese, maxime perchè non haveva con che substentar le guardie et diffese, poste per lui in la detta cittade, se partì esso Schandarbegh da casa sua et venne ala detta città de Ragusa cum lettere della vostra sanctitade, per le qual essa sanctitade exhortava el rezimento della detta cittade ad aiutar et subvenir el detto Schandarbegh." The text has been printed again by Radonić, *Djuradj Kastriot Skenderbeg*, p. 21. The Ragusan documents are also given in summaries (*régestes*) in B. Krekić, ed., *Dubrovnik (Raguse) et le Levant*, Paris and The Hague, 1961, this one being no. 1209, p. 370.

The pope had just granted the plenary indulgence of the jubilee to Ragusei, who (fulfilling the spiritual conditions) would give to the Knights of Rhodes one-third of what they would have had to spend by remaining the required two weeks in Rome to visit the four principal churches at least once daily (Arch. Segr. Vaticano, Reg. Vat. 392, fols. 98^r–103^v, esp. fols. 98^v–99^r, dated 6 November, 1450). Since the privilege covered Ragusei dwelling in the entire Levant, the sums would probably be great. The purpose of the Ragusan embassy to Nicholas V was to have the grant to the Knights revoked and to secure it for the defense of Ragusa itself, but the pope was offered a fourth of the amount in question. In this connection the ambassador was to inform the pope of the multiple expenses which Ragusa had to undergo against the Turks (subsidies to Hungary, the subvention of Scanderbeg, their own fortifications, etc.).

On Scanderbeg's success against Murad II, *cf.* also Chalcocondylas, bk. VII (Bonn, pp. 351, 353–55), who thinks the siege of Croia in 1450 preceded the second battle of Kossovo in 1448; Barletius, *Vita*, 1st ed., Rome, 1509, bk. VI, fols. LXXII–LXXXIV; ed. Zagreb, 1743, pp. 161–91, where Murad's death is erroneously placed during the siege of Croia: *Croia morte Amurathis tunc nobilior quam Argos olim Pyrrhi morte reddita*! (*edd. citt.*, fol. LXXXIV; p. 191). Raynaldus, *Ann. eccl.*, ad ann. 1450, no. 15, vol. XVIII (1694), pp. 370–71, follows Barletius; K. Hopf, "Griechenland im Mittelalter," in J. S. Ersch and J. G. Gruber, eds., *Allgemeine Encyklopädie*, vol. 86 (repr. II), p. 125; F. S. Noli, *Geo. Castrioti Scanderbeg*, New York, 1947, pp. 42–44, 199–200, an odd but useful book; Babinger, *Maometto*, pp. 105–6; and see esp. Pall, "Marino Barlezio," in *Mélanges d'histoire générale*, ed. Const. Marinescu, II (Bucharest, 1938), 208–9, where most of the relevant sources are collected for the five months' siege of Croia in 1450. Unfortunately Athanase Gegaj, *L'Albanie et l'invasion turque au XVe siècle*, Louvain and Paris, 1937, pp. 77–80, had not discovered that the "Anonymous of Antivari" was an invention of Biemmi, nor had Noli even by 1947.

[82] Francesco Cerone, "La Politica orientale di Alfonso di Aragona," in *Arch. stor. per le province napoletane*, XXVIII (1903), 171–81, and *cf.* Radonić, *Djuradj Kastriot Skenderbeg*, nos. 37–38, pp. 22–24. Besides Alfonso V's assertion of suzerainty over Scanderbeg and the latter's father-in-law George Arianiti Topia Golem Comninović, whom we have already noted as one of the most important of all the Albanian chieftains (see above, note 26), Alfonso also gave recogni-

gether as lord and vassal, and two years after the king's death Scanderbeg described to Giovanni Antonio del Balzo Orsini, prince of Taranto, supporter of the renewed Angevin claim to Naples and archenemy of Alfonso's son Ferrante, the great benefits he had received "from that holy and immortal king of Aragon, whom neither I nor any of my vassals can recall without tears . . . , because you must remember that the counsels, subsidies, favor, and holy works of that angelic king were what preserved and defended me and my vassals from the oppression and cruel hands of the Turks, our enemies and those of the Catholic faith. . . ."[83]

Although Europe did well to honor Scanderbeg, one of the greatest soldiers and most honorable men of his time, his exploits were but an assurance of things hoped for, and for generations no one was to see the diminution of Turkish power in the Balkans. The worst was yet to come. On Wednesday morning, 3 February, 1451, Sultan Murad II died of apoplexy in a drunken debauch, bringing to a close his reign of thirty years. Both Ducas and Chalcocondylas have paid tribute to his love of peace and justice, indicating that his victories had been virtually thrust upon him by Christian treachery and provocation,[84] an appraisal one need hardly accept, but certainly Murad II was less cruel and cold-blooded than his more famous son, Mehmed II, who assumed control of the Ottoman empire for the second time. And now Mehmed's elders and advisers were no longer in a position to restrain his ambition to attempt the conquest of Constantinople.

Whatever the hopes and fears of leaders and lesser folk in the East, there was as yet a normality to the routines of life. One still made the pilgrimage to the Holy Sepulcher in Jerusalem. A French noble, for example, a subject of good King René [of Naples, duke of Anjou], wanted to make the pilgrimage, but he had arrived in Venice with six or eight companions some six days after the departure of the regular pilgrim galley. After a long wait on the lagoon, he addressed a petition to the Senate, which responded favorably to his request on 21 September, 1450. The unnamed noble was allowed to sail with the Beirut galleys, which were leaving shortly for the Levant. The skippers of the galleys were directed to provide him with passage "at a reasonable price, as has often been done for similar persons in the same situation."[85]

The Beirut galleys went by way of Modon (or Coron), Crete, and Cyprus. Their route lay beyond the usual reach of the Ottoman arm during this period. The Venetian Archives, however, also take us to the sultan's court, as when on 8 July, 1451, the Doge Francesco Foscari issued a commission to Lorenzo Moro, who was being sent as an envoy to Mehmed II. Moro was instructed

> that since one of our citizens, Alemanto, a factor of the nobles, the late Francesco and his brother Marco Ruzini, has had to do with the magnificent lord Nerio Acciajuoli, who is lord of Thebes and Athens, from whom the Ruzini should receive a large sum of money, as you will be fully informed . . . , we wish that since the aforesaid lord Nerio is a subject of the . . . most serene

---

tion as vassals to the Ducagin family, to Simon Zenevisi, and to some of Simon's subjects in 1454–1455 (Const. Marinesco, "Alphonse V, roi d'Aragon et de Naples, et l'Albanie de Scanderbeg," *Mélanges de l'École roumaine en France*, Paris, 1923, esp. pp. 48–53, 83–84, 88 ff., and *cf.* pp. 112–13). On the family of the Arianiti, besides F. Babinger's monograph on *Das Ende der Arianiten*, Munich, 1960, note the genealogical table in Hopf, *Chron. gréco-romanes* (1873), p. 535. On 13 April, 1451, Pope Nicholas V granted Scanderbeg the plenary indulgence of the jubilee year in a special bull honoring his heroic services to Christendom and taking some account of the needs of Albania (Arch. Segr. Vaticano, Reg. Vat. 397, fols. 4^v–6^r, and *cf.* Radonić, *op. cit.*, pp. 24–25).

[83] V. V. Makušev, in the *Monumenta historica slavorum meridionalium*, II (Belgrade, 1882), p. 121, reprinted by Radonić, *Djuradj Kastriot Skenderbeg*, p. 120, doc. dated at Croia on 31 October, 1460. The letter was written to Prince Giovanni of Taranto in answer to a letter which Scanderbeg had received from him dated 10 October (Makušev, II, 118–20, reprinted by Radonić, *op. cit.*, p. 119–20), protesting against the assistance Scanderbeg was rendering to King Ferrante in the Aragonese-Angevin war (1459–1464) for the throne of Naples (*cf.* Pastor, *Hist. Popes*, III [5th ed., London, 1949], 74–75, 120–23, 338, and *Gesch. d. Päpste*, II [repr. 1955], 60, 95–97, 262). Scanderbeg says he will stand by Ferrante, who will win in the end, his affairs being far less grievous than those of Scanderbeg himself when in 1450 the Turks besieged Croia, "la quale hogi è de Casa de Aragona et de Soa Maestà" (Makušev, *op. cit.*, II, 122). Prince Giovanni's protest was directed against Scanderbeg's sending an Albanian cavalry force into southern Italy in September, 1460, on which see below, Chapter 8, p. 231.

[84] Ducas, chap. 33 (Bonn, p. 228); Chalcocondylas, bk. VII (Bonn, p. 375); *cf.* Sanudo, *Vite de' duchi*, in *RISS*, XXII (1733), col. 1137E; Babinger, *Maometto*, pp. 107–8; and Jos. von Hammer-Purgstall, *Geschichte des osmanischen Reiches*, I (repr. Graz, 1963), 489 ff.

[85] Arch. di Stato di Venezia, Senato Mar, Reg. 4, fol. 3^v.

emperor of the Turks, you should make every possible effort both with the most serene emperor himself and in other quarters, as shall seem advisable to you, to see that the said lord Nerio or his heirs, if he is not alive, should pay this debt to our aforesaid nobles and make them quiet and content, as is just and proper. And, in short, you must give them all possible assistance to achieve the settlement of this debt.[86]

This text provides a glimpse into the affairs of Nerio II Acciajuoli, duke of Athens (1435–1439, 1441–1451), who may or may not have been dead by July, 1451. If he was, it seems unlikely that his widow Chiara Giorgio (Zorzi) and her lover Bartolommeo Contarini,[87] Venetians both, were any more concerned than Nerio had been to make a "just and proper" settlement of the debt to the Ruzini.

Another document from the Venetian series Senato Mar gives us some insight into conditions in the south Moreote village of Xereni, where the serfs were obliged to serve the Correr *secundum leges et consuetudines despotatus*. In recent years we have been cautioned to regard the term "despotate" as denoting the dignity of an office rather than the territorial circumscription ruled by a despot. Nevertheless, a resolution of the Senate (dated 10 June, 1452), which takes us to within a year of the fall of Constantinople—the great tragedy of Nicholas V's reign—shows us that by now "despotate" had come to mean a Greek principality, in this case the principality of the Morea:

. . . The nobles Pietro Correr, son of the late Ser Giovanni, and Filippo Correr, son of the late Ser Paolo, procurators, possess in the dependencies of Coron and Modon a certain village [*caxale*] called Xereni, the inhabitants of which, as serfs [*pariche*, *πάροικοι*], are held to serve our said nobles, and because they do not obey [these manorial dictates], our Signoria wrote on 17 July of last year to the government of Modon and Coron that they must force the . . . serfs to serve the said nobles according to the laws and customs of the despotate. And yet, because the said letter was not written by this council [the Senate], it has not been put into due effect. The motion is [therefore] carried that the aforesaid letter must be sent again to the . . . authorities of Modon and Coron and to their successors, and by the authority of this council it is ordered that they must observe it and have it observed inviolably.[88]

Despite the inevitable fact of change, the social process varied little from earlier generations. The pilgrim galleys still sailed to the Holy Land, the Latin lordlings in Greece did not pay their debts, and the Greek peasantry resisted manorial service to absentee landlords in Venice. The Turks had often invaded the Morea, but they had not yet conquered it. The Aegean islands had been harried since long before the memory of anyone then living, but the Venetians were still dominant. There was a sameness to life in the Levant, as Greeks and Latins, Turks and Mamluks fought with one another, and went their own ways.

Nicholas V went his own way also. It is pointless to defend him against the charge that through most of his reign he neglected the well-being of eastern Christendom in his preoccupation with his own affairs and those of Italy. In 1450, to be sure, he welcomed at the Curia an Ethiopian embassy, of which little is known, although its purpose may have been to effect "une entente avec les chrétiens d'Occident . . . en vue de se retourner contre l'ennemi commun: l'Islam."[89] Certainly there is something to be said on Nicholas's behalf. The Greeks remained obdurate schismatics. There was little or no co-operation, against the Turks, between the imperial government of Constantinople and the corrupt court of the "empire of Trebizond," with which the Genoese had been at constant odds for more than thirty years.[90] Although the policy of the government in Constantinople was cautious and conciliatory, even in the capital itself the Grand

---

[86] Sen. Mar, Reg. 4, fol. 67v [68v].

[87] *Cf.*, K. M. Setton, *Catalan Domination of Athens, 1311–1388*, rev. ed., London, 1975, pp. 209–10, and *Los Catalanes en Grecia*, Barcelona, 1975, pp. 181–83, 195–96.

[88] Sen. Mar, Reg. 4, fol. 128r [129r], doc. dated 10 June, 1452. On the title "despot," see Lucien Stiernon's review of Božidar Ferjančić, *Despoti u Vizantiji i južnoslovenskim Zemljama* [*Despots in Byzantium and the Lands of the South Slavs*], Belgrade, 1960, in the *Revue des études byzantines*, XXI (1963), 291–96.

[89] C.-M. de Witte, "Une Ambassade éthiopienne à Rome en 1450," *Orientalia Christiana periodica*, XXII (1956), 286–98, and in this connection note Lucas P. Desager, "Lettre inédite du patriarche copte Jean XI au pape Nicolas V (1450)," in the *Mélanges Eugène Tisserant*, II (1964), 41–53 (Studi e testi, no. 232).

[90] Iorga, *Notes et extraits*, I, 243–44, 268, 272 ff., 304, 464, 476–77, and III, 68, 132, 216–18, 234–36, 245–47, 259; Wm. Miller, *Trebizond*, London, 1926, pp. 77–80, 91–94; Nicolas Bănescu, "Le Conflit entre Gênes et l' empire de Trébizonde à la veille de la conquête turque (1418–1449)," *Studi bizantini e neoellenici*, V (1939), 4–10 (Atti del V Congresso internazionale di studi bizantini [Rome, 1936]).

Duke Lucas Notaras, one of the most upright and distinguished of the Byzantine grandees, was alleged to entertain a preference for "the Turkish turban to the Roman tiara."[91]

Even on the verge of disaster, however, the pope seems to have been almost as much concerned about the petty lapses of the Latins resident in Greece as he was about the whole freedom of Orthodoxy from the oncoming Turkish tide. On 6 September, 1448, the pope wrote the Dominican inquisitor and the provincial in Greece:

> It has come to our attention that in places which are subject to Catholics in Greece, many Catholics under pretext of the Union [of 1439] are improperly going over to the Greek rites. We have been most astonished at this, and do not cease to be so, not knowing what it is that has shifted them from the custom and rites in which they were born and brought up. Although the rites of the Eastern Church are laudable, it is not permissible to intermingle the rites of the Churches, and the sacrosanct Council of Florence has never permitted it. Therefore we, in whom despite our unworthiness God has placed the care of all such things, desiring to provide a quick remedy lest the evil keep spreading, do strictly enjoin upon each and both of you . . . that by the apostolic authority you entirely forbid the commingling of rites in all the aforesaid places when you visit them in accordance with your duty, and if it should be necessary, you are to summon the secular arm to assist you.[92]

In a most interesting and revealing communication to the Emperor Constantine XI, dated 27 September, 1451, the pope acknowledged the receipt of a letter from the emperor and commended the Byzantine envoy who had brought it. The issue was the difficulty and inexpediency of promulgating in Constantinople the Florentine decree of Union (of 6 July, 1439). In firm but courteous tones the pope remonstrated with Constantine for the failure publicly to announce and to abide by the decree. "Receive, then, my dearest son, what we are about to say as from a loving heart . . . addressing you truly and freely." Stressing the necessity of ecclesiastical unity and authority for salvation and peace among Christians, the pope said there was one Church, of which Rome was the head: "Outside the Church there is no salvation: he who was not in Noah's ark perished in the flood. . . ." Turkish depredation and domination in Greece were the judgment and visitation of God for the sin of schism, "which arose in the time of Pope Nicholas I and of which Photius was the author" [in the ninth century]. According to the pope, this schism had now endured for almost five centuries,[93] and during all this time the Church of Constantinople had failed in its obedience to Rome. All the world had watched Constantine's brother, the Emperor John VIII, accept by his signature and by his presence the decree of Union at Florence. Now a dozen years had passed; the union had not been put into effect; and the same excuses were always advanced to explain the unwarrantable delay. "The Greeks cannot really assume that the Ro-

[91] Ducas, chap. 37 (Bonn, p. 264): "*κρειττότερόν ἐστιν εἰδέναι ἐν μέσῃ τῇ πόλει φακιόλιον βασιλεῦον* Τούρκων *ἢ καλύπτραν Λατινικήν*." The traditional rendering of the quotation is misleading. *Cf.* H. Evert-Kappesowa, "La Tiare ou le turban," *Byzantinoslavica*, XIV (1953), 245–57: "Je préfererais voir régner dans cette ville le turban du Sultan à la tiare du Pape" (*ibid.*, p. 245). Notaras's alleged statement means, however, that he would prefer to see a wearer of the turban dominant in Constantinople rather than one who wore a western "hat;" use of the word "tiara" implies an anti-papal sentiment which Notaras doubtless felt, but which Ducas does not specifically attribute to him. It is unlikely that Notaras made any such statement although it presumably represents the view of some of the anti-unionist party in the capital.

[92] Raynaldus, *Ann. eccl.*, ad ann. 1449, no. 10, vol. XVIII (1694), p. 359. On 2 October, 1457, Calixtus III was to appoint Simon de Candia, a Dominican, as *inquisitor heretice pravitatis in provincia Grecie* (Reg. Vat. 449, fols. 163ᵛ–164ʳ, by mod. stamped enumeration).

[93] Nicholas V was separated from the time of Photius by almost six centuries, and his interpretation of the Photian schism was a simplification of history which had been current in the West from the close of the eleventh century. Throughout the later years of his reign Pope Nicholas I (858–867) refused to acknowledge the imperial deposition of the Patriarch Ignatius in Constantinople and the election of Photius as his successor in November and December, 858 (see J. B. Bury, *History of the Eastern Roman Empire*, London, 1912, chap. VI, esp. pp. 192–99). Subsequently, in a reversal of political fortune, Photius was condemned at the fourth (pro-Ignatian) Council of Constantinople (869–870), the decrees of which were later rejected by Pope John VIII (880) when Rome and Constantinople became reconciled after Photius's second elevation to the patriarchal throne. Toward the end of the eleventh century, however, the anti-Photian council of 869–870 became recognized as oecumenical in the West, largely by accident, because certain of its canons condemning simony and lay interference in ecclesiastical affairs were very useful to the Gregorian reformers, and by this time there was renewed schism between Rome and Constantinople (from in fact 1009). After the council of 869–870 had been recognized by Rome as the Eighth Oecumenical Council, there developed the western "legend" of the second Photian schism (according to Fr. Francis Dvornik, *The Photian Schism*, Cambridge, 1948, *passim*, esp. pp. 309–49), but Photius seems to have remained in communion with Rome throughout his second patriarchate.

man pontiff and the whole Western Church . . . are so bereft of intelligence as not to realize why in this delay the excuses keep coming—they understand, but they bear with it. . . ." There was no alternative, it would seem, to the Greeks' observing the full import of the Florentine decree (to which they had given an almost unanimous acceptance in 1439). "But if, however, you refuse to maintain this decree among your people," the pope informed Constantine, "you will compel us to make provisions which look both to your salvation and to our honor."[94]

It was an unfortunate answer, but its lack of charity must be set against the background of centuries of embittered relations between the Greeks and Latins. Nicholas V could not know that the Byzantine empire was now to survive no longer than its emperor, whose days were severely numbered. The pope had had problems and aspirations, fears and hopes of his own. On 19 January, 1449, he had proclaimed a jubilee for the following year,[95] when untold thousands of pilgrims flocked to Rome, to be decimated by a violent outbreak of the plague and to witness the pope's timorous flight (on 15 July) from the city whither he had called them.[96] During the jubilee, however, the needs of Hungary were kept in mind, and a special indulgence was proclaimed for the archbishops, bishops, abbots, and other prelates, the barons, knights, nobles, and lesser folk of the kingdom, with special mention of John Hunyadi. They were dispensed from the visit to Rome and the principal basilicas of the city to earn the plenary remission of sins, because they had to defend the country against the Turks, "so that the rest of its inhabitants . . . might be able to live in sweet security without fear and peril. . . ."[97]

---

[94] Raynaldus, *Ann. eccl.*, ad ann. 1451, nos. 1–2, vol. XVIII (1694), pp. 375–76, where the letter is dated 11 October (1451); Hofmann, *Epistolae pontificiae*, III (1946), no. 304, pp. 130 ff., who dates the letter 27 September, and prints the Greek version from Sp. P. Lampros, *Palaiológeia kaì Peloponnesiaká* [in Greek], IV (Athens, 1930), 49–63, where it is dated (p. 63) "the fifth day before the Kalends of October" [27 September]. On the background see Gill, *The Council of Florence* (1959), pp. 377–80, and note Pastor, *Hist. Popes*, II, 248–51, and *Gesch. d. Päpste*, I (repr. 1955), 601–3, who approves of the pope's reply. *Cf.* Nicholas V's later recollection of his (sparse) assistance to the emperor after Constantinople had fallen, as given by Manetti in the so-called "testament" of the pope (*Vita Nich. V*, III, in *RISS*, III-2, col. 953); Ducas, chap. 36 (Bonn, pp. 252–53); Critobulus, *De rebus gestis Mechemetis II*, I, 39, ed. K. Müller, *FHG*, V-1 (Paris, 1870), 84a, and ed. V. Grecu, Bucharest, 1963, p. 109, who says the pope had planned to send thirty ships. According to Critobulus, *loc. cit.*, Nicholas did send three galleys (see, below, pp. 117–18), which arrived in Constantinople on 20 April, and made their way heroically through the Turkish blockade (for the sources see Müller, *loc. cit.*, note). In Reg. Vat. 393, fols. 124r–125r, I find a reservation to the church of Coron made in favor of the eleven-year-old Venetian Antonio Andrea Venier, dated at Rome on 29 April, 1450, which was hardly the way to provide for the Latin Church in Greece, and *cf.* fols. 125r–127v.

[95] Raynaldus, *Ann. eccl.*, ad ann. 1449, no. 15, vol. XVIII (1694), pp. 362–63.

[96] Pastor, *Hist. Popes*, II, 74–104, much revised in *Gesch. d. Päpste*, I (repr. 1955), 433–62; for the flight of Nicholas V from Rome, see the latter work, I, 445, and *cf.* the English edition, II, 86–88; note the *Ann. Forolivienses*, ad ann. 1450, in *RISS*, XXII (Milan, 1733), col. 223E; on the jubilee, *cf.* Raynaldus, *Ann. eccl.*, ad ann. 1450, nos. 1 ff., vol. XVIII (1694), pp. 363 ff.

[97] Raynaldus, *Ann. eccl.*, ad ann. 1450, no. 6, vol. XVIII (1694), pp. 365–66, bull dated 12 April; Pastor, *Hist. Popes*, II, 244, and *Gesch. d. Päpste*, I (repr. 1955), 597–98. The Hungarians could gain the benefits of the indulgence by paying a three days' visit to the cathedral church of Grosswardein (Hungarian Nagyvárad, Rumanian Oradea; *cf.*, below, Chapter 5, note 44) as well as to certain other designated churches and by contributing one-half the sum which the journey to Rome and the required fifteen days' residence in the city would have cost them. There is no statement in the bull that the sums thus paid by the faithful in Hungary would be used for the crusade.

The bull is contained in one of the many registers in the charge of Pietro da Noceto (Petrus de Noxeto), who was a *nobilis et notabilis persona* in his time (see the Sen. Secreta, Reg. 19, fols. 92, 94v, docs. dated 10 and 12 November, 1451). Pietro da Noceto was the secretary of Nicholas V and Calixtus III, and good friend and correspondent of Aeneas Sylvius. On 14 November, 1451, Pietro, "papal secretary and citizen of Venice," was granted a letter patent (from the Doge Francesco Foscari) according him and his brother Jacopo the right to purchase Venetian state bonds and to own property in Venice (R. Predelli, ed., *Regesti dei Commemoriali*, V [1901], bk. XIV, no. 210, p. 66). Pietro was living in the Vatican palace in December, 1453 (Eugène Müntz, *Les Arts à la cour des papes pendant le XVe et le XVIe siècle*, 3 vols., Paris, 1878–82, I, 131).

For the bull in question, see the Arch. Segr. Vaticano, Reg. Vat. 391, fols. 252v–254r: "Indulgentia pro nobilibus et prelatis Regni Hungarici . . ." [in margin of fol. 252v]: ". . . pro parte . . . nobilis viri Johannis de Hunniad, gubernatoris ac rectoris . . ." [fol. 253r]. A special bull dated 12 April, 1450, was sent to honor Hunyadi and extend to him and his family "omnium peccatorum suorum remissio plenaria" under the same conditions as those noted above (*ibid.*, fol. 249). (The enumeration of folios in this register is somewhat confused, owing to corrections having been made at several points.) The registers of Nicholas V contain a number of such special letters of indulgence for the jubilee (*cf.* those to King Casimir IV of Poland in Reg. Vat. 393, fols. 17r–18r, dated at Rome, 7 December, 1450; to Queen Margaret of England, *ibid.*, fols. 122v–123r, dated at Assisi, 5 October, 1450; and to Duke Philip of Burgundy, *ibid.*, fols. 360v–361v, dated at Rome, 1 February, 1451, "anno, etc., MCCCCL, Kal. Februarii, [pontificatus nostri] anno quarto").

A dilettante rather than a scholar, petulant sometimes and irritable, Nicholas V was withal an honest man. Fair-minded in his dealings with others, devoted to his friends, and a great lover of fine books and fine buildings, he was a generous and appreciative patron of the arts, who spent the great sums which accrued from the jubilee of 1450 in beautifying the city of Rome and stocking his newly founded Vatican Library with hundreds of manuscripts in handsome bindings, often of crimson velvet with silver clasps. The munificence of his gifts to Giannozzo Manetti, who wrote his biography,[98] as well as to Niccolò Perotti, Francesco Filelfo, Lorenzo Valla, Poggio Bracciolini, Pier Candido Decembrio, and other devotees of humanism evoked the admiration (and the ire) of the Christian world.

One of the favorite popes of Gregorovius, Nicholas V's love of learning has endeared him to most scholars who have studied his career. Always shrinking from physical violence and timid of the hurly-burly of life, Nicholas showed himself during the eight years of his pontificate one of the boldest planners and most indefatigable builders in the long history of Rome. He restored many famous churches and palaces, rebuilt the Acqua Vergine and improved the city's water supply, repaired and fortified the bridges over the Tiber, rebuilt the walls of the Aurelian circuit, and finally proposed under the influence of Leone Battista Alberti a stupendous reconstruction of the Leonine City with a new S. Peter's, a vast papal palace, ecclesiastical and other residences, broad squares, streets, colonnades, porticos, and shops—a complete renovation of the Vatican. Although these last projects awaited the papacy of Julius II, with other ideas and other architects, for their partial fulfillment, Nicholas accomplished a remarkable amount of building in the time at his disposal, ridding Rome of hundreds of thousands of tons of rubble and débris, and unfortunately pillaging the Coliseum, the Forum, and other ancient sites for blocks of marble and travertine as if they were mere quarries. He helped destroy the old Rome as he began the creation of a new one.

Nicholas V stands at the close of the middle ages and the beginning of a new era. In the abdication of Felix V (on 7 April, 1449), the conciliarists' candidate for the papal throne, Nicholas triumphed over the last of the anti-popes. With his own hands he crowned Frederick III of Hapsburg emperor in an elaborate ceremony in S. Peter's, the last of the imperial coronations in Rome (on 19 March, 1452). After a half-dozen years of satisfying achievement as pontiff and as patron of scholars, painters, and architects, however, Nicholas found the year 1453 beginning badly for him with the revelation of a reckless conspiracy against his authority engineered by Stefano Porcari, who was put to death with some of his followers in January.[99] The conspiracy made a profound impression upon the pope as it did upon all Italians; he was saddened by the event, made rather moody and suspicious; he suffered a good deal from the gout, and was often unable to grant audiences for weeks at a time. He was ill-prepared, mentally and physically, for the blow which was about to fall.

[98] *Cf.* Francesco Pagnotti, "La Vita di Niccolò V scritta da Giannozzo Manetti," *Archivio della R. Società romana di storia patria*, XIV (1891), 411–36.

[99] Pastor, *Hist. Popes*, II, 218–39, and append., nos. 12–16, pp. 507–19, and *Gesch. d. Päpste*, I (repr. 1955), 274–91, and append., nos. 43–49, pp. 832–40. On the coronation of Frederick III, see Franz Wasner, "Tor der Geschichte: Beiträge zum päpstlichen Zeremonienwesen im 15. Jahrhundert," *Archivum historiae pontificiae*, VI (1968), 142–53, with the text (of the papal ceremonial diarist) describing the event, and on Frederick's career, Alphons Lhotsky, "Kaiser Friedrich III.: Sein Leben und seine Persönlichkeit," in his *Aufsäftze und Vorträge*, II (1971), 119–63, cited above in Chapter 2, note 56.

4. THE SIEGE AND FALL OF CONSTANTINOPLE (1453)

FROM THE TIME of his second accession to the throne of his fathers in February, 1451, Sultan Mehmed II set about the fulfillment of his dream of conquering Constantinople. The extent of his ambition was not yet clear, however, and his personality still remained an enigma to his contemporaries. In April the Emperor Constantine XI sent one Andronicus Leontaris on an embassy to Venice, Ferrara, Rome, and Naples, to seek assistance against the new sultan whose youth, it may have been assumed, would provide both Greeks and Latins with an opportunity to proceed against the Turks. By early June (1451) Leontaris had reached Venice, where one of his objectives becomes clear when on the eleventh the Senate declined to accept an impost which the emperor wished to impose on merchandise as well as a restriction which he proposed to place on the export of hides from Constantinople.[1] There is no word of emergency in the documents, and Leontaris apparently brought no warning of especial danger to the enfeebled Byzantine "empire."[2]

Toward the end of June (1451) the Venetian Senate was itself preparing to dispatch two embassies to the East. Lorenzo Moro was going as the Republic's envoy to Mehmed II, and Francesco Venier as envoy to Ibrahim Beg, the Gran Caramano in Asia Minor, the chief Levantine enemy of the Ottomans. Ibrahim Beg thought he saw an opportunity in Mehmed's accession, and was already endeavoring to stir up trouble in Germiyan and the coastal emirates of Aydin and Menteshe.[3] Lorenzo Moro was, however, to console Mehmed for the loss of his father and to congratulate him upon his attainment of the sultanate. He was also to preach peace to Mehmed, especially in Bosnia, and (among other assignments) to press for payment of the debt which Nerio II Acciajuoli (a Turkish subject for all that he was *dominus Stives et Sitines*) owed the commercial firm and family of the Ruzini. Upon leaving the Ottoman court, Moro was to proceed to Constantinople, where he was directed to lodge a vigorous remonstrance against the unlawful activities of Constantine XI's brothers in the Morea. The Despot Thomas Palaeologus had occupied *plura territoria* in the region of Modon, as the Despot Demetrius had done in that of Nauplia, Venetian territories of course, and the numerous protests of the Signoria had never produced anything but "bona verba sine ullo effectu." Moro was to make it clear to the emperor that Venice would no longer tolerate the occupation of lands and the usurpation of rights belonging to her citizens and her subjects. Furthermore, since Moro would doubtless reach Constantinople before Andronicus Leontaris's return home, Constantine might ask him about the Venetian response to the requests which Leontaris had made to the Signoria in the emperor's name. If this should happen, Moro was to reply in the words of the senatorial resolutions (of 11 and 12 June), of which he was given a copy, to the effect that the emperor's proposals were not in accord with the "antiquissima amicicia et

---

[1] Arch. di Stato di Venezia, Senato Mar, Reg. 4, fol. 58v [59v]. N. Iorga, *Notes et extraits pour servir à l'histoire des croisades au XVe siècle*, IV (Bucharest, 1915), no. XXVII, p. 46, gives Constantine XI's letter, dated 10 March, 1451, recommending Andronicus Leontaris to Borso d'Este, marquis of Ferrara. On Leontaris's mission to Rome, see Joseph Gill, *The Council of Florence*, Cambridge, 1959, pp. 377–80, and on Constantine XI's desire to tax foreign merchandise (the *sansaria* or *sensaria*), note Iorga, *Notes et extraits*, III (Paris, 1902), 254–55.

[2] After the departure of Amadeo VI of Savoy in June, 1367 (see above, Volume I, Chapter 13), the Byzantine government gradually lost its tenuous hold upon the southwestern shore of the Black Sea until, during (and even before) the reign of Bayazid I, the "empire" was reduced almost to the city of Constantinople. Byzantine authority extended northward again, however, as a result of the territorial concessions made to Manuel II by the Emir Suleiman and thereafter by Sultan Mehmed I, Bayazid's sons, as one result of the civil wars of the Ottoman succession which followed the Turkish defeat at Ankara in late July, 1402. From the time of Mehmed I's final victory (in 1413) until the beginning of the year 1453 the Byzantines seem to have remained in precarious and intermittent control of the coastline of the Black Sea as far north as Mesembria, and of the northern shore of the Sea of Marmara as far west as Heraclea. The subject is obscure, and the sources are sketchy, but see the attempt at clarity in A. Bakalopulos, "Les Limites de l'empire byzantin depuis la fin du XIVe siècle jusqu'à sa chute (1453)," *Byzantinische Zeitschrift*, LV (1962), 56–65.

[3] For whatever his evidence may be worth, note the account in Ducas, *Hist. byzantina*, chap. 34 (Bonn, pp. 233–37; ed. Vasile Grecu, *Ducas, Istoria turco-bizantină [1341–1462]*, Bucharest, 1958, pp. 291, 293, 295), of the attempts by the Gran Caramano and even of Constantine XI to profit by Mehmed's accession to the throne.

benivolentia" which had long existed between the Palaeologi and the Republic.[4]

Francesco Venier was to begin his eastward voyage, along with Moro, in the galley *Barbadica*, which would take him to Candia in Crete. Another galley would convey him to Cyprus, to the court of King John II, who had been at bellicose odds with the Gran Caramano. Venier was to learn the details of the "differentiae et discordiae existentes inter [Johannem] et dictum Caramanum," and thereafter make his way into Caramania to try to make peace between Ibrahim Beg and the Cypriotes. On his return journey he was to report the extent of his success (or failure) to John in Cyprus. By the end of December, 1451, Venier was still somewhere in Caramania or Cyprus (or en route home), and the Senate wrote the colonial government in Crete to locate him and speed him on his way to the Adriatic "et inde ad presentiam nostram." Hard pressed by both the Caramano and the soldan of Egypt, John had been unable to pay his debts to Venice and to various Venetians. Peace with the Caramano would free John from one source of expense and apprehension, and then perhaps he would settle some of the claims against him. This was the purpose of Venier's mission, as far as the documents reveal it.[5] His commission contains no reference to the Turks. If Ibrahim Beg suggested that Venice make a move against Mehmed II, Venier very likely replied that he was without authority to deal with the proposal, but he would convey to his government any message that Ibrahim Beg might wish to send. As far as Venice was concerned, the Turks seemed hardly more of a problem than they had been for decades.

All the while, however, Mehmed II was nurturing the passion of his boyhood—the taking of Constantinople—which was to win him the title of Conqueror (*Fātiḥ*), and make him the outstanding prince and the pride of the house of Osman. It was incumbent upon Mehmed, as a warrior for Islam (*ghāzī*), to begin his reign with a victory over the infidel Christians. What worse enemy was there than the Greek emperor and the Greek metropolis, now set in the very midst of Ottoman territory, the cynosure of Orthodox churchmen, Frankish crusaders, and Latin merchants? When he became sultan, Mehmed could pursue his ambition without let or hindrance from anyone, including the grand vizir, Khalil Pasha, who was reputedly a friend of the Greeks. For months the attention of Europe now became fastened on the shores of the Bosporus, and indeed few events have caused more contemporary excitement or subsequent speculation than the Ottoman siege and seizure of Constantinople.

Another Byzantine embassy was sent to Venice, Florence, Rome, "et ad alias potentias Italie," but now with solemn warnings of the extent of Turkish preparations. The Venetians agreed to send supplies to Constantinople, but they wanted to see what the other powers would do before promising the Greeks armed assistance. They reminded the ambassador that the war in Lombardy, to which we shall come in the next chapter, restricted their earnest desire to help the threatened city. They addressed strong pleas, nevertheless, to Pope Nicholas V and the Curia Romana for quick action against the Turk, promising to make every contribution they could to such an enterprise. The Senate voted to send appeals also to the Emperor Frederick III as well as to the kings of Aragon and Hungary, imploring their aid as necessary for the salvation of Constantinople, "informing them furthermore of the provisions that we have taken on our part, and stating that these are by no means sufficient for so great a crisis."[6]

---

[4] Sen. Mar, Reg. 4, fols. 67^r–68^r [68^r–69^r], Moro's commission dated 8–9 July, 1451, and *cf.* fol. 58^v [59^v]. The instructions which Moro received with reference to Leontaris's embassy were couched in the following terms: "Verum si forte per eius Majestatem tibi fieret ulla mentio de capitulis que a nobis petiit pro parte sue Serenitatis spectabilis dominus Andronicus Leondari orator suus, volumus ut responsiones per nos factas capitulis antedictis et unicuique eorum honestare et iustificare debeas cum illis verbis que in predictis responsionibus, quarum copiam tibi dari fecimus, continentur, et aliter sicut prudentie tue expediens visum fuerit, procura[re] que animum suum contentum et satisfactum reddere" (*ibid.*, fol. 68^r [69^r]).

[5] On Venier's embassy to the Gran Caramano in 1451, see Sen. Mar, Reg. 4, fols. 53^v [54^v], 54^r [55^r], 60^r [61^r], 66^v [67^v], 68 [69], 98^r [99^r], and Sen. Secreta, Reg. 19, fol. 50^r. *Cf.* Louis de Mas Latrie, *Documents nouveaux servant de preuves à l'histoire de l'île de Chypre* (from the *Mélanges historiques*, vol. IV [Paris, 1882]), Famagusta: Éditions l'Oiseau, 1970, p. 370, and Geo. Hill, *A History of Cyprus*, III (Cambridge, 1948), 508–13.

[6] Sen. Secreta, Reg. 19 [1450–1453], fol. 122^r, dated 14 February, 1452 (Ven. style 1451); *ibid.*, fol. 170^r, 16 November, 1452; fol. 184^v, 4 February, 1453 (Ven. style 1452), a letter of the Senate to Nicholas V; and fol. 187^r, 24 February, 1453 (Ven. style 1452). These documents are all published in Enrico Cornet, ed., *Giornale dell'assedio di Costantinopoli di Nicolò Barbaro, P.V.*, Vienna, 1856, append., pp. 67–73. The original numbering of the folios

During the spring and summer of 1452 Mehmed II built Rumeli Hisar (the "Rumelian Castle," as it was later called) on the European side of the Bosporus across the strait from Anadolu Hisar, where the ruins of the older fortress of Bayazid I "the Thunderbolt" still stand. At this point Europe is less than half a mile from Asia. Here the two castles have stood as guardians of the seaway for more than five centuries, great stretches of walls and towers still remaining of Rumeli Hisar (restored in 1953), which the sultan's forces constructed in a mere three or four months, "the most heavily fortified castle in the world," says Critobulus, "and the most secure and famous."[7] Mehmed spent months in gathering together a great army and a fleet. According to Sphrantzes, he formally declared war on Byzantium as early as June, 1452, when he sent an army to invade the environs of the city, capturing the suburban residents. After the completion of Rumeli Hisar on 31 August, he left there and himself appeared under the walls of the Greek capital on a tour of inspection of its fortifications, departing thence for Adrianople on 3 September.[8] The imperial government in Constantinople spent the winter taking such measures as it could to prepare the city for the coming assault. Walls were strengthened, and at least one abandoned foss or moat reopened from the Golden Horn.

One Niccolò Barbaro, a Venetian ship's physician or surgeon, who got caught in the city during the siege, has left us a full account of the disaster in the dated, day-to-day entries in his diary. Aid came to the city, as Barbaro

---

in this important register corresponds to the modern enumeration.

During the course of the siege the Venetian Senate authorized issuance of a commission to Bartolommeo Marcello (on 8 May, 1453) to go to Constantinople to confer with Constantine XI and with Mehmed II "ut per omnem modum procuremus pacificare Teucrum cum sua Serenitate [imperiali] et ponere statum suum in tranquilo et securitate . . ." (Sen. Mar, Reg. 4, fol. 187 [188], published by Sime Ljubić, *Listine*, X [Zagreb, 1891], 7). The Venetians claimed "iura et iurisditiones" in the Greek capital, as indeed they had, and Marcello was to explain to Mehmed: "Deliberavimus armare aliquas galeas et naves nostras et eas mittere Constantinopolim non pro inferendo guerram vel novitatem sue Excellentie sed ut associent galeas nostras Romanie et ipsam civitatem tanquam rem nostram deffendant et conservent, quod cum omni iure et honestate facere possumus . . ." (Reg. cit., fol. 187^v [188^v]). Marcello's mission was quite impossible. He did go to Constantinople later on, however, as we shall see, but under very different circumstances. *Cf.* in general R. Guilland, "Les Appels de Constantin XI Paléologue à Rome et à Venise pour sauver Constantinople (1452–1453)," *Byzantinoslavica*, XIV (1953), 226–44, who adds little new, and M. M. Alexandrescu-Dersca Bulgaru, "L'Action diplomatique et militaire de Venise pour la défense de Constantinople (1452–1453)," *Revue roumaine d'histoire*, XIII-2 (1974), 247–67.

[7] Michael Critobulus, *De rebus gestis Mechemetis II*, I, 11 (ed. K. Müller, *Fragmenta historicorum Graecorum* [*FHG*], V-1 [Paris, 1870], pp. 60b–62a; ed. V. Grecu, *Critobul din Imbros: Din domnia lui Mahomed al II-lea, anii 1451–1467*, Bucharest, 1963, pp. 53, 55). Laonicus Chalcocondylas, bk. VIII (Bonn, pp. 380–81; ed. E. Darkó, II-2 [Budapest, 1927], 147), says the castle was built in three months. Both Ducas, *Hist. byzantina*, chap. 34 (Bonn, pp. 241–46), and the Pseudo-Sphrantzes, III, 3 (Bonn, pp. 233–34; ed. V. Grecu, *Geo. Sphrantzes . . . în anexă Pseudo-Phrantzes . . .* , Bucharest, 1966, p. 378), describe the armed conflict with the Greeks while Rumeli Hisar was being constructed. *Cf.* Geo. Sphrantzes, *Chron. minus* (*PG* 156, 1060BC; ed. Grecu [1966], p. 94), and Barbaro, *Giornale*, ed. Cornet, pp. 1–2, also published by P. A. Dethier, in *Monumenta Hungariae historica*, XXII, pt. 1 (1872), pp. 694–95; and for other sources, see Müller's notes, *op. cit.*, pp. 60–61. Ducas, chap. 34 (Bonn, p. 246, lines 20–21), states that the castle was erected, mounted with cannon capable of shooting stone balls weighing more than 600 pounds, and garrisoned with a troop of 400 men "all within four months." Actually 5,000 workmen built the castle from 15 April to 31 August, 1452 (*cf.* F. Babinger, *Maometto il Conquistatore*, Turin, 1957, p. 128), on which note the Ottoman historian Khoja (Sa'd-ad-Dīn) Efendi, in N. Moschopoulos, "Le Siège et la prise de Constantinople selon les sources turques," *Le Cinq-Centième Anniversaire de la prise de Constantinople* (in *L'Hellénisme contemporain*, 2 ser., VII, 1953), pp. 31–32, and E. J. W. Gibb, trans., *The Capture of Constantinople from the Tāj-ut-tevārīkh* [*"The Diadem of Histories"*], *written in Turkish by Khōja Sa'd-ud-Dīn*, Glasgow, 1879, p. 12.

There is a brief account of the siege by Admiral Luigi Fincati, "La Presa di Costantinopoli (Maggio 1453)," in the *Archivio veneto*, XXXII (1886), 1–36, old but still useful, and a recent book on the subject by Sir Steven Runciman, *The Fall of Constantinople (1453)*, Cambridge, 1965. An invaluable anthology of the sources, with Italian translations and extensive notes, has lately been published by Agostino Pertusi, *La Caduta di Costantinopoli*, 2 vols., Verona, 1976: I, *Le Testimonianze dei contemporanei*, and II: *L'Eco nel mondo*. Professor Pertusi's introductions to the wide range of (often improved) texts he has selected for inclusion are most useful. I want to thank him for sending me these two volumes, for although this chapter was written long before their publication, I have had time to study them and make appropriate additions to the notes before the present volume went to the press.

[8] Sphrantzes, *Chron. minus* (*PG* 156, 1060C; ed. Grecu, pp. 94, 96); Pseudo-Sphrantzes, III, 3 (Bonn, pp. 234–35; ed. Grecu, pp. 378, 380); *cf.* Chalcocondylas, bk. VIII (Bonn, p. 381, lines 10–11; ed. Darkó, II, 147, lines 18–19). Barbaro, *Giornale*, ed. Cornet, p. 2; ed. Dethier, pp. 695–96, says that Mehmed II came with 50,000 men. I have of course followed Sphrantzes' *Chron. minus* rather than the *Chron. maius* of the Pseudo-Sphrantzes [the late sixteenth-century compiler Macarius Melissenus-Melissurgus], which dates Mehmed's departure from Rumeli Hisar on 28 August and his withdrawal to Adrianople on 1 September.

indicates, haphazardly and even unintentionally, with the arrival of some Venetian, Genoese, and Cretan ships, mostly merchantmen. Among the defenders whom chance thus brought to the scene were Gabriele Trevisan, commander of two light Venetian galleys, and Giacomo Coco, skipper of a Venetian galley from Trebizond, both of whom were to play important roles in the coming struggle. With the approach of winter Isidore of Kiev, the "cardinal of Russia," arrived on the Bosporus with two hundred men, including gunners and crossbowmen, both to defend the city and to commemorate the union of the Churches, as was done on 12 December (1452) in a ceremony which, to the disgust of the anti-unionists, Constantine XI attended in Hagia Sophia. The beginning of Barbaro's diary is full of these matters, with a record of the men and vessels available for defense when the Turks closed in upon the city.[9]

Toward the end of January the Genoese soldier Giovanni Giustiniani-Longo arrived with two large galleys. He had on board 400 men in armor (κατάφρακτοι) enrolled in Genoa, besides his sailors, and had recruited

[9] The sources differ as to the number of western ships still in the harbor of Constantinople by the spring of 1453 (*cf.* Müller's note to Critobulus, I, 24, 3, in *FHG*, V-1, p. 73). In any event Barbaro, *Giornale*, ed. Cornet, pp. 3–4; ed. Dethier, pp. 698–99, shows that two large Venetian galleys from Caffa got safely through the narrow strait under Rumeli Hisar despite cannonading from its walls, and under Girolamo Morosini arrived on 10 November, 1452 (E. Pears, *The Destruction of the Greek Empire*, London, 1903, p. 217, is quite wrong). Three large Venetian (merchant) galleys under Alvise Diedo also came from Tana to Constantinople, where their escort of two light galleys, commanded by Gabriele Trevisan, had already put into port from Venice with orders to return home within ten days of the arrival in Constantinople of a galley coming from Trebizond (Leonardo of Chios, in Philip Lonicer, *Chronica turcica*, II [Frankfurt am Main, 1578], 91, mentions the five galleys [he calls them triremes] of Diedo and Trevisan). On 4 December, 1452, the galley from Trebizond sailed safely into the harbor of Constantinople under Giacomo (or Jacopo) Coco, who was to play a heroic role in the defense of the city (Barbaro, ed. Cornet, p. 4; ed. Dethier, pp. 699–700).

Although the Venetian captains and merchants were anxious to depart, the Emperor Constantine XI detained them to help defend the city, in which he was aided by the intelligent and courageous Venetian bailie, Girolamo Minotto, who in mid-December won over the majority of the influential members of the Venetian colony in Constantinople, at a meeting of the Council of Twelve (*Conseio di Dodexe*) in the church of S. Maria, on which see Barbaro, ed. Cornet, pp. 8 ff. Trevisan was especially hard to convince. A literal-minded seaman, he had his orders, and was going to obey them, but he had to yield to a decision of the leaders among his compatriots in the city. According to the Venetian Senate, in a statement of 8 May, 1453, they had recently been informed "quod galee nostre viagii Romanie simul cum duabus galeis nostris subtilibus rettente fuerunt in Constantinopoli propter ea que divulgata erant de apparatibus sue Serenitatis [i.e., Mehmed II] terra marique ad expugnationem civitatis Constantinopolitane . . ." (Sen. Mar, Reg. 4, fol. 187^{v} [188^{v}], the commission issued to Bartolommeo Marcello and then canceled, referred to above in note 6).

There would seem to have been eight Venetian galleys participating in the Christian operations against the Turks. Nevertheless, Critobulus, I, 24, 3 (ed. Müller, p. 73b; ed. Grecu, p. 85), says there were six galleys (he calls them triremes, i.e., ships with three lengths of oars). A ninth Venetian ship escaped from the city under its skipper Piero Davanzo on 26 February, 1453 (Barbaro, ed. Cornet, pp. 13–14; ed. Dethier, pp. 717–18). According to Barbaro (see below), there were three Cretan ships in the harbor of Constantinople, as the Pseudo-Sphrantzes, III, 3 (Bonn, p. 238; ed. Grecu, pp. 382, 384), also notes in his "catalogue of ships:" "There were the following vessels—three from Liguria [Genoa], one from Iberian Castile . . . , [one] from Provence, and three from Crete, one coming from the city of Candia [Chandax] and the other two from Cydonia, all well equipped for warfare. . . ." (There were more than three Genoese ships in the harbor.) Leonardo of Chios, in Lonicer, *Chron. turcica*, II, 89, also mentions three Cretan ships. All ships being requisitioned by the emperor, their departure required a special license, which he would not grant. In November, 1452, however, eight Cretan ships engaged in the wine trade had come to Constantinople, six of which set sail with a northeast wind under cover of night on 26 February (1453), when Piero Davanzo made his own illegal exit from the harbor. Barbaro says that by the defection of these seven ships 700 men were lost to the defense (ed. Cornet, p. 13).

On 26 January, 1453, Giovanni Giustiniani-Longo arrived in Constantinople with two Genoese ships, while the previous October Isidore of Kiev, cardinal of Sabina, had arrived in the city with his two hundred men, intent upon church union (Barbaro, ed. Cornet, p. 3; ed. Dethier, p. 698). While Barbaro puts the unionist ceremony in Hagia Sophia on 13 December (1452), Ducas, chap. 36 (Bonn, p. 255), dates it on the twelfth, as do Isidore and Leonardo of Chios.

Isidore was accompanied by Archbishop Leonardo of Mytilene, a native of the island of Chios; both Isidore and Leonardo of Chios are important sources for the siege and fall of Constantinople. They had come in a Genoese ship, which had waited at Chios for another ship on its way to Caffa, both ships being commandeered by the Byzantine government (*cf.* Ducas, chap. 36, ed. Bonn, pp. 252–53). Barbaro mentions them together several times. Leonardo's account of the siege and fall of Constantinople (in the form of a letter dated 16 August, 1453, to Pope Nicholas V) has also been published in the *Patrologia graeca*, vol. 159 (1866), cols. 923–41. It became widely known through the Italian version in Francesco Sansovino's *Historia universale dell'origine et imperio de' Turchi* (1568) as well as in his *Annali turcheschi* (1571–73), which latter work is the basis of the "anonymous" Greek chronicle (Bibl. Apost. Vaticana, Cod. Barberini gr. 111) published by G. Th. Zoras, *Chronicle* a number of others in Chios and Rhodes, making his total force about 700 men. Critobulus reports a rumor that Giustiniani had been invited to come to Constantinople by the emperor, who was said to have promised him the island of Lemnos if the Christians proved successful in their opposition to the Turks. Ducas describes the splendid reception accorded Giustiniani, and adds that the cession of Lemnos was guaranteed by a chrysobull.[10] The hardy Genoese soldier was put in general charge of the city's defense, receiving the rank of *protostrator*. On 2 April the great iron chain set in wooden blocks was extended across the mouth of the Golden Horn to prevent the entry of enemy ships into the inner harbor.[11] The young sultan and the Ottoman army were just reaching the environs of the capital.

Mehmed II is said to have left Adrianople for the shores of the Bosporus on Friday, 23 March;[12] Critobulus states that the march took

---

of the Turkish Sultans . . . [in Greek], Athens, 1958, pp. 79 ff., and *cf.* Zoras, *On the Conquest of Constantinople* [in Greek], Athens, 1959, pp. 105 ff. On this so-called chronicle, note Gyula Moravcsik, in the *Byzantinische Zeitschrift*, XLIV (1951), 430–34, and *Byzantinoturcica*, 2 vols., Berlin, 1958, I, 296–99, and see esp. Elizabeth A. Zachariadou [now Mrs. N. A. Oikonomides], *The Chronicle of the Turkish Sultans (in the Barberini Greek MS. 111) and the Italian Original* [in Greek], Thessaloniki, 1960. Miss Zachariadou's book cleared up a long-lived puzzle as to the date (after 1573) and the major source (Sansovino) of the Greek chronicle. Although a better (but incomplete) text of Leonardo of Chios, with an Italian translation, is now available in Pertusi, *Caduta di Costantinopoli*, I (1976), 120–71, it has seemed best to retain the references to the edition in Lonicer's *Chronica turcica*, and check the latter text against that given by Pertusi. Likewise I have retained the references to Cornet's edition of Barbaro's diary of the siege, Martène and Durand's edition of Tedaldi, etc., and checked these and other texts against those in Pertusi, adding occasional references to the latter.

Barbaro (ed. Cornet, pp. 20, 36) indicates that nine or ten of the larger ships in the harbor guarded the iron chain stretched on buoys across the mouth of the Golden Horn. Of these ships five were Genoese, three from Crete, one apparently from Ancona, and one belonged to Constantinople. Barbaro also states that there were seventeen ships in the inner harbor (ed. Cornet, p. 20). An exact count of the vessels available for the defense of the harbor and city is impossible (the emperor had at least five galleys). Leonardo of Chios, in Lonicer, *Chron. turcica*, II, 91, line 22, says there were thirty ships in the harbor; Jacopo Tedaldi, a Florentine merchant who was in the city throughout the siege, gives thirty-nine (Edm. Martène and Urs. Durand, eds., *Thesaurus novus anecdotorum*, I [Paris, 1717, repr. New York, 1968], cols. 1820–21). On Tedaldi (or Tetaldi), note the rather speculative article of M.-L. Concasty, "Les 'Informations' de Jacques Tedaldi sur le siège et la prise de Constantinople," *Byzantion*, XXIV (1954), 95–110. Tedaldi's text may also be found in P. A. Dethier, ed., *Monumenta Hungariae historica*, XXII, pt. 1 (Istanbul, 1872), pp. 891 ff. For the opening of the foss or moat from the Horn, see Barbaro, ed. Cornet, p. 15; ed. Dethier, *ibid.*, pp. 721–22.

[10] Critobulus, I, 25 (ed. Müller, *FHG*, V-1, p. 74; ed. Grecu, pp. 85, 87); Ducas, chap. 38 (Bonn, pp. 265–66); Barbaro, *Giornale*, ed. Cornet, p. 13; ed. Dethier, p. 717, who indicates that Giovanni Giustiniani's whole force amounted to 700 men; Pseudo-Sphrantzes, III, 3 (Bonn, pp. 241–42; ed. Grecu, p. 386). Giovanni was a member of the family of the Giustiniani-Longhi, long resident on the island of Chios (*cf.* Ch. Hopf, *Chroniques gréco-romanes*, Berlin, 1873, repr. Brussels, 1966, p. 517, geneal. tables). On his arrival in Constantinople, see the preceding note and Leonardo of Chios, in Lonicer, *Chron. turcica*, II, 87. While Critobulus, *loc. cit.*, states that Giustiniani arrived with 400 men in armor, Leonardo says there were only 300 Genoese with him on the landward wall on the last day of the siege (*op. cit.*, p. 93, and Pertusi, *Caduta di Costantinopoli*, I [1976], 148), although he had earlier stated that Giustiniani had come "cum . . . armatis circiter quadringentis" (*ibid.*, p. 132).

The Longhi were a separate branch of the Giustiniani, the latter being actually an association of families (*albergo*) formed in March, 1364, which had adopted the family name of the Giustiniani for various political and social reasons. Such an alliance or union of families, which enabled the smaller to compete with the larger kinship groups, was a peculiarly Genoese institution (*cf.* Philip P. Argenti, *The Occupation of Chios by the Genoese*, I [Cambridge, 1958], 134, 332–34). At one time or another there were 120 families in the *albergo* of the Giustiniani (Argenti, ed., *Hieronimo Giustiniani's History of Chios*, Cambridge, 1943, p. 387).

[11] Chalcocondylas, bk. VIII (Bonn, p. 384, lines 6–13; ed. Darkó, II, 150, lines 10–17); Barbaro, *Giornale*, ed. Cornet, p. 15; Ducas, chap. 38 (Bonn, p. 268, lines 2–6); Pseudo-Sphrantzes, III, 3 (Bonn, p. 238, lines 6–8; ed. Grecu, p. 382, lines 26–28); Sa'd-ad-Dīn, *Tāj-ut-tevārīkh*, trans. E. J. W. Gibb, p. 24. The chain was employed only five times as part of the city's defenses (in 717–718, 821, 969, 1203, and 1453); see the detailed account of R. Guilland, "La Chaine de la Corne d'Or," in the Ἐπετηρὶς Ἑταιρείας Βυζαντινῶν Σπουδῶν, XXV (1955), 88–120. The well-known Turkish traveler Evliya Chelebi (d. 1669) wrote an account of the siege and fall of Constantinople in his *Seyāḥatname*, vol. I, chap. 10, which is less interesting as a historical source than as a record of the later Turkish tradition (and of Evliya's imagination). There is a French translation of the text by H. Turková, "Le Siège de Constantinople d'après le Seyāḥatname d'Evliyā Čelebi," in *Byzantinoslavica*, XIV (1953), 1–13, and *ibid.*, XVII (1956), 125–27. On the Turkish historians and (it would appear) their rather limited value for evidence on the siege and fall of Constantinople, see Alessio Bombaci, *La Letteratura turca*, 2nd ed., Florence and Milan, 1969, esp. pp. 351 ff., and Pertusi, *Caduta di Costantinopoli*, I (1976), pp. XLV–XLIX, 304 ff., and II, 254 ff.

[12] Feridun-Bey, *Münşaat-i-Selātin*, I (Istanbul, 1848), p. 239, cited by A. D. Mordtmann, *Belagerung u. Eroberung Constantinopels durch die Türken im Jahre 1453*, Stuttgart and Augsburg, 1858, p. 44, and K. Müller, note on Critobulus, I, 23, 1, in *FHG*, V-1, p. 71. The texts of Critobulus and Sphrantzes (see the following notes) are better reconciled, however, if we assume that Mehmed left

ten days;[13] and Sphrantzes gives 4 April as the date of his arrival.[14] Barbaro informs us that on 5 April, between eight and nine o'clock in the evening, Mehmed encamped with 160,000 men two and one-half miles from the western, landward walls which went in a majestic line from the Golden Horn to the Sea of Marmara. On the sixth he came to within a mile of the walls; it was a Friday, and after the prayer the siege began.[15]

The taking of Constantinople by the Turks is one of the notable events of the fifteenth century, and Mehmed II's eight-week investment of the city is one of the most famous sieges in history. It marked also the start of a new era in warfare, for the Turks employed huge cannon on a more extensive scale than that to which Europeans had hitherto been accustomed. Mehmed began operations by establishing a number of batteries along the landward or west walls. He pitched his own tent opposite the "military" Gate of S. Romanus [now Sulukule Kapisi],[16] as the old Pempton ("fifth military gate"?) was apparently called during the period of the siege. It is located in the valley of the river Lycus. The janissaries were for the most part encamped between the sultan's tent and the walls, opposite the northern stretch of the Mesoteichion ("middle wall"), the most vulnerable part of the whole range of the westward fortifications. Details of the siege, as given in the contemporary accounts, are sometimes not easy to reconcile with the topography of the area. The "Mesoteichion" was apparently well to the south of the Gate of Charisius [the modern Adrianople Gate, Edirne Kapi]; at its northern end it descended into the Lycus valley at the Pempton, to which the name of S. Romanus seems to have been given by the time of the siege. The Gate of S. Romanus, properly so named, was a civil gate a bit farther south [now Top Kapi or "Cannon Gate"]. It took its name from a nearby church. The landward walls contained both "civil" and "military" gates, although this distinction is not to be found in the fifteenth-century texts. The civil gates, used by the public in time of peace, led into and out of the city over bridges which were removed upon the likelihood of attack. The landward approach to the city was protected by a high inner wall (the μέγα τεῖχος) and a lower outer wall (the προτείχισμα). Outside the lower wall was a broad walkway (περίβολος), shielded by a crenelated parapet, beyond which lay the foss or moat some sixty feet wide and twenty feet deep. The double walls and foss ran from the

Adrianople on 25 or 26 March. Details of some importance are provided by a rather late Russian account, *Povest' o sozdanii i o vziatii Tsaregrada*, first published by I. I. Sreznevskii, and translated into French by Ph. Ant. Dethier, as the "Anonymus Moscovita," in the *Mon. Hung. hist.*, XXII, pt. 1 (1872), pp. 1053–1122. Used freely by Chedomil Mijatovich, *Constantine [XI]*, London, 1892, pp. 150 ff., 233–34, the text has been reappraised by N. Iorga, "Une Source négligée de la prise de Constantinople," *Bulletin historique de l'Académie roumaine*, XIII (Bucharest, 1927), 59–128, in connection with a Rumanian version of the eighteenth century, and *cf.* Pertusi, *Caduta di Costantinopoli*, I (1976), 261 ff.

[13] Critobulus, I, 23, 1 (ed. Müller, *FHG*, V-1, p. 71b; ed. Grecu, pp. 83, 85).

[14] Sphrantzes, *Chron. minus* (*PG* 156, 1060D; ed. Grecu, p. 96, lines 10–11), and *cf.* the Pseudo-Sphrantzes, III, 3 (Bonn, p. 237, lines 7–9; ed. Grecu, p. 382, lines 10–11), who gives 2 April as the date of Mehmed's arrival, and also reckons the beginning of the siege from this date since he represents the Emperor Constantine as saying, on the evening of 28 May in his final address to the army and the Byzantine court, that Mehmed had then maintained his day-and-night investment and bombardment of the city for fifty-seven days (*ibid.*, III, 6, p. 273, lines 8–11; ed. Grecu, p. 416, lines 15–17). (Since my references to the Bonn edition of the Pseudo-Sphrantzes precede those I give to Grecu's edition, I have retained the chapter numbers in the Bonn edition, which Grecu has unnecessarily altered—the present reference, for example, appears in the latter's edition as bk. iii, chap. 8.) Sphrantzes' date (4 April) is in accord with that of Barbaro (*cf.* the following note).

[15] Barbaro, *Giornale*, ed. Cornet, p. 18; Ducas, chap. 36 (Bonn, p. 263, lines 8–10); Müller, note to Critobulus, I, 23, 1, in *FHG*, V-1, p. 71; and *cf.* Leonardo of Chios, in Lonicer, *Chron. turcica*, II, 86. According to Barbaro, Mehmed encamped at the first hour, which in late March and early April began between eight and nine P.M. Jacopo Tedaldi says that Mehmed came up to the city on 4 April, and that the siege began on the fifth (Martène and Durand, *Thesaurus novus anecdotorum*, I, cols. 1819 ff.).

[16] Critobulus, I, 23 (ed. Müller, *FHG*, V-1, pp. 71b–72a; ed. Grecu, pp. 83, 85); Pseudo-Sphrantzes, III, 3 (Bonn, p. 237, lines 9–10; ed. Grecu, p. 382, lines 11–12); Chalcocondylas, bk. viii (Bonn, p. 385, lines 3–5; ed. Darkó, II-2, 151, lines 5–7). Ducas, chap. 37 (Bonn, p. 263, lines 2–3), says that Mehmed pitched his tent opposite the Gate of Charisius (see below); from the rise on which the tent was placed it might in fact be described as "over against the Gate of Charisius" (κατέναντι τῆς πύλης τοῦ Χαρισοῦ). For topographical details of the city, see the excellent work of R. Janin, *Constantinople byzantine*, 2nd ed., Paris, 1964; the course of the siege can be followed on the large plan (no. i) in the portfolio of maps at the end of Janin's volume. Smaller plans are easily accessible elsewhere (ee. g., in Pears, *Destruction of the Greek Empire*, opp. p. 335; Steven Runciman, *The Fall of Constantinople [1453]*, Cambridge, 1965, opp. p. 89; and Pertusi, *Caduta di Costantinopoli*, I [1976], pp. 332–33). Other sources indicate that the sultan's tent—and his heaviest cannon—were set opposite the Gate of "S. Romanus" (see below).

Sea of Marmara north to the Golden Horn, a distance of four miles, but the great inner wall was in some disrepair. The outer wall, which was protected by the parapet and foss, had been kept up, and so the emperor and his Greek advisers decided to concentrate upon the defense of the outer wall, as had been done in 1422 when Murad II had attacked the city.[17] They lacked sufficient forces to man both walls.[18]

The sources give us various estimates of the size of Mehmed's army, ranging from Chalcocondylas's figure of 400,000 to Niccolò Barbaro's of 160,000,[19] and even the latter figure is doubtless too large. But the size of Mehmed's cannon was more fearsome than the numbers of his army. Three cannon seem to have been especially formidable, of which one had been cast at Adrianople by a Hungarian or Rumelian founder named Urban, who had first offered his services to the Byzantine government.[20] In February and March, 1453, this cannon had been drawn from Adrianople to Constantinople by sixty strong oxen yoked to thirty wagons with 200 men on either side to steady the huge gun (ἡ χωνεία) lest it fall. Fifty artisans went before the wagons with 200 workmen to construct or strengthen bridges and level off the roads, the whole operation requiring two months.[21] The awe-struck Critobulus has described in detail the methods employed by the founders in casting the large cannon—"this is a new invention of the Germans or the Celts," he says, "about a hundred and fifty years old or a little more, a very ingenious and well-contrived weapon."[22] According to Barbaro and Leonardo of Chios the largest cannon, whether Urban's or not, shot a stone ball 1,200 pounds in weight.[23] Such cannon balls more than seven feet in circumference are still to be seen in Istanbul, where the ruined walls in the area between the so-called palace of Porphyrogenitus or Tekfur Saray (Tekfursarayi̊)[24] and the Gate of Charisius, at the so-called S. Romanus Gate (the old Pempton) in the Lycus valley, and near the Triton ("third military gate"?) bear witness to the places where Mehmed concentrated his heaviest artillery. Tedaldi states that the Turkish cannon (*bombardes*) "fired from one hundred to one hundred and twenty shots each day, and [the siege] lasted fifty-five days; since one reckons that they used a thousand pounds of gunpowder every day, in

[17] Chalcocondylas, bk. VIII (Bonn, p. 384, lines 21–24; ed. Darkó, II-2, 150–51). On Murad II's siege in the summer of 1422, *cf.* above, p. 12, and Chalcocondylas, bk. V (Bonn, pp. 227–33; ed. Darkó, II-1 [Budapest, 1923], 6–12); C. N. Sathas, *Documents inédits relatifs à l'histoire de la Grèce au moyen âge*, I (Paris, 1880, repr. Athens, 1972), no. 79, pp. 120–21, 122, dated 26 August, 1422; and Ducas, chaps. 28 (Bonn, p. 189, lines 20–23), and 29 (p. 197, line 5). Murad II had also employed cannon against the city, but they did not achieve the devastating results of 1453. On the westward wall, see Ernest Mamboury, *Istanbul touristique*, Istanbul, 1951, pp. 430–31, and especially Janin, *Constantinople byzantine* (1964), pp. 265–83, and *cf.* pp. 347, 406, 420–21, where no mention is made, however, of the fifteenth-century confusion between the Pempton and the "civil" Gate of S. Romanus.

[18] Leonardo of Chios, in Lonicer, *Chron. turcica*, II, 93, 95, who believed that more effort should have been made to rebuild the damaged parts of the higher, inner wall, which he says ought to have been made a second line of defense.

[19] Chalcocondylas, bk. VIII (Bonn, p. 383, lines 13–15; ed. Darkó, II-2, 149, lines 21–22): λέγεται κτλ.; Barbaro, *Giornale*, ed. Cornet, p. 18: ". . . fo Turchi zerca zento e sesanta milia." *Cf.* Critobulus, I, 23 (ed. Müller, *FHG*, V-1, pp. 72b–73a; ed. Grecu, p. 85), 300,000; Ducas, chap. 39 (Bonn, p. 283), over 260,000, but elsewhere Ducas (chap. 38, p. 267, lines 6–7) says that eyewitnesses placed the number at more than 400,000. Leonardo of Chios, in Lonicer, *Chron. turcica*, II, 86, informs us that there were more than 300,000, among whom were 15,000 janissaries. Sphrantzes, *Chron. minus* (*PG* 156, 1060D; ed. Grecu, p. 96, line 14), puts the Turkish land forces at 200,000, but the Pseudo-Sphrantzes, III, 3 (Bonn, p. 240, lines 16–17; ed. Grecu, pp. 384, 386), at 258,000. Isidore of Kiev sets them at 300,000 (Pertusi, *Caduta di Costantinopoli*, I [1976], 68, 88, 94, 108), as does Henry of Soemmern (*ibid.*, II, 82; Iorga, *Notes et extraits*, III [1902], 310).

The author of the *Threnos* ("Lament") for Constantinople, ed. Adolf Ellissen, *Analekten d. mittel-und neugriechischen Literatur*, III (Leipzig, 1857), pp. 208–12, verses 749–79, gives a total of 217,000 men (147,000 from Europe, 70,000 from Asia), among whom were 15,000 janissaries (cited and correctly reckoned by Müller, note to Critobulus, *FHG*, V-1, p. 73). Tedaldi, in Martène and Durand, *Thes. novus anecdotorum*, I, col. 1820AB, states that Mehmed had 200,000 men; Adam de Montaldo, ed. Karl Hopf, in P. A. Dethier, *Monumenta Hungariae historica*, XXII, pt. 1 (1872), pp. 46–47, gives the total of Mehmed's forces "on land and sea" as 240,000. *Cf.* Feridun Dirimtekin, *İstanbul' un fethi* [*The Conquest of Constantinople*], Istanbul, 1949, pp. 64–72, and Pertusi, *Caduta di Costantinopoli*, I (1976), pp. XIX–XXI, LXXIII.

[20] Ducas, chap. 35 (Bonn, pp. 247–49); Chalcocondylas, bk. VIII (Bonn, pp. 385–86; ed. Darkó, II, 151–52).

[21] Ducas, chap. 37 (Bonn, p. 258). According to Chalcocondylas, bk. VIII (Bonn, p. 382, lines 20–21; ed. Darkó, II, 149, lines 6–8), the large cannon had to be drawn by seventy yokes of oxen and two thousand men. On the size of the various cannon, note Pertusi, I, pp. XXII–XXIII, LXXIV–LXXV, 229, and II, pp. 82, 84.

[22] Critobulus, I, 29–30 (ed. Müller, *FHG*, V-1, pp. 76a–78b; ed. Grecu, pp. 93, 95, 97). The Greek historians, like all their contemporaries, were stupefied by Mehmed's cannon, which they call by various names (ἑλέπολις, τηλεβόλος, πετροβόλος, βουμπάρδη, etc.).

[23] Barbaro, *Giornale*, ed. Cornet, p. 21; ed. Dethier, p. 736; Leonardo of Chios, in Lonicer, *Chron. turcica*, II, 88; see also Müller's notes to Critobulus, in *FHG*, V-1, pp. 76–77, and *cf.* p. 70. Urban's cannon is said to have exploded, killing its founder, and required recasting, but the sources are inconsistent in their reports.

[24] Tekfur means *kyrios*, "lord," and was the title by which the Turks referred to the Byzantine emperor.

fifty-five days they used up fifty-five thousand pounds, and there were also ten thousand culverins."[25] The informed visitor to Istanbul can easily reconstruct in his imagination some of the major episodes of the siege from the present-day condition of the landward walls. One may walk along the walls today from the fortress of the Seven Towers (Yedikule) on the south to the palace of Porphyrogenitus on the north in less than three hours even as he pauses to consult notes, to take photographs, or in the mind's eye to repeople with the attackers and defenders of five centuries ago what were empty fields and sparsely settled areas until the recent, rapid growth of the population of Istanbul.

During the first days of the siege Mehmed assigned his commanders to their posts—Zagan Pasha to the region of Pera and the eastern shore of the Golden Horn; Karaja Beg, to the landward walls north of the Charisius Gate; Ishak Pasha and Mahmud Pasha, the latter of whom was soon to become the grand vizir, to the walls between Top Kapi and the Marmara. Mehmed took his stand with Khalil Pasha at the northern end of the Mesoteichion opposite the so-called S. Romanus Gate, against which the three chief cannon were usually trained as probably the weakest section of the walls. The Ottoman fleet under the Bulgarian renegade Balta-oghlu kept a watch along the sea walls from the Golden Gate (at the south end of the landward walls) all the way along the Marmara coast to Neorion at the entrance to the Horn, where he was to break, if possible, the iron-and-wooden boom and force his way into the harbor.[26] Critobulus attests the success of Mehmed's constant cannonading of the Mesoteichion, and says that he filled the foss with stones, wood, earth, and other débris to facilitate the approach to the great breaches appearing in the walls.[27] Barbaro locates for us the four chief batteries which were established before Tekfur Saray on the north, the Pegé (modern Silivri Kapi) on the south, and the Charisius and S. Romanus Gates in the center; it is clear that both sides centered their best efforts on the S. Romanus, "la più debel porta de tuta la tera."[28] Here Mehmed placed the cannon which

---

[25] Tedaldi, in Martène and Durand, *Thesaurus novus anecdotorum*, I, col. 1820BC.

[26] Critobulus, I, 27–28 (ed. Müller, *FHG*, V-1, pp. 75a–76; ed. Grecu, pp. 89, 91), who gives the fullest account of the disposition of the Turkish forces; Ducas, chap. 37 (Bonn, p. 263); Chalcocondylas, bk. VIII (Bonn, pp. 383–84; ed. Darkó, II, 149–50); Pseudo-Sphrantzes, III, 3 (Bonn, pp. 237–38; ed. Grecu, p. 382); and *cf.* N. Iorga, *Gesch. d. osman. Reiches*, II (Gotha, 1909), 19–21. The sources vary concerning the size of Mehmed's fleet no less than of his army, from well over 400 ships to 145, the smallest figure given by a western source again being that of Barbaro (the sources and figures are collected in Müller, note on Critobulus, I, 22, 2, in the *FHG*, V-1, p. 71). Barbaro, *Giornale*, ed. Cornet, p. 21; ed. Dethier, pp. 737–38, says: "La dita armada del Turco fo vele cento e quaranta cinque fra galie e fuste e parandarie e bergantini, ma ne iera galie dodexe compie, fuste grose ne iera da setanta in otanta, parandarie da vinti in vinti cinque, tuto el resto si iera bregantini." *Cf.*, *ibid.*, ed. Cornet, p. 24; ed. Dethier, p. 743.

According to Leonardo of Chios, Mehmed assembled from Asia Minor, Thrace, and Pontus some 250 vessels (which he calls *fustae*), including sixteen regular galleys (*triremes*) and seventy light galleys (*fustae*), the remainder being true fuste with a single bank of oars, *reliquae fustae unius banchoremis* (Pertusi, *Caduta di Costantinopoli*, I [1976], 136). Henry of Soemmern informs us that Mehmed's fleet was made up of 220 "galeae, inter parvas et magnas" (*ibid.*, II, 82; Iorga, *Notes et extraits*, III [1902], 310). Ducas, chap. 38 (Bonn, p. 268, lines 1–2), believed that the Turkish fleet consisted of 300 triremes (galleys), biremes (fuste), and transports. The fusta was a long, fast galley-like vessel with about two dozen oarsmen (see above, Volume I, p. 264, note 24, with refs.). It is often called a bireme by the Greek historians. The parandaria was a heavy transport, and the brigantine a light, fast boat, in larger models a favorite of the corsairs. It is interesting to note, however, that the Turkish historian 'Ashîk-Pasha-Zade says that Mehmed II had only seventy ships (N. Moschopoulos, in *Cinq-Centième Anniversaire de la prise de Constantinople* [*L'Hellénisme contemporain*, 2nd ser., VII, 1953], p. 28). In one passage Tedaldi gives the size of the Turkish fleet as about 110–128 galleys, galiots, fuste, and other vessels (Martène and Durand, *Thes. novus anecdotorum*, I, col. 1820C), and elsewhere as 240 "ships" (*nefs*), galleys, and galiots (*ibid.*, I, 1823DE). Although Tedaldi's account is useful, as that of an eye-witness, it is confused and confusing, as are the wildly differing estimates of the size of the Turkish fleet given in the various sources (Pertusi, I, p. LXXVI).

[27] Critobulus, I, 31 (ed. Müller, *FHG*, V-1, p. 79; ed. Grecu, p. 99). The cannon were doing so well that Mehmed is said to have stopped his engineers' efforts to cut passages under the walls as a needless expense (on the success of the cannon, *cf. idem*, I, 34, ed. Müller, pp. 80a–81b; ed. Grecu, p. 103). The mining operations continued, however (Pseudo-Sphrantzes, III, 3, ed. Bonn, p. 244; ed. Grecu, p. 388). Barbaro speaks of them in the *Giornale* almost to the very end of the siege (*cf. Giornale*, ed. Cornet, p. 41; ed. Dethier, pp. 782–84). The mines were dug, as Leonardo of Chios tells us, by "fossores, quos ex Novo Brodo [in southern Serbia] conduxerat magistros . . . [Theucrus, i.e., Mehmed II]" (Pertusi, *Caduta di Costantinopoli*, I [1976], 132, 134, and *cf.*, *ibid.*, p. 394 [note 10]). Seven mines were discovered between 16 and 25 May.

[28] Barbaro, *Giornale*, ed. Cornet, p. 21. The identification of the Gate of S. Romanus, where the final break was to come, has caused some difficulty. In the siege of 1453 one is chiefly concerned with three civil and two military gates. The civil gates are: 1) the Charisius or modern Adrianople Gate (Edirne Kapi); 2) Top Kapi or "Cannon Gate," which had been commonly known as the Gate of S. Romanus until some time before the siege; and 3) the Pegé (Πηγή or Gate of the Springs, now called the Silivri

shot stone balls weighing twelve hundred pounds.

On the other side the Emperor Constantine XI and Giovanni Giustiniani also took their position at the Gate and Tower of S. Romanus. Against the masses of Turks, among whom were some 12,000 highly trained and determined janissaries, they had discouragingly few men for service on the walls. Early in the siege the emperor ordered a survey made of all the manpower and equipment available in the city. All laymen and monks capable of bearing arms were to be included in the census. When the records of the local commanders and municipal authorities were turned in, the emperor gave them to the historian Sphrantzes to compute the totals quietly in his own home. It was a sad report that Sphrantzes had to make: there were about 4,773 Greeks and about 2,000 foreigners in the city who could be employed for its defense. Some nobles and commoners had fled the city before its investment, but not very many. The population within the walls at this time was probably between 40,000 and 50,000.[29] The emperor and Sphrantzes concealed the results of the census, which would have been damaging to morale.[30] Subsequent reinforcements may have increased the number of the city's defenders to about 6,000 Greeks and almost 3,000 Latins: these at any rate are the figures given by Leonardo of Chios.[31] There was probably little need to conceal the census computed by Sphrantzes. The empty stations on the walls could speak for themselves, and the Florentine merchant, Jacopo Tedaldi, who witnessed the siege, observed that there might be 6,000 or 7,000 soldiers in the city but no more.[32]

The Greeks and Italians behind the ancient walls of Constantinople fought with a heroism and endurance worthy of a happier result than they were to experience. Niccolò Barbaro's diary records three large-scale attacks by the Turks, who tried on 18 April, 7 May, and

Kapi). The military gates are: 1) the Pempton and 2) the Triton. When Barbaro, *loc. cit.*, refers to the Pegé, he seems to mean the Triton, which shows the effects of severe bombardment.

Although there is no question that the present Top Kapi had long been called the Gate of S. Romanus, both the Greeks and the Italians appear to have transferred this name to the military gate of the Pempton when as a civil gate the Top Kapi was closed before the siege began—the Pempton seems very clearly to be the gate called S. Romanus in the sources (for which see the references partially collected in Müller's note in *FHG*, V-1, pp. 72–73, but the reader should be guided in his interpretation of the texts by Pears, *Destruction of the Greek Empire*, pp. 238–45, 429–35). For the sources relating to the number, location, and size of the Turkish batteries, see Müller, *op. cit.*, note on p. 79.

[29] See A. M. Schneider, "Die Bevölkerung Konstantinopels im XV. Jahrhundert," in the *Nachrichten der Akademie der Wissenschaften in Göttingen, Philol.-Hist. Kl.*, IX (1949), 233–44, esp. p. 237. The population of Byzantium at its height has doubtless been much exaggerated. The area within the Theodosian walls had never been entirely occupied. There were extensive open spaces throughout the twelfth century. Besides the dwellings of the masses of the inhabitants, much land was taken up by the imperial palaces and those of the aristocracy, quarters for the soldiery, public squares and public buildings, the hippodrome, numerous churches, monasteries, vineyards and grain fields, warehouses, magazines, barns, and stables, open cisterns, orchards, vegetable gardens, and other open and cultivated fields, the vineyards always being conspicuous within the city walls. In a learned and sensible article David Jacoby, "La Population de Constantinople à l'époque byzantine: Un problème de démographie urbaine," *Byzantion*, XXXI (1961), 81–109, has sought to show that even at its height the population of Byzantium never exceeded 400,000 as an absolute maximum.

[30] Actually Sphrantzes, *Chron. minus* (*PG* 156, 1060D; ed. Grecu, p. 96, a better text), gives the number of Greeks as "4,773 without the foreigners, of whom there were scarcely an additional 200" (*͵δψογ' ἄνευ τῶν ξένων μόλις ὄντων σ' ἢ μικρόν τι πρός*), where 200 has presumably been read for 2,000 (͵β). The text of this passage in the *Chron. minus* appears in *PG* 156, 1060D, precisely as it does in the first edition of Angelo Mai, *Classici auctores*, IX (Rome, 1837), *ad finem*, p. 65. The Pseudo-Sphrantzes, III, 3 (Bonn, pp. 240–41), gives 4,773 Greeks and some 2,000 foreigners (*ibid.*, p. 240, lines 19–20; ed. Grecu, p. 386, lines 2–3), which latter figure I have retained in the text. *Cf.* Ducas, chap. 38 (Bonn, pp. 275–77), on the paucity of men, the ruined walls, and the despair of the city. On the disposition of the Christian forces, at the gates and along the walls, to repel the Turkish attacks, note Pertusi, *Caduta di Costantinopoli*, I (1976), pp. LXXI–LXXII.

Sphrantzes' *Chron. minus* (*PG* 156, 1061; ed. Grecu, p. 96) records nothing that happened in Constantinople from the time of his reckoning the totals of the Greek forces until the capture of the city by the Turks on 29 May (1453), leaving a gap which Macarius Melissenus-Melissurgus, the "Pseudo-Sphrantzes," has filled in from whatever source or sources (in the Bonn edition this added material extends from pp. 240–41 to p. 288 and in Grecu's edition from p. 386 to p. 430).

[31] Leonardo, in Lonicer, *Chron. turcica*, II, 93, and in Pertusi, *Caduta di Costantinopoli*, I (1976), 146.

[32] Tedaldi, in Martène and Durand, *Thes. novus anecdotorum*, I, col. 1820F: "En icelle cité ly avoit entour de trente à trente-six mille hommes, et six à sept mille combattans, et non plus." Tedaldi's text is also given in Dethier, *MHH*, XXII-1, no. 9, p. 896. Ducas, chaps. 38 (Bonn, p. 266, lines 13–14), and 39 (p. 286, lines 7–9), says the defenders of the city were outnumbered twenty to one, and that all together they did not exceed 8,000 (chap. 39, p. 287, lines 15–16), which is of course not consistent with the figures he gives for the Turkish army, but would fit Barbaro's figure of 160,000 Turks.

12 May to force their way into the city through the gaps their cannon had made in the walls.[33] Critobulus says that minor assaults were a daily routine.[34] The defenders also had some cannon, but their largest one exploded when it was first fired. The bombardier was suspected of collusion with the Turks, and subjected to a judicial inquiry for treason, although the charge was dismissed for lack of evidence. In any event the Greeks and Italians found they could not use cannon safely. The recoil shook the walls and caused damage, proving in fact to be a greater danger to those who fired the cannon than to the Turks.[35] Now there occurred, however, a thrilling and heartening episode, which must have seemed to the besieged inhabitants like an answer to their prayers for deliverance from the terror which beset them.

Three large Genoese ships and an imperial grain transport from Sicily or the Morea,[36] the former having been delayed for weeks at Chios by northerly winds, sailed into the Marmara one night. On the following morning, 20 April, their approach was reported by Turkish scouts. Mehmed's entire fleet left its base at Diplokionion (the modern Beşiktaş), on the western shore of the Bosporus above Pera, to go in pursuit of them. The four ships made steadily for the great boom across the Golden Horn, where the Greek and Italian vessels on guard were prepared to assist them. The hopeful eyes of thousands watched from the walls of the city, the roof-tops, and other heights. The wind unexpectedly died down, however, probably when the ships had reached the turn under the walls of the ancient acropolis (Seraglio Point, Sarayburnu). For two or three hours the Genoese and Greeks fought off from their tall vessels the unremitting attacks of a sea full of Turkish ships (in one another's way) under the Bulgarian admiral Balta-oghlu, who had already failed in a costly attempt to enter the Horn, and knew that his life might depend upon the outcome of this battle. The Turks had begun the attack with every confidence of victory. Sultan Mehmed himself

[33] For these three attacks, see Barbaro, *Giornale*, ed. Cornet, pp. 22–23; ed. Dethier, pp. 739–41 (on 18 April), Cornet, pp. 36–37; Dethier, pp. 771–73 (on 7 May), and Cornet, p. 39; Dethier, p. 777 (on 12 May). Barbaro's diary is not entirely consistent with the other sources (see Müller's note in *FHG*, V-1, p. 81). Critobulus, I, 35–36 (ed. Müller, *loc. cit.*; ed. Grecu, pp. 103, 105), and the Pseudo-Sphrantzes, III, 3 (Bonn, pp. 246–47; ed. Grecu, pp. 390, 392), both seem to be describing the Turkish attack of 18 April, which came after the destruction of the Tower of S. Romanus by cannon fire (to the sultan's amazement, says the Pseudo-Sphrantzes, Giustiniani restored the essential fortifications in a single night). The Turks had also built a tall wooden turret which they pushed up against the wall at the place where the Tower of S. Romanus had been destroyed, and the besieged are said to have burned this turret during the night.

Several such turrets were set against the walls of the city in the course of the siege. The Pseudo-Sphrantzes calls this one a "taker of cities" (ἑλέπολις). He very definitely places this attack just before the naval battle of 20 April (see below) when an imperial grain transport and three Genoese ships entered the Golden Horn in the face of the whole Turkish armada. Barbaro, *Giornale*, ed. Cornet, pp. 26–27, however, places the destruction of the Tower of S. Romanus (and its repair and the building of a palisade to replace the ruined outer wall) on 21 April, at which time the Turks would have been successful (he says) if they had attacked "with a mere ten thousand men." On 22 April, according to Barbaro, Mehmed decided to have recourse to his naval force (of 145 vessels), which was stationed at the Two Columns (Diplokionion), at the northern entrance to the Golden Horn, and there followed the dragging of seventy-two Turkish fuste overland into the harbor under the fortifications of Pera (to which we shall come shortly)—within the iron-and-wooden boom which had been stretched across the entrance to the harbor.

All this is quite at odds with the account in the Pseudo-Sphrantzes, who represents Mehmed as up bright and early the day after the attack (when the Tower of S. Romanus collapsed), ready to renew his attempt to take the city. This whole passage in the Pseudo-Sphrantzes (III, 3, pp. 244–47; ed. Grecu, pp. 388, 390) certainly suggests the Turks' building (and the Christians' destroying) a great wooden turret, which Barbaro, *Giornale*, ed. Cornet, pp. 42–43; ed. Dethier, pp. 785–88, dates to 18 May (*cf.* the Anonymus Moscovita, chap. 11, in Dethier, *MHH*, XXII-1, pp. 1086–88; Zorzo Dolfin, *Chron.*, *ibid.*, nos. 58, 61, pp. 1011, 1013; and Tedaldi, *ibid.*, no. 14, p. 898, also in Martène and Durand, *Thes. novus anecdotorum*, I, col. 1821C). A. G. Paspates, *Siege and Capture of Constantinople* [in Greek], Athens, 1890, repr. 1939, pp. 133–34, and Pears, *Destruction of the Greek Empire*, pp. 192–94, have employed the Pseudo-Sphrantzes text in this connection, actually assuming a gross error in his chronology, which is probably the case. (Incidentally Barbaro, *loc. cit.*, does not mention the burning of the turret, which he calls a *bastion*, and seems to imply that it stood during the remainder of the siege, which is in accord with the account of Tedaldi, in Martène and Durand, *Thes. novus anecdotorum*, I [1717, repr. 1968], cols. 1821C and 1823A, where "le chastel be bois" is mentioned in the last assault of 29 May.)

[34] Critobulus, I, 36, 2 (ed. Müller, *FHG*, V-1, p. 81b; ed. Grecu, p. 105), especially against the places where the walls were broken down.

[35] Chalcocondylas, bk. VIII (Bonn, p. 389; ed. Darkó, II, 154).

[36] The imperial government in Constantinople purchased a good deal of grain from Sicily (*cf.* Const. Marinescu, "Contribution à l'histoire des relations économiques entre l'Empire byzantin, la Sicile et le royaume de Naples de 1419 à 1453," *Studi bizantini e neoellenici*, V [1939], 209–19, from the *Atti del V congresso internazionale di studi bizantini* [Rome, 1936]).

watched the contest from the Pera (Galata) shore of the Horn. In fact, the four ships were drifting toward him as those aboard fought for their lives. Just when it seemed that Turkish expectations of success were justified, the south wind returned in splendid gusts, filling the Christians' sails and moving their harassed vessels under the protective walls of the acropolis. To the fury of the sultan, who shouted directions and imprecations from the shore, Balta-oghlu ordered the northward withdrawal of his ships. That night the four vessels were brought within the chain, with the aid of Gabriele Trevisan and his two light galleys, and Constantinople had more men and supplies and additional units for guard duty along the boom.[37]

The exasperating failure of his fleet to capture the four Christian vessels on 20 April may well have hastened somewhat the execution of a plan which Mehmed had been entertaining for some time. This was to transport a sizable part of his fleet from the base of Diplokionion on the Bosporus overland to the Golden Horn. According to Barbaro, this remarkable feat was accomplished on 22 April. About seventy vessels were hauled on various rollers and gliders over a carefully prepared roadbed from a place near Tophane (south of Diplokionion) up the eastern slope of the hill of Pera and down again on the west into a small bay, which Critobulus calls Cold Springs (*ἐν τῷ κόλπῳ τῶν Ψυχρῶν Ὑδάτων καλουμένῳ*), in the modern district of Kasim Pasha just across from the midway point between the ancient Byzantine acropolis and the Palace of Blachernae. It was all done, says the Pseudo-Sphrantzes, "in a single night;" if so, it bespeaks the vast manpower which the sultan had brought to the siege.[38] Mehmed had entered the inner harbor of Constantinople by the back door; secured his lines of communication with the Diplokionion and Rumeli Hisar; exposed the northern wall of the besieged city to attack; and thoroughly intimidated the Genoese in well-fortified and independent Pera. This was a development which the Greeks and Italians in Constantinople, says Critobulus, "could never have anticipated, and they were frightened out

[37] The naval battle of 20 April is described by Critobulus, I, 39–41 (ed. Müller, *FHG*, V-1, pp. 84a–86a; ed. Grecu, pp. 109, 111, 113); Barbaro, *Giornale*, ed. Cornet, pp. 23–25; Ducas, chap. 38 (Bonn, pp. 268–70); Chalcocondylas, bk. VIII (Bonn, pp. 389–90; ed. Darkó, II, 154–55); Leonardo of Chios, in Lonicer, *Chron. turcica*, II, 90–91; and Pseudo-Sphrantzes, III, 3 (Bonn, pp. 247–50; ed. Grecu, pp. 390, 392, 394).

The usual discrepancies appear in these sources. Chalcocondylas says that two Christian ships were involved, one Genoese and the other Byzantine; Critobulus, three large merchantmen (ὁλκάδες) "from Italy," sent by the pope [Nicholas V], and does not mention the Byzantine grain transport; Ducas, one Byzantine grain ship from the Peloponnesus and four Genoese merchantmen; Pseudo-Sphrantzes, three Genoese ships, which after leaving Chios met a Byzantine ship from Sicily; and Barbaro, Pusculus, and Leonardo of Chios say much the same thing. Barbaro, p. 24, says the actual fight lasted close to three hours. Pears, *Destruction of the Greek Empire*, p. 258, incorrectly identifies Leonardo as "archbishop of Chios:" Leonardus Chiensis was the archbishop of Mytilene (Lesbos); according to Eubel, II, 198, he died before 3 December, 1459, and was succeeded by one Benedetto, O.S.B. With some inaccuracy G. Ostrogorsky, *History of the Byzantine State*, trans. Joan Hussey, Oxford, 1956, pp. 506–7, has written: "The Golden Horn was barred by a heavy chain which all Turkish efforts had failed to break, and it was as a result of such an attempt that a naval battle broke out on 20 April in which the imperial fleet won the day"[!].

[38] Critobulus, I, 42–43 (ed. Müller, *FHG*, V-1, pp. 86b–88b; ed. Grecu, pp. 115, 117), says there were 67 ships; Barbaro, *Giornale*, ed. Cornet, pp. 27–28 (see above, note 26), 72 fuste; the Pseudo-Sphrantzes, III, 3 (Bonn, pp. 251–52; ed. Grecu, pp. 394, 396), comments on the diversity of the equipment used by the Turks in transporting the ships overland, and is forced to admire the remarkable "strategem;" Ducas, chap. 38 (Bonn, pp. 270–71), 80 "biremes" (fuste), and who ever saw or heard of such a thing? making the land as navigable as water; Chalcocondylas, bk. VIII (Bonn, p. 387; ed. Darkó, II, 153), 70 ships; Leonardo of Chios, in Lonicer, *Chron. turcica*, II, 89, seventy biremes; Henry of Soemmern, ed. Iorga, *Notes et extraits*, III (1902), 310, seventy *naves*; and for additional sources see Müller's notes to Critobulus, *loc. cit.* A. D. Mordtmann, *Belagerung u. Eroberung Constantinopels* (1858), pp. 57–60, rightly follows Barbaro amid the disagreement among the sources. Sa'd-ad-Dīn, trans. E. J. W. Gibb (1879), pp. 24–25, says that the ships were moved over the hill (of Pera) on greased wooden rollers. *Cf.* Iorga, *Gesch. d. osman. Reiches*, II, 25–26.

According to Tedaldi, Zagan Pasha had "seventy to eighty galleys as well as other armed fuste" dragged overland from Diplokionion into the inner harbor of the Golden Horn, which he calls the *mandraquin*, i.e., in Greek *mandraki* (enclosure, harbor), "which is between the two cities" of Pera and Constantinople (Martène and Durand, *Thes. novus anecdotorum*, I, col. 1820D). When put together, the Turkish and Christian naval forces did not amount to seventy to eighty actual galleys. The galley was a very heavy and very expensive vessel, as scores of Venetian documents constantly remind us. Nevertheless, we are informed by one Samile, who calls himself a "Bladick oder Bischoff," in a letter dated 6 August, 1453, to Oswald, burgomaster of Hermannstadt (Rumanian Sibiu, Hungarian Nagyszeben, the capital of Transylvania), Mehmed's forces "dragged with their own hands two hundred galleys over land for a distance of about two miles, and then let them down in that part of the sea which lies between the two cities [of Pera-Galata and Constantinople]" (the German text in Iorga, *Notes et extraits*, IV [1915], 66, with an Italian translation in Pertusi, *Caduta di Costantinopoli*, I [1976], 229).

of their senses by the unexpectedness of the sight, and lapsed into depression and a feeling of utter helplessness, not knowing what to do from now on. . . ."[39]

Something had to be done. Niccolò Barbaro describes a council of war held by the Venetian leaders in Constantinople on 23 April, at which Giustiniani was probably present although Barbaro makes no mention of him. Various plans were discussed for destroying the Ottoman fleet in the cove on the northern shore of the Horn where the Turks, even though they would not come out and fight, were a menace to the Italian and Greek ships behind the boom or "chain," for they might emerge at any hour. We have already noted that Barbaro says the Turks had seventy-two fuste in the cove. Ducas says eighty. It was finally decided in the council that Giacomo Coco, master of the Venetian galley from Trebizond, should try to burn the Turkish fleet in a nocturnal attack. The bold Coco, who had volunteered to do the job, wanted to get at it immediately, but when the Genoese in Pera learned about it, according to Barbaro, they said they wanted to participate in the undertaking. Their request was granted. They took several days to get ready (24–28 April). It is strange that the Genoese in Pera should have learned about the plan so quickly, even though they were doubtless in constant touch with their compatriots in Constantinople. The Venetian Barbaro, who hated the Genoese and dishonestly magnifies the part played by the Venetians throughout the entire siege, charges that the podestà of Galata revealed the impending attack to Sultan Mehmed, who prepared a hot reception for his assailants.

In the early morning hours of 28 April, before it was light, two heavy transports, loaded with bales of cotton and wool (to break the impact of the stone cannon balls if they were hit), pulled out of the harbor near the northern end of the iron-and-wooden chain. They were to serve as a buffer for two large galleys and three swift fuste which followed with a number of smaller boats, called brigantines, full of gunpowder, pitch and other incendiary materials, including Greek fire. Their quiet progress toward Cold Springs was too slow for the impatient Coco, who pulled out of line in his fusta, anxious for glory, says Barbaro. As Coco prepared to launch his attack, however, the silence was suddenly broken by the thunderous blasts of Turkish cannon. Coco's ship was immediately hit twice, and the second time she went straight to the bottom with all aboard, "in less time than it would take to say ten paternosters," *quanto che saria a dir diexe paternostri*.[40] If we may believe Barbaro, all Coco's crew were drowned.

In the meantime the Venetian captain Gabriele Trevisan, in charge of one of the galleys, had been advancing slowly and cautiously. Baffled by the sudden explosions, he did not know what had happened. It was impossible to see, for visibility was impeded not only by the darkness but also by the clouds of smoke issuing from the Turkish cannon and billowing from the cotton and wool on the transports which had also been hit. Trevisan's uncertainty was quickly resolved when his own ship was struck. She did not sink, however, and the crew finally managed to get her back to her anchorage. The Turkish fleet now joined the fray, all seventy-two fuste says Barbaro, trying to capture the two transports, but the men aboard them prevented their seizure by fighting off the attacks for an hour and a half in a contest "that was truly like hell itself." It had been a costly venture. The Christians had lost one or two ships and perhaps some eighty men, and had managed to destroy only one Turkish ship.

The Turks had captured a number of Italians and Greeks who had swum to the Pera (Galata) shore, some of them presumably from Coco's fusta. When morning came, we are told, Mehmed had forty of them put to death in plain sight of their relatives and companions who watched from the city walls. By way of recompense the Emperor Constantine is alleged to have ordered that two hundred and sixty Turkish prisoners then held in the city should be hanged from the defense towers on the walls. The sources tend to agree that the Genoese in Pera had in one way or another warned the Turks although the story told by Barbaro in this regard is extremely suspect. We can imagine that the Venetians were not slow to charge their

---

[39] Critobulus, I, 43, 1 (ed. Müller, *FHG*, V-1, p. 87b; ed. Grecu, p. 117).

[40] This expression is not to be regarded merely as picturesqueness of speech (Barbaro, *Giornale*, ed. Cornet, p. 31; ed. Dethier, p. 760); it actually denoted a means of reckoning brief periods of time. Medical recipes were in fact prepared in the fourteenth and fifteenth centuries by boiling the ingredients or letting them stand or applying a caustic to a wound for the space of so many *paternosters* or *avemarias* (*cf.* D'Arcy Power, *Treatises of Fistula . . . by John Arderne*, London, 1910, p. XXIX, in Early English Text Society, no. 139).

ancestral enemies with treachery. On the other hand the Genoese declared that the whole affair had been badly managed from the start. The trouble was that the Venetians simply lacked the acquaintance of the Genoese with such matters (so the jibes of the Genoese are reported); Giacomo Coco had not known what he was about; the rest of the Venetians had displayed the same lack of experience; and here lay the cause of the disaster. On one occasion, however, before there was an exchange of blows, the emperor is said to have hurried to the scene of the quarrel, and succeeded in making a sort of peace between the two groups: "I beg you, my brothers, remain at peace. The war outside the walls is enough for you. Do not fight among yourselves, for the mercy of God!"[41]

The last days of Constantinople present a historical drama of great poignancy, in which the chief actors on the Christian side inevitably evoke a warm sympathy and admiration because of

---

[41] Barbaro, *Giornale*, ed. Cornet, pp. 28–33; ed. Dethier, pp. 754–63; Leonardo of Chios, in Lonicer, *Chron. turcica*, II, 91–92, whose account is rather like that which appears in the Pseudo-Sphrantzes, III, 4 (Bonn, pp. 256–58; ed. Grecu, pp. 400, 402), who has added details. In the present context, *cf.* Tedaldi, in Martène and Durand, *Thes. novus anecdotorum*, I, col. 1821AB, and Chalcocondylas, bk. VIII (Bonn, pp. 387–88; ed. Darkó, II, 153). Marino Sanudo, *Vite de' duchi*, in L. A. Muratori, ed., *RISS*, XXII (Milan, 1733), col. 1149B, says that thirty-three men were executed by Mehmed. Barbaro's account is very hostile to the Genoese throughout; his charge of their treachery might be discounted but for other evidence. Almost two years later, however, in a letter to Philip the Good of Burgundy, Isidore of Kiev put in a good word for the Genoese as having aided the defenders of Constantinople throughout the siege (see the text in Pertusi, *Caduta di Costantinopoli*, I [1976], 108, letter dated 22 February, 1455, and *cf.*, below, note 95).

Ubertinus Pusculus (Pusculo) of Brescia, the epic poet of the siege (*Constantinopoleos libri IV*), reports that, as the Christian ships first began to move toward their objective, a light flared from atop the Tower of Galata, apparently as a signal to the Turks (bk. IV, vv. 585–88, 610 ff., ed. Ad. Ellissen, *Analekten*, III [Leipzig, 1857], *Anhang*, pp. 72–73). Pears, *Destruction of the Greek Empire*, p. 260, says that "Critobulus and Pusculus each affirm that Mahomet had information from Galata;" but he gives no reference to Critobulus, for there is none to give, and Critobulus says no such thing (see below). The Pseudo-Sphrantzes, III, 3 (Bonn, pp. 256–58; ed. Grecu, pp. 400, 402), says nothing of Genoese treachery, and attributes the Christians' failure to bad luck and God's punishment for their sins (he notes that they destroyed only one Turkish trireme), but Leonardo of Chios (in Lonicer, *Chron. turcica*, II, 88, 92), who was a Genoese, seems to hint at treachery to the Christian cause from Galata: "O Genuenses iam quodammodo cicurati, sileo ne de meis loquar, quos externi cum veritate dijudicant. . . . Sed quid dicam, beatissime pater [Pope Nicholas V]? accusarene quempiam licet? silendum mihi est." The Genoese Adam de Montaldo, ed. Hopf, in Dethier, *MHH*, XXII-1, no. 16, p. 48, denies there was any treachery. The evidence in Ducas and Critobulus may be more difficult to use than Pears suspected. The Pseudo-Sphrantzes is not without a certain willingness to gloss over Latin misdeeds, and his sources are always open to question.

Although Ducas, chap. 38 (Bonn, pp. 277–79), appears to be alluding to the nocturnal attempt of Giacomo Coco, whom he does not name, to burn the Turkish fleet, for he says that "the Genoese of Galata, learning of what was being done, informed the Turks" (p. 277, lines 13–14), he has dated the whole episode on 4 May, since on the following day, *ἡμέρας οὖν γενομένης* (p. 278, lines 7–8), the Turks sank by cannon-fire in the harbor of Galata a Genoese merchantman loaded with cargo and preparing to leave for Italy (*cf.* Pseudo-Sphrantzes, III, 4, ed. Bonn, p. 259; ed. Grecu, p. 402), an event which Barbaro, *Giornale*, ed. Cornet, pp. 35–36; ed. Dethier, pp. 769–70, informs us occurred on 5 May. Ducas next describes the building of a bridge, which Barbaro places on 19 May. Ducas seems in fact to be concerned (as he says) with an attempt of the Genoese Giustiniani on the Turkish fleet, and so is Critobulus, I, 44 (ed. Müller, *FHG*, V-1, p. 88; ed. Grecu, pp. 117, 119), who says that Giustiniani tried to confine the Turkish ships in the cove of Cold Springs by arraying a heavy transport and three triremes (galleys) in battle order, but lost a trireme to the Turkish cannon, and had to withdraw the other ships to a safe distance. Actually, however, if we are to take Critobulus literally, this trireme was lost on 25 or 26 May, for he goes on to say (I, 45, 1) that "during these same days . . . three or four days before the battle" (*κατὰ δὲ τὰς αὐτὰς ἡμέρας. . . . Πρὸ γὰρ τριῶν ἢ τετάρων ἡμερῶν τοῦ πολέμου. . . .*) certain portents of disaster occurred in the city.

Since Critobulus is generally well informed, it would seem that he is not here describing the events of 28 April. This passage of Critobulus has often been used as a source for these events, as by A. G. Paspates, *Siege and Capture of Constantinople* [in Greek], Athens, 1890, repr. 1939, pp. 119–23, who shows, however, considerable facility for misreading texts. Paspates, for example, after actually quoting a sentence from Ducas's description of Giustiniani's attempt on the Turkish fleet (*op. cit.*, p. 120, note 19), which he attributes to "Phrantzes," states that no author except Critobulus mentions Giustiniani in this connection (p. 121, note 20). L. Bréhier, *Le Monde byzantin*, I: *Vie et mort de Byzance*, Paris, 1947, p. 520, also assumes that when Critobulus says Giustiniani, he means Coco, having obviously acquired this impression from Pears and from G. Schlumberger's *Le Siège, la prise et le sac de Constantinople*, Paris, 1914, pp.179–80, whose book is largely based upon that of Pears. The latter, however, has taken pains with the chronology, and places Critobulus's portents of disaster just before 26 May (*op. cit.*, pp. 296–97).

One need not be surprised at Barbaro's failure to mention Giustiniani's action against the Turkish fleet. He consistently deprecates the contribution of Giustiniani and the Genoese to the siege (which exceeded that of the Venetians), and actually states that the Venetians were posted at the critical S. Romanus gate, which we know was defended by Giustiniani and the Genoese. It must be noted, however, that Giustiniani also took part in the attempt to burn the Turkish ships on 28 April (*cf.* Leonardo of Chios, in Lonicer, *Chron. turcica*, II, 92, and in Pertusi, *Caduta* their determination to fight on in the face of hopeless odds. Some time after about half the Turkish fleet had been drawn over the peninsula of Pera from the Bosporus to the Golden Horn, Mehmed II constructed a bridge across the Horn near the northern corner of the city walls (below the Byzantine region of Cynegion, the modern Ayvan Saray), thus exposing the whole range of the city's weakly defended fortifications along the Horn to the constant danger of direct assault.[42] The bombardment of the landward walls was incessant, with its deafening roar of explosion and the sickening crash of the huge stone balls as they struck the ancient walls and the hastily improvised palisade which Giustiniani had thrown up before the threatened gate of S. Romanus. All day long the Turks shot at the walls, and all night long the Greeks and Italians struggled to repair them.

If the Venetian commanders and their sailors had been most reluctant to remain in the city in the days before the siege began, as the early portions of Barbaro's diary make only too clear, they were making up for it now in their fight "prima per l'amor de Dio e poi per honor de la cristianitade." Although the Genoese community in Galata professed neutrality in the struggle and even friendship for the Turk,[43] their sympathies were entirely with the besieged. Their countryman Giustiniani was the very heart of the Christian defense. The fate of Galata seemed clearly bound up with that of Constantinople. As the Venetians resisted the Turks from the walls of the Greek capital, however, some of them doubtless regarded themselves as fighting for the preservation of Galata. This was an awkward position for Venetians to be in; it must be admitted that they fought rather for their lives than for the preservation of the city; and yet no one should disparage the valiant effort of Coco and Trevisan to destroy the Turkish ships in the harbor. The Venetians probably had just cause for complaint against the Genoese, whose merchants from Galata traded with the Turks by day and the Christians by night. Of course they did it for profit, but they gave information picked up in the Turkish camp to the Christians as they sold them badly needed supplies. Mehmed knew what was going on, but much preferred the alleged neutrality of the Genoese to their armed opposition on behalf of Constantinople. Also some of them were very useful to him, for it seems most probable that he first learned of the projected Venetian attack upon his ships in the Horn, planned for and attempted on 28 April, from a Genoese source. Security was poor on both sides, for Tedaldi states that Christians in the Turkish army shot notes over the city walls to inform the Greeks and Italians of the decisions taken at the last meetings of the Ottoman high command before the great assault on the walls on 29 May.[44] It would be interesting to know how many Greeks, Italians, Germans, Hungarians, and other Christians, especially technicians, were serving in Mehmed's army and in his fleet. Not all Christians were laboring "for the honor of God and Christendom."

On 3 May at midnight the Venetians had dispatched a small, swift vessel with a dozen men aboard, disguised as a Turkish corsair, according to Barbaro, to find the Venetian fleet under the captain-general Jacopo Loredan and

---

di Costantinopoli, I [1976], 142, and *cf*. pp. 354–55). Pusculus, bk. IV, vv. 606–7, ed. Ellissen, p. 73, places him on one of the transports in Coco's brave fiasco, but I suspect that Critobulus may be describing and Ducas alluding to another (and later) offensive against the Turkish ships in which a different strategy was employed. Ducas accuses the Genoese of treacherously informing the Turks of Giustiniani's impending attack, which is clearly a confusion with Coco's attempt upon Mehmed's fleet. In fact the confusion of the sources makes certainty of detail impossible.

[42] According to Leonardo of Chios, in Lonicer, *Chron. turcica*, II, 89–90, the Pseudo-Sphrantzes, III, 3 (Bonn, pp. 251–52; ed. Grecu, pp. 394, 396), and Pusculus, *Constantinopolis*, bk. IV, vv. 572–73, ed. Ellissen, p. 72, the bridge was built after the transport of the Turkish ships to the Horn (which happened on 22 April, according to Barbaro). *Cf*. Critobulus, I, 27, and 43 (ed. Müller, *FHG*, V-1, pp. 75, 88; ed. Grecu, pp. 89, 91, 117). Chalcocondylas, bk. VIII (Bonn, p. 388, lines 9 ff.; ed. Darkó, II, 153, lines 25 ff.), places the construction of the bridge after the Venetian failure to burn the ships (which happened on 28 April, according to Barbaro); Barbaro, *Giornale*, ed. Cornet, pp. 43–44; ed. Dethier, pp. 788–89, dates the bridge to 19 May; and Ducas, chap. 38 (Bonn, p. 279, lines 11–12), places it after the Turkish sinking by cannonfire of the Genoese merchantman on 5 May (another date fixed by Barbaro).

Ubertino Pusculo (Pusculus), cited above and elsewhere in this chapter, was an eyewitness of the events he describes in his *Constantinopoleos libri IV*, which he dedicated to Pope Nicholas V. He had been living in Constantinople for some time before the siege. A native of Brescia and *utriusque linguae doctus*, Pusculo later taught Greek in the city of his birth.

[43] *Cf*. Ducas, chap. 38 (Bonn, pp. 278–79), to which other references could easily be added; the quotation comes from Barbaro, *Giornale*, ed. Cornet, p. 5; ed. Dethier, p. 702, *et alibi*.

[44] Tedaldi, in Martène and Durand, *Thes. novus anecdotorum*, I (1717, repr. 1968), cols. 1821E–1822AB.

carry to him the last appeal of an empire now gasping for breath. Twenty days later, on the twenty-third, the men came back, ran the Turkish gauntlet through the Marmara, and were admitted within the boom to report their sad failure to locate the fleet.[45] Their return, possibly to death, shows something of the spirit which now existed within the walls of the beleaguered city, inspired by the heroic examples of Constantine XI and Giustiniani, whose tasks were made the more difficult by the endless quarrels among the defenders, the results of fatigue, strained nerves, and generations of hostility between Greeks and Latins, Genoese and Venetians. Always on hand somewhere were the Grand Duke Lucas Notaras, Cardinal Isidore of Kiev, Archbishop Leonardo of Mytilene, the historian George Sphrantzes, the Venetian physician Niccolò Barbaro, and dozens of others whom the contemporary records have identified as active participants in the defense of the city, and with every century that has passed since then the pious labor of historians has dutifully recalled their names to the readers of later times. Worthy as that task may be, however, it is not the one which we have set ourselves in this volume, and some interesting episodes in the siege must be omitted from these pages. On 7 May and again on the twelfth, as we have noted, the Turks made heavy assaults on the landward walls, but the defenders repulsed the attacks,[46] and day after day thereafter they discovered and destroyed tunnels which the Turks were digging under the walls. These mining operations were concentrated, as Barbaro informs us, at the northern end of the westward fortifications, in the area of the Gate of Caligaria (now Egri Kapi), near the Comnenian palace of Blachernae, where there was no foss or outer wall.[47] And so the grim contest dragged on to its inevitable conclusion, because, as Barbaro says more than once, "God wanted to prolong the taking of the city."

Sultan Mehmed II received reinforcements from Asia. Every day seemed to increase his strength and redound to his advantage. The plight of the besieged grew worse. The disaffected and disgruntled murmured in the streets and squares of the city, according to the Pseudo-Sphrantzes, even maligning the emperor, and doubtless the sultan had not overlooked the value of a fifth column within the crumbling walls. On 24 May the knowledge became general in the city that Mehmed was planning an all-out attack on the twenty-ninth both by land and by sea. Giustiniani embarked

[45] Barbaro, *Giornale*, ed. Cornet, pp. 34–35, 46–47; ed. Dethier, pp. 766–69, 794–95. Since under his entry of 3 May Barbaro mentions both the dispatch of the men to search for the Venetian fleet and their return to Constantinople twenty days later, it is clear that his diary was later recast. In his entry under 12 April he knew the siege would end on 29 May (ed. Cornet, p. 22). All through the diary his comments make it clear that, as the defense continued from week to week, the author knew that the city was going to fall. Barbaro undoubtedly kept a sketchy diary from day to day, but wrote up the account we now have after his return to Venice. Although the introductory paragraph of the diary is obviously a later addition, it sets the tone of the whole work, a sketch of the siege of Constantinople "dal principio fino al finimento del aspra e passionevole presa soa."

Although on 3 May the Venetians in Constantinople doubtless sent out a small vessel to locate the fleet somewhere in the Aegean (since Barbaro says so), Loredan's commission as captain-general of the sea is dated 7 May, 1453, by which date he had not left Venice (Sen. Secreta, Reg. 19, fols. 193^v–194^v): "Nos Franciscus Foscari Dei gratia dux Venetiarum, etc. Committimus tibi nobili viro Jacobo Lauredano dilecto civi et fideli nostro quod . . . vadas et sis . . . capitaneus noster generalis maris curamque et gubernationem totius classis nostre, quam ob reverentiam Dei, honorem Christianorum, et conservationem civitatis Constantinopolis paravimus, prudentie et fidei tue committimus. . . ." Note Iorga's summary of the text in his *Notes et extraits*, III (1902), 283–85; Thiriet, *Régestes*, III (1961), no. 2922, p. 185; and *cf.* Sanudo, *Vite de'duchi*, in *RISS*, XXII (1733), col. 1148, and Pastor, *Hist. Popes*, II, 261–62, and *Gesch. d. Päpste*, I (repr. 1955), 610–11. Actually it was almost a month later (on 3 June) before the Venetian fleet, with Loredan aboard, had even reached Negroponte, where the first Venetian refugees from the sack of Constantinople were already arriving (Pertusi, *Caduta di Costantinopoli*, I [1976], 348 [note 29]). *Cf.* Zorzo Dolfin, *Assedio e presa di Costantinopoli*, ed. G. M. Thomas, in *Sitzungsber. d. k. bayer. Akad. d. Wissen. zu München*, II (1868), 36: "Le gallie tre de Romania et le do gallie sotil . . . tirate fuora del porto circa a mezo di [i.e., about midday on 29 May] feceno vela et in 4. zorni [i.e., on 3 June] perveneno a Negroponte dove trovono M. Jacomo Loredan capitano zeneral cum otto gallie che aspettavano tempo de andar a dar soccorso a Constantinopoli, et per quella sapeno Constantinopoli esser prexo dal Turco adi 28. [*sic*!] Mazo 1453 al levar del sole. . . ." Dolfin's source is Jacopo de'Languschi.

[46] *Giornale*, ed. Cornet, pp. 36–37; ed. Dethier, pp. 771–73 (on 7 May), and Cornet, p. 39; Dethier, p. 777 (on 12 May). On 20 May the bombardment of the walls was very heavy, and on the twenty-first the Turkish armada at Diplokionion made an ineffective attempt on the boom across the harbor (*op. cit.*, ed. Cornet, pp. 44–45).

[47] *Cf.* Janin, *Constantinople byzantine*, p. 283. The name Caligaria is said to have been derived from a manufactory of military boots (*caligae*) located in the area. According to Tedaldi, Turkish miners dug fourteen tunnels under the walls (Martène and Durand, *Thes. novus anecdotorum*, I, col. 1821BC).

upon a last, incredible spurt of energy. He requested the Grand Duke Notaras to give him the cannon which were mounted on the northern walls along the Golden Horn, where they were doing little good, so that they might be employed on the palisade before the S. Romanus gate where the chief attack was expected. Notaras refused to give up his cannon, however, on the grounds that he needed them where they were, and in the heated altercation which followed, Giustiniani called him a useless oaf, an accursed fool, and the enemy of his own fatherland, to which Notaras replied in kind. Again the emperor had to calm ruffled spirits and restore peace before the two leaders would go about their business. The Pseudo-Sphrantzes, who tells this story, pays the highest tribute to the indomitable Giustiniani, who alone in that last week caused fear in the Turkish ranks and inflicted losses on them. The Pseudo-Sphrantzes is pro-Latin, and (like Sphrantzes himself) is hostile to Notaras. Nevertheless, whatever hope of ultimate safety there was in the city was placed in Giustiniani. In these last days a rumor spread through the Turkish camp that a fleet was on its way from Italy to Constantinople, and even that John Hunyadi was coming with a great Hungarian army to break the siege. Now Mehmed II became the object of muttered abuse among his forces on the part of those who believed the reports, which of course proved false, for no Christian prince, as the good Sphrantzes himself later complained with understandable bitterness, sent either a foot-soldier or a farthing to assist the Greeks and their Latin comrades in Constantinople.[48]

Mehmed II, having been informed that a squadron of Italian ships had already reached Chios,[49] realized that he had reached the crossroads. He is also said to have been worried by the appearance of certain celestial phenomena which he superstitiously interpreted as signs of adverse fortune. A council of war was summoned at which the question was discussed of a great attack or the abandonment of the costly siege. Khalil Pasha, the grand vizir and the most notable figure in the army after the young sultan, had apparently never approved of this vast undertaking against Constantinople, for fear that it might bring about a coalition of western powers which would drive the Turks from Europe. He urged withdrawal from the Bosporus, lest something worse than the failure of the siege should happen. But Zagan Pasha, the rival and enemy of Khalil Pasha, argued otherwise, saying that Alexander the Great (all this according to the Pseudo-Sphrantzes) had conquered the world with a smaller army than Mehmed now had before Constantinople. He did not believe that any fleet was coming from the West, where political dissension made united action almost impossible. Even if a fleet actually should come, the sultan's army would still outnumber the westerners by more than four to one. Mehmed, who is said to have been much encouraged by Zagan Pasha's stand, directed him to go among the troops and sound out their attitude, which he did, and when he returned, he reported that they were eager to fight.[50]

It was now the evening of 27 May, and Sultan Mehmed II ordered that all through the night and the following day fires should be lighted, and the army should fast. On the

[48] Sphrantzes, *Chron. minus* (*PG* 156, 1063AB; ed. Grecu, p. 102), who notes that the Serbs sent both men and money to assist the Turks; Pseudo-Sphrantzes, III, 4, and IV, 2 (Bonn, pp. 261–64, 326; ed. Grecu, pp. 404, 406, 408, 472); and *cf.* Lodrisio Crivelli (Cribellus), *De expeditione Pii papae secundi in Turcas*, bk. I, in *RISS*, XXXIII (1733), cols. 49–50, and ed. G. C. Zimolo, in the new Muratori, *RISS*, XXXIII, pt. v (1948–50), pp. 49–50, on Giustiniani's quarrel with Notaras, which became widely known. Leonardo of Chios (in Lonicer, *Chron. turcica*, II, 94–95) states that, after Giustiniani's attack upon Notaras, the latter became more remiss in his efforts for the city's defense, and that the Greeks resented the fact the Latins would get the credit if the city were saved. Paspates, *Siege and Capture*, p. 136, has garbled the quarrel of Giustiniani and Notaras.

[49] Critobulus, I, 47 (ed. Müller, *FHG*, V-1, p. 89b; ed. Grecu, p. 121).

[50] Pseudo-Sphrantzes, III, 4 (Bonn, pp. 264–68; ed. Grecu, pp. 406, 408, 410, 412), who also reports that Khalil Pasha secretly informed the Emperor Constantine what had gone on in the council of war, and encouraged him to hold out, because the fortune of war was always doubtful (ed. Bonn, p. 269; ed. Grecu, p. 412). Leonardo of Chios (in Lonicer, *Chron. turcica*, II, 95–96) says the same thing, and is doubtless the Pseudo-Sphrantzes' source. The charge of treason against Khalil Pasha appears to be true; three days after the taking of Constantinople, Mehmed II had him imprisoned; and he was executed at Adrianople on 10 July, 1453 (Sa'd-ad-Dīn, trans. E. J. W. Gibb [1879], p. 35; Babinger, *Maometto* [1957], pp. 145, 164–65, and *cf.* pp. 84–87). At the time of his execution Khalil Pasha had been the grand vizir of the Ottoman empire (the sixth to hold the office) for some years, having been appointed by Murad II before 1443. He belonged to a family which had entertained close relations with the Byzantine court (*Encycl. of Islām*, I [1908], 834, under Čendereli, and esp., *ibid.*, II [1965], 445, under Djandarlî).

evening of the twenty-eighth[51] he called together all his officers and subalterns both in the army and in the fleet to encourage them to do their best in the great assault which was to come on the following day. Critobulus gives us the fullest version of his supposed speech. Mehmed reminded his men of the fabulous wealth of the city they would conquer the next day. There were vast treasures awaiting them, he said, in the palaces, the homes of the nobility, and above all in the many churches; aristocratic men and boys to be enslaved; beautiful women to be taken as wives, enjoyed as slaves, or put up for sale; and handsome buildings, houses, and gardens in the city which they could look forward to securing for themselves. "Now I give over to you for rapine and plunder this great and populous city, the royal capital of the old Romans, which has advanced to the height of prosperity, good fortune, and fame, and has become the head of the civilized world. . . ." As they could see for themselves (ὡς ὁρᾶτε), the foss before the parapet had been all filled in, and the landward walls had been broken down in three places, through which not only the heavy infantry but even the cavalry could easily pass. The besieged were few and badly armed. Two or three men were guarding a tower. A single man had to protect three or four crenelations (ἐπάλξεις). The Italians were unlikely to fight very long or hard, he said, to defend a city and property that belonged to others. The Turks would attack in relays, always fresh; the defenders would be fighting continuously without food, drink, or rest. Mehmed urged the officers to be courageous and obedient. He would himself lead the attack (according to Critobulus), and would see what each of them did. Then dismissing them, he kept their leaders longer to explain his detailed plans for the disposition of their forces. The admiral Hamza Beg, who had replaced the unfortunate Balta-oghlu, was to harass the sea walls along the Marmara, land men on the shores, and try to scale the walls with ladders. Zagan Pasha was to attack the wall along the Golden Horn, using the seventy ships or so within the harbor. Karaja Beg was to attack the northern part of the great landward walls where they were in ruins; Ishak Pasha and Mahmud Pasha, the long southern section where less damage had been done through the weeks of bombardment. The old Khalil Pasha, the grand vizir, and Saruja Pasha were to attack, on either side of the sultan, the ruined area of the Gate of S. Romanus, where Giustiniani's palisade was not expected to withstand an assault in mass. "And now go back to your tents and your divisions. Good luck! Have something to eat and get some sleep"![52] Although the points which Critobulus emphasizes in this long speech were probably those which the sultan made in his appeals to the army, the form of the speech is as un-Moslem as possible. Critobulus knew his Turks; he was writing for western readers. The brief address which the Pseudo-Sphrantzes puts in the sultan's mouth has a much more Moslem cast, and promises a three days' sack of Constantinople. Whatever the nature of the sultan's speech or speeches to his men, the hour of decision was past, and that of action had come.

On the eve of the last assault the Emperor Constantine delivered his final address, an *oratio imperii funebris*, to the nobility and the soldiers who had participated in the last Christian procession in the city. The Turk had had them under siege for fifty-two days, he said, and had battered their walls with cannon. They were not to yield to fear, however, and should put their trust in God's protection, their own strength, and their drawn swords. The Turkish horde would attack with barbarous screams

[51] *Cf.* Pseudo-Sphrantzes, III, 5 (Bonn, p. 269, lines 6–13; ed. Grecu, p. 412, lines 10–16); Tedaldi, in Martène and Durand, *Thes. novus anecdotorum*, I, col. 1822BC. Barbaro, *Giornale*, ed. Cornet, pp. 48–49; ed. Dethier, pp. 798–99, mentions the constant Turkish bonfires which almost turned darkness into daylight from the first hour of the night of (he says) 26 May "to encourage the people in the camp." The weird Turkish cries could be heard as far as the Anatolian shores, "che sun mia dodexe luntan dal campo" (according to him). He also says that on the twenty-eighth Mehmed ordered "a son de trombeta" all his commanders to their posts for the whole day under pain of death, "e questo perchè . . . el signor Turco vuol dar doman la bataia zeneral a questa dolente cità." Oddly enough, Tedaldi says the Turks had no trumpets, but used "tambours," drums (*op. cit.*, I, 1822C).

[52] Critobulus, I, 48–51 (ed. Müller, *FHG*, V-1, pp. 89b–92a; ed. Grecu, pp. 123 ff.). The speech is imaginary, modeled after Thucydides, of whom it contains at least two reminiscences. The Pseudo-Sphrantzes, III, 5 (Bonn, pp. 269–70; ed. Grecu, pp. 412, 414), has composed a briefer speech, with a picture of the Moslem heaven which awaited those who lost their lives, and indicates that the sultan promised the army on oath that Constantinople would be plundered for three days, and that every soldier could keep his own spoils. Chalcocondylas, bk. VIII (Bonn, pp. 392–93; ed. Darkó, II, 157), also reports a speech to the janissaries, promising rewards for victory; *cf.* the poet Pusculus, bk. IV, vv. 819–55, ed. Ellissen, pp. 77–78, and Leonardo of Chios, in Lonicer, *Chron. turcica*, II, 96–97.

under a cloud of arrows. They were wild beasts, but the defenders were men, and if they fought with courage, the beasts would be repulsed. The Turk had surrounded Galata with a pretext of peace. Now he threatened "to take the city of the great Constantine, your ancestral home, the refuge of Christians, the bulwark of all Greeks, and to profane God's sacred churches by stabling his horses in them." With a special appeal to the Genoese and the Venetians, Constantine turned to the soldiers, "And you, my fellow soldiers, obey your commanders. Understand that this is the day of your glory. If you shed your blood, you will win the crown of martyrdom and everlasting renown!"[53] But God seems to have been on the side of the heavier battalions,[54] unmoved by the sad ceremony in Hagia Sophia on the evening before the city's fall.[55] Only the alert angel of death heard that litany of heroic sacrifice to freedom.

When the Greeks and Italians took their stand upon the enclosure (περίβολος) between the (lower) outer wall and the exterior parapet, they locked the gates leading into the city. There was to be no retreat. The outer wall and Giustiniani's palisade would stand or they would fall with it. They could only succeed or die.[56] From Hagia Sophia the emperor had returned to the palace of Blachernae, where with grave courtesy he asked forgiveness of all who were there. Some of those present are said to have been overcome with emotion by the scene: "Even if a man were made of wood or of stone, he could not have avoided grief." About midnight of 28–29 May the emperor rode out from the palace to inspect the landward walls. The defenders were all at their posts that night on the walls and in the towers. The gates were locked. It was impossible to enter or leave the city. We are informed that Sphrantzes went with the emperor. When they returned to Caligaria, at the first cockcrow, they dismounted and went up into a tower. They were in the northwest corner of the city, between Blachernae and the "palace of Porphyrogenitus" (Tekfur Saray). Below them could be heard with frightening distinctness the noise of the Turks preparing for the attack. The men on the walls waited in silence. Leonardo of Chios, who was probably somewhere nearby, mentions the sounds of cannon being made ready, the rumbling of carts, and the racket of those moving the scaling ladders into prescribed positions. The guards in the tower told the emperor that the noise had been going on all night. The shores were full of a like activity. About the sound of the second cockcrow, with no sign of a signal being given, the attack began. The start of this day was like that of many others during the weeks now past, but the end was, alas, to be very different. At this point Sphrantzes is said to have left his beloved master, probably never to see him again.[57]

[53] Leonardo of Chios, in Lonicer, *Chron. turcica*, II, 97–98; Pseudo-Sphrantzes, III, 6 (Bonn, pp. 271–79; ed. Grecu, pp. 414, 416, 418, 420, 422), reports a longer and yet very similar speech, but refers to the fact that the "sultan has had us under siege for fifty-seven days." (Although Grecu has numbered the books in his edition of the Pseudo-Sphrantzes as in the Bonn edition, he has numbered the chapters differently, on which see above, note 14.)

[54] *Cf.* Critobulus, I, 46 (ed. Müller, *FHG*, V-1, p. 89; ed. Grecu, p. 121); Pusculus, bk. IV, v. 1024, ed. Ellissen, p. 81: ". . . Auxilium deus ipse negavit." At the conclusion of his epic Pusculus added these verses concerning himself (the scansion needed a little more attention):

Brixia me genuit civem: Ubertinum Puscula honesta
Gens tulit—haec ausus talia qui cecini.
Me Constantini studiis urbs dulcis habebat,
Cum cecidit bello: barbara praeda fui.

[55] *Cf.* Pseudo-Sphrantzes, III, 7 (Bonn, p. 279; ed. Grecu, p. 422); Anonymus Moscovita, in Dethier, *MHH*, XXII-1, p. 1113.

[56] Andrea Cambini, *Commentario . . . della origine de'Turchi, et imperio della casa ottomanna*, ed. 1538, bk. II, fol. 20r, lines 16–20; *cf.* Leonardo of Chios, in Lonicer, *Chron. turcica*, II, 98: ". . . valvis urbis, ne quisquam retrocederet, clausis. . . ."

[57] Pseudo-Sphrantzes, III, 7 (Bonn, pp. 279–81; ed. Grecu, pp. 422, 424), whose source one would give much to know; *cf.* Leonardo of Chios, in Lonicer, *Chron. turcica*, II, 98. Both Pseudo-Sphrantzes, *loc. cit.*, and Barbaro, *Giornale*, ed. Cornet, pp. 49 ff.; ed. Dethier, pp. 799 ff., indicate that, after the preparations of 27–28 May, Mehmed II launched the final attack upon the city in the early morning hours of the twenty-ninth. According to Critobulus, I, 54 (ed. Müller, *FHG*, V-1, p. 92b; ed. Grecu, p. 133), a signal for this attack was given by trumpet blasts on (Monday) afternoon, 28 May, when the Turks had the western sun at their backs and the besieged had it shining in their eyes. Ducas, chap. 39 (Bonn, pp. 282–83), says that Mehmed began the attack on Sunday evening, 27 May, giving the besieged no rest that night, and continued his harassment, but rather less severely, until the following afternoon (the twenty-eighth) when he deployed his troops for the kill, giving the signal in the evening at the second hour, which would appear more or less in accord with Critobulus. Here, however, it seems better to follow Barbaro, who was in the city throughout the siege, in placing the last assault in the early morning hours of the twenty-ninth. The Pseudo-Sphrantzes says much the same thing (III, 8, ed. Bonn, p. 288, lines 17–19; ed. Grecu, p. 430, lines 22–24), although he also regards the attack as beginning in a general way on Sunday, the twenty-seventh, observing that the enemy finally took Constantinople "on the third day." On the events which led up to and included the fall of the city, from

Sultan Mehmed began by sending against the landward walls his poorest troops, the expendable masses of bashi-bazuks, among whom were large numbers of Christian irregulars who hoped to share in the rich pillage which victory would bring.[58] Both Barbaro and the Pseudo-Sphrantzes note that the purpose of this motley horde was to tire the defenders (and diminish their supplies of ammunition), and yet there was nothing for them to do but expend the strength and ammunition necessary to stop the wild onset. The bashi-bazuks came on by the thousands, their approach covered by volleys of arrows, stones, crossbow bolts, and cannon balls. Over the foss they charged, many of them carrying ladders which they placed against the parapet. They attacked on a broad front from the palace of Porphyrogenitus to the region south of the S. Romanus gate, where Giustiniani and the Genoese fought valiantly to hold the palisade against the undisciplined but strong attacks.

The bashi-bazuks were driven on by Turkish troops drawn up behind them. Maiming or death awaited them whether they ventured too far east or west of the foss. They tried to climb the parapet on ladders and on one another's shoulders. The ladders were pushed backwards from the parapet, and crashed to the ground amid the screams of the attackers and the triumphant shouts of the defenders, who threw stones down upon their assailants, so that few of those who reached the walls escaped with their lives. It was still too dark to see clearly. The roar of cannon, the blare of horns and trumpets, the screeching and cursing of men, the bells ringing the alarm on the walls and in the nearby churches, all caused a fearful din. After some two hours of vigorous, even courageous assault, more than once involving hand-to-hand fighting, the bashi-bazuks were allowed to withdraw, their numbers decimated and their ardor subdued. There had been frightened laggards among them, but they had served well their purpose of tiring the bodies, daunting the spirits, and disordering the ranks of the intrepid Greeks and Italians on the broken walls.

Before the defenders could derive much satisfaction from their successful repulse of the bashi-bazuks, Mehmed ordered out the more determined and disciplined troops of his Anatolian division, which had been stationed through most of the siege on the southern (right) end of the Turkish lines, opposite the Gate of Regium (or of "Polyandros," the modern Yenimevlevihane Kapi). The Anatolians moved northward over the hills into the Lycus valley, poised for attack against the northern Mesoteichion. The great cannon was directed against the palisade, causing it severe damage. It was not yet light. The alarm bells were ringing frantically, summoning all men to their posts. Women, children, and the aged carried stones to the defenders. The Anatolians made their way in large numbers to the parapet, placing their ladders against it, and trying to climb up and over it. Their best efforts were not enough; the Greeks and Italians drove them

---

27 May to about noon and somewhat later on the twenty-ninth, see Barbaro, ed. Cornet, pp. 49–57; ed. Dethier, pp. 799–821; and *cf.* Critobulus, I, 54–68 (ed. Müller, *FHG*, V-1, pp. 92b–98b; ed. Grecu, pp. 133 ff.); Pseudo-Sphrantzes, III, 7–8 (Bonn, pp. 280–90; ed. Grecu, pp. 422–32); Ducas, chap. 39 (Bonn, pp. 282–96); and Chalcocondylas, bk. VIII (Bonn, pp. 393–99; ed. Darkó, II, 158–63). Sphrantzes, *Chron. minus* (*PG* 156, 1061AB; ed. Grecu, pp. 96, 98), says suspiciously little about the siege of which he was an eyewitness; one would like to believe at this point that Macarius Melissenus-Melissurgus, the author or redactor of Pseudo-Sphrantzes' text, had access to an expanded memoir of Sphrantzes, the emperor's friend and last companion.

In this last connection, see Margaret Carroll, "Notes on the Authorship of the 'Siege' Section of the Chronicon Maius of the Pseudo-Phrantzes, Book III," *Byzantion*, XLI (1971), 28–44, and XLII (1972), 5–22, who believes that Macarius Melissenus (or rather Melissurgus) did in fact have a more detailed version of Sphrantzes' memoir in hand when he produced the *Chronicon maius*. She makes capital of the strange omission from both the *Chronica minus* and *maius* of any mention of the several embassies exchanged between Constantine XI and Mehmed from the latter's accession in 1451 to March, 1453, although we find one or more of these embassies referred to by Leonardo of Chios, Critobulus, Ducas, and Chalcocondylas, whom Macarius used in his description of the siege. Mrs. Carroll also dwells on the hostility shown by Sphrantzes in the *Chronicon minus* for Lucas Notaras, which animus receives even more extensive expression in the *Chronicon maius*, although Macarius could hardly have entertained any personal enmity for Notaras a century and a quarter after the events he describes. Macarius's account contains many convincing, circumstantial details which it is hard to believe he could have invented unless he were a novelist of immense talent. On Macarius, see the first volume of this work, Chapter 13, note 206.

[58] According to Barbaro, *Giornale*, ed. Cornet, pp. 51–52; ed. Dethier, p. 805: "Questo Signor Turco [Mehmed II] si fece far tre schiere de le sue zente, a cinquanta millia persone per schiera; una schiera si iera de Cristiani [the bashi-bazuks!], i qual steva per forza in nel campo; la seconda schiera si iera de zente menuda . . . [the Anatolian division]; la terza schiera si iera tuti ianizari . . . homeni zernidi e valenti a la bataia, e driedo questi ianisari si iera tuti i subasi, e driedo questi si iera el Signor Turco."

back to the foss.[59] The besieged had exerted an almost superhuman effort, and now the force of the Anatolians' attack was spent. The hours had been full of terror and passed slowly for those in the city.

More than once Barbaro observes that the continuous bombardment of the landward walls was like "something from the other world," *una cossa de l'altro mondo*.[60] The city had also been under constant attack elsewhere, however, as Critobulus emphasizes in his biography of Sultan Mehmed. The Turkish admiral, Hamza Beg, was ranging the Marmara walls, shooting at them from the decks of his ships, looking for a weak spot to exploit. Zagan Pasha had crossed the bridge over the Golden Horn to attack the city's northern walls from the harbor. While his infantry climbed up toward the walls along the Horn, archers and fusiliers covered them with a barrage from his ships which sailed back and forth in the Horn, doubtless well protected from the Christian vessels in the harbor by the Turkish cannon mounted on the Galata shore. Zagan Pasha's men, however, were quite unable to scale the city walls. In the meantime Karaja Beg's division had struck across the foss at the northern stretch of the landward walls between Tekfur Saray and the Gate of Charisius or Adrianople, where previous cannonading had made a serious breach, but they were vigorously opposed by a Genoese contingent under the three brothers Bocchiardi. Ducas says that fifty Turks got into the city at this point, but his account is not without some measure of confusion.[61] The defenders had done incredibly well, and Critobulus reports that Mehmed was indignant at the failure of the successive Ottoman attacks. Now it was time for the élite corps of heavy infantry and especially for the redoubtable janissaries.[62]

Mehmed sent the janissaries into the attack with chosen infantrymen, bowmen, lancers, and members of his own bodyguard without allowing the besieged a moment's respite. They came, says Barbaro, "not as Turks but as lions," with terrible cries and trumpet blasts. This also was like "something from the other world," the noise being heard as far as the shores of Anatolia, which Barbaro says were a dozen miles from the Turkish camp. Terror gripped all the inhabitants of the city. The bells were ringing, both those in the churches and the special alarms on the walls. Prayers were addressed to God to spare Constantinople the rule of pagans. The great Turkish cannon which shot stones weighing 1,200 pounds was still directed at the palisade before the S. Romanus gate. The janissaries attacked in a fury, especially in this area, and "the fierce battle lasted until daybreak." Barbaro improperly assigns the spirited defense of the S. Romanus gate and the palisade to the Venetians, but every eyewitness saw Giustiniani and the Genoese repelling the Turks at this focal point of attack. "It was of no avail, however," says Barbaro, "because the eternal God had already rendered his judgment that this city should pass into the hands of the Turks."

At an hour before dawn, which would be about 4:00 A.M., the great cannon was fired again, with a foul abundance of powder, which sent black smoke billowing around the battered palisade, part of which now came down. Dust rising from the débris mingled with the smoke, and "one could hardly see a thing," *quaxi non se vedeva nula*. The heavy infantrymen and janissaries plunged through the smoke, and about three hundred of them cut and thrust their way into the enclosure behind the parapet, *dentro dai*

[59] Pears, *Destruction of the Greek Empire* (1903), p. 338, says that in the attack of the Anatolian division 300 Turks climbed over the parapet into the peribolos (near the S. Romanus gate). He is confusing this attack with that of the janissaries and heavy reserves, which came later: Barbaro, *Giornale*, ed. Cornet, p. 52; ed. Dethier, p. 807, specifically says that the Anatolian troops, whom he identifies only as "la segonda schiera," did not succeed in penetrating the walls, *e non poder* [*intrà*].

[60] *Giornale*, ed. Cornet, p. 50; ed. Dethier, p. 801.

[61] According to Ducas, chap. 39 (Bonn, pp. 282, 285–86), just before the Turks finally broke through into the city in mass, they effected an entry by an unguarded postern gate, known as the Circus Gate (Kerkoporta), which was below one end of the palace of Porphyrogenitus (Tekfur Saray), on which *cf.* Müller's note to Critobulus, I, 60 (*FHG*, V-1, pp. 94–95); Pears, *Destruction of the Greek Empire*, pp. 341–44; and esp. Janin, *Constantinople byzantine*, pp. 282–83.

[62] Critobulus, I, 56–57 (ed. Müller, *FHG*, V-1, p. 93; ed. Grecu, pp. 135, 137); on Zagan Pasha, *cf.* Barbaro, *Giornale*, ed. Cornet, p. 56; ed. Dethier, pp. 817–18; on the Genoese brothers Paolo, Troilo, and Antonio Bocchiardi, *cf.* Leonardo of Chios, in Lonicer, *Chron. turcica*, II, 93. According to Barbaro, *loc. cit.*, the Turkish armada under Hamza Beg raised anchor at Diplokionion and sailed at "one hour before daybreak" (daybreak would come about 5:00 A.M. in May) toward the boom or "chain" across the entrance to the harbor, which they found well guarded by the ten Christian ships stationed there. Troilo and Antonio Bocchiardi [Buciardi, Buzzardi] were still active in February, 1461 (R. Predelli, ed., *Regesti dei Commemoriali*, V [Venice, 1901], bk. xv, no. 73, pp. 142–43).

barbacani, but in a fierce struggle the Greeks and Italians on the peribolos closed in on them and killed most of them. While the exhausted defenders were congratulating themselves on this success, the monstrous cannon spoke again, belching forth black smoke, under the concealment of which the Turks charged again, "like dogs . . . all of them mad."[63] They pressed so hard upon one another that within a quarter of an hour, we are told, more than 30,000 Turks had climbed the parapet (*dentro dai barbacani*), and soon there were 70,000 of them in the enclosure, presumably in the long section of the peribolos before the S. Romanus gate. (Both figures are absurd.) Although many Turks had been killed by the stones thrown upon them from above, there was no halting the onslaught once they had reached the upper level of the enclosure.

The stars were fading in the heavens, says the Pseudo-Sphrantzes, and it was becoming lighter. In the east was seen the reddish glow of morning. As night gave way to day, the Christians had so far managed to drive back the first attacks. As Leonardo of Chios puts it, "Tenebrosa nox in lucem trahitur, nostris vincentibus,"[64] but now "our men" were no longer winning. The attacks of the janissaries, ready and rested, were too heavy, and "our men" were weary beyond endurance. At this critical point in the battle Giustiniani was wounded, apparently by an iron or lead bolt from a crossbow. Critobulus says the bolt went through his breastplate; he fell in his tracks, and was promptly removed to his tent in serious condition (κακῶς ἔχων). His men were stunned by the blow, and thought only of getting him aboard one of his galleys and clearing out themselves. The Emperor Constantine tried to dissuade them from leaving the walls, but they went anyway, armor and all, hurrying to put Giustiniani on one of the galleys and seeking safety aboard ship themselves.[65]

As usual in most matters relating to the siege, our authorities differ concerning the details of Giustiniani's fateful withdrawal from the palisade. According to Leonardo of Chios (and the Pseudo-Sphrantzes), Giustiniani quietly abandoned his post when he was injured, in a strange reversal of his previous steadfastness. He wanted a physician, and left the scene of combat without a word of reassurance to those with him and without turning over his command to a lieutenant, who might have tried to prevent the panic which ensued as a result of his departure. The Emperor Constantine is said to have been in the peribolos at this time and, learning the cause of the too obvious consternation, apparently hurried after Giustiniani: "My brother, why have you done this? Return to your station. This wound is but a trifle. Go back, for now there is the more need of you. The city is depending upon you for salvation!" The Pseudo-Sphrantzes says that Giustiniani made no reply to the emperor's remonstrance, but left the walls, and made his way to Pera (Galata), where he died in the bitterness of self-reproach and the scorn of others.[66] The fame which he had

[63] Barbaro, *Giornale*, ed. Cornet, p. 54, ed. Dethier, p. 810: ". . . come cani . . . tuti in furia. . . ."

[64] Pseudo-Sphrantzes, III, 7 (Bonn, p. 281, lines 4–7; ed. Grecu, p. 424, lines 4–5); Leonardo, in Lonicer, *Chron. turcica*, II, 98. (In Constantinople on 29 May the sun rose at 6:23 A.M.) *Cf.* Pusculus, bk. IV, v. 889, ed. Ellissen, p. 78.

[65] Critobulus, I, 58 (ed. Müller, *FHG*, V-1, p. 94b; ed. Grecu, pp. 137, 139). The sources contain their usual variations. Pusculus, bk. IV, v. 975, ed. Ellissen, p. 80, says that Giustiniani was wounded in the upper arm (*percussus glande lacertum*); Pseudo-Sphrantzes, III, 7 (Bonn, p. 283, lines 17–19; ed. Grecu, p. 426, lines 9–10), in the right foot; Ducas, chap. 39 (Bonn, p. 284, lines 14–15), in the back of the hand. Chalcocondylas, bk. VIII (Bonn, p. 395, lines 2–3; ed. Darkó, II, 159, lines 11–12), also says he was wounded in the hand, and Leonardo of Chios, in Lonicer, *Chron. turcica*, II, 98, places the wound *sub asella*, "below the armpit." In any event it seems unlikely that all the three hundred Genoese stationed at the palisade with Giustiniani could have withdrawn with him "armor and all." *Cf.*, Leonardo of Chios, *ibid.*, II, 93: "Iuxta ergo se eodem capitaneo [Iustiniano] cum tercentis commilitonibus Genuensibus posito, splendidis refulgentibus armis . . . circa illam partem murorum Sancti Romani reparatorum, ubi magis urgebat pugna, Imperator stetit."

[66] Pseudo-Sphrantzes, III, 7 (Bonn, pp. 283–84; ed. Grecu, p. 426). For material relating to the Latins, the Pseudo-Sphrantzes (or rather Macarius Melissenus-Melissurgus) drew heavily upon Leonardo of Chios's letter to Pope Nicholas V. Leonardo was a Genoese of Chios, like Giustiniani, but speaks in obvious disapprobation of the latter's withdrawal from the palisade: "Inter haec malo urbis fato, heu Iohannes Iustinianus sagitta sub asella configitur: qui mox inexpertus iuvenis sui sanguinis effusione pavidus perdendae vitae concutitur. Et ne pugnatores qui vulneratum ignorabant virtute frangantur, clam medicum quaesiturus ab acie discessit. Qui si alium suo loco surrogasset, salus patriae non periisset. Pugnam inter haec arduam committunt. Imperator ut vidit deesse capitaneum ingemiscens quo scilicet ierit percunctatur. Nostri ut se vident sine duce resilire e locis incipiunt. Teucri convalescunt, horror nostris incutitur," etc. (in Lonicer, *Chron. turcica*, II, 98–99, with a slightly different text in Pertusi, *Caduta di Costantinopoli*, I [1976], 160, and on the whole episode see, *ibid.*, pp. 362–63). In a well-known address delivered before Alfonso V of Aragon in Naples in late January, 1454, Niccolò Sagundino says that Giustiniani was wounded twice, *duobusque acceptis vulneribus* (Pertusi, II, 134).

gained by fortitude, observes the Pseudo-Sphrantzes, he thus lost by cowardice.[67]

According to Ducas, however, Giustiniani could not bear the pain and told the emperor that he was going to one of his ships for treatment, and would return with all speed.[68] Leonardo of Chios, who gives us a full account of Giustiniani's leaving the palisade, informs us that he answered the emperor's appeal to remain with the request, "Give my man the key to the gate." It was opened, and Giustiniani and a number of his followers crowded through it: "The captain fled to Pera, and afterwards sailed to Chios, but departed this life ingloriously as a result either of his wound or of grief."[69] Giustiniani's departure was the end of the defense. Exhausted men left their posts on the walls and fled. Almost everyone thought of the ships in the harbor as the only remaining means of escape. The Emperor Constantine was killed, as were most of those who stood by him to the end.[70]

Now the Turks got into the city, especially through the little gate which had been opened to permit Giustiniani's withdrawal.[71] Soon they were streaming in by the thousands, intent upon pillage, through the Gate of Charisius as well as that of S. Romanus, killing all whom they encountered. According to Ducas, the Turks slew about 2,000 men. They had believed that the defenders of the city numbered at least 50,000, but if they had realized that this number was in fact only about 8,000, they would not have killed any one.

For this people is so avaricious that if a father's murderer fall into their hands, they release him

---

The Pseudo-Sphrantzes reports the emperor's speech to Giustiniani from Leonardo, *loc. cit.*, "At ille salutis, gloriae, suique oblitus, uti altam quidem primo magnanimitatem, ita posthac pusillanimitatem ostendit. Debuit enim, si poterat, vulneris dolorem sufferre, non recedere: si vir erat a seipso, vel saltem alium qui stetisset, loco sui surrogare," etc. *Cf.* Adam de Montaldo, ed. Hopf, in Dethier, *MHH*, XXII-1, pp. 49–50, 55. Tedaldi, in Martène and Durand, *Thes. novus anecdotorum*, I, col. 1822F, notes that at the time of the final Turkish attacks the city had placed its hope in Giustiniani's valiance. Pusculus, bk. IV, vv. 976–78, ed. Ellissen, p. 80, says that Giustiniani left his post after being wounded, either from fear of the Turks or because of the acuteness of his pain:

Ac se subripuit pugnae, navesque petivit,
Sive metu Teucrum seu vulnere abactus acerbo,
Deseruitque locum. . . .

[67] Pseudo-Sphrantzes, III, 4 (Bonn, p. 263, lines 17–18; ed. Grecu, p. 406, line 32).

[68] Ducas, chap. 39 (Bonn, p. 284, lines 17–20), who also declares that Giustiniani was on shipboard when he learned of the Turkish entry into Constantinople and of the emperor's death (*ibid.*, pp. 295–96). The dishonest Barbaro, *Giornale*, ed. Cornet, p. 55; ed. Dethier, p. 813, says that Giustiniani fled to his ship, broadcasting the fact that the Turks had entered the city: "Vedando questo [the Turkish penetration of the parapet in force], Zuan Zustignan, zenovexe da Zenova [actually he was from Chios], se delibera de abandonar la sua posta [*per esser ferito de freza* is written by a later hand in the margin of the MS.], e corse a la sua nave, che iera stà messa a la cadena. . . ." *Cf.* Tedaldi, in Martène and Durand, *Thes. novus anecdotorum*, I (1717, repr. 1968), col. 1823A, who says that Giustiniani was "blechié d'une couleuvrine, s'en parti pour se faire mediciner, et bailla sa garde à deux gentils hommes Jennevois," but that the men on the walls fled before the Turkish attack, "et ainsi les Turcs entrerent en Constantinople à l'aube du jour, le XXIX jour de May."

[69] Leonardo, in Lonicer, *Chron. turcica*, II, 99. Giustiniani was buried on the island of Chios in the church of S. Domenico (in the Castro). His funerary inscription is apparently known only from Hieronimo Giustiniani's *History of Chios* [*Istoria di Scio, scritta nell'anno 1586*], edited from the MS. in the Archivio di Stato di Roma, Fondo Giustiniani, Busta 130, fasc. 3, by Philip P. Argenti, Cambridge, 1943, p. 418: "Fu sepolto [il Giustiniano] in la chiesa di Santo Dominico a man sinistra intrando appresso nella gran porta della nave del tempio in una sua capella nella quale avanti la presa dell'Isola si vedea la sua sepultura, in marmore elevata, con questo epigramma: 'Hic iacet Joannes Justinianus, inclitus vir ac Genuensis patricius Chiique maunensis, qui in Constantinopolis expugnatione a principe Turchorum Mehemet, serenissimi Constantini Orientalium ultimi Christianorum imperatoris magnanimus dux, lethali vulnere icto interiit, anno a partu Virginis M.IIII V [*sic*], VIII Kal. Augusti.'" S. Domenico, later called S. Maria del Castello, was within the precincts of the castle of Chios; after the Turkish occupation, in 1566, it was converted into a mosque. On the Latin churches and monasteries in the Castro, *cf.* Aimilia K. Sarou, Τὸ Κάστρον τῆς Χίου, Athens, 1916, pp. 46, 93 ff., 100, 104–5. Giustiniani's inscription is no longer extant (*cf.* F. W. Hasluck, "Latin Monuments of Chios," *Annual of the British School at Athens*, XVI [1909–1910], 155; Argenti, *Occupation of Chios*, I [1958], 203, note; 368; 559).

[70] Critobulus, I, 60 (ed. Müller, *FHG*, V-1, p. 95b; ed. Grecu, pp. 139, 141); Sphrantzes, *Chron. minus* (*PG* 156, 1061B; ed. Grecu, pp. 96, 98); Pseudo-Sphrantzes, III, 9 (Bonn, pp. 290–91; ed. Grecu, p. 432); Ducas, chaps. 39 (Bonn, pp. 286–87, 296), 40 (p. 300); Chalcocondylas, bk. VIII (Bonn, p. 395; ed. Darkó, II [1927], 159–60); Barbaro, *Giornale*, ed. Cornet, p. 57; ed. Dethier, p. 820; Leonardo of Chios, in Lonicer, *Chron. turcica*, II, 99; Pusculus, bk. IV, vv. 1007–16, ed. Ellissen, *Analekten*, III, *Anhang*, p. 81; Tedaldi, in Martène and Durand, *Thes. novus anecdotorum*, I, col. 1823C. Sa'd-ad-Dīn, trans. E. J. W. Gibb (1879), pp. 30–31, has no difficulty imaging an unworthy end for the last Byzantine emperor, "that monarch of evil custom;" his account of the decapitation of the emperor, however, is rather like that of Pusculus.

[71] Critobulus, I, 60–61 (ed. Müller, *FHG*, V-1, p. 95b; ed. Grecu, pp. 139, 141, 143), and *cf.*, below, the letter of Angelo Giovanni Lomellino, podestà of Pera, to his brother; G. M. Angiolello, *Hist. turchesca*, ed. Ion Ursu, Bucharest, 1909, pp. 19–20; and Sp. P. Lambros [Lampros], *Ecthesis chronica*, London, 1902, pp. 12–16, a sixteenth-century source.

for gold—how much the more, then, one who has done no injury, but has himself been injured by the Turk! After the war I talked with many Turks who told me "how in fear of those in the front ranks we slew those whom we met, but if we had known there was such a dearth of men in the city, we would have sold them all like cattle!"[72]

The Turks immediately began their frantic search for gold, jewels, and other valuables. Ducas indicates that among the first monasteries to be looted were those of S. John the Baptist called the "Petra" and of S. Salvator in Chora (Kariye Jami), which lay just within the Gate of Charisius.[73] It was now about 6:00 A.M. or shortly thereafter, and some two hours later the Turks reached the fora of Taurus and Constantine.[74] The imperial and Latin standards had been lowered, and the banner of the crescent raised over the captured towers and over at least one of the historic columns in the city. As the terrified inhabitants fled before them, the victors broke into all the monasteries and the shops, looking for loot. The women, including nuns, were rounded up, and loaded on the Turkish ships or dragged off to the camp outside the walls for safer keeping. To stake out a house and its contents as his possession, a Turk would raise his banner (*bandiera*) over it, and "as other Turks saw that banner raised over it," says Barbaro, "no one of them would think of entering the house, but went on looking for a house which had no banner. . . ." Banners were also raised over the monasteries and churches, according to Barbaro, and "I think that throughout Constantinople there would have been found 200,000 [!] such banners over all the houses. . . ."[75] Turks as well as Christians were slain, and the bodies were thrown into the Marmara where they floated, says the Venetian diarist, "as melons float through the canals."

The Byzantine historians found in the fall of Constantinople and the tragic end of the empire a subject worthy of their pens, and in the fulsome tradition of Byzantine rhetoric they dilate upon the atrocities of that ghastly morning of 29 May. Critobulus declares that the Turks killed the inhabitants of the city in a senseless slaughter, venting their rage upon defenseless men, women, and children for the hardships of the siege and the insults which had been hurled at them from the walls. The treatment of the women was appalling, and the old men, boys, priests, and nuns were savagely manhandled and dragged off into slavery, while "ten thousand other crimes were committed" (*ἄλλα μύρια εἰργασμένα δεινά*).[76] The churches were robbed of gold and silver chalices, precious reliquaries, and robes embroidered with gold, jewels, and pearls. The holy tables were wrenched from their foundations and overturned. Relics were desecrated. Even the graves of those long dead were opened in the expectation of gain or the desire for ghoulish sport. Critobulus informs us that sacred and divine books, as well as those on profane learning and philosophy, were consigned to the fire, trampled under foot, or sold for a song as a gesture of contempt for their contents.[77] According to Ducas, books without

---

[72] Ducas, chap. 39 (Bonn, pp. 287–88; ed. Grecu [1958], p. 361).

[73] Ducas, chap. 39 (Bonn, p. 288, lines 3–6).

[74] *Cf.* Chalcocondylas, bk. VIII (Bonn, p. 397; ed. Darkó, II, 161), who says there was a Greek legend that, when invaders reached the Forum Tauri, they would be driven back, and Ducas, chap. 39 (Bonn, pp. 289–90), who tells a similar story.

[75] *Giornale*, ed. Cornet, p. 57; ed. Dethier, pp. 819–20. Dethier is unduly harsh in his judgments on Barbaro, for whom he entertained an almost personal antipathy. Undoubtedly Barbaro makes a number of ridiculous statements, and his misrepresentation of the facts is sometimes scandalous, especially in his denigration of the Genoese and in his mendacious accounts of Venetian exploits. As a physician on a Venetian galley in the harbor, Barbaro was probably not in the city very much. Nevertheless, he remains our best source for the siege of Constantinople, especially for the chronology of events. He must have treated many a man injured in action, but oddly enough he never once refers in his entire diary to his activities as a physician. He was a person of some consequence, and had daily access to good sources of information. On the whole his figures are rather less fantastic than those of most of our other authorities, but in the present passage of course he has 40,000 more banners flying than his previous estimate of the size of the Turkish army (160,000 men). On the Conqueror's grants of houses to Turks, Greeks, and others, and his imposition of rents on "state-owned" land and properties, see Halil Inalcik, "The Policy of Mehmed II toward the Greek Population of Istanbul and the Byzantine Buildings of the City," *Dumbarton Oaks Papers*, XXIII–XXIV (1969–70), 231–49.

[76] Critobulus, I, 61 (ed. Müller, *FHG*, V-1, p. 96a; ed. Grecu, pp. 141, 143). Tedaldi, in Martène and Durand, *Thes. novus anecdotorum*, I, col. 1823B, says that the Turks "mistrent à mort tout ce qu'ils faisoient à eulx resistance." On the Turkish desecration of crosses torn from the walls of churches, violation of women, mocking of the Christian faith, etc., see Leonardo of Chios, in Lonicer, *Chron. turcica*, II, 100.

[77] Critobulus, I, 62 (ed. Müller, *FHG*, V-1, p. 96b; ed. Grecu, pp. 143, 145). The Franciscans lost their library in Constantinople, and Leonardo of Chios, archbishop of Mytilene, bought two of their missals, a breviary, and some other books from the Turks! (Pastor, *Hist. Popes*, II, append., no. 22, pp. 524–25, and *Gesch. d. Päpste*, I [repr. 1955], append., no. 55, pp. 843–44), a fact which Leonardo does not mention in his letter to Nicholas V on the fall of Constantinople.

number were loaded on carts and scattered to the east and west. Ten books were sold for a single nomisma—Aristotles, Platos, the theologians, and every kind of book. Gold and silver bindings were torn from the most beautiful gospels, which were then sold or thrown away.[78] The Turks searched in the churches and shrines, old vaults and tombs, underground porticos, cellars, and cisterns, hidden retreats and caves, and in every place where valuables might be concealed or people hiding.[79] There was no escaping.

In those first hours of peril and horror the poor inhabitants of the city thought only of celestial aid. Men and women, monks and nuns, fathers and mothers carrying infants flocked into the great church of Hagia Sophia. The portals were locked against the invading infidel. Now only a miracle could save those who sought refuge in the church which they had called "but yesterday and the day before a pit and altar of heretics," the resort of unionists and Catholics. For the pro-Latin historian Ducas the plight of the populace was the judgment of God being rendered on those who had been saying only a few days before that it would be "better to fall into the hands of the Turks than those of the Franks." Shortly after 7:00 A.M., the Turks reached Hagia Sophia in their wild career of carnage. They broke open the locked doors with axes, entered with drawn swords, and enslaved the multitude like so many sheep. Beautiful nuns, the mistress with her maidservant, the master with his slave, the archimandrite with his doorkeeper, young men and nobly born girls—all were dragged off to places of safekeeping by the plundering Turks, who returned a second and even a third time to get more of this human booty, with none to gainsay them. Words fail the eloquent Ducas as he recalls the dreadful scene. The gold and silver vessels were stolen, the icons and holy table desecrated, and the famous church stripped bare. Here was the fulfillment of the prophecy of Amos (3:15), "And I will smite the winter-house with the summer-house; and the houses of ivory shall perish, and the great houses shall have an end, saith the lord."[80]

When it was clear that the Turks had captured the city, Angelo Giovanni Lomellino, the Genoese podestà of Pera, closed the gates of Galata on the harbor side. In doing so, he shut in Alvise Diedo, Venetian captain of the galleys from Tana; Bartolo Furian, armorer of the same galleys; and the diarist Barbaro, *el miedego de le galie*, to whose partisan account we owe a good deal of our knowledge of the last days and hours of Byzantium. The Venetians had gone over to Galata to consult with the podestà when there was no longer any hope of the city's withstanding the attacks of the early morning hours of the twenty-ninth. Barbaro as usual accuses the Genoese of treachery, saying that they intended to turn over the Venetian galleys and their cargoes to the Turks. Diedo talked his way out, however, and he and his companions rejoined their ships, which were already under sail, preparing to leave without the captain. Breaking the iron-and-wooden chain with axes, they sailed into the Marmara and anchored near Diplokionion, where the Turkish fleet had itself been stationed only hours before. They waited a little while for any Venetian merchant who might reach them, but Barbaro says that none managed to do so. The Florentine merchant Jacopo Tedaldi, however, who has also left us a brief account of the siege, reached the Venetian ships, presumably before they had passed beyond the chain. Having been fighting on the wall near where the Turks entered the city, Tedaldi succeeded in escaping to the shore, removed his clothes, and swam out to the galleys, which took him aboard.[81]

---

[78] Ducas, chap. 42 (Bonn, p. 312). After his escape to Candia on the island of Crete, Isidore of Kiev discussed the literary losses with the Venetian humanist Lauro Querini (Quirini), who wrote Nicholas V from Candia on 15 July (1453) that 120,000 Greek manuscripts (*librorum volumina*) of works both sacred and profane were destroyed in the sack of Constantinople (Agostino Pertusi, "Le Epistole storiche di Lauro Quirini sulla caduta di Costantinopoli e la potenza dei Turchi," in P. O. Kristeller, K. Krautter, A. Pertusi, G. Ravegnani, H. Roob, and C. Seno, *Lauro Quirini umanista: Studi e testi*, Florence, 1976, p. 227, cited by Pertusi, *Caduta di Costantinopoli*, I [1976], 381 [note 25]).

[79] Critobulus, I, 66 (ed. Müller, *FHG*, V-1, p. 98a; ed. Grecu, p. 147). On the Turks' desecration of the tombs in their search for plunder, note the address (in 1455?) of Giacomo Campora, bishop of Caffa, to Ladislas Postumus of Bohemia and Hungary, in Pertusi, *Caduta di Costantinopoli*, I (1976), 192, 194.

[80] Ducas, chap. 39 (Bonn, pp. 289–93); *cf.* Leonardo of Chios, in Lonicer, *Chron. turcica*, II, 100, who is briefer but no less rhetorical than Ducas; Critobulus, I, 66, 2 (ed. Müller, *FHG*, V-1, p. 98a; ed. Grecu, p. 147); Pseudo-Sphrantzes, III, 8 (Bonn, pp. 289–90; ed. Grecu, pp. 430, 432); Chalcocondylas, bk. VIII (Bonn, p. 397; ed. Darkó, II, 161). Cardinal Isidore of Kiev also wrote a *Lamentatio* on the fall of Constantinople, which has been published by P. A. Dethier, in the *Monumenta Hungariae historica*, XXI, pt. 1 (1872), pp. 687–95 (*cf.*, below, note 95).

[81] Tedaldi, in Martène and Durand, *Thes. novus anecdotorum*, I, col. 1823CD: "Les gallées Venitiennes de voyage de Romanie et de Trapesonde demourerent là jusques à

At midday Diedo set sail with the Tana galleys. Girolamo Morosini followed in his galley. Then the Trebizond galley got under way, but she had trouble because she was short 164 men, who had been drowned, killed by cannon-fire, and otherwise lost in the fighting. Gabriele Trevisan's light galley sailed; he was left behind as a Turkish prisoner. A galley from Candia under Zaccaria Grioni also set out, but was quickly captured by the Turks. Three other vessels from Candia, armed merchantmen, sailed off with the Venetians, and with a favorable (north) wind passed through the Dardanelles to safety, arriving in Crete a month later. The crews of the Turkish ships were sharing in the pillage of the fallen city. "Within the harbor there remained fifteen ships of the Genoese, the emperor, and the Anconitans, including all five galleys of the emperor, which had been disarmed, and all the other vessels in the harbor remained there, both ships and galleys, which could not get away, all being captured by the Turks." Besides these fifteen, however, seven Genoese ships, which had been near the chain, did escape, as well as another from Pera, setting sail in the evening, hours after the hasty departure of the Venetians, whose valor the loyal Barbaro praises from one end of his diary to the other.[82] It must have been in one of these seven Genoese galleys that Giustiniani lay, wounded and heart-broken, dying upon arrival at Chios.

The battle for Constantinople had lasted from well before dawn until about noontime, after which the Christians were generally imprisoned rather than killed. According to a note added to the text of Barbaro, "sixty thousand prisoners were taken, and the Turks found infinite riches."[83] Leonardo of Chios states that, after the

midy, attendans pour sauver aucuns Chrestiens, dont il en est venu ung, entre lesquieulx fut cestuy Jacques Tedaldy, qui estant sur le mur en sa garde de la part où entrerent les Turcs, senti leur entrée bien deux heures après. Ainsi gagna la mer et se dépouilla et entra jusques aux gallées, qui le receurent." Since the Turks entered the city at various places, after breaking through at the Gates of S. Romanus and Charisius, it would be hard to say where Tedaldi was stationed on the walls.

[82] *Giornale*, ed. Cornet, pp. 57–59; ed. Dethier, pp. 821–24; *cf.* Tedaldi, in Martène and Durand, *Thes. novus anecdotorum*, I, col. 1123D, and Ducas, chap. 39 (Bonn, p. 297). Zaccaria Grioni was ransomed from the Turks in July, 1453. On his way back to Crete he was detained for debts by the Genoese at Chios (see M. Manoussakas, "Les Derniers Defenseurs crétois de Constantinople d'après les documents vénitiens," *Akten des XI. Internationalen Byzantinisten-Kongresses* [1958], Munich, 1960, pp. 333–34). The masters of the other three Cretan vessels were Greeks (Peter Sgouros, whose uncle George owned the vessel; Antonios Yalinas ['Υαλινᾶς]; and Antonios Philomatis), while the ship of another Venetian, Giovanni Venier, appears also to have got away safely (*cf.* Manoussakas, *art. cit.*, pp. 335–39, and R. Browning, "A Note on the Capture of Constantinople in 1453," *Byzantion*, XXII [1952], 381–84). Besides these, other vessels also escaped the Turks (Pertusi, *Caduta di Costantinopoli*, I [1976], 368 [note 180]). Yalinas, *notabilis homo maris*, lost almost all his possessions in the fall of Constantinople. On 26 December (1453) the Venetian Senate directed the colonial government of Crete to assist him to pay his debts to certain Jews, who must not be allowed more than ten per cent interest (Thiriet, *Régestes*, III [1961], no. 2950, p. 193). Three years later (on 16 November, 1456) Antonios Philomatis (Filomati) and his brother Markos were authorized by the Senate to purchase 40,000 measures of wheat in Apulia for shipment to Crete, where there was a very serious shortage (*ibid.*, III, no. 3026, p. 214).

[83] *Giornale*, ed. Cornet, p. 59; ed. Dethier, p. 825. The Venetians' losses alone were 200,000 ducats, to which must be added another 100,000 ducats lost by their compatriots of Candia (Zorzo Dolfin, *Assedio e presa di Costantinopoli*, ed. G. M. Thomas, in *Sitzungsber, d. k. bayer. Akad. d. Wissen. zu München*, II [1868], 37; Sanudo, *Vite de'duchi*, in *RISS*, XXII, col. 1151A; W. Heyd, *Histoire du commerce du Levant au moyen-âge*, trans. Furcy Raynaud, II [Leipzig, 1886, repr. 1967], 308–9). Tedaldi, *Thes. novus anecdotorum*, I, col. 1823E states, "On estime que le butin de Constantinople vault aux Turcs quatre millions de ducas. . . ." Tedaldi, however, sets the Venetian loss at 40–50,000 ducats; that of the Florentines, 20,000; that of the Anconitans, more than 20,000; while the Genoese loss was beyond calculation (*cf.* Heyd, *loc. cit.*). Some forty-seven Venetians were killed or captured (*cf.* Sanudo, *op. cit.*, col. 1150B, and the lists of names appended to Barbaro's diary, which present problems that need not be considered here). On the captives and the casualties, however, see Pertusi, I, 405–6, and on the losses sustained by the Italian states, *ibid.*, pp. 413–14.

According to A. D. Mordtmann, *Belagerung u. Eroberung Constantinopels* (1858), pp. 95–96, the Turks used to say of a rich man, for many years after the fall of the city, that he was "at the sack of Constantinople." Chalcocondylas, bk. VIII (Bonn, pp. 398–99; ed. Darkó, II, 162–63), speaks of the wealth that fell into Turkish hands. Anti-Greek sentiment in the West gave rise to some tall tales of Constantinopolitan avarice in the face of danger, such as that the city fell because the Greeks were unwilling to hire troops although one woman was later found to be hoarding 150,000 ducats' worth of jewels, silver, money, and clothes, and a man was concealing 80,000 ducats (*Cronica di Bologna*, ad ann. 1453, in Muratori, *RISS*, XVIII [1731], col. 701D; *Corpus chronicorum bononiensium*, in the new edition of the *RISS*, XVIII, pt. I, tom. 4, pp. 187a, 188b). *Cf.* L. Crivelli, *De expeditione Pii papae secundi in Turcas*, bk. I, in *RISS*, XXIII (1733), col. 55, and in the new *RISS*, XXIII, pt. V (1948–50), 59–60; note also the addendum to Niccolò Barbaro's diary, made by Marco Barbaro (*Giornale*, ed. Cornet, pp. 65–66).

S. Antonino of Florence relates that, while Constantinople was beset by the Turks, the Greeks sent envoys to Pope Nicholas V, imploring him for aid in men and money, which he refused, believing it unfair to burden Italy, already exhausted by wars, with further taxation to help the Greeks, whom he knew to have plenty of money to hire mercenaries, but who were devoid of all patriotism and so intent upon city had been subjected to pillage for three days, the booty was carried off to the Turkish camp, and that 60,000 Christians had been put in fetters.[84] Critobulus reports that some 4,000 Greeks and foreigners (ξένοι) lost their lives during the entire siege and final assault on the city, and that rather more than 50,000 persons were taken captive, including 500 from the defending army.[85] The population of Constantinople, however, was probably closer to 40,000 than to 50,000 in the mid-fifteenth century.

The Turks had emptied the city and largely destroyed it. According to Critobulus, even Mehmed II was moved to tears: "What a city, he said, we have given over to pillage and desolation!"[86] There were probably almost as many personal tragedies as there were people in the city. Bitter memories and recriminations long outlived those who had been involved in the disaster. The Grand Duke Lucas Notaras, first minister of the Byzantine state, who had been opposed to the union of the Churches, emerges a villain in our largely pro-Latin sources. Leonardo of Chios charges him with trying to curry favor with the young sultan by accusing the Grand Vizir Khalil Pasha of treasonable correspondence with the Emperor Constantine. In fact Notaras is said to have turned over to the sultan some of the letters which the grand vizir had sent, thus destroying the Greeks' one influential friend in the Ottoman camp. Leonardo adds, however, that Notaras paid the price of his wickedness. Having lost his two elder sons in the siege, he now saw a third, a youngster, slain before his very eyes, after which he was himself beheaded with some other Byzantine nobles. The Venetian bailie in Constantinople, Leonardo continues, Girolamo Minotto, and his son were both executed. Catarino Contarini, *vir humanissimus*, and another six Venetian nobles would also have been done to death if they had not managed to assure the Turks of 7,000 gold ducats' ransom. The Aragonese-Catalan consul was killed with two members of his staff or of his family.[87] As

preserving their private wealth that they lost everything, including freedom: after the siege great private treasures were found, but the Greeks had been blinded by avarice (see Raynaldus, *Ann. eccl.*, ad ann. 1453, no. 1, vol. XVIII [Cologne, 1694], p. 404). Undoubtedly the Greeks tried to conceal wealth, as the Pseudo-Sphrantzes accuses Notaras of doing (III, 9, ed. Bonn, p. 291, lines 15–20; ed. Grecu, pp. 432, 434), but it is surprising to find Pastor, *Hist. Popes*, II, 274, and *Gesch. d. Päpste*, I (repr. 1955), 621, being taken in by this anti-Greek propaganda.

Although Zorzo Dolfin says that after the fall of the city Nicholas V ordered five galleys to be armed in Venice *a sue spese* against the Turks (ed. Thomas, *op. cit.*, p. 38, and ed. Dethier, *MHH*, XXII-1, p. 1046), a Venetian document of 10 April, 1453, shows that the pope had been trying to arm his five galleys for some time before that date (Sen. Secreta, Reg. 19, fol. 192^r, and G. B. Picotti, "Sulle Navi papali in Oriente al tempo della caduta di Costantinopoli," *Nuovo Arch. veneto*, n.s., XXII [1911], 420–21, 438–39). Dolfin also observes that Nicholas V offered a plenary indulgence to whoever took up arms against the Turks, "ma è pocho soccorso in tanto bisogno."

[84] Leonardo, in Lonicer, *Chron. turcica*, II, 100: "Traducitur ad papiliones omnis substantia et praeda, vinctique omnes ad sexaginta milia funibus Christiani captivantur." Sa'd-ad-Dīn, trans. Gibb, p. 31, reports that "for three days and nights there was with the imperial permission [of the sultan] a general sack; and the victorious troops, through the richness of the spoil, entwined the arm of possession round the neck of their desires. . . ." Following Runciman, *The Fall of Constantinople* (1965), p. 148, however, Inalcik, "The Policy of Mehmed II . . . ," *Dumbarton Oaks Papers*, XXIII–XXIV, 233, believes that Mehmed "put an end to the pillage on the evening of the first day."

[85] Critobulus, I, 67 (ed. Müller, *FHG*, V-1, p. 98b; ed. Grecu, p. 149). The *Chronica bononiensia*, ad ann. 1453, in the new *RISS*, XVIII, pt. I, tom. 4, pp. 186a, 187b, state that ". . . furono morti da tre milia homini de amedoe le parte," according to a Franciscan report received in Bologna (*Cron. di Bologna*, in *RISS*, XVIII [1731], col. 701B, and *cf.* Dethier, *MHH*, XXII-1, p. 940).

[86] Critobulus, I, 68 (ed. Müller, *FHG*, V-1, p. 98b; ed. Grecu, p. 149).

[87] Leonardo, in Lonicer, *Chron. turcica*, II, 100–101, and *PG* 159, col. 943AB; *cf.* Pseudo-Sphrantzes, III, 9 (Bonn, p. 293, lines 13–14; ed. Grecu, p. 434, line 33), who says that the Catalan consul's two sons were executed with him. According to our other sources (see the following note), Notaras also had two sons who were put to death with their father. *Cf.* Crivelli, *De expeditione Pii P. II*, bk. I, in *RISS*, XXIII (1733), col. 55; new edition, in *RISS*, XXIII, pt. V (1948–50), 60, on Notaras; Critobulus, I, 76 (ed. Müller, *FHG*, V-1, pp. 103b–104a; ed. Grecu, p. 167), on Khalil Pasha; Zorzo Dolfin, *Assedio e presa di Costantinopoli*, from Dolfin's *Cronaca*, ed. G. M. Thomas, in *Sitzungsber. d. k. bayer. Akad. d. Wissen. zu München*, II (1868), 32–33 (also in Dethier, *MHH*, XXII, pt. 1), who had read Leonardo of Chios.

The Venetian Senate believed the bailie Girolamo (or Geronimo) Minotto to be alive on 17 July, 1453, when the following resolution was passed (Sen. Mar, Reg. 4, fol. 201^v [202^v]): "Cum omnibus notus sit miserabilis casus nobilis viri Ser Jeronimi Minoto, qui erat baiulus Constantinopolis, qui sicut habetur ductus est captivus in Turchia cum uxore et uno filio et perdidit omnem facultatem suam, et unus eius filius deliberaverit ire ad procurandum redemptionem et liberationem suam et sit res pia dare sibi omnem favorem et comoditatem possibilem, considerato hoc miserabili casu, vadit pars quod filius dicti Ser Jeronimi vadat pro ballistario super hac galea subtili cuius est patronus nobilis vir Ser Petrus Arimundo in numero duorum balistariorum ordinariorum qui accipi debent pro dicta galea: De parte 163, de non 0, non sinceri 0." On 28 August, however, having learned that Minotto and one of his sons had been put to for the proud Notaras, who can say what the truth may have been? Ducas and Chalcocondylas tell a moving story of Notaras's boldly refusing to surrender the younger of two surviving sons to Mehmed's abnormal lust, preferring death for himself and his family to Turkish infamy. Mehmed ordered the immediate execution of father and sons.[88] Very likely Critobulus was right when he affirmed that the siege and sack of Constantinople were more terrible than those of Troy and Babylon, Carthage, Rome, and Jerusalem.[89]

The podestà of Pera, Angelo Giovanni Lomellino, had reason to be frightened. He sent messengers to Sultan Mehmed to offer him the keys to Galata. The sultan accepted them and received the inhabitants of the Genoese colony as his subjects. Mehmed appointed a Turkish governor, confiscated the property of those who had fled, and ordered the demolition of the towers and landward walls of Galata. The inhabitants obeyed and accepted the status of slaves, writes Leonardo, for safety's sake, disregarding their instructions from Genoa (whatever they may have been), and now the sultan "is pulling down the tower, at the height of which stood the cross of Christ, from which it took its name." Those who had been free and kept the peace were now slaves. Their future lay with Pope Nicholas V, to whom Leonardo wrote his long letter on the fall of Constantinople and addressed his plea to avenge the terrible injuries inflicted upon the Christians by the Turks.[90]

The Turkish occupation of Pera is vividly described in a letter written by the podestà Angelo Giovanni Lomellino to his brother on 23 June, 1453, less than a month after the fall of Constantinople:

> Noble and most dear brother: If I have not written before this, and do not herewith answer the letters I have received from you, do pardon me, because I have been and am unceasingly in such melancholy and so preoccupied that I prefer death rather than life. I am certain you have learned before this of the unexpected fall of Constantinople, taken by the lord Turk on the twenty-ninth of last month, a day that we had been looking forward to with keen anticipation, because it seemed to hold certain victory for us. The lord [Turk] gave battle all night and on all fronts, and he was met courageously at every point. To put it briefly, however, in the morning Giovanni Giustiniani . . . left his gate, withdrawing to the sea, and the Turks entered by that very gate, where no resistance was offered—indeed, in this miserable fashion not even a village should have been lost!
>
> I want to believe this comes of our sins. Considering my nature, just imagine how I am now. God give me patience. [The Turks] gave the city over to a three days' sack. You have never seen such suffering. They took an inestimable booty. I sent in defense of the city all the mercenaries from Chios and all those sent from Genoa as well as a good many citizens and burgesses from here [Galata] and, what concerns us more at this point, our [nephew] Imperiale and our family retainers. For my own part I have done as much as I could, God knows, for I have always recognized that, if Constantinople were lost, we should lose this place too. . . .

The podestà notes that some of the Genoese had saved themselves by flight. Others had been captured on the palisades. The rest had been obliged to remain in Galata, because the captains of the ships had been unwilling to wait for people who wanted to escape: "When I saw, however, that things had reached such a pass, I preferred to lose my own life rather than to leave this land. If I had gone, this place, thus abandoned, would have been sacked." The

death by the Turks, the Senate voted the dead bailie's daughter a dowry of 1,000 gold ducats if she married or 300 if she entered a convent. His other children and his wife—she must have escaped or been ransomed—were each to receive a pension of twenty-five ducats a year (Iorga, *Notes et extraits*, III [1902], 289, and note Pertusi, *Caduta di Costantinopoli*, I [1976], 369–70).

[88] Ducas, chap. 40 (Bonn, pp. 303–6), at length, and Chalcocondylas, bk. VIII (Bonn, pp. 401–3; ed. Darkó, II, 164–66); see also Critobulus, I, 73 (ed. Müller, *FHG*, V-1, p. 102; ed. Grecu, pp. 159, 161, 163); Pusculus, bk. IV, vv. 1070–74, ed. Ellissen, p. 82; Leonardo of Chios, *loc. cit.*; Adam de Montaldo, ed. Hopf, in Dethier, *MHH*, XXII-1, p. 53; *cf.* Babinger, *Maometto* (1957), pp. 155–58, and J. I. Kotsonis, "Loukas Notaras" [in Greek], in *Aktines*, no. 139 (Athens, 1953). According to the poet Pusculus, bk. I, vv. 434–439, ed. Ellissen, p. 21, Notaras was not of noble birth as commonly stated: ". . . olim pisciculos vendebat avus. . . ." Two Cantacuzeni were also executed after the Turkish occupation of Constantinople (D. M. Nicol, *The Byzantine Family of Kantakouzenos* [*Cantacuzenus*] *ca. 1100–1460*, Washington, D.C., 1968, nos. 68–69, pp. 179–81).

[89] Critobulus, I, 68 (ed Müller, *FHG*, V-1, p. 99; ed. Grecu, pp. 151, 153). On the fortunes of "Istanbul" during the half century or so following the conquest, see the article of Inalcik referred to above in note 75.

[90] Leonardo, in Lonicer, *Chron. turcica*, II, 101–2, letter dated at Chios on 16 August, 1453; on the surrender of Pera, *cf.* Tedaldi, in Martène and Durand, *Thes. novus anecdotorum*, I, col. 1823B; Critobulus, I, 67 (ed. Müller, *FHG*, V-1, p. 98a; ed. Grecu, p. 149). L. T. Belgrano reprints Leonardo's letter to Nicholas V, from Philip Lonicer's *Chronica turcica* [1578], in the *Atti della Società ligure di storia patria*, XIII (1877–84), no. CL, pp. 233–57. An improved text, with an Italian translation, is given in Pertusi, *Caduta di Costantinopoli*, I (1976), 124–71.

podestà sent ambassadors to Mehmed II with handsome gifts, the keys to Galata, and a request that the peace which obtained between the Turks and the Genoese might be observed. There was no immediate reply. In the meantime the frantic podestà tried to maintain quiet in the terrified colony, and implored the skippers [*patroni*] of the ships to remain all the next day, because he was sure that, if the sultan was not provoked, he could secure the desired peace from him. The skippers were unwilling to take the chance, and sailed at midnight.

> When in the morning the lord [Turk] received the news of the departure of the ships, he informed my ambassadors that he wanted an unconditional surrender [*terra libera*]—we could scarcely save ourselves and our personal property—for he said that we did everything possible to save Constantinople, and that we were the reason why the Turks had not taken the place on the first day. Certainly they spoke the truth. We were in the gravest danger.

Despite the extreme difficulty peace was made with the Turk in the name of the burgesses of Galata. The podestà now kept behind the scenes, possibly in order not to appear to commit Genoa to the terms imposed by the sultan. The podestà did, however, pay a visit to the sultan, who entered Galata twice; ordered most of the defenses, including the Tower of Santa Croce, to be demolished; took all the cannon; "and he intends to take all the munitions and all the arms of the burgesses."

Mehmed also had an inventory made of all the goods and property of the merchants and burgesses who had fled. If they returned, their possessions would be restored; if not, they would be confiscated. The fugitives, who seem to have congregated at Chios, were notified of this fact. Mehmed had just withdrawn to Adrianople, whither he had had Khalil Pasha sent, having taken his wealth from him (Khalil was to be executed on 10 July). The Venetian bailie and his son had been beheaded along with seven other Venetians; so had the Catalan consul with another five or six Catalans. "Just think whether we have been in danger." Mehmed had placed one of his men (Angelo Giovanni calls him a *sclavus*) over Galata, and a *subashi* and a *kadi* with about 1,500 janissaries in Constantinople. He was said to be demanding the *kharaj* or poll-tax levied on non-Moslems (*carrachium*) from Chios, Caffa, and other Genoese possessions. He was making claims on the despot of Serbia. "Finally he has achieved such arrogance as a consequence of the capture of Constantinople that it seems he will soon make himself master of the whole world, and states publicly that in less than two years he plans to come to Rome. . . ."[91]

Sultan Mehmed had provided, at the beginning of June, 1453, for the Genoese community of Galata by a firman which spared the town (*κάστρον*), and permitted the inhabitants to retain their homes, shops, and warehouses, vineyards and mills, merchandise and ships. Their wives and children were not to be taken away, their sons being made exempt from the *devshirme* or tribute of boys for the service of the sultan. The residents of Galata could also keep their churches, but were forbidden to build new ones, and as usual they were prohibited from ringing church bells. No Turks, however, were to live in Galata except officials of the Porte. The residents were to have freedom of trade, and the Genoese ready access to their erstwhile colony. They were to be free of *corvées*, but had to pay the poll-tax (*kharaj*) exacted of non-Moslem subjects of the Porte. Although they could elect a sort of chairman (*protogeros*) of their local board of trade, Galata had become a Turkish town, and Genoa had no prospect of recovering it.[92]

---

[91] This letter was first published by the orientalist Silvestre de Sacy, "Pièces diplomatiques tirées des Archives de la République de Gènes," in *Notices et extraits des manuscrits de la Bibliothèque du Roi et autres bibliothèques*, XI (Paris, 1827), 75–79. It was later republished by P. A. Dethier and K. Hopf, in the *Monumenta Hungariae historica*, XXII, pt. 1 (1872), pp. 647–55, and by L. T. Belgrano, in the *Atti della Società ligure di storia patria*, XIII (1877–84), no. CXLIX, pp. 229–33. Angelo Giovanni suggested to his brother that an embassy be sent from Genoa to deal with the sultan. His nephew Imperiale was captured in Constantinople, but he had been unable to secure his release, "quia dominus [Mehmed] vult habere aliquos Latinos in curia sua" (an interesting fact on which Babinger, *Maometto*, p. 171, comments). He had not yet written to the doge, "non habendo animum." On Angelo Giovanni Lomellino [not Zaccaria], note Pertusi, *Caduta di Costantinopoli*, I (1976), 39–40, 355 (note 75).

[92] The Greek text of the firman is given, after the edition by Jos. von Hammer-Purgstall, in F. Miklosich and J. Müller, eds., *Acta et diplomata graeca medii aevi*, III (Vienna, 1865, repr. Aalen, 1968), 287–88, and by Belgrano, in *Atti della Società ligure*, XIII, 226–29; there is a Venetian translation in Zorzo Dolfin, *Assedio e presa di Costantinopoli*, ed. G. M. Thomas, in the *Sitzungsber. d. k. bayer. Akad. d. Wissen.*, II (1868), 34–36, and *cf.* J. W. Zinkeisen, *Gesch. d. osman. Reiches in Europa*, II (Gotha, 1854), 26–28.

An original Greek text of the firman of 1453 is preserved in the British [Museum] Library (MS. Egerton, no. 2817), where it has been hanging framed on the wall of one of the exhibition rooms for more than sixty years. It is dated 1 June A.M. 6961–A.D. 1453, and bears the sultan's

In retrospect perhaps no event in the history of the fifteenth century seems more certainly inevitable than the Ottoman occupation of the Greek capital on the Bosporus. In 1453 the city had stood as a tiny island in an Ottoman sea. For a full hundred years, ever since the Turks had seized Gallipoli in 1354, their power had been expanding, their influence extending, throughout the entire Balkan peninsula. Over the years tens of thousands of Turks had moved into southeastern Europe, where they fought and won, went about their daily affairs and died, leaving their impact upon the life, language, and literature of the Balkan peoples. The latter took their revenge of the invaders by reviling them in folk songs of lament and heroism, prophecies, chronicles, and lives of saints and princes. In the popular as well as in the learned literature of the later fifteenth century (and thereafter) the fall of Constantinople was always a pre-eminent theme.[93]

In the meantime, however, except for the sad lot of the inhabitants of the fallen city, most people continued their usual humdrum lives of hardship and of want. The fortunate discovery by Jean Darrouzès of eight letters dated from 29 July to 13 December, 1453, provides us with a fleeting glimpse into the affairs of the Greeks in the months that followed the Ottoman occupation of Constantinople. The chief actor in the petty lay and ecclesiastical dramas depicted in these letters is an otherwise unknown Nicholas Isidorus, who was serving Mehmed II as a Greek "judge" (κριτής) in the erstwhile Ottoman capital of Adrianople. The requests made of him by his Greek correspondents, however, make clear that they were seeking his financial assistance and the employment of his influence rather than the exercise of his authority (if any) as a judge, whatever *krités* may have meant in the present context. While it was hard to find the ransom for a captive being held by a "merciless and unyielding Moslem" (Μουσουλμάνος . . . ἀνιλεὴς καὶ ἀσυγκατάβατος), and there is more than one reference to the fall of Constantinople in these letters, most of them illustrate the dreary continuance of life and its problems as being much the same after as before

---

official signature (*tughra*) at the top, with the signature of Zagan Pasha at the bottom. Being the first treaty made by the sultan with an Italian state after the conquest of Constantinople, the grant of privileges to the Genoese of Galata is a most important document. In fact it was to constitute for more than four centuries the juridical foundation upon which were to be built the rights enjoyed by Roman Catholics in the Ottoman empire, forming the major precedent for later treaties between the sultan and the Christian powers, especially France, which from 1536 (as we shall see in the next volume) became the chief protector of Roman Catholics under the Porte.

The firman of 1453 was formally renewed for the first time, with some modifications of content, in March, 1613, by Sultan Ahmed I. For re-editions of the Greek text and commentaries, see N. Iorga, "Le Privilège de Mohammed II pour la ville de Péra (l-er juin 1453)," in the *Bulletin historique de l'Académie roumaine*, II (Bucharest, 1914), 11–32, where a number of other Ottoman-Christian treaties are also republished, and E. Dalleggio d'Alessio, "Le Texte grec du traité conclu par les Génois de Galata avec Mehmet II, le ler juin 1453," Ἑλληνικά, XI (1939), 115–24; "Traité entre les Génois de Galata et Mehmet II," *Échos d'Orient*, XXXIX (1940), 161–75; and "Listes des podestats de la colonie génoise de Péra (Galata) . . . ," *Revue des études byzantines*, XXVII (1969), 151–57. The Turkish disposition of the affairs of Galata is rather inaccurately described by Pears, *Destruction of the Greek Empire* (1903), pp. 371–72, but see Heyd, trans. Furcy Raynaud, II, 310–13, with refs., and the works cited by Dalleggio d'Alessio.

The Genoese community was located not only in Pera, but (after 1475) also in the area of Salma Tomruk, called "Kaffa Mahalessi," when Mehmed II settled the inhabitants of Caffa near the Adrianople Gate (Edirne Kapi) in the northwestern part of Istanbul. The community developed into the "nation latine de Constantinople," under the religious authority of the Apostolic Delegation. It numbered almost 14,000 persons by the mid-nineteenth century, but had fallen to about 3,400 by 1927, when it was suppressed as a sort of juridical entity (see Dalleggio d'Alessio, "La Communauté latine de Constantinople au lendemain de la conquête ottomane," *Échos d'Orient*, XXXVI [1937], 309–17, and in general *cf.* Ernest Mamboury, *Istanbul touristique*, Istanbul, 1951, pp. 92–101).

Some twenty-five years after the Turkish occupation of the city there were, according to the census of 1477, some 8,951 Moslem households in Istanbul proper and 535 in Galata; 3,151 Orthodox-Greek households in Istanbul and 592 in Galata; and, all together, 3,095 households of Armenians, Latins, and Gypsies (Inalcik, "The Policy of Mehmed II . . . ," *Dumbarton Oaks Papers*, XXIII–XXIV, 247). According to "Bishop" Samile's letter of 6 August, 1453, to Oswald, the burgomaster of Hermannstadt (see above, note 38), Mehmed had already by that date transferred 30,000 persons by sea to Istanbul and the area roundabout (Iorga, *Notes et extraits*, IV [1915], 67; Pertusi, *Caduta di Costantinopoli*, I [1976], 230, and *cf.*, *ibid.*, p. 426).

[93] *Cf.* I. Dujčev, "La Conquête turque et la prise de Constantinople dans la littérature slave contemporaine," in *Byzantinoslavica*, XIV (1953), 14–54; *ibid.*, XVI (1955), 318–29; and, *ibid.*, XVII (1956), 276–340; V. Grecu, "La Chute de Constantinople dans la littérature populaire roumaine," *ibid.*, XIV (1953), 55–81; J. Irmscher, "Zeitgenössische deutsche Stimmen zum Fall von Byzanz," *ibid.*, XIV, 109–22; A. Vaillant, "Les Langues slaves méridionales et la conquête turque," *ibid.*, XIV, 123–29; G. Th. Zoras, "Orientations idéologiques et politiques avant et après la chute de Constantinople," *L'Hellénisme contemporain*, 2nd ser., VII (29 May, 1953), 103–23, esp. pp. 108 ff.; G. Megas, "La Prise de Constantinople dans la poésie et la tradition populaires grecques," *ibid.*, VII, 125–33.

"the seizure of the wretched city" (ἡ ἅλωσις τῆς ἀθλίας πόλεως).[94]

Constantinople was wretched, but Mehmed II was not. He seemed to have climbed to the top of the world in two months. He had realized the ancient Moslem ambition of conquering the greatest city in the Levant. He was soon to set about repopulating it. There can be no doubt that he aspired to world domination, as Angelo Giovanni had informed his brother; Leonardo of Chios warned Pope Nicholas V that Mehmed was boasting that he would soon be appearing in the Adriatic on his way to Rome.[95] Jacopo Tedaldi also speaks of his desire to rule the world, and notes that he fed his ambition by reading the histories of Alexander and Caesar, and was full of inquiries about Venice, Rome, and Milan, "et d'autres choses que de guerre ne parle. . . ."[96] Although after his great victory Mehmed had returned to Adrianople, which had been the Ottoman capital for almost a century, he would soon be establishing his court and his government in the newly acquired city. Constantinople, however, was no longer the city of Constantine. It became Turkish Istanbul, a city of oriental bazaars, grey domes, and white minarets, tombs, little cemeteries, black cypresses, and turbanlike vines growing atop crumbling walls.

---

[94] J. Darrouzès, "Lettres de 1453," *Revue des études byzantines*, XXII (1964), 72–124. George Scholarius, then the monk Gennadius, is mentioned in one of these letters (*ibid.*, pp. 101, 122–23).

[95] Leonardo, in Lonicer, *Chron. turcica*, II, 101. After his flight from Constantinople, Cardinal Isidore of Kiev took refuge for a while on the Venetian island of Crete, from which in July, 1453, he addressed letters to Nicholas V (Iorga, *Notes et extraits*, II, 522–24), Cardinals Bessarion and Capranica, the Doge Francesco Foscari, and the Florentines (for references to the texts see Georg Hofmann, "Quellen zu Isidor von Kiew als Kardinal und Patriarch," *Orientalia Christiana periodica*, XVIII [1952], 143–48, who gives the text of Isidore's letter to the Florentines, dated 7 July, with a brief description of the horrors of the Turkish sack of the city, and *cf.* F. Babinger, "Veneto-kretische Geistesstrebungen . . . ," *Byzantinische Zeitschrift*, LVII [1964], 70–71).

For good texts, with Italian translations, of Isidore's letters to Nicholas V (from Candia in Crete, dated 6 and 15 July, 1453) and to Bessarion (also dated 6 July, in which he informs Bessarion that he had arrived on the Bosporus on 26 October, 1452 [*cf.*, above, note 9]; declares that Mehmed had had an army of 300,000 men and a fleet of 220 vessels, as he also says in his letter of 15 July to Nicholas V; reports that he was himself wounded by an arrow on the left side of the head; and gives a dramatic picture of the siege and sack of Constantinople), as well as for the letter of lamentation addressed to Christendom at large (*universis et singulis Christi fidelibus*, dated 8 July), and the letters to Francesco Foscari (26 July) and to Philip the Good of Burgundy (from Rome, dated 22 February, 1455), see Pertusi, *Caduta di Costantinopoli*, I [1976], 58–111. In the letter to Philip, Isidore again states that Mehmed had assembled 300,000 men and 220 vessels for the siege of Constantinople. He also defends, as stated above in note 41, the conduct of the Genoese during the siege.

[96] Mehmed's ambition and his interest in Italy are well known, but Tedaldi's text is interesting (Martène and Durand. *Thes. novus anecdotorum*, I, col. 1824AB): ". . . courageux et ardant de seignourer et converser tout le monde: voire plus qu'Alexandre, ne César, ne aultre vaillant qui ait esté allegué qu'il a plus grande puissance et seignourie que nul d'eulx n'avoit: et tousjours faisoit lire leur histoire, demande où et comment est posé Venise, combien loing de terre ferme, et comme on y puet entrer par mer et par terre. . . . Pareillement demande de Romme où elle est assise, et du duc de Milan et de ses vaillans: et d'autres choses que de guerre ne parle. . . ." Tedaldi offers a program for the expulsion of the Turk from Europe (*ibid.*, cols. 1824–25).

When Cardinal Isidore returned from the East, he reported that Mehmed seemed more powerful than Caesar, Alexander, "or any other prince who has ever aspired to dominion over the world." His treasure in coined money was immense; he had 230 ships, and could build as many more as he chose; he also had 30,000 horsemen and many footsoldiers, with apparently no limit to possible additional recruitments. See the dispatch dated 22 November, 1453, of Leonardo de'Benvoglienti, Sienese envoy to Venice (in Pastor, *Hist. Popes*, II, 288–89, note, and *Gesch. d. Päpste*, I [repr. 1955], 634, with addenda to the note), who says that Mehmed "intende presto venire in Italia."

5. PERILS AND PROBLEMS AFTER THE FALL OF CONSTANTINOPLE (1453–1455)

THE FALL of Constantinople seems to have made as great an impression both in Europe and in the East as the fall of Rome had almost a thousand years before. The news reached Venice on Friday, 29 June, while the Grand Council was in session. A fast vessel, a *grippo* from Corfu, bringing letters from Lepanto, put in at the wooden landing-stage on the Bacino. People were standing by their windows and on the balconies, "waiting between hope and fear to learn the import of the news, whether of the city of Constantinople or of the galleys of Romania." They were anxious for news of a father, a son, or a brother. The letters were presented to the Signoria, presumably in the Sala del Collegio. The word spread immediately through the Grand Council that Constantinople had been taken, and that everyone above six years of age had been killed. All balloting in the Council was postponed. There were cries and groans, wringing of hands and beating of breasts. As one wept for the assumed death of a relative, another lamented the loss of his property on the Bosporus. When silence was achieved, by order of the Signoria the secretary of the Ten, Lodovico Bevazan, read *ad alta voce* (presumably in the Sala del Maggior Consiglio) a letter from the colonial government of Corfu, "la qual avisava haver per lettere da Nepanto exaudito Constantinopoli esser prexo." Lamentation gave way to recrimination, and everyone accused the Signoria and the Collegio of negligence, and blamed "those who had written falsely from Constantinople that the Turkish army was not coming. . . ."[1]

On the same day, at about 11:00 A.M., a certain Battista de' Franchi and one Piero Stella wrote the doge of Genoa, Pietro di Campofregoso, and the "officials of Romania" of the news which they had just learned at the ducal palace in Venice. During that very hour a *grippo* had arrived from Corfu with (they said) two letters, one from the castellan of Modon and the other from the bailie in Negroponte. On 28 May, or so they informed the doge, the sultan had taken Pera by force of arms at about eleven o'clock in the morning, killing everyone except the children. On the twenty-ninth he had captured Constantinople, and again he had slain everyone. Two large Venetian galleys and a light galley had escaped miraculously with all aboard, but the letters from Modon and Negroponte contained no word of the Genoese ships in the Golden Horn. The Venetians were in such utter despair that Battista de' Franchi and Piero Stella had not yet ventured to ask for copies of the letters.[2]

---

[1] Zorzo Dolfin, *Assedio e presa di Costantinopoli*, ed. G. M. Thomas, in *Sitzungsber. d. k. bayer. Akademie d. Wissenschaften zu München*, II (1868), 36–37, also in P. A. Dethier, ed., *Monumenta Hungariae historica*, XXII, pt. 1 (Istanbul, 1872), pp. 1043–44; Marino Sanudo, *Vite de'duchi*, in L. A. Muratori, ed., *RISS*, XXII (Milan, 1733), col. 1151A; Ludwig von Pastor, *History of the Popes*, II, 271–72, and *Geschichte der Päpste*, I (repr. 1955), 619; F. Babinger, *Maometto il Conquistatore*, Turin, 1957, p. 159; and *cf.* N. Iorga, *Gesch. d. osman. Reiches*, II (Gotha, 1909), 39 ff. On the "incredibilis dolor" in Venice, see Giov. Simoneta, *Res gestae Fr. Sfortiae*, bk. XXIII, in *RISS*, XXI (Milan, 1732), col. 645AB, and ed. Giovanni Soranzo, in the new Muratori, *RISS*, XXI, pt. 2, pp. 378–79.

[2] Arch. di Stato di Firenze, Dieci di Balìa: Carteggi, Responsive, Reg. 22 [old classification: Classe X, dist. 2, no. 22], fol. 261: The letter was written "ex Venetiis adi XXVIIII a hore XIIII" [on 29 June, 1453, at about 11:00 A.M.]. Battista de' Franchi and Piero Stella began with an apology for the lamentable news which their letter would bring to Genoa, ". . . perche noi vi facciamo noto come nella presente hora cè venuto grifo da Corfu mandato pel bali di decto luogo a questa illustrissima Signoria con due lettere, una del castellano di Modone et laltra del bali di Negroponte, le quali contengono questo effecto: El signore de'Turchi adi XXVIII di Maggio avendo avuto Pera per forza alle XIIII hore et amazato ogniuno et maschi et femine excepto che i fanciulli piccoli, et adi XXVIIII del decto mese avendo avuto Costantinopoli et nel medesimo modo amazato ogniuno. Due galee grosse de Venitiani et una sottile miracolosamente fuggirono quasi con tutti gli huomini fediti. Delle navi nostre non cè nessuna mentione. Questa cipta [città] è in maximi lamenti, et non abbiamo avuto ardire de cercare le copie delle lettere, per la quale cosa non piglino admiratione le Signorie vostre se abbiamo scripto confusamente et maximamente essendo in tanta angustia et dolore, non avendo provato mai simili cose per cagione del damno cosi publico come privato nella roba et nelle persone. . . ." *Cf.*, *ibid.*, fol. 263, a letter of the Florentine ambassador Niccolò Soderini to the Florentine Dieci, dated at Genoa on 8 July, 1453, alluding to this letter.

Soderini had written the Signori Dieci on 29 May [!], 1453, that Constantinople appeared likely to fall to the Turks (fol. 249^v). On 10–11 July he informed his government that many persons in Genoa were unwilling to believe that the Turks had actually taken Constantinople and Pera, and that the news which came his way was still too confusing to allow him to reach a conclusion as to what had

The next day, on 30 June, the Venetian government wrote Pope Nicholas V

although we assume, most blessed father, that both by letters of the reverend father, the lord archbishop of Ragusa [Jacopo Venier of Recanati], your papal legate here, as well as from other sources your Holiness has probably been able to learn before this of the horrible and most deplorable fall of the cities of Constantinople and Pera.[3]

Actually the pope had not yet been informed. The news reached Bologna on 4 July,[4] and Rome on the eighth. The popular preacher, Fra Roberto da Lecce, made the announcement to the people. Rome was for weeks the scene of deep lamentation as well as of rumors that Constantinople had not fallen or that the Turks were already preparing for an attack on Rome.[5]

On 18 July (1453) the Venetian Senate notified the papal legate, Archbishop Jacopo of Ragusa, who was busy with the prospect of a crusade, that their Greek and Levantine possessions, which had enjoyed upwards of two centuries of peace [!], were neither fortified nor equipped to face the great peril in which they found themselves, and that, if they should be lost, the Turk would have no difficulty entering Apulia.[6] About the same time (on 19 July) Cardinal Guillaume d'Estouteville wrote Francesco Sforza, duke of Milan, that the latter knew of course

really happened. Couriers had reached Genoa about 5:00 P.M. on the eleventh, *a hore XX*, from Venice and from Naples, each bearing letters confirming the Turkish victory. It was still some time before the facts were given credence in Genoa, where there was much wishful thinking, partly occasioned by Genoa's difficulties with Naples (fols. 258^r, 259^r, and *cf.* fols. 260 ff., 278).

[3] Arch. di Stato di Venezia, Senatus Secreta, Reg. 19 [1450–1453], fol. 202^r, cited by Pastor, *Gesch. d. Päpste*, I, 619, note; the text has been published by Sime Ljubić, ed., *Listine* [*Documents*] *o odnošajih izmedju južnoga slavenstva i mletačke republike*, vol. X (Zagreb, 1891), pp. 13–14 (in the Monumenta spectantia historiam slavorum meridionalium, vol. XXII); *cf.* F. Thiriet, *Régestes des délibérations du Sénat de Venise concernant la Romanie*, III (Paris and The Hague, 1961), no. 2928, p. 187.

On 30 June, 1453, the Venetian Senate also debated whether to allow the departure of commercial vessels for Syria until more certain news could be had from Constantinople (Sen. Mar, Reg. 4, fol. 197^r [198^r], and *cf.*, *ibid.*, fol. 201^v [202^v], docs. dated 17 July). The stir caused by the ghastly news has naturally left its imprint upon the documents (*ibid.*, fols. 197^v [198^v] ff.). On 12 July two envoys from Negroponte appeared before the Signoria, stating that the city and the island lacked the arms and munitions wherewith to put up a defense against the Turks, should the need arise. The Senate responded promptly to the needs and fears of the Negropontines, and gave orders that arms be sent them, including ten small cannon to mount upon the city walls. The decision was made also to send immediately an "engineer" with the requisite skill and experience to put the walls and breastworks of the city into shape for an emergency (fol. 200^v [201^v]). From this time on, a Turkish attack upon Negroponte remained the Senate's worst fear.

[4] *Corpus chronicorum bononiensium*, ed. Albano Sorbelli, in the new Muratori, *RISS*, XVIII, pt. 1, vol. IV, pp. 189a, 190b.

[5] Pastor, *Hist. Popes*, II, 272–73, and *Gesch. d. Päpste*, I, 619–20. On the Franciscan friar Roberto Caracciolo da Lecce, who gave a series of pentecostal sermons on the fall of Constantinople, note Agostino Pertusi, *La Caduta di Costantinopoli*, 2 vols., Verona, 1976, I, pp. XXXVIII–XXXIX, and II, 510.

[6] Arch. di Stato di Venezia, Sen. Secreta, Reg. 19 [1450–1453], fol. 205^r, doc. dated 18 July, 1453. The Venetians claimed to be very sympathetic to the representations of the legate: ". . . Verum dicimus quod quoniam preteritis mensibus ante casum urbis Constantinopolis hinc expedivimus non nullas galeas nostras pro favore et succursu urbis eiusdem, misimus etiam cum eisdem galeis unum oratorem nostrum ut proficisceretur ad dominum Teucrum ut se interponeret et operaretur quicquid boni posset pro concordia facienda inter serenissimum dominum imperatorem Constantinopolitanum et ipsum Teucrum, et etiam ut si quid per nos agendum esset cum Teucro ob favores datos Constantinopoli per galeas nostras Romanie et aliter id fieri posset ita quod per viam pacis, si ita fieri posset, res ille transirent.

"Supervenit autem inopinatus casus amissionis urbis eiusdem de quo tamen cordialiter doluimus quantum facile satis diiudicari potest. Remanserunt captivi in ea clade XL nobiles nostri aliique cives et mercatores nostri in bono numero ultra multos Cretenses et alios subditos nostros ita ut ultra quingenti ex nostris illic remanserint. Cupimusque multum illos qui vivi superfuerunt posse redimere ne pereant. Consideravimus etiam quod civitates et loca nostra Gretie et illarum partium nostrarum que ab annis CC citra, ut ita dixerimus, in pace vixerunt nec fortificate nec munite sunt per modum quod in magno et evidenti periculo constitute sunt, et si (quod absit) amitterentur, non est dubium quod valde, habiliter, ac comodissime absque alia contradictione hostis iste crucis cum potentia sua in Apuliam se transfretare posset cum magno periculo nominis Christiani. Nos vero ut iste impetus, si fieri possit, aliquanto contineatur, iussimus prefato oratori nostro quod det operam eundi ad presentiam Teucri tam pro redimendis captivis nostris predictis quam etiam pro componendo res illas ut non procedat ad expugnandum et occupandum terras et loca nostra predicta pro evitando tantum excidium tantumque inconveniens quantum occurrere posset. . . ."

The letter closes with a statement of the necessity of achieving peace and union among the Christian powers to help meet the Turk, *crudelissimus hostis*, and thanks the pope for his promise to send five galleys into Levantine waters, which should be done as soon as possible. Note the Venetian claim, in the text quoted above, that more than 500 subjects of the Republic were taken captive by the Turks in the fall of Constantinople. Venetian subjects (*subditi*), however, were not citizens (*cives*). Greeks and *gasmuli* had often been given Venetian "naturalization papers," which had made them "subjects," and had enabled them to escape the buyer's half of the Byzantine customs duties (see Volume I, p. 239, note 71, and *cf.* Thiriet, *Régestes*, III, no. 2933, p. 188, which document, however, presents Greeks as acting "au nom de Vénitiens" in a different context).

about the Gran Turco's having taken Constantinople "although now some people are trying to say that it has been miraculously recovered, which is possible but not probable." The pope looked upon the catastrophe as the "shame of Christendom" (*vergogna de la christianitade*), and was in agreement with his advisers that, if possible, peace must be established in Italy. (The Venetians, as we shall note, had given far more attention during the winter of 1452–1453 to their war with Milan than to the plight of Constantinople.) To this end Cardinal Domenico Capranica had just left for Naples as legate to Alfonso V of Aragon-Catalonia, and Cardinal Juan de Carvajal was to leave the next day for Florence, Milan, and Venice.[7] Years later Marino Sanudo, learned historian of the doges of Venice, summed up the situation:

> The news of the loss of Constantinople caused a great terror among Christians, and the pope immediately sent word to the Signoria that the Venetians should arm five galleys against the Turks at his expense, and he launched the crusade. Those who went in an armada or by land against the Turks should receive the full benefits of the jubilee. If any soldier refused recruitment and declined to go, he was excommunicated. The Senate decided to send an ambassador to the lord Turk to demand of him our men who were taken prisoners in Constantinople, because we had a just peace [*buona pace*] with him. Bartolommeo Marcello was elected; he accepted the commission and went. It was also decided that Jacopo Loredan, captain-general of the sea, should go with twelve galleys to protect Negroponte.[8]

Although Sanudo has got his facts somewhat out of order, they are substantially accurate.

The Venetian envoy Bartolommeo Marcello reached Istanbul safely, and labored there to good effect, apparently finding Sultan Mehmed easy to deal with, *avendo impetrato tutto da lui benignamente*. When Marcello returned in the mid-year of 1454, he brought with him the well-known Turco-Venetian peace of 18 April. Mehmed sent one of his "slaves" back with him to receive the doge's oath if the Signoria found the terms satisfactory. They were quite satisfactory, for the new treaty was largely a confirmation of the one made on 10 September, 1451.[9] In April, 1454, the peace of Lodi, to which we shall come presently, had effected the

---

[7] L. v. Pastor, *Acta inedita historiam pontificum romanorum . . . illustrantia*, I (Freiburg im Breisgau, 1904), no. 22, pp. 35–36; on Carvajal's difficult mission, see Simoneta, *Res gestae Fr. Sfortiae*, bk. XXIII, in *RISS*, XXI, cols. 645–46, and ed. G. Soranzo, in the new Muratori, *RISS*, XXI, pt. 2, p. 379; Cristoforo da Soldo, in the so-called *Istoria bresciana*, *RISS*, XXI, cols. 882D–888, and ed. Giuseppe Brizzolara (who notes that in the oldest MSS. Cristoforo's work is called simply *Cronaca*), in the new Muratori, *RISS*, XXI, pt. 3, pp. 123–31, on the warfare in northern Italy, leading to the peace of Lodi in April, 1454, when Francesco Sforza made peace "che'l si possa resistere al impeto del Turco" (*ibid.*, p. 129, line 22).

See in general Enrico Carusi, "La Legazione del Card. D. Capranica ad Alfonso di Aragona (Napoli, 29 luglio–7 agosto 1453)," *Archivio della R. Società romana di storia patria*, XXVIII (1905), 473–81; there is a sketch of Capranica's career in M. Morpurgo-Castelnuovo, "Il Cardinal Domenico Capranica," *ibid.*, L11 (1929), 1–146, with twenty-one documents, and on Capranica's (unsuccessful) mission to Naples, *ibid.*, pp. 55–57. On the peace that was eventually made at Lodi (on 9 April, 1454), see below, but Cristoforo da Soldo notes, "Hor perchè cadauno sapia che questa Italia non pò stare senza guerra."

On Carvajal's dedication to the *bellum in Turcos*, note Card. Jacopo Ammanati, *Ep.* 41, in ed. Frankfurt of Pius II's *Commentarii* (1614), p. 483, and Ammanati's own *Commentarii*, *ibid.*, pp. 354–55.

[8] *Vite de' duchi*, in *RISS*, XXII (Milan, 1733), col. 1151B; *cf.* Zorzo Dolfin, ed. Thomas, in *Sitzungsber. d. k. bayer. Akad.*, II, 38. Sanudo's chronology is a bit awry. Already on 10 April, 1453, the Senate had written Pope Nicholas V (Sen. Secreta, Reg. 19, fol. 192[r]), "Habuimus nuper literas a reverendissimis dominis cardinalibus, vicecancellario [Francesco Condulmer, d. 30 Oct., 1453] et Sancti Marci [Pietro Barbo, later Pope Paul II], quibus nos cerciores faciunt Beatitudinem vestram pro sua innata clemencia ut occuratur tantis malis et periculis que parari videntur opem ferre civitati Constantinopolitane constituisse et triremes quinque in hac nostra civitate armari facere. . . ." The pope had decided to arm his five galleys long before the fall of Constantinople (*cf.* Thiriet, *Régestes*, III, nos. 2917, 2927, pp. 184, 186–87).

Furthermore, on 8 May the Senate had directed Loredan "quoniam non deveniente Teucro ad pacem vel treuguas cum serenissimo domino Imperatore Constantinopolis posset occurere quod mitteret ex gentibus et navigiis suis contra civitatem et insulam nostram Nigropontis, volumus quod in hoc casu cum galeis nostris tibi commissis provideas ad bonam securitatem et tutellam civitatis et insule Nigropontis sicut sapientie tue melius et utilius videbitur" (Sen. Secreta, Reg. 19, fol. 194[v]). Well before the Turkish victory on the Bosporus, therefore, the Senate had provided for the defense of Negroponte but, it would seem, not adequately (*cf.*, above, note 3).

[9] G. M. Thomas (and R. Predelli), *Diplomatarium veneto-levantinum*, II (Venice, 1899, repr. New York, 1965), no. 209, pp. 282–84, and note V. V. Makušev, *Monumenta historica slavorum meridionalium*, II (Belgrade, 1882), 226–27, doc. dated 18 June, 1454. Thomas does not give the text of the treaty of 18 April, 1454, his latest document being the Venetian pact with Ibrahim Beg, the Gran Caramano, dated 12 February, 1454, a diplomatic move on the part of the Venetians which presumably hastened Mehmed's willingness to make peace with the Republic, since Ibrahim Beg was one of his chief enemies. An envoy of Ibrahim Beg was active in Rome a little later (Makušev, II, 195–96, doc. dated 16 August, 1455).

pacification of Italy,[10] and the Venetians found themselves free from the onerous burdens of war both at home and abroad. Marcello was sent back to Istanbul to discuss the modification of certain articles, and since by the terms of the treaty the Venetians were allowed to maintain a bailie on the Bosporus to preside over their commercial colony, Marcello was appointed to the post with an annual salary of 1,000 ducats.

According to Sanudo, Venice had been under the huge (annual) expense of 550,000 ducats for her Italian wars, and for an armada of forty-five galleys and eight other ships the captain-general Jacopo Loredan had wanted an additional 120,000 ducats a year. By the treaties of Lodi and Istanbul, Venice was relieved of much of this expense. By the terms of 18 April, 1454, the Porte and Signoria swore to maintain with each other "peace and friendship" (*la pace et amicizia*), with full respect for the rights and properties of both the signatories. As in the agreement of 1451, Venice was assured protection for her citizens' ships and goods throughout the Ottoman domain, free entry into and exit from ports, including that of Istanbul, and the right to buy and sell, "and they shall be safe on the sea and on land," promised Mehmed, "as was customary before, in the time of my father." The Venetians were only obliged to pay a two per cent sales tax, and they granted to Turkish merchants the same rights in Venetian ports as they were to enjoy in those of the sultan. Both powers pledged themselves not to assist each other's enemies, to which the Venetians cheerfully assented some seven months after the papal announcement of a crusade. From the Venetian standpoint it seemed to be a good peace and to meet the needs of the Republic if not those of Christendom.[11]

It was one thing to negotiate a treaty, as Heyd has observed, "but the situation was much more attractive on paper than in reality." In Ottoman Istanbul the Venetians lived in an atmosphere of perennial disturbance. The

[10] See, below, pp. 156–57.

[11] The full text and historical background are given by Sanudo, *Vite de' duchi*, in *RISS*, XXII, cols. 1153–58; Thiriet, *Régestes*, III, nos. 2923, 2932, 2934–36, 2946, 2955–56, pp. 186 ff.; *cf.* S. Romanin, *Storia documentata di Venezia*, IV (Venice, 1855), 254, 527 ff.; J. W. Zinkeisen, *Gesch. d. osman. Reiches in Europa*, II (Gotha, 1854), 33–37; W. Heyd, *Histoire du commerce du Levant au moyen-âge*, trans. Furcy Raynaud, II (Leipzig, 1886, repr. Amsterdam, 1967), 315–17; Pastor, *Gesch. d. Päpste*, I (repr. 1955), 626–28; F. Babinger, *Maometto il Conquistatore* (1957), pp. 175–76. Bartolommeo Marcello served as Venetian bailie in Istanbul for two years, being replaced in 1456 by Lorenzo Vitturi (Thiriet, *Régestes*, III, nos. 2969, 3016, pp. 198, 211). We may also note that in the treaties of 1451 and 1454 Venetian suzerainty was recognized over the duchy of Naxos, which was not to pay tribute to the Turk (Thomas and Predelli, *Dipl. ven.-levantinum*, II, no. 209, p. 383, from the peace of 10 September, 1451; note also Sanudo, *op. cit.*, col. 1155C, and R. Predelli, ed., *Regesti dei Commemoriali*, V [1901], bk. XIV, no. 204, p. 65, misdated 1461, and no. 288, pp. 91–92).

The commission, issued in the name of the Doge Francesco Foscari to Bartolommeo Marcello, "about to go as bailie to Constantinople," is dated 16 August, 1454, and may be found in the Sen. Secreta, Reg. 20, fols. 29^v–30^r [30^v–31^r], with a brief summary in Thiriet, *Régestes*, III, no. 2976, p. 200. It is an important document. Marcello was to press for the Turkish observance of the peace which obtained between the Republic and the Porte, and to protest against Turkish depredation of Venetian territory. The Venetian government had instructed its own officers in critical areas strictly to maintain the peace, "sed sicut ex Corphoo et Nigroponte sumus informati post dictam pacem per Teucros ex Barga et Nepanto quam plures anime abducte fuerunt et multa damna illata, et ex insula Nigropontis non nulle anime per unam fustam Turcorum fuerunt accepte cum derobatione bonorum subditorum nostrorum, et quoniam credimus quod hec processerunt contra mentem et scitum Excellentie sue quam non dubitamus velle pacem ipsam servare, instabis quod anime abducte relaxentur et quod damna restituantur sicut iustum et debitum est et quod ordinet per modum quod omnes sui a damnis nostrorum se de cetero abstineant."

Venice wanted to retain the northern Sporades (Skyros, Skiathos, and Skopelos) because of their proximity to Negroponte (Euboea). If Domenico Gattilusio, lord of Mytilene (Lesbos), or his envoy was at the Porte asking for the return of the islands to his rule, Marcello was to dissuade him: "Ad partem vero insularum Schyri, Schinti, et Scopuli per formam capitulorum pacis nulla fit mentio quod restituantur fueruntque insule ille accepte tempore guerre quo tempore accipi potuerunt promisimusque hominibus dictarum insularum quod eos pro dominio nostro tenebimus et conservabimus et nulli alio domino dabimus, propterea non videmus, salvo jure et honore nostro, posse ipsas insulas alicui dare licet vellemus in longe maioribus quam de his minimis et miserabilibus insulis complacere sue Excellentie sicque non dubitamus quod dominatio sua pro eius summa sapientia et magnitudine animi bene contenta et satisfacta remanebit. Et cum his et aliis pertinentibus rationibus et verbis instabis et procurabis, sicut de prudentia tua confidimus, quod desistat a petitione dictarum insularum quia nostre mentis est quod ipse insule nobis remaneant. Et si dominus Methelini [Domenico Gattilusio, d. 1458] vel nuntius suus esset ad portam Theucri solicitando restitutionem dictarum insularum sibi suadebis cum illis verbis et rationibus que tue prudentie videbuntur quod velint desistere ab hac petitione et potius caripendere benevolentiam nostram quam tres scopulos prout sunt dicti tres."

The commission continues with Marcello's instructions to the effect that: "Iustificata materia insularum dices prefato domino quod pro observatione et implemento capitulorum pacis designavimus et misimus te in bailum nostrum Constantinopolis et misissemus etiam galeas nostras iuxta solitum. Sed quoniam in tempore convenienti ad nos non rediisti nostras galeas mittere non potuimus sed ex Venetiis,

Turks were hardly civilized, and the merchants of S. Mark often looked back with strong nostalgia to the good old days of Byzantium. At any moment the sultan might indulge in some fit of passion or brutality. However conciliatory the policy of the home government, the Venetians found it hard to get along with the warlike Turks, who looked with disdain upon merchants of patrician families as mere hucksters. If the Venetian bailie in Istanbul received an unusually large salary, he earned it. Considering the conflict of interest which, given the sultan's insatiable ambition, was certain to obtain between the Porte and the Signoria, the bailie could not be sure any morning that he would not spend the night in prison. The fate of Girolamo Minotto was always before him. The Venetians could lament the passing of the Byzantine empire almost as much as the Greeks.[12]

The recovery of Constantinople rather than of Jerusalem now became the crusading ideal of such Europeans as were moved to contemplate war against the infidel. There were a good many of them. The significance of the Turkish victory

---

Creta, et aliis omnibus locis nostris ordinavimus quod naves et navigia cum mercatoribus vadant Constantinopolim iuxta solitum et in futurum servabitur consuetudo." He was to make the customary presents of cloth of gold, silk, and other gifts to the high officials of the Porte; report fully and clearly on conditions in Constantinople four days after his arrival; attend to several other important matters; and finally look to the release of Venetian prisoners in Turkish hands —"Sicut scis, restant adhuc captivi in manibus Teucrorum non nulli Veneti et fideles nostri inter quos est Victor Trivisano de la Barba; ipsorum liberationem procurabis sicut melius et utilius cognoveris et maxime dicti Victoris cuius pater providit de pecuniis necessariis ad illius redemptionem."

Marcello's duties, as he departed for Constantinople "in baylum et rectorem nostrorum Venetorum exercendo regimen tuum ibidem et in illis locis que tenebat Imperator Constantinopolis a die quo applicueris illuc usque ad duos annos," are defined in detail in the Senato Mar, Reg. 5, fols. 49^v–51^v [50^v–52^v], doc. dated 16 August, 1454, with a concise summary in Thiriet, *Régestes*, III, no. 2976, pp. 200–1. Upon his return to Venice, Marcello passed through Ragusa in April, 1456, bringing the news of vast Turkish preparations for a campaign "ad expugnanda Danubii loca" (to be directed against Belgrade, for which see below, Chapter 6). The Ragusei reported the fact to John Hunyadi on 15 April (J. Gelcich and L. Thallóczy, eds., *Diplomatarium ragusanum*, Budapest, 1887, no. 342, p. 592). A Turkish envoy accompanied Marcello upon the latter's return home (Sen. Secreta, Reg. 20, fol. 89^r [90^r], doc. dated 19 May, 1456).

[12] *Cf.* Heyd, *Hist. du commerce*, trans. Furcy Raynaud, II (1886, repr. 1967), 317–18. There was some intellectual activity at the court of Mehmed II, especially in his later years. An assessment of his interest in western culture usually begins with a discussion of Ciriaco of Ancona's presence at the Porte (see above, Chapter 2, note 113). Most of the Ottoman soldiers and tax officials with whom the Venetian merchants dealt were a crude and grasping lot. Although the names are known of various literati and scholars at the Ottoman court, to whom Mehmed sometimes gave pensions and offices, their intellectual achievements were very modest indeed.

In a most engaging but rather misleading article Emil Jacobs, "Mehemmed II., der Eroberer, seine Beziehungen zur Renaissance und seine Büchersammlung," *Oriens*, II (1949), 6–30, has depicted Mehmed's cultural interests and the intellectual life of the court circle around him in too glowing colors. Jacobs believed that Mehmed, "der treueste Repräsentant des alten Osmanentums," had acquired "ein Verständnis für die zeitgenössische Bildung des Abendlandes" (*ibid.*, p. 9). He gives a good deal of attention to Ciriaco, whom he erroneously believes to be the Kyrízis of Francesco Filelfo's letter of 11 March, 1454 (pp. 14–15), which has already claimed our attention in Chapter 2. Certainly more influence was exerted on Mehmed by his Italian Jewish physician Yakub Pasha than by the diplomats and humanists who came for (usually) brief periods to the Porte. At a later date (in July, 1469), for example, the Venetian Senate thought that Yakub Pasha, "Master Jacomo the Physician" (see below, p. 296), whose name is linked with that of the Grand Vizir Mahmud Pasha, might help prevail upon Mehmed to make peace with the Republic during a terrible phase of the Turco-Venetian war (Sen. Secreta, Reg. 24, fols. 34^v and 36^r). On this interesting figure, apparently more important than any humanist at the Porte, see Babinger, "Ja'qūb-Pascha, ein Leibarzt Mehmed's II., Leben und Schicksale des Maestro Jacopo aus Gaeta," *Aufsätze u. Abhandlungen*, I (1962), 240–62 (first published in the *Rivista degli studi orientali*, XXVI [Rome, 1951], 87–113); note also Bernard Lewis, "The Privilege Granted by Meḥmed II to his Physician," *Bulletin of the School of Oriental and African Studies*, University of London, XIV–3 (1952), 550–63; and *cf.* E. Birnbaum, "Ḥekim Ya'qūb, Physician to Sultan Meḥemmed the Conqueror," *Harofé Haivri: The Hebrew Medical Journal*, I (1961), 250–222 [*sic*].

Few works of notable value were produced in Istanbul in the fifteenth century, very little originality being shown in belles-lettres, grammar, theology, philosophy, law, or the sciences (*cf.* Babinger, *Maometto*, pp. 685–720). Mehmed's interest in western "culture," as was noted by Jacopo Tedaldi, Jacopo de' Languschi, Niccolò Sagundino, the Pseudo-Sphrantzes, and others, was to learn enough of Europe to facilitate further conquests in the West (Babinger, "Mehmed II., der Eroberer, und Italien," in *Aufsätze u. Abhandlungen*, I [1962], 178–86). He wanted to know how Alexander and Caesar had conquered the world, but he was no "prince of the Italian Renaissance," addicted to humanism (*idem*, *Maometto*, pp. 740–42). To be sure, Persian copyists, miniaturists, and binders produced some fine books at Mehmed's court, but the sixteenth century was the great era of bookmaking and manuscript illumination (*ibid.*, pp. 682–83). Highly intelligent without doubt, Mehmed practiced a religious tolerance which did him honor. He was in fact intrigued by Christian theology, but probably had a less extensive knowledge of "foreign" languages than has usually been assumed (Ch. G. Patrinelis, "Mehmed II the Conqueror and His Presumed Knowledge of Greek and Latin," *Viator*, II [1971], 349–54). On the whole Heyd, II, 317, seems not without reason in stating that "chez les Turcs, prince et peuple étaient encore . . . loin de la civilisation. . . ."

of 29 May, 1453, quickly penetrated even into the dream world of chivalric forms and ceremonials which one still found at the court of Burgundy, and on 17 February, 1454, Duke Philip the Good and the Knights of the Golden Fleece took the most solemn crusading vows at Lille amid the gorgeous and (to us) melodramatic spectacles attending the celebrated Feast of the Pheasant.[13]

If the Venetians viewed the Turkish success with dismay, the Genoese did so with terror. Mehmed II's occupation of Pera (Galata) had come at a low point in the checkered fortunes of Genoa, which could do nothing but fear for the future of Caffa and the trading company or *mahona* of Chios. Since the state had only the slenderest resources, and was at war with Naples, it was preposterous to think of making war also on the Porte. It was difficult even to find the funds necessary to send an embassy to Istanbul. On 11 March, 1454, however, two envoys were finally appointed, Luciano Spinola and Baldassare Maruffo, whose instructions were to proceed without delay to Istanbul, stopping first at Chios and then at Pera, in order to learn all they could of conditions at the Ottoman court and of the sultan's general mood, as a guide to how much they might ask for, and with what chance of success. Once in the sultan's presence, they were to congratulate him on the occupation of Constantinople, which under his domination might now look forward to a new era of prosperity! If their previous consultations at Chios and Pera had been at all hopeful, they were to make a special plea for Pera, which without its own defenses would inevitably perish, being unsafe as a resort for merchants and as a depot for merchandise. They were to try to gain the return of Pera to Genoa and to secure permission for the repair of its walls and towers, for only thus could Mehmed hope to see the place again become a rich market for precious stones, fine cloths, silks, and other agreeable items. They were, however, not to discuss the possibility of a tribute, if the sultan brought up the question, unless there seemed a reasonable chance of his restoring Pera to the Republic. Should they be able to secure no concession at all from him, they were to solicit his mercy for the inhabitants of Pera, whose own prayers they were also to transmit to him. In the (highly unlikely) event of their success, the two envoys were to draw lots to see which one of them would take over the office of podestà and assume the task of refortifying Pera. They were also to secure in writing, if they could, the sultan's guarantee of freedom for Genoese trade and shipping as well as access to the Black Sea, where Caffa now hung like a ripe apple on the tree. Permission to export wheat from Ottoman territories was another request. The commission given Spinola and Maruffo represented the triumph of wishful thinking over common sense, and after consulting with their compatriots at Chios, Pera, and Adrianople, as Heyd suggests, very likely the poor envoys never presented their petition to the sultan at all, which would also have been in keeping with their instructions. Maruffo died on the return journey, and Spinola later gave the poor state of his health as the reason for declining to return to Istanbul on a second such mission.[14]

Spinola's reluctance again to face the Gran Turco was no greater than that of his government, which had surrendered Caffa and all its other possessions on the Black Sea to the Bank

[13] G. du Fresne de Beaucourt, *Histoire de Charles VII*, V (Paris, 1890), 395–97; Otto Cartellieri, *The Court of Burgundy*, trans. Malcolm Letts, New York, 1929, pp. 136–53; Constantin Marinesco, in *Comptes rendus de l'Académie des Inscriptions et Belles-Lettres*, Paris, 1951, p. 136; Armand Grunzweig, "Philippe le Bon et Constantinople," *Byzantion*, XXIV (1954), 47–61; Richard Vaughan, *Philip the Good: The Apogee of Burgundy*, London, 1970, pp. 143–45, 266–67, 297–99, 358 ff.; and Yvon Lacaze, "Politique 'méditerranéenne' et projets de croisade chez Philippe le Bon: De la chute de Byzance à la victoire chrétienne de Belgrade (mai 1453–juillet 1456)," *Annales de Bourgogne*, XLI (1969), 5–42, 81–132.

[14] Amedeo Vigna, "Codice diplomatico delle colonie tauro-liguri durante la signoria dell'Ufficio di S. Giorgio [1453–1475]," in *Atti della Società ligure di storia patria*, VI (Genoa, 1868), docs. II, XXXVIII–XXXIX, CXVII, pp. 21–23, 118–22, 297–301, and esp. L. T. Belgrano, "Documenti riguardanti la colonia di Pera," *ibid.*, XIII (1877–84), no. CLIV, pp. 261–70, where note the importance of Francesco Drapperio (p. 263), on whom see above, pp. 79, 94–95, and below, note 19. *Cf.* also V. V. Makušev, *Monumenta historica slavorum meridionalium*, II (Belgrade, 1882), 14–15, letter dated 13 March, 1454, of the Doge Pietro di Campofregoso and the Council of the Anziani to Sultan Mehmed II; Heyd, *Histoire du commerce*, trans. Furcy Raynaud, II, 313–15, 387; Philip P. Argenti, *The Occupation of Chios by the Genoese*, I (Cambridge, 1958), 203–5. For conditions in the Genoese colonies of Pera and the Black Sea, see Vigna, in *Atti*, VI, nos. I, XXI–XXII, XXXIII ff., CXXXVIII, CLI, *et alibi*, and on Genoese commercial enterprise both at home and abroad, see Jacques Heers, *Gênes au XVe siècle: Activité économique et problèmes sociaux*, Paris, 1961, who gives some attention to the colonies at Pera and on the Black Sea as well as to Francesco Drapperio.

of S. George (*Uffizio di S. Giorgio*) in an irrevocable grant, made in the Palazzo Pubblico in Genoa shortly after noontime on Thursday, 15 November, 1453. The Bank of S. George acquired Caffa and the other colonies in full sovereignty, with the rights of naming all officials, legislating for the inhabitants, and trying under its jurisdiction even capital cases. The Bank, founded in 1407, disposed of larger resources than did the impoverished Republic of Genoa. The directors (*protectores*) of the Bank began most vigorously to see to the repair of the fortifications and the reform of the administration of Caffa (and Samastri also). The constant danger, however, to men and ships having to run the gauntlet under the cannon of Rumeli Hisar and Anadolu Hisar, as well as the great expense involved in such difficult and distant operations, soon diminished the directors' ardor for justice, efficiency, and the honor of S. George. The stockholders had to be considered. The Bank had been obliged to reduce its dividend from seven to four per cent, and the inhabitants of Caffa apparently paid the Porte from year to year a tribute of 3,000 Venetian ducats, which an embassy sent from the colony had negotiated for 1454–1455.[15]

Important enough before the fall of Constantinople, the city and island of Chios became (after the Turkish occupation of Pera) the chief Genoese outpost in the Levant. There was therefore every reason for the *mahonesi* solemnly to warn the Genoese Doge Pietro di Campofregoso and the Council of the Anziani, in the autumn of 1454, that as the Republic's ships and merchandise were more and more concentrated in the island, the danger from the Turks would become all the greater "unless the city [of Chios] were fortified with stronger walls and battlements, and protected by a larger garrison." Considering the Turks' striking power both on land and at sea and Sultan Mehmed II's audacity and greed, the refortification of Chios and its harbor facilities had become a grave necessity. Fear of the sultan, however, had already imposed the most terrible financial burdens on the *mahona*. The intolerably large annual tribute which the island company had to pay the Porte made it quite impossible to provide for the proper defense of Chios from current revenues. Conditions had become such that the commune of Genoa should itself be extending a helping hand. There was pressing need, we are told, of a financial subvention for the preservation of Chios, but the *mahonesi* realized that the home government was faced with its own perils and problems, and so dared not ask for the help which the state of emergency actually demanded. The *mahonesi* therefore proposed as an alternative, however inadequate it might be, the fuller employment of local resources in the public interest—increasing the import duty paid by foreigners and also the tax on wine; doubling the government brokerage fees on all purchases, sales, and exchanges; removing the Latin burghers' exemption from the *kharaj* (*caragium*), which was levied on all property to help meet the Turkish tribute; and further requiring from the Latin burghers an annual contribution of food (*provisio victualium*), such as the Greeks, Jews, and others were obliged to make, notwithstanding the burghers' previous exemption from this impost.[16] On 18 December, 1454, after two days' examination of the *mahonesi's* petition, the doge and Anziani granted all their requests, which were confirmed by the treasury officials on the following day, and registered by the chancellor on the twentieth.[17] It was necessary to do something, but of course there was little to do. The Genoese hold on Chios would be relinquished whenever the Ottoman sultan should decide that the time had come.

For a while it seemed as though the time had come in the spring and summer of 1455 when the Turkish admiral Hamza Beg, after raids upon the Hospitaller strongholds at Rhodes and elsewhere,[18] directed his large fleet toward the

[15] *Cf.* Heyd, *Hist. du commerce*, trans. Furcy Raynaud, II, 382–90, and for the sources see Vigna, "Codice diplomatico," in *Atti della Società ligure di storia patria*, VI, nos. III–IV, pp. 24–43, docs. dated November, 1453, and Sil. de Sacy, "Pièces diplomatiques," in *Notices et extraits des manuscrits de la Bibliothèque du Roi et autres bibliothèques*, XI (Paris, 1827), 81–89. The revenues of Caffa "and those parts" were estimated at more than 30,000 pounds (Vigna, *op. cit.*, p. 25). On 22 April, 1455, Nicholas V's successor Calixtus III was to grant the Genoese "all and singly," who would fight against either the Turks or the Tatars to help hold threatened Caffa for the directors of the Bank of S. George, the plenary remission of all sins, as outlined in Nicholas's declarations with respect to the jubilee year (Arch. Segr. Vaticano, Reg. Vat. 436, fols. 3^r–5^r, and 269^r–270^v, by mod. stamped enumeration, and *cf.* Reg. Vat. 439, fols. 174^v–175^v, doc. of the following November referring to that of 22 April). On the Bank of S. George, which survived until 1797, see Heers, *Gênes au XVe siècle*, esp. pp. 97 ff.

[16] Argenti, *Occupation of Chios*, II (1958), 302–4.

[17] *Ibid.*, II, 304–5; vol. I, pp. 422–23.

[18] On the problems of the Hospitallers in the years immediately after 1453, see R. Valentini, "L'Egeo dopo

harbor of Chios, which was rather better defended than the *mahonesi's* petition of 1454 might have led the Genoese government to believe. Although Hamza Beg landed troops on Chios, lacking cannon and siege tackle, he did not attack the town walls nor the harbor installations, but he demanded the payment of 40,000 ducats which the *mahonesi* were alleged to owe Francesco Drapperio for alum delivered to Chios. Drapperio, a Genoese resident in Galata, whom we have met as Ciriaco of Ancona's friend, had long been a favorite of the Porte. He appears to have assigned the debt, which the *mahonesi* claimed already to have satisfied, to the sultan.[19]

Drapperio was in fact on board a Turkish vessel calmly watching Hamza Beg's ineffective effort to collect the money. After ravaging parts of the island and taking two reluctant Chian envoys into custody, Hamza Beg sailed on to Cos (Stanchio, Istanköy), where he laid unsuccessful siege to the highland castle for three weeks. Cos was a dependency of the Hospitallers, whose persistent refusal to pay tribute to the Porte earned them Mehmed II's lifelong enmity. Accomplishing nothing against the defenders of Cos, Hamza Beg finally set sail for Gallipoli, again weighing anchor off Chios, where he demanded that the *mahonesi* send envoys to Adrianople to settle the question of their debt to Drapperio. He landed some forces on the island; they became embroiled with the inhabitants; and in the encounter the Turkish flagship was sunk. The ship was Hamza Beg's own property, but the fact helped little to assuage the wrath of Mehmed II, who removed him from the naval command, and appointed Yunus Pasha in his place. Chios was spared a full-scale Turkish attack when the *mahonesi* agreed to pay an increased tribute and an indemnity of 30,000 ducats, which seems like a steep price for the ship which the Turks had lost as a consequence of their own aggression. Toward the end of the year 1455, however, the two Phocaeas on the Anatolian coast, the chief source of alum for the European market, were taken by the Turks, who sacked them with their customary thoroughness.[20]

During the anxious months of waiting for Mehmed II's next move, the *mahonesi* addressed an appeal from Chios to Rome on 14 August, 1455, reminding the pope, now Calixtus III, of the terror under which they lived. The Turkish fleet had just been sent against them. It was going to return in greater strength, "and that this will happen, we have learned through no idle rumor but from informed authorities." The *mahonesi* would stand by the Christian cause with steadfast hearts:

> But what is our strength? How will so small a colony be defended without the common help of Christendom?—and yet, however small, we think its importance is not unknown to all Christians overseas. Its fall would carry most of them to the same destruction. Amid these perils which we share with other Christians we take refuge in your Holiness. . . .

The *mahonesi* expressed a touching if somewhat

---

la caduta di Costantinopoli nelle relazioni dei Gran Maestri di Rodi," *Bullettino dell' Istituto storico italiano per il medio evo e Archivio Muratoriano*, LI (1936), 137–68, with four documents, and in the present context note, *ibid.*, pp. 148–51.

[19] Drapperio was not always prompt, it would seem, in the payment of his own debts. Four years before this (on 8 July, 1451), when Lorenzo Moro was being sent as Venetian envoy to the new sultan, Mehmed II, among the charges he received from the Senate was that of getting Mehmed or the pashas at the Ottoman court to force Drapperio to pay what he owed one Giovanni de Mercato Novo, a Venetian citizen, who had done business with Drapperio through a factor named Domenico de Magistris. Moro's commission indicates that a *magna summa pecuniarum* was involved, and describes Drapperio as a "Genoese and subject of the sultan," *Januensis et subditus dicti imperatoris Turchorum* (Arch. di Stato di Venezia, Sen. Mar, Reg. 4, fol. 67^{v} [68^{v}]). Amedeo Vigna, "Codice diplomatico," *Atti della Società ligure di storia patria*, VI, 221, note, says that "Drapperio" (*drappo*, cloth; *drappiere*, draper, mercer) seems not to be a Genoese surname, and that Francesco was a Jew, which might explain his friendliness with the Turks and his apparent indifference to his Christian compatriots. He was the chief financial figure in the eastern alum trade during the fifth decade of the century (Marie-Louise Heers, "Les Génois et le commerce de l'alun à la fin du moyen âge," *Revue d'histoire économique et sociale*, XXXII [1954], 36–42, 49 ff.).

[20] On the indemnity, see Ducas, *Hist. byzant.*, chap. 45 (Bonn, p. 335); in addition to the ship it was, of course, intended to cover the Turkish loss of life. The annual tribute for Chios was now set at 10,000 ducats. In a second expedition of the same year the Genoese station of New Phocaea, together with its alum works, was taken by the Turks (on 1 November, 1455), as we learn from Critobulus, II, 5 (ed. Karl Müller, in *Fragmenta historicorum graecorum* [*FHG*], V-1 [Paris, 1870], p. 108b, and ed. V. Grecu, *Critobul din Imbros: Din domnia lui Mahomed al II-lea, anii 1451–1467*, Bucharest, 1963, p. 179), as well as from Ducas, chap. 44 (Bonn, pp. 333–34), in some detail.

Old Phocaea soon followed New Phocaea into Turkish hands. See in general Vigna, "Codice diplomatico," *Atti della Società ligure*, VI, 220 ff.; W. Heyd, *Hist. du commerce*, trans. Furcy Raynaud, II, 319–20; Babinger, *Maometto* (1957), pp. 202–6, 208; Argenti, *Occupation of Chios*, I, 208–9; and esp. Wolfgang Müller-Wiener, "Kuşadasi und Yeni-Foça: Zwei italienische Gründungsstädte des Mittelalters," *Istanbuler Mitteilungen*, XXV (1975), 399–420.

rhetorical confidence in the aged pontiff's divine mission to save them and redeem the faith by massing western arms against the Turks. The *mahonesi* were pleading for the rescue not of schismatic Greeks, but of ancient Christians of Italian stock, who had ever been faithful to the sacrosanct Church of Rome, and who (whether deserted by their fellow Christians or not) were prepared to fight until the end.[21] On 28 November, 1455, Calixtus III granted to those who supported themselves for six months in the defense of Chios the indulgence and plenary remission of sins which had been bestowed on pilgrims to Rome in the jubilee and on crusaders in the Holy Land.[22] The pope made no mention of his intention to send a fleet into Levantine waters against the Turks. The customary privileges of the crusading indulgence did not fit very well the requirements of the *mahonesi*. There were more attractive ways to win the indulgence than by giving half a year to garrison duty in Chios, to the patrol of lonely shores, or to service aboard the *mahona's* galley.

The attention of Europe had been fastened upon Constantinople. The Genoese worried about Pera and Caffa, and the Venetians about Negroponte, but there had been another important theater of Turkish military operations in the Morea. While Mehmed II had been making preparations for the siege of Constantinople, he had sent the old general Turakhan Beg and the latter's two sons, Ahmed Beg and Omar Beg, to invade the Morea in October, 1452, directing them to remain there all winter to prevent the Despots Thomas and Demetrius from coming to the assistance of their brother Constantine XI.[23] The Hexamilion was taken again, with considerable losses on both sides, and partially destroyed. This was the fifth Turkish invasion of the Morea and the fifth destruction of the Hexamilion in less than thirty years, the previous occasions being in 1423, '31, '46, and '50.[24]

After forcing his passage through the Isthmus of Corinth in October, 1452, Turakhan Beg had traversed the Argolid and southern Arcadia, going by way of Mantineia, Tripolitza, and Tegea, past Megalopolis, all the way to the rich plains of ancient Messene at the foot of historic Mount Ithome. Killing or capturing all the inhabitants who did not escape him, he despoiled the beautiful countryside in a brutal razzia. As a diversion to prevent the Moreote despots from sending aid to the beleaguered capital, it was quite successful, although a Turkish contingent under Ahmed Beg was ambushed in a mountain pass near Mycenae by a force under Matthew Asan, whose sister Zoe had married the Despot Demetrius. Ahmed Beg was captured and sent to Demetrius at Mistra, where he was imprisoned. The Pseudo-Sphrantzes concludes his account of these events with the sad notice that "on 17 January [1453] . . . there was born the heir of the Palaeologi and of this small spark of the Roman empire, the lord Andreas Palaeologus, son of the porphyrogenite Despot Thomas."[25] Andreas's later history was to be as sad as the political circumstances attending his birth.

The fall of Constantinople had produced consternation in the Morea, and it would be hard to say whether the despots were the more reassured or frightened by the accounts they received from some of the notable refugees who managed to reach their peninsular domain in safety. Among these was the diplomat and historian George Sphrantzes, who had lost his

---

[21] Cod. Barberini lat. 3210, fols. 115–16, published by Argenti, *Occupation of Chios*, II, 427–28, and by Vigna, "Codice diplomatico," *Atti della Società ligure*, VI (1868), no. CXLVIII, pp. 353–54, from Raynaldus, *Ann. eccl.*, ad ann. 1455, no. 33, vol. XVIII (Cologne, 1694), p. 443.

[22] Reg. Vat. 439, fols. 220r–221; wrongly dated in Argenti, *op. cit.*, II, 430–31. Numerous documents relating to Calixtus III's crusading efforts are given by Vigna, in *Atti*, VI, esp. pp. 505 ff.

[23] Pseudo-Sphrantzes, III, 3 (Bonn, p. 235; ed. V. Grecu, *Geo. Sphrantzes . . . în anexă Pseudo-Phrantzes*, Bucharest, 1966, p. 380), and *cf.* Geo. Sphrantzes, *Chron. minus* (*PG* 156, 1060D; ed. Grecu, p. 96); Laonicus Chalcocondylas, bk. VIII (Bonn, p. 381; ed. E. Darkó, II-2 [Budapest, 1927], 148). This expedition is not mentioned by either Ducas or Critobulus.

[24] For the Turkish assaults on the Hexamilion in 1423, 1431, and 1446, see above, pp. 38, 95b, 96–97; for that in 1450, see Chalcocondylas, bk. VII (Bonn, p. 378; ed. Darkó, II-1 [1923], 144–45), and *cf.* in general Wm. Miller, *Latins in the Levant*, London, 1908, pp. 387, 410, 412–14, and 425.

[25] Pseudo-Sphrantzes, III, 3 (Bonn, pp. 235–36; ed. Grecu, p. 380), from Sphrantzes, *Chron. minus* (*PG* 156, 1060D; ed. Grecu, p. 96); Chalcocondylas, bk. VIII (Bonn, pp. 381–82; ed. Darkó, II, 148); *cf.* Critobulus, I, 19 (ed. Müller, *FHG*, V-1, pp. 69–70; ed. Grecu, pp. 79, 81), and Chas. Hopf, *Chroniques gréco-romanes*, Berlin, 1873, repr. Brussels, 1966, geneal. tables, p. 536. On this expedition, note also Franz Babinger, "Turakhān Beg," *Encyclopaedia of Islām*, IV (1924–34), 877, where it is wrongly dated October, 1453.

wife and children, sold into slavery by the Turks,[26] and who had apparently served the late Emperor Constantine XI with love and loyalty to the last hours of the latter's life. Another refugee to reach the Morea, after a sojourn in Crete, was Cardinal Isidore of Kiev, of whom Chalcocondylas says: "If the sultan had known this man, that he was Cardinal Isidore, he would have killed him and not let him escape, but thinking that he was dead by now, he had paid no attention to the matter."[27] Pope Pius II later recalled that Isidore, who became cardinal bishop of Sabina, escaped from Constantinople by changing clothes with a corpse, "leaving his cowl and the red hat on the dead man" (*cuculla et rubenti pileo supra mortuum dimissis*), whose head was mounted on a pike and paraded through the city and the Turkish camp "per ignominiam contemptumque Sedis Apostolicae."[28]

The terrible news from the Bosporus undoubtedly added much to the confusion that commonly existed in the Morea. According to Chalcocondylas, the two despots were preparing to flee to Italy with the most important Greek dignitaries of the Morea when Sultan Mehmed made peace with them.[29] If they paid the annual tribute, they could apparently retain their sovereignty, which they chose to do, but now a storm of discontent against their feeble rule broke out in the Morea. By the late summer of 1453 some 30,000 Albanians had revolted against the despots, aroused by one of their chieftains, Peter Boua "the Lame," who was a member of the family of the Boua Spatas, once despots of Arta and Lepanto. The Albanians offered to submit to Venice; it was said they had raised the banner of S. Mark. The Republic answered their appeal with alacrity and appointed one Dr. Niccolò da Canale on 17 October, 1453, as its high commissioner to the Albanians, who were to be urged "to be bold and of stout heart and to proceed manfully until the coming of the said commissioner."[30] Although Canale's appointment and this encouragement of the Albanian insurrection apparently passed the Senate by a large majority, it is not clear what if anything was done in consequence of this action. The coming months, moreover, saw a considerable modification of Venetian views, for occupation of a large part of the Morea would inevitably embroil them in war with Sultan Mehmed, which they certainly did not want.

In an elaborate commission of 16 and 19 July, 1454, the Doge Francesco Foscari directed another envoy, the famous Vettore Capello, to go to Modon, where he should notify both the despots and the Albanians of his arrival for the purpose of negotiating with them. He was instructed to acquaint himself thoroughly with the state of affairs in the Morea and by what means and methods peace might be re-established between the contending parties. Capello was also to investigate the extent of the Despot Thomas's violation of Venetian rights and territories, request an audience of Thomas, and explain

> that because of our very great affection for his illustrious forebears, we have suffered deep distress on his Excellency's behalf and on behalf of all his family for the death of the most serene lord, the emperor of Constantinople, and for the grievous fall of that famed city—but recognizing now the many uncertainties and perils hanging over him and all the Morea, because no one can doubt that if the war continues between their Excellencies and the Albanians, the country will be reduced to such condition that it must needs pass into the hands of others with the complete ruin and destruction of his state, we have decided not to postpone any longer the sending of our embassy, which we have not been able to send up to this time because of other occupations and our many commitments. . . .

Capello's task was then defined in these terms:

---

[26] Sphrantzes, *Chron. minus* (*PG* 156, 1061CD; ed. Grecu, p. 98); Pseudo-Sphrantzes, IV, 1 (Bonn, pp. 309–10; ed. Grecu, p. 458), and *cf.*, *ibid.*, chap. 14 (Bonn, pp. 383–84, 385; ed. Grecu, pp. 522, 524).

[27] Chalcocondylas, bk. VIII (Bonn, p. 399; ed. Darkó, II, 163), who informs us that the inhabitants of the Greek islands fled when they had learned of the fall of Constantinople, and those of the Morea, including the despots, hastened to the sea, contemplating flight.

[28] Pius II, *Commentarii*, bk. XI, Frankfurt, 1614, pp. 299–300, trans. Florence Alden Gragg, in *Smith College Studies in History*, vol. XLIII (Northampton, Mass., 1957), pp. 746–47 [on which see below, Chapter 7, note 13].

[29] Chalcocondylas, bk. VIII (Bonn, p. 406; ed. Darkó, II, 169).

[30] C. N. Sathas, ed., *Documents inédits relatifs à l'histoire de la Grèce au moyen-âge*, I (Paris, 1880, repr. Athens, 1972), nos. 145–48, pp. 215–17; Stefano Magno, *Estratti degli Annali veneti*, ed. Hopf, *Chron. gréco-romanes*, p. 199, and geneal. tables, p. 531; Chalcocondylas, bk. VIII (Bonn, pp. 406–7; ed. Darkó, II, 169–70); D. A. Zakythinos, *Le Despotat grec de Morée*, I (Paris, 1932, repr. London, 1975), 247 ff; and in general see J. Ch. Poulos, "The Settlement of the Albanians in Corinthia" [in Greek], in the Ἐπετηρὶς τοῦ μεσαιωνικοῦ Ἀρχείου, III (Athens, 1950), 31–105, esp. pp. 75 ff.

> You are to interpose yourself in our name [between the contestants] and provide for and insist upon concord and agreement with respect to all existing differences between his Excellency [Thomas] and the most illustrious lord Demetrius, his brother, and the Albanians, and to contrive a sound peace and harmony between them. . . .

After trying to secure Thomas's subscription to peace, Capello was to go next to Demetrius, and finally to the chiefs of the Albanians. In any event "we wish that you take particular care before or after the conclusion of the said peace, as shall seem better to you, that all our places, villages, lands, and jurisdictions of Modon, Coron, and Nauplia should be fully restored to us, as is just and most proper." Various difficulties were anticipated if one or more of the contending parties should be unwilling to make peace. Such were Venetian fears and suspicions of the Genoese and Catalans that sixteen members of the Senate wanted Capello to try peacefully to acquire, by purchase or otherwise, such important seaports as Glarentza, Patras, Corinth, and Vostitza (Lagusticia, Logostiza), if there should be any danger of their falling into the hands of "another maritime power." A majority of the Senate was opposed, however, to the acquisition of more places that would require defense, and so this proposal was not incorporated in Capello's instructions.[31]

While Vettore Capello went from place to place in the Morea, circumspectly fulfilling the instructions in the doge's commission as well as those he received from home after his arrival, Sultan Mehmed intervened to help the despots suppress the Albanian insurgents. No few Greeks had joined the Albanian uprising, taking advantage of the situation to seek their own profit in the peninsular war against the Palaeologi. The chief of these was Manuel Cantacuzenus, a descendant of the imperial family which had established the despotate of Mistra. Manuel, who was lord of Maina, took the Albanian name Ghin; his wife Maria called herself Cuchia; and the Albanians proclaimed him despot (1453–1454). Turakhan Beg's son Omar was sent into the Morea, but remained only long enough to score a small victory over the Albanians, and then withdrew, gaining the freedom of his brother Ahmed as a reward for his services from the Despot Demetrius.[32] Doubtless the Porte saw much value in the Albanians' continued hostility to the Palaeologi, for it would make the latter more tractable and very likely make their payment of the annual tribute more prompt. The immediate repercussions of the Albanian revolt had redounded to the discredit of the Palaeologi, who could not suppress it, but if allowed to continue indefinitely in a Turkish satellite state such as the Morea had become, the revolt would ultimately reflect on the sultan's own power to preserve order.

Omar Beg's military gesture was not sufficient to discourage the Albanians and re-establish peace in the Morea, especially since Giovanni Asan, the bastard son of Centurione II Zaccaria, last of the Frankish princes of the Morea (d. 1432), came forward as a new aspirant to power. The Albanians flocked to his standard as Manuel Cantacuzenus faded into the turbulent background. Giovanni Asan was the brother-in-law of the Despot Thomas, who had married Caterina Zaccaria, legal heiress of Achaea, in 1430; he had now escaped from imprisonment in the castle of Chloumoutsi, where Thomas had confined him after an uprising in 1446 during the Turkish invasion. Quite a stir was caused by Giovanni's appearance in the arena, and Chalcocondylas recounts the events of 1454 at length. It looked as though an Albanian principality might be set up in the peninsula under this last Latin prince of Achaea, who took his father's name, Centurione. The Albanians had already appealed to the Porte, recognizing Turkish suzerainty and promising a large annual

---

[31] Sathas, *Docs. inédits*, I, no. 149, pp. 218–23. The Venetian Senate had an especial fear of Genoese meddling in the Morea (*ibid.*, no. 150), but Capello was reminded by letter after his arrival in the Morea that Venice had no territorial ambitions in the peninsula, and wanted only to see peace maintained (no. 151). The handsomely written archival copy of Capello's commission of 16–19 July, 1454, from which Sathas published the document, may be found in the Sen. Secreta, Reg. 20, fols. 23^v–25^v [24^v–26^v]. Nicholas V was showing, at this time, a rather belated anxiety to proceed against the Turks, having even dispatched galleys to the East (*cf.* his letter to the doge of Venice, dated 9 March, 1454, in Arch. Segr. Vaticano, Arm. XXXIX, tom. 6, fol. 8^v, by mod. stamped enumeration).

[32] Chalcocondylas, bk. VIII (Bonn, p. 407; ed. Darkó, II, 170); Sphrantzes, *Chron. minus* (*PG* 156, 1064; ed. Grecu, pp. 104, 106); Pseudo-Sphrantzes, IV, 14 (Bonn, p. 383; ed. Grecu, p. 522); Ioann. Cartanus, *Anthos*, in Hopf, *Chron. gréco-romanes*, p. 267; Theod. Spandugnino, *Tratt*[*at*]*o della casa d'Ottomano* [under Giov. Musachi], *ibid.*, pp. 330–31; and for Manuel Cantacuzenus's alleged descent from the Emperor John VI, see Hopf, *op. cit.*, geneal. tables, p. 536, and esp. D. M. Nicol, *The Byzantine Family of Kantakouzenos (Cantacuzenus), ca. 1100–1460*, Washington, D.C., 1968, pp. 201–3.

tribute. The despots, however, sent Demetrius's brother-in-law Matthew to the Porte with a second request for assistance, and this time the sultan sent Turakhan Beg himself with a large army. Accompanied again by his two sons, the old warrior arrived in October (1454), declaring that, since the inhabitants of the Morea regarded the Turks as their enemy, one of the two despots must at all times be seen with the Turkish forces as an assurance to the people. First, Demetrius joined the Turks in an attack upon a strongly fortified place called Borbotia. The Albanians, fearing apparently both assault and siege, withdrew from the place at night, leaving an alleged 10,000 men and women behind them. Next, Thomas, the younger of the brothers, assisted Turakhan Beg in attacks upon Ithome and nearby Aetos. The latter place had recently acclaimed Prince "Centurione," and was obviously an important center of the resistance to the Palaeologi. It produced another thousand captives. The Albanians had never intended, however, to make war on the Porte, a considerable undertaking. They now capitulated with the understanding that they might keep the lands, horses, and beasts of burden they had seized in the course of their revolt. Quiet returned to that harassed land, long ravaged by war, plague, and famine.[33] Before his departure Turakhan Beg summoned the two despots to him for another conference, urged them to rule together in harmony, do justice to their subjects, and suppress evil and sedition. Then, having extended his hand to them in friendship, he left the country.[34] But harmony and justice were words that Demetrius and Thomas did not understand.

The European abandonment of Constantinople to the Turks had shaken the conscience of the West. As Pope Nicholas V had said, it was the "shame of Christendom," and contemporaries were well aware that an important change had taken place in world history. Shocked by the fall of the city, Cardinal Bessarion wrote from Bologna on 13 July, 1453, to Francesco Foscari, the doge of Venice, recounting the tragedy of the event, and appealing to the Republic to take up arms against the Turks with the Christian princes, lest the Greek islands, central Europe, and Italy should in their turn come under attack.[35] There were doubtless many thoughtful people who realized the importance of these recent events as fully as Aeneas Sylvius Piccolomini, onetime publicist and orator at the Council of Basel, and for years thereafter observant diplomat and knowledgeable secretary of the German imperial chancery. Never a profound thinker, Aeneas Sylvius was well informed, and his views possess an especial significance, because within a few years he was to become S. Peter's successor and to make the crusade the chief object of his papacy.

Aeneas was bishop of his native Siena at this time, and happened to be with Frederick III and the imperial court at Graz in Styria when news of the fall of Constantinople reached him. The Turkish menace had probably been on everyone's mind, but on 17 April, 1453, Aeneas had written Cardinal Juan de Carvajal from Wiener Neustadt: "We hear nothing about the Turk. Would that we might never hear anything! for there is no word of him unless he is up to some harm."[36] On the same day he wrote in the same vein to Cardinal Nicholas of Cusa: "Concerning the Turk I neither hear anything nor want to do so, for whenever word comes

[33] In the general famine of 1456, for example, grain for bread, when obtainable at all, sold for more than thirty *nomismata* for a five-pound weight (*πεντάλιτρον*), on which *cf.* the *Chronicon breve*, ad ann. 1456 (following Ducas, in Bonn corpus, p. 520).

[34] Chalcocondylas, bk. VIII (Bonn, pp. 407–13; ed. Darkó, II, 170–76); Sphrantzes, *Chron. minus* (*PG* 156, 1064; ed. Grecu, pp. 104, 106); Pseudo-Sphrantzes, IV, 14 (Bonn, pp. 384–85; ed. Grecu, pp. 522, 524). For the family of Giovanni Asan ("Centurione") and his relationship to the Despot Thomas, *cf.* Hopf, *Chron. gréco-romanes*, geneal. tables, pp. 502, 536, and Wm. Miller, *Latins in the Levant* (1908), pp. 391–92, 428–30.

[35] Bessarion's letter is published in *RISS*, XXV (Milan, 1751), cols. 35–38, and H. Vast, *Le Cardinal Bessarion*, Paris, 1878, pp. 454–56; *cf.* L. Mohler, *Kardinal Bessarion*, I (Paderborn, 1923), 275–76. Mohler's book is important, but contains a good many errors throughout. In his brief account of the fall of Constantinople (p. 273), for example, we may note that Giovanni Giustiniani was a Genoese, not Venetian, that he went to assist the city with two ships, not five, etc. There are brief sketches of Bessarion's career, with bibliographical data, by L. Labowsky, in the *Dizionario biografico degli italiani*, IX (1967), 686–96, and Antonio Coccia, in the *Miscellanea francescana*, LXXIII (1973), 265–93. Raoul Manselli, "Il Cardinale Bessarione contro il pericolo turco e l'Italia," *ibid.*, LXXIII, 314–26, adds nothing new. Bessarion's letter of 13 July, 1453, to Francesco Foscari may be found also in Mohler, III (Paderborn, 1942), 475–77. Mohler's volumes were reprinted at Aalen in 1967.

[36] Rudolf Wolkan, ed., *Der Briefwechsel des Eneas Silvius Piccolomini*, in the Fontes rerum austriacarum [*FRA*], II. Abt., vol. 68 (Vienna, 1918), *Ep.* 69, p. 140.

of him, it portends evil for Christendom."[37] Indeed it did, and such word had reached him by 12 July at Graz, where the court had been since late May: "Here we have horrible news," he wrote, "of the loss of Constantinople—if only it were false!"[38]

The news was not false. On the same day (12 July) Aeneas wrote his fellow humanist Nicholas V:

> I grieve that S. Sophia, the most famous church in all the world, has been ruined or polluted. I grieve that saints' basilicas without number, built with wondrous skill, should lie beneath the desolation or defilement of Mohammed. What shall I say of the countless books, as yet unknown to the Latins, which were there [in Constantinople]? Alas, how many names of great men will now perish! Here is a second death for Homer and for Plato too. Where are we now to seek the philosophers' and the poets' works of genius? The fount of the Muses has been destroyed. Well might we wish that sufficient talent were vouchsafed us to deplore this calamity with fitting words! . . .
>
> Men used to say that there was no such danger as was alleged, that the Greeks were lying, scheming to get money—they used to say that all the perils were imagined, the fears empty. Your Holiness has done what he could. There is nothing for which you can be blamed, but posterity without knowledge of the facts will attach this disaster to your name when it has learned that Constantinople was lost in your time. . . . Now we see one of the two lights of Christendom extinguished. We behold the seat of eastern empire overthrown, all the glory that was Greece blotted out. . . . Now Mohammed reigns among us. Now the Turk hangs over our very heads. The Black Sea is closed to us, the Don has become inaccessible. Now the Vlachs must obey the Turk. Next his sword will reach the Hungarians, and then the Germans. In the meantime we are beset by internecine strife and hatred. The kings of France and England are at war; the German princes fight amongst themselves. Rarely is all Spain quiet; our own Italy is without peace. . . .
>
> How much better we might turn this abundance of arms and unceasing warfare against the enemies of the faith. I know not, most blessed father, to whom more than to your Holiness this responsibility belongs. You must rise up; write to the kings; send legates; warn, exhort the princes and the communities [of Europe] to assemble in some place of meeting or to send thither their envoys. Right now, while the evil is fresh in mind, let them hasten to take counsel for the Christian commonwealth. Let them make a peace or truce with their fellow Christians, and with joined forces take up arms against the enemies of salvation's cross![39]

The letters of Aeneas Sylvius and Frederick III to Pope Nicholas V show that the report which reached the imperial court of the fall of Constantinople carried with it the information that the Turks had slain 40,000 persons and reduced even more to slavery.[40] The disaster filled men's thoughts, and in a bull promulgated on 30 September, 1453, the distressed pontiff summoned all the Christian princes to a crusade against the Turks and their ruler, Mehmed, "son of Satan, perdition, and death."[41] In the weeks

---

[37] *Ibid.*, *Ep.* 70, p. 141. Aeneas Sylvius and Nicholas of Cusa had a common interest in German affairs which served to some (slight) extent to draw them together, and their relationship forms the major theme of Erich Meuthen's study of *Die letzten Jahre des Nikolaus von Kues: Biographische Untersuchungen nach neuen Quellen*, Cologne, 1958.

[38] Wolkan, ed., in *FRA*, II. Abt., vol. 68, *Ep.* 108, p. 188, to Stefano Caccia di Fara in Rome. The news had been brought to Graz by travelers from Serbia (*Ep.* 112, p. 207) and from Venice (*Ep.* 114, p. 217).

[39] *Ibid.*, *Ep.* 109, pp. 200–1, a better text than that in Pius II, *Ep.* 162, *Opera quae extant omnia*, Basel, 1551, repr. Frankfurt a.M., 1967, pp. 715–16. In August a false rumor reached Graz from Venice that the Christians still held Constantinople, but it was soon dispelled by reports from various sources (Wolkan, ed., in *FRA*, II. Abt., vol. 68, *Epp.* 126–27, pp. 230, 231). References to the fall of the city and to the Turks now become especially frequent in Aeneas Sylvius's correspondence (*cf. Epp.* 112, 114, 121, 124–28, 133–39, 141, 147, 152–53, 163, 165, 167, etc.), where there are many interesting letters from the latter part of 1453 and the early months of 1454, especially *Ep.* 153 to Leonardo de' Benvoglienti, then Sienese ambassador to Venice; *Ep.* 274 to Gregorio (Goro) Lolli, Aeneas's cousin and fellow student at the University of Siena (1423–1431), on conditions in Austria and Germany; and *Ep.* 280 from Giovanni Cirignano to Aeneas, on the political situation in Italy. On Aeneas's years of service with Frederick III and his yearning to return home to Italy, the *hortus mundi*, see Alphons Lhotsky, "Aeneas Silvius und Österreich," in *Aufsätze und Vorträge*, III (Munich, 1972), 26–71, esp. pp. 69–71.

[40] Wolkan, ed., *Ep.* 109, *ibid.*, p. 199; Raynaldus, *Ann. eccl.*, ad ann. 1453, no. 8, vol. XVIII (1694), p. 408. In Frederick's letter, however, the text as given in Rayn., *loc. cit.*, *hominum quadraginta millia caesa sunt,* differs from that in Wolkan's better edition, *hominum pleraque milia cesa sunt* (*Ep.* VII, p. 577); Aeneas Sylvius, however, does say *quadraginta et amplius milia personarum illic occisa referuntur* (*Ep.* 109); manuscripts do vary, but in any case Aeneas wrote not only his own letter, but Frederick's also! (Although I have tried throughout this study to adhere closely to the sources, I have commonly omitted detailed notices of minor textual variations.)

[41] Raynaldus, *Ann. eccl.*, ad ann. 1453, nos. 9–11, vol. XVIII (1694), pp. 408–10; *cf.* Pastor, *Hist. Popes*, II, 275–76, and append., no. 20, p. 522, and *Gesch. d. Päpste*, I (repr. 1955), 622–23, and append., no. 53, p. 842.

and months that followed, papal emissaries equipped with the usual letters of credence were sent to the Italian courts as well as to those farther afield to acquaint the princes with what the pope and cardinals had decided in consistory as to the steps to be taken against the Turk and to solicit their financial assistance and general support for the crusade, *haec tam pia et sancta res*, which the pope had launched.[42]

The Emperor Frederick III called for a crusading assembly to meet at Regensburg in the spring of 1454, to which Philip of Burgundy came with great ceremony,[43] as well as a few of the German princes, including Duke Ludwig [IX] of Bavaria-Landshut and the Margrave Albrecht Achilles of Brandenburg-Ansbach. The emperor remained in Austria, however, for he feared the German diets, and sent Aeneas Sylvius to Regensburg as his chief spokesman. Nicholas V had a papal suspicion of anything resembling a council, and although he sent the bishop of Pavia as his legate, he did little to add to the effectiveness of the meeting.[44] At a session of the privy council, when Aeneas Sylvius and others had urged Frederick to attend the assembly of Regensburg in person, the indolent, short-sighted emperor had frankly stated his position:

> Certainly I should like to be on hand at the congress since nothing is closer to my heart than to take counsel for the common good. It is hard, nevertheless, to look after general interests at one's own peril. I admit that as individuals we ought to aid the commonwealth, but I see no one anxious to put the advantage of another before his own. Why mention the [imperial] electors to me? It does not escape me how much anxiety they entertain for the common good! I'll go to Regensburg. They'll stay at home! . . .[45]

When it was known that Frederick was not going to Regensburg, Aeneas wrote Cardinal Carvajal from Wiener Neustadt on 11 April, 1454, two or three days before the imperial envoys left for the assembly, "I fear that in German fashion because of the emperor's absence we shall only get another diet out of this one, but we hardly know what the evening may bring!"[46] Five weeks or so later Aeneas wrote the priors of Siena from Regensburg that

> this would have been a great assembly if the emperor had come, but his Majesty was necessarily detained at home because of the uprisings in Hungary [which had served Frederick as well as any other

---

[42] *Cf.* the papal letter of 24 November, 1453, to Marquis Lodovico II Gonzaga of Mantua (Arch. di Stato di Mantova, Arch. Gonzaga, Busta 834): "Nicolaus episcopus, servus servorum Dei, dilecto filio et nobili viro Ludovico marchioni Mantue. Salutem et apostolicam benedictionem. Ut intelligat nobilitas tua quid per nos unacum venerabilibus fratribus nostris Sancte Romane Ecclesie cardinalibus ordinatum sit atque statutum circa provisiones faciendas contra Teucrum, Christi nominis inimicum, comisimus nonnulla dilecto filio Stephano Cacie [on whom note Walther von Hofmann, *Forschungen zur Geschichte der kurialen Behörden vom Schisma bis zur Reformation*, 2 vols., Rome, 1914, II, 185], iuris utriusque doctori, archidiacono Taurinensi, cubiculario et nuncio nostro, presentium exhibitori, tue Excellentie nostri parte referenda qui eandem ad plenum de omnibus informabit et litteras nostras superinde confectas ostendet, hortamur ergo tuam nobilitatem ut velit sibi tanquam nobis plenam fidem adhibere auxiliaque et favores oportunos ad hanc tam piam et sanctam rem peragendam impendere quemadmodum in eadem plene confidimus et speramus. Datum Rome apud Sanctum Petrum anno Incarnationis dominice millesimo quadringentesimo quinquagesimo tercio, octavo Kal. Decembris, pontificatus nostri anno septimo."

[43] Richard Vaughan, *Philip the Good*, London, 1970, pp. 296–302, and on the Burgundian background, see also Armand Grunzweig, "Philippe le Bon et Constantinople," *Byzantion*, XXIV (1954–55), 47–61.

[44] Aeneas Sylvius wrote a "history" of the famous but futile diet of Regensburg in the form of a letter to John Vitéz, bishop of Grosswardein (Hungarian Nagyvárad, now Oradea in western Rumania), chancellor of the kingdom of Hungary (*Ep.* 291, ed. Wolkan, in *FRA*, II. Abt., vol. 68, pp. 492–563; ed. J. D. Mansi, *Pii II . . . orationes*, 3 vols., Lucca, 1755–59, III, 1–84); *cf.* Raynaldus, *Ann. eccl.*, ad ann. 1453, no. 13, vol. XVIII (1694), pp. 410–11, and ad ann. 1454, nos. 1–2, pp. 418–19; N. Iorga, *Notes et extraits pour servir à l'histoire des croisades au XVe siècle*, IV (Bucharest, 1915), pt. 3, nos. 13–14, pp. 88–91, and *cf.* no. 17, and Georg Schrötter, *Dr. Martin Mair: Ein biographischer Beitrag zur Geschichte der politischen und kirchlichen Reformfrage des 15. Jahrhunderts*, diss. Munich, 1896, pp. 45–56.

References are frequent in Aeneas's correspondence from 1 January, 1454, to the coming diet at Regensburg (*Epp.* 211–14, 216, 221, 224, 229–30, 234, 236, 240–44, 253, 256–58, etc.), but he had his reservations: "De Ratisponensi dieta, etsi spem bonam multi gerunt, non tamen futuri certitudo ulla est apud homines . . ." (*Ep.* 267, ed. Wolkan, *op. cit.*, p. 455, to Cardinal Carvajal, dated at Wiener Neustadt, 4 March, 1454). Aeneas also composed Frederick III's letter to the pope outlining Frederick's intentions at the coming diet of Regensburg, summoned for the feast of S. George (23 April), and requesting that a cardinal legate be sent to assist him (ed. Wolkan, *ibid.*, *Amtliche Schreiben*, *Ep.* XIII, pp. 595–602, dated at Wiener Neustadt, 1 January, 1454). *Cf.* also *Epp.* XIV, XV, XVI, etc., to the king of France, the duke of Burgundy, the duke of Modena, etc., also written by Aeneas. Young King Ladislas of Bohemia and Hungary was not represented at Regensburg, although the Hungarian realm was much threatened by the Turks, and Ladislas was in close touch with Rome concerning the crusade (Iorga, *Notes et extraits*, IV, pt. 3, nos. 5, 7–8, pp. 81 ff.)

[45] Aen. Syl., *Ep.* 291 (*de Ratisponensi Dieta*), ed. Wolkan, in *FRA*, II. Abt., vol. 68, pp. 499–500.

[46] *Ibid.*, *Ep.* 272, p. 460.

pretext might have done]. In attendance at this meeting have been the great dukes Philip of Burgundy and Ludwig of Bavaria; the Margrave [Albrecht Achilles] of Brandenburg; the cardinal of S. Pietro in Vincoli [Nicholas of Cusa]; the papal legate, Bishop [Giovanni Castiglione] of Pavia; the envoys of the emperor, the king of Poland, the duke of Savoy, the electoral princes, and other lords and cities in Germany—those who had promised to come from Italy have not appeared. . . .[47]

On the same day (19 May, 1454) Aeneas wrote his friend Heinrich Senftleben in Rome,

Although you have heard from others of the dissolution of this diet, nevertheless I want you to learn from me what happened here. . . . From this diet, as is our custom, another diet has been born, which is to be held in Frankfurt on the feast of the nativity of the Virgin [8 September], where, if it can be done, the plans [*capitula*] devised here for the defense of Christendom are to be completed, for all have agreed that an army is to be raised against the Turks: but on the methods of recruiting troops we have met with difficulty and dissension. . . .[48]

Provision had been made at Regensburg for the next diet, which was in fact to be held on the feast of S. Michael [29 September] at Nuremberg, if Frederick III decided to come in person. Otherwise the place of meeting was to be Frankfurt. The emperor's decision as to his attendance, and so the choice of sites for the diet, was requested promptly. If he was not going to appear himself, he was to send representatives with full powers to act on his behalf. "I think that within a few days the emperor's edict will go out," Aeneas Sylvius wrote Cardinal Carvajal on 1 June, 1454, "by which the princes will be ordered to convene at Nuremberg; the emperor's appearance will be promised; God knows whether he will go or not." If he did not go, everyone's effort would be in vain, and the whole business would be ludicrous. If he did go, Aeneas had high hopes for the future.[49] In other words, a diet held at Nuremberg had a chance of organizing an effective crusade. One held at Frankfurt was foredoomed to failure.

The letters of Aeneas Sylvius are among the more fascinating literary productions of a century rich in the variety of its life and letters. The writer of a historical synthesis, however, must select only letters which illustrate the main flow of events and resist the ever pleasant temptation to follow Aeneas into the lesser byways of his time. He was a keen observer, a shrewd appraiser of men and their motives. If we may be permitted to cite one or two more of his letters relating to the attempt to organize a crusade for the recovery of Constantinople, we may note his letter of 5 July, 1454, to his old friend and fellow citizen, Leonardo de' Benvoglienti, written from Wiener Neustadt between the diets of Regensburg and Frankfurt. In this he extolled Philip of Burgundy, "a prince to be praised above them all." Philip had put the interests of the Christian commonwealth above his own concerns, "and he promised that he would go in person against the Turks if the emperor, the king of Hungary, or some other great prince would lead an army [eastward]." Aeneas spoke of the coming diet of Frankfurt, for which the date was still given as

[47] *Ibid.*, *Ep.* 281, p. 479, dated 19 May, 1454. The diet of Regensburg had just been dissolved. Friedrich II, margrave and elector of Brandenburg (1440–1471), seems not to be mentioned in Aeneas Sylvius's many letters from the years 1453–1454; the reference is always to his younger brother *Albertus marchio Brandenburgensis* (*Epp.* 49, 61, 90, 135, 147, 160, 168, 172–75, 291). Aeneas Sylvius, as Pope Pius II, later expressed his admiration for the Margrave Albrecht, "vir celsi animi et rei militaris peritissimus, qui et in Hungaria et in Bohemia et in Polonia et in omni Germania militavit. . . . Achillem plerique Theutonicum vocavere . . ." (*Commentarii*, bk. III, Frankfurt, 1614, p. 91, lines 19 ff., and *cf.* Pastor, *Gesch. d. Päpste*, II [repr. 1955], 77, 124). Note also Erich Meuthen, "Nikolaus von Kues auf dem Regensburger Reichstag (1454)," in the *Festschrift für Hermann Heimpel*, II (Göttingen, 1972), 482–99.

Since the Poles were at armed odds with the Teutonic Knights and had also to defend themselves against the Tatars, they were not likely to join a crusading alliance against the Turks (*cf.* Şerban Papacostea, "La Moldavie, état tributaire de l'empire ottoman au XVe siècle: Le Cadre international des rapports établis en 1455–1456," *Revue roumaine d'histoire*, XIII-3 [1974], 445–61). The Polish king, Casimir IV, was suzerain of Moldavia, which paid tribute to Mehmed II, and during the 1450's (and '60's) neither Casimir nor the voivodes of Moldavia had any intention of becoming embroiled with Mehmed. Later on (from 1470) Stephen the Great of Moldavia turned against the Turks.

[48] Aen. Syl., *Ep.* 282, ed. Wolkan, in *FRA*, II. Abt., vol. 68, p. 480, from Regensburg. Aeneas also notes that "principes absente imperatore negligentiores sunt." *Cf.* also *Epp.* 283, 290, and esp. *Ep.* 291.

[49] *Ibid.*, *Ep.* 290, p. 490, from Wiener Neustadt, and see also *Ep.* 291, p. 551. Aeneas adds, "Therefore, if our lord the pope has the expedition at heart, if he desires Christianity to be safe from Turkish attack, let him take heed and make every effort to see that the emperor attends the diet at Michaelmas. I have wanted to say this as my duty, although I do not doubt that the advice is of small consequence since it comes from me." There was little love lost between Aeneas and Nicholas V, who refused to make Aeneas a cardinal, although he had appointed him bishop of Siena on 23 September, 1450 (C. Eubel, *Hierarchia catholica medii aevi*, II [1914, repr. 1960], 235).

29 September. Leonardo had written Aeneas that many delegates should have been summoned from Italy to attend the diet of Regensburg. Indeed, Leonardo had thought of this assembly as being like that of Constance, not to say Basel, which had lasted for twenty years. "But our diet [at Regensburg]," as Aeneas hastened to agree,

> has been over and done with after a month. Another has been called. Once more there are being summoned here, from Italy, King [Alfonso V] of the Aragonese, the Venetians, Genoese, Florentines, Sienese, and Lucchesi. Count Francesco [Sforza], although he has not been invested [by the emperor] with the Milanese duchy, is also being summoned, as are the duke of Modena and the marquises of Mantua, Montferrat, and Saluzzo. Now we shall see how great the ardor of our Italians is going to be. Letters are also being dispatched to the kings of France, England, Bohemia, Hungary, Poland, Denmark [*Dacia*], Sweden, Norway, and Scotland to send delegates to the diet. The German princes are being ordered to attend, the cities to send their representatives.

Such activity and planning were all very well, but Aeneas had little hope of success:

> I should prefer that my own opinion prove wholly wrong; I should prefer the name of a false rather than a true prophet. . . . Christendom has no head whom all may obey. Neither the supreme pontiff nor the emperor is given his due. There is no reverence, no obedience. Like characters in fiction, figures in a painting, so do we look upon the pope and the emperor. Every city-state has its own ruler. There are as many princes as houses. . . . What order will there be in the army? what military discipline? what obedience? who will feed so many people? who will understand the different languages? who will hold in check the different customs? who will endear the English to the French? who will get the Genoese to join with the Aragonese? who will reconcile the Germans with the Hungarians and the Bohemians? If you lead a few men against the Turks, you are easily defeated. If you lead many, you are confounded![50]

The diet met at Frankfurt in October, 1454. Frederick III did not appear; Aeneas Sylvius was no false prophet. Although rather more largely attended than the diet of Regensburg, that of Frankfurt displayed from the beginning a poorer spirit, at least from a crusading standpoint. There were a number of important personages present, among them Albrecht Achilles of Brandenburg-Ansbach, the Margrave Karl of Baden, and the electors (archbishops) of Mainz and Trier. Again the papal legate was the bishop of Pavia, Giovanni Castiglione, whose Latin address to the diet was translated into German by Bishop Ulrich of Gurk. Envoys represented the king of Hungary, the dukes of Burgundy, Savoy, and Modena, the lord of Mantua, and others; the German dukes of Austria, Bavaria, and Brunswick sent envoys, as did a number of cities and towns, among them Cologne. Fra Giovanni da Capistrano had left his preaching mission at Olmütz in Moravia to urge the crusade upon the assembly; a popular preacher, he made a deep impression on the people, but the princes were little affected by his eloquence. The whole course of the diet was disrupted by strong differences of opinion, intrigues, and dissension.

The pope and the emperor were accused of promoting the crusade in order to get money from Germany (the bishop of Pavia was collector of the ecclesiastical tithe), and it was widely agreed that the internal reform of both the German church and state was the indispensable first step toward a crusade. Although a reformer himself, Albrecht Achilles saved the diet from becoming a complete travesty by supporting the proposal that a German army of 10,000 horse and 30,000 foot soldiers should be sent the following year to aid the Hungarians, provided an Italian fleet set sail concurrently to attack the Turks by sea. Another diet, however, was to be held at Wiener Neustadt in February, 1455, to confer directly with the emperor (Neustadt was his home and favorite seat), at which time arrangements were to be made for the recruitment of the promised German troops and for the necessary reforms to be instituted in the legal, financial, and ecclesiastical structure of the

---

[50] Aen. Syl., *Ep.* CXXVII, in *Opera quae extant omnia*, Basel, 1551, repr. Frankfurt a. M., 1967, pp. 654–57, misdated "MCCCCXLIIII," not in Wolkan. *Dacia* is common for *Dania* in texts of this period. On Palm Sunday (14 April, 1454) King Christian I of Denmark had sent the Emperor Frederick III his regrets for not being able to attend the diet of Regensburg (*ibid.*, *Ep.* CXXVIII, pp. 658–59). Writing from the Castel Nuovo in Naples, however, on 1 April, Alfonso V of Aragon-Catalonia urged the Sacred College to action, and declared himself ready to embark on a crusade to rewin "Greece" for Christendom, observing at the same time: "Sed haec communis culpa sit—dum enim alii alios intuemur ante Constantinopolis calamitatem, si quis in eius defensionem arma capiat et obsistere iniuriae conetur, illa civitas interim capta est, et illa omnis Graecia concidit . . ." (*ibid.*, *Ep.* CXXIX [misnumbered CXXXIX], pp. 659–60). That was indeed why Constantinople had fallen, but no one was likely to take Alfonso's written pledge to go on the crusade any more seriously than Philip of Burgundy's sworn vow to do so. They would both wait to see *quis alius arma capiat*.

empire. Frankfurt had been a trial to the imperial envoys; Aeneas Sylvius had delivered a two-hour address to the diet, urging at least a renewal of the commitments made at Regensburg. On 28 October, 1454, at the close of the meetings at Frankfurt, Capistrano wrote Nicholas V in high praise of Aeneas, "who certainly in this diet both by his remarkable and lengthy oration as well as by his excellent advice has conducted himself with such ability, prudence, and distinction that nothing more could be expected."[51]

While these events were taking place in Germany, the peace which Aeneas Sylvius had longed to see established in Italy was finally arranged. It had taken a long time, and a brief review of the background will not be entirely out of order. At mid-point in the century a diplomatic revolution had occured which bound Florence to the duchy of Milan. For years the two mercantile republics, Venice and Florence, had been allied against Milan whose duke, Filippo Maria Visconti, was prone to invade the Veneto and Tuscany whenever the opportunity presented itself. The Florentine humanists' predilection for republicanism, born of their classical studies, had played some part in forging and maintaining the alliance with Venice. Increasingly, however, the Florentines were becoming commercial rivals of the Venetians in the Levant. The imperiled Byzantine government felt impelled to favor the latter, while Florentine agents were showing much skill in winning the approval of the Turks.[52] The Florentines were striving to build up their merchant marine, a development which the Venetian Senate watched with some misgivings.

Naples, once the Guelf ally of Florence, had found few adherents on the Arno since the turbulent days of King Ladislas (d. 1414), the son of Charles III of Durazzo. With the triumph of Alfonso V of Aragon-Catalonia on the Neapolitan scene, the northern duchy and the southern kingdom might have continued to work together. Alfonso had become the friend and supporter of Filippo Maria (in 1435), but he wanted nothing to do with the upstart Sforza. As the Florentines drew closer to Milan, Alfonso cast friendly glances toward the Venetians, with whom he made an alliance against Sforza, the new duke of Milan, in October, 1450. The various factors which had produced this new balance of power in Italy are well known and have often been described.[53]

Italian politics had been vastly complicated when Filippo Maria died in August, 1447, leaving the Milanese succession in doubt. Chief among the various claimants to the duchy (or parts of the duchy) was the enterprising condottiere Francesco Sforza, who had married Filippo Maria's illegitimate daughter Bianca. Sforza soon won out.[54] Among the contenders

[51] Luke Wadding, *Annales Minorum*, XII (3rd ed., Quaracchi, 1932), 236 (ed. Lyon, VI [1648], 105; ed. Rome, XII [1735], 203); J. Radonić, ed., *Acta et diplomata ragusina*, I, pt. 2 (Belgrade, 1934), no. 251, and esp. no. 253, pp. 579–81, doc. dated 15 March, 1455 (previously published in Gelcich and Thallóczy, *Diplomatarium ragusanum* [1887], no. 324, pp. 571–73), and *cf.* no. 255; Iorga, *Notes et extraits*, IV, pt. 3 (1915), nos. 25–26, pp. 101–3, where the summary given of the document in the Bayerische Staatsbibliothek, MS. 5,333, fols. 1 ff., is faulty or the text itself is in error: "le duc de Bourgogne . . . , le duc de Savoie, les seigneurs de Modène, de Ferrare et de Mantoue . . ." (p. 102). The lord of Ferrara, the Marquis Borso d'Este, was in fact the duke of Modena and Reggio, having been raised to this dignity in the spring of 1452 by Frederick III as the latter was returning home from Rome after his imperial coronation (Pastor, *Gesch. d. Päpste*, I [repr. 1955], 510–11). Lodovico II Gonzaga was the marquis of Mantua. Capistrano had been engaged on a remarkable tour of preaching throughout southern and eastern Germany, Poland, and Bohemia since 1451 (Pastor, *ibid.*, I, 482–86, and *cf.* the interesting item in Alex. Apponyi, *Hungarica*, I [Munich, 1903], no. 179, pp. 142–48).

[52] Florentine influence at the Porte grew rapidly after about 1460 (*cf.* Babinger, "Mehmed II., der Eroberer, und Italien," *Aufsätze u. Abhandlungen*, I, 188 ff.).

[53] *Cf.* the brief sketch, with a good bibliography, by Vincent Ilardi, "The Italian League, Francesco Sforza, and Charles VII (1454–1461)," *Studies in the Renaissance*, VI (1959), esp. pp. 129–43, and on the extant archival collections for the diplomatic history of the period, especially in Italy, see Ilardi, "Fifteenth-Century Diplomatic Documents in European Archives and Libraries," *ibid.*, IX (1962), 64–112. As an addendum to Ilardi's survey of the Florentine sources (*ibid.*, pp. 79–85), we may note that a large number of letters, many of them originals, relating to European and especially Italian affairs during the critical years 1451–1454 may be found in two bound volumes in the series of *Responsive* in the Arch. di Stato di Firenze, Dieci di Balia: Carteggi, Responsive, Regs. 21–22 [old classification: Classe X, dist. 4, no. 22, and dist. 2, also no. 22]. Here are many letters of Dietisalvi di Nerone, Angelo Acciajuoli, Francesco Ventura, Geronimo Machiavelli, Donato de' Donati, Niccolò Soderini, and others, describing the progress of the Italian war, the peace maneuvers, the descent of Frederick III into Italy and his coronation at Rome, etc., and weighing the interests of the various states in the peninsula.

[54] After Filippo Maria's death the Milanese established the short-lived Republic of S. Ambrose, which Francesco Sforza brought to an end, assisted by a famine in which many of the inhabitants perished, "morti de fame per le

for the ducal title was, allegedly, Alfonso V, whose naval armament combined both the Aragonese-Catalan and Neapolitan fleets, which (along with that of Venice) threatened the commercial future of Florence in the Mediterranean. The Venetians tried to add as much Milanese territory as possible to their *terra ferma*, but Sforza held his own against them with unyielding determination, and launched a vigorous campaign of anti-Venetian propaganda. He was supported by Cosimo de' Medici, who had come to realize that Florentine interests were going to be better served thereafter by Milanese despotism than by Venetian republicanism. Cosimo's policy, which meant the abandonment of the Venetian alliance, encountered the opposition of Florentine statesmen and humanists like Neri Capponi and Giannozzo Manetti, whose views on foreign affairs followed more traditional patterns.

When Charles VII of France afforded virtual recognition to Francesco Sforza as duke of Milan, the first sovereign in Europe to do so, the new alliance struck by Sforza and Cosimo de'Medici acquired solidity (in 1451–1452). The cleavage at the French court between Charles VII and his namesake Charles of Orléans (the son of Giangaleazzo Visconti's daughter Valentina) proved most helpful to Sforza and Cosimo. Orléans had wanted to press the Visconti claim to Milan, now rendered impossible by the royal recognition of Sforza.

Angelo Acciajuoli, who went on three missions to France (in 1451–1453) and negotiated with Charles VII on behalf of Cosimo de' Medici and Francesco Sforza, encouraged the French to reassert the old Angevin claim to Naples against their common enemy Alfonso.[55] (We have already encountered Angelo Acciajuoli as the Byzantine Emperor John VIII's guide to Pistoia, Prato, and Peretola in 1439.) The French acceptance of Sforza as duke diminished the danger from Venice, but the French claim to Naples was inevitably a source of anxiety to Alfonso. The Medici became enamored of the French alliance which was, after all, part of the tradition of old Florence. As for Sforza, he was obviously better off with France as a friend than as an enemy. France, however, was now emerging victorious from the Hundred Years' War. There remained, to be sure, other problems for the French to solve, especially those relating to Burgundy. If the Medici had not encouraged French interest in Italy, others would have done so. The Angevin claim to Naples and the Orléanist to Milan made such interest inevitable, however long direct intervention might be postponed.

During the reign of Nicholas V the papacy, which had not yet recovered from the long years of schism and conciliarism, was unable to play a decisive role in the diplomatic drama. Nicholas might have worked for peace, nonetheless, more vigorously than he did, although the conflicting territorial interests of the Italian states seemed insusceptible to any resolution but that of force. Francesco Sforza was wary of the French connection, for everyone knew of Charles VII's desire to recover Genoa, which (as we have seen in the preceding volume)

---

strate," on which see Alessandro Colombo, "L'Ingresso di Francesco Sforza in Milano e l'inizio di un nuovo principato," *Archivio storico lombardo*, XXXII (4th ser., III, 1905), 297–344, and, *ibid.*, IV (1905), 33–101, with seven documents dated from 22 February to 22 March, 1450.

The Emperor Frederick III claimed the Milanese duchy by escheat as a vacant fief, refusing to recognize the succession through a female line (either through Gian Galeazzo's daughter Valentina Visconti to her son, the poet Charles d'Orléans [1391–1465], or through Bianca Maria Visconti to her husband Francesco Sforza). Alfonso V asserted his right to the duchy on the basis of a will which Filippo Maria was believed to have left, bequeathing the Milanese duchy to him. See B. Buser, *Die Beziehungen der Mediceer zu Frankreich während der Jahre 1434–1494 in ihrem Zusammenhang mit den allgemeinen Verhältnissen Italiens*, Leipzig, 1879, pp. 27 ff., 358 ff., an old but still most useful book. On some of the problems which Alfonso faced at this time, including the possibility of war with Venice, note Amedeo Miceli di Serradileo, "Sul Temuto Assalto veneziano alle coste ioniche della Calabria nel 1447 e 1449," *Archivio storico per la Calabria e la Lucania*, XL (1972), 113–27, and see in general Ernesto Pontieri, *La Calabria a metà del secolo XV et le rivolte di Antonio Centelles*, Naples, 1963, chaps. II–III.

There seems no reason to doubt that Filippo Maria had designated Alfonso V as his heir. Alfonso's own intentions appear somewhat ambiguous, however, inasmuch as he assumed the role of defender of the Ambrosian Republic against Francesco Sforza and the Venetians (see Aurea Javierre Mur, "Alfonso V de Aragón y la República Ambrosiana," *Boletín de la Real Academia de la historia*, CLVI-2 [Madrid, 1965], 191–269, with twenty-four documents, and especially Alan F. C. Ryder, "Alfonso d'Aragona e l'avvento di Francesco Sforza al ducato di Milano," *Archivio storico per le province napoletane*, n.s., XLI [LXXX, 1962], 9–46, with several documents). Alfonso lacked the military strength to make himself a decisive force in northern Italy.

[55] Paul M. Kendall and V. Ilardi, eds. and trans., *Dispatches with Related Documents of Milanese Ambassadors in France and Burgundy, 1450–1483*, 2 vols., Athens, Ohio, 1970–71, I [1450–1460], nos. 1–19, pp. 3–131, docs. dated from 10 September, 1451, to 21 April, 1453.

France had held from 1396 to 1409. Sforza thus had more reason to fear France than the Florentines did. Neither the Angevins nor the Orléanists had any claim to Florence. If, however, the Venetians could add much of Lombardy to their own great resources, they would dominate the northern part of the peninsula.[56] Cosimo had come to see in his friend Sforza the best means of preventing that possibility. But Venice was determined to push her western border to the river Adda, and on 16 May, 1452, she declared war on Sforza and Florence. The Senate believed that the French were not yet in any position to take action. Alfonso of Naples promptly joined his Venetian allies on 4 June. The following April (1453) the Florentines induced René, duke of Anjou, to cross the Alps on Sforza's behalf, to the discouragement of the Venetians. Both Sforza and the Florentines were vague in their offers to support René's ambition to conquer Naples. Alfonso was concerned, but hardly alarmed, although Sforza had enjoyed considerable success against the Venetians, and René was not inactive.

Suddenly came the news of the fall of Constantinople, and Venice had a hundred reasons for wanting to make peace. After some difficulty and disagreement with his alleged friends, René of Anjou withdrew north of the Alps, decidedly unhappy, but Charles VII believed that René had not pushed hard enough, and was apparently not seriously affronted. Cosimo and Sforza had won their game, and the latter was now recognized as the fourth duke of Milan.

Nicholas V summoned a congress of the Italian powers to convene in Rome. Both the contestants and the authorities of the minor states sent their ambassadors, who debated and aired the differences of their principals from November, 1453, to the following March. The congress failed to settle anything,[57] and indeed Nicholas had done little to help it achieve the peace which he had doubtless hoped would make possible a crusade against the Turks.[58]

Francesco Sforza desired peace, however, as much as the Venetians did, and what the diplomats had been unable to accomplish in Rome was brought about by the Augustinian friar Simonetto da Camerino, who served as a secret mediator between Milan and the Republic. Owing largely to the efforts of the indefatigable friar, suddenly and unexpectedly Sforza and the Serenissima suspended their hostility to each other. With the flowers of spring came the peace of Lodi (on 9 April, 1454).[59] Writing to Sforza on 21 April, Frate Simonetto told him of the joy which reigned in Venice as a consequence of the peace, and ended his letter with an exhortation to the duke to arm galleys against the Turks, as was being done at Venice.[60] The new allies were later

[56] On the Venetian government's policy of "imperialist" expansion westward and the propaganda of the Sforzeschi and Florentines to combat it, note Nicolai Rubinstein, "Italian Reactions to Terraferma Expansion in the Fifteenth Century," in J. R. Hale, ed., *Renaissance Venice*, London, 1973, 197–217.

[57] See especially Federico Antonini, "La Pace di Lodi ed i segreti maneggi che la prepararono," *Archivio storico lombardo*, 6th ser., LVII (1930), 233–96, with eighteen documents, and *cf.* Leopoldo Pagani, "L'Ambasciata di Francesco Sforza à Nic[c]olò V per la pace con Venezia (da documenti del R. Archivio di Stato in Milano, 1453–1454)," *ibid.*, 5th ser., XLVII (1920), 82–96; Carlo Canetta, "Il Congresso di Roma nel 1454," *ibid.*, IX (1882), 129–35.

[58] *Cf.* Pastor, *Hist. Popes*, II, 289–95, and *Gesch. d. Päpste*, I (repr. 1955), 634–38. Nicholas was taking some steps against the Turks. A tithe was being collected from the Italian clergy and laity for the "exaltation and preservation of all the Christian faithful and the destruction and desolation of all the infidels." The accounts were kept from January, 1454, to January, 1455, by one Francesco di Benedetto of Borgo S. Sepolcro, with numerous payments recorded through the Medici (Arch. Segr. Vaticano, Introitus et Exitus, Reg. 426, fols. 85^r–91^v, 100^v–101^r). In 1453–1454 the Lombard humanist Lampo Birago composed and dedicated to Nicholas his *Strategicon adversum Turcos*, in which he describes the pope as having been ardent for the crusade, *et nunc ingenti spiritu ad bellum idque iustissimum* (Agostino Pertusi, "Le Notizie sulla organizzazione amministrativa e militare dei Turchi nello 'Strategicon adversum Turcos' di Lampo Birago [c. 1453–1455]," in the *Studi sul medioevo cristiano offerti a Raffaello Morghen*, II [Studi storici, fascc. 88–92, Rome, 1974], 692).

[59] Cristoforo da Soldo, *Istoria bresciana*, in *RISS*, XXI (1732), cols. 882DE–883, 886–88, and ed. Brizzolara, in the new Muratori, *RISS*, XXI, pt. 3, pp. 123, 127–30; Sanudo, *Vite de'duchi*, in *RISS*, XXII, cols. 1151E–1153A; C. Canetta, "La Pace di Lodi (9 aprile 1454)," *Rivista storica italiana*, II (1885), 516–64; Antonini, in *Arch. stor. lombardo*, LVII, esp. pp. 245–72. The text of the "pace perpetua" of 9 April is summarized in Predelli, *Regesti dei Commemoriali*, V (1901), bk. XIV, nos. 282–83, pp. 87–90.

[60] Antonini, *op. cit.*, p. 277. A few days after the peace of Lodi, Jacopo da Recanati, archbishop of Ragusa, also wrote Sforza to congratulate him on the peace which had just been made. He also stated, "Si anchora che ho speranza, essendo unita Italia, facilmente se porra obviare et reprimere le crudelità de pessimo animo del Turco, contro lo quale non dubito che la Sanctità di Nostro Signore [Nicholas V] fara qualche buona provisione, et questa illustrissima Signoria [Venice] ce fara omni sfor[c]io possibile. Supplica la Excellentia vostra che lei anchora una con li altri principi Christiani vogli porre mano a si pesta, sancta et laudabile impresa . . ." (V. V. Makušev, *Monumenta historica slavorum meridionalium*, II [Belgrade, 1882], 84–86, doc. dated at Venice on 14 April, 1454).

joined by Cosimo de' Medici and the Florentines (on 30 August), and finally by the reluctant Alfonso of Naples (on 26 January, 1455), who had been supporting Venice. When Pope Nicholas V in a further agreement went along with the others for the preservation of peace in Italy (on 25 February, 1455), the millennium appeared to have been reached. The peace was supposed to last for twenty-five years. The formation of the Italian League of the five powers was publicly announced in Rome on 2 March, and again there was widespread rejoicing in the peninsula. An equilibrium had actually been achieved. With Venice held in check by Milan in the north, and Naples by the papacy in the south, Florence tried to maintain the political balance by commonly supporting Milan against Venice, which was much the strongest single state in Italy.[61] Now the pope could turn his undivided attention to the expedition against the Turks, as he immediately informed Francesco Sforza on 28 February, 1455,[62] and indeed it did seem that the political situation in Italy had become unusually favorable for the crusade against the Turks.

Unfortunately for the Christian cause, however, no such progress was being made in the north. In February, 1455, as decided at Frankfurt, the third diet had assembled at Wiener Neustadt, where the timid Frederick III had to leave his gardens and aviaries for the unpleasant deliberations of the small gathering of notables, dominated by Archbishop Jacob von Sirk of Trier, who represented all the other electors. Jacob von Sirk pressed for the "reforms" which would have still further weakened the emperor's feeble grasp of the reins of government in the highly feudalized empire. The margraves of Brandenburg-Ansbach and Baden had come again; many cities had sent their deputies; the king of Naples had sent envoys; and of course Aeneas Sylvius and the bishop of Pavia were both present, and urged the crusade upon the diet. Ladislas of Bohemia and Hungary came as close as Vienna, while his envoys pressed an appeal for aid against the Turks before Frederick at Neustadt, reminding his Majesty that the imperial office imposed this noble responsibility on him, that the opportunity was at hand, and that there was need for action. The emperor had himself summoned the diets. He must try to fulfill the high purpose for which he had summoned them.

While the pope carried the keys, the emperor bore the shield of Christendom. More than twenty months had passed since the fall of the eastern empire. Further delay could be fatal, for as time passed Christian strength was being diminished, and that of the Turks increased. The campaigning season was approaching. The Hungarians did not blame the emperor for past delays; certainly proper preparation was essential for so great an undertaking. Besides this, the Hungarians had been obliged to make a truce with the Turks, but the last day of the truce had recently passed: "We freely promise our aid and best effort," the Hungarian spokesman said. "We are absolutely ready to respond to whatever is wanted of us. We are directed to arm twenty thousand men, and we will arm them well. We are asked to allow the passage of the army through our lands, and we grant it most willingly. We are requested to supply food for the army on the march, and we will do so in great abundance!" The Hungarian made a good speech: "Now you will show clearly whether you are truly Christian, truly Augustus. . . . Behold how heaven and earth, God and man implore you: do not frustrate the just hope that so many peoples have placed in you. . . ."[63]

Frederick III was not to be moved by oratory, however, and he doubtless assumed that everyone knew he was quite prepared to frustrate any crusading hopes that might be placed in him. His mind had probably wandered as the Hungarian envoy spoke, even as it had probably wandered when on 25 February his own advocate, Aeneas Sylvius, had delivered "eine schöne getzirde latteinische Red" before the delegates in the castle of Neustadt. Interminable discussions and sometimes heated wrangling continued all through March. Time was taken to consult the young Ladislas and his advisers in Vienna. The decisions of Frankfurt were reviewed. The question of the Italian fleet was

---

[61] Pastor, *Hist. Popes*, II, 295–300, and *Gesch. d. Päpste*, I (repr. 1955), 638–41; see especially Giovanni Soranzo, *La Lega italica (1454–1455)*, Milan, n.d. [1924], with nine documents; and *cf.* Iorga, *Notes et extraits*, IV, pt. 3 (1915), no. 31, pp. 104–5. On Alfonso's ratification of the peace on 26 January, note Predelli, *Regesti dei Commemoriali*, V, bk. xv, nos. 13–14, pp. 121–25, and on Nicholas V's ratification, *ibid.*, no. 15, p. 125.

[62] Iorga, *Notes et extraits*, IV, pt. 3, no. 11, p. 87. Iorga seems to have thought this document belonged in the year 1454, but *pridie Kl. Martii pontificatus nostri anno octavo* is 28 February, 1455 (Nicholas V was crowned on 19 March, 1447 [Pastor, *Gesch. d. Päpste*, I, 393], which is therefore the first day of his first year).

[63] Iorga, *Notes et extraits*, IV, pt. 3, no. 36, pp. 106–10.

raised. The affairs of the empire were thoroughly ventilated, and on 5 April the formal sessions of the diet were adjourned until the twelfth, when Frederick summoned Archbishop Jacob of Trier and the envoys of the absent electors at ten o'clock in the morning, and then kept them waiting for three hours, to Jacob's great annoyance. But the news had just arrived of Nicholas V's death in Rome on the night of 24–25 March. Frederick therefore proposed that, owing to the uncertainty which now existed with respect to the Italian fleet, it would be better to postpone plans for the expedition until the following spring (1456). He would in the meantime carry on negotiations with the new pope and the Italian states and seek to restore peace in the empire. The diet then broke up, as it had begun, in bickering.[64]

The advocates of the crusade in Germany had at least one great weapon which their dread enemy, Mehmed II, lacked, and they employed it against him as effectively as they could. This was the newly devised printing press, which was made to serve Christian interests against Islam. The political and social disunion of the empire, however, the rapacious individuality of the German princes, and the incompetence, timidity, and indecisiveness of Frederick III prevented the full realization of the power of the press. But the printers certainly helped propel the vast ecclesiastical program of anti-Turkish propaganda which had been set in motion in Germany. The importance of the press in this connection will be better appreciated perhaps by our gathering together some illustrations of its use at this point rather than by putting them at those places in the text to which a strictly chronological treatment would assign them.

At Mainz in 1454–1455, for example, during the period of the diets held at Regensburg, Frankfurt, and Neustadt to promote the crusade, Johann Gutenberg's types were employed in printing broadsides to advertise Nicholas V's encyclical letters of plenary indulgence for those who assumed the Christian burden in the war against the Turks and contributed to the defense of imperiled Cyprus.[65] Indulgences were sold in the Rhineland on printed forms, with blank spaces left for the insertion of names and dates, the earliest known examples of "job printing." The press was now employed, also for the first time, in what was almost news reporting, for as Europe feared the loss of Cyprus to the Turks, someone, very likely Gutenberg himself, published the famous nine-page pamphlet, *Eyn manung der cristenheit widder die durken (A Warning to Christendom against the Turks)*. The *Manung*, prepared in the form of a calendar or almanac, addresses stirring appeals for action against the Turks to Nicholas V, Frederick III, the emperor of Trebizond, the king of Inkerman (in the Crimea), the Ragusei, Albanians, and Bulgarians, Dalmatians, Croats, Wends, and all their fellow Christians, the kings of France and England, Castile and Navarre, Bohemia and Hungary, Portugal and Aragon, Denmark, Sweden, and Norway, the archbishops

---

[64] Iorga, *Notes et extraits*, IV, pt. 3, nos. 37–38, pp. 111–16, and *cf.* nos. 39–40, 42, 47. On the three diets of Regensburg, Frankfurt, and Wiener Neustadt, *cf.* G. Voigt, *Enea Silvio de'Piccolomini als Papst Pius der Zweite* . . . , 3 vols., Berlin, 1856–63, II, 108–35; M. Creighton, *Hist. Papacy*, II (London, 1882), 315–25; Schrötter, *Dr. Martin Mair* (1896), pp. 39–93; Pastor, *Hist. Popes*, II, 300–5, and *Gesch. d. Päpste*, I (repr. 1955), 642–45; and the Ragusan documents in Gelcich and Thallóczy, *Dipl. ragusanum*, nos. 324–25, 327, pp. 572–74, 576. Jacob von Sirk, archbishop of Trier, had gone to Rome during the jubilee of 1450 (Pastor, *Gesch. d. Päpste*, I, 447). He was in the city in May, at which time a long series of grants and confirmations of privilege was made to him, which may be found in the Arch. Segr. Vaticano, Reg. Vat. 392, fols. 222–46 (by original foliation).

[65] Konrad Haebler, ed., *Einblattdrucke des XV. Jahrhunderts*, Halle a. S., 1914, nos. 482–89, pp. 121–22; W. A. Copinger, *Supplement to Hain's Repertorium bibliographicum*, pt. II, vol. 2 (London, 1902), p. 504; L. Hain, *Repertorium bibliographicum*, II (Stuttgart and Paris, 1831), nos. 11753–54, p. 487. On the famous broadsides of Nicholas V's indulgences of 1454–1455, which were printed with the types employed in both the 42- and the 36-line Bibles, issued under the authority of Paulinus Chappe (Zappe), see also the *Gesamtkatalog der Wiegendrucke*, VI (Leipzig, 1934), nos. 6555–56, cols. 420–24. Chappe was a Cypriote noble, ambassador and commissioner of King John II of Cyprus, appointed to administer the three years' crusading indulgence (1452–1455) declared by the pope against the Turks (N. Paulus, *Gesch. d. Ablasses im Mittelalter*, III [Paderborn, 1923], 198–99; Geo. Hill, *A History of Cyprus*, III [Cambridge, 1948], 523–24). Although only the Germans were equipped to print them, these letters of indulgence were sent to all the states in Europe (Pastor, *Hist. Popes*, II, 247, and append., no. 7, pp. 503–5, and *Gesch. d. Päpste*, I [repr. 1955], 599–600, and append., no. 38, pp. 830–31). On 30 May, 1452, the pope granted King John of Cyprus one-half the return from the sale of indulgences in France to help rebuild the walls of Nicosia (Raynaldus, *Ann. eccl.*, ad ann. 1452, no. 15, vol. XVIII [1694], p. 401). The first set of bulls on behalf of King John may be found in Reg. Vat. 396, fols. 167^v–173^v, including the *indulgentia per totum orbem* and that relating to Nicosia (fols. 170^v–172^r): these bulls are all dated "Rome apud S. Petrum anno . . . MCCCCL primo pridie Idus Augusti, pontificatus nostri anno quinto" (12 August, 1451).

and bishops, the military orders, and all the other lords, prelates, and cities of Christendom. Among the great landmarks in the early history of typography, as well as the first book ever printed in a vernacular language, the *Manung* appeared in Mainz toward the end of the year 1454, presumably, between the diets of Frankfurt and Neustadt.[66]

About seven years later, in the same city of Mainz, Gutenberg's successors, Johann Fust and Peter Schöffer, printed Pius II's bull *Dudum in conventu*, dated at Tivoli on 4 September, 1461, imposing a clerical tithe to help prosecute the coming war against the Turks[67] (he had preached the crusade at Mantua two years before). Again and again as the years passed, preachers of indulgence, ecclesiastical administrators, bailies, commissioners, and other authorized persons sought to enlist popular support for the war against the Turks by having recourse to the wonderful instrumentality of the press. Some of the chief printers of the day multiplied for wide distribution the briefs, bulls, and other documents, in Latin, German, and Italian, by which Sixtus IV, Innocent VIII, and Alexander VI announced the financial and other impositions for the crusade and the accompanying "plenary remission of all sins."[68]

Although it is too early in our narrative to consider the religious problem in Germany and the indulgence hawkers, who were to evoke the ire of Martin Luther (and to whom we shall come in the following volume), one may be permitted the belief that until the time of Sixtus IV, at least, the funds gained by the sale of indulgences in Germany and central Europe were in fact largely expended on the crusade, whether as subsidies granted to the Hungarians or directly on papal fleets for service in the Levant. It seems unlikely that the amounts collected in Germany met more than a fair portion of the Curia's expenses in combatting the Turk. The higher clergy in Germany, recruited largely from the nobility, were independent and anti-Italian. They were also exploitive of their own people, and their rapacity added to the growing anti-clericalism. It is undeniable, of course, that the papacy made heavy demands upon the German archbishoprics and bishoprics in the *servitia communia* and in other charges. Pluralism was rife, contrary to the canon law of cumulation. There were many conciliarists in Germany to whom the papal victory over the Council of Basel was a grave disappointment.

The conciliarists nurtured for decades a deep and understandable resentment of German money going to Rome whether by crusading tithe or by indulgence, and it would not be difficult to show (it has been shown often enough) that the ecclesiastical commissioners of the indulgence were grasping and employed the most questionable tactics. They went quite beyond the instruction of the people and the sale of the indulgence (*Ablassverkauf*) to the crudest advertising and its "hawking" like some article of commerce (*Ablasskrämerei*). But we are not here concerned with the sources of Nicholas V's money for his building programs, of Paul II's for his jewel collection, or of Sixtus IV's for his Italian wars. Ironically enough, papal efforts to collect funds through indulgences for the protection of Hungary, Carniola, Carinthia, Styria, and Germany itself against the Turk actually redounded to the disadvantage of Rome in the very areas that the papacy was anxious to assist. This is not to suggest, of course, that

---

[66] The original of the *Manung* was reproduced in a facsimile edition by J. Neuhaus, *Das erste gedruckte Buch Gutenbergs in deutscher Sprache*, Copenhagen, 1902, with notably inadequate historical notes and commentary (from the only copy known to be extant, in the Bayerische Staatsbibliothek).

[67] Haebler, *Einblattdrucke*, no. 1199, p. 321; Copinger, *Supplement*, II-2, p. 409. Pius II's bull of 22 October, 1463, was often printed (Hain, *Rep. bibliogr.*, I [1826], nos. 261–63, p. 31). The works of Pius II were very interesting to the Germans and central Europeans, and were often reprinted from the later fifteenth century (*cf.* Alex. Apponyi, *Hungarica*, I [1903], nos. 4–5, 9, 11, 41–46, 59, etc.), as were various *Turcica* (*ibid.*, nos. 10, 55, 58, 62, 69, 75, 78, 87, 102, etc.). Some important examples are listed in a catalogue of the antiquarian bookseller Jacques Rosenthal, *Einblattdrucke . . ., 1455–1519*, Katalog 92, Munich, no date.

[68] Haebler, *Einblattdrucke*, nos. 1–41, 91, 106–7, 108, 111, 357–75, 378–82, 406–11, 421–29, 477, 510, 535–44, 553–54, 562, 565–66, etc., etc., and *cf.* nos. 1007–15, etc. Frequently reprinted in 1489, the *Modus promerendi indulgentias sacrae Cruciatae* reads, with variations: "Quo ad tres [or quatuor] facultates principales. Quarum prima est iubileus. Primo pro iubileo et remissione plenissima omnium peccatorum obtinendis necessarium est christifideles confiteri qua confessione facta illos oportet de bonis suis secundum suam devotionem et facultatem ad iudicium sui confessoris aut alicuius alterius boni viri propriis manibus distribuere et ponere. . . . [and concludes:] Sint ergo solliciti commissarii avisare de omnibus istis omnes et singulos penitentiarios et habeant illis istas instructiones perfecte declarare. Cetera suppleant discretiones commissariorum sed horum nihil omittant sub penis in bullis contentis" (*ibid.*, no. 1014). Certainly a good deal was left to the judgment of the confessor and the discretion of the officials. On the printing of Calixtus III's crusading bull of 20 (or 29) June, 1456, see below, Chapter 6, note 101.

the abuses were not real, of long standing, far too numerous and persistent, and often accompanied by a cavalier cynicism. But complaints were quite as numerous as the abuses, and for an example let us turn to a contemporary source —an eloquent denunciation of the failings both of the pope and of the Curia. It comes from Dr. Martin Mayr, chancellor of the archiepiscopal elector of Mainz.

On 31 August, 1457, Mayr wrote to congratulate Aeneas Sylvius upon the latter's receipt of a cardinal's hat. Mayr expressed pleasure in this advancement of a friend who could now render him assistance if he needed it, but he was disturbed that Aeneas's promotion should have come in such evil times:

> To my lord the archbishop complaints are frequently brought concerning the Roman pontiff [Calixtus III], who observes the decrees of neither the Council of Constance nor that of Basel, and does not regard himself as bound by the commitments of his predecessor [Nicholas V]. Rather he seems to hold our [German] nation in contempt and to be exhausting us completely. It is a known fact that the elections of prelates are set aside, and that benefices and dignities of every grade are reserved for cardinals and protonotaries. Even you yourself have obtained reservation to three provinces of the German name by this device, which up to now is without precedent and quite unheard of. Expectancies are granted without number. Annates . . . are demanded with no allowance of time, and it is public knowledge that they are extorted, even beyond what is due.
>
> The governance of churches is not given to the one who deserves it more but to the one who offers more for it, and new indulgences are granted every day to scrape up money. Collections of tithes are ordered because of the Turks, with no consultation of our prelates. Cases which should have been handled and settled in the places [of their origin] are dragged off indiscriminately to an apostolic court, and a thousand ways are thought up by which the Roman See with its finely-wrought talent extracts gold from us—from the barbarians! Hence our nation, once illustrious, which by its valor and blood secured the Roman empire, and was mistress and queen of the world, is now reduced to penury and made a servant and taxable subject. Lying in squalor, she has been lamenting her lot and poverty these many years. But now, as though awakened from sleep, our nobles have begun to consider the remedies with which they may meet this dreadful plight, and have decided to throw off the yoke entirely and reclaim their ancient liberty. It will be no small loss to the Curia Romana if the princes of the Roman empire give effect to what they are now thinking. The more I rejoice in your new dignity, the more I am grieved and tormented that this trouble should be developing in your time.[69]

Martin Mayr's frank expression of German nationalism and of estrangement from Rome is hardly a unique text. Trouble was indeed developing in Aeneas Sylvius's time, and German self-consciousness was to be intensified by events. German dislike of the Italian increased, and German hostility to the Curia Romana assumed dangerous proportions. The warning signs of this disaffection were not sufficiently heeded in Rome, where wit was mistaken for wisdom and too many complaints had for too long been dismissed with the usual shrug of Italian shoulders. The final break came three generations later, causing spiritual lesions that have never been healed.

---

[69] Pius II, *Opera quae extant omnia* (1551, repr. 1967), p. 1035, dated "MCCCCVII" by a typographical error (one of the many in this volume); *cf.* Voigt, *Enea Silvio*, II (1862), 232–33; Pastor, *Hist. Popes*, II, 417–18, and *Gesch. d. Päpste*, I (repr. 1955), 734–35; Albert Werminghoff, *Nationalkirchliche Bestrebungen im deutschen Mittelalter*, Stuttgart, 1910, pp. 106–8 (Kirchenrechtliche Abhandlungen, Heft 61).

6. CALIXTUS III AND THE SIEGE OF BELGRADE, MEHMED II AND ALBANIA (1455–1458)

SULTAN MEHMED II's spectacular victory on the Bosporus had added immeasurably to the woes and burdens of Pope Nicholas V, who died on the night of 24–25 March, 1455, after several serious and prolonged illnesses.[1] On his deathbed Nicholas delivered a well-known apologia for his papacy, which Giannozzo Manetti has reported in unlikely detail. The pope defended not only his vast building program but also his efforts on behalf of Constantinople, lamenting the unfairness and shortsightedness of his many critics.[2] But certainly neither Nicholas nor the Curia could take satisfaction in the results of papal policy in the Levant, as Mehmed II was organizing his military successes for profit. During the summer of 1454 a Turkish fleet of fifty-six vessels had sailed into the Black Sea; attacked the grain port of Moncastro, which resisted their assault manfully; captured Sebastopolis, at the mouth of the Phasis (Rioni) river in ancient Colchis; and appeared on 11 July under the walls of Caffa, which was forced to pay tribute, as we have seen. The fleet also imposed a tribute upon the defenseless population of Gothia in the Crimea.[3] Aeneas Sylvius was quite right. Whenever one heard about the Turks, it was bad news.

A military people little given as yet to industry or large-scale commerce, the Turks lived on their conquests. While broadsides warning Christians against the Turks were being printed in Europe, the Serbs, Greeks, Latins, and others in the conquered territories in the East were experiencing to bitter fullness the dire fears constantly voiced by the western preachers. Mehmed imposed an annual tribute of 12,000 ducats (*nomismata*) on Serbia; 10,000 or 12,000 on the Greek "despotate" of the Morea; 6,000 on Chios; 3,000 on Mytilene (Lesbos); and unspecified sums on Trebizond and the rest of the Pontic region.[4] In the despotate of the Morea

[1] Arch. Segr. Vaticano, Acta Consistorialia (1439–1486), in Arm. XXXI, tom. 52, fol. 57[v], by mod. stamped enumeration: "Anno a nativitate Domini MCCCCLV[o] die lune, que fuit XXIIII[a], mensis Martii hora quinta [vel] circa sextam noctis [about 1:00 A.M.] sanctissimus dominus noster dominus Nicolaus divina providentia papa Quintus suum diem clausit extremum, cuius anima requiescat in pace." Selections from the Acta Consistorialia, including this passage (in very abridged form), may be found in Conrad Eubel, *Hierarchia catholica medii aevi*, II (1914, repr. 1960), 26 ff., 30. As recorded in Arm. XXVIIII, fol. 4[r], Nicholas V died "die lune vicesima quinta mensis Martii anni supradicti [1455, in which year, however, 25 March fell on a Tuesday, not a Monday] circa horam quintam noctis cum dimidia animam Deo reddidit, cuius corpus in Vaticano in basilica Sancti Petri de urbe honorifice sepultum fuit. . . ."

[2] Gian. Manetti, *Vita Nich. V*, II, in L. A. Muratori, ed., *RISS*, III-2 (Milan, 1734), cols. 947–57; *cf.* O. Raynaldus, *Annales ecclesiastici*, ad ann. 1455, nos. 10–16, vol. XVIII (Cologne, 1694), pp. 431–34; L. v. Pastor, *History of the Popes*, II, 166–67, and esp. pp. 305–18, with append., nos. 26–28, pp. 529–33, and *Gesch. d. Päpste*, I (repr. 1955), 514–15, and esp. pp. 645–56, with append., nos. 59–61, pp. 846–48. Already before 7 March Nicholas V had informed his secretary Pietro da Noceto "in qual locho el voleva esser sepelito," as the Milanese ambassadors informed Francesco Sforza (Pastor, *Acta inedita historiam pontificum Romanorum . . . illustrantia*, I [Freiburg im Breisgau, 1904], no. 25, p. 39, lines 27 ff.), and on 14 March the Florentines had informed their ambassador in Venice "chel sancto padre è si gravemente malato che si dubita che in pochi dì non passi di questa vita" (*ibid.*, I, no. 26, p. 40).

[3] W. Heyd, *Histoire du commerce du Levant au moyen-âge*, 2 vols., Leipzig, 1885–86, repr. Amsterdam, 1967, II, 383. The Turks had already ravaged Gothia in 1446 when Murad II had sent a fleet against Colchis (Laonicus Chalcocondylas, bk. v, in ed. Bonn, pp. 260–61, and ed. Eugen Darkó, II-1 [Budapest, 1923], 37–38).

[4] Ducas, *Hist. byzantina*, chap. 42 (Bonn, p. 314; ed. Vasile Grecu, *Ducas: Istoria turco-bizantină [1341–1462]*, Bucharest, 1958, p. 395), and *cf.*, *ibid.*, chap. 45 (Bonn, p. 339, line 4; ed. Grecu, p. 423, lines 27–28). Grecu gives marginal references to pages in the Bonn edition of Ducas; I rarely cite his edition in the present volume. While Ducas puts the Moreote tribute at 10,000, Chalcocondylas, bk. VIII (Bonn, p. 414; ed. Darkó, II-2 [1927], 176), gives it as 12,000 ducats: ". . . ἣν δὲ αὐτοῖς [the inhabitants of the Morea] ὁ ἐπέτειος φόρος μύριοι καὶ δισχίλιοι χρυσίου στατῆρες."

According to Critobulus of Imbros, when the Despots Thomas and Demetrius were faced, after the fall of Constantinople, with a revolt of the Albanians (in 1453–1454, on which see above, Chapter 5), they appealed to Sultan Mehmed for aid, promising to pay him an annual tribute of 6,000 gold staters (*De rebus gestis Mechemetis II*, III, 1, ed. Karl Müller, *Fragmenta historicorum graecorum* [*FHG*], V-1 [Paris, 1870], p. 120a; ed. V. Grecu, *Critobul din Imbros, Din domnia lui Mahomed al II-lea, 1451–1467*, Bucharest, 1963, p. 215). Aeneas Sylvius, *De Europa*, 12, in *Opera quae extant omnia*, Basel, 1551, repr. Frankfurt a. M., 1967, p. 405, puts the tribute at 17,000 gold pieces after the suppression of the Albanian uprising. Andrea Cambini, *Commentario*, ed. 1538, p. 22, gives the same figure ("di pagarli [Mehmed II] lanno diciasette migliaia di ducati conditions were especially bad. We have already paid some attention to the Albanian revolt which had followed the Greek loss of Constantinople. Now there were even demands from the Greek nobility for direct dependence on the Porte rather than on the Despots Thomas and Demetrius. Sometimes the two brothers contemplated flight from their harassed dominions, and at others apparently set themselves the unpopular task of raising the Turkish tribute, which the Greeks paid no more willingly than the Albanians, believing that much of the tribute money would stick to the fingers of the despots. There could be little confidence in these last Palaeologi. A once rich society was declining rapidly into chaos. There had been too much war, and the future looked even blacker than the past. The Greek population in the Morea waited fearfully for the inevitable. Everyone knew what was coming; the only question was when it was coming.

After the fall of Constantinople Pope Nicholas V had turned hopeful eyes toward Alfonso V "the Magnanimous," whose power extended from the banks of the Ebro in Spain to the shores of the Adriatic and to Albania, and whose influence was felt in Cyprus, Rhodes, and Egypt. Despite grandiose promises Alfonso did less than he might have done, although Pastor does him an injustice when he says that "neither now nor later did Alfonso ever raise a hand in defense of Christendom."[5]

After the death of Nicholas V, the position of Alfonso seemed to be unexpectedly strengthened when on 8 April, 1455, fifteen cardinals elected the Catalan canonist Alfonso Borgia (Alonso de Borja) as Pope Calixtus III. Actually the great Cardinal Bessarion had almost been awarded the tiara, receiving eight votes early in the conclave, but the opposition of Alain de Coëtivy, the cardinal of Avignon, and of Lodovico Trevisan, the worldly cardinal of Aquileia, cost the long-bearded Greek humanist the election which he might have won if he had been a more effective politician.[6] The electors being divided by constant pressures from the opposing factions of the Orsini and Colonnesi, Calixtus III was made pope as a compromise candidate, who at seventy-seven years of age was believed to be too old to last long.[7] Since the new pope had once been the secretary of King Alfonso, and had served him in various diplomatic connections, there was widespread fear that his election would endanger the peace of Lodi and the newly formed Italian League.

On 8 April the cardinal of Aquileia had

---

doro . . ."). According to the Rabbi Joseph Ben Joshua Ben Meir, *Chronicles*, trans. C. H. F. Bialloblotzky, 2 vols., London, 1836, I, 281, the Despots Thomas and Demetrius promised to pay the sultan an annual tribute of 17,000 "pieces of gold."

[5] Pastor, *Gesch. d. Päpste*, I (repr. 1955), 629–30: "Alfonso . . . rührte weder jetzt noch später eine Hand zum Schutze der Christenheit." In actual fact, during the summer of 1455, Alfonso V dispatched a thousand foot to Scanderbeg "in Albania per defensione de quelle terre," most of whom were killed in the Turkish invasion, ". . . e hano tra morti e presi da cinque in sey milia Cristiani" (V. V. Makušev, *Monumenta historica slavorum meridionalium*, II [1882], 148–51, docs. dated 8 and 14 August, 1455). Alfonso had apparently intended to send Scanderbeg 1,200 foot and five hundred horse (*ibid.*, p. 227, doc. dated 22 May, 1455), but may have found himself unable to spare so large a cavalry force (*cf.* below, note 127, for further reference to these documents). See in general Ernesto Pontieri, *Alfonso il Magnanimo, re di Napoli (1435–1458)*, Naples, 1975, pp. 262–63, 318–25, and esp. "Alfonso I d'Aragona e la 'crociata' di Callisto III," in the *Atti della Accademia nazionale dei Lincei, Rendiconti*, Cl. di scienze morali, etc., 8th ser., XXIX (1974), 61–68, for a simple statement of the reasons why Alfonso, although a "son of the Spain of the reconquista," abandoned his (apparent) plans to move against the Turks on a grand scale.

[6] According to the letter of Roberto di Sanseverino to Francesco Sforza, duke of Milan, written from Bologna on 17 April (1455), as given in F[rancesco] Petruccelli della Gattina, *Histoire diplomatique des conclaves*, 4 vols., Paris, 1864–66, I, 269, from a document in the Arch. di Stato di Milano, Carteggio di Roma; Pius II, *Commentarii*, bk. I, Frankfurt, 1614, p. 24, and note the addendum to this passage in Jos. Cugnoni, ed., *Aeneae Silvii . . . opera inedita*, in the *Atti della R. Accademia dei Lincei*, anno CCLXXX (1882–83), 3rd ser., *Memorie della classe di scienze morali, storiche e filologiche*, VIII (Rome, 1883), p. 498, *ex cod. man.*, p. 33, inc. "Ecquid scimus" [which passage was omitted from the printed edition of Pius II's *Commentarii*], on Cardinal Alain's questioning the sincerity of Bessarion's conversion to Latin Catholicism; *cf.* the English translation of the Commentaries by Florence Alden Gragg, in the *Smith College Studies in History*, XXII (1936–37), 75–76, which work has the merit of including the passages excised from the printed text; Raynaldus, *Ann. eccl.*, ad ann. 1455, no. 17, vol. XVIII (1694), p. 434; Pastor, *Hist. Popes*, II, 323–24, and *Gesch. d. Päpste*, I (repr. 1955), 659–60; Ludwig Mohler, *Kardinal Bessarion als Theologe, Humanist und Staatsmann*, 3 vols., Paderborn, 1923–42, repr. Aalen and Paderborn, 1967, I, 267–68.

[7] Raynaldus, *Ann. eccl.*, ad ann. 1455, no. 17, vol. XVIII (1694), p. 434; Pastor, II, 319–26, and *Gesch. d. Päpste*, I (repr. 1955), 656–61; Arch. Segr. Vaticano, Acta Consistorialia, in Arm. XXXI, tom. 52, fol. 57^v: "Creatio domini Calixti papae Tertii: Anno predicto [1455] die vero Martis octava dicti mensis [Aprilis] circa horam quintadecimam reverendissimus in Christo pater et dominus, dominus Alfonsus, etc., Quatuor Coronatorum presbyter cardinalis Valentinus, assumptus fuit ad summi apicem apostolatus et vocatus Calixtus Tertius . . ." (not in Eubel). *Cf. Arm.* XXVIIII, fol. 4^r, by mod. stamped enumeration, and J. B. Saegmüller, *Die Papstwahlen und die Staaten von 1447 bis 1555 (Nikolaus V. bis Paul IV.)*, Tübingen, 1890, pp. 82–84.

written Lodovico II Gonzaga, the marquis of Mantua, that the cardinals had elected Alfonso Borgia, the former cardinal of Valencia, as pope about 10:00 A.M. that morning (*circha le XIV hore*), and expressed the hope "that by his singular goodness and virtue this election will be helpful to all Christendom."[8] The Venetians, Florentines, and Genoese, however, were gravely concerned that the balance of power in the peninsula would be upset. Antonio Guidobono, the Milanese ambassador in Venice, informed Duke Francesco Sforza in a letter dated 12 April that "in this city [Venice] most people are very dissatisfied, both because this dignity has gone from the Italians and also because it seems to everyone that his Majesty, the king of Aragon, may have the Church at his disposal as he wishes, and will thereby become more arrogant than ever."[9] The Milanese ambassador in Genoa, Giovanni de la Guardia, sent a similar report to Sforza from Liguria on 14 April: the election of Calixtus III was most displeasing to the Genoese, because the Catalans were their long-standing enemies, and because it seemed to have been contrived "per gli favori de la Sacra Regia Maestà del re de Ragona. . . ."[10] On the following day (15 April), however, the Genoese Doge Pietro di Campofregoso wrote Calixtus of the vast, incredible joy which his compatriots took in the election of one whose far-famed and wondrous virtues had made him known throughout the world, a proper pastor for those troubled times in which the savagery of the Turks was ever growing, and who alone seemed likely to bring about peace among the crowned heads of Europe as well as to arouse the laggards and arm them against the infidels.[11] Other documents of the time strike a similar note, and certainly the brief reign of Calixtus III, who was a native of Valencia and imbued with the Spanish spirit of the *reconquista*, was marked by a sincere if ineffectual dedication to the crusade against Mehmed II and the Turks.

Calixtus III was crowned on 20 April, 1455, the ceremonies being disrupted by factional strife.[12] Embassies soon arrived, however, to congratulate the new pope upon his accession to the throne. Serving on them were distinguished citizens sent from Lucca, Siena, Bologna, Florence, and Venice. Alfonso V of Naples and Frederick III of Germany also sent ambassadors, the latter being especially represented by the untiring Aeneas Sylvius. The anti-Turkish war was uppermost in men's minds. The Venetian ambassadors were instructed to give Calixtus the urbane assurance "that, when we see that the other Christian powers are moving in force against the Turks, we also shall be found following in the footsteps of our forebears, with that same good disposition which we have evinced in the past."[13] The Venetians

---

[8] Pastor, *Acta inedita*, I, no. 27, p. 41.

[9] *Ibid.*, I, no. 28, pp. 41–42.

[10] *Ibid.*, I, no. 29, p. 42: "ex Ianua die XIIII aprilis 1455."

[11] *Ibid.*, I, no. 30, pp. 42–43. The Doge Pietro also requested the confirmation of his young brother Paolo as archbishop of Genoa, for although elected to the office three years before, Paolo had never been accorded the title, owing to his youth. *Cf.* the Genoese letter to the College of Cardinals, dated 28 April, 1455 (*ibid.*, I, no. 32, p. 44). For the Florentine letters of congratulation, see Cesare Guasti, *Due Legazioni al sommo pontefice per il comune di Firenze presedute da Sant' Antonino arcivescovo*, Florence, 1857, pp. 34–35, cited by Pastor, *Gesch. d. Päpste*, I (repr. 1955), 664, note 2, who also quotes a brief passage from a Venetian letter of 20 April (in the Sen. Secreta, Reg. 20, fol. 58^{v} [59^{v}]) to the effect that Calixtus III's election must be regarded as a celestial rather than human act, and letters cannot express the immense joy and pleasure which the statesmen of the Serenissima have derived from it. On the same day, the Senate wrote Pietro Barbo, the cardinal of S. Marco, of their great satisfaction in Calixtus's election and in his crusading vow, of which Barbo had sent a copy to Venice (*ibid.*, fol. 59^{r} [60^{r}]): "Ea omnia nobis profecto fuere gratissima." *Cf.* Marino Sanudo, *Vite de' duchi*, in *RISS*, XXII (Milan, 1733), col. 1158DE.

[12] Arch. Segr. Vaticano, Arm. XXXI, tom. 52, fols. 57^{v}–58^{r}, by mod. stamped enumeration; Pastor, *Hist. Popes*, II, 337–39, and *Gesch. d. Päpste*, I (repr. 1955), 671–72; *Acta inedita*, I, no. 31, pp. 43–44.

[13] Sen. Secreta, Reg. 20, fols. 61^{v}–62^{r}[62^{v}–63^{r}], from the commission dated 6 June, 1455, issued in the name of the Doge Francesco Foscari to Pasquale Malipiero, Triadano Gritti, Jacopo Loredan, and Lodovico Foscarini, the Venetian envoys being sent to Rome, as an embassy of obedience to Calixtus III: ". . . Quando eritis Rome dabitis operam adeundi conspectum summi pontificis, et exhibitis litteris nostris credentialibus factisque devotis et filialibus recommendationibus Beatitudini sue . . . declarabitis summum gaudium ineffabilemque letitiam quam suscepimus cum primum intelleximus Sanctitatem suam ad summi pontificatus apicem esse assumptam, persuasimus namque nobis ac certissimum tenuimus hanc eius electionem divinam potius quam humanam fuisse. . . .

"Si per id tempus quo stabitis Rome summus pontifex qui, ut intelligere potuistis, multum inclinatus esse videtur ad exterminium Theucrorum requireret seu diceret vobis quicquam de his rebus Theucrorum velletque intelligere nostram intentionem si et nos cum aliis potentiis favores nostros huic impresie prestaturi sumus, contenti sumus et volumus quod sue Beatitudini respondeatis in ea modesta et pertinenti forma verborum quam magis utilem iudicabitis: Quod quando videbimus alias potentias Christianas contra Teucros potenter se movere, nos quoque imitantes vestigia maiorum nostrorum repperiemur illius bone dispositionis cuius per elapsum fuimus."

A month later, on 7 July, the envoys were again directed to repeat this statement to the pope, with whom were well aware how unlikely the prospect was of the "aliae potentiae Christianae" moving in force against the Turks, despite the already famous vow which Calixtus frequently made to give his whole effort, "even to the shedding of his own blood," to the recovery of Constantinople, the liberation of the enslaved Christians in the East, and the destruction of the diabolical sect of the wicked and perfidious Mohammed.[14]

The world had changed since the old days of Urban II, but in the aged pope's breast there beat the heart of a true crusader. The Franciscan Gabriele da Verona wrote Fra Giovanni da Capistrano from Rome:

> This new pope is always talking, always thinking about the expedition [against the Turks]. Fra Lodovico da Bologna, a layman, who has just now come from Jerusalem, and is well versed in Turkish affairs, often talks with the pope, sometimes for two hours. Fra Valentino da Treviso has ready access to him, as often as he wants; the pope likes to listen to him, and consults him frequently, for he speaks well and informedly about these matters. The pope conducts other affairs with a single word, but this matter which relates to the faith he thinks about and concerns himself with continually. He is always discussing it, turning it over in his mind; he hardly sleeps and eats, and people are all wondering at such great enthusiasm in so old a man for this arduous and difficult business. Everything he can get, he turns to this account. I was present once while he was at the table, and seeing the golden salt-cellar, which had belonged to his predecessor Nicholas, he cried, "Take it away, take it away! Use it against the Turk; earthenware is good enough for me!" He has stripped a great number of books of their gold and silver ornamentation—Nicholas had put these books in the Vatican Library, for he was a great student of the fine arts and a most assiduous collector of books—and he has converted this spoil into money for use [against the Turks]. He is said to have had 200,000 ducats when he was elevated to the papacy; he has spent these and almost another 60,000, which Nicholas left, in preparing a fleet and enlisting troops.[15]

On 14 April (1455) Calixtus sent King Ladislas Postumus of Bohemia and Hungary, who was still a boy, an announcement of his elevation

---

they had by now had an audience, and whom they had found burning with the desire to proceed against the perfidious Turk (*ibid.*, fols. 65^{v}–66^{r} [66^{v}–67^{r}]). The pope was hampered, however, in his own efforts to initiate a campaign against the Turks by the expense he was put to in opposing the hostilities of the condottiere Jacopo Piccinino, who had recently invaded the region of Siena (Pastor, *Acta inedita*, I, nos. 34–35, pp. 45–47). On the embassies, *cf.* Raynaldus, *Ann. eccl.*, ad ann. 1455, nos. 20–24, vol. XVIII (1694), pp. 435–38. Venetian sources for these years, especially the Sen. Secreta, Reg. 20 [1453–1459], contain many references to Piccinino. On 14 April, 1455, the pope had directed all his temporal vicars to exclude Piccinino from the states of the Church (Arch. Segr. Vaticano, Reg. Vat. 436, fol. 1).

[14] Raynaldus, *Ann. eccl.*, ad ann. 1455, no. 18, vol. XVIII (1694), p. 435; Pastor, *Hist. Popes*, II, 346, and *Gesch. d. Päpste*, I (repr. 1955), 678–79; Luke Wadding, *Annales Minorum*, ed. J. M. Fonseca, XII (3rd ed., Quaracchi, 1932), 284.

[15] Gabriele da Verona, quoted in Wadding, *Ann. Minorum*, XII (1932), 336. Calixtus III himself wrote Dionysius Széchy, archbishop of Gran (Esztergom) and cardinal-priest of S. Ciriaco, on 5 August, 1456, that up to the preceding 31 May the crusade had cost him, *Deo teste*, more than 150,000 ducats (Arch. Segr. Vaticano, Arm. XXXIX, tom. 7, fol. 25^{r}, by mod. stamped enumeration). *Cf.*, *ibid.*, fol. 43^{v}.

A decade later Gabriele da Verona was appointed by Pope Paul II inquisitor in Bohemia, ". . . ad extirpationem heresium et precipue nephande Hussitarum septe . . . per Boemie regnum et partes illi adiacentes . . ." ("datum Rome apud Sanctum Marcum, anno etc., MCCCCLXVI, tertiodecimo Kal. Aprilis, [pontificatus nostri] anno tertio," i.e., 20 March, 1467, because according to the style of the Incarnation the new year began on 25 March), for which document see Reg. Vat. 519, fol. 250^{v}, by mod. stamped enumeration, and *cf.* the bull against the Hussites addressed to Gabriele on 15 March, 1467, "datum Rome apud Sanctum Marcum, anno etc., MCCCCLXVI, Idus Martii, pontificatus nostri anno tertio" (*ibid.*, fols. 235^{r}–236^{v}). As is well known, the Bohemian king, George of Poděbrady, was declared a heretic and "deprived" of his kingdom and possessions by Paul II, all his vassals being released from their oaths of allegiance to him on 23 December, 1466 (Pastor, *Hist. Popes*, IV, 140–41, and *Gesch. d. Päpste*, II [repr. 1955], 404–5; F. G. Heymann, *George of Bohemia, King of Heretics*, Princeton, 1965, pp. 437–39). On 14 May, 1467, Paul II again pronounced the most solemn declaration of excommunication against him in the bull "Ad Romani pontificis Christi in terris vicarii," *datum Rome apud S. Marcum, anno etc., pridie Idus Maii, pont. nostri anno tertio* (also in Reg. Vat. 519, fols. 236^{v}–237^{v}), and a crusade was announced against him on the following day, the fifteenth (*ibid.*, fols. 237^{v}–241^{r}). Papal efforts against George were unavailing, however, and he was still unbeaten and unreconciled to Rome when he died on 22 March, 1471 (Pastor, IV, 146, and *Gesch. d. Päpste*, II, 409; Heymann, *George of Bohemia*, pp. 584–85 and ff.). The contemporary texts show the importance of Gabriele da Verona during this period, when Paul II's concern with the Hussite king (as we shall see) was to be an impediment to the crusade, and the Venetians were to lose Negroponte.

On the family and the extraordinary career of Fra Lodovico [Severi] da Bologna, see the important article of Angelo Bargellesi Severi, "Nuovi Documenti su fr. Lodovico da Bologna, al secolo Lodovico Severi, nunzio apostolico in Oriente (1455–1457)," in the *Archivum Franciscanum historicum*, LXIX (1976), 3–22, with three new documents—a (spiritual) grant made by Lodovico to certain members of his family, dated 19 November, 1455, and two bulls of Calixtus III, misdated by Severi 22 December, but properly dated 22 November, 1457. On Lodovico, see below, Chapter 7, note 80.

to the papal throne, and declared his resolution, even to the shedding of his own blood if need be, "that those most hideous enemies of the Christian name [the Turks] should be entirely expelled not only from the city of Constantinople, which they have recently occupied, but also from the confines of Europe."[16] This was encouraging news, and on 21 July the Hungarian leaders wrote Calixtus from Buda that, "since our world was struck with terror by the infidels, we believed that we could hardly bear at the time the sad and unexpected death . . . of Pope Nicholas V," who had won the commendation of the Christian world by his pastoral care of the imperiled Hungarians. They had been consoled, however, by the news of Calixtus's accession to the throne. Their grief had given way to joy, for a worthy successor had been found who would protect Christendom, recover Constantinople, and expel the Turks from Europe:

> How very much indeed the pitiable condition of Christians now has need of your Holiness's protection, . . . can be the more fully understood from the report which the legate of the Apostolic See has just brought back from the diet of Neustadt, where after the loss of valuable time and the deception of our hopes only this was accomplished—that our enemy might rejoice that nothing was accomplished![17]

On 15 May, 1455, Calixtus confirmed his predecessor's crusading bull of 30 September of the year before, explaining some of its doubtful provisions, and abrogating all the indulgences which had been granted since the Council of Constance unless they related to the crusade. He set 1 March, 1456, as the date of the departure of "all the Christian princes and peoples,"[18] and appointed or sent legates to Hungary, Germany, Poland, England, and France.[19] On 8 September

[16] N. Iorga, *Notes et extraits pour servir à l'histoire des croisades*, IV (Bucharest, 1915), pt. 3, no. 45, p. 118. The pope's determination to expel the Turks from Constantinople was well known in Europe (*cf.* Lorenzo Bonincontri, *Ann.*, in *RISS*, XXI [Milan, 1732], col. 158). Ladislas Postumus was to die in Prague in November, 1457, just short of eighteen years of age, awaiting his forthcoming marriage to Madeleine, the daughter of Charles VII of France. He was to be succeeded as king of Bohemia by the Utraquist (Hussite) George of Poděbrady, who had been regent during Ladislas's minority. Matthias Corvinus, son of John Hunyadi, the late regent of Hungary, succeeded to the latter kingdom. The fortunate young Matthias had been prisoner of Ladislas, who had executed John Hunyadi's elder son László. Ladislas had inherited Austria from his father, King Albert II, and at his death the duchy went to his cousin, Frederick III, head of the house of Hapsburg, whose previous landed possessions had been chiefly Styria and Carinthia. On Ladislas's eventful career from about February, 1455, until his death, see Heymann, *George of Bohemia*, pp. 125–48.

[17] Wadding, *Ann. Minorum*, XII (1932), pp. 294–95 (ed. Lyon, VI [1648], pp. 151–52; ed. Rome, XII [1735], p. 254).

[18] By the bull *Ad summi pontificatus apicem*, published in part in Raynaldus, *Ann. eccl.*, ad ann. 1455, no. 19, vol. XVIII (1694), p. 435. The complete text may be found in the Reg. Vat. 436, fols. 161^r–163^r, by mod. stamped enumeration (earlier foliation, 163^r–165^r), the first of the eighteen registers of Calixtus III *de Curia* (Regg. Vatt. 436–53). The first folia of each register contain, as is usually the case, an index of its contents (*rubricellae*). An abridged index of the eighteen volumes and a small number of selected documents may be studied in Arm. XXXI, tom. 59, which I have not, however, found very useful. *Cf.* the *Sussidi per la consultazione dell' Archivio Vaticano*, I (Rome, 1926), 73 (Studi e testi, no. 45). There is also a complete (and beautifully written) copy of the bull *Ad summum* [*sic*] *pontificatus apicem* in Arm. XXXII, tom. 12, fols. 75^r–80^v. This is a very useful collection of briefs, bulls, and certain other documents relating to the crusades from Celestine III to Leo X. Pastor, *Gesch. d. Päpste*, I (repr. 1955), 683, note 1, describes this volume as being "ohne bestimmten Standort" in the Archives, but in fact the armorial assignment of the volume (XXXII, tom. 12) is carefully lettered on the spine in the same ink and hand as the title (which Pastor cites) "Pontif. Bullae pro Subs. Terrae Stae. et de Bello Turcis infer."

[19] Raynaldus, *Ann. eccl.*, ad ann. 1455, nos. 25–27, vol. XVIII (1694), pp. 439–40, and *cf.* Pastor, *Gesch. d. Päpste*, I (repr. 1955), 681–82. Dionysius Széchy, cardinal archbishop of Gran, was appointed legate *de latere* to Hungary (Arch. Segr. Vaticano, Reg. Vat. 438, fols. 79^v, 129); Juan de Carvajal, cardinal of S. Angelo "in Pescheria," whose anti-Utraquist mission to Prague in April and May, 1448, had failed miserably, was to go to Germany, Hungary, and Poland (*ibid.*, fols. 212^r–213^v, 233^v–234^v, *et alibi*); Nicholas of Cusa to England and Germany (*ibid.*, fols. 189, 215^r–218^r, *et al.*); and Alain de Coëtivy to France (*cf.*, *ibid.*, fols. 118^r–119^r, 171^r–172^r, by mod. stamped enumeration). The numerous faculties granted Carvajal were so important as to cause a scribe to write "Facultates Cardinalis Sancti Angeli" on the vellum wrapper to Reg. Vat. 442, where see fols. 99^r–109^v, 245^r–246^v, and 247. On 27 August, 1457, *sexto Kal. Septembris*, Carvajal was granted certain faculties of dispensation and absolution (Reg. Vat. 449, fols. 133^v–135^r). Carvajal was an able and eminent figure despite his badly managed mission to Bohemia, on which note Lino Gómez Canedo, *Un Español al servicio de la Santa Sede, Don Juan de Carvajal, cardenal de Sant' Angelo, legado en Alemania y Hungria*, Madrid, 1947, pp. 22, 105 ff., 113–19, and see Heymann, *George of Bohemia* (1965), pp. 36–41. On Carvajal's Hungarian mission, which lasted from 1455 to 1461, see Gómez Canedo, *op. cit.*, pp. 153 ff., and on these legations in general, *cf.* Sanudo, *Vite de'duchi*, in *RISS*, XXII, col. 1159AB.

Calixtus III devoted especial pains to trying to win Charles VII of France over to the Crusade, but his efforts were quite in vain (*cf.* Arm. XXXIX, tom. 7, fols. 41, 50^v–51^r, 69^r–70^r, 105^r–106^r, 137^r–138^r). In a letter of 28 May, 1457, Calixtus informed Charles of his decision to present him

Calixtus himself bestowed the cross upon two of these legates, Cardinals Alain de Coëtivy and Juan de Carvajal, who were going to France and Hungary respectively, as well as upon Pedro de Urrea, the archbishop of Tarragona, who was being sent against a Turkish fleet which was ravaging the islands and mainland shores of the Aegean and Ionian Seas. Bishop Giovanni Castiglione of Pavia witnessed the ceremony in S. Peter's, and wrote of it the following day to Francesco Sforza: "His Holiness performed the act with great devotion and many tears. He has the most ardent desire to proceed against the Turk, and it is a great pity that he should be obstructed in his efforts, especially on account of Jacopo [Piccinino]," the condottiere, who was then menacing the papal states and the territories of Siena.[20] The activities of Piccinino were a dangerous and irritating distraction, but Calixtus concentrated upon the crusade with the most dogged determination.

The crusade received, nevertheless, numerous setbacks in Calixtus's brief reign. Pedro de Urrea, archbishop of Tarragona, whom the pope had made captain-general of the fleet which was to protect the islands and shores of the Ionian Sea and the Aegean, had been the apostolic legate in Aragon, Catalonia, and Valencia. He was to play in years to come an important part in the affairs of the Aragonese crown. Urrea had sixteen "triremes" under his command; ten more were being built; and the pope had additional ships in the harbor of Ancona.[21] Urrea was assigned two members of knightly orders as commanders of the fighting forces, Antonio Olzina and Antonio Frescobaldi.[22] They never sailed against the Turks. They joined the fleet of King Alfonso V in waging war upon the Genoese, the traditional enemies of Aragon-Catalonia. They also attacked the Venetians. Calixtus finally denounced them as traitors and their betrayal of the faith as an outrage to Christendom. He remonstrated with Alfonso, "O king of the Aragonese, help Pope Calixtus, do not leave him alone, and God will make your reign a long one. Otherwise you will feel His wrath!"[23] On 15 April, 1456, the

with the golden rose (*ibid.*, fols. 96^v–97^r, and *cf.* fol. 102), on the significance of which see Anna Hedwig Benna, "Zur kirchlichen Symbolik: Goldene Rose, Schwert und Hut," *Mitteilungen d. Österreichischen Staatsarchivs*, IV (Vienna, 1951), 54–62.

[20] Pastor, *Hist. Popes*, II, 349–50, and append., no. 35, pp. 539–40, and *Gesch. d. Päpste*, I (repr. 1955), 681–82, and append., no. 68, pp. 851–52; Raynaldus, *Ann. eccl.*, ad ann. 1455, nos. 28–29, vol. XVIII (1694), pp. 440–41, who gives Pedro de Urrea's commission, dated 20 September, 1455: Calixtus was sending him with "no mean fleet," "quia perfidum Turcum . . ., maritimis quoque auxiliis aedificata atque constructa non exigua classe, nunc insulas Aegei atque Ionii marium, nunc continentem, . . . invadere, diripere, impugnare . . . ac barbarica crudelitate vastare intelligeremus. . . ."

The date of Carvajal's departure from Rome on his mission is fixed by an entry in the Acta Consistorialia (1439–1486), ad ann. 1455, in Arm. XXXI, tom. 52, fol. 58^r: "Recessus domini cardinalis Sancti Angeli: Anno et pontificatu predictis [1455 de tempore Calixti III] die vero XXV. Septembris, que fuit dies Iovis, fuit factum consistorium secretum, et reverendissimus dominus cardinalis Sancti Angeli recessit legatus in Alamaniam et Ungariam de mane per portam Sancte Marie de Populo" (and *cf.* Eubel, *Hierarchia catholica*, II [1914, repr. 1960], 31a). Carvajal's mission to Hungary and Germany, as observed in note 19 above, was to last until 1461 (see the work already cited, of Lino Gómez Canedo, *Don Juan de Carvajal, cardenal de Sant' Angelo* [1947], pp. 15, 22–23, 153 ff.).

[21] Arch. Segr. Vaticano, Arm. XXXIX, tom. 7, fol. 28^r (older enumeration, fol. 25), an undated letter (probably April, 1456) to the doge and council of Genoa. After congratulating the Genoese on their reported efforts against the Turks, Calixtus described his own untiring concern "ut classis nostra expediatur et legatus noster cum ea ad partes orientales maturo tempore enavigare possit: itaque triremes quas hic fabricari facimus per totum mensem Maii proximi absolventur eruntque decem omni armamentorum genere validissime instructe: Est eciam in mari venerabilis frater archiepiscopus Terraconensis legatus noster cum triremibus XVI: una cum illis que iam sunt habemus insuper in portu Anconitano aliqua navigia bello navali apta quas[!] prope diem versus orientem emitti faciemus facimusque alios opportunos apparatus ut pecunie et commeatus suppleant. Adeo autem incitati in hanc rem sumus ut nulla festinatio nobis non tarda videatur. Vos autem bene sapienterque fecistis capere consilium de mittendis sagittariis in subsidium Lesbi [MS. *lesti*] Lemnique insularum et de comportando frumento pro Caphensi populo ut contra barbarorum impetus muniti sint quoad adventu classis nostre ex periculo liberentur. . . ." *Cf.* Matteo Sciambra, Giuseppe Valentini, and Ignazio Parrino, *Il "Liber brevium" di Callisto III, la crociata, l'Albania e Skanderbeg*, Palermo, 1968, no. 2, p. 69 (on this work, see below, note 25).

[22] Antonio Olzina, *miles ordinis militie Sancti Jacobi de Spata*, had been recipient of a grant from Nicholas V in the mid-summer of 1451 (Reg. Vat. 396, fols. 278^v–279^r), and in May, 1455, Calixtus had assigned to Antonio Frescobaldi, a Hospitaller, funds owing to the Apostolic Camera "ad armandum quatuor galeas et unam navim in portu Pisano" (Reg. Vat. 436, fol. 38^v). On 23 May, 1455, Olzina, *familiaris noster . . . duarum gallearum patronus*, was granted a safe-conduct or *littera passus* (Reg. Vat. 436, fol. 102, by mod. stamped enumeration). *Cf.* in general Pio Paschini, "La Flotta di Callisto III (1455–1458)," in *Archivio della R. Società romana di storia patria*, LIII–LV (Rome, 1930–32), 180–82.

[23] Raynaldus, *Ann. eccl.*, ad ann. 1456, nos. 11–12, vol. XVIII (1694), p. 457; Pastor, *Gesch. d. Päpste*, I (repr. 1955), 693–94. The pope's words are from an undated letter to Jaume de Perpinyà (Arch. Segr. Vaticano, Arm. XXXIX, tom. 7, fol. 9^v).

pope removed Urrea, Olzina, and Frescobaldi in an indignant bull of deposition for their attacks upon fellow Christians "and for the perpetration of many other unspeakable acts."[24] Disappointing as this experience was, it seemed only to make the pope work harder than ever to launch an offensive against the Turks.

Preachers of the crusade, sellers of indulgences, and collectors of tithes were sent throughout the length and breadth of Europe, from Norway and Sweden to Corsica and Sicily, from Portugal to Poland, and from Ireland and Scotland to Germany and Dalmatia.[25] The mendicant friars were much employed as preachers, especially the Franciscans. One of the more interesting documents is a letter addressed by Calixtus III to the Dominican Giovanni de Curte, papal nuncio in the March of Ancona.[26] The pope reminded Fra Giovanni of the horrors of the Turkish capture of Constantinople, and informed him that a tithe was being levied "throughout the entire Christian world" on all ecclesiastical incomes. The friar was to consult, however, with the bishops of the March or with their vicars as to its imposition. In each city one or two collectors were to be chosen to receive the tithes and keep a record of the full names of those who paid and of the amounts they paid. In fact these records were to be kept in duplicate as a safeguard against loss or pilfering. Full ecclesiastical penalties were to be meted out to recalcitrant clerics, who might be deprived of their benefices, fined, turned over to the secular arm, and imprisoned. Popular preachers were to be enlisted who would properly expound the contents of the papal letters respecting the tithes to the people, exhorting them to contribute to the defense of the faith or to join, if they could, the forthcoming expedition against the Turks.

With the advice and counsel of the bishops or their vicars, the papal letter continues, Fra Giovanni was to place in the sacristy of each

[24] Pastor, *Hist. Popes*, II, append., no. 38, pp. 544–45, and *Gesch. d. Päpste*, I (repr. 1955), append., no. 71, p. 854. There are numerous references to Olzina and to the archbishop of Tarragona in an important volume of Calixtus III's briefs in the Vatican Archives (Arm. XXXIX, tom. 7), e.g., fol. 37^{v}, where the scandalous conduct of the archbishop is denounced to Lodovico Trevisan, the cardinal of Aquileia, to whom his galleys were given in order that they might see the service in eastern waters for which they were intended. Eight years later, however, Frescobaldi was appointed by Pius II his crusading commissioner for Ancona: ". . . Dilecto filio Antonio de Frescobaldis, priori prioratus Pisarum Hospitalis Sancti Johannis Hierosolimitani commissario nostro salutem, etc. Cum nuper nos de tua industria rerumque experientia plurimum confidentes pro perficiendis non nullis galeis et aliis navigiis ac quampluribus aliis rebus ad apparatum classis nostre maritime contra Turchos pertinentibus conducendis et peragendis te commissarium nostrum ad civitatem nostram Anconitanam et alia loca . . . destinaverimus ac deputaverimus, . . . auctoritate apostolica tenore presentium concedimus," etc. [granting administrative faculties for the preparation of the papal fleet], doc. in Reg. Vat. 519, fols. 62^{v}–63^{r}, "datum Rome apud Sanctum Petrum, anno etc., millesimo CCCCLXIII, sexto Idus Januarii, pontificatus nostri anno sexto" (8 January, 1464). *Cf.* Paschini, "La Flotta," pp. 192–204, 212, 216–17, who dates the final removal of Urrea, Olzina, and Frescobaldi from their commands on 20 March, 1457 (*ibid.*, p. 204).

[25] *Cf.* Pastor, *Gesch. d. Päpste*, I (repr. 1955), 683–85. There are numerous letters to *collectores* in the volume of briefs referred to in the preceding note (and often cited in these pages). On Calixtus III's crusading efforts, see the brief but densely packed article by Matteo Sciambra, Giuseppe Valentini, and Ignazio Parrino, "L'Albania e Skanderbeg nel piano generale di crociata di Callisto III (1455–1458)," in the *Bollettino della Badia greca di Grottaferrata*, new series, XXI (1967), 83–136, who give in appendices lists of the names of crusading legates, nuncios, collectors of funds, and preachers. Their archival researches have led them to conclude that Calixtus spent (or expected to spend?) a "minimal total" of 639,000 ducats on the crusade, and committed thereto some 750,000. Their study is based chiefly but not exclusively on the volume of briefs in question (Arm. XXXIX, tom. 7, which I used years ago in the Vatican Archives), of which they have prepared a valuable *edizione in regesto*, i.e., Italian summaries of the texts, with selected briefs given in the original Latin (*Il "Liber brevium" di Callisto III, la crociata, l'Albania e Skanderbeg*, Palermo: Centro internazionale di studi albanesi, 1968)—there are in all 436 briefs covering the period from 4 May, 1456, to 28 June, 1458.

On the papal registers in Calixtus's time and curial and scribal practices in signing, dispatching, copying, and preserving bulls, briefs, and other texts (corrections, erasures, cancellations; expectancies, nominations to ecclesiastical offices and benefices; the Camera and Chancery; papal secretaries, abbreviators, *scriptores*, and other officials; and the role of the pope in the Vatican setting), see Ernst Pitz, *Supplikensignatur und Briefexpedition an der römischen Kurie im Pontifikat Papst Calixts III.*, Tübingen, 1972. Calixtus made his nephew Rodrigo Borgia (later Alexander VI) vice-chancellor on 1 May, 1457, and hence head of the Chancery, after the office had been vacant for four years (*ibid.*, p. 39).

[26] This letter, dated 1 September, 1455, is briefly noted, although not published, by Raynaldus, *Ann. eccl.*, ad ann. 1455, no. 27, vol. XVIII (1694), p. 440, but see the following note. On the financial participation of Genoa and the Bank of S. George in the crusade and the sale of indulgences in the area to the south of the city (for the maintenance of Caffa on the Black Sea), note Jacques Heers, "La Vente des indulgences pour la croisade, à Gènes et en Lunigiana, en 1456," *Miscellanea storica ligure*, III (1963), 69–101. Funds were collected in the coinages of Genoa, Florence, the Holy See, Milan, Ferrara, Venice, Bologna, Siena, Savona, Savoy, Catalonia, France, and the Genoese island of Chios, indicating the wide variety of coins in local circulation and the apparent ease of monetary exchange in the mid-fifteenth century.

cathedral or other important church a chest with four locks and keys, one key being held by the local bishop, the second by the friar himself, the third by the two collectors, and the fourth by two grave and good citizens of the community. All the funds collected were to be deposited in this chest, with a notary on hand to make another record of the names of those who paid and the amounts in question, so that everyone might be assured that all the money being collected would be expended solely for the needs of the faith. The extent of these precautions suggests that at other times and other places there had been serious abuses, as we know well from other sources. Finally, the pope informed Fra Giovanni and all other nuncios who received similar letters that he was going to arm and maintain at least fifteen galleys (*triremes*) or, if such a naval force was forthcoming from other sources, to spend the funds on a land army.[27]

Despite Pope Calixtus's precautions funds were secreted by ecclesiastical agents. False collectors and false preachers arose to take the opportunities for peculation.[28] Glancing ahead for a moment we may note that on 28 December, 1456, the pope wrote the bishop of Arezzo that he had been informed of the theft of funds collected as part of the crusading tithe by a certain Leonardo, a priest of Arezzo, while he was serving as vicar in the church of Sarsina. Leonardo was to be apprehended, "wherever he might be," imprisoned, and forced to return the money he had stolen. The bishop was reminded that any negligence on his part to effect Leonardo's arrest would incur ecclesiastical censure.[29] In a brief of 26 March, 1457, the pope, while commending the diligence of Guillem Ponç de Fenollet (then in Barcelona), expressed strong disapproval of certain financial irregularities in the Catalan diocese which had come to his attention.[30] Conditions were no better in various other areas. There was embezzlement of crusading funds in the territories of the Genoese republic, for example, and in a letter of 26 May (1457) Calixtus ordered his commissioners in Genoa to arrest and call to account those guilty of such grave impropriety.[31] Less than two months later (on 15 July) Calixtus wrote the bishop of Feltre, "Not without displeasure have we learned that a certain John de Revo, falsely representing himself as a nuncio and commissioner of the Apostolic See, has been preaching the crusade throughout the whole duchy of Austria, and without authorization of the Apostolic See granting unheard-of indulgences whereby he is said to have purloined from the devout and ignorant people of those parts money and a substantial quantity of goods."[32] It was an exasperating but constantly recurring problem, and on 4 December of the same year (1457) the pope wrote Cardinal Lodovico Trevisan, complaining of the wretched friars who were "in malum exemplum plurimorum et perditionem bonorum Cruciate."[33]

Although in the meantime the response to the crusade was sometimes discouraging, there had been a few bright colors in the picture. Thus Cardinals Bessarion, d'Estouteville, Trevisan, Capranica, Orsini, and Barbo, who had been appointed as a commission to promote the *sanctum bellum*, could write the Marquis Lodovico II Gonzaga of Mantua on 15 February, 1456, thanking him for the thousand ducats or

[27] Pastor, *Acta inedita*, I (1904), no. 36, pp. 47–51, dated 1 September, 1455; *cf.* also Pastor, *Gesch. d. Päpste*, I (repr. 1955), 685. The text may be found in the Reg. Vat. 438, fols. 59^r–60^v.

[28] *Cf.* Pastor, *Gesch. d. Päpste*, I (repr. 1955), 686.

[29] Arch. Segr. Vaticano, Arm. XXXIX, tom. 7, fol. 57: "Intelleximus fidedigna relatione quendam Leonardum presbyterum Arretinum dum exerceret officium vicariatus ecclesie Saxinatensis cum certa pecuniarum quantitate, quas ex decima Cruciate perceperat, aufugisse. Quare volumus et fraternitati tue presentium tenore committimus et mandamus ut dictum Leonardum, ubicumque sit, capi facias et carceribus mancipari cogasque eum ad restitutionem dictarum pecuniarum faciendam officialibus deputatis Cesenne aut dilecto filio Francisco Coppino commissario nostro, in qua re si negligens fueris aut tardus, indignationem nostram incurres et deinde ad acriora contra te procedemus. Datum Rome, etc., die XXVIII Decembris MCCCCLVII [*sic*, but dated *a nativitate* (25 December) the year is 1456] [pontificatus nostri] anno secundo."

[30] Arm. XXXIX, tom. 7, fols. 76^v–77^v, in reply to a letter from Fenollet dated at Barcelona on 24 February, 1457.

[31] A. Vigna, "Codice diplomatico delle colonie tauroliguri," in *Atti della Società ligure di storia patria*, VI (Genoa, 1868), doc. no. 349, pp. 738–40, and *cf.*, *ibid.*, pp. 698–99.

[32] Arm. XXXIX, tom. 8, fols. 7^v–8^r, letter of 15 July, 1457, to the bishop of Feltre, *in spiritualibus et temporalibus vicarius et officialis generalis*: "Non absque displicentia percepimus quendam Johannem de Revo se falso nuntium et apostolice sedis commissarium asserentem perque universum Austrie ducatum predicare sanctam cruciatam et inauditas absque sedis apostolice facultate concedere indulgentias ex quibus a devotis ignarisque personis illarum partium pecunias et bona quam plurima dicitur surripuisse. . . ."

[33] Arm. XXXIX, tom. 7, fol. 135^r, in reply to a letter from Cardinal Lodovico, dated at Rhodes 12 October, 1457.

so collected in his territories and for his announced intention of equipping a galley for service against the Turks. They inquired of the Marquis Lodovico whether his galley would be ready for the following 1 April, by which time Pope Calixtus had indicated his legate should take charge of the papal fleet. They also wanted to know whether the marquis would be willing to maintain the vessel at his own expense for the duration of the crusade.[34] On the same day (15 February, 1456) Calixtus himself addressed a further appeal to the marquis, to whom (he said) the cardinals were also writing, to inform the Holy See as soon as possible and as precisely as possible "when and how much and what sort of support" he was going to give the papal fleet which was being prepared for service against the Turks in eastern waters. It was necessary to know, for the cardinal legate was to sail with the fleet on the coming 1 April.[35] The legate in question was the well-known Lodovico Trevisan, cardinal patriarch of Aquileia, who had already written the marquis on 17 December, 1455, that "on this day" the pope had chosen him, with the unanimous agreement of the Sacred College, apostolic legate and commander "of all the fleet which is being prepared against the Turks."[36]

Lodovico Trevisan, along with Alain de Coëtivy, had been largely responsible for Calixtus III's unexpected elevation to S. Peter's throne. Quite understandably, therefore, he had enjoyed a large influence at the Curia for some weeks thereafter.[37] The humanist Lodrisio Crivelli states that Lodovico had "thought he could use the poor old man as he wished." Establishing himself in the Vatican, Lodovico had begun to take over, but very soon made himself offensive both to the pope and to the latter's ambitious relatives. Lodovico was removed from the papal palace, and was for a while in considerable danger, says Crivelli, until he perceived the extent of the pope's attachment to the crusade. Then Lodovico offered to go on the expedition, to the pope's delight, for the wily cardinal had had much experience of arms in the time of Eugenius IV. He was also very rich. Indeed some people believed that he was going to give up his great treasures to help the crusade "as a memorable

[34] Pastor, *Acta inedita*, I (1904), no. 37, pp. 51–52. The Venetians apparently agreed to send Cardinal Lodovico Trevisan 3,000 ducats a year to help support the papal fleet (Arm. XXXIX, tom. 7, fol. 53^v). On 16 March, 1457, the Ragusei wrote King Ladislas Postumus of Hungary (and Bohemia) that the Franciscan friar Mariano da Siena, Trevisan's crusading deputy in Ragusa (Dubrovnik) and Dalmatia, was granting the "apostolic indulgence of all sins" to those who contributed three ducats to assist Christian efforts against the Turks. His success had been sufficient to collect, it was believed, about 4,000 ducats in Ragusa alone as well as an unspecified sum from the rest of Dalmatia.

The Ragusei gave some emphasis to the constitutional fiction that their city still lay under the jurisdiction of the Hungarian crown (Mariano was preaching the crusade *in hac Serenitatis vestre civitate . . . quamquam civitas predicta regni Maiestatis vestre membrum sit*). They assumed that the funds were to be used to support Trevisan's fleet, which was then in Rhodian waters (see, below, p. 188), but they much preferred that all the money be diverted to support a (Hungarian) expedition against the Turks on land. The money would thus pass into the hands of Cardinal Carvajal rather than into those of Trevisan (see J. Gelcich and L. Thallóczy, eds., *Diplomatarium ragusanum*, Budapest, 1887, no. 347, pp. 594–95). Naturally Ladislas tried to get the money sent to Hungary, but Calixtus III intervened, threatening the Ragusei with excommunication if they did not turn it over to the apostolic nuncio John Navarre, who was sent to Ragusa to collect it (*ibid.*, nos. 351–52, pp. 598–600). The Ragusei did not, however, turn the money over to the nuncio until 7 February, 1458, by which time they had learned for sure of Ladislas's death the previous November (no. 355, p. 603).

[35] Arch. di Stato di Mantova, Arch. Gonzaga, Busta 834: ". . . Nos certe ad huius nostri apparatus faustam expeditionem omni studio, cura et vigilantia intenti sumus optamusque ut omnes quicquid ad eam subsidii sint allaturi sine mora conferant cum effectu cum decreverimus iam quod noster legatus ad Kal. Aprilis cum tota classe navigationi et bello feliciter gerendo sit accinctus. Datum Rome . . . sub anulo piscatoris die XV Februarii MCCCCLVI, pontificatus nostri anno primo." No one enjoyed paying the crusading impost, and at this time we find Pietro de'Tebaldeschi da Norcia, the senator of Rome, complaining of the tithe the pope had levied on his salary (A. Cappelli, "Un Senatore di Roma nel 1456," *Archivio storico lombardo*, 3rd ser., XX [ann. XXX, 1903], 195–99, esp. p. 198, a letter of 11 February [1456] to Francesco Sforza, duke of Milan).

[36] Pastor, *Hist. Popes*, II, 368, and append., no. 36, pp. 540–41, and *Gesch. d. Päpste*, I (repr. 1955), 696, and append., no. 69, p. 852, who (as noted elsewhere in this volume) inaccurately calls Trevisan "Scarampo;" Niccola della Tuccia, *Cronaca di Viterbo*, ed. Ignazio Ciampi, Florence, 1872, p. 187. On 29 December, 1455, the Venetian Senate wrote Cardinal Lodovico: "Reverendissimo domino cardinali, patriarche Aquilegiensi, camerario: . . . Novimus litteris reverendissime dominationis vestre nuper nobis redditis electionem factam per pontificem maximum unanimi voto et consensu Sacri Collegii . . . de reverendissima persona vestra in legatum apostolicum generalemque gubernatorem et capitaneum tocius maritime classis contra hostes fidei instruende . . .," after which come the usual flattering expressions of confidence and affection (Arch. di Stato di Venezia, Sen. Secreta, Reg. 20, fol. 76^r [77^r]).

[37] *Cf.* Pastor, *Hist. Popes*, II, 323–25, 330, and *Gesch. d. Päpste*, I (repr. 1955), 659–61, 664, with refs. to the sources.

and highly laudable example." This was not, however, Lodovico's intention. According to Crivelli, Lodovico was in fact unwilling to sail with the fleet when the time came, because Calixtus had promised he would outfit thirty galleys, although only seven were actually made ready for action. Thereupon Calixtus is said to have summoned a secret consistory at which he assailed the cardinal "with the bitterest words," and threatened him with an ecclesiastical tribunal. Lodovico assumed command of the fleet.[38] Probably little could be expected, however, of an expedition whose commander discounted its chances of success even before he sailed.

Calixtus III's preparations for the fleet in 1455–1456 are recorded in some detail in a register preserved in the Roman State Archives.[39] The Sienese banker Ambrogio Spanocchi was entrusted with the expenditure of funds. Pedro (Pere) Torres of Barcelona was appointed *executor operum dictarum galearum*, and as *provisores operum galearum* Giovanni Jacobi of Rome and Niccolò da Fabriano were each paid five florins a month. The first order of payment (*mandatum*), dated 22 October, 1455, provided twenty florins to two caulkers; a mandatum follows authorizing payment of eighteen florins for 1,000 pounds of iron to make nails and other fixtures for the galleys. Charges for pitch, hemp, and timber are all carefully noted as well as expenditures for 760 stone cannon balls and 9,000 smaller balls for hand-guns, together with the costs of helmets, breastplates, lances, crossbows, arrows, swords, axes, chains, and anchors, banners and tents, biscuits and writing paper. It was easy, although expensive, to equip the fleet, but quite another matter (as the pope was soon to discover) to send it into effective action in eastern waters against the Turks.

In the meantime Calixtus III was having other troubles, especially in the war with the condottiere Jacopo Piccinino in central Italy. Although the unpredictable Alfonso of Aragon-Catalonia and Naples had taken the cross with a theatrical flourish on 1 November, 1455,[40] he was supporting Piccinino against both Siena and the papacy. In June, 1455, Calixtus had informed the Venetian envoys in Rome that the war with Piccinino had already cost him more than 70,000 ducats, "which would have been better expended against the Turk," but that Piccinino had to be eliminated as a threat to the peace of Italy, because peace was the indispensable prelude to the crusade.[41] While

---

[38] Lodrisio Crivelli (Cribellus), *De expeditione Pii papae secundi in Turcas*, bk. I, in *RISS*, XXIII (Milan, 1733), cols. 56E–57D, and ed. G. C. Zimolo, in the new Muratori, *RISS*, XXIII, pt. 5 (1942, 1948–50), pp. 64–65. The size of Lodovico Trevisan's fleet remains uncertain. He may have had ten galleys to start with (see below, note 100). Crivelli's account of Lodovico's reluctance to embark for the eastward voyage because of the inadequacy of the fleet, and of Calixtus's threat to take action against him, is quite plausible, but there seems to be no confirmation either in the diplomatic correspondence or in the consistorial records (*cf.* Pastor, *Gesch. d. Päpste*, I [repr. 1955], 696, note 2).

[39] Arch. di Stato di Roma, Mandata pro classe conficienda: Diversorum Calixti III, vol. 831, fols. 193 ff., on which see Pastor, *Gesch. d. Päpste*, I (repr. 1955), 696–97, and esp. P. Paschini, "La Flotta di Callisto III," *Arch. della R. Soc. rom. di storia patria*, LIII–LV (1930–32), 184 ff., 190–91. From November, 1455, to August, 1456, Ambrogio Spanocchi of Siena, acting as the financial agent of the Holy See, received some 49,076 gold florins and paid out some 45,369 for Trevisan's fleet. When the final accounting of the funds took place at Mantua on 20 June, 1459, Spanocchi thus owed the Apostolic Camera about 3,707 florins. The interested reader will find the details summarized in the following paragraph.

The financial accounting is given in the Arch. Segr. Vaticano, Introitus et Exitus, Reg. 432, fols. 79^r–101^r, by mod. stamped enumeration, "in questo libro sara scritta tutta l'entrata e uscita de che si ricieveranno e pagheranno per la fabricha de le galee [che] si fanno contro lo Turcho, tenuto per me Francesco Ghinucci da Siena in nome d'Anbrosio Spannochi, deputato depoxitario de detta fabricha" (*ibid.*, fol. 79^r). During the period specified, Ambrogio Spanocchi received funds totaling 49,076 gold florins *de camera*, 13 shillings (*solidi*), and 6 pence (*denarii*) in Roman money (fol. 88^r), and expended, for the most part "per mandato del camarlengo," 45,369 florins, 17 solidi, 9 denarii, "et sic introitus superat exitum in florenis auri similibus [i.e., de camera monete Romane] tribus milibus septingentis sex, solidis quadragintaquinque, denariis novem [3,706 fl., 45 sol., 9 den.] dicte monete, salvo tamen calculo veriori in quibus quidem III m. DCCVI, soll. XXXXV, den. VIIII predictus Ambrosius remanet Camere Apostolice debitor et efficaciter obligatus. . . . Mantue in Camera Apostolica die vicesima mensis Iunii MCCCCL [!], pontificatus sanctissimi d. n. domini Pii divina providentia Pape II anno primo" (fol. 101^r).

In the Introitus et Exitus, Reg. 459, fols. 8^r–16^v, there is a record of the collection and disbursement of funds "in adiutorium armate contra Turchos" (fol. 9^r) from April to July, 1456, by Ambrogio Spanocchi, Alessandro Miraballi, Tommaso Spinelli, and others. As always in the history of the medieval and Renaissance papacy, the financial records are incomplete, but I doubt whether Calixtus spent a "minimal total" of 639,000 ducats on the crusade, for which estimate see above, note 25.

[40] Pastor, *Gesch. d. Päpste*, I (repr. 1955), 689–90, and *cf.* Raynaldus, *Ann. eccl.*, ad ann. 1455, no. 30, vol. XVIII (1694), pp. 441–42.

[41] Letter of Bartolommeo Visconti, bishop of Novara, to Francesco Sforza, dated at Rome, 29 June, 1455, in Pastor, *Acta inedita*, I (1904), no. 34, pp. 45–46; *cf.* Pastor, *Hist. Popes*, II, 360, where the letter is misdated 1456 in

Alfonso had the effrontery to propose that Piccinino be made commander of an army which the Italian League should maintain against the Turks, the condottiere actually tried to burn the papal fleet then being outfitted for service in the East.[42]

In view of Alfonso's support of Piccinino, however, there was little that the Sienese and Calixtus could do against him; they had to buy him off, and in September, 1456, Piccinino withdrew from Sienese territory into the Neapolitan kingdom.[43] Once again Calixtus could give his full attention to preparations for the anti-Turkish war.

Certainly the pope's full attention was needed. As the Ragusei had written John Hunyadi, still called by courtesy the "lord governor of Hungary," on 11 June, 1455, the savage ruler of the Turks had already added (in the lust and ambition of his imagination) all Christendom to his dominion, "and he is burning with the desire to conquer the world."[44] Again and again the published documents from Ragusa bear witness to the fear and trembling inspired by the Gran Turco, whose forces spread havoc with their constant raids into Albania, Bosnia, and Serbia, Wallachia and Transylvania. The Ragusei wrote letter after letter, emphasizing the Turkish peril, to King Ladislas Postumus of Hungary (and Bohemia), John Hunyadi, Ulrich of Cilli, and other nobles and high ecclesiastics. News of the sultan's especial displeasure so terrified the Ragusei that, as they informed Ladislas, they were "utterly bereft of judgment."[45]

The fear of Turkish domination was as widespread in the Balkans and in Greece as it was in Italy and in Hungary. Turakhan Beg had imposed a form of peace upon the Morea by repressing the Albanians and intimidating the despots. The Greeks, however, like the Ragusei, were pinning their slender hopes on receiving aid from the West. Thomas Palaeologus sent the humanist John Argyropoulus, "master of arts and medicine," to Pope Calixtus, whose passion for the crusade almost equaled his flagrant nepotism. In a letter of 15 March, 1456, the pope recommended Argyropoulus to Francesco Sforza, "as one who has always been a Catholic and a champion and defender in Greece of the union achieved [between the Churches]—besides he is most learned in both languages and endowed with many virtues."[46] As Calixtus noted in his letter, Thomas was the "brother of the late emperor of the Greeks." After the fall of Constantinople Thomas sometimes tried to mend his rapacious ways. His relations with the Venetians were improved slightly, but only slightly, by the exchange of embassies.[47] Ambassadors could come and go, and so they did. No matter how eloquent and distinguished, they secured little aid for the imperiled Morea. Francesco Sforza, for one, still had all he could do without adding the Turk to his other problems. Italy and the West had lost confidence in papal intentions. Crusading tithes and sales of indulgences were unfortunately, and at this time wrongly, regarded as mere devices to enrich the pope, the cardinals, and the whole curial establishment in Rome.

The failure of King Ladislas the Jagiellonian at Varna (in 1444) and of John Hunyadi at Kossovo (in 1448) had made the "apostolic kingdom" of Hungary, always the scene of much internal dissension, appear less the Christian march against the Turk than his avenue of approach into the heart of Europe. Despite occasional successes against the Turks, bad news came constantly from central Europe. The important mining city of Novo Brdo, located in the mountainous area between Kossovo and the Morava river, was subjected to a determined Turkish siege led by Sultan Mehmed II himself. George Branković, the despot of Serbia, had secured its return from the Turks more than a decade before (1444–1455), after the treaty of Adrianople, but the young sultan

the text, and *ibid.*, p. 362, where it is dated both incorrectly and correctly in the second note, as it is in the *Gesch. d. Päpste*, I (repr. 1955), 691, note 3.

[42] Raynaldus, *Ann. eccl.*, ad ann. 1456, no. 6, vol. XVIII (1694), p. 454; Pastor, *Hist. Popes*, II, 362–63, and *Gesch. d. Päpste*, I (repr. 1955), 691–92.

[43] Pastor, II, 364, and *Gesch. d. Päpste*, I, 693.

[44] Gelcich and Thallóczy, *Diplomatarium ragusanum* (1887), no. 332, p. 581.

[45] *Ibid.*, no. 353, p. 601, letter dated 14 November, 1457: ". . . ut consilii prorsus inopes simus. . . ."

[46] Sp. P. Lampros, *Palaiológeia kaì Peloponnesiaká*, IV (Athens, 1930), 247, and *cf.* Giuseppe Cammelli, *I Dotti bizantini e le origini dell' umanesimo*, II: *Giovanni Argiropulo*, Florence, 1941, pp. 75–76. The letter is dated at S. Peter's in Rome, "MCCCCLV, idibus Martii, pontificatus nostri anno primo," i.e., 15 March, 1456 (O.S. 1455): Calixtus III was consecrated pope on 20 April, 1455.

[47] Arch. di Stato di Venezia, Sen. Secreta, Reg. 20, fols. 76^r ff., 80^r–81^r, 107^v, 108, 110^v–111^v, 127^r [77^r ff., 81^r–82^r, etc.], docs. dated from the end of December, 1455, to June, 1457.

had decided to retake the city. After forty days of assault Novo Brdo surrendered, at the beginning of June, 1455, and more than three hundred of its stoutest youths were enrolled in the ranks of the janissaries. The prosperity of the place was largely destroyed, and its fame gradually forgotten. While its memory was fresh, however, its capture by the Turks made a profound impression.[48]

Hungarian diets might pass resolutions to take the offensive against the Turks and make perennial appeals to the pope and the emperor, but the lack of peace in the kingdom and of confidence in its government rendered effective action unlikely. Hunyadi had been regent (*gubernator*) of the realm from 1446, during the minority of Ladislas Postumus, but had resigned the office in 1452, although most Hungarians still looked upon him as their true governor. Ladislas was a boy, of small account. He fell wholly under the influence of Count Ulrich of Cilli, who hated Hunyadi more than he did the Turk. Ladislas was filled with hostility toward his imperial cousin Frederick III, who had profited from the years of tutelage over him, and so there was no hope of their co-operating against the Porte. Indeed Ladislas would have preferred to injure Frederick rather than the Turk, an ambition which also seemed rather easier of fulfillment. The papal legate, Juan de Carvajal, could not establish harmony between the two rulers, who however trivial in themselves had a symbolic importance for the crusade by virtue of their exalted titles. Calixtus was busy throughout these weeks and months, raising money (as we have seen) by the imposition of tithes and by other devices to support the *cruciata publicata contra Turchas*.[49] Tithes and the profits of usury were collected from the Jews to assist "in this sacred work against the savage Turk, for his defeat and for the exultation of the Christian faith."[50]

---

[48] We owe the details to the so-called *Memoirs of a Janissary (Pamiętniki Janczara)*, chap. 27, trans. Renate Lachmann (with additional notes by C.-P. Haase and G. Prinzing), *Memoiren eines Janitscharen oder Türkische Chronik*, Graz, Vienna, and Cologne, 1975, pp. 112–13 (Slavische Geschichtsschreiber, VIII), according to which the alleged author, the Serbian Constantine Michailović of Ostrovica, was among the group of 320 young men and 704 (or 74!) women seized by the Turks in Novo Brdo (*cf.* the unsatisfactory edition of the *Pamiętniki Janczara Polaka*, chap. 27, in P. A. Dethier, ed., *Monumenta Hungariae historica*, XXII, pt. 1 [Istanbul, 1872], pp. 1249–50, with a French translation, *ibid.*, XXII-2, pp. 335–36). The "memoirs" appear to be an amalgam of various texts (plus the figments added in the Polish redaction). They survive in a dozen or more manuscripts in Czech (as the *Kronika Turecká* or *Turkish Chronicle*) and especially in Polish (as the *Pamiętniki Janczara* or *Memoirs of a Janissary*). The original seems clearly to have been written in Czech (see Lachmann's introduction to the German translation and Angiolo Danti, "Contributi all' edizione critica dei *Pamiętniki Janczara*," *Ricerche slavistiche*, XVI [1968–69], 126–62, with bibliographical addenda in Pertusi, *Caduta di Costantinopoli*, I [1976], 254–55). The Czech text of the "memoirs," with an English translation by Benjamin Stolz and an historical commentary by Svat Soucek, has recently been published by the University of Michigan (*Konstantin Mihailović, Memoirs of a Janissary*, Ann Arbor, 1975).

On the siege of Novo Brdo and the events leading up to it, see Critobulus, II, 8–9 (ed. Müller, *FHG*, V-1 [1870], pp. 110–11; ed. Grecu, pp. 185, 187), and *cf.* F. Babinger, *Maometto il Conquistatore*, Turin, 1957, pp. 196–97. For Mehmed II's regulations on the exploitation of the mines of Novo Brdo, see especially Nicoară Beldiceanu, *Les Actes des premiers sultans . . .*, I: *Actes de Mehmed II et de Bayezid II du MS. Fonds Turc Ancien 39* [*de la Bibl. Nationale*], Paris, 1960, nos. 3–6, pp. 68–73, and *cf.* nos. 15–16, pp. 84–85, with full bibliography.

[49] *Cf.* the brief of 7 January, 1456, to the Marquis Lodovico II Gonzaga of Mantua (of which I have seen a dozen other examples) in the Arch. di Stato di Mantova, Arch. Gonzaga, Busta 834: "Dilecte fili, nobilis vir, salutem et apostolicam benedictionem. Commisimus dilecto filio Francisco Coppino iuris utriusque doctori, Camere Apostolice clerico et secretario nostro, nonnulla exequenda circa colligendas et transmittendas pecunias et alias res occasione decimarum et cruciate publicate contra Turchas quemadmodum in litteris nostris superinde confectis plenius continentur, quocirca nobilitatem tuam in domino exhortamur ut eidem Francisco plenam in premissis fidem adhibeat, assistendo eidem auxiliis, consiliis et favoribus oportunis. Datum Rome apud Sanctum Petrum sub anulo piscatoris die VII Januarii MCCCCLVI, pontificatus nostri anno primo. Io. Aurispa." The brief still has the red wax seal attached, with the legend "Calistus Papa III." *Cf.* also the brief dated 20 September, 1457, expressing the pope's satisfaction with the success of Francesco Coppini's mission in Mantua, "et quoniam eundem Franciscum ob causas predictas [circa causas decimarum et sanctissime cruciate] et alias nonnullas ad partes illas remittimus, devotionem tuam hortamur in domino ac requirimus ut eidem Francisco . . . credat et assistat favoribus oportunis. . . ."

[50] Arch. di Stato di Mantova, Arch. Gonzaga, Busta 834, a brief of 29 January, 1456, to the Marquis Lodovico: ". . . Quoniam dilectum filium Antonium Mariam de Tuscanis, iuris utriusque doctorem, secretarium nostrum, ad nobilitatem tuam contra Iudeos nuncium apostolicum ducimus destinandum, idcirco Excellentiam tuam hortamur in domino ut pro nostra et Sedis Apostolice reverentia ad decimas et usuras ab ipsis Iudeis exigendas et in hoc sancto opere contra illum crudelissimum Turchum pro ipsius depressione et fidei Christiane exaltatione convertendas dicto Antonio Marie tales prebeas favores prout speramus atque confidimus quod littere apostolice superinde confecte eum ferventi auxilio tuo sine mora debitum sortiantur effectum. Quicquid enim nobilitas tua in hac re erga ipsum Antonium Mariam fecerit, nobis et Sedi Apostolice profecto facies. Datum Rome . . . sub anulo piscatoris die XXVIIII Januarii millesimo CCCCLVI, pontificatus

A great diet was assembled at Buda on 6 February, 1456. Carvajal described papal preparations for the fleet which would attack the Turkish empire at its very center as well as the aid which was expected from King Alfonso V and from Duke Philip of Burgundy. A plenary indulgence was offered to every soldier who would bear arms against the Turks. It was at this diet, on 14 February, that Carvajal bestowed upon the famous Minorite friar Giovanni da Capistrano a cross sent by the pope, and gave him a special papal brief to preach the crusade.[51] The diet declared a levy of a golden florin on every farmhouse, and began to make provision for feeding and sheltering the many crusaders who, it was presumed, would be passing through Hungary on their way east. King Ladislas attended the diet, which on 6 April finally resolved to take the field against the Turks in August, but on the following day, alas, the news came that Mehmed II was already moving toward the Danube.[52]

After the capture of Novo Brdo, Sultan Mehmed had spent the winter of 1455–1456 planning a still larger expedition against Serbia and Hungary. He regarded the latter country, despite its internal difficulties, as his most formidable enemy in Europe, since Venice was willing to keep the peace for commercial reasons. The Turks believed the chief obstacle to their conquest of Hungary was the strong fortress of Alba Greca or Belgrade on the Danube. When this had been taken, the road would be open to Buda. Western contemporaries and some modern historians have reported, with much exaggeration, that more than 150,000 men had been mustered in the plains between Istanbul and Adrianople, and that the sultan had prepared a fleet of some two hundred river boats to be sent up the Danube and assembled at Vidin.[53] A German source of late August, 1456, says, however, that Mehmed had no more than twenty-one ships![54] The ships

nostri anno primo." Another brief on the same subject, to be found in the same *busta*, was addressed to Lodovico on 16 March, 1456, ". . . misimus ad partes illas . . . Antonium Mariam . . . ut a Iudeis in dominio tuo comorantibus decimas exigat et alias subventiones. . . . Datum Rome . . . sub anulo piscatoris die XVI Martii anno domini MCCCCLVI, pont. nostri anno primo."

[51] Giovanni da Tagliacozzo, *Relatio de victoria Belgradensi*, 2, in Luke Wadding, *Annales Minorum*, 3rd ed. by J. M. Fonseca, XII (Quaracchi, 1932), 752 (and *cf.*, *ibid.*, ad ann. 1456, p. 396). Fra Giovanni's *relatio* is in the form of a letter dated at Udine on 22 July, 1460, to the Franciscan preacher Jacopo della Marca (on whom see, below, p. 208, note 33). The text in the older editions of Wadding is poor, but Fr. Fonseca has reproduced the better text established by L. Lemmens, in the *Acta Ordinis Minorum*, fasc. I–XI (1906), which was reprinted as a book (with title abbr.) *Victoria mirabilis divinitus de turcis habita . . . descripta per fr. Ioannem de Tagliacotio* . . ., Quaracchi, 1906. (I cite this text from the new Wadding, XII, Addenda, pp. 750–96.) Besides this long letter Tagliacozzo has left two other accounts of the siege of Belgrade (dated 28 July, 1456, six days after the end of the siege, and 15 September, 1457), on which *cf.* J. Hofer, in the *Hist. Jahrbuch*, LI (1931), 169–70, 207–8 (see the following note). On the background of events in Germany and Hungary, note Gómez Canedo, *Don Juan de Carvajal* (1947), pp. 128–58.

[52] *Cf.* Carvajal's letter to Francesco Sforza, duke of Milan, dated at Buda on 17 April, 1456, in L. Thallóczy and A. Áldásy, eds., *Monumenta Hungariae historica*, XXXIII (Budapest, 1907), doc. DXXIX, pp. 463–64. The older sources relating to the siege of Belgrade are collected in Wadding, *Annales Minorum*, ad annum 1456, XII (Rome, 1735), 315 ff., and 3rd ed., vol. XII (1932), pp. 365 ff. (and *cf.* the preceding footnote). A full list of almost all the known sources is given with a penetrating discussion of them by Johannes Hofer, "Der Sieger von Belgrad 1456," *Historisches Jahrbuch d. Görres-Gesellschaft*, LI (Cologne, 1931), 163–212; see also Hofer's book *Giovanni da Capestrano: Una vita spesa nella lotta per la riforma della Chiesa*, L'Aquila, 1955, pp. 644–87; and *cf.* Babinger, *Maometto*, pp. 212–25, and esp. "Der Quellenwert der Berichte über den Entsatz von Belgrad am 21–22 Juli 1456," *Sitzungsberichte d. Bayer. Akad. d. Wissenschaften*, Philos.-hist. Kl., Munich, 1957, Heft 6. On Turkish preparations for the siege of Belgrade (as reported in Ragusa, where the intended object of the sultan's attack was still unclear as of mid-April, 1456), note Gelcich and Thallóczy, *Diplomatarium ragusanum* (1887), nos. 338, 340, and 342, pp. 587, 589, 592.

[53] Aeneas Sylvius, *Historia bohemica* (written in June, 1458), 65, in *Opera quae extant omnia*, Basel, 1551, repr. Frankfurt a. M., 1967, p. 137; Giovanni da Tagliacozzo, *Relatio*, 5, in Wadding, *Annales Minorum*, XII (1932), 755: ". . . Nam centum sexaginta millia, multi autem dicunt ducenta millia, Turcorum bellantium de electioribus et fortioribus illuc [to Belgrade] convenerunt;" and on the Turkish fleet Fra Giovanni says (chap. 6, *ibid.*, p. 757): ". . . Sexaginta quatuor galeas cum multis scaphis atque naviculis in servitium galearum . . . deducebant . . ., in quibus galeis homines diversae linguae variaeque nationis in bello navali exercitati erant." *Cf.* Raynaldus, *Ann. eccl.*, ad ann. 1456, no. 14, vol. XVIII (1694), p. 459a; Wadding, XII (1932), 389, 434; L. Kupelwieser, *Die Kämpfe Ungarns mit den Osmanen bis zur Schlacht bei Mohács, 1526*, Vienna and Leipzig, 1895, pp. 124–25, "ein Heer von 150,000 Mann;" this figure appears also in the first edition of Pastor, *Hist. Popes*, II, 390, but he reduced it to 100,000 in the last edition (*Gesch. d. Päpste*, I [repr. 1955], 713); R. Nisbet Bain, "The Siege of Belgrade by Muhammad II . . .," *English Historical Review*, VII (1892), 240, 244; Babinger, *Maometto*, pp. 214–15; Hofer, *Giovanni da Capestrano* (1955), p. 660, note 128. Estimates of the Turkish army ranged as high as 400,000.

[54] Iorga, *Notes et extraits*, IV (1915), pt. 3, no. 73, pp. 145–46, doc. dated 25 August, 1456: "Item Eur Gnad sol wissen, von der Niderleg wegen der Turken, daz ich, der durch ain warhafften underricht bin, der die Sach alle mit

were easier to count than the men. If Mehmed maintained as many as thirty thousand men at the siege of Belgrade, he did well.

Hunyadi was active throughout June and early July, moving from place to place, seeking ships enough to impede the progress of the Turkish flotilla up the Danube and forces enough to relieve the investment of Belgrade, when the Turkish army should arrive and put the city under siege. He planned to concentrate his forces at Kovin, which faces the Morava's entrance into the Danube, the usual point of departure for Hungarian expeditions against the Turks. It was the best place to halt the westward course of the Turkish galleys and transports. Hunyadi asked Carvajal to send to Kovin all those who had taken the cross, and on 22 June (1456) he addressed an appeal from Temesvar (Timişoara) to the German towns in Transylvania, informing them that the sultan's army was only four days' march south of the Danube. But he was unable to assemble an army at Kovin,[55] and once again the Serbian despot George Branković remained aloof from danger, preferring for obvious reasons neutrality to hostile involvement with the Turks.

Belgrade had never been in greater peril. Giovanni da Capistrano was said to have given the cross to 27,000 men in Hungary alone, and Carvajal and other preachers to an additional 13,000, not counting the crusaders enrolled in Germany. Weeks would pass, however, before most of these were ready for service on the banks of the Danube; in the meantime the Gran Turco was advancing with astonishing speed. Capistrano was recalled from his preaching mission. He entered the fortress of Belgrade on 2 July with about 2,500 men, welcomed by the sounds of music and the shouts of the inhabitants. Hunyadi had directed that Capistrano should leave some of his men in Belgrade, and join him at Kovin with the rest. Michael Szilágyi, Hunyadi's brother-in-law and the commandant of Belgrade, advised against the idea, however, on the grounds that it was already too late, and Capistrano was needed more in Belgrade. But after a mass, a sermon, and a meal, Capistrano set off downstream on the Danube with three boatloads of soldiers. (Kovin is about forty miles from Belgrade.) Almost as soon as Capistrano had departed, Szilágyi learned that the Turkish flotilla had got west of Kovin without Hunyadi's being able to intercept it. Although he notified Capistrano promptly, the latter was determined to join Hunyadi with his men. Suddenly, however, a beautiful, cloudless day disappeared into a violent storm, we are told, and Capistrano and his men had to return to Belgrade that night by land.[56]

About the time of Capistrano's return there also arrived in Belgrade a number of other crusaders from Peterwardein (Petrovaradin), sent by Francesco de' Oddi, bishop of Assisi, Cardinal Carvajal's chief agent in Hungary.[57] On 3 July Capistrano wrote Francesco from Belgrade that within the hour he had received letters from him and the crusaders together with the munitions they brought, *li quali me sono stati gratissimi*. The Turks, he informed Francesco, held all the Danube below Belgrade, "et ogy aspectamo da loro la obsidione ad questo castello." The Christian commonwealth, the Catholic faith, the native population, and the kingdom of Hungary were exposed to imminent danger; John Hunyadi was engaged every day in hand-to-hand battles with the Turks, but who could resist such a great army unless others came to his aid? Capistrano asked the good bishop of Assisi to inform Carvajal of the terrible situation in order that the cardinal legate might again appeal to King Ladislas and the ecclesiastical and secular princes "che vogliano prestare favore et subsidio ad resistere ad questo gran periculo," because there was no longer time for them to sleep and enjoy their ease. The hour had come to arise from slumber. If the king of Hungary

---

seinen Augen gesehen hat, von erst so hat der Turk zu disem Zug uber hundert tausent Man nye gehabt. Item er hat auch nye mer dann ains und zwanczig Schiff gehabt. . . ." According to an eyewitness, then, Mehmed did not have more than 100,000 men nor more than twenty-one ships, and we are also informed that "er hat alle sein Leut uber Landt bracht." Our source, however, has allowed Mehmed too many men and too few ships.

[55] Hofer, *Giovanni da Capestrano*, pp. 652–53, and *cf.* Thallóczy and Áldásy, *MHH*, XXXIII (1907), nos. CCLXIX–CCLXX, p. 203, letters from Antonio Guidobono, Milanese envoy in Venice, to Francesco Sforza (dated 18 June), and from Hunyadi to the Germans in Transylvania (22 June). Of the latter document only a Hungarian summary is given. Temesvar (in Hungarian) and Timişoara (in Rumanian), in western Rumania at the base of the triangle formed by the nearby borders of Hungary and Yugoslavia, is the social center of a polyglot area of Rumanians, Magyars, Germans, Serbs, gypsies, and Jews, survivors of the long "balkanized" history of their city and their lives.

[56] Hofer, *Giovanni da Capestrano*, pp. 653–56; Giovanni da Tagliacozzo, *Relatio*, 4, in Wadding, *Annales Minorum*, XII (1932), 754–55.

[57] Hofer, *Giovanni da Capestrano*, pp. 650, 656–57.

and the other princes, barons, and prelates of the realm did not want personal visits from the Turks, if they were willing to defend their dominions, let them come to Belgrade or at least send their military forces! Otherwise they would soon have to drive the Turks from their very homes. Belgrade was the place to resist them, to do battle with them, lest they who were already masters of the Danube make themselves masters of Hungary also. Francesco was to write Carvajal to try day and night to arouse the king and the other lords to come to the aid of Belgrade. Capistrano could not write just then to Carvajal "per la grande afflictione, dolore et fatiga, quali sostengo . . .," and so he urged Francesco to do so for him.[58]

On the very day that Capistrano wrote Francesco de' Oddi, Saturday, 3 July, advance units of Turkish cavalry came within sight of Belgrade.[59] Before the siege had got under way, however, Capistrano decided again to leave the city. He wanted to maintain the connection of Belgrade with the countryside to the north and west, whence supplies and reinforcements must come. The Turks were slow in establishing their blockade along the Danube. On 4 July, then, Capistrano left Belgrade, taking four friars with him; he promised to return shortly with crusaders enough to astound the Christians and confound the Turks. In the meantime Hunyadi had moved from Kovin up the left bank of the Danube to the area opposite Belgrade, waiting in an agony of expectation for the arrival of more Hungarian troops. By 7 July the main body of Mehmed's army appeared under the walls of Belgrade. The plain and the hilly landscape to the south of the city were so covered with white tents that there seemed to have been a "recent snowfall." The Turkish army was divided into two parts. The sultan's pavilion, with its green banner flying, was pitched among the European troops toward the right bank of the Danube. A pasha was encamped along the right bank of the Sava with the Anatolian troops which formed the left wing of the army.[60]

On 10 July (1456) Cardinal Carvajal wrote Francesco Sforza from Buda, urging him to send immediately the troops which he had promised, guaranteeing them *pieno et valido salvoconducto* from the emperor, the king of Hungary, and the count of Cilli as soon as they entered Albania. When Sforza's troops had reached the German border, Carvajal would send people to meet them. The bishop of Assisi was active recruiting and receiving crusaders (*pellegrini*). Capistrano was preaching. There was great hope, almost a certainty, of concord being established between the emperor and the king of Hungary. Carvajal would send Sforza other news as events occurred, but he knew it would not be necessary to write often, "because we understand that his Holiness writes often and informs your Excellency, whom God be pleased to keep safe forever." Before dispatching his letter Carvajal then added as a postscript

> that the Turk has on the Danube two hundred large galleys, not counting many other small boats, and on land 200,000 men. To resist them we have sent many who have taken the cross, and every day we are sending them, but it amounts to almost nothing in comparison with the multitude [of the enemy]. The most illustrious lord John [Hunyadi] . . . has pitched his camp opposite the Turk's, but it is quite unequal in strength to that of the Turk![61]

Belgrade was probably one of the strongest fortresses in Europe. Located at the confluence of the Danube and the Sava, it stood high on the right bank of both rivers. In 1433 the

[58] Thallóczy and Áldásy, *MHH*, XXXIII (1907), doc. DXXXI, pp. 465–67, "ex castro Albandor die tertia Iulii MCCCCLVI."

[59] Giovanni da Tagliacozzo, *Relatio*, 5, in Wadding, *Annales Minorum*, XII (1932), 755, begins the siege of Belgrade on 3–4 July: "Mane autem . . ., scilicet tertia die mensis, ecce, Turcorum exercitus apparere coepit." *Cf.* Hofer, in *Hist. Jahrbuch*, LI, 187, 194, and *Giovanni da Capestrano*, p. 657. The Hungarian historian Antonio Bonfini erroneously supplies 13 June as the date (*Historia pannonica*, Cologne, 1690, decad. III, bk. 8, p. 351, also in Wadding, XII, 389): "A Turcis . . . Alba [Greca] obsidetur, quod Idibus Iuniis accidisse ferunt," which might seem to be confirmed by a dispatch which the Sienese envoys sent from Naples on 3 July to the effect that already the "Turchi . . . erano achampati a Belgrado" (Pastor, *Gesch. d. Päpste*, I [repr. 1955], 724, note) except that ambassadors often sent inaccurate information based on rumor and hearsay to their governments, and of course the statements of Capistrano, Tagliacozzo, and other eyewitnesses or participants more than suffice to fix 3–4 July as the beginning of the siege, which could not be certainly known in Naples for another two weeks or more.

[60] Taken from Hofer, *Giovanni da Capestrano*, pp. 658–59.

[61] Thallóczy and Áldásy, *MHH*, XXXIII, doc. DXXXII, pp. 467–69, "[datum] ex Buda die X Iulii MCCCCLVI." Actually the Turkish flotilla may have consisted of 64 galleys and various other ships, making a total of some 200 vessels (according to Hofer, *Giovanni da Capestrano*, p. 660). If Sforza could not send all the troops he had promised, Carvajal wanted at least part of them to leave Italy by mid-August (*MHH*, XXXIII, 469), which seems rather a late date in view of the critical situation in Belgrade.

Burgundian knight Bertrandon de la Broquière had visited Belgrade on his way back from the Holy Land, and was much impressed with its strong position and elaborate defense works.[62] In 1440 Sultan Murad II had failed to take the city in a siege which had lasted six months. Karaja Beg is said now to have advised Mehmed to learn from his father's experience and place Belgrade under siege without attempting to take the city by assault. He wanted the young sultan to employ his army on a westward march to conquer all the "Slavonian" territory between the Sava and the Drava, thus pretty much isolating Belgrade from the hinterland which sustained it. Mehmed rejected the idea. He would take the city in two weeks, and observe the fast of Ramadan in Buda within two months.[63]

The sultan's artillery was soon set up against the walls and defense towers of Belgrade. All the Turks' cannon and most of the other siege engines were manned by Italians, Germans, Bosnians, Slavs, and even Hungarians. As usual renegade European engineers placed their skill and knowledge at the sultan's disposal, eager for their own profit at whatever cost of life or liberty to their fellow Christians under attack. At the approach of the Turks King Ladislas had left Buda on the pretext of a hunt and fled to Vienna. The Hungarian nobles, divided in their allegiance between Ulrich of Cilli and John Hunyadi, were slow to respond to the crusade. "There was no one in Hungary taking up arms against the Turks: the king and the barons stayed at home."[64] To the conquerors of Constantinople the fortifications of Belgrade doubtless looked like the work of a fortnight, and the rumble of Turkish cannon was soon resounding from Belgrade to Szeged.[65] The Turks held the besieged city in a tight grip as their land forces were deployed along the walls and their fleet was moored outside the harbor.

At length some Magyar barons did hasten with their followers to join Hunyadi, in whom everyone placed such hope as there was of seeing Belgrade saved from destruction by the Turks, whose preparations had been made on a gigantic scale. They had brought guns, spingards, and siege machinery of all kinds. Their equipment included twenty-two huge cannon, each of which measured twenty-seven feet in length, transported to Belgrade with no less ingenuity than expense. There seemed to be no limit to the number of smaller cannon.[66] The Turks had also brought with them seven special mortars, "by which in wondrous fashion they hurled huge, round stones on high to kill people day and night, with no stopping, both in the fortress and in the city." Although such stones were hurled unceasingly into crowded quarters, Giovanni da Tagliacozzo informs us, they killed only one woman, "which I think was no small miracle, since at night no one could take precautions against them." In the daytime they could be seen, their trajectory calculated, and their point of impact avoided. The Turks set up vast tents. Their banners were "incomprehensible" to Fra Giovanni, "but the insignia of the Gran Turco had a half moon on a green field." Enormous numbers of camels, oxen, and buffaloes from Asia Minor, Serbia, and Bosnia had carried "arrows, bows, and provisions." The awe-struck friar was fascinated by the paraphernalia of the Turkish camp, and mentions the various kinds of carts and wagons which had carried the cannon. He also notes the musical instruments, ceremonial books and garments, the mills for grinding grain, ovens for baking bread, and the various vessels to hold an infinity of things. The Turks had thought of everything, for they had even brought packs of dogs to consume the Christian corpses, of which they obviously anticipated large numbers. Indeed they seemed to have come not to besiege a fortress but to occupy Hungary itself and other realms as well. In

---

[62] Bertrandon de la Broquière, *Le Voyage d'outremer*, ed. Chas. Schefer, Paris, 1892, pp. 211–14 (in the Recueil de voyages et de documents pour servir à l'histoire de la géographie, XII).

[63] Hofer, *Giovanni da Capestrano*, p. 662, and Thallóczy and Áldásy, *MHH*, XXXIII, doc. DXXXIII, p. 470.

[64] Giovanni da Tagliacozzo, *Relatio*, 2, in Wadding, *Annales Minorum*, XII (1932), 753, and on the European gunners in the Turkish army, *ibid*., chap. 11, p. 759.

[65] According to Bonfini, *Hist. pannonica* (1690), decad. III, bk. 8, p. 352, and in Wadding, *Annales Minorum*, XII (1932), 390, who also informs us of the flight of Ladislas and the court "simulata venatione," which was of course most damaging to the crusading effort, for the prelates and barons regarded themselves as thus relieved of their own oaths to take the field against the Turks (Hofer, *Giovanni da Capestrano*, p. 652).

[66] According to another Franciscan, Niccolò de Fara, who like Tagliacozzo was a companion of Capistrano, Mehmed II had converted the church bells of Constantinople into cannon (Wadding, XII [1932], 420). The bells were offensive to the Moslems (*cf*. Khoja Sa'd-ad-Dīn, *The Capture of Constantinople from the Tāj-ut-tevārīkh*, trans. E. J. W. Gibb, Glasgow, 1879, p. 33). The Turks are alleged to have had about two-hundred cannon before Belgrade.

fact Tagliacozzo and his fellows were told by deserters from the Turkish camp that the sultan had vowed by the Prophet Mohammed and by his own life that within two months he would take Hungary and would dine in Buda.[67]

According to Fra Giovanni da Tagliacozzo, Hunyadi had witnessed the assemblage of a motley army of some 60,000 men, most of whom had flocked to the standard of the cross in a mass movement of about ten days. Capistrano preached to them in unremitting frenzy, urging them to confess their sins, for the pope had granted all who fought for the faith the plenary remission of all sins. The ardent defender of orthodoxy proved also to have the practical mind of a soldier: "Whoever will take their stand with us against the Turks, are our friends! Serbs, schismatics, Vlachs, Jews, heretics, and whatever infidels will side with us in this storm, these let us embrace in friendship. Now it is against the Turks, against the Turks that we must fight!" Hunyadi's alleged 60,000 men were townsmen and peasants, paupers and priests, students, monks, mendicants, and hermits, most of them inexperienced and inadequately armed, but fired with a fanatical determination by the impassioned sermons of the old Franciscan preacher. Actually this was not Hunyadi's army but Capistrano's. Hunyadi had no faith in them. Against the Turkish armaments these crusaders had swords, cudgels, slings, shepherds' staffs, and shields, as well as some ballistas, bows, guns, lead spingards, and grappling hooks.[68] But this "army" certainly fell far short of the estimate of the good friar of Tagliacozzo. Hunyadi seems to have had very few men under his direct command, although there may have been four thousand well-armed and effective troops on the Christian side.[69]

Fra Giovanni says that there were no horses except those which carried provisions. Hunyadi had managed to get together, however, about forty or fifty river boats (to take the smallest estimate), on which he placed his more resolute followers. It was on these men that he would have to depend to help him gain access to the inner harbor and fortress of Belgrade, set in a complicated terrain on an isthmus at the confluence of the Danube and the Sava. Swift currents with strong whirlpools ran along two sides of the steep height on which the city and fortress were built; the landward side was to the southeast, and was protected by high rocks and well-contrived walls. Hunyadi arranged by messenger that the boats in the harbor of Belgrade should be outfitted and manned by the townsmen, hardy merchant seamen, who were, says Tagliacozzo, "in aqua doctissimi certatores, nec terga vertunt," stout fighters and reliable haters of the Turk, although deficient in Catholic doctrine.[70]

Hunyadi had planned his attempt to enter Belgrade by water for 14 July; conditions in the city had become desperate, and it was a matter of do or die. News of Sultan Mehmed's tremendous preparations and the huge stores of food and material he had moved to the front in unending supply trains had evoked the gravest fears in Europe for the future of Hungary. Although as usual the sultan had tried to keep his military objective secret as long as possible, all Europe knew by this time that it was Belgrade, and in most quarters the city was doubtless presumed to be lost. Pope Calixtus III, as we shall see, had been working furiously week after week, and was sending a fleet into eastern waters with the intention of harrying the Turkish coasts and even of attacking Istanbul itself. But other European princes did nothing to help, merely looking on with calm indifference if they were far from the scene, or listening in frightened apathy, if they lived near the Hungarians, to the loud explosions of cannon shot that burst against the walls of Belgrade. This cannonading went on day after day, the largest cannon being disposed in three groups of batteries, the countless smaller ones being placed in between them to keep up a protective fire. The towers were conspicuous targets, and their battlements were demolished faster than they could be repaired. Fra Giovanni assures us that "within the space of ten days almost all the

[67] Giovanni da Tagliacozzo, *Relatio*, 5–6, in Wadding, *Annales Minorum*, XII (1932), 755–57.

[68] Giov. da Tagliacozzo, *Rel.*, 19–22, *ibid.*, pp. 765–67.

[69] Critobulus, II, 18, 4 (ed. Müller, *FHG*, V-1 [1870], p. 115b; ed. Grecu [1963], p. 201), places the number of troops at four thousand as does Peter Eschenloer, municipal chronicler of Breslau (Hofer, in *Hist. Jahrbuch*, LI, 195, note 80, and *cf.* p. 211).

[70] Giov. da Tagliacozzo, *Rel.*, 14, in Wadding, *Annales Minorum*, XII (1932), 761, says that Hunyadi collected almost two hundred river boats (*naviculae*), and arranged for the manning of forty similar boats in the harbor of Belgrade. Note also Babinger, *Maometto*, p. 216, and in the *Sitzungsber. d. Bayer. Akad. d. Wissen.*, 1957, Heft 6, p. 17, where a plan of the topography of Belgrade is given, taken from L. Kupelwieser, *Die Kämpfe Ungarns mit den Osmanen* (1895), opp. p. 128.

walls of the citadel were leveled to the ground." There still remained, however, the inner towers of the citadel, he says, which apparently means that the fortifications of the castle which stood on a rock in the city were withstanding the bombardment better.[71] But it was clear that unless a large relief force appeared soon, Belgrade would fall to the Turks.

Hunyadi and Capistrano conferred in Slankamen, some miles to the north of Belgrade, and had difficulty in agreeing upon a plan of action. George Branković states in a letter of 13 July (1456) that Hunyadi had been collecting river boats at Slankamen, where the Theiss meets the Danube, and that many crusaders were gathering there. Branković claimed to be ready to assist Hunyadi in every way he could, but he took no decisive step in that direction. He also stated that there was famine in the Turkish host, where a florin of gold would not buy bread enough for five men for a day. Horses had nothing to eat but the grass they found in the fields. Men were getting sick and dying every day.[72] He was, however, describing conditions in Belgrade quite as much as—or more than—those in the Turkish camp.

The size of the Turkish host and the Conqueror's reputation were causing panic in Italy. On 28 July Francesco Sforza wrote Jacopo Calcaterra, his envoy in Rome, how he had just learned that an agent of Carvajal, passing through Venice on his way to Rome, had said that the Turk had reinforced both his land and naval forces to the extent that he now had 300,000 men engaged in the siege of Belgrade! The agent was also quoted as stating that the Hungarians could not help the besieged. The fear was that they would make an accord with the Turk, "who says that he wants nothing else from the Hungarians and Germans than a [free] passage into Italy, and accordingly offered to give them hostages."[73] Hunyadi may well have thought of securing as favorable a peace with the sultan as he could before the siege had progressed much farther. Capistrano may have prevailed upon him to place confidence in God's help and his own efforts. In any event he went on with his plans to relieve the mounting pressure upon Belgrade. He would go down the Danube from Slankamen. His forces may by this time have numbered 18,000 men.[74]

Hunyadi completed his preparations during the night of 13–14 July. Early the next morning his miscellany of ships and determined men were sailing down the swift current of the Danube toward a line of Turkish ships strung across the river just above its junction with the Sava at Belgrade. The land forces of the crusade marched with Hunyadi and Capistrano down the right bank of the Danube, keeping pace with their ships as well as they could. The Turkish ships were fastened together by chains, an iron-bound barrier against the Hungarian fleet's approach to the city. The Turks greeted the small oncoming forces with derision, confident of victory, but were attacked in the rear by the boats from Belgrade, which put out of the harbor to combine their attack with that of their fellow Christians coming down the river. The fourteenth of July was a Wednesday, a day the Turks regarded as ill-omened, and they were right. After Hunyadi's vessels had struck the Turkish cordon, the battle lasted for five hours as the Christians tried to break the line. Their heroic efforts were finally rewarded. The iron barrier was broken in several places. Three large Turkish galleys were sunk with all aboard; four other ships were captured with all their equipment; the rest were either driven ashore or reached their earlier moorings. More than five hundred Turks had lost their lives.[75]

Hunyadi entered Belgrade with his best troops on 15 July. Capistrano went with him. The connection of the city with the northern hinterland was restored, a necessity for bringing in provisions. The Danube, says Fra Giovanni da Tagliacozzo, had been restored to the Christians. The presence of Hunyadi and Capistrano gave new life to the defense. The walls were re-

---

[71] Giov. da Tagliacozzo, *Rel.*, 11, in Wadding, *Annales Minorum*, XII (1932), 759. On the *castrum tripartitum* of Belgrade, with its three distinct areas of defense, see, *op. cit.*, chap. 32, *ibid.*, pp. 774–75. On papal activity during the period of the siege, see Pastor, *Gesch. d. Päpste*, I (repr. 1955), 720–23.

[72] Thallóczy and Áldásy, *MHH*, XXXIII, doc. CCLXXIII, p. 205. The report of Urban Vignatus, the bishop of Sebenico (Šibenik), on the Dalmatian coast, also speaks of the famine and high cost of bread in the Turkish camp (*ibid.*, doc. DXXXIII, p. 470).

[73] Thallóczy and Áldásy, *MHH*, XXXIII, doc. CCLXXVIII, p. 210.

[74] Hofer, *Giovanni da Capestrano*, pp. 664–66.

[75] Giov. da Tagliacozzo, *Rel.*, 14–15, in Wadding, *Annales Minorum*, XII (1932), 761–62, and *cf.* Hofer, *Giovanni da Capestrano*, pp. 666 ff. On Wednesday, as a day of ill omen among the Turks, note Babinger, "Der Quellenwert der Berichte über den Entsatz von Belgrad," *Sitzungsber. d. Bayer. Akad. d. Wissen.*, 1957, Heft 6, p. 5, note 2.

paired after a fashion, and apparently maintained for a few days. During the siege of Constantinople the Turks had shot at the walls all day, and the Christians had repaired them all night. At Belgrade, however, the Turks clearly found the torrid blasts of the cannon intolerable in the heat of mid-July. They shot at the walls all night, and the defenders labored to repair them all day in the merciless sun.[76] The siege of Belgrade is almost as interesting, almost as important, as that of Constantinople.

The Turkish army was encamped south and east of Belgrade, around the landward walls. The main body of Hungarians and crusaders was located to the southwest, across the Sava from the Turks. After the defeat of his ships on the Danube, Sultan Mehmed raked the outer walls of the city incessantly with cannon-fire. Three great breaches were made, which could not be repaired, and Mehmed prepared for the grand assault. He chose the evening of 21 July, another Wednesday. Despite the near destruction of his flotilla the preceding week, the superstitious sultan still regarded Wednesday as his lucky day. Most Turks thought of it as the worst of the seven days, and events were again to confirm their prejudice against the mid-week. The preliminary cannonading had been so thorough, however, that a few days later Hunyadi reported with pardonable exaggeration that Mehmed had converted the "fortress into a field."[77]

The long-awaited Turkish attack now came in the early evening of 21 July, after the terrible heat of the day had passed, and men could fight in armor without nearly suffocating. The defenders drove back the first assaults, but as the fighting continued, some seven hundred Turks are said to have mounted the ramparts and entered Belgrade. They believed they had captured the city. Five banners were set up on the ruined outer walls. There was consternation among the nobles in the inner fortress; they had put their valuables on the ships, and now many of them wanted to flee. More and more Turks were streaming over the battered ramparts, and were soon attacking the bridge which led into the second area of defense in the city. The Christians contested every foot of ground. They fought the janissaries from door to door and street to street. The horrible struggle went on for hours. The wide spaces between the outer walls and the castle were swarming with Turks, and so were the moats below the walls. But Hunyadi and the Hungarian command had apparently caught the invaders in an ambuscade. The defenders proved to be far more numerous on the outer walls than the triumphant Turks, intent upon pillage, had observed, and they began to throw lighted bundles of dry branches impregnated with sulphur upon their enemies, both those within the walls and those in the moats below. The action was sudden and concerted; it was also unexpected. Now there seemed to be more crusaders than the Turks had reckoned on; they emerged from the castle, and slew those whom the fires had not killed or maimed with ghastly torment. By this time the dawn had come, and with it the hot, bright sunshine of 22 July, the feast of S. Mary Magdalene.[78]

The janissaries had been especially hard hit. The moats were full of Turkish corpses; within the walls the streets and passageways were blocked by the infidel dead. Tagliacozzo informs us, however, that hardly sixty Christians had won the crown of martyrdom in the battle although a good many more than this number had been wounded.[79]

When Hunyadi made a tour of inspection early in the morning of 22 July, he was astonished at the extent of the Christian success, and observed that a strong blow had been

---

[76] *Cf.* Giov. da Tagliacozzo, *Rel.*, 26, in Wadding, *Annales Minorum*, XII (1932), 769: ". . . quidquid ex machinis Turcorum in nocte ruebat, in die reparabant [sc. Christiani]."

[77] Iorga, *Notes et extraits*, IV, pt. 3, no. 68, p. 134, doc. dated 24 July, 1456, and *cf.* Thallóczy and Áldásy, *MHH*, XXXIII, doc. CCLXXVII, p. 208: "In tantum enim castrum per ictus bombardarum destruxit [sc. imperator Turcorum], quod ipsum castrum non castrum sed campum dicere possumus, quod usque ad terram murus castri est destructus" (from Hunyadi's report to the Hungarian King Ladislas Postumus). This is one of three letters of Hunyadi concerning the Christian victory (Hofer, in *Hist. Jahrbuch*, LI, 172–74). One of these letters is dated 23 July, and the other two on the twenty-fourth. They are rather vague as to his precise role in the final battle for Belgrade, a fact which in view of the sources giving Capistrano the credit for the Christian victory has helped feed controversy, on which see below.

[78] Giov. da Tagliacozzo, *Rel.*, 29–33, in Wadding, *Annales Minorum*, XII (1932), 771–76. Throughout Tagliacozzo's *relatio* Capistrano is the hero of the siege of Belgrade, and constantly restores the flagging spirit and ebbing courage of Hunyadi, who is said to have taken refuge on board a ship, as Hofer, *Giovanni da Capestrano*, pp. 675–76, also believes.

[79] Giov. da Tagliacozzo, *Rel.*, 35, in Wadding, *Annales Minorum*, XII (1932), 777.

struck for Hungarian freedom. He remembered Varna and Kossovo, however, and gave orders that no one in Belgrade should venture out of the walls against the Turks. The sailors were ordered not to transport anyone over either the Danube or the Sava. Hunyadi expected another Turkish attack, and he feared that the credulous horde of "crusaders" which had followed Capistrano would be slaughtered. Thousands of these simple folk were encamped across the Sava. They were probably waiting for a miracle, and were not to be disappointed. A commotion arose among them; standards were raised; shouts were heard. Capistrano was among them. In the meantime on the other side of the river a small body of Christian archers, who had climbed a hill outside the walls in defiance of Hunyadi's orders, was seen by a band of Turkish cavalry, which charged them and was repulsed by arrows. Across the Sava, Capistrano raised his voice among the crusaders: "This is the day of victory for which we have waited! Let us go across and climb up [to the city]! Don't fear the Turks; we can eat them up like bread!" He then chose two of his attendant friars, Giovanni da Tagliacozzo and Ambrogio Aquilano, and with his standard-bearer was taken across the narrow Sava by two sailors in a small boat. Weary from fasting and his night-long vigils, Capistrano began the steep ascent from the river bank to the moats beneath the broken walls of the city. He must have made his way up more slowly than his five companions. For many days he had hardly eaten or slept. It was about one o'clock in the afternoon.[80] A number of persons outside the walls saw him, and "soon they are running to him joyfully as to a father;" others came from the city to see him, despite Hunyadi's prohibition against venturing outside the walls. The crowd got bigger and bigger. Now Capistrano saw the burned corpses of the Turks piled up in the moats and ditches, "and he considered the great peril which all Christendom had escaped the night before." Clasping his hands together and raising his eyes to heaven in prayer, he said that God, who had granted their efforts such an auspicious beginning, would help them to finish what they had begun.

The Turks at the cannon emplacements could see the growing crowd. They feared an attack. By this time, says Tagliacozzo, about 2,000 people were milling around Capistrano. Holding his staff, on which he had inscribed the name of Jesus, the great preacher began to move toward the nearest Turkish batteries. He walked slowly, crying Iesu! Iesu! A thousand men followed him. The terrified Turks withdrew from these cannon to the second line of batteries. The incredible advance continued beyond it to the third line, behind which was the sultan's own encampment. The crusaders had pushed the Turks back beyond their cannon, which they promptly seized. None of the cannon, we are told, had been ready for firing; the iron keys were still in the *foramina*, to which the torch was applied to shoot them. It was all most remarkable, and Tagliacozzo admits that there was more than one account of how Capistrano and the crusaders with him had accomplished their feat.

Meanwhile the force with Capistrano had grown to about three times its original size, but the eager old man, who had fed his soul on dreams of martyrdom for forty years, now pushed on ahead of them all, to the consternation of the friars who tried to keep up with him. Before the Turkish counterattack, Capistrano climbed to the top of a small eminence, so the enemy could see him and the crusaders hear him. He urged his followers into battle to fight for the imperiled faith, telling them to resist the Turks, not kill them, "for the pious father craved the conversion and humiliation of the Turks, but not their death." In the thick of battle he refused the protection of a shield. Tagliacozzo says the Christians turned the captured cannon against the Turks, "and perhaps Mary Magdalene, on whose day these things happened, attended the cannon with fire and stone!" This battle, like the one on the Danube a week before, lasted about five hours, and ended in the rout of the Turks and the victory of the crusaders. There was immense jubilation in Belgrade and the Christian camp that night. Mehmed the Conqueror had suffered a stunning defeat, the news of which would soon be reverberating throughout Europe.

[80] Giov. da Tagliacozzo, *Rel.*, 36–38, in Wadding, *Annales Minorum*, XII (1932), 778–80: "Hora erat quasi decima sexta" (p. 780). If Tagliacozzo is reckoning the first hour in contemporary Italian fashion from sunset, the sixteenth hour is obviously not, as Hofer puts it, "schon vier Uhr nachmittag" (*Hist. Jahrbuch*, LI, 178), which hardly leaves sufficient time for all that follows. *Cf.* also Hofer's *Giovanni da Capestrano*, p. 680. In July the sixteenth hour would be about 1:00 P.M. (*cf.* B. M. Lersch, *Einleitung in die Chronologie*, 2 vols., 2nd ed., Freiburg im Breisgau, 1899, I, 9).

The Turks hastily buried such of their dead as they could before they began their terrified and disorderly retreat, leaving behind vast stores of military equipment and supplies. The sultan was carried off in a carriage, wounded in the left leg or the left thigh. A hundred and forty other carriages or carts removed other Turkish notables who had been wounded, some of whom would be buried along the road to Sofia. The defeated Turkish army continued its retreat by forced marches for ten days. Before abandoning the camp at Belgrade, however, they had destroyed or burned such equipment as they could to prevent its falling into Christian hands. They burned all the galleys which had survived the naval battle on the Danube and all the munitions which they had stored in the church of S. Mary Magdalene, and they burned the church as well. On the following morning, nevertheless, amazed Christians, including Hunyadi and his staff, toured the Turkish camp taking stock of what was left to them as the spoils of victory—the twenty-two giant cannon and innumerable small ones, wagons and carts, building materials, shields, bucklers, guns, various utensils, clothes, ornaments, books (of which Tagliacozzo got one), as well as cattle, oxen, camels, and buffaloes. There too they saw with grim satisfaction the graves and unburied bodies of countless Turks who would never ride herd on Christians again. Hunyadi had the cannon carried into Belgrade with great solemnity, amid joyous festivities, "and there to this very day they are located to the astonishment and admiration of all who see them."[81]

It is obvious that Giovanni da Tagliacozzo did not assign a hero's role to John Hunyadi. In his reports of 28 July, 1456, and of 15 September, 1457, as well as in the long letter to Jacopo della Marca (dated 22 July, 1460), Fra Giovanni indicates that the hesitant Hunyadi remained safely on board a ship which moved back and forth between the Danube and the Sava during both the terrible night of 21–22 July and the Christian attack on the afternoon of the twenty-second, coming back into the fortress of Belgrade only after the Turkish withdrawal had begun.[82] There is a good deal of confusion in the sources, some of which describe a Hungarian sortie in force from the city when Hunyadi saw an opportunity to capture or destroy Mehmed II's cannon. This attack is said to have followed an earlier, ill-advised venture of the

---

[81] Giov. da Tagliacozzo, *Rel.*, 38–47, in Wadding, *Annales Minorum*, XII (1932), 780–89. The Turkish losses were immense, as we know from the Genoese noble Jacopo de Promontorio de Campis (1410?–1487?), who spent a full twenty-five years as a merchant at the Ottoman court (eighteen years in the time of Murad II and seven in that of Mehmed II). Jacopo was himself present at the siege of Belgrade, *ala quale impresa et zuffa col dicto Gran Turcho era presente in persona lo prenominato Domino Iacobo suo mercatante*, which in view of the poverty of the Ottoman chronicles gives some importance to his brief account of the disaster which Mehmed suffered at Belgrade (Franz Babinger, "Die Aufzeichnungen des Genuesen Iacopo de Promontorio-de Campis über den Osmanenstaat um 1475," *Sitzungsber. der Bayer. Akad. d. Wissen.*, Philos.-hist. Kl., 1956, Heft 8, pp. 24–28, 87). Jacopo wrote twenty years after the events he describes (in 1475 or a bit later), after he had gone back to Genoa to live out his retirement at home. He informs us that Mehmed went to Belgrade "in persona . . . con magno exercito con tutto suo perforzo di tutta Turchia et Grecia di armigeri et pedestri azapi." He remembered best, however, the sultan's terrible losses —twenty-eight, not twenty-two, large cannon (*bombarde grosse*), one hundred galleys, and more than 13,000 men —the whole venture having cost him more than 500,000 ducats (*ibid.*, pp. 84–87, and *cf.* Babinger, "Der Quellenwert der Berichte über den Entsatz von Belgrad," *ibid.*, 1957, Heft 6, pp. 61–66).

Jacopo states that Mehmed was wounded twice, and an undated letter of Pope Calixtus III to Alfonso V of Portugal, who had promised a fleet for service against the Turks, notes the reports that Mehmed had been wounded and had lost more than half his army in the retreat from Belgrade (Arch. Segr. Vaticano, Arm. XXXIX, tom. 7, fols. 28^v–29^r, addressed "Carissimo in Christo filio. A. Portugallie regi illustri"): "Nam post eas litteras, quarum copiam Serenitati tue misimus super felici victoria quam deus nobis et populo Christiano . . . mirabiliter concessit, pluribus modis per litteras dilecti filii Cardinalis Sancti Angeli legati nostri et dilecti filii nobilis viri Comitis Johannis Vayvode ac fratris Johannis de Capestrano certiores facti sumus ultra dimidiam partem copiarum Turchi concisam et profligatam esse ipsumque Turcum strage ac iactura suorum perculsum et, ut a pluribus dicitur, saucium ac concilii inopem incertumque et animo labantem ad propria remeasse. Quapropter numquam tanta oportunitas fuit invadendi eius regnum et Constantinopolitane urbis recuperande, pro quo tuam Celsitudinem hortamur ut sanctum propositum tuum contra Turcum ipsum cum classe tua navigandi execucioni mandes. . . ." *Cf.*, *ibid.*, fol. 40^v, and note Sp. P. Lambros [Lampros], ed., *Ecthesis chronica*, London, 1902, pp. 33–34. B. X. Coutinho, "L'Idée de croisade au Portugal au XVe siècle," *Miscellanea historica in honorem Alberti de Meyer*, 2 vols., Louvain and Brussels, 1946, II, 737–47, adds little or nothing to the subject.

[82] *Cf.* Hofer, in *Hist. Jahrbuch*, LI, 170–72. A German report of September, 1456, also places Hunyadi aboard a ship on the Sava on these critical days (*ibid.*, pp. 178–79, 208, and *cf.* p. 185). Hunyadi's own three letters announcing the victory of Belgrade are vague as to the nature of his activity during the two critical days (pp. 172–74, 207). Capistrano also wrote three letters, to Pope Calixtus III, dated 22 and 23 July and 17 August, 1456 (pp. 174–76, 207), but refers to Hunyadi's part in the battle of Belgrade only in the first of these, which is translated below in the text.

"crusaders" against the Turks, from which, however, they were called back by Capistrano in time to escape disaster, the two actions apparently proving quite a distraction to the Turks, who at first found it difficult to understand the Christians' objective. Such is the account of the Hungarian historian Bonfini, who tried to combine the conflicting reports into a single unified account in which Hunyadi emerges as the hero of the siege of Belgrade, always setting an example for the whole Christian host both in word and deed.[83] According to Hofer, Bonfini, who took his cue from Aeneas Sylvius and Hunyadi's ambiguous dispatches, is actually the author of the legend of the Hungarian hero's exploits at Belgrade.[84] In these pages, however, we are under no necessity to enter into or take sides on the controversial issues involved.

In this connection Aeneas Sylvius wrote two years or so after the siege of Belgrade:

> Capistrano has given no account of Hunyadi and Hunyadi none of Capistrano in the letters which they wrote concerning the victory either to the Roman pontiff or to their friends. Each claimed that God gave the Christians victory through his own effort. The human mind craves honor, and shares sovereignty and wealth more easily than glory. Capistrano could hold property in contempt, scorn pleasures, subdue desire, but he could not spurn glory.[85]

Whether the chief credit should go to Capistrano or Hunyadi, Belgrade was an inspiring success for Christendom and a notable setback for Islam.

If John Hunyadi, remembering Varna and Kossovo, could see no hope of saving Belgrade and could put no faith in the inexperienced and undisciplined horde of crusaders who had followed Capistrano, one can hardly blame him. On the evening of 22 July, immediately after the conclusion of the Christian attack upon the Turkish camp, Capistrano wrote the first of his three letters to Calixtus III on the events which took place at Belgrade. He wrote briefly and quickly, he says, tired upon his return from the battle:

> We were in such tribulation and placed in such terrible difficulties that everyone thought no further resistance could be offered to the power of the Turks, and the commander Hunyadi himself, in truth the terror of the Turks and the stalwart champion of the Christians, believed the fortress of Belgrade had to be abandoned, for so strongly and incessantly did the savage Moslems attack the citadel and hammer at the walls with so many cannon and fight so fiercely against our men that our strength failed us and the best soldiers were overcome with terror. But in the midst of tribulation the Lord restored us to life, for when the savage enemy had been expelled from the city and craftily withdrew in order to lay snares for our men as they ventured out, albeit the lord Hunyadi ordered that none of our soldiers should leave the fortress, the crusaders took no heed of his command, but rushing upon the enemy, they put themselves in grave danger. But I, the least of your Holiness's servants, when from the walls I was unable to recall them, went down into the battlefield, and running to and fro, I called them back at first, then en-

---

[83] Bonfini, *Hist. pannonica* (1690), decad. III, bk. 8, pp. 352–54, also in Wadding, *Annales Minorum*, XII (1932), 391–93. Hofer, in *Hist. Jahrbuch*, LI, 182–86, could be right in believing that Hunyadi's great fame secured a wider currency in Europe for his reports than those of the Franciscans and of certain German eyewitnesses of the events at Belgrade, and that to the single attack upon the Turks by the crusaders was added a second attack by Hunyadi, possibly as a consequence of the mistaken assumption of Aeneas Sylvius (*Historia bohemica*, 65, in the *Opera quae extant omnia*, Basel, 1551, repr. Frankfurt a. M., 1967, p. 138) that Hunyadi personally went about the city directing its defense throughout the night of 21–22 July: ". . . Huniades modo huc, modo illuc cum globo militum currere, instaurare ordines, pro fessis validos, pro sauciis integros sufficere, imperatoris ac militis officium exequi."

In view of Hunyadi's reputation it is easy to see why Aeneas should assume that this must have been the way Hunyadi conducted himself at the siege, but Aeneas knows nothing of a sortie by the Hungarians under Hunyadi, nor do the Hungarian historians Johannes Thuróczi and Petrus Ranzani, who make little or no distinction between the Hungarians and the "crusaders" (who incidentally, according to Aeneas Sylvius, *loc. cit.*, were largely German and most hostile to Hunyadi and the Hungarians), and assign a subordinate role in the battle of Belgrade to Capistrano, who merely assists the Christian cause by his prayers. The conflict between the pro-Capistrano and pro-Hunyadi sources has usually been resolved by supposing that each leader led an attack of his own followers upon the Turks. Bonfini, *loc. cit.*, mistakenly assigns the battle of Belgrade to 6 August. On the alterations made in Wadding's text of Tagliacozzo in favor of Hunyadi, see Hofer, *art. cit.*, pp. 188–89, who gives Capistrano the chief credit for the relief of Belgrade and the defeat of the Turks in his work on *Giovanni da Capestrano*, pp. 682–87, 696–97. To no small extent, however, Hofer's biography of Capistrano is an *apologia pro vita eius*. There is, on the other hand, a rather harsh judgment of the friar in Heymann, *George of Bohemia*, pp. 69–76, 78–80, 119–20, who is understandably indignant at Capistrano's persecution of the Jews in Breslau.

[84] Hofer, in *Hist. Jahrbuch*, LI, 186–88.

[85] Aeneas Sylvius, *Europa*, 8, in *Opera quae extant omnia* (1551, repr. 1967), p. 403, who also observes that the three authors of the victory at Belgrade were all named John —Carvajal, Hunyadi, and Capistrano.

couraged them, and drew them up in order, so they would not be surrounded by the enemy. Finally the Lord, who can bring deliverance to a few as well as to many, mercifully gave us the victory and caused the flight of the Turks' huge army, and our men got possession of all their cannon and diabolical machines wherewith they thought to make all Christendom subject to themselves. . . .[86]

The cardinal legate Juan de Carvajal also saw the hand of God in the Turkish defeat, and while in a letter of 29 July to Francesco Sforza he pays tribute to Hunyadi's ability and prudence, he says the *gubernator* lacked sufficient forces to proceed against the Turks. It was the poor crusaders who did the fighting. Capistrano called to Jesus and was heard.[87] Certainly it had been a remarkable victory, and best understood by its Christian participants as a mark of divine favor.

In another letter to the pope (of 17 August) Capistrano wrote that the Serbian despot, George Branković, had reported to Carvajal and to him that more than 24,000 Turks had been killed in the battle of Belgrade, adding among other things that the time had come to recover the Holy Land and Jerusalem, Greece and eastern Europe.[88] News of the Christian victory had reached Rome by 6 August, and set off tremendous celebrations. All Europe rejoiced, and most of the contemporary chroniclers noted the happy event with evident satisfaction. A dispatch of the Milanese ambassador, Jacopo Calcaterra, to Francesco Sforza, dated 24 August, 1456, describes a private audience with Pope Calixtus which lasted from about 4:00 to 7:30 P.M., in which the pope talked constantly of the victory in a most jubilant mood, "praising and commending to the stars the name of the illustrious voivode John [Hunyadi] as one of the most glorious men who have been born for the last three hundred years or are at present living in the world. . . ."[89]

Sweet as the memory of Belgrade always remained, Pope Calixtus did not have cause for long rejoicing. About three weeks after the Turkish defeat, John Hunyadi died of the plague on 11 August, 1456, at Semlin (Zemun) near Belgrade, where his elder son László took over his command. Ten weeks after Hunyadi, Giovanni da Capistrano died also, on 23 October, at Ilok on the Danube, worn out by his exertions at Belgrade. László Hunyadi inherited his father's strife with the partisans of King Ladislas Postumus and Ulrich, count of Cilli. Having agreed to surrender Belgrade to the king and Cilli, László admitted them to the castle, but raised the drawbridge before the full force of their retinues could enter. The following day (on 9 November, 1456) Cilli was slain, and Ladislas Postumus found himself almost a

---

[86] Capistrano's first letter on the victory of Belgrade to Calixtus III is dated "Ex Nanderalba [Belgrade] in festo sanctae Mariae Magdalenae [22 July, 1456], ipso die gloriosissimae victoriae," and is given in Wadding, *Annales Minorum*, XII (1932), 429–30.

[87] Carvajal's letter is dated at Ujlak on 29 July, 1456, and is published by Thallóczy and Áldásy, *MHH*, XXXIII (1907), doc. CCLXXIX, pp. 210–11, on which *cf.* Hofer, *Hist. Jahrbuch*, LI, 176, 209. Letters of the Venetian Senate, dated 5 and 12 August, 1456, to Carvajal and Hunyadi express jubilation over the victory of Belgrade (Sen. Secreta, Reg. 20 fols. 98–99 [99–100]), attributing it to Hunyadi's talent, courage, and prudence (*ibid.*, fol. 99ᵛ [100ᵛ]). Since the texts of these letters lack the cross, which was entered in the left-hand margin of a register to indicate that an act was put into effect, the letters were probably never sent (the texts are given in Sime Ljubić, *Listine*, X [Zagreb, 1891], 94–95, and *cf.* p. 97). The Venetians did, however, send an envoy to acknowledge the thrilling news of Hunyadi's victory, "felicissima nova victorie sue de imperatore Turcorum turpiter cum multa suorum strage et tormentorum [cannon] et ceterarum munitionum suarum amissione in fugam converso que animos nostros tanto gaudio tantaque leticia affecit tantumque erexit ut exprimere difficile sit" (Sen. Secreta, Reg. 20, fol. 99ʳ [100ʳ], and *cf.* fols. 101ᵛ, 103ʳ).

Calixtus III in a letter dated at S. Maria Maggiore in Rome on 25 August, 1456, sent Capistrano a most generous statement of appreciation for the friar's part in the victory at Belgrade (Arch. Segr. Vaticano, Arm. XXXIX, tom. 7, fol. 42ᵛ), reserving even higher praise for the brilliant leadership which he attributes to Cardinal Carvajal (*ibid.*, 43ᵛ). Calixtus commonly lauds both Capistrano and Hunyadi without trying specifically to assess the contribution of each (*ibid.*, 47ʳ, *et alibi*). On Carvajal's activities before the siege (and after the relief) of Belgrade, see Gómez Canedo, *Don Juan de Carvajal* (1947), pp. 165–74.

[88] Capistrano also outlines a brief program for a crusade (in Wadding, *Annales Minorum*, XII [1932], 430–32); the letter contains a flattering reference to Hunyadi, who had died of the plague six days before.

[89] Pastor, *Hist. Popes*, II, 403–4, and append., no. 43, pp. 548–50, and *Gesch. d. Päpste*, I (repr. 1955), 724–25, and append., no. 76, pp. 856–57: ". . . Steti secho solo chel non zera altra persona da le XX hore [about 4:00 P.M. in August] per fina ale XXIII et meza. . . ." Calixtus also excoriated the failure of the Hungarians to take part in the defense of Belgrade, "dicendo che tuta [questa victoria] hera stata del prefato Zohanne Vayvoda acompagnato da li poveri e soli cruciati. . . ." *Cf.* the joyous letters of Calixtus to the Doge Francesco Foscari of Venice, Charles VII of France, and the Florentine government in the Arch. Segr. Vaticano, Arm. XXXIX, tom. 7, fols. 22–24. In August the pope wrote [S.] Antonino, the archbishop of Florence, that he looked forward "not only to the recovery of Constantinople but also to the liberation of Europe, Asia, and the Holy Land" (*ibid.*, fol. 26ᵛ, and *cf.* fol. 29ʳ, *et alibi*).

prisoner. The latter was allowed freely to depart, however, assuring László that he did not regard him as responsible for Cilli's death. A few months later Ladislas struck back at the Hunyadis, as a result of an alleged conspiracy; László and his younger brother Matthias Corvinus were both arrested in Buda. László was given a trial in which the verdict was a foregone conclusion. He was beheaded in March, 1457,[90] and Matthias Corvinus remained a prisoner until Ladislas's own death the following November. In the meantime Ladislas and his archenemy Frederick III struggled for the lands of the heirless Cilli. The turmoil in Hungary was linked to that in Serbia, where the Despot George Branković, who had married one daughter to Cilli and another to Murad, had recently died at the age of eighty (on 24 December, 1456). There was dissension among his children.[91] Clearly there was no hope of exploiting the victory at Belgrade and organizing a crusade in the eastern lands which had the most to fear from the Turks.

Throughout this period Pope Calixtus III had been continuing his own efforts against the Turks. By the late spring of 1456 he had ready, at a cost of some 150,000 ducats,[92] a fleet of sixteen galleys over which, as we have seen, he had placed as captain-general and admiral the reluctant Lodovico Trevisan, the cardinal of Aquileia, who was also made legate to Sicily, Dalmatia and Macedonia, Greece, the islands of the Aegean, Crete, Rhodes, Cyprus, and the provinces of Asia, as well as governor of such places as he might seize from the Turks.[93] Calixtus had done his best, but the going was never easy. In March, 1456, the Venetian Senate had declined to allow a tithe to be collected from the Jews for Lodovico's coming expedition on the grounds that when the other Christian powers, especially those north of the Alps, had arranged to proceed against the Turks, Venice would join the general crusade and would require for its own expenses both the ecclesiastical and the Jewish tithes.[94] Apparently no help would be forthcoming from the richest state in Italy.

In late April (1456) Calixtus III wrote Francesco Sforza of his "unbelievable anxiety to send out our legate with the fleet against the evil Turk," and urged Sforza to assist in the collection of the tithes and other imposts in the duchy of Milan, "so that as much

[90] Aeneas Sylvius, *Historia bohemica*, 66–68, in *Opera quae extant omnia* (1551, repr. 1967), pp. 139–40; Pastor, *Gesch. d. Päpste*, I (repr. 1955), 730–31; Heymann, *George of Bohemia* (1965), pp. 134–37. There is a garbled account of Cilli's murder and László Hunyadi's execution in Jacopo de Promontorio de Campis (Babinger, in the *Sitzungsber. d. Bayer. Akad. d. Wissen.*, 1956, Heft 8, pp. 87–89, and, *ibid.*, 1957, Heft 6, pp. 66–68).

[91] The Despot George Branković left three sons at his death. The two elder, Gregory and Stephen, had been blinded by the Turks. In the fall of 1457 Gregory and his sister the Sultana Mara, Murad II's widow, sent information from Adrianople to Ragusa—as apparently they did from time to time—and, as usual, the Ragusei sent the information on to the king of Hungary (Gelcich and Thallóczy, *Diplomatarium ragusanum* [1887], no. 353, pp. 600–2). Lazar, the third son, succeeded his father in an unsteady reign of hardly more than a year, being constantly harassed by Michael Szilágyi, Hunyadi's brother-in-law and now the governor of Belgrade. Lazar died on 20 January, 1458, leaving no male heirs (*cf.* N. Iorga, *Gesch. d. osman. Reiches*, II [Gotha, 1909], 80–81; Babinger, *Maometto*, pp. 226–27, 239). The papacy tried to bring Serbia within its sphere of influence. A letter of Calixtus, dated 15 March, 1458, sending Cardinal Lodovico Trevisan a summary of the news, reports that "despotus . . . Rassie, qui nullo relicto herede mortuus est, terras suas Cardinali Sancti Angeli legato nostro pro nobis et Apostolica Sede tradi et consignari mandavit et, ut credimus, iam illas nominibus predictis accepit" (Arch. Segr. Vaticano, Arm. XXXIX, tom. 7, fol. 155^r^). On 3 April the pope again informed Lodovico of Carvajal's efforts to secure the lands of the deceased despot for the Holy See (*ibid.*, fol. 158^v^). While Carvajal labored "viriliter et potenter" for the Church, Calixtus appeared to find a decided lack of such enterprise in Lodovico.

[92] According to a letter of 5 August, 1456, addressed "dilecto filio Dionisio tituli S. Kyriaci in Termis presbytero Cardinali Strigoniensi" [Dionysius Széchy, cardinal archbishop of Gran], "Nos autem iam ab ultima die Maii proxime elapsi [31 May, 1456], ut ante obtulimus, classem nostram cum legato nostro ad partes orientales emisimus hostes mox vexaturam, in qua paranda et armanda deo teste iam supra CL ducatorum milia expendimus facturique omnia sumus que in dies magis augere votum nostrum in conspectu dei et hominum profutura putemus" (Arch. Segr. Vaticano, Arm. XXXIX, tom. 7, fol. 25^r^, by mod. stamped enumeration, and *cf.* the *Schedario Garampi: Vescovi*, vol. 63 [archival *Indice*, vol. 507], fol. 17). *Cf.*, above, note 15.

[93] Raynaldus, *Ann. eccl.*, ad ann. 1456, no. 13, vol. XVIII (1694), p. 458, where the letter of appointment is given (17 December, 1455), to which Raynaldus adds: "Amplificata alio diplomate eius fuit potestas, quo legatio ipsi in Sicilia, Dalmatia, Macedonia, Graecia universa, Aegei maris insulis, Creta, Rhodo, Cypro, regnisque et provinciis Asiaticis data est, praefectusque omnibus locis, quae hostibus eripuisset. . . ." *Cf.* Alberto Guglielmotti, *Storia della marina pontificia*, II (Rome, 1886), 253–55, who translates Cardinal Lodovico's letter of 26 April, 1456, to Giovanni da Capistrano (from Alph. Ciacconius, *Vitae pontif. romanorum*, II [Rome, 1677], 920), announcing that the fleet was ready to sail "within a few days."

[94] Pastor, *Acta inedita*, I (1904), no. 38, pp. 52–54, doc. dated 8 March, 1456.

money may be had as possible and sent to us, for funds are badly needed for this sacred expedition, which we are preparing with all our heart for the defense of the Christian religion."[95] About two weeks or so later (in May) the pope wrote the French King Charles VII of his "overwhelming and inexpressible desire to avenge the injuries which the Turks have inflicted on [our] sacrosanct religion," and asserted his belief that the king was also prepared to aid the faith. "But because with each passing hour our heart takes fire and burns for so sacred a cause, and this care alone remains fixed in our mind, we cannot but continually incite all Catholic princes to so salutary, so holy, and even so divine an undertaking. . . ." The growth of Turkish power had to be stopped, the pope wrote, and it could be if Christendom would arouse itself from its negligent attitude toward the East.

> And because we have been informed by letters, of which we send your serene Highness a copy, from our beloved son Juan [de Carvajal], cardinal of S. Angelo and legate of the Apostolic See, that the Turks have decided to cross the Danube with an innumerable army and to attack the kingdom of Hungary, we have thought that the best plan (and a necessary one) to divide and diminish their strength [will be] to send our legate with a fleet to the East, so that the enemy forces, when they want to aid their own people assailed by our fleet, may be withdrawn from Hungary. . . .

The pope had no doubt that Cardinal Lodovico's fleet would set sail "at the end of this month . . ., and we would that the capture of our own person might suffice to stop the defeat and dishonor of the faith, for God knows we willingly offer ourselves. . . ." The pope concluded his letter by exhorting Charles not to delay the collection of the tithes and the preaching of the crusade, "so that funds may not be lacking to this divine work. . . ."[96] He wrote in similar terms to King Alfonso V, urging him to have in readiness the fifteen galleys which he had promised to arm, so that they might be able to sail with Cardinal Lodovico and the papal fleet into Levantine waters.[97]

It was on the last day of May, 1456, that Cardinal Lodovico received the crusader's cross from the pope's own hands.[98] The next morning, accompanied by the cardinals, he boarded his flagship, which was moored with the other galleys on the Tiber by the Borgo S. Spirito and along the Ripa Grande. He remained with the fleet for ten days, not sailing for Ostia until 11 June.[99] For whatever reason, he had not left

---

[95] Pastor, *Acta inedita*, I, no. 39, p. 54, dated 27 April, 1456, and *cf.* the undated papal letters to Sforza and the archbishop of Milan in Arch. Segr. Vaticano, Arm. XXXIX, tom. 7, fol. 20ʳ.

[96] Pastor, *Acta inedita*, I, no. 40, pp. 55–56, probably to be dated about mid-May, 1456; and *cf.* the pope's letter to the Emperor Frederick III, in Raynaldus, *Ann. eccl.*, ad ann. 1456, no. 16, vol. XVIII (1694), p. 460a. Despite frequent papal exhortations and the legatine mission of Cardinal Alain de Coëtivy of Avignon, Charles VII did nothing for the crusade, in which connection the pope had a good deal of trouble with the University of Paris (Pastor, *Hist. Popes*, II, 377–82, somewhat revised in *Gesch. d. Päpste*, I [repr. 1955], 702–6, and *cf.* Raynaldus, ad ann. 1456, nos. 1–5, vol. XVIII, pp. 452b–454a). The papal letters to Charles VII and Frederick III, dated 1456 (but with blanks left for the day and month), are preserved in the Vatican Archives, Arm. XXXIX, tom. 7, fols. 4ᵛ–5 and 4ʳᵛ respectively by mod. stamped enumeration. Numerous letters were sent at the same time to other princes, the Florentines, and Bishop Giovanni Castiglione of Pavia (*ibid.*, fols. 6–9). Sciambra, Valentini, and Parrino, *Il "Liber brevium" di Callisto III* (1968), pp. 53–55, 71 ff., date these letters in July, 1456.

[97] Raynaldus, *Ann. eccl.*, ad ann. 1456, no. 10, vol. XVIII (1694), p. 456b: "Quapropter Serenitatem tuam iterato instantissimeque hortamur, ut omnino det operam, quod XV ille galee, quas alias pollicita est armare, in apparatu sint, ut cum prelibato legato et reliqua classe nostra navigare possint." The papal letter is in Arm. XXXIX, tom. 7, fol. 5. At the same time the pope wrote John Soler, his ambassador in Naples, that all Christians must be aroused from their slumber, and directed him to urge Alfonso "ut XV illas triremes parari armarique quam raptissime faciat omni postposita excusatione" (*ibid.*, fol. 6), adding: "Nos enim ita ex hac re mente animo pendemus ut donec audiamus classem predictam orientales partes attigisse nullo modo quiescere possumus." Another undated letter to Alfonso is given at this point in the register (*ibid.*, fol. 6). On Alfonso's promised fifteen galleys, see also, *ibid.*, fols. 20ᵛ–21ʳ, 38ʳ.

[98] Raynaldus, *Ann. eccl.*, ad ann. 1456, no. 12, vol. XVIII (1694), p. 458a: "Nos die S. Petronillae [31 May] Ludovicum tituli S. Laurentii in Damaso presbyterum Cardinalem nostrum et Apostolicae Sedis legatum contra Christi et Christiani nominis inimicos, ipso etiam devotissime suscipiente, crucesignavimus. . . ." On 13 May, 1456, Isidore, the "Ruthenian cardinal," left Rome on a two months' crusading mission to Venice (Acta Consistorialia [1439–1486], in Arch. Segr. Vaticano, Arm. XXXI, tom. 52, fol. 58ᵛ, with abbreviated text in Eubel, *Hierarchia*, II [1914, repr. 1960], 31b). The papal registers furnish constant evidence of the intense activity in the Curia at this time.

[99] The dates are fixed by entries in the invaluable Acta Consistorialia, Arm. XXXI, tom. 52, fol. 58ᵛ: "Recessus domini camerarii Cardinalis Aquilegiensis: Anno a nativitate ut supra [1456] die vero prima mensis Iunii reverendissimus dominus camerarius Cardinalis Aquilegiensis de mane recessit de secreto consistorio legatus de latere per mare contra Teucros associatus a dominis cardinalibus usque ad galeas que erant in Ripa Tiberis in urbe. Non tamen discessit de Ripa tunc sed die undecima dicti mensis per Tiberim ivit ad Hostium versus Neapolim." *Cf.* Eubel,

Ostia by 20 June when he addressed a letter to the Marquis Lodovico Gonzaga "from the mouth of the Tiber aboard the fleet."[100] It was on the twentieth also that Calixtus III promulgated the "anti-Turkish" bull which, when sent to Germany, was printed in both Latin and German to secure it a wider distribution. This bull was, oddly enough, to acquire far more importance in the history of typography than in that of the crusades.[101]

Lodovico Trevisan must have sailed for Naples very soon after 20 June. The promulgation of the papal bull may have hastened his departure. Long a servitor of the royal house of Aragon-Catalonia, Calixtus III had naturally placed his chief reliance on Alfonso V, who had been collecting the crusading tithe from his various dominions. Alfonso had so far promised more than he had done for the Christian cause in the East, preferring to employ his resources against Genoa. Lodovico expected to be joined in Naples by the fifteen galleys which Alfonso had promised for the crusade. Now there was a long delay at Naples, which Lodovico doubtless found quite tolerable as he waited for Alfonso to provide the ships. But as the weeks passed, Calixtus became understandably impatient, and sent the Catalan Jaume de Perpinyà to Naples, directing him as soon as he arrived there to insist upon Lodovico's immediate departure with the papal fleet even if the king's galleys were not ready.[102]

The pope wrote in the most urgent tones to Lodovico himself:

> If our fleet invades the Turkish shores and seacoast territories as soon as possible, the troops and striking force of the enemy, gathered for an attack upon Hungary, will be withdrawn and divided. On the speed of the fleet, therefore, the safety of the Hungarian kingdom depends, nay, the safety of all Christianity, because if Hungary is crushed—which God forbid!—Christendom will be in the gravest and most certain peril.

Hierarchia, II, 31b; P. Paschini, *Lodovico Cardinal Camerlengo*, Rome, 1939, p. 184; and Pastor, *Gesch. d. Päpste*, I (repr. 1955), 697–98. Note also Paschini, "La Flotta di Callisto III," *Arch. della R. Soc. rom. di storia patria*, LIII–LV (1930–32), 207 ff.

An interesting register in the Archivio Segreto Vaticano, bearing the old enumeration "2008" (*Calist. III, Diversor. Cam., 1455–1458*, now Arm. XXVIIII [XXIX], tom. 28), is more than half filled with records of the wide range of Cardinal Lodovico's activities in Rome right up to 31 May, 1456 (to fol. 180ʳ), the day before he boarded his ship on the Tiber. From 4 June the business of the Camera was transacted in the name of George, *vicecamerarius* and bishop of Lausanne (fols. 180ᵛ–181ʳ ff.). George had been appointed *vicecamerarius* on 14 March, 1456 (Reg. Vat. 465, fol. 166, by mod. stamped enumeration, "datum Rome apud Sanctum Petrum, anno etc., MCCCCLV [i.e., in the year of the Incarnation, or according to the 'Florentine style'], pridie Idus Martii, pontif. nostri anno primo"). Before this, on 21 April, 1455, he had been made castellan of the castle of S. Angelo: "Venerabili fratri Georgio episcopo Lausanensi, Castri nostri Crescentii alias dicti Sancti Angeli de urbe castellano nostro" (Reg. Vat. 465, fol. 16). He held the castellany of S. Angelo for almost a year, until he was forced to give it up on the night of 15 March, 1456, when the Borgia family and their Catalan supporters secured control of the city of Rome (Pastor, *Gesch. d. Päpste*, I [repr. 1955], 771, and note 1). Reg. Vat. 465 is the first of three registers of Calixtus III relating to appointments (*Officiorum liber primus, Anno I–II–III*), the others being Regg. Vatt. 466–67. (There are almost forty Regg. Vatt. from the brief reign of Calixtus III.) From 6 April, 1458, we have an order of "Georgius, ep. Lausanen., vicecamerarius," relating to the acquisition of lumber for oars, for galleys then being constructed against the Turks (Arm. XXIX, tom. 28, fol. 273).

[100] Cardinal Lodovico addressed two letters to Lodovico II Gonzaga dated 13 and 20 June, 1456, "ex ostio Tiberis super classem," which are preserved in the Archivio Gonzaga (in the State Archives in Mantua), on which *cf.* Pastor, *Gesch. d. Päpste*, I (repr. 1955), 698, note 2; 709, note 5. According to Guglielmotti, *Storia della marina pontificia*, II (1886), 255–56, the papal fleet consisted of at least twenty-five ships, carrying 5,000 soldiers, a thousand mariners, and 300 cannon; Paschini, *Lodovico Cardinal Camerlengo*, p. 184, says that the cardinal commander, on 1 June, "prese il possesso delle dieci galee già pronte." Urrea had had sixteen galleys under his command, and ten more were under construction, besides the papal ships at Ancona, as we learn from an undated letter of Calixtus III (Arch. Segr. Vaticano, Arm. XXXIX, tom. 7, fol. 28ʳ, probably in April, 1456, on which see, above, note 21). In an undated letter to Cardinal Carvajal, which I assume should be assigned to the last few days in June, Calixtus III wrote ". . . legatum nostrum emisimus qui die ultima Maii triremes conscendit Neapolimque se contulit . . ." (Arm. XXXIX, tom. 7, fol. 10ᵛ), which was finally the case. The pope's assurance to Carvajal that the fleet had departed would certainly be encouraging to the Hungarians—"itaque, dilecte fili, confide et bono animo fortique sis: Deus non relinquet causam suam" (*ibid.*), and Carvajal could pass on this assurance to the king and court at Buda.

[101] The bull *Cum hiis superioribus* [*annis*] may be found in Reg. Vat. 457, fols. 226ᵛ–229ʳ, "datum Rome apud Sanctum Petrum anno incarnationis dominice millesimo quadringentesimo L sexto, duodecimo Kalend. Iulii, pontificatus nostri anno secundo" [20 June, 1456], on the importance of which, see Paul Schwenke and Hermann Degering, *Die Türkenbulle Pabst Calixtus III.: Ein deutscher Druck von 1456 in der ersten Gutenbergtype*, Berlin, 1911. The text is described as "bulla oracionis contra infideles pro victoria populi Christiani" (in the rubric to Reg. Vat. 457, fol. 5ᵛ); it is actually dated 29 June (*tercio Kal. Iulii*) in the archival copy (*ibid.*, fol. 229ʳ), presumably the day it was entered into the register.

[102] Arch. Segr. Vaticano, Arm. XXXIX, tom. 7, fols. 9–10, 33, 33ᵛ–34ʳ, 37, and *cf.* Pastor's account of the delayed departure of "Scarampo" from Naples (*Gesch. d. Päpste*, I [repr. 1955], 699).

The pope also warned Alfonso directly that the fate of Hungary might be hanging on the appearance of the papal fleet in Levantine waters, "so that his Majesty may not wonder if we have made the legate hasten off with just a small fleet,"[103] while Lodovico was told that in Sicily he would receive money and the ships which had been entrusted to Pedro de Urrea, archbishop of Tarragona, for the Aegean expedition he had never made.[104]

Pope Calixtus's command and the crisis in Hungary finally impelled Lodovico's departure from Naples on 6 August (1456).[105] The letter of the Milanese ambassador Jacopo Calcaterra to Francesco Sforza, which we have already noted as reporting the pope's elation over Hunyadi's victory at Belgrade, also contains a statement of Calixtus's extreme annoyance with the procrastinating Lodovico. The letter informs us, furthermore, although the claim may well be doubted, that King Alfonso had finally turned over to the cardinal the fifteen galleys he had promised for the expedition.[106] At least Alfonso furnished some ships. No sooner had Lodovico set out for Sicily than Calixtus was all for hastening him on to Istanbul to help effect the diversion of the Turks from Hungary,[107] and plans were being made in Rome to build still more ships to add as reinforcements to Lodovico's fleet, which the pope knew was hardly sufficient for the large hope he entertained of distracting the Turk from his Hungarian campaign.[108] Before the remarkable Christian victory of 21–22 July, 1456, the papal fleet was badly needed in the area of the Dardanelles, where an attack might encourage Mehmed II to abandon the idea of laying siege to Belgrade. With the Turkish defeat at Belgrade, however, Calixtus believed that his fleet was more than ever needed in Levantine waters: Turkish power had received its death blow in Mehmed's failure against Hunyadi and Capistrano. The recovery of Constantinople was in sight, even the extermination of Islam and the recovery of the Holy Land![109]

---

[103] There are selections from the papal letters in Raynaldus, *Ann. eccl.*, ad ann. 1456, no. 13, vol. XVIII (1694), p. 459a; the pope wrote Alfonso *manu propria* (Arch. Segr. Vaticano, Arm. XXXIX, tom. 7 fols. 25^v–26).

[104] See Calixtus III's undated letters to Jaume de Perpinyà in Arm. XXXIX, tom. 7, fol. 10^r, and to Cardinal Lodovico (*ibid.*, fol. 33).

[105] The date is known from a dispatch of Aeneas Sylvius, Galgano Borghese, and Bernardo de'Benvoglienti, dated at Naples on 6 August, 1456 (Bibl. Com., Siena, Cod. A., III, 16, cited by Pastor, *Gesch. d. Päpste*, I [repr. 1955], 700, note 2): "El rev. patriarcha questa sera si parti. . . ." On 4 July, 1456, however, Calixtus wrote Cardinal Alain de Coëtivy: "Misimus enim legatum Cardinalem Camerarium nostrum cum incredibili celeritate qui iam in mari est et quam citissime versus orientem vela dat littoraque hostium invadet ut per hoc eorum potentia ex Hungaria distrahatur . . ." (Arch. Segr. Vaticano, Arm. XXXIX, tom. 7, fol. 12^r). On 6 August Calixtus again appealed to the Neapolitan king for assistance, reminding him of the grave responsibility which the peril of Hungary imposed on his "mediocris classis" (*ibid.*, fol. 26^r), and on the eighteenth he wrote to Cardinal Lodovico expressing the greatest pleasure in his departure with the fleet to Sicily (*ibid.*, fol. 34^v). *Cf.* Paschini, "La Flotta," pp. 209–14.

[106] Pastor, *Gesch. d. Päpste*, I, append., no. 76, pp. 856–57, doc. dated at Castro Giubileo on 24 August, 1456: "E la M^{ta} del Re li ha dato quele XV. gallee li haveva promisso. . . ."

[107] Pastor, I, append., no. 73, p. 855, letter of Calixtus III to Jaume de Perpinyà, mid-August, 1456: "Optamus enim ut illico cum classe ad Constantinopolim se conferat . . ." (from Arch. Segr. Vaticano, Arm. XXXIX, tom. 7, fol. 13^r, mod. stamped enumeration). *Cf.*, *ibid.*, fols. 13^v–14^r, a letter to John Soler on the same general theme, written partly in Catalan. Although after the Christian success at Belgrade, Calixtus often gave expression to his hope of reconquering Constantinople, Asia Minor, and the Holy Land, his first thought was generally for Catholic Hungary, Albania, and Bosnia. His attitude towards the Greeks was that of his predecessor Nicholas V, as was doubtless to be expected, and as is shown in his bull of 3 September, 1457, directed to the Greek clergy: ". . . statuimus et ordinamus quod ex nunc in antea omnes et singuli presbyteri et sacerdotes greci ubilibet existentes infra missarum solempnia nomen Romani pontificis in loco deputato alta et intelligibili voce exprimere ac pro ipsius et Sancte Romane Ecclesie incolumitate statuque pacifico orare teneantur . . ." (Reg. Vat. 449, fol. 133, by mod. stamped enumeration, previously fol. 130). I find this bull also in Arm. XXXI, tom. 59, fols. 82^v–84^r, by mod. enumeration.

[108] *Cf.* Pastor, *Gesch. d. Päpste*, I, 700.

[109] In an undated letter, apparently from early September, 1456, Calixtus wrote Cardinal Lodovico (Arch. Segr. Vaticano, Arm. XXXIX, tom. 7, fol. 31^v; older enumeration, fol. 28^v): "Credimus Circumspectionem tuam intellexisse felicissimum novum quod novissime ex Hungaria nobis allatum est quo de gloriosa victoria Hungariorum contra pessimos Turchos divina potencia obtenta certiores facti sumus: arbitramur quo gaudio eo magis exultavit cor nostrum quod de felici tuo recessu ex Neapoli certiores facti etiam fuimus ita ut divino consilio quo sine dubio res iste gubernantur factum putemus ut uno tempore crudelissimi hostes navali et terrestri pugna profligati essent. Et tu cum classe nostra ad eorum maritimas terras vastandas proficisceris. Quare, dilecte fili, exsuscita te ipsum tuamque prudentiam omnibus cognitam in hoc divino opere ostende ex quo tuum nomen inmortalitati donabitur. Nunc omnes promende sunt vires, nunc maxime instandum est hosti perculso et fugato incertoque quo se vertat. Numquam facilius eius regnum occupari potuit. Deus animum et vires suggerit populo suo. Vide qualem eventum dedit inclinatus orationibus plebis sue quas ut tua Circumspectio scit cum maxima devotione per universum orbem Christianum fieri

From Sicily the papal fleet sailed, presumably by way of Modon or Coron, to the island of Rhodes, where money and supplies were delivered to the Hospitallers. In February or March, 1457, Cardinal Lodovico was given the charge of reforming the convent of the Hospitallers at their island center. The officials in the Curia Romana seem to have had some trouble drafting the text of the cardinal's commission.[110]

Lodovico then moved on into the northern Aegean where the old Genoese family of the Gattilusi had suffered severe losses during the preceding year. Early in 1456, before the expedition to Belgrade, Sultan Mehmed had taken away from Dorino II Gattilusio the mainland city of Aenos, by the mouth of the Maritsa, as well as the nearby islands of Imbros and Samothrace. The historian Critobulus was installed by the Turks as governor of his native Imbros. Next, Niccolò, the harsh lieutenant of his brother Domenico Gattilusio of Mytilene (Lesbos), had been expelled from Lemnos, which also received a Turkish commandant. Of the seven possessions which the Gattilusi had held in the Aegean region, only the island lordship of Lesbos now remained to them. Domenico held it on a very precarious tenure, for which he paid the Porte an annual tribute of four thousand gold pieces. Failing to convince either Domenico or the Genoese *mahonesi* on Chios to refuse the further payment of the Turkish tribute, Lodovico now occupied Lemnos without any difficulty; took over Samothrace; and finally seized Thasos after an attack upon the fortress in the harbor. He placed garrisons on the three islands, from whose ramparts the banner of the keys of S. Peter now floated for a few years. Lodovico is also reported to have won a notable victory over a Turkish fleet at Mytilene in August, 1457, when he captured more than twenty-five Turkish vessels.[111]

Lodovico's successes led the Despot Thomas Palaeologus to suspend payment of the Moreote tribute to the sultan, which was soon to bring his rule in the peninsula to an inglorious con-

---

ordinavimus. . . ." As always in letters of this period papal hopes ran high. The Asian as well as European territory which the Turks had occupied could now be rewon, etc.

It was all a dream, for according to "le nove recevute da Constantinopoli scripte del mese de Decembre [1456]" the Turks were doing very well under their young sultan and his young pashas: "Questo Signor e de grandissimo animo et presto a fare le sue provisione, non vole contrasto a la sua opinione, et per fare quello, chel vole, ha allevato duoi zoveni bassa de sua etade, li quali in tute cose lo seguitano. Item ha facto suo capitaneo de mare Janisbei [Yunus Pasha], zovene de XXV anni, animoso, allevato con lui da puto in suso, et a tempo novo usira con potente armata dicese per tuore Trebesunda, Caffa et altri lochi del mare maiore. Il dicto Signor gli ha promesso in dicta armata zulie XXX in XL, havemo speranza chel usira male per lui. . . . Dapoi la venuta de questo Signore, questi cani vano dicendo: a Roma, a Roma! poi diceno, in Puglia, in Puglia! Ogni giorno fa fare edifiei et munitione da offendere et maxime bombarde . . ." (V. V. Makušev, *Monumenta historica slavorum meridionalium*, II [1882], 89–90).

[110] On 11 February, 1457, the charge of reforming the Hospitallers' convent was issued to Cardinal Lodovico, "datum Rome apud Sanctum Petrum anno incarnationis dominice MCCCCLVI, tertio Idus Februarii, pontificatus nostri anno secundo" [the new year of the Incarnation begins on 25 March] (Reg. Vat. 444, fols. 23^{r}–25^{v}, by mod. stamped enumeration), the bull being rewritten and redated (in the margin of fol. 23^{r}), with a note of the change and the new date 14 March, 1457, recorded by the papal secretary G. de Vulterris. Calixtus tried to keep his fleet and its headquarters at Rhodes well equipped (*cf.* Arm. XXXIX, tom. 7, fols. 80^{v}–81^{v}, 83^{v} f., 86^{r}, 87^{v}, 89^{v}, 90^{r}, 91^{r}, 125^{v}–126^{r}, 135^{v}–136^{r}, 154^{v}–156^{r}, 157, 159^{r}, 160^{v}, *et alibi*). In a letter to Lodovico dated 4 December, 1457, the pope stated that ". . . proximo . . . mense Augusti et ultimis diebus eiusdem mensis expedivimus hic tres galeas bene armatas . . ." (*ibid.*, fols. 134^{v}–135^{r}, and *cf.* fols. 120^{r}–121^{v}, 122). Note also Const. Marinescu, "L'Île de Rhodes au XVe siècle et l'Ordre de Saint-Jean de Jérusalem d'après des documents inédits," in the *Miscellanea Giovanni Mercati*, V (1946), 399–401 (Studi e testi, no. 125), where Lodovico Trevisan is called "Scarampo."

On Turkish aggression in the Aegean and the debt-laden Hospitallers' fear of Mehmed II, who was demanding an annual tribute of 2,000 ducats from them (which they refused to pay), see R. Valentini, "L'Egeo dopo la caduta di Costantinopoli nelle relazioni dei gran maestri di Rodi," *Bullettino dell'Istituto storico italiano per il medio evo e Archivio Muratoriano*, LI (1936), 137–68, with four documents dated from 1453 to 1462. Incidentally, the Grand Master Jean de Lastic (1437–1454) and the Convent at Rhodes seem to have believed the rumor that Mehmed had had 600,000 men at the siege of Constantinople! (*ibid.*, doc. I, p. 160). Nevertheless, they refused to pay the tribute (doc. II, p. 162) to the sultan, who had set out "suis gestis Alexandri Magni gesta superare" (doc. III, p. 163).

[111] Arch. Segr. Vaticano, Arm. XXXIX, tom. 7, fol. 126^{v}, letter of Calixtus III dated 24 September, 1457, to Guillem Ponç de Fenollet. The text is inaccurately given as thirty (instead of twenty-five) Turkish vessels captured, in Sciambra, Valentini, and Parrino, *Il "Liber brevium" di Callisto III* (1968), p. 174. *Cf.* Raynaldus, *Ann. eccl.*, ad ann. 1457, nos. 31–32, vol. XVIII (1694), pp. 490b–91, and Pius II, *Asia*, 74, in *Opera quae extant omnia* (1551, repr. 1967), pp. 355–56 (the chap. is misnumbered, and the text poor). On 31 August, 1457, Calixtus had written the Emperor Frederick III that Lodovico's fleet was defending Rhodes, Cyprus, Lesbos, Chios, and all the Christian islands of the East, which could not have resisted the continued Turkish attacks without such assistance (Paschini, *Lodovico Cardinal Camerlengo*, p. 186, and see also "La Flotta," pp. 218 ff.).

clusion. Lodovico also harried the coasts of Cilicia, Syria, and Egypt, but his costly expedition probably did the Christians in the East more harm than good by arousing against them the vengeful wrath of Mehmed II, who soon set about the reconquest of the three islands he had lost.[112] Henceforth, for decades, life in the Aegean was disrupted by almost continuous warfare, punctuated by piracy, between the Ottoman government and the Hospitallers of Rhodes.[113] Lodovico had hardly done more than enhance his own prestige when he returned to Italy a few months after death had claimed the aged Calixtus III (on 6 August, 1458).[114]

Lodovico had remained at Rhodes until November (1457). Upon his return to Italy he disembarked at Taranto. After spending some time in Apulia, where conditions were deteriorating because of the death of Alfonso V (on 27 June, 1458),[115] he went on to Naples and thereafter to Monte Cassino in January (1459). He stayed at the abbey for several days, but appears to have arrived in Rome before the end of the month.[116] By 16 March he had rejoined

[112] Mehmed also took Lesbos, in 1462 (Valentini, "L'Egeo dopo la caduta di Costantinopoli," doc. IV, pp. 166–67, and Wm. Miller, "The Gattilusj of Lesbos," *Essays on the Latin Orient*, Cambridge, 1921, repr. Amsterdam, 1967, pp. 340–49).

[113] *Cf.* Elizabeth A. Zachariadou, "Contribution [Συμβολή] to the History of the Southeastern Aegean . . . 1454–1522," *Κέντρον βυζαντινῶν ἐρευνῶν, Βασιλικὸν ἵδρυμα ἐρευνῶν: Σύμμεικτα*, I (Athens, 1966), 184–230, with the texts of eleven Ottoman firmans from the monastery of S. John on the island of Patmos.

[114] On the activities of Cardinal Lodovico in the East, see also Critobulus, *De rebus gestis Mechemetis II*, II, 23; III, 10, 15 (ed. Müller, *FHG*, V-1 [1870], pp. 118–19, 126a, 129a; ed. Grecu [1963], pp. 211, 213, 235, 245); Ducas [who was the secretary of Domenico Gattilusio, lord of Lesbos], chap. 45 (Bonn, p. 338; ed. Grecu [1958], p. 423); and Chalcocondylas, bk. IX (Bonn, pp. 469–70; ed. E. Darkó, II-2 [1927], 225). Critobulus describes how by diplomacy he saved from the Latins his native island of Imbros, which both Ducas and Chalcocondylas incorrectly state was taken by Lodovico. Calixtus III was also not well informed when he wrote on 2 January, 1457 (in Raynaldus, *Ann. eccl.*, ad ann. 1457, no. 10, vol. XVIII [1694], p. 486b): "Ad XXIX [diem mensis] Decembris [1456] accepimus litteras a classe nostra, quemadmodum tres insulas Turcorum expugnasset, et ad obedientiam sanctae matris Ecclesiae reduxisset, scilicet Mitilenum [Lesbos], Taxum [Thasos], et Staliminum [Lemnos], quae conficiunt circa LX millia animarum." (Lesbos was of course already under Latin dominion.) Calixtus III's letter of 2 January, 1457, was written to the young King Ladislas Postumus of Hungary; one may find the archival copy of the original text in Arch. Segr. Vaticano, Arm. XXXIX, tom. 7, fols. 58^{v}–59^{r}, whence Raynaldus transcribed the quotation relating to Lodovico's conquest of the three islands from the Turks.

Note also Sanudo, *Vite de'duchi*, in *RISS*, XXII (1733), col. 1159B; K. Hopf, "Griechenland im Mittelalter," in J. S. Ersch and J. G. Gruber, *Allgemeine Encyklopädie*, vol. 86 (Leipzig, 1868, repr. New York, 1960, II), 152–53; Pastor, *Hist. Popes*, II, 372–76, 438–39, and append., no. 45, pp. 551–52, and *Gesch. d. Päpste*, I (repr. 1955), 698–702, 751–52, and append., no. 78, p. 858; Iorga, *Gesch. d. osman. Reiches*, II, 68–71, 85–86; Paschini, *Lodovico Cardinal Camerlengo*, pp. 185–87; Babinger, *Maometto*, pp. 209–11, 231–32; Wm. Miller, "The Gattilusj of Lesbos," *Essays on the Latin Orient*, Cambridge, 1921, pp. 334–41; Const. Marinescu, "Le Pape Calixte III (1455–1458), Alfonse V d'Aragon, roi de Naples et l'offensive contre les Turcs," *Bulletin historique de l'Académie roumaine*, XIX (1935), 77–97.

Paolo Brezzi, "La Politica di Callisto III: Equilibrio italiano e difesa dell'Europa alla metà del sec. XV," *Studi romani*, VII (1959), 37, states that the fleet of Cardinal "Scarampo" forced the capitulation of the Acropolis at Athens in June, 1458, and took Corinth [from the Turks] in August. He has read too rapidly Massimo Petrocchi, *La Politica della Santa Sede di fronte all'invasione ottomana (1444–1718)*, Naples, 1955, pp. 35–36, who is referring to the Turks under Mehmed II, not the Christians under Trevisan! Brezzi has passed on his error to Michael Mallett, *The Borgias*, London, 1969, p. 72.

[115] Alfonso was succeeded in the Neapolitan kingdom by his natural son Ferrante I, and in Aragon-Catalonia and Sicily by his brother John II (d. 1479). The latter got along very badly with his son Charles, prince of Viana, whose turbulent career complicated the affairs of Sicily as well as of Aragon-Catalonia until his death in 1461 (see Jaime Vicens Vives, "Trayectoria mediterránea del príncipe de Viana [1458–1461]," in the review *Príncipe de Viana*, XI [1950], 211–50). In June, 1468, John II made his other son Ferdinand king and co-regent of Sicily, and although Ferdinand's activities in Sicily were curtailed by his marriage the following year to Isabella of Castile, his interest in Italian affairs increased with the years, as we shall see (*cf.* Vicens Vives, *El Príncipe Don Fernando [el Católico], rey de Sicilia*, Saragossa, 1949).

[116] Costantino Corvisieri, ed., *Notabilia temporum di Angelo de Tummulillis da Sant'Elia*, Livorno, 1890, p. 78: ". . . Patriarcha Aquilegensis a legatione contra Turchos . . . primo actinsit portum Taranti . . .; postea venit in Apuliam . . ., et inde venit Neapolim per certos dies; postea de mense Januarii venit in abbatiam Casinensem et ibidem commoratus est pluribus diebus, deinde accessit Romam." *Cf.* Paschini, *Lodovico Cardinal Camerlengo*, p. 188, and "La Flotta di Callisto III," *Arch. della R. Società rom. di storia patria*, LIII–LV (1930–32), 251. Paschini has dated Cardinal Lodovico's arrival "a Roma l'otto marzo."

He had been in Rome, however, for some days when on 8 February (1459) he wrote the Marquis Lodovico II Gonzaga (Pastor, *Hist. Popes*, III, 63, note, revised in *Gesch. d. Päpste*, II [repr. 1955], 51, note 3, a letter from the Gonzaga Archives in Mantua): "Significamus vobis nos post varios casus ac pericula que hactenus terra marique perpessi fuimus, tandem concedente altissimo, ad almam urbem Romam redisse atque in ea ad presens esse sanos atque incolumes." I find a very similar letter, also dated "ex urbe Roma die VIII Februarii 1459," from Cardinal Lodovico to Francesco Sforza in the Arch. di Stato di Milano, Arch. Visconteo-Sforzesco, Potenze Estere [Fondo Sforzesco], Cart. 48 (tit. "Roma"), where there are numerous other the Curia at Siena, where he gave a depressing report on the dangers which Rhodes and the other Christian islands faced from impending Turkish attacks. Calixtus III had made an immense effort. It was not his fault that little was accomplished.

A crusade which would stop the Turkish advance was quite beyond anything the papacy could achieve without the full support of the western powers.[117] Such support had been impossible to secure, despite Calixtus's repeated appeals to the rulers of Germany, Poland, France, Burgundy, Denmark and Norway, Portugal, and most of the Italian states. The crusading tithes were widely collected in Europe, but apparently only a small portion of these funds reached Rome. Little or no help came from Milan, Venice, or Florence; Mantua did what it could; but Federigo da Montefeltro prohibited the collection of imposts for the crusade in Urbino.[118] Federigo served as apostolic vicar in the temporal affairs of his

---

letters from Lodovico to Francesco and Bianca, at least one signed in Lodovico's own hand. Calixtus's successor, Pius II, wrote Cardinal Lodovico a note of congratulation on his safe return (Arch. Segr. Vaticano, Arm. XXXIX, tom. 9, fol. 15^{r}, dated at Perugia on 13 February, 1459): "Dilecte fili, salutem, etc. Intelleximus Circumspectionem tuam Romam incolumem applicuisse, quod nobis plurimum placuit et tibi congratulamur. . . ."

The date of Lodovico's return to Rome is thus inaccurately given as 8 March, 1459, in the usually reliable Acta Consistorialia, in Arm. XXXI, tom. 52, fol. 61^{v}: "Adventus domini camerarii : Anno a nativitate Domini MCCCCLVIIII, die vero octava mensis Martii, reverendissimus in Christo pater et dominus, dominus Ludovicus cardinalis camerarius domini nostri papae, veniens de partibus Rodi ubi fuit legatus, intravit urbem, et die XVI mensis Martii intravit Senas ubi papa [Pius II] erat cum Curia et ex[inde] incipit participare, etc." (with an abridgment of the text in Eubel, *Hierarchia*, II [1914, repr. 1960], 32b, and on the "participation" [*incipit participare*] of the cardinals in the *servitia communia*, see A. V. Antonovics, "A Late Fifteenth-Century Division Register of the College of Cardinals," *Papers of the British School at Rome*, XXXV [n.s., XXII, 1967], 87–101). That Lodovico rejoined the Curia at Siena on 16 March is apparently quite correct.

On 30 March Pius II wrote Matteo Contarini, the patriarch of Venice, from Siena that Cardinal Lodovico, recently returned from the East, had reported to him that Rhodes and the islands which the papal fleet had just recovered from the Turks were in grave danger. Pius therefore directed that some 25,000 ducats, which had allegedly been collected in the interests of the crusade from the Venetian territories "in Dalmatia and beyond," should now be employed to assist a papal project for the protection of the islands from the Turks until further steps could be taken at the coming diet of Mantua for the Christian offensive against the Porte (*Pii II brevia*, in Arm. XXXIX, tom. 9, fol. 30, "datum Senis penultimo Martii anno primo").

[117] Pope Pius II in 1461 summed up Cardinal Lodovico's expedition thus (*Asia*, 88, in *Opera quae extant omnia*, Basel, 1551, repr. Frankfurt a. M., 1967, p. 370): "Calixtus tertius Papa . . . classem non parvam in auxilium Rhodiorum misit, quae diu apud eos morata plures Turcarum naves praelio superatas dimersit, et corpora hominum palo suffixit [!]. Staliminumque insulam Lemnum olim appellatam et Taxum et Nembrum [but we have noted that Lodovico did not occupy Imbros] et alias quasdam minoris nominis Turcarum imperio ademit: nec Aegyptios quiescere permisit, neque Syrios neque Cilicias. Sed mortuo Calixto dissoluta classe, Ludovicus Cardinalis Aquileiensis, qui ei praefectus erat, Romam rediit, Rhodo et omni oriente nostri [*sic*] religionis cultore in discrimine summaque desperatione relicto: Et acquisitae insulae ad hostes rediere, cum nos intestinis Italiae motibus et subditorum seditionibus occupati, longinqua prospicere non possemus, praesertim cum Roma ipsa in periculo esset, non solum baronibus per circuitum, sed aliquibus Romanis civibus, res novas molientibus et ecclesiasticae potentiae insidiantibus." Conquests abroad were certainly impossible without peace at home. Pius repeated this passage, almost word for word, in his *Commentarii*, Frankfurt, 1614, p. 205.

[118] *Cf.* Pastor, *Hist. Popes*, II, 376–86, revised in *Gesch. d. Päpste*, I (repr. 1955), 701–9, and Calixtus's letter of 4 December, 1457, to Cardinal Lodovico (Arch. Segr. Vaticano, Arm. XXXIX, tom. 7, fol. 134^{v}, *et alibi*). The correspondence was extensive and the problems numerous (*cf.*, *ibid.*, fols. 132^{r}–133^{v}, a hopeful letter to Cardinal Carvajal). Although for obvious reasons I have regarded northern European and Polish affairs as lying generally outside the scope of this study of papal relations with the Levant, the popes made every effort to collect money for the crusade in these areas. Polish interests were naturally more closely connected with the anti-Turkish enterprise than those of Scandinavia.

The papal registers furnish much information on crusading activity in Poland. On 20 April, 1455, for example, Calixtus appointed Nicholas Spitzinuri (whose name occurs in the registers with different spellings), cantor of the church of Cracow and *decretorum doctor*, as collector and receiver general of the Holy See in Poland (Reg. Vat. 465, fols. 31^{r}–32^{r}); on 21 December following, Calixtus granted him the faculty of giving absolution to those who rendered military service in the war against the Turks or contributed money thereto (Reg. Vat. 440, fols. 89^{r}–90^{r}). Similar grants had been made to Spitzinuri by Nicholas V five years before (Reg. Vat. 393, fols. 297^{r}–300^{r}, docs. dated "anno, etc., MCCCCL, quinto Idus Ianuarii," i.e., 9 January, 1451). Spitzinuri's activity continued into the reign of Pius II, who informed the Polish episcopacy in a letter of 24 August, 1459, ". . . disponimus enim auxiliante deo pro viribus nostris frenare superbiam et insolentiam horum perfidorum Turcorum propter quod iam plurimas in terrestribus et maritimis expeditionibus expenere [*sic*] pecunias non desinimus . . ." (Arm. XXXIX, tom. 8, fols. 67^{v}–68^{r}, where a letter of the same tenor is also addressed to King Casimir IV of Poland, and *cf.* fol. 68^{v}, a letter to Spitzinuri himself). On 17 May, 1465, Paul II appointed Spitzinuri a general collector for the Holy See in Poland, ". . . Romane Ecclesie ac camere apostolice inibi debitorum et debendorum collector ac generalis receptor usque ad nostrum et dicte sedis beneplacitum," the papal concern being especially for the "oblata et data pro Cruciata in subsidium contra Turchum" (Reg. Vat. 542, fols. 65^{r}–67^{r}, by mod. stamped enumeration).

county. When he refused to allow the official announcements of the crusade to be published in his domain or to authorize the collection of tithes or alms, the pope threatened him with the penalty of "excommunication and eternal malediction."[119]

The city of Perugia had promised to contribute four thousand florins to assist Calixtus in the costly effort to prosecute the war against the Turk, but the pope was disappointed in his expectation that the priors, nobles, and citizens would be "as prompt in paying as in promising." Months after their pledge, when Calixtus wrote them in remonstrance on 5 July, 1457, they had still made no move toward converting their commitment into cash.[120] The future looked good for the Turk, "for the enemy of the Christian religion does not sleep," wrote Calixtus, "but even now threatens the kingdom of Hungary with a strong army, and unless he should be met in time, certainly the people of Christendom will be struck with the greatest calamity."[121]

To avert this calamity the pope and the Curia Romana worked unceasingly. For the pope to have kept the equally tireless Cardinal Carvajal informed of every detail of the effort would have exhausted the papal supply of paper: "si singula scriberemus, non sufficeret papirus!"[122] The papal supply of money was more easily exhausted, however, and the collection of the crusading tithe was often made difficult by the failure of the clergy to pay their share.[123] As a Catalan, Calixtus had a special knowledge of ecclesiastical conditions in the three kingdoms of Aragon, Valencia, and Majorca, and of course in the rich principality of Catalonia. The records of his reign show the constant pressure he exerted upon his countrymen to pay their full share of the costs of the projected crusade as he tried to reform the tithe-collecting and the keeping of accounts.[124] As usual, the Florentine bankers were eager to handle funds collected by the pope for the crusade to which their fellow citizens made so small a contribution. Thus on 10 April, 1457, Calixtus wrote Carvajal that he had sent him three thousand ducats by the Medici bank, and more would be coming in due time.[125] Be that as it

[119] Arm. XXXIX, tom. 7, fol. 115r, doc. dated 26 July, 1457, addressed "nobili viro Frederico comiti Urbini in temporalibus vicario nostro."

[120] Arm. XXXIX, tom. 7, fols. 110r–111r.

[121] Letter of Calixtus to Fra Roberto da Lecce, papal nuncio and collector in the duchy of Milan, dated 19 April (1457), in Arm. XXXIX, tom. 7, fol. 88r: ". . . Non enim dormit inimicus Christiane religionis, sed iam im[m]inet regno Hungarie cum valido exercitu, et nisi occurratur in tempore, certe maxima calami[ta]te Christianus populus afficietur."

[122] Arm. XXXIX, tom. 7, fol. 83v, letter to Carvajal, dated 10 April, 1457 (*ibid.*, fol. 84v).

[123] *Cf.*, for example, Calixtus III's letter of 7 July, 1457, to Fra Roberto da Lecce (Arm. XXXIX, tom. 7, fol. 109r): "Per litteras dilecti filii nobilis viri ducis Mediolani et tuas plene intelleximus difficultatem quam facit clerus ille in solvenda decima presenti. . . ."

[124] *Cf.* the various letters to John Soler and Guillem Ponç de Fenollet in Reg. Vat. 441, fols. 18v–21v, *et alibi*. In Reg. Vat. 439, fols. 3r [index], 82r–84v, we may note the appointment of Soler and Guillem Ponç de Fenollet [ffenollet] as "collectores decime in regnis Cathalanis" —"constituuntur nuntii pro decimis colligendis in regnis Aragonum, Valentie, et Maioricarum et principatu [Cathalonie]"—the document begins with the recollection of the occupation of Constantinople by the perfidious Turks, and is dated at S. Peter's in Rome 12 September, *secundo Idus Sept.*, 1455.

On 25 October, 1455, Guillem Ponç de Fenollet [de Fonolleto], canon of the church of Barcelona and *decretorum doctor*, was appointed collector-general for the Apostolic See in Aragon (Reg. Vat. 465, fols. 121v–123), and on 15 May, 1456, was made an apostolic notary (*ibid.*, fol. 176v). Guillem Ponç was an active and trusted servitor of the Catalan pontiff; his name occurs often in the papal registers, but no further notice need be taken of him here. On the last day of February, 1456, the Catalan Antoni Ferrer (Ant. Ferrarii) was appointed a special nuncio to collect tithes owed to the Apostolic Camera in a number of German provinces, in Burgundy, and in England (Reg. Vat. 441, fols. 21v–22v). Calixtus's constant employment of Catalans in the papal service is too well known to require documentation. Although a letter of 26 April, 1458, informs us that a crusading tithe of 50,000 florins had been imposed on the Spanish kingdoms (Arm. XXXIX, tom. 7, fol. 161v), it seems doubtful that the Holy See actually received any appreciable portion of this sum.

[125] Arm. XXXIX, tom. 7, fol. 84r: "Subventionem quam tibi deputavimus statutis terminis eam facere non ommittemus, prout hactenus non ommisimus, et proximis diebus per banchum de Medicis tibi misimus tria milia ducatorum pro tempore quo fuimus usque ad mensem Septembris proxime futurum. . . ." *Cf.*, *ibid.*, fol. 129v, letter to Cosimo de' Medici dated 1 November, 1457. This register (Arm. XXXIX, tom. 7) contains numerous documents relating to the collection of the crusading tithe from various European countries as well as from most of the Italian states, and often mentions the Florentine banking houses of the Pazzi and the Miraballi as handling funds intended for the crusade (e.g., fol. 109): ". . . ex pecuniis decime et cruciate per te collectis in bancho illorum de Pazis tria milia et illorum de Miraballis quatuor milia ducatorum dedisti et consignasti qua re nihil gratius nobis facere potuisti . . . ," letter to Agostino, abbot of Casanova, nuncio and apostolic collector, dated 6 July, 1457, and *cf.*, *ibid.*, the pope's letter of 8 July concerning the receipt of 3,000 ducats from the "societas illorum de Miraballis." Note also Gelcich and Thallóczy, *Diplomatarium ragusanum*, nos. 351–52, pp. 598, 599, concerning Jacopo and Pietro de' Pazzi, whose agent in Ragusa was Martino Clarini. In this year (1457) Jacopo was one of the richest men in Florence (*cf.* Raymond de Roover, *The Rise and Decline of the Medici Bank, 1397–1494*, New York, 1966, pp. 29–30), and his family flourished until the Pazzi conspiracy in 1478.

might, there seemed never to be money enough to match the resources of Mehmed II.

No one, however, either in Rome or elsewhere could question Calixtus III's determination to furnish the imperiled Christians in the East with such help as he could find in the West. On 30 June, 1457, the pope wrote his secretary Lodovico de Narnia that God would bear witness to his daily anxiety for the progress of the crusade, the exaltation of the faith, and the destruction of the sect of Mohammed. He did what he could and more than he could, but most of the European princes were slow and laggardly in their response to the needs of Christendom.[126] Papal exhortations received of course much more attention from eastern rulers, whose lands and people were exposed to constant attack by the Turks. Earlier in the month (on 4 June, 1457) Calixtus had written Scanderbeg to persist without discouragement in his role as a strong athlete and true defender of the Christian faith, for God would no more desert Scanderbeg than he had Hunyadi the year before. In both 1455 and '56 the Turks had invaded Albania, and were now sending a huge army against Scanderbeg and his frightened people.[127]

On 20 June (1457) Calixtus informed Cardinal Carvajal that King Stephen Thomas of Bosnia had just sent two Franciscans as envoys to Rome with the royal assurance that he was planning to take the field against the Turks, and that he had discontinued the tribute which he had been paying each year to Sultan Mehmed II. Carvajal was to assist the king to the fullest possible extent in his laudable resolution to oppose Mehmed's advance toward the Adriatic.[128] Stephen Thomas did actually attack and

---

[126] Arch. Segr. Vaticano, Arm. XXXIX, tom. 7, fol. 106[r], by mod. stamped enumeration.

[127] Arm. XXXIX, tom. 7, fol. 99[v], by mod. stamped enumeration, dated 9 June, 1457, "Georgio Castrioto Scandarbeg." The pope acknowledged the receipt of two letters from Scanderbeg, informing him "de adventu perfidorum Turcorum ad expugnationem terrarum tuarum, ex quo significas te non parvo timore perculsum . . ." (*ibid.*). On 26 July, 1455, an Albanian army of 14,000 men, including Catalan contingents sent by Alfonso V of Naples, was badly defeated at Berat ("Belgrado") by strong Turkish forces alleged to have numbered *da circha 40,000 cavalli . . . , e hano tra morti e presi da cinque in sei milia Cristiani* (J. Radonić, *Djuradj Kastriot Skenderbeg*, Belgrade, 1942, nos. 95–97, pp. 54–55, docs. dated 8, 14, 22 August, 1455, reprinted from V. V. Makušev, in the *Monumenta historica slavorum meridionalium vicinorumque populorum*, II [Belgrade, 1882], 147–51, and *cf.* M. Barletius, *De vita et gestis Scanderbegi*, 1st ed., Rome, *ca.* 1509, bk. VIII, fols. XCVIII[v]–CII[r]; ed. Zagreb, 1743, pp. 225–33, who describes the battle in full and rather unreliable detail). *Cf.* Francisc Pall, "Marino Barlezio," in *Mélanges d'histoire générale*, ed. C. Marinescu, II (Bucharest, 1938), 210–211, and see in general Joseph Gill, "Pope Callistus III and Scanderbeg the Albanian," *Orientalia Christiana periodica*, XXXIII (1967), 534–62, with seventeen documents from the Arch. Segr. Vaticano.

For details concerning the Albanian defeat at Berat (on 26 July, 1455), see F. Pall, "I Rapporti italo-albanesi intorno alla metà del secolo XV," in the *Archivio storico per le province napoletane*, LXXXIII (3rd ser., IV, 1966), docs. I–II, pp. 153–57, and *cf.*, *ibid.*, pp. 141–42. This article, *ibid.*, pp. 123–226, with eighty-eight documents from the Arch. di Stato di Milano, is one of the most valuable studies relating to Scanderbeg which has appeared in recent years. An entry in the Neapolitan treasury accounts for 28 August, 1455 (by which time the extent of the defeat at Berat was fully understood in Naples), would seem to indicate that Alfonso V was preparing to send Scanderbeg more assistance immediately (Camillo Minieri Riccio, "Alcuni Fatti di Alfonso I. di Aragona . . . [1437–1458]," *ibid.*, VI [1881], 432, from the Cedole della Regia Tesoreria, no. 29, fol. 276[v]): "E [Alfonso] fa consegnare a Giovanni Catalano contestabile de'balestrieri e de'fanti *che spedisce in Albania contro il Turco* lo stendardo che à fatto costruire dal suo arazziere Cirillo Gallinaro e dal suo pittore Leonardo Bruzzo. . . ."

[128] Arm. XXXIX, tom. 7, fol. 104[r] (and *cf.* fols. 112[v]–114[v]): "Calistus, etc. Dilecte fili, salutem. Venere ad nos proximis diebus dilecti filii Britius de Pannonia et Demetrius de Albania, fratres Ordinis Minorum, missi a carissimo in Christo filio nostro [Stephano Thome], Rege Bosne illustri, et multa nobis retulerunt de fide et devotione ipsius regis erga nos et religionem Christianam et de optimo ac laudabili proposito sue Serenitatis prodeundi viriliter in Turcos et expugnationem eorum pessime nationis et quod iam ipse rex desiit pendere tributum quod hactenus ipsi tyranno Turcorum dare consuevit. . . ." On 30 April, 1455, King Stephen and his family had been taken under the special protection of the Holy See (Reg. Vat. 436, fols. 23[v]–24[r], 32).

On 24 June, 1457, Giovanni Castiglione, bishop of Pavia, who had received the red hat in mid-December (1456), wrote Francesco Sforza from Rome: "Havemo qui novelle che Monsignore el Cardinale di Sancto Angelo [Carvajal] è partito de Buda per andare in Bosna: el Re de Bosna desydera pigliare la croce et fare tuto il suo sforzo contra il Turcho . . ." but Castiglione had small hope of Carvajal's accomplishing anything in Bosnia, and (as he told the pope) "seria meglio che dicto Monsignore di S. Angelo fusse rimasto . . ." (Makušev, *Monumenta historica slavorum meridionalium*, II, 199, and note also p. 217). About eleven weeks later (on 7 September) Castiglione wrote that the Turks had occupied almost all the lowlands of Albania. Scanderbeg had fled into the mountain fastnesses. The pope was allegedly sending him some money "per alcuna sua consolatione" (*ibid.*).

A year before this (in June, 1456), two envoys of Stephen Thomas, "Dei gratia rex Bossine, etc.," had requested aid and counsel of the doge and Signoria of Venice, "ad providendum et resistendum perverse voluntati huius scevissimi tyranni imperatoris Turcorum, qui totaliter intendit extorquere a nobis regnum nostrum: Et quamvis hucusque sue insatiabili voluntati ac suorum predecessorum satisfecerimus plurimis occupy a few Turkish strongholds in Serbia, but early in 1458 he reached an agreement with Mehmed, who appears to have ratified Stephen's possession of the major portion of his conquests in return for a tribute of nine thousand ducats.[129] Although a good Catholic in the kingdom of the Bogomils, Stephen Thomas was no crusader. He also failed to understand that one could not fight with the Turk and make peace with him as self-interest, opportunity, or convenience might suggest. A few years later Stephen's son and successor, Stephen Tomašević, last of the Bosnian kings, was to lose his life as a result of his father's ambition.

During these years, however, the eyes of the Curia Romana like those of Europe at large were often fixed upon Scanderbeg who, casting about everywhere for aid, appealed to Francesco Sforza, duke of Milan. Sforza replied on 20 June, 1456, expressing his sympathy for the Albanian's plight, *maximum imminens vestre Celsitudini periculum . . . quod a nephandissimo Turcorum rege contra provinciam illam vestram videtur preparari.* He sent Scanderbeg no aid, however, merely reminding him that Calixtus III had already dispatched the papal fleet, under the cardinal legate Lodovico Trevisan, against the Turks and that Alfonso V of Aragon-Naples was preparing "with all his might" for an offensive against the sultan both on land and at sea.[130]

Already gravely concerned over the traitorous relations of various prominent Albanians with the Turks, Scanderbeg again witnessed an almost overwhelming invasion of his country by the Turks in the midsummer of 1457. On 31 July the Doge Francesco Foscari was informed that Scanderbeg, abandoned by all his chieftains, had apparently fled into the mountains before a Turkish army of some eighty thousand men, which was said to represent "tuta la possanza del Gran Turco."[131] On 11 September (1457) Pope Calixtus wrote Scanderbeg that he had received the indescribably bad news from the Albanian emissary who had been sent to Rome. He promised Scanderbeg funds from the money collected for the crusade in the region of Ragusa and in Dalmatia, although the hard-pressed kings of Hungary and Bosnia were also seeking funds from this source for employment against the Turks.[132] Paying the

---

pecuniis cum maximo detrimento nostro nostrorumque subditorum, nunquam tamen gravavimus aliquos Christianos principes." The sultan was, however, no longer content with money. He was demanding four Bosnian castles, one of which (*unum castrum videlicet Bystrychky*) was only a day's journey from the Venetian cities of Spalato (Split), Traù (Trogir), Sebenico (Šibenik), and Zara (Zadar). The Senate allowed Stephen Thomas to recruit, at his own expense, up to one hundred crossbowmen (*ballistarii*) in Venetian Dalmatia, and granted him and all who might come with him (but God avert the necessity!) refuge in Venetian territory (Arch. di Stato di Venezia, Sen. Secreta, Reg. 20, fols. 93ᵛ–94ᵛ [94ᵛ–95ᵛ], the Senate's responses to the Bosnian envoys being dated 14 June, 1456, and *cf.* fols. 140ᵛ [142ᵛ], 153 [155]).

[129] Iorga, *Gesch. d. osman. Reiches*, II (1909), 108. Stephen Thomas aspired to rule over Danubian Serbia. Toward the end of the year 1458 his son and namesake, Stephen Tomašević, was betrothed to Helena, only daughter of Lazar, the late despot of Serbia. The marriage took place on 1 May, 1459, thus effecting the dynastic union of Bosnia with Danubian Serbia. Mehmed II, however, could not abide the Bosnian ambition, and with the Turkish occupation (in July, 1459) of the important city of Semendria, at the confluence of the Morava and the Danube, the Stephens' almost imperial dream collapsed. Helena withdrew to Hungary and thereafter to Italy, where she lived under papal protection, dying in a nun's garb in 1474. *Cf.* Iorga, *op. cit.*, II, 108–9; Chalcocondylas, bk. IX (Bonn, pp. 459–60; ed. Darkó, II, 216–17). Semendria is the modern Smederevo.

[130] Pall, "I Rapporti italo-albanesi," *Arch. stor. per le province napoletane*, LXXXIII (1966), doc. III, pp. 157–59. Francesco Sforza had no intention of becoming embroiled with Mehmed II (*cf.* Luigi Fumi, "Il Disinteresse di Francesco I Sforza alla crociata di Calisto III contro i turchi . . . ," *Archivio storico lombardo*, XXXIX [4th ser., XVII, 1912], 101–111). There is an interesting but rather rapid survey of Milanese relations with the Ottoman sultans in Franz Babinger, "Relazioni visconteo-sforzesche con la corte ottomana durante il secolo XV," in the *Atti del Convegno la Lombardia e l'Oriente* [June, 1962], Milan, 1963, pp. 8–30. As for Francesco Sforza, at the time he received Scanderbeg's appeal, he was concentrating on building up the duchy he had acquired a half-dozen years before. Georges Peyronnet, "Il Ducato di Milano sotto Francesco Sforza (1450–1466): Politica interna, vita economica e sociale," *Archivio storico italiano*, CXVI (1958), 36–53, provides an instructive, succinct sketch of Sforza's internal policy—an efficient administration, patronage of the arts, attention to public works and irrigation, promotion of agriculture, viticulture, and industry, and the further development of commerce —all rather remarkable in an unlettered condottiere. Scanderbeg recognized the suzerainty of Alfonso V, "cuius nos vasalum esse et capitaneum istis in partibus," as Scanderbeg wrote Francesco Sforza from Croia on 18 July, 1456, "vestram Celsitudinem latere non credimus" (Pall, *op. cit.*, doc. IV, p. 161).

[131] V. V. Makušev, *Monumenta historica slavorum meridionalium*, II (1882), 113–14, report of Marco Diedo, bailie and captain of Durazzo, on whom *cf.* Hopf, *Chron. gréco-romanes* (1873, repr. 1966), 390–91.

[132] In a somewhat abusive but not irrelevant article Stavri N. Naçi, "À propos de quelques truchements concernant les rapports de la papauté avec Skanderbeg durant la lutte albano-turque (1443–1468)," *Studia Albanica*, V-1 (Tirana, 1968), 73–86, holds certain historians up to opprobrium on the grounds that "ils firent mettre la

highest tribute to Scanderbeg's valor and well-earned fame, Calixtus said, "Nemo enim est tam ignarus rerum qui non summis laudibus ad celum te extollat, et de tua nobilitate tanquam de vero athleta et propugnatore nominis Christiani non loquatur. . . ." To aid the Albanian athlete and champion the pope even thought of diverting Cardinal Lodovico Trevisan's fleet or part of it, if necessary, from operations in the eastern Mediterranean. In any event Scanderbeg had only to hold on until the coming winter, after which a vast army would be proceeding against the sultan's forces in response to the pope's warnings, prayers, and tears to effect the complete destruction of "that mad dog and serpent, the Turk." Scanderbeg would see wonders performed, and could console himself for his losses by the happy sight of the Turks defeated and in flight. Calixtus made no vain boast, for God would aid their cause. The victorious spectacle of Belgrade was held up to Scanderbeg as the hope and expectation of the future: "Magna hec fuerunt, sed maiora restant que deus faciet pro tutela populi sui." The land and sea would soon be swarming with Christian troops to exterminate the pestiferous Turk, and so it well behooved Scanderbeg, "as an unconquered soldier and athlete of Christ," to sustain with his accustomed courage the Turkish attack, which would soon "be reduced to nothing." In the meantime, however, Calixtus was sending John Navarre, a papal shield-bearer (*scutifer*), into Dalmatia to collect the promised funds and convey them to Scanderbeg, with whom John might remain as long as the latter wished to keep him.[133] Calixtus's expectations of the future proved to be justified, surprisingly enough, for in September, 1457, Scanderbeg descended upon the great Turkish army in the region of Mount Tomor (Maj'-e-Tomorrit, eleven miles east of Berat), and taking the invaders quite by surprise won a remarkable victory over them.[134]

---

livrée religieuse à la lutte des Albanais pour la liberté, ils transformèrent Skanderbeg en croisé, et les fruits de l'héroisme populaire furent censés d'être les fruits de l'aide en argent de la papauté" (p. 78), although over the quarter-century of his struggle against the Turks Scanderbeg hardly received more than 20,000 ducats from the Holy See (according to Naçi), which sum would not have provided for the continuous maintenance of twenty armed men, at three to five ducats per man in monthly wages (pp. 81–82 ff.). Actually, however, Albania was one part of a long Christian front opposed to the Turks, which included Hungary, Styria, Carinthia, Carniola, Croatia, Bosnia, Dalmatia, Serbia, Rhodes, and the Aegean islands under Venetian and Genoese domination (*cf.* the article, referred to above in note 25, by Sciambra, Valentini, and Parrino, in the *Bollettino della Badia greca di Grottaferrata*, n.s., XXI [1967], 83–136).

[133] Arch. Segr. Vaticano, Arm. XXXIX, tom. 7, fols. 122^v–123^r, by mod. stamped enumeration, dated 11 September, 1457, "Georgio Castriotti Scandarbech Albanie domino," published by A. Theiner, ed., *Vetera monumenta historica Hungariam sacram illustrantia*, II (Rome, 1860), no. 472, pp. 303–4. *Cf.* also the pope's letters to King Stephen of Bosnia, Cardinal Carvajal, Scanderbeg, the rector and council of Ragusa, and others including the doge of Venice, in Arm. XXXIX, tom. 7, fols. 123^v–125^v, 141^v, and 142^r–143^r.

On 10 September (1457) the pope had appointed John Navarre papal commissioner for the crusade in Albania and Dalmatia, "considerantes quot labores et discrimina perpessi hactenus sint et in dies patiantur carissimi in Christo filii nostri, Hungarie et Bosne reges illustres necnon dilectus filius nobilis vir Georgius Castrioti dictus Scandarbech Albanie dominus, qui prope soli oppositi sunt furori barbarorum et Turchorum . . ." (Reg. Vat. 449, fol. 172^r, and publ. by A. Theiner, ed., *Vetera monumenta Slavorum meridionalium historiam illustrantia*, I [Rome, 1863], no. 604, p. 427). Having learned of the terrible Turkish irruption into Albania, the pope directed John to proceed there with all haste to take charge of the tithes and other funds collected for the crusade in the cities of Ragusa and Antivari as well as throughout all Dalmatia: ". . . Decem mille ducatis de Camera exceptis qui de mandato nostro mercatoribus societatis de Pazis [the Florentine banking firm of the Pazzi family] apud illas partes moram trahentibus consignari debent et ex dictis pecuniis omnino, nisi iam consignati fuerint, consignari mandamus ratione maioris summe de qua mercatores predicti pro hoc sancto opere nobis subvenerunt: a quibuscumque collectoribus . . . depositariis et aliis, apud quos quovis modo [pecunie] sunt et esse contingent, habere procures easque in partes tres equas dividas, quarum unam prefato regi Hungarie, alteram regi Bosne, tertiam vero memorato Scandarbech aut eorum procuratoribus effectualiter consignes . . ." (*ibid.*).

The pope was especially anxious that Scanderbeg receive his share of the available funds as soon as possible because of the perilous state of Albanian affairs. Provision was also made at this time for the restoration and support of two important churches in Albania, and a *littera passus* was granted to Paul, abbot of the monastery of S. Maria de Trefandena (Reg. Vat. 449, fols. 172^v–174^r). In an undated document, toward the end of 1455, Calixtus had appointed one Jacobus de Cadaporto, "archidiaconus ecclesie Quironensis," collector of the tithe in Dalmatia (Reg. Vat. 440, fols. 71^v–72^v).

[134] On 24 September, 1457, Calixtus wrote Guillem Ponç de Fenollet, the apostolic collector in Aragon, ". . . et in Albania et ubique victoria adeo continue nobis datur contra perfidos Mahometicos . . ." (Raynaldus, *Ann. eccl.*, ad ann. 1457, no. 31, vol. XVIII [1694], p. 491a). *Cf.* Hopf, "Griechenland im Mittelalter," in Ersch and Gruber, *Allgemeine Encyklopädie*, vol. 86 (1868, and repr. New York, 1960, II), 134–35; Iorga, *Gesch. d. osman. Reiches*, II, 84; F. S. Noli, *Geo. Castrioti Scanderbeg*, New York, 1947, pp. 52–53, with refs. on pp. 205–6. Despite Cardinal Lodovico Trevisan's naval successes and Scanderbeg's defeat of the Turks in Albania (which had led Calixtus to see "victory everywhere"),

Scanderbeg was not only one of the most remarkable soldiers of the fifteenth century. He was also a political realist. The historian who studies the documentary sources relating to his career finds constant evidence of the clarity of Scanderbeg's vision. Like the popes, he had a simple view of what were proper relations with the Turks. One always fought with them, making peace (when possible) only to gain time for further preparations for war. However much the Venetians, Genoese, and Moreote Greeks might try to weigh the pros and cons of peaceful co-existence with the Turks, Scanderbeg believed that the ultimate price of such a peace would be degrading servitude. Whatever sense of honor the earlier sultans may have entertained, Mehmed II was unimpeded by moral scruples. A ruthless egotist, an arrogant dreamer, he attached no value to human life and had small regard for the dignity of others. The ruler of a slave state, his idea of world conquest was simply the enslavement of mankind. Long the enemies of imperial ambition, whether manifesting itself in Byzantium or in Germany, the popes could only find the Gran Turco doubly repulsive both as a conqueror and as an infidel. It is no wonder they turned to Scanderbeg as their champion. His political ambition was confined to Albania, where he was trying to construct a centralized state, ousting the quarreling chieftains from their mountain strongholds. But they too had the highlanders' attachment to independence, and they often appealed to the Gran Turco to help them against the tyranny of Scanderbeg. There was a difference, however, between these two Albanian views of freedom. The chieftains looked back with nostalgia upon a chaotic past, and Scanderbeg looked forward to the establishment of a centralized Christian state. Turkish domination would succeed in giving the Albanians the worst of both worlds, at least in Scanderbeg's opinion, imposing the arbitrary rule the chieftains feared and detaching Albania from the *respublica Christiana*, the commonwealth of Europe.

---

the government of Ragusa saw no diminution of Mehmed II's power. On 14 November, 1457, the Ragusei wrote King Ladislas Postumus of Hungary: "Hostem ferocissimum [i.e., Magnum Turchum], terra marique victorem et rebus nostris infestissimum, timemus et in dies ad ruinam nostram expectamus . . ." (Gelcich and Thallóczy, *Diplomatarium ragusanum* [1887], no. 353, p. 601; J. Radonić, ed., *Acta et diplomata ragusina*, I, pt. 2 [Belgrade, 1934], no. 267, p. 604).

7. PIUS II, THE CONGRESS OF MANTUA, AND THE TURKISH CONQUEST OF THE MOREA (1458–1461)

SULTAN MEHMED II had set the Moreote tribute at 10,000 or 12,000 ducats a year, as we have seen, but by 1457 it had become three years in arrears. Although Turkish emissaries were sent into the Morea to demand the tribute, it was still not forthcoming, and Mehmed now gave the Despots Thomas and Demetrius the alternatives of paying the annual assessment on their domains or surrendering the Morea to him. According to Critobulus, the despots collected ample sums from the Albanians to pay the tribute, but spent the money on themselves. Entertaining undue hopes of the naval expedition sent by Pope Calixtus into eastern waters under Cardinal Lodovico Trevisan, the brothers had held off until it was too late. In April, 1458, Mehmed set out from Adrianople (Edirne) with a large army recruited in Asia Minor, Macedonia, and Thessaly. Arriving in Thessaly, he stopped for some days to rest his army, wait for more troops, and give envoys from the despots a chance to appear with the tribute. Critobulus says that if envoys had come, bringing the tribute and asking for peace, the sultan would have given up the expedition, "for he had other urgent matters to attend to" (εἶχε γὰρ ἄλλα τὰ κατεπείγοντα). No envoys came from the despots, however, and the order to advance was given.

Traversing the plains of Thessaly, the Ottoman army came through the pass of Thermopylae, skirted Lake Copais, and encamped in Boeotia in the valley of the river Asopus, in the region of Plataea. While his scouts were reconnoitering the roads and passes through Mount Cithaeron to the south, envoys arrived from Thomas with 4,500 ducats. They had come too late. Mehmed took the money, and remarked with derision that he would arrange terms of peace when he arrived in the Morea. He reached the Isthmus of Corinth on 15 May, "as the grain was ripening," says Critobulus, and went through the Hexamilion without opposition. He spent some time trying to bombard the fortress built on the towering rock of Acrocorinth, its one approach girt with triple walls, but finding his efforts futile, he laid waste the surrounding fields and vineyards, and left a division of his Anatolian forces behind to invest the fortress and starve its garrison into submission.[1] Within a few days the Turks occupied all the other strong places in Corinthia.

Advancing into the Morea, Mehmed took the road to Nemea, then turned west through the district of Phlius, beyond which he laid siege to an Albanian town called Tarsus, on the road from ancient Pellene to Pheneus (Phonia, west of Mount Cyllene). Tarsus soon surrendered, giving up a group of three hundred boys for possible enrollment in the janissaries. The local chieftain, Doxas or Doxies, defended the stronghold of Phlius valiantly with a force of Greeks and Albanians until Mehmed cut off their only source of water, whereupon they even tried to bake bread with the blood of slaughtered beasts of burden. While they were seeking terms for surrender, the Turks forced an entry through an unguarded section of the wall and reduced the defenders and other inhabitants to slavery. Next Mehmed attacked and took the castle town of Akova.[2] Going on to the town

[1] According to Critobulus, *De rebus gestis Mechemetis II*, III, 3–4 (ed. K. Müller, *Fragmenta historicorum Graecorum* [*FHG*], V-1 [Paris, 1870], p. 122a; ed. V. Grecu, *Critobul din Imbros: Din domnia lui Mahomed al II-lea*, Bucharest, 1963, pp. 219, 221, 223), the Anatolian troops were left before Corinth under the grand vizir, Mahmud Pasha, whom we shall meet often in the following pages. Wm. Miller, *Latins in the Levant*, London, 1908, p. 432, has followed Critobulus without question, not noticing that Mahmud must have been in Serbia at this time (Chalcocondylas, bk. IX, ed. Bonn, pp. 443 ff.; ed. E. Darkó, II-2 [Budapest, 1927], pp. 202 ff.; and Geo. Sphrantzes, *Chron. minus*, in *Patrologia Graeca*, vol. 156, col. 1065C; ed. Grecu, *Geo. Sphrantzes . . . în anexă Pseudo-Phrantzes*, Bucharest, 1966, p. 108). *Cf.* Fr. Babinger, *Maometto il Conquistatore*, Turin, 1957, pp. 240–41.

On 3 June, 1458, Roberto di Sanseverino, having reached Durazzo on his way eastward (on a pilgrimage to Palestine), wrote Francesco Sforza, duke of Milan, "che el Turcho ha havuto la Morea . . . , e stimase che dicto Turcho debia andare a canpo a Nigroponte o veramente a Croya contra de Scandarbeco longe de qui diece miglia" (Francisc Pall, "I Rapporti italo-albanesi intorno alla metà del secolo XV," *Archivio storico per le province napoletane*, LXXXIII [3rd ser., IV, 1966], doc. v, pp. 162–64). There was some fear that Mehmed might employ his forces, after the Moreote campaign, against Venetian Negroponte or against Scanderbeg, who was said to be "ten miles" from Durazzo.

[2] Chalcocondylas, bk. IX (Bonn, p. 445, line 15, *Akribe* [*Akrivi*]; ed. Darkó, II-2, p. 204, line 22, *Akobe* [*Akova*]); Sphrantzes, *Chron. minus* (*PG* 156, 1065D; ed. Grecu, p.

of Roupele, where both Greeks and Albanians had sought refuge, as the Turkish cavalry scoured the countryside, the Turks tried for two days to storm the place. Its frightened defenders resisted the onslaught so strenuously that Mehmed was ready to give up the attempt to take Roupele when they finally surrendered. The population was spared but sent to Istanbul, which the sultan was trying to repopulate. But at Roupele the Turks seized twenty Albanians who had been allowed to withdraw from Tarsus on their given word not to bear arms against the sultan again. Mehmed had these poor wretches put to death after breaking their hands and feet.

Continuing his southward course past Arcadian Orchomenus, where remains of a medieval fortress still repay a hard climb to the summit of the hill, Mehmed entered the region of Arcadian Mantineia. He had with him Manuel "Ghin" Cantacuzenus, whom the Albanians had proclaimed "despot" in 1453. Cantacuzenus failed, however, to convince the people of Pazanike to lay down their arms, and being suspected of treachery by the Turks, he fled, going eventually to Hungary (where he died some years later). Mehmed soon reached Tegea in the heart of the peninsula. Now the despots fled to the coast, Thomas to Laconian Mantineia (Mandinie) and Demetrius to Monemvasia (ancient Epidaurus Limera). Mehmed would have liked to take this famous fortress, according to Chalcocondylas, but yielded to the advice he received not to attempt it. It was well off the beaten track, and the terrain of southeast Laconia would make it difficult and dangerous to reach. Instead he attacked the hilltop fortress of Mouchli (near Tegea), where again he cut off the water supply, and the town surrendered after a three-day siege.[3]

Moving northwest across country toward Patras, Thomas's capital, along steep and nearly impassable roads, Mehmed ravaged the whole area through which he went. The inhabitants of Patras fled before him, some of them crossing the strait to Lepanto (Naupactus); the garrison, fearing his cannon, surrendered, and their lives were spared. Impressed with the region of Patras, both the site of the city and the fertility of the soil, Mehmed offered all the inhabitants who would return immediately both the restitution of their property and some years' exemption from taxes. According to Critobulus, he now sent part of his army to overrun Elis and Messenia, "and to pillage them thoroughly and to bring him all the booty" (III, 5). He himself advanced upon Corinth, taking Vostitza, the ancient Aegium, on the way. Corinth had been under siege for many weeks. The sultan's army was weary. The Turkish depredation of the preceding May had stripped the area of feed for horses, cattle, and beasts of burden. Since Matthew Asan, the governor of Corinthia, refused to surrender, Mehmed decided to try renewed cannonading and an assault.

The besiegers battered down a part of the wall and the first gate on the southwest slope of Acrocorinth with cannon which they mounted on the pointed rock of Penteskuphi a mile southwest of the fortress. According to Chalcocondylas, one of the stone cannonballs missed the wall, demolished the garrison bakery, killed a man, somehow cleared the northern parapet in its amazing trajectory, and destroyed the naval warehouse in the lower town—a cannonball weighing nine hundred pounds (seven talents) being shot over a mile and a half (fourteen stadia)! When the order for the assault was given, the main attacking force scampered up the steep ascent which winds around the rocks on the west slope. They made their way through the first gate in the ruined outer wall to the second gate, from which they were turned back in hand-to-hand fighting and especially by the volleys of great stones hurled down from the walls and towers above them by the defenders. Despite his determination to remain

---

108) and Pseudo-Sphrantzes, *Chron. maius*, IV, 15 (Bonn, p. 387, line 7; ed. Grecu, p. 526, line 17), Akova. Akova (Matagrifon) was one of the dozen great Frankish baronies, dating from the early period of the conquest.

[3] Mouchli is located between Tripolis and Argos. According to the *Libro de los fechos*, ed. and trans. A. Morel-Fatio, Geneva, 1885, par. 485, p. 106, it was first established by the Greeks in 1296 as an outpost against the Franks. The name Mouchli was derived from that of a monastery founded in 1281 in Constantinople; it is mentioned in Andronicus II's chrysobull of 1314, and again in Italian sources of 1398. Mouchli was still a Byzantine frontier post against the Franks in 1417. In 1458, on the occasion of its capture by Mehmed II, described in the text, the painter Digenis fled from the city to Crete. In the earlier Turkish period Mouchli was, after Corinth, the chief fortress in the Morea, but it was deserted by the early eighteenth century. There are numerous scattered remains on the site today, the most important being those of a church dedicated to the Virgin. See E. Darkó, "*Περὶ τῆς ἱστορίας καὶ τῶν μνημείων τοῦ* Μουχλίου," *Πρακτικὰ τῆς* 'Ακαδημίας 'Αθηνῶν, VI (1931), 22–29. When I visited the tall, dome-like hill of Mouchli (in 1960), its lower reaches were under cultivation, its upper portions abandoned to goats and travelers who like to climb.

before Acrocorinth until he had taken the citadel, Mehmed ordered a retreat from the gates, deciding that hunger would be his best weapon after all. He could afford to wait, for the raiding party he had dispatched to Elis and Messenia had returned, bringing back, according to the report Critobulus had heard, fifteen thousand sheep, oxen, and horses, as well as four thousand captives. The latter were sent to the Bosporus to help populate the suburbs of Istanbul. The sheep and cattle would support the army for the long siege that seemed necessary. If Mehmed's army had had difficulties, conditions in Acrocorinth had become desperate.

The embattled Corinthians were well led. Their commander, Matthew Asan, was governor not only of their city and fortress, but also of "no small part of the Peloponnesus."[4] He was the brother-in-law of the Despot Demetrius, as we have noted, and was undoubtedly the military mainstay of the government at Mistra. Matthew had been absent in the Venetian colony at Nauplia when he first learned of the Turkish investment of Corinth. He had hurried back (Critobulus says Demetrius sent him) to try to save one of the finest fortresses in the Levant. He climbed the little-known and precipitous path up the north wall of Acrocorinth under the cover of night with seventy men, each of whom carried such grain and supplies as he could. When these slender provisions were exhausted, there was much grumbling among the inhabitants of the citadel, which seems to have been identical with the city, for few people dwelt in the lower town at this time. Some of them finally went to the metropolitan of Corinth, who shared their fears and sympathized with their complaints. While Matthew urged the populace to stand firm, the metropolitan sent a messenger to the sultan, telling him of the lack of food and indicating that persistence would bring him success. Mehmed then informed Matthew that friends within the walls had apprised him of the defenders' plight. He called on him to give up Acrocorinth. Most of the garrison had lost heart. Further resistance would merely make the terms of surrender more onerous without saving the citadel. On 6 August Matthew admitted the Turks to Acrocorinth on condition that the inhabitants might continue to live there without let or hindrance and merely pay tribute. At the same time he arranged a peace for the despots, who were to pay, according to Critobulus, three thousand ducats (*nomismata*) each year. They were also to cede to the Porte all the cities and castles the sultan had taken as well as all the territory his forces had entered, which Critobulus estimates at about one-third of the Morea.

The remainder of the peninsula should belong to the despots, but since the sultan held Patras, Vostitza, and Kalavryta, Thomas had lost his capital and two of his chief cities. The Turkish acquisition of Acrocorinth was an absolutely irremediable loss for both brothers. Matthew met them at Trype, near the mouth of the Langada Gorge, and presented them with Mehmed's terms. They found no alternative to acceptance, although Sphrantzes was shocked by the loss of Corinth, "the head on the Moreote body," and complains that the cities which the great Constantine Dragases had won were ceded by Thomas to the sultan "as though they were garden vegetables." Mehmed left four hundred janissaries behind as a garrison in Corinth, well provided with food, arms, and cannon. He repaired and garrisoned such other captured cities as he believed essential to his continued domination of the areas in which they were located. Some fortresses he demolished, sending their inhabitants to Istanbul to reside in the suburbs of the city, to which he had just transferred from Adrianople the capital of the Ottoman empire. At the end of the summer Mehmed withdrew from the Morea, leaving Turakhan's son Omar Beg as governor of the new Turkish province of the Morea. He went on to Athens, Plataea, Chalcis (Negroponte), Pherae (Velestinon), and finally back to Adrianople.[5] He had desolated the Morea.

[4] *Cf.* Chalcocondylas, bk. VIII (Bonn, p. 413, lines 18–19; ed. Darkó, II-2, p. 176, lines 6–8).

[5] The account in the text seeks to effect a synthesis of the following sources: Critobulus, III, 1, 3–9 (ed. Müller, *FHG*, V-1, pp. 120–26; ed. Grecu [1963], pp. 215 ff.); Chalcocondylas, bks. VIII, IX (Bonn, pp. 414, 442–52 and ff.; ed. Darkó, II-2, 176, 202–11 and ff.); Sphrantzes, *Chron. minus* (*PG* 156, 1065D–1066AB; ed. Grecu [1966], pp. 108, 110); Pseudo-Sphrantzes, IV, 15 (Bonn, pp. 387–88; ed. Grecu [1966], pp. 526, 528); Ducas, *Hist. byzantina*, chap. 45 (Bonn, pp. 339–40; ed. Grecu, *Istoria turco-bizantină [1341–1462]*, Bucharest, 1958, pp. 423, 425, 427); *Chronicon breve*, ad ann. 1458 (in the Bonn edition of Ducas, pp. 520–21); Ioann. Cartanus, *Anthos*, ad ann. 1457–1458, ed. Hopf, *Chroniques gréco-romanes* (1873, repr. 1966), pp. 267–68; and Stefano Magno, *Estratti degli Annali veneti*, *ibid.*, p. 200. *Cf.* Hopf, "Griechenland im Mittelalter," in Ersch and Gruber, *Allgemeine Encyklopädie*, vol. 86 (1868; repr. vol. II [1960]), p. 127; Wm. Miller, *Latins in the*

In October, Mehmed sent an envoy to Demetrius, asking for the hand in marriage of his daughter Helena, the despot's only child, and making clear that his refusal to send the girl to the Ottoman court to enter the sultan's harem would mean war. The same envoy then sought out Thomas at Pontiko, exacted an oath of vassalage from him, and arranged for the surrender of the castles which Thomas had to give up according to the terms agreed upon the preceding August.[6] Even as the envoy departed, Thomas began to repent of his docility.

Historians both medieval and modern have believed that the bellicose despot Thomas now brought about the complete destruction of the Morea, abetted by a born intriguer, Nicephorus Lucanes. The latter had caused much agitation in the Morea ever since the beginning of the Albanian revolt when, a fellow prisoner of Giovanni "Centurione" Asan in the castle of Chloumoutsi (Clermont), he had helped plan Centurione's escape and supported his futile attempt to seize power from Thomas in 1453–1454. Now in January '59 the energetic Lucanes, whom Sphrantzes calls the "plague of the Morea" (Μορεοφθόρος), persuaded Thomas to attack his brother Demetrius and to rebel against Sultan Mehmed, "and to eat like so many vegetables the oaths which he had rendered them a little while before."[7] But the background of the final Graeco-Turkish contest, which was to extinguish the last remnants of Palaeologian authority in the Morea, is rather more complicated, for example, than the late William Miller has represented it in his well-known study of the *Latins in the Levant*.

The Despot Thomas had been the heavy loser in 1458, and so he had the more cause to try to restore the political conditions which had existed in the Morea before Mehmed's invasion. Undoubtedly Thomas was ill-advised and reckless, and released a flood which he was powerless to control and which finally swept him away. Undoubtedly too the predatory Greek magnates and officials did all they could to stir up the troubled waters in which they were forever casting their own nets. They were also to be swept away in the deluge. Zakythinos has observed, however, that the two despots represented "two different aspects of the Greek mentality of the epoch."[8] Demetrius lacked the will to resist the Ottoman advance, and may well have been ill-disposed toward the Latins, although we know he sent embassies to France, Ferrara, Florence, the papacy, and Milan, in each case doubtless asking for assistance against the Turks, but apparently doubting that western Christians would aid their eastern brethren *in hac calamitosa aetate nostra*.[9] Demetrius obviously

Levant (1908), pp. 431–35; D. A. Zakythinos, *Le Despotat grec de Morée*, I (Paris, 1932, repr. London, 1975), 256–60; A. Bon, in *Corinth*, III-2 (1936), Am. Sch. Class. Stud. at Athens, Cambridge, Mass., pp. 143–45; Babinger, *Maometto*, pp. 242–47.

Although Chalcocondylas (ed. Darkó, II-2, 210, lines 14–15) says that Mehmed II put the final tribute at five hundred ducats (*stateres*) after the fall of Corinth, Critobulus's sum of 3,000 seems more likely (III, 7, ed. Grecu, p. 231, line 1). The siege of Corinth appears to have lasted almost three months, from 15 May, 1458 (Sphrantzes, *Chron. minus*, in *PG* 156, 1065CD; ed. Grecu, p. 108) to 6 August (*Chron. breve*, *loc. cit.*). Critobulus represents the siege as lasting four months (τετράμηνον), but may be counting inclusively like the ancients (III, 7, ed. Grecu, p. 229, line 4).

On 4 August (1458) the Venetians took precautions for the protection of their citizens and subjects overseas "cum per litteras que habentur ex Corphoo et Mothono exercitus Turchorum persistat in provintia Amoree [the Morea] quam dietim oppugnant, occupant, et dissipant . . ." (Arch. di Stato di Venezia, Sen. Mar, Reg. 6, fol. 80ᵛ [81ᵛ]). The colonial government of Corfu was informed "quod si exercitus Turchorum forte, quod absit, occupasset provinciam Amoree aut in ea persisteret, unde illi provincie et per consequens insule nostre Nigropontis et ceteris locis nostris Levantis periculum imineret, . . . supracomiti [certain galley commanders, concerning whom the senatorial resolution of 4 August was passed] se conferant cum omni possibili celeritate ad reperiendum capitaneum nostrum Culfi . . . ," to help deal with the emergency if necessary (*ibid.*, fol. 81ʳ [82ʳ], and *cf.* fol. 83 [84] on Scanderbeg). Mehmed II's years of success made a profound impression upon contemporaries. Note the list of the conquests of this *Signore horribile, crudele, insano, gaino* [inhuman, gruesome] *et maligno Turcho* compiled in 1475 by Jacopo de Promontorio [*cf.* above, Chap. 6, note 81], in Franz Babinger, "Die Aufzeichnungen des Genuesen Iacopo de Promontorio-de Campis über den Osmanenstaat um 1475," *Sitzungsber. d. Bayer. Akad. d. Wissen.*, Philos.-hist. Kl., 1956, Heft 8, pp. 81 ff.

[6] Sphrantzes, *Chron. minus* (*PG* 156, 1066AB; ed. Grecu, p. 110); Pseudo-Sphrantzes, IV, 16 (Bonn, pp. 388–89; ed. Grecu, p. 528); Chalcocondylas, bk. IX (Bonn, p. 455; ed. Darkó, II-2, 213).

[7] Sphrantzes, *Chron. minus* (*PG* 156, 1066CD; ed. Grecu, p. 110); Pseudo-Sphrantzes, IV, 16 (Bonn, pp. 388–89; ed. Grecu, p. 528), Πελοποννησιοφθόρος.

[8] Zakythinos, *Despotat grec de Morée*, I (1932, repr. 1975), 261.

[9] *Cf.* the letters of Demetrius in Sp. P. Lampros, *Palaiológeia kaì Peloponnesiaká*, IV (Athens, 1930), 196–204. Pope Calixtus III informed Francesco Sforza, duke of Milan, in a letter of 23 February, 1456, that Demetrius's envoy, Franculius Servopoulos, was ". . . catholicus, et tam grecis quam latinis litteris eruditissimus" (*ibid.*, p. 206). On 7 November, 1458, a papal safe conduct (*littera passus*) was granted to "Fraculinus Servopuli," described as *miles Constantinopolitanus* (Arch. Segr. Vaticano, Reg. Vat. 468, fol. 343ʳ).

had no desire to risk annihilation, however noble the cause. He preferred to live as a tribute-paying vassal of the sultan to whom he would be bound by the ties of his daughter's projected marriage. In justice to Demetrius we must remember that when he searched the horizon for an ally, he never found one, and he could never hope to win by fighting. Thomas pursued to a greater extent the western policy of the Palaeologi. He favored church union and Latin alliances as the only possible defense against the Turks. His wife was a westerner, Caterina Zaccaria, the heiress of old Centurione, the last Frankish prince of Achaea. Both despots certainly had deficiencies of character that would have made failure easy for them to achieve under favorable circumstances, but the roles they were assigned in the Turkish conquest of the Morea called for their destruction.

In early August, 1458, Calixtus III died in Rome. About two weeks later Cardinal Aeneas Sylvius Piccolomini of Corsignano was elected Pope Pius II, being consecrated on 3 September. Pius loved his birthplace no less than his family, and Corsignano became Pienza during his pontificate.[10] On 20 August (1458) the Sacred College had written his grace of Liége and other bishops, announcing the death of Calixtus and the election of Cardinal Aeneas, who by his character, wisdom, religious life, and other virtues (we are told), as well as by his outstanding accomplishments in sacred and humane letters and in every kind of intellectual endeavor, seemed called by divine judgment to the governance of the Church.[11]

---

[10] *Cf.* Eugène Müntz, *Les Arts à la cour des papes pendant le XVe et XVIe siècle: Recueil de documents inédits*, 3 vols., Paris, 1878–82, I, 300–5. On Pius's birthplace, see Enzo Carli, *Pienza, la città di Pio II*, Rome: Monte dei Paschi di Siena, 1966, with beautiful illustrations and copious notes. In the Pieve di S. Vito (of Corsignano) the visitor may still see the font at which both Pius II and his nephew Pius III were baptized. The biographical sketches of Pius II (who was born on 18 October, 1405) by his friends and admirers Giovanni Antonio Campano, whom he made bishop of Cotrone (1462–1463) and Teramo (1463–1477), and Bartolommeo Platina, humanist and librarian of the Vaticana under Sixtus IV, have been edited with a rich annotation by Giulio C. Zimolo, *Le Vite di Pio II*, in the new Muratori, *RISS*, III, pt. 3 (Bologna, 1964). Platina wrote his life of Pius shortly after the latter's death; Campano, who died in 1477, wrote his after the Turkish occupation of Negroponte (Euboea) in 1470, to which he refers (*ibid.*, p. 78). The two works are compared and contrasted by their editor Zimolo, "Il Campano e il Platina come biografi di Pio II," in Domenico Maffei, ed., *Enea Silvio Piccolomini, Papa Pio II: Atti del convegno per il quinto centenario della morte . . .*, Siena, 1968, pp. 401–11.

The works of Georg Voigt, *Enea Silvio de' Piccolomini als Papst Pius der Zweite und sein Zeitalter*, 3 vols., Berlin, 1856–63, and Ludwig v. Pastor, *Geschichte der Päpste*, II (repr. 1955), 5–289, still provide us with the most substantial treatments of Pius II's career. Voigt is unsympathetic toward him, both before and after his elevation to the papacy. Pastor has rejected Aeneas, and embraced Pius. There are semi-popular lives of Pius in English by William Boulting (London, 1908), Cecilia M. Ady (London, 1913), and Rosamond J. Mitchell (London, 1962). Gioacchino Paparelli, *Enea Silvio Piccolomini (Pio II)*, Bari, 1950, is thoughtful and readable, as is Eugenio Garin, "Ritratto di Enea Silvio Piccolomini," *Bullettino senese di storia patria*, 3rd ser., LXV (ann. XVII, 1958), 5–28, reprinted in his *Ritratti di umanisti*, Florence, 1967, pp. 9–39. Berthe Widmer, *Enea Silvio Piccolomini, Papst Pius II*, Basel and Stuttgart, 1960, has written a good brief life of Pius, with extensive selections from his works (the Latin texts accompanied by German translations), in which she gives at least some slight attention to the Ottoman empire and the Crusade. Three years later she followed this book with a monograph on *Enea Silvio Piccolomini in der sittlichen und politischen Entscheidung*, Basel and Stuttgart, 1963, in which she is not concerned with eastern affairs. From the flood of recent literature on the first Piccolomini pope, I would note chiefly Giuseppe Bernetti, *Saggi e studi sugli scritti di Enea Silvio Piccolomini, Papa Pio II . . .*, Florence, 1971, and C. Ugurgieri della Berardenga, *Pio II Piccolomini, con notizie su Pio III e altri membri della famiglia*, Florence, 1973 (Biblioteca dell' Archivio storico italiano, vol. XVIII).

[11] Arch. Segr. Vaticano, Arm. XXXI, tom. 52, fol. 5^r^. The precious Acta Consistorialia (1439–1486) thus record Pius II's election and coronation (*ibid.*, fol. 61^r^, not in Eubel, *Hierarchia*, II [1914, repr. 1960], 32): "Creatio Pii pape Secundi: Anno predicto [1458], die vero XVIIII^a^ eiusdem mensis [Augusti], circa horam XVI^am^ [about noontime, but the sources vary as to the hour of Pius's election, on which *cf.* Pastor, *Gesch. d. Päpste*, II (repr. 1955), 11, note 1, who always records details of this sort] reverendissimus in Christo pater et dominus, dominus Eneas . . . , Sancte Sabine presbyter cardinalis Senensis, assumptus fuit ad summi apicem apostolatus et vocatus Pius Secundus et associatus de conclave quod factum fuit in capella palatii usque ad altare Sancti Petri et reductus in palatium cum omnibus cardinalibus. Coronatio Pii pape Secundi: Anno predicto, die vero tertia mensis Septembris, qui [*sic*] fuit dies dominica, sanctissimus dominus noster Pius divina providentia papa Secundus fuit coronatus in gradibus Sancti Petri et deinde ascendens equum album associatus [here a blank space is left in the MS. where we should expect 'ab omnibus reverendissimis dominis'] cardinalibus in pontificalibus cum consueta sole[m]pnitate ivit ad Sanctum Ioannem Lateranensem."

A letter of 20 August, 1458, sent by the Sacred College to Marquis Lodovico II Gonzaga of Mantua told him of the election of the "reverendissimus . . . dominus Eneas tituli Sancte Sabine presbyter cardinalis Senensis vulgariter nuncupatus. . . ." Giving Cardinal Aeneas the usual praise, the letter includes the doubtful statement that he was elected "incredibili animorum consensu" (Arch. di Stato di Mantova, Arch. Gonzaga, Busta 834). On 4 September Pius II him-

Humanist, diplomat, traveler, and statesman, Pius II seems to have been the only pope to write his memoirs (he called them *Commentarii*) while he occupied S. Peter's throne. Pius had long been interested in the Greek world and, despite the frivolities of his youth, had for years lived in deep concern over the Turkish advance into Europe.[12] Soon after his coronation he announced that he would hold at Mantua or Udine on 1 June, 1459, a congress of all the great powers to organize a crusade against the Turks. The Venetians, however, fearing to disrupt their political and economic relations with the Ottoman empire, were unwilling to allow the congress to meet in Udine, and so Mantua was selected as the site.[13] Pius's good friend

---

self informed the marquis of his election (*ibid.*), ". . . ipsi fratres [cardinales] licet potuissent in alios maioris meriti consentire, tandem . . . unanimiter vota sua nos . . . nescimus quo occulto sed tremendo nobis Dei iudicio ad celsitudinis apostolice fastigium concorditer elegerunt." This *occultum sed tremendum iudicium* made a profound impression upon its beneficiary.

Aeneas Sylvius had been ordained a priest on 4 March, 1447 (see Angelo Mercati, "Aneddoti per la storia di pontefici: Pio II, Leone X," in *Archivio della R. Società romana di storia patria*, LVI–LVII [Rome, 1933–34], 363–65), a date which always eluded Pastor, *Gesch. d. Päpste*, I (repr. 1955), 351–52, note. On Aeneas Sylvius's election as Pius II on 19 August, see Pastor, *Acta inedita* I (Freiburg im Breisgau, 1904), nos. 64–65, pp. 90–95, docs. dated 19 and 20 August, 1458, and *Gesch. d. Päpste*, II (repr. 1955), 9–11. It is worth noting that Benozzo Gozzoli painted numerous banners, flags, and even the cardinals' benches used in the ceremonies attending Pius's coronation on 3 September (Müntz, *Les Arts à la cour des papes*, I, 263, 330).

[12] We may observe, for example, that in an oration which Pius had delivered as Aeneas Sylvius more than twenty years before (1436) at the Council of Basel as to the choice of a site for the oecumenical council which was to discuss the prospect of church union (Aeneas advocated Pavia as the best place for the Greeks and Latins to meet), he had made especial note of the plight of the Greeks in subjection to the overwhelming power of the Turkish empire (J. D. Mansi, ed., *Sacrorum conciliorum nova et amplissima collectio*, XXX [repr. Paris, 1904], 1098C–1099). This oration, like Pius's others, may also be found in Mansi, ed., *Pii II. P. M. . . . orationes politicae et ecclesiasticae*, 3 vols., Lucca, 1755–59, I, 5 ff. (with the passage relating to Greek subjection to the Turks on pp. 11–12), and *cf.*, *ibid.*, pp. 163–81.

[13] The most interesting source for the six-year reign of Pius II is his own *Commentarii*, in thirteen books, which the English reader may easily employ in the useful translation of Florence A. Gragg, published in the *Smith College Studies in History*: Book I appeared as vol. XXII, nos. 1–2 (1936–37); bks. II–III as vol. XXV (1939–40); bks. IV–V, vol. XXX (1947); bks. VI–IX, vol. XXXV (1951); and bks. X–XIII, vol. XLIII (1957). The pagination is continuous. This translation is said to be based upon an unpublished edition of the Codex Reginensis lat. 1995 (Pius's original text) in the Bibl. Apost. Vaticana; it is complete, while the printed Latin texts of the original are all mutilated, as indicated below in this note. An Italian translation of the *Commentarii* has recently appeared in Siena, the work of Giuseppe Bernetti, *Pio II (Enea Silvio Piccolomini), I Commentari*, 4 vols., 1972–74. It is based upon a study of the Cod. Corsinianus 147 (on which see below) as well as the Cod. Reginensis 1995, each volume being equipped with an informative introduction.

Of particular interest for the present chapter is the work in two books of the humanist Lodrisio Crivelli (Cribellus) of Milan, whom Pius II made a papal secretary on 17 October, 1458 (Arch. Segr. Vaticano, Reg. Vat. 515, fol. 109), *De expeditione Pii P. II in Turcas*, in *RISS*, XXIII (Milan, 1733), cols. 25–80, and ed. G. C. Zimolo, in the new Muratori, *RISS*, XXIII, pt. 5 (Bologna, completed in 1950). On the rather unhappy career of Crivelli, poet as well as Greek scholar, see Ferdinando Gabotto, "Ricerche intorno allo storiografo quattrocentista Lodrisio Crivelli," *Archivio storico italiano*, 5th ser., VII (1891), 267–98, who gives the text of several of Crivelli's letters, and Leslie F. Smith, "Lodrisio Crivelli of Milan and Aeneas Silvius, 1457–1464," *Studies in the Renaissance*, IX (1962), 31–63, who provides us with the text of six of Crivelli's poems.

On 9 December, 1458, Pius renewed his predecessor's declaration of the crusading tithe, in a bull to be found in Reg. Vat. 469 (vol. II of Pius's letters *de Curia*), fols. 86^v–87^r, and *cf.* the bull dated 5 July, 1459, in Reg. Vat. 471, fols. 302^r–303^r, ". . . ad executionem indulgentiarum pro defensione ipsius fidei contra dictos Turchos concessarum . . . ;" etc., etc. The *convocatio Pii papae II ad dietam Mantue vel Utini celebrandam*, as sent to King Charles VII of France and the German imperial electors, appears as the first document in the volume of *Pii II brevia: Ann. I, II, et III (1458-59-60)*, in Arm. XXXIX, tom. 9, fol. 4, by mod. stamped enumeration (originally fol. 1), and *cf.* the pope's letters to Cardinal Carvajal, fols. 6^v–7^r, 8^r–9^r; the Emperor Frederick III, fol. 9; etc., etc. Late copies of various *opuscula* of Pius II may be found in the Vatican Archives, Miscellanea, Arm. XII, tomm. 3–4 (=Bibl. Apost. Vaticana, Codd. latt. 12,255–56), together with texts of Platina on Sixtus IV, Volaterrano, Infessura, and a few other items, but there seems to be nothing in these two volumes not elsewhere available in better form.

Also *cf.* in general Mansi, *Concilia*, XXV (repr. Paris, 1902), 105–34, a poor section, and, *ibid.*, XXXII, 203–66; Raynaldus, *Ann. eccl.*, ad ann. 1458, nos. 1–5, 14–19, vol. XIX (Cologne, 1693), pp. 1–2, 4–5; Marino Sanudo, *Vite de'duchi di Venezia*, in *RISS*, XXII (Milan, 1733), cols. 1166E, 1167; K. J. Hefele, *Histoire des conciles*, ed. and trans. H. Leclercq, VII, pt. 2 (Paris, 1916), 1291 ff.; Pastor, *Hist. Popes*, III (repr. 1949), 19, 21–24, 45 ff., 240 ff., and *Gesch. d. Päpste*, II (repr. 1955), 15, 16–19, 39 ff., 220 ff.

Since frequent reference will be made in the following pages to Pius II's *Commentarii*, his most important literary work and one of the chief sources for his reign, some account should probably be taken of its peculiar history, even at the risk of wearying the informed reader who chooses to pursue this note to the end. Following Julius Caesar, whose title *Commentarii* he adopted, Pius wrote his memoirs in the third person, a fact which was to play its part in the now well-known attempt to conceal his authorship. In the edition of the *Commentarii* printed at Rome in 1584 and reprinted in 1589, as well as in that printed at Frankfurt in 1614, one Johannes Gobellinus (of Linz), vicar of the Church of Bonn, is given on the title page as the author of the work (. . . *a R. D. Ioanne*

Gobellino Vicario Bonnen. iamdiu compositi, et a R. P. D. Francisco Bandino Picolomineo Archiepiscopo Senensi ex vetusto originali recogniti). Gobellinus, however, identifies himself in Cod. 147 (35-G-6) in the Bibl. Corsiniana in Rome [at the Accademia de' Lincei, Via Lungara, 10] merely as a copyist, as Voigt clearly showed him to have been (*Enea Silvio*, II [1862], 336–41, and see Pastor, *Gesch. d. Päpste*, II [repr. 1955], 33–38, and append., no. 65, pp. 754–56). *Cf.* also Giuseppe Lesca, "I Commentarii . . . d'Enea Silvio de'Piccolomini," in the *Annali della R. Scuola normale superiore di Pisa*, Filos. e Filologia, vol. X (della serie XVI, 1894), pp. 22–24 [of whose work Pastor, II, 756, note 2, had a low opinion, although it is of some use], and especially Hans Kramer, "Untersuchungen über die 'Commentarii' des Papstes Pius II," in *Mitteilungen des Österreichischen Instituts für Geschichtsforschung*, XLVIII (Innsbruck, 1934), 83–86.

It has long been clear that Francesco Bandini de' Piccolomini, archbishop of Siena (1529–1588!), also named on the title pages of the printed editions, must assume the responsibility for this imposition on the learned world (Kramer, "Untersuchungen," pp. 86–91, although I can hardly agree with Kramer that Pius II himself wanted to conceal his authorship of the *Commentarii*, allowing only the Piccolomini family to share in the secret [*ibid.*, pp. 85–86]). Bandini was the great-grandson of Pius II's sister Laudomia, and the grandnephew of Pius III. Although about 1566 Bandini was prepared to print the *Commentarii* under the name of Pius II, and had received a license to do so (Kramer, *op. cit.*, pp. 88–89), he changed his mind, and published the work under the name of Gobellinus. The deliberate fraud was part of an effort to protect Pius II's reputation against the attacks of Protestant critics during the later years of the Catholic Reformation. The work was moreover severely and carefully edited (clearly by Bandini himself, for his letter to Pope Gregory XIII, printed in his edition of 1584, p. 3, states that Gobellinus's *Commentarii* was his favorite reading). Bandini prepared the work for the press by recasting or removing many of Pius II's frankest observations on the people and events he described. The first edition (1584) was printed, directly or indirectly, from Cod. 147 (35-G-6), now in the Corsiniana, where the passages to be excised were marked for the printer (*cf.* also Voigt, II, 341); from this edition those of 1589 (Rome) and 1614 (Frankfurt) were reprinted. The passages omitted from the first twelve books of the *Commentarii* are published in Jos. Cugnoni, *Aeneae Silvii Piccolomini . . . opera inedita*, in the *Atti della R. Accademia dei Lincei*, CCLXXX (1882–83), 3rd ser., *Memorie della classe di scienze morali, storiche e filologiche*, VIII (Rome, 1883), pp. 496–549. Book xiii, not given in the printed texts of the *Commentarii*, has been published by Voigt, II, 359–77. *Cf.* Pastor, *Gesch. d. Päpste*, I (repr. 1955), 659–60, note 2; it was Pastor (see, *ibid.*, II [repr. 1955], append., no. 65, pp. 754–56) who discovered or rather rediscovered the original MS. of Pius's work in the Bibl. Apost. Vaticana, Codex Reginensis lat. 1995.

Although Pius II wrote some of this MS. in his own hand, he usually dictated his entries in the work to his secretary, Agostino Patrizzi (or Patrizi), who is mentioned in bk. xi (Engl. trans., pp. 754–55; ed. Frankfurt, 1614, p. 303, lines 55–56) as taking such dictation; in the original MS., Cod. Reg. lat. 1995, the passage occurs on fol. 523^{r}: "Pius in cubiculo suo pro consuetudine dictare aliquid ceperat Augustino Patricio scribente. . . ." On 1 April, 1464, Patrizzi was appointed an *abbreviator litterarum apostolicarum* (Arch. Segr. Vaticano, Reg. Vat. 516, fols. 258^{r}–259^{r}). Since he had been in close personal attendance upon the pope long before this, however, the appointment was designed to confirm his status in view of the recent reorganization of the college of (seventy) abbreviators or to add to his income. Patrizzi's handwriting has been identified as that in which most of the MS. is written (Kramer, "Untersuchungen," pp. 62–69). From all this it is quite obvious why Raynaldus, *Ann. eccl.*, thinks he is citing Gobellinus when he is of course quoting Pius's own words; unfortunately Gobellinus is still sometimes cited as a historian, for example by Zakythinos, *Despotat grec de Morée*, I, 264–65. Various aspects of Patrizzi's career are explored in Rino Avesani, "Per la Biblioteca di Agostino Patrizi Piccolomini, vescovo di Pienza," in the *Mélanges Eugène Tisserant*, VI, pt. 1 (Città del Vaticano, 1964), 1–37, esp. pp. 3–31 (Studi e testi, no. 236).

In July, 1959, and May, 1970, I examined for myself Cod. Reg. lat. 1995 in the Vaticana. A quarto volume, it is of quite manageable size and weight, containing 595 fols. (1190 pages), in an eighteenth-century leather binding, a paper MS. with several different watermarks including crossed arrows imposed upon a circle, a column, scissors, and a hunting horn suspended on a crossed cord. The first twelve folios (with a separate enumeration) give the *rubrice* of the first twelve books of the *Commentarii*. Book i begins with fol. 1^{r}, and bk. xii concludes with fol. 584^{v} and the notice that the twelfth and last book is fortunately finished (see below), after which comes the Greek word Τέλος. The MS. is written in several hands, most of them quite legible. In the margins are various additions, corrections, guide words to the text, and notations of special emphasis. Following a fine humanist hand there begins a section in Pius II's own hand (fols. 35 ff.), which runs to the conclusion of bk. i, where a group of blank pages were left (fols. 61^{v}–68^{v}) for a continuation that was never added. Special notice should be taken of the directions given to the copyist on fol. 189^{v}: "pone hec ultra ad hoc signum ⊹ ," which marks a passage to almost the middle of fol. 191^{v}. The same sign reappears at the middle of fol. 238^{r} with directions for replacement of the marked passage at this point: "vide supra et pone que sunt ad hoc signum usque quo reperies aliud in hunc modum ⊹ ." These directions are in Pius's own hand. His coronation is recorded on fol. 69^{r}.

The paper of Cod. Reg. 1995 is of the same general quality throughout despite the different watermarks. It was all manufactured in Italy, and was being used in Rome during the years 1459–1464, on which *cf.* C. M. Briquet, *Les Filigranes*, ed. Allan Stevenson, 4 vols., Amsterdam, 1968: for the crossed arrows ("deux flèches en sautoir"), see vol. III, no. 6303; the column ("colonne"), *ibid.*, no. 4411; the scissors ("ciseaux"), no. 3685; and the hunting horn ("huchet"), nos. 7686 (too early) and 7693, which occurs throughout the MS., including book xiii, but the precise *huchet* is not given among the watermarks even in the new Briquet. On fol. 584^{v} appears the annotation, "Comentariorum Pii Secundi Pont. Max. liber duodecimus et ultimus feliciter finitus," but Pius obviously changed his mind and added bk. xiii, the genuineness of which is no longer doubted. Although Campano refers to twelve books (*Vita Pii II*, ed. G. C. Zimolo, in the new Muratori, *RISS*, III-3 [1964], 71–73), Platina knew of the thirteenth (*ibid.*, p. 119, lines 15–16): "Commentariorum de rebus a se gestis libros XII scripsit, tertiumdecimum incohavit." Book xiii was an afterthought (fols. 585^{r}–595^{v}). It is in the hand of Agostino Patrizzi, however, and on the same paper stock as a good proportion of the preceding twelve books (with the watermark of the hunting horn).

In July, 1959, I also examined Cod. 147 (35-G-6) of Pius's

Albrecht Achilles, margrave of Brandenburg, was the uncle of the Marchioness Barbara of Hohenzollern, wife of Lodovico II Gonzaga, who had been ruling the small state of Mantua for some fifteen years.[14] The pious Aeneas could be sure of a warm welcome at Mantua, on the banks of the Mincio, where Vergil was born, and so could the cardinals and the Italian and German princes, on whom rested the papal hopes for a crusade.

Shortly before leaving Rome on the long, slow journey to Mantua, Pope Pius established a new religious order of knights to be known under the name of Our Lady of Bethlehem. Based upon the model of the Hospitallers at Rhodes, its headquarters were to be at Lemnos; its purpose, the protection of Christians against the Turks in the northern Aegean. It is not clear, however, whether knights were ever actually enrolled under the red cross of its banner.[15]

Commentarii in the Bibl. Corsiniana in Rome. This MS. has the following title page (in a later hand): "Commentariorum Pii Papae II, Libri XII a Johanne Gobellino de Lins Vicario Bonnensi exscripti, anno MCCCCLXIV, divo Pio II pont. max. volente. MS. di cart. 431." It is a very handsome MS., especially prepared for the pope. A carefully inscribed preface, following the title page, states:

"Il tomo membranaceo in foglio di carte 431 con l'effigie del Pontefice Pio II nella prima lettera iniziale in principio, la quale è un S. con l'arme di Casa Piccolomini giù a basso, e con una testa barbata, nel mezzo in principio, coperta di un berettone rosso, contiene i *libri XII de Comentarj latini* delle cose operate dal medesimo Pontefice Pio II, opera mentovata dagli scrittori, che di lui parlano. Questa però viene falsamente attribuita a Giovanni Gobellino, vicario di Bonna nella diocesi di Colonia, e poi segretario del medesimo Pontefice Pio II; e l'errore è provenuto da Francesco Bandini Piccolomini, arcivescovo di Siena, il quale diede alle stampe in Roma questi Comentarj presso Domenico Basa nel 1584 in forma quarta, dedicandogli al Pontefice Gregorio XIII come opera di Giovanni Gobellino, e non di Pio II, nella qual cosa l'arcivescovo fece un grandissimo errore, perchè il Gobellino non attribui mai a sestesso quest' opera, mentovata dal Platina, come propria di Pio II, e non di altri. Nel Giornale de'letterati d'Italia pubblicato in Venezia, si parla di questo affare nel tomo XIV, pag. 367. Ma il presente Codice sopra tutti gli altri mette in chiarissima luce questa verità, mentre nel fine di esso si legge, che il Gobellino fù copista, e non autore del codice dei Comentarj di Pio II. Le parole del chirografo sono queste:

"*Divo Pio Secundo Pontifice Maximo volente, Johannes Gobellini de Lins, Vicarius Bonnensis Coloniensis Dioecesis, hoc opus anno Domini MCCCCLXIIII, die XII mensis Junii excripsi foeliciter*. [This note is written in small red capitals on fol. 431ᵛ.] Dunque il Gobellino non compose questi Comentarj, ma solamente gli copiò, e trascrisse, *excripsi*. Perciò questo codice è molto stimabile, perchè finisce di decidere questa letteraria controversia, e facilmente ancora potrà servire a migliorare l'edizione I di Roma, la quale fu replicata ancora in Francfort nel 1614 insieme con le lettere del Cardinal Papiense."

Gobellinus had a beautiful hand, obviously the reason why he was chosen for the task; he employed few abbreviations, and the text is as easily read as print. The first folio is magnificently rubricated and decorated in red, blue, and gold, with minor shades of yellow, green, and brown. The initial letters of the first words of each book are also handsomely illuminated. A number of passages were marked for deletion sometime after Gobellinus had finished copying the work, presumably by Bandini a century later. The MS. has the following explicit (fols. 426ᵛ–427ʳ): "Hec habuimus que ad annum sextum pontificatus sui nondum exactum de rebus eius scriberemus, in libros digestis duodecim quorum ultimus pridie Kal. Ianuarias finem accepit anno ab incarnato verbo MCCCCLXIII: [and in red capitals:] Comentariorum Pii Secundi Pontificis Maximi liber XII et ultimus feliciter finit." After this comes (fol. 427ʳ): "Io. Antonii Campani episcopi Aprutini [Teramo] epistola de operibus Pii Secundi Pontificis Maximi iudicium faciens" [*inc.* "Campanus Iacobo Cardinali Papiensi: Percurri nuper comentarios Pii pontificis rerum a se gestarum . . ."]. In this letter Campano states that, although Pius had given him a free hand to edit the *Commentarii*, he had not done so, thus anticipating and refuting Voigt, II, 338–40, on which *cf.* Kramer, "Untersuchungen," pp. 82–83.

In a discerning review of some recent works on Pius II, Remo Ceserani, in the *Giornale storico della letteratura italiana*, CXLI (ann. LXXXI, Turin, 1964), 265–82, has sketched the history of both Cod. Reginensis 1995 and Cod. Corsinianus 147, the two most important MSS. of the *Commentarii* (*ibid.*, pp. 273–75), of which he is preparing or has by this time prepared a new edition. On the history of these two MSS., note also Kramer, "Untersuchungen," pp. 61, 83–88. Finally we must note a brief but important article by Giuseppe Bernetti, "Ricerche e problemi nei Commentarii di Enea Silvio Piccolomini," *La Rinascita*, II-7 (1939), 449–75, reprinted almost without change in his *Saggi e studi sugli scritti di Enea Silvio Piccolomini* (1971), pp. 31–52. Bernetti has some interesting reflections on Pius's memoirs, especially that the account (in bk. VIII) of the ceremonies attending the reception of the head of S. Andrew in Rome in April, 1462 (with which the present chapter ends) is actually "l'origine, il nucleo primo" of the Commentaries. Bernetti believes that Pius, having written this section, got on quickly with the rest of the work, writing or rather dictating bks. I–XII between Easter of 1462 and Christmas of 1463 (*Saggi e studi*, p. 32), and dictating but not completing bk. XIII between April and June, 1464 (*ibid.*, p. 39, note 6). Ceserani, *art. cit.*, p. 277, pretty much agrees with this dating. In other words, Pius wrote his memoirs in 1462–1463; he did not keep a diary of events as they occurred from year to year.

[14] *Cf.* B. Widmer, *Enea Silvio* (1960), p. 103.

[15] Raynaldus, *Ann. eccl.*, ad ann. 1459, nos. 2–3, vol. XIX (1693), p. 15; J. W. Zinkeisen, *Gesch. d. osman. Reiches in Europa*, II (Gotha, 1854), 237–38; Voigt, *Enea Silvio*, III (1863), 652; Hefele and Leclercq, *Hist. des conciles*, VII-2 (1916), 1292; Pastor, *Gesch. d. Päpste*, II (repr. 1955), 39; Erich Meuthen, *Die letzten Jahre des Nikolaus von Kues*, Cologne, 1958, pp. 47–48, and doc. no. 17, pp. 155–57, with notes. On the fraudulent crusading order formed by the Frenchman Gerard, see Pius II, *Comm.*, bk. XII, Engl. trans., pp. 790–92; ed. Frankfurt, 1614, pp. 322–23. A Societas Jesu Christi was also organized "propriis sumptibus arma capere expeditionemque inire in Turchos hostes Christiani nominis immittendam," as stated in a curial letter of Pius to the members of the new society (Arch. Segr. Vaticano, Reg. Vat. 469, fol. 486ʳ, dated 15 January, 1459), on which *cf.* Pastor, II, 39–40, note. Pius issued a further bull in

Pius left Rome on 22 January, 1459, and after an elaborate, ceremonial journey through Assisi and Perugia, Siena and Florence, Bologna and Ferrara, he arrived in Mantua on 27 May.[16] He has devoted the entire second book of his *Commentaries* to a description of his itinerary and to the various historical and other reflections which the sight of the many cities and towns, through which he passed, recalled to mind. On 1 June, as planned, the congress was opened with an address by the bishop of Coron, who in a long oration deplored the unhappy state of the Church, and explained the pope's reasons for seeking to assemble representatives of the chief European powers to take action against the Turks. After this, when the congregation was about to withdraw, the pope raised his hand for silence, and spoke "with misery in his eyes" according to Crivelli. He lamented the fact that, although the Turks did not hesitate to die for a vile faith, Christians were unwilling to undergo the least expense or hardship for the gospel.[17]

The congress got off to a poor start. Actually its first and only general session did not take place until 26 September, for the envoys arrived tardily, most of them invested with inadequate powers by the indifferent princes of Europe. The outlook was dismal, but the pope refused to be discouraged. The Emperor Frederick III was constantly intriguing against John Hunyadi's son Matthias Corvinus, whom Pius had recognized as king of Hungary. Frederick had had himself declared king of the disputed land (in March, 1459). Pius warned him, however, "that since this kingdom has hitherto been the shield of all Christendom, and we have always enjoyed a comfortable security while it fought our battles, do not doubt that dire destruction would descend upon us all if this road were opened to the barbarian multitude" [of Turks].[18]

---

commendation of this society on 29 June, 1459 (Reg. Vat. 471, fols. 201ᵛ–202ᵛ), but the "societas" never amounted to anything. Pius's preoccupation with the crusade is sketched in Else Hocks, *Pius II. und der Halbmond*, Freiburg im Breisgau, 1941, esp. pp. 55 ff., which gives no references to the sources, and seems to be based on an inadequate bibliography.

[16] An important register in the Vatican Archives (Arm. XXXIX, tom. 8) contains the following calendar of events (fol. 28ᵛ):

> Dominus Calistus papa III obiit die VI Augusti 1458.
> Dominus Pius papa II creatus die XVIIII dicti mensis Augusti.
> Die XXII Ian. MCCCCLVIIII dominus Pius recessit de urbe.
> Die XXVI dicti mensis intravit Spoletum et exivit XXVIIII eiusdem.
> Die prima Febr. MCCCCLVIIII intravit Perusium et exivit XVIIII.
> Die XXIIII Febr. intravit Senas et exivit XXIII Aprilis 1459.
> Die XXV Aprilis intravit Florentiam et exivit V Maii.
> Die nona Maii intravit Bononiam et exivit XVI eiusdem.
> Die XVII dicti mensis intravit Ferrariam et exivit XXV eiusdem.
> Die XXVII Maii 1459 intravit Mantuam.

By way of commentary on this schedule we may note that in a letter dated at Perugia on 9 February, 1459, Pius indicated his intention of leaving for Siena on the twentieth (*Brevia*, in Arm. XXXIX, tom. 9, fol. 14ᵛ): "Ad vicesimam Februarii hinc discedemus Senas. . . ." He was at Corsignano on 22 February (*ibid.*, fols. 17ᵛ, 18ʳ), and at Siena on the twenty-fifth (fol. 18ʳ); another letter, if properly dated, was written from Siena on 24 February (fols. 19ᵛ–20ʳ), the day of his arrival. The first register here referred to (Arm. XXXIX, tom. 8) bears the old enumeration 2804, a reminder of the sad losses which the Vatican Archives have suffered.

[17] Pius II, *Comm.*, bk. III, Engl. trans., pp. 191–92; ed. Frankfurt, 1614, pp. 60–61; Crivelli, *Expeditio in Turcas*, in *RISS*, XXIII (1733), cols. 66B, 77–78, and ed. G. C. Zimolo, in the new Muratori, XXIII-5 (1948–50), 80 ff., 98 ff.; *cf.* Raynaldus, *Ann. eccl.*, ad ann. 1459, no. 42, vol. XIX (1693), pp. 26–27; Lesca, "I Commentarii," pp. 90 ff.

[18] Raynaldus, *Ann. eccl.*, ad ann. 1459, no. 15, vol. XIX, p. 18, and see Pius II's letters to Cardinal Carvajal and the Emperor Frederick III on the necessity of leaving Matthias Corvinus at peace while he tried to defend himself against Turkish attacks (*Brevia*, in Arch. Segr. Vaticano, Arm. XXXIX, tom. 9, fols. 28ʳ–29ʳ). The quotation in the text comes from the letter to the emperor, dated at Siena on 2 April, 1459 (fol. 29ʳ). On 13 April, Pius wrote the emperor justifying his recognition of Matthias as king of Hungary, as Calixtus III had already done—"non ergo aut juste aut honeste poteramus eum regio nomine spoliare . . ." (*ibid.*, fol. 32ʳ, and *cf.* Pius's letter to Carvajal on the fourteenth of the month, fols. 32ᵛ–33ʳ, *et alibi*, and a notable letter to Carvajal from Mantua on 5 November, *ibid.*, fols. 89ᵛ–91ʳ). On Calixtus III's full approval of Matthias Corvinus's accession to the Hungarian throne, "quod bonum felixque sit ad regni ipsius pacem et tranquillitatem perpetuamque totius Christianitatis felicitatem," see Arm. XXXIX, tom. 7, fol. 165ᵛ, and *ibid.*, fols. 167, 168ʳ–169ᵛ, 170 ff. Most of these letters (of March, 1458) had urged their recipients to work for the destruction of the perfidious Turk.

The strife between Frederick and Matthias was very hard to settle (Arm. XXXIX, tom. 9, fols. 54ᵛ–55ᵛ, papal letters of 6 July, 1459, to the two principals). This register contains numerous letters on the problems which Frederick was introducing into the threatened *regnum Hungariae*, to which I shall make little further reference since they are for the most part only indirectly related to the "eastern question." Although Pius II certainly found Frederick exasperating to deal with, a genuine friendship existed between them (*cf.*, *ibid.*, fols. 74ᵛ–75ᵛ, *et alibi*). Conditions

Pius II had spent years in central Europe (as we have seen) where he had represented the emperor at various diets and other meetings. He had met most of the important princes, and knew some of them well. His knowledge of German, Bohemian, Austrian, Hungarian, and Polish affairs was doubtless one of the main reasons for his elevation to the papal throne. No one at the Curia Romana knew better than he the extent to which internecine strife exposed Hungary, Carniola, Carinthia, and Styria to Turkish attack. At the time of the congress of Mantua there was an uneasy peace north of the Alps, but one could never be certain when the lid might blow off the cauldron.

There had been a congress of the German princes, held in the city of Cheb (Eger) in April, 1459, just before Pius's assembly at Mantua. Its purpose had been the maintenance of peace. Despite its apparent success, however, strong tensions still existed. Eventually they would lead to war. The Hohenzollerns (in the margraviates of Brandenburg) and their Wettin allies (in the duchies of Saxony) were pitted against the Wittelsbachs (in the Palatinate and Bavaria-Landshut). Although Duke William of Saxony had been obliged to recognize, at Cheb, the Hussite George of Poděbrady's accession to the throne of Bohemia—which William had claimed as husband of the late King Ladislas Postumus's elder sister, Anna of Hapsburg—there was abundant dissatisfaction in Catholic circles at the "heretic" king's good fortune. The Emperor Frederick III and King Casimir IV of Poland both claimed the Hungarian succession, and so (as we have noted) the youthful Matthias Corvinus's possession of S. Stephen's throne was still uncertain.

To glance ahead for a moment, the future was to be no better than the past. From the fall of 1459 to about the spring of 1461 George of Poděbrady was to contribute to the political confusion in Germany by trying, with the aid of that perennial busybody Martin Mayr, to get himself elected king of the Romans. He wanted, he said, to help bring about "reform" in the empire, which was faring badly under Frederick III, whom Pope Nicholas V had crowned emperor in Rome (in March, 1452). Poděbrady pictured himself as exercising the regency of the empire (under the Emperor Frederick) as he had exercised the regency of Bohemia for some years during the minority of Ladislas Postumus. It was a vainglorious illusion. Economic conditions were in almost as sad a jumble as the political situation. In many parts of the empire the roads and rivers were unsafe for trade and travel. Tolls were numerous and often heavy. The imperial coinage was corrupt. Germany, then, was not well off, but what of France? As Pius II reviewed the past and pondered the future on his way to Mantua, what were indeed his thoughts of France?

King Charles VII was certainly no crusader. Besides, the French were too interested in making René of Anjou king of Naples to campaign against the faraway Turks at the behest of a pope who had just accorded the royal title to Alfonso V's illegitimate son Ferrante.[19] On 14 July, 1459, Pius II wrote Charles that he was receiving word almost daily from Hungary, Bosnia, Albania, and the Morea as well as from numerous other Christian territories in the Levant that nothing was more damaging to Christian interests in those areas than the

---

were very critical throughout the summer of 1459, and on 25 July Pius wrote Stefano de'Nardini from Mantua that the road into Hungary lay open to the Turks after the Christian loss of Semendria (Smederevo): ". . . hoc presertim tempore in quo sicut devotio tua intellexisse iam debuit Zendren. opido [*sic*] amisso secundum vulnus Christianitati inlatum est, et Turcis liber in Ungariam patet excursus . . ." (*ibid.*, fol. 59ᵛ). Stefano de'Nardini of Forlì (Forliviensis) had been appointed *orator et nuntius* to Germany a few months before—while Pius was in Florence (from 25 April to 5 May, 1459, according to the itinerary in Arm. XXXIX, tom. 8, fol. 28ᵛ)—with the very difficult mission of making peace among the German princes (see the bull "datum Florentie, anno etc., MCCCCLVIIII [no day given], pontificatus nostri anno primo" in Reg. Vat. 471, fol. 107, and *cf.* fol. 108). Shortly after his accession Matthias Corvinus sent an envoy to Scanderbeg (J. Gelcich and L. Thallóczy, *Diplomatarium ragusanum*, Budapest, 1887, no. 365, p. 613), obviously to discuss the crusade.

[19] Calixtus III seems to have harbored a strong hostility toward his former patron Alfonso V of Naples and Aragon-Catalonia (d. 27 June, 1458). For obvious reasons he found it expedient to conceal his sentiments during Alfonso's lifetime, but after the latter's death he absolutely refused to recognize Ferrante as king of Naples. Pius II's accession brought about a complete change in papal policy, with subsequent rewards for the Piccolomini family in the southern kingdom. *Cf.* N. M[engozzi], "Il Pontefice Pio II e l'aragonese Ferdinando I, re di Napoli," *Bullettino senese di storia patria*, XX (1913), 263–80, with nine documents [from August, 1458, to February, 1460] drawn from Arm.-Ad. Messer, *Le Codice aragonese: Contribution à l'histoire des Aragonais de Naples*, Paris, 1912, who publishes 358 documents from a Paris MS., running from 1 July, 1458, to 20 February, 1460.

interminable and intolerable delay of the western powers to take some decisive step on behalf of their threatened co-religionists in the East.[20] Charles was unmoved.[21] Diplomatic etiquette might require that a papal brief be sent to King Henry VI of England, but that gentle monarch of uncertain mind had already seen the Yorkists victorious at S. Albans in May, 1455, the first of a dozen battles in the disastrous Wars of the Roses, which were to remove England from the international scene for thirty years. Ferrante of Naples, who had helped elect the pope, and needed his support against the French, sent an embassy, of course; Philip the Good of Burgundy finally dispatched his nephew John of Cleves to Mantua with a large retinue. John exacted concessions from the pope, and departed, leaving unimportant representatives behind him and promising that Burgundy would contribute or hire six thousand men for service in Hungary.[22]

At long length Francesco Sforza came, also with a most impressive retinue. He nurtured an incessant fear of the French re-entering Italy. He had no difficulty, however, prevailing upon Pius II to support Ferrante of Naples against another Angevin attempt to occupy the south Italian kingdom, as a result of a rebellion which had just broken out against Ferrante (in August, 1459).[23] The duke of Milan would contribute all his resources to the projected war against the Turks insofar as conditions in Italy would allow him (but just how far would they in fact allow him?).[24] Following the personal ap-

[20] Pius II to Charles VII, doc. dated 14 July, 1459, in *Brevia*, in Arch. Segr. Vaticano, Arm. XXXIX, tom. 9, fol. 58: ". . . Accedunt nuntii pene quottidiani ex Ungaria, Bosna et Albania, et Peloponesso multisque aliis fidelium locis ad nos venientes quorum testimonio satis certum habemus nichil rebus Christianorum calamitosius esse quam tarditatem hanc tantam ferendi auxilii. . . ."

[21] *Cf.*, *ibid.*, fols. 84r–86r, and esp. fols. 93r–94r, 112r–113r, 116r–117v. Charles's attention was not to be deflected from western affairs, especially the Angevin claim to Naples.

[22] Pius II, *Comm.*, bk. III, Engl. trans., pp. 206–17; ed. Frankfurt, 1614, pp. 65–70, deals at length with the embassy which Philip sent to Mantua under John of Cleves. Most of books VI and VII of Pius's *Commentarii* is devoted to the affairs of Germany, France, England, Spain, Naples, Cyprus, and Savoy, with historical analyses of the chief problems of these countries up to the time of his pontificate. Philip of Burgundy had been the center of papal hopes, having at first promised to come to Mantua in person: *cf.* Pius's letter to Philip, dated at Florence on 3 May, 1459 (*Brevia*, in Arch. Segr. Vaticano, Arm. XXXIX, tom. 9, fols. 35r–36r): ". . . Confidimus te veniente venturos esse complurimos principes qui alioquin libentius domesticum otium amplectentur. . . ." On the coming of John of Cleves to Mantua, *cf.*, *ibid.*, fols. 61v–62r, papal letters of 29 July, 1459, *et alibi*, as fol. 73. Although he became pro-Yorkist, Pius tried through his legates Francesco Coppini, bishop of Terni, and Jean Jouffroy, bishop of Arras, to see peace established in England, whence he hoped to draw men and money for the crusade (see Constance Head, "Pope Pius II and the Wars of the Roses," *Archivum historiae pontificiae*, VIII [Rome, 1970], 139–78).

In the Archivio di Stato di Milano, Arch. Visconteo-Sforzesco, Potenze Estere, Cart. 48 ("Roma"), is an undated schedule of current preparations for the crusade (which an archivist has assigned to January, 1459, although the annotations obviously extend over more than a year), the original text being revised by a second but contemporary hand. It is said of the king of England: "Nihil adhuc certi promissit [and the second hand adds:] neque etiam ad hoc videtur intendere." The following note appears concerning the king in Spain: "Pugnat contra Granatenses neque ei contra Turchos facilis expeditio est [and the second hand adds:] nec futura speratur." And of the Venetians it is stated: "Cum certam regum et principum terra marique paratam expeditionem viderunt, aderunt et ipsi cum valida classe [and the second hand has crossed out the words "nec postremi Christianorum erunt," replacing them by the following:] quam interim satis lente preparare videntur, et forsitan inter postremos erunt!"

[23] *Cf.* Ernesto Pontieri, *Per la Storia del regno di Ferrante I d'Aragona, re di Napoli: Studi e ricerche*, 2nd ed., Naples, 1969, pp. 92 ff., 231–36.

[24] Pius II, *Comm.*, bk. III, Engl. trans., pp. 217, 219, 223–26, 252, 254; ed Frankfurt, 1614, pp. 70, 72–73, 82–83. On 16 September (1459) Pius wrote in answer to the pro-Angevin prince of Taranto, from whom he had just received a letter, that ". . . nichil aliud respondere habemus nisi molestas esse nobis vestras dissensiones . . ." (Arch. Segr. Vaticano, Arm. XXXIX, tom. 9, fol. 81r). With some reason Francesco Sforza feared the French, who would not relax the interest they had acquired in the duchy of Milan through the marriage (in 1387) of Valentina Visconti, daughter of Gian Galeazzo, to Louis, duke of Touraine and later of Orléans, the brother of King Charles VI of France. As we have noted, Francesco Sforza's wife Bianca Maria Visconti, daughter of Duke Filippo Maria, was illegitimate, which gave the then duke of Orléans, Charles, son of Valentina and Louis, an excellent claim to Milan, which in fact Charles's own son, Louis XII of France, was later to vindicate (in 1499–1500). In 1459, however, both Pius and Francesco Sforza could agree on a policy aimed at keeping the French out of Italy, for the Angevin reoccupation of Naples could well be followed by the Orléanist capture of Milan. The papacy would then be between the upper and nether millstones (*cf.* Voigt, *Enea Silvio*, III, 64–66, and Chr. Lucius, *Pius II. und Ludwig XI. von Frankreich, 1461–1462*, Giessen diss., Heidelberg, 1913).

On the return journey from Mantua to Rome, Pius stopped off in Florence, where he explained to the pro-French Cosimo de'Medici "that he was protecting Italy as long as he protected Ferrante" (. . . *tueri se Italiam dum Ferdinandum tueretur*, in the *Comm.*, bk. IV, Frankfurt, 1614, p. 96, lines 46–47). Although relating to the turn of events a few years later, the report which the Milanese ambassador to Rome, Otto del Carretto, sent his master Francesco Sforza on 12 March, 1462, is one of the most illuminating documents we have on Pius's Italian policy (Pastor, *Acta inedita*, I [1904], no. 125, pp. 150–62): Despite his assurances in the *Commentarii* that he never wavered, and that pearance of Francesco Sforza in Mantua, various Italian states sent embassies, including Florence, Siena, Lucca, and Bologna. After unconscionable delays the Venetian Signoria finally sent an embassy with great pomp, but the genial Doge Pasquale Malipiero, who was more devoted to peace and the pursuits of love than to war, especially with the Turks, would not think of using his influence to promote a crusade that might fail.[25] The Venetians had no intention of risking their fortresses and commercial stations in the Morea and the Aegean by courting the hostile attention of the Turks, whose virtual conquest of the Morea in 1458 had caused abiding alarm in the Senate. Arms were being sent to Coron and Modon, Nauplia and Negroponte, where the castellans and other Venetian officials were put on a constant alert.[26] Despite an abundance of fine words, the Venetians would make no commitment to the war against the Turks.[27]

The pope had found the preliminaries to the congress hard going. Most of the cardinals had been disaffected from the beginning, as Pius emphasizes in his *Commentaries* (especially bks. II–III). Little help could be expected from the two French members of the college. Among the Italians Jacopo de' Tebaldi and Lodovico Trevisan were complaining openly, as Pius knew well,[28] and Lodovico soon returned to the "dear" city of Rome, but Bessarion and Torquemada encouraged the pope and supported him devotedly. The cardinals were especially distressed with Mantua, a dull city, a marshland, where the air was said to be pestilential, the weather too hot, the food poor, the wine flat, and "nothing was to be heard except the frogs."[29] Pius's relations with the strong-minded Lodovico Trevisan were far from cordial. A year or so later (on 18 September, 1460) he was to reply ironically to Lodovico's excuse of gout and a "contraction of nerves" for not accepting a legatine mission to the court of King Ferrante of Naples: "As we have already written you, we were not of the opinion that your feet were essential, nor did the present necessity require agility and strength of limbs: our assumption was that King Ferrante and our affairs had need of your ability and experience. . . ."[30] Few popes have left upon the archival registers of their reigns such clear marks of personality as has the humanist Pius II.

The conquest of Constantinople had shaken the political structure of central Europe to its foundations, and the impress had been no less great upon Italy. Popular interest in Greece

---

he encouraged Milan to cleave to the alliance with Ferrante of Naples throughout the Angevin-Aragonese war in Italy, we find the pope fearful that his policy had in fact foundered, and the ambassador urged him to stand firm!

[25] *Cf.* Pius II, *Comm.*, bk. III, Engl. trans., pp. 232–33, 250–51, 254; ed. Frankfurt, 1614, pp. 75, 82, 83; Pastor, *Acta inedita*, I, nos. 77, 81, 83, 85–86. *Cf.* also the pope's letter of 28 July (1459) to the Florentines, in the volume of his *Brevia* in Arch. Segr. Vaticano, Arm. XXXIX, tom. 9, fol. 61: "Requisivimus devotionem vestram sepius ut oratores ad conventum hunc Mantuanum mittere non differretis . . . :" the pope believed the Italian powers should set a good example for the *ultramontani*, and note, *ibid.*, fols. 68r–69r, 71v. Among the letters to the doge of Venice on the Republic's delay in sending envoys to Mantua, see that of 3 August (fol. 71r).

[26] *Cf.* Arch. di Stato di Venezia, Sen. Mar, Reg. 6, fol. 118r [119r], a resolution of the Senate dated 6 April, 1459: "Quia civitas nostra Coroni, ut litteris regiminis illius habetur, munitionibus vacua est, tutelle cuius que a nostro dominio magni facienda est sit providendum his precipue temporibus quibus Theucer Amoream adeptus est, vadit pars quod auctoritate huius consilii mitti debeant per patronos nostri Arsenatus Coronum per primum passagium . . . munitiones que suprascriptis patronis Arsenatus solvantur de pecuniis depositi quod in procuratia fieri debet," and there follows a list of the *bombardae*, *sclopeti*, *springardae*, *ballistae*, etc., to be sent to Coron (*ibid.*, fol. 118v [119v]). A month later, on 7 May (1459), the Senate agreed that "civitas nostra Neapolis Romanie, ut notum est, in faucibus Theucrorum est," and arms and artillery were listed for shipment to Nauplia (fol. 121v [122v]). On 17 August the Senate voted to strengthen the defenses of Negroponte (fol. 138r [139r], and *cf.* fol. 174r [175r], docs. dated 20 May, 1460). In the spring of 1460 the Senate approved of continuing (rather slight) financial assistance to Scanderbeg, "cum . . . ipse utilis [sit] et ad conservationem status nostri ipsarum partium plurimum conferat" (fol. 165r [166r], dated 4 April). Various other documents in this register bear witness to the precautions taken by the Venetians to protect their territories from Turkish attack. Giuseppe Valentini, "La Crociata di Pio II dalla documentazione veneta d'archivio," *Archivum historiae pontificiae*, XIII (1975), 249–82, has published an invaluable list of Venetian documents relating to the "crusade" in the time of Pius II (as he has also done for the reigns of Pius's immediate predecessors, for which see above, Chapter 2, note 99).

[27] Pius II, *Comm.*, bk. III, Engl. trans., esp. pp. 257–59; ed. Frankfurt, 1614, p. 85; Cugnoni, *Opera inedita*, pp. 512, 513, the deleted passages on the Venetians.

[28] *Cf. Comm.*, bk. III, Engl. trans., pp. 193–94; ed. Frankfurt, 1614, p. 61; Cugnoni, *Opera inedita*, p. 511, on the disaffection of Lodovico Trevisan.

[29] Pius II, *Comm.*, *loc. cit.*; Pastor, *Gesch. d. Päpste*, II (repr. 1955), 50–52; and *cf.* Hefele and Leclercq, *Histoire des conciles*, VII-2 (1916), 1299.

[30] Arch. Segr. Vaticano, Arm. XXXIX, tom. 9, fols. 143v–144r ("datum Corsignani, XVIII Septembris, anno tertio"): "Nos, dilecte fili, sicut antea scripsimus, pedibus tuis opus esse non putabamus, nec presens necessitas agilitatem membrorum et robur querebat: ingenio tuo et usu rerum quem habes indigere regem Ferdinandum et res nostras arbitrabamur. . . ."

was widespread; there was an eastern vogue in art. While the Congress of Mantua was sitting, Benozzo Gozzoli was painting the marvelous murals of the Magi in the little chapel of the Palazzo Medici-Riccardi in Florence, showing the entry of the Byzantine Emperor John VIII and the Patriarch Joseph II into Florence to attend the famous council of twenty years before, among the handsomest and best preserved paintings of the Italian Renaissance. Court poets and humanists wrote much about the Turkish danger. As Greece grew poorer, the splendor of the Byzantine past was recalled with the more poignancy. Cardinal Bessarion was very active at Mantua, at the height of his influence, employing all his eloquence and prestige to help launch the crusade against the Turks. In his youth Bessarion had spent some years as a monk in the Morea, which he now saw was going the way of Constantinople. His only hope was that the Europeans would discharge their obligation to Christianity and rescue their Greek co-religionists from the coming onslaught of Islam.

If the western envoys arrived at Mantua with a studied reluctance, there was all too much urgency in the manner of those who came from Albania, Bosnia, and Ragusa, Cyprus, Rhodes, Lesbos, and the hard-pressed Morea.[31] Besides the official envoys various prominent Greeks had appeared at the papal court. Having sought safety in Italy, they now sought support at the Curia. Among them were nobles of the highest rank, even some from Constantinople, who had managed in one way or another to escape capture when the city had fallen a half dozen years before. On 30 May, 1459, for example, Pope Pius II granted an indulgence under certain conditions to those who would give alms to relieve the desperate plight of Demetrius and Michael Leontaris, once magnates of the highest dignity and authority at the Byzantine imperial court, now reduced to poverty and buffeted by the capricious turns of outrageous bad fortune. Each new arrival at the Curia probably had a tale to tell even more piteous than that of his predecessor. Pius expressed the sincerest sorrow for those whom the misfortunes of life had degraded from high rank and great possessions to the sad status of refugees and virtual beggary.[32]

From Ferrara on the way to Mantua, Pius II had written on 19 May, 1459, to the well-known Franciscan preacher Jacopo della Marca, papal nuncio in the March of Ancona, whom he had appointed to preach the crusade in that area,[33] telling him of a grant of plenary in-

[31] Pius II, *Comm.*, bk. III, Engl. trans., p. 200; ed. Frankfurt, 1614, p. 63; on the Congress of Mantua, note also Campano, *Vita Pii II*, ed. G. C. Zimolo, in the new Muratori, *RISS*, III-3 (1964), 28, 36–40, 52, and Platina's life of Pius, *ibid.*, pp. 106–7, 109; and *cf.* Pastor, *Gesch. d. Päpste*, II (repr. 1955), 56–57. On the pope's interest in church union and his attitude toward the eastern Orthodox churches, *cf.* the brief article of Fr. Georg Hofmann, "Papst Pius II. und die Kircheneinheit des Ostens," *Orientalia Christiana periodica*, XII (1946), 217–37.

[32] Arch. Segr. Vaticano, Reg. Vat. 471, fol. 202^v, "datum Mantue, anno etc., MCCCCLVIIII, tertio Kal. Iunii, pontificatus nostri anno primo." The letter is an "indulgentia pro benefacientibus Demetrio et Michaeli, militibus Constantinopolitanis." Pius says that ". . . cum itaque post illud miserabile excidium civitatis Constantinopolitane ad nostram presentiam venerint dilecti filii nobiles viri Demetrius et Michael Leontarii milites quorum progenitores, sicut fidedigna relatione percepimus, et supra nominati quoque apud olim Romeorum imperatores in eadem civitate Constantinopolitana maxime auctoritatis et potentie extitere quique ob innumerabiles et eroicas virtutes, splendorem sanguinis, et munificentiam, auctoritatem et maximas divitias totius Grecie lumen et ornamentum habebantur et post imperatorem, dum in humanis ageret, nemini cederent: Nunc vero everso imperio et civitate huiusmodi in tirannidem Turchorum redacta supradicti rerum egeni et ab omnibus destituti in erumnis versantur et varietatum fortune experimentum in se patiuntur nec vitam suam substentare valent nisi fidelium suffragia et elemosine piarum personarum eisdem subministrentur. . . ."

[33] Jacopo della Marca was a Minorite professor, who had preached for some forty years in Italy and Hungary. Three years later, in the spring of 1462, he was to provoke a tremendous renewal of the dispute between the Franciscans and Dominicans concerning the blood of Christ, to which Pius II devotes a large part of bk. XI of his *Commentarii* (Engl. trans., pp. 703–29; ed. Frankfurt, 1614, pp. 278–92, and *cf.* Voigt, *Enea Silvio*, III, 591–93, and Pastor, *Gesch. d. Päpste*, II [repr. 1955], 197–98). Although both the pope and a majority of the cardinals favored the Dominican position, "it did not seem best to issue an official statement at the time for fear of offending the great body of the Minorites, whose preaching against the Turks was needed" (*Comm.*, bk. XI, Engl. trans., p. 729). Jacopo della Marca (1391–1476) was canonized on 10 December, 1726. He is the subject of a considerable literature (for the older publications, see U. Chevalier, *Répertoire: Bio-bibliographie*, II [Paris, 1907], col. 2321), and documents relating to him are easily found in the Vatican Archives (e.g., Arm. XXXIX, tom. 7, fols. 84^r, 94, 95). Jacopo was sent to Hungary to preach after Capistrano's death. *Cf.* Ludwig Mohler, *Kardinal Bessarion als Theologe, Humanist and Staatsman*, I (Paderborn, 1923, repr. Aalen, 1967), 287, who does not seem to recognize his importance. Fra Jacopo was among those to whom Calixtus III's commission of 19 January, 1456, was issued "contra Iudeos," whereby the tithes to be paid by the Jews as well as the restitutions of usury were to be applied to the war against the Turk:

"Novit ille qui nichil ignorat [i.e., Deus] quod nos

dulgence to all who would serve in the Morea for a year at their own expense.[34] On the following day his Holiness wrote again to Fra Jacopo, informing him that "our venerable brother Bessarion, bishop of Tusculum, called the cardinal of Nicaea, will write you about the aforesaid matters at our request, and you are to accord him in everything the undoubting trust you would give our own self."[35] Bessarion had become the cardinal protector of the Franciscans eight months before this.[36] His letter to Jacopo, dated at Ferrara on 20 May, is a very important document.

Bessarion described the Morea to Jacopo as a large country with a coastline of some eight hundred miles, a very fertile land, which produced in abundance bread, wine, meat, cheese, wool, cotton, flax, silk, the scarlet kermes (*chremisinum*), grain, and the berries from which dye is made. A single ducat bought 1,400 lbs. of grain; wine cost nothing; meats were cheap; hay and straw were available for horses without number; "so that besides the inhabitants and natives of the place that country can support fifty thousand horsemen without having to seek food from any other source." In the preceding year (1458) the Turks had come with eighty thousand horsemen, a great number of footsoldiers, and a vast baggage train. They remained in the Morea for five months, and enjoyed food in plenty. After their departure everything was still very cheap, "such is the huge abundance of all things. . . ." "Likewise, besides the cities in the Morea there are about three hundred walled towns [*terrae muratae*], strongly fortified, animals beyond count, and a great multitude of people." The location of the Morea gave it easy access to Italy, Sicily, Crete, and the other islands, Asia Minor, Illyricum, Macedonia, and other Christian countries. If Christians held it, they could concentrate troops there for attacks upon the Turks, to the obvious advantage of Christendom when the Turks were a threat. The Turks, however, had occupied most of the Morea the year before, coming with a huge military force, and aided by the treachery of some evil men; a few places had held out, and in these the lords of the land had taken refuge, two brothers of the late Emperor Constantine.

---

quamquam immeriti ad summi apostolatus apicem assumpti inter cetera iusta et honesta desideria nostra nil magis optamus neque magis in corde nostro tenemus quam ut veneranda fides nostra Christiana prospere conservetur et nostro presertim tempore feliciter augeatur ac perfidissimus ille Machomectus Turchorum dux, iniquissimus redemptoris nostri crudelissimus hostis et nefandissimus Christiane religionis perturbator, cum eius superbia deprimatur ac illius temeritas pariter et superbia conteratur. Cum autem ad obviandum ne hec crudelissima belua suas perversas cupiditates explere valeat ad recuperandum etiam terras et civitates, presertim illam insignem olim civitatem Constantinopolitanam, ac ecclesias quas hic omnium scelerum artifex detinet occupatas, plurimis militum et gentium armorum copiis tam terrestribus quam maritimis ac maximis opus sit impensis et quamplura diversorum hominum auxilia ad ipsius Turchi depressionem et fidei Christiane exaltationem sint plurimum oportuna, nos matura consideratione cogitantes quod decime per Iudeos solvende necnon usure per eosdem Iudeos restituende in nullo magis pio neque magis pro ipsa fide nostra Christiana necessario opere quam contra illum sceleratissimum Turchum deputari aut converti possent, decimas et usuras huiusmodi in hoc sancto opere convertendas deputantes, et ut in subsidium ac ipsius fidei Christiane exaltationem et illius crudelissime fere depressionem convertantur, de nostre potestatis plenitudine tenore presentium decernentes te de cuius sincera fide et integritate plenam in domino fiduciam optinemus . . . contra Iudeos . . . decimarum et usurarum collectorem et executorem nostrum ad hoc cum potestate substituendi vel delegandi ydoneos viros religiosos cuiuscumque ordinis specialiter deputamus ac tibi per apostolica scripta committimus et mandamus quatenus prefatos Iudeos ad solvendum decimas omnium bonorum suorum que detinent mobilium et immobilium necnon ad restituendum omnes et singulas usuras quas hactenus usque in presentem diem quomodolibet receperunt seu recipient in futurum et quas in dicto sancto opere converti volumus auctoritate apostolica harum serie cogas et compellas invocato ad hoc si opus fuerit auxilio tam brachii ecclesiastici quam secularis . . ." (Reg. Vat. 440, fols. 119v–120r, 121v). The fairly full citation of this single document may serve as an illustration of various others to the same effect. *Cf.* Gelcich and Thallóczy, *Diplomatarium ragusanum*, no. 356, p. 604, a letter of the Ragusei to Fra Jacopo, dated 7 February, 1458.

[34] Sp. P. Lampros, *Palaiológeia kaì Peloponnesiaká*, IV (Athens, 1930), 251–53; Luke Wadding, *Annales Minorum*, XIII (3rd ed., Quaracchi, 1932), 134–35 (ed. Lyon, VI [1648], 436–37; ed. Rome, XIII [1735], 117–18). (I have commonly cited the third edition of Wadding's *Annales*, edited by J. M. Fonseca and published at Quaracchi, which gives cross-references to the Roman edition.) Pius II was at Ferrara from 17 May to the twenty-fifth (Arch. Segr. Vaticano, Arm. XXXIX, tom. 8, fol. 28v, and *cf.* Pastor, *Gesch. d. Päpste*, II [repr. 1955], 48–49).

[35] Lampros, *Pal. kaì Pel.*, IV, 253–54; also in Wadding, *Annales Minorum*, XIII (1932), 135.

[36] Wadding, *Annales Minorum*, XIII (1932), 72 (ed. Lyon, VI [1648], 415–16; ed. Rome, XIII [1735], 63). Pius II appointed Bessarion protector of the Franciscans on 10 September, 1458, after the death of Cardinal Domenico Capranica. Two letters dated "ex palatio residentie mee Rome A.D. MCCCCLXII, die XX Aprilis" (in Arch. Segr. Vaticano, Arm. XXXV, tom. 135, fols. 127r–128r) show Bessarion concerned with details of his position as protector of the order, which must have taken a fair amount of his time and caused him numerous headaches.

This year, in the month of January just passed, God had raised the spirit of one of these lords, the Despot Thomas Palaeologus of the Morea. He had taken up arms against the infidels for his own freedom and that of his people. Within two months he had recovered all the lost places (according to Bessarion!), "a great and wonderful and miraculous thing it was and is, and one which gives us hope of great things for the future, provided we know how to use this opportunity well." Sultan Mehmed had lost his awesome reputation and suffered grievous losses, but he would return in anger and in great might. The Christians in Greece needed help, which they had asked of the pope, who had promised it. His Holiness and Bessarion were placing their hopes in the diet to be held at Mantua. In the meantime aid was desperately needed in the Morea. Jacopo was to enroll crusaders to embark at Ancona on a ship which the pope would furnish. Good men were needed with arms and funds for a year, fifty or at least forty ducats of their own or in contributions from others. Jacopo was to grant a plenary indulgence both to those who went on this crusade themselves and to those whose gifts made it possible for others to go. Speed was essential. It would be far better to send five hundred or four hundred or even three hundred men right away than many thousands too late. Jacopo was to send his recruits to Ancona, where the papal ship would be ready to transport them immediately to the Morea. Bessarion closes his letter with an urgent appeal to the good friar to take this matter to heart, for he would be rendering Christendom an inestimable service in which they would all find rich fruits and consolation.[37]

Bessarion's statement that a few hundred troops now might be better than thousands later was his own idea. His emotions tended to get the better of his mind when he pondered the Turkish problem. When the Despot Thomas's envoys arrived in Mantua, bringing the pope sixteen Turkish captives, they also said that a small Italian army would be able to drive the Turks from their land, but perhaps they were afraid of asking for too much. When the question was raised in the consistory, the pope indicated that in his opinion such a force would not accomplish anything.[38] No one in his generation had a better grasp of the facts of international life than he; his *Europa* shows how well he knew both the Greeks and the Turks, their past history and contemporary circumstances.

Time was necessary, however, to organize even a small force, and in July, 1459, Pope Pius wrote to the Greek magnates and the chiefs of the Albanian tribes in the Morea of the joy he felt in their rebellion against the Turks and their return to the authority of the Despot Thomas, *ad vestrum catholicum principem dilectum filium nostrum*. The pope spoke of Thomas with the highest praise. He appealed to both the Greeks and the Albanians to keep faith with him and manfully to resist the Turks, "fighting for your native land, your wives, children, your own homes, churches, and places of burial, and above all for the very religion of our Lord Jesus Christ founded by his very precious blood, and do not hesitate for Him to give your life and shed your blood, Who spared not His own blood for us and for our salvation. . . ."[39] We may assume that the Greek translation was as stirring as the original text, and still doubt that it made any impression upon those to whom it was addressed.

Discouraging as the outlook was, a small body of three hundred footsoldiers was finally recruited. Bianca Maria Visconti, wife of Francesco Sforza, duke of Milan, who was active at the Congress of Mantua, supplied one hundred of these at her own request. Pius II equipped the other two hundred "although he did not approve of building great undertakings on so weak a foundation: but he could not disappoint Bessarion, who had set his heart on it."[40] Bianca's

[37] Lampros, *Pal. kaì Pel.*, IV, 255–58; Wadding, *Annales Minorum*, XIII (3rd ed., 1932), 135–37; Mohler, *Kard. Bessarion*, III, 490–93. In 1422 a Venetian commission reported to the Signoria that the Morea, *la quale è di maggiore entrata che l'isola di Candia*, contained more than 150 castles; was 700 miles in circumference; produced gold, silver, and lead; and was a source of silk, honey, wax, grain, poultry, and currants (Sanudo, *Vite de'duchi*, in *RISS*, XXII, col. 943). In a letter sent from Mantua on 2 June, 1459, Pius II informed the European princes that the Morea was in revolt against the Turks (Arch. Segr. Vaticano, Arm. XXXIX, tom. 9, fol. 41ʳ).

[38] Pius II, *Comm.*, bk. III, Engl. trans., p. 195; ed. Frankfurt, 1614, p. 61; and *cf.* Raynaldus, *Ann. eccl.*, ad ann. 1459, no. 46, vol. XIX (1693), pp. 27–28.

[39] Raynaldus, *Ann. eccl.*, ad ann. 1459, no. 47, vol. XIX (1693), p. 28.

[40] Pius II, *Comm.*, bk. III, Engl. trans., pp. 195–96; ed. Frankfurt, 1614, pp. 61–62; Bibl. Apost. Vaticana, Cod. Reg. lat. 1995, fol. 119ʳ: ". . . Bissarionem noluit contristari. . . ." Raynaldus, *Ann. eccl.*, ad ann. 1459, no. 46, vol. XIX, pp. 27–28; Wadding, *Annales Minorum*, XIII (1932), 133; Voigt, *Enea Silvio*, III, 57–58; Hefele and Leclercq, *Hist. des conciles*, VII-2 (1916), 1301–2; Pastor, *Gesch. d. Päpste*, II (repr. 1955), 56–57.

forces were placed under the command of Giannone of Cremona (or Crema), and the others under that of the pope's countryman Dotha of Siena, a political exile from his native city. On 14 July, 1459, Pius had written a laudatory letter to the Despot Thomas, giving thanks to God that such a champion had emerged as the times required. While congratulating Thomas upon his initial victory over the Turks, the pope urged him to fortify with proper garrisons the places he had rewon and to take whatever other measures might be necessary for their defense, "and since you ask assistance of us to protect your dominion, we are sending you for now as a sign of our good will three hundred and fifty footsoldiers, dependable men with experience in war and thoroughly capable, over whom have been set as commanders Giannone of Cremona and Ser Dotha of Siena—and these we have instructed to obey your Excellency in all things. . . ." The pope further stated that, when some agreement had been reached with the princes at Mantua, he would see to the sending of forces to hold the lands of the Moreote despotate against the Turks. Thomas was therefore urged to persevere in his sacred undertaking, being assured of the divine and papal assistance soon to be made manifest.[41]

Soon after the arrival of the Milanese and papal soldiers in the Morea, the Despot Thomas wrote a letter full of heartfelt thanks to Francesco Sforza for the valuable services of Giannone, whom Thomas cannot praise too much.[42] Some time later, on 2 October, 1460, Francesco answered him in sad recognition of the desperate conditions in Greece, but expressed the hope that eventually Pope Pius II and the Italian powers would come to the aid of afflicted Greece and render the Turks their due in punishment. He also promised that the resources of the Milanese duchy, such as they were, would never be lacking to assist the Morea. He rejoiced that Giannone and his troops had been so useful, "although he has not been able to provide the protection or advantages which your present necessity requires and for which we could most earnestly wish. . . ."[43]

The Despot Thomas had promptly attacked Patras in conjunction with his Italian auxiliaries, and had succeeded in taking the lower city by

---

[41] Arch. Segr. Vaticano, Reg. Vat. 471 [*Pii II de Curia, anno I, tom. IV*], fol. 349: "Pius, etc. Dilecto filio excellenti principi Thome Paleologo Porphirogenito despoto Amoree salutem, etc. Intelligentes pridem tuam precipuam animi magnitudinem, fortitudinem, atque constantiam et alias bellicas et eroicas virtutes quibus usus novissime adversus Turcos victoriam reportasti, gratias in primis Deo agimus quod hiis presertim temporibus talem pugilem habeamus qualem presens conditio postulat et requirit. Commendamus itaque tuam Excellentiam et invictissimum animum et veris laudibus extollimus, et licet necessarium esse minime arbitremur te hortari ad hoc sanctum opus Deo plurimum acceptum, tibi ac statui tuo necessarium, et apud Christianos homines summe commendabile, cum ad id tua sponte ardentissimum esse sciamus, hanc tamen hortationem pro magnitudine rerum adiecimus ut nec potissime tuis viribus incumbas, nam cum loca tui dominii per hostes fidei, vi et armis superiori tempore subacta tua virtute nuper recuperaveris, antequam illi aliqua in perniciem tui status moliri possent, eorum consilia preveniendo loca ipsa oportunis presidiis premunire et cetera ad tutelam locorum huiusmodi et illorum oppugnationem necessaria efficere debes, et quia subsidium a nobis exposcis quo tuum dominium tutari valeas, impresentiarum pro signo nostre bone voluntatis mittimus trecentos quinquaginta pedites fidos et expertos bello ac valentes veros quibus prefecti sunt dilecti filii Zeno de Crema miles et Ser Dota de Senis.

"Hiis itaque mandavimus ut in omnibus tue Excellentie pareant et ita in vinculum iuramenti prestiti et fidelitatis debite per presentes stricte precipimus ut tibi obedientissimi sint et tuam in cunctis faciant voluntatem eosque itaque benigne recipere et pertractare ac commendatos habere placeat, ceterum quia inpresentiarum in civitate Mantuana, loco diete per nos institute, personaliter permanemus exspectantes ut Dei et fidei cause prodesse possimus postquam conclusio aliqua cum Christianis principibus habita fuerit, oportuna presidia adhibere curabimus que ad tutelam tuarum regionum conferre poterunt. Hanc igitur sanctam expeditionem alacri animo assummas tibi enim recte agendi [*sic*] assistet omnipotens Deus adiutor et defensor Christianorum in tempore tribulationis, qui te succumbere nullo modo permittet et tuam potentiam augebit et nos quoque tue generositati non deerimus prout re ac effectu oportuno tempore demo[n]strare intendimus. Datum Mantue, anno etc., MCCCCLVIIII, pridie Idus Julii, pontificatus nostri anno primo."

[42] Lampros, *Pal. kaì Pel.*, IV, 242–43. The letter is in Italian and undated; it was probably sent in the late summer of 1459. Lampros believes that the despot's letter, presumably written in Greek, was very likely translated by Francesco Filelfo, who was then in Milan (*ibid.*, introd., p. 26). Filelfo accompanied Francesco Sforza to the Congress of Mantua in September, 1459 (Pius II, *Comm.*, bk. III, Engl. trans., p. 225; ed. Frankfurt, 1614, p. 73; and *cf.* Voigt, *Enea Silvio*, III, 63–64). According to Pius II, Dotha had been a notary and was not a very good soldier (*Comm.*, bk. III, Frankfurt, 1614, pp. 61–62, and bk. X, p. 259): ". . . Dota, cuius ante meminimus, centurio peditum, non tam miles audax quam notarius olim peritus. . . ."

[43] Lampros, *Pal. kaì Pel.*, IV, 244–45. Giannone had accompanied the Greek embassy from Monemvasia, which earlier in the year (1460) had offered the city to Pope Pius, lest it fall into the hands of the Turks (*Comm.*, bk. IV, Engl. trans., pp. 321–22; ed. Frankfurt, 1614, pp. 103–4, and see below, pp. 224–25). In a letter to Bessarion dated at Corsignano on 12 September, 1460, the pope notes his acceptance of the city and his hope that it may provide the means "ad recuperandam Peloponessum" (*Brevia*, Arch. Segr. Vaticano, Arm. XXXIX, tom. 9, fol. 142).

storm. He could not take the citadel, however, and soon the Greeks and Italians were quarreling. Rivalries and jealousies, and perhaps disputes over the rewards accruing from their slender victories, made further co-operation too difficult. The Italians, very few in number, were probably appalled to learn at such close quarters how many Turks had entered the Morea, and the odds against victory being absurd, they withdrew from the troubled land, leaving it to its fast approaching fate.[44]

On 26 September, just four months after his arrival in Mantua, Pope Pius addressed the only general session of the congress in a three-hour oration in which he inveighed against the atrocities of the Turks; recalled the glorious exploits of the First Crusade, with its Godfreys and Bohemonds; and finally offered to accompany the new crusaders into the very battlefield if they wished him to do so. After the pope, Bessarion spoke in the same vein, praising Pius, assuring him of the cardinals' willingness to pledge their full support in the great enterprise, and recalling the dreadful plight of the Greeks and the sacrilegious horrors perpetrated by the Turks in Christian churches.[45] The assembled envoys now went on record with a unanimous decision for war against the Turks. Thereafter the pope dealt with the various embassies in groups, gathered by nations, starting with the Italians. When Francesco Sforza suggested that the Italian and other western states furnish the money, and the countries neighboring upon the Turkish empire furnish the troops, because they knew the Turks best, his proposal met with much favor. When Sigismondo Malatesta's turn came to speak, however, he took strong exception to it on the grounds that those who lived nearest to the Turks were the most afraid of them. Sigismondo expressed great confidence in Italian soldiers and commanders, horses, and equipment: "Therefore I urge that the others contribute money and the Italians wage the war." Pius then said that he too would prefer Italian soldiers if other peoples could supply the necessary funds, but only Italy could do that, and then he added, not without irony: "Nor have we generals who would be willing to campaign outside Italy. Here they wage war without risk of their lives and with great profit; battles with the Turk are bloody and the only prizes to be won are souls, which our soldiers hold very precious while they are within the body but very cheap outside it."[46]

The pope was indefatigable in his efforts to stimulate resistance against the Turks. On 16 November, 1459, he wrote reassuringly to Leonardo III Tocco, the despot of Arta, that the latter's envoy Bernardo Colelli had reported at Mantua on the losses which Leonardo and his harassed subjects were suffering at the hands of the perfidious Turk. Leonardo was to stand firm, however, because Pius hoped to contrive the Turk's expulsion from Europe.[47]

---

[44] Pius II, *Comm.*, *loc. cit.*; Raynaldus, *Ann. eccl.*, ad ann. 1459, no. 48, vol. XIX (1693), p. 28; Wadding, *Annales Minorum*, XIII (1932), 133; *Tre lettere inedite di Messer Giovanni Mignanelli, oratore della repubblica di Siena alla corte di Papa Pio II*, Pisa, 1869, p. 9, cited by Pastor, *Gesch. d. Päpste*, II (repr. 1955), 56–57; Zinkeisen, *Gesch. d. osman. Reiches in Europa*, II (1854), 193–200; Voigt, *Enea Silvio*, III (1863), 57.

[45] J. D. Mansi, ed., *Pii II P. M. . . . orationes politicae et ecclesiasticae*, II (Lucca, 1757), 9 ff., and Mohler, *Kard. Bessarion*, I, 288–89.

[46] Pius II, *Comm.*, bk. III, Engl. trans., p. 255; ed. Frankfurt, 1614, p. 84. On Pius's contempt for the Italian soldiery of his time, see, *ibid.*, bk. IV, p. 100: "Perfida est nostri temporis militia, quae stipendio veluti mercaturae utitur lucro, quod ne deficiat bellum producit," etc. The pope says that he spoke for three hours at the general session of the congress, and that "Bessarion cardinalis graecus . . . non pauciora quam pontifex verba fecit . . ." (*ibid.*, bk. III, p. 82, lines 47–48). On the course of events at the congress from the general session of 26 September, 1459, to its conclusion and the departure of the pope on the following 19 January, see Hefele and Leclercq, *Hist. des conciles*, VII-2 (1916), 1304–21, 1334, and Pastor, *Gesch. d. Päpste*, II (repr. 1955), 63–79.

Referring to Murad II's victory at Varna fifteen years before, the Venetian Senate reminded Pius on 11 October, 1459, that Mehmed II was a far more dangerous adversary than his father had been: "Non era [Murad] si gran signore come costui [Mehmed] ne si feroce ne di tanta reputatione. . . ." While his father had given himself over to pleasure, Mehmed's chief enjoyment was the "exercise of arms and the enlargement of his empire:" "A nui pareria che la suo Sanctità facesse ogni instantia et solicitudine possibile con la Maestà del Re de Franza, Ingeltera, Spagna et Portegallo, siche almeno quella de Franza con alcuni de quelli altri qual fosse piu ardenti a tal gloriosa imprexa dovesse mettere potentemente le mane et non abandonarla fino a guerra finita . . ." (Arch. di Stato di Venezia, Sen. Secreta, Reg. 20, fols. 192^v–193^r [194^v–195^r], from a letter to the Venetian envoys Orsato Giustinian and Lodovico Foscarini, who would convey the Senate's warning to the pope).

[47] Pastor, *Acta inedita*, I (1904), no. 88, p. 119. This letter to Leonardo Tocco occurs in a small collection of Pius II's correspondence in a late fifteenth-century octavo volume in the Bibl. Laurenziana in Florence, which now bears the binder's title *Leonardi Arretini quaedam* (Plut. LXXXX, super. cod. 138, selections from Bruni's works occupying the second half of the volume, fols. 52 ff.), no. 46, fol. 23^r: "Leonardo de Spoto [for Despoto] Arthe. . . . Datum Mantue, die XVI Novembris, [pontificatus nostri] anno II."

Two weeks later, on the twenty-ninth, the pope wrote the Mantuan bishop, Galeazzo Cavriani, the governor of Rome, and the vice-treasurer Jacopo de' Mucciarelli that Leonardo Tocco would do his part against the Turks, and therefore "we have granted him one of our galleys which have been built at Rome."[48]

The envoys from Germany and France reached Mantua only in late October and November (1459). The French were impossible to deal with, their meetings with the pope being full of the Angevin claims to Naples; the Germans were so divided among themselves that adherence to a common cause seemed quite beyond expectation. The envoys of the Emperor Frederick and the other German princes advanced various grandiose and impracticable proposals, but on 19 December agreed to contribute to the crusade the thirty-two thousand infantry and ten thousand cavalry which had previously been promised to Pope Nicholas V. Final arrangements were to be made with papal legates in two diets, one of which was to be convoked in Nuremberg, and the other in Austria, for it was necessary to conclude a peace between Frederick and Matthias Corvinus, "der sich nennet ein koenig zu Hungerrn," as well as to obtain free passage through Hungary.[49] Months before, on 1 June, the opening day of the congress, Pope Pius had made a special appeal to the inhabitants of Nuremberg. All the Morea was in revolt, he had told them, determined not to submit again to the Turkish yoke if only western Christians would assist them. If help did not reach them in time, however, the Moreotes would be forced to return to their former servitude. The expected envoys had not come (as we have noted); he was old and tired; the patrimony of the church claimed his attention; it would not be his fault if the enterprise failed, for he could not bear the burden alone.[50] At last, however, it appeared as though he should not have to bear the burden alone.

Much depended on the legatine mission to Germany, and on 2 January, 1460, Cardinal Bessarion was appointed in a secret consistory. On 14 January a three years' crusade against the Turks was proclaimed, and a plenary indulgence provided for all who would serve in the armies for eight months, and also for the members of all convents and monasteries which would support for eight months one fighting man for every ten of their religious.[51] In a

---

[48] Pastor, *Acta inedita*, I, no. 89, p. 119. Pius also ordered that Leonardo be sent 3,000 florins from Bologna (*ibid.*, no. 95, p. 122, letter dated at Macereto, 13 May, 1460).

[49] N. Iorga, *Notes et extraits*, IV (Bucharest, 1915), pt. 3, doc. no. 96, pp. 166–68; *cf.* Mansi, *Concilia*, XXXV, col. 115; Raynaldus, *Ann. eccl.*, ad ann. 1459, nos. 66–70, vol. XIX (1693), pp. 34–35. According to the general form of the papal briefs prepared in this connection, the two diets were needed "ad componendum differentias inter principes et magnates et cetera facienda ad expeditionem exercitus oportuna," doc. dated 22 December, 1459, in Arch. Segr. Vaticano, Arm. XXXIX, tom. 9, fol. 94^v, and *cf.* fols. 95^r–96^r, 98, where mention is made of the 10,000 *equites* and 32,000 *pedestres* as well as of making peace between Frederick and Matthias Corvinus, etc. *Cf.* Pastor, *Gesch. d. Päpste*, II (repr. 1955), 76, and Mohler, *Kard. Bessarion*, I, 290–92.

In the meantime Cardinal Carvajal had been continuing his efforts to make peace between Frederick and Matthias Corvinus. There had been no cessation in the Turkish attacks which had beset Matthias since his accession to the throne. *Cf.* Pius II's letter to Carvajal, dated at Mantua on 11 June, 1459 (Arm. XXXIX, tom. 9, fol. 47^r): "Ex litteris tue Circumspectionis in Nova Civitate [Wiener Neustadt] ultimo datis intelleximus que de tenenda inter imperatorem et regem Ungarie dieta deque novo ac repentino Turcorum adventu significas: fuerunt nobis hec nova satis molesta et dolemus." Note the letters of the same date to Frederick III and the Venetians (*ibid.*, fols. 48^r–49^r) and those of almost a year later, dated at Siena on 25 April, 1460, to Carvajal and Frederick (*ibid.*, fols. 185^v–187^r): ". . . Iterum atque iterum rogamus tuam Excellenciam ut omnibus tuis desideriis quamquam etiam iustissimis orthodoxam nostram Christiane religionis fidem et eius defensionem maxime nunc dum periculum immineat, ut decet religiosissimum imperatorem pro Dei et tua gloria et cunctorum tibi subdictorum salute, anteponas . . ." (to Frederick, fol. 186^v). A letter to Carvajal, dated 2 May, 1461 (*datum Rome II Maii anno III*) noted the expectation of another Turkish siege of Belgrade, ". . . Turchum magnis apparatibus ad obsidendam Nandoralbem venturum . . ." (fol. 211^r).

Pius II, *Comm.*, bk. III, Engl. trans., pp. 259–73; ed. Frankfurt, 1614, pp. 85–90, describes his dealings with the French, English, and German embassies. The statement in the English translation (p. 273) that, in addition to the 32,000 infantry, the Germans had promised Nicholas V 40,000 cavalry is erroneous. The Latin text reads (p. 90, lines 29 ff.): "Convenerunt tandem omnes in unam sententiam Germanorum legati, eumque pontifici exercitum promisere, qui pridem Frankfordiae sub Nicolao praeside promissus fuerat, id est pedites duo et triginta millia, *equites decem millia*. . . ." Both in this passage and in his final speech at the congress Pius refers to a German total of 42,000, including both infantry and cavalry, *Germani exercitum pollicentur duorum et quadraginta millium bellatorum* . . . (p. 92, lines 34–35).

[50] Iorga, *Notes et extraits*, IV, pt. 3, doc. no. 98, pp. 168–69, and *cf.* nos. 100, 113, 115, pp. 171, 180, 181.

[51] Raynaldus, *Ann. eccl.*, ad ann. 1460, nos. 5–7, 18–20, vol. XIX (1693), pp. 41–42, 44–45; Aug. Theiner, ed., *Vetera monumenta historica Hungariam sacram illustrantia*, II (Rome, 1860), nos. 528–31, pp. 348–51; Pastor, *Gesch. d. Päpste*, II (repr. 1955), 77–78; Mohler, *Kard. Bessarion*, I. 294.

letter dated 15 January Pope Pius informed Bessarion that he would participate in the expedition himself if his health permitted; he had granted crusading indulgences more ample than those of his predecessors; and had decreed a general tithe of clerical goods, without excepting his own apostolic goods or those of the cardinals. Bessarion was to have the power of raising and organizing armies, collecting the tithe, naming preachers for the crusade, pronouncing ecclesiastical sentences, and taking money deposited in churches. There was to be no exemption from the responsibility of assisting eastern Christendom against the Turks, not even for the mendicant orders.[52]

In his last address to the assembly at Mantua, Pius said: "The seventh month has already passed . . . , and we are in the eighth. This is the end of the congress at Mantua, which we do not dissolve, but have decided to transfer with us wherever we take our Curia. . . ." He gave thanks for the achievements of the congress. "But someone is probably saying, What good has been done here? What should Christians hope for or the Turks fear?" His detractors would say that nothing had been accomplished in this congress, which Pius had felt he had to call, because he lacked, he said, the lofty spirit of Eugenius IV, the sublime mind of Nicholas V, and the vast courage of Calixtus III. They had declared war on the Turks by themselves, armed soldiers, and equipped fleets, but "we have believed that the Roman Church can by no means sustain so great an effort of war by herself alone. . . . We have thought that common problems should be solved by common counsel. . . ." He had thought when he came to Mantua that more would be done, he said candidly, for what the princes had promised was not the most that could be done, nor was it the least. "Another might exaggerate with fine words; it is for us to tell the plain and simple truth. . . ." Then, summarizing the commitments of the princes with a marked literary skill, he reckoned an army of some eighty thousand men as promised to the cause, "and he who thinks that this is not enough either has no knowledge of military science or puts no hope in the Lord."[53] Before he left Mantua (on 19 January, 1460), Pius promulgated the famous bull *Execrabilis*, condemning an appeal from the pope to a general council, for not only was the practice canonically repugnant to him, but he foresaw it would be employed as a device to avoid payment of the Turkish tithes.[54]

---

[52] Iorga, *Notes et extraits*, IV, pt. 3, no. 108, p. 177. On 18 January, 1460, Pius II wrote Matthias Corvinus that ". . . mittimus ad nationem germanicam in executionem sue pollicitationis venerabilem fratrem nostrum Bissarionem episcopum Tuscullanum S. R. E. cardinalem Nicenum, nostrum et apostolice sedis legatum: curabit Circumspectio sua pacem vel treguas inter dissidentes illic stabilire; curabit promissum exercitum fieri. . . ." Bessarion was also to try to compose the dissension between the Emperor Frederick and Matthias (always an important consideration in these documents), and the pope reminded the latter that he now had a fine opportunity "non solum ad liberandum regnum Hungarie ex quottidianis hostium incursibus, sed ad parandam tibi et posteris commendationem perpetuam . . ." (*Brevia*, in Arch. Segr. Vaticano, Arm. XXXIX, tom. 9, fol. 100ʳ, and published in Theiner, *op. cit.*, II, no. 530, p. 350).

[53] Mansi, *Concilia*, XXXV, cols. 113–16; *cf.* Hefele and Leclercq, *Hist. des conciles*, VII-2, 1319–20. Pius even manages graceful allusions to the Venetians and Charles VII of France despite their failures to make any commitment. In March, 1462, after the death of Charles, his son and successor Louis XI offered to lead an army of 70,000 men against Sultan Mehmed II if the pope would help him to regain Genoa and abandon Ferrante of Naples in favor of the Angevins (Pastor, *Gesch. d. Päpste*, II [repr. 1955], 117–18, 119–20), but his sincerity was more than suspect.

[54] The bull *Execrabilis et pristinis temporibus* was promulgated on 18 January, 1460, the day before the pope's departure from Mantua: Raynaldus, *Ann. eccl.*, ad ann. 1460, nos. 10–11, vol. XIX (1693), pp. 42–43, corrected by Voigt, *Enea Silvio*, III, 101–3; Hefele and Leclercq, *Hist. des conciles*, VII-2, 1320–21; Pastor, *Gesch. d. Päpste*, II (repr. 1955), 79–81; and especially G. B. Picotti, "La Pubblicazione e i primi effetti della 'Execrabilis' di Pio II," *Archivio della R. Società romana di storia patria*, XXXVII (1914), 5–56. Mohler, *Kard. Bessarion*, I, 292, is mistaken in setting 14 January as the day on which Pius left Mantua. *Cf.* Pius II, *Comm.*, bk. III, Engl. trans., pp. 276–79; ed. Frankfurt, 1614, pp. 91–93 (the texts of Pius's speech differ somewhat); Raynaldus, ad ann. 1460, nos. 12–13, vol. XIX, p. 43.

When Pius II left Mantua on 19 January, 1460, Cardinal Nicholas of Cusa withdrew from the Curia to resume his battles with the local clergy in his episcopal see of Brixen (Bressanone), where Duke Sigismund of the Tyrol was his most powerful and dangerous opponent (Cusa ended his days in this bitter strife, on which see Pastor, *Hist. Popes*, III, 178–212, revised in *Gesch. d. Päpste*, II (repr. 1955), 138–64). Bessarion departed for Germany. Note the interesting entries in the Acta Consistorialia (1439–1486), in Arch. Segr. Vaticano, Arm. XXXI, tom. 52, fol. 61ᵛ: "Recessus domini Sancti Petri [Nich. of Cusa] a Mantua euntis versus suam ecclesiam [Brixinensem] et non participat [i.e., does not share in the collegial fees after his departure]. Anno a nativitate Domini MCCCCLX°, die vero sexta mensis Februarii, reverendissimus dominus meus, cardinalis Sancti Marci [Pietro Barbo, later Paul II], retulit michi [i.e., the clerk of the Sacred College], qualiter reverendissimi domini cardinales dixerant sibi tanquam camerario collegii quod reverendissimus dominus cardinalis Sancti Petri a die XVIIII

The historian Flavio Biondo had accompanied Pius from Rome to Mantua, taking with him the manuscript of his *Roma triumphans*, "with the hope of being able to complete his work," as the late Bartolomeo Nogara has said, "more easily in the quiet of Siena and the city of the Gonzagas than in Rome." Flavio had spent almost four years on the *Roma triumphans*, and he did in fact finish it at Mantua. In his brief dedicatory epistle to the pope Flavio expressed the confident belief that God would crown with glory and mankind with applause the expedition *quam paras in Turcos*, and that the Italians, French, Spaniards, and Germans whom Pius was inspiring to go on the crusade would learn from his *Roma triumphans* the lessons of endurance which imitation of the valor of the ancient Romans would teach them.[55]

Despite the assurance of Flavio Biondo, the outlook was not encouraging. Much would depend upon Bessarion's mission to Germany. Although Pius wanted the Emperor Frederick to take at least nominal leadership of the crusade, he was naturally not so naive as to assume that the Frederick he knew could ever emulate his namesake Barbarossa. The emperor, however, had long been the central figure in Aeneas Sylvius's views of temporal sovereignty in Europe. In two early treatises, the *Pentalogus de rebus ecclesiae et imperii* (1443) and *De ortu et auctoritate imperii romani* (1446), he had glorified the imperial authority as the divinely ordained center of Christian secular society.[56] His experience of the conciliarists' disunion at Basel had made a lasting impression on him. He came to believe that Europe needed unity of authority as much as the Church needed unity of doctrine. He became what might be called a conservative, opposed to church councils and suspicious of other representative assemblies. Also the failure of conciliarism had discouraged and disillusioned the ecclesiastical reformers themselves, who had little to offer Europe after their unsuccessful revolution at Basel.

It was hard for Pius to stop thinking in terms of the *imperium et sacerdotium*. The universalist claims of the papacy and the empire had become almost categorical imperatives. Never a profound thinker, Pius could hardly divest himself of the political tradition of the later middle ages. He had been for some years as much an imperialist as Dante, who could preserve his illusions because he never had to discharge the practical responsibilities of high office. Although Aeneas Sylvius had seen much of Europe in his travels, as pope he was loath to think in terms of national states, especially since the crusade would have to be an international undertaking. He was only too unhappily aware of the pride and prestige of the French nation, to which he appealed in urging the crusade upon Charles VII, but the universality of the papacy's spiritual claims too easily suggested a similar recognition of the temporal authority of the empire. If, however, the spiritual claims of the pope had suffered no abatement or diminution through the years, obviously the universality of imperial authority, which had never been a historical fact, was a

---

mensis Januarii quo sanctissimus dominus noster recessit de Mantua non deberet participare quia ibat ad suam ecclesiam. Ita quod retulit scripsi./ Recessus domini Niceni legati de latere euntis versus Alamanias et non participat: Item retulit michi idem reverendissimus dominus cardinalis Sancti Marci camerarius quod reverendissimus dominus cardinalis Nicenus legatus de latere yens versus partes Alamanie a die XVIIII mensis Januarii quo discessit sanctissimus dominus noster de Mantua in antea non participabat de communibus et minutis serviciis." (The last phrase supplies the expansion and shows the meaning of the recurring formula "non participat" in the Acta.) Nicholas of Cusa returned to the Curia on 28 May, 1460 (*ibid.*, fol. 62^v): ". . . die vero XXVIII mensis Maii reverendissimus in Christo pater, dominus noster Cardinalis Sancti Petri ad Vincula, veniens de partibus Alamanie intravit Senas [where Pius II then was] et incipit participare" (*cf.* the highly abbreviated entries in Eubel, *Hierarchia catholica*, II [1914, repr. 1960], 32, 33). About ten weeks later (on 8 August) Duke Sigismund of the Tyrol was excommunicated, and German ecclesiastical affairs were soon in a turmoil.

On the bitter contest between Nicholas of Cusa and Sigismund, into which Pius was inevitably drawn, see Edmond Vansteenberghe, *Le Cardinal Nicolas de Cues (1401–1464): L'Action—la pensée*, Paris, 1920, repr. Frankfurt am Main, 1963, pp. 144–53, 166–210, and Andreas Posch, "Nikolaus von Cusa, Bischof von Brixen, im Kampf um Kirchenreform und Landeshoheit in seinem Bistum," in Nikolaus Grass, ed., *Cusanus-Gedächtnisschrift*, Innsbruck and Munich, 1970, pp. 227–50, esp. pp. 237 ff., 242 ff. The bibliography relating to Nicholas of Cusa is immense (*cf.* the *Mitteilungen und Forschungsbeiträge der Cusanus-Gesellschaft*, I [Mainz, 1961], 95–126, III [1963], 223–37, etc.).

[55] *Blondi Flavii Forliviensis de Roma triumphante*, Basel, 1559, p. 1, and on this work note B. Nogara, *Scritti inediti e rari di Biondo Flavio*, Rome, 1927, pp. CXLIX ff., 192–93 (Studi e testi, no. 48).

[56] *Cf.* in general John B. Toews, "Dream and Reality in the Imperial Ideology of Pope Pius II," *Medievalia et humanistica*, fasc. XVI (Sept. 1964), 77–93, and B. Widmer, *Enea Silvio* (1960), pp. 44 ff., and *Enea Silvio Piccolomini in der sittlichen und politischen Entscheidung* (1963), pp. 135 ff.

chimera which no realistic statesman could pursue.

It was a pity, of course, because the international crusade required an international leadership, but there was no imperial plenitude of power, there was no international *imperium*, and was there no secular leadership for the great crusade of which Pius dreamed? In trying to organize an expedition against the Turks, it was necessary to take account of the Hapsburg emperor's *Hauspolitik*, the princes' territorial ambitions, and the niggardliness of the German diets as well as the French king's Italian policy and the internecine warfare which preserved old hostilities and constantly stimulated new ones. Pius probably realized that a crusade on the grand scale was beyond anything that his generation could achieve. But, then, who had yet devised a better way of trying to meet the Turkish menace on the eastern fronts? Pius's hopes, such as they were, went with Bessarion to Germany.

Chance could hardly have assigned Cardinal Bessarion a worse time to go to Germany, where a war had begun between the houses of Wittelsbach and Hohenzollern, and the princes were for some time too busy fighting one another to fight the Turks.[57] Although Bessarion found the princes and the cities violently at odds among themselves, elaborate and impracticable plans were being discussed for a great expedition against the Turks. The emperor assured the cardinal by letters and later in person of his devotion to the noble cause enunciated at Mantua, but few of the great personages came to the supposedly important diets held at Nuremberg, Worms, and Vienna. It was a difficult mission for Bessarion. He was then about sixty, his health was poor, and he found the northern winter especially severe. He arrived in Nuremberg on 28 February, 1460, and on the following 11 July the pope wrote the citizens of Augsburg that his legate was working day and night.[58]

After Bessarion's departure from Mantua, he had kept the pope well informed concerning his itinerary and the progress of their affairs in Germany. The Hungarians suffered constantly from Turkish incursions. King Matthias Corvinus could only view with alarm the imperial machinations against him. Document after document, easily to be found in Pius II's registers in the Vatican Archives, still bears witness to the efforts made by the Curia to arrange peace between the grasping emperor and the young king. The pope's position was difficult. The Emperor Frederick III had once been his patron and had long been his friend. The ability of Matthias to hold his own against the Turks and even against the Magyar nobility was still uncertain. Pius, however, did support Matthias firmly against Frederick and, fearing that the Hungarians might be forced into another truce with the Turks, he pledged forty thousand ducats from the papal treasury in the spring of 1460, only too aware that the sum was insufficient, but it was apparently

---

[57] On Bessarion's legatine mission to Germany, *cf.* Pastor, *Hist. Popes*, III, 158–76, 194, 198–99, revised in *Gesch. d. Päpste*, II (repr. 1955), 124–37, 151–52, 154–55; Hefele and Leclercq, *Hist. des conciles*, VII-2 (1916), 1337; Voigt, *Enea Silvio*, III, 215–21; Mohler, *Kard. Bessarion*, I, 293–303.

[58] Iorga, *Notes et extraits*, IV, pt. 3, no. 116, p. 181; for the elaborate German plans, *cf.*, *ibid.*, no. 105, pp. 175–76; and note Pius II, *Comm.*, bk. v, Engl. trans., pp. 366–68; ed. Frankfurt, 1614, pp. 125–26, and bk. vii, Engl. trans., p. 497; ed. Cugnoni, *Opera inedita*, p. 530; Raynaldus, *Ann. eccl.*, ad ann. 1460, nos. 21–23, vol. XIX (1693), p. 46 (from Platina); nos. 77–81, *ibid.*, pp. 60–61; and nos. 84–89, pp. 62–63. On the date of Bessarion's arrival in Nuremberg (28 February), see the attempt to establish his itinerary (which Pastor and Mohler had also tried to do) in Erich Meuthen, "Zum Itinerar der deutschen Legation Bessarions (1460–1461)," *Quellen und Forschungen aus italienischen Archiven und Bibliotheken*, XXXVII (1957), 328–33. The diet of Nuremberg was held in the great hall of the Rathaus. Bessarion made a plea for peace among the Christian princes (*Pax eligenda est, non bellum!*), so that they might have done with diets, and take up arms against the Turks (Mohler, *Kard. Bessarion*, III [1942, repr. 1967], 377 ff.): "Iam tempus est ut omissis verbis ad rem veniamus. Armis, armis, inquam, opus est, viri praestantes, non verbis . . ." (*ibid.*, III, 384). His eloquence proved fruitless. The Margrave Albrecht Achilles of Brandenburg-Ansbach was locked in strife with Duke Ludwig of Bavaria-Landshut.

Bessarion left Nuremberg on or about 18 March, and went on to Worms, where he arrived late for the diet, and met the same contentious indecision. He returned to Nuremberg, where he remained until about 24 April, and then went on to Vienna, where the next diet and further disappointment lay before him. See Günther Schuhmann, "Kardinal Bessarion in Nürnberg," in the *Jahrbuch für Fränkische Landesforschung*, XXXIV–XXXV (*Festschrift für Gerhard Pfeiffer*, 1975), 447–65, with summaries of thirteen documents (from the Nürnberger Stadtarchiv) issued by Bessarion between 14 March and 23 April, 1460, and a summary of Bessarion's letter (dated at Lyon on 21 June, 1472, five months before his death) to the burgomaster and town council of Nuremberg, asking them to extend a kindly welcome to the Byzantine princess Zoe Palaeologina, who would soon pass through Nuremberg on her way from Rome to Moscow (see below, pp. 318–19).

all that he could manage, with his other commitments, for the coming summer.[59]

A particularly important diet was to be held in May (1460) under the auspices of the Emperor Frederick in Vienna, where Bessarion arrived on the fourth. Frederick gave him a gracious welcome, but no princes had come, only some envoys, neither instructed nor empowered to commit their principals to significant action. Bessarion had to accept another long and galling postponement. The diet was not formally opened until just after the middle of September, at which time not one of the electoral princes had yet come in person, while many cities were quite content to be unrepresented.[60] On the fourteenth of the month Bessarion saw Frederick, the latter's chancellor, and the imperial council in a preliminary session. Three days later the discouraging business got under way, and extended well into October. Actually the diet of Vienna was a rather impressive affair. Although the electoral princes of Saxony and Brandenburg had not bothered to send representatives, a dozen or so lesser princes finally came. Ten archbishops and bishops appeared. One hundred and ten cities had been invited to send deputies; thirty-four of them sent about eighty persons to speak for them. Of speaking, in fact, there was no end. The Germans made promises, and drew up many resolutions.[61]

Bessarion's legation was but one of the pope's endeavors to launch a crusade. Cardinal Juan de Carvajal had been in Hungary about four years. Other legates had been sent to France, England, Scotland, Scandinavia, Castile, Catalonia, and elsewhere. A tremendous effort was expended. The results were a shocking disappointment. Pledges were made in various places; oaths were taken; and many documents drafted. Now in Vienna, on 4 October, the Emperor Frederick declared himself ready to follow the decisions of Mantua, but the delegates of the princes and the cities insisted upon taking counsel together, appointing as their spokesman Heinrich Leubing, who represented Diether von Isenburg, the anti-papal archbishop of Mainz, and Leubing proved adept at raising difficulties.[62] Further consideration of the expedition was said to be necessary. The emperor warned the delegates of the danger of delay. General declarations were made in favor of the crusade, which Bessarion said were fine, "dummodo facta verbis aliquando respondeant!" The German ecclesiastical electors were bound by the promises which had been made for them at Mantua, Bessarion reminded the assembly; the duke of Burgundy had just renewed

---

[59] See the letter of Pius II to Bessarion, in Arch. Segr. Vaticano, *Pii II brevia*, Arm. XXXIX, tom. 9, fols. 204^v–205^r, dated at Macereto on 5 May, 1460: "Venerabilis frater. Salutem, etc. Post discessum tuum a nobis quam plures a te litteras habuimus ex quibus itineris tui et rerum in Germania gestarum progressum cognovimus. Laudamus in primis diligentiam tue Circumspectionis que sine ulla exceptione laboris in exequendis mandatis nostris fideliter est operata. . . . Videntes tamen non posse in presenti estate maiora presidia illi regno [Ungarie] prestari ex Italia ut suffragium aliquod ad reprimendos Turchorum incursus ei adesset, promisimus XL milia ducatorum ex Camera nostra apostolica . . ." (fol. 205^r). In the letter which follows in the register (13 June, 1460), the pope writes, "Letamur Circumspectionem tuam incolumem pervenisse ad imperialem Celsitudinem et de rebus Alamanie non malam spem hinc cepisse: hoc enim aliquantulum nos recreavit anxios tam diuturna malorum contumacione. Non dubitamus quin diligencie tue sit ascribendum quicquid inde boni sequetur [*sic* for sequatur] . . ." (fol. 205).

[60] For the opening of the diet on 17 September, see Pastor, *Gesch. d. Päpste*, II (1955), 127–28, and Mohler, *Kard. Bessarion*, I, 300; for the date of Bessarion's arrival in Vienna (4 May), Mohler, *ibid.*, I, 298. Iorga, *Notes et extraits*, IV, pt. 3, no. 117, p. 182, doc. dated 16 September, 1460, says "les séances commencent le vendredi (18), à une heure après-midi," but in September, 1460, the eighteenth fell on Thursday, not Friday. For Bessarion's problems, *cf.* Pope Pius's letters to him and to the Emperor Frederick in July, 1460 (*Brevia*, in Arm. XXXIX, tom. 9, fols. 121^v–123^v and 133). Hope for German participation in the crusade had increased by the fall of 1460 when the pope wrote Bessarion (*VI Oct.*, *anno tertio*): "Cooperante Deo tempestas illa que Alamaniam totam comprehenderat in tranquilitatem conversa est; princeps [*sic*, in the register, for *principes*] qui tantis inter se odiis armati surrexerant pacem recipientes quietem nunc agunt nec ulla in parte nationis sicut nobis refert vestigium belli apparet. Laus Deo qui tanto beneficio Christianitatem affecit. . . . Facultatem nunc habet Germania in defensionem arma convertere . . ." (*ibid.*, fol. 194). Pius now wished that the Count Palatine Frederick might become "vicecapitaneus belli contra Turcos" (letter to the Emperor Frederick of 11 October, fols. 195^r–196^r): the emperor, who had been appointed commander-in-chief at Mantua, might remain as a figurehead.

[61] *Cf.* Mohler, *Kard. Bessarion*, I, 300–2.

[62] Diether von Isenburg's campaign against the papacy and its leadership of the projected crusade continued with increased momentum through much of the year 1461 (Pius II, *Comm.*, bk. VI, Engl. trans., pp. 413–23; ed. Frankfurt, 1614, pp. 143–48). He charged that the entire effort was simply a scheme to extort money from the Germans, and that "the Italians do not hate the Turks as much as they do us" (*non tam Turcas quam nos Itali oderunt*), which passage was omitted from the Frankfurt edition of 1614 (at p. 143, line 40), but is published by Cugnoni, *Opera inedita*, p. 529.

his offer of six thousand men (for service in Hungary); the king of Bohemia was having the crusade preached in his domains; and the Hungarians were said to have promised twenty thousand men despite the war in their country.

Bessarion said it would take sixty to seventy thousand men to retake Constantinople and drive the Turks out of Europe. The pope and the Italians would provide the fleet. If Germany would supply the forty-two thousand men requested, the undertaking could get started. There was no need to spend so much time on matters of secondary importance, to worry about aid from France and the details of the expedition, such as the route, the commanders, the length of the campaign, and what should be done in case of defeat. There had been so many diets, all poorly attended; nothing had come of them except "bona verba et magniloquentia." The Turks continued to make progress. The summer had passed, and the Greeks had lost the Morea; the sultan had subjected more than forty fortified towns; many Greeks had been killed, and thirty thousand prisoners taken. Hungary had been devastated; more than twenty thousand persons had been carried off into captivity. If Hungary passed under the Turkish yoke, it would soon be Germany's turn. These months had been a great trial to Bessarion. He was tired and irritable, discouraged and ill. At one point in his discourse before the assembly he stated with much animation: "We need arms, arms I tell you, and strong men, not words; an army well supplied, not neat and polished oratory; we need the enduring strength of soldiers, not the bombast of fine speeches!"[63]

The delegates to the diet, however, could not make firm commitments. Their principals would of course do all that lay in their power. The decisions of past assemblies, even that held at Mantua, bound only those who had been represented, not "the German nation, half of which has not yet come together" to discuss the problem. Another diet was necessary, to which the emperor must come, for only in this way could decisions be reached on the proposals made at Mantua.[64] In vain did Bessarion protest that this was no answer. The emperor had said many times that, although he might send representatives to such a diet, he would not come in person. There was no dealing with the German evasions and maneuvers, and nothing had been accomplished when the delegates went home. At the insistence of Pius II, however, Bessarion spent almost another year in the uncongenial north.[65] After the pope himself gave up hope of enlisting German manpower for the crusade, Bessarion was to attempt the restoration of harmony between Vienna and Buda. Although no peace of long duration was possible, the truce of Laxenburg was finally negotiated (on 6 September, 1461). About three weeks later Bessarion set out from the imperial court for Italy, delighted to leave the barbarians, "hostile to Greek and Latin by nature," and to be rid of the riots of tipsy students in Vienna. He reached Bologna on 23 October, and arrived in Rome on 20 November.[66]

---

[63] Iorga, *Notes et extraits*, IV, pt. 3, no. 118, pp. 182–87; Voigt, *Enea Silvio*, III, 223–31; Iorga, *Gesch. d. osman. Reiches*, II (1909), 96; Pastor, *Gesch. d. Päpste*, II (repr. 1955), 127–28, 131–32. Mohler, *Kard. Bessarion*, III, 384–98, gives the full text of Bessarion's discourse. (In his first volume Mohler did not use, for some reason, Iorga's invaluable *Notes et extraits*.)

[64] Iorga, *Notes et extraits*, IV, 187; Voigt, *Enea Silvio*, III, 228–29; Pastor, *Gesch. d. Päpste*, II (repr. 1955), 132–33; Mohler, *Kard. Bessarion*, I, 302.

[65] Note Pius II's long letter to Bessarion, "datum Rome, IIII Novembris, anno tertio [1460], among the *Brevia*, in Arm. XXXIX, tom. 9, fols. 196^{v}–199^{r}, and *cf.* fols. 260^{r}–262^{v}.

[66] Bessarion had already left Vienna when on 28 September, 1461, he wrote Jacopo Ammanati a touching letter, expressing great relief at the prospect of his return to Italy and giving voice to no little complaint about the financial hardship under which the journey was placing him (Arch. Segr. Vaticano, Arm. XXXIX, tom. 10, fol. 18^{r}, by mod. stamped enumeration): "Reverende in Christo pater, amice et frater honorande: Usi iam sumus dulcissimo fructu laboris vestri. Nam quemadmodum intelligetis ex litteris quas scribimus ad sanctissimum dominum nostrum venimus ad Maiestatem imperialem et obtinuimus ab ea bonam et gratam licentiam redeundi ad pedes sanctissimi domini nostri, quod etiam antea fecissemus nisi iudicavissemus impium et parum gratum sanctissimo domino nostro si res Maiestatis sue in eo periculo in quo hac tempestate fuerunt relinqueremus. Nunc vero rebus suis in tuto positis subito venimus ad Maiestatem suam a qua habita grata licentia iter nostrum ad vos domino concedente continuabimus. . . ." Because of his poor health, however, he would have to travel slowly, "nec speramus ante finem Novembris istuc posse pervenire. . . ." He expected the waters of La Porretta at Bologna to help him, but financial matters were also weighing on his mind: "Ceterum significamus paternitati vestre quod in discessu nostro ex Wienna fuit necesse ut ad ex[s]olvenda debita que contraxeramus et parandum viaticum in Italiam acciperemus mutuo sexcentos ducatos quos promisimus solvere Venetiis ubi tamen solvendi modum non habemus nisi sanctissimus dominus noster pro sua pietate nobis providerit . . . ," etc., etc. Bessarion relied upon Ammanati's influence with

While the diplomats were wrangling at Mantua, Vienna, and elsewhere, the "Gran Turco" Mehmed II was on the move. On 20 June, 1459, three weeks after the opening of the Congress of Mantua, Semendria (Smederevo) had opened its gates to Mehmed. Within the next few months all Serbia finally succumbed, with very little resistance, to the Ottoman armies. The fall of the northern despotate was accompanied by the enslavement of many thousands of Serbs. While his soldiers were completing the conquest, Mehmed had learned of Thomas's uprising in the Morea, being probably first informed by the envoy of Demetrius seeking aid against his brother. Chalcocondylas seems to imply that Mehmed was at Skoplje (Üsküb) when he heard the news.[67] In any event he left the suppression of the revolt to his Moreote commanders, for the time being, although he had to make two important changes in their ranks. Chalcocondylas repeats a rumor current at the time that Omar Beg, the governor of Thessaly and the Morea, who sometimes inhabited the old palace of the Acciajuoli on the Acropolis in Athens, was encouraging Thomas's dangerous defection. This is very unlikely. It would appear, however, that Omar Beg's indifference or negligence had allowed the situation to get out of hand. The sultan now sent Hamza Zenevisi, "the Falconer," an Albanian convert to Islam,[68] to replace him; upon his arrival Hamza took Omar Beg into custody together with the latter's father-in-law, Ahmed, who had served as his lieutenant in the Morea. The country was in a sadly turbulent state. Thomas's evil genius, Nicephorus Lucanes, had found fertile soil for his rebellious schemes. Critobulus dwells on the grasping and treacherous ways of the Greek magnates and officials, lining up first with one of the despots and then with the other, and keeping them in a state of sustained hostility toward each other.[69]

The Despot Thomas had laid siege to Patras with the aid of the Italian troops which Pope Pius and the Duchess Bianca Maria of Milan had sent to his assistance. Hamza had no difficulty in relieving the city, however, for Thomas and his army abandoned the siege at his approach, withdrawing to "Megalopolis, now called Leondari," where the Moreote army was mustered with the apparent intention of doing battle with the Turks when they arrived. The sultan's troops moved south along the coast of Elis, turned inland at the latitude of Ithome, and headed for Leondari,

---

the pope to extricate him from the embarrassment of pledging all his personal property in Venice as a guarantee for the loan. In the MS. this letter is dated "XXVIII Septembris;" the first figure of the numeral has been largely erased. Pastor, *Gesch. d. Päpste*, II (repr. 1955), 136–37, note, dates it the twenty-eighth; Mohler, *Kard. Bessarion*, I, 303, the eighteenth. Mohler, *op. cit.*, III, 507–8, gives a careless transcription of Bessarion's letter [of 28 September] to Ammanati, which he still dates the eighteenth.

Jacopo Ammanati, who later added the name Piccolomini to his own, was the protégé and secretary of Pius II, who made him bishop of Pavia, despite the opposition of Francesco Sforza, duke of Milan (Raynaldus, *Ann. eccl.*, ad ann. 1460, no. 55, vol. XIX [1693], p. 54), and finally made him a cardinal on 19 December, 1461 (*Comm.*, bk. VII, Engl. trans., p. 503; ed. Frankfurt, 1614, p. 184, lines 11–12). On his career, see Giuseppe Calamari, *Il confidente di Pio II, Cardinale Jacopo Ammannati Piccolomini*, 2 vols., Rome and Milan, 1932.

For Bessarion's arrival in Bologna on 23 October, 1461, see the *Cronica di Bologna*, in *RISS*, XVIII (Milan, 1731), col. 741D, and in the new Muratori, *Corpus chronicorum bononiensium*, *RISS*, tom. XVIII, pt. 5, vol. IV (1924–39), pp. 289a, 290b. He reached Rome on Friday, 20 November (1461), according to the Acta Consistorialia in Arch. Segr. Vaticano, Arm. XXXI, tom. 52, fol. 63r: "Adventus domini cardinalis Niceni: Anno predicto [1461], die vero Veneris, XX mensis Novembris, reverendissimus dominus, meus dominus Nicenus cardinalis, episcopus Sabinensis, veniens de legatione sua de Alamania intravit urbem et pernoctavit illa die in Sancta Maria de Populo. Die Sabbati in crastinum fuit receptus in consistorio generali et incepit participare" (*cf.* Eubel, II, 33a). Sanudo, *Vite de'duchi*, in *RISS*, XXII, col. 1168, says that Bessarion was back in Venice in December, 1461, as papal legate "per la materia della Crociata," being made an honorary citizen and enrolled in the Maggior Consiglio on the twentieth of the month. *Cf.* in general Voigt, *Enea Silvio*, III, 232–33; Pastor, *Gesch. d. Päpste*, II (repr. 1955), 136; Mohler, *Kard. Bessarion*, I, 303.

The quotation on the Germans' natural hostility to Greek and Latin comes from Platina (*Panegyricus Bessarionis*, in *PG* 161, col. CXII): "Inter exteras gentes, Graecis et Latinis natura infestas, periclitatum est saepius dum temulenti et armati non solum in agris, sed in urbibus grassantur; Viennae autem potissimum, ubi gymnastici quavis licentia et petulantia utuntur."

[67] Chalcocondylas, bk. IX (Bonn, pp. 456–57; ed. Darkó, II-2 [1927], 214–15). Mehmed's return, later on, to the region of Adrianople and Istanbul is, however, indicated by a passage in Critobulus, III, 20, 2 (ed. Müller, *FHG*, V-1 [1870], p. 132b; ed. Grecu [1963], p. 255).

[68] On Hamza's family, *cf.* Hopf, *Chron. gréco-romanes* (1873, repr. 1966), geneal. tables, p. 531, and "Griechenland im Mittelalter," in Ersch and Gruber, *Allgemeine Encyclopädie*, vol. 86 (1868, repr. 1960, vol. II), p. 129; Iorga, *Gesch. d. osman. Reiches*, II (1909), 84, 92, who confuses Hamza Zenevisi with Scanderbeg's nephew Hamza Castriota; Babinger, *Maometto* (1957), pp. 237, 264–65.

[69] Critobulus, III, 19 (ed. Müller, *FHG*, V-1, p. 131; ed. Grecu, pp. 251, 253); Chalcocondylas, *loc. cit.*, ed. Bonn, p. 470; ed. Darkó, II-2, 226.

where they found Thomas's forces deployed in the hills. Upon perceiving the situation, the Turks debated whether to entrench themselves in their position or to push on to Mouchli, as they had intended. But Yunus Beg, a cavalry commander, seeing how badly dispersed Thomas's forces were, put them to flight in the first charge, killing about two hundred of them. The rest took cover in Leondari, which the Turks subjected to a brief siege, and where famine and plague made their appearance. Burdened by the prisoners they had taken in the province of Achaea after freeing Patras, the Turks went on to Mouchli, leaving Yunus Beg to assist Demetrius in Mistra.[70]

Although Lucanes had been confident of taking Corinth by a conspiracy which his agents were supposed to be hatching within the walls of the fortress,[71] the capture of Kalavryta was Thomas's only military success against the Turks. It was conceivably in Kalavryta that the sixteen Turks were captured whom Thomas sent with his embassy to Pius II in the summer of 1459. The despot did not do things by halves. As he attacked the Turks, he undertook an even more vigorous war against Demetrius to deprive his feeble brother of his share of the Palaeologian inheritance in the Morea. Demetrius apparently instructed the stalwart Matthew Asan, then on an embassy to Sultan Mehmed, to solicit aid of the sultan, who looked forward to receiving the princess Helena in his harem. Critobulus reports a story circulating at the Porte and in the northern Aegean that Demetrius had offered to exchange all his Moreote possessions for other holdings, presumably the islands of Lemnos and Imbros, under the sultan's direct dominion. It looked, however, as though Demetrius would soon have little to exchange. The commanders of some of his chief fortresses declared their independence of his tottering regime. He thus lost the hilltop castle of Karytaina and that of S. George to the south of it; Bordonia and Kastritza near Sparta; as well as Kalamata, Zarnata, Leuktron (Beaufort), and most of the peninsula of Maina, which last places were occupied by Thomas. Demetrius besieged Leondari and even Akova, and found in George Palaeologus and Manuel Bouchales commanders to help him press the campaign against Thomas, who broke the siege of Leondari, however, and sent Demetrius and his commanders scurrying for cover at Mistra. The Albanians joined the fray, looting what they could and changing sides, says Sphrantzes, "twice a week." The poor inhabitants of the Morea experienced untold misery. The Turkish forces in Corinth, Amyclae, and Patras took their opportunity in the confusion to send out raiding parties, capturing and killing people, laughing at the despots and the magnates, whose swords were drawn against one another. Sphrantzes, who served Thomas through this period, beheld with his own eyes the complete and senseless ruination of Arcadia.[72]

The two despots, belatedly recognizing the peril to which their strife exposed their people and their lands, came together in the church of Kastritza and swore by oaths to live in amity with each other. The metropolitan of Sparta celebrated the eucharist in their presence. When he held up before the congregation the elements of the sacrifice, saying "In fear of God come unto me and in faith . . . ," the brothers came forward and vowed to keep the peace. A common danger, however, does not always produce concord. The two despots viewed their problems and those of the Morea very differently, as we have seen, Demetrius finding it quite possible to live under Turkish hegemony and his brother being quite unable to do so. This time it was Demetrius, according to the information Sphrantzes received, who disrupted the unaccustomed harmony to which the brothers had pledged themselves at Kastritza. Relying on the prospect of Turkish aid, he renewed the war, and the poor inhabitants of the Morea knew yet again the harsh exactions of an undisciplined soldiery bent upon plunder.[73]

Chalcocondylas relates that Sultan Mehmed appointed the Christian renegade Zagan Pasha, who had been governor of Gallipoli, to the high command over Thessaly and the Morea, after the removal of Omar Beg. Zagan Pasha had achieved quick fame when, some time before this, he had captured Morezina, the most

[70] Chalcocondylas, bk. IX (Bonn, pp. 457–59; ed. Darkó, II-2, 214–16).

[71] *Cf.* Chalcocondylas, bk. IX (Bonn, p. 456; ed. Darkó, II-2, 214).

[72] Critobulus, III, 14, 2–3; 15, 3; 19, 4–6 (ed. Müller, *FHG*, V-1, pp. 128a, 129a, 132a; ed. Grecu, pp. 241, 245, 253); Sphrantzes, *Chron. minus* (*PG* 156, 1066–1067D; ed. Grecu, pp. 110, 112, 114); Pseudo-Sphrantzes, IV, 16 (Bonn, pp. 388–92; ed. Grecu, pp. 528, 530, 532), who credits the Albanians with changing sides "three times within a week."

[73] Sphrantzes, *Chron. minus* (*PG* 156, 1068CD; ed. Grecu, pp. 116, 118), and *cf.* Pseudo-Sphrantzes, IV, 16 (Bonn, p. 394; ed. Grecu, p. 534).

notorious pirate on the Aegean Sea. Now Zagan Pasha went with an army into the Morea, in March, 1460, heading straight for the town of Palaeo-Achaea on the Gulf of Patras. Thomas was bombarding the place, but departed hastily at the approach of Zagan Pasha. The Italians sent by Pope Pius and the Duchess Bianca Maria participated in this engagement also, according to Chalcocondylas, who adds that the Greeks had prepared a cannon for their attack on Achaea, but enjoyed little success with it, because they lacked an experienced bombardier (τηλεβολιστής), and the rest of their siege tackle was inadequate for the capture of a city. Thomas retreated southward, overran Laconia (it was now that he seized Kalamata from Demetrius), and laid siege to Mantineia, which according to Chalcocondylas he was also unable to take.[74] At this point Thomas, who saw no future in his petty victories and dwindling resources, sent envoys to Mehmed to sue for peace.

Without the active intervention of the Venetians, one could not hope for success against the Turks. Shortly before his departure from Mantua, Pius II had sent Gregorio Lolli, the companion of his youth, on a mission to the Signoria to discuss the Republic's participation in the proposed expedition against the eastern enemy.[75] The Senate laid down the Venetian terms on 15 January, 1460. Pius was to grant the Signoria all the moneys accruing from the collection of tithes, twentieths, and thirtieths as well as the proceeds from the sale of indulgences and the preaching of the crusade. These funds were to be used to outfit and maintain the Venetian fleet. Pius also had to promise that Ragusa, Ancona, Rhodes, and Mytilene, or certain other states should furnish ten well-armed galleys to serve under the captain of the fleet and remain in service "usque ad finem belli." Venice would prepare her fleet for action against the Turks as soon as an army should be raised in Hungary of at least seventy thousand warriors, of whom fifty thousand must be mounted (*equites*). The Venetians were to have and to hold under the Holy See, *sub perpetuo et libero vicariatu seu feudo*, all the cities, castles, and other places which their forces might seize from the enemy. The pope would provide without charge, from the March of Ancona or from other sources, the grain and fodder which the fleet would need. Furthermore, if the Turks should attack Venetian territory—Dalmatia was always vulnerable—before the Christian expedition got under way, Pius must agree to make immediately available to the Signoria the tithes and indulgences, "and besides his Holiness promises [the agreement was supposed to state] to give and to pay to the said most illustrious Signoria every month eight thousand ducats for the protection of the places . . . belonging to the Signoria on land bordering upon territories of the Turk."[76]

It was hard to deal with the Venetians on the Turkish question unless they found themselves in immediate danger. When in February, 1460, Pius in his turn sought to collect the "decime, predicationes, et indulgentie" from Venetian territories, his emissary met with the Senate's courteous but firm refusal to allow such levies or collections. To the claim that such avails were "res ecclesiastice" and should not be denied, the Senate replied (on 1 March) that Venice was eager to comply with all possible papal requests, especially when they concerned the "sancta expeditio contra Turcum." The faithful sons of S. Mark were as anxious as anyone to help exterminate the common enemy of Christendom.

. . . We assure his Holiness, the supreme pontiff, that when the affairs of Christendom are set in order

[74] Chalcocondylas, bk. IX (Bonn, p. 471, lines 14–16; ed. Darkó, II-2, 227, lines 1–2).

[75] Sen. Secreta, Reg. 20, fol. 204 [206], doc. dated 15 January, 1460 (Ven. style 1459): "Venit ad nos magnificus doctor dominus Gregorius Lolius orator et nepos Romani pontificis et longo ordine verborum explicavit nobis summum desiderium quod Beatitudo sua ab ipso principio assumptionis sue ad summum pontificatum continue habuit et habet ad expeditionem contra Turcas, declarando modos hucusque per Sanctitatem suam circa hoc servatos et adventum suum ad dietam Mantue et reliqua gesta hactenus per Beatitudinem suam, deinde descendit ad praticas habitas cum oratoribus nostris in Mantua pro maritima classe paranda et ad capitula porrecta per oratores nostros, subindeque ad reformationes factas per Sanctitatem prefatam ad ipsa capitula, quas non dubitabat oratores nostros misisse nobis, concludens quod cum summus pontifex, qui infra breves dies ex Mantua recessurus est, intendat videre finem huiusce rei, instituit mittere ipsum oratorem ad nos quoniam non disponit amplius sic stare et quod habebat facultatem et mandatum concludendi et sigillandi nec desistendi pro rebus parvis devenire ad conclusiones, hortando ac astringendo nos plurimum multis efficacibus verbis ut pro honore Dei et Christiane religionis sequi velimus vestigia maiorum nostrorum ut summus pontifex non habeat materiam aliter providendi. . . ."

[76] Sen. Secreta, Reg. 20, fols. 204^v–205^r [206^v–207^r], doc. dated 15 January, 1460 (Ven. style 1459). Negotiations continued with Lolli, but the Venetian Senate refused to make any significant concessions (see, *ibid.*, fols. 206^v ff., 208 ff.).

and a land army has been raised, we have every intention of honoring wholeheartedly our obligation to prepare and send our fleet against the Turks. For our part we shall omit nothing that can relate to our duty and their destruction. In getting this fleet ready, however, we shall need not only the funds accruing from the tithes, preaching, and indulgences, but more, very much more, as can be readily imagined, and these funds we shall take from our own resources to assure a successful outcome for this sacred undertaking.

The Senate reminded Pius, through his emissary, that he had graciously conceded the tithes and indulgences to the Germans and to others. Venice needed such funds for her own preparations when the time came. But if the tithes were to be collected now, the Turk would immediately declare war on Venice "with manifest peril to our overseas possessions and to so many thousands of souls." Furthermore, if the Germans and Hungarians were to learn that the tithes and indulgences were being collected in Venetian territory, and were being sent elsewhere (presumably to Rome), they would assume that Venice was not going to build and equip a fleet, and would relax their own efforts against the Turks. This would be a tragedy for Christendom.[77] Pius understood the Senate's answer.

While Thomas Palaeologus sought peace in the Morea, Mehmed II was turning his attention eastward. He wanted to march against Uzun Ḥasan of Diyār-Bakr (Amida) in Mesopotamia, who after the death of Ibrahim Beg, the "Gran Caramano," was to be Mehmed's chief enemy in the East. Uzun Ḥasan had married Theodora, called the Despina-Khātūn, daughter of the Emperor John IV Comnenus ("Kalojoannes") of Trebizond.[78] An anti-Ottoman alliance had been formed between Uzun Ḥasan and John IV. The former lived in perennial fear of the Gran Turco, and John had just been forced to recognize Turkish suzerainty over Trebizond and agree to an annual tribute of three thousand gold pieces.[79] It was about this time, however, that John died, leaving a boy as his heir. Since the circumstances demanded a stronger rule than a boy could provide, John's experienced brother David ascended the imperiled throne as co-emperor. Nevertheless, the alliance of Uzun Ḥasan and the Grand Comneni lost most of its effect. Had the eastern powers which feared the Porte been able to reach an accord with the western states for a concerted attack upon the Ottoman empire, Mehmed might conceivably have been in serious danger, but no such league was practicable in the fifteenth century.[80]

---

[77] Sen. Secreta, Reg. 21, fol. 1r [2r], and *cf.* fols. 4v–5r [5v–6r], a friendly letter of 21 April, 1460, from the Venetian government to Mehmed II, although they had constant trouble with the Turks in Modon, Coron, and Lepanto (*ibid.*, fol. 29 [30], doc. dated 22 January, 1461 [Ven. style 1460]).

[78] Wm. Miller, *Trebizond: The Last Greek Empire*, London, 1926, pp. 88–89. Domenico Trevisan, onetime Venetian bailie at Istanbul (1553–1554), refers to John IV's daughter as ". . . Fiordispina di Calò Janni cristiano, imperatore di Trebisonda e di tutto il Mar Maggiore . . ." (in E. Albèri, ed., *Relazioni degli ambasciatori veneti al Senato*, ser. III, vol. I [Florence, 1840], p. 168, cited by Miller). She is sometimes, but incorrectly, called Catherine: Khātūn means "lady." *Cf.* also G. Berchet, *La Repubblica di Venezia e la Persia*, Turin, 1865, pp. 1–2, 7, 99–100, 108, concerning "la despota Teodora mojer de Ussun Cassan. . . ." On Theodora's marriage to Uzun Ḥasan (in 1458), see A. Bryer, "Greeks and Türkmens . . . ," *Dumbarton Oaks Papers*, XXIX (1975), append., no. II, following p. 148.

[79] *Cf.* Ducas, chap. 42 (Bonn, p. 314; ed. Grecu [1958], p. 395); Chalcocondylas, bk. IX (Bonn, pp. 461, 466–67; ed. Darkó, II-2, 218, 222–23).

[80] On the remarkable false embassy of alleged Persians, Georgians, Armenians, and others (to form an east-west alliance against the Porte), which was led by Lodovico da Bologna, a Franciscan Observantine, an impostor and a charlatan (but also a missionary to the East!), see Pius II, *Comm.*, bk. V, Engl. trans., pp. 371–74; ed. Frankfurt, 1614, pp. 127–28; Voigt, *Enea Silvio*, III, 643–49; Pastor, *Gesch. d. Päpste*, II (repr. 1955), 224–26; Miller, *Trebizond*, pp. 98–99; Babinger, *Maometto*, pp. 278–85. For a time in 1460–1461 this "embassy" hoodwinked the courts of Rome, France, and Burgundy.

Perhaps not every aspect of this general embassy was fraudulent, however, for on 14–15 December, 1460, the envoy of the Emperor David Comnenus of Trebizond, Michele Alighieri, alleged to have belonged to the family of Dante, negotiated an (authorized?) pact between Florence and Trebizond as a member of Lodovico da Bologna's outlandish troupe (see Giuseppe Müller, ed., *Documenti sulle relazioni delle città toscane coll'Oriente cristiano e coi Turchi*, Florence, 1879, pt. I, docs. 136, 138–39, pp. 185–89), whereby the Florentines were to receive a quarter (*fondaco*) in Trebizond, with a consulate and chapel, paying merely a two per cent import duty and nothing on exports. All Florentine merchants, ships, and goods were to be protected by a general safe-conduct revocable only on six months' prior notice. Although the Florentines contemplated the voyage to Trebizond (and Caffa) both before and after the time of this treaty (*cf.*, *ibid.*, pt. II, docs. 12, 17, pp. 296, 302), little came of the intention as the Osmanlis converted the Black Sea into a Turkish lake.

There is a letter (of doubtful authenticity) dated 22 April, 1459, which the Emperor David of Trebizond is alleged to have sent Duke Philip of Burgundy, urging the duke to attack the Turks through Hungary while an oriental alliance attacked from the East (*cf.* Miller and Babinger, cited above). As an inducement Philip was offered the crown of Jerusalem. In the Vatican Library an interesting miscellany of Greek and Latin texts (Cod. Reg. lat. 557) contains this letter: "*Epistola Imperatoris Trapesundarum ad ducem Burgundie*: . . . Vale in Christo, data Trapesunde in

At this time, nonetheless, serious consideration was being given in the Curia Romana to the possibility of an east-west alliance. Mehmed II wanted to make a strong show of force in the East to hold Uzun Ḥasan in check and to add to his fear of the Porte. Mehmed was therefore not unwilling to return to the *status quo ante bellum* in the Morea, provided Thomas gave up the siege of such Turkish strongholds as he was then trying to take; restored those he had succeeded in taking; paid immediately a tribute of three thousand ducats; and appeared before a Turkish emissary in Corinth within twenty days. These terms were acceptable to Thomas, but, owing to the ill-advised refusal of his subjects to help him, he could not raise the money. This was the last straw. Mehmed put off the projected expedition against Uzun Ḥasan, and in May, 1460, he gathered his forces for a final campaign in the Morea.[81]

In twenty-seven days Mehmed marched from Adrianople to Corinth, where Critobulus says he had expected the Despot Demetrius to come to him within three days. The despot did not appear, however, having sent Matthew Asan in his stead with many gifts. Asan was given a long private audience which Mahmud Pasha also attended, but the sultan had decided upon the liquidation of Greek authority in the Morea and was not to be dissuaded therefrom. He had Asan arrested the day after his arrival. Mehmed now invaded the territory of Demetrius, not that of his enemy Thomas; from Argos he sent Mahmud Pasha by night with a considerable force to Mistra, where he arrived at dawn and invested the city. Demetrius remained in the castle on the hill. Mahmud Pasha sent to him Thomas, the son of Katabolenos, the sultan's Greek secretary, who tried to persuade him to give up the city, the capital of the "despotate" and the center of Hellenism in the Morea for two hundred years. Demetrius said that Asan must first be released to bring him written pledges (*πιστά*), presumably of his safety and of what he would receive in exchange for his domain. Critobulus says the whole performance was a farce, designed for public consumption.[82] Mahmud Pasha gave the letter of guarantee to Asan to take to Demetrius; with him went Hamza Zenevisi, who was a friend of the despot. Demetrius returned with them to the encampment of Mahmud Pasha, who received him with due honors, and on 30 May took over the city and castle of Mistra.

Sultan Mehmed appeared the next day, according to Critobulus, and immediately summoned the Despot Demetrius, who came gravely apprehensive as to the next move. Mehmed honored him by rising from his seat to greet

---

palatio nostre residentie, A. D. MCCCCLIX, die XXII Aprilis." This MS. also contains an "*Epistula ducis Georgiane ad ducem Burgundie*: . . . Vale in Christo, data in Carcethe anno MCCCCLIX;" an "*Epistula regis Persarum ad ducem Burgundie*: . . . Vale in Christo [!], data in castris nostris prope tentorium, anno MCCCCLIX, die V Novembris;" and a list of the "Nomina oratorum orientalium qui personaliter fuerunt cum duce Burgundie" (Reg. lat. 557, fols. 108^{v}–110^{r}). Pius II's letter of 13 January, 1461, stands at the head of this oriental correspondence: "*Papa* [*Pius II*] *duci Burgundie oratores commendat principum Asie*: . . . datum Rome apud Sanctum Petrum anno Incarnationis dominice MCCCCLIX [*sic!*], Idibus Januarii, pontificatus nostri anno III." (January of Pius II's third year falls in 1461.) The alleged ambassadors of the Asiatic princes arrived in Rome in December, 1460, bringing their letters. Lodovico da Bologna was their guide and served as interpreter. At first they easily imposed upon Pius II, who sent them to France and Burgundy with letters of recommendation. He also paid their expenses. As time passed, however, suspicions arose, and upon their return to Rome, they were regarded as impostors, which Lodovico's subsequent conduct did much to confirm (*cf.* Pastor, *Gesch. d. Päpste*, II [repr. 1955], 226, and esp. Babinger, *Maometto*, pp. 283–85, and Anthony Bryer, "Lodovico da Bologna and the Georgian and Anatolian Embassy of 1460–1461," *Bedi Kartlisa*, XIX–XX [Paris, 1965], 178–98).

Although known to Nicholas V and Calixtus III, Lodovico da Bologna first occurs (I think) in the registers of Pius II on 5 October, 1458, upon the occasion of his return from a year's sojourn in the East: "Pius, etc. Dilectis filiis, populis et universitatibus Christianorum, qui Franchi appellantur, in regione Asie et Georgiaranie constitutis, salutem, etc. Reversus ad nos dilectus frater Ludovicus de Bononia ordinis Sancti Francisci, nuntius noster, qui apud vos anno preterito fuit, nobis retulit . . . ," etc. (Arch. Segr. Vaticano, Reg. Vat. 468, fol. 383^{r}, by mod. stamped enumeration), "datum Rome apud Sanctum Petrum, anno etc. MCCCCLVIII, tertio Non. Octobris, pont. nostri anno primo." *Cf.*, *ibid.*, fol. 383^{v}, for the (canceled) beginning of a letter from Pius to Lodovico, and note fol. 384^{r}, two letters to the Franciscan friars Michele da Milano and Antonio di Cena, indicating Pius's intention of sending Lodovico back to the East (these letters gave Michele and Antonio permission to visit the Holy Land, each with two companions of their order). Various texts (from 1457 to 1465) relating to Lodovico da Bologna are given in Luke Wadding, *Annales Minorum*, ed. J. M. Fonseca, vol. XIII (Quaracchi, 1932), pp. 30–32, 69–70, 174–80, 425, but Wadding's comments are colored by his assumption that Johannes Gobellinus wrote Pius II's *Commentarii*, and that Lodovico was "a Gobellino indigne traductus" (p. 425). See above, Chapter 6, note 15.

[81] Chalcocondylas, bk. IX (Bonn, pp. 470–72; ed. Darkó, II-2, 226–28).

[82] Critobulus, III, 20, 4–6 (ed. Müller, *FHG*, V-1, pp. 132b, 133a; ed. Grecu, pp. 255, 257): ". . . *Σκηνὴ καὶ ὑπόκρισις ἦσαν καὶ πλάσμα. . . . Ταῦτα δὲ πάντα . . . ἐς τὸ φανερὸν μὲν ἐπλάττοντο, ἄλλα δ'ἦσαν ἐν ἀπορρήτοις καὶ βεβουλευμένοι καὶ πράττοντες.*"

him as he entered the tent, extended his right hand, seated him at his side, and addressed him with kind words to allay his fears and reassure him as to the future.[83] Sphrantzes reports Mehmed as saying:

> Since your affairs, O despot, have come to this pass, it is impossible for you to rule this place any longer. Nevertheless, since we have decided to have you as our father and to marry your daughter, surrender this place to us; you and your daughter come away with us; and we shall bestow another place upon you for your maintenance and well-being.[84]

Mehmed then sent to Monemvasia, where Demetrius's wife and daughter were staying, and demanded their surrender of the Monemvasiotes, who turned over the unhappy despoina and Helena, but refused to give up the city and fortress, allegedly informing the officers of the sultan and despot who had come to take over, that the strong position of Monemvasia was a gift of God, and whenever He wished the place to become Turkish, "His will be done!" In the meantime, however, they would not surrender the gift of God to the sultan. Mehmed is said to have admired the courageous reply. The bold governor of Monemvasia, one Manuel Palaeologus, recognized the Despot Thomas as lord of the city. When the latter presently sought refuge in Italy, the threatened inhabitants had to look elsewhere for someone to govern and defend them against the Turks.[85]

Following the Despot Thomas's advice, the Monemvasiotes sent an embassy to the Curia Romana in the late summer of 1460, urging Pope Pius to accept the cession of their city. "The Pope was so moved," Pius informs us in his *Commentarii*, "that he wept as he reflected on the uncertainty of earthly things. . . . He then dispatched a prefect [Gentile de' Marcolfi of Spoleto] to administer justice and replenish the city's grain supply, which was utterly exhausted."[86] Vatican documents fix the chronology of papal appointments. On 27 February, 1461, Pius confirmed all the grants and privileges which the Monemvasiotes had previously possessed, and thereafter appointed Gentile de' Marcolfi governor of their city and its dependencies. The Monemvasiotes were to yield all fortified places to him and give him their unqualified obedience.[87] On 10 July (1461) Pius

---

[83] Critobulus, III, 20, 7 (ed. Müller, *FHG*, V-1, p. 133a; ed. Grecu, p. 257).

[84] Sphrantzes, *Chron. minus* (*PG* 156, 1068D–1069A; ed. Grecu, pp. 116, 118); Pseudo-Sphrantzes, IV, 16 (Bonn, p. 395; ed. Grecu, pp. 534, 536); *cf.* Chalcocondylas, bk. IX (Bonn, pp. 472–73; ed. Darkó, II-2, 227–28).

[85] Pseudo-Sphrantzes, IV, 16 (Bonn, pp. 396–99; ed. Grecu, pp. 536, 538), showing the special interest of the author [Macarius Melissenus-Melissurgus] in Monemvasia. *Cf.* Sphrantzes, *Chron. minus* (*PG* 156, 1069AB; ed. Grecu, p. 118), very brief; Chalcocondylas, bk. IX (Bonn, p. 476; ed. Darkó, II-2, 231), also without any embellishment of the circumstances attending the refusal to surrender Monemvasia; and in general, Zakythinos, *Despotat grec de Morée*, I (1932, repr. 1975), 267–74.

[86] Pius II, *Comm.*, bk. IV, Engl. trans., pp. 321–22; ed. Frankfurt, 1614, pp. 103–4, placed by Pius among events occurring before the summer of 1460; Raynaldus, *Ann. eccl.*, ad ann. 1460, nos. 56–59, vol. XIX (1693), pp. 54–56; Magno, *Estratti*, ed. Hopf, *Chron. gréco-romanes*, pp. 203–4. On 27 February, 1461, Pius addressed a bull to the Monemvasiotes (Arch. Segr. Vaticano, Reg. Vat. 479, fols. 292^v–293^r, by mod. stamped enumeration, and *cf.* the following note):

". . . Paucis ante mensibus venerunt ad presentiam nostram dum in civitate Senensi cum nostra Romana Curia residebamus, in frequenti audiencia assistentibus ibidem venerabilibus fratribus et dilectis filiis nostris Sancte Romane Ecclesie cardinalibus et diversarum civitatum archiepiscopis, episcopis et prelatis ac regum et principum quorundam oratoribus, dilecti filii . . . vestri oratores viri honesti et graves . . . , dedicionem facientes et homagium tanquam vero et indubitato vestro domino pro nobis et successoribus nostris imperpetuum tam in spiritualibus quam [in] temporalibus, tactis ambabus manibus sacrosanctis evangeliis, genibus coram nobis flexis in forma per Apostolicam Sedem servari consueta fidelitatis iuramentum prestiterunt, supplicando eciam quod vobis privilegia vestra que hactenus sub dispositis [i.e., the despots of the Morea] aut aliis quibuscumque dominis vestris in temporalibus habuistis ac etiam in spiritualibus dignaremur in omne tempus robur habitura confirmare nostra et Apostolice Sedis auctoritate . . . [which Pius said he proceeded to do on 9 September, 1460, when Monemvasia thus became a papal possession, and now on 27 February, 1461, to give effect to the Monemvasiotes' homage he was sending Gentile de'Marcolfi of Spoleto to take over the city, the fortress, and its dependencies]. Datum Rome apud Sanctum Petrum anno, etc., millesimo CCCCLX, tercio Kal. Martii, pontificatus nostri anno tercio" [i.e., 1461].

On 28 February (1461) Pius granted a safe-conduct (*littera passus*) for "Janonus de Crema miles et Gentilis de Malcolfis de Spoleto ac Johannes [de] Hanglis, dilecti filii nobilis viri Thome Paleologi dispoti Achaye illustrissimi oratores," obviously to facilitate their return to the Morea, "datum . . . pridie Kal. Martii, pontificatus nostri anno tercio" (*ibid.*, fol. 293^v). Gentile de'Marcolfi's letter of appointment as *generalis gubernator et vicarius* is also dated 28 February (1461) in this register. He was to exercise full jurisdiction in the city and fortress, ". . . nostra civitas Monabassie in Peloponesso quam nuper sub nostro et Romane Ecclesie temporali dominio de fratrum nostrorum Sancte Romane Ecclesie cardinalium consilio pariter et assensu recepimus" (*ibid.*, fol. 229^r).

[87] See the preceding note, and *cf.* Arch. Segr. Vaticano, Miscellanea, Arm. IX, tom. 15 (Collett. per Città, Terre, e Luoghi: Lett. M e N), fols. 150^r–155^v, where two copies are given of Marcolfi's bull of appointment, "datum Rome apud S. Petrum anno etc. 1460 [O.S.], III Kal. Martii, pontificatus nostri anno tertio."

appointed the Portuguese soldier Lope de Valdaro as *capitaneus civitatis Monobasie*. He was to take the oath of fealty to the Holy See in the proper form, which oath of office was to be administered by the papal chamberlain, Cardinal Lodovico Trevisan, or the latter's lieutenant.[88]

Eleven days later, on 21 July (1461), Pius replaced Marcolfi with Francis of S. Anatolia, abbot of the monastery of S. Niccolò of Osimo. Francis was to govern Monemvasia and its dependencies as well as all the places in the area which should be freed from the infidels within a year. The terms of the abbot's commission show that the pope entertained high expectations of him.[89] But the Monemvasiotes, despite papal confirmation of the great privileges which they had enjoyed for generations under the Byzantine emperors, found neither contentment nor a sense of security under the banner of S. Peter's keys, and in 1462 they accepted the rule of the Venetian republic.[90]

Sultan Mehmed spent four days at Mistra (31 May–3 June, 1460), adding to the fortifications, and upon his departure left behind him a garrison of four hundred men. Thence he went on, taking Demetrius with him, to the town of Bordonia, which fell to him without a struggle, because the frightened *archontes* had fled. Next he came to a castle town on the slopes of Taygetus, called Kastrion by Critobulus, and identified as Kastritza by Sphrantzes. The town was built on an inaccessible height, its sole approach blocked by a triple wall, against which the janissaries launched at least one or two strong attacks in vain. The Pseudo-Sphrantzes says that the inhabitants surrendered with the understanding that they might preserve their rights and customs, to which the sultan agreed, promising to add further benefits to those they already possessed. When they emerged from the citadel, however, the sultan ordered some of the men beheaded, and others impaled, and had their leader flayed alive. Critobulus says nothing of the sultan's alleged violation of his pledge (and there is no word of such treachery either in Sphrantzes' short chronicle or in Chalcocondylas), but states that the citadel fell in the second day's assault, and the defenders, being driven into a narrow pathway and lacking food and water, surrendered unconditionally. Of four hundred chosen men in the citadel only three hundred had survived the Turkish attacks. The sultan ordered the immediate execution of all these, the enslavement of the women and children, and the destruction of the town.[91]

---

[88] Reg. Vat. 516 [*Pii II Officiorum Ann. III–VI, lib. II*], fol. 32ʳ by mod. stamped enumeration: "Pius etc. Dilecto filio Luppo de Valdaro laico portugalensi civitatis nostre Monobasie capitaneo. . . . Volumus autem quod antequam officium huiusmodi incipias exercere in manibus dilecti filii Ludovici tituli Sancti Laurentii in Damaso presbyteri cardinalis camerarii nostri [Lodovico Trevisan] vel eius locumtenentis de officio ipso fideliter exercendo prestare debeas in forma debita iuramentum. Datum Rome apud S. Petrum anno etc. millesimo CCCCLXI sexto Idus Iulii pont[ificatus] n[ostri] anno tercio." *Cf.* the rubric (fol. 2ʳ): "Lupus de Valdaro constituitur capitaneus civitatis Monobasie," and note also the Miscellanea, Arm. IX, tom. 15, fol. 150ʳ.

[89] Reg. Vat. 516, fols. 37ᵛ–39ʳ, "datum Rome apud Sanctum Petrum anno etc. MCCCCLXI, XII Kal. Augusti, pont[ificatus] nostri anno tertio." Pius apparently placed much confidence in Francis of S. Anatolia, ". . . et ut indubitanter credimus fluctuum turbines sedare et iustitie terminos colere, superbos humiliare et rebelles, ac inobedientes compescere et errantes ad rectam semitam poteris . . . ," etc. (*ibid.*, fol. 38ʳ). The intrepid Francis of S. Anatolia, *abbas Auximanus, gubernator Monobasie*, went to Monemvasia, where Bariša Krekić, "Monemvasia under Papal Protection" [in Serbocroatian, with a French summary], *Zbornik Radova Vizantološkog Instituta*, VI (*Recueil des travaux de l'Académie serbe des sciences*, LXV, Belgrade, 1960), 129–35, has found traces of his activities in the Archives of Ragusa (Dubrovnik).

On 19 July, 1461, Pius appointed John Navarre as governor *in temporalibus* of the Greek island of "Staliminus," i.e., Lemnos (Reg. Vat. 516, fol. 33ʳ, "datum Rome apud Sanctum Petrum anno etc. MCCCCLXI, quarto decimo Kal. Aug., pontificatus nostri anno tertio"). Paul II canceled John Navarre's appointment on 1 March, 1465, as indicated by a marginal note in the register.

[90] Magno, *Estratti*, ed. Hopf, *Chron. gréco-romanes*, p. 204. According to Raynaldus, *Ann. eccl.*, ad ann. 1462, no. 35, vol. XIX (1693), p. 120, Monemvasia was occupied by the Turks between the period of papal and that of Venetian domination: ". . . at dissipata sunt ea consilia [i.e., the failure of the pope's plan to exploit Monemvasia as a beachhead for sending 10,000 German troops into the Morea] in Turcicam iterum missa Monobassia servitutem, quam deinde recuperatam a Venetis, iterumque a Turcis, quibus hactenus paret expugnatam. . . ." On 12 August, 1462, however, the Venetian Senate answered point by point a petition presented to the Signoria by the Despot Thomas. Monemvasia was then obviously in Venetian hands, but Thomas still retained a lively interest in the place (Arch. di Stato di Venezia, Sen. Secreta, Reg. 21, fols. 103ᵛ–104, published by Sime Ljubić, *Listine*, X [Zagreb, 1891], 222–24).

[91] Critobulus, III, 21 (ed. Müller, *FHG*, V-1, pp. 133–34; ed. Grecu [1963], pp. 257, 259); Sphrantzes. *Chron. minus* (*PG* 156, 1069B; ed. Grecu [1966], p. 118), also makes no mention of Mehmed's violating a pledge at Kastritza. Chalcocondylas, bk. IX (Bonn, pp. 473–74; ed. Darkó, II-2 [1927], 228–29), describes the janissaries' capture of the lower town (which he identifies as Kastria), their successful assault upon the citadel, and the slaughter of its three hundred defenders, but knows of no violation of the sultan's pledge, which seems to be an invention of

The Turks occupied Leondari with no trouble, because the terrified inhabitants had fled westward to the much stronger town of Gardiki, which commanded a pass through Taygetus called Zugos. Having his usual offer of surrender rejected, Mehmed decided to starve the inhabitants of Gardiki and their numerous guests out of the impregnable height. But a shortage of food and water, the merciless heat of summer, the fearfully crowded conditions, and the lack of any help in prospect induced the poor wretches in the citadel atop the narrow rock to surrender after a single day's siege. According to the very doubtful account of the Pseudo-Sphrantzes, the sultan having again given his assurance that no one would be harmed or enslaved, nevertheless had all the men, women, and children herded together in a little field, had them tied up, and ordered them to be slain. Not a single one of the refugees from Leondari survived the slaughter, says Chalcocondylas, who states that he had been informed by people who lived in the area that the sultan had about six thousand persons put to death after the capture of Gardiki. Although obviously appalled at the sultan's cruelty, Chalcocondylas says nothing of a broken pledge, nor do Sphrantzes and Critobulus. The leading family of Gardiki, the Bouchaleis, would have suffered the same fate if the beylerbey, Mahmud Pasha, had not appealed to the sultan on their behalf. The wife of Manuel Bouchales, apparently leader of the clan, was Mahmud Pasha's cousin. They ill repaid his kindness. When they were leaving, he furnished them with an escort to Pontiko on the west coast, but before they boarded a ship they found there, they killed all the members of the escort, and then sailed for Corfu and thence to Naples.[92]

In the meantime Sultan Mehmed continued his career of conquest, taking the towns and castles of S. George, Karytaina, Androusa, and Ithome. There was no further resistance. After the horror of Gardiki the governors of the Moreote fortresses sent envoys to the sultan, offering him the surrender of their charges, among others a place called Salvarium and also Kyparissia, known as Arcadia in the middle ages, a well-fortified city, the naval arsenal of the region. Assembling the men and women of both these places to the number of ten thousand, Mehmed seemed to be about to kill them, but finally sent them to Istanbul to be settled in the suburban areas. Little was left of the "despotate" of the Morea.[93]

The Despot Thomas had been quite unable to protect his portion of the despotate against the overpowering Turkish onslaught. He lacked the troops and resources for an effective resistance. His small Italian force, of little consequence anyway (as Pius II had foreseen), had already been dispersed. Its members had lived for a while by plundering the country they were supposed to defend, and had finally disappeared. When Thomas saw there was no hope of combatting the Turk, and no safety in the Morea except in Venetian territory, he left his southern stronghold of Kalamata on the Messenian Gulf and made his way to Navarino.[94] Mehmed now paid a visit to Coron and thereafter crossed the western prong of the Morea to Modon. The Venetian authorities, including presumably Mauro Caravallo and Giovanni Bembo, the castellans and provveditori of Coron and Modon respectively, urged Thomas to leave the Venetian port of Navarino and not attempt resistance there. They offered him ships on which to get away. He went to Marathi, and learning that Mehmed was pitching his camp near Navarino, he set sail with his wife Caterina, his children, and a number of Moreote nobles from the harbor of Porto Longo for Corfu, where he arrived on 28 July. The historian Sphrantzes arrived by another ship on 2 August, undecided whether to go on to Crete or to the monastery of S. Nicholas, founded by his

the Pseudo-Sphrantzes [Macarius Melissenus-Melissurgus], IV, 18 (Bonn, p. 405; ed. Grecu [1966], pp. 542, 544), surreptitiously inserted into his expansion of Sphrantzes' text.

[92] Pseudo-Sphrantzes, IV, 18 (Bonn, pp. 405–6; ed. Grecu, p. 544); Sphrantzes, *Chron. minus* (*PG* 156, 1069CD; ed. Grecu, pp. 118, 120); Chalcocondylas, bk. IX (Bonn, pp. 474–75; ed. Darkó, II-2, 229–30); Critobulus, III, 22 (ed. Müller, *FHG*, V-1, p. 134; ed. Grecu, pp. 259, 261).

[93] Sphrantzes, *Chron. minus* (*PG* 156, 1070; ed. Grecu, pp. 120, 122), and *cf.* Pseudo-Sphrantzes, IV, 19 (Bonn, pp. 407–8; ed. Grecu, p. 546); Chalcocondylas, bk. IX (Bonn, p. 475; ed. Darkó, II-2, 230).

[94] According to Sphrantzes, *Chron. minus* (*PG* 156, 1070B; ed. Grecu, p. 120), Thomas went to Navarino from Kalamata (*cf.* Pseudo-Sphrantzes, IV, 19, ed. Bonn, p. 407, lines 16–18; ed. Grecu, p. 546, lines 9–11). Wm. Miller, *Latins in the Levant* (1908), p. 449, and Babinger, *Maometto* (1957), p. 267, both state that Thomas went to Navarino from Mantineia, which Chalcocondylas says Thomas had failed to take (see above, note 74). Thomas had taken refuge in Mantineia during the Turkish invasion of 1458.

maternal grandfather near Berrhoea in Macedonia.

The Venetians renewed their pacts with Sultan Mehmed and made themselves appear as hospitable as they could. The Turkish cavalry still invaded the region of Navarino, however, captured some Albanians, and killed a number of Venetian subjects. Mehmed himself rode up to the walls of Modon, according to Chalcocondylas, and when some of the inhabitants approached him "with a flag of truce" (ὡς ἐπὶ σπονδαῖς), he had them put to death. The sultan soon withdrew to the northwest corner of the peninsula, where Zagan Pasha had been busily at work in Achaea and Elis. He had occupied Kalavryta with the apparent collusion of its commander, the Albanian chieftain Doxas, who had fought against Mehmed two years before at Phlius, and was now flayed alive by the sultan's order. Sphrantzes believed that Doxas deserved his punishment, having failed to keep faith with the despots, with the sultan, and even with God.[95]

Zagan Pasha had also captured the old Frankish castles of Chloumoutsi and Santameri ("of S. Omer"), the latter being just north of the mountain of the same name. At Santameri, Zagan Pasha had violated the terms of surrender he had granted, killing and enslaving the inhabitants, to the indignation of Sultan Mehmed, who finally understood that the terror and despair of the Greeks and Albanians might serve as well as courage in leading them to reject assurances of safety which they were afraid to trust. The sultan had the liberation of the captives taken at Santameri announced throughout the camp, and removed Zagan Pasha from the high command in the Morea, replacing him by Hamza Zenevisi.[96]

Leaving the Morea at the end of the summer, Mehmed took the Despot Demetrius and the latter's wife and daughter with him as far as Livadia, where he left Demetrius, the women, and most of the army to travel at a slower pace. He went on with his personal following to Adrianople, where he arrived in mid-autumn. Demetrius soon followed him to the court and, according to Critobulus, Mehmed promptly made generous provision for him, granting him the islands of Imbros and Lemnos as well as parts of Thasos and Samothrace. Actually most of the inhabitants of these islands had been transported to Istanbul, "but the total annual revenue of these islands," says Critobulus, "was 300,000 [aspers] in the small silver coinage of the realm."[97] Mehmed also gave him the town of Aenos, at the mouth of the Maritsa, with its rich salt works which produced another 300,000 aspers. Besides these grants Mehmed directed that each year Demetrius should re-

---

[95] Chalcocondylas, bk. IX (Bonn, pp. 444, 477–78; ed. Darkó, II-2, pp. 203–4, 231–33); Sphrantzes, *Chron. minus* (*PG* 156, 1070D–1071A; ed. Grecu, p. 122); and *cf.* Pseudo-Sphrantzes, IV, 19 (Bonn, p. 409; ed. Grecu, p. 548).

[96] Chalcocondylas, bk. IX (Bonn, pp. 477–79, 481; ed. Darkó, II-2, 231–34, 235).

[97] Critobulus, III, 24, 4 (ed. Müller, *FHG*, V-1, p. 135b; ed. Grecu, p. 265). The asper, a small silver coin of Byzantine origin, weighed originally about a gram (=15.4 grains). It was later called the akçe by the Turks, who minted it as the basic unit of Ottoman imperial currency until its displacement in the seventeenth century by the *para* (by which time the asper weighed no more than 0.13 grams of silver). To start with, ten aspers appear to have been worth about one Venetian ducat, but the silver content of the asper was constantly diminished, and so its purchasing power persistently declined. In the time of Mehmed II a ducat was worth 40–50 aspers; in the sixteenth century it finally became worth about 80. An asper was about a quarter of a *dirham* (from the Greek *drachma*), the unit of silver currency employed in the eastern provinces of the old Caliphate (*cf.* the notices in K. H. Schäfer, *Die Ausgaben d. Apostolischen Kammer unter Johann XXII.*, Paderborn, 1911, pp. 89, 115, and see especially Friedrich von Schrötter, *Wörterbuch der Münzkunde*, Berlin and Leipzig, 1930, pp. 145–48). Three dirhams equaled a *dinar* (from the Latin *denarius* but based upon the Byzantine *solidus*), the Arabic gold unit of currency, weighing about 4.25 grams of gold (=65.45 grains). Twelve aspers therefore equalled a dinar, the latter term being no longer used after the beginning of the fifteenth century, although it has been restored as the name of the basic unit of modern Yugoslav, Iraqi, and other currencies (*cf.* the *Wörterbuch d. Münzkunde*, pp. 139–42). On the whole, however, in Ottoman trade with the Italian states monetary values were commonly reckoned in terms of ducats and florins.

On the revenues of the Ottoman empire and its system of coinage, see Babinger, *Maometto*, pp. 655–66, and for the various coins see, under their names, the *Encycl. of Islām*; C. H. Philips, ed., *Handbook of Oriental History*, London, 1951; *Wörterbuch d. Münzkunde*, under *akçe* and *asper* and esp. *dinar* and *dirhem*; Franz Babinger, "Zur Frage der osmanischen Goldprägungen im 15. Jahrhundert unter Murâd II. und Mehmed II.," and "Contraffazioni ottomane dello zecchino veneziano nel XV secolo," both studies reprinted in Babinger's *Aufsätze und Abhandlungen zur Geschichte Südosteuropas und der Levante*, 2 vols., Munich, 1962–66, II, 110–26; Babinger, "Die Aufzeichnungen des Genuesen Iacopo de Promontorio-de Campis . . ." [on the military personnel, seraglio, court, and revenues of the Ottoman empire in 1475], in the *Sitzungsber. d. Bayer. Akad. d. Wissen.*, Philos.-hist. Kl., 1956, Heft 8, pp. 62–72; and Speros Vryonis, "Laonicus Chalcocondyles and the Ottoman Budget," *International Journal of Middle East Studies*, VII (1976), 423–32.

ceive in three installments an additional 100,000 aspers from the mint at Adrianople, which gave Demetrius (according to Critobulus) an annual income of 700,000 aspers.[98] Later Sphrantzes heard a report that Demetrius, being "old and sick," retired on a pension of fifty thousand aspers a year. Mehmed spent the winter of 1460–1461 in Istanbul, thus concluding a remarkable decade in Ottoman history. Critobulus says that Mehmed had captured about two hundred and fifty fortified cities, castles, and towns in the Morea.[99] Demetrius spent his last years under the biblical name of David in a monastery at Adrianople, where he died in 1470. His poor wife, an Asanina, soon followed him to the grave. Their daughter, the unfortunate princess Helena, had died of the plague shortly before her father. The unknown rhetorician who composed a lament in her honor could not find tears enough to bemoan her passing.[100]

When Thomas Palaeologus fled before the Turks, he brought with him the head of S. Andrew, which had long been preserved in the metropolitan Church of Patras. He arrived in Ancona on 16 November, 1460, and then, at the invitation of Pope Pius II, he made his way to Rome. On 9 March, 1461, the Mantuan ambassador in Rome wrote the Marchioness Barbara,

> Last Saturday, which was the seventh of this month, the despot of the Morea came here. He is certainly a handsome man with a fine, serious look about him and a noble and quite lordly bearing. He must be about fifty-six years old. He wore a caftan of black camlet with a white furlike hat lined with black velvety satin with a band around it. I understand that he had seventy horse and as many foot, all the horses being borrowed save three which are his own. . . .

Pius received him in a consistory held in the Camera del Pappagallo in the east wing of the Vatican Palace. He gave him a pension of 300 ducats a month, to which the cardinals added another 200. Thomas was at first assigned the papal palace near the Church of SS. Quattro Coronati, and thereafter was given an apartment in the Ospedale di S. Spirito. On Laetare Sunday (15 March, 1461) the pope presented him with the golden rose as a mark of esteem and in recognition of the tragedy which had befallen him.[101]

Thomas was prevailed upon to surrender the head of S. Andrew to Pope Pius II, and on 12 April, 1462, in emotional ceremonies replete with tears and sermons, Cardinal Bessarion turned the precious relic over to the pope. The presentation took place on a wooden tribune erected on the city side of the Ponte Molle (now the Piazza Card. Consalvi), where a small chapel of S. Andrew and a lengthy inscription in the little cemetery of the Pellegrini still recall the dramatic reception of S. Peter's brother into Rome.[102] Thousands wit-

---

[98] Chalcocondylas, bk. IX (Bonn, p. 483; ed. Darkó, II-2, 237), states that Mehmed gave Demetrius the city of Aenos and the revenue from its salt works as well as a pension of about 600,000 aspers (ἐς ἑξήκοντα μυριάδας ἀργυρίου) from the Porte. *Cf.*, *ibid.*, Bonn, p. 494; ed. Darkó, II-2, 247.

[99] Critobulus, III, 23, 3 (ed. Müller, *FHG*, V-1, p. 135a; ed. Grecu [1963], p. 263).

[100] Sphrantzes, *Chron. minus* (*PG* 156, 1072D, 1075BC, 1078AB; ed. Grecu [1966], pp. 134, 142), and *cf.* Pseudo-Sphrantzes, IV, 19, 22–23 (Bonn, pp. 413–14, 427–29, 449; ed. Grecu, pp. 552, 566, 568, 586), whose unlikely tales of Demetrius's later years seem to be taken seriously by Miller, *Latins in the Levant*, p. 452. On Helena, see Lampros, *Palaiológeia kaì Peloponnesiaká*, IV (1930), introd., pp. 22–23, 221–29 (a rhetorical monody lamenting her tribulations and her death). Actually she was never married to Mehmed; the Pseudo-Sphrantzes calls her "sultana" (ἀμήρισσα), but Sphrantzes does not. More than once in 1460–1461 the Venetians tried to make the fall of the Greek despotate of the Morea an object lesson to quarreling Balkan princelings (*cf.* Ljubić, *Listine*, X, 164, 165), but the lesson was lost on them (*ibid.*, pp. 227–29), and within a couple of years the "most serene king of Bosnia" was no more (*ibid.*, pp. 247, 250–52).

[101] Pastor, *Hist. Popes*, III, append., no. 43, p. 403, and *Gesch. d. Päpste*, II (repr. 1955), append., no. 42, p. 728, Bonatto's letter of 9 March, 1461, to the Marchioness Barbara [von Brandenburg] of Mantua, the wife of Lodovico Gonzaga. In the English translation of Pastor's text (vol. III, p. 249) Thomas's arrival in Rome is incorrectly dated 7 May. *Cf.* Pius II, *Comm.*, bk. V, Engl. trans., pp. 377–78; ed. Frankfurt, 1614, p. 130, lines 13–19. On Thomas Palaeologus's dress, as described by Bonatto, *una turcha de zambeloto* [camlet] *negro cum uno capello biancho peloso fodrato de cetanino* [satin] *velutato negro cum una cerata intorno*, Pastor reminds us of the discussion of the Levantine trade in satin and camlet in W. Heyd, *Hist. du commerce du Levant*, trans. Furcy Raynaud, 2 vols., Leipzig, 1885–86, repr. Amsterdam, 1967, II, 701–5.

[102] The text of the inscription may be found in Vincenzo Forcella, *Iscrizioni delle chiese e d'altri edificii di Roma dal secolo XI fino ai giorni nostri*, 14 vols., 1869–84, XII, pt. XXIII, no. 245, p. 213: "Pius II. Pont. Max. sacrum beati apostoli Andree caput ex Peloponneso advectum his in pratis excepit et suis manibus portavit in urbem anno salutis MCCCCLXII pridie Idus Aprilis [12 April] que tunc fuit secunda feria [Monday] maioris hebdomade atque idcirco hunc titulum erexit et universis Christifidelibus qui eadem feria imposterum hunc locum visitaverint et quinquies Christo Domino adorato intercessionem Sancti

nessed the event, and thereafter long processions conveyed the sacred head to the Vatican basilica, where Pius later built the round chapel of S. Andrew. Pius was to be buried in this chapel, which disappeared in the demolition of old S. Peter's. He regarded the acquisition of the relic as one of the chief events of his reign. The ceremonies attending the reception of the relic doubtless appealed to him as effective propaganda for the crusade which had been proclaimed at Mantua.

Extensive preparations had been made in advance of the ceremonies. The crumbling steps to the Vatican basilica were replaced, a wooden loggia for the papal benediction was built over the top landing of the steps, and the houses which encroached upon the piazza were removed to clear the stage for S. Andrew's solemn entrance into the basilica. The tombs of long-dead popes were taken from the nave of the basilica and put along the walls to create space and passageways for the throngs who would attend S. Andrew's welcome to the site of S. Peter's martyrdom.

In their sermons at the reception of the relic both Pius and Bessarion expressed the fervent hope that, with the expulsion of the Turks from Greece, S. Andrew might some day return to his home in Patras. At long length in September, 1964, five centuries after the ceremonies of 1462, to which Pius devotes almost the whole first half of the eighth book of his *Commentaries*, Cardinal Augustin Bea headed a papal mission which duly returned the relic in its original silver-gilt reliquary to the Metropolitan Constantine of Patras. As for poor Thomas Palaeologus, he had found a refuge in Rome, where for a while he was wined and dined by the cardinals, but his appeals to various states for help to regain the lost despotate always went unheeded. He was beset by a constant melancholy, and died almost forgotten on 12 May, 1465, in the lodgings prepared for him in the Ospedale di S. Spirito near the Vatican.[103]

During the early period of his residence in Rome, Thomas Palaeologus had made no small impression upon the Curia, and besides the head of S. Andrew he seems to have left behind

---

Andree pro communi fidelium salute imploraverint plenariam omnium peccatorum in forma ecclesie consueta perpetuo duraturam indulsit remissionem anno pontificatus sui quarto."

[103] Pius II, *Comm.*, bk. VIII, Engl. trans., pp. 523–41; ed. Frankfurt, 1614, pp. 192–202; Campano, *Vita Pii II*, ed G. C. Zimolo, in the new Muratori, *RISS*, III-3 (1964), 56–57, with notes; Pastor, *Hist. Popes*, III, 249–52, 258–61, and *cf.* pp. 302–3, revised in *Gesch. d. Päpste*, II (repr. 1955), 227–29, 233–36, and *cf.* pp. 211–12; Hopf, "Griechenland im Mittelalter," in Ersch and Gruber's *Allgemeine Encyklopädie*, vol. 86 (1868; repr. 1960, II), p. 131b; Sp. P. Lampros, "The Translation [ἀνακομιδή] of the Head of S. Andrew from Patras to Rome" [in Greek], Νέος Ἑλληνομνήμων, X (1913), 33–112; Zakythinos, *Despotat grec de Morée*, I (1932, repr. 1975), 287–90, not without error; and especially Ruth Olitsky Rubinstein, "Pius II's Piazza S. Pietro and St. Andrew's Head," in Domenico Maffei, ed., *Enea Silvio Piccolomini, Papa Pio II* . . . , Siena, 1968, pp. 221–43.

The account of the reception of S. Andrew's head, called the *Andreis*, occurs separately in Cod. Vat. lat. 5667, fols. 19–40, "Andreis idest Hystoria de receptione capitis Sancti Andreae." This MS. was prepared by order of Cardinal Francesco Piccolomini, later Pius III, for Jacopo Silveri Piccolomini, who had requested it (the latter died before the cardinal could send it to him). Remo Ceserani, in the *Giornale storico della letteratura italiana*, CXLI (ann. LXXXI, Turin, 1964), 279–81, has noted that the "Andreis" fills a *sesternio* of the Cod. Reginensis lat. 1995, fols. 349^{r}–366^{v} [365^{v}?], written in an unknown copyist's hand (with the preceding and following pages in that of Patrizzi), suggesting the insertion of the account of the translation of S. Andrew's head as a unit into the text of the *Commentarii*. The strange fact is that in the letter which Cardinal Francesco wrote on 23 February, 1464, as he got ready to send Jacopo Silveri the MS., he seems to say that the *Andreis* had been (should we say?) written, edited, or prepared by Alessio de' Cesari, bishop of Chiusi (1438–1462) and archbishop of Benevento (d. 31 July, 1464): Francesco apologizes for the delay in sending the MS. containing certain works of Pius II. He had been too preoccupied with various affairs and frequent consistories. Finally, however, he had found the time to have the works in question copied (*conscribi*), "adiecta etiam Andreide domini Alessii episcopi clusini patrui tui."

Since the style of the so-called *Andreis* seems unmistakably Pius's, Ceserani assumes that de' Cesari edited the text, putting Pius's two orations and that of Bessarion as well as the hymn by Agapito de' Rustici and other material all in the proper place. Among the various opuscula of Pius II relating to the Crusade, in the Arch. Segr. Vaticano, Miscellanea, Arm. XII, tom. 3 (=Bibl. Apost. Vaticana, Cod. Vat. lat. 12,255), fols. 61^{r}–82^{v}, by mod. stamped enumeration, one may also find the *Historia de receptione capitis Sancti Andree*, which is attributed to Pius II in the index to the MS. on fol. 2^{r}. On the importance of the *Andreis* in the structure of the *Commentarii*, note the observations of G. Bernetti, referred to above, at the conclusion of note 13.

The return of the relic of S. Andrew to the Church of Patras is described in the *New York Times*, 24 and esp. 27 September, 1964, where both fact and typography are garbled. When the sacred relic was taken to S. Peter's on 14 April, 1462 (the thirteenth seems to have been washed out by rain), Bessarion preached a sermon from the high altar to the throng which had crowded into the basilica. He ended by making S. Andrew appeal to Pius II (*Comm.*, bk. VIII, ed. Frankfurt, 1614, p. 202, lines 15–19): ". . . te Deus incolumem cum felicitate diutissime conservet sedis Petri gubernacula cum summo decore et moderatione tenentem, et tibi pro sua pietate praestet him a curious memorial which still exists in fine condition at the Vatican. Thomas is said to have been the model for Paolo Romano's statue of S. Paul which stood, with a like statue of S. Peter, at the foot of the steps leading to the front portals of the Vatican basilica, from the time of Pius II to that of Pius IX, when the two statues were replaced by the colossal stone figures of the apostles, done by de Fabris and Tardolini, which now stand on either side of the approach to the basilica. In 1847 the old statues of Peter and Paul, for the latter of which (as we have just said) Paolo Romano is alleged to have copied the features of the Despot Thomas, were removed to the entrance to the sacristy of S. Peter's and thence to the Museo Petriano. Within the last few years they have been moved again, this time to the vestibule of the upper rooms prepared for the Synod of Bishops, in the north wing of the old palace (built by Nicholas V), rooms which Sixtus IV converted into the Vatican Library. The two statues in question have been variously attributed to Mino da Fiesole, Mino del Reame, and Paolo di Mariano [Romano], "the first and only important sculptor in the Rome of the Quattrocento."[104] Years ago, however, Eugène Müntz published excerpts, from the papal financial accounts, recording payments to Paolo Romano for the statue of S. Paul, "honorabili viro magistro Paulo Mariani scultori de Urbe . . . pro parte eius salarii et mercedis sculturae per eum factae statuae sancti Pauli ponendae super scalis . . . basilicae [S. Petri]."[105] Both the pedestal of S. Paul's statue and that of S. Peter's still bear the arms of Pius II, Turkish crescents on a cross, the symbol of his dedication to the Crusade.

gratiam ut qui cum magna me gloria in hac urbe in praesentiarum accepisti cum maiori in patriam aliquando reducas, quemadmodum magno cum affectu tua sponte heri pollicitus fuisti!"

As is well known, and we shall have further occasion to note, Pius II died in Ancona, where his viscera (*praecordia*) were buried in the cathedral Church of S. Ciriaco, as an inscription in the choir still attests. His body was taken to Rome, however, and buried in a low tomb in the Cappella di S. Andrea at the Vatican. Immediately, in 1464, his nephew Cardinal Francesco Todeschini-Piccolomini, later Pope Pius III, built near the tomb the handsome monument which was transferred in 1614 to the Church of S. Andrea della Valle, where it still exists, but is placed so high above the pavement of the nave that it is hard to see. The remains of Pius II were exhumed on 13 November, 1608, and after temporary burial were also removed to S. Andrea della Valle in 1623 by Cardinal Alessandro Peretti. The original inscription which Cardinal Francesco Todeschini-Piccolomini put upon the monument, after rehearsing the great achievements of his uncle Pius II, states that the latter ". . . relatus in urbem est patrum decreto et hic conditus [i.e., in the no longer existent Cappella di S. Andrea in S. Peter's] ubi caput Andreae Apostoli ad se Peloponneso advectum collocari iusserat. . . ." The inscription which (in 1623) Cardinal Peretti put on the monument, as it now exists in S. Andrea della Valle, also recalls Pius II's acquisition of the relic of S. Andrew for the Vatican basilica. See Renzo U. Montini, *Le Tombe dei Pape*, Rome: Istituto di Studi Romani, 1957, pp. 285–89, for references, the inscriptions, and a picture of the monument, on which the sculptor has depicted the translation of S. Andrew's head to the Vatican, as described in Pius II's *Commentaries*.

[104] Pastor, *Gesch. d. Päpste*, II (repr. 1955), 211–12, and see the recent brochure *Il Restauro delle aule di Niccolò V e di Sisto IV nel Palazzo Apostolico Vaticano*, Città del Vaticano: Direzione Generale dei Servizi Tecnici del Governatorato Vaticano, 1967. Miller, *Latins in the Levant* (1908), p. 454, mistakenly believed that "every visitor to Rome unconsciously gazes on his [Thomas Palaeologus's] features, for on account of his tall and handsome appearance he served as a model for the statue of St. Paul, which still stands at the steps of St. Peter's." (The statue was removed, as noted above, from its place before the basilica in 1847.) Zakythinos, *Despotat grec de Morée*, I, 289, repeats Miller's mistake.

[105] E. Müntz, *Les Arts à la cour des papes*, I (1878), 246–49, 280. The first payment for the statues of SS. Peter and Paul is recorded under 11 March, 1461, for "marmi per le scale di San Pietro . . . per costo di una petra di marmo per fare due figure, cioe S. Pietro e S. Paulo per le scale, fl. 20" (*ibid.*, p. 279). This was four days after the first arrival of Thomas Palaeologus in Rome. See in general R. O. Rubinstein, "Pius II's Piazza S. Pietro and St. Andrew's Head," in *Enea Silvio Piccolomini, Papa Pio II* (1968), pp. 230–35.

8. PIUS II, THE CRUSADE, AND THE VENETIAN WAR AGAINST THE TURKS

ALTHOUGH more than one passage in Pope Pius II's *Commentarii* was penned with guile, there cannot be the slightest doubt of his genuine and indeed overriding devotion to the crusade. The problems he had to face, however, seemed insurmountable. There were difficulties enough in Italy where, besides the four important states of Milan, Venice, Florence, and Naples, there were about a score of lesser *signori* and *signorie* very much attached to their independence. Most of the Italian states, large and small, entertained justifiable suspicions of one another. They protected themselves from their rivals and neighbors by an elaborate and sometimes inconsistent balance-of-power diplomacy in which Pius was necessarily as much involved as any other of the various princes. The greatest single danger faced by the papacy, however, was the possibility of the French re-entering the peninsula in force to oust Ferrante from Naples and to re-establish the old Angevin kingdom of "Sicily."

Every political event or military episode which occurred in Italy of sufficient importance to distract the pope's attention from the crusade had its bearing upon the Christian defense against the Turks. Giovanni Antonio del Balzo Orsini, prince of Taranto, had come to nurture such animus against King Ferrante of Naples as to work vigorously for his replacement by the Angevin claimant to the Neapolitan throne. A number of the (Italian) feudal families in the kingdom, now remembering the erstwhile French regime almost with nostalgia, had never taken very amicably to domination by the Catalans. But a south Italian war was something which Pius II did not want, and on 3 February, 1459, he wrote Prince Giovanni of Taranto, urging him to compose his differences with King Ferrante.[1] On 27 February Pius informed Francesco Sforza, the duke of Milan, that he was receiving news daily from the papal legate in the kingdom of Naples to the effect that relations between Ferrante and the prince of Taranto were getting steadily worse, and that he believed war was imminent.[2] This was a most inopportune development, for Pius was then occupied in securing forces to serve against the Turks.[3] We need not stop to consider the many papal briefs dealing with Ferrante's difficulties in the south with the prince of Taranto and the Angevin party.[4] Despite Pius's efforts and admonitions, the war came. It proved to be a long struggle (1459–1464), hampering his attempts to organize a crusade until the end of his pontificate. His support and that of Francesco Sforza—Florence and Venice remained neutral—assured Ferrante of the throne. Scanderbeg, always a loyal servitor of the Catalan royal house in Naples, sent an Albanian cavalry force into southern Italy in September, 1460.[5] On 10 October Prince Giovanni of Taranto wrote a letter of protest to Scanderbeg, whose interesting reply we have already had occasion to note.[6]

At the beginning of September of the following year (1461) Scanderbeg himself crossed the Adriatic to Apulia.[7] His force is said to have consisted of about one thousand horse and two thousand infantry. He served a full five months in Italy in opposition to the condottiere Jacopo Piccinino, Pius II's *bête noire*; the prince of Taranto; and Jean d'Anjou; and he may well

[1] Arch. Segr. Vaticano, Arm. XXXIX, tom. 9 [*Pii II brevia*], fol. 14.

[2] *Ibid.*, fols. 18^v–19^v, letter written from Siena.

[3] *Cf.* the letter of 24 February (1459) to the legate in Rome, *ibid.*, fols. 19^v–20^r.

[4] *Cf.*, *ibid.*, fols. 21^v–22^r, 23, 25^v–26^v, etc., 165^v–166^r, a letter from the pope to Scanderbeg, dated 29 June, 1460, and 166^v, etc.

[5] Francisc Pall, "I Rapporti italo-albanesi intorno alla metà del secolo XV," *Archivio storico per le province napoletane*, LXXXIII (3rd ser., IV, 1966), doc. no. VI, pp. 164–66, letter of Jacopo Perpinià [i.e., Jaume de Perpinyà, on whom see above, p. 186b] to King Ferrante of Naples, dated at Barletta on 17 September, 1460. Reference has already been made to Pall's article [see above, Chapter 6, notes 127, 130], which contains eighty-eight documents from the Milanese Archives, ranging from July, 1455, to July, 1467 (all but the first eight documents dating from the years 1461–1467).

[6] See, above, Chapter 3, note 83, and Achille Ratti [later Pope Pius XI], "Quarantadue Lettere originali di Pio II relative alla guerra per la successione nel reame di Napoli . . . ," *Archivio storico lombardo*, 3rd ser., XIX (ann. XXX, 1903), 263–93, with (as indicated by the title) forty-two briefs covering the period from 29 May, 1460, to 23 April, 1463. *Cf.* G. Lesca, "I Commentarii . . . d'Enea Silvio Piccolomini," *Annali della R. Scuola normale superiore di Pisa*, Filos. e Filologia, vol. X (della serie XVI, 1894), pp. 106–28.

[7] Pall, "I Rapporti italo-albanesi," docs. XXV–XXIX, pp. 176–79, dated 31 August to 10 September, 1461.

have saved the Neapolitan kingdom for Ferrante. In early February, 1462, he was recalled to Albania by the approach of the Turks.[8]

During the course of the south Italian war the French made various efforts to assist the Angevins and more than one gesture to the pope. On 27 November, 1461, at a meeting of the royal council in Tours the new king of France, Louis XI, abrogated the Pragmatic Sanction of Bourges, thus allegedly restoring French obedience to the Holy See, in an effort to win Pius to support of the Angevin claims to Naples (or at least to neutrality while Louis made good these claims by force of arms).[9] A few months later Louis made another bid for papal acquiescence in the French designs upon Naples. In March, 1462, French envoys to the Holy See formally announced in a public consistory, over which the pope presided, that Louis XI "would send to Greece against the Turks forty thousand cavalry and thirty thousand archers, a force which could easily drive Mahomet from Europe and recover a second time Syria and the most holy sepulchre of Christ"—provided the kingdom of Naples were restored to the house of Anjou and Genoa returned to French domination. Pius knew insincerity when he saw it, however, and in his reply to the envoys "touched as briefly as possible on the chimerical and fanciful and meaningless offer of seventy thousand fighting men, so as not to seem to be taking nonsense seriously."[10]

The failure of the Congress of Mantua had been discouraging, and so were the affairs of Naples. The Turks had taken Trebizond in the late summer of 1461, as we shall note, dealing a last blow to Greek Orthodoxy. Nevertheless, Mehmed II's well-known curiosity concerning Christian doctrine had suggested to more than one westerner that he might conceivably be converted to the true faith. Following in the

---

[8] The correspondence between Scanderbeg and the prince of Taranto is given in an imaginary form in Pius II, *Commentarii*, bk. VI, Engl. trans. by Florence A. Gragg (in *Smith College Studies in History*, vols. XXII, XXV, XXX, XXXV, and XLIII [1937–57], with continuous pagination), pp. 458–60; ed. Frankfurt, 1614, pp. 166–67. Marinus Barletius, *Historia de vita et gestis Scanderbegi*, 1st ed., Rome, *ca.* 1509, fols. CXXII ff., devotes his entire tenth book to Scanderbeg's efforts on Ferrante's behalf in the Neapolitan kingdom in 1461 (ed. Zagreb, 1743, pp. 282 ff.).

We do not lack trustworthy sources for the Albanian expeditions of 1460–1461: Pall, "I Rapporti italo-albanesi," docs. VII–IX, XI–LX, pp. 167–201, dated from 14 October, 1460, to 11–12 February, 1462, with much detail; V. V. Makušev, *Monumenta historica slavorum meridionalium*, II (Belgrade, 1882), 156, reprinted by J. Radonić, *Djuradj Kastriot Skenderbeg*, Belgrade, 1942, pp. 123–24, dispatch of the Milanese envoy Antonio Guidobono from Venice, dated 12 August, 1461, on the alleged numbers of Albanian troops ready to set out for Apulia; Giov. Pontano, *De bello neapolitano*, bk. II, in *Opera omnia*, II (Venice, 1519), 279–82; Giov. Simoneta, *Res gestae Francisci Sfortiae*, bk. XXVIII, ad ann. 1461, in *RISS*, XXI (Milan, 1732), cols. 728E–729A, and ed. Giov. Soranzo, in the new Muratori, *RISS*, XXI, pt. 2, pp. 448–49; Raynaldus, *Ann. eccl.*, ad ann. 1460, no. 60, vol. XIX (1693), p. 56, and ad ann. 1461, no. 3, p. 70; and see for the whole background the detailed study of Emilio Nunziante, "I Primi Anni di Ferdinando d'Aragona e l'invasione di Giovanni d'Angiò," in *Arch. stor. per le province napoletane*, XX (1895), esp. pp. 495, 501, and XXI (1896), notes on pp. 517, 521, 525, 527, and 529; F. S. Noli, *Geo. Castrioti Scanderbeg*, New York, 1947, pp. 57–62, 207–13; and esp. F. Pall, "Marino Barlezio," in *Mélanges d'histoire générale*, ed. Const. Marinescu, II (Bucharest, 1938), 212–16. Voigt, *Enea Silvio*, III (1863), 158–59, and K. Hopf, "Griechenland im Mittelalter," in J. S. Ersch and J. G. Gruber, eds., *Allgemeine Encyklopädie*, vol. 86 (1868, repr. New York, 1960, II), p. 153, used insufficient sources.

However much legend has marred the historical portrait of Scanderbeg, his valor was justly praised by contemporaries, and his exploits against the Turk were almost epic in their proportions. No one knew this better than the cautious statesmen of Ragusa. On 4 April, 1461, by a vote of thirty-one to two, the Ragusan Senate instructed the rector and his council to offer Scanderbeg a refuge "for his family in our islands if it should happen that he is harried by the Turks, which God forbid" (J. Gelcich and L. Thallóczy, eds., *Diplomatarium ragusanum*, Budapest, 1887, p. 749, and *cf.* pp. 751–54, 756, 758, 766–67, 774–75, 780, 783–84, and 786, for important details concerning Scanderbeg during the last half-dozen years of his life). The political and religious background of Scanderbeg's career is sketched in Stavro Skendi, "Il Complesso Ambiente dell'attività di Skanderbeg," in the *Atti del V convegno internazionale di studi albanesi*, XI (1968, publ. Palermo, 1969), 83–105.

[9] There is a handsomely inscribed copy of the abrogation of the Pragmatic Sanction in Pius II's *Liber rubeus diversorum memorabilium*, in Arch. Segr. Vaticano, A. A., Arm. I–XVIII, no. 1443, fols. 36^v–37^v: ". . . Abroganda sit ipsa Pragmatica pellendaque a regno nostro, quippe que adversus tuam sedem, omnium ecclesiarum matrem, ab inferioribus prelatis lata sit. . . ."—". . . datum Turonis sub magno sigillo nostro, die XXVII mensis Novembris, A.D. MCCCCLXI, et regni nostri primo. . . ." Despite revocation of the Pragmatic Sanction the royal government did not appreciably relax its control of the French Church, on which *cf.* P. Bourdon, "L'Abrogation de la Pragmatique et les règles de la chancellerie de Pie II," *Mélanges d'archéologie et d'histoire*, XXVIII (1908), 207–24.

[10] Pius II, *Comm.*, bk. VII, Engl. trans., pp. 510–11; ed. Frankfurt, 1614, p. 187; Jos. Cugnoni, *Opera inedita* (1883), p. 535, for the passage omitted from the Frankfurt edition. Note also the letter of the Milanese ambassador, Otto del Carretto, to Francesco Sforza dated at Rome on 15 March, 1462, in Ludwig v. Pastor, *Acta inedita*, I (Freiburg, 1904), no. 127, p. 162: ". . . che lassandoli il regno de Napoli et Genoa, voglino mandare contra il Turcho XXX mila cavalli et XL mila fanti. . . ." *Cf.*, *ibid.*, no. 132, pp. 170–71.

footsteps of Ramón Lull, John of Segovia, Nicholas of Cusa, and especially Juan de Torquemada, Pius believed for a little while that in dealing with Islam recourse to reason might be preferable to the employment of arms. During a period of almost inexplicable fantasy and aberration, apparently late in the year 1461, he wrote his long *Letter to Mehmed (Epistola ad Mahumetem)*. He actually seems to have thought that Mehmed might be converted if only he could be made to understand that Christ was the redeemer. Continued warfare with Christian Europe would lead the Turks to disaster. For eighty years they had been fighting the Hungarians, and could never get beyond the Sava and the Danube. "Una te gens tuasque vires agitat!" But what about the valiant Spanish, the mighty French, the many Germans, the strong English, the daring Poles, and the rich, powerful, and militarily skillful Italians? "Quid facias, si tibi cum Italis aut Gallis aut Germanis res fuerit, amplissimis et robustissimis populis?"

Christianity was the only Ottoman road to ultimate success and prosperity. Let Mehmed take his predecessor Constantine as his model.

> Sic procul dubio et tu clarissimus eris si nobiscum sapiens Christum colas et Constantinum imiteris: sicut Romani cum Constantino Christiani facti sunt, ita et Turchi fient tecum, *eritque tuum regnum super omnia quae sunt in orbe et nomen tuum nulla aetas silebit*. Latinae te litterae et graecae et barbarae celebrabunt.

Pius thus promised Mehmed world dominion, but still greater things lay ahead. He had spoken only of earthly power and human glory. "Caduca haec et fluxa sunt. . . ." Everything in this world comes to an end. Men die, kingdoms are overthrown, fame fades. There were better things to be sought, above all salvation in Christ. Although the extant manuscripts make it clear that Pius's *Epistola ad Mahumetem* had some circulation in Europe, it was certainly never sent to Mehmed. Further reflection doubtless impressed him with its utter impracticability. He never alludes to it in the *Commentaries*, and his thoughts soon returned to the Crusade.[11]

Amid the multiple distractions of his reign Pius had done little to organize an expedition against the Turks. Indeed, as he remarked to a small group of six loyal cardinals whom he summoned for consultation in early March, 1462,

> My brethren, perhaps you, like almost everyone else, think that we are neglecting the common weal because since our return from Mantua we have neither done nor said anything toward repulsing the Turks and protecting religion, and that too though the enemy has pressed us harder every day. We have been silent; we do not deny it. We have done nothing against the enemies of the Cross; that is evident. But the reason for our silence was not indifference but a kind of despair. Power, not will, has been lacking. . . .[12]

The Neapolitan problem had not been his only concern. From the beginning of his reign Hungary had claimed his frequent attention. Matthias Corvinus's hold upon the throne had been constantly threatened by the intrigues and attacks of the Emperor Frederick III, who was only effective when he was causing trouble.

About two months before Pope Pius's meeting with the six cardinals, the Venetian Senate had passed a resolution on 4 January, 1462, with 162 affirmative votes (to a mere eight negative and three neutral votes) to write his Holiness on a matter of extreme importance. They agreed in fact to send him a copy of a letter dated 15 December (1461) which they had recently received from their secretary Pietro Tommasi, whom they kept as a resident envoy at the Hungarian court. Pietro had written the doge and Signoria *circa materiam Turchorum* after having addressed Matthias Corvinus before a congregation of prelates and barons of the realm, all in accord with the instructions which he had received (through the doge) from the Senate. The Hungarians needed a subsidy to maintain the defense of their country against the Turks. They also required papal intervention to make the Emperor Frederick III cease his activities against Matthias Corvinus. Otherwise

---

[11] Franco Gaeta, "Sulla 'Lettera a Maometto' di Pio II," *Bullettino dell'Istituto storico italiano per il medio evo e Archivio Muratoriano*, LXXVII (Rome, 1965), 127–227, with the text of the *Epistola ad Mahumetem* on pp. 195–227, and *cf.* Gaeta, "Alcune Osservazioni sulla prima redazione della 'Lettera a Maometto'," in Domenico Maffei, ed., *Enea Silvio Piccolomini, Papa Pio II* . . . , Siena, 1968, pp. 177–86. The text of Pius's letter to Mehmed has also been published with a translation by Giuseppe Toffanin (Naples, 1953); it has been widely known for centuries, having been made available in Pius's so-called *Opera omnia*, Basel, 1551, repr. Frankfurt a. M., 1967, *Ep.* CCCXCVI, pp. 872–904. *Cf.* G. Paparelli, *Enea Silvio Piccolomini*, Bari, 1950, pp. 319–324: "Fallita la crociata del latino, non restava che preparare . . . quella delle armi." A reference to the fall of Trebizond in the first redaction of Pius's letter to Mehmed seems to fix the date of its composition between October and December, 1461 (Gaeta, *art. cit.*, 1965, p. 196: ". . . Trapezuntem in deditionem habuisti . . .").

[12] Pius II, *Comm.*, bk. VII, Engl. trans., p. 515; ed. Frankfurt, 1614, p. 189.

they would be obliged to make peace with the Turks, which would be an obstacle to the "sacred expedition" which a papal envoy had been discussing with the Senate.[13]

In their cautious way the Venetians were reconsidering their Turkish policy. They had been provoked by Turkish attacks upon Coron and Modon, and had sent an emissary to the sultan to protest this unwarranted aggression. Matthias Corvinus had heard tell of this emissary. When therefore the Senate wrote Pietro Tommasi (on the same day as they wrote the pope), they asked him to explain the reason for this mission to the Porte. He was also to state that the Signoria had been in close touch with the pope, who had sent an envoy to the lagoon to discuss the crusade. His Holiness had a burning desire to organize an expedition against the Turks. He had already set about making plans, and was trying to prevail upon the Christian princes to do their part in the sacred enterprise. The king and the barons in Hungary could rest assured that the Venetian government would do everything possible to bring their difficulties with Frederick III to an end.[14] In the time of Matthias Corvinus's father, John Hunyadi, the Hungarians had been the bulwark of Christendom. Venice wanted to keep them employed against the Turks.

Despite the pose which Louis XI had struck, no one saw a crusader in him.[15] Although the Florentines and even the Venetians seemed willing to play a dangerous game of chance with the French, Francesco Sforza was unalterably opposed to the Angevin designs upon Naples.

---

[13] Arch. di Stato di Venezia, Sen. Secreta, Reg. 21, fol. 74^v [75^v], dated 4 January, 1462 (Ven. style 1461): "Accepimus his diebus litteras secretarii nostri quem tenemus apud regiam Maiestatem Hungarie et quia vise sunt nobis non vulgaris ponderis et momenti spectabili oratori Sanctitatis vestre ostendendas atque tradendas censuimus. Ceterum considerato discrimine rerum pro magnitudine incumbentis periculi si forte subsidii desperatione rex et barones illius regni adducti inducias aut aliquod aliud concordie genus cum communibus Christiane fidei et religionis hostibus inirent non alienum existimavimus exemplum ipsarum litterarum etiam ad vestram Beatitudinem.

"Intelliget Sanctitas vestra pro sua mirabili sapientia quo in cardine res illius versentur. Nec dubitamus quin pro sua singulari in rem Christianam dilectione paternique officii cura cogitationes et consilia sua huc conversura sit ut impresentiarum omni celeritate et diligentia ad aliquod particulare subsidium veniatur quo mediante rex ille et regnum illud paulo erectioribus animis ab omni pestifera et pernitiosa concordia cum hoste naturali et implacabili ineunda absterreantur atque spei pleni et auxilio freti adversus hostiles impetus et vafros conatus se tueantur donec Salvatore et Domino nostro Jesu Christo opitulante opera, consilio et auctoritate Beatitudinis vestre comparatis regum et principum fidelium auxiliis ad expeditionem sanctissimam generaliter veniatur. . . ." The Hungarians were also disquieted by what they regarded as the likely prospect of further machinations by the Emperor Frederick III against King Matthias Corvinus: Pius must intercede with the emperor lest the latter drive Matthias and the Hungarian barons into some sort of peace or truce with the Turks, which would free their hands to deal with him.

Actually, as an "elected king" without a hereditary claim to the Hungarian throne, Corvinus had trouble with some of his own magnates as well as with the emperor and various German princes. He cast himself, however, in the role of the defender of Catholicism in central Europe (and in 1468 he went to war against the Utraquists in Bohemia), seeking always to enhance his reputation in the West, which meant that he usually had to restrict his activities against the Turks to the defense of his own realm. *Cf.* Frederick G. Heymann, *George of Bohemia, King of Heretics*, Princeton, N.J., 1965, esp. pp. 484–86, and Karl Nehring, "Herrschaftstradition und Herrschaftslegitimität: Zur ungarischen Aussenpolitik in der zweiten Hälfte des 15. Jahrhunderts," *Revue roumaine d'histoire*, XIII–3 (1974), 463–71, and note below, p. 295.

[14] Sen. Secreta, Reg. 21, fol. 74^v–75^r [75^v–76^r], also dated 4 January, 1462: ". . . Interim vero per summum pontificem omnis accuratissima opera omneque ardens studium adhibetur ad provisiones necessarias faciendas et ad excitandos principes Christianos ad sanctam expeditionem, et ex his que iampridem scripsimus Beatitudini sue huc se contulit unus eius orator cum quo continue sumus, et omnia operamur pro provisionibus faciendis et ut principaliter succuratur rebus illis Hungarie omnia possibilia facere non desistimus, et similiter ut omnis opera quamprimum adhibeatur quod dissensiones vigentes inter regnum illud et imperatorem omnino tollantur. . . ."

Since Pietro Tommasi had been questioned at the Hungarian court about a report that Venice had sent an emissary to Sultan Mehmed, the Senate informed him: "Ad Turchum vero nuntium nostrum mittere coacti fuimus solum [m]odo propter multas novitates, violentias et damna que inferebantur et inferri non cessant subditis nostris Coroni ac Mothoni per turchos subassi finitimos illis terris et locis nostris, et non alia causa. Si quid aliter vulgatum est, id penitus a veritate declinat!"

The Venetians always played it safe, however, and if, when Pietro Tommasi received the present letter, Matthias Corvinus had already made a truce or a peace with the sultan, Pietro was to tell him nothing of what was going on in Venice and Rome (*quod nihil Serenitati sue nec aliis de predictis dicere debeas*). On 22 January (1462) the Senate defeated a motion to send a special envoy to the pope to discuss with him the perils threatening Bosnia as well as Hungary (*ibid.*, fol. 75^r [76^r]). On Venice, the Turks, and Pius II, see in this register, fols. 76, 78, 80, 83–84, 86^r, 88, 89^v, 90^r, 92 ff., etc. Snatches from Tommasi's dispatches from Buda to Venice concerning the *grandi apparati fatti per el Turcho*, the *infiniti danni e spolii . . . [che] . . . detti Turchi in la Schiavonia commesseno*, and the *andamenti del exercito Turco* are given in V. V. Makušev, *Monumenta historica slavorum meridionalium*, II (Belgrade, 1882), pp. 215–25, docs. dated from February, 1457, to June, 1462.

[15] Nevertheless, on 22 January (1462), the Venetian Senate wrote Louis at some length concerning the "pericula Turchorum gravissima imminentiaque toti Christiane religioni" (Sen. Secreta, Reg. 21, fols. 75^v–76^r [76^v–77^r]).

He never for a moment forgot that Louis XI's distant cousin, the poet prince Charles of Orléans, had a strong claim to the ducal throne of Milan through his mother, Valentina Visconti. Pius II himself, although he occasionally wavered under the pressure of misfortune, was equally opposed to allowing the French to regain a foothold in Italy, for reasons we have already noted. Support had to be found for the crusade, however, and whence was it to come?

When in March, 1462, Pius summoned the six cardinals to confer with him, he told them of the thoughts and plans which had for some time been taking shape in his mind: "We have spent many sleepless nights in meditation, tossing from side to side and deploring the unhappy calamities of our time." His heart swelled, he said, and his blood boiled with rage as he thought of the Turks' insolence and their continuing destruction of eastern Christendom:

> We longed to declare war against the Turks and to put forth every effort in defense of religion, but when we measure our strength against that of the enemy, it is clear that the Church of Rome cannot defeat the Turks with its own resources. . . . We are far inferior to the Turks unless Christian kings should unite their forces. We are seeking to effect this; we are searching out ways; none practicable presents itself. If we think of convening a council, Mantua teaches us that the idea is vain. If we send envoys to ask aid of sovereigns, they are laughed at. If we impose tithes on the clergy, they appeal to a future council. If we issue indulgences and encourage the contribution of money by spiritual gifts, we are accused of avarice. People think our sole object is to amass gold. No one believes what we say. Like insolvent tradesmen we are without credit. Everything we do is interpreted in the worst way, and since all princes are very avaricious and all prelates of the Church are slaves to money, they measure our disposition by their own.

During his silent days and nights Pius had been searching for a solution to this problem, however, and he now informed the six cardinals that he believed it was to be found in Burgundy. Shortly after the fall of Constantinople, Duke Philip the Good had taken the most solemn vow to go on a crusade against Sultan Mehmed II if only one of the greater monarchs of Europe, whom it would not be beneath his dignity to follow, would first embark on the same sacred enterprise. Almost a decade had passed. No such leader had appeared, and so the pope himself, "a greater than king or emperor, the Vicar of Christ," proposed at this time to lead the crusade which Burgundy was bound by oath to join. The king of France would be ashamed to send fewer than ten thousand men, since he was openly promising seventy thousand. Public opinion would oblige the Germans, English, and Spanish to send sizable contingents. The Hungarians would not fail the pope; the crusade was their own cause. Pius was confident that, when the time came, the Venetians would furnish the fleet. The Albanians, Bosnians, Serbs, Vlachs, and Bulgarians would rise to the occasion when they saw the mighty host of crusaders reconquering Greece from the Turks. Such was Pius's plan, to go on the crusade himself. After some days' deliberation the six cardinals expressed their approval, declaring the idea worthy of the pope, "who like a shepherd did not hesitate to lay down his life for his sheep."[16]

As Pius had emphasized to his cardinal confidants, a commitment from Venice would be essential from the start, for neither the Burgundians nor the French could be expected to join the expedition if they could not rely on Venetian transport. One might indeed hope for Venetian co-operation, for on 10 December, 1461, the Republic had enrolled the threatened King Stephen Tomašević of Bosnia and his heirs among the Venetian nobility, and ten days later the same honor had been accorded Cardinal Bessarion, who had gone to Venice as papal legate "per la materia della Crociata."[17] After his conference with the cardinals the pope

---

[16] Pius II, *Comm.*, bk. VII, Engl. trans., pp. 515–18; ed. Frankfurt, 1614, pp. 189–91; Raynaldus, *Ann. eccl.*, ad ann. 1462, no. 33, vol. XIX (1693), p. 119; Voigt, *Enea Silvio*, III, 676–77; Pastor, *Gesch. d. Päpste*, II (repr. 1955), 241–42, where the Doge Pasquale Malipiero (1457–1462) is incorrectly called Prospero.

About a year and a half later, in September, 1463, Pius made a long speech at a secret consistory in which he addressed the assembled cardinals in much the same fashion as he spoke to the six chosen members of the College (*Comm.*, bk. XII, Engl. trans., pp. 822–26; ed. Frankfurt, 1614, pp. 339–41). It is interesting to note that in this address Pius set the annual income of the Holy See at less than 300,000 ducats, of which half was expended every year on garrisons, mercenaries, the administration of papal territories, and the Curia Romana (*ibid.*, p. 339, lines 12–16). There was no need for the Venetian Senate in January, 1463, to emphasize to Pius the necessity of winning the support of the Christian princes and the other powers for the success of the crusade (Arch. di Stato di Venezia, Sen. Secreta, Reg. 21, fol. 135, published by Sime Ljubić, ed., *Listine* [*Documents*] *o odnošajih izmedju južnoga slavenstva i mletačke republike*, vol. X (Zagreb, [1891]=*Monumenta spectantia historiam slavorum meridionalium*, vol. XXII, pp. 231–32, and *cf.* p. 257). Pius was only too well aware of that fact.

[17] Marino Sanudo, *Vite de' duchi di Venezia*, in *RISS*, XXII (Milan, 1733), col. 1168CD; *cf.* Sen. Secreta, Reg. 21, fols. 69 ff.

wrote a letter on 8 March, 1462, in his own hand to the Doge Pasquale Malipiero,[18] and although the Venetian reply of 19 March was rather vague, it contained a pledge of support in the projected war against the Turks. Promising to preserve the secrecy which Pius wished to be kept for the present, the spokesmen for the Serenissima sent their solemn assurance that his plans would be revealed only to those whom the necessities of state required to be consulted. With words of the highest praise for Pius's "glorious" intention of going on the crusade himself, the Venetians professed to believe that his example would arouse the other princes from their slumber; make them take counsel for the safety of their states; bind Philip of Burgundy to his famous promise "proficisci personaliter et bellum gerere contra Turcos;" and force the king of France to send at least ten thousand men upon the expedition. Peace must be established, however, as Pius well knew, between the Emperor Frederick III and King Matthias Corvinus, to free the latter's western frontiers and make it possible for him to invade Serbia (Rascia) or some other Turkish territory.[19]

On the following day, 20 March (1462), the Senate wrote the pope again, sending news of the needs and intentions of Corvinus, which had just been received in a letter dated 4 March from the Venetian envoy at the Hungarian court.[20] Corvinus required a cavalry force of four thousand men for service against the Turks. Despite the expense which the Republic had been put to in maintaining an unusually large fleet, always necessary because of the continual crises in the Levant, as well as in providing garrisons for Venetian territories exposed to Turkish attack, the Republic would be willing nevertheless to pay a reasonable part of the costs involved in thus strengthening Hungary against the Porte.[21] This was a very good beginning. Although it was well understood in Rome that the Doge Pasquale Malipiero would postpone war with the Porte as long as possible, all informed observers in the Levant knew that war was inevitable. Malipiero died, however, on 5 May, 1462, after a reign of almost five years. A week later (on the twelfth) Cristoforo Moro was elected his successor. The cultivated Malipiero reminded Kretschmayr of an abbé of the *ancien régime*, but he was far superior to the avaricious and hypocritical Moro, whose failure of courage when the crusade seemed almost to be in the offing soon won him the contempt and reprobation of his contemporaries.[22]

The Venetians had not allowed the papal congress of 1459 to be held in Udine, and they had of course refused permission for the crusade to be preached anywhere in their territories. There were too many observers in northern Italy ready to report all anti-Turkish activities to the Porte. Now that the Venetians were seriously preparing for war, they might seem to be hampering their own efforts by the complete secrecy upon which they insisted. But they were naturally much afraid of attacks upon their fortresses and commercial outposts in the

[18] *Cf.* Pastor, *Gesch. d. Päpste*, II (repr. 1955), 242. Unfortunately Rudolf Wolkan's *Briefwechsel des Eneas Silvius Piccolomini* (Vienna, 1909–18) does not reach the period of Pius II's papacy. Chr. Lucius, *Pius II. und Ludwig XI. von Frankreich*, Heidelberg, 1913, pp. 60–66 (Heidelberger Abhandlungen zur mittleren und neueren Geschichte, no. 41), believes that the impetus was given to papal leadership against the Turks by the Venetians, "denn im Januar 1462 beschloss der Rat, einen Spezialgesandten [nach Rom] zu schicken," to urge the pope to preach the crusade. Lucius's source is the "*Monumenta Hungariae historica*, I, doc. no. 70," which he quotes (on p. 61, note 1). The text may be found in the Sen. Secreta, Reg. 21, fol. 75ʳ [76ʳ], dated 22 January (1462), but the Senate did *not* pass this resolution: it was defeated *de parte* 44, *de non* 64, *non sinceri* 10, and in fact no special envoy was sent to the Curia Romana.

[19] The Venetian answer to Pius II's letter of 8 March, 1462, is preserved in the Sen. Secreta, Reg. 21, fols. 80ʳ–80ᵛ, dated 19 March, 1462, from which I have drawn the summary in the text. The document has been published in part by Pastor, *Acta inedita*, I, no. 131, pp. 169–70. *Cf.* in general the (Venetian) sources published by Ljubić, *Listine*, X, 204–11.

[20] If Pius did not already possess all this information, the Venetians would write him at greater length (Sen. Secreta, Reg. 21, fols. 80ᵛ–81ʳ): "At scimus Beatitudinem vestram pro sua admirabili sapientia et rerum omnium intelligentia omnia longe melius intelligere quam nos referre possemus. . . . Si unquam pro nostra sententia necessarium fuit rebus Hungarie providere, id impresentiarum est! . . ."

[21] *Ibid.*, fol. 81ʳ: ". . . quamquam ut notissimum est magnis gravissimisque expensis impliciti sumus tum in classe nostra maritima contra Turchos, quam longe potentiorem solito instruximus, tum in muniendis terris nostris partium Orientis finitimis Turcho gentibus et presidiis, erimus tamen contenti contribuere illam partem istius expense que decens et honesta fuerit. Salutiferum hoc necessariumque remedium saluti rerum Hungarie et Christianorum esse tenemus. Sapientissima est Sanctitas vestra remque istam que iudicio nostro celeritatem requirit cum aliis potentatibus Italie disponere poterit ut melius utiliusque cognoverit." *Cf.* also the Senate's letter to the pope of 30 March (*ibid.*, fol. 84ʳ–84ᵛ), to the same general effect. On 22 April the Senate wrote the pope of the necessity of keeping the Republic's commitments secret (fol. 86ʳ).

[22] *Cf.* Heinrich Kretschmayr, *Geschichte von Venedig*, II (Gotha, 1920, repr. Aalen, 1964), 366–67.

Levant. For them war against the Turk would have to be all or nothing. They wanted either a great crusade to be supported by the major states in Europe with every likelihood of success or the scrupulous preservation of peace to help insure Venetian colonies in the East against large-scale Turkish attacks. Their stations at Negroponte, Lepanto, and Nauplia, Modon and Coron, as well as in Crete and the Archipelago, exposed them to the ever-present possibility of easily mounted attacks upon a wide front, too wide in fact for them to cope with. For years the Venetians had been playing the pacific game of defense, always expensive, while the aggressive Turk had struck here and there at Christian territories in the Levant, wherever a maximum of opportunity could mean a minimum of expense. Each new Turkish conquest had added both to the aggressor's desire and to his resources with which to strike another blow. The Venetians sought material gain through peace and commerce, the Turks through war and plunder. It had been all very well, in Venetian opinion, for the popes to preach crusades and for the princes to make promises—it was Venice which stood to lose the most if the crusade failed. Now the Turk's ambition had grown so great, however, his hostility so pronounced, that even the cautious majority in the Venetian Senate could clearly see that war was coming.

The Ottoman advance seemed irresistible in the East as well as in the West. Sultan Mehmed II's forces occupied Amastris (Amasra) on the Black Sea in the summer of 1459, taking it from the Genoese, who were unable to offer resistance, and two years later the sultan embarked on another memorable campaign into Asia Minor. Having removed the ruler of Sinope on his eastward march, Mehmed agreed to a peace, after one or two hostile encounters, with Uzun Ḥasan, whose family had been princes of Diyār-Bakr (Amida) in northern Mesopotamia from before the time of Timur the Lame. Uzun Ḥasan had been ruler of the Turkoman tribe of the "White Sheep" (Ak-Koyunlu) from 1454, and was now embarked upon a very successful career of conquest against the states lying around his hereditary fief of Diyār-Bakr. About 1458 he had married, as we have seen, the beautiful "despoina" Theodora (Despina-Khātūn), shortly before the death of her father, the Emperor John IV of Trebizond ("Kalojoannes"), promising the latter his assistance against the Ottomans when it should be needed.[23]

When the time to keep his promise had come, however, Uzun Ḥasan, with troubles at home, had sent his mother Sāra-Khātūn, one of the most influential figures in the Turkoman world, to Sultan Mehmed to intercede for him. The price of peace was abandonment of his ally and relative, the Emperor David Comnenus of Trebizond. After a continuous if not always proud history of more than two and one-half centuries, the "empire" of Trebizond (now mostly confined to the city and its surrounding region) gave up in the late summer of 1461, offering little resistance to Mehmed and the grand vizir Mahmud Pasha. The negotiations for its surrender were carried on by the unscrupulous George Amiroutzes, the treasurer or head of the imperial wardrobe (*protovestiarios*) of Trebizond.[24] Owing to the part he played in

---

[23] Chalcocondylas, bk. IX (Bonn, p. 490; ed. E. Darkó, II-2 [Budapest, 1927], 243); G. B. Ramusio, *Delle Navigationi et viaggi*, II (Venice, 1559, and later editions), fol. 84; Wm. Miller, *Trebizond: The Last Greek Empire*, London, 1926, pp. 88–89; and see, above, Chapter 7, note 78, for Theodora. The chief rivals of the Turkoman "White Sheep," who were orthodox, were the very heterodox "Black Sheep" (Kara-Koyunlu), who held Persia, and over whom Uzun Ḥasan finally triumphed (in 1466–1467), whereby his power to oppose the Osmanlis was greatly increased. On 16 October, 1459, Pius II wrote to Ibrahim Beg, the Gran Caramano, recalling the good will he had manifested toward Christians and his relations with the papacy in the time of Calixtus III, urging the Caramano to persevere in his opposition to Mehmed II and prepare for war against the Ottoman empire, ". . . sic ut, cum Christianus exercitus venerit, possis eodem tempore hostem invadere . . ." (*Brevia*, in Arch. Segr. Vaticano, Arm. XXXIX, tom. 9, fol. 87r).

[24] Critobulus, *De rebus gestis Mechemetis II*, IV, 1–9 (ed. Karl Müller, *Fragmenta historicorum graecorum* [*FHG*], V-1 [Paris, 1870], pp. 137–43; ed. Vasile Grecu, *Critobul din Imbros: Din domnia lui Mahomed al II-lea, anii 1451–1467*, Bucharest, 1963, pp. 269–89); Chalcocondylas, bk. IX (Bonn, pp. 460–61 [on the occupation of Amastris], 485–98; ed. Darkó, II-2, 217–18 [Amastris], 238–49); Ducas, *Hist. byzant.*, chap. 45 (Bonn, pp. 340–43; ed. V. Grecu, *Ducas: Istoria turco-bizantină [1341–1462]*, Bucharest, 1958, pp. 427, 429, 431); Pseudo-Sphrantzes, *Chron. maius*, I, 32, and IV, 20 (Bonn, pp. 94, 413–14; ed. V. Grecu, *Geo. Sphrantzes . . . în anexă Pseudo-Phrantzes*, Bucharest, 1966, pp. 232, 552 [as we have already noted, Grecu has altered the Bonn edition's chapter divisions]); *Historia politica* (Bonn, pp. 36–38); letter of Geo. Amiroutzes to Bessarion, dated 11 December, 1461, in Migne, *PG*, 161, cols. 723–28 (on which see Sp. P. Lampros, "The Capture of Trebizond and Venice" [in Greek], Νέος Ἑλληνομνήμων, II [1905], 324–33, and *idem*, "Amiroutzes' Letter on the Capture of Trebizond" [in Greek], *ibid.*, XII [1915], 476–78, and XIV [1917], 108);

the city's surrender, Amiroutzes, a cousin of Mahmud Pasha, won the favor of Sultan Mehmed, who had added almost the entire northern coastline of Asia Minor to his now vast domain.

After an extraordinarily difficult but finally successful campaign against Vlad III Dracula, later known as "Tepes" ("the Impaler"), the notorious voivode of Wallachia (Vlachia), in the spring and early summer of 1462,[25] Sultan Mehmed crossed over into Asia Minor at the end of August. He made his way with a small body of janissaries to the northern shore of the ancient Gulf of Adramyttium, opposite the island of Lesbos. Soon Mahmud Pasha arrived with a large fleet. Mytilene was taken in mid-September, after a brief resistance, and the rest of the island promptly surrendered. Although the sources vary in detail, they tend to say much the same thing. Mahmud and the sultan apparently agreed to accept the terms of surrender proposed by Niccolò Gattilusio, the lord of Lesbos, that the Turks should spare both life and property, *salvando le teste et l'havere*.[26] Mehmed spent four days on the island, during which time he ordered some four hundred Latins to be sawed in half, thus sparing his victims' heads according to the pact he had made with them.[27] With a feeling of accomplishment, doubtless, Mehmed then returned to his camp on the mainland, leaving Mahmud to deport the most promising third of the Mytilenians to Istanbul; another third was given as slaves to the janissaries and other troopers; the fortunate remainder, the poor, the aged, and the infirm, were allowed to remain in their city and to retain such property as they had. *Salvò le teste et salvò l'havere*. The last ruler of the family of the Gattilusi—Niccolò, the successor and murderer of his brother Domenico—was sent to Istanbul, where he was soon imprisoned and put to death.[28] Was there

---

Lampros, ed., *Ecthesis chronica*, London, 1902, pp. 25–27; Sanudo, *Vite de'duchi*, in *RISS*, XXII, col. 1159; and *cf.* N. Iorga, *Notes et extraits*, IV (Bucharest, 1915), pt. 3, doc. no. 180, p. 271 (a confused report, which should be dated 1473 if its reference to Uzun Ḥasan as being fifty years of age is correct); Fr. Babinger, "La Date de la prise de Trébizonde par les Turcs (1461)," *Revue des études byzantines*, VII (1949), 205–7.

Two years later (on 30 August, 1463), when Venice had finally been provoked into war with the Porte, the Senate would seek an alliance with Uzun Ḥasan against their common enemy (Ljubić, *Listine*, X, 269, and *cf.* pp. 277, 314). See also Wm. Miller, *Trebizond*, London, 1926, pp. 97–112; V. Minorsky, "Uzun Ḥasan," *Encyclopaedia of Islām*, IV (1924–34), 1066; *cf.* J. H. Kramers, "Tarabzun," *ibid.*, IV, 661–62, and Chrysanthos, metropolitan of Trebizond (later of Athens), "The Church of Trebizond" [in Greek], in Ἀρχεῖον Πόντου, IV–V (Athens, 1933, also published separately in 1936), 318–25, 387. David Comnenus and most of his male relatives were executed in the prison fortress of the Seven Towers in Istanbul on 1 November, 1463. As late as 1500, however, the eldest son of Uzun Ḥasan by the Despina-Khātūn was recognized in the West as a claimant to the empire of Trebizond—"ad quem qua materno jure Trapezuntis imperium spectat, quod anno abhinc quadragesimo parens communis hostis occupaverat . . ." (Iorga, *Notes et extraits*, V [1915], doc. no. 363, p. 328).

[25] On Vlad Dracula, *cf.* Pius II, *Comm.*, bk. XI, Engl. trans., pp. 738–40; ed. Frankfurt, 1614, pp. 296–97; Raynaldus, *Ann. eccl.*, ad ann. 1462, no. 29, vol. XIX (1693), pp. 117–18; F. Babinger, *Maometto il Conquistatore*, Turin, 1957, pp. 304–13, 519–20; and especially Radu Florescu and Raymond T. McNally, *Dracula: A Biography of Vlad the Impaler*, New York, 1973, pp. 90–110, with a good outline of the sources (Chalcocondylas, the Turkish chronicler Enveri, the so-called "memoirs" of Constantine of Ostrovica, etc.), *ibid.*, pp. 197–201. *Cf.* the letter of the Venetian Senate, dated 28 June, 1462, to Niccolò Sagundino, then at the Curia Romana, containing news of Vlad Dracula's flight before the sultan's attack "in partes Valachie" (Ljubić, *Listine*, X, 217).

Vlad "Dracula" (*Draculea*) was the son of Vlad II Dracul (the Dragon or the Devil). He put up an almost incredible resistance to the Turkish invasion of 1462. Abandoned by most of his boyars, however, he had to give up his armed opposition to the Turks in July. Making his way to Braşov (Kronstadt), at the foot of the Transylvanian Alps, where King Matthias Corvinus was then encamped, Dracula was taken into custody (on 26 November, 1462) and removed to Buda. Thereafter he spent a dozen years as a captive, more or less, of the Hungarians (1462–1474). Released to continue the war against the Turks, Dracula began an offensive in the summer of 1476, in alliance with the Hungarian magnate Stephen Báthory, Stephen the Great of Moldavia, and Vuk Branković of Serbia. Seeking to recover Wallachia, he occupied Tîrgovişte and Bucharest (Bucureşti) in November, 1476. A month or so later, Vlad was dead, either assassinated or killed in an encounter with the Turks. His head was sent to Mehmed II in Istanbul, and he passed from history into legend.

[26] *Ducae historia italice interprete incerto* (in the Bonn edition of Ducas, p. 512).

[27] R. Valentini, "L'Egeo dopo la caduta di Costantinopoli nelle relazioni dei gran maestri di Rodi," *Bullettino dell'Istituto storico italiano per il medio evo e Archivio Muratoriano*, LI (1936), doc. no. IV, p. 167: According to an encyclical letter, dated 4 November, 1462, from the Grand Master Pedro Ramón Zacosta to the Hospitallers in Italy and the kingdom of Sicily, ". . . Theucer cunctos Latinos medios truncari precipit, servata cum domino Lesbiorum vite pactione. Abscinduntur ense viri latini fere quadringenti, demum tripartita preda sibi, militibus et piratis [i.e., the soldiers and sailors in the Turkish expeditionary force], archiepiscopum latinum [Benedictum] et sacerdotes, utpote pecudes venales effectos, et universum populum in Constantinopolim duci iubet. . . ." *Cf.* Chalcocondylas, bk. X (Bonn, p. 526, lines 9–11; ed. Darkó, II-2, 273, lines 23–25), who says the sultan ordered three hundred "pirates" to be cut in two.

[28] Critobulus, IV, 11–14 (ed. Müller, *FHG*, V-1, pp. 144–46; ed. Grecu [1963], pp. 295, 297, 299, 301, 303,

no way of stopping the Turkish advance? Anxiety grew into apprehension on the island of Rhodes, from which the Hospitallers made an appeal for support to the whole of western Christendom.[29]

The Gattilusi had been a Genoese family of economic as well as of political importance in the Aegean world. For two centuries the Genoese had, with few setbacks, controlled the export of alum not only from the mines of Old and New Phocaea (*le Foglie*), on the Gulf of Smyrna, but also from those of inland Anatolia, Thrace, and the Greek islands. The Gattilusi had been heavily involved in both the mining and marketing of alum, the magic ingredient which made possible almost every refinement of the textile industries in Italy, England, and Flanders. As we have already seen (in Chapter 5), the Turks had occupied the two Phocaeas late in the year 1455. Alum continued to flow westward, however, into the European dyeworks, to the large profit of the Turks. Christendom had thus been helping to provide the Porte with the financial means for further conquests, for the price of alum rose from year to year, reaching unprecedented heights by the time of the Turkish occupation of Lesbos. The island of Chios had become the center of much of the alum trade. After the fall of Constantinople, however, Mehmed II had exacted a tribute of six thousand ducats from the *mahonesi*; in 1456 he raised it to ten thousand, and the following year he demanded thirty thousand. The Genoese lost their monopoly, and the alum trade of Chios was ruined.

It is small wonder, therefore, that when in 1461 Giovanni da Castro discovered huge deposits of alum at Tolfa, near Civitavecchia, he could come to Pius II, whom he knew well, and announce:

> Today I bring you victory over the Turk. Every year he wrings from the Christians more than 300,000 ducats for the alum with which we dye wool various colors. For this is not found among the Latins except a very small quantity. . . . But I have found seven mountains so rich in this material that they could supply seven worlds. If you will give orders to engage workmen, build furnaces, and smelt the ore, you will provide all Europe with alum and the Turk will lose all his profits. They will accrue to you and thus he will suffer a double loss. There is an abundance of wood and water there. You have a harbor nearby in Civitavecchia where ships may be loaded to sail to the west. Now you may equip a war against the Turks. These mines will supply you with the sinews of war, i.e., money, and take them from the Turks.[30]

---

with alterations in the text); Chalcocondylas, bk. x (Bonn, pp. 523–27; ed. Darkó, II-2, 271–74); Ducas, chap. 45 (Bonn, pp. 345–46; ed. Grecu [1958], pp. 433, 435). Ducas's Greek text and the Italian version of his work (Bonn, pp. 511–12) both end with Mehmed's capture of Lesbos in September, 1462. The Italian version contains a number of picturesque details lacking in the original, a few of them being drawn from Critobulus. Benedetto, archbishop of Mytilene (Lesbos), who had held his see from December, 1459 (Eubel, II, 198), described the Turkish occupation of the island in a rhetorical letter to Pius II (ed. Hopf, *Chron. gréco-romanes* [1873, repr. 1966], pp. 359–66, where the letter is erroneously attributed to Leonardo of Chios): Benedetto urged peace in Christendom, especially among the Italians, to make possible an expedition "against this Cerberus, who has absorbed almost the whole community of [eastern] Christians."

Cf. Arch. di Stato di Venezia, Sen. Secreta, Reg. 21, fols. 114^v and 124^v; Domenico Malipiero, *Annali veneti dall'anno 1457 al 1500* [as abridged by Francesco Longo], in the *Archivio storico italiano*, VII, pt. 1 (1843), 11; Stefano Magno, *Estratti degli Annali veneti*, ed. Hopf, *Chron. gréco-romanes*, p. 201; Pius II, *Comm.*, bk. x, Engl. trans., pp. 633–34, and note p. 637; ed. Frankfurt, 1614, pp. 243–44, and note p. 245, lines 32 ff.; Hopf, "Griechenland im Mittelalter," in Ersch and Gruber, *Allgemeine Encyklopädie*, vol. 86, repr. vol. II, p. 143; Iorga, *Gesch. d. osman. Reiches*, II (1909), 118–19; Pastor, *Gesch. d. Päpste*, II (repr. 1955), 237–38, 243; Babinger, *Maometto* (1957), pp. 314–18; Wm. Miller, "The Gattilusj of Lesbos (1355–1462)," in *Essays on the Latin Orient*, Cambridge, 1921, repr. Amsterdam, 1964, pp. 341–49.

[29] By a brief of 24 February, 1463, Pius II recommended to Marquis Lodovico II Gonzaga "Sergius de Serpando, . . . conventus [Rhodi] armiratus ac . . . magistri et conventus orator et locumtenens noster," who was on a mission with other knightly envoys of the convent of Rhodes to all the European princes on behalf of the imperiled Order (Arch. di Stato di Mantova, Arch. Gonzaga, Busta 834). Sergio di Seripando was admiral of the Hospital from 1462 to 1465 (*cf.* B. Waldstein-Wartenberg, *Rechtsgeschichte des Malteserordens*, Vienna and Munich, 1969, pp. 118–19). Papal briefs of 16 February, 11 April, and 14 April, 1464, in the same busta in the Mantuan Archives, also relate to the Turkish danger in the Levant and the necessity of the crusade, "id unum opus mente agitamus, id totis sensibus sumus complexi, et quod antea inauditum est, proprium corpus pro salute ovium nobis commissarum exponere decrevimus . . . ," as Pius states in his brief of 14 April, in which he requests of Lodovico safe passage and assistance for all crusaders who set out from or traverse the marquisate of Mantua, including freedom from taxes and chance tallages of all kinds (*ibid.*): "Vectigalia et gabelle non exigantur ab eisdem, nec passus fluminum aut portarum seu portuum et stafarum solvere compellantur nec etiam bulletas accipere pro passu teneantur."

[30] Pius II, *Comm.*, bk. VII, Engl. trans., p. 506, which I have corrected from the Frankfurt edition (1614), p. 185. On the alum trade, see M.-L. Heers, "Les Génois et le commerce de l'alun à la fin du moyen âge," *Revue d'histoire économique et sociale*, XXXII (1954), 31–53 [to which reference has been made earlier in this volume], and Jean

Pope though he was, Pius was skeptical of this gift from heaven, but Giovanni da Castro was not exaggerating his find. The mines at Tolfa were soon in production. In 1463 Pius forbade Christian merchants to import eastern alum into Europe. Following Giovanni da Castro's advice, Pius and his successors resolved to employ the revenues from Tolfa solely for the crusade (*allume della crociata*). The alum trade became a sacred monopoly of the Holy See, and infringement upon the papal commerce allegedly became a sin of such a serious nature that an ordinary confessor could not grant the offender absolution.[31]

In the spring of 1463 Sultan Mehmed's conquest of Bosnia exposed Venetian-held Dalmatia, the city of Ragusa, and the Adriatic ports of Italy to Turkish attacks.[32] Relations between the Porte and the Serene Republic had been strained for some time. The prospects for peace were not improved when (as we have just noted) the Doge Pasquale Malipiero died in May, 1462. He had been the leader of the party of appeasement. The choice of Cristoforo Moro to succeed him caused rejoicing in the Curia. Pius II and Bessarion professed to see in Moro a defender of the imperiled faith, and the letters of at least thirteen cardinals are extant congratulating him on his elevation to the dogate.[33] Although Malipiero's

---

Delumeau, *L'Alun de Rome, XVe–XIXe siècle*, Paris, 1962, pp. 15–21; and *cf.* below, Chapter 9, note 14. The discovery of alum at Tolfa was made at the beginning of the year 1461 (not 1462), as shown by Giovanni da Castro's agreement of 30 April, 1461, with the town officials of Corneto "super inventione et confectione certarum minerarum aluminis quas ipse Johannes [de Castro] sperat reperire posse *seu reperisse* in territorio Cornetano et alibi. . . ." On 20 July (1461) the Camera Apostolica approved the convention which Giovanni had made with Corneto, placing an impost and excise on the mining and sale of the alum, and Pius II approved of the arrangements by a bull of 23 August (1461). For the text of the cameral approval of 20 July (Arch. Segr. Vaticano, Div. Cam., Reg. 29, fols. 207–12), which incorporates the vernacular text of Giovanni's convention with Corneto (*che esso si persuade e dice credere trovare o havere trovato . . . habundantissime 'lumiere . . .*), see Pietro Sella, "La Prima Concessione per l'allume della Tolfa," *Quellen und Forschungen aus italienischen Archiven und Bibliotheken*, XXXIII (1944), 252–59.

[31] Delumeau, *L'Alun de Rome*, pp. 23 ff.; Raymond de Roover, *The Rise and Decline of the Medici Bank (1397–1494)*, New York, 1966, pp. 152–56 and ff.

[32] *Cf.* the two interesting letters written by Cardinal Francesco Gonzaga to his father Lodovico II, the first dated at Rome on 22 June, 1463, and the second at Tivoli on 1 July (in Pastor, *Acta inedita*, I [1904], nos. 141–42, pp. 183–85), which state that Mehmed has conquered all Bosnia with an army of 200,000 persons, "and many hold that, unless the Turk is strongly opposed, in less than a year and a half he will take a great part of Italy. . . ." Cardinal Francesco left Rome for Mantua on 14 November, according to the Acta Consistorialia, in Arch. Segr. Vaticano, Arm. XXXI, tom. 52, fol. 65^{r}.

The last king of Bosnia, Stephen Tomašević (1461–1463), was executed in late May, 1463, by Mehmed although the grand vizir, Mahmud Pasha, had given the king a written guarantee of safety in the sultan's name, in order to secure possession of Stephen's person and the fortress of Ključ. Stephen's stepmother, Queen Catherine, escaped to Ragusa, and from 1466 lived in Rome as a pensioner of the papacy, to which she bequeathed Bosnia (unless her son Sigismund, a convert to Islam, should return to Christianity). Her will is published in A. Theiner, ed., *Vetera monumenta slavorum meridionalium historiam illustrantia*, I (Rome, 1863), 509–11. The funeral monument of *Catharina regina Bosnensis* may still be seen, perfectly preserved, in S. Maria d'Aracoeli on the Campidoglio (on the east end of the north pillar, facing the high altar). It records the date of her death (on 25 October, 1478): ". . . obdormivit Romae anno Domini MCCCCLXXVIII die XXV Octobris [*sic*], monumentum ipsius scriptis positum." *Cf.* Voigt, *Enea Silvio*, III, 684–85; Iorga, *Gesch. d. osman. Reiches*, II, 120–21; Pastor, *Gesch. d. Päpste*, II (repr. 1955), 238–40; Babinger, *Maometto*, pp. 324–35; and Pietro Balan, *Delle Relazioni fra la Chiesa cattolica e gli slavi della Bulgaria, Bosnia, Serbia, Erzegovina*, Rome, 1885, pp. 92–98.

Stephen Tomašević had warned Pius II that the Turkish onslaught was coming, and that Mehmed II "will aim at Italy, which he aspires to rule" (*Comm.*, bk. XI, Engl. trans., pp. 740–42; and on the Turkish occupation of Bosnia, pp. 768–70; ed. Frankfurt, 1614, pp. 297–98, 311–12; Cod. Reg. lat. 1995, fols. 512^{v}–513^{v}, 533^{v}–535^{r}); Giovanni Maria Angiolello, *Hist. turchesca*, ed. Ion Ursu, Bucharest, 1909, p. 29; and *cf.* Raynaldus, *Ann. eccl.*, ad ann. 1462, nos. 30–32, vol. XIX (1693), p. 118; ad ann. 1463, nos. 14–16, *ibid.*, p. 127; and on the death of Catherine, ad ann. 1478, nos. 42–45, pp. 278–79, where her will is published in part.

On 23 March, 1462, Pius II had granted King Stephen the right to a portable altar (Reg. Vat. 484, fol. 268^{v} by mod. stamped enumeration, "datum Rome apud Sanctum Petrum anno, etc., MCCCCLXI, decimo Kal. Aprilis, pontif. nostri anno quarto"), and a month later he sent Luca de'Tolenti as an apostolic nuncio on a mission to the counts of Segna (Senj) as Turkish attacks were awaited in Bosnia, Dalmatia, and Istria (Reg. Vat. 485, fol. 248, dated 24 April, 1462). Stephen had warned the pope: "Ego tempestatem primus expecto; post me Hungari et Veneti suam sortem manebunt, nec Italia conquiescet: sic stat consilium hostis" (MS. cit., fol. 513^{r}). *Cf.*, in general, Iorga, *Gesch. d. osman. Reiches*, II, 110–22. Note Stephen's last, pitiable appeal to Venice (and the papacy) of 28 February, 1463 (Ven. style 1462) in Ljubić, *Listine*, X, 237–38, and *cf.*, *ibid.*, pp. 247, 250–52, etc.—after the fall of Bosnia the Turk had reached "ad hostium et fores Italie" (p. 251). On the fall of Bosnia, see also the Venetian letters to the Republic's envoy in Rome, in *MHH*, *Acta extera*, IV (Budapest, 1875), nos. 133, 137–38, pp. 211, 216–19, etc. The ancient sect of the Bogomils had contributed to the internal weakness of Bosnia, and had facilitated the Turkish conquest.

[33] Pastor, *Gesch. d. Päpste*, II (repr. 1955), 242–43, where (as stated above) Pasquale Malipiero is mistakenly called Prospero; Domenico Malipiero, *Annali veneti*, in *Archivio storico italiano*, VII, pt. 2 (1844), 654; Sanudo, *Vite de'duchi*,

party continued to recommend diplomacy and forbearance in dealing with the Ottoman government, a minor incident now provoked the war which was doubtless inevitable between the military and commercial empires, whose interests were in obvious conflict. Both powers had agreed in the peace of September, 1430 (negotiated after the Venetians had lost Thessalonica to the Turks), to the extradition of traitors and the reciprocal return of escaped slaves, stolen property, and the like,[34] a provision which the Turks had not observed with much scrupulosity through the years, although it had been renewed in the Turco-Venetian treaty of 1454. Now, however, an Albanian slave belonging to the Turkish commandant (subashi) of Athens is said to have escaped to Coron (in 1462), having robbed his master of 100,000 aspers. He secured asylum in the house of Girolamo Vallaresso, Venetian councillor at Coron, who is said to have received some of the stolen money. Owing to the runaway's alleged conversion to Christianity, the request for his return to the Athenian commandant was denied.[35] According to Critobulus, Omar Beg, who had been restored to his Greek command because of his signal services against Vlad Dracula on the Danube, now launched a surprise attack upon Lepanto, which he nearly captured in November, 1462.[36] Isa Beg, who had succeeded Zagan Pasha as governor of the Morea, attacked Argos, which he took easily on 3 April, 1463, with the assistance of a Greek priest, whose hatred of the Latins apparently exceeded his fear of the Turks.[37]

Following the loss of Argos the Venetian Senate began making final preparations for the expected war with the Gran Turco, and on 17 May, 1463, responded favorably to a Hungarian embassy which sought Venetian aid against the Porte, "setting forth the power and greatness of the Turk and the dangers threatening the kingdom of Hungary and Christianity." The Senate acknowledged King Matthias Corvinus's courteous expressions of friendship and respect; emphasized the Republic's entertainment of similar sentiments toward his Majesty; and promised him a subvention of three thousand ducats a month for six months, with the assurance that the subvention would be continued for a longer period if the needs of his kingdom for defense against the Turks required it. The Venetians also took the opportunity to remind the king of their own great expenses in maintaining the Republic's fleet against the Turk and in garrisoning their Levantine terri-

---

in *RISS*, XXII, col. 1168E, who notes that "alle sue esequie fu l'illustre Chir Tomado Despoto della Morea della casa Paleologo, scacciato dal Turco, e venuto in questa terra;" Andrea Navagero, *Storia veneziana*, in *RISS*, XXIII (Milan, 1733), col. 1121, etc.; Pius II, *Comm.*, bk. x, Engl. trans., pp. 639–40; ed. Frankfurt, 1614, pp. 246–47. The magnificent *promissio*, "quam fecit popolo pro ducatu," of Cristoforo Moro on his election as doge (dated 12 May, 1462), probably executed by Leonardo Bellini, is now preserved in the British Library (Add. MS. 15,816, *cf.* fols. 4^v–5 ff.).

[34] G. M. Thomas and R. Predelli, eds., *Diplomatarium veneto-levantinum*, II (Venice, 1899, repr. New York, 1965), no. 182, pp. 343–45, dated at Adrianople 4 September, 1430; *cf.* Predelli, ed., *Regesti dei Commemoriali*, IV (1896), bk. xii, no. 140, p. 164, dated 4 September, 1430.

[35] Sanudo, *Vite de'duchi*, in *RISS*, XXII, col. 1172A, who dates the slave's escape in 1463, in which he is followed by Babinger, *Maometto*, p. 336 (but see the following note); Malipiero, *Annali veneti*, in *Archivio storico italiano*, VII, pt. 1 (1843), 12–13, or his editor, places the event in 1462.

[36] Critobulus, IV, 16 (ed. Müller, *FHG*, V-1, p. 148; ed. Grecu, p. 309), who says that Omar Beg was then "ὁ Πελοποννήσου καὶ τῆς ἄλλης Ἑλλάδος σατράπης," but Isa Beg seems to have succeeded Zagan Pasha as governor of the Morea (*cf.* Chalcocondylas, bk. x, Bonn, p. 545, lines 8–9; ed. Darkó, II-2, 289, lines 25–27). *Cf.* Navagero, *Storia veneziana*, in *RISS*, XXIII, col. 1121D, and Sanudo, *loc. cit.*, who seems to be wrong in putting the escape of the slave from his Turkish master in Athens in 1463, because this event clearly precedes Omar Beg's attack upon Lepanto, which is precisely dated in November, 1462, by Sphrantzes, *Chron. minus* (*PG* 156, col. 1073A; ed. Grecu [1966], p. 128), and *cf.* Pseudo-Sphrantzes, IV, 20 (Bonn, p. 414; ed. Grecu, p. 554), as perceived by Hopf, in Ersch and Gruber, *Allgemeine Encyklopädie*, vol. 86, repr. vol. II, p. 154, and note Pastor, *Gesch. d. Päpste*, II (repr. 1955), 244, and Wm. Miller, *Latins in the Levant*, London, 1908, p. 465.

Nevertheless, the story of Vallaresso's reception in Coron of the escaped slave belonging to the Turkish commandant of Athens is not quite above suspicion. It may represent a retelling of the fact that Vallaresso was already charged at this time (1461–1462) with harboring three slaves of Mahmud Pasha who had escaped with 30,000 aspers' worth of the grand vizir's property, for which the Venetian Senate appears to have made restitution (Arch. di Stato di Venezia, Sen. Secreta, Reg. 21, fol. 83^v, doc. dated 29 March, 1462, and, *ibid.*, fols. 109^v–111^r, dated 22 September, 1462, and Sen. Mar, Reg. 7, fol. 56^v, dated 30 March, 1462). *Cf.* Roberto [S.] Lopez, "Il Principio della guerra veneto-turca nel 1463," in the *Archivio veneto*, 5th ser., XV (1934), 48–49.

[37] The precise date is given in the *Chronicon breve*, ad ann. 1463 (Bonn, p. 521); Chalcocondylas, bk. x (Bonn, p. 545; ed. Darkó, II-2, 289), who calls Isa Ἰησοῦς; Navagero, *Storia veneziana*, in *RISS*, XXIII, col. 1121; and *cf.* the anonymous secretary of Sigismondo Malatesta (Lorenzo Gambuti?) in C. N. Sathas, ed., *Documents inédits relatifs à l'histoire de la Grèce au moyen âge*, VI (Paris, 1885, repr. Athens, 1972), 95. According to Angiolello, *Hist. turchesca*, ed. Ursu, p. 29, Argos was taken "per mezzo d'un popa greco."

tories against his ubiquitous assaults and imperial ambitions.[38]

The Venetians suffered further damage in raids directed against the region of Coron and Modon. Alvise (or Luigi) Loredan, captain-general of the sea, was then in the Aegean with nineteen galleys. He tried to arrange for the restoration of Argos and, being refused, requested large reinforcements for an assault upon the island of Lesbos, which the Turks had occupied.[39] When the issue was debated in the Venetian Senate, Vettore Capello advocated war in an impassioned address, reported by Chalcocondylas: Sending an embassy to the Ottoman court to seek the return of Argos and to compose the differences between the Republic and the Porte would be interpreted as a sign of weakness. It would be an invitation to further Turkish aggression. Mehmed's visit to Negroponte (in 1458) had been to examine the defenses with a view to attacking the city and the island at some later time. Venice should send an army against this barbarian, who was always increasing his strength as he marched from one conquest to another. War was inevitable. The peace party was flirting with self-destruction. War would show the Turk the extent of Venetian power, and nothing else would stop his advance. Hesitation and delay had caused the loss of Constantinople, the Morea, and now Bosnia. Capello laid a large measure of responsibility for these misfortunes squarely on Venetian shoulders. It was widely stated throughout Europe that Venice had sacrificed eastern Christendom to commercial

---

[38] Arch di Stato di Venezia, Sen. Secreta, Reg. 21, fol. 152: "Quod reverendo patri, domino episcopo Vesprimiensi [Veszprém in Hungary], ac magnifico comiti Stephano Segne, etc., oratoribus serenissimi Hungarie regis, qui ad presentiam nostram venerunt explicantes potentiam et magnitudinem Turci ac pericula imminentia regno Hungarie et Christianitati si huic hosti, qui omni conatu suo contra regnum ipsum se direxerit, succumbere compelletur. Commemoraverunt quoque magnam affectionem et confidentiam quam regia majestas Hungarie in nos repositam habet; successive petierunt instanter auxilia nostra terrestria ut resistere possint; tertio loco dixerunt quod cum ad Romanum pontificem profecturi sint, presidia sua imploraturi, similiter petebant consilium et favorem nostrum iuxta quod ut retulerunt habuisse in mandatis a serenissimo rege procedent, etc., sicut per serenissimum dominum ducem huic consilio relatum est. [The etc.'s are in the original.] Respondeatur: [fol. 152^{v}:]

"Quod gratissimo animo intelleximus r[everendam] p[aternitatem] et magnificentiam suas sique regia majestas Hungarie de nobis confidentiam capit, id quippe amplissime facere potest, qui sumus semperque esse intendimus serenitati sue singulari benivolentia et amore devincti. Adducimusque Deum nostrum in testem semper nos calamitatibus regni illius tantum indoluisse quantum exprimi posset tum ex ardore fidei et honoris Christiane religionis tum ex precipua affectione nostra in regiam celsitudinem suam. . . . Nos vero dudum studia nostra convertimus ut per Beatitudinem suam, que caput est Christianorum, regno Hungarie auxilia conferrantur habemusque impresentiarum ob id specialiter penes pontificem maximum oratorem nostrum, nec dubitamus per appulsum dominationum suarum ad urbem Sanctitatem suam quam huic rei bene dispositam esse scimus provisuram esse, nosque in hoc etiam nihil apud eum pretermissuri sumus ut effectus iste sequi habeat.

"At quoniam magnificentie sue in specie auxilia terrestria nostra petunt dicimus quod licet maximis expensis simus impliciti tam in classe nostra quam continue tenemus contra Turchum et maxime nunc multo potentiorem solito quam in muniendis terris nostris finitimis hosti gentibus et presidiis, cupidi tamen honoris et commodi serenissimi regis conamur libenter suis beneplacitis satisfacere sumusque contenti contribuere majestati sue ducatorum III. milia in mensem per menses sex, et ulterius si ex opportunitatibus regni illius respectu Turchorum opus esse videbimus quod subsidium nostrum per magis longum tempus fieri habeat, non estimantes minus pericula regni ipsius quam nostra declarabimus in hoc etiam serenitati sue per veros effectus quantum sibi affecti sumus.

"Circa partem consilii pro suo accessu ad sanctissimum pontificem, dicimus quod sapientissimi sunt nec opus habent consilio nostro, sed hortamur magnificentias suas ut bono animo vadant ad Romanum pontificem commemorentque gravissima pericula regni et Christianitatis ac solicitent auxilia conferenda presertim portionem debitam Beatitudinis sue in qua re etiam orator noster, ut diximus, nihil de possibilibus ommissurus est." After transcribing this document in the Venetian Archives, I found it published in *MHH*, *Acta extera*, IV (1875), no. 129, pp. 206–7: I retain my text because it differs considerably from that given in the Hungarian *Acta extera*. Venetian diplomatic relations with Hungary were extremely close at this time; see the numerous documents, *ibid.*, IV, nos. 123 ff., pp. 196 ff. By mid-April, 1463, the Venetian government had been informed "de magnanima deliberatione . . . Regie Majestatis coadunandi exercitum suum exeundique in castra adversus hostes fidei" (*ibid.*, no. 126, p. 200).

[39] Sanudo, *Vite de' duchi*, in *RISS*, XXII, cols. 1171E–1172. Loredan had apparently wanted to attack Lesbos for some months, as indicated in a letter dated at Florence on 12 October, 1462, and sent by the Milanese ambassador Nicodemo Tranchedini da Pontremoli to Francesco Sforza (Pastor, *Acta inedita*, I, no. 135, pp. 172–73), but had been restrained by the home government. On the Turkish occupation of Lesbos, see above, notes 27–28, and on the ambassador, note Piero Parodi, "Nicodemo Tranchedini da Pontremoli, genealogista degli Sforza," *Archivio storico lombardo*, 5th ser., XLVII-1 (1920), 334–40.

Leonardo Tocco of S. Maura sent his brother on an embassy to Venice at this time to make clear to the Signoria the "malae et periculosae conditiones status sui." Leonardo implored the Venetians to send him two hundred foot soldiers and supplies, lest his lands and Christian subjects should pass "ad manus Turcorum." The Senate voted to give him four hundred ducats and one hundred men to serve for six months (Sen. Secreta, Reg. 21, fols. 118^{r}, 119, docs. dated 16 and 26 October, 1462).

advantages. The Republic must take up arms against the Porte in alliance with the Hungarians and the papacy, reconquer the Morea, and thence move into Ottoman territory while the Hungarians were launching an attack from the Danube. If Venice would not defend her Levantine possessions, she would lose them. The alternative to war was dishonor and defeat. It was an eloquent speech, and Capello had his way. Although there were a good many in the Senate opposed to the inevitable risks and expenses of the course he advocated, a declaration of war against the Ottoman government was passed by a small majority on 28 July, 1463.[40]

Vettore Capello's position had certainly been strengthened by the presence in Venice of Cardinal Bessarion, whom Pius II had dispatched as legate of the Apostolic See on 5 July, 1463,[41] to carry assurances of papal support to the Senate and make known the pope's intention of again summoning the Christian princes to arms against the Turks.[42] Bessarion had arrived in Venice on the twenty-second, going by way of Bologna.[43] He was received with extreme deference by the highest officials of the Republic, among whom, however, he still found a good deal of indecision. Although they were glad to get permission to levy the crusading tithes, twentieths, and thirtieths, which they had directed their ambassador in Rome to request for them, they had been hesitant to proclaim a state of war between Venice and the Porte. On 26 July Bessarion wrote the pope:

> I do not perceive and I can only marvel why these gentlemen are so reluctant to express their willingness to break with the Turks since at this point they have expended the greatest sums both on the fleet and the land forces which they have got ready and continue to get ready, even transporting men into the Peloponnesus. Besides it is common knowledge that they are in fact perfectly willing to make the break; actually many people think that their captain [Loredan] has already done so. Also they have decided to send a subsidy to the Ragusei; they have sent an envoy to the Hungarians; and now they are sending another to other powers north of the Alps. They do all this openly whereas before, as your Holiness knows, they feared even the appearance of this sort of activity. They probably have their reasons for not wanting to come out into the open.[44]

The Venetians had to make war on the Turks, Bessarion

---

[40] Chalcocondylas, bk. x (Bonn, pp. 545–51; ed. Darkó, II-2, 289–95); *cf.* Pastor, *Gesch. d. Päpste*, II (repr. 1955), 244–45; Babinger, *Maometto*, pp. 337–38; Arch. di Stato di Venezia, Sen. Secreta, Reg. 21, fols. 168^r–171^v (there is no entry in the Sen. Mar, Reg. 7, fols. 126^r–127^r, between 19 July and 1 August, 1463); and see especially the detailed study of R. S. Lopez, "Il Principio della guerra veneto-turca . . . ," *Archivio veneto*, 5th ser., XV (1934), 4–131, with thirty-two documents and two other texts. On Venetian preparations for the war and the extensive revenues with which the Senate planned to support their efforts against the Turks, see Malipiero, *Annali veneti*, in *Archivio storico italiano*, VII, pt. 1 (1843), 11–14, summarized in Lopez, *art. cit.*, pp. 56–57.

[41] The date of Bessarion's departure from Rome is fixed by the Acta Consistorialia, Arch. Segr. Vaticano, Arm. XXXI, tom. 52, fol. 64^v: "Anno a nativitate Domini MCCCCLXIII, die V mensis Iulii, reverendissimus dominus Cardinalis Portuensis [a slip of the pen, for Bessarion was cardinal-bishop of Tusculum] Nicenus nominatus recessit de Roma legatus de latere apud Venetias ad solicitandum armatam contra nephandissimum Turcum et participat de communibus et minutis servitiis usque ad eius reditum in Roma secundum quod retulit mihi [i.e., to the clerk of the College] reverendissimus dominus Sancti Marchi [Pietro Barbo, nephew of Eugenius IV, later Paul II] ad presens regens officium camerariatus officii in absentiam domini Sancti Petri in Vincula [Nicholas of Cusa], camerarius preffati collegii" (*cf.* Eubel, *Hierarchia*, II [1914, repr. 1960], 33b).

[42] Pius II, *Comm.*, bk. XII, Engl. trans., p. 777; ed. Frankfurt, 1614, p. 315; Cod. Reg. lat. 1995, fol. 538^r.

[43] See the following note, and *cf. Ann. bononienses*, ad ann. 1463, in *RISS*, XXIII (Milan, 1733), col. 893E. Bessarion arrived in Bologna on 18 July, departing on the following morning for Venice (*Cronica di Bologna*, in *RISS*, XVIII [Milan, 1731], col. 752AB, and *Corpus chronicorum bononiensium*, in the new Muratori, *RISS*, XVIII, pt. 1, vol. IV, pp. 313a, 314b). He had been the papal legate in Bologna from 1450 to 1455, and had fulfilled his long mission there with rare success (Pastor, *Gesch. d. Päpste*, I [repr. 1955], 429–31, and append., no. 32, p. 826).

[44] Arch. Segr. Vaticano, Arm. XXXIX, tom. 10, fol. 3, by mod. stamped enumeration ("datum Venetiis die XXVI Iulii, MCCCCLXIII"): "Sanctissime ac beatissime pater. . . . Veni huc die XXII presentis; exceptus fui cum honore ob reverentiam Apostolice Sedis. Sequenti die exposui breviter causam legationis mee; expressi dolorem et anxietatem vestre Beatitudinis de calamitate Christianorum et promptitudinem animi ac optimam voluntatem ad subveniendum. Dixi missum me a Sanctitate vestra propter duo principaliter: primo ut in hac expeditione atque expensa quam faciunt, eos auctoritate vestre Beatitudinis pro viribus iuvarem; secundo ut una tractaremus de generali expeditione et bello aperto cum hostibus gerendo. . . . Non video, beatissime pater, nec satis mirari possum cur isti domini ita difficiles sint in dicendo se velle cum Turcis rumpere cum maximos hucusque sumptus fecerint et in classe et in terrestribus copiis quas et paraverunt et continue parant ac in Peloponnesum traiiciunt. Preterea communis fama est apud omnes eos omnino rumpere velle: imo multi opinantur capitaneum eorum iam rupisse. Item decreverunt mittere subsidium Ragusinis; miserunt oratorem ad Ungaros; mittunt nunc alium ad alias potentias ultramontanas; et hec omnia faciunt aperte cum antea, sicut scit Sanctitas vestra, umbram etiam istarum rerum formidarent. Fortasse aliqua ratione id fateri nolunt. . . ."

Three days later, however, in his report of the twenty-ninth, he had the satisfaction of writing the pope that war had formally been declared at midnight on the twenty-eighth.[45]

The crusade had become the major fact in Bessarion's life and while in Venice, his favorite Italian city, he had instructions prepared for those who were to preach the crusade. These instructions are dated 24 August and 1 September, 1463. Bessarion's first concern was that no one should be allowed to impede the *predicatores crucis*, whose efforts were to be upheld, if occasion should arise, by "ecclesiastical censures and other remedies of law, even invoking (if need be) aid of the secular arm." A hundred days' indulgence was granted to those who in a penitent mood heard the preachers. The reasons for preaching the crusade were threefold: to publicize the terrible injuries the Turks had visited upon Christendom, to seek aid for Christians reduced by the Turks to servitude, and to build up the defenses of the West, "lest that which still remains to us should pass into Turkish hands." The Gran Turco's ambition had been aroused to conquer "all the world and especially Italy." Every day he acquired another kingdom and increased his power.[46]

The Venetians must carry on the war they had just begun, and ". . . those who have lived evil lives up to now, who have been guilty of murder, theft, rapine, arson, and every kind of crime, now have the opportunity of fighting in such fashion that not only will they incur no punishment for these crimes, but will even secure the full remission of all their sins and attain to the life eternal! . . ." Crosses of red cloth were to be fastened by pins to the garments of newly won crusaders who could later have the *signum salutiferum* sewn in place. A special prayer accompanied the ceremony of taking the cross. Those who served in the crusade for six or eight months were to receive the "plenissima omnium peccatorum suorum remissio." Monks and nuns in the cloisters of every order could gain the same indulgence by outfitting one armed man for every ten members of their monastery or convent. Crusaders, their families, and their properties were to be under the special protection of the Holy See. Each preacher was to see that a suitable chest was placed in a major church in every city or town for receiving the funds to be collected. As usual, there were to be three keys, one each to be kept by the local ordinary or his vicar, by the rector of the church, and by the preacher himself. Special processions, litanies, and prayers were prescribed to advance the sacred cause. The preachers were authorized to hear confessions of crusaders and grant them absolution. Among those from whom the indulgence was to be withheld, however, were heretics, simoniacs, and public sinners, those who cheated on the crusading tithes, transported arms to the Turks, or sought to impede or dissuade crusaders from the grand emprise, usurers who would make neither restitution nor financial compromise, and other such gentry as lay beyond the Christian pale.[47]

The crusade was now preached in Piazza S. Marco before a great multitude. Tithes, twen-

---

concludes, or their expenditures of 50,000 ducats would have been wasted. The full text of this letter may be found in Adolf Bachmann, *Urkundliche Nachträge zur österreichisch-deutschen Geschichte im Zeitalter Kaiser Friedrich III.*, Vienna, 1892, no. 12, pp. 18–21 (Fontes rerum austriacarum, II. Abteilung: Diplomataria et acta, vol. 46); L. Mohler, *Kard. Bessarion*, III, 516–19; and G. Palmieri, "Lettere del Bessarione relative alla crociata contro il Turco," in *Il Muratori*, III (Rome, 1894), 61–66. Th. N. Vlachos, "Bessarion als päpstlicher Legat in Venedig im Jahre 1463," *Rivista di studi bizantini e neoellenici*, new ser., 5 (XV, 1968), 123–25, adds nothing new.

[45] Arch. Segr. Vaticano, Arm. XXXIX, tom. 10, fol. 4^r ("datum Venetiis die XXVIIII Iulii MCCCCLXIII"): Bessarion describes the meetings of the Venetian Senate from Monday through Thursday (25–28 July, 1463), "et ita heri tertia hora noctis [about 12:00 P.M. in July] decreverat in consilio rogatorum et unanimi omnium consensu concluserat bellum indicere Turco: volui hoc statim significare Sanctitati vestre ad consolationem eius et sacri collegii totiusque curie sue: spero iam dato hoc principio omnia feliciter successura." Bachmann, *Urkundliche Nachträge*, no. 13, p. 21, summarizes this letter briefly, but does not publish the text, which appears in Mohler, *Kard. Bessarion*, III, 519–22, and Palmieri, "Lettere del Bessarione," *Il Muratori*, III (1894), 97–100. From the session on Monday, 25 July, a declaration of war by the Senate must have seemed likely (Sen. Secreta, Reg. 21, fols. 169–70; Ljubić, *Listine*, X [1891], 260; Lopez, "Il Principio della guerra," p. 113–14).

[46] Arch. Segr. Vaticano, Arm. XXIX, tom. 31, fols. 19 ff., published by L. Mohler, "Bessarions Instruktion für die Kreuzzugspredigt in Venedig (1463)," *Römische Quartalschrift*, XXXV (1927), 337 ff., and see Pio Paschini, "Due Polizze d'indulgenza del 1463–1464 rilasciate nel territorio del Friuli-Istria," *Memorie storiche forogiuliesi*, VIII (1912), 304–5.

[47] Mohler, "Bessarions Instruktion," *Röm. Quartalschr.*, XXXV, 341–48. Each crusading preacher was allowed five ducats a month as compensation for maintenance. On the obligations and rewards involved in taking the cross during the first two centuries of crusading history (with canonical implications for later periods), see James A. Brundage, *Medieval Canon Law and the Crusader*, Madison, Milwaukee, and London, 1969.

tieths, and thirtieths were imposed, and collectors appointed. Nevertheless there were dark clouds on the eastern horizon, as Bessarion had to inform the Curia:

It has been reported to me recently by nobles here in Venice that the Rhodians [the Knights of S. John] have entered into a peace with the Turks. I could not believe it, but from Chios the day before yesterday I received letters from one of my friends, who is a prudent person and well informed. Among other things he writes, not without bitterness, that the fact is true, and he dwells on what a disgrace it is to all Christians and how much damage is resulting from it in those parts. They are paying the Turk as a tribute (but calling it a gift, not a tribute) 3,000 ducats, and now they have given him 5,000 in presents. . . . Here the Senate has dealt with Scanderbeg in this fashion. They are now sending him a gift of 4,000 ducats for next summer. In the early spring they will send him five hundred horsemen and the same number of foot-soldiers. Over there [in Albania], they will furnish him with subsidies for about ten thousand men who may carry the war to the Turk. . . .[48]

As Scanderbeg contemplated his role in the coming offensive, however, he appears to have harbored some doubt as to the possible outcome. Thinking of his own future, he had sent an embassy to Venice, and had requested the assurance that, if the Turks should succeed in driving him out of Albania, the Signoria would give him lands in Venetian territory "in order that he might be able to live with the hope of returning to his own state." His envoys received the rather vague assurance that the Republic would certainly do so.[49]

Since the Congress of Mantua there had been endless discussions of the crusade and much complaint among the people about the crusading levies. After Pius II's departure from Mantua, he had stopped briefly in Bologna in late January, 1460. Thereafter, at the beginning of the Lenten season, a papal brief had been read in the church of S. Petronio in Bologna to the effect that every layman, male and female both, should pay a thirtieth of his or her income, and that priests should pay a tithe. The assessment was to run for three years. According to the chronicle of Bologna, everyone who refused to pay it was to be denied confession and communion: "Therefore many men, being unwilling to pay such sums, neither confessed nor took communion. This tax was not levied

---

[48] All this comes from a letter to Cardinal Jacopo Ammanati, dated at Venice on 28 August, 1463, in Arch. Segr. Vaticano, Arm. XXXIX, tom. 10, fol. 8: ". . . nam cum superioribus diebus declarassent se domini Veneti apertos hostes Turci, heri qui fuit dies XXVIII mensis publice in eum indictum est bellum [but see below]: predicata enim fuit cruciata in platea Sancti Marci cum summa omnium expectatione et gaudio, dominio et me presente cum incredibili populi multitudine. Decime, trigesime et vigesime decrete sunt et iam instituti exactores. Indulgentie et absolutiones et dispensationes publicate et omnes modi ad pecunias colligendas edicti. . . . Relatum est mihi nuper hic a proceribus urbis Rhodienses iniisse pacem cum Turco. Non potui fidem adhibere, verum litteras ex Chio nudius tertius accepi a quodam amico qui prudens est et rerum expertus: quibus inter cetera non sine animi amaritudine scribit id verum esse: et quanta inde Christianis omnibus ignominia, quantum partibus illis detrimentum sequatur exponit. Solvunt Turco tributum, nomine tamen doni non tributi, tria milia ducatorum, et nunc donarunt ei in muneribus quinque milia. . . . Hic senatus composuit cum Scandabeo hoc modo. Mittunt ei nunc quatuor milia ducatorum dono pro futura hyeme. Primo vere mittent hinc equites quingentos et pedites totidem. Illinc vero prestabunt ei subsidia hominum suorum circiter decem milia, qui una cum suis Turco bellum inferant. . . ." This letter is dated (fol. 8^v) at Venice on 28 August, 1463, which is not in accord with the statement in the text to the effect that "yesterday, which was the twenty-eighth of the month, war was publicly declared against the Turk."

I have no explanation for this discrepancy (which Pastor passes over in the *Gesch. d. Päpste*, II [repr. 1955], 247–48, and append., no. 58, pp. 741–42, where a somewhat careless transcription of the text is given [not in the English translation]). Conceivably, Bessarion began the letter on 29 July after he had written to the pope, put it aside, and then finished it a month later. Mohler, *Kard. Bessarion*, I, 313, note 3, noticed the problem: "Das Datum dieses Briefes (28. August) ist wahrscheinlich in 29. Juli zu ändern," but the date at the conclusion of the letter, "datum Venetiis XXVIII Augusti, MCCCCLXIII," does not look like a mere slip of the pen. Bachmann, *Urkundliche Nachträge* (1892), no. 14, pp. 21–22, gives a brief summary of this letter, but publishes none of the text, which is available in Mohler, III, 522–24, and had previously been published by Palmieri, "Lettere del Bessarione," *Il Muratori*, III, 101–3. On Venetian aid to Scanderbeg, see also *MHH*, *Acta extera*, IV, nos. 144–45, pp. 231, 233, and on Bessarion's complaint against the Hospitallers, *cf.* in general Z. N. Tsirpanlis, "Friendly Relations of the Knights of Rhodes with the Turks in the Fifteenth Century" [in Greek], *Byzantinische Forschungen*, III (Amsterdam, 1968), 191–209.

[49] Arch. di Stato di Venezia, Sen. Secreta, Reg. 21, fol. 178, dated 20 August, 1463: The Albanian embassy had requested the Venetian Signoria, on Scanderbeg's behalf, "che essendo expulso del suo paese li sia deputado qualche vostro luogo e terra cum la provisione se convegni al Signor chel possi viver cum speranza de tornar in suo stado . . . ," to which the Senate replied that, since the pope and the Christian princes were uniting in the crusade, they could not imagine things reaching such a pass, "sed nihilominus in satisfactionem prefati domini [Scanderbegi] dicimus quod, si forte occurreret casus predictus, certus sit quod loca nostra sua semper reputari poterunt et Magnificentie sue taliter providebimus quod de nobis poterit merito contentari."

in any city except Bologna.[50] Note, you who read, that the pope said he wanted such payments to make war on the Turk, and this was not the truth, because he did otherwise. It was sheer robbery."[51]

Whatever the attitude of Bologna, by the time of Bessarion's mission in the summer of 1463 the Venetians could see the need of supporting the crusade. Ten years had passed since the fall of Constantinople; the Turks had become an ever greater threat to Venetian colonies in the Levant. Victory would mean relief from constant fear and frustration, possibly an increase of wealth in the Republic and still finer buildings on the Grand Canal. Perhaps Venetian ambition went even further, and the urbane tradesmen on the lagoon themselves shared some of the ideas which Pius II attributes to Ottone de' Niccolini, the Florentine ambassador to the Curia:

Your Holiness, what are you thinking of? Are you going to wage war on the Turks that you may force Italy to be subject to the Venetians? All that is won in Greece by driving out the Turks will become the property of the Venetians who, after Greece is subdued, will lay hands on the rest of Italy. . . . You are helping them in this by aligning your arms with theirs against the Turks and you do not see into what an abyss you are hurling Italy. You are weaving a net of perpetual slavery for your country. To say nothing of the losses to Italy, what will become of the Church of Rome?

Niccolini was not unhappy that Venice was finally at war with the Porte. In his opinion both powers threatened the well-being of Italy, and should be left to exhaust each other, which would be all to the good. To this Pius, who was no lover of the Venetians, answered:

. . . We admit that the Venetians, as is the way of men, covet more than they have; that they aim at the dominion of Italy and all but dare to aspire to the mastery of the world. But if the Florentines should become the equals of the Venetians in power, they would also have an equal ambition for empire. It is a common fault that no one is satisfied with his lot. No state's lands are broad enough. . . . Would you rather obey Venice or the Turks? . . . We urged the Venetians to wage war in defense of religion. They have obeyed. Now when they ask aid, shall we refuse? . . . It is enough for us that if Venice conquers, Christ will conquer.[52]

In the conversation which Pius II thus reports he had with the Florentine ambassador Niccolini (in late September, 1463), the latter was merely rehearsing the well-known views of old Cosimo de' Medici on Florentine foreign policy. Ever since the accession of Francesco Sforza to power in Milan (with the aid of Medici funds), Cosimo had adhered to an alliance with Milan against the excessive strength of Venice. If the Turk weakened Venice, so much the better for

[50] This statement is untrue. Papal nuncios and collectors were sent to Scandinavia and Lithuania, the Germanies and Italy, England, Scotland, and Ireland, and the Spanish kingdoms of Aragon, León, and Castile (see Pastor, *Gesch. d. Päpste*, II [repr. 1955], 222).

[51] *Cronica di Bologna*, ad ann. 1460, in *RISS*, XVIII (Milan, 1731), cols. 732E–733B, and *Corpus chronicorum bononiensium*, in the new Muratori, *RISS*, XVIII, pt. 1, vol. IV, pp. 271–72.

[52] Pius II, *Comm.*, bk. XII, Engl. trans., pp. 812–15, but for other sentiments of Pius concerning Venice, see bk. XI, pp. 743–46; ed. Frankfurt, 1614, bk. XII, pp. 334–35 (*hoc satis est nobis, quoniam vincente Veneto Christus vincet*), and *cf.* bk. XI, *ibid.*, p. 299, and for the omitted portions of the text excoriating the Venetians, see Jos. Cugnoni, *Opera inedita* (1883), pp. 541–43. Perhaps, however, the Venetians were not as great a menace to Italy as the Florentine ambassador believed (*Comm.*, bk. XII, Engl. trans., pp. 816–17; ed. Frankfurt, 1614, pp. 335–36). The ambassador in question, Ottone or Otto de' Niccolini (1410–1470), played an important role in the diplomacy of the mid-fifteenth century (*cf.* Pastor, *Acta inedita*, I, no. 184, p. 279, lines 7–8, and no. 159, p. 218, lines 20–21).

Niccolini was a lawyer, and had been a member of the Florentine embassy sent to Rome in the spring of 1455 to congratulate Calixtus III on his election to the papacy (Pastor, *Gesch. d. Päpste*, I [repr. 1955], 673–74). In 1467–1468 the "magnificus dominus Otho Lapi de Nicolinis, eques et legum doctor, orator, sindicus, procurator, et mandatarius," was the chief legal adviser and representative of Florence at the general conferences which produced the "pax Italica" and Confederation a few years after Pius II's death (see Arch. Segr. Vaticano, A. A., Arm. I–XVIII, no. 1443, fols. 77^r, 85^v, 86^v, *et alibi*). Although I have made no attempt to collect archival references concerning Niccolini, my notes reveal several mentions of him, as in a letter of the Florentine historian and diplomat Matteo Palmieri, written to the Signori Dieci on 25 February, 1467 (Arch. di Stato di Firenze, Dieci di Balia: Carteggi, Responsive, Reg. 23, fol. 329 [330]). Since Leona C. Gabel, in her notes to Florence A. Gragg's translation of Pius II's *Commentaries*, in *Smith College Studies in History*, XLIII (1957), 812, note 100, has "not been able to identify this Florentine envoy," she thinks that, inasmuch as Pius addresses him as "my very dear Ottone," this speech was probably made by Ottone or Otto del Carretto, the Milanese envoy to the Curia!

Friend of the Medici, Strozzi, Pazzi, Acciajuoli, Marsilio Ficino, John Argyropoulus, and other humanists, correspondent of Francesco Sforza and Federigo da Montefeltro, member of the Dieci di Balia, Ottone di Lapo de' Niccolini became "gonfalonier of justice" in his native Florence in the fall of 1458. There is a sketch of his life by Ginevra Niccolini di Camugliano, *The Chronicles of a Florentine Family, 1200–1470*, London, 1933, pp. 179–355.

the Turk. Good Christian as he was, Cosimo doubtless felt his mind and his emotions at odds on the question of the crusade. Cosimo could not, however, be sympathetic to Pius's attempts to strengthen the papal hold upon the Romagna and Umbria, which enveloped Tuscany on the north, east, and south. An alliance with Milan against Venice, an entente with Naples against the papacy, such tended to be the foreign policy of the Medici for about half a century. The burghers on the Arno wanted peace in Italy, which was good for business and safer for them, but they also wanted domination over Tuscany (including Lucca and Siena), and they sometimes found these two objectives inconsistent with each other. But however complex their position might become in this respect, the Medicean party in Florence were quite sure that they did not wish to participate in a crusade against the Gran Turco, who might be able to liquidate the Venetian empire in the Levant. They would make only such contribution to the cause as public opinion and occasional pangs of conscience might require of them.

It is clear, then, that the crusade was not going to be popular in Italy if a Christian victory over the Turk was also to be a Venetian victory. Bessarion's mission in the summer of 1463 was viewed with some suspicion. The Brescian chronicler Cristoforo da Soldo informs us that while in Venice Bessarion did what the Signoria told him to do (and certainly he got along well with the Venetians, whom he admired). Cristoforo indicates that the crusade was widely preached in northern Italy; the more one paid, the greater his indulgence; and in fact twenty ducats would buy a plenary indulgence. The exhortations of the preachers accomplished little in Brescia, however, and there were few who paid, for the whole effort seemed like a "trick to get money" (*cattaria de dinari*). At the carnival season of 1464 a Franciscan friar named Roberto appeared in Brescia, a very effective preacher, but he could not get the inhabitants to pay the charge. He set a period of fifteen days after which those who had not paid would incur the ban of greater excommunication, and this was to include priests, friars, and all parishioners. Roberto's given period ended on Friday, 16 March, 1464. Very few had paid up. Accordingly on the following Sunday, the eighteenth, Roberto preached from the pulpit in the Duomo, and pronounced a malediction on everyone who had refused to pay as well as on any priest or friar who should grant absolution to any such offender. "The excommunication and malediction were little respected by the people of Brescia, and especially by those who had any understanding, because they were well aware that he had no authority to declare such an excommunication." But the lesser folk were afraid, and many of them did finally pay the thirtieth part of their income.[53]

Having long hesitated to take on the Gran Turco, the Venetians now hoped to conquer the entire Morea, which was said to be worth 300,000 ducats a year in tolls and customs. Most contemporaries believed that the Venetians cared only for their commercial interests, not for the fate of eastern Christendom. This was certainly the view of Pope Pius II, who informs us in some detail of the Venetian preparations. Large cavalry forces as well as infantry were sent into the Morea from Italy. Three thousand archers were recruited from Crete, many Albanians were enrolled, and Pius estimates that the Venetian "army could go into battle with more than thirty thousand fighting men." Loredan's fleet was heavily reinforced. "The alleged object of the war," the pope informs us, "was to avert aggression and defend the Christian religion. [The Venetians] accused the Turks of taking Argos and sacking Lepanto in violation of the treaty." He adds, however, in two interesting and characteristic passages (which were deleted from the printed editions of his *Commentarii*):

> None of these considerations impelled the Venetians to arm so strong a fleet and incur such heavy expense. Traders care nothing for religion nor will a miserly people spend money to avenge it. The populace see no harm in dishonor if their money is safe. It was lust for power and insatiable greed of gain that persuaded the Venetians to equip such forces and undergo such expense. . . . [The Venetians considered only that the Morea was one of the centers of the world's commerce, producing an abundance of wine, wheat, and all the other necessities of life.] They were possessed with the desire of conquering a very rich province. They spent money to get more money. They followed their natural instincts. They were out for trade and barter. This course was urged upon them by an overcrowded city which could no longer endure itself. Those they call nobles, who have control of the

[53] Cristoforo da Soldo, *Istoria bresciana*, in *RISS*, XXI (Milan, 1732), cols. 898–99, and ed. Giuseppe Brizzolara, in the new Muratori, *RISS*, XXI, pt. 3 (1938–42), 144. The friar in question was probably Roberto Caracciolo da Lecce.

government, had increased to a remarkable degree, though all are slaves to the sordid occupations of trade. They thought they ought to send out a colony and that there was no better place to found one than the Peloponnese. These were their real reasons for equipping a fleet; all others were pretended. He is a fool who thinks a people can be persuaded to noble deeds unless it is to their material advantage.[54]

The Venetian view was doubtless that attributed to the Doge Leonardo Donato, about a century and a half later, in the contest with Pope Paul V over the growth of ecclesiastical properties in Venice, to the effect that the citizens of the Republic were just as good Christians as the pope (*Siamo Cristiani quanto il papa*).

The Venetians appeared to be making a good beginning, now that they had gone to war against the Turks. They appointed the young Marquis Bertoldo d'Este, a relative of the ruling family of Ferrara and Modena, commander-in-chief of the land forces in the Morea. Argos was retaken in early August with little difficulty,[55] and the lion banner of the evangelist floated again over the picturesque height of the Larissa. The Hexamilion remained the symbol of security against the Turks, the Maginot of the Morea, not only for the Greeks, but even, at first, for the Venetians. It was a vain thing for safety, however, having been rebuilt and destroyed some eight or nine times in the forty years from 1423 to 1463. In the first two weeks of September of the latter year the Venetians reconstructed it with great blocks of stone, employing, it is said, thirty thousand men to do so; 136 defense towers were built at intervals along its six-mile length; and an altar dedicated to S. Mark was placed in the center of the wall, which was further protected by a deep moat. The Venetians now began the siege of Corinth. Omar Beg soon appeared before the Hexamilion, but had to withdraw from the range of Venetian cannon. There were a number of engagements between the Venetians and the Turkish forces south of the great wall. On 20 October, however, the Venetians were badly defeated, and Bertoldo d'Este was mortally wounded, hit in the head by a stone. He died before Corinth on 4 November, 1463. The siege of the city had to be abandoned. The Venetians withdrew to the Hexamilion and Nauplia.[56]

Omar Beg, *flambulare della Morea*, who had not dared to attack the Hexamilion with his own inadequate troops, had appealed for reinforcements. He was now awaiting the arrival of Mahmud Pasha, whose chances of taking the wall he nevertheless considered doubtful. In fact he advised Mahmud Pasha not to continue his advance, but to inform the sultan that a great undertaking lay before them. He reported that he had himself approached very close to the Venetian army, and had seen more than two thousand (small) cannon and four hundred bombardiers, as well as archers and shield-bearers. Such a force was certainly not going to allow a Turkish encampment in the Isthmus. An Albanian messenger from Turkish-held Corinth, however, made his way to Mahmud in Thessaly to urge his continuing southward, for the Venetians did not expect an attack. Mahmud decided to take the chance. He had already determined to come as far as Livadia in Boeotia. As soon as he got there, he received the astonishing news that the Venetians had abandoned the Hexamilion.

That evening he made preparations for his advance. During the night he withdrew from the region of Plataea, going through the passes of Cithaeron under the cover of darkness. By the break of dawn he had reached the Isthmus, just in time to see the Venetian ships putting

[54] Pius II, *Comm.*, bk. XII, Engl. trans., pp. 775–76; ed. Frankfurt, 1614, pp. 314–15; Cugnoni, *Opera inedita*, pp. 544–45; *cf.* Voigt, *Enea Silvio*, III, 695; Pastor, *Gesch. d. Päpste*, II (repr. 1955), 245.

[55] The Venetian recapture of Argos is dated 5 August by the *Chronicon breve*, ad ann. 1463 (Bonn, p. 521); this chronicle is generally reliable, but Malatesta's secretary seems to date the event on the third (Sathas, *Docs. inédits*, VI, 95).

[56] See the account left by Malatesta's secretary, in Sathas, *Docs. inédits*, VI, 96; Chalcocondylas, bk. x (Bonn, p. 558; ed. Darkó, II–2, 300–1); Malipiero, *Annali veneti*, in *Arch. stor. italiano*, VII–1 (1843), 15; Cristoforo da Soldo, in the so-called *Istoria bresciana*, in *RISS*, XXI, cols. 895–96, and ed. G. Brizzolara, in the new Muratori, *RISS*, XXI, pt. 3 (1938–42), 140–41; *Corpus chronicorum bononiensium*, ad ann. 1463, in *RISS*, XVIII, pt. 1, vol. IV, pp. 319a, 320b; Sanudo, *Vite de'duchi*, in *RISS*, XXII (1733), cols. 1172–73, 1179C; Navagero, *Storia veneziana*, in *RISS*, XXIII, cols. 1121–23. Vallaresso, who deserted to the Turks, was exchanged by them for the son of an officer of the Porte, and was hanged as a traitor in Venice in November, 1463 (Sanudo, *op. cit.*, cols. 1173–74). On the Hexamilion, *cf.* Pius II, *Comm.*, bk. XII, Engl. trans., p. 830; ed. Frankfurt, 1614, p. 343; Cod. Reg. lat. 1995, fols. 576^v–577^r, and Ljubić, *Listine*, X (1891), 277. On Bertoldo d'Este, see Lopez, "Il Principio della guerra," pp. 53 ff., 64 ff., 79 ff., and on Bertoldo's death, *ibid.*, pp. 96–99.

out to sea. Depressed by their recent defeat, their troops afflicted with dysentery, the Venetian high command had decided to fall back on Nauplia. Mahmud Pasha thus found the Isthmus deserted. He camped there for a brief while, and then pushed on to Argos by way of Corinth. The Hexamilion was destroyed. Having been built partly without mortar, it was easier to tear down than to erect. The remains of the Venetians' Isthmian camp were plundered, and Turkish horsemen and janissaries pursued the straggling Venetian troops to Nauplia. Here the Turks were repulsed with heavy losses by a sortie which one Giovanni della Tela led out from the city. Mahmud's troops, however, recovered Argos in the first attack. Chalcocondylas says that they captured the Venetian garrison of seventy men, who were sent to the sultan in Istanbul. According to Critobulus, Mahmud sent all the inhabitants of Argos to add to the population of Istanbul and razed the Moreote town. A Turkish garrison was presumably placed in the Larissa on the hilltop. Mahmud's troops also moved into the southern part of the Morea. Various towns and fortresses which had been prepared to recognize the authority of Venice quickly reverted to the Ottoman allegiance. Mahmud and the main body of the army went through the territory of Tegea as far as Leondari. Isa Beg was removed from command over the Morea. Zagan Pasha was restored and sent to Patras and a number of other places in the northern part of the peninsula, to see to their fortifications and stock them with food and other necessities. Mahmud Pasha next ordered Omar Beg to take command of the army, which then contained some twenty thousand men, and to attack the Venetian territory in the south. The Republic's whole establishment in the Morea was probably saved by the advent of winter.[57]

According to Chalcocondylas, Omar Beg raided the district of Modon with the army which was now placed under his command, captured a small town, and sent some five hundred prisoners to Mahmud Pasha, who had been summoned back to Istanbul by Sultan Mehmed.[58] The five hundred prisoners were also sent to Istanbul, where Mehmed had them all cut in two, a barbarity which in his case need not excite undue incredulity. Our source is Chalcocondylas, however, who lived and wrote in Athens, far from the scene of this hideous mass execution. He may very well be doing no more than recounting a tale which was abroad at this time, and indeed there is a sequel to the tale (λέγεται δέ . . .). An ox is said to have gone among the severed bodies with a mournful lowing, and to have put the two halves of one body together, although they had been lying a considerable distance apart. What was even more remarkable, on the following day, when the two halves of this body were again separated, the ox sought them out from all the rest of the carnage, and again put them together. The superstitious sultan, who had seen the second (and more astounding) miracle with his own eyes, ordered the two halves of this body to be buried, and the ox to be placed in the imperial garden of the Seraglio to live a life of ease as the harbinger of an uncertain future. The sultan believed that he saw in this unusual event a sign of good fortune for the people to which the poor victim had belonged. There was no way of telling, however, whether he had been a Venetian or an Albanian.[59] Apparently he was not a Greek and obviously he could not have been a Turk.

On 12 September, 1463, the Venetians and King Matthias Corvinus of Hungary committed themselves to a crusade, and on 19 October the statesmen of the Republic formed an alliance against the Turks with Pope Pius II and Duke Philip the Good of Burgundy for a period of three years.[60] In the preceding

---

[57] See Malatesta's secretary in Sathas, *Docs. inédits*, VI, 96–97, where on 4 November (1463) the Venetians are reported to have captured two Turkish spies, who under torture said that Mahmud Pasha ("Daut Bassà") was within eight days of the Hexamilion with an army of 80,000 men; Chalcocondylas, bk. x (Bonn, pp. 559–61; ed. Darkó, II–2, 301–3); Critobulus, IV, 16 (ed. Müller, *FHG*, V–1, pp. 148b–149; ed. Grecu [1963], pp. 311, 313), and V, 1–2 (ed. Müller, pp. 150–151a; ed. Grecu, pp. 315, 317); *cf.* Kretschmayr, *Gesch. v. Venedig*, II (1920, repr. 1964), 371–72; Babinger, *Maometto* (1957), 338–40.

[58] *Cf.* Malatesta's secretary, in Sathas, *Docs. inédits*, VI, 97, lines 40–41.

[59] Chalcocondylas, bk. x (Bonn, pp. 561–63; ed. Darkó, II–2, 303–5); *cf.* Raynaldus, *Ann. eccl.*, ad ann. 1464, no. 11, vol. XIX (1693), p. 155.

[60] Sanudo, *Vite de' duchi*, in *RISS*, XXII, cols. 1174–76; Navagero, *Storia veneziana*, in *RISS*, XXIII, col. 1124. The text of Matthias Corvinus's accord with Venice (of 12 September, 1463) is given in Ljubić, *Listine*, X, 272–74, *cf.* pp. 281–82, and see *MHH*, *Acta extera*, IV (1875), nos. 149–50, 152, pp. 240 ff. In January, 1464, the Venetian Signoria is said to have made Pius II a wholly incredible offer of supplies, cannon, cuirasses, spingards, lances and galleys (according to a [late fifteenth-century?] MS. in the

July, Corvinus had finally made peace with the Emperor Frederick III of Germany who, as we have seen, himself coveted the Hungarian throne. Corvinus had then pledged the full use of all his resources to the war against the Turks, undoubtedly reassured by the fortunate turn his affairs were taking. The Venetians now undertook to arm forty galleys for an offensive.[61] In late September, Corvinus entered Bosnia with an army of about four thousand men, making his way without serious opposition to the city of Jajce. The lower city fell to him after four days, although the janissaries in the upper fortress had to be starved into surrender, but surrender they finally did on 16 December. Most of the captives were offered the alternatives of enrollment in the Hungarian army or their free departure without weapons. Corvinus spared the Turkish garrisons everywhere. The commander of the garrison of Jajce and four hundred chosen prisoners were carried off to Hungary, where they furnished spectacular evidence of the victory over the Turks. During the course of his campaign Corvinus sent an envoy to Venice, seeking funds wherewith to continue his success. The Senate expressed regret that they could not help him; since they had entered the war their land forces and the fleet were costing them more than 600,000 ducats when figured on an annual basis.[62] Such, at least, was the envoy told. With or without the help of the Republic, however, Corvinus is said to have taken sixty places in Bosnia, many of them fortified. It was widely believed that the victory had restored Bosnia to Christendom and assured the future of the Herzegovina.[63] This was not so, but in July and August, 1464, the fortress of Jajce withstood a terrible siege conducted under the personal command of Sultan Mehmed II, who had to throw his heavy cannon into the river, abandon his baggage, and retreat toward Sofia, upon the news of Corvinus's advance from the Sava. A new Turkish army, however, was quickly assembled at Sofia. The sultan set over it Mahmud Pasha, before whom Corvinus in his turn was soon in northward flight. Bosnia had been largely depopulated. It remained for the most part in the hands of the Turks, who launched repeated but vain attacks upon Jajce (which in 1472 became the capital of Nicholas Ujláky, whom Corvinus made the ruler of a new Bosnian kingdom). Some of Mehmed II's difficulty in 1464 was ill health. Like his father, he now showed a strong tendency to fat. Intemperance and the hardships of constant campaigning were beginning to leave their ineffaceable marks upon his constitution. When he returned to Istanbul at the close of that summer of defeat, he remained within the capital for more than a year.[64]

Bibl. Apost. Vaticana, Cod. lat. 5994, fols. 86^v–87^r, which contains the following fantasy):

"Ad laudem et memoriam illustrissimi dominii Venetorum: In nomine domini nostri Jesu Christi: Questa e la offerta che fa la Signoria de Venetia de Jenaro 1464 alo santissimo papa Pio Secundo contra el Turco. In prima: Per grano e biscotti ducati tridicimilia./ Item bombarde grandi settanta che getta la petra de libre cinquecento./ Item bombarde picchole quattrocentoquaranta [corrected from centoquaranta milia!] che butta la petra de libre ottanta./ Item corazze dacciaio settemilia./ Item spingharde quattordici milia./ Item dui navi piene de lance, che ciaschuna nave portaria cento botti./ Item una nave de polve da bombarda che portaria ottanta botti./ Navi quattro de verrottoni et frezze che ciaschuna portaria settecento ottanta botti . . . [quantities of equipment and tools are listed as well as:] Item fantarie a piede da dece ale dodici milia. . . ./ Item gentedarme a cavallo seimilia. . . ./ Item galee pachate infino a Natale ottantasei./ Item ultra le navi et tutte la cose scritte de sopra ducati, 1,000,000 che fanno un milione. . . ."

[61] Raynaldus, *Ann. eccl.*, ad ann. 1463, nos. 1–12, vol. XIX (1693), pp. 123–26, and no. 51, *ibid.*, p. 137; Ljubić, *Listine*, X, 273; Voigt, *Enea Silvio*, III, 683–84; Pastor, *Gesch. d. Päpste*, II (repr. 1955), 248.

[62] Arch. di Stato di Venezia, Sen. Secreta, Reg. 21, fols. 194^v–195^r, doc. dated 13 October, 1463: ". . . Ad partem favorum pecuniarum vellemus profecto et in hoc et in omnibus regie Maiestati complacere posse, sed sicut per oratorem nostrum dici fecimus Serenitati sue per ingressum nostrum in bello cum Turco sumus ad presens in expensis ducatorum sexcentorum milium et ultra in anno tam in gentibus armigeris et peditibus ex Italia missis et quos incessanter mittimus contra comunem hostem quam in potentissima classe quam continue fortificamus contra ipsum hostem: Hinc est quod . . . non sit nobis possibile facere quod vellemus. . . ."

[63] Iorga, *Gesch. d. osman. Reiches*, II, 124–25; Babinger, *Maometto*, pp. 340–42; and see the documents in Ljubić, *Listine*, X, 277, 313, 316–17.

[64] Critobulus, V, 4–6 (ed. Müller, *FHG*, V–1, pp. 151b–153; ed. Grecu [1963], pp. 319 ff.); Malipiero, *Annali veneti*, in *Arch. stor. italiano*, VII, pt. 1 (1843), 32–33. Francesco Filelfo, serving Francesco Sforza as a secretary in Milan, emphasizes Mehmed II's ill health in a letter to the Doge Cristoforo Moro on 15 March, 1464: "Mahometus ob vitae intemperantiam victusque luxuriam membris est adeo mollibus atque dissolutis ut vix equo insistat; nam quo pacto ephippiis erecto corpore insideat, qui homo temulentus morbo comitiali quam saepissime corripiatur, et ea sit enervatione articulorum, ut ne stapedibus quidem satis queat inniti" (cited by Raynaldus, *Ann. eccl.*, ad ann. 1464, no. 20, vol. XIX [1693], p. 157). On the fighting in Bosnia, *cf.* Raynaldus, *loc. cit.*, no. 63, p. 168; Iorga, *Gesch. d. osman. Reiches*, II, 126–27, 177; Babinger,

Early in the year 1464 the Republic of S. Mark made changes in its chief commands both on land and sea. Sigismondo Pandolfo Malatesta, the tyrant of Rimini, whom Pius II regarded as the "prince of wickedness,"[65] but a good soldier, was made captain-general of the land forces in the Morea, while Orsato Giustinian replaced Alvise Loredan, who was ill, as admiral in the Aegean. Giustinian was ordered to occupy Mytilene if he could.[66] The Senate planned to keep the Turks busy on all fronts. On 5 April (1464) they informed Giustinian that they were recruiting *gentes armigerae et pedites* in large numbers to send into Albania as soon as possible, to fight along with Scanderbeg and the anti-Turkish chieftains.[67] On the same day they wrote Alvise Foscarini, their envoy to the Holy See, that they had recently learned from Jacopo Zane, their vice-consul in Naples, that Scanderbeg had gone to the court of King Ferrante, and would soon be visiting the pope. Foscarini was to pay Scanderbeg an official call, if and when he came to the Curia Romana, do him especial honor, and assist the pope to hurry him on his way to Venice, where it was understood he was also planning an appearance. The sooner he came to Venice, the sooner he could return to Albania, where his presence would be much needed in the coming offensive against the Turks.[68]

As he had been instructed, Orsato Giustinian attacked the island of Lesbos in April and May, laying siege to the city of Mytilene for six weeks, until Mahmud Pasha with a large Ottoman fleet forced his precipitate withdrawal (on 18 May, 1464).[69] Giustinian made another attempt upon Lesbos in the following month, but this also failed. In early July he sailed to Modon, where he died on the eleventh, a thoroughly discouraged man. Already the war was taking its toll of Venetian commanders. Jacopo Loredan was appointed to his post, and set out for Rhodes with forty-two galleys. From the haven of the Hospitallers he ranged the eastern Aegean up to Tenedos, making an impressive demonstration of force at the mouth of the Dardanelles, which accomplished nothing.[70]

Maometto, pp. 343–45. In 1475 Nicholas of Ujlak came to Rome, ostensibly for the jubilee of indulgence alone, but very likely to appeal to Pope Sixtus IV for aid against the Turks (*cf.* Pastor, *Gesch. d. Päpste*, II [repr. 1955], 515–16).

[65] Pius II, *Comm.*, bk. I, Engl. trans., p. 80, and bk. II, pp. 167–70 (most of Pius's invective against Malatesta in these passages being omitted from the Frankfurt edition, pp. 26, 51–52, see Cugnoni, *Opera inedita*, pp. 80, 509); and without further reference to the Frankfurt edition or Cugnoni, see bk. III, Engl. trans., p. 254; IV, 325, 331; V, 364, 374–76, 380; VII, 504–5; VIII, 541; X, 647–63 (on the family of the Malatesta); *et alibi*—Pius hated Sigismondo beyond all men of his time. His references to him are generally entertaining if not edifying; on the process Pius instituted against him, *cf.* Erich Meuthen, *Die letzten Jahre des Nikolaus von Kues*, Cologne, 1958, pp. 282–83. Since abusive references to Sigismondo in the letters of Pius are not relevant to any significant aspect of this study, I have kept no record of those I have found in the Vatican registers, but *cf. Brevia*, in Arm. XXXIX, tom. 9, fols. 241^v–242^r, dated (apparently) 10 August, 1461, to the doge of Venice; fols. 242^v–244^r, also to the doge; etc. On the general background of Pius's hostility to Sigismondo, see A. A., Arm. I–XVIII, no. 1443, fols. 40^r–44^r, by mod. stamped enumeration. There are numerous documents relating to Pius's pursuit of Sigismondo in the Arch. di Stato di Milano, Arch. Visconteo-Sforzesco, Potenze estere [Fondo Sforzesco], Cart. 49 (tit. "Roma," 1460–1461).

In early March, 1464, Malatesta came to Venice to arrange with the Signoria the terms of his service in the Morea (Arch. di Stato di Venezia, Sen. Secreta, Reg. 22, fols. 3^v–4^r [5^v–6^r], dated 13 March): "Venit huc, ut est notum, magnificus dominus Sigismundus Pandulfus qui conductam et capitaneatum Amoree ei oblatum acceptavit. . . ." We need not be concerned with the details of his condotta, the initial terms being altered for his benefit on the morning of the fifteenth, when he appeared in person before the Signoria (*ibid.*, fol. 4^r [6^r]).

[66] Sanudo, *Vite de' duchi*, in *RISS*, XXII, col. 1179; Navagero, *Storia veneziana*, in *RISS*, XXIII, col. 1123; Raynaldus, *Ann. eccl.*, ad ann. 1464, no. 65, vol. XIX (1693), p. 168. On 5 March the Senate reconsidered, but did not alter previous instructions to Giustinian to attack the island of Lesbos, *in facto Mithilenarum* (Sen. Secreta, Reg. 22, fol. 2^v [4^v]). Twelve days later (on 17 March) Giustinian, *capitaneus generalis maris*, was informed by the Senate: "Conduximus in capitaneum nostrum generalem terrestrem in partibus Amoree magnificum dominum Sigismundum de Malatestis, qui cum equitibus II. millia vel circa de mense Aprilis proximi in Dei nomine itineri se committet venturus in illam provinciam Amoree ut simul cum aliis gentibus et viribus nostris fieri possit honor creatoris nostri . . ." (*ibid.*, fol. 6^v [8^v]).

[67] Sen. Secreta, Reg. 22, fol. 10^r [12^r].

[68] *Ibid.*, Reg. 22, fol. 10 [12]. On Scanderbeg's movements, at least after Mehmed II raised the siege of Jajce (on 22 August, 1464), see Fr. Pall, "I Rapporti italo-albanesi," *Archivio storico per le province napoletane*, LXXXIII (3rd ser., IV, 1966), doc. no. LXII, p. 203, a letter of the condottiere Antonio da Cosenza to the Doge Cristoforo Moro, written from Valle Carda in Albania on 17 September, 1464.

[69] Critobulus, V, 7 (ed. Müller, *FHG*, V-1, p. 154; ed. Grecu [1963], pp. 329, 331).

[70] Two years later, in the third year of the war, Andrea Duodo, who knew well the area of the Dardanelles, wrote Vettore Capello of the vanity and danger of trying to conduct a war in the northern Aegean and making attempts on the straits, from which only damage but never victory could ensue for Venice (see his detailed program *Pro bello Peloponnensi* in Sathas, *Docs. inédits*, VI, 104–5, in which he alludes to Loredan's showy gesture). Duodo advocates the

The Venetians had appointed Sigismondo Malatesta to the command of their land forces in the Morea only when it was quite clear that no other Italian condottiere of note would accept the post. They feared the impression which his appointment would make upon the Curia Romana. Pius II was anxious to keep Malatesta in the straitened circumstances to which he had been reduced, and was not above bestowing Malatesta lands upon the Piccolomini. The time and money he had devoted to his struggle with Malatesta had been an impediment to his plans for the crusade. It was feared in Rome that Malatesta would try to use his new position and the assurances he was receiving from the Venetians to help rebuild his shattered fortunes in Italy as well as to fight the Turks in the Morea. His commission was to last for two years. He departed for his command at the end of June, about two months later than he had promised the Signoria. Although constantly beset by his enemies, who were always abetted by the Piccolomini, Malatesta had managed to send ahead of him into the Morea 1,400 horses for his men-at-arms, 400 mounted crossbowmen, and 300 infantry. He must have arrived in the Morea in mid-July (1464), although the chronicler Malipiero says that he landed at Modon on 8 August.[71] His forces were later increased in size, but their effectiveness declined with each passing month, owing to lack of supplies, encounters with the Turks, and the near-famine conditions which the war soon brought to the Morea. Malatesta never had a sufficient military establishment to do what the Republic expected of him.[72] He had reason to be dissatisfied with the Serenissima's conduct of its military affairs, and proved unable or unwilling to get along with Andrea Dandolo, provveditore of the Morea.[73]

Although Malatesta made a number of attacks upon Turkish positions and occupied a few places, including the lower city of Mistra (on 16 August, 1464), his attempt to take the hilltop castle of the Villehardouin and the Palaeologi failed. He retreated to Modon in the late autumn, upon receiving the news that Omar Beg was on his way to break the Italian siege. Later Malatesta went to Nauplia, where he became ill. He had removed from Mistra the body of the Platonic philosopher George Gemistus Pletho. He later buried Pletho in a handsome sarcophagus at the cathedral of Rimini, the old church of S. Francesco, which Leone Battista Alberti had transformed in 1450 into the Tempio Malatestiano.[74] This

defense of Venetian possessions in the Levant and concentration upon the conquest of the Morea (*ibid.*, pp. 105 ff.). Although he proposes adequate numbers of ships and men, money, and supplies for the war against the Turks, he also cautions reason and moderation: "E le gran cose non si fa tanto con numero de zente, quanto per conseio e sapientia" (p. 107). During the first year of the war Venice had offered Matthias Corvinus a subsidy of 60,000 florins for an expedition against the Turks, "eunte maiestate sua cum exercitu suo extra regnum suum contra perfidos Turcos . . ." (Sen. Secreta, Reg. 22, fol. 2^{r}, publ. by Ljubić, *Listine*, X, 299, and *cf.* pp. 301, 311 ff.).

[71] Malipiero, *Annali veneti*, in *Archivio storico italiano*, VII–1 (1843), 32; *cf.* Ant. G. Mompherratos [Monferrato], Σιγισμοῦνδος Πανδόλφος Μαλατέστας: Πόλεμος Ἑνέτων καὶ Τούρκων ἐν Πελοποννήσῳ κατὰ τὰ ἔτη *1463–1466*, Athens, 1914, p. 28, and especially Giovanni Soranzo, "Sigismondo Pandolfo Malatesta in Morea e le vicende del suo dominio," *Atti e memorie della R. Deputazione di storia patria per le provincie di Romagna*, 4th ser., VIII (Bologna, 1918), 211–80, esp. pp. 212–27. Malatesta's secretary in Sathas, *Docs. inédits*, VI, 98, says that Malatesta landed in the Morea on 13 July (1464), which seems quite likely.

[72] Malatesta never had as many as 4,000 men, all told, both horse and foot, in the Morea (*cf.* Soranzo, *op. cit.*, p. 229).

[73] Dandolo's commission, drafted in the name of the Doge Cristoforo Moro and dated 17 March, 1464, is to be found in the Sen. Secreta, Reg. 22, fol. 5 [7]. Besides the various instructions he received, Dandolo was sent into the Morea with 10,000 ducats, of which 8,000 were in gold. Before his departure he was given an additional 1,000, of which 480 were for six months' salary and the remaining 520 for expenses. At the same time he received sixty-eight bolts of cloth of various colors (all under the lead seal of S. Mark) which he was to deliver to the Venetian captain-general of the sea "if he was in those parts:"

"Si vero idem capitaneus noster inde abesset, volumus tibique mandamus ut habita collatione cum regimine nostro Mothoni de fide et meritis cuiusque tam Grecorum quam Albanensium medietatem eiuscemodi pannorum inter eos nostri dominii nomine dono distribues ut in devotione et fide sua ardentius perseverent ac de bono in melius pro statu nostro partium ipsarum se exerceant. Medietatem vero pannorum scarlatinorum finorum distribues inter Sp. Nicolaum Griza et suos, Petrum Buam et suos, Nicolam Rali et suos, et Michaelem Rali et suos, et Cumino et suos. Reliquam vero medietatem servabis usque adventum ipsius capitanei nostri cui eos assignabis" (*ibid.*, fol. 5^{r} [7^{r}]). Apparently fine cloth went farther than gold in the Morea.

[74] Malatesta's secretary in Sathas, *Docs. inédits*, VI, 98; Theodore Spandugnino, *ibid.*, p. 100; Ces. Clementini, *ibid.*, pp. 93–94; Sanudo, *Vite de'duchi*, in *RISS*, XXII, cols. 1181, 1182; Ljubić, *Listine*, X, 320, doc. dated 13 January, 1465 (Ven. style 1464), from the Sen. Secreta, Reg. 22, fols. 58^{v}–59^{r} [60^{v}–61^{r}], noting the withdrawal of Malatesta's forces from Mistra, on which *cf.* G. Soranzo, in the *Atti e memorie*, etc., VIII, 231–33, 279–80. For Malatesta's activities against the Turks and his many difficulties in 1465, see Soranzo, *ibid.*, pp. 259–70, and on the reburial of Gemistus Pletho, see Corrado Ricci, *Il Tempio Malatestiano*, Milan,

was more than the sentimental gesture of a patron of art and humanism toward a famous scholar, whom Malatesta had once tried to entice to Rimini. Pletho had been known personally to the Malatesti from the time, more than forty years before, when Cleopa Malatesta of Pesaro had married the Despot Theodore II of Mistra (1407–1443), brother of the last emperor, Constantine XI.[75]

Sigismondo Malatesta had not been a success in the Morea. According to Angiolello, Malatesta had been deprived of the support of the Venetian fleet during the siege of Mistra (in October, 1464), when the admiral Loredan was ordered from Moreote waters to Rhodes as a consequence of trouble with the Hospitallers. His failure to take the castle of Mistra—*che la terra era già presa*—was attributed to this fact.[76] After eighteen hard months in the Morea, Malatesta was finally released from Venetian service, and departed for Italy on 25 January, 1466. He was in Venice the following March; returned to Rimini (with Pletho's bones) on 14 April; and was called the following month to Rome, where Pius II's successor, the Venetian Paul II, received the excommunicate with every honor as an athlete of Christ, awarding him the golden rose as Pius presumably turned in his grave. Actually Malatesta had done what he could in the Morea. The vacillating policy of the Venetians had failed to provide him with men and provisions.[77] At the time of his departure Venetian affairs in the Morea were in a sorrier plight than they had been when he arrived. Malatesta was not, however, responsible for the deterioration of the Venetian position in the turbulent peninsula.

We can follow the course of this deterioration in the most interesting and detailed reports of Jacopo Barbarigo, who succeeded Andrea Dandolo as Venetian provveditore in the Morea to advise Malatesta in prosecuting the war against the Turkish forces under Omar Beg. Barbarigo's reports extend from 5 June, 1465, to just after the middle of March, 1466.[78] He watched Omar Beg's movements with great attention. From week to week, almost from day to day, he sent word to the home government concerning them. Now the Turkish commander was at Mouchli, then on a raid or laying siege to some Venetian stronghold, and finally came the news that he had gone to Athens, owing to the severe shortage

---

1925, pp. 291–95, and François Masai, *Pléthon et le platonisme de Mistra*, Paris, 1956, pp. 364–65. The epitaph on Pletho's tomb is dated 1465. The Tempio was severely damaged in 1943–1944, Rimini being an important position in the German line of defense against the allied advance.

[75] *Cf.* Sp. P. Lampros, *Palaiológeia kaì Peloponnesiaká*, IV (Athens, 1930), 102–3, 143, 144–75, 176, where monodies of Nicephorus Cheilas and Plethon as well as Bessarion's epitaph on the Despoina Cleopa are given; G. Müller, *Documenti sulle relazioni delle città toscane coll'Oriente cristiano e coi Turchi*, Florence, 1879, pt. 1, doc. no. 102, p. 150, and *cf.* pp. 479–80; Ducas, chap. 20 (Bonn, p. 100; ed. Grecu [1958], p. 137); Chalcocondylas, bk. IV (Bonn, p. 206; Darkó, I [1922], 193); Sphrantzes, *Chron. minus* (*PG* 156, 1043D–1044A; ed. Grecu [1966], p. 50, lines 28–30), and *cf.* Pseudo-Sphrantzes, II, 10 (Bonn, p. 158; ed. Grecu, p. 300, lines 35–37). Cleopa was also buried at Mistra, in the Zoodotou monastery (Sphrantzes, *loc. cit.*, and Miller, *Latins in the Levant* [1908], p. 415), but her grave has not been identified in excavations of Hagia Sophia, presumed to have been the *katholikón* of the monastery. *Cf.* Hopf, *Chron. gréco-romanes* (1873, repr. 1966), geneal. tables, p. 536; Chas. Yriarte, *Un Condottiere au XVe siècle: Rimini, Études sur les lettres et les arts à la cour des Malatesta*, Paris, 1882, pp. 261–63, 449; D. A. Zakythinos, *Le Despotat grec de Morée*, I (1932, repr. 1975), 189–91, 299–302. (Cleopa died in 1433.) The daughter of Theodore II of Mistra, Helena Palaeologina, had married King John II of Cyprus in 1442. Helena's ambition and hostility toward the Latin Church plunged John's kingdom into sixteen years of violence and fruitless intrigue (Geo. Hill, *A History of Cyprus*, III [Cambridge, 1948], 527–44).

[76] Angiolello, *Hist. turchesca*, ed. Ursu (1909), pp. 32–33.

[77] *Cf.* Mompherratos, Σιγισμοῦνδος Πανδόλφος Μαλατέστας, pp. 46–50. The date of Malatesta's departure from the Morea is noted in a dispatch of the Venetian provveditore Jacopo Barbarigo, addressed to the home government on 18 February, 1466 [Ven. style 1465] (Sathas, VI, doc. no. 82, p. 87, lines 24–25, the full reference to this work being repeated below). Note also what we might regard as Malatesta's final discharge in Sen. Secreta, Reg. 22, fols. 142^v–143^r [144^v–145^r], dated 18 March, 1466; "Quod magnifico domino Sigismundo de Malatestis ad ea que petiit et exposuit, viz. commendari per nostras litteras summo pontifici, item quod si eum dominatio nostra vult ad servitia sua promptus reperitur ire et ad partes orientis et ponentis, etc. Sin minus, dignetur saltem dominatio nostra ei declarare que via sibi gratior esset, quoniam illam capiet, et quod aliis qui opera et servicio suo uti vellent, commendamus, etc. Item de gentibus suis que in Amorea remanserunt . . . , respondeatur: " that Venice would be pleased to recommend him to the pope, and was quite content that he should return to Italy and to his home (in Rimini); that his obligations to Venice were duly discharged, and the Senate would be quite willing to recommend him to others; that those of his troops in the Morea who wished to remain in Venetian service might do so, and the others return to Italy: At the same time, however, the Senate wrote to the Venetian provveditore in the Morea to enrol for further service only the best troopers and to let the others go.

[78] Jacomo (or Jacopo) Barbarigo, *Dispacci della guerra di Peloponneso*, in C. N. Sathas, ed., *Documents inédits relatifs à l'histoire de la Grèce au moyen âge*, VI (Paris, 1884, repr. Athens, 1972), nos. 1–87, pp. 1–92.

of food and fodder in the Morea (according to a dispatch from Coron on 14 October, 1465). Through the early months covered by Barbarigo's reports so many men-at-arms lost their lives in one way or another that the Venetian command usually had an excess of horses (and little fodder). The troops, both horse and foot, went unpaid and were demoralized; the provveditore had trouble with the Republic's lesser condottieri, their subalterns, and the "constables." Barbarigo took only a slightly more sanguine view of life and affairs in the Morea in the earlier than in the later months of his residence there:

"When I consider the affairs of this province," he wrote the Doge Cristoforo Moro on 25 July, 1465 (in a letter actually intended, of course, for the Senate), "as they have gone up to the present, and the state in which they still are, I can only feel the deepest distress that so much money and effort have been expended with such slight utility to your Highness. . . ." If the doge were the master of the Morea, however, he might account himself also *signor de tuta Gretia*. From the resources of the Morea alone an occupying power could support ten thousand men, both horse and foot, but the Republic's feeble forces were unable either to extend Venetian hegemony in the peninsula or to maintain their present position in the face of Turkish strength. It was all very well to entertain the hope in Venice that, if the Hungarians took the field in force, Malatesta and Barbarigo might do great deeds in the Morea:

> I want to point out to your Highness that, if the most serene king of Hungary should set out for Constantinople with no larger force than we have in this country, we shall not be able to accomplish any more than we are doing, for Omar Beg with a thousand Turks and some peasants, considering the places he holds, is easily strong enough to prevent our even appearing [in the field]. It is my nature to express my feelings openly because, as your Highness knows, I cannot hold one opinion in my heart and express another. . . .

In Barbarigo's opinion the Venetian armada, under the command of the captain-general Jacopo Loredan, should remain in Moreote waters, and not go off to the Dardanelles (and not even to Negroponte). It could tie down many Turks, and cost the sultan men and money he might prefer to employ in Anatolia or against the Hungarians. It was thought that Matthias Corvinus might take the field in August; in Anatolia the sultan must turn his attention to the troubled affairs of Caramania and the well-known hostility of Uzun Ḥasan.[79] The Turks could not send out a fleet this year. Omar Beg's people kept spreading rumors abroad. The Venetians should not take them seriously and lose "grandissimo fructo in questa Amorea." His Highness would excuse Barbarigo if the latter spoke too frankly. He was trying to save the Venetian forces in the Morea. He wanted the Senate to send out two thousand horse and three thousand foot next February, so that they might arrive in March or at the beginning of April, and "forthwith close the Hexamilion," *ad uno tracto ad serare l'Eximilia*. He needed foodstuffs and other supplies, "which are necessary, as your lordship will understand." If the Hexamilion were made secure, the Moreotes could sow and reap their crops. They would feel safe and willingly pay their taxes as in the time of Greek rule in the peninsula. It would be far better to go to this expense now than to spend and spend for nothing. The needed troops could come with the *muda* in March.[80] He wanted the recruitment not of "el ragazo," but of "el saccomano," for the latter was almost as valuable as a man-at-arms in the Morea. The *saccomani* were fast-moving "raiders," equipped with cuirass, helmet, and light arms; without them, Barbarigo was certain, the Venetians were going to get nowhere at all. If the Senate decided not to meet his requests, it would be well to find some "via honesta" to make peace with the Turks.

There were many notable persons among the Greeks and Albanians who had proved their loyalty to the Republic. They should all be treated alike, according to their merits. Some of the leaders of the *stradioti* were so poor, however, that they could not remain in the field and support their families. Barbarigo therefore requested permission to distribute a thousand ducats a year among such leaders.

---

[79] In early August, 1464, Ibrahim Beg, the Gran Caramano, had died at the castle of Cavalla (Kevele), near Konya, and his seven sons, six of them legitimate offspring of his marriage with a sister of Murad II, all quarreled among themselves for the succession. Although the situation required Mehmed's attention, it did not yet require his presence (*cf.* Babinger, *Maometto* [1957], pp. 397–99).

[80] The Venetian *muda* was a commercial convoy (the term was also used to describe the set period during which a convoy might be loaded), on which see F. C. Lane, "Fleets and Fairs: The Functions of the Venetian Muda," in *Studi in onore di Armando Sapori*, I (Milan, 1957), 651–63, reprinted in *Venice and History*, Baltimore, 1966, pp. 128–41.

Venice would save twice this sum in the long run. The enrollment of more *stradioti* would become easier, and even those who had been obliged to serve the Turks would be drawn back to their allegiance to S. Mark.[81]

Omar Beg had found it easy to confine Malatesta's forces to Venetian fortresses and outposts. Malatesta complained unendingly of the lack of money, good troops, and supplies. If Loredan would stay in Moreote waters with his thirty galleys, Omar Beg's forces would be immobilized, and could not maintain themselves by raids into Venetian territories. The Morea was becoming a scene of ruined and abandoned villages. Grapes, figs, and olives could not be gathered in safety when the time should come to do so. In late June Barbarigo had had a serious riot on his hands; three hundred infantry, *chi morivano da fame*, demanded money. He promised to pay them something the next day. One of the condottieri, Francesco da Tiano, told Barbarigo and Malatesta "that his footsoldiers and men-at-arms were at his throat every day, saying that they were dying of hunger, and that in eight months they had had only two and one-half months' pay. . . ." Francesco and his company wanted to be paid every month if they were to serve Venice; otherwise they should be given their discharge (*licentia*), "and they would go with God." They had conquered Mantineia and saved Maina for Venice. They had got no money for it, "ma pur una bona letera nè da la illustrissima Signoria vostra nè da gentilhomo da Veniexia," not even a word of thanks.

As for Francesco da Tiano, a well-known condottiere, he had had his fill of Venice and the Morea. He had lost his son and his brother. Now he was alone. His company was wasted; his money was gone. He was getting old, and had neither lands nor possessions. He had done his best, and had been ill rewarded for his efforts. He had sent his notary (*cancellier*) to Venice to ask for his discharge, "et non voleva più star in questo paexe." In two whole years he had not received even "una minima subvention" to maintain his company. He had watched them sell their arms, their boots, their lives in vain. He had watched them die of hunger. He had had enough.[82]

Sigismondo Malatesta wanted to accomplish something in the Morea, but nothing could be done with the starveling troops at his command. He could depend on Barbarigo to send another appeal to Venice for men and money, "perche questo signore he rimasto solo con Francesco da Othiano, ne altri ce che sia da conto."[83] Of all Sigismondo's sub-commanders or military contractors in the Morea only Francesco da Tiano was "of any account." Finally the well-fed nobles who gathered in the senate chamber in the doge's palace in Venice decided to do something for Francesco, and about the end of the first week of August (1465) Barbarigo could tell Francesco that the Senate had voted him an annuity of 300 ducats for life, "unde grandemente ringratiava quella [i.e., Celsitudine vostra, the doge, in whose name the Senate's letter was sent] di tanto beneficio. . . ."[84] But what of the poor Greeks and Albanians? how were they faring when Francesco's company was so badly off? There were many Greeks and Albanians who claimed to have served Venice for three years without receiving their due, *et in parte dixe el vero*. Barbarigo gave them the usual assurance "that in conquering this country, as is to be hoped by the grace of God, your Highness will repay all his servitors."[85]

Occasionally some report of action relieves Barbarigo's dreary appeals to the home government. Having urged Malatesta to undertake a raid on either Mistra or Karytaina "to give some reputation to this army," Barbarigo was glad to write the doge on 8 July (1465) that at about 6:00 P.M. on the fourth "this lord set out with about five hundred horse and foot, together with about four hundred mounted stradioti." On the following day they reached Karytaina, and launched an attack upon the Turks, "and they killed about forty of them, took fifteen alive, ten pavilions [tents], 120 horses, 600 cattle, 2,000 capons, 100 sumpters, and plenty of mules, pigs, and other things belonging to the Albanians and Turks, and many persons from Karytaina, both men and women, . . . have come back here. This evening or in the morning milord will be here with all the booty."[86]

Barbarigo had occasion on 12 August (1465)

[81] Sathas, VI, no. 27, pp. 26–29, dispatch of 25 July, 1465.

[82] Sathas, VI, no. 15, pp. 15–16, dated 26 June, 1465; G. Soranzo, "Sigismondo. . . ," *Atti e memorie . . . per le provincie di Romagna*, VIII (1918), 254–55.

[83] Sathas, VI, no. 22, p. 22, lines 9–11, dated 11 July, 1465.

[84] Sathas, VI, no. 28, p. 30, lines 34 ff., dated 3 August, and no. 30, pp. 31–32, dated 10 August, 1465.

[85] Sathas, VI, no. 18, p. 18, apparently dated 6 July, 1465.

[86] Sathas, VI, no. 20, p. 20.

to write the doge that Sigismondo Malatesta had been pleased by a ducal letter, *tal humane lettere*, which had just been delivered to him. Sigismondo had expressed his gratitude, saying that he had been, was, and would continue to be the good and faithful son and servitor of the Signoria. He was very worried, however, because he had heard from Venice that his brother Domenico Malatesta Novello was close to death, and that there was no hope of his recovery. Sigismondo feared that Pius II's successor, Pope Paul II, would try to seize Cesena while he was fighting the Turks. He asked Barbarigo to write the doge immediately, requesting that firm steps be taken to prevent any such move on Paul's part. The loss of the city would be the "total ruin" of his house. The Malatesti had held Cesena (he said) for more than three hundred years. Barbarigo added his own plea to Sigismondo's, recalling the long loyalty of the Malatesti to Venice "et boni portamenti de questo signore a questa impresa."

Sigismondo wanted to request leave to go to Italy for the winter season, so that he could the more fully inform the Signoria (he said) of the pressing needs of the Venetian expeditionary force in the Morea. He would return in the spring. He was naturally thinking of Cesena. Barbarigo told him that the Senate would not grant the *licentia*, and that it would be a grave impropriety to ask for it. If Sigismondo should leave the Morea, everyone would believe for certain that "this enterprise was to be abandoned," and everything would be turned upside down, *che tuto anderia sottosopra*. Sigismondo said he would accept Barbarigo's counsel, and would send one of his chief retainers, Ser Marioto, to attend to matters in Venice. Marioto was thus going for two reasons, *una per el facto de Cesena, l'altra per le cosse necessarie a questa imprexa*, and on both scores Barbarigo recommended him most warmly to the doge and Senate.[87]

If Sigismondo feared a papal move against Cesena by Paul II, who did not dislike him, one can imagine with what anxiety he had begun the Moreote campaign in the reign of Pius II, who loathed him. The Malatesti were indeed in danger of losing Cesena, however, and during a period when Sigismondo was ill (and rumor had it that he had died), his disinherited son Roberto, Paul II, and Venice all coveted the possessions of the family, Rimini itself as well as Cesena. Malatesta Novello died on 20 November (1465). Roberto occupied Cesena briefly, and then had to surrender it to Paul II's troops in return for territorial concessions of less importance. Paul then laid claim to Rimini. It is small wonder that Sigismondo wanted to return home.[88]

As time went on, Barbarigo decided that it would be too costly to man the Hexamilion. In dispatches of 10 and 25 November (1465) and the following 22 January he urged the fortification of Glarentza, which may never have been restored from the ruins to which Constantine Dragases had reduced it thirty-five years before. Glarentza would supply a center for attacks upon the Turks from Patras to Kalamata. Barbarigo reported also that by 25 November, after six months in the Morea, he had received only 18,000 ducats to cover the manifold charges which his office obliged him to meet.[89] Indeed the constant and crippling shortage of funds, as he complained in letter after letter, had filled his woebegone troops with disaffection and moved them every day to desertion. As for Sigismondo Malatesta, Barbarigo's instructions had been to co-operate with him, which he had tried to do. When from early November, however, Venetian intelligence had reported that there were few Turkish forces in the Morea, and one could go anywhere with a hundred horse,[90] Barbarigo felt there was no longer any

[87] Sathas, VI, no. 31, pp. 32–33, dated 12 August, 1465, and see nos. 42, 62, pp. 43, 65–66.

[88] Soranzo, "Sigismondo . . . ," *Atti e memorie . . . per le provincie di Romagna*, VIII (1918), 239–52, 258, 264, 270–77, and note Ian Robertson, "The Return of Cesena to the Direct Dominion of the Church after the Death of Malatesta Novello," *Studi romagnoli*, XVI (1965), 123–61. When Sigismondo died in October, 1468, he left Rimini to his wife Isotta degli Atti and their son Sallustio. Roberto gained control of the city, however, with the help of the triple alliance of Milan, Florence, and Naples. He eliminated Isotta and Sallustio in 1470, and fought for and received papal recognition as hereditary vicar of Rimini in 1473. A decade of regency followed Roberto's death (in September, 1482), after which his profligate son Pandolfo succeeded to the vicariate until Cesare Borgia occupied Rimini in the fall of 1500 (see P. J. Jones, "The End of Malatesta Rule in Rimini," in E. F. Jacob, ed., *Italian Renaissance Studies*, London, 1960, pp. 217–55, esp. pp. 244 ff.). Although this did not extinguish Malatesta claims to Rimini, it ended their effective rule.

[89] Sathas, VI, nos. 59, 62, 75, pp. 63, 66–67, 79–80.

[90] Sathas, VI, no. 57, p. 61, lines 6–7, dispatch dated at Modon on 8 November, 1465: ". . . in questo paise non se trovano al presente Turchi, se puol andar per tuto con cento cavalli. . . ." In Venice the failure of the Moreote campaign was being blamed on Malatesta (Soranzo, "Sigismondo," *Atti e memorie*, VIII, 261–62).

excuse for Malatesta's inaction. But he remained inactive; he wanted to return home to attend to his affairs; and Barbarigo was glad when the condottiere finally sailed for Italy. With the advent of spring in 1466, Barbarigo learned of Vettore Capello's appointment as captain-general to replace Jacopo Loredan, and rejoiced in the change being made in the eastern naval command. He would have been as glad as Malatesta to leave. A burden would have been lifted from his tired shoulders (as he had written from Modon on 21 October, 1465), "because I do not intend that it should ever be said in the future that in the time of Jacopo Barbarigo the Morea was lost—or Modon and Coron."[91] Destiny was to spare him that ignominy. The Morea was not to fall in his time; but, as we shall see in the next chapter, he was to fall defending the Morea.

When the Turco-Venetian war began, Pius II looked upon it as part of the crusade which he had preached at Mantua. In following the first stage of the war, which was to last a long time (1463–1479), we have got beyond the reign of Pius, to which we must now return. We must also note some of the people at the Curia Romana, whose literary talents were employed as publicists for the crusade. They drafted the crusading bulls and briefs, and some of them were presumably responsible for various poems and prophecies relating to the Turks. They were all admirers of Greek literature, even when they did not know the language, and like Aeneas Sylvius himself most of them were doubtless stunned by the fall of Constantinople.

The humanists had had close relations with the Byzantine world from the end of the preceding century when in 1395 Jacopo Angeli da Scarperia had gone to Constantinople to study Greek. He had been followed in later years by other students and seekers after Greek manuscripts—Guarino da Verona, who spent five years in the East (1405–1410); Giovanni Aurispa, who made two notable trips to Constantinople, bringing back some two hundred and fifty Greek manuscripts; and Francesco Filelfo, who lived and studied in Constantinople for seven years (1420–1427), coming back to Italy with a Greek wife and with manuscripts of some forty different Greek authors. The list could easily be expanded. Most humanists, especially when they were Greek scholars, were publicists for the crusade. For years Filelfo, for example, made speeches and wrote letters to the popes and princes urging united action against the Turks.

Fear of the Turks in fact comprised one of the few areas of agreement among the humanists. Their value as lay preachers of the crusade must not be forgotten as one considers the patronage which the popes afforded them. Humanist secretaries and abbreviators at the Curia drafted the stirring appeals which the popes addressed to Christendom. The attention which Nicholas V lavished on such scholars is well known. Calixtus III, as a benighted canonist, is alleged to have neglected them. We may observe, however, that the reappointment of Poggio Bracciolini, *civis Florentinus*, as a papal secretary was one of the first acts of Calixtus's reign, coming in fact on 20 April, 1455, the very day of his coronation.[92] If Poggio had not been a model of literary probity, he was obviously a useful man to have around. On 5 March, 1457, Calixtus appointed Andreas of Trebizond, son of the well-known George, a papal secretary, after which his name appears constantly in the registers. The letter of appointment has words of praise for George, who still held a secretarial post.[93] If humanist expectations of lucrative

[91] Sathas, VI, no. 52, p. 57, lines 12–13; Mompherratos, *op. cit.*, p. 42; and *cf.* Malipiero, *Annali veneti*, in *Archivio storico italiano*, VII-1 (1843), 37: "A' 9 de fevrer [1466] è stà fatto capitanio general Vettor Capello in luogho de Giacomo Loredan. A' 20 d'avril, Vettor Capello ha tolto l'armada per consegnada, e dopo visitati i luoghi della Signoria, è andà con 25 galie in golfo de Salonichi. . . ." Capello's commission, issued in the name of the Doge Cristoforo Moro, is dated 25 April, 1466 (Sen. Secreta, Reg. 22, fols. 152^v–153^v [154^v–155^v]). Loredan had been seeking release from the captaincy-general for months (*ibid.*, fol. 116^r [119^r], motion put to the Senate on 13 September, 1465): "Quoniam nobilis vir Jacobus Lauredano capitaneus generalis maris pluribus litteris suis maxima instantia postulat quod attenta etate sua et conditione persone, que non sine manifesto suo periculo hac hyeme stare posset foris, dignemur sibi de successore providere, vadit pars quod . . . eligi debeat unus capitaneus generalis maris loco prefati Ser Jacobi . . . ," but after two votes in the Senate the motion had been defeated *de parte* 64, *de non* 74, *non synceri* 9.

[92] Arch. Segr. Vaticano, Reg. Vat. 465, fol. 43, "datum Rome apud Sanctum Petrum, anno etc., MCCCCLV, duodecimo Kal. Maii, pontif. nostri anno primo." The document commends Poggio, "qui annis ut asseris amplius quadraginta dicte [Apostolice] Sedis secretarius fuisti in nostris et Romane ecclesie obsequiis exercendis" (fol. 43^v).

[93] Reg. Vat. 465, fols. 245^v–246^r, by mod. stamped enumeration: ". . . ut te favoribus apostolicis prosequamur, hinc est quod nos te, qui etiam litterarum apostolicarum scriptor et familiaris noster existis, premissorum obsequiorum et virtutum tuarum intuitu specialibus favoribus prosequi cupientes sperantesque quod tu per vestigia dilecti filii

employment at the Curia were sometimes disappointed, one reason was doubtless that there were fewer positions available than applicants seeking them. Other persons than humanists and their sons inevitably received a good many of the appointments to papal notariates and secretarial positions. Thus we find that on 25 August, 1457, Calixtus appointed James, the illegitimate son of King John II of Cyprus, a papal notary.[94] This appointment had less to do with the crusade than with Cypriote politics. John had sought confirmation of his son as archbishop of Nicosia, to which the papacy never consented, although for some time James enjoyed the revenues of the see. A few years later James [II] became the king of Cyprus (1464–1473) by ousting his half-sister Charlotte. Pius II supported Charlotte's legitimist claims, but Paul II recognized James, who in 1468 was to marry Caterina Corner (Cornaro), from whom the island kingdom was to pass to Venice in 1489.[95]

Pius II is often accused of neglecting the humanists, although he was a generous patron of architects, builders, painters, sculptors, goldsmiths, copyists, miniaturists, embroiderers, and other skilled artisans. He was undoubtedly an extreme nepotist, as the three volumes of his *Officia* in the Vatican Archives (Regg. Vatt. 515–517) amply attest, and it has been said that "his predilection for Corsignano [Pienza, his birthplace] was the corollary of his nepotism."[96] To be sure, Pius always remained a good humanist, self-conscious and anxious for distinction. But neither the man nor his career as pope can be described by a simple formula. If he was a "humanist," he was also a good deal more. His untiring quest for adventure, fondness for travel, and hunger for knowledge (all so manifest in the *Commentarii*) imposed marked limits upon his introspectiveness. He devoted little time to exploring his own ego. Desire for recognition gradually gave way before his determination to press the Turkish war. Election to the papacy had obviously won him a secure niche in the temple of fame. He was resolved to show himself equal to the great challenge of his time. Of course in his mind's eye he could always cast himself in the role of the Christian champion against the infidel, but he was well aware that his failure as a crusader would add little luster to his name. He knew that historians award the palm to those who succeed, not to those who fail. The Turkish peril is the main theme of the *Commentarii*, just as it was the major preoccupation of his reign.[97]

Whether Pius II really neglected the humanists of his day remains unclear. Pastor has wisely cautioned us that "the last word on Pius II's attitude towards the literati still cannot be said: for this the pertinent manuscript material has not yet been sufficiently explored."[98] Pius wanted harmony in the Curia. His appointment of humanists was limited to those who pursued the so-called curial humanism, which eschewed the

---

Magistri Georgii Trapezuntii, genitoris tui, qui etiam secretarius et familiaris noster existit quique tam nostro quam nonnullorum predecessorum nostrorum Romanorum pontificum temporibus officium secretariatus fideliter, diligenter, et laudabiliter exercuit et exercet . . ." ("datum Rome apud Sanctum Petrum, anno etc., MCCCCLVI, tertio nonas Martii, anno secundo"). The letter is dated in the year of the Incarnation, which begins on 25 March. George of Trebizond, however, "un cervello poco equilibrato," came to fancy himself a Turcophil (and an admirer of Mehmed II), which landed him in the Castel S. Angelo for a while (Angelo Mercati, "Le Due Lettere di Giorgio da Trebisonda a Maometto II," *Orientalia Christiana periodica*, IX [1943], 65–99).

Passing far beyond the western hopes for the union of the Churches, George of Trebizond had advocated the amalgam of Christianity and Islam, believing in the likelihood of Mehmed II's coming dominance over Europe. His contemporary Jacopo de' Languschi in fact attributed to Mehmed II the idea of world unity under his own rule (as given in the chronicle of Zorzo Dolfin, *Assedio e presa di Costantinopoli*, ed. G. M. Thomas, in *Sitzungsber. d.k. bayer. Akad. d. Wissen. zu München*, II [1868], 7): ". . . uno dice dover esser lo imperio del mundo, una fide, una monarchia." There were no few westerners who, like George of Trebizond, were willing to serve the Turk as well as the Holy See. In July, 1453, in his tract *On the Truth of the Christian Faith*, George had written Mehmed, "Θαυμάζω τὸ κράτος καὶ τὴν ἐξουσίαν, ἣν ἔδωκέ σοι ὁ Θεός" (see Agostino Pertusi, *La Caduta di Costantinopoli*, II: *L'Eco nel mondo*, pp. 68–79).

[94] Reg. Vat. 465, fol. 286 ("datum Rome apud Sanctum Petrum, anno etc., MCCCCLVII, octavo Kal. Septembris, pontif. nostri anno tertio," with a letter of the same date to the bishop of Nicosia): "Dilecto filio Magistro Jacobo clerico, carissimi in Christo filii nostri Johannis Cypri regis illustris nato, notario nostro salutem . . . te in nostrum et apostolice sedis notarium auctoritate apostolica recipimus et aliorum nostrorum et dicte sedis notariorum consortio favorabiliter aggregamur. . . ."

[95] Geo. Hill, *Hist. of Cyprus*, III (1948), chaps. IX–XII, esp. pp. 530–31, 536 ff., 550 ff., 592–94, 620 ff., 631 ff.; Jean Richard, "Chypre du protectorat à la domination vénitienne," in *Venezia e il Levante fino al secolo XV*, Florence, 1973, pp. 657–77, esp. 668 ff.

[96] E. Müntz, *Les Arts à la cour des papes*, I (Paris, 1878), 228.

[97] *Cf.* Gerhart Bürck, *Selbstdarstellung u. Personenbildnis bei Enea Silvio Piccolomini*, Basel and Stuttgart, 1956, esp. pp. 1–4, 29–40, 53–67 (Basler Beiträge zur Geschichtswissenschaft, vol. 56).

[98] Pastor, *Gesch. d. Päpste*, II (repr. 1955), 30.

avowal of republicanism and the defense of liberty. In this he resembled both his predecessors and his successors, and it must be acknowledged that in Pius's dealings with the Sienese government, for example, as in almost every political opinion expressed in the *Commentarii*, he reveals a strongly aristocratic, anti-democratic mentality. No commune beset by civil disturbance could make its contribution to the crusade. Papal secretaries with a humanist bent had long chosen safe subjects for their literary compositions. They extolled the Christian *contemptus mundi*, and discussed among themselves the place of pleasure in the virtuous life. They discoursed upon the evils of avarice, the pitfalls of ambition, and the advantages of a poverty they were anxious to avoid. Privy to the *secreta papae*, they knew the dangers of involvement in the strife-torn politics of the period. Like their successors in the Curia today most of them tried to avoid public expressions of political opinion. From reign to reign papal patronage changed more than papal politics, and secretaries were as easily dismissed as appointed. Competition for office was keen and sometimes unscrupulous. Offices might be purchased, and often were, the salary being an annuity until death or dismissal.

Fear and frustration led the humanist secretaries into contention. Sometimes they attacked one another's moral character as well as Latin style, dipping their pens into the black ink of invective. On the whole, however, they performed their duties well although the archival registers were less well kept at the Vatican and in the Castel S. Angelo than in Venice, where a stronger discipline was maintained in the chancery and other offices of state. The crusade was always a safe subject for an essay, a sermon, or an oration, and papal scriptors and secretaries were drawn to an exercise which commanded attention on all solemn occasions. For years, indeed for generations, neither the writers nor their audiences seemed to weary of these crusading preachments.

Voigt has compiled a considerable list of scholars and literati who appealed in vain to Pius II for the patronage which Nicholas V had dispensed with sometimes uncritical largesse.[99] Committed to the crusade, and to costly building programs at Pienza and Siena, Pius lacked the money which Nicholas had found available for princely gifts to the humanists. Himself a writer of true talent and a man of spirit, Pius was unlikely to reward the poetic effusions of a Giannantonio Porcellio with much money or approval, while he could hardly be expected to pay tribute to the effrontery of Filelfo.[100] Nevertheless, among his early appointments we find that of the famous Giannozzo Manetti as a papal secretary on 27 November, 1458.[101] A month before this he had appointed another humanist, Lodrisio Crivelli of Milan, as a papal secretary (17 October).[102] Pius's cousin Gregorio Lolli, the son of his aunt Bartolommea, did not receive an appointment until 28 September, 1459.[103] Lolli remained close to the pope

[99] Voigt, *Enea Silvio*, III, 606–19; and *cf.* Müntz, *Les Arts*, I, 224; Pastor, *Hist. Popes*, III, 37–41,revised in *Gesch. d. Päpste*, II, 28–33. Voigt, *loc. cit.*, does note, however, that of the older generation of distinguished humanists only Beccadelli and Filelfo were left. There were good reasons for Pius's withholding large sums of money and patronage in various other cases.

[100] Filelfo had hailed Pius II's accession as the sunrise dispelling the darkness (Voigt, *Enea Silvio*, III, 606–7), but sent him a list of errors which had unfortunately marred one of his works, observing that, if he (the great Filelfo) were in Rome, Pius's literary reputation would be better protected. The pope replied through Ammanati that, to be sure, he was only human. Amid so many preoccupations he doubtless wrote things with which the idle might find fault, but it so happened that he was not the author of the poem in which Filelfo had found the false quantities! For the rest, Ammanati indicated that, if Filelfo lived in poverty, the pope's nephews and the Curia were not much better off; war consumed the papal revenues; and besides many poets, historians, and philosophers had been poor. Ammanati lectured Filelfo on the Christian virtues, which the old rascal was not likely to appreciate (*Epistolae Iacobi Picolomini Cardinalis Papiensis*, Milan, 1521, fol. 11). Filelfo did come to Rome, but was not welcomed very warmly, and later greeted the news of Pius's death with a poetic appeal to the muses to rejoice (Carlo de' Rosmini, *Vita di Francesco Filelfo da Tolentino*, II [Milan, 1808], 320). Shortly thereafter, however, the Sacred College learned that Francesco Sforza, duke of Milan, had imprisoned Filelfo and the latter's son Mario because of their attacks upon Pius's memory, for which gesture of filial respect for the deceased pontiff a note of thanks to Sforza was drafted in the name of the College (Arch. Segr. Vaticano, Arm. XXXIX, tom. 10, fol. 26, by original enumeration). On the career of Pius's friend and protégé Ammanati, see Giuseppe Calamari, *Il Confidente di Pio II: Card. Iacopo Ammannati-Piccolomini (1422–1479)*, 2 vols., Milan, 1932.

[101] Reg. Vat. 515, fol. 99, "datum Rome apud Sanctum Petrum, anno etc., MCCCCLVIII, quinto Kal. Decembris, pontif. nostri anno primo."

[102] Reg. Vat. 515, fol. 109, "datum Rome apud Sanctum Petrum, anno etc., MCCCCLVIII, sexto decimo Kal. Novembris, pontif. nostri anno primo." *Cf.* Voigt, *Enea Silvio*, III, 614.

[103] Reg. Vat. 515, fols. 201^{v}–202^{r}, "datum Mantue, anno etc., MCCCCLVIIII, quarto Kal. Octobris, pontif. nostri anno secundo." Gregorio Lolli de' Piccolomini of Siena, doctor of laws, was appointed a "scriptor litterarum apostolicarum."

throughout his reign, and his name figures prominently in the registers.

Pius was always the friend and admirer of the learned antiquarian Flavio Biondo of Forli, whose *Roma triumphans* he received in dedication. On 1 January, 1463, Pius appointed Gasparo, Flavio's son, as a papal secretary in the place of his beloved father, who had served the papacy for some thirty years.[104] Gasparo's name still stands in many registers; he proved to be as attentive to duty as his father had been. His handwriting can be identified from a signed note of a decade later.[105] In the meantime death had removed Giannozzo Manetti and Poggio Bracciolini from the curial service (they both died in October, 1459). On 29 March, 1464, however, Poggio's son Battista Poggio, a master of arts and a canon of Florence, received appointment as an "abbreviator of apostolic letters."[106] Three days later (on 1 April) Agostino Patrizzi (Patrizi), a Sienese, received a similar appointment.[107] Patrizzi, an old friend of the pope, his private secretary, and constant companion, formed with the humanist Jacopo Ammanati, the poet Giannantonio Campano, "Goro" Lolli, and a few others an inner circle among whom Pius lived his life from day to day. The original manuscript of Pius's *Commentarii*, now preserved in the Vatican Library (Cod. Reg. lat. 1995), is largely in Patrizzi's handwriting. No one knew better than Patrizzi and Lolli, Ammanati and Campano, Pius's dedication to the crusading ideal. They lived it with him month after month until it must have become a part of the fabric of their lives as it was of his.[108] Although some historians have found it hard to accept Pius and reject Aeneas, the crusade was not the pope's "humanistic effort to achieve immortality." The Turk was the archenemy of the faith; Pius was therefore the archenemy of the Turk. Furthermore, his support

---

[104] Reg. Vat. 516, fols. 135^v–136^r. Gasparo's appointment contains a tribute to his father ("datum Rome apud Sanctum Petrum, anno [ab incarnatione dominica] MCCCCLXII ['Florentine style'], Kal. Ianuarii, pontificatus nostri anno quinto"): "Grata familiaritatis obsequia diu nobis prestita prout prestare perseveras, necnon fidei sinceritas, morum honestas et vite integritas laudabilisque institutio in quibus per annos ante triginta sub aliquibus Romanis pontificibus, predecessoribus nostris, et demum sub nobis Romane Ecclesie servivisti promerentur ut votis tuis quantum cum deo possumus annuamus: exhibita siquidem nobis tue petitionis narratio continebat te qui in secundo anno felicis recordationis Eugenii IIII, predecessoris nostri, notarius camere nostre apostolice ab ipso creatus fuisti postquam id officium sub vicecamerario et thesaurario ac aliis officialibus camere apostolice similiter cum aliis notariis tunc temporis existentibus ultra annum unum exercueras ab eodem Eugenio IIII in suum secretarium apostolicum creatum deputatumque fuisse. . . ." *Cf.*, *ibid.*, fols. 166^v–167^v, dated at Rome on 9 June, 1463, and note Voigt, *Enea Silvio*, III, 609–10, who does not know of Gasparo's appointment on 1 January, 1463. I do not know whether or not the Tommaso Biondo di Stefano de'Rinucci ("dilecto filio Thome Blondo Stephani de Rinutiis, canonico Pistoriensi, accolito nostro salutem . . ."), who was appointed a papal acolyte and chaplain on 4 February, 1464, was a relative of the Biondi (Reg. Vat. 517, fol. 2^v). On 24 October, 1466, Paul II conferred upon Gasparo the "officium custodie et magistri registri camere apostolice" (Reg. Vat. 542, fol. 186, by mod. stamped enumeration), again with a recollection of Flavio's devotion to the papacy.

[105] Reg. Vat. 517, fol. 26^v, note dated 16 September, 1473.

[106] Reg. Vat. 516, fols. 257^r–258^r, "datum Senis, anno, etc., MCCCCLXIIII, quarto Kal. Aprilis, pontif. nostri anno sexto." Battista Poggio's appointment takes the same form as that of Patrizzi given in the following note. We may also observe here that on 10 February, 1466, Paul II appointed Battista to the "officium lectorie et taxatorie in bullaria litterarum apostolicarum" (Reg. Vat. 542, fols. 103^v–104^r, "MCCCCLXV, quarto Idus Februarii, pontificatus nostri anno II"), and on 10 January, 1468, appointed him "in capellanum nostrum et . . . Camere [Apostolice] clericum numerarium" (*ibid.*, fols. 200^v–201^r, by mod. stamped enumeration, "MCCCCLXVII, quarto Idus Ianuarii, pont. nostri anno IV").

[107] Reg. Vat. 516, fols. 258^r–259^r ("datum Senis, anno etc., MCCCCLXIIII, Kal. Aprilis, pontif. nostri anno sexto"): "Dilecto filio magistro Augustino Patritio, presbytero Senensi, litterarum apostolicarum abreviatori, cappellano secreto et familiari nostro salutem, etc. Grata familiaritatis obsequia que nobis hactenus impendisti et adhuc sollicitis studiis impendere non desistis necnon vite ac morum honestas aliaque laudabilia probitatis et virtutum merita quibus personam tuam tam familiari experientia quam etiam fidedignorum testimoniis iuvari percepimus nos inducunt ut te specialibus favoribus et gratiis prosequamur, cum itaque nuper nos ex certis arduis animum nostrum moventibus causis numerum abreviatorum litterarum apostolicarum qui preter dilectos filios abreviatores litterarum ipsarum de maiori cancellarie apostolice presidentie sive porro existentes incertus et magnus esse consueverat ad septuaginta dumtaxat computatis hiis qui in dicta [p]residentia sive porro existunt abbreviatorum numerum reduxerimus ac officium septuaginta abbreviatorum huiusmodi de novo instituerimus prout in aliis nostris inde confectis litteris plenius continetur [see this same register, fols. 201^r–203^v, for the establishment of a general staff of seventy *abbreviatores participantes*] necnon numerus ipse nondum repletus sit, sed plura adhuc loca de eisdem septuaginta vacare noscantur [then there was room for some humanists!], nos volentes te qui etiam continuus commensalis noster existis premissorum obsequiorum et meritorum tuorum intuitu favore prosequi gratioso motu proprio . . . te in earundem litterarum abreviatorem auctoritate apostolica recipimus ac officium abreviatoris huiusmodi . . . tibi conferimus. . . ."

[108] *Cf.* a letter of Campano to Ammanati, dated 15 March, 1475, in Arch. Segr. Vaticano, Arm. XXXIX, tom. 10, esp. fol. 206^v.

of the crusade is hardly to be rationalized in terms of political motivation, for although leadership of the crusade would certainly help raise the fallen prestige of the papacy, it was not likely to secure papal hegemony in Italy.

Pope Pius II's determination to go himself overseas on the crusade, come hell or high water, presents one of the nobler pictures of the Quattrocento. In early July, 1463, he had summoned a congress of the Italian powers, to which came representatives of Venice and Naples, Milan and Florence, Mantua and Modena, Siena, Bologna, and Lucca. Although Genoa, Savoy, and Montferrat sent no representatives, the duke of Burgundy did, and this was more to the point. The Burgundian mission was headed by Guillaume Filastre, the bishop of Tournai, and got a fervent reception at the Curia Romana. In a public consistory, on 22 October (1463), Pius promulgated his declaration of war against the Turks in the bull *Ezechielis prophetae*, which Goro Lolli read to the assembly. The pope reviewed the Christian setbacks in the East and the cruel advance of the Turks, and set forth to the world at large his decision to go on the expedition. Pius had heard the mutterings and murmurings of men, ". . . Quid ages in bello senex, aegrotus sacerdos? non est bellare tuum, nec potes nec debes ferire gladio. . . . Tuum est iusta bella gerentibus benedicere." He did not himself propose to shed Turkish blood, but religion was in peril:

> We shall do battle with the power of speech, not the sword. We shall aid warriors with our prayers. We shall take our stand on the tall deck of a ship or on some nearby height of land, bless our soldiers, and render the enemy accursed. . . . This we can do and this we will do to the fullness of our strength. The Lord will not despise the contrite and humble heart![109]

Determination to see the crusade get under way had come to mark almost every move and utterance of the pontiff, who a month before (on 23 September, 1463) had addressed the cardinals in a secret consistory, emphasizing that, with the achievement of peace in Italy, a great expedition against the Turks was at long last a practicable undertaking. He had said some of the things which would be published in the bull *Ezechielis prophetae*, but had also made a number of observations which he would not have wished to broadcast to the world: "The priesthood is looked down upon," he told the cardinals,

> and the clergy have an evil name. Men say we devote our time to pleasure, accumulate money, serve ambition, ride fat mules and fine horses, keep lengthening the fringes of our gowns, and go about town with fat cheeks under the red hat and broad cowl, keep dogs for hunting, squander large sums on actors and parasites, and spend nothing in defense of the faith! They do not entirely misrepresent the facts: there are many among the cardinals and other members of the Curia who do these things. If we are willing to confess the truth, the luxury and arrogance of our court are excessive. This is why we are odious to the people, so that we are not listened to when we speak the truth!

Respect for the clergy must be restored by the same means that had built the great authority of the Church: "abstinence, chastity, innocence, zeal for the faith, religious fervor, contempt for death, and desire for martyrdom have set the Roman Church over all the world."[110]

Pius believed there was no better means than the crusade to effect the moral redemption of the Curia as well as that of Christendom. Envoys were promptly dispatched to the Venetians, Hungarians, and Burgundians, upon whom Pius believed he could depend for the crusade, and also to Austria, Bavaria, and

---

[109] Raynaldus, *Ann. eccl.*, ad ann. 1463, nos. 29–40, vol. XIX (1693), pp. 131–35, the bull *Ezechielis prophetae*; *cf.* Pius II, *Comm.*, bk. XII, Engl. trans., p. 835; ed. Frankfurt, 1614, p. 344, esp. lines 3–12; Pastor, *Hist. Popes*, III, 317, 320–34, and *Gesch. d. Päpste*, II (repr. 1955), 246–47, 249–59, with numerous references to archival sources. The long bull *Ezechielis prophetae* is given in its entirety in a MS. in the Bibl. Apost. Vaticana, Cod. Reg. lat. 557, fols. 104ʳ–108ʳ ("Bulla de profectione pape in Turchos et de prerogativis eiusdem passagii"), "datum Rome apud Sanctum Petrum, anno Incarnationis dominice MCCCCLXIII, XI Kal. Novembris, pontificatus nostri anno sexto." (The quotation in the text occurs at fols. 105ʳ–105ᵛ.) I note another copy in the Miscellanea, Arm. XII, tom. 4 (=Bibl. Apost. Vaticana, Cod. Vat. lat. 12,256), fols. 55ʳ–73ʳ, by mod. stamped enumeration, and it also appears in Aeneas Sylvius Piccolomini, *Opera quae extant omnia*, Basel, 1551, repr. Frankfurt, a. M., 1967, ep. CCCCXII, pp. 914–23.

[110] J. D. Mansi, ed., *Pii II . . . orationes*, II (Lucca, 1757), 175, and *cf.* Voigt, *Enea Silvio*, III, 687–90. Although this address (inc. *Sextus agitur annus*) is reported in the 1614 Frankfurt edition of Pius's *Commentarii*, pp. 336–41, the passage relating to the cardinal and curial clergy's way of life is omitted. I have made the translation from the text in Mansi; an English version is also given in Pius II, *Comm.*, bk. XII, Engl. trans., p. 823; the passage is not to be found in Cugnoni, *Opera inedita* (1883), pp. 544 ff. Pastor, *Hist. Popes*, III, 321, note, 324, and *Gesch. d. Päpste*, II (repr. 1955), 249, note 4, 252, seems to be right in dating the address on 23 September, 1463.

Franconia; Prussia, Poland, Saxony, and the Rhineland; England, Scotland, and Scandinavia; France, the Spains, and Savoy.[111] Although the response of Europe was doubtful from the beginning, Pius persisted in his intention. The Venetians were already at war. Philip of Burgundy, who regarded recovery from a

[111] Pius II, *Comm.*, bk. XIII, Engl. trans., pp. 845–49; ed. Voigt, *Enea Silvio*, II (1862), 359–65. Francesco Sforza promised a Milanese force of 2,000 cavalry and 1,000 infantry; Borso d'Este, duke of Modena, two galleys; Lodovico Gonzaga, marquis of Mantua, whose son was a cardinal, also two galleys; the Bolognese and Sienese each promised another two galleys; and the Lucchese, one. The Florentines marked time, but Cosimo de' Medici as a private citizen offered one galley. The Genoese agreed to help. Seven cardinals promised to equip one ship each. The pope committed himself to furnish at his own expense ten galleys, four large transports, and some smaller ones, as well as a number of *fuste* (light galley-like vessels). Naples could do little, as a result of the recent Aragonese-Angevin war, but Ragusa would send two galleys; the Knights of Rhodes, three; and Scanderbeg, who had been obliged to make peace with the Turks, assured the pope that he would not fail the Christian host. *Cf.* Pastor, *Acta inedita*, I (1904), no. 178, p. 266; no. 181, p. 274. The size of the commitments of the various Italian states in Pius II's list is in approximate accord with their own annual revenues and financial position in the later fifteenth century (Adolf Gottlob, *Aus der Camera Apostolica des 15. Jahrhunderts*, Innsbruck, 1889, pp. 256–58). By Italian standards the Balkan defenders of Christendom against the Turks were very poor. Scanderbeg kept relatively small sums of money in Ragusa (Gelcich and Thallóczy, *Diplomatarium ragusanum* [1887], pp. 746–47).

Two detailed plans for the Christian fleet may be found in Arch. Segr. Vaticano, Arm. XXXIX, tom. 10, fols. 256ʳ–257ᵛ:

"Summario per larmata del mare a dare a n[ostro] s[ignore] (Pius II) galee XXV et II nave grosse oltra altre tante extraordinarie che sequiranno larmata, et de tutto el numero dele dicte armate n[ostro] s[ignore] non pagarà senon galee XII et II navi grosse con homini mille che satisfaranno al bisogno come più oltre evidenter se monstrara, etc.:/ Et primo la insula de Cypro . . . galee II;/ la insula de Rhodi . . . galee III;/ la insula de Chio . . . galee II;/ la insula de Mitilino . . . galee III;/ el Duca delarcipelago . . . galea I;/ la comunita de Ragusia . . . galee II. Summa galee XIII.

"Dechiarando le sopradicte galee XIII, i segnori de dicti lochi armaranno facilimamente, pero che la colta se metterà generalmente per le loro insule et pagesi, la quale aquesta facendo pagaranno alegramente i populi per francarse questa volta dal pericolo de'Turchi che quotidie li desfanno, et nulla spenderanno li segnori de loro borse, anzi avanzaranno, etc."

There follows a statement relating to the cost of another twelve galleys at 600 ducats a month for four months (*28,800* ducats, for which the text erroneously provides 28,000); two ships (*nave dui grosse*) with a thousand men, i.e., five hundred on each ship, at a monthly rate of three ducats a man for four months (*12,000*); and the rental of the two ships, at 400 ducats each or 800 for the two, for four months (*3,200*). Bolts for crossbows, powder for the cannon, and other things would cost *1,000* ducats. The total of the sums in italics is obviously 45,000. It is recorded in the text as 44,200 ducats.

Besides the foregoing expenses, a subsidy of *46,000* ducats was contemplated for Albania (fol. 257ᵛ):

"Per lo exercito dalbania veramente cavalli mille Italiani utili a ducati IIII el mese per homo per mesi IIII vale . . . . ducati XVI m.

"Et per fanti mille V. c. [millecinquecento] a ducati dui e mezo el mese per mesi IIII . . . . ducati XV m.

"Et per subventione ad Scandarbech, el quale ussirà acampo con homini XV m. del suo exercito . . . . ducati XV m.

"Summa ducati XLVI m."

These plans were optimistically made (fol. 257ᵛ): "Dechiarando che dicto exercito como se move ala giornata vanno acquistando lalbania et la Walachia bassa sottoposite al Turco per modo che avanti che siano gionti al confino de la Grecia saranno multiplicati in triplo oltra li crucesignati che saranno passati d'Italia et daltri pagesi, etc.: Summa summarum, ducati LXXXX m. ii c." The text thus gives a total of 90,200 ducats, but addition of the figures italicized above comes to *91,000*. The costs of the expedition could be in part met by the booty, *Deo dante*, which the galleys might take by putting various places to sack and also by taking advantage of the exchange discounts available in the Levant on Italian ducats (fol. 256ᵛ).

"Le supradicte galee XII mettendo banco in Ancona se armaranno pur de ciurme Venetiane si bene como ad Venegia, dechiarando che oltre ale sopradicte galee XXV ordinarie e navi due grosse ut supra, Venetiani ad ogni modo ne haveranno XV che tengono fora armate per conservatione de soi lochi de Levante . . ." [continued on fol. 257ᵛ]. These twenty-five galleys plus fifteen from Venice make a total of forty galleys, not counting various *fuste* and corsairs' galleys as well as the vessels of "altre nationi che sequiranno larmata . . . contra Turchi," all of which would add "another fifty sail besides the aforesaid forty galleys, and yet we do not pay for any except the twelve," the first thirteen galleys being paid for by Cyprus, Rhodes, Chios, etc., and the last-mentioned fifteen by Venice.

"Ad fare la empresa con Venetiani et darli galee Lᵗᵃ et nave X con fanti IIII m. a ducati II et mezo per homo per mesi quatro," etc. In the second plan a fleet of fifty galleys was thought essential, and since the Aegean islands and Ragusa were providing thirteen, and Venice fifteen (making a total of twenty-eight), it would be necessary to find the funds for twenty-two: "Resta fino alla summa de Lᵗᵃ galee XXII se hanno a pagare." Twenty-two galleys, at 600 ducats a month each, would cost *52,800* ducats, which figure is given in the text. Ten ships with 4,000 infantry, not counting the ship rental (*nave X con fanti IIII m., non pagando el corpo dele navi . . .*), at two and one-half ducats a man for four months, would cost *40,000* ducats, the figure given in the text. Six hundred mariners, at four ducats a man for four months, would cost *9,600* ducats, which is also the figure given in the text. Adding the *46,000* ducats' subsidy for Albania, as in the first plan, we reach an overall total of 148,400. In the text, however, it appears as "summa summarum duc. CLXVIII m., IIII c.," i.e., 168,400, the numeral X (I assume) having been placed after rather than before the L. At least 140,000 ducats are anticipated to meet these costs —100,000 from the Venetians, 30,000 from the tithe being levied on ecclesiastical benefices, and 10,000 from the assessment (*per la colletta*) on the Jews (fols. 256ᵛ–257ʳ). This text being, alas, one of a number which I transcribed before discovering that they had already been published, I have reduced my quotations to the most important excerpts. The full text may be found in Enrico Carusi, strange illness as a warning from heaven and as an opportunity to fulfill his crusader's vow, assured the Curia he would delay no longer.[112] The pope, the doge, and the duke were all advanced in years and infirm, which fact doubtless caused comment both in the western chanceries and in the East. When Sultan Mehmed II learned of the papal decree of October, 1463, he is alleged to have said that he would spare the poor old men the trouble of a long voyage by taking the field first and seeking them out in their own homes: "There, if they will, they shall contend with me about empire."[113] It had been the Venetian view for some time that such a contest was inevitable. A few months before (on 28 June, 1463), the Senate had written King Alfonso V of Portugal in unanimous agreement that their "ghastly enemy, the Turk, has driven himself to such an extraordinary pitch of arrogance and lust for power that almost the whole world seems not to be containing him!"[114]

The Turk and the crusade filled Italian diplomatic correspondence during the busy winter of 1463–1464. The Italian states were much concerned about money and the balance of power in the peninsula. A letter of the Milanese envoys at Rome, Otto del Carretto and Agostino de' Rossi, to Francesco Sforza makes devastatingly clear the difficulty, perhaps the impossibility, of organizing a crusade against the Turks. The problem was principally that of the general antipathy to Venice, which alone in the eyes of contemporaries stood to profit from a Christian victory in the East.[115] This was not an object

"Preventivi di spese per la spedizione contro il Turco al tempo di Pio II," *Archivio Muratoriano*, XIII (1913), 273–79, esp. pp. 278–79, where Carusi has, however, attempted no analysis of the financial vagaries. Had he done so, I am sure that he would have bettered my effort.

[112] Pius II, *Comm.*, bk. XII, Engl. trans., pp. 793, 805, 809–11; ed. Frankfurt, 1614, pp. 323, lines 28 ff.; 329–30, and 331–33. For the illness of Philip, *cf.* Pastor, *Acta inedita*, I, no. 142, p. 185, letter of Cardinal Gonzaga to his father, dated at Tivoli, 1 July, 1463. Actually, of course, the Burgundians found serious reasons for delay, and Philip never embarked on the crusade (*Comm.*, bk. XIII, pp. 852–56; ed. Voigt, *Enea Silvio*, II, 369–73).

After Pius's death, however, Philip apparently continued to think of an eastern expedition in which he quite naturally wished to associate the Hospitallers on the island of Rhodes, to whom in 1465 he gave 10,000 *écus d'or*. The Grand Master Pedro Ramón Zacosta promptly expended the money on Fort S. Nicholas, which stands just north of the walled town on an ancient mole, the site on which medieval tradition and modern scholarship have placed the ancient Colossus of Rhodes (Archives of the Order at Malta [abbreviated elsewhere as AOM], *Libri Bullarum [1465–1466]*, fol. 160, published by Albert Gabriel, *La Cité de Rhodes*, I [Paris, 1921], 144–45, doc. dated at Rhodes on 20 June, 1465). Zacosta expected the tower and bulwark of the fort to be completed within two years. *Cf.* also Gabriel, I, 79–87.

[113] Pius II, *Comm.*, bk. XIII, Engl. trans., p. 849; ed. Voigt, *Enea Silvio*, II, 865, lines 6–11.

[114] Arch. di Stato di Venezia, Sen. Secreta, Reg. 21, fol. 164ʳ, published in Ljubić, *Listine*, X (1891), 258: "Exercuit in tantam insolentiam tantamque dominandi libidinem immanissimus hostis Turcus ut totus pene orbis eum non capere videatur. . . ."

[115] Pastor, *Acta inedita*, I, no. 148, pp. 188–93, dated 24 September, 1463: Pius II was seriously intent on the crusade, and was now bound to continue in the project since he had apparently secured Philip of Burgundy's commitment thereto: "Noy consideramo la Santità Sua molto ardente a questa impresa, sì per l'officio suo, sì perchè già havea fatta tal promessa a lo illustre duca de Borgogna, che non era possibile a Sua Santità per alcun rispetto desistere da quella" (*ibid.*, p. 189). Francesco Sforza's hostility to Venice prevented his supporting the crusade, which was forcing the pope into the hands of the Republic, whose success in the war would inevitably mean an enhancement of power in Italy. It was obvious that the duke of Burgundy and his western allies would not seek to acquire islands in the Aegean or lands in Greece and the Balkans: ". . . et essendosi già la Santità de Nostro Signore intesa con Venetiani e datosi a loro, se ben volessemo poy noy far altre intelligentie circa questo fatto, non potria Sua Beatitudine farlo e tutta la gloria saria de Venetiani et cossi tutto il guadagno e conquisto saria loro, perchè nè il duca de Borgogna nè altri signori ultramontani cerchaveno d'aquistar ysole nè provintie in oriente e ne seguirebe tuto il contrario de quello noy cerchamo; per la qual cosa a noy pareva de haver ben gran riguardo a non desperare Sua Santità de nostri presidii [!], si che se precipitasse in man de Venetiani . . . ," etc.

The Milanese plan, then, was to deceive the pope into the belief that Sforza would assist the crusade (as he had no intention of doing) in order to retain influence at the Curia and be in a better position to frustrate Venetian ambition. The ambassadors outlined a number of obstacles in the way of financing the expedition, and came to the question of who would lead it. Here they believed the interests of Burgundy and Venice came happily into conflict: "Poy se vegnerà ad intender chi sia il superior de lo exercito et non credemo ch'el duca de Borgogna vogli star sotto il capitaneo de Venetiani nec contrario. Poy circa l'aquisto se farà, nam contribuendo altre potentie in digna quantità più che Venetiani, s'è già ragionato, maxime per questi ambasiatori de Borgogna che ogni cosa, che se acquistarà, se aquisti a nome de Christo sotto il vexillo de la croce de Christo, per lo qual si fa la guerra, e lo vicario de Christo habi ad haver tal aquisto in suo arbitrio et ordinare quello li parà ragionevole e più expediente per la conservatione et augmento de la fede christiana; la qual cosa credemo Venetiani non consentirano e potria esser cagione, . . . vero de confunder et impedire questa impresa . . . ," etc. (*ibid.*, pp. 190–91).

The idea of papal dominion over territories conquered from the Turks would be certain to appeal to Pius II, who (as the ambassadors note) was not too partial to the Venetians (as a half-dozen extensive passages in the *Commentarii* make amply clear), and so another impediment was found to Venetian progress, "et così non hariano tutto il guadagno. . . !" An experienced diplomat, however, Pius was fully a match for the urbane sharpsters with whom he was dealing. In a letter of 16 November to Francesco Sforza the envoys defended toward which Milan and Florence could work with any satisfaction. There was widespread fear that the wealthier Italian states were going to be asked to pay a large proportion of the costs. The Florentine Signoria, for example, complained to its envoy in Rome that, while the Hungarians, Germans, and other nations bordering on Turkish territories lacked funds themselves, they obviously believed that there was an inexhaustible treasury in Italy.[116] When Pius II asked the Sienese representative at the Curia, Leonardo de' Benvoglienti, whether he had yet received his government's response to the request for the crusading tax of the thirtieth (levied on the income of the laity), he replied that he had not, doubtless because of the difficulty of holding meetings of the council with a number of the citizens absent from Siena owing to fear of the plague. In the course of their conversation, Pius told him: "We do not want to touch the money. Collect it yourselves and spend it on whatever shall seem to the citizenry most effective against the Turks, either on galleys or on something else as you choose!"[117]

The Mantuan ambassador, Giacomo d'Arezzo, wrote the Marquis Lodovico II Gonzaga of a papal audience held for cardinals and resident ambassadors in Rome on 6 October, at which Pius outlined the half-dozen prime requisites for launching a successful war against the Turks —recognition of the enterprise as a crusade, election of a single commander, choice of a definite time and place of assembly, adequate financing, transport, and supplies, and definite rates of monetary exchange. When, however, Pius asked the ambassadors the replies of their governments to the request for the thirtieth,

> only the Lucchese ambassador answered that he had had the reply, and that his community was willing to pay it freely and of good will: likewise the Bolognese ambassador spoke, saying that, although he had not got the reply, his Holiness being able to command the Bolognesi as his subjects, he did not doubt that the request would be obeyed. All the others replied that, in brief, they expected the answer. . . .[118]

So it went week after week.

On 25 January, 1464, the Milanese ambassador, del Carretto, had an audience with the pope, who chided him with Francesco Sforza's delay in rendering the promised assistance to the crusade while, in view of the amicable relations between the pope and the duke of Milan, the latter should have been the first to help and to set a good example to the others. The ambassador assured him of Sforza's good will and ultimate intentions,

> but that in truth things are not as easy to carry out as to think and talk about, and at this point I told him of many reasons for our difficulties, such as the famine in the land and the fear of plague, which prevents trade and commerce; likewise because of this fear of plague the entry of his Holiness's nuncio into [Milanese] territory has been delayed, and for the same reason preaching, congregations, and other things which help the expedition are being prohibited. . . .[119]

---

themselves against Sforza's charge that they had been negligent in their duty to keep him informed of the pope's affairs, but they agreed "che la Sanctità de Nostro Signore habi usata molta arte e simulation con essa [i.e., vostra Excellentia] in queste pratiche de la dieta [of Mantua]. . . !" (*ibid.*, no. 171, p. 246). Although the interests of the papacy and Milan corresponded with respect to Naples, they clashed on Venice. The reasons for this are obvious and have been noted elsewhere in this volume. On the whole it seems to me that in all the backstairs diplomacy of the years 1458–1464 Pius II, whatever his lapses of sincerity, played the straightest game, and was almost alone in his willingness to make sacrifices for eastern Christendom. On Milanese relations with the papacy, note in general Pastor, *Acta inedita*, I, nos. 154, 159–61, 163, 171 (cited above), 178–79.

The Florentines entertained the same fears of Venetian aggrandizement as a result of a successful crusade as did Francesco Sforza. They saw many difficulties in financing the crusade, and had been constantly trading with the Turks. Now they had become worried about their merchants and ships in Turkish waters (*ibid.*, nos. 150–51, 156–57, 162, 165, 169, 172, 174). They promised to "do their duty and preserve their honor when they were sure of the safety of their ships" (no. 174, p. 259). Certainly no contemporary doubted the genuineness of Venice's fear of the Turk as the Republic was slowly moving toward war with the Porte in the spring and early summer of 1463. Every successive document attests this fear (*cf.* Ljubić, *Listine*, X, 238–39, 250–52, 257–59, etc.): the concern of the other powers was obviously the predictable course of Venetian policy in the event of victory over the Turk.

[116] Pastor, *Acta inedita*, I, no. 150, p. 198, doc. dated 1 October, 1463.

[117] *Ibid.*, no. 153, p. 206, doc. dated 9 October, 1463, and *cf.* nos. 166 and 170, in which the pope says much the same thing to Benvoglienti on 12 November, now indignant that his fellow countrymen have not yet begun to collect the tithes from the clergy, the thirtieth from the laity, and the twentieth levied on the property of the Jews.

[118] *Ibid.*, no. 155, pp. 211–12, dated 10 October, 1463.

[119] Otto del Carretto to Francesco Sforza, letter dated at Rome, 25 January, 1464, in Pastor, *Acta inedita*, I, no. 179, p. 268. The pope also asked the ambassador about the rumored Milanese alliance with France against Venice, which would have been most detrimental to the crusade. Del Carretto denied knowledge of any such arrangement between Sforza and Louis XI (*ibid.*, pp. 270–71).

As a matter of fact, the plague had been serious. The reports of other ambassadors refer to it often, Benvoglienti of Siena constantly expressing fear of it on both his own account and that of his family.

The diplomatic correspondence of the last two years of Pius II's reign is instructive and even entertaining to read. The historian may follow in detail an endless variety of petty maneuvers and a long series of evasive statements all couched in terms of profoundest filial devotion to the pope and of undying dedication to the cause of Christendom against the infidel. Rarely has the diplomatic profession exercised with such adroitness the fine art of courteous prevarication or explained away the failure to keep promises with so many ingenious excuses. Jealousy, self-interest, and shortsightedness overcame religious scruple, overcame the feeling of humanity for eastern Christians oppressed by the Turks, and overcame even a concern for the common safety of the Italian states themselves. One must in justice acknowledge the awkwardness of the position in which Milan and Florence found themselves. They could only deplore the very thought of the Venetians' occupying the whole Morea, *nobilissima provincia*. And the word was current in Rome by early November, 1463, that the Turkish fortress of Corinth had fallen, and that Venice was mistress of the Morea.[120] How in fact could Milan and Florence support the crusade without increasing the power of Venice to incontestable supremacy in the peninsula and so to domination over themselves? They never discovered the answer to this question, which was, however, as great a problem for the papacy as for the rulers of Milan and Florence. But Pius II had reached a solution in his own mind, as he indicated in response to the protests of the Florentine ambassador Niccolini. Ironic as it might seem, the Venetians were doing the Lord's work, and it was marvelous in his eyes.

Pius intended to do his share of the work, too, and on 11 November, 1463, he wrote Antonio Bertini, bishop of Foligno, apostolic nuncio and collector in the Milanese duchy, that the resources of all Italy were to be taxed for the equipment of the crusading fleet and the army, and this on the advice of the cardinals and with the consent of various princes, prelates, and ambassadors, who had recently convened in Rome to consider this matter. We have already noted this congress, which had opened on 22 September, and ended a month later with the promulgation of the bull *Ezechielis prophetae*, launching the crusade. A tithe was to be collected for three years from all ecclesiastical incomes in Italy and adjacent regions, the pope informed Antonio; a thirtieth of lay incomes was to be exacted, and a twentieth of the property as well as of the incomes of the Jews, however obtained by them, including the profits of usury. In person or by deputy Antonio (like other recipients of such letters) was to collect the stated imposts from all persons and corporations owing them, whatever the dignity or lowliness of their station.[121] The still unused

[120] Benvoglienti to Siena, 5 November, 1463 (Pastor, *Acta inedita*, I, no. 166, p. 237): "Novelle altre con ci sono, se non che li Venitiani anno preso Corintho de la Morea, e puòsi hora dire interamente sieno signori de la Morea. La quale è un gran facto, nobilissima provincia, di giro 700 miglia, tutta circuita dal mare. . . ." There follows a description of the rebuilding of the Hexamilion with 128 towers, the wall being constructed partly with mortar, partly dry, and partly diked with great ramparts—"cosa stupenda a udire in sì breve tempo, che pare dell'uopere Romane antiche." Unfortunately for the Venetians the rumor that they had taken Corinth was untrue.

[121] Arch. Segr. Vaticano, Reg. Vat. 519 [*Pii II et Pauli II, S. Cruc., tom. IV*], fols. 6^v–7^r ("datum Rome apud Sanctum Petrum, anno etc., millesimo CCCCLXIII, tertio Idus Novembris, pontificatus nostri anno sexto"): "Cum pro apparatu expeditionis maritime et terrestris exercitus adversus Turchos, Christiani nominis hostes acerrimos, a quibus Christiano populo clades innumerabiles et dampna quam plurima continuo inferuntur, de consilio venerabilium fratrum nostrorum Sancte Romane Ecclesie cardinalium, accedente etiam consensu plurimorum principum et dominorum aliorumque prelatorum ac oratorum diversorum dominorum et comunitatum in hac nostra alma urbe propter hanc causam nuper convocatorum et congregatorum, unam integram decimam secundum verum valorem omnium fructuum, reddituum et proventuum quorumcumque beneficiorum ecclesiasticorum in tota Ytalia et partibus illi adiacentibus consistentium [replacing the phrase "in toto orbe terrarum," which was deleted] triennio durante ac trigesimam partem omnium fructuum et proventuum annuorum a laicalibus personis et a Iudeis vigesimam portionem omnium suorum bonorum, fructuum, reddituum et proventuum ac pecuniarum quarumcumque undecumque et quomodocumque etiam per usurariam pravitatem ad eorum manus provenientium portiones persolvendas sub certis terminis, modis et formis exigendas, levandas et colligendas imposuerimus, prout in aliis nostris super inde confectis litteris latius continetur, ea propter fraternitatem tuam de qua specialem in domino fiduciam obtinemus receptorem, collectorem et exactorem huiusmodi decime, vigesime et trigesime ac quarumcumque aliarum pecuniarum et bonorum ratione indulgentie seu cruciate conferendorum in civitatibus, terris et locis in dominio predicto consistentibus, constituentes ac deputantes per apostolica scripta committimus et mandamus quatenus adiunctis tibi aliis collectoribus iuxta formam dictarum litterarum nostrarum deputatis seu

archival sources for the history of Pius II's momentous reign are extensive. Voigt did not have access to the Vatican Archives. Indeed, no biographer of Pius has attempted a systematic search of the available material in the Vatican. Unpublished texts of importance can be chosen almost at random. The narrow proportions of this study limit the amount of detail which may be recorded in illustration of Pius's efforts to send (indeed himself to lead) the expedition which eastern Christians needed so desperately. Had the king of France or the duke of Burgundy possessed half his dedication to the "sacred work," the subsequent four centuries of Balkan history might have had a different complexion.

Such was the general cynicism of the Italian courts that the ambassadors to the Curia in Rome could hardly believe in Pius II's own sincerity. They suggested various motives to their governments to help explain his determination not only to promote the crusade at any cost but to go himself as a crusader to the East, even if it meant his virtual martyrdom to an impracticable ideal. On 12 November, 1463, the Venetian Doge Cristoforo Moro wrote Pius of how great a boon the papal resolution to go on the crusade and the inspired legation of Cardinal Bessarion had been to the Republic as the hideous Turk thirsted after the slaughter of Christians. In an unctuous tone the doge assured the pope that he would go too, although his health was far from robust and his age was advanced.[122] But one can easily read between the lines of the doge's letter. He really did not expect Pius to go. However, the Sienese ambassador, Leonardo de' Benvoglienti, who watched Pius struggle month after month, weighed down by ill health and the most painful attacks of gout, assessed him differently. Writing to the Sienese government on the same date (12 November, 1463), trying to get the pope's own native city to levy and collect the crusading imposts, Benvoglienti paid a long tribute to Pius: "I truly believe that God has sent this holy pontiff for the safety of His Christian people, deserted by all other Christian princes in such a great scourge as this fearful drive of the Turks, who have already occupied one realm after another in a brief time, and have converted Christians by force into in-

---

deputandis ad civitates, terras et loca huiusmodi personaliter accedas atque ipsam decimam integram secundum verum valorem fructuum ab omnibus et singulis ecclesiis, monasteriis, hospitalibus, cenobiis et aliis piis locis ecclesiasticis secularibus et quorumcumque ordinum regularibus virorum et mulierum eorumque prelatis, capitulis, conventibus, collegiis, plebanis, rectoribus, canonicis aliisque ecclesiasticis personis cuiuscumque status, gradus, ordinis et preheminentie aut conditionis existant etiam si patriarchali, archiepiscopali, episcopali, abbatiali aut quavis alia prefulgeant dignitate etiam sub quavis verborum forma exemptis et non exemptis ac insuper trigesimam a laicalibus personis utriusque sexus ac a Iudeis vigesimam iuxta earumdem litterarum formam petere, exigere, levare et colligere cures . . ." etc., etc. *Cf.*, *ibid.*, fols. 23^{v}–24^{v}, doc. dated 3 February, 1464.

There are many bulls relating to the *decima*, *tricesima*, and *Iudeorum vicesima* for the years 1463–1464, in this same register [Reg. Vat. 519]—fols. 5^{v}–6^{v}: ". . . Iudeis omnibus et singulis in tota Ytalia et partibus adiacentibus constitutis vigesimam partem omnium bonorum suorum, fructuum, reddituum et proventuum ac pecuniarum . . .," etc.; fols. 9^{r}–10^{v}; 16^{r}–16^{v}; 17^{r}–18^{r}: ". . . decimeque et trigesime ac vigesime in subsidium Christianorum contra immanissimos Turchos per nos indicte et aliorum subsidiorum collectoribus;" fol. 23^{r}: ". . . in suffragium expeditionis quam contra Turchos paramus unam decimam super ecclesiasticis beneficiis et trigesimam super laicorum et vigesimam super Iudeorum proventibus et redditibus . . . imposuerimus . . . ;" esp. the two documents on fols. 40^{v}–45^{r}; etc., etc.

A letter of Pius II *ad futuram rei memoriam*, dated 11 November, 1463, states: ". . . Cum itaque nuper decreverimus opitulante domino classem contra eosdem Turchos et alios Christi nominis inimicos parare et personaliter ad expeditionem huiusmodi proxima estate accedere ac propterea omnibus et singulis qui ad hoc sanctum opus personaliter se contulerint aut bellatorem seu bellatores eorum sumptibus destinaverint sive pro facultatum suarum viribus pias elemosinas erogaverint, plenam omnium peccatorum suorum remissionem sub certis modo et forma tunc expressis duxerimus concedendam prout in nostris inde confectis litteris plenius continetur . . . ," etc., "datum Rome apud Sanctum Petrum anno Incarnationis dominice MCCCCLXIII, tertio Idus Novembris, pontificatus nostri anno sexto" (Reg. Vat. 519, fol. 30^{v}).

[122] Arch. Segr. Vaticano, A. A., Arm. I–XVIII, no. 1443, fol. 44: ". . . Nec ulla ex parte deerimus: opibus, viribus ullis nostris, aut sanguini non parcemus pro Christi gloria proque salute nominis Christiani. Adhortatur nos Sanctitas vestra et admirabili sapientia sua nobis persuadet ut cum persona propria sanctam expeditionem complecti velimus et cum Beatitudine vestra et illustrissimo duce Burgundie proficisci; id etsi ratione senectutis et etatis nostre iam ingravescentis difficillimum esse noscamus, quando presertim haud robusti sed inhabiles satis sumus, in[h]erere tamen cupidi Sanctitatis vestre iussis collocantesque voluntatem et dispositionem nostram omnem in summo creatore nostro personam nostram Beatitudini vestre libero et prompto animo oblatam facimus obviam sibi accessuri et profecturi cum ea et illustrissimo duce Burgundie. Nichilque demum pretermissuri eorum omnium que vires patientur nostre ut tam sanctum, tam celeste, tamque gloriosum opus auxiliante Deo feliciter perfici possit. Datum in nostro ducali palatio die XII mensis Novembris, ind. XII, MCCCCLXIII." It may be noted that the doge promised to go on the crusade with the pope *and the duke of Burgundy*; very likely the doge still doubted the pope's true intention.

fidels. . . ." Pius had expended endless industry, care, and money on Hungary. He had been the mainstay of Matthias Corvinus, who had been harassed by internal dissension as well as by the Turkish offensive. His resolution to go on the crusade in person had buoyed up the Venetians and committed the Burgundians. Were it not for Pius the Turks would have wrought greater havoc than the Goths. Now there was hope of success in the war against the Turks, says Benvoglienti, "and I believe there has not been for long years a more glorious pontiff than this one!"[123] He was right, quite right.

At the beginning of August, 1463, Francesco Filelfo had addressed a rhetorical exhortation to the Venetians to pursue with unrelenting fervor the war against the Turks, whose successes and alleged moral degradation he described almost with relish.[124] Francesco Sforza warned the pope, however, that Mehmed II could put 300,000 men in the field and had various Moslem allies, who in their own interest could not allow the destruction of the Ottoman empire.[125] Although in time the further discouraging news came of yet another Burgundian delay, supposedly imposed this time by Louis XI of France, the pope with the support of eight cardinals continued with his plans for personal participation in the crusade, leaving Philip to face the obloquy of having failed religion in this period of direst need.[126] In the meantime, however, both the pope and the Venetians were proceeding with their plans for an offensive against the Turks, in the expectation of Philip's playing an important part in that offensive.

Acting on behalf of the Senate (on 2 March, 1464), the Doge Cristoforo Moro wrote Dr. Niccolò da Canale, the Venetian ambassador to the French court, that the road to a Christian victory lay through Hungary. A powerful army was obviously required. Such was, however, the "paupertas et depopulatio" of Matthias Corvinus's harassed kingdom that he needed money, much money,

> by means of which he can proceed in force against the enemy, and although we are caught up in the heaviest expenses, we have nonetheless offered his serene Highness 60,000 ducats for this year, a modest sum and quite insufficient for gathering an army to serve against the enemy. . . . The supreme pontiff and we are striving with might and main to get everything ready to set out personally on this expedition, and on land and sea alike we are sparing neither resources nor strength. We trust that the most illustrious lord duke of Burgundy has done and will do the same thing, so that in accord with our agreements he may also join in this venture. . . . In the

[123] Pastor, *Acta inedita*, I, no. 170, p. 243, and *cf.* nos. 173–74, 176 (the Sienese were not even sending money to their ambassador: "sto con spese et senza denari," p. 261). Benvoglienti's high opinion of Pius II was certainly shared by the Albanian humanist of the next generation, Marinus Barletius, *Historia de vita et gestis Scanderbegi*, 1st ed., Rome, *ca.* 1509, bk. XI, fol. CXLIII; ed. Zagreb, 1743, pp. 332–33.

On 22 April, 1464, the Sienese government finally provided for a salary of fifty ducats a month for the captain of the [two] galleys which the commune had promised to add to the crusading fleet (Arch. di Stato di Siena, Pergamene Bichi [vol. containing nos. 101–200], no. 138, with the old inventory no. 246): "Magnifici et potentes domini, domini priores gubernatores comunis et capitaneus populi civitatis Senarum, una cum spectabilibus vexilliferis magistris, quorum nomina inferius notata sunt [among the fourteen names is that of 'Leonardus de Benvoglientibus'] . . . decreverunt declarare et declaraverunt quod salarium sive stipendium illius spectatissimi viri qui eligetur capitaneus galearum, quas magnificum comune Senarum mictit contra perfidissimum Turchum et inimichum Christiane fidei ad requisitionem summi pontificis Pape Pii . . . , sit quinquaginta ducatorum pro quolibet mense. . . ."

In a resolution of 29 June, excoriating Mehmed II and praising their fellow citizen (*concivis*) Pius, the Sienese appointed Giovanni de' Bicchi captain of their galleys to go on the crusade with "Pius Secundus . . . qui . . . in occursum eiusdem immanis draconis furoribus ire personaliter constituit . . ." (*ibid.*, no. 140, with the old inventory no. 248). Three weeks before his death Pius wrote to Giovanni de' Bicchi (on 24 July, 1464), ". . . Pervenimus iam Deo volente ad civitatem nostram Anconitanam propter quod significandum tibi duximus adesse tempus ut ad nos venias executurus mandata dilectorum filiorum nostrorum Senensium . . ." (*ibid.*, no. 128, with the old inventory no. 232, the original brief addressed on the back, "Dilecto filio Johanni Bico, equiti Senensi").

[124] Raynaldus, *Ann. eccl.*, ad ann. 1463, nos. 52–56, vol. XIX (1693), pp. 137–38.

[125] *Ibid.*, no. 45, vol. XIX, p. 135, letter dated at Milan on 25 October, 1463.

[126] Pius II, *Comm.*, bk. XIII, Engl. trans., p. 857; ed. Voigt, *Enea Silvio*, II, 374–75; Raynaldus, *Ann. eccl.*, ad ann. 1464, nos. 3–9, vol. XIX (1693), pp. 153–55, and nos. 25–30, pp. 158–59. On French interference in Philip of Burgundy's plan to lead his troops in person, *cf.* Pastor, *Acta inedita*, I, no. 182, p. 275; no. 184, p. 278; no. 187, pp. 281–82; esp. no. 188, pp. 283–86, a Milanese report dated 27 April, 1464, concerning the instructions of Louis XI's embassy to Pius II, refusing to let his vassal Philip go to Greece on the crusade; and note also nos. 189–90, 192. Philip is said, nevertheless, to have been preparing to go with Pius on the crusade as late as June, 1464 (Richard Vaughan, *Philip the Good*, London, 1970, pp. 216–18, 368–72, and see above, note 112). Relations between Pius II and Louis XI were very bad (*cf.* the report of the Milanese ambassador, Albrico Malletta, to Francesco Sforza, dated at Paris, 26 May, 1464, Pastor, *ibid.*, no. 192). The French were constantly pressing for a council to be held at Lyon to rectify the affairs of the Church.

Morea our affairs are going well enough. All the "arm" of Maina, which forms a large part of that province, remains in fidelity and obedience to us. Our people are making war upon the Turks in that area to free Christians from the torment of the enemy. What we have just learned by letter, dated 13 February, from our government at Corfu about the conflict with the flambulari of the Morea, you will see from a copy of the letter which we send you herewith. . . .[127]

Although the Venetians preached a good crusading sermon, there can be no doubt that their prime objective was the conquest of the Morea. And if successful, they had no intention of returning any part of the peninsula to the Palaeologi. They objected to the Despot Thomas Palaeologus's being cast in the role of a crusader. On 17 May (1464) the Senate (or rather the doge) acknowledged the receipt of letters dated the seventh and the ninth from Lodovico Foscarini, their ambassador to the Curia Romana. Pius II had left Siena to go to Rome "ut inde ad statutum tempus Ancone esse possit." Among other matters of interest Foscarini had informed the Senate that the Despot Thomas was with Pius, to whom he had presented the arm of S. John and other relics. It was believed in Venice that Thomas had every intention of sailing with the papal fleet to the Morea. The Senate had considered this possibility, however, as the doge now wrote Foscarini, and if the latter had the slightest suspicion that this was likely to happen,

we want you to be sure to go as soon as possible into the presence of the Roman pontiff and, with such fitting and suitable words [of remonstrance] as shall recommend themselves to your discretion, you will tell his Holiness that, as he knows well, we have undertaken by ourselves, for a whole year now, the campaign in the Morea with colossal expense and peril to ourselves . . . to free [the Morea] from the servitude and tyranny of the enemies of our faith. Since we have heard that the Despot Thomas alleges he is going into the Morea, which could produce terrible and incongruous scandals, we want to ask his Holiness and, as his obedient sons, most faithfully to request that for the good of the undertaking he deem it important, by whatever means shall seem best . . . to his Holiness, to take steps to insure that the said despot does not set out for the Morea. . . .

The Venetians also objected strongly to Asan Zaccaria's going into the Morea, and Foscarini was so to inform the pope, who (according to Zaccaria) wanted him to accompany the crusaders. If Zaccaria went, the Senate was certain that "inconvenientia et divisiones" would inevitably be the result, and the expedition would be getting off to a bad start.[128]

Pius II took the cross on 18 June, 1464, in S. Peter's. He left Rome the same day for distant Ancona, whence he intended to go by the Adriatic to Brindisi and Lecce and thereafter into the Morea. He went up the Tiber to Otricoli (it was easier for him to travel by water),[129] and thence by land to Narni, Terni (*Interamna*), Spoleto, and Assisi, where he arrived on 3 July. Old beyond his years, very tired, and deathly ill, he traveled slowly. The heat was oppressive; sometimes the roads were crowded. He reached Fabriano on 7 July. At Loreto he dedicated a golden chalice at the stone cottage of the Virgin, and on 19 July he finally reached Ancona.[130] By this time Pius had been joined by eight cardinals. He took up residence in the episcopal palace,[131] which stood on the high bluff in the far north of the city, beside the cathedral church of S. Ciriaco, where the stone lions which Pius knew still guard the beautiful portal. From the palace he could look out upon the sparkling waters of

[127] Sen. Secreta, Reg. 22, fol. 1^r [3^r], and *cf.* the commission of the same date (2 March, 1464) issued in the doge's name to Francesco Giustinian, who was going to Hungary as a special envoy to attend the coronation of Matthias Corvinus (*ut intersis coronationi regie Maiestatis*), to whom he was to repeat the Republic's offer of 60,000 ducats [or florins], "quod offerre deberet [i.e., Giovanni Emo, the Venetian ambassador at Buda] serenissimo regi florenos LX m. nomine nostro, eunte Maiestate sua cum exercitu suo extra regnum suum contra perfidos Turcos" (*ibid.*, fols. 1^v–2^r ff., and note fols. 11^r, 17^v, 29^r).

[128] Sen. Secreta, Reg. 22, fol. 14^r, doc. dated 17 May, 1464. The Senate did not want either the Despot Thomas or Asan Zaccaria to go even to Ancona, for if they did, dissension would certainly impede the crusade: "Notissime enim sunt consuete partialitates et divisiones Grecorum et Albanensium quoniam quidam unum alii aliud sentiunt cupiuntque, sique idem despotus et Assanius proficiscerentur ad partes illas certum teneri posset quod sequerentur errores priores prioribus qui difficillimam et ut ita dixerimus quodammodo impossibilem redderent impresiam illam . . ." (*ibid.*, fol. 18^r).

[129] Acta Consistorialia, in Arch. Segr. Vaticano, Arm. XXXI, tom. 52, fol. 66^r: "Die lune XVIII Iunii anno a nativitate Domini MCCCCLXIIII sanctissimus dominus noster, dominus Pius papa II, discessit ab urbe Romana dirigens se ad Anchonam ad preparandum arma contra nephandissimum Turchum: fuit asociatus per omnes cardinales usque ad Pontem Mollem ubi intravit navem que ivit per aquam usque ad Utriculum, etc." (*cf.* Eubel, II, 34b). Pius left his nephew, Cardinal Francesco Todeschini Piccolomini, as his *legatus in urbe (loc. cit.)*.

[130] Card. Jacopo Ammanati, *Ep.* 41, in ed. Frankfurt of Pius II's *Comm.* (1614), pp. 482–85; Ammanati's own *Commentarii*, *ibid.*, pp. 354–56; Pastor, *Hist. Popes*, III, 353–57, and *Gesch. d. Päpste*, II (repr. 1955), 273–76, with refs. to other sources.

[131] *Cf.* Malipiero, *Annali veneti*, in *Archivio storico italiano*, VII–1 (1843), 29: "El papa era alozado in vescovado su'l monte. . . ."

the Adriatic and search the horizon for the first appearance of the galleys expected from Venice. Rebuilt toward the end of the last century, the episcopal palace at Ancona was destroyed during the war of 1939–1945. Its place has been taken by a small museum, on the front wall of which an inscription now recalls the site as that of Pius II's death. And so indeed it was.

The plague had come to Ancona in the midsummer of 1464 although so far few had died of it. It seemed unlikely to the Mantuan ambassador that the pope would remain in the city, but the doge of Venice was expected in fifteen or twenty days. Some companies of Catalan, Spanish, Saxon, and French crusaders were on the way or had already arrived. By now the heat was insupportable; no one liked Ancona; prices were high, and there was a greater lack of water than of wine.[132] Although the pope's health had been reported better on 10 July,[133] it was as clear to the cardinals as to his physicians that, if he persisted in his resolution to go on, death would soon overtake him. Most of the cardinals became less concerned about the crusade than about the conclave which would soon be electing his successor.

The city and the Curia were full of rumors that the Turk had pitched his camp within thirty miles of Ragusa, which he threatened to destroy if the government sent the pope the two ships it had promised him; that the territory of Ragusa was already being plundered; and that the Ragusei lacked a sufficient supply of grain to withstand a siege. Pius ordered a shipment of grain to the city, whither he proposed himself to sail with the aged Juan de Carvajal, the cardinal of S. Angelo, to break the Turkish siege. Four days later, however, word came of the Turkish withdrawal. The papal court was now awaiting the arrival of the Venetian fleet with the Doge Cristoforo Moro on board.[134] The doge was finally forced to come after at first refusing because of his age, but Vettore Capello had told his serene Highness that if he would not accompany the crusade willingly, he would be forced to do so, "because we hold more dear the well being and honor of this land than your own person!" (as we learn from Marino Sanudo). The archival records bear eloquent witness to the widespread dissatisfaction which the doge's craven conduct caused throughout the city as well as in the Senate.

Although Pius II had arrived at Ancona some two weeks before, and was waiting for the Venetian contingent to join the crusading fleet, Moro had not sailed by the beginning of August. He had boarded his galley on 30 July, however, at which time the news had been immediately dispatched to the Venetian ambassador at the Curia. And now Moro still procrastinated to the extreme annoyance of his fellow citizens, who saw themselves disgraced in the eyes of the Christian world by the pusillanimity of their doge. On 1 August, therefore, a motion was carried in the Senate to the effect

> that four nobles from the Collegio must go immediately to the most serene lord doge, and with all pertinent and appropriate words they must respectfully and effectively request his Highness in God's name to bestir himself this very night and hurry to Ancona with all possible speed, reminding his Excellency that this is the universal desire not only of this entire Council but of the whole city as well, because of the vast importance of the matter and of the peril of censure and dishonor which we all, along with his Excellency, could easily incur as a consequence of this delay.[135]

As August came on, the gloom deepened in

---

[132] Giacomo d'Arezzo to Lodovico Gonzaga, from Ancona, 21 July, 1464 (Pastor, *Acta inedita*, I, no. 198, p. 311, and *cf.* no. 200, p. 321); on two thousand Saxon crusaders, "qui se reduxerunt versus Anchonam," see the letter of the Venetian Senate to the Republic's ambassador to the Holy See, dated 21 June, 1464, in Ljubić, *Listine*, X (1891), 305.

[133] Pastor, *Acta inedita*, I, no. 196, p. 309, lines 6–7; Pius was not well, however, on the twenty-second (no. 199, p. 320); *cf.* the letter of the Venetian Senate to their ambassador, dated 23 July (1464), in Ljubić, *Listine*, X, 308.

[134] Pastor, *Acta inedita*, I, nos. 167–68, pp. 238–39, has published the decrees of the Venetian Senate and Maggior Consiglio, dated 8 and 9 November, 1463, respectively, announcing the doge's personal participation in the crusade. *Cf.*, *ibid.*, nos. 173, 175, 180, and 185–86. On the activities of Nicholas of Cusa with respect to the crusade in June and July, 1464, there is much error in the works of older scholars (J. W. Zinkeisen, F. A. Scharpff, A. Jäger, G. Uzielli, and J. Marx, and some inadequacy in Pastor, *Gesch. d. Päpste*, III [repr. 1955], 274, 286–87), for which see Erich Meuthen, *Die letzten Jahre des Nikolaus von Kues*, Cologne, 1958, pp. 122–25, and doc. 93, pp. 302–4. Cusa is said to have died on 11 August of this year (for the contemporary reports, *cf.* Meuthen, *op. cit.*, p. 305). I note, however, that the contemporary Acta Consistorialia, in Arch. Segr. Vaticano, Arm. XXXI, tom. 52, fol. 66^v, put Cusa's death on 12 August: "Obitus domini Sancti Petri in Vincula: Die XII Augusti, anno a nativitate Domini MCCCCLXIIII, pontificatus domini Pii anno VI, obiit in civitate Tudertina bone memorie dominus Nicolaus Sancti Petri in Vincula cuius anima quiescat in pace" (*cf.* Eubel, II, 34b).

[135] Sen. Secreta, Reg. 22, fol. 28^v [31^v], doc. dated 1 August, 1464. The doge still lingered a while longer, to the exasperation of the Senate (*ibid.*, fol. 29). There is no entry in the Senatus Secreta between 13 and 20 August.

Ancona. Pius was very sick; his physicians said, of a *febre fleumatica*; "and they indicate that, if he puts to sea, he will not live two days."[136] With every passing day his condition became worse. On 12 August the doge sailed into the harbor of Ancona with a dozen galleys.[137] Three days later Pius II died, and the doge set sail on the eighteenth for Istria and thence to Venice.[138] There was to be no crusade.

Pius II's death had frustrated the highest purpose of his life. It was perhaps as well for his memory and for Europe. His efforts were doomed to failure. Had he been more successful, thousands might have lost their lives in the eventual unsuccess. It was not that the so-called crusade had become a political and social anachronism. Popular support for the anti-Turkish war waxed and waned with the times; it had fallen to a low ebb in Pius's day, owing partly to the mutual enmities and conflicting interests of the princes and especially to the widespread hostility to Venice. When Aeneas Sylvius, the opportunist whom heaven had raised to the papal throne, contrasted his rich estate in the Vatican palace with the poverty of his home in Corsignano, he could not help but think of what he owed the Almighty. His dedication to the crusade appears to have been a forlorn but sincere attempt to pay that debt.

---

[136] The Milanese ambassador, Paganino, to Francesco Sforza, from Ancona on 1 August, 1464 (Pastor, *Acta inedita*, I, no. 201, p. 322, also on the Turks at Ragusa). Paganino notes the arrival in Ancona of Bessarion "con una galea ben armata." On Pius II's increasing illness, *cf.*, *ibid.*, nos. 202–3.

[137] Pastor, *Acta inedita*, I, no. 203, pp. 328–29.

[138] Ammanati, *Ep.* 41, in ed. Frankfurt of Pius II's *Comm.* (1614), pp. 487–89, and Ammanati's own *Commentarii*, *ibid.*, pp. 359–61; Pastor, *Acta inedita*, I, no. 204, p. 329; Campano, *Vita Pii II*, ed. G. C. Zimolo, in the new Muratori, *RISS*, III-3 (1964), 85–87, and Platina's life of Pius, *ibid.*, pp. 110–11; Sanudo, *Vite de'duchi*, in *RISS*, XXII (1733), cols. 1174, 1180–81 (the wife of the Doge Cristoforo Moro was Sanudo's grandfather's sister, *ibid.*, col. 1180C), but the text of the *Vite*, as printed, erroneously dates the pope's death on 13 August and the doge's return to Venice on the sixteenth; *Corpus chronicorum bononiensium*, ad ann. 1464, in the new Muratori, *RISS*, XVIII, pt. 1, vol. IV, pp. 325a, 336, and 329a, 339, with the wrong date (18 July) of Pius's arrival in Ancona; Cristoforo da Soldo, in the so-called *Istoria bresciana*, *RISS*, XXI (1732), col. 900, and ed. G. Brizzolara, in the new Muratori, *RISS*, XXI, pt. 3, p. 146; Giov. Simoneta, *Res gestae Fr. Sfortiae*, bk. xxx, in *RISS*, XXI, cols. 763–64, and ed. G. Soranzo, in the new Muratori, *RISS*, XXI, pt. 2, p. 478; *Ann. forolivienses*, ad ann. 1464, in *RISS*, XXII (1733), col. 226E; Raynaldus, *Ann. eccl.*, ad ann. 1464, nos. 38–51, vol. XIX (1693), pp. 161–65, who does not mention the arrival of the Venetian fleet just before the death of Pius II. *Cf.* Malipiero, *Annali veneti*, in *Archivio storico italiano*, VII-1 (1843), 30–31, who also says that the doge left Ancona on 16 August; Pastor, *Hist. Popes*, III, 368 ff., and *Gesch. d. Päpste*, II (repr. 1955), 284 ff.; Kretschmayr, *Gesch. v. Venedig*, II (1920, repr. 1964), 372–73; Babinger, *Maometto* (1957), pp. 351–55.

The Acta Consistorialia, Arch. Segr. Vaticano, Arm. XXXI, tom. 52, fol. 66^{v}, put the pope's death on 14 August: "Obitus domini Pii pape Secundi: Die XIIII Augusti, anno ut supra [1464, the preceding entry recording the death of Nicholas of Cusa], vigilie Assumptionis Virginis Marie tertia hora noctis [about 11:00 P.M.] . . . obiit bone memorie dominus Pius papa Secundus in civitate Anchonitana ubi venerat ad preparandum bellum navale contra Turchum, et corpus suum fuit delatum Romam et sepultum in basilica Sancti Petri" (*cf.* Eubel, II, 34b). Other sources place Pius's death on 15 August (Pastor, *Gesch. d. Päpste*, II, append., no. 64, p. 753, and note; see also below, Chapter 9, note 1). Pius was actually buried in the Cappella di S. Andrea, which he had built. His tomb and monument were later removed to the Church of S. Andrea della Valle (*cf.* above, Chapter 7, note 103), which now occupies the site of the old Palazzo Piccolomini in Rome.

Since we have seen a good deal of the militant Cardinal Lodovico Trevisan, we may note that he died on 22 March, 1465, according to the Acta Consistorialia, fol. 67^{r}: "Obitus Cardinalis Aquilegiensis et camerarii: Die Iovis XXII^{a} Martii hora tertia noctis anno 1465 pontificatus domini Pauli anno primo. Reverendissimus d. Ludovicus episcopus Albanensis et patriarcha Aquilegiensis et apostolice sedis camerarius obiit Rome et sepultus in Sancto Laurentio in Damaso, cuius anima requiescat in pace" (*cf.* Eubel, II, 34b). Contrary to the Acta, however, in 1465, the twenty-second of March fell on a Friday, not a Thursday.

9. PAUL II, VENICE, AND THE FALL OF NEGROPONTE (1464–1471)

AFTER PIUS II's death the cardinals hurried back to Rome, where they had agreed the conclave should be held to elect his successor. Although the sources contain the usual conflicting data, the cardinals apparently entered the conclave during the evening of 29 August, 1464. The conclave was held in the Chapel of S. Niccolò da Bari, under frescoes by Fra Angelico, across the long Aula Prima from the Capella Maior in the Vatican Palace. According to an election capitulation to which all the cardinals except Lodovico Trevisan subscribed, they agreed to carry on the war against the Turks to the extent that the resources of the Church would make possible. They also agreed to apply the revenues of the alum mines at Tolfa to the "inchoata expeditio in Turcos." The next day, 30 August, the handsome Pietro Barbo, a rich Venetian, a nephew of Eugenius IV, was elected pope as Paul II after a single scrutiny. From the window in the sacristy of the Chapel of S. Niccolò, behind the left wall of the apse, the joyful news was announced to a satisfied crowd which had assembled below in the Cortile del Maresciallo.[1]

Although known as the cardinal of Venice, Paul II was not well disposed toward his native city, which in May, 1459, had objected so vio-

---

[1] Acta Consistorialia, in Arch. Segr. Vaticano, Arm. XXXI, tom. 52, fol. 66v: "Dies ellectionis pape Pauli Secundi: Die penultima Augusti, anno ut supra [1464], hora terciarum unico scrutinio fuit electus in summum pontifficem reverendissimus in Christo pater dominus Petrus tituli Sancti Marchi Venetus nuncupatus et imposuit sibi nomen novum—Paulus papa Secundus." He was crowned on Sunday, 16 September (*ibid.*). In a bull dated 11 September (*tertio Id. Septembris*), 1464, Paul II notified the Marquis Lodovico II Gonzaga of Mantua—among many others—of his election by a single cast of ballots after the death of Pius II:

"Cum . . . verus Jesu Christi vicarius in sede Petri hactenus sedens in civitate nostra Anchonitana, ad quam pro expeditione in Turchos supra vires etatis et valitudinis sue personaliter se contulerat, decimo octavo [after an erasure, a correction was made, resulting in the date 15 August] Kal. Septembris ex hac peregrinatione ad celestem patriam migraverit, . . . nos una cum venerabilibus fratribus nostris . . . cardinalibus . . . Rome in palatio apostolico apud basilicam beati Petri Apostolorum principis loco ad id consueto [i.e., the Chapel of S. Niccolò da Bari] . . . conclave ingressi sumus, ubi in primo scrutinio missa Spiritus Sancti celebrata deus . . . ita . . . effecit ut . . . nos tunc tituli Sancti Marci presbyterum cardinalem ad hanc supremam honoris atque auctoritatis sedem concorditer [venerabiles fratres nostri] erexerint . . ." (Arch. di Stato di Mantova, Arch. Gonzaga, Busta 834). Paul promised to bend his efforts "maxime ad reprimendam Turchorum rabiem" (*ibid.*). Incidentally, a bull of the same date (11 September) was sent also to Lodovico's wife Barbara of Brandenburg, announcing Paul's election and again correcting the date of his predecessor's death to *decimo octavo Kal. Septembris*, 15 August, 1464 (*ibid.*).

On the background and the date of Paul's election, see Ludwig v. Pastor, *Hist. Popes*, IV (repr. 1949), 3–11, and *Gesch. d. Päpste*, II (repr. 1955), 293–99; J. B. Saegmüller, *Die Papstwahlen und die Staaten von 1447 bis 1555*, Tübingen, 1890, pp. 92–96; *cf.* Marino Sanudo, *Vite de' duchi di Venezia*, in *RISS*, XXII (Milan, 1733), col. 1181B; Raynaldus, *Ann. eccl.*, ad ann. 1464, nos. 51–56, vol. XIX (1693), pp. 165–67. According to Jacopo Ammanati, *Commentarii*, in ed. Frankfurt of Pius II's *Comm.* (1614), pp. 367, 368, 371, ". . . Et conclavi iam constituto sexto Calendas Septembris [27 August] . . . recluserunt se omnes [cardinales] ad novam electionem in anteriores Pontificiae Vaticanae aulas [the correct date, however, seems to be 29 August]. . . . Mane patres omnes . . . in cellam Beati Nicolai, quae ad dexteram primae aulae est, silentio convenere. . . . Pro pontifice habebatur Petrus [in Barborum nobili familia ortus]. . . . [The cardinals, including Paul, had agreed that:] Quisquis patrum ad pontificatum esset assumptus inchoatam expeditionem in Turcos, quantum Romanae Ecclesiae paterentur opes, continuare proventumque aluminis ad eam rem integrum adhibere. . . ."

The *cella Beati Nicolai* (possibly built in the time of Boniface VIII, 1294–1303), to which Ammanati refers, was the Chapel of S. Niccolò da Bari, which (together with the frescoes by Fra Angelico) was demolished by Paul III in 1538, when he built the present stairway leading down to the Cortile del Maresciallo. This chapel, the *capella parva S. Nicolai*, has usually been confused with the *capella parva superior* (built by Nicholas V, with the still extant and well-known frescoes by Fra Angelico)—Pastor, for example, always confused the Chapel of S. Nicholas with that of Pope Nicholas on the upper floor.

The Chapel of S. Niccolò da Bari was across the Aula Prima, as Ammanati calls it (now the Sala Regia), from the old Capella Maior, which Sixtus IV replaced with the Sistine Chapel. When the Chapel of S. Niccolò disappeared, its functions were transferred to the Cappella Paolina, which Paul III built on the south end of the Aula Prima or Sala Regia. See Franz Ehrle and Hermann Egger, *Der Vaticanische Palast in seiner Entwicklung bis zur Mitte des XV. Jahrhunderts*, Città del Vaticano, 1935, pp. 103–9, 124–25. All twelve popes from Calixtus III to Paul III (from 1455 to 1534) were elected in the Chapel of S. Niccolò da Bari (*op. cit.*, p. 126). Note also Deoclecio Redig de Campos, *I Palazzi Vaticani*, Bologna, 1967, pp. 37–41, 49–51, 127–31, and in general, Christoph L. Frommel, "Antonio da Sangallos Cappella Paolina: Ein Beitrag zur Baugeschichte des Vatikanischen Palastes," *Zeitschrift für Kunstgeschichte*, XXVII (1964), 1–42.

lently to his nomination as bishop of Padua that he had finally been forced to relinquish the see.[2] The Venetians were no fonder of him than he of them. On 5 September (1464) the Senate set about choosing an embassy of obedience of ten nobles to go to Rome to congratulate Paul upon his elevation to the apostolic throne. Several of those chosen in the first selection of names refused to go and paid the usual penalty of declination.[3] Officially, of course, the Senate chose to greet Paul's election with rejoicing, *incredibili, ut par est, gaudio et leticia affecti*.[4]

The time should have been opportune for a Venetian offensive against the Porte, for the Turks seemed to be tired of overmuch fighting, the janissaries were disaffected, and Sultan Mehmed II was mostly confined to his palace in a poor state of health through 1464–1465. Paul promptly declared his dedication to the crusade. In a brief to Marquis Lodovico Gonzaga, dated 22 September (1464), he reaffirmed his intention of continuing his predecessor's efforts against the impious Turks. He also stated that he had chosen Cardinals Guillaume d'Estouteville and Juan de Carvajal as commissioners for the crusade, with financial oversight and responsibility for the undertaking. He urged Lodovico not to let his devotion to the crusading ideal cool in the least, for nothing was more acceptable to God than the struggle against Islam.[5] This was the prevailing sentiment in the Sacred College. Under a commitment made to the wavering Doge Cristoforo Moro in late August, after Pius II's death and before Paul's election, the cardinals had sent some forty thousand ducats *de camera* to Matthias Corvinus, the king of Hungary, "pro subventione sancte expeditionis adversus impium Turcum."[6]

Toward the end of September (1464) an envoy of Uzun Ḥasan was preparing to leave Venice, where he had been for some time. Uzun Ḥasan, onetime lord of Diyār-Bakr (the classical Amida and Turkish Diyarbakîr) and prince of the Turkoman Ak-Koyunlu (White Sheep), had become the ruler of Persia. The envoy had brought letters from his master, proposing an alliance against the hated Sultan Mehmed, whose aggressiveness had caused no less dismay among his eastern enemies than among the Italians and the Hungarians. The delighted Senate made haste to speed Uzun Ḥasan's envoy on his way to Syria "in the Beirut galleys," whence he might return home and carry the Venetian acceptance of Uzun Ḥasan's proposal to catch the forces of the Ottoman sultan in a vast pincers' movement. The Senate assured Uzun Ḥasan that the new pope, *capo e principe de' Christiani*, was seeking every means of effecting the sultan's ruin.[7]

---

[2] Sanudo, *Vite*, in *RISS*, XXII, col. 1166; Pastor, *Hist. Popes*, IV, 93–98, and *Gesch. d. Päpste*, II (repr. 1955), 366–69; G. B. Picotti, *La Dieta di Mantova e la politica de'Veneziani*, Venice, 1912, p. 374. On Paul's career, see in general Giuseppe Zippel, ed., *Le Vite di Paolo II di Gaspare da Verona e Michele Canensi*, in the new Muratori, *RISS*, III, pt. 16 (Città di Castello, 1904). The third book of Gaspare da Verona's life of Paul II appears no longer to be extant. The fifth book has been recently published, with a translation, by Avery Andrews and Susan Fowler, "The 'Lost' Fifth Book of the Life of Pope Paul II by Gaspar of Verona," *Studies in the Renaissance*, XVII (1970), 7–45.

A lover of history and archaeology, collector of antiquities and ancient coins, Paul has been rescued from the pit of ignorance, obscurantism, and hostility to belles-lettres, to which Platina and the Pomponiani tried to consign him, on which see Eugène Müntz, *Les Arts à la cour des papes pendant le XVe et le XVIe siècle*, 3 vols., Paris, 1878–82, of which the second volume is devoted entirely to Paul and his pontificate; Pastor, *Hist. Popes*, IV, 36–78, and *Gesch. d. Päpste*, II (repr. 1955), 318–54; Roberto Weiss, *Un Umanista veneziano, Papa Paolo II*, Venice: Fondazione Giorgio Cini, 1958; and A. J. Dunston, "Pope Paul II and the Humanists," *Journal of Religious History*, VII (Sydney, 1972–73), 287–306.

[3] Arch. di Stato di Venezia, Sen. Secreta, Reg. 22, fol. 35^r [37^r].

[4] Sen. Secreta, Reg. 22, fols. 43^v [45^v], 44^r [46^r], 45^v–46^r [47^v–48^r], 49^r ff. [51^r ff.].

[5] Arch. di Stato di Mantova, Arch. Gonzaga, Busta 834, "datum Rome apud Sanctum Petrum sub annulo piscatoris die XXII Septembris, MCCCCLXIIII . . . ," the brief being partly destroyed.

[6] Sen. Secreta, Reg. 22, fol. 37^v [39^v], doc. dated 23 September, 1464, and note, *ibid.*, fol. 38^v [40^v].

[7] Sen. Secreta, Reg. 22, fols. 38^v–39^r [40^v–41^r], doc. dated 26 September, 1464: "Quod orator domini Usoni Cassani, qui ad presentiam dominii fuit, quam primum expediri debeat ut cum galeis Baruti ad partes Syrie se transferat et inde ad dominum suum reverti. . . . [The envoy was to be given rich gifts of scarlet and other cloths to take back to Uzun Ḥasan's court.] Domino vero Usono Cassano scribatur in hac forma . . . : Nui havemo ricevuto le sapientissime et benivole lettere de la illustrissima Signoria vostra et inteso etiam quanto abocha saviamente ha referito Mametavazach vostro secretario et ambassador de la optima dispositione e mente de la Excellentia vostra de far insieme cum nui contra l'otoman commune et accerrimo inimico, et molto ne ha piacuto intender questa opinion et mente de la vostra Celsitudine . . . , perche l'otoman per la sua superbia et ambitione non studia nè desydera altro con tuti i suo pensieri ch'a devorar et opprimer tuti i signor del mondo et specialmente i suo vicini . . . et acresser la potentia e tyrrania soa—pertanto se conviene a la vostra excellentissima signoria animosa et sapientissima in questo tempo che nui et gli altri principi christiani se ritrovamo contra de lui in guerra dal canto vostro con tuta vostra potentia prestissimamente movervi e venir a sua ruina e desfatione per propria vostra salute et de tuti altri perche

As plans and proposals were being entertained in Rome, Venice, and Buda for a western offensive against the Turks, Mehmed II apparently made a feint to divide his Christian opponents. We learn of it from a letter of 13 January, 1465, from the Venetian Senate to their ambassador at the royal court in Hungary:

> By your . . . letter [of the preceding 17 November] we have learned of the request which you state was made to the most illustrious lord king [Corvinus] in the Turk's name for a safe-conduct to be issued to two of his envoys in order to negotiate a peace and of the aforesaid king's denial [of the request] . . . . We reply that his Majesty seems to us to have made a prudent decision and quite properly to have reached the same conclusion as we have necessarily done ourselves after diverse attempts and requests for peace from the said Turk—through the chancellor our bailie in Constantinople last year, later by way of Greece, and now by way of Albania and through Scanderbeg. We have always assumed and do assume that these are artful gestures and wary moves on the part of the Turk not for the purpose of peace but the better to satisfy his lust for power. . . .[8]

Scanderbeg continued to fight while occasionally exchanging futile peace feelers with the Turks. Although his relations with Venice were not entirely friendly, the Republic was always willing to co-operate with him to the detriment of the Turk.[9] Every success he achieved in Albania redounded to the ultimate advantage of S. Mark. The Turkish overtures for peace were belied by reports which Venice had been receiving from the Levant. On 30 April, 1465, the Senate wrote Dr. Niccolò da Canale, their new ambassador to the Curia Romana, that a dispatch from the colonial government of Crete, dated 29 March, as well as letters from the Venetian captain-general of the sea, indicated that Sultan Mehmed was putting together a fleet *magno studio omnique conatu suo* for an attack upon the Republic's armada in eastern waters and her towns and territories in Greece and the islands. This information was said to be confirmed by a letter written from Constantinople by a "certain Greek captive of the Turks" to one Niccolò Corner, a Venetian noble in Crete, where the colonial government had apparently based its dispatch also upon word received in Candia from a "Constantinopolitan noble," who is described as a friend of Cardinal Bessarion (*qui alias stetit cum reverendissimo domino cardinale Niceno*).[10] Like

---

remanendo questo Othoman ne le sue force e signoria ne la vostra Excellentia ne alcun altro signor se po reputar signor nel stato suo.

"El novo santissimo pontefice, capo e principe de Christiani, fa et e per far ogni di piu a ruina del ditto Ottoman. Questo medesimo fa lo illustrissimo ducha de Borgogna et molti altri principi et signor christiani. . . . [Venice had a powerful armada at sea, and an army in the Morea and in Albania. The king of Hungary was carrying on an *acerbissima guerra* against the Ottoman Turks.] Nè e possibile che ditto Othoman possi per modo alcun farvi alcun obstaculo et resistentia. Et pero quanto piu presto la Excellentia vostra se movera, tanto piu presto et facilmente otenira tuto el stato suo in quelle parte. . . ." *Cf.*, *ibid.*, fols. 64^{r}, 131^{v}–132^{r}. Venice also had an alliance with the Gran Caramano (fols. 66^{v}, 67^{v}–68^{r}).

[8] Sen. Secreta, Reg. 22, fols. 58^{v}–59^{r} [60^{v}–61^{r}], doc. dated 13 January, 1465 (Ven. style 1464). About two weeks later, on 29 January, the Senate wrote again to the Venetian ambassador in Buda concerning these peace feelers from Mehmed II, who had recently made a rather more convincing approach through Leonardo III Tocco of S. Maura (*ibid.*, fol. 62^{v} [64^{v}], letter perhaps not sent to Buda):

"Scripsimus vobis sub die XIII presentis [the letter given above in the text] in responsionem vestrarum, et inter cetera diximus quod diversis modis tentati fueramus de pace cum Turco et presertim per medium domini Scanderbegi et quod suspicione non carebamus quod iste essent de consuetis astuciis et fallaciis Turci quodque de hoc noticiam daretis, sicut affectioni et unioni nostre convenit regie Serenitati Hungarie, cui etiam si quid ultra haberemus, id significaremus quemadmodum tenemus eam pari animo erga nos semper esse facturam, sequentes itaque hoc institutum nostrum volumus et mandamus vobis cum nostro consilio Rogatorum [the Senate] quod adeatis presentiam Serenitatis sue, dicendo sibi quod per viam Orientis novissime etiam diversis modis requisiti sumus de hac pace et presertim per medium magnifici domini Leonardo [III], despoti de Sancta Maura, et quamquam ut diximus dubitandum sit de artibus hostis istius consyderato tamen quod tot modis et mediis nos de re ista tentari fecit, forsitan esse potest quod revera cupidus est devenire ad pacem, unde ut magis ultra verum intelligi possit et etiam respectu persone prefati domini Sancte Maure, licet hactenus alicui requisitioni nobis facte noluerimus aures accommodare, melius esse existimavimus respondere sibi post generalia quod quoniam Turcus tales conditiones pacis offeret que non solum omnem occasionem et materiam iniuriarum et belli tollant, sed etiam habeant rationem dignitatis et lige inter Serenitatem suam et nos vigentis ac etiam aliorum principum christianorum tunc cum Maiestate sua ei respondebimus. De qua re cum simus cum regia Maiestate sua indissolubili charitate, benivolentia et federe coniuncti et perpetuis temporibus esse intendamus, statuimus Serenitati sue dare noticiam et si quid ultra in futurum habebimus id pro consueto more nostro Maiestati sue notum faciemus. De quanto autem habebitis a Serenitate sua subito reddetis nos vestris litteris certiores." Note also fols. 63^{r}, 64^{v}, 66, 74^{v} ff., 122^{r}–123^{r}, 145 ff. [65^{r} ff.].

[9] Sen. Secreta, Reg. 22, fols. 136^{v} [138^{v}], 143 [145], docs. dated 21 February and 18 March, 1466.

[10] Sen. Secreta, Reg. 22, fol. 81^{r} [83^{r}], doc. dated 30 April, 1465, and note fols. 84^{r}, 85^{v}–86^{r}. Canale's commission as Venetian ambassador to the Curia is dated 9 April (*ibid.*, fols. 77^{v}–78^{v}). On 8 March, 1469, he was appointed captain-general of the sea (Sen. Secreta, Reg. 24, fols. 1^{v}–3^{r}), to his ultimate grief, on which see below, pp. 292 ff.

Scanderbeg, Venice had no alternative but to continue the grim struggle against the Turks.

Paul II was also prepared to go on with his predecessor's crusading plans, but he was as practical as any Venetian tradesman when it came to the problem of financing the war. Although his relations with Venice left something to be desired, like those of many another pope before and after him, he appreciated the plight of his fellow countrymen in the East. On the whole he tried to avoid a serious break with the Republic, lest the latter should make peace with the Turks, who were said to be willing to do so, as Paolo Barbarigo, the Venetian bailie in Istanbul, could attest from a personal interview he had had in February, 1465, with the grand vizir Mahmud Pasha. Sultan Mehmed had just ordered Barbarigo's release from imprisonment as a gesture of amity, and Mahmud had expressed surprise that the Republic should have been carrying on persistent warfare with the Porte.[11]

The Venetians were interested, even hopeful, but they required the cession of the Morea and Lesbos as well as the recognition of Hungarian suzerainty over much of Bosnia, terms to which Mehmed could hardly be expected to consent (especially since, as subsequent events were to show, the sultan would accept peace with Venice only at a price which the Senate must refuse to pay). While the Venetians spent their money on a fleet which won no battles and conquered no territory, and on a general who rescued a philosopher's body from the Turks, Mehmed spent his time building a palace in Istanbul and continuing the embellishment of his new capital as well as studying Greek philosophy and Ptolemy's *Almagest* with George Amiroutzes and perhaps with George of Trebizond.[12]

Although Paul II did something for the crusade, he certainly lacked his predecessor's greathearted devotion to the cause. Cardinal Jacopo Ammanati could write with much truth of his old friend Pius II:

> One cannot say whether he was more fortunate in death or in life. He attained the supreme pontificate

[11] Sen. Secreta, Reg. 22, fol. 86^{r} [88^{r}], a letter of the Senate dated 10 May, 1465, to Barbarigo in Istanbul: "Havemo intexo per vostre lettere de XIII de Febraro tenute fino a di XVI la liberation vostra seguita de ordine del Signor Turco et le parole usate con vui circa di questo per Mamutbassa, la qual liberation ne è stata molto grata et è de mente nostra che vui regratiate el ditto Mamutbassa de le humane parole et bone opere sue. Verum perche inter alia ne scrivete Mamutbassa haver monstrado meravegliarse con vui de la guerra senza cason per nui tolta commemorando el far de la pace, etc., semo contenti che vui sie con esso Mamutbassa dicendoli che come è manifesto provocadi et astreti devenissemo ad questa guerra con el Signor Turco si per la novita fatta contra Argos come per altre molte violentie et damni inferidi a luogi et subditi nostri.

"Al presente dicemo che quando el si promova [*propona*, *ibid.*, fol. 91^{r}, where the text also occurs] condition de pace le qual toia via la occasion et materia de la guerra et habia etiam rispecto a la liga che nui havemo con el serenissimo re de Hongaria, alhora pertinenter responderemo et voremo bona pace. De quanto el prefato Mamutbassa ve rispondera, volemo che [*volemo che* omitted on fol. 91^{v}] per bon messo ne date [*darete*, fol. 91^{v}] aviso, dechiarandone tute condition et particularita porete haver per piu intelligentia nostra."

This letter, which seems to have been accepted by the Senate on a second ballot on 8 June, 1465 (by a vote *de parte* 96, *de non* 0, *non sinceri* 2), was apparently not sent to Barbarigo. The text lacks the upright cross in the left margin which indicates that an action voted on was actually put into effect. As presented to the Senate on both 10 May and 8 June a word of appreciation was included for the efforts of the Italian Jewish physician Yakub Pasha ("Messer Jacomo Medego") on behalf of Venice. The Senate was going to try to find some "libri de medicina" for Yakub (*ibid.*, fols. 86^{r}, 91^{v}), on whom see above, Chapter 5, note 12.

[12] Critobulus, V, 9–10 (ed. Karl Müller, in *Fragmenta historicorum graecorum* [*FHG*], V-1 [Paris, 1870], pp. 155–56; ed. V. Grecu, *Critobul din Imbros*, Bucharest, 1963, pp. 333, 335, 337); for the terms on which Venice would (happily) make peace, see Sime Ljubić, *Listine*, X (Zagreb, 1891), 327, doc. dated 3 July, 1465, and *cf.*, *ibid.*, pp. 328, 331–32, 344, *et alibi*, but esp. pp. 360–61. On the relations of Amiroutzes with Mehmed II, see Adolf Deissmann, *Forschungen u. Funde im Serai*, Berlin and Leipzig, 1933, pp. 25–36, and *cf.* F. Babinger, *Maometto il Conquistatore*, Turin, 1957, pp. 363–71, 725. Although responsible for some notable structures, Mehmed II was actually not a great builder; he did employ a number of western painters, especially Gentile Bellini, and some bronze miniaturists, but no western architects of note (*cf.*, *ibid.*, pp. 679–80, and Chapter 5, note 12, on Mehmed's intellectual interests and cultural contacts with Italy). Inevitably he was affected by the artistic vogue of his time.

Life in the late Quattrocento was informed by art to an extent not always easy to realize. In a collection of letters, for example, of the Frangipani lords of the island see of Veglia (modern Krk, across the head of the Adriatic from Venice) a letter of one Elisabetta Morosini, dated at Veglia on 11 May, 1471, to the brothers Pietro and Marco Morosini di Paolo, reads: ". . . We pray you dearly, Messer Marco, to be willing by the friendship which we understand you have with the painters Gentile and Giovanni Bellini to persuade them to teach the fundamentals of design to our Father Domenico [*che i vogliano insegnar la rasom del desegno a pre domenego nostro*] . . . ," and if the Bellini should prove unwilling to do so, perhaps some other "benevolent painter" could be found to instruct Domenico, who might then return to Veglia to paint in the popular style of the Venetian school (see the note by F. S., in *Nuovo Archivio veneto*, 2nd ser., II [Venice, 1891], 382).

by his own inner resources [*virtute sua*] and achieved eternal glory in religion and in genius. He met a death than which, if you but look at the world, none could be more sublime. . . . He died for truth and for the redemption of an enslaved people, offering himself as a sacrifice to God and leaving an example to priests of what they should be for their own people. . . .[13]

It was not, however, an example which the papal merchant of Venice could follow. But Paul II did what he could, after his fashion, and established at the beginning of his reign a special commission for the crusade, to which Cardinals Bessarion, Guillaume d'Estouteville, and Juan de Carvajal were appointed. The commissioners were to receive the profits from the papal monopoly of the alum mines at Tolfa, "seven mountains of alum" (discovered early in 1461), as well as most of the income from indulgences and the crusading tithes, which funds they were to expend on the war against the Turks. Despite wearisome diplomatic exchanges nothing was accomplished, for the Italian states refused to subscribe to the levies proposed by the commissioners, who tried to assess the requirements of the crusade after consultation with the hard-pressed Venetians.[14]

The Florentines are a case in point, and one example may serve for several. On 16 May, 1465, Paul II appealed to the Signoria for their contribution to assist the Hungarians against Mehmed II, the "common enemy and calamity of Christians." The pope stated that at the recent meeting of the Italian powers, when he had asked for help against the Turks, the Florentine representative had agreed to give two thousand ducats a month,[15] "although this seemed a small sum to all present and doubtless far less than your most prosperous state should have pledged." (Florence had in fact been asked for fifty thousand a year.) King Matthias Corvinus had written of the desperate need to stem the ever-rising Turkish tide, and the pope assured the Floren-

---

[13] Ammanati, *Ep.* XLI, in Pius II, *Commentarii*, Frankfurt, 1614, p. 489, lines 19 ff., to Cardinal Francesco Todeschini Piccolomini (later Pope Pius III), also cited in Raynaldus, *Ann. eccl.*, ad ann. 1464, no. 45, vol. XIX (1693), p. 163.

[14] On the alum mines of Tolfa and their importance for the crusade, see Augustin Theiner, ed., *Codex diplomaticus dominii temporalis S. Sedis*, III (Rome, 1862, repr. Frankfurt am Main, 1964), nos. CCCLXV, CCCLXX–CCCLXXII, CCCLXXIX, CCCXCI, CCCXCIII–CCCXCIV, CCCXCVIII, pp. 419–20, 423–25, 434–36, 451–55, 456–59, 463–67; Adolf Gottlob, *Aus der Camera Apostolica des 15. Jahrhunderts*, Innsbruck, 1889, pp. 278–300; Pastor, *Hist. Popes*, IV, 80–81, and *Gesch. d. Päpste*, II (repr. 1955), 355–56; A. Guglielmotti, *Storia della marina pontificia*, II (Rome, 1886), 318–22; G. Zippel, "L'Allume di Tolfa e il suo commercio," in *Archivio della R. Società romana di storia patria*, XXX (1907), esp. pp. 14–51, 389 ff., 402 ff., 416–18, 431 ff., with refs. to both printed and archival sources; and in general Jean Delumeau, *L'Alun de Rome, XVe–XIXe siècle*, Paris, 1962 (see above, Chapter 8, notes 30–31). The profits derived from alum were actually used for many purposes other than the "Cruciata," which almost gave its name to the papal monopoly in alum. The Camera Apostolica is believed at times to have received from eighty to one hundred thousand ducats a year from the concessions it granted to mine the alum, which was widely used in the fifteenth century for the dyeing of cloth, the preparation of leather, glass-making, tanning, and even in medicines. Grants from the alum fund supported some famous papal pensioners in Rome such as the exiled despot of the Morea, Thomas Palaeologus, his son Andreas and the latter's wife Caterina, Queen Catherine of Bosnia, and the exiled despot of Arta, Leonardo Tocco, as well as many others (Gottlob, *op. cit.*, pp. 292–94).

The crusading plan of the year 1464 involved a realistic schedule of payments by the Italian states, with the papacy and Venice each providing 100,000 ducats (Sen. Secreta, Reg. 22, fols. 63 [65], 78^r [80^r], 102^v [104^v] and 104 [106]); Naples, 80,000; Milan, 70,000; Florence, 50,000; Modena, 20,000; Siena, 15,000; Bologna, 15,000; Mantua, 10,000; Lucca, 8,000; and Montferrat, 5,000 (Ammanati, *Ep.* LIV, in Pius II, *Commentarii*, Frankfurt, 1614, p. 506; *MHH*, *Magyar Diplomacziai Emlékek: Acta extera* of the reign of Matthias Corvinus, II [Budapest, 1877], 233–34, document incorrectly assigned to the year 1471). The lesser states like Siena and Mantua assumed that the greater powers would prevent the Turkish entry into Italy and were extremely loath to pay their share of any assessment for the common good. The larger states imposed unacceptable conditions upon their compliance with the commissioners' plan.

The appointment of Lorenzo de' Medici's father, Piero di Cosimo, and his associates in the Medici bank as *alme urbis thesaurarii* on 16 September, 1464, may be found in Arch. Segr. Vaticano, Reg. Vat. 542 [*Pauli II Officiorum lib. I, anno I*], fols. 8^v–9^r. On the sixth of the following November, Piero and the bank were appointed *pecuniarum Sancte Cruciate depositarii* (*ibid.*, fol. 23): "Volumus autem quod in dispendiis pecuniarum prefatarum mandatis venerabilium fratrum nostrorum Bessarionis Tusculani, Guillelmi Hostiensis, et Johannis Portuensis, episcoporum Sancte Romane Ecclesie cardinalium, per nos super premissis deputatorum absque aliqua contradictione parere debeatis. . . ." The Pazzi and Ricasoli, also Florentines, served as *depositarii* too, but apparently had nothing to do with the special crusading fund (*cf.*, *ibid.*, fols. 2^v–3^r). Zippel, "L'Allume di Tolfa," pp. 437–62, publishes a number of important documents relating to the "Cruciata;" see also Delumeau's careful study of *L'Alun de Rome*, and *cf.* R. de Roover, *The Rise and Decline of the Medici Bank (1397–1494)*, New York, 1966, pp. 152–64, and František Beneš, "Depositeria generale della crociata," *Československý Časopis historický*, XIV–5 (Prague, 1966), 738–57, with fifty-four documents relating to Bohemia from the reign of Paul II, in Czech summaries or the original Latin text.

[15] *Cf.* Ammanati, *Ep.* XCV, in Pius II, *Commentarii*, Frankfurt, 1614, p. 532, which letter also gives details of the financial recalcitrance of the other Italian states.

tines that Hungarian strength was simply unequal to the task. The subvention of Hungary was in fact the defense of Italy. The pope warned against delay (*bis dedit qui cito dedit*). If the Signoria had difficulty producing the whole sum, "which we can hardly believe, we pray you at least give half of it now" [i.e., 12,000 ducats]. On 1 June the Signoria replied, acknowledging the Florentine commitment and commending the elegance of the papal style as well as the soundness of the papal reasoning, "but many and grave difficulties are arising which make it so hard for us that we cannot see how action can be taken on your wish and our own desire, which is always attendant upon a pontiff's wish." The price of grain was high; the fear of plague had laid the city low; and there were other troubles too. The Signoria did not therefore fear to ask his Holiness to hear with kindly ears their plea to be excused, for necessity impelled them to request this consideration of the supreme pontiff, whose most devoted sons they were.[16] The insincerity of the letter vies with its urbanity; Pius II had become all too familiar with the meaning of such communications. The Florentines were not going to assist the Venetians to remove any chestnuts from the fire, but when such a letter might be received from any one of a dozen states in Italy, and rejoinders less courteous perhaps from half a dozen kings and princes in western Europe, it was only too clear that no great crusade, such as Pius II had envisaged, was going to take place during the pontificate of Paul II.[17]

Although cities in the papal states were as reluctant as those elsewhere to pay the crusading tithes, Paul II managed to send very substantial sums to Matthias Corvinus to assist the Hungarians against the Turks. The bookseller Vespasiano da Bisticci, a well-informed contemporary observer, says that Paul II sent Corvinus some 80,000 ducats in the year 1465 alone.[18] According to the accounts of the "Cruciata" preserved in the Archivio di Stato in Rome, the commission for the crusade did in fact turn over to the Hungarian envoys 57,500 gold florins from the fund produced by the alum monopoly on 23 May, 1465,[19] and another grant was made on 28 April, 1466, of 10,000 Hungarian ducats.[20] Nevertheless, bitter complaints were being voiced in the Venetian Senate that in neither Rome nor the Veneto was the high clergy doing its share in the war against the Turks, which was almost impoverishing the Republic.[21] The costs of war exceeded the profits of trade. On 26 September, 1465, the Senate informed Paul that, as Venice fought almost alone against the Turks, the expense of maintaining her forces on land and sea had exceeded the burdensome total of 700,000 ducats in a year.[22]

During the early spring of 1465 the Venetians and the Hospitallers, the Turks' chief Christian opponents in the eastern Mediterranean, came to blows in a conflict which seemed likely to play into Sultan Mehmed's hands. At that time certain Venetian galleys sailed from Alexandria to Rhodes, as they frequently did, but on this occasion they had on board a number of Moorish merchants (*plerique mercatores mauri*), who had valuable wares with them. The Venetians had been obliged to take the Moors on board "lest besides the terrible war we are carrying on with the Turk we should also provoke against ourselves the hatred of the soldan [of Egypt]" (as the Senate found it necessary to explain to King Edward IV of England on 9 September, 1465), "to whom we knew the Turk had sent envoys to [persuade him to] declare war upon us." As the Venetian galleys were approaching the harbor of Rhodes, Pedro Ramón Zacosta, the grand master (1461–1467), attacked them with several Hospitaller galleys and other armed vessels. Some Venetians were wounded in the encounter, some even killed. Their galleys were

[16] Giuseppe Müller, ed., *Documenti sulle relazioni delle città toscane coll'Oriente cristiano e coi Turchi*, Florence, 1879, pt. I, no. 153, pp. 202–3, docs. dated 16 May and 7 June, 1465.

[17] After "six months' effort" Paul II realized this fully (Raynaldus, *Ann. eccl.*, ad ann. 1465, nos. 1–2, vol. XIX [1693], p. 170, and *cf.* Müller, *op. cit.*, pp. 498–99).

[18] A. Mai, *Spicilegium romanum*, I (Rome, 1839), 297: ". . . [la sua Santità] mandò al Re d'Ungaria circa ducati ottanta mila, e composesi con detti ambasciadori dare ogni anno una certa somma di danari. . . ." In July, 1466, Paul II wrote Philip of Burgundy that in the preceding year he had sent the Hungarians 100,000 gold florins (Raynaldus, *Ann. eccl.*, ad ann., no. 3, vol. XIX [1693], p. 178): ". . . aureorum millia centum anno proximo ad Hungaros misimus."

[19] Liber depositarii S. Cruciate, fol. 40, cited by Gottlob, *Aus der Camera Apostolica*, p. 291.

[20] Gottlob, *loc. cit.* The Hungarians received additional sums in later years.

[21] *Cf.* Sen. Secreta, Reg. 22, fols. 129r/130r [132r], 160r [162r], dated 28 May, 1466: ". . . Clerici vero in causa hac sancte fidei preter ius omne divinum atque humanum in ocio atque tranquillitate quiescunt, et a longo tempore citra nihil solverunt ex decimis sive factionibus quas ab hac urbe condita citra solvere consueti sunt. . . ."

[22] Sen. Secreta, Reg. 22, fols. 117/118v–118/119r [120v–121r]: "Urgent insuper stipendia terrestris exercitus atque navalis supplementorumque mittendorum, que excedunt iam summam ducatorum septingentorum millium in anno . . ." [fol. 121r by mod. enumeration].

seized as though they were spoils of war. The Moors were thrown into Rhodian prisons. Very quickly matters went from bad to worse.

When word of the Moors' capture spread through Syria and Egypt, where there were many Venetian merchants as well as Venetian consuls in Damascus and Alexandria, the soldan ordered all citizens and subjects of the Republic to be seized and brought in chains to Cairo. They were being held *duris carceribus*, and threatened with death, for the soldan held Venice responsible for the Moors' plight. Getting no satisfaction from the grand master despite repeated efforts to deal with him—"at this point, most serene king, we cannot in silence pass over the fact that, although the grand master declares himself to be a champion of the faith, his heart is far removed from such a purpose"—the Senate ordered the Venetian captain-general of the sea, Jacopo Loredan, to suspend all activity against the Turks and proceed at once to Rhodes, where (peaceably if possible) he was to secure the freedom of the Moors.

Sailing to Rhodes, Loredan tried for three whole days by letters and envoys to persuade the grand master to release the Moors and to return their goods, but contrary to the advice of many of the Knights, the grand master refused to do so, "with incredible pertinacity and avarice," although the lives and properties of so many Venetians were then hanging in the balance. At last, however, peaceful arrangements were made between the persistent captain-general and the recalcitrant grand master. The Moors were released, and their goods, or such as could be found, were given back to them. Before "concord and agreement" had made this possible, however, the Venetians had found it necessary to effect a landing on Rhodes. The Senate expressed courteous regret if in the process anything had happened which was displeasing to his Majesty. Edward IV had written to Venice, at the instance of the Hospitallers in England, to protest against the Venetian incursion into the island stronghold.

The Senate reaffirmed the propriety and justice of their action, noting that the Moors had now returned to their homes. The release of the Venetians from the prisons in Cairo, however, and the restitution of their goods were not going to be achieved without the greatest expense to the Republic. A Venetian ambassador had been sent to the soldan, "but there is no doubt that in the usual barbaric fashion he will require of us a great sum of money to rescue our people from their awful predicament," very likely many thousands of ducats. If the most reverend lord prior of the Hospital in England had had a fuller knowledge and a more accurate account of the events at Rhodes, he would certainly have refrained from making any complaint against Venice. Indeed, if the lord prior had himself been at Rhodes, his wisdom and authority would have shown the way to an entirely pacific solution.[23]

The Senate had indeed sent an envoy, Filippo Correr, to the soldan's court to protest against the injustice then being done to the Republic's citizens and subjects. Even the apparent threat to give up the Venetian consulates in Damascus and Alexandria and to order the abandonment of Mamluk lands by all Venetian merchants failed to secure full satisfaction from the soldan's government.[24] The matter dragged on interminably. While the Venetians fought with the Turks, they had to haggle and remonstrate with the Mamluks. Seven years later (on 22 July, 1472), a well-known Venetian diplomat, Giovanni Emo, received a ducal commission to go by way of Modon to Alexandria and thence to Cairo to the court of the soldan, to whom he was again to protest against the injuries and losses which the Venetian merchants had suffered in Mamluk territory, where even the Republic's consul in Damascus had been ignominiously beaten. Emo was also to take up the "matter of the pepper which is given to our people, soggy and full of sand and pebbles" (*humefactum et terra lapidibusque plenum*), and to request punishment for those "who in the person of our consul have injured our Signoria" so that no such offense would be committed in years to come. He was also to request restitution for the merchants' losses.[25]

---

[23] Sen. Secreta, Reg. 22, fol. 115/116 [118], doc. dated 9 September, 1465. The Senate also wrote to the earl of Warwick and to the prior and preceptor of the Hospital in England (*ibid.*, fols. 115^{v}–116^{r}). As we have already noted, Loredan was trying to give up the captaincy-general of the sea at this time, but the Senate voted not to replace him (*ibid.*, fol. 116^{r}) until 7 February, 1466 (fol. 133^{v}/134^{v} [136^{v}]). Finally on 25 April Vettore Capello was elected his successor (fols. 152^{v} ff. [154 ff.]), and the war against the Turks was pressed more vigorously. The soldan of Egypt was aẓ-Ẓāhir Saif-ad-Dīn Khushkadam (1461–1467).

[24] Sen. Secreta, Reg. 22, fols. 92^{v}–96^{r} [94^{v}–98^{r}], docs. dated 15 to 21 June, 1465. Correr was at least authorized to make such a threat (*ibid.*, fols. 94^{r}, in next to the last paragraph, and 96^{r}, where the Senate's letter to the soldan ends with the statement that ". . . a nui è intollerabile poder più patir tante violentie et damni, come più compidamente lo ambassador nostro referira a la vostra Serenità . . .").

[25] Sen. Secreta, Reg. 25, fols. 142^{v}–143^{r} [151^{v}–152^{r}].

In the early spring and summer of 1466 Sultan Mehmed II led a large army into Albania against Scanderbeg, but failed to take the mountain fortress of Croia by siege. It was a costly expedition. The Turks are said to have built the castle of Elbasan in a month,[26] and Elbasan soon proved its worth by resisting an Albanian attack the following spring. From about the middle of May, 1466, word was spreading that Scanderbeg had been defeated, and that some 14,000 Christians had been killed in a disastrous encounter with the Turks. One can still feel the atmosphere of alarm in the dispatches. Even the Florentines were distressed by the disquieting news. Piero de' Medici, son and successor of the great Cosimo, was said to have felt grief and shed tears for the Turkish attack upon Albania, offering Paul II aid through his father's old friend, Timoteo Maffei, the humanist prior of the canons regular of Fiesole and later archbishop of Ragusa (1467–1470).[27] The defeat of Scanderbeg would have been a blow to Venice, and the Medici were not given to weeping for the misfortunes of Venice.

The death of Francesco Sforza, duke of Milan, on 8 March, 1466, threatened to upset the balance of power in Italy. In Rome and Milan and Florence one feared for the peace of Italy, and watched every move being made in Venice and Naples. The Venetian Senate assured an Albanian envoy in early July, 1466, however, that they would furnish Scanderbeg with all the support they possibly could. They were gratified by his defense of Croia, "and as to the money he asks for, we certainly wish that we could satisfy . . . [him] to the fullest extent of his desire, but we must inform him that we have been incurring huge and intolerable expenses both on land and at sea, and not only in Albania and Dalmatia, but in the Morea, Negroponte, and other points in the east." Scanderbeg had complained of the inadequacy of the assistance which Venice had sent him, to which the Senate replied that, besides the infantry they had promised him, they had also sent the condottiere Cimarosto with his troop of experienced men. The condottiere's death had certainly caused confusion in the ranks, but before he died he had complained to Venice

> that his troop had been badly treated by his lordship's subjects, quite without his lordship's intention, as we know, but this has been the chief reason that other Italian troopers in our employ have been loath to go into Albania. But to return to the question of money, we reply that although, as has been stated, we are burdened in many ways with insupportable expenses, nevertheless in deference to his lordship we shall try for the present to have two thousand ducats sent to him from here, and we shall order that another thousand ducats be given to him by our commissioner in Albania.[28]

Although they had to keep preparing for war, most members of the Venetian Senate found some solace in discussions of peace. Few of them, however, could agree on how to bring the war to an end. On Monday, 28 July (1466), a motion was passed in the Senate

> that tomorrow and Wednesday all the members of the Collegio must convene and stay together, and they cannot leave as long as the most serene lord doge remains: nothing can be discussed or dealt with in the Collegio except the aforesaid matter [peace with the Turks] under a penalty of ten pounds for anyone [disregarding this injunction]. . . . On Thursday this council [the Senate] will be convoked. All are required to take part, as shall seem best to every member in accordance with his opinion of the mode and method of arriving at a peace or truce with the Turk. . . . And in this council [the Senate] nothing can be done unless this matter is first cleared for action.[29]

---

[26] *Cf.* Johannes Adelphi, *Die Türckisch Chronica von irem Ursprung, Anefang und Regiment*, Strassburg, M. Flach, 1513, unnum. fol. 7^v (=sign. B–i): "Darnach im LXV[I] iar do zog der Türck wider in Albania, und bauwet ein schöne stat in XXXI tagen . . . ," and see the article by Franz Babinger, referred to in the following note.

[27] Pastor, *Hist. Popes*, IV, 86, and append., no. 14, pp. 480–81, and *Gesch. d. Päpste*, II (repr. 1955), 360, and append., no. 79, p. 761, letter from Maffei to Piero de'Medici, dated at Rome on 15 May (1466); C. Eubel, *Hierarchia*, II (1914, repr. 1960), 220. On the building of Elbasan, see Fr. Babinger, "Die Gründung von Elbasan," *Mitteilungen des Seminars für Orientalische Sprachen*, XXXIV (1931), 94–103, reprinted in his *Aufsätze und Abhandlungen zur Geschichte Südosteuropas und der Levante*, I (Munich, 1962), 201–10. According to the longer of two commemorative inscriptions at Elbasan, the square fortress with its great corner towers was built in twenty-five days (*ibid.*, pp. 204–6). Documents relating to Scanderbeg's struggle with the Turks in 1466 are conveniently assembled in J. Radonić, *Djuradj Kastriot Skenderbeg*, Belgrade, 1942, pp. 179–94, and *cf.* S. Ljubić, *Listine*, X, pp. 359–84, *passim*.

[28] Sen. Secreta, Reg. 22, fol. 173^r [175^r], doc. dated 7 July, 1466. A month earlier (on 7 June) the Senate had urged King Ferrante of Naples, always the friend of Scanderbeg, to send him infantry and archers "cum magnificus Scandarbegus et res Albanie et per consequens Christianitatis in maximo periculo constitute sint" (*ibid.*, fol. 166^r [168^r], and *cf.* fols. 170^r, 179^v, and Reg. 23, fol. 57^r, dated 28 July, 1467).

[29] Sen. Secreta, Reg. 22, fols. 175^v–176^r [177^v–178^r]. The motion passed unanimously (*de parte* 132, *de non* 0, *non sinceri* 0), but letters addressed on 7 August to Francesco

Reports reaching the Curia Romana brought with them a sense of almost irremediable disaster. Paul II made another appeal to the great powers, writing Philip of Burgundy late in the year 1466:

My dearest son: Scanderbeg, stalwart athlete of Christ, ruler of the great part of Albania, who has fought for our faith for more than twenty years, has been attacked by vast Turkish forces and now defeated in battle, stripped of all his dominion, and driven defenseless and destitute to our shores. The Albanians, his fellow warriors, have been put to the sword, some of them reduced to abject slavery. The towns, which hitherto have resisted the attacks of the Turks on our behalf, have now come under their sway. The neighboring peoples, who dwell on the Adriatic, are terrified by the nearness of their danger. Everywhere panic, grief, death, and captivity are before our very eyes. It is terrible to hear what great turbulence has overtaken everything. It is a tearful sight to watch the ships of fugitives putting in at Italian ports. Families in want, robbed of all they had, driven from their homes, huddle everywhere on the shores. Stretching out their hands to heaven, they fill our hearts with their lamentations. Evils without number encompass them, but the Turkish ruler, victorious, proud, monstrous, equipped with greater forces than ever before, rushes forward to claim one land after another.[30]

Though the pope's letter to Philip of Burgundy did not exaggerate the terror and misery caused by the Turks in Albania, he was mistaken in the belief that Scanderbeg had been defeated. Mehmed had in fact withdrawn from the siege of Croia in June, 1466, toward Durazzo, spreading death and destruction before him. He left Balaban Beg before Croia, however, with orders to maintain the investment of the fortress until he had taken it by attack or starvation. Meanwhile a severe plague had been ravaging Thessaly, Macedonia, and Thrace, extending into Asia Minor. It caused a high mortality in Istanbul where, according to Critobulus, the gravediggers could not keep up with the deaths of more than six hundred persons a day. Mehmed delayed his return to the capital (in 1466), marching northward after his withdrawal from Albania into the Danube region north of Sofia, between Vidin and Nicopolis, where he spent the autumn in the mountains, returning to Istanbul only when the plague disappeared with the advent of winter.[31] Critobulus's valuable but somewhat confused account of the career of Mehmed II closes with a description of the plague of 1466.

Late in the year Scanderbeg made a hurried journey to Italy to seek aid directly of Ferrante in Naples and of Paul II in Rome. Although the Ragusan Senate had been prepared in May (1466) to provide Scanderbeg with gunpowder, saltpeter, and sulphur, on 2 November they voted to send a delegation of three nobles to ask "that he not come to Ragusa *ob bonum respectum*," which means for fear of the Turks.[32] On 27 November, Agostino de' Rossi, the Milanese ambassador in Rome, wrote Duchess Bianca Maria and her son Galeazzo Maria Sforza that Scanderbeg had lost "all his state except for Croia." He had arrived in Apulia, and would go first to Ferrante and then come to Rome to request the support he needed.[33] On 14 December the Mantuan ambassador to the Vatican, Giovanni Pietro Arrivabene, described Scanderbeg's coming to Rome: "The lord Scanderbeg arrived here Friday [12 December, 1466], and the households of the cardinals were sent out to meet him. He is a man of advanced age, past sixty; he has come with few horses, a poor man. I understand he will seek aid."[34]

Venier, the Venetian ambassador to Matthias Corvinus, show that the Senate had no clearer idea after the unusual sessions than before them, of how to achieve peace with the Turks, for the terms must be acceptable to both Venice and Hungary: ". . . Et quoniam non dubitamus quin tractatio pacis, tum propter conditiones quas Maiestas sua petit et nos etiam petimus tum propter naturam Turci, habitura sit multum difficultatis" (*ibid.*, fols. 177ᵛ–178ʳ [179ᵛ–180ʳ]).

[30] The letter was written for Paul II by Jacopo Ammanati, *Ep.* CLXIII, in Pius II, *Commentarii*, Frankfurt, 1614, pp. 588 ff.; Raynaldus, *Ann. eccl.*, ad ann. 1466, no. 2, vol. XIX (1693), p. 178; for the date (toward the end of 1466), see F. Pall, "Marino Barlezio," in *Mélanges d'histoire générale*, ed. C. Marinescu, II (Bucharest, 1938), 219, note 1. On 2 June, 1466, the Venetians had accused the Ragusei of selling supplies to the Turks "toto hoc bello" (Ljubić, *Listine*, X, 366).

[31] Critobulus, V, 11–12, 16–19 (ed. Müller, *FHG*, V-1, pp. 156b–158b, 159b–161; ed. Grecu, *Critobul din Imbros* [1963], pp. 339 ff., 349 ff.), who tries to make Mehmed's Albanian expedition appear as successful as possible, declaring that the Turks took 20,000 Albanians captive (chap. 11, ed. Müller, p. 157b; ed. Grecu, p. 343). On the plague and Mehmed's intention of spending the winter near Sofia, *cf.* Radonić, *Djuradj Kastriot Skenderbeg*, no. 336, p. 192, doc. dated 9 October (1466).

[32] J. Gelcich and L. Thallóczy, eds., *Diplomatarium ragusanum*, Budapest, 1887, pp. 774, 780.

[33] F. Pall, "I Rapporti italo-albanesi intorno alla metà del secolo XV," *Archivio storico per le province napoletane*, LXXXIII (3rd ser., IV, 1966), doc. no. LXIII, p. 204, and note no. LXIV.

[34] Pastor, *Hist. Popes*, IV, 88, note, and *Gesch. d. Päpste*, II (repr. 1955), 361–62, note 4; Pall, "I Rapporti italo-albanesi," no. LXV, pp. 206–7; Malipiero, *Annali veneti*, in *Archivio storico italiano*, VII, pt. 1 (1843), 38;

Agostino de' Rossi and his fellow ambassador in Rome, Lorenzo da Pesaro, kept the Milanese court well informed of what they learned at the Curia. They watched Paul II very closely. After all, he was a Venetian. Since Francesco Sforza's death there was widespread fear that the Italian peace might not be maintained. The anti-Medicean exiles from Florence had gathered in Venice, where the condottiere Bartolommeo Colleoni was being encouraged to proceed against the Medici. The Venetians were believed to have designs on Milanese territory. They would have liked to make peace with the Turks, and were having some difficulty with their ally Matthias Corvinus, whose forces had seized a strategic pass near Spalato (Split) "contro voluntà et a despecto de Venetiani." The Venetians were trying to conceal their annoyance. They had to put up with this evidence of Hungarian ambition because of the Turkish war, but it was understood in Rome "che ne hanno amaro il stomacho." The pope was trying to preserve the peace and to keep the Venetians in line. He told the envoys at the Curia of the huge sums he had expended on the Turkish war and of the continuing necessity to provide Matthias Corvinus and Scanderbeg with subsidies. According to the latter, the Turks had raided the Venetian territories in Dalmatia at the time of his departure from Albania. They had taken more than four thousand captives as well as much booty, which made it clear that there was little immediate likelihood of a peace or truce between the Republic and the Porte. The pope had sent his fellow countryman Bertuccio Contarini to the Venetians, "adiungendoli che non se fidano de fare ni pace ni tregua col Turcho per innovare guerra in Italia."[35]

The Milanese ambassadors in Rome wrote Duchess Bianca and Galeazzo Maria that Paul II had directed Scanderbeg to write the Albanian envoy in Venice of "how the pope refuses to give him any subvention to be used against the Turk in Albania unless he first sees such security in Italy that there is no likelihood of war here, and that all the other Italian powers are in accord on this, except that the Venetians seem rather to be holding back. One can, therefore, affirm that this whole matter depends upon them. . . . And Scanderbeg has himself written to this effect and sent the letter off to Venice." The ambassadors believed that Paul would give Scanderbeg "some subsidy, but only a small one."[36] On 7 January, 1467, Cardinal Francesco Gonzaga wrote his father, Marquis Lodovico, that a secret consistory had been held that morning on the matter of aiding Scanderbeg: Paul II had said that he would give five thousand ducats, but was unwilling to give more on the grounds that he had to provide for his own affairs, expressing apprehension of certain possible developments. Cardinal Latino Orsini then began to say that his Holiness had no cause for fear from any source, but the pope turned on him in anger with the information that he knew for certain Ferrante of Naples was planning an attack upon the states of the Church. On the twelfth Cardinal Gonzaga wrote his father again that he had attended another secret consistory that morning concerning "the affairs of Scanderbeg, to whom there will be given only the five thousand ducats."[37]

Scanderbeg remained in Rome for another month or more, waiting for a subvention from the pope,

> but his Holiness apparently wants to see what shape the affairs of Italy are going to take, because if there is to be a war, he intends that his first expenditure should be for his own protection. On the other hand, he says that he still wants to know what contribution his Majesty [Ferrante] is willing to make. [The pope] has written to [Ferrante] and is awaiting his reply in order to find out whether what the king will do [for Scanderbeg], together with the pope's assistance, will be sufficient for the needs of Albania so as not to throw the money away! In the meantime Scanderbeg is much aggrieved and well nigh desperate.

---

and *cf.* Marinus Barletius, *Historia de vita et gestis Scanderbegi*, 1st ed., Rome, 1509, bk. XII, fol. CLIII^r; ed. Zagreb, 1743, p. 357a: ". . . Scanderbeg interim . . . sine mora sagulo gregali et vilissimo admodum habitu indutus ad urbem Romanam pro ope et auxilio a summo principe patrumque collegio implorando profectus est: Erat enim eo tempore Paulus II Pontifex maximus." The house where Scanderbeg is said to have stayed in Rome may be found at 114–118 Vicolo Scanderbeg (at the foot of the Quirinal) on the Piazza Scanderbeg. His picture over the main doorway of the house is accompanied by the inscription: "Geor. Castriota a Scanderbeg princeps Epiri ad fidem iconis rest. an. Dom. MDCCCXLIII" (the building was commemorated as his alleged residence in 1843).

[35] Pall, "I Rapporti italo-albanesi," nos. LXIV–LXVIII, pp. 205–9, docs. dated from 10 to 19 December, 1466. Within a few years the Venetians sorely regretted their estrangement from Corvinus and Colleoni's meddling in the affairs of Florence (Malipiero, *Annali veneti*, ad ann. 1470, in *Archivio storico italiano*, VIII, pt. 1 [1843], 59).

[36] Pall, "I Rapporti italo-albanesi," nos. LXVIII–LXX, pp. 209–11, docs. dated from 19 to 31 December, 1466.

[37] Pastor, *Hist. Popes*, IV, 88–90, and append., no. 18, pp. 482–83, and *Gesch. d. Päpste*, II (repr. 1955), 361–63, and append., no. 83, p. 763, who insists, however, that generous treatment was accorded the "champion of Albania." Gonzaga's letters are reprinted in Radonić, *Djuradj Kastriot Skenderbeg*, pp. 194–95.

The ambassadors of the king of Hungary were also in Rome, seeking their annual subvention from the Holy See for the "impresa del Turcho." So were the Grand Master Pedro Ramón Zacosta and a large number of Hospitallers, for the chapter general of the Order was being held in Rome (from 12 December, 1466, to 7 February, 1467). The Hospitallers were said to be 200,000 ducats in debt. A levy had allegedly been imposed upon the fighting friars "to pay three-quarters of their incomes every year," which was supposed to be enough to discharge the debt in three years. An accounting of the Order's funds now revealed, however, that they had spent all their incomes, and their debts had increased to 250,000 ducats. Consequently it was decided that each "frate" should pay one-half of his income for the next five years, which was thought to be enough to reestablish the Order's solvency, "provided God does not will the debt's increase, as happened the first time."[38] Five days after the conclusion of the chapter general Paul II issued the bull *Quamvis ex commisso* (on 12 February, 1467), outlining the manifold debts of the Order, providing for an overall financial reform, and requiring payment in full within five or six years. Ten days thereafter the Grand Master Zacosta died (on 22 February), as tired of debts as he was of the Turks.[39]

Lorenzo da Pesaro and Agostino de' Rossi reported to the Milanese government on 24 January (1467) that, while Scanderbeg was "almost desperate, with little hope of getting assistance from the pope for Croia and Albania," Paul II was losing interest in his plight. One Paolo Contarini, a Venetian, had told the pope that it was not necessary to go to further expense to defend Croia, "because the Signoria of Venice has taken the place under their protection and will take care to guard it well, and their infantry and other forces are within [the fortress]." Scanderbeg was said to understand the sinister intentions of Venice, and threatened to surrender Croia and the rest of Albania to the Turks.[40] Although the ambassadors' dispatch was anti-Venetian enough to please Duchess Bianca and Galeazzo Maria, it remains suspect in the light of the Venetian documents.

Scanderbeg had already remained overlong in Rome. Croia was still holding out against the Turks. Paul II, however, showed small signs of giving him the five thousand ducats he had spoken of at the consistory of 7 January. He was, to be sure, willing to assign him part of the feudal dues (the *census*) which the Neapolitan kingdom was supposed each year to pay the Holy See. Certain of the cardinals had persuaded Scanderbeg to remain a while longer. They offered him their own money, and told him that another consistory would soon be held, at which the cardinals believed Paul might be induced to grant him the needed subsidy.

The consistory was in fact held on 13 February (1467). The question of assistance to Scanderbeg must have arisen immediately. Paul II now stated that he was prepared to contribute two thousand ducats to the Albanian cause, to which certain of the cardinals remonstrated, saying that his Holiness should provide at least seven or eight thousand. Paul said in reply that he was willing for the cardinals to lend Scanderbeg some such sum, and he would see to its repayment from the revenues of the alum mines [at Tolfa]. The idea did not appeal to the cardinals since Paul was known to have "il dinaro in capsa."[41]

The Milanese ambassadors informed their government on the same day (13 February) that so far "Scandarbecho povereto" had got almost nothing from the pope, who had hardly paid his living expenses. But Paul was sending him back to Ferrante with a so-called grant of 7,500 ducats to be paid from the Neapolitan *census*,

---

[38] Pall, "I Rapporti italo-albanesi," no. LXXI, pp. 211–12, dated 16 January, 1467.

[39] Gaspare da Verona, *De gestis tempore . . . Pauli II*, ed. G. Zippel, in *RISS*, III, pt. 16 (1904), 44, and Michele Canensi, *De vita et pontificatu Pauli II, ibid.*, pp. 145–46. Zippel, pp. 185–88, gives the text of the bull *Quamvis ex commisso*, "datum Rome apud S. Marcum pridie Idus Februarias anno ab incarnatione Domini MCCCCLXVI, pontificatus nostri anno tertio" [12 February, 1467], which he misdates 14 February. *Cf.* Zippel, "Ricordi romani dei Cavalieri di Rodi," *Archivio della R. Società romana di storia patria*, XLIV (1921), 186–88.

On 2 July, 1956, an urn containing the remains of the Grand Master Zacosta was transferred from S. Peter's to the church of S. Maria on the Aventine. After a requiem mass on 3 July the urn was placed in a niche behind the main altar, where a plaque commemorating Zacosta's *translatio* now preserves the original text of the funerary stele in the Vatican grottoes (*cf.* the *Bulletin officiel du grand magistère de l'Ordre S. M. H. de Malte*, III [July–Aug. 1956], 5).

[40] Pall, "I Rapporti italo-albanesi," no. LXXII, p. 213. On 11 March (1467), however, Agostino wrote that the Venetian government was then appealing to the pope to assist Scanderbeg (*ibid.*, no. LXXX, p. 219). On the Venetian establishment in Albania and its governance, see the careful study of Giuseppe Valentini, "Dell'amministrazione veneta in Albania," in Agostino Pertusi, ed., *Venezia e il Levante fino al secolo XV*, 2 vols., Florence, 1973–74, I–2, 843–910.

[41] Pall, "I Rapporti italo-albanesi," nos. LXXIV–LXXV, p. 214, dated 11 and 13 February, 1467, and *cf.* no. LXXVIII, p. 216.

provided Ferrante would add thereto the same amount from his own funds (*de li soy*). Aside from this, according to the Milanese ambassadors, Scanderbeg had got nothing, and even this was "una cosa in aere," because the amount of the *census* was itself an unsettled question. As Scanderbeg prepared to leave Rome for Naples, he received depressing news from Albania, "como tutti li homeni de quelle terre . . . stavano desperati et malissimo contenti."[42]

After almost five weeks, dismal weeks, at the Curia the Albanian "champion" took the road to Naples. On 14 February (1467) Lorenzo da Pesaro wrote Duchess Bianca and Galeazzo Maria: "Scanderbeg departed today, in despair, for he has not received any money from the pope. A cardinal gave him two hundred ducats . . . . In jeering tones he said the other day to a cardinal that he would rather make war on the Church than on the Turk!"[43]

Five days later, on the nineteenth, Lorenzo and his colleague Agostino de' Rossi sent Bianca and Galeazzo a few further details: Scanderbeg had left Rome, "saying that he did not believe one could find greater cruelty anywhere in the world than among these priests!" His departure had been delayed, because he did not have money enough to pay his bill at the inn (*hostaria*) where he had been staying. The cardinal of S. Sisto, however, gave him two hundred ducats, of which he had only forty left as he was setting out for Naples. At the last moment, hearing of how poor Scanderbeg actually was, Paul II finally sent him 2,300 ducats, "and so he went away."[44]

Ferrante of Naples was more generous than the pope, promptly providing Scanderbeg with money, provisions, and arms.[45] The Venetians, despite the reports of the Milanese envoys, gave assurance of their continued support. Upon returning home, Scanderbeg took the field with a considerable army for a last encounter with Balaban Beg, who had in the meantime received strong reinforcements and again put Croia under siege. Scanderbeg harried the Turks day and night. In the spring of 1467, probably in April, he defeated a body of auxiliary troops being sent to Balaban, even capturing the latter's brother Yunus, who was in command of them. At the same time Balaban was himself killed by gunshot in a frantic attack upon Croia, and the Turks hastily abandoned the siege, withdrawing in frightened disorder into Macedonia.[46]

Agostino de' Rossi had informed Duchess Bianca and Galeazzo Maria on 11 March (1467) that the news had reached Rome the Turks were preparing "grandi armate" for attacks upon the Christians by both land and sea, although it was still unclear where they would seek to perpetrate their "ruina."[47] The Turkish objective

---

[42] Pall, "I Rapporti italo-albanesi," no. LXXVI, p. 215.

[43] Pall, "I Rapporti italo-albanesi," no. LXXVII, p. 216: ". . . Ello beffando disse l'altro dì a uno cardinale che nante voria fare guerra alla ghiesa che al Turcho!"

[44] Pall, "I Rapporti italo-albanesi," no. LXXVIII, pp. 216–17: ". . . con dire non credere se potesse trovare la mazore crudelitate al mondo cha in quisti preti. . . ." The cardinal of S. Sisto was Juan de Torquemada. He died on Monday, 26 September, 1468, according to the Acta Consistorialia, in Arch. Segr. Vaticano, Arm. XXXI, tom. 52, fol. 71^v (*cf.* Eubel, *Hierarchia*, II [1914, repr. 1960], no. 283, p. 36, and p. 65), and see Pietro Egidi, ed., *Necrologi e libri affini della provincia romana*, I (Rome, 1908), 300 (Fonti per la Storia d'Italia, XLIV).

[45] Franc. Trinchera, *Codice aragonese*, vol. I (1467–1468), Naples, 1866, nos. 22, 66, pp. 33, 90.

[46] Balaban Beg held Croia under siege through the winter of 1466–1467 (Radonić, *Djuradj Kastriot Skenderbeg*, no. 350, p. 196, doc. dated 18 February, 1467). He failed in an attack upon Croia in April, 1467, being wounded by gunshot (*de primo schiopeto*) and dying shortly thereafter (*ibid.*, nos. 359–60, p. 198, docs. dated 10 and 20 May, 1467). His brother had just been captured (*ibid.*, no. 359, p. 198a, repr. from V. V. Makušev, *Monumenta historica slavorum meridionalium*, II [Belgrade, 1882], 29–30). A Venetian chronicle (the *Cronica Zena*) notes under the date 7 September, *1466* (after Capello's attack upon Athens and Barbarigo's failure at Patras, on which see below), that the news had just arrived in Venice from Scutari "come . . . Scandrabecho havea roto Balaban-Bassa et tagliado molti Turchi a pezi" (ed. N. Iorga, *Notes et Extraits*, IV [Bucharest, 1915], 211); since Balaban Beg was still very much alive in April, 1467, Radonić, *op. cit.*, no. 379, p. 205, puts this text without comment under the date 7 September, *1467*. Apparently the provveditore of Scutari merely confirmed the fact of Balaban Beg's defeat in April, 1467, in a letter which reached Venice on the following 7 September. Accurate information was difficult to get, and such repetitions of news some months old were apparently always welcome.

Barletius, *De vita et gestis Scanderbegi*, 1st ed., Rome, 1509, bks. XI–XII, fols. CXLIII^v–CLIV^r; ed. Zagreb, 1743, pp. 334–61, knows a good deal about the events of 1466–1467, including the capture of Balaban's brother and Balaban's own death in his final desperate assault upon Croia (*edd. citt.*, fol. CLIV^v; pp. 360–61). Raynaldus inaccurately places these events under the year 1465 (*cf. Ann. eccl.*, ad ann. cit., nos. 16–19, vol. XIX [1693], pp. 173–74). Pastor, *Gesch. d. Päpste*, II (repr. 1955), 363, rightly places this defeat of Yunus and Balaban Beg in the spring of 1467, as of course does Pall, in the *Mélanges d'histoire générale*, II, 219–20. *Cf.* Babinger, *Maometto* (1957), pp. 373–74, 382–83, and Pall, "Les Relations entre la Hongrie et Scanderbeg," in *Revue historique du Sud-Est européen*, X (1933), 138–41.

[47] Pall, "I Rapporti italo-albanesi," no. LXXX, p. 219.

was to be Albania. Sultan Mehmed II returned in the summer with another great army. Thousands fled in terror from the Adriatic coast to Italy, leaving behind them all they owned. Durazzo was almost uninhabited except for military personnel. The city was well provisioned, however, and its walls strong. Mehmed made no serious attempt to take it, although a large Turkish cavalry force pillaged the surrounding country. Croia was in grave danger through most of July, but soon the sultan and his army were departing eastward. The Turkish campaign of 1467 had been even less effective than that of the previous year. The Albanians and their Venetian allies still held Croia. But another grim visitation of the plague occurred in 1467 also, and again the sultan spent the winter in the Balkan mountains before returning to Istanbul, apparently in February, 1468.[48] In fact the plague returned almost year after year, adding to the fearful hardships which Turkish depredation and a harsh administration imposed upon the poor inhabitants of the Balkans.

Venetian naval and military undertakings during 1466 proved hardly more successful than those of the Turks. In late April, Vettore Capello, leader of the war party on the lagoon, replaced Jacopo Loredan as captain-general of the sea. Capello set sail with twenty-five galleys for the Venetian ports in the Levant, and thence for the Gulf of Thessalonica and the northernmost Aegean, where he seized the islands of Imbros, Thasos, and Samothrace. It was a good beginning. Next he headed for the Athenian harbor of Piraeus with a fleet now consisting of twenty-eight galleys. He attacked Athens, and effected the surrender of Ligourio, northeast of Nauplia, which Jacopo Barbarigo, provveditore of the Morea, had reported in a dispatch of 17 November (1465) as having been captured by the Turks. Capello sent news of his victories in several letters to the doge (or rather to the Senate), the last coming from Coron on 18 July (1466), to which he received in reply the highest commendation for the signal services he was rendering the Republic on both land and sea (dated 5 September).[49]

Capello had indeed made a brilliant beginning. For a while it looked as though he might recover the city of Athens, which Venice had held for some years (1394–1402/3) between the reigns of Dukes Nerio I Acciajuoli and his illegitimate son Antonio I. The Turks had occupied the lower city on 4 June, 1456, and the Acropolis shortly thereafter.[50] They had found the almost impregnable fortress useful as a command post, and possession of Piraeus must have aided their activities in the Aegean. As we noted in the

---

[48] Some of the sources for the Turkish invasion of Albania during the summer of 1467 are collected in Radonić, *Djuradj Kastriot Skenderbeg*, pp. 199–206, and note Ljubić, *Listine*, X, 389–400; on the return of Mehmed II to Istanbul, see Radonić, *op. cit.*, pp. 211–12; *cf.* also Barletius, *Vita*, 1st ed., Rome, 1509, bk. XIII, fol. CLVI, and ed. Zagreb, 1743, pp. 364–66; *cf.* Hopf, "Griechenland im Mittelalter," in J. S. Ersch and J. G. Gruber, *Allgemeine Encyklopädie*, vol. 86 (Leipzig, 1868, repr. New York, 1960, vol. II), p. 157; Pastor, *Gesch. d. Päpste*, II (repr. 1955), 363; Babinger, *Maometto*, pp. 383–85, 389; and on the areas of Albania under Turkish control by March, 1467, see Halil Inalcik, "Les Régions de Kruje et de la Dibra autour de 1467, d'après les documents ottomans," *Studia Albanica*, V-2 (1968), 89–102, esp. pp. 95 ff.

[49] Arch. di Stato di Venezia, Sen. Secreta, Reg. 22, fol. 186ʳ [188ʳ]: "Capitaneo generali maris: Accepimus his superioribus diebus complures litteras vestras, et postremas ex portu Coroni XVIII Julii prope preteriti obsignatas, que nostro dominio gratissime fuerunt. Cum illis intellexerimus vos insulas Embros, Thiassos, Samothraciaque feliciter magnanimeque optinuisse, direptionem postea urbis Athenarum et deditionem demum Ligurii, optimi oppidi commodissimique in Peloponeso [but Barbarigo in Sathas, VI, 64, had described Ligourio as a weak castle.]. Que omnia tum pro nostri dominii existimatione tum pro vestra commendatione iocundissima nobis extiterunt. Vestram proinde virtutem et animi magnitudinem non possumus non parum cum nostro Rogatorum consilio commendare. Quod felix faustumque victorie initium rebus nostris bene favente Deo feliciores successus polliceri videtur: quemadmodum in illius ineffabili clementia speramus! . . ."

The Senate also informed Capello that they had sent him two large cannon to replace a very big one which had been ruined in earlier operations (*quam fractam vestris litteris significastis*) as well as 12,000 ducats. Although the Signoria appreciated Capello's plans for arming galleys during the coming winter for use against the Turk when the early spring came, his desires apparently exceeded the state's resources: ". . . Et quia ad presens non possumus vobis tot pecunias mittere quot exarmamento ipsarum X galearum satisfaciant, volumus vobisque mandamus ut pro summa ducatorum XXX millia, quos vobis hac de causa mittimus, ad exarmandum mittere debeatis illum galearum numerum quarum refusuris cum iamscriptis pecuniis satisfacere posse videbitis, in quarum numero volumus esse quatuor de magis veteribus satisfactioni refusurarum quarum usque suum a vobis discessum ita providebitis quod quando hic erunt nullum stadium seu molestiam habeamus. Mittemus preterea vobis de tempore in tempus de aliis pecuniis pro exarmamento aliarum galearum usque iamscriptum numerum X galearum quas exarmari decrevimus."

[50] For the sources, see K. M. Setton, in *A History of the Crusades*, III (1975), 272–73, notes 174–75, drawn from Setton, *Los Catalanes en Grecia*, Barcelona, 1975, pp. 183 and 196–97, notes 93–94, and *cf. Catalan Domination of Athens*, rev. ed., London, 1975, pp. 209–10.

previous chapter, Omar Beg had retired to Athens in the early fall of 1465, during his contest with Sigismondo Malatesta and Jacopo Barbarigo, because Athens was then better supplied with food and fodder than was the Morea.[51]

Capello had landed his troops on the Attic shore, and marched them before daybreak the four miles to Athens (on 12 July, 1466, according to Stefano Magno). He took the lower town, apparently without serious opposition. Sparing the Greek population, he burned the Turkish ships in Piraeus. He could not dislodge the Turkish garrison from the Acropolis, however, and withdrew in early August from Athens to Old Patras,[52] which Barbarigo had been trying to take with two thousand men, the remains of the armies of Bertoldo d'Este and Sigismondo Malatesta. When success had seemed attainable, Omar Beg had suddenly appeared, unseen and unexpected; Malatesta's secretary says that he had twelve thousand horsemen with him; driving the Venetian forces into the sea, Omar Beg took about one hundred prisoners and killed about six hundred in the battle. The prisoners were later put to death in Istanbul.[53] Barbarigo was killed in the encounter, and his body was impaled by the Turks at Patras. Some days later Capello arrived on the scene, too late to help Barbarigo, but determined to avenge him. Attacking Omar Beg at Patras, Capello was defeated with heavy losses. His reports to the Senate, written from Patras on 9 and 15 August, were no longer in jubilant tones, and on 7 September (1466) the senators answered him in far less happy tones than those of their preceding letter, sent only two days before. They lamented the death of Barbarigo and his brave companions, but reminded Capello that such were the fortunes of war. He must bear defeat with patience, strive to preserve the honor and reputation of the Republic, and guard well (as he had written he was doing) the safety of the men and fleet entrusted to his charge.[54]

The worst news coming from the East, however, was not the report that the Turkish fleet would soon be sailing from the Bosporus. It was the now persistent illness of Vettore Capello. The Senate feared that he could no longer manage (*quod . . . idem capitaneus personam suam exercere non posset*). If he was rendered *hors de combat*, the Venetian fleet and the fortunes of the Republic were on the rim of an abyss. On 25 March (1467), therefore, the Senate voted to replace him. The new captain-general should receive the same salary and be subject to the

[51] Jacopo Barbarigo, *Dispacci della guerra di Peloponneso*, in C. N. Sathas, ed., *Documents inédits relatifs à l'histoire de la Grèce au moyen âge*, VI (Paris, 1884, repr. Athens, 1972), no. 47, p. 51, lines 30–34, dispatch dated 14 October, 1465.

[52] On Vettore Capello's capture of Athens, see Stefano Magno, *Estratti degli Annali veneti*, ed. Hopf, *Chron. gréco-romanes* (1873, repr. 1966), p. 204: ". . . Venne [Vettore Capello] con galie 28 alle marine dell'antiqua e bella cittade de Greci Athene in nella provincia d'Acaia in nella region d'Attica chiamada al presente Setines, distante dalla marina mia 4, et adì 12 detto avanti zorno . . . ," he attacked Athens and took the city, etc. Capello's capture of Athens (*Setines*) is also described in the *Cronica Zena*, ed. N. Iorga, *Notes et extraits*, IV, 209–10. (In commenting on "Setines" in this text, Iorga writes that "il ne peut pas être question d'Athènes," which is precisely what it is, as the chronicler Malipiero, *Annali veneti*, in *Arch. stor. italiano*, VII, pt. 1 [1843], 37, knew well.) *Cf.* Geo. Sphrantzes, *Chron. minus* (*PG* 156, 1074C; ed. V. Grecu [1966], p. 132, lines 9–13), and Pseudo-Sphrantzes, *Chron. maius*, IV, 22 (Bonn, p. 425; ed. Grecu, p. 564, lines 16–20); Navagero, *Storia veneziana*, in *RISS*, XXIII (Milan, 1733), cols. 1125–26; Sanudo, *Vite de'duchi*, in *RISS*, XXII, col. 1183A, represents Capello's course as directly from Venice to Negroponte and the assault on Athens; Marcantonio Coccio Sabellico, *Historiae rerum venetarum*, ed. Venice, 1718, decad. III, bk. VIII, pp. 730–31. The historian Sabellico had his admirers in the Venetian Senate (Sen. Secreta, Reg. 33, fols. 9ʳ [19ʳ], 15ʳ [25ʳ], docs. dated 27 April and 3 June, 1486).

[53] Critobulus, V, 13 (ed. Müller, *FHG*, V-1 [1870], pp. 158b–159a; ed. V. Grecu, pp. 345, 347); C. N. Sathas, ed., *Documents inédits*, VI (1884, repr. 1972), 99, lines 31 ff.

[54] Sen. Secreta, Reg. 22, fol. 187ʳ [189ʳ]: "Ser Victori Capello, capitaneo generali maris: Nudius tertius [on 5 September] ad vos scripsimus quantum tunc usque novimus oportere: postea vero accepimus litteras vestras datas nono Augusti preteriti et successive XV mensis eiusdem contra Patrassium, ex quibus intelleximus accessum vestrum ad locum illum modosque observatos et demum inopinatum casum occursum quondam viro nobili Jacobo Barbadico, provisori nostro, ac spectabili quondam Michaeli Rali et Andree de Molino supracomito aliisque viris et gentibus nostris. Et respondentes cum nostro consilio Rogatorum dicimus: quod licet de casu predicto magnam displicentiam susceperimus ob interitum ipsius provisoris et aliorum nostrorum et reputationem rerum nostrarum illarum partium, sicut etiam vos ad nos scripsistis cum tamen isti sint de casibus qui adversante fortuna contingere solent, patienti animo ferendi sunt adhibendaque sunt studia et cogitamina cuncta nostra et vestra ad relevationem et conservationem honoris et reputationis nostre ut tandem propiciante clementissimo Domino, Deo nostro, contra perfidissimum hostem istum honor et gloria reportari possit. Quod autem in litteris ipsis vestris scribitis in omnibus rebus gerendis vos cum omni optimo respectu et securitate gentium et classis nostre processurum esse, maximopere nobis placet, nam consideratis artibus et fallaciis Turcorum non possumus satis laudare, commemorare et mandare vobis quod in hoc precipue sitis vigilans et intentus." There follow financial and military details as in the letter addressed to Capello on 5 September.

same conditions as had attended Capello's election.[55]

Five days later (on the thirtieth) the senators acknowledged that "it is manifest to this entire council and to all the city with what courage, greatness of heart, and diligence the noble Vettore Capello has conducted our affairs." The decision to proceed with the election of his successor had been made necessary because of the fear that he could no longer carry on, but now several letters, some of them in his own hand, had brought the reassuring word that he was recovering from his fever, and that within a few days he would go back aboard his galley to resume command of the fleet. If this proved to be the case, it would be unwise to replace him, and "therefore the motion is carried that the election of a new captain should be postponed for eight days and for as much longer as shall seem advisable to the Signoria and to the Collegio, so that upon the receipt of further news, which we should have within the aforesaid period, it may be possible to take more appropriate action."[56]

A week later everyone in Venice knew that Capello was dead.[57] Everyone knew that he was irreplaceable, but a new captain-general had to be elected. Capello's successor was to receive one hundred ducats a month salary and the usual perquisites. Upon notification of his election he was to reply within twenty-four hours; declination of the charge would entail a fine of one thousand ducats. Jacopo Loredan was re-elected to the post, and he accepted.[58]

Capello's defeat at Patras had been the last important event in his life. Ordering the survivors of his battered force back on board the galleys, he had sailed through the Archipelago to Negroponte, where he became ill. On 13 March, 1467, he died of a heart attack, *che i Greci chiamano "cardiaco."*[59] Sanudo reports that during the last five months of his life, after his defeat by the Turks, Capello was said never to have been seen smiling.[60] In recent years his tomb has been put back over the main portal of the church of S. Elena in Venice, where his body was interred after its return home. He kneels before S. Elena; the tomb stands behind them. The powerful rendering of Capello's figure, with the realistic portrayal of his features, is one of the finest works of the sculptor Antonio Rizzo (if indeed it is by him). The inscription reads: "D. IM. Victor Cappellus imperator maritimus maximis rebus gestis III et LX annos natus ab anno salutis MCCCCLXVII, III Idus Marcias in Euboia perrit, hic eius ossa, in caelo anima."

Capello's illness and concern for their fleet had not been the sole preoccupations of the Senate through these worrisome days. A deliberation of 30 March (1467) identifies a further problem, and casts a stark light on the failure of the crusading ideal to mould the mind of merchants and to alter the so-called spirit of capitalism:

> As is common knowledge, although we are involved in this desperate war with the Turk, the Anconitans never cease to sail with their trading ships [*naves*] and other vessels [*navigia*] to the Dardanelles and Constantinople, where they are now planning to send, among others, a ship of seven hundred light "tons" [*butarum VII c.*]. Not only do they carry on trade with the Turks, whereby we suffer grave damage, but they even transport arms and munitions, by means of which the war is waged against us the more easily and effectively. There is the further peril that their ships are received and armed against us by the Turks, and so we must face these additional hazards.

The motion was therefore made and passed in the Senate that the Collegio should send a secretary to Ancona to declare in appropriate and no uncertain terms

> that, owing to the losses and dangers aforesaid, . . . we are unwilling that their trading ships and vessels should continue to sail to the Dardanelles and Constantinople as long as the aforesaid war shall last, and that from now on we are making it known to the . . . commune [of Ancona] that if their ships set out for these places, and are captured by our fleet or [other] ships, we shall regard them as being subject to confiscation [*capi potuisse*], as the spoils of a just and righteous war.[61]

---

[55] Sen. Secreta, Reg. 23, fol. 29^v [31^v].

[56] Sen. Secreta, Reg. 23, fol. 30^r [32^r]. The motion was passed, as the upright cross in the left margin indicates, by a vote *de parte* 109, *de non* 48, *non sinceri* 8.

[57] Sen. Secreta, Reg. 23, fol. 33^v [35^v], doc. dated 7 April, 1467, seems to contain the Senate's first notice of Capello's death: "Quoniam ob casum quondam viri nobilis Victoris Capello capitanei nostri generalis maris, cui parcat clementissimus dominus deus noster, attentis maxime his, que undique referuntur de classe Turcorum que dicitur exitura strictum, pro evidentissimo commodo nostri status summe necessarium est cunctis dilationibus postpositis eligere et quam citissime expedire unum capitaneum nostrum generalem maris. . . ."

[58] Sen. Secreta, Reg. 23, fols. 33^v–34^r [35^v–36^r].

[59] Malatesta's secretary, in Sathas, VI, 99; *Cronica Zena*, ed. Iorga, *Notes et extraits*, IV, 210, 211, 212.

[60] *Vite de'duchi*, in *RISS*, XXII, col. 1184B.

[61] Sen. Secreta, Reg. 23, fol. 30^r [32^r], the motion being passed *de parte* 130, *de non* 14, *non sinceri* 16. In the middle ages, as in antiquity, the size of a ship was reckoned in terms of its "tunnage" or tonnage, i.e., its capacity to carry wine, the Venetian *buta*, *botta* or *botte*

On 6 April (1467) the Senate could recall with satisfaction the decision of a week before to send a secretary to warn the Anconitans against further traffic with the Turks. The news had just come that a large Anconitan ship had left port some time before, passed through Ragusan waters, and was then heading for the Dardanelles. It was further stated that among other cargo (including munitions) she had aboard 1,500 sacks of ship's biscuit (*sacchi M Vc. biscocti*), which were clearly intended for the Turkish fleet then being readied for action in the arsenal at Istanbul. The Turks would certainly retain the Anconitan ship (or so it was stated), and arm it also for action against the Venetians. Letters were, therefore, to be sent to the captain-general by the next galley to leave the lagoon (and by other means as well) telling him that he must try to intercept the ship, and seize the biscuit and munitions she was carrying. If it seemed expedient, the captain-general was also to seize the ship.[62] Within hours the news must have reached Venice that the captain-general Vettore Capello was dead, but the provveditori with the fleet would try to see that the Senate's orders were carried out.

Every spring one debated the same question in Venice: Where was the Turk going to strike? In Jacopo Loredan's commission of reappointment as captain-general of the sea the Doge Cristoforo Moro began with the statement that Mehmed II's preparation of a powerful fleet as well as a land army was widely assumed to have Negroponte as its objective. Loredan was therefore to hasten to Modon and thence to Negroponte. He received ten thousand ducats for expenditure on the fleet, especially on the older galleys, "and we shall take care to send you other funds from time to time." He would also have the money which had been in Capello's possession when he died. Negroponte must be held at all cost. It was the "shield and base of our state in the East." Loredan was also to convey two thousand ducats to the colonial government of Corfu for the purchase of grain and the production of ship's biscuit for the fleet, and another thousand to the Venetian officials at Negroponte for the same purpose. He was to prevent as best he could the Anconitan trade in supplies and munitions with Istanbul, and finally (among other instructions) he was directed to take 1,500 ducats, in addition to the sums already mentioned, to Paolo Priuli, the newly appointed provveditore in the Morea, "for the purchase of horses for the lord Girolamo de Novello,"[63] one of Malatesta's successors.

Shortly after the reappointment of Loredan as captain-general, Dr. Niccolò da Canale, who had recently served as the Venetian ambassador to France and thereafter to the Holy See, was named provveditore of the city and island of Negroponte (on 26 April, 1467). He was to receive a salary of 100 ducats a month, and to take with him a notary of the chancery, who might have one servant, "and you will have eight servants, all at the expense of our Signoria." His instructions, like those of Loredan, were to hold the city and island at all cost, and the commission he received from the doge directed him:

> If by chance, which God forbid, the captain-general of the sea should fall ill or suffer some infirmity so that he should be unable to carry on or if he should die, we order you . . . , if some one of the aforesaid contingencies should occur, at once to embark as captain of the galleys of our fleet . . . , assuming the responsibility of the said captaincy until . . . the captain-general shall regain his former health. . . .[64]

The Venetian suspicion that Sultan Mehmed was contemplating an attack upon Negroponte was wholly justified. The attack would not come, however, until a few more years had passed. And when it came, unfortunately for Venice and for

("butt"), weighing about 640 kg. (1,411 lbs. or .63 long ton), on which see F. C. Lane, "Tonnages, Medieval and Modern," *Economic History Review*, 2nd ser., XVII (1964), 213–33, reprinted in *Venice and History*, Baltimore, 1966, pp. 345–70, esp. pp. 349, 352–53, 357–58, 366.

[62] Sen. Secreta, Reg. 23, fol. 33^{r} [35^{r}].

[63] Sen. Secreta, Reg. 23, fols. 35^{r}–36^{v} [37^{r}–38^{v}], dated 15 April, 1467, and *cf.* fol. 41^{v} [43^{v}]. A few weeks earlier the Venetian Senate had been preparing to send the condottiere Girolamo de Novello with five hundred horse and "a goodly number of foot" to add to the defenses of the Morea, while Paolo Priuli was to go to Modon with 8,000 ducats to hold a muster of troopers in Venetian employ and to recruit up to five hundred additional stradioti "at the usual rate of pay" (*ibid.*, fol. 30^{v} [32^{v}], doc. dated 21 March, 1467, and "registrata hic, quod non fuit data in tempore," for the text should have been entered at fol. 29^{v} [31^{v}]).

[64] Sen. Secreta, Reg. 23, fols. 39^{v}–40^{r} [41^{v}–42^{r}], but note fols. 64^{v} ff., 71^{r}, 75^{v}–76^{r}, 80^{r} [66^{v} ff., etc.], which show that the Senate also entertained the forlorn hope that Canale might manage "negotia pacis cum Turcho." In June, 1468, Canale was sent on a mission to Bartolommeo Colleoni (*ibid.*, fols. 118^{r}–119^{r}, 119^{v}, 127^{r} [120^{r} ff.]), who was long in Venetian employ. Colleoni figures prominently in the senatorial documents of these years. His fame today rests largely upon his equestrian statue by Andrea Verrocchio and Alessandro Leopardi in the Campo SS. Giovanni e Paolo in Venice.

him, Canale would in fact be captain-general of the sea.

In the meantime, as the Anconitans carried on their traffic with the Turks, the Venetians had the satisfaction of capturing some of their vessels. On 7 September (1467) the Senate voted to have them sent to Venice with all their cargo except for the ship's biscuit, which the captain-general could reserve for the needs of his own crews. The Senate also wanted all the written evidence relating to the Anconitans' shipping "contraband" (*res vetitae*) to Istanbul,[65] and on the twenty-second of the month they explained their action to the Florentine government, which was itself not above trading with the Turk. Actually the Anconitan vessels had been sailing from Istanbul to Italy when they were captured, but the Anconitans had been (according to the Venetian Senate) shamelessly shipping to Istanbul "arms, powder, and all sorts of munitions which the enemy lacks."[66] A year later (on 2 September, 1468) the matter came up again before the Senate. An Anconitan envoy had arrived in Venice, and had appealed to the Signoria "that we should be willing to have certain contraband and other goods restored by the office of *avogadori del comun*, and also to allow his fellow citizens . . . of Ancona . . . to have their merchandise removed to Rimini." The Senate replied that the matter was no longer in their hands, but the envoy might, if he so wished, take his case to the avogadori and the other officers of state concerned.[67]

When the war began, Venetian merchants had been imprisoned, and some had been executed by the Porte. A few had braved untold dangers to protect their commercial interests in the Ottoman empire. As the years passed, Venetian trade with subjects of the Porte was being reduced to nothing. The revenues of the state suffered accordingly. Venice bore the brunt of the costs of the offensive against the Turks both in subsidies to Matthias Corvinus and in her own efforts on land and sea. The statesmen of the hard-pressed Republic could not arrange peace with Mehmed II, who probably preferred a condition of war, being constantly abetted by the Florentines and Genoese in the capital, who were not made unhappy by the continuing discomfiture of Venice.[68] To a Venetian embassy which proposed peace on the basis of each party's retaining what it then possessed, Mehmed returned a blank refusal, demanding the return of the islands of Imbros and Lemnos as well as the payment of an annual tribute by the Republic,[69] which was, of course, unwilling to accept any such mark of inferiority.

The Venetians had found no allies in western Europe. Only mutual necessity bound the Hungarians and Albanians to them. The papacy was usually ready to help any person or power hostile to the Turks, and yet the popes had only money, which was to be sure the *nervus belli*, although the Venetians had almost three times the income of the papacy, in more normal times at least.[70] There were few who loved Venice except the Venetians. Their admirer Bessarion still did all he could to prosecute the war against the Turks, but Pius II had held them in disdain, and even their own countryman Paul II was at constant odds with them. Paul was also a true Venetian. He did not want to invest too heavily in Scanderbeg's efforts against the Turks until he could be sure that his money would be profitably employed. The unpopularity of the Venetians was not confined to the Italian peninsula, as Louis XI had made clear to Pius II when he sent him the troublesome embassy in the spring of 1464, which by royal command had postponed Philip of Burgundy's departure on the crusade until the restoration of peace between France and England. Louis XI's ambassadors had been instructed to state as his opinion

that this enterprise was honorable neither to the pope nor to the duke of Burgundy—thus to undertake it with true tradesmen [the Venetians], insolent and common, who do not wage this war for reverence of God, but on their own account and with the special purpose of defending themselves against the Turk

[65] *Ibid.*, Reg. 23, fol. 70ᵛ [72ᵛ]: "Quod mandetur capitaneo generali maris ut mittere huc debeat naves Anchonitanorum captas per capitaneum navium armatarum [of which there were four with Loredan's galleys, as the Senate had informed their ambassadors in Rome on 2 June, for which see fol. 44ʳ] simul cum omnibus mercantiis et bonis que in eis erant quando capte fuerunt excepto biscoto et cum omni processu et examinationibus factis et cum omnibus litteris et scripturis ad declarationem veritatis circa res vetitas conductas Constantinopolim opportunis et necessariis."

[66] *Ibid.*, Reg. 23, fol. 73ʳ [75ʳ], and *cf.* fols. 83, 85ᵛ, 88ᵛ, 92ʳ [85, 87ᵛ, etc.].

[67] Sen. Secreta, Reg. 23, fol. 130ʳ [132ʳ]. The Venetians kept the port of Ancona under constant surveillance. On 27 September (1468) the Senate allowed Paul II to export grain from Ancona (*ibid.*, fol. 132 [134]).

[68] *Cf.* Sanudo, *Vite*, in *RISS*, XXII, cols. 1183–84.

[69] Critobulus, V, 15 (ed. Müller, *FHG*, V–1, p. 159; ed. Grecu, pp. 347, 349).

[70] *Cf.* Gottlob, *Aus der Camera Apostolica*, pp. 257–58.

and of making great gain with the money of the pope and of the duke of Burgundy: they would have to serve in the armada, as desired by the Venetians, who are more powerful on the sea than the pope and the duke of Burgundy because of their ships and their overseas dominion; if the Venetians were doing this for love of God, they would have done many years ago what they want to do now, especially when the pope was at Mantua for this purpose, and they would not have allowed the defeat of the prince of the Morea, nor of the king of Bosnia, whom they have allowed to be ruined by the occupation of their states, just as they did with Constantinople![71]

The reputation of the Venetians for self-seeking was widespread, and it increased their difficulties in securing aid against the Turks. When the Venetian envoy Giovanni Gonela stopped off at Milan on his way to Genoa in October, 1467, Duke Galeazzo Maria Sforza had something to say to him about the unpopularity of his countrymen. Seeking out the duke to take leave of him, Gonela found him at chapel. Galeazzo Maria dismissed his attendants, and spoke to Gonela frankly in private:

I told you yesterday . . . part of what I want to tell you before you depart, [but] I wish to say these few words to you in addition. You Venetians have certainly behaved very badly, having the finest state in Italy, not to be content with it, and to disturb the peace and state[s] of others. If you knew the ill will which all men everywhere have against you, your hair would stand on end, and you would let everyone live [at peace] in his own state. Do you think that these Italian powers which have banded together are friendly to one another? Certainly not! But necessity has led them to get together, constrained by the fear they have of you and of your power. Everyone will do his utmost to clip your wings. . . .

Believe me, I am telling you the truth. . . . Let everyone lead his own life, leave him alone. . . . [The Venetians have forced him into an alliance with King Ferrante of Naples, "who is my mortal enemy!"] You have spent money enough, and you have made others spend it. You preach peace, and make as much war as you can. . . . [Venice has alienated Paul II, himself a Venetian; Ferrante urges the duke to break with Venice; and the Florentines and Genoese, like the other Italian states, are biding their time.] The *signori* have a great advantage over the *signorie*, because the latter must rely on others, and the signori are always on their own. A signore counts for more and does more with fifty thousand ducats than a signoria with a hundred thousand, because a signore sees what his soldiers do, and the soldiers do all they can in the presence of their lords. . . . You are free to have peace or war.

If you want peace, you'll have it. If you want war, you'll have the most dangerous war you have had in [all] your days. You are alone, and have all the world against you, not only in Italy, but even beyond the mountains. Be assured that your enemies are not sleeping. Take good counsel, for by God you need it! I know what I am saying. You have a splendid state, and a larger income than any power in Italy. Don't squander it—*dubius est eventus belli*. . . .[72]

Galeazzo Maria knew whereof he spoke. The rulers of the Italian states, including Paul II, had had the jitters since the death of Galeazzo Maria's father the year before. On 9 March, 1467, for example, Paul had addressed a bull to Marquis Lodovico Gonzaga and to all the chief powers in the peninsula, warning them that Francesco Sforza's removal from the scene might well upset the political equilibrium in Italy. He urged them all (and he doubtless had his native Venice especially in mind) "ut pacem italicam servarent." The Turkish danger increased with every passing day. "Without doubt," Paul wrote Gonzaga, "it is common knowledge that, unless the Italian peace [*fedus*] remains firm and stable, ruin hangs over not only all Italians, but even all Christians." Nicholas V had with great wisdom confirmed the peace [of Lodi], and Paul had

[71] Albrico Malletta, Milanese ambassador at the French court, to Francesco Sforza, dated 27 April, 1464 (Pastor, *Acta inedita*, I [1904], no. 188, p. 284). Actually the Venetians did not want either Pius II or the duke of Burgundy to go with the crusading fleet; in fact they wanted the pope to stay home and use the money he was spending on his *aparato* to send men of arms into Albania. They also wanted the pope to send Matthias Corvinus 100,000 ducats, and reduce his own naval and military preparations accordingly, but Pius said he could not help the Hungarians with money, requiring 214,000 ducats for his own expenses even before he put to sea, being obliged to pay his galleys six months in advance, purchase munitions, and meet other expenses, let alone the cost of administering the states of the Church in his absence. Although Pius stated that it was beneath the papal dignity to go "con mancho compagnia" (and he insisted on going), it is clear that he wanted a large force at his disposal since his faith in the Venetians was also limited. In any event Venice wanted both the pope and the duke of Burgundy to concentrate on the land forces, contrary to the implication of Louis XI, whose views concerning the Venetians, however, were in general accord with the pope's own (*ibid.*, nos. 177–78, pp. 263–66). In purely military terms the Venetian plan made better sense, but Pius was obviously thinking of the administration of conquered territory, and was unwilling to leave all the Morea, the ports, and the islands to Venice, after the crusaders' land armies had grappled with the Turks in the highlands of Albania and Bosnia!

[72] Malipiero (according to Gonela's own report), *Annali veneti*, ad ann. 1467, in *Archivio storico italiano*, VII, pt. 1 (1843), 215–18, and note pp. 221–24, and Kretschmayr, *Gesch. v. Venedig*, II (1920, repr. 1964), 373–74, 635.

himself approved it. It was the necessary shield of Italy, and must be preserved with unremitting vigilance. The Turk was always on the horizon. Despite the impelling necessity of the crusade, there were those who were prepared to disrupt the peace of Italy—a pestilential, detestable thought—but Paul did not for a moment doubt that the marquis shared his view of the crying need to maintain peace. He exhorted Lodovico (and the other powers) to do everything possible to keep the *pax universalis italica*, without which the peninsula would fall prey to unspeakable discord.[73]

The Turkish peril was something the Venetians understood. No one knew better than they that Paul II was not exaggerating, or at least not exaggerating very much. In a ducal commission dated 2 June (1467), naming Pietro Morosini and Giovanni Soranzo as special envoys to the Holy See, the appointees were instructed to inform the pontiff

> that it has always been our desire to maintain . . . ambassadors at the court of his Holiness, and in fact the reason why the Curia Romana has not had our ambassadors on hand at this time has merely been our wish not to detract from the dignity . . . of this most reverend father and lord cardinal legate [Juan de Carvajal], who in all his actions displays so much wisdom and consideration that he has deservedly won the esteem of our entire city, but now in truth under the pressure of developments in Turkey, we have decided to delay no longer and to send our ambassadors to you.

Morosini and Soranzo were to inform the pope that Albania was in fearful peril "because of the Turk's approach to that province with a most powerful army" which, according to various reports reaching Venice, had already drawn close to the Albanian borders.

The Senate was exasperated as well as apprehensive, for "although that most barbarous and crafty enemy . . . has made a show of intending to leave the Hellespont with a large fleet, so that we had to counter his gruesome efforts by making provision for the expansion of our fleet by a larger number of galleys than heretofore . . . and to fortify all our maritime holdings with hired soldiery at very great and indeed unbearable expense," the sultan had actually not been concentrating his efforts upon arming his galleys, but had obviously been planning the invasion of Albania. He realized all too clearly the importance of Albania *ad res italicas*, and he was aiming at the occupation of Durazzo. "Although despite the incredible expense of our fleet," as the Venetian ambassadors were to tell the pope,

> and of the forces we have sent to the Peloponnesus, Negroponte, and our coastal possessions, we have not stopped sending infantry in large numbers into Albania and assisting the magnificent lord Scanderbeg; nevertheless, we know very well that greater strength and more effective units are required to repress so great an attack—and a danger that threatens all Christendom.
>
> And therefore you will beg his Holiness . . . to deem worthy of consideration, with his accustomed prudence and exceeding wisdom, this [sad] state of affairs . . . and quickly to provide those salutary remedies which the magnitude of the peril demands. For when [the sultan] has occupied the coast of Albania, which God forbid, nothing else remains but for him to cross over into Italy, whenever he wishes, for the destruction of all Christendom![74]

---

[73] Arch. di Stato di Mantova, Arch. Gonzaga, Busta 834, "datum Rome apud Sanctum Marcum, anno incarnationis dominice millesimo quadringentesimo sexagesimo sexto, septimo Id. Martii, pontificatus nostri anno tertio." In 1467–1468, following prolonged negotiations, Paul II helped to secure a general peace in Italy, which was to be the prelude to an expedition against the Turks, ". . . volens inherere vestigiis felicis recordationis domini Nicolai pape Quinti sue Sanctitatis predecessoris, qui publicam Italie pacem tunc etiam confectam inivit, contraxit, recepit, acceptavit, benedixit, approbavit, et confirmavit ut commodius rei publice Christianorum adversus impios Turchos consuli faciliusque expeditioni excercitus [*sic*] Christianorum contra eosdem Turchos intendi valeat et possit . . ." (Arch. Segr. Vaticano, A. A., Arm. I–XVIII, no. 1443, fol. 46ᵛ, *cf.* 45ʳ, *et alibi*). For the general instrument of peace, full documentation relating to the negotiations, and the Neapolitan, Venetian, Milanese, and Florentine declarations, together with the statements attesting entry into the peace by Modena and Siena, the conditions of ratification by the high contracting parties, the instruments of the new Italian Confederation, etc., see MS. cited, fols. 45ʳ–98ʳ, which illustrates the political structure of Italy at this time in the fullest possible detail.

[74] Sen. Secreta, Reg. 23, fol. 44ʳ [46ʳ], and *cf.* fol. 56ᵛ [58ᵛ], dated 24 July, 1467, a letter (which was not sent) to the Venetian ambassadors in Rome: "Scripsimus iam vobis et noticiam dedimus de novis gravibus et periculosis que ex Albania accepimus, ubi Turcus ipse cum potentissimo exercitu reperitur et ultra miserabiles cedes et horribiles crudelitates quibus usus est et utitur quotidie in ea provincia, igni et ferro omnia vastando ac immanissime perdendo gentem illam, irrumpere intentat in agros et oppida nostra et in primis occupare urbem Dyrachii quo sibi muniat viam et transitum in Italiam!" Note also, *ibid.*, fols. 92ᵛ–93ᵛ [94ᵛ–95ᵛ]. Venice had thus a desperate need for additional funds, much more than the two tithes which Paul II had allowed to be levied on ecclesiastics, and which the abbot of S. Gregorio had been deputed to collect, but above all there was need of haste in making the collections and putting them to use against the Turk (fols. 56ᵛ, 133ᵛ [58ᵛ, 135ᵛ]).

The Venetian captain-general Jacopo Loredan was probably relieved by Sultan Mehmed's concentration upon Albania. Loredan was competent and experienced, but he lacked Vettore Capello's dash and daring. Although he was prepared to follow orders, Loredan was freed of a grave responsibility by the senatorial decision (of 22 July, 1467) that the fleet should not operate for long off the straits of Gallipoli and should not make a landing on the island of Mytilene.[75] The Venetians were fastening their attention upon Albania, where Mehmed was trying once more to take Croia. Although he was unable to force the surrender of the fortress, and had to withdraw after the customary depredation of the land, Turkish raiding parties could now reach the Adriatic coast whenever they wished from Bosnia. The Herzegovina was ravaged. Ragusa was in danger. The long campaign may have been too strenuous for the aging Scanderbeg. He died on 17 January, 1468, at Alessio (Lesh), where he was buried in the cathedral church of S. Niccolò (later transformed into a mosque).

News of Scanderbeg's death reached Venice before 13 February, by which time all Albania was *in magno tumultu et trepidatione*. Paulus Angelus, the archbishop of Durazzo (1460–1469), was in Venice at the time, having come as an envoy on Scanderbeg's behalf. He had been there for some time. The Senate regarded him as a good and faithful friend, and wanted him to hurry back to Albania to use his influence with Scanderbeg's widow, son, retainers, and subjects to try to introduce some order into the confusion. The Senate voted the archbishop two hundred and twenty ducats, which he apparently claimed the Republic owed him, and voted to send him on his way with the assurance that his labors would be well rewarded. They wanted him to work with Francesco Capello, the newly appointed Venetian provveditore in Albania, where they voted also to send another two hundred foot and one hundred artillerymen (*ballistarii ac sclopeterii*),[76] who might be more useful than the archbishop.

A decade later Mehmed II removed Scanderbeg's body when, as we shall see, the Turks overran Albania (in 1478), and conquered from the Tocchi the last shreds of the Epirote despotate and county palatine of Cephalonia (in 1479).[77] We have already noted the Venetian acquisition of much of the Dalmatian coast by purchase from King Ladislas of Naples (in July, 1409), to which the Republic gave effect by force of arms in the years that followed, until by 1420–1422 the lion banners of the evangelist were floating over the fortifications of most of the strategic ports along the eastern shores and islands of the Adriatic.[78] Sometimes it looked as though the Ragusei might again fall under Venetian domination as they had in 1205. They retained their independence, however, under the nominal suzerainty of Hungary. If they found life precarious, they did not find it

---

[75] Sen. Secreta, Reg. 23, fol. 55r [57r], doc. dated 22 July, 1467, the doge (actually the Senate) to Loredan: "Accepimus his diebus nonnullas litteras vestras . . . quibus, quamquam occurrentia iuxta accuratam consuetudinem vestram nobis diligenter significastis deque profectione vestra ad angustias Calipollis, vestram solitam virtutem et diligentiam plurimum commendantes cum nostro Rogatorum consilio vobis respondemus: Et primo ad partem expeditionis adversus Mithilinum eiusmodi rem per conditiones temporum et rerum nostrarum ad presens nobis difficillimam videri. Ad secundam vero partem exponendarum turmarum et hominum istius classis nostre in terram dicimus ob pericula que facile accidere possent nos vestram sententiam laudare vobiscumque in opinione concurere." A year later the Senate was still discussing the projected attack upon Mytilene (*ibid.*, fol. 116r [118r], dated 25 June, 1468).

[76] Sen. Secreta, Reg. 23, fol. 94 [96], a resolution of the Senate dated 13 February, 1468 (Ven. style 1467): "Sicut per litteras vicerectoris nostri Dyrachii intelligitur, mortuus est magnificus quondam Scandarbegus ob cuius obitum universa illa provincia in magno tumultu et trepidatione est constituta, unde necessario est providendum conservationi tam locorum prefati quondam domini Scandarbegi quam nostrorum, propterea: Vadit pars quod cum omni possibili celeritate expediatur hinc ut in provinciam illam redeat reverendus dominus archiepiscopus Dyrachii, qui apud nos diu stetit orator nomine prefati quondam domini Scandarbegi, et est persona multum prudens et nobis statuique nostro fidelis et devota. Habet preterea et apud uxorem et filium ceterosque tam familiares quam subditos prefati quondam domini Scandarbegi creditum et auctoritatem, cuius presentia et consilio sperandum est res illas facilius dirigi et stabiliri posse. Et quoniam reverenda paternitas sua habere debet, ut asserit, a nostro dominio ducatos circa 220, captum sit quod denarii predicti eidem domino archiepiscopo dari debeant, et bonis verbis hortetur ut alacriter vadat et operetur sicut est consuetus, quoniam dominium nostrum erga eum utetur gratuitate et ita ut laborum et fidelium operationum suarum merito poterit contentari. . . ." *Cf.*, *ibid.*, fol. 100r [102r].

[77] *Cf.* Iorga, *Gesch. d. osman. Reiches*, II (Gotha, 1909), 140–41, 185–89; Pastor, *Gesch. d. Päpste*, II (repr. 1955), 363–64; Babinger, *Maometto* (1957), pp. 390–91, 540; Pall, in *Mélanges d'histoire générale*, II (1938), 221–22. The documentary texts bearing upon Scanderbeg's death may be found in Radonić, *Djuradj Kastriot Skenderbeg*, pp. 208–11; *cf.* Barletius, *De vita et gestis Scanderbegi*, 1st ed., Rome, 1509, bk. XIII, fols. CLVIv–CLIX; ed. Zagreb, 1743, pp. 366–73; and note Frano Prendi, "Le Lieu de sépulture de Skanderbeg," *Studia Albanica*, V-1 (1968), 159–67.

[78] See Volume I, pp. 403–4.

hopeless. Ragusa was an important midway point between Christendom and Islam, and the "argosies" carried goods for sale into both western and Turkish ports. The well-known palace of the rectors (the *knežev dvor*) was rebuilt at this time (in 1468), and now begins the long series of Ragusan writers from Ilija Crijević to Junija Palmotić, who for some two centuries wrote epics and dramas, songs and lyrics, pastorals and eulogies in Serbocroatian, Italian, and Latin. Strongly influenced by Italian culture, these writers often made the Turks their theme.

As the prospects for peace in Italy improved, Paul II pledged his continued allegiance to the crusade in a bull prepared *ad futuram rei memoriam* (on 22 February, 1468). He lamented the "calamitous situation of our times and the barbarous, unrelenting pressure of the Turks upon the Christians" (*calamitosa modernis temporibus conditio et seva contra Christicolas ingensque Turchorum perseveratio*). He wished to put the resources of the Holy See at the disposal of those who could use them in defense of the faith and the faithful. Indeed, he said that, since the death of his predecessor Pius II, he had spent no small part of those resources—200,000 florins in fact—on subsidies to assist the Hungarians, the despots of the Morea and Arta, the lord Scanderbeg in Albania, and "many other magnates, provinces, and peoples." Like Christ whose vicar he was, Paul would shed his own blood for the Christian cause, and he held up as the model of a Christian prince Francis II, duke of Brittany (1458–1488), upon whose aid he knew he could depend.[79]

By the middle of May, 1468, it was known in the Venetian Senate that Mehmed II had crossed over into Anatolia on a campaign against Uzun Ḥasan. For a brief while this suggested some relief and relaxation for those aboard the Venetian fleet. Many senators even thought that the captain-general Loredan should be allowed to return home.[80] But the memory of Vettore Capello prevailed in the Senate, and the war party had its way. Two weeks later (on 3 June), the doge wrote Loredan:

> Never, in everyone's judgment, has there been a more promising and favorable period than at present for embarking upon an expedition against the Turk, the fierce enemy of our faith. The opportunity has been divinely granted to us at this time when, besides the poor conditions in his domains and especially the plague, he is far away in distant lands in Asia [Minor], from which he cannot return for many days and months. His whole army, furthermore, will probably come back in poor condition. Consequently, placing our hope in the clemency of Almighty God and relying upon your courage and experience, we wish and, with the Senate, we order that . . . after receiving the twenty thousand ducats we are sending you, . . . communicating with our provveditore in the Morea, and seeking also the advice of our faithful Count Mechra . . . , you must consider embarking upon such an expedition as you shall deem both honorable and expedient.

To insure success in the undertaking Loredan was to recruit from Crete, Corfu, and other Venetian territories whatever men he thought might be needed. He was to use part of the twenty thousand ducats he would soon receive, for the enrollment of more stradioti, so that he would have two thousand of them ready for action. The Signoria was going to send him immediately some four hundred foot soldiers under three or four constables. Jacopo Venier, the captain of the Gulf (the Adriatic), would be instructed to leave two galleys for the protection

---

[79] Reg. Vat. 540 [*Pauli II, de Curia, lib. II*], fols. 16^v–20^v, "datum Rome apud Sanctum Marcum, anno etc., millesimo quadringentesimo sexagesimo septimo, octavo Kal. Martii, pont. nostri anno quarto:" "Cupientesque pro eiusdem fidei defensione et Christianorum salute non solum exponere nostras et Sedis Apostolice facultates nostre dispositioni commissas, quarum partem non exiguam a tempore obitus sancte recordationis Pii immediati predecessoris nostri tam pro dilectorum filiorum Ungarorum subsidio quam nobilium virorum despoti Moree, Scanalbec domini in Albania, et despoti Arte ac aliorum quamplurimorum magnatum, provintiarum et populorum subventione rebusque aliis ad hanc rem conferentibus saluti fidelium oportunis usque ad summam ducentorum millium florenorum liberaliter errogavimus, sed et si opus fuerit immitatione illius cuius vicariatum licet immeriti tenemus in terris proprium effundere sanguinem et incommoda quecumque subire eo equidem ferventius quo dilectum filium nobilem virum Franciscum Britannie ducem nobis et Apostolice Sedi devotissimum obsequentissimumque et pro fidei eiusdem zelatorem ad significationem nostram de premissis certiorem effectum inter alios catholicos principes huic nostro pio atque laudabili desiderio spontaneum adiutorem et cohoperatorem indubie habere speramus . . ." (*ibid.*, fols. 17^v–18^r).

[80] Sen. Secreta, Reg. 23, fol. 113 [115], dated 19 May, 1468: "Quoniam variis et diversis viis intelligitur Turcum transisse in Natoliam causa eundi contra Usum Cassam cumque iustum et conveniens sit ut nobili viro Jacobo Lauredano, procuratori, capitaneo nostro generali maris, qui diu ad multum fuit extra, concedatur licentia repatriandi . . . :" there were two votes on the proposal (*de parte* 75, *de non* 1, *non sinceri* 2 and 79-0-4), but there is no cross in the left-hand margin of the register opposite this entry, and Loredan was not granted the *licentia repatriandi*, as the next letters addressed to him make abundantly clear. He held the post for about six more months.

of the Venetian strongholds and stations on the Albanian coast, and to sail eastward with his other galleys to place himself under Loredan's command.[81]

Within a few days a letter went off to Rome, describing this golden opportunity to strike at the Porte while the sultan was absent in Anatolia. Victory over the Turk had been divinely ordained to come in Paul II's time, as the Doge Cristoforo Moro wrote his Holiness on the Senate's instruction, and they must not allow success to slip from their fingers.[82] Paul also saw a golden opportunity in this news from the East, as is clear from the Senate's response to the pope's answer:

> With our usual devotion and filial respect we have received your Holiness's brief dated the second of the present month with reference to the two tithes which your Holiness has on other occasions allowed us to collect each year from ecclesiastics. Your Holiness states in his brief that he has [previously] conceded the two tithes in order that the Turk might be driven from Albania . . . , but that now, since the Turk himself is far away . . . , we ought to be content with only one tithe.

To be sure, the Senate replied, the Turk was far away, but his power was still so great that he could strike at and destroy Christians wherever in the Levant he chose. Indeed, the pope must have heard that Turkish forces had just attacked Andros, killed the lord of the island, sacked the city, and carried off a huge number of the inhabitants. Thousands upon thousands of Turks had recently carried their deadly raids as far westward as Segna (Senj) and Zara, *fores scilicet Italie*, laying waste everything with fire and sword and carrying off an incredible booty in cattle and captives. Venice was fighting the Turks alone; she desperately needed both tithes.[83]

Paul granted the double tithe again, and the Senate thanked him on 8 October with new tales of Turkish raids and atrocities in Croatia and Dalmatia.[84] Despite all the rhetoric, neither the Venetians nor the Hungarians had been in any position to make an effective attack upon the Porte during the absence of the sultan, who returned to Istanbul at the end of November (1468), having achieved the conquest of much of Caramania.[85]

Stefano Magno also recalls the attack upon the island of Andros. A Turkish squadron of eleven long, light runners (*fuste*) had issued from the port of Miletus ("Palatia"), intending to attack Lemnos, but had been unable to disembark armed men. Four of the fuste, however, had sailed for Andros, which they took by storm, killing Giovanni Sommaripa, the lord of the island, and thirteen others, carried off seventy prisoners, and piled up booty said to have been worth fifteen thousand ducats. Magno also gives us a Venetian tally, dating from this period (1467–1468), of some 121 Moreote castles, of which more than fifty are said to have been in Turkish hands, and more than forty in ruins. Twenty-six belonged to Venice, but nine of these are described as being ruined.[86]

Repetitive scenes of death and destruction made life an intolerable hardship for the Greeks, Serbs, Hungarians, and others on the periphery of Turkish power, for expansion was always the order of the day during Mehmed II's long reign of thirty years. Another disaster for the Christians lay just ahead, and it was going to involve the Venetians as well as the Greeks. On 8 March, 1469, Niccolò da Canale received the heavy charge of captain-general of the sea, and

> because both by letters and by various other means we have word that the Turk, cruelest enemy of Christ's name, is preparing a strong fleet and a powerful land army to attack our city of Negroponte as well as Nauplia in Romania, we wish and order you,

---

[81] Sen. Secreta, Reg. 23, fols. 115^v–116^r [117^v–118^r], the ducal letter being a resolution of the Senate, dated 3 June, 1468, and passed by a vote *de parte* 108, *de non* 2, *non synceri* 1, and *cf.*, *ibid.*, fol. 116^r [118^r], letters of 25 June.

[82] Sen. Secreta, Reg. 23, fol. 116^v [118^v], dated 7 June, 1468: ". . . Mahumetes, iste tyrranus Turcorum, . . . conflato ingenti exercitu atque universe Grecie viribus contractis traiecit Ellespontum, penetravit in Asiam. Deseruit Europam dira peste et fame pene confectam. Nec inde rediturus est nisi multos post menses et aut fractus (quod superi dent!) aut omnino de via fessus et defaticatus cum toto exercitu. Et postea [non] dubitandum est in hac facie rerum quin, si Christiani velint, evadant victores et de insolentissimo hoste pulcherrimum triumphum ferant. Credimus procul dubio divinitus reservatam esse temporibus Sanctitatis vestre huiusmodi victoriam, quam vestra Beatitudo negligere non debet . . . ," and *cf.* fol. 120 [122].

[83] Sen. Secreta, Reg. 23, fol. 133^v [135^v], doc. dated 15 September, 1468, of which the text may be found in Ljubić, *Listine*, X (1891), 413, and *cf.* J. Adelphi, *Türckisch Chronica* (1513), unnum. fol. 8^v (=Bii).

[84] Sen. Secreta, Reg. 23, fol. 137^r [139^r], and on the danger to Dalmatia, *ibid.*, fol. 150 [152].

[85] *Cf.* Babinger, *Maometto* (1957), pp. 396–401, and note Halil Inalcik, "Mehmed the Conqueror (1432–1481) and His Time," *Speculum*, XXXV (1960), 424.

[86] Magno, *Estratti degli Annali veneti*, ed. Hopf, *Chron. gréco-romanes* (1873, repr. 1966), pp. 205–6.

owing to the extreme importance of this matter, to hasten your voyage with all possible speed . . . to Modon and Negroponte in order to meet, with your customary prudence and valor and with the help of God's clemency, the perils which could well be in store for us there. . . .

Canale was reminded that, both in the defense of Negroponte and in any other emergency he might encounter, he was to request the aid of galleys and other ships not only from Venetian territories, "but also from the most serene king of Cyprus [James II], who has offered and promised us not merely his galleys but all sorts of assistance and support, and likewise from the Knights of Rhodes and any others, as may seem best to you in case of need. . . ."[87]

The war between Venice and the Porte had gone on year after year, a grim and toilsome business. Although Mehmed II had had serious distractions in Asia Minor, he had not taken up the Venetian overtures for peace. During the summer of 1469 Niccolò da Canale commanded a fleet of some twenty vessels on a raiding expedition along parts of the Macedonian shore, striking at the environs of Thessalonica and brutally sacking the city of Aenos. He had less success on the coast of Asia Minor, but making his way around the Morea, Canale occupied Vostitza on the Gulf of Patras. Mehmed now put the redoubtable Mahmud Pasha, who had been temporarily out of favor at the court, in charge of the Ottoman fleet, which was being built up in the most determined fashion.[88] Mehmed was infuriated by the sack of Aenos, and was now moved to undertake a great venture which he had long had in mind. This was the capture of the great city and island of Negroponte, perhaps the chief Venetian center and naval base in the Levant.

In the fifteenth century the Hussite was the unwitting, unwilling ally of the Turk, like the Lutheran in the sixteenth. There were few in the Curia Romana who did not regard the heretic as worse than the infidel, and who were not ready to transfer manpower and resources from the eastern fronts to wherever in Christendom the Holy See was meeting heretical opposition. The insistence upon receiving the eucharist in "both species," the wine as well as the bread, marked even the most moderate Utraquists as nonconformists. Failure to abide by a papal declaration of faith or discipline, however, posed a threat to the doctrine of papal absolutism in religious matters, which Pius II had propounded in the bull *Execrabilis*.

In the early spring of 1462 Pius had declared invalid the Compacts of Basel (promulgated at Jihlava in July, 1436), upon which the Czech Estates and the Council of Basel had hoped to build a religious peace, and through which they had expected to effect the return of Bohemia

---

[87] Sen. Secreta, Reg. 24, fols. 1^v–3^r [10^v–12^r], and on 27 October, 1469, the Senate wrote Canale that "speramus fore ut res nostre ita per vos administrentur quod aut victoria aut bona et honorabilis pax secutura sit" (*ibid.*, fol. 62^r [71^r]).

[88] Mahmud Pasha (Angelović) was for almost twenty years one of the most important figures at the Porte and in the entire Ottoman world. He was born in Serbia, probably at Kruševac, midway between Belgrade and Sofia. His father Michael, who belonged to the noble Greek family of the Angeli of Thessaly, lived at Novo Brdo, and married a Serb; the latter was captured (about 1427) by the Turks, and brought to Adrianople, where her son (Mahmud) was converted to Islam and trained for the Ottoman service under Murad II (*cf.* Babinger, *Maometto*, pp. 179–80). He first came into prominence in 1451 at the accession of Mehmed II, whom he had apparently known for some years. Mahmud Pasha took part in the successful siege of Constantinople, but he did not (as sometimes stated) succeed Khalil Pasha as grand vizir in the summer of 1453 (Khalil was executed, it would appear, on 10 July). According to Halil Inalcik, Mahmud was appointed to the grand vizirate in 1456 (see his review of Babinger's life of Mehmed II, in "Mehmed the Conqueror [1432–1481] and His Time," *Speculum*, XXXV [1960], 412, 413–14). Mahmud Pasha was engaged in the internal strife of his compatriots in Serbia in 1458. According to Critobulus, he also joined Mehmed II in the invasion of the Morea about the same time, which is not the case (on Mahmud's two invasions of Serbia, see Inalcik, "Mehmed the Conqueror," pp. 419–21). Mahmud distinguished himself in the Ottoman campaigns against Sinope and Trebizond (in 1461), Wallachia (1462), and Lesbos (1462); expelled the Venetians from the Hexamilion (1463); fought against the Bosnians and Hungarians (1463, 1464); but lost favor with Mehmed during the Anatolian campaign (in July, 1468), and was removed from the grand vizirate, serving as governor of Gallipoli. Restored to the position of grand vizir (1472–1473), he was again dismissed after the campaign against Uzun Ḥasan, the Turkoman ruler of Mesopotamia (see, below, pp. 315–16), and was thereafter imprisoned and put to death by the ungrateful sultan in the midsummer of 1474. He occupies a prominent place in the works of the Ottoman chroniclers (J. H. Kramers, in the *Encycl. of Islām*, III [1928–36], 136–37; Fr. Babinger, *Geschichtsschreiber d. Osmanen u. ihre Werke*, Leipzig, 1927, p. 25; and esp. Inalcik, "Mehmed the Conqueror," in *Speculum*, XXXV, 408–27, *passim*). Soldier and statesman, builder of mosques and schools, Mahmud Pasha won glowing praise for his personal qualities from Critobulus, I, 77 (ed. K. Müller, *FHG*, V-1, p. 104; ed. V. Grecu, *Critobul din Imbros* [1963], p. 169). *Cf.* J. Adelphi, *Türckisch Chronica* (1513), unnum. fol. 8^v (=sign. Bii), and Babinger, *Maometto*, pp. 403–5, 408, 411.

to the fold of Catholicism. The negotiators of the Compacts had watered down the more rigid demands the Hussites had made in the Four Articles of Prague, but communion *sub utraque specie* had been assured at least to all adults in Bohemia who wanted to receive the chalice. The Holy See had never confirmed the Compacts, however, and Pius's uncompromising rejection of them had prepared the way for a renewal of warfare between those of the wine and those of the wafer. The war finally came in the spring of 1467, during the reign of Paul II. In rejecting the Compacts Pius had also declined to accept the obedience of George of Poděbrady, king of Bohemia, unless George forbade, throughout the kingdom, the laity's access to the chalice. For George to have done so would have produced civil war in Bohemia, while the alternative inevitably led to a break with Rome. In the meantime, to enhance his position in Europe and to forestall papal action against him, George made a pact of mutual assistance with Casimir IV of Poland at Glogau in Silesia (in May and June, 1462), part of their agreement being to protect each other against the Turks. With doubtful sincerity George tried to cast himself in the role of crusader, and that summer he sent Antoine Marini, a Frenchman, to Venice with the proposal that a league of princes—the kings of France, Bohemia, Poland, and Hungary, the dukes of Burgundy and Saxony, and the doge and signory of Venice—be formed "for the ruination and extermination of the common enemy." While commending Marini's project in the most laudatory terms, the Senate believed that the pope should be brought into the plan, for the authority of the Holy See would add greatly to the success of the undertaking.[89]

Similar proposals had often been made in the past, and would often be made in the years to come. This one was more detailed—and pro-Poděbradian historians have tried to make it appear more important—than most of those which had been advanced previously. The Holy See was not included in the Bohemian project, which the Curia Romana did not take seriously, however, and so did not regard itself as being faced with a choice between George the crusader and George the fautor of heretics.

By the bull *Profecturos adversus* [*sacrosancte religionis hostes*], promulgated in a public consistory on 16 June, 1464, Pius II had stated that it would be difficult to fight successfully the enemies of the faith on the outside (*foris*) while being attacked by those on the inside (*intus*). Heresy, which bred schism, was not less perilous and detestable than the damnable perfidy of the Turks. The latter could only slay bodies; the heretics destroyed souls. In Bohemia there were those who had fallen into the heresy of the Waldensians, denying the primacy of the Roman See. This unspeakable heresy had returned under the influence of John Hus, whose followers were called Hussites and Taborites. George of Poděbrady, *qui nunc se gerit pro rege Bohemie*, had been born and raised among them, and was said still to adhere to their heresy and to show no desire to reject it. Reviewing the history, as he saw it, of the Councils of Constance and Basel, Pius dwelt on the Compacts and on the Utraquists' (to him) offensive insistence on the "communion of the chalice," which Pius regarded as an *ad hoc* concession made by the conciliarists at Basel, ill advised at the time and no longer admissible. George had taken Prague *per arma et insidias*, the first of his numerous

---

[89] Sen. Secreta, Reg. 21, fols. 101v–102r, doc. dated 9 August, 1462: "[Spectabilis miles dominus Antonius Gallicus, orator] serenissimi domini regis Bohemie, qui ad presentiam nostram venit et sub litteris credentialibus regis eiusdem longo ordine verborum declaravit nobis optimam dispositionem fervensque propositum domini sui regis ac regis Pollonie ad procedendum magnanime contra Turcum, nepharium hostem nominis Christiani, commemoravitque ligam et intelligentiam faciendam esse inter hos principes Christianos, viz. regem Franchorum, reges ipsos Bohemie et Pollonie, regem Hungarie, ducem Burgundie, ducem Saxonie, et nos dominiumque nostrum, quibus potentatibus unitis procedendum erat ad ruinam et exterminium istius comunis hostis, sicut facile fieri poterat . . . ," of which proposal the Senate expressed the highest possible approval (by a vote *de parte* 128, *de non* 0, *non sinceri* 1), although they believed the pope should be made a member of the league for obvious reasons:

"Commemoramus quoque et laudamus non obstantibus his que idem spectabilis orator dixit nobis quia summus pontifex in hanc intelligentiam intervenire deberet, nam cum sit caput et princeps Christianorum dubitari non debet quod eius auctoritas multum conferet huic rei et erit magni momenti his que agenda erunt. . . ." The text of this document has been published by Franz Palacky, ed., *Urkundliche Beiträge zur Geschichte Böhmens und seiner Nachbarländer im Zeitalter Georg's von Podiebrad (1450–1471)*, Vienna, 1860, no. 295, pp. 289–90 (Fontes rerum austriacarum, II. Abt., Diplomataria et acta, vol. XX). An engineer and inventor, Marini was a native of Grenoble in Dauphiné; presumably of Italian origin, he was well known in Venice. See N. Iorga [Jorga], "Un Auteur de projets de croisades: Antoine Marini," *Études d'histoire du moyen âge dédiées à Gabriel Monod*, Paris, 1896, pp. 445–57, and on the Poděbradian project, F. G. Heymann, *George of Bohemia* (1965), pp. 297–313.

crimes; he had accepted the heretic John Rokycana as archbishop of Prague. The two of them may even have been guilty, as rumor had it, of poisoning Ladislas Postumus, king of Hungary and Bohemia, who had died after an illness of sixty hours. *Veritas in obscuro erat*, but such was the prelude to the Hussites' raising George to the throne of Bohemia. Charging him now with probable heresy, Pius cited George to appear "before us wherever we may be within one hundred and eighty days" to answer *super delictis et excessibus* and to submit to the judgment of the Holy See.[90] Sixty days later Pius was dead, and the citation lapsed, but not for long.

On 2 August, 1465, Cardinals Bessarion, Carvajal, and Berardo Erolo renewed Pius's citation of George of Poděbrady in Paul II's name, for "Georgius a dictis heresibus suis et erroribus minime est conversus." Nay, he was descending ever deeper into the mire of perfidy, and daily contemplating worse and worse outrages against the faith and the faithful.[91] Four days later, on the sixth, Paul II authorized Rudolf von Rüdesheim, bishop of Lavant (in Carinthia), his legate in the Silesian city of Breslau, to release all George's vassals and subjects from whatever oaths of fealty they had sworn or acts of homage they had done him. All alliances with him were forbidden, including marriages with his sons and daughters. He was declared beyond the pale, an utter outcast.[92]

Civil war finally broke out in Bohemia in the spring of 1467, when George faced a clique of Catholic barons led by Zdeněk of Sternberg, the disaffected Catholic burghers of Breslau and Pilsen, and the papal legates Lorenzo Roverella and Rudolf von Rüdesheim, the latter of whom became the bishop of Breslau in April, 1468. George also faced the hostility of the Emperor Frederick III and (most important of all) the long latent, formidable enmity of Matthias Corvinus, king of Hungary. As the pope was Corvinus's ally against the Turkish infidel, so was Corvinus the papal ally against the Bohemian heretic.

Not without some provocation George of Poděbrady's son Victorin invaded Austria in January and February, 1468, and Matthias Corvinus responded promptly to Frederick III's urgent call for help. Corvinus's army, acting in conjunction with imperial troops and those of the rebellious Czech barons, entered southern Moravia in April. Mehmed II had already crossed the Bosporus and embarked on his campaign in Caramania, with the complete assurance that his western fronts would not be attacked, despite the Venetian appeal to Paul II to seize the marvelous opportunity for an attack upon the Turks in Europe while the sultan was absent in Asia Minor. Almost a year of dismal, desultory warfare now began in central Europe, in lands that would be exposed to Turkish attack soon after the close of the century. Following a period of truce, during which the anti-Podĕbradian barons elected Corvinus king of Bohemia (in most irregular fashion), George struck back more vigorously at his enemies. The Czechs defeated the Hungarians near the Moravian town of Hradiště (Radisch) on 2 November, 1469, but the struggle went on, and Corvinus did not abate his claim to the crown of S. Wenceslas. In fact Corvinus also wanted to be elected king of the Romans, to serve as colleague and heir apparent of Frederick III, an idea which the latter did not find appealing, and so the new allies were soon enemies again.

To glance ahead for the sake of completeness, George of Poděbrady's death in March, 1471, brought Corvinus only slightly closer to the Bohemian throne. Ladislas [II] of Poland, the teen-aged son of Casimir IV, was elected George's successor. The contest continued, however, until the peace of Olomouc (Olmütz in Moravia) in 1478, which left Ladislas's royal presence (and title) undisturbed in Bohemia, and left Corvinus (also with the title king of Bohemia) in possession

[90] The text of the bull *Profecturos adversus* is given in Jos. Cugnoni, ed., *Aeneae Silvii Piccolomini . . . opera inedita*, in the *Atti della R. Accademia dei Lincei*, CCLXXX (1882–83), 3rd ser., *Memorie della classe di scienze morali, storiche e filologiche*, VIII (Rome, 1883), *Epistolae*, no. LXXI, pp. 461–70. For details of the consistory, see Hermann Markgraf, ed., *Politische Correspondenz Breslaus im Zeitalter Georgs von Podiebrad*, Breslau, 1874, nos. 253A–253B, 254, pp. 77–83, 87–90 (Scriptores rerum silesiacarum, vol. IX). The citation was repeated shortly before Pius's death, at Ancona (*ibid.*, nos. 253C, 257, pp. 83–87, 91–93). Neither as Aeneas Sylvius nor as pope did Pius II distinguish between the radical Taborites ("Waldensians") and the moderate Utraquists, who merely demanded access to the chalice (granted them by the Compacts), on which note Howard Kaminsky, "Pius Aeneas among the Taborites," *Church History*, XXVIII (1959), 281–309.

[91] Markgraf, *Politische Correspondenz Breslaus* (1874), no. 303, pp. 135–39, and note in general nos. 259 ff.

[92] *Ibid.*, no. 308, pp. 143–45. With orthodoxy beset by the Hussites in Bohemia and by the Fraticelli in Rome itself—as Paul II saw the situation—it is not strange that he struck at the "Pomponiani" of the so-called Roman Academy. *Cf.* L. Fumi, "Eretici in Boemia e fraticelli in Roma nel 1466," in the *Archivio della R. Società romana di storia patria*, XXXIV (1911), 117–30, with five letters of Agostino de' Rossi, the Milanese envoy to the Curia Romana.

of Moravia, Silesia, and even Lusatia. Ironically enough, when Corvinus died in April, 1490, Ladislas succeeded him in Hungary, where his weak and incompetent rule until 1516 helped prepare the way for the Turkish victory at Mohács a decade later, and Hungary became "the graveyard of Europe."[93]

In the meantime the Venetian Senate had been watching with discouragement and disapproval the internecine warfare among the Christians to the north. On 16 March, 1469, upon instructions from the Senate, the Doge Cristoforo Moro wrote Francesco Sanudo, the Venetian ambassador to the Curia Romana, that the news from Hungary clearly suggested that Matthias Corvinus's ill-advised "undertaking" (*impresia*) against George of Poděbrady was not merely a very difficult but actually a quite impossible affair. With a little persuasion Corvinus could easily be induced to give up his war against the Czechs—according to the doge's letter—and turn his arms against the madness and ferocity of the Turk. Sanudo must therefore explain to Paul II that Sultan Mehmed, "already the near neighbor of Italy" (*vicinus iam Italie finibus*), was driving off hordes of Christians every day into slavery. Mehmed's forces had so devastated and depopulated the lands of the counts of Segna (Senj) that it was grievously evident that, unless the counts received armed assistance soon, the Turks would be occupying castles and towns, with irreparable damage to Christendom and especially to Italy, which was after all "contiguous to and conjoined with the state of the aforesaid counts [of Segna]." Sanudo must try to persuade the pope to look to the perils and problems of the poor Christians who dwelt just across the narrow stretch of the northern Adriatic. The Venetians wanted the "undertaking" then being carried on against the king of Bohemia to be given up for a while. Corvinus should reach an understanding with the Emperor Frederick III, and employ his resources against the Turks. It would be far better for him to defend his own kingdom than to suffer Turkish attacks for the dubious purpose of assailing the Czechs.[94]

While the Venetians believed, quite correctly, that Corvinus would have found a better use for his men and money in enlarging the Hungarian defense against the Turks than in attacking the Poděbradians, the Senate had tired of its own defense against the Turks. The war party had diminished in strength since the death of Vettore Capello. There was a desire to come to terms with Mehmed II, if possible, but the Republic had no representative at the Porte. Once more, therefore, in July, 1469, the Senate turned to David [Mavrogonato] "the Jew," a Venetian subject of Candia, who had tried to help them on a previous diplomatic mission. David was now to go to Istanbul "without any indication that your going arises from our wish or knowledge" (*senza alcuna demostration che questa tua andata sia de nostra volunta ne saputa*). Since David was on good terms with the grand vizir Mahmud Pasha and with Mehmed's physician, the Italian Jew Yakub Pasha, "Master Jacomo the Physician," it appeared conceivable that he might open the door to further negotiations.[95]

---

[93] *Cf.* in general J. V. Polišenský, "Bohemia, the Turk and the Christian Commonwealth," *Byzantinoslavica*, XIV (1953), 82–108. On George of Poděbrady's (alleged) final reconciliation with the Vatican, despite the crusade which had been published and preached against him (*cruciata . . . contra ipsum publicata et predicata*), and (alleged) receipt of absolution just before his death, see the interesting document published by Otto Eduard Schmidt, "Des Böhmenkönigs Georg von Podiebrad Lösung vom Kirchenbann und sein Tod: Nach der neugefundenen Urkunde über die Aussagen des sächsischen Gesandten Nicolaus von Köckeritz von 20. Oktober 1495," in the *Neues Archiv für sächsische Geschichte*, LIX (Dresden, 1938), 39–65.

[94] Sen. Secreta, Reg. 24, fol. 4^{v} [13^{v}], doc. dated 16 March, 1469. The Venetians were eager for Corvinus and Frederick III to come to terms with each other (*ibid.*, fols. 22^{v}, 27^{v}–28^{r} [31^{v}, 36^{v}–37^{r}]). Sanudo's commission as ambassador to Rome was issued on 11 November, 1468 (*ibid.*, Reg. 23, fols. 143^{v}–145^{r} [145^{v}–147^{r}]).

On the collection of funds throughout southwestern Germany, through the sale of the crusading indulgence during the last year of Paul II's reign and later, *contra hereticos Bohemos et pro subsidio catholicorum pugnatorum contra eos*, see K. A. Fink, "Der Kreuzablass gegen Georg Podiebrad in Süd- und Westdeutschland," *Quellen und Forschungen aus italienischen Archiven und Bibliotheken*, XXIV (1932–33), 207–43, where the interested reader may find the financial records of Angelo de' Cialfi, canon of Camerino and a papal collector in Germany, who presented his final accounts to the Camera Apostolica on 9 February, 1474.

[95] Sen. Secreta, Reg. 24, fols. 34^{v} [43^{v}] and 36^{r} [45^{r}], dated 14 and 21 July, 1469. Occasionally the Turkish government seemed to hold out the palm of peace, as on 10 November when the Senate voted that "non est spernenda practica pacis cum Turcho oblata per subassi Argirochastri regimini nostro Corphoy . . ." (*ibid.*, fol. 65^{r} [74^{r}]).

David had tried to serve both Venice and the Porte as an envoy of peace in 1466 (*ibid.*, Reg. 23, fols. 11^{r}–12^{r} [13^{r}–14^{r}]), at which time as almost always the Senate was anxious "devenir a treugue cum el Signor Turco, possendo haver quelle" (*ibid.*, fol. 13^{r} [15^{r}], doc. dated 4 November, 1466, *et alibi*). His activities are well known for the decade

Throughout the summer and fall of 1469 the Venetians watched the Hungarians almost as closely as they did the Turks. The Senate wanted peace, and for various reasons was not satisfied with Giovanni Emo, the Republic's ambassador to Matthias Corvinus. On 25 September (1469) the doge or rather the Senate acknowledged the receipt of Emo's dispatches of 22 and 28 August and 5 September concerning his attempts to follow their instructions. Emo had described his *colloquia* with Corvinus, Archbishop John Vitéz of Gran (Esztergom), and Bishop Albert Hangacs of Veszprém "super negotio Turcorum."

The Senate believed that Emo had talked too freely, and warned him that, when he found himself involved in such conversations, he must speak with such reserve and caution

> that by your words the right and authority are not taken from us, which we have had from the king, of making a peace or truce with the Turk by ourselves alone—without his Majesty. Seeing that you have handled this matter differently [from your instructions] and contrary to our wish and intention, we have accordingly wanted to send you this reminder. Furthermore, since you have alluded to the financial subvention we gave his royal Majesty against the Turks, you must bear in mind and understand . . . the vast, rather the intolerable, expenses with which we are at present burdened both on land and on the sea. . . .

It was quite impossible for Venice to give Matthias Corvinus another financial subsidy at this time, and so when the talk turned to money, Emo must be most circumspect. He must also regard his present instructions as absolutely secret. Among other matters the Senate had directed Emo to speak to Corvinus of the lords of Segna (Senj) in terms of the highest commendation, "and you were to ask his . . . Majesty in our name that he should be willing to caution the captain of his forces in that area not to molest the said magnificent lords [of Segna]. We have been waiting . . . to learn how much you have accomplished in this connection, and what his . . . Majesty has replied to you. . . ." And the Senate made clear by further instructions that, so far, they were not pleased with Emo's conduct of his mission.[96]

By the following spring, however, the Senate had come to think rather better of Emo's efforts, congratulating him upon the manner of his defense of the Republic against certain *sinistra informatio* which had reached the ears of Matthias Corvinus, and expressing pleasure that the latter was dealing kindly and fairly with Count Stefano de' Frangipani of Segna.[97]

The county of Segna was a line of defense against the Turks, as it remained for years after Mohács, when it was to become a refuge for Slavs fleeing before the Turks. The refugees were known as Uskoks (Italian *Uscocchi*). Under the Hapsburgs the Uskoks would take to the sea as corsairs, becoming a menace to Venetian shipping as well as a thorn in the Turkish side. In 1469 the Venetians wanted to protect the counts and natives of Segna (who had just fallen under Hungarian domination) as allies, however small, against the Turks. No allies were too small to be useful, for the Turkish war was apparently consuming the resources of the Venetian state more rapidly than trade and taxes could replace them. Negroponte was in obvious danger, and its defense would be costly.

Paul II was said recently to have had bulls published (the Senate seems to have been a little doubtful)

> in certain cities and towns, especially in ours, . . . prohibiting under ecclesiastical censure navigation to the lands and marts of the infidels, and yet because he appears to agree that in this matter we should follow the custom of our forebears, who used to seek a license from the supreme pontiffs of the past for the voyage to the lands of the infidels, the motion is

---

1460–1470, on which see David Jacoby, "Un Agent juif au service de Venise: David Mavrogonato de Candie," *Thesaurismata*, IX (Venice, 1972), 68–96. On the physician Yakub Pasha (Jacopo da Gaeta), see above, note 11, and Donado da Lezze [actually Gian Maria Angiolello], *Historia turchesca (1300–1514)*, ed. Ion Ursu, Bucharest, 1909 [1910], pp. 64, 66.

[96] Sen. Secreta, Reg. 24, fol. 55 [64], doc. dated 25 September, 1469. The Senate approved the form of their letter to Emo *de parte* 148, *de non* 1, *non sinceri* 0. Venice constantly opposed the Hungarian pressure on Segna (*ibid.*, fols. 82ᵛ, 86ᵛ, 89ʳ, 90ᵛ, 112ʳ).

[97] Sen. Secreta, Reg. 24, fol. 90ᵛ [99ᵛ], doc. dated 17 March, 1470, the Senate to Emo: "Litteras accepimus vestras ex Viena dierum ultimi Februarii, 2, 3, et 4 mensis instantis et quecumque scripsistis distincte cognovimus laudamusque consuetam vestram diligentiam et prudentiam servatosque modos in proponendo et respondendo regie Celsitudini ad omnia occurrentia et criminationes de nobis factas purgando et dilluendo advertendoque regiam Celsitudinem a credulitate cuiusvis sinistre informationis. . . . Inter cetera autem gratissimum nobis fuit intelligere quod regia Sublimitas benigne indulgenterque egerit cum magnifico Comite Stefano de Frangepanibus eique et reliquum statum suum et illesum dimittens et portionem suam civitatis Segne restituere contenta sit et hoc idem facere reliquis fratribus eius disposita appareat et policeatur. . . ."

made [in the Senate] that the Collegio may write about this to our ambassador at the Curia in whatever suitable form shall seem best to the Collegio to obtain from his Holiness the license for the [eastward] voyages, for as long a period of time as shall prove possible.

Trade with the Moslem Levant must help to pay for the war with Moslem Turkey, and the Senate passed the resolution by 103 affirmative votes (*de parte*), with 16 opposed (*de non*), and eleven neutral or uncommitted votes (*non sinceri*). Nevertheless, the motion seems not to have been put into effect.[98]

As the Venetians now hoped and worked for peace in Italy, much of the senatorial correspondence was directed toward the formation and maintenance of a league of the peninsular and European states which might assist Venice against the Turks, and which would in any event leave the Republic free to defend her interests in the Levant. Letter after letter stressed the Turkish peril. Finally a note of panic entered the Senate's dispatch of 8 March, 1470, to Francesco Giustinian, now their ambassador to the Curia. The Senate had already learned, before the eighth, of the *maximi Turcorum apparatus* which threatened the Venetian colonies in the East, as they informed Giustinian, but only on that day had they been informed of the extent of the danger, which they described in a postscript to their dispatch of the eighth, the text of which had already been approved by the Senate before the bad news had reached the lagoon.[99]

Day after day came fearful reports from the East of the Gran Turco's gigantic preparations on land and sea "ad perniciem Christianorum." Everyone expected the first attack to be directed against Venetian territories, "and he will spew forth his venomous slime against us." The Republic's failure to resist the onslaught would leave the Turks swarming through the Aegean, ravaging the defenseless shores and depopulating the islands, "pro libidine vagando et debachando." As the Senate wrote Giustinian at the Curia Romana on 15 March, 1470, they had often urged upon Paul II the absolute necessity of a *pax Italica* (although, as we have seen, Venice had been regarded as the power most likely to break the Italian peace after the death of Francesco Sforza). Now the need for papal leadership and for action was desperate. The pope was the helmsman of Christendom, the Senate told Giustinian, and his guidance toward the port of peace in Italy would be the peninsula's only shelter from the rising waves and gathering tempest of a Turkish invasion.[100] If the Arsenal had been as well equipped with men, munitions, and galleys as the Venetian secretariat was with tropes and imagery, the Senate might have had less to fear from the Turks.

By 7 July (1470) the Senate could see the writing on the wall, and wrote Giustinian (and Andrea Vendramin and Lodovico Foscarini, who had joined him on the Roman mission) to seek an audience with Paul II immediately upon receipt of the present letter. They were to give Paul the Republic's most reverent thanks for his paternal help and especially for his offer of part of the proceeds of the alum mines of Tolfa [*sua oblatio aluminum*], which the Senate wanted signalized by bulls making the grant without conditions. "Add, moreover, in refutation of those who have been trying maliciously to minimize the seriousness of our perils, that the Turk has sent a fleet of three hundred and fifty sail under Mahmud Pasha out from the Dardanelles, and that he himself has also come with a huge and

---

[98] Sen. Secreta, Reg. 24, fol. 64^v [73^v], doc. dated 3 November, 1469, but since no cross was inscribed in the left-hand margin of the register, opposite this text, we may assume that no action was taken as a consequence of this resolution.

[99] Sen. Secreta, Reg. 24, fols. 87^r, 87^v–88^r [96^r, 96^v–97^r]: "Post scriptas accepimus litteras quas quidam civis noster veniens ex Constantinopoli scribit ex Parentio ad unum nobilem nostrum et per illas ultra multas et alias vias intelleximus Turchum magna solicitudine parare classem suam et terrestrem exercitum ut statum aggrediatur nostrum, quas litteras vobis mittimus presentibus introclusas ut illas summo pontifici ostendatis, et subiungite nos cogitatus omnes nostros, studia, et vires convertisse ad augumentum classis nostre et ad reliquias necessarias provisiones pro defensione status nostri, cum cuius salute et periclitacione salus et periclitatio reliquorum Christianorum coniuncta est. Et quoniam huiusmodi Turci apparatus duas habet extimes[c]endas conditiones, celeritatis alteram incredibilis et numero alteram viriumque longe maiorum quam non solum antehac fecerit sed ne nuntiatum quidem est ut nos antevertat si poterit et opprimat—quod absit—nobis quoque necessarium est maturare provisiones nostras supra quam possibile vix sit et vires undecumque et comodocumque contrahere nostras et non solum pro fortificanda augendaque classe in quo nihil reliqui facimus sed pro mittendis etiam ad loca nostra presidiis quibus tuta ab impetu rabieque hostili esse possint. Et hec omnia singilatim que vobis scribimus et hanc inter cetera particulam summo pontifici declarate." The dispatch was approved: *De parte* 167, *de non* 0, *non synceri* 0. On the same day the Senate voted to send an additional 8,000 ducats immediately to the captain-general Canale (*ibid.*, fol. 88^r).

[100] Sen. Secreta, Reg. 24, fol. 90 [99].

powerful army to lay siege to the city of Negroponte."[101]

Mehmed's forces were said to exceed one hundred thousand men. As for the number of his guns, cannon, and siege machines, they were said to be "of such and such size and strength," *tanta et talia*, and although the figures given for them were reliable (according to the Senate), they surpassed all possibility of belief. All thoughts of trade and commerce, lading and brokerage fees were put aside. The Venetians were arming galleys, ships, and transports of every sort, and sending them off with foot soldiers, crossbowmen, and munitions to Niccolò da Canale, the captain-general of the sea. "And we are squeezing not merely money from every source but even blood, so to speak, from our very veins to aid the aforesaid city, if it is possible, lest such a slaughter and calamity fall upon all the Christians [in Negroponte] as would prove irreparable if the city, which God forbid, should be stormed by that fierce and rabid enemy."

Whatever the Venetians tried to do, however, would be of no avail unless the pope and the other Christian princes joined them *potenter et celeriter* in one vast movement against the Turks. This was the message which Giustinian, Vendramin, and Foscarini must din in the papal ears *sedulo et continue*. Mehmed's success at Negroponte would give him control of the sea, and would be the prelude to a Turkish invasion of Italy. No description, however eloquent, of the plight of the Negropontini which the Venetian envoys might give the Curia could depict the reality of the impending danger. Rhodes, Cyprus, and the other island strongholds in Christian hands were caught in the same storm. For them as for her own possessions Venice would do her utmost, but her strength was unequal to the immensity of the task.[102]

Throughout the long months of 1469–1470 the Venetians had been urging, and finally almost desperately urging, the formation of a *liga generalis* in Italy both to assure their position in the peninsula, as they fought the Turks in Greece and the islands, and to secure from the Christian allies some sort of assistance against the common enemy of Christendom.[103] Their efforts appeared to have led to success when on 9 July (1470) the peace of Lodi and the league of 1454 were revived.[104] It was too late.

---

[101] For the source, see the following note. With reference to the revenues from the mines at Tolfa, we may observe that on 1 February, 1469, the papal vice-chamberlain had undertaken the sale of 18,000 *cantara* of alum over a three-year period to one Bartolommeo Zorzi of Venice, son of the late Luca, 6,000 cantars a year for three years, each cantar to be 150 lbs. Roman: the agreement was negotiated in the name and for the benefit of the commission of cardinals for the crusade:

"In Dei nomine amen. A.D. MCCCCLXVIIII, indictione secunda die vero prima mensis Februarii, pontificatus sanctissimi in Christo patris et domini nostri, domini Pauli divina providentia pape Secundi anno quinto. Infrascripta sunt pacta, conventiones, et capitula inita, facta, firmata et conclusa inter reverendissimum . . . dominum Vianesium prothonotarium Bononiensem sanctissimi domini nostri pape vicecamerarium de licentia et voluntate, ut asseruit, reverendissimorum in Christo patrum et dominorum, domini Bissarioni [*sic*], episcopi Sabinensis, Niceni; domini Guillelmi, episcopi Ostiensis, Rothomagensis; domini Johannis, episcopi Portuensis, Sancti Angeli, Sancte Romane Ecclesie cardinalium commissariorum super negotiis Sancte Cruciate deputatorum . . . et spectabilem et generosum virum dominum Bartholomeum Georgio [*sic*], patricium Venetum, pro se ipso suisque in posterum heredibus et successoribus . . . , quorum capitulorum in vulgari ydiomate pro maiore ipsorum intelligentia conscriptorum tenor sequitur de verbo ad verbum et est talis videlicet: Inprimis el reverendissimo Monsignor vicecamarlengo predicto come e dicto di sopra nel predicto nome promette dare et vender al nobil homo mesier Bartholomeo Zorzi da Vinesia, quondam mesier Luca, cantara disdotto milia de alumi conducti et navigati a Vinesia a risego de la camera apostolica in anni tre proximi advenire, principiando a Pasqua proxima anno uno et avanti al piacere del dicto mesier Bartholomeo, cioè ogni anno cantara seimilia et cadauno cantaro sintenda essere di libre centocinquanta Romane: et quale alume per lui o soy commessi se habbi ad vendere in Venesia nel Golfo da terra et da mare, Friuli, Marcha Trivisana, Lombardia, et de la da le Alpe, nel dominio de lo Imperadore et del duca d'Austria, Romagna fino a Fano," etc., etc. (Arch. Segr. Vaticano, A.A., I–XVIII, no. 1443, fols. 98^v–100^v). (The alum concession was called the *apaltus*, *lo apalto*.)

[102] Sen. Secreta, Reg. 24, fols. 117^v–118^r [121^v–122^r], doc. dated 7 July, 1470, "oratoribus nostris in Curia."

[103] *Cf.* Sen. Secreta, Reg. 24, fols. 9, 11^v ff., 16^v–17^r, 19^r, 37^r, 38^r, 47^v, 49 ff., 56^v–57^r, 60 ff., 66^r, 69^v ff., 75 ff., 83^v ff., 90^r, 91 ff., 99 ff., etc. [18, 20^v ff., etc.].

[104] Sen. Secreta, Reg. 24, fol. 119^r [123^r], doc. dated 20 July, 1470, the Senate to Andrea Vendramin and Lodovico Foscarini, Venetian envoys in Rome: ". . . Et deinde per litteras nobilis viri Bernardi Iustiniano militis, oratoris nostri in Neapoli, scriptum erat de reformatione et renovatione lige inter regem [Ferrante of Naples], ducem [Galeazzo Maria Sforza of Milan], et Florentinos *die nono mensis presentis*; postea vero accepimus litteras ab oratore nostro predicto datas Neapoli nono et decimo dicti mensis, quibus nos certiores fecit de successu et refirmatione dicte lige cum capitulo et facultate reformandi et renovandi ligam generalem Italie Nicolai pontificis maximi et insuper de optima mente illius serenissimi regis ad quietem et pacem Italie et ad honorem Dei et bonum Christiani nominis, offerendo se ad renovationem predicte lige." *Cf.*, *ibid.*, fols. 120^r ff., 171^v [124^r ff., 175^v].

Within three days Venice was to suffer one of the major disasters of her history—the fall of Negroponte to Mehmed II—and final confirmation of the league by the high contracting parties did not come until 22 December, 1470.[105]

As fears rose from day to day in the Venetian Senate, but the full extent of the disaster was not yet known, the somewhat more cheerful news came that King Ferrante had offered the Venetian ambassador at his court ten galleys as the Neapolitan contribution to the Christian cause.[106] Ten galleys would indeed be a splendid afforcement of the Republic's naval strength, if Ferrante actually made them available, but even if he did, everyone knew that the whole Venetian empire (if such it was) in the Levant, *universus status noster Levantis*, would still be in terrifying danger. Since the Turkish fleet had left the Dardanelles, the Cretans had been living in fear and trembling. To reassure them it was proposed in the Senate (on 31 July, 1470) that the condottiere Andreono da Parma should be sent directly to Candia with his company, but the motion received only fourteen votes *de parte*, and so was defeated. It was then moved, and carried by 157 votes *de parte* (with no word of dissent), that Andreono should sail to Modon to place himself under the orders of the captain-general Niccolò da Canale, "who would provide for the city and island of Crete and our other possessions, as it is part of his charge and he has his orders and the freedom to act."[107]

The vote to assign Andreono da Parma's mercenaries to Modon had doubtless been hastened by the arrival of painful news from the East. On that same Tuesday afternoon or early evening of 31 July (1470) the Senate approved the dispatch of the following letter to the Emperor Frederick III, King Ferrante of Naples, Matthias Corvinus of Hungary, Galeazzo Maria Sforza of Milan, Borso d'Este of Modena (Ferrara), the Florentine republic, and other princes and states:

> Today the report has been brought to us from Naupactus [Lepanto], our city in Aetolia, that Christ's monstrous enemy the Turk has finally taken by storm the city of Negroponte, to which he had laid siege . . . with an army of incredible size, and that he has visited every form of cruelty upon his victims, in keeping with his foul and fearsome character. Nevertheless, we are neither shattered by this loss nor broken in spirit, but rather we have become the more aroused and are [now] determined, with the advent of these greater dangers, to augment our fleet and to send out fresh garrisons in order to strengthen and maintain our hold on our other possessions in the East as well as to render assistance to the other Christian peoples, whose lives are threatened by the implacable foe. . . .[108]

According to a letter of one Geronimo Longo, a Venetian galley commander, the Turkish fleet had set out from the Dardanelles on 3 June (1470), with 300 sail, of which 108 were said to be galleys, 60 transports, and the rest *fuste*. The report was that there were 70,000 men on board. The fleet was heading westward toward the Venetian island of "Egripo" or Negroponte (Euboea), and as the Venetian Senate knew well, Mahmud Pasha was in command. Longo, who was at the time with the Venetian armada in the Aegean, informs us that Mahmud occupied Imbros (on 5 June), but failed to take Lemnos (8–12 June). He then sailed on to Skyros, where

---

[105] Arch. Segr. Vaticano, Arm. XXXIX, tom. 12, fols. 61^v, 66^v–67^r; Arch. di Stato di Venezia, Sen. Secreta, Reg. 24, fols. 174^r, 176^v–177^r [178^r, 180^v–181^r], and see below, p. 307b.

[106] *Ibid.*, Reg. 24, fol. 121^r [125^r], doc. dated 24 July, 1470, the Senate to Ferrante: ". . . Iamque accepimus periocundo animo oblationem regiam vestram de triremibus auxiliaribus mittendis prefecto classis nostre utpote huic tempestati et necessitati Christiane religionis convenientissimam." A week later (on 31 July) the number of galleys is specified as ten (fol. 122^r [126^r]).

[107] Sen. Secreta, Reg. 24, fol. 121^v [125^v], doc. dated 31 July, 1470, the votes being *de parte* 157, *de non* 0, *non synceri* 0.

[108] Sen. Secreta, Reg. 24, fol. 122^r [126^r], doc. dated 31 July, 1470, a copy of the letter sent to Ferrante of Naples. The text was approved in the Senate by a vote *de parte* 162, *de non* 0, and *non synceri* 0. On the same day the Senate wrote the Venetian envoys in Rome, ". . . unde cognoscetis miserabilem expugnationem et excidium civitatis nostre Nigropontis qua ingentissima iactura quales sint futureque sint reliquarum rerum nostrarum et universe Christianitatis conditiones nemo est qui perspicere non cognoscat" (*ibid.*).

As the days passed, the disaster of Negroponte was confirmed on all sides, as the Senate wrote their envoys on 10 August, "ut amplius dubitandum non sit truculentissimum Christi hostem . . . complanasse . . . et facilem sibi stravisse viam ad invadendam Italiam tum terra tum etiam mari et ad delendam penitus extinguendamque Christianam religionem: que trepidatio, qui pavor sit in omni insula et ora maritima Orientis nemo est sensus particeps qui non intelligat. . . . Estote igitur cum summo pontifice . . . , instate ut ad conclusionem unionis et generalis Italie confederationis omni remota cunctatione devenire dignetur ut quisque pro viribus et facultatibus communi cause opitulari possit. Et non solum intestine sedentur discordie sed diffidentie etiam et ranchores posthabeantur et negligantur . . ." (*ibid.*, fol. 125^r [129^r]), to all of which Paul II returned a "clement and benign response" (fol. 126^r), just as various other powers expressed their sorrow and distress at the blow which had fallen upon Venice (fols. 126^v, 128, 135^v–136^r, 170^r).

he sacked the northern village of S. George (on 13 June), but could not take the well-defended fortress. Further reflection soon led Longo to revise his initial estimate of the size of the Turkish fleet:

At first I judged it to be of 300 sail. Now I believe there are 400, divided in this way: 100 galleys, 150 fuste, two galleasses, a ship of 500 "tons" [*bote*], and the rest transports. The sea looked like a forest. It seems incredible to hear tell of it, but to see it is something stupendous! . . . Negroponte is in danger, and if it falls, our whole state in the Levant will be lost as far as Istria. . . .[109]

After his unsuccessful attempt on Skyros, Mahmud Pasha rounded Capes Doro, Mantelo, and Karysto (on the southern end of the island of Negroponte), and sailed up the channel, taking the castle of Styra (Stura), which lay just across the strait from Marathon. On 15 June (1470) his fleet anchored within sight of ancient Aulis in the bay of "Burchio" (the later Bourkos), near the Negropontine Giudecca. The troops aboard the galleys and transports were disembarked in the cove of Millemoza, hard by the city of Negroponte. On the eighteenth the land army, under Sultan Mehmed himself, arrived on the scene, and the long-awaited and long-feared siege began. Niccolò da Canale, the Venetian captain-general, who had been following the Turkish fleet (at a safe distance) with aimless indecision, suddenly sailed off to Crete, where he frightened the inhabitants almost to death, for they mistook his approach for that of Mahmud and the Turks.[110]

Nevertheless, the defenders of Negroponte rejected Sultan Mehmed's demand for surrender (on 25 June). Giacomo Rizzardo, who was an eyewitness of the events he describes, says that the sultan offered the inhabitants of Negroponte ten years' exemption from all imposts, and to such gentlemen as possessed a villa he was willing to give two. The bailie Paolo Erizzo and the captains or commissioners Alvise Calbo and Giovanni Bondumier could be assured of lives of ease either at Negroponte or in Istanbul, for the sultan knew that they could not return to Venice if they surrendered their Euboeote charge. The offer had been made through Mahmud Pasha and the renegade interpreter Domenico Demunessi. The latter were told that Venice had made the city her own; the contest would be over in ten or a dozen days; then they would see who was to have the city. Speaking through a subaltern, the bailie ended his refusal to give up the city to Sultan Mehmed with an insult that the sultan was not likely to forget: "Tell your lord to go and eat swine's flesh, and then come and meet us at the foss!"[111]

With these words the die was cast, and the Turkish cannon began battering the city walls. Two thousand Turkish horse scoured the island, killing all Greeks and Latins over fifteen years of age, "e fecero schiavi li altri." According to the account given in Malipiero's *Annali veneti*, 14,000 Turks perished in the first assault upon the city; 16,000 in the "seconda battaglia," which took place on 30 June; and 5,000 in the third attack, which came on 5 July. On the day of the third attack treachery was discovered within the beleaguered walls when an old woman revealed that Tommaso Schiavo, the Dalmatian condottiere with 500 foot under his command, intended to betray the city to the Turks that very night. The conspirators were promptly slain, and Tommaso's body was soon dangling by the feet from the balcony of the bailie's palace.

The colonial government of Negroponte now sent off two messengers to the captain-general Canale, imploring him for help. One of the messengers got safely through the Turkish lines; the other was captured, and was done to death by impalement. The Turks launched their fourth assault on 8 July. It is said to have cost them 15,000 casualties, "so that the lord Turk, seeing that his forces were doing badly, sent word to all his domains that, leaving one [able-bodied] man in each household, all others should come to help in this undertaking."

Mehmed was not to need further reinforce-

[109] Domenico Malipiero [as abridged by Francesco Longo], *Annali veneti dall'anno 1457 al 1500*, in the *Archivio storico italiano*, VII, pt. 1 (1843), 49–52, gives the text of Longo's (undated) letter to his brothers Leonardo and Francesco in Venice. On the three brothers, see, *ibid.*, p. 63.

[110] Malipiero, *Annali veneti*, in *Arch. stor. italiano*, VII–1, 53: "I feudatari, che erano in la terra, tolsero le cose preciose che haveano, le mogier e i fioli, e fuzirono ai casali e ai monti. . . . [In Venice] si biasma el general che'l sia andà in Candia con l'armada, e che'l habbia lassà Negroponte assedià. . . ." Canale is said to have informed the Venetian government that when his armada was increased in strength to "100 galleys, large and light, together with ten ships, he would go to seek out the Turkish fleet." He spent three days in Candia for the recaulking of his galleys (*ibid.*, p. 55).

[111] L. Fincati, "La Perdita di Negroponte (luglio 1470)," *Archivio veneto*, XXXII, pt. 2 (new ser., anno XVI, 1886), 292–93, and see Giacomo Rizzardo, *La Presa di Negroponte fatta dai Turchi ai Veneziani nel MCCCCLXX*, Venice, 1843, pp. 9–11 (*cf.*, below, note 118).

ments, for the Venetians were reaching the end of their resistance. On 11 July, two hours before dawn, the Turks began moving all the manpower aboard their fleet onto the shoreline of the little bay of Burchio at the point where ten cannon had razed the walls of the Negropontine Giudecca. They filled the moats with "barrels full of dead bodies" (*botti piene di corpi morti*). With the approach of darkness they began the fifth and final attack, concentrating their strength upon the landward walls, for in the area to the east of the city they had room to muster their forces.

"Those within could not resist," as we learn from the account in Malipiero, "because they had no relief force, and so on the morning of 12 July, two hours after daybreak, the Turks entered Negroponte." The Venetians fought on all day, however, from the piazza into the barricaded streets. They preferred to die "sword in hand in defense of their fatherland than to fall into the hands of the Turks." Mehmed came into the devastated city on the fourteenth. "In the last assault 27,000 Turks were killed, so that in five assaults 77,000 of them lost their lives. Of the Venetians, according to this report, 6,000 died in the city and on the island."[112]

Almost a century ago the Italian admiral Luigi Fincati, whose learning was relieved by common sense, estimated the population of the city of Negroponte (with its walled enclosure of sixteen hectares) at about 2,500 inhabitants. Adding at the most some 300 refugees (for there were far better places on the island in which to seek shelter from the Turks), plus 300 crossbowmen from Crete, the 400 mercenaries who had recently arrived, and the 500 infantry under Tommaso Schiavo, there could not have been more than 4,000 persons of all ages and conditions in Negroponte during that memorable July of 1470. Although the chronicles of Bologna set the size of Mehmed's land army at "300,000 persons,"[113] Fincati knew that "reducing it to 20,000 would still be an exaggerated figure and beyond what was needed."[114]

Certainly Mehmed had troopers enough for a general massacre, once the Turks had got into the city. Alvise Calbo fell fighting in the piazza. Giovanni Bondumier was slain in the house of Paolo Andreozzo, who lived to tell the tale. The bailie Paolo Erizzo had surrendered the castle built midway in the channel when Mahmud Pasha and the interpreter Demunessi promised him the safety of those who had taken refuge behind its drawbridges. Mehmed, however, ordered their execution; their bodies were thrown into the channel. Erizzo was tied between two boards and sawn in half. The Turkish conquest was complete. Mehmed ordered the return of his fleet to the Dardanelles, and shortly after the middle of July he began his own return march to Istanbul by way of Thebes, Thessaly, and Thessalonica. Canale kept track of Mahmud Pasha's return to Istanbul at the same cautious distance as he had followed the *kapudan pasha* to Negroponte. Mahmud remarked on the courtesy of the Venetian escort, "e ben trattado dall'armada della Signoria."[115]

---

[112] Malipiero, *Annali veneti*, in *Arch. stor. italiano*, VII–1, 56–58; Rizzardo, *La Presa di Negroponte*, pp. 11–15, on the treachery of Tommaso Schiavo; *cf.* the *Chronicon breve*, ad ann. 1470 (following Ducas, in Bonn corpus, pp. 521–22); Sanudo, *Vite de'duchi*, in *RISS*, XXII (1733), cols. 1190–91; Navagero, *Storia veneziana*, *RISS*, XXIII (1733), 1128–29; Stefano Magno, *Estratti degli Annali veneti*, ad ann. 1470, ed. Hopf, *Chron. gréco-romanes* (1873, repr. 1966), pp. 206–7; *Corpus chronicorum bononiensium*, in the new Muratori, *RISS*, XVIII, pt. 1, vol. IV, pp. 390–93, a detailed account in general but not in precise accord with that in Malipiero.

There is a notice concerning Tommaso Schiavo in the Arch. di Stato di Venezia, Sen. Mar, Reg. 9, fol. 2^v, and many documents relating to the Turkish problem and its perils are to be found in this register, especially fols. 8^v, 21^v, 30^v, 34^v, 36^v, 40, 45^v (doc. dated 4 June, 1470, on the Turkish preparations *ad oppugnationem Nigropontis*), 49^r (also on Negroponte), 66^r, 67^v, 72^r, 73^r, 78^v, 89^r, 94^r, docs. dated 1469–1471.

[113] *Corpus chronicorum bononiensium*, in *RISS*, XVIII, pt. 1, vol. IV, p. 391. Jacopo dalla Castellana (see below, note 118) says that Mehmed came by land with 300,000 men, and that 60,000 had come aboard the Turkish fleet, "che volea dire CCCLX milia persone per mare e per terra." Jacopo was in the city throughout the siege.

[114] Fincati, "La Perdita di Negroponte," p. 291, and *cf.* pp. 297–98.

[115] Malipiero, *Annali veneti*, in *Arch. stor. italiano*, VII–1, 63–64. Gian Maria Angiolello, who became a slave and servitor of the sultan when Negroponte was taken, reports that on 13 July Mehmed ordered all the prisoners who wore beards to be rounded up, and had them beheaded (Giovanni Maria Angiolello, *Historia turchesca [1300–1514]*, ed. Ion Ursu [who attributes the work to Donado da Lezze], Bucharest, 1909 [1910], p. x). Angiolello, on whom see below, note 118, also gives the itinerary of Mehmed's return to Istanbul. He was at Thebes on 28–29 July, 1470, went to Athens on the twenty-ninth, and thereafter passed through Livadia, Salona (Amphissa), Boudonitza (on 1 August), Zeitounion (Lamia), Neopatras (Hypate), Domokos (on 3 August), Larissa, Platamona (on the ninth), Thessalonica (on the eleventh), Serres (on the thirteenth), Kavalla (on the sixteenth), and Demotica (on the twenty-second), reaching Istanbul on 5 September (*cf.* Babinger, *Maometto* [1957], pp. 418–20).

About the time the last attack was getting under way (on 11 July) Niccolò da Canale had suddenly appeared in the channel of Talanda, having rounded the northern end of the island. By coming this way he had added two days to his voyage from Crete, and he had avoided contact with the Turkish fleet, which was in the channel to the south of the (no longer existent) mid-stream castle of Negroponte. Canale's route suggests timidity rather than tactics. Had he attacked and destroyed the Turkish bridge of boats linking the island of Negroponte to the mainland, he might conceivably have broken the siege. He is said to have come with fifty-two galleys, a *galia grossa*, and eighteen "ships" (*nave*), but to have decided to await the reinforcement of his fleet before bringing relief to Negroponte.[116] By the next day it was too late. Making the gesture of an attack upon the Turkish bridge of boats, he withdrew in despair, and the fate of Negroponte was sealed.

Niccolò da Canale was a doctor of laws, more given to books than to battles. His election to the captaincy-general had been the Senate's mistake. If Canale was a failure in the high command, his galley commanders (*sopracomiti*) were also a sad lot. As the Senate presently acknowledged, corruption was rife in the Venetian naval forces. The galley commanders entered on the enrollment lists the names of men who never served. Many of them had even become surreptitious merchants, carrying goods for sale from port to port contrary to Venetian law and custom. When it came to recruiting crossbowmen, they took on cooks, vintners, and servants (. . . *circa ballistarios in quorum numero scriptos esse intelleximus choquos, caniparios, famulos*).[117] Before surrendering his command to his successor Pietro Mocenigo, however, Canale actually did make an ill-planned and rather costly attempt to retake Negroponte. His attacking force was cut to pieces by Turkish cavalry. Failure was inevitable, partly because, as Malipiero says, "no one in the armada gave them any help."[118]

In the fall of Negroponte, Venice had suffered almost her worst loss of the entire fifteenth century. The city had been, after Crete, her chief naval station in the Aegean. The Turks quickly acquired the rest of the island, and Omar Beg returned to the Morea, allegedly with 25,000 troops. Vostitza, the modern Aigaion (Aegium), soon surrendered to the Turks. When the commandant and the garrison in the town of Kalamata had abandoned the fortress, Giacomo Marcello, the provveditore, ordered the crew of his galley to burn the place, lest the Turks seize it and hold it against the Venetians.[119] One piece of bad news after another reached Venice that summer. And Malipiero sadly observed, "Now it does indeed seem that the greatness of Venice has been brought down, and our pride has been swept away."[120]

---

[116] Malipiero, *Annali veneti*, in *Arch. stor. italiano*, VII–1, 55; Rizzardo, *La Presa di Negroponte*, pp. 18 ff. Canale had left Candia in Crete on 25 June. According to the *Corpus chronicorum bononiensium*, in *RISS*, XVIII, pt. 1, vol. IV, p. 393b, there were forty-five galleys and seven large ships in the Venetian armada upon Canale's arrival at Negroponte, but he feared too close an approach to the Turks "per l'impeto delle bonbarde."

[117] Sen. Secreta, Reg. 24, fol. 130v [134v], from the commission of Pietro Mocenigo, who was appointed to succeed Canale as captain-general of the sea on 30 August, 1470: ". . . Certificati sumus *magnam partem supracomitorum nostrorum* fraudare non solum homines suos multis modis, sed etiam dominium nostrum et multos continue tenere homines scriptos qui re vera non serviunt. Mandamus tibi efficaciter et expresse ut ad huiusmodi perniciosam et periculosam corruptellam et latrocinium occulos dirrigas et omnem adhibeas diligentiam ne fiat. Et si quem per huiusmodi modum fraudantem inveneris, punias accerrime, depone et priva si tibi videbitur supracomitaria . . . ," and *cf.* Fincati, "La Perdita di Negroponte," pp. 300–1, who refers to this text (with a wrong archival reference).

[118] Malipiero, *Annali veneti*, in *Arch. stor. italiano*, VII–1, 64: ". . . perchè nessun dell'armata no ghe dava favor, e cosi l'assalto è reussido vano." On the Turkish capture of Negroponte, see also Filippo Luigi Polidori, "Due Ritmi e una narrazione in prosa di autori contemporanei intorno alla presa di Negroponte fatta dai Turchi a danno dei Veneziani nel MCCCCLXX," in the *Archivio storico italiano*, app. to vol. IX (1853), pp. 397–440, who gives the texts of two poems, *Il Pianto de Negroponte*, *ibid.*, pp. 403–8, and *La Persa di Nigroponte*, pp. 409–32, as well as the account (in prose) of Fra Jacopo dalla Castellana, *Perdita di Negroponte*, pp. 433–40. Jacopo was an eyewitness (*cf.* pp. 439, 440). He adds many interesting details to the account in Malipiero, and also makes various absurd statements. Another eyewitness, Giacomo Rizzardo, *La Presa di Negroponte*, ed. Emmanuele Antonio Cicogna, Venice, 1844, has left us a more substantial account. Gian Maria Angiolello of Vicenza, who lost his brother in the siege, was himself captured, and survived to write the valuable *Historia turchesca*, ed. I. Ursu (1909), in which note pp. 35–37, 158, on Negroponte (see Fr. Babinger, "Angiolello," in the *Dizionario biografico degli italiani*, III [Rome, 1961], 275–78). See above, Chapter 3, note 54.

Besides the excellent article by Fincati, "La Perdita di Negroponte," *Arch. veneto*, XXXII (1886), 267–307, shorter accounts of the Turkish occupation of Negroponte may be found in Wm. Miller, *Latins in the Levant* (1908), pp. 470–79; Iorga [Jorga], *Gesch. d. osman. Reiches*, II (1909), 147–49; H. Kretschmayr, *Gesch. v. Venedig*, II (1920, repr. 1964), 377–78, 635; and Babinger, *Maometto* (1957), pp. 411–19.

[119] Malipiero, *Annali veneti*, in *Arch. stor. italiano*, VII–1, 65.

[120] *Ibid.*, pp. 58–59.

On 18 August (1470) the Senate sent the Venetian envoys at the Curia Romana a description of the fall of Negroponte, based upon a letter of 18 July from the captain-general Canale as well as upon other letters from various galley commanders, who all wrote to the same sad effect. The terrific impact of Turkish cannon balls had almost leveled to the ground the thick walls and heavy ravelins of the city. After numerous fierce encounters of the defenders with the Turks, the captain-general had approached the city with the larger part of the fleet, with the intention of destroying a bridge which the Turks had built across the upper end of the Euboeote canal (*in parte superiori canalis*). The Turkish response was immediate. Before dawn on 11 July the opposing sides entered a "prelium . . . generale et omnium atrocissimum . . . , quod pertinacissime et audacissime utrimque pugnantibus per diem illum totum et in sequentem noctem duravit." There was no defeating, no resisting the Turks, whose manpower had been assembled from every province in the Ottoman empire, near and far. They had 150,000 men, according to the Senate, and their strength increased with every passing hour as new arrivals enlarged their numbers. The Venetian and Negropontine defenders of the city were killed, wounded, and exhausted beyond endurance. The Turks finally surged over the battered walls and bulwarks about the first hour of the day, on the twelfth. Men, women, and children above ten years of age were slaughtered. It was not a bloodless victory for the Turks, however, for many of them were killed, and the Venetian cannon sank their galleys and set them afire. The miserable end of Christian Negroponte, according to the Senate, would prove the beginning of still greater ills for Christendom.

The Venetian envoys at the Curia were instructed to stress the gravity of the situation to Paul II, who was after all a Venetian. Not only the shores of Italy but those of the whole Mediterranean were now exposed to attack since the Christian stronghold of Negroponte had been lost to the enemy. Nuncios and legates should be sent to the emperor, the king of Hungary, the king of Poland, and other princes on the eastern front who could launch an attack *commode et valide* upon the Turks. The problems in Bohemia must be set aside for a while. The pope should also send legates to the king of France, the duke of Burgundy, "and even to England and Spain."[121] These requests were met with assurances at the Curia,[122] but there was little that Paul II could do to assist Venice or to impede the Turks.

The Venetian diplomatic correspondence, like that of most states in the Quattrocento, is usually couched in religious terms. The Ottoman sultan is *crudelissimus* or *immanissimus Christiani nominis hostis*, and there are frequent references to the *respublica Christiana* and to *fides Catholica servanda*. The Venetians looked upon themselves (however reluctantly) as the defenders of Christianity against Islam, and so they were. Whenever they could, they tried to avoid warfare, but in war as in business they wanted not to lose. Victory might produce a profit; defeat always entailed a loss.

The captain-general Canale, though he had served Venice well as a diplomat, was a loser, and he had certainly proved himself to be a timid and inept commander. Many members of the Senate now wanted to elect a new captain-general of the sea immediately as well as two provveditori to serve with him.[123] Within less than two weeks it was done. Pietro Mocenigo was chosen to succeed Canale (on 30 August); his ducal commission instructed him to hasten to take over his command. Marino Malipiero and Lodovico Bembo were to go with him as "provveditori, companions, and counsellors," and "in hac . . . celeri navigatione," which they were to undertake on such short notice, they were to stop off at Corfu, Modon, and Coron to encourage by their presence and counsel the officials and subjects of the Republic, in whom the loss of Negroponte had inspired obvious terror.[124]

From his boyhood in Venice, Paul II had always understood the importance of Negroponte to the Republic. As pope he realized only too well the significance of its loss to Christendom. Between 14 and 18 September, 1470, he wrote to the marquises Lodovico Gonzaga of

---

[121] Sen. Secreta, Reg. 24, fols. 127v–128r [131v–132r]: ". . . Sedanda sunt aut interim dimittenda negotia Boemie ut huic incomparabiliter maiori incendio provideri possit. . . ." *Cf.*, *ibid.*, fols. 138r, 159v, and 172v [142r, 163v, 176v].

[122] *Ibid.*, Reg. 24, fols. 129v–130r [133v–134r].

[123] Sen. Secreta, Reg. 24, fol. 127r [131r], dated 18 August, 1470: ". . . Quanta negligentia et ignavia amissa sit in conspectu capitanei et classis nostre miserima civitas nostra Nigropontis omnibus iam palam est."

[124] *Ibid.*, Reg. 24, fols. 130–31, 135v, 137 [134–35, 139v, 141].

Mantua and Guglielmo Paleologo of Montferrat, as well as to King John II of Aragon-Catalonia and Dukes Borso d'Este of Modena (Ferrara) and Amadeo IX of Savoy. The recipients of his briefs had doubtless learned, he stated, of the frightful progress of Sultan Mehmed II, who had stormed the fine city of Negroponte by land and sea with an overpowering armament and with the ghastly cruelty to be expected of his inborn ferocity. Mehmed wanted and was working for nothing else than the utter extinction of the Christian name by every barbarity of which he was capable. He was striving not only for the subjugation of the lands of his Christian neighbors, but also for the conquest and ruination of Italy, *provinciarum nobilissima*. The peril was tormenting Paul, as he wrote the princes, "beyond all belief" (*supra quam credibile res sit ipsa*). All the Italian states must unite in opposition to the enemy, and then the other Christian powers would help them.

Various Italian ambassadors had already come to Rome in this connection. Paul was awaiting the others with vast impatience, and he implored those to whom his briefs were addressed

> that immediately upon reading the present letter you send us . . . as your envoy an upright, God-fearing man, who is bent upon preserving the Christian commonwealth, with ample authority to negotiate and conclude a general league in Italy, for as the Italian failure to reach an accord feeds the Turkish tyrant's audacity and encourages his advance, just so will all his courage be dispelled when he learns that the armed might of the Italians has been conjoined by common agreement. . . . Beloved sons, there must be no delay, because our enemy, who seems to desire nothing more than the bloody extermination of all Christendom, [is] already at our throats, grows stronger every day, and fresh from the victory he has had, he is strengthened in his resolve, so that every slightest delay affords him the opportunity for our common destruction. . . .[125]

The Florentines and King Ferrante of Naples had already sent their envoys to the Curia. The Milanese "orator" was expected shortly. But just when Italy needed peace so badly, it seemed as though war might lie ahead. The Florentine and Neapolitan envoys had informed Paul II that the Venetian government had recently decided to alter the course of the Mincio and deflect its waters into another channel. Lodovico Gonzaga, marquis of Mantua, and Galeazzo Maria Sforza, duke of Milan, were highly exercised by the Venetian proposal, which (as Paul informed the Doge Cristoforo Moro on 17 September) could hardly have come at a worse time. As the Venetians ought to know, the *respublica Christiana* had probably not been in such parlous need of peace and co-operation for a thousand years. Paul beseeched the doge and the Signoria, therefore, if the report of their designs upon the Mincio was true, to lay aside all thought of the project and to aid the Curia in establishing in Italy such a peace as would make it possible to ward off the danger and to preserve the "pristine majesty" of Christendom.[126]

Venice obviously had more serious concerns than the alteration of the course of the Mincio. Her commerce in the Levant was threatened. In a letter of 8 October, 1470, to Charles the Bold, the duke of Burgundy, the Senate dwelt again on the *magnitudo et atrocitas* of Sultan Mehmed's occupation of Negroponte, which was (they said) one more step toward his invasion and destruction of all the Christian islands in the

---

[125] Arch. Segr. Vaticano, Arm. XXXIX, tom. 12 [*Liber brevium de Curia anni septimi D. Pauli papae II*], fol. 2, by mod. stamped enumeration, "datum Rome apud Sanctum Petrum, etc., die XVIII Septembris 1470, [pontificatus nostri] anno septimo." The original of the brief sent to Lodovico Gonzaga, "datum Rome apud Sanctum Petrum sub annulo piscatoris die XIIII Septembris, MCCCCLXX, pontificatus nostri anno septimo," is preserved in the Arch. di Stato di Mantova, Arch. Gonzaga, Busta 834. The Mantuan copy of this brief may be found, *ibid.*, Busta 85, B. XXXIII, no. 13, fols. 23^v–24^r, where it is dated 18 September, together with Lodovico Gonzaga's reply dated 16 October, indicating that a Mantuan embassy was being sent to Rome to discuss the proposed league against the Turks.

[126] Arch. Segr. Vaticano, Arm. XXXIX, tom. 12, fol. 3, by mod. stamped enumeration. This register contains two briefs, also dated 17 September, 1470, to Duke Galeazzo Maria, urging caution and the maintenance of peace in Italy despite the Venetians' alleged intention to deflect the course of the Mincio. Paul informed the duke that he had written to the Venetians "hortando et monendo," and hoped that the allegation would prove groundless (*ibid.*, fols. 3^v–4^r). The important problem facing Christendom was the Turkish advance, and the Italian powers must unite to meet the peril: "Ita enim expedit pro gloria salvatoris nostri amplianda, pro liberanda republica Christiana, pro victoria fidelium consequenda, proque insania perfidissimi inimici nominis Turchi comprimenda: non decet nobilitatem tuam tam sanctum et tam necessarium et pium ac commune opus perturbare, quod omnes Catholici principes summopere affectant: plura enim scribenda essent in hanc rem . . ." (fol. 4^r): "Quanto magis id nunc facere debemus et tenemur quoniam Turchum communem hostem immanissimum ad Italiam subiugandam suo nefandissimo imperio festinare videamus ut illa subacta ceteras Christianitatis nationes subiugare posset . . ." (fol. 4^v). On Paul II's concern with the Turkish problem, see, *ibid.*, fols. 12^r, 77^v–78^r, 78^v, 87^v, 88, 90^v–91^v, 101, 106, *et alibi*.

eastern Mediterranean.[127] The Senate was especially worried about Crete, *que est caput status nostri Levantis*,[128] the chief depot in transit for the Republic's trade with Egypt and Syria. Peace was more important, at least for the time being, than the Mincio, for Venice needed freedom from strife in Italy to employ her resources against the Turks in the East.

On 16 October (1470), however, the Senate could report an interesting development to their ambassadors at the Curia Romana:

Two envoys have come into our presence these past days from the most illustrious ladies Maria [Sultana Mara], stepmother of the lord Turk, and Catherine, widow of the late magnificent count of Cilli [Ulrich, who was slain by the Hungarians at a conference in the fortress of Belgrade in November, 1456]. Both are daughters of the late most illustrious lord despot of Serbia [George Branković, d. 1456]. The envoys stated on behalf of both ladies that, before the Turk moved against Negroponte, they tried on their own initiative to induce him to make peace with us, for both ladies are Christians, and are well disposed toward Christians and especially toward us. The Turk had replied to them that it was the wrong time for such a peace, because of the vast expense he had incurred and the preparations he had made for the campaign on which he had decided to embark.

After the storming of Negroponte, however, the ladies again of their own accord had tried to persuade the aforesaid Turk to make peace. He has informed them that, if we send someone to him for the negotiations, he will be ready to reach a settlement with us. He was willing and has authorized that the aforesaid envoys come to us at Venice and inquire of our wishes, offering a safe-conduct in case we should decide to send someone to him and to come to an agreement with him. We have made our reply to the said envoys, as you will see from the enclosed copy [of our text], and our desire and instructions to you are that you communicate all this to his Holiness, the supreme pontiff. . . .

Add also that we understand very well that this is one of the usual cunning tricks of the Turk, in whom we believe that absolutely no trust should be placed, for he yearns for the destruction of our faith and religion. Considering the present state of affairs, however, it has seemed best to us to play his own game of pretense [*secum dissimulare*] and to go along with him. . . .[129]

On the same day (16 October, 1470) the Senate approved a second letter to the Venetian ambassadors at the Curia, directing them to warn Paul II that the peninsular peace must be confirmed and the Italian league renewed. An expedition against the Turks would require more time and preparation than present circumstances would seem to allow. The weeks were flying by, and unless a fleet was ready by the following summer, of such size and strength as to match the enemy's forces, one could only fear for the future of Italy.[130] The Venetians were forever identifying their lot in the Levant with the well-being of Italy. Although the Curia generally agreed with them, the other states in the peninsula did not. The Senate was not entirely wrong, however, for Mehmed II did entertain designs upon Italy, as the events of a decade later were to show. In the meantime suspicions and hostilities continued so to confound relations among the Italian states that in late October (1470) Paul II stated that, if conditions in the peninsula became intolerable for the Holy See, he would leave Italy and go to Avignon![131]

Despite the Venetian Senate's distrust of the Turk, by the end of November (1470) two envoys, Niccolò Cocco and Francesco Capello, having been duly elected, were preparing to leave for the Porte in response to the embassy of the Serbian princesses. According to their instructions, they were to go by way of Corfu, where they would await their safe-conduct or passport to enter Turkish territory. From Corfu they should proceed to Istanbul by land or sea, as indicated by the text of their passport. They were to explain to the sultan "that although fortune, in whose grasp lies the determination of all human affairs, has allowed that we should have been drawn into war with his Excellency, nevertheless our intention has always been and is sincerely to live at peace with his Excellency, as we have done for many generations with his most illustrious forebears." Honorable and appropriate terms of peace could simply be "that each should hold and possess what he holds and possesses at present . . . ," and the peace should include "all the lords of the Aegean archipelago as well as the most serene king of Cyprus; the most reverend lord, the grand

[127] Sen. Secreta, Reg. 24, fol. 145^r [149^r], and *cf.* the letter of 11 October to Louis XI of France, *ibid.*, fols. 146^v–147^r [150^v–151^r].

[128] *Ibid.*, Reg. 24, fol. 149^r [153^r].

[129] Sen. Secreta, Reg. 24, fol. 150 [154], doc. dated 16 October, 1470, and *cf.*, *ibid.*, fol. 148^r [152^r]. On the circumstances leading to the death of Count Ulrich of Cilli, see F. G. Heymann, *George of Bohemia* (1965), pp. 130–35, and for the embassy of the Serbian princesses, see Malipiero, *Annali veneti*, in *Arch. stor. italiano*, VII-1, 67.

[130] Sen. Secreta, Reg. 24, fol. 150^r [154^r].

[131] *Ibid.*, Reg. 24, fol. 156^v [160^v], doc. dated 3 November, 1470: ". . . summo pontifice dicente . . . se Italiam deserturum et concessurum Avinionem. . . ."

master of Rhodes, with the Order [of the Hospitallers]; and the most illustrious lord of S. Maura."[132] Peace would be doubly welcome, for reports from all the Venetian territories in the Levant foretold a serious shortage of grain, which carried with it the threat of famine.[133]

Upon his return to Venice, Niccolò da Canale had been brought to trial by the "advocates of the commune." He was charged with the failure to make a serious attempt to aid Negroponte and then, when the city had clearly been lost, with the fatuous effort to recover it, "mettendo in evidentissimo periculo tanto numero de valenti huomini cum tuta larmada a lui commessa." He was found guilty, and sentenced to exile and confinement at Portogruaro in Friuli.[134] Six or seven weeks after Canale's trial, his friend Paul II intervened on his behalf (on 24 December, 1470), urging the Doge Cristoforo Moro and the Senate to rescind the measures taken against him on the grounds of his past services to the Republic and of his devotion to the Holy See.[135] Two months later, on 20 February (1471), Paul wrote again, complaining of the doge's failure to answer his previous letter. He was grieved and astonished at the doge's silence. Having now a fuller knowledge of the facts, Paul was more convinced than ever of Canale's innocence of negligence or of any other adjudicable failing. He renewed his plea for Canale's release, and hoped this time for a speedy reply to his letter.[136] His efforts were unavailing. Canale died in his Friulan exile.

By the standard of the times Canale's punishment was hardly severe. Mehmed II was as likely as not to execute an incompetent or unsuccessful commander. Venice might well have yielded to Paul II's solicitous regard for Canale, however, for the Italian peace the Senate had been pleading for throughout the past year and longer had finally been confirmed. As Paul wrote the papal governor of Bologna on 24 December (1470),

> by the grace of the Holy Spirit on the twenty-second day of the present month . . . we have concluded, renewed, blessed, and entered into a league of all the powers in Italy, placing our hope in the Lord that from this confederation, union, and league there will come an expedition against [the Turk], the monstrous common enemy of the Christian faith, so that this great peril and crisis may be met by combining our strength.[137]

The peace of Lodi (of 1454) had been restored, the so-called Italian league revived. The news reached Venice quickly. Paul II was talking of an expedition against the Turk, but Niccolò Cocco and Francesco Capello were on the road to Istanbul to make peace with the Porte if they could. The Senate approved new instructions, sent as usual in the doge's name, to "our orators to the Turk," telling them (on 2 January, 1471)

> . . . how by letters from our ambassadors in the city of Rome we have been informed that on the twenty-second of this past December, with divine assistance, Pope Nicholas V's general league of Italy has been restored . . . and reshaped—between the supreme pontiff and all the other Italian powers—a development which we have all yearned for, and one certainly most advantageous for the affairs of

---

[132] Sen. Secreta, Reg. 24, fols. 164ᵛ–166ʳ [168ᵛ–170ʳ], doc. dated 27 and 29 November, 1470: ". . . Diximus vobis . . . ut ex Corphoo ad Portam accedatis sive per terram sive per mare prout fueritis per salvumconductum assecurati. . . . [The envoys' instructions provided:] quod . . . exponere debeant quod licet fortuna, in cuius potestate rerum humanarum omnium conditiones posite sunt, permiserit ut cum illius Excellentia ad bellum devenerimus, intentio tamen nostra semper fuit et est cum illius Excellentia in pace sincero animo vivere quemadmodum cum illustrissimis illius maioribus per multa secula viximus. . . . Et si vobis responderetur ut vos illius [pacis] conditiones proponeretis, dicetis nobis honestum conveniensque videri pro diuturnitate stabilitateque pacis ipsius . . . quod quisque teneat possideatque que ad presens tenet et possidet. . . . In qua quidem pace includantur adherentes colligati et commendati nostri soliti, hoc est omnes domini Egeopelagi ultra quos includantur quoque serenissimus rex Cypri, reverendissimus dominus magnus magister Rhodi cum illa Religione, illustrissimus dominus Sancte Maure. . . ." *Cf.*, *ibid.*, fol. 185 [189].

[133] Sen. Mar, Reg. 9, fol. 73ʳ, doc. dated 7 December, 1470: "Quante importantie sit res frumentaria statui nostro maritimo in hoc ardenti bello Turcorum nemo est qui non intelligat. Nam ab universis nostris civitatibus Levantis habentur littere que nuntiant maximam futuram esse in illis penuriam frumentorum. . . ."

[134] Fincati, "Perdita di Negroponte," pp. 305–7.

[135] Arch. Segr. Vaticano, Arm. XXXIX, tom. 12, fols. 62ᵛ–63ʳ: "Dilecto filio nobili viro Cristoforo Mauro Venetiarum duci: Nigropontis expugnatio cum a nobis non sine ingenti dolore primo audita fuit, paucis post diebus, accepimus te et nobilem istum Senatum tuum statuisse ut dilectus filius Nicolaus de Canali, qui maritime classi tue preerat cuique ob rem tandem infeliciter gestam id factum vitio potissimum dari videbatur, publico decreto in vincula coniectus ad vos usque deveheretur. . . ."

[136] *Ibid.*, fols. 99ᵛ–100ʳ.

[137] Arch. Segr. Vaticano, Arm. XXXIX, tom. 12, fol. 61ᵛ by mod. stamped enumeration. A similar notice was sent to the governors of all the other papal cities. *Cf.* also Paul's brief letter to the Doge Cristoforo Moro in Venice, "datum Rome apud Sanctum Petrum, die II Januarii, 1471, [pontificatus nostri] anno VII" (*ibid.*, fols. 66ᵛ–67ʳ).

Christendom. Since, as you see, after your departure [from Venice] things have changed, it is necessary for us to hold off a while on our decision [*deliberatio*], and therefore it is our desire and that of the Senate and our instructions to you that, if upon your receipt of the present letter you have not left Corfu and have not begun your journey to betake yourselves into the presence of the lord Turk, as we believe it reasonable to suppose, you are to stop and delay your departure until we write you otherwise.

If a messenger has arrived with a safe-conduct, you will excuse yourselves, either owing to the late arrival of the safe-conduct itself, on which account it would be necessary for you to write us and await our answer, or owing to the feigned illness of either one of you—or, finally, you might entertain doubt concerning some article in the aforesaid safe-conduct, expressing your doubt in courteous and diplomatic terms. If by chance, however, you have already left Corfu, so that this letter has overtaken you along the way, we wish . . . that, when you find yourselves in the presence of the lord Turk, you try to negotiate a peace with his Excellency with that stipulation and condition which we have included in your commission, namely that each of us should retain what he possesses at present and acquire nothing further. . . .

If the lord Turk should be unwilling [to accede to this], however, state our position in such terms as to keep his Excellency from making a decision, being quite careful to assert the necessity of writing to us. In other ways and by appropriate means you will be able to learn his ultimate requirements so that these negotiations for peace may not be given up entirely. You will keep us informed by rapid post.[138]

There was some feeling in the Senate that Cocco and Capello should proceed to the Porte, whatever the point at which a letter might reach them, but proponents of this view apparently could not muster votes enough to secure the passage of their motion.[139] On 22 March (1471) the Senate informed Vettore Soranzo, their ambassador in Naples, that the Florentines had suddenly raised wholly unexpected objections to "subscribing to the instrument of renewal of the general league." Thus peace in Italy seemed likely to be jeopardized at precisely the time when Mehmed II was summoning to Istanbul all available horse and foot from Canina and Valona, which was a sure sign (in the Senate's opinion at least) that a Turkish armada would soon be leaving Istanbul.[140]

In the meantime, although Paul II had been doing his literary best to help the Venetians, they thought he was capable of larger financial exertions on their behalf. Paul was, nevertheless, doing something. On 18 January, 1471, he wrote Élias de Bourdeilles, the archbishop of Tours, that the latter's epistle of the preceding 17 October had been enormously encouraging, wholly concerned as it was "circa reprimendam rabiem ac vexonias furias Turchorum." Upon receiving the news of the catastrophe of Negroponte, Paul had described its attendant horrors and outlined his fears for the future to his venerable brother of Tours and other members of the episcopate. In his turn Élias had apparently organized processions to implore the mercy of the Almighty and to move Louis XI to take action against the Turkish dragon, for the salvation of Christendom. Indeed, Élias had made a direct and public appeal to his Majesty before a distinguished gathering, which had included the king's confessor Jean Bochart, the bishop of Avranches, and Louis had in fact (as Élias had written on 17 October) proposed to take up arms "pro defensione ac salute populi Christiani." Nothing could become his royal Majesty more, Paul now wrote, than to undertake a crusade which would win him immortal merit in heaven and abiding glory on earth. Paul wanted Élias to continue his pressure on Louis XI to embark upon the sacred enterprise, and declared himself willing (in the usual words) to shed his own blood and to give his own life "if it should prove necessary," but, alas, "the Turkish monster grows larger from hour to hour before our very eyes. . . ."[141]

On the whole the Venetians found Paul II's efforts to prosecute the war against Mehmed II inadequate and his financial provisions unworthy of the vicar of Christ, who seemed to them to be deserting the Christian cause and

---

[138] Sen. Secreta, Reg. 24, fol. 174^r [178^r], doc. dated 2 January, 1471, with the upright cross in the left-hand margin of the register, indicating that the Senate approved both the text of the letter and its dispatch to Cocco and Capello.

[139] *Ibid.*, Reg. 24, fols. 176^v–177^r [180^v–181^r], docs. dated 15, 16, and 23 January, 1471.

[140] *Ibid.*, Reg. 25, fols. 7^v–8^r [16^v–17^r], with a similar letter to Antonio Priuli, the Venetian envoy in Florence (*ibid.*, fol. 8, and *cf.* fols. 9, 11^r [18, 20^r]).

[141] Arch. Segr. Vaticano, Arm. XXXIX, tom. 12, fols. 67^v–68^r: ". . . Crescit illud Turchorum monstrum in horas ante oculos, atque utinam Itali sufficerent ad resistendum: faciemus autem favente Altissimo pro viribus quod poterimus. . . . Datum Rome apud Sanctum Petrum [die] XVIII Januarii, 1471, [pontificatus nostri] anno septimo."

exposing his flock to the approaching wolf.[142] They shared the merchant mentality, Paul and his compatriots. While they deplored the losses they were sustaining in the war with the Turks, he deplored the expenditure of his resources on the war. The Senate tried by unending repetition to convince Paul that the sultan was an indescribable peril to Italy and to Christendom, and that, if Venice did not soon receive large help from the Holy See and the other Italian powers, she could not possibly hold her own in the unequal contest.[143] In fact the Senate now wanted, as a minimum from the pope, the immediate grant of 50,000 ducats without strings attached and, in addition, all the revenues accruing to the Holy See from the alum mines at Tolfa. Although instead of waiting for the proceeds from the sale of alum, they would prefer a specified sum of money, "which would be better for us as being more certain and expeditious, and although this entire amount [the 50,000 ducats plus the income from the sale of alum] is not that which the magnitude of the problem requires, as we have often stated, nevertheless it is prudent to want the things we can [get] since we cannot [get] the things we want. . . ."[144] Actually Paul had already made the requested *aluminum donatio*, but there was such disagreement as to the price and manner of sale that the grant did the Venetians little good, and their remonstrances and complaints continued.[145]

During 1470–1471 Paul II had occasion more than once to remind Charles the Bold of Burgundy of the papal assignment to the crusade of the profits from the alum mines at Tolfa. Although Charles had made an agreement with the pope (on 5 May, 1468) that only alum belonging to the Holy See would be allowed into his dominions, two years had passed since this commitment was made. Now there seemed to be some further postponement in the offing before the papal alum could be sold at its set price in the duchy of Burgundy and its dependencies. Paul feared that such delay would be damaging to the projected crusade.[146] One was less concerned about the crusade in Flanders than in Italy.

The Scottish bishops, being even farther removed from the Turkish menace, apparently showed little enthusiasm for the crusade and shied away from the costs. In January (1471) one of their number was threatened with excommunication for his failure to transmit to the Camera Apostolica "certain sums of money" which had been collected in accordance with Pius II's *bulla cruciate*. Paul demanded immediate satisfaction of the bishop's debt to the Camera, "because our faith is in the direst peril."[147]

One felt the peril in the Levant. After the Turkish seizure and sack of Negroponte fear had entered every Christian household in the Aegean, making its way also into the palace of the grand master and the auberges of the Knights at Rhodes. A letter of Paul II to the Grand Master Giovanni Battista Orsini and the Convent, dated 20 January (1471), gives us a glimpse into conditions on the island:

We have received your letter . . . , and gathered clearly enough that you are doubtful and apprehensive about the city of Rhodes because of the power and increasing impetus of the terrible Turks. Certainly we must fear, but not so as to cease the search for aid and remedies. Not at all. We shall have to move with greater care and speed. Do not fail yourselves [*nolite vobis ipsis deesse*], but take heart. We are managing, along with the Italian and other Christian powers, to take such steps . . . as will contain the great attack [you fear]. We shall always help that city, which we love as our own, to the fullest extent of our ability. But since we understand

---

[142] Sen. Secreta, Reg. 24, fol. 177^v [181^v], dated 23 January, 1471 (Ven. style 1470), the Senate to the Venetian envoys at the Curia Romana.

[143] *Ibid.*, fols. 178^v–179^r [182^v–183^r], doc. dated 25 January, 1471: ". . . Sed nisi ab Sanctitate summi pontificis reliquisque Italicis potentatibus adiuvemur, impossibile est ut tantum sustineamus impetum." *Cf.*, *ibid.*, fols. 181^r [185^r], 182^v [186^v], and Reg. 25, fol. 20^r [29^r].

[144] *Ibid.*, Reg. 24, fol. 184^r [188^r], dated 13 February, 1471, to the Venetian envoys at the Curia.

[145] *Ibid.*, Reg. 25, fol. 1^v [10^v], dated 2 March, 1471, "oratoribus nostris in Romana Curia."

[146] Arm. XXXIX, tom. 12, fol. 17^v, dated 18 October, 1470: ". . . Novit Excellentia tua nos dedicasse ipsum alumen sancte cruciate et tuitioni fidei orthodoxe: novit item, ut putamus, quam gravia pericula ab infidelibus Turchis quotidie magna immineant. . . ." *Cf.*, *ibid.*, fols. 32^v–33^r, a letter dated 2 November, 1470, to the abbot of S. Giorgio in Venice: ". . . totum alumen nostrum . . . pro expeditione contra Turchos," and note fol. 100, letter dated 18 February, 1471, again to Charles the Bold, and esp. fol. 102^r, on the pope's annoyance with the delays in the sale of Tolfan alum in Charles's territories. See in general Adolf Gottlob, *Aus der Camera Apostolica des 15. Jahrhunderts*, Innsbruck, 1889, esp. pp. 287 ff., and Raymond de Roover, *The Rise and Decline of the Medici Bank (1397–1494)*, New York, 1966, pp. 154–58 and ff., with the notes, *ibid.*, pp. 438 ff.

[147] Arm. XXXIX, tom. 12, fol. 88, "datum [Rome apud Sanctum Marcum die V Januarii, 1471, anno septimo]."

that the towers of [Fort] S. Nicholas, of the Harbor, and of the Mole are not being so well and diligently guarded as they should be, and that, furthermore, the city has not been well fortified along the moats, we have wanted to warn you to take every precaution against negligence and too little concern in this matter. . . .

Paul ordered that the towers be put under a vigilant system of watch and ward, *sub diurna ac nocturna custodia*, and that stores of munitions be gathered against an emergency. The fortifications were to be strengthened along the moats, "and there must be no delay here, but haste!"[148]

The defenses of Rhodes would be built up under Orsini's renowned successor Pierre d'Aubusson, and they would be needed, but the Knights still had a decade to prepare for the great assault which already seemed inevitable. In the meantime Paul II continued to write letters of hopeful assurance to whomever he could find in conflict with the Turks. On 10 February (1471), for example, he encouraged the Albanian chieftain John Balsichi to continue in his resistance to the infidel oppressor and in his devotion to the Christian faith. John should not be deterred in his opposition to the sultan because of the proximity of the Turks to his homeland. It was to be hoped, indeed expected, that God would not allow Christendom to live much longer "in this persecution, tribulation, and fear, but [that] he will soon free us from the clutches of this dragon, crush him, and confound him by his power." An alliance had been formed throughout Italy (*universalis liga Italie*) in order to organize an expedition against the "perfidious dog" Mehmed. There was no need for John to yield to Turkish blandishments or to fear. In steadfastness he would find salvation as well as security.[149]

Since by 28 February, 1471, the Turkish safe-conduct for Cocco and Capello had not yet reached them in Corfu, as far as was known in Venice, on 1 March the Senate wrote the two envoys to return home, for it would be unbecoming to the dignity of the Republic for them to wait any longer.[150] Since the remote chance of getting out of the war by negotiation now seemed unlikely of fulfillment, the Senate took much interest in the arrival of another embassy from Uzun Ḥasan, whose envoy dilated on his master's power and desire to proceed against the Turk, in which noble enterprise, needless to say, he received the enthusiastic encouragement of the Senate.[151] But shortly before 11 March the news came from Corfu that the Turkish safe-conduct had finally arrived, and that Cocco and Capello had set out for the Porte. The Venetian envoys in Rome and Naples, however, were instructed to inform both the pope and King Ferrante that the Senate intended to press on with all vigor and vigilance the organization of their fleet for an expedition against the Turk,[152] whose own preparations for a renewed assault upon the Christian strongholds in the Levant were nearing completion.[153]

The gathering clouds did not preclude all hope of sunshine. Paul II wanted to believe that something worthwhile might even come of the Emperor Frederick III's personal attendance at a diet he was summoning to meet in Regensburg on S. George's day (23 April, 1471). Frederick

[148] Arm. XXXIX, tom. 12, fols. 88^v–89^r, "datum Rome apud Sanctum Petrum, anno etc., MCCCCLXX, tertiodecimo Kal. Februarii, pontificatus nostri anno septimo" [1471]. The general reform of the convent at Rhodes was being considered at this time (*ibid.*, fol. 94). On 12 March (1471) Paul wrote the Hospitallers again, assuring them of his efforts to save their island bulwark: "Dilecti filii [magister et conventus Hospitalis Sancti Johannis Ierosolimitani Rhodi commorantes] salutem, etc. . . . Hortamur vos in domino ut huic rei fidei fortibus ac intrepidis animis incumbatis. . . . Vobis non deerimus et conabimur Christianos ac Catholicos principes, sicuti conati sumus, ut contra ipsum rabidissimum canem Turchum pro potentia eorum insurgant inducere ita ut aliqua bona et utilis expeditio fiat . . ." (fol. 113^r). Orsini was the grand master of the Hospital from 1467 until his death in 1476, when he was succeeded by Pierre d'Aubusson.

[149] Arm. XXXIX, tom. 12, fols. 95^v–96^r, "datum Rome apud Sanctum Petrum [die] X Februarii, 1471, [pontificatus nostri] anno septimo."

[150] Sen. Secreta, Reg. 24, fol. 187^r [191^r].

[151] *Ibid.*, Reg. 25, fols. 2^r–3^r [11^r–12^r], docs. dated 2 and 7 March, 1471, and fols. 24^r ff. [33^r ff.], dated 18 May, 1471: "Quod orator illustrissimi domini Ussoncassani expediatur et cum eo insimul vadat nobilis vir Catarinus Geno orator noster designatus ad ipsum dominum et vadat cum infrascripta commissione," and there follows the commission of Zeno, who was to express the Senate's sympathy to Uzun Ḥasan for the injuries he had suffered as a result of Mehmed II's perfidy and intolerable lust for world domination, to encourage him in his determination to take up arms against the Ottomans, and to remind him that Venice had also been driven "to take up arms both by land and by sea to resist [the Turk's] insatiable appetite to destroy [us] all!" Note also, *ibid.*, fols. 57^v–58^r, 60^v ff., 63^v, 121^r ff., 123^v, 126^v, 134, 143 [66^v–67^r, 69^v ff., 72^v, etc.].

[152] Sen. Secreta, Reg. 25, fols. 3^v, 4^r [12^v, 13^r], dated 11 March, 1471, and *cf.* fol. 42 [51].

[153] *Ibid.*, Reg. 25, fols. 4^v–5^r [13^v–14^r], 7^r [16^r], docs. dated in March, 1471. *Cf.* V. L. Ménage, "Seven Ottoman Documents . . . ," in S. M. Stern, ed., *Documents from Islamic Chanceries* (1965), pp. 82–83, 101–6.

might bestir himself, for the Turks were not sparing his own hereditary lands.[154] And indeed in early June the news came that Mehmed II had invaded Frederick's lands, with "vastation grandissime nel paixe de lo imperador." The Venetian government rushed forces from the region of Vicenza to the frontiers of Friuli and Istria "in order to meet the aforesaid Turks if they should advance any farther."[155] In September the Senate recalled Niccolò Cocco from Istanbul, where Capello had died, for the sultan's terms were beyond the price the Republic was prepared to pay for peace.[156]

Lamenting the "misunderstanding" which had arisen between Venice and the Porte during the course of Cocco's mission, the Senate wished to continue the effort to make peace with the Turks by sending another ambassador to Istanbul.[157] The secretary Marco Aurelio was chosen for the assignment.[158] On 21 April (1472) the Senate came to the conclusion, after weeks of indecision, that Aurelio should proceed to Corfu to await further orders. One Theodore, envoy of the Turco-Serbian princess Mara and the countess of Cilli, was to go with him. They both went to Corfu, but Aurelio's instructions and his departure for Istanbul were delayed while the Senate waited for news of Uzun Ḥasan's offensive against Mehmed II, to which we shall return in the following chapter. Niccolò Cocco was finally allowed to come home from Corfu, where he had been ordered to remain on his way back from Istanbul, so that he might give Aurelio whatever useful information he had acquired on the Bosporus.[159]

On 31 August, 1472, the Senate finally voted that no more time should be lost in formulating Aurelio's commission so that, in the event of his Turkish safe-conduct's arriving, he could make his way to the Porte. The matter was to be decided the next day, but whatever terms if any were finally accepted by the Senate are not recorded in the Senatus Secreta.[160] The fact need not concern us unduly, however, since on the following 12 December, Aurelio was recalled to Venice from Corfu, *ob rerum maximam factam mutationem*,[161] there being little point in a mission to Istanbul, for Mehmed was preparing a great offensive against Uzun Ḥasan, to whom the Senate had sent the intrepid Caterino Zeno as an envoy, and for whom they were trying vigorously to raise help by arranging that a Christian fleet should strike the Turks in the west as Uzun Ḥasan attacked them from the east. The records of the Senate suggest that the Venetians did everything they could, considering the distances involved and the difficulties of communication, to assist Uzun Ḥasan in one of the greater military ventures of the time.[162]

---

[154] Arch. Segr. Vaticano, Arm. XXXIX, tom. 12, fols. 106^v–107, and *cf.*, *ibid.*, fols. 130^r, 173, 174^v–175^r, and 179, the last reference being to a letter dated 20 July, 1471, six days before Paul II's death (*cf.*, *ibid.*, fol. 290^r, the note with which this register ends: "Paulus papa II obiit die XXVI Iulii, 1471, pont. sui anno septimo").

[155] Sen. Secreta, Reg. 25, fol. 29^r [38^r], doc. dated 10 June, 1471, and fol. 29^v [38^v], dated the seventh, and note also fols. 30^v–31, 32^r, 33^v, 35^r [39^v–40, etc.]. There was another Turkish incursion into imperial territory a year later (fols. 143^v, 155, 159).

[156] *Ibid.*, Reg. 25, fols. 56^r–57^r [65^r–66^r], a letter authorized by the Senate on 6 September, 1471, to be sent in the doge's name to Cocco, and note fol. 79 [88], another letter to Cocco, dated 26 November.

[157] *Ibid.*, Reg. 25, fols. 109 ff. [118 ff.], 112^r [121^r].

[158] Some members of the Senate wanted Aurelio to be given the following instructions (on 12 March, 1472): "Marce, ut meminisse debes et potes de integro perspicere per introclusas scripturas omnis difficultas et causa non facte ab oratoribus nostris pacis conclusionis fuit ob brachium Mayne et Croyam ab Turco petitam et ab nobis dari recusatam. Nam de Stalimine et Schiro [Lemnos and Skyros] contentabamur et circa pecunias credimus quod res facilius aptari potuisset. Et eiusdem sumus propositi et intentionis ut quoniam quidem Staliminem et Schirum semel obtulimus ad illas iterum promittendas descendas, et similiter quantitatem pecuniarum, ad ducatos scilicet XXV usque L m., solvendam in annis quinque per ratam, et insta quantum potes ut vel melioribus si potes vel ad extremum his saltem conditionibus ad conclusionem devenias. Et facta per te omni experientia non obtinendo si intelligeres posse adiunctas etiam insulas Schiati et Scopuli [Skiathos and Skopelos] facere conclusionem illas offer et adiunge . . . ," but Aurelio was not to agree to the cession of either Maina or Croia, and other proposals being made, it was finally voted that, owing to the importance of the matter, a decision should be postponed to a later session (*ibid.*, Reg. 25, fol. 114 [123]).

[159] *Ibid.*, Reg. 25, fols. 122^v [131^v] and 133 [142], docs. dated 21 April and 13 June, 1472.

[160] *Ibid.*, Reg. 25, fol. 147^v [156^v]: ". . . Vadit pars quod cras pro hac materia vocari debeat hoc consilium [Rogatorum], ad quod omnes venire teneantur, et qui ponere possint partem pro conscientia uniuscuiusque sua."

[161] *Ibid.*, Reg. 25, fol. 170^r [180^r], and note fols. 156^r, 168^v–169^v, 171^v [165^r, etc.].

[162] On Venetian relations with Uzun Ḥasan and Caterino Zeno's embassy, an ample record is to be found in the Sen. Secreta, Reg. 25, fols. 148^v, 149^v–150^r, 151–54, 157, 160, 161^v, 162^v, 163–164^r, 167–168^v, 171^v–178^r, 180–183^r [157^v, etc., by mod. enumeration], docs. dated from 12 September, 1472, to 11 February, 1473 (Ven. style 1472). Zeno's mission to Persia during these years (1472–1473) is among the famous adventures of the fifteenth century (*De i Commentarii del viaggio in Persia di . . . Caterino Zeno . . . et delle guerre fatte nell'imperio persiano, dal tempo*

By this time, Pope Paul II was no more. After presiding over a six-hour consistory, and then enjoying three melons at dinner, he had died during the night of 26 July, 1471,[163] having seemingly been in the best of health. Six months before his unexpected end, after consultation with the commission of cardinals which had charge of funds to promote the crusade (they met in Bessarion's house), Paul had pledged a fourth of his revenues, which (he said) would amount to 50,000 ducats a year, to the war against the Turks. This we know from a letter of 17 January (1471) which Cardinal Francesco Gonzaga sent to his father, Marquis Lodovico II of Mantua. Except for the income from the papal alum monopoly (the "Cruciata"), which was already assigned to the crusade, the pope claimed that his total receipts did not exceed 200,000 ducats, and as an instance of his good faith he had offered to open to the ambassadors of the Italian states the papal account books, both his own and those of his predecessors. This offer did not satisfy the diplomatic corps, however, especially the Venetians, who believed the pope should sell all his jewels and devote all his revenues to the crusade, reserving only enough for bare existence. The hard-pressed Venetians also wanted the cardinals to give up one-half of their revenues for the war against the Porte. They thought "that his Holiness should specify how many galleys he was willing to maintain for the enterprise, saying that they did not want this offer of money nor of the fourth [of the papal income]: because the hour was late the matter was postponed for another consistory. . . ."[164]

Paul's passing from the troubled scene, however, entailed the election of a new pope. New plans would have to be made, new commitments secured from the Holy See. Without doubt Paul had had the crusade at heart from the first weeks of his pontificate. He had seen the Turks strike harder blows at Latin territories than his predecessor had witnessed. Nevertheless, he had insisted that all he could afford to give the valiant Scanderbeg was a subsidy of five thousand ducats, and even this amount was not forthcoming in full. The fall of Negroponte had made a profound impression on him, as on all his contemporaries, but at his death he left a treasure of pearls, jewels, gold, silver, precious ornaments, and ancient coins, which the Milanese envoy to the Vatican estimated at about a million ducats. Paul had himself stated in a consistory held not long before his death that he would spend half a million ducats on the crusade if the princes of Europe would go together on an expedition against the Turks,[165] but he knew well they would not go.

Venice wanted the Greek cardinal Bessarion to succeed Paul II. On 1 August (1471), the very day that news of Paul's death reached the lagoon, the Senate wrote Alvise Donato, their ambassador to Federigo da Montefeltro of Urbino, expressing their immense regard for Federigo, and assuming as well as enlisting his

---

di Ussuncassano in quà, libri due . . . , Venice, 1558; G. B. Ramusio, *Delle navigationi et viaggi . . .* , Venice, 1559, and later editions (with same foliation); Charles Grey, trans., *A Narrative of Italian Travels in Persia, in the Fifteenth and Sixteenth Centuries*, London, 1873, pp. 5–65, esp. 11–40 [published with Wm. Thomas (who was executed at Tyburn on 18 May, 1553, for high treason) and S. A. Roy, trans., *Travels to Tana and Persia, by Josafa Barbaro and Ambrogio Contarini*, London: Hakluyt Society, 1873]). On Caterino Zeno (Zen) and his son Pietro (born about 1453), see Pietro Donazzolo, *I Viaggiatori veneti minori: Studio bio-bibliografico*, Rome, 1929, pp. 48–49, 88–89, 370 (Memorie della R. Società geografica italiana, XVI).

[163] A letter from the College of Cardinals, announcing the death of Paul II, reached Venice on 1 August, on which day the Senate wrote the College: "Accepimus hoc die et hora litteras reverendissimarum dominationum vestrarum nuntiantes nobis acerbum nuntium mortis summi pontificis domini Pauli Pape II ac hortantes ad Italie tranquillitatem et pacem Sancteque Romane Ecclesie statum felicem . . ." (Sen. Secreta, Reg. 25, fol. 49^r [58^r]).

[164] Pastor, *Hist. Popes*, IV, 190–93, and append., nos. 42 and 29, pp. 504–5, 497–98, and *Gesch. d. Päpste*, II (repr. 1955), 444–46, and append., nos. 107 and 94, pp. 778–79, 773–74.

[165] Pastor, *Gesch. d. Päpste*, II (repr. 1955), 461–62. After the death of Paul II the pamphleteers accused him of avarice (*cf.* Raynaldus, *Ann. eccl.*, ad ann. 1471, no. 64, vol. XIX [1693], pp. 232–33). According to one of the first anti-Turkish bulls of Paul II's successor, Sixtus IV, *Quamvis ad applicanda ecclesiarum omnium commoda* (dated 31 December, 1471), Paul had spent some 200,000 florins in subsidies for the Hungarians, the despot of the Morea, Scanderbeg, the despot of Arta, and other Christian magnates and peoples under Turkish assault (Arch. Segr. Vaticano, Arm. XXXI, tom. 62, fol. 17^v, by mod. stamped enumeration): ". . . usque ad summam ducentorum milium florenorum liberaliter erogavit [fe. re. Paulus, predecessor noster]. . . ."

assistance in achieving the election of the Greek cardinal,[166] who had almost ascended S. Peter's throne in 1455.

Bessarion was, as everyone knew, the most strenuously anti-Turkish member of the Sacred College.

[166] Sen. Secreta, Reg. 25, fol. 49^{r} [58^{r}]: "Vestris litteris et ante obitum summi pontificis et post illius decessum intelleximus prudentissimas opiniones et memorationes istius illustrissimi domini cuius exactam virtutem et rerum experientiam et in nos affectionem et devotionem maximi semper fecimus. Secum igitur receptis presentibus estote et illi gratias uberes agite nostro nomine tam de suis fidelissimis sapientissimisque memorationibus quam de liberalissimis oblationibus et de opera postremo adhibita ut pontificatus sit [*sic*] in reverendissimum dominum Cardinalem Nicenum, ceterorum omnium optimum et ad rerum temporumque conditiones accomodatissimum, cadat. . . . Et Excellentiam suam certificate quod pridie quam litteras vestras acciperemus per litteras privatas ex urbe nuntium obitus pontificis Pauli acceperamus et eodem die ac ferme hora expedivimus unum tabellarium nostrum cum litteris ad Collegium reverendissimorum dominorum cardinalium, ad ipsum reverendissimum dominum, et ad cardinales venetos—et unicuique servata convenienti modestia et diversa scribendi forma pro uniuscuiusque conditione—efficaciter scripsimus et declaravimus ardentissimum in hac materia desiderium nostrum. . . ."

On 14 August (1471) the Senate sent congratulations to Francesco della Rovere upon his election to the papacy as Sixtus IV (see the following chapter); the letter is recorded, *ibid.*, Reg. 25, fol. 50^{v} [59^{v}], with the note "qùod prefatus Sixtus IIII creatus fuit papa die Veneris 9 Augusti." Thereafter the Senate set about the election of certain nobles to go to Rome as an embassy of obedience (*ibid.*, fols. 51^{v}, 71 ff. [60^{v}, 80 ff.]). They were to stress the Turkish peril and the vast expense to which Venice had been put year after year in carrying on a war for the protection of Christendom.

10. SIXTUS IV AND THE TURKISH OCCUPATION OF OTRANTO (1471–1480)

THE TIMES were bad, and would soon get worse. The Venetians had already suffered their severest blow of the war in the loss of Negroponte. The Genoese feared for the survival of their distant colony at Caffa, and the future of their settlement at Chios was in doubt. The Hospitallers at Rhodes had always to reckon with the possibility of a large-scale Turkish attack. The Neapolitans would soon feel the powerful thrust of the sultan's relentless aggression. The new pontiff would have to give much attention to eastern affairs.

On 9 August, 1471, a conclave of eighteen cardinals raised a Franciscan theologian to the throne, Francesco della Rovere, cardinal priest of S. Pietro in Vincoli. He took the name Sixtus IV.[1] For some years he had had a reputation as a reformer, and at first he seemed anxious to maintain peace in Italy in order to protect Latin interests in the Levant. He was a friend of Galeazzo Maria Sforza, duke of Milan, who had helped to secure his election, and Lorenzo de' Medici came to Rome himself as head of a Florentine embassy to extend greetings and do obeisance to Sixtus, who made the Roman branch of the Medici bank the financial agents of the Holy See.[2] Sixtus had been elected amid reports and rumors of Turkish depredation, especially in Styria, and a Venetian embassy which arrived in Rome on 28 November emphasized the Turkish peril. Sixtus was well aware of his responsibility in this regard, but the hostility between Sultan Mehmed II and Uzun Ḥasan, the powerful Turkoman lord of the Ak-Koyunlu (White Sheep), who then ruled from Cappadocia to Persia, appeared to promise well for the future. Venetian diplomats were doing their best to enlist Uzun Ḥasan's aid

---

[1] On the election, see the Acta Consistorialia [1439–1486], in Arch. Segr. Vaticano, Arm. XXXI, tom. 52, fols. 75^v–76^r, by modern stamped enumeration: ". . . Anno a nativitate Domini MCCCCLXXI die vero X [actually on the ninth] . . . mensis Augusti circa horam quintamdecimam [about 11 A.M.] reverendissimus in Christo pater et dominus, dominus Franciscus tituli Sancti Petri in Vincula presbiter cardinalis Saonensis asumptus fuit ad summum apicem apostolatus et vocatus Sixtus Quartus, et associatus fuit de conclavi quod factum fuit in cappella palatii [i.e., the Chapel of S. Niccolò da Bari] usque ad altare Sancti Petri [et] reductus in palatium cum omnibus cardinalibus, ut est moris. Anno predicto die vero XXV predicti mensis Augusti que fuit dies dominica sanctissimus dominus noster Sixtus divina providentia papa Quartus fuit coronatus in gradibus Sancti Petri . . . ," and in general see Pastor, *Hist. Popes*, IV, 201 ff., and *Gesch. d. Päpste*, II (repr. 1955), 453 ff., with relevant documents in the appendices. Sixtus was "grosso di corpo e di capo, ma sottile d'ingegno" (*Diario di Papa Sisto IV*, in Bibl. Apost. Vaticana, Urb. lat. 1641, fol. 2^r). For the "capitulations" of 7 August, prepared in the conclave which elected Sixtus, see Ubaldo Mannucci, "Le Capitolazioni del conclave di Sisto IV (1471)," *Römische Quartalschrift*, XXIX (1915), 73–90. The first pledge of the assembled cardinals was that whoever was elected pope would prosecute the war against the Turks to a successful conclusion, and would employ the revenues accruing from the alum beds at Tolfa for this and for no other purpose (*ibid.*, p. 83).

[2] *Cf.* Adolf Gottlob, *Aus der Camera Apostolica des 15. Jahrhunderts*, Innsbruck, 1889, p. 111. Lorenzo and Giuliano de' Medici served the papacy as general *depositarii* from August, 1471, until some time in 1475, and in financial matters one dealt largely "cum honorabilibus viris Laurentio et Juliano de Medicis et sociis mercatoribus Romanam Curiam sequentibus pecuniarum Camere Apostolice depositariis" (*cf.* the numerous entries for 1471–1472 in *Sixti IV Introitus et Exitus Camere Apostolice Augusti Septembris et Octobris 1471 ad Julium 1472*, in Arch. Segr. Vaticano, Reg. 487, fols. 1 ff., 100^r, 117^v, 130^v, 140^v, 148^v, 149^r, 156, 162^v, 170^r, 184^r, 191^v, 199^r). One-third of the proceeds of the alum beds at Tolfa was going to the Medici, and two-thirds to the "camera and crusade" (*ibid.*, Arm. XXXI, tom. 62, fols. 46^r–48^r, by mod. stamped enumeration, bull dated 17 June, 1472). As of 27 April, 1473, the Holy See owed the Medici bank 54,000 ducats (*ibid.*, fols. 55^v–57^r). On 1 August, 1474, Sixtus borrowed 22,000 florins from Guglielmo and Giovanni de' Pazzi (fols. 85^v–86^v), but was still doing business in 1475 with the Medici, to whom he then owed 20,000 florins (fols. 113^r–114^r, "datum Rome apud Sanctum Petrum anno incarnationis dominice MCCCCLXX quinto, pont. nostri anno quarto," with no month given). The bottom fell out of the alum market in 1474–1475 (see Gottlob, *Aus der Camera Apostolica*, p. 288), and papal revenues were reduced; the Medici suffered a sharp decline in income, and for political reasons Sixtus IV broke with them at this time. On papal attempts to establish a monopoly in the sale of alum in Europe, and the part played therein by the Medici bank, see Raymond de Roover, *The Rise and Decline of the Medici Bank, 1397–1494*, Cambridge, Mass., 1963, repr. New York, 1966, pp. 152–64. As de Roover notes, the effort of the papacy to arrogate to itself and certain associates the exclusive right to sell alum to Christians was probably contrary to canon law (*Decreti secunda pars*, causa XIV, quest. IV, can. IX, ed. Aem. Friedberg, *Corpus iuris canonici*, I [Leipzig, 1879, repr. Graz. 1955], col. 737: "Turpe lucrum sequitur, qui minus emit, ut plus vendat"). On the decline of the Medici bank, which barely survived until the expulsion of the family from Florence, see de Roover, *op. cit.*, pp. 220–24, 358 ff.

against the Porte. In a secret consistory on 23 December, Sixtus established five anti-Turkish legations *de latere*, for the dispatch of Bessarion to France, Burgundy, and England; Rodrigo Borgia to Spain; Angelo Capranica to Italy; Marco Barbo to Germany, Hungary, and Poland; and Oliviero Carafa to the kingdom of Naples, where he was to command a fleet.[3]

A week later Sixtus published an encyclical letter (on 31 December, 1471), urging the united action of Christendom against the common foe. He expressed his heartfelt grief that the "most truculent race of the Turks, followers of the impious dog Mohammed, had risen rabidly against the Christian faith." They had occupied Christian countries in both Asia Minor and the Balkans, had taken Constantinople and many other lands and cities of the Byzantine empire, and were still thirsting for Christian blood. Their strength had grown with their conquests; they had swept with fire and sword through Hungary even into inner Germany. Sixtus recounted the atrocities of the Turks with lugubrious eloquence, and lamented the fall of Negroponte. The ambition of the Turk was to blot the name of Christian off the face of the earth.[4] Europe hardly took note of his warning, and made little response to his legations.

Despite the Christian propaganda for a new crusade, Mehmed II was more concerned with the clouds gathering on his eastern frontier than with Sixtus IV's preparations against him. Mehmed could never feel secure in his western conquests until he had destroyed the now swollen power of the Turkoman ruler Uzun Ḥasan, with whom the Venetians were in close and constant contact. By 1469 Uzun Ḥasan had come to control a great state which included Cappadocia, Armenia, Kurdistan, Mesopotamia, and western Persia, and the Ottoman subjugation of the other Turkish states of Asia Minor had made conflict with him inevitable. Three envoys of Uzun Ḥasan were at the Curia Romana in August, 1471, when the papal treasurer paid out to them 400 "florins Venetian," worth 415 florins *de camera*, the disbursement being made by order of Sixtus,[5] who received two Turkish envoys the following November, and ordered a similar diplomatic subvention paid to them.[6] A year later, on 6

---

[3] Acta Consistorialia, in Arch. Segr. Vaticano, Arm. XXXI, tom. 52, fol. 77^{r}, by mod. stamped enumeration, entry dated "die lune XXII decembris 1471" (but Monday fell on 23 December in 1471): "Idem sanctissimus dominus noster in dicto consistorio secreto creavit quinque legatos de latere cardinales per universas provincias et regna mundi ad requirendum reges, principes et alios Christianos ad defensionem fidei Chatolice contra nefandissimum Turcum qui nomini Yesu infensus est . . . ," on which *cf.* Pastor, *Hist. Popes*, IV, 219, and *Gesch. d. Päpste*, II (repr. 1955), 467, and on the papal legates note also Marino Sanudo, *Vite de' duchi di Venezia*, in *RISS*, XXII (Milan, 1733), 1196C, and D. Malipiero, *Annali veneti*, ad ann. 1471, in *Archivio storico italiano*, VII-1 (1843), 69–70. Bessarion went to France in the summer of 1472, finding the intractable Louis XI very unsatisfactory to deal with; without proceeding to England, he returned to Italy where he died at Ravenna on 18 November, 1472 (Pastor, *Gesch. d. Päpste*, II, 467–69). Borgia was little more successful in Spain, and Marco Barbo spent more than two unavailing years in Germany, Poland, and Bohemia, the most critical area of all in Europe's defense against the Turks (*ibid.*, pp. 469–71). On Borgia's protracted legation to Spain (and Naples), see Arch. Segr. Vaticano, Reg. Vat. 680, fols. 1^{r}–10^{v}, documents dated on and after 21 March, 1473 (Florentine style 1472), and those dated from 30 June, 1476, to 13 August, 1477, in Reg. Vat. 679, fols. 31^{v}–33^{v}, relating to the levy of a crusading tithe in Spain; fols. 67^{r}–68^{r}, 69^{r}–70^{r}, on the previous publication in Castile and León of the "sancta cruciata et plenissima peccatorum indulgentia omnibus Christi fidelibus . . . ;" fols. 105^{r}–107^{r}, concerning Ferrante of Naples, from whom one expected to receive much support; and on the crusade against the Moors in the kingdom of Granada, see the bull *Superne dispositionis*, dated at Rome on 1 December (corrected from 1 September), 1475, *ibid.*, fols. 77^{r}–80^{r}. On the faculties granted Barbo as he began his mission, see Reg. Vat. 680, fols. 34^{r}–68^{r}, 77^{v}–81^{v}, 85–86 and ff., by mod. stamped enumeration. Raynaldus, *Ann. eccl.*, ad ann. 1472, nos. 5 ff., vol. XIX (1693), pp. 238 ff., gives numerous letters and details concerning these embassies.

[4] Arch. Segr. Vaticano, Arm. XXXI, tom. 62, fols. 14^{v}–16^{v}, "datum Rome apud Sanctum Petrum, anno incarnationis dominice MCCCCLXXI, pridie Kal. Ianuarii, pontificatus nostri anno primo," and *cf.* Raynaldus, *Ann. eccl.*, ad ann. 1471, no. 72, vol. XIX (1693), pp. 234–35; much the same letter was published again on 17 February, 1472 (*ibid.*, ad ann. cit., nos. 18–19, p. 240).

[5] Arch. Segr. Vaticano, Introitus et Exitus, Reg. 487, fol. 97^{v}, by mod. stamped enumeration: "[Exitus] Augusti MCCCCLXXI: Pro tribus oratoribus Somcassani: Die XX eiusdem [mensis] prefatus dominus thesaurarius de mandato et per manus ut supra dedit et solvit tribus oratoribus Somcassani florenos venetos quadringentos, valentes de Camera quadringentos et quindecim, quos sanctissimus dominus noster eis dono dari mandavit ut apparet per mandatum factum die XVIIII eiusdem: fl. CCCC XV."

[6] Intr. et Ex., Reg. 487, fol. 126^{v}: "Exitus Novembris MCCCCLXXI: Duobus Turcis oratoribus: Die XXII dicti [mensis] dominus thesaurarius de mandato et per manus ut supra solvit duobus Turcis oratoribus florenos de camera centum octo et bol. XL [i.e., 40 bolognini or 'baiochi,' papal pence], quos dominus noster papa eis donari mandavit, per mandatum factum XXI eiusdem: fl. C VIII, bol. XL." On the coins in question, *cf.* Friedrich von Schrötter, *Wörterbuch der Münzkunde*, Berlin and Leipzig, 1930, pp. 54b, 81.

November, 1472, Sixtus wrote the Marquis Lodovico II Gonzaga of Mantua that the sultan was forever thinking of how he might vent his hatred upon Christians and effect their destruction. Mehmed was said even to be planning an attack upon Italy in the spring of 1473, but his Holiness placed his hope in God and in Uzun Ḥasan to wear down the common enemy, and he had recently been assured by a Turkoman emissary that Uzun Ḥasan had gathered together huge forces for this noble purpose.[7]

The Ottoman embassy to the Curia Romana had doubtless sought to fasten papal attention upon Italy (which was usually easy to do), probably by threats of one sort or another, and by putting the Italian states on the defensive, to weaken any offensive action which they might launch against the Ottoman western front. But to secure such a diversion of Mehmed II's strength was the reason for Uzun Ḥasan's embassies to the Curia. Communication was slow because of the long distances the Turkoman envoys had to travel, and the news they brought the Curia was likely to be out of date and no longer pertinent by the time of their arrival. As always Mehmed moved when he had the advantage, and after extensive preparations he marched into Anatolia in October, 1472, accompanied by his two sons, Mustafa and Bayazid Chelebi. He apparently spent the winter in encampment near Amasya. The Ottoman army was enormous, for it is clear the sultan entertained no little respect for Uzun Ḥasan's effectiveness in the field. After an initial setback on the banks of the Euphrates near the important fortress of Erzinjan (on 1 August, 1473), Mehmed met and defeated Uzun Ḥasan in a decisive battle near Bashkent (about 11 August). Mahmud Pasha advised against the pursuit of the defeated Turkoman, because the Ottomans would be hard put to maintain control over the lands they had still to conquer. Mehmed agreed to the withdrawal of his forces westward, but subsequently regretted it and again removed Mahmud Pasha from the grand vizirate and, having other grievances against him, put the great pasha to death soon after their return to Istanbul.[8]

In the meantime, during the years 1471–1472, Pope Sixtus had spent more than 144,000 gold florins on the fleet which Cardinal Oliviero Carafa was to lead on the crusade. He had also formed accords with both Venice and Naples, which were to furnish fleets for the coming effort against the Turks. Cameral disbursements for the papal fleet exceeded 72,000 gold florins in each of these two years.[9] In early

[7] Arch. di Stato di Mantova, Arch. Gonzaga, Busta 834, brief dated 6 November, 1472: [Sixtus IV appealed to Lodovico Gonzaga to lend all his efforts to the crusade against the Turk:] ". . . Nos et fecimus hactenus pro viribus. . . . Habemus quoque spem in domino deo nostro quod eius insti[n]ctu potentissimus princeps Zuncassan hostem communem debilitabit et atteret. Habet enim ad hoc ingentes copias instructas, sicut per suum nobis oratorem nuperrime declaravit et iam intelleximus eum principium rei bene gerende dedisse." *Cf.*, *ibid.*, another brief to Lodovico dated 13 November, 1473, on the "insignis princeps Zuncassan Christianorum amicus." On 31 July, 1472, at the behest of King Ferrante, Sixtus had granted merchants of the kingdom of Naples the right to trade in the Mamluk ports of Egypt, Syria, and the Holy Land, although (as always) they were not to deal in articles of contraband, "exceptis ferro, armis, lignaminibus, et aliis prohibitis" (Reg. Vat. 546, fols. 10^r–11^r, by mod. stamped enumeration).

[8] For the failure of Uzun Ḥasan's efforts against Mehmed II and for the execution of Mahmud Pasha, see especially Giovanni Maria Angiolello, *Hist. turchesca*, ed. I. Ursu, Bucharest, 1909, pp. 38–63, on which *cf.* N. Di Lenna, *Archivio veneto-tridentino*, V (1924), 13–17. At this time (1472–1473) Angiolello was in the Ottoman army, in the service of the sultan's son Mustafa Chelebi, whom rumor accused Mahmud Pasha of poisoning, but "jo Zuan Maria dico questo esser falso, perch'io in quel tempo era al servitio del detto signor Mustafa, et gli stava in casa, et me trovai con lui . . ." (Angiolello, p. 63). The contest of Uzun Ḥasan with the Ottomans made a great impression upon Europe and the Mediterranean world (*cf.* Joannes Adelphi, *Türckisch Chronica*, Strassburg, 1513, unnum. fols. 8^v–9^r [=B-ii-iii], and M. A. Halevy, "Les Guerres d'Étienne le Grand et de Uzun-Hassan contre Mahomet II, d'après la 'Chronique de la Turquie' du candiote Élie Capsali [1523]," *Studia et acta orientalia*, I [Bucharest, 1958], 189–98, esp. 193 ff.). The battle of Bashkent is described in the Ottoman chronicle of 'Ashîk-Pasha-Zade (trans. R. F. Kreutel, *Vom Hirtenzelt zur Hohen Pforte*, Graz, 1959, pp. 250–56), on whom see Alessio Bombaci, *La Letteratura turca*, 2nd ed., Florence and Milan, 1969, pp. 347–51. On the eastern background of events, note Halil Inalcik, "Mehmed the Conqueror (1432–1481) and His Time," *Speculum*, XXXV (1960), 423–25.

[9] *Cf.* the bulls *Quamprimum fuimus* (9 April, 1472), *Etsi dispositione superna* (20 February, 1473), and *Cum inter cetera* (27 April, 1473) in the Arch. Segr. Vaticano, Arm. XXXI, tom. 62, fols. 41^r–42^v, 50^v–53^v, and 55^v–57^v, the last of which undertakes to repay Lorenzo and Giuliano de' Medici the sum of 54,000 gold ducats *de camera* spent on the fleet. Numerous bulls in this register are concerned with ways to finance the crusade, especially through tithes, receipts for alum, and impositions of a twentieth on the Jews.

Sixtus IV's expenditures on Carafa's fleet for the critical year 1472 may be followed, as an illustration of the sources, in Arch. Segr. Vaticano, Intr. et Ex., Reg. 487, fol. 171^v, by mod. stamped enumeration: "Exitus Maii MCCCCLXXII: Dicta die [quarta] dominus thesaurarius de mandato sibi die 30 Aprilis facto per manus depositariorum

June, 1472, Carafa sailed from Ostia for Naples, and thence on to Rhodes, where the naval forces of Venice and Naples were being assembled. The Christian armada is said to have reached a grand total of about eighty-seven galleys and fifteen transports, more than half of them being Venetian. As a display of strength to reassure Uzun Ḥasan and his allies in Caramania (Karaman), the Venetians recovered from the Ottomans the castle towns of Silifke (Seleucia), Sequin (or Sechin, ancient Syedra), and Corycus, which were repossessed by Kasim Beg, the lord of Caramania, whom Mehmed II had driven from his lands.

The crusaders attacked Satalia (Adalia) on the southern coast of Asia Minor in August, 1472, breaking the chain which was supposed to block entry into the harbor; they burned the warehouses near the waterfront and the suburbs, but could not take the town, which was strongly fortified. The Neapolitans, finding themselves in continual disagreement with the Venetians, withdrew their fleet from the expedition, and returned home. The commander of the Venetian squadron was Pietro Mocenigo, soon to become the doge. With Carafa he launched a successful attack upon the important, but badly defended, town of Smyrna (on 13 September, 1472). Although Carafa wanted to hold the town as a center for later operations, the Venetians burned it to the ground, and mounted two hundred and fifteen Turkish heads on their ships as a grim symbol of their destruction of the Ottoman garrison. Thereafter Mocenigo and Carafa got along less well, and the expedition rendered very little genuine assistance to Uzun Ḥasan. No attack was made upon Istanbul although Mehmed was absent therefrom, as we have noted, on his notable campaign against Uzun Ḥasan. Mocenigo had assisted, months before, in the bold scheme of a certain Antonello, who succeeded in setting fire to the Turkish arsenal at Gallipoli in February, 1472, but apparently he made no attempt to enter the Dardanelles in force at any time during the expedition.[10]

[the Medici] solvit reverendissimo domino Cardinali Neapolitano [Carafa] florenos similes [i.e., de camera] septem millia septingentos septuaginta septem, bologninos XXV, in ducatis venetis auri VII m., in deductionem stipendiorum classis contra Turcum: fl. VII m., VII c., LXXVII, 25" [7,777 florins, 25 bol., de camera = 7,000 gold ducats Venetian, paid to Carafa on 4 May, 1472]. On 9 May Carafa received 1,555 florins, 40 bol., "in ducatis venetis MCCCC" (*ibid.*, fol. 173ᵛ); on 20 May, 1,041 florins, 48 bol. (fol. 179ʳ); on 22 May, 2,777 florins, 50 bol. (fol. 179ᵛ); and on 25 May, 24,001 florins: ". . . rev. dominus thesaurarius de mandato sibi facto 23 eiusdem [mensis] per manus depositariorum solvit reverendissimo domino Cardinali Neapolitano classis contra Turcum legato florenos vigintiquatuor milia unum pro valore XXIII m. XXVIII florenorum auri in auro de camera pro residuo et complemento 72,000 florenorum auri in auro qui ei dantur pro integro stipendio classis contra Turcum pro isto anno et qui 72,000 florenorum auri in auro constituunt summam florenorum de camera LXXV m.: fl. XXIII m. I" (fol. 180ᵛ). As stated in this account, and as noted by Gottlob, *Aus der Camera Apostolica des 15. Jahrhunderts*, p. 291, the 72,000 florins in question amounted to 75,000 cameral florins. On 30 May Carafa received still another 333 florins (fol. 183ᵛ). Various other persons received substantial sums for the lease of a vessel "ad usum classis contra Turcum" (fols. 181ʳ, 183ᵛ), and on 27 June (1472) ". . . rev. dominus . . . vicethesaurarius de mandato facto die 9 eiusdem per manus depositariorum solvit Pisis rev. domino P[hilippo de Medicis] archiepiscopo Pisano florenos tria millia ducentos octo pro reparatione et instructione galearum cruciate que Pisis parantur . . .: fl. III m., CC, VIII" (fol. 190ᵛ).

On the collection of grain in the region of Fabriano "pro fulciendis et muniendis navibus que Ancone parantur contra Turcum," see R. Sassi, "Il Contributo di Fabriano alla guerra di Sisto IV contro i Turchi," *Atti e memorie della R. Deputazione di storia patria per le Marche*, 5th ser., I (Ancona, 1937), 73–119.

[10] Malipiero, *Annali veneti*, ad ann. 1472, in *Arch. stor. italiano*, VII-1 (1843), 71–86, describes something of the Venetian diplomatic relations with Uzun Ḥasan; says that the Venetian, papal, Neapolitan fleet consisted of 85 galleys (p. 74); and relates the bold exploit of Antonello, a Sicilian (pp. 84–86): "L'incendio durò 10 zorni, che'l no se potè estinguer; e fo giudicado che'l danno havesse importà 100,000 ducati." On Antonello, *cf.* Franz Babinger, *Maometto il Conquistatore* (1957), pp. 473–75, and on the devastation of Smyrna, Stefano Magno, *Annali veneti*, in Ch. Hopf, *Chroniques gréco-romanes* (1873), pp. 207–8. A. Navagero, *Storia veneziana*, in *RISS*, XXIII (Milan, 1733), cols. 1131, 1132–33, 1134–37, gives a good deal of attention to the rivalry of Mehmed II and Uzun Ḥasan, doubtless reflecting the strong Venetian interest in making an effective alliance with the latter, and of course Raynaldus, *Ann. eccl.*, devotes much space to Uzun Ḥasan in his entries for the early 1470's.

On the satisfaction which the Venetian government took in the destruction of Smyrna, see the Arch. di Stato di Venezia, Sen. Secreta, Reg. 25, fols. 161ᵛ–162ʳ [171ᵛ–172ʳ], dated 27 October, 1472, the Senate to the captain-general of the sea and the provveditori of the Venetian fleet: "Per viam Corcyre plures litteras vestras accepimus quibus solito studio, cura, et diligentia nos facitis certiores de cladibus ac depopulationibus illatis per vos proxime Smyrnis et aliis locis hostilibus deque nuntiis ad vos perlatis de adventu serenissimi domini Ussonassan. Non possumus certe non vehementer letari et magnam capere voluptatem ex iis que strenue et fortiter gessistis adversus nostros hostes, immo hostes nostre religionis et Christiani nominis. . . ."

A. Guglielmotti, *Storia della marina pontificia*, II (Rome, 1886), 342–72, has exploited the older literary sources, among which we may note the references to Carafa's fleet in Stefano Infessura, *Diaria rerum romanarum*, ad ann.

As the new year approached, and the winter became more severe, the Venetian fleet withdrew to Nauplia and Modon, while Carafa returned to Italy with the papal galleys. He entered Rome on 23 January, 1473, bringing with him some Turkish prisoners and some pieces of the chain which had blocked the entrance to the harbor of Satalia. Throughout the eventful campaign of 1472, during which the crusaders harried the long coasts of southern and western Asia Minor, no Ottoman fleet was sent into the Aegean to oppose them. The Ottomans generally played a cautious game in naval warfare, knowing when to seek an engagement and when to avoid one, and Babinger reminds us that from the battle of Gallipoli (29 May, 1416) to that of Lepanto (7 October, 1571) they were never seriously defeated at sea.[11] The pieces of Carafa's chain were mounted over the main portal of S. Peter's, where they remained until the reconstruction of the basilica in the following century. Later on, they were put over the door leading to the Archives of the Basilica, to the right of the sacristy,[12] where they may still be seen. Sixtus IV paid heavily for the souvenir.

Sixtus sought support for the crusade wherever he could find it, and for a while he thought he had found it in Russia. Zoe Palaeologina, younger daughter of the late Despot Thomas, had been living in Rome for some years, in a house on the Campus Martius, as a ward of the Holy See. Efforts had already been made (and had failed) to marry her off to Federico Gonzaga, son of the cautious Marquis Lodovico of Mantua, and to James II of Lusignan, the rather unstable king of Cyprus. She had no dowry except what the pope might provide. Through Italian emissaries, however, Ivan III, the grand prince of Moscow, had become interested in her, and eventually (on 25 May, 1472) his envoys appeared before a secret consistory in Rome to claim Zoe as his bride. A week later, on 1 June, she was married by proxy to Ivan, who (it was hoped) might render assistance against the Turks, and even perhaps entertain proposals for the union of the Roman and Russian Orthodox Churches.[13]

In any event, when Zoe left Rome on 24 June for the long journey to Moscow by way of

---

1472, ed. O. Tommasini, Rome, 1890, p. 76, and Cardinal Jacopo Ammanati, *Diario concistoriale*, ad ann. 1472 (attributed by Muratori to Jacopo [or Giacomo] Gherardi da Volterra), in *RISS*, XXIII-3 (Città di Castello, 1904), 143, who says that the papal flotilla contained 18 galleys (*triremes*) and two transports (not 24 galleys and six transports, as stated by Guglielmotti, II, 342–43, 353), and that the Venetians provided 56 ships (Guglielmotti says 46 galleys and six transports), and King Ferrante of Naples, 30 ships (Guglielmotti says 20, 17 galleys and three transports). The Hospitallers later added two galleys. It would be difficult to ascertain precisely the size of the Christian fleet which eventually saw service in the Aegean. Ammanati, *loc. cit.*, recounts how Sixtus IV blessed the standards and crews of four of Carafa's galleys drawn up in the Tiber on 28 May, 1472, the feast of Corpus Domini, and describes the scene again in a letter written from Rome on the following day to Cardinal Marco Barbo (*Epistolae Iacobi Picolomini Cardinalis Papiensis*, in *Pii Secundi P.M. Commentarii*, Frankfurt, 1614, *Ep.* CCCCXLIX, p. 766). *Cf.* C. Eubel, *Hierarchia catholica medii aevi*, II (1914, repr. 1960), 38a, from the Acta Consistorialia.

[11] Raynaldus, *Ann. eccl.*, ad ann. 1472, nos. 1–5, 40–43, vol. XIX (1693), pp. 237–38, 244, and ad ann. 1473, nos. 1–2, p. 248; Babinger, *Maometto*, pp. 461–64; Pastor, *Hist. Popes*, IV, 226–28, and *Gesch. d. Päpste*, II (repr. 1955), 472–74; and *cf.* Mocenigo's later report to the Venetian Senate (Raynaldus, ad ann. 1474, no. 13, vol. XIX, p. 255). See also Michele Paone, "Il Cardinale Oliviero Carafa e la Terra d'Otranto," in *Atti del congresso internazionale di studi sull' età aragonese* [held at Bari, 15–18 December, 1968], Bari, n.d., pp. 613–19, who seems to think that Satalia is in Africa (p. 614).

[12] Guglielmotti, *Storia della marina pontificia*, II, 370; Pastor, *Gesch. d. Päpste*, II, 474.

[13] Ammanati, *Diario concistoriale*, ad ann. 1472, *RISS*, XXIII-3 (1904), 141–42, 143–44, describes in detail the appearance of the Italian-led embassy from "Alba Russia" and Zoe's marriage by proxy in S. Peter's basilica. Sixtus IV was generous both to Zoe and to her brother Andreas. On 10 December, 1477, recalling that their father, the Despot Thomas, had brought Pius II the revered head of S. Andrew from the city of Patras, *munere regio*, Sixtus granted Andreas full possession of the house in the Campus Martius, where the latter was still living five years after his sister had gone to Russia: ". . . motu proprio . . . quandam domum sitam in regione Campi Martii de urbe ad nos et cameram nostram apostolicam legitime pertinentem et spectantem quam nunc inhabitas . . . absque alicuius census, fictus vel canonis seu alterius cuiusvis oneris solutione cum omnibus et singulis eius ingressibus, egressibus, ortis, edificiis, iuribus, et pertinentiis suis . . . tenore presentium perpetuo concedimus, donamus, et assignamus . . . ," the grant carrying with it the right to transmit the property to his heirs (Arch. Segr. Vaticano, Reg. Vat. 583, fols. 89^v–91^r, by mod. stamped enumeration). Two years later, on 9 October, 1479, when Andreas was himself planning a visit to Russia from which he would not be likely to return to Rome before the end of 1481, Sixtus granted him the continuation (during his absence) of his annual pension of 1,800 gold ducats *de camera*, which was being paid from the revenues of the alum beds at Tolfa (for which see Reg. Vat. 563, fols. 122^r–123^r, bull dated 6 July, 1474). Andreas needed the money "pro expensis quas te in peregrinatione huiusmodi subire oportet." To allay Andreas's apprehension concerning the future, Sixtus assured him that the pension would also be continued upon his return to Rome and the Curia. The bull was issued *gratis*, and was collated by Flavio Biondo's son Gaspare, who had a long tenure as a papal secretary (Reg. Vat. 594, fol. 183).

northern Italy and Germany, Sixtus prepared for her safe passage by sending ahead letters of praise and protection to the cities and princes through whose territories she would travel.[14] As is well known, the papacy had been generous to Zoe's father, granting him a monthly pension, which was continued after his death for the benefit of his children. A painting in the Ospedale di S. Spirito in Saxia (near the Vatican), which Sixtus IV rebuilt and enlarged, also recalls the pope's generosity to Zoe's brother Andreas as well as to Leonardo III Tocco, fugitive despot of Arta, to whom Paul II had made grants of several thousand gold florins in 1465–1467 "as assistance in the war against the Turks."[15] As the inscription states under the painting, which commemorates Zoe's marriage to Ivan, Sixtus gave her a dowry of 6,000 gold ducats together with other presents to help her start life anew in the frozen north, from which no help was sent against the Turks. Zoe immediately re-embraced Orthodoxy, and church union was only discussed vaguely, with small intention of any true commitment to the Latin Church.[16]

Although fat and homely, Zoe was intelligent and came to exercise great influence in Moscow, where she was known as Sophia. Her marriage with Ivan III began a new era in the history and political ideology of Russian Orthodoxy. Ivan III became the heir of Byzantium, the protector of all Orthodox Christians, and twenty years later (in 1492) the Metropolitan Zosimus hailed the prince of Moscow as "sovereign and autocrat of all Russia, the new Czar Constantine of the new city of Constantine, Moscow." Moscow succeeded Constantinople as the "third Rome," and the Muscovite Church became the center of the true faith, emulating in the ecclesiastical domain the grand prince's new claims to universal authority. Muscovy soared on the wings of Byzantium. Ivan III adopted the double-headed eagle of the Palaeologi as his

---

[14] Fr. P. Pierling, *La Russie et le Saint-Siège*, I (Paris, 1896, repr. 1967), 161–62, and Pastor, *Gesch. d. Päpste*, II (repr. 1955), 474–75, know of copies of the "safe conduct" (*littera passus*), which Sixtus IV gave Zoe, from the archives at Modena, Bologna, Nuremberg, and Lübeck, but seem to have missed the copy in the Vatican. Since neither writer gives a text, I provide one herewith (Arch. Segr. Vaticano, Reg. Vat. 660, fol. 314, by mod. stamped enumeration): "Littera passus pro Zoe nata Thome Paleologi: Sixtus episcopus, servus, etc. Universis et singulis presentes litteras inspecturis salutem et apostolicam benedictionem. Cum dilecta in Christo filia nobilis mulier Zoe nata insignis memorie Thome Palaeologi, Constantinopolitani imperii legitimi successoris, quam post cladem Constantinopolis Peloponessique depopulationem e manibus immanissimorum Turchorum elapsam apostolica sancta sedes ad quam confugit gremio pietatis excepit et semper in honore habendam censuit ad virum cui nuper nobis auctoribus desponsata fuit impresentiarum cum nostra benedictione proficiscatur ad dilectum videlicet filium nobilem virum Johannem Volodomirie, Muscovie, Novoguordie, Pascovie, etc. magnum ducem, clare memorie Basilii olim magni ducis natum, nos qui eandem Zoen tam clara ortam sobole in visceribus gerimus caritatis, cupientes ipsam cum quacumque sua comitiva cumque familiaribus tam pedestribus quam equestribus salvis bonis et rebus etc. sine clausula mercimonii, sine numero, et sine terminatione temporis etc. . . . Datum Rome apud Sanctum Petrum anno, etc. millesimo quadringentesimo septuagesimo secundo, undecimo Kalendas Iulii, pontificatus nostri anno primo" [21 June, 1472]. (N. Iorga, *Notes et extraits*, IV [Bucharest, 1915], doc. CCXXXII, p. 324, publishes a somewhat different text from the archives of Nuremberg.) On 22 June, 1472, Sixtus also authorized issuance of a *littera passus* to an "envoy" (*orator*) of Zoe's two brothers, Andrea and Manuel, "pro eorum peragendis necessariis negotiis ad diversas mundi partes" (Reg. Vat. 681, fol. 273ʳ).

Zoe left Rome with a large retinue on 24 June (1472), and reached Moscow on 12 November. Along the way she spent from 10 to 14 August in Nuremberg, where she was most hospitably received by the burgomaster and the town council (Günther Schuhmann, "Die 'Kaiserin von Konstantinopel' in Nürnberg," in *Archive und Geschichtsforschung: Studien zur fränkischen und bayerischen Geschichte Fridolin Solleder zum 80. Geburtstag dargebracht*, Neustadt a.d. Aisch, 1966, pp. 148–74, esp. pp. 157–65).

[15] Pierling, *La Russie et le Saint-Siège*, I, 116–75, in full detail; Pastor, *Hist. Popes*, IV, 193–94, 229–30, and *Gesch. d. Päpste*, II (repr. 1955), 446–47, 474–75; Alex. Eck, *Le Moyen-âge russe*, Paris, 1933, pp. 424 ff.; Raynaldus, *Ann. eccl.*, ad ann. 1470, no. 9, vol. XIX (1693), p. 209, and ad ann. 1472, nos. 48–49, *ibid.*, pp. 245–46; and the note in Arch. Segr. Vaticano, Miscell., Arm. VI, tom. 39, fol. 352, from the late seventeenth century. Paul II had also been generous to the exiled Palaeologi (Gaspare da Verona, *De gestis tempore . . . Pauli II*, ed. G. Zippel, in *RISS*, III, pt. 16 [1904], 59, lines 29–32, and Michele Canensi, *De vita et pontificatu Pauli II*, *ibid.*, pp. 138–39, with note 1). There is a brief sketch of papal relations with Russia and central Europe in Oscar Halecki, "Sixte IV et la chrétienté orientale," *Mélanges Eugène Tisserant*, II (Città del Vaticano, 1964), 241–64 (in the Vatican series Studi e testi, 232); see also Halecki's book *From Florence to Brest (1439–1596)*, Rome, 1958, pp. 100 ff. (Sacrum Poloniae Millennium, vol. V).

[16] The inscription under the painting in the Ospedale di S. Spirito reads as follows: "Andream Palaeologum Peloponnesi / et Leonardum Toccum Epiri Dynastia / a Turcarum Tyranno Exutos / Regio Sum[p]tu Aluit / Sophiam Thomae Palaeologi Filiam / Ruthenorum Duci Nuptam / Cum Alys Muneribus / Tum Sex Mille Aureorum Dote Auxit." I remember with much pleasure a long afternoon's visit to the Ospedale in May, 1957, when Pietro de Angelis, librarian of the Lancisiana, gave me a conducted tour of the famous hospital, and showed me the fifteenth-century *Liber Fraternitatis S. Spiritus*, containing Sixtus IV's handsome grants to the Hospital, which was first established on its present site by Innocent III.

standard, introduced the imperial ceremonial into his court, and built palaces and churches in Moscow, which he tried to make worthy of the new dignity which Zoe had bestowed upon him.[17] Under these circumstances the Curia Romana could expect no help from Russia against the Turks, and events soon made clear that the hopes entertained of the Turkoman ruler were doomed to a like disappointment.

Uzun Ḥasan had lost little territory as a result of his defeat in August, 1473, and he had promptly informed the Venetians of his intention to resume his attack upon the Ottoman sultan.[18] Sixtus IV did what he could to assist the Turkoman cause, which he identified with that of the Italian states. On 2 October, 1474, for example, he wrote the Marquis Lodovico of Mantua and various other Italian princes that Uzun Ḥasan's hostility to Mehmed had served them all well, and could be even more useful in the future. If he should cease his pressure upon the Ottoman empire, however, the Italian peninsula and all Christendom would be in manifest danger. To ensure their own safety, therefore, the Christians must maintain Uzun Ḥasan in his resolve to continue the war against Mehmed, "because in all likelihood no such opportunity as this will ever offer itself again." Once more a Turkoman envoy had come to the Curia, urging

> that the Christians attack the Turk with a land army, and [Uzun Ḥasan] promises, if this is done, that he will again descend upon the Turk with a powerful army, and that he will not give up the war until the Turk has been destroyed. Uzun Ḥasan's envoy is insisting upon a response since he wishes to return to his prince, not mollified with words, but certain of what the Christians will really do.

Sixtus feared that if the Christian powers did not grasp this opportunity, Uzun Ḥasan would be forced to make a pact with Mehmed, which would obviously be to the extreme detriment of Christendom.

"We are ready to do as much as our strength makes possible," Sixtus wrote the marquis of Mantua, "and would that we could bear this weight alone, because we would burden no one. Our resources are not sufficient, however, and therefore it is necessary that we have recourse to your Excellency and the other Italian powers." He implored Lodovico to send to the Curia an envoy *cum pleno mandato* to confer with the representatives of the other Italian states and rulers (to whom he was sending similar briefs) on the financing of an expedition to go by land against the Turks. They might wish to support the crusading efforts of King Matthias Corvinus of Hungary or prefer to strike at the Turk in some other way, but plans should be made quickly, "so that we may know how to give a definite reply to the [Turkoman] envoy and his prince."[19] On 23 October (1474) Lodovico answered Sixtus that in accordance with the papal request he was appointing his son, Cardinal Francesco Gonzaga, as his envoy to deal with matters relating to the proposed expedition against the Turks. Francesco was to have full authority to commit the marquis to the crusade.[20] It was a courteous reply and a safe one, for it seemed unlikely that the Italian states would again move in unison against the Turks for some time, not after the expedition of 1472, which had cost Rome, Venice, and Naples far more than its rather slender results had justified.

The urgency and the frequency of Pope Sixtus IV's appeals for action against the Turks belie any assumption that his letters were indited merely for the record. In a brief of 1 July, 1475, he continued his importunities to the marquis of Mantua for aid against the Turks. The Doge Pietro Mocenigo had just sent the worrisome news from Venice that the sultan was planning a large expedition to avenge the recent Turkish defeat in Moldavia, and the pope was anxious for Lodovico to realize that not only Moldavia but all Europe was in danger. He requested an appropriate subsidy from Mantua to be sent to those who bore the brunt of Turkish enmity along the eastern front.[21] On

---

[17] *Cf.* Eck, *Le Moyen-âge russe*, pp. 357, 425–27, 432 ff.; Pierling, *La Russie et le Saint-Siège*, I, 225–28; Halecki, *From Florence to Brest*, pp. 100, 104–5, 108–9, 112–13; Wm. K. Medlin, *Moscow and East Rome*, Geneva, 1952, pp. 78 ff.

[18] G. Berchet, *La Repubblica di Venezia e la Persia*, Turin, 1865, pp. 137–39, translation into Italian of a letter from Uzun Ḥasan to the doge of Venice, "data ala nostra porta die primo lune mensis Augusti VIII^{c} LXXVII a Machometo citra" (Arch. di Stato di Venezia, Commemoriali, Reg. 16, no. 48, fols. 76^{v}/77^{v}–77^{r}/78^{r} [78^{v}–79^{r}]), and *cf.* R. Predelli, *Regesti dei Commemoriali*, V (1901), bk. XVI, no. 65, pp. 212–13.

[19] Arch. di Stato di Mantova, Arch. Gonzaga, Busta 834, brief of 2 October, 1474, and *cf.*, *ibid.*, the papal brief of April, 1475, for the collection of tithes in Mantuan territories "propter apparatus maximos" to be prepared against the Turks.

[20] Arch. Gonzaga, Busta 85, BXXXIII, no. 13, fol. 60.

[21] Arch. Gonzaga, Busta 834, brief of 1 July, 1475, and *cf.* the (damaged) brief to Lodovico dated 12 September, 1475. Stephen the Great, prince of Moldavia, to whom Sixtus

17 September (1475) Sixtus wrote the marquis again, demanding the immediate dispatch of a Mantuan envoy to the Curia. He had previously asked that an envoy be sent by 1 November, but *imminentia pericula* would not allow so long a delay (the news had just reached Rome that the Turks had taken the Genoese colony of Caffa in early June).[22] Similar letters were sent to other Italian rulers (*et aliis hoc idem scribimus*),[23] but they bestirred themselves no more than did the marquis of Mantua.

If Uzun Ḥasan really expected further help from the West, he was disappointed. He had other reasons for disappointment, even in his own family, for he was obliged to suppress a revolt by one of his sons and to march against his brother Uwais. In 1475–1476 the plague ravaged Persia; the campaign against the Ottomans was first postponed and then abandoned. Venice and the papacy did what they could to keep alive in Uzun Ḥasan's mind the idea that a simultaneous attack from east and west would eventually crush Mehmed II as though between two millstones, but Venetian policy suffered a severe blow when Uzun Ḥasan died at Tabriz in early January, 1478. His death was an important factor in the Republic's decision to make peace with the Porte a year later.[24]

Sixtus looked everywhere for money with which to combat the Turks, and lamented the colossal expense the Church faced in seeking to stem their aggression. In the bull *Catholice fidei defensionem* of 1 December, 1475, he stated that Sultan Mehmed II was elated by the continuing Turkish destruction of Christian life and property, and that he was exerting himself to the full to effect the subjugation of the remaining areas of Christendom which he had not yet overrun. The revenues of the Holy See were not adequate to provide the necessary protection. All the faithful must give their support lest there be any relaxation of the long-continued papal effort against the infidel. The kings of Castile and León had employed a third part of the tithes against the Moslems in Granada, but for some time they had been giving these funds to various ecclesiastical and lay persons and for various ecclesiastical and lay purposes. All such improper diversions of the income from these "thirds" must cease, and restitution must be made to the parish churches from which the collections had been made. Sixtus pointed out, however, that if the income from these thirds were divided into two equal parts, one of them might be used "for the defense of the orthodox Church and for an expedition against the Turks for two years" (but it must be channeled through the Camera Apostolica), and the other half would remain in the parishes for maintenance of the fabric of their churches. The crusade would thus receive no little impetus without marked disadvantage to the churches which had long been deprived of this revenue. Sixtus therefore decreed *motu proprio* that the thirds should be divided between the Camera (for use against the Turks) and the parish churches of Castile and León (for the maintenance of their fabrics), with the usual declaration of penalties against those persons, lay or ecclesiastical, who might seek to contravene or frustrate his decision.[25]

---

alludes in his brief of 1 July, defeated the Turks near Rahova (Rahovitsa), northwest of Galati (Galats), on 10 January, 1475, on which note Pastor, *Hist. Popes*, IV, 285, and *Gesch. d. Päpste*, II (repr. 1955), 519, and R. Rosetti, "Stephen the Great of Moldavia and the Turkish Invasion," *Slavonic Review*, VI (1927–28), 86–103. On the importance of Stephen's career in the history of eastern Europe, see Şerban Papacostea, "La Politique extérieure de la Moldavie à l'époque d'Étienne le Grand: Points de repère," *Revue roumaine d'histoire*, XIV-3 (1975), 423–40.

[22] *Cf.* W. Heyd, *Histoire du commerce du Levant*, trans. Furcy Raynaud, II, (1886, repr. 1967), 399–404, and on the fall of Caffa, note below.

[23] Arch. Gonzaga, Busta 834, brief dated 17 September, 1475, and *cf.*, *ibid.*, the (damaged) brief of 30 September, with which Sixtus sent Lodovico a copy of a letter from Matthias Corvinus dilating on the Turkish threat: ". . . Itaque considera, dilectissime fili, quam aperta immineant pericula nisi nosmet ipsos excitemus et salutaria remedia quamprimum adhibeamus, quod te pro viribus tuis non dubitamus esse facturum." These appeals were unceasing; *cf.*, *ibid.*, the briefs dated 17 March, 1476, and 18 February, 1477.

[24] On the evidence concerning Uzun Ḥasan, furnished by Angiolello's *Historia turchesca*, see N. Di Lenna, in the *Archivio veneto-tridentino*, V (1924), 28–30; V. Minorsky, in *Encycl. of Islām*, IV (Leiden, 1934), 1066–68, and *cf.* p. 588 (on Tabriz); Barbara von Palombini, *Bündniswerben abendländischer Mächte um Persien (1453–1600)*, Wiesbaden, 1968, pp. 16–31; note also Navagero, *Storia veneziana*, in *RISS*, XXIII, col. 1144AB, and J. Gelcich, and L. von Thallóczy, *Diplomatarium relationum reipublicae ragusanae cum regno Hungariae*, Budapest, 1887, no. 385, pp. 630–31 (abbr. *Dipl. ragusanum*).

[25] Arch. Segr. Vaticano, Reg. Vat. 679, fols. 80ʳ–81ᵛ, by mod. stamped enumeration, and *cf.* the authorization dated 1 September, 1475, to collect the anti-Turkish tithe "in regnis Ioannis Aragonum regis illustris" (*ibid.*, fols. 84ʳ–85ᵛ). On 1 March, 1476, Sixtus wrote Bishop Domenico Camisati of Rieti, his legate in Germany, Hungary, Poland, and Bohemia, about the necessity for both princes and prelates to put aside their personal rancor "ad suscipiendum et magno animo prosequendum Christiane reipublice defensionis negocium adversus immanissimos Turchorum

Of the western powers Venice had the most at stake in the Levant, and sustained the heaviest losses in the long war with the Porte. The Genoese suffered also, however, when the Turks took over their rich colony at Caffa in the Crimea (in June, 1475), and soon thereafter occupied Tana on the Sea of Azov. The loss of life at Caffa was accompanied by the wholesale confiscation of money and merchandise.[26] Old and New Phocaea had already been cruelly ravaged twenty years before (in 1455) by the Turkish admiral Yunus Beg, after which the profits of the alum trade had of course declined.[27] Genoa now had little to show for some three and a half centuries of effort in the Levant.[28] But the day was passing when the Venetians could take much pleasure in Genoese misfortune, and considering that it was the Turks who gained thereby, the Venetians had small cause for satisfaction. It was as Pius II's old friend, Cardinal Jacopo Ammanati, wrote a fellow member of the Sacred College, Francesco Gonzaga—Europe was in a dangerous turmoil, with the Christian princes rattling their arms in one another's ears. "The sack of Caffa has filled us with grief." The pope had written to the princes. What else could he do?[29]

There was, to be sure, still one important Genoese settlement left in the Levant. For almost a century after the fall of Caffa the Genoese *mahonesi* held on to the island of Chios (until the Turks forced them out in April, 1566). Their revenues from farming the Chian taxes, duties, and imposts, the local soap factory, the sale of wine and silk, and the production of something over two hundred cases of mastic each year hardly sufficed to pay the administrative costs of the island. The rapacity of the officials, the speculations of the bankers, and the depredations of pirates gave life the quality of a constant crisis. The *mahonesi*, belonging to noble families, exerted some political influence in Genoa, which was constantly obliged to assist them in the confused conduct of affairs in Chios, where the local coinage was likely to be corrupt, justice to go awry, the food supply to be mismanaged, taxes manipulated, and the fortifications neglected. There were frequent grounds for disagreement and misunderstanding. The *mahonesi* were in a business which they hoped the Genoese state would buy from them, but the home government could never find the money to redeem the rights it had mortgaged at the time of the conquest, for which the first *mahonesi* had paid. Until the last two decades or so of the *mahonesi*'s possession of Chios, by which time the Genoese

---

impetus" (*ibid.*, fols. 15r–16v), and on the following 7 May he wrote Bishop Niccolò Sandonnino of Modena, his legate in France and Brittany, Burgundy and Savoy, "sane inter cetera desideria cordis nostri incrementum vere fidei et animarum salutem ac commissi nobis gregi[s] dominici libertatem supremis [desideramus] affectibus, hoc precipue tempore quo notissima fidelium pressura et sevissima Turchorum persecutio imminet . . ." (*ibid.*, fols. 20r–21r).

[26] Raynaldus, *Ann. eccl.*, ad ann. 1475, nos. 23–27, vol. XIX (1693), pp. 261–62; Heyd, II, 400–6, whom Babinger, *Maometto* (1957), pp. 505–9, follows rather closely. Pastor, *Gesch. d. Päpste*, II (repr. 1955), 519, notes that the fall of Caffa (6 June) was known in Rome by September. It was a crushing blow to the morale of the *mahonesi* of Chios, on which *cf.* Philip P. Argenti, *Occupation of Chios*, I (Cambridge, 1958), 226–29. Angiolello, *Hist. turchesca*, ed. Ursu, pp. 72–80, is well informed on the fall of Caffa, which made a deep impression on the Curia Romana, ". . . nuper expugnata splendidissima ac populosa urbe Caffa dilectorum filiorum populi Ianuensium dicioni subiecta cum multorum Christi fidelium strage et bonorum omnium illius incolarum detractione . . ." (from the bull *Dum attenta meditatione*, dated 1 March, 1476 [according to the *stile fiorentino*, 1475], in Arch. Segr. Vaticano, Reg. Vat. 679, fol. 90r, and *cf.*, fol. 147r). As the years passed, Sixtus IV tried to ransom some of the unfortunates who were captured by the Turks "annis superioribus in calamitate et direptione civitatis Caffensis" (Reg. Vat. 550 [*Sixti IV Bull. secret. "apud Trapezuntium,"* tom. V], fol. 118, by mod. stamped enumeration, bull dated 18 September, 1479).

[27] *Cf.* Argenti, *Occupation of Chios*, I, 210, 509; Babinger, *Maometto*, pp. 207–9, 404. On the Phocaeas, see Wolfgang Müller-Wiener, "Kuşadasi und Yeni-Foça: Zwei italienische Gründungsstädte des Mittelalters," *Istanbuler Mitteilungen*, XXV (1975), 399–420, to which reference has been made above.

[28] From about 1415 the Levantine trade of the Genoese (and that of the Catalans) had decreased steadily, despite an occasional good year, while that of Venice appears to have increased by about one-third in the course of the century. See the somewhat speculative but important article of Eliyahu Ashtor, "The Volume of Levantine Trade in the Later Middle Ages (1370–1498)," *The Journal of European Economic History*, IV-3 (Rome, 1975), 573–612, and (in general) Ashtor, "The Venetian Supremacy in Levantine Trade: Monopoly or Pre-Colonialism?" *ibid.*, III-1 (1974), 5–53. The economic institutions and commercial history of Genoa are dealt with in some detail by Jacques Heers, *Gênes au XVe siècle*, Paris, 1961.

[29] Arch. Segr. Vaticano, Arm. XXXIX, tom. 10, fol. 159r, by mod. stamped enumeration, dated 29 July, 1475, and *cf.* Giuseppe Calamari, *Il Confidente di Pio II: Card. Iacopo Ammannati-Piccolomini*, 2 vols., Milan, 1932, II, 530–31. On the MS. in question, see Frank-Rutger Hausmann, "Armarium 39, tomus 10 des Archivio Segreto Vaticano: Ein Beitrag zum Epistolar des Kardinals Giacomo Ammannati-Piccolomini (1422–1479) und anderer Humanisten," *Quellen und Forschungen aus italienischen Archiven und Bibliotheken*, L (1971), 112–80.

position had become almost ludicrous in the face of Turkish power, the Republic seems always to have planned this redemption of an authority which it had never exercised. For more than two centuries, therefore, the *mahona*, a joint-stock company, collected the revenues of Chios through its own treasurers (*massarii*). The stockholders, many of whom were resident on Chios, made a living from the company, and that was all they cared about until they could sell their rights to the state.

The stockholders in the *mahona* held 38 major shares (*carati grossi*, each divisible into eight *carati piccoli*, of which there were thus 304). Three *carati grossi* comprised a basic twelfth (*duodenum*) of the *mahonesi*'s total investment (which was actually 12⅔ *duodena*). Appointments to most of the lucrative positions on the island (the appointees served the *mahona* rather than the state) were assigned by lot to the holders of the basic *duodena*, which were however subdivided into large and small *carati* held by a considerable number of different persons belonging for the most part to the so-called family of the Giustiniani. It was from these shareholders or from persons of their own choice that the officers in question were chosen. Membership in the *mahona* thus not only yielded a profit (in theory at least), the amount varying with the number of *carati* held, but also provided a job which paid a salary in most cases larger than the income derived from the stockholder's shares in the company.[30] The tendency to make hay while the sun shone was very strong, for the Turks cast a longer shadow over the affairs of the island with each passing decade, and no one knew when the clouds would finally produce the storm.

There were two reasons for Genoa's holding on to Chios long after possession of the island was a source of any profit. First, Chios was the last remnant of the Genoese colonial empire; pride made its relinquishment very difficult. Secondly, the *mahonesi* cherished the prolonged hope that some day the state would redeem, for the often stated sum of 152,250 *lire*, the rights farmed out to them in the series of leases or conventions which formed the charter of their company. Genoa never had money enough to do so, and through the last years of the *mahona* the home government apparently took little interest in Chios, which might be occupied by the Turks at almost any time. The resident *mahonesi*, in turn, took little interest in Genoa except as a possible source of help in raising the tribute (and making "gifts") of some 12,000 ducats which had to be delivered promptly each year to the Porte.[31] Later on, the tribute might be allowed to fall a full three years in arrears (as in 1534–1536), but in one way or another it seems generally to have been made up and eventually paid in full. For generations the Turks tolerated the *mahona* in Chios, although more than once (as in 1534 and 1552) they refused to countenance the sending of the podestà from Genoa. Presumably the pashas in Istanbul believed that a tribute of 10–12,000 ducats a year, with no cost or problems of administration, was more than they could have wrung from the inhabitants if they had taken direct possession of the island.

Life was not unpleasant on Chios. On the whole the Greeks were well treated, in accordance with the agreement between the admiral Simone Vignoso and the leaders of the Byzantine community at the time of the conquest in 1346. The Jews had fewer legal rights, but were less abused than in many other places. Latin women enjoyed in Chios as in Genoa a comparatively favorable status. The robust and uncertain lives which their husbands led on the sea have left the names of numerous widows in the Chian documents in the Genoese archives. The laws concerning intestacy in Chios, as in Genoa, were full of complicated specificities that need not concern us here.

The *mahonesi* enjoyed sizable dividends during the earlier period of their exploitation of Chios and the Phocaeas. Their fiscal agents or treasurers (*massarii*) took over the revenues which had previously been paid to the Byzantines, from whom Vignoso had taken the island. These fiscal agents were elected by the shareholders of the *mahona*, and could enlist the aid of both the podestà and the castellans in bringing pressure to bear upon recalcitrant taypayers. They collected the fines imposed in the law courts; the old Byzantine land tax or *akrostichon*; various excises

[30] Argenti, *Occupation of Chios*, I, 126–46, 408, 411–4. Argenti has followed various sales and transfers of stock as well as the general operation of the *mahona* in sometimes minute detail.

[31] Argenti, *Occupation of Chios*, I, 210, 238–39, 268–69, 655–56; II, 318: ". . . domini Mahonenses . . . solverunt annuatim regi turcorum ducatos decem milia auri venetos per certa tempora et deinde solverunt et solvunt duodecim milia pro caraihio sive tributo . . ." (from doc. dated 1482).

(*gabelle*); and a multiplicity of other duties and imposts. The Greek inhabitants were for some time subject to an onerous poll tax (*kapnikon*), which might amount to six *hyperperi* a year, enough to cause emigration from the island; the poll tax was removed, however, in March, 1396, and an annual hearth tax of two *hyperperi* was substituted for it, certain groups of workers being exempted since they had to pay other taxes. There were special taxes on silk, wine, vinegar, domestic animals, real estate, some kinds of personal property, and the employment of weights and measures; imposts were laid on the milling of grain, even on gambling (*commerchium baratarie*); and a special levy of one, later three, per cent was collected on imports and exports, being known as the "drictus Chii . . . impositus pro expensis faciendis ob metum Turchorum." The *drictus* was levied almost surreptitiously for defense against the Turks; to do away with the necessity of explaining the charge, Turks were exempted from paying it.[32]

The soil of Chios was not unfertile, yielding figs, oranges, lemons, nuts, oil, wax, and even some cotton and grain. The *mahona* held monopolies in mastic, alum, pitch, and salt. The production of mastic was limited and carefully supervised to keep up both the health of the plants and the price; in the sixteenth century, however, when annual production was probably more than 25 per cent smaller than it had been in the previous century (a decline from about 430 to about 300 quintals a year),[33] the mastic trade is said to have grossed some 30,000 ducats a year.[34]

The profits made in the alum mines of Phocaea are well known to all economic historians of the medieval Levant. In 1480–1481, at the time of the Turkish attacks upon Rhodes and Otranto, some of the *mahonesi* were engaged in the alum trade with the Turks, which incensed Pope Sixtus IV, who was trying to organize a crusade. By briefs of 30 September, 1480, addressed to the *mahonesi*, the doge and "ancients" of Genoa, and the vicar of the church of Chios, Sixtus renewed the prohibition against the *negotiatio aluminum Turcorum* under the penalty of excommunication. The Chian traffic in Turkish alum not only brought profit to the Porte, but it was inconsistent with the defense of Chios, and was detrimental to the sale of papal alum from the beds at Tolfa, the proceeds of which were reserved for the crusade. The pope ordered that all Turkish alum on Chios should be sequestered and held until he gave further word as to its disposition.[35]

It was much easier for the pope to declare such a prohibition at the Curia than for the *mahonesi* to observe it on Chios. They could not avoid trading with the Turks; they naturally wanted to avoid trouble with them. Alum remained a problem, but there were of course other products they could turn into money. Pitch was distilled from turpentine, a product of the terebinth tree, which was grown on Chios; it was used for caulking the seams in ships and probably for waterproofing under slate roofing and tiles. Hides were tanned and dyed on the island. The silk industry was apparently quite important, employing numerous weavers; woolen cloth was produced also, although it is not clear whether many sheep were kept on the island or not. Be all this as it may, Chios was more important as a trading station and depot in transit than as a producing area or manufacturing center. A brisk trade was carried on with England, Flanders, and Spain as well as with the home government, Greece, Syria, Egypt, and the Ottoman empire. Asiatic drugs and spices were transshipped from Chios to the chief ports of western Europe. Loss of the island was not to improve the economy of the home government, and was to destroy the last remnants of Genoese prestige in the East.

If the Venetians could find small cause for satisfaction in the Genoese loss of Caffa, they could find no more in the parlous state of affairs in Italy. Sixtus IV would soon throw the peninsula into turmoil in the interests of his nephew Girolamo Riario, who on 17 January,

[32] Argenti, *Occupation of Chios*, I, 424–27.

[33] The late medieval quintal (about 110 lbs. avoirdupois) was apparently only about one-half the weight of the modern quintal (in the metric system 100,000 grams = 220.46 lbs. avoirdupois). The cantar or (long) hundredweight seems to have been the same as the quintal; mastic was usually shipped in cases of two cantars, which would have weighed about 220 lbs. avoirdupois when full. *Cf.* in general Argenti, *Occupation of Chios*, I, 521–24, which I find somewhat confused.

[34] Argenti, *Occupation of Chios*, I, 484–87.

[35] Biblioteca Nazionale Centrale di Firenze, Bibl. Magliabecchiana, MS. II–III 256, fols. 55^v–56^v, a collection of Sixtus IV's briefs from August, 1481, to August, 1482.

1473, was betrothed to Caterina Sforza, a natural daughter of Galeazzo Maria, the duke of Milan, and upon whom with the duke's connivance he bestowed Imola as a papal vicariate in the following autumn.[36] Florence had more reason than Venice, however, to wonder whither Sixtus's nepotistic policy would lead. Since it was well known that Riario also aspired to lordship over Faenza and Forlì, Lorenzo de' Medici had become very fearful of the pope's maneuvers. It was not to the ambitions of Sixtus and the Riari as such that Lorenzo took exception, but if the pope could bring Umbria and the Romagna under effective control, he would have Tuscany between the upper and nether millstones. A century before this, after the military Cardinal Albornoz's consolidation of the states of the Church, the Florentines had conducted the so-called War of the Eight Saints against Pope Gregory XI, lest he should accomplish what his successor Sixtus now seemed to be envisaging. It was always possible that Florence, old home of the Parte Guelfa, might again take up arms against the papacy.

Dissension was beginning, and on 2 November, 1474, Venice entered with Milan and Florence into a twenty-five-year pact, being soon joined by the duchy of Ferrara. Sixtus IV refused to become a party to the league, which declared its purpose to be the preservation of peace in Italy. Although he wrote the Marquis Lodovico Gonzaga on 11 April, 1475, that it ill became the supreme pontiff, "who is the universal father of all," to form an alliance with any particular league,[37] he could have explained his declination in less abstract terms. He believed the league designed to constrict the Holy See in the full governance of the states of the Church, and saw in it an obstacle to the continued practice of his nepotism. King Ferrante of Naples, also suspicious of the league, was drawn more closely to the pope, whom he visited for three days in Rome toward the end of January, 1475, possibly returning for another two days in mid-February. Ostensibly they discussed the necessity of organizing a new Italian alliance against Mehmed II, but undoubtedly they also considered the meaning of the north Italian league, which they both interpreted as contrary to their interests.[38]

It is neither easy nor necessary for the modern historian to fix the blame for the coming struggles in Italy upon any one or two of the participants. These struggles did, however, invite the eventual entry of the French and Spanish into the peninsula, and sadly diminished the long-continued prosperity of Italy. Venice was in a particularly awkward position through these years, for she was not only at war with the Porte, but was very unpopular throughout Italy and distrusted throughout Europe, as Mehmed II well knew. As trouble loomed on the Italian horizon, the Turk was preparing to move westward. On 5 February, 1476, Sixtus IV issued the bull *Quamvis ad amplianda* imposing a tithe (with the full assent of Charles the Bold) upon the harassed faithful in the duchy of Burgundy and Charles's other possessions "because of the calamitous condition of the times . . . and the vast Turkish offensive" (*calamitosa moderni temporis conditio . . . ingensque Turchorum persecutio*). Sixtus deplored Mehmed's uninterrupted success under the banner of Satan, the invasion of Albania, the fall of Caffa, and the slaughter and enslavement of the faithful throughout the Balkans. The arrogant Turk was again preparing powerful

[36] Pier Desiderio Pasolini, *Caterina Sforza*, 3 vols., Rome, 1893, I, 45–46, and III, docs. 52–59, pp. 21–26, on the betrothal (somewhat by chance) of Girolamo and Caterina, and *ibid.*, I, 48–49, and III, docs. 64–67, p. 29, on the county of Imola, the restitution of which to the states of the Church Sixtus had to purchase from the duke of Milan for 40,000 ducats. *Cf.* Pastor, *Gesch. d. Päpste*, II (repr. 1955), 490–91. According to a papal brief dated 18 January, 1474, addressed to the Marquis Lodovico II of Mantua, "Dilectus filius nobilis vir Hieronymus vicecomes nepos secundum carnem noster possessionem civitatis nostre Imolensis quam nuper de consilio venerabilium fratrum nostrorum Sancte Romane Ecclesie cardinalium in vicariatum ei concessimus adire quam primum debet, et quia persone nostre assistit continue, per se ipsum non potest . . . ," and so Girolamo Riario planned to send a lieutenant to Imola (Arch. di Stato di Mantova, Arch. Gonzaga, Busta 834).

[37] Arch. di Stato di Mantova, Arch. Gonzaga, Busta 834: "Superioribus diebus cum dilectorum filiorum nobiliorum virorum Petri Mozenici Venetiarum et Galeatii Marie Mediolani ducum necnon reipublice Florentine oratores ad nos venissent postulantes ut ligam quam inter se fecerant et in qua locum ingrediendi nobis reliquerant ingredi vellemus, adduximus multas rationes quibus eis ostendimus non decere summum pontificem, qui omnium universalis pater est, particulari alicui lige confoederari . . . ," after which Lodovico was instructed in the meaning and function of the papal *ligandi et solvendi potestas*. This brief is also preserved in a Mantuan archival register, where it was recorded with Lodovico's courteous but rather noncommittal reply (*ibid.*, Busta 85, fols. 72^v–73^r).

[38] Pastor, *Hist. Popes*, IV, 272, 278–80, 284–85, and *Gesch. d. Päpste*, II (repr. 1955), 507–8, 513–14, 518–19.

armies and fleets to subject all Christendom "if he can" (*si possit*), with obvious peril to the faithful and the faith.[39]

While the Turk maintained pressure on the eastern front, the peace of Italy rested in precarious balance. The strength of the Milanese duchy in the north held in equipoise the ambition rife in the southern kingdom of Naples. From the time of the conqueror Charles I (1266–1285), the rulers of Naples, Angevins and Aragonese alike, appear to have held an exaggerated idea of the power and resources of their domain, as indeed did most of their contemporaries in Italy and elsewhere in Europe. An imperious and bureaucratic regime, the kingdom was organized to play international politics. If the supply of cereals was low, the grain trade was a royal monopoly, and export could be made, for example, to Venice or withheld, as expediency suggested at any given time. But after Robert the Wise, who died in 1343, the Neapolitan government tended to be incompetent and was constantly beset by internal strife. The peasants lived on fruit, chestnuts, wine, and such little meat and grain as they could get.

Located in the fertile plains of Lombardy, well watered by the Po, the Milanese duchy did not have the same problem of putting food on the table as the Venetians, who depended much on imports. Milanese policy could easily be based on political desire instead of economic necessity. In the eighth decade of the fifteenth century, however, the duke of Milan, Galeazzo Maria Sforza, despicable as he may have been personally, was the mainstay of peace in Italy, but on the morning of 26 December, 1476, he was assassinated at the church of S. Stefano by three young Milanese nobles, students of the humanist Cola Montano, who were allegedly fired by the study of the ancient classics to rid the state of a tyrant.[40] Whatever his failings, Galeazzo Maria's political vision seems to have been broader than that of Lorenzo de' Medici. To Sixtus IV his death meant the end of peace in Italy. The pope sent briefs to all the Italian powers on 1 January, 1477, urging them to keep the peace as well as deploring the *insperata mors* of Galeazzo Maria,[41] and during that year it was kept for the most part although Florence, Venice, and Milan maintained their dangerous alignment against the papacy and Naples, to which powers Siena adhered in fear of Florence.[42] Italy was like a volcano which might erupt at any time.

In the East, however, the contest with the Porte went on without abatement. On 15 February, 1476, Matthias Corvinus had taken the Turkish fortress of Shabats (Šabac) after a thirty-day siege, capturing the garrison of about 1,200 janissaries, and thereafter had advanced as far as Semendria (Smederevo), but the enthusiastic support of Sixtus IV and the Venetians, who were in whole-hearted agreement in their anti-Turkish sentiment, was offset by the refusal of the Emperor Frederick III to render any assistance at all. Frederick would still not allow Matthias to acquire ships and arms in his territories without paying tolls and customs duties. He made no effort even to halt the raids of German knights into north Hungarian territory, let alone the continual and deadly raids which the Turks launched from Bosnia through Croatia into the old duchies of Carniola and

---

[39] Arch. Segr. Vaticano, Reg. Vat. 679, fols. 147^r–150^r, by mod. stamped enumeration. In this bull Sixtus also emphasizes that, ever since the death of his predecessor Paul II, no small part of the resources of the Apostolic See had been spent in subsidies to the Hungarians, the despot of the Morea, the Albanian princes, the despot of Arta, "and very many other magnates, provinces, and peoples" (*ibid.*, fols. 147^v–148^r). As for Charles the Bold of Burgundy (d. January, 1477), although he liked to cast himself in the role of a crusader, he never began serious preparations for an expedition against the Turks (*cf.* R. J. Walsh, "Charles the Bold and the Crusade . . . ," *Journal of Medieval History*, III [1977], 53–86).

[40] Allegretto Allegretti, *Diari sanesi*, in *RISS*, XXIII (Milan, 1733), cols. 777–78, who shows that the assassins had personal reasons also; Malipiero, *Annali veneti*, in *Arch. stor. italiano*, VII-1 (1843), 245; Sigismondo de'Conti (da Foligno), *Le Storie de'suoi tempi dal 1475 al 1510*, 2 vols., Rome, 1883, I, 17; *cf.* Bernardino Corio, *L'Historia di Milano*, Venice, 1554, pp. 22^v–25^v; and see in general Vincent Ilardi, "The Assassination of Galeazzo Maria Sforza and the Reaction of Italian Diplomacy," in Lauro Martines, ed., *Violence and Civil Disorder in Italian Cities, 1200–1500*, Berkeley, Los Angeles, London, 1972, pp. 72–103.

[41] Such a brief may be found in the Arch. di Stato di Mantova, Arch. Gonzaga, Busta 834, addressed to Lodovico Gonzaga: "Debuit iam ut opinamur nobilitas tua intellexisse insperatam mortem insignis memorie Galeazmarie ducis Mediolani quam nos pluribus ex causis maxime vero propter quietem Italicam vehementer dolemus . . . ," and *cf.*, *ibid.*, the brief dated 1 February, 1478. Hoping that Lodovico might prove a stabilizing force in northern Italy, the pope conferred the golden rose on him by a brief dated 31 March, 1477 (*ibid.*, Busta 834, and Busta 85, BXXXIII, no. 13, fols. 79^v–80^r).

[42] *Cf.* Pastor, *Hist. Popes*, IV, 290–99, and *Gesch. d. Päpste*, II (repr. 1955), 524–31.

Carinthia. The enterprise of the Turks was extraordinary. Greece suffered no less than central Europe. Although a Turkish attack upon the stout walls of Naupactus (Lepanto) had failed in July, 1476, Naxos was sacked in the following year, and in 1479 an ecclesiastical source depicts the island diocese of Naxos and Paros as being largely in Turkish hands.[43]

To the Venetians the war seemed endless, among the darkest months and years in the history of the Republic. They had increasing grounds for apprehension, as we have seen, in the tense political situation in Italy, and it must be added that they constantly added to the tension by seeking to compensate for their losses in the Levant by making territorial gains in the peninsula. Turkish raiders carried their merciless depredations into Istria and Friuli (in 1477), and the fires of burning woods, farmhouses, and villages were visible in Venice from atop the campanile in the Piazza S. Marco. The long sweep of Friuli south of Forogiulio (Cividale), Udine, and Pordenone is an almost indefensible flatland protected only by the easily bypassed height of Conegliano in the northwest. There was reason for the fear which struck the Venetians, who had to manage alone while Matthias Corvinus again became embroiled in war with Frederick III, and gave up trying to check the constant westward attacks of the Turks and their Bosnian *saccomanni*.[44] When the Venetians sought by diplomacy to end the war in which they were losing so much and gaining so little, their endeavors were in vain, for Sultan Mehmed II with patent insincerity insisted upon almost impossible conditions of peace, and, when his terms were accepted, imposed still further conditions or changed his mind. In June, 1478, the great Albanian fortress of Croia (Krujë), Scanderbeg's stronghold, surrendered to Mehmed after a siege of more than a year. Despite the sultan's assurance that their lives would be spared, many of the inhabitants were killed. They had had no alternative to surrender, having been reduced, according to the Italian chroniclers Navagero and Angiolello, to devouring their horses, dogs, "and anything else they could eat."[45] (The Turks held Croia, the "White Castle," for more than four centuries.) Further north, Drivasto (Drisht) and Alessio (Lesh) were taken, but the Venetian garrison and the terrified inhabitants of Scutari (Scodra, Shkodër) resisted, with a fortitude born of desperation, the frightful siege which began in May, 1478, and was still unconcluded when peace was finally made between the Republic and the Porte at the beginning of the following year. Scutari was then given

---

[43] Navagero, *Storia veneziana*, in *RISS*, XXIII, cols. 1146E–1147, 1149C, on Lepanto; C. Eubel, *Hierarchia*, II (1914, repr. 1960), 200: [Niccolò da Gaeta, archbishop of Naxos and Paros] "non obtulit servitia communia nisi illos solitos 10 fl. pro balista, quia ecclesia Pariensis a Turcis pro maiori parte occupata dicitur." *Cf.* Raynaldus, *Ann. eccl.*, ad ann. 1476, nos. 4–9, vol. XIX (1693), pp. 265–66; Wm. Miller, *Latins in the Levant*, pp. 611–12; Babinger, *Maometto*, pp. 512–17, 526–27. On Matthias's difficulties in dealing with Frederick III, *cf.* A. Bachmann, *Urkundliche Nachträge zur österreichisch-deutschen Geschichte im Zeitalter Kaiser Friedrichs III.*, Vienna, 1892, nos. 251, 264, 371, and esp. 416, and for the Turkish war in Bosnia against the Hungarians in 1476–1477, see Angiolello, *Historia turchesca*, ed. Ursu (1909), pp. 93–96.

[44] On the Turkish incursions which reached deep into Friuli, threatening Pordenone on 11 November, 1477; the terrible fear of the invaders throughout Sixtus IV's reign and for years thereafter; and the long war between Frederick III and Matthias Corvinus, which came to an end only with the latter's death in April, 1490, see Giuseppe Vale, *Itinerario di Paolo Santonino in Carintia, Stiria e Carniola negli anni 1485–1487 (Cod. Vat. lat. 3795)*, Città del Vaticano, 1943, esp. pp. 21–36, with a rich bibliography. Santonino's itinerary contains frequent references to churches and villages, "que in Turcorum excursione omnes [ville] incendio consumpte fuere" (*ibid.*, p. 154), "tempore quo Turcorum exercitus regionem omnem incendio et preda vastavit" (p. 164, and *cf.* pp. 166, 199, 202, 207, 208 note 2, 211, 216, 217, 219 [referring to an army of 15,000 Turks], *et alibi*).

A number of Sixtus IV's anti-Turkish briefs addressed to Duke Ercole I d'Este of Ferrara are preserved in the Archivio di Stato di Modena, Cancelleria marchionale [dal 1393] poi ducale [dal 1471] Estense, Carteggio di principi e signorie, Roma, Busta 1293A/8, nos. 65, 73, and 86 (on behalf of Uzun Ḥasan), 93 and 94 (on the fall of Caffa in 1475), 103, 105, 111, 116, and 119 (on the impelling need of a subsidy for Corvinus). A brief of 17 January, 1478, stresses the danger of the Turkish incursions into Friuli (*in agro Foroiuliensi, ibid.*, no. 125), and another of 27 April again sought Ferrarese assistance for the hard-pressed Corvinus (no. 127). Two years before this, by a brief of 21 April, 1476, Sixtus had rejected a request of Louis XI of France to hold a general council in Lyon "ob utilitatem et reformationem reipublice Christiane" in alleged accord with the decree of Constance. Sixtus denied the validity of the decree, stating that general councils required the assurance of all the Christian princes "ut personaliter interessent," besides which there was too much dissension and hostility among the princes to hold a council, and that if such dissension continued, the Turk would eventually seize the rest of Europe and try to destroy Christianity: the most Christian king of France should know that a crusade was necessary, not a council (no. 104).

[45] Navagero, *op. cit.*, col. 1153C; Angiolello, *Hist. turchesca*, ed. Ursu, pp. 97–102.

up to the Turks as one of the stipulations in the treaty.[46] The Venetians had held the fortress for more than eighty years. Like Croia it now passed under Turkish dominance for more than four centuries (in 1913 it was incorporated in the new Albania, after the triumph of the short-lived Balkan league over Turkey).

Some sixteen years of war between Venice and the Porte came at long last to an end on 25 January, 1479, in the peace negotiated in Istanbul by the diplomat Giovanni Dario, who had been accorded extraordinary powers by the Venetian Senate, of which he was the secretary. The Venetians now formally ceded to the Porte both Scutari and Croia, the islands of Lemnos and Negroponte, and the rough promontory of Maina in the southern Morea; they agreed to return within two months their own conquests in the Morea to the Porte, which in its turn undertook to restore to the Republic some of the lands the Turks had occupied in the Morea, Albania, and Dalmatia. The Venetians also bound themselves to pay within two years the sum of 100,000 gold ducats, which Bartolommeo Zorzi and Girolamo Michiel, lessees of the Turkish alum mines, still owed the Porte when they fled from Istanbul after the outbreak of war, promising also the annual payment to the Porte of 10,000 ducats in return for the general right of free trade within the Ottoman empire and exemption from both import and export duties. Venice was to be allowed to maintain a bailie in Istanbul with civil authority over his fellow citizens resident in the Ottoman capital.[47]

Minor territorial problems still remained unsolved, however, especially in the Morea, where the local Turkish pashas, *flambulari*, judges, and *subashis* disputed with Bartolommeo Minio, the Venetian provveditore and captain of Nauplia, what belonged to Venice and what to the Porte. The defection of the Albanian captain Theodore Bua, who joined the great uprising of Corcondilo Cladas (Korkodeilos Kladas) in Maina, produced much anxiety among the Venetian officials in the Morea. The insurgents threatened the newly made peace by their continued attacks upon the Turks. Cladas, who had been one of the last of the Moreote chieftains to give up the struggle to save the Morea from the Turks twenty years before,[48] and had served the Serenissima well during the late war, now refused to accept the Venetian cession of Maina to the Porte in accord with the treaty of January, 1479.[49] The insurgents fared badly,

---

[46] *Cf.* Navagero, *op. cit.*, cols. 1141–43, 1153–55, 1158E–59E, 1161–62, on Scutari, and on Croia, *passim*; for the treaty, see the text and note which follow; Marinus Barletius, *De obsidione Scodrensi*, in Philip Lonicer, *Cron. turcica*, III, Frankfurt a. M., 1578, fols. 231–71, the best source for the siege of Scutari. *Cf.* Iorga, *Gesch. d. osman. Reiches*, II (Gotha, 1909), 187 ff. The historian Marinus Barletius, a native of Scutari, lived through the Turkish siege of 1478, and has left a very vivid account of it (see F. Pall, "Marino Barlezio," in *Mélanges d'histoire générale*, ed. Const. Marinescu, II [Bucharest, 1938], 139–41, *et alibi*). For other sources relating to the siege, *cf.* Pall, *op. cit.*, pp. 198–99, and see Angiolello, *Hist. turchesca*, ed. Ursu, pp. 102–7.

[47] Franz Miklosich and Jos. Müller, eds., *Acta et diplomata graeca*, III (Vienna, 1865, repr. 1968), 293–98, Greek texts of Turkish documents dated 7 to 29 January, 1479; Navagero, *Storia veneziana*, in *RISS*, XXIII, cols. 1151–60, 1161–62, and *cf.* cols. 1168DE–69A, in detail; *Diarium parmense*, ad ann. 1479, in *RISS*, XXII (Milan, 1733), cols. 309, 338C; Sanudo, *Vite de'duchi*, *ibid.*, col. 1210CD; Raynaldus, *Ann. eccl.*, ad ann. 1478, nos. 40–41, vol. XIX (1693), p. 278; Angiolello, *Hist. turchesca*, ed. Ursu, p. 108. Alessio Bombaci, "Nuovi Firmani greci di Maometto II," *Byzantinische Zeitschrift*, XLVII (1954), 298–319, publishes for the first time thirteen letters in Greek from Mehmed II to the Doge Giovanni Mocenigo (from 23 September, 1479, to 30 April, 1481), all from the *Liber graecus*, a sixteenth-century parchment register in the Arch. di Stato di Venezia, Miscellanea, atti diplomatici e privati, B. 45, on which see Bombaci, "Il 'Liber graecus,' un cartolario veneziano comprendente inediti documenti ottomani in greco (1481–1504)," in Fritz Meier, ed., *Westöstliche Abhandlungen: Rudolf Tschudi zum 70. Geburtstag überreicht . . .*, Wiesbaden, 1954, pp. 288–303, esp. pp. 291 ff. The register in question contains 112 documents, of which seventy-six are or were in Greek (most of them accompanied by an Italian translation, some of them extant only in translation)—there are twenty-six letters of Mehmed II, and fifty-eight of Bayazid II.

On the conclusion of the peace of 1479, see Fr. Babinger, *Johannes Darius (1414–1494), Sachwalter Venedigs im Morgenland, und sein griechischer Umkreis*, Munich, 1961, pp. 84 ff. For the later stages of the war and the peace, note also Miller, *Latins in the Levant*, pp. 479 ff.; H. Kretschmayr, *Gesch. v. Venedig*, II (1920, repr. 1964), 381–82, and for the sources, *ibid.*, pp. 634–35; Babinger, *Maometto*, pp. 528–50.

[48] Sphrantzes, *Chron. minus* (*PG* 156, 1070AB; ed Grecu, pp. 120, 122), and Pseudo-Sphrantzes, IV, 19 (Bonn, p. 407; ed. Grecu, p. 546). "Crocondilo Clada" is mentioned several times in the dispatches of Jacopo Barbarigo (1465–1466), in C. N. Sathas, ed., *Documents inédits relatifs à l'histoire de la Grèce au moyen âge*, 9 vols., Paris, 1880–90, repr. Athens, 1972, vol. VI, often cited above, in Chapter 8.

[49] On 8 January, 1481, the Senate wrote Sultan Mehmed, "Havemo intexo per lettere de la vostra illustrissima Signoria quello che anche per avanti era pervenuto cum molta molestia a nostra noticia del movimento et novitate facta per el Clada grecho perfido et rebelle . . ." (Sen. Secreta, Reg. 29, fol. 154^r [164^r]), and on the same day they

however, when Cladas and Theodore Bua fell out with each other; the latter returned to Venetian territory and was imprisoned at Monemvasia; while Cladas was finally obliged to flee before a Turkish army which dared to ascend the waterless heights of Kakaboulia against him. Escaping to Naples, Cladas entered the service of King Ferrante, for whom he later fought in Epirus by the side of Scanderbeg's son Giovanni. Bartolommeo Minio had other troubles. The Turkish *flambulario* of Negroponte raided the northeastern shores of the Morea. Minio protested to the Venetian bailie in Istanbul, remonstrating also with the aged Omar Beg, who in 1482 caused the obstreperous governor's replacement by a more peaceable successor.[50]

At the beginning of August, 1479, a Jewish envoy of Sultan Mehmed II arrived in Venice to invite the Doge Giovanni Mocenigo to attend the circumcision of one of his grandsons, and to ask him to send a good portrait painter, *un bon depentor che sapia retrazer*, to Istanbul.[51] Pleading the pressure of his official duties, the doge declined the sultan's invitation to the ceremony, but the Signoria promptly selected the painter Gentile Bellini to gratify the sultan's second request. With his expenses paid by the state, Bellini left Venice in one of the *galie di Romania* on 3 September. He arrived in Istanbul about the end of the month, and remained at the Ottoman court for some fifteen months (until mid-January, 1481). The great palace at Istanbul was finally finished. Mehmed wished to have the walls adorned by an Italian master of approved talent. Bellini not only painted the famous portrait of Mehmed (dated 25 November, 1480), now in the National Gallery in London, but also decorated the walls of the new palace with erotic scenes, which the tired sultan could contemplate with the recollection of pleasures

---

wrote Vettore Soranzo, Venetian captain-general of the sea, directing him to take steps "ad persequendum in omni actione et omni demonstratione displicentie nostre ex temeraria rebellione illius Clade et sequatium suorum et in studio conservande pacis nostre" (*ibid.*, fols. 154^{v} [164^{v}] and ff., and see refs. in following note to Sathas, *Docs. inédits*, I).

[50] See the detailed and most instructive dispatches of Minio, from 12 November, 1479, to 25 March, 1483, in Sathas, *Docs. inédits*, VI, pp. 117–213. The title *pasha*, of disputed derivation, denoted the highest honor in the Ottoman empire; the *flambulario*, *flamburar*, of the Venetian documents was the Ottoman *sanjak-beyi*, the governor of a military district (*sanjak*), a subdivision of the pasha's province (*eyālet*, *pashalik*, later called *vilāyet*); the judge was a *qāḍī*, *kadi* (*cf.* Minio's reference, for example, to *i Caddi de la Charitena, Calavrita et Argos*, *ibid.*, p. 142, lines 27–28); and the *subashi* (Ven. *subassi*) was the commandant of a town or castle in which he exercised the functions of a security officer or chief of police. On the officers of the Ottoman army and court at this time, military corps, pay, functions, and the like, see Şerif Baştav, *Ordo Portae: Description grecque de la Porte et de l'armée du Sultan Mehmed II*, Budapest, 1947, who has published from Bibl. Nat., MS. grec no. 1712, fols. 424^{v}–26^{v}, part of a treatise on Ottoman military personnel written between 1473 and '81. Baştav's commentary is useful. Much more detailed (and much more important) is the survey of Ottoman offices and the empire in Angiolello, *Hist. turchesca*, ed. Ursu, pp. 123–64, which comes from the generation following the *Ordo Portae*. On these matters see also Agostino Pertusi, "Le Notizie sulla organizzazione amministrativa e militare dei Turchi nello 'Strategicon adversum Turcos' di Lampo Birago (c. 1453–1455)," in the *Studi sul medioevo cristiano offerti a Raffaello Morghen*, II (*Studi storici*, fascc. 88–92, Rome, 1974), 677–87, 693–99. Birago describes briefly the military and provincial organization of the Ottoman state, Turkish arms and armor, available manpower, etc. (and had outlined plans for an expedition to recover Constantinople).

On Venetian affairs in the Morea in 1480–1481, and especially the uprising of Cladas, see also Sathas, I, docs. 184–94, pp. 271–81, and *cf.* no. 198, pp. 303–4 (dated May, 1485), always indicative of Venetian efforts to keep the peace with the Turks. Sathas has also published from the British Museum, Add. MS. 8586, and the Biblioteca del Museo Civico Correr, MS. Cicogna 3533, extracts relating to the history of Greece (1479–1497), from the Venetian chronicle of Stefano Magno (*Docs. inédits*, VI, 214–43). His transcription is careless.

Stefano Magno, the son of Andrea, was born about 1499. He died on 14 October, 1572. His manuscript, *Annali veneti [e del mondo]*, is preserved in five volumes in the Bibl. Correr in Venice, MSS. Cicogna 3529–33. The first volume deals with the origins of the patrician houses in Venice, with the dates of their admission to the Maggior Consiglio; they are alphabetically arranged according to the first letter of the family names, usually one family to a page, with coats of arms in color. Magno's compilation covers the years from 697 to 1498 (vols. II–V), but the years 1193–1366, 1389–1477, and 1482–1484 are lacking, and the year 1481 is represented by only 14 lines of text. He provides an extraordinary coverage, in entries given year by year, of events almost everywhere in Europe and the Levant, with especial attention to Venice and Friuli, Italy, central Europe, Turkey, Albania, Syria, Egypt, Persia, Spain, Tunis, and the Barbary Coast, and never misses a Turkish invasion into Christian territory. Volume IV deals with the years 1478 to 1481—the Turkish inroads into Friuli, the siege of Croia, and Dario's negotiation of the peace of 1479. The huge bulk of Magno's manuscript and the problem of determining his sources have unfortunately been obstacles to the publication of the *Annali veneti*, which remains one of the more important literary sources for the last two decades of the fifteenth century.

[51] Malipiero, *Annali veneti*, ad ann. 1479, in *Arch. stor. italiano*, VII-1 (1843), 123; Louis Thuasne, *Gentile Bellini et Sultan Mohammed II, notes sur le séjour du peintre vénitien à Constantinople*, Paris, 1888, p. 10 and note 2.

in which failing health, gout, and corpulence must have made indulgence very difficult. These paintings were removed from the palace by Mehmed's son and successor Bayazid II, no admirer of his father. They were sold for paltry sums at the bazaar in Istanbul, where the portrait of Mehmed was acquired by a Venetian merchant. Four centuries later it came into the possession of Sir Austen Henry Layard (1817–1894), British ambassador to the Porte and a good friend of the Turks, passing after his widow's death to the National Gallery (in 1917).[52]

Despite the grievous losses of the long war, Venice still held Lepanto, which stood like a sentinel on the northern shore of the Corinthian Gulf; Nauplia, with the dependent castle of Thermisi, *una fortezza inespugnabile*, where there were rich salt pans opposite the island of Hydra, and the fortified tower called Kastri, which was nearby, as well as the ruined fort of Civeri, across the narrow bay from Nauplia; Monemvasia, with its rugged hinterland of Vatika; the twin ports of Modon and Coron, always the "eyes" of the Republic in the Morea; and the islands of Corfu, Cerigo, and Crete, Aegina, Tenos, and Mykonos, as well as a few others in the southeastern Aegean. However much the peace of January, 1479, might be protested by Matthias Corvinus and lamented by Sixtus IV, the truth undoubtedly was that Venice had reached the point where she could no longer carry on the ruinous war.

The worst fears of Matthias Corvinus were not realized, although Turkish *saccomanni* did overrun Carniola and harass Hungary. In October, 1479, Stephen Báthory, the voivode of Transylvania, and Paul Kinizsi, the ban of Temesvar (Timişoara), defeated a large Turkish army in the "Field of Bread" (Kenyérmezö) on the Maros river, achieving one of the most remarkable victories in the long annals of Hungarian opposition to the Turks. There was no way to stop the Turkish devastation, however, and through the following summer some 16,000 raiders again pillaged Carniola, Carinthia, and Styria, taking great numbers of prisoners, including five hundred ecclesiastics.[53] The reader who looks upon the history of these years as merely a tedious record of death and destruction should pause for a moment to consider what it must have meant to live through them.

It may well be that the inhabitants of the Greek mainland, the Morea, and the Aegean islands were not always and immediately worse off under the Turks than they had been under the Graeco-Latin dynasts or the Venetian Signoria. It has also been claimed that the mountain roads in Serbia and Bosnia were safer after the Turkish conquests than in the earlier years of the local robber barons. Turkish destructiveness is too well attested for disbelief, however, and the later decades of the fifteenth century are a tragic chronicle of the terrible depredation wrought by the Turks' light cavalry (the *akinji* or *saccomanni*). We may well doubt that "it really seemed in the time of the Conqueror that the Byzantine security of the glorious past had returned, the *pax romana*, and that all might enjoy it."[54] Even the

---

[52] Angiolello, *Hist. turchesca*, ed. Ursu, pp. 120–21, with refs.; Thuasne, *Gentile Bellini et Sultan Mohammed II*, pp. 38–57; Franz Babinger, "Ein weiteres Sultansbild von Gentile Bellini?" in the *Sitzungsberichte der Österreichischen Akademie der Wissenschaften*, Philos.-hist. Kl., CCXXXVII-3 (1961), offprint of 16 pp. with plates, and *ibid.*, CCXL-3 (1962), offprint of 20 pp. with plates; "Ein vorgeblicher Gnadenbrief Mehmeds II. für Gentile Bellini (15 Jänner 1481)," *Italia medioevale e umanistica*, V (1962), 85–101. Layard excavated Nimrūd and Nineveh intermittently between 1845 and 1850 for the trustees of the British Museum, and served as his government's envoy to Istanbul from 1877 to 1880.

[53] Raynaldus, *Ann. eccl.*, ad ann. 1479, nos. 26–29, vol. XIX (1693), pp. 284–85; Iorga, *Gesch. d. osman. Reiches*, II, 181–82; Babinger, *Maometto*, pp. 555–60, 594–95. The documents published or summarized by Iorga, *Notes et extraits*, IV (1915), nos. CCXIV–CCC, pp. 312–76, and V (1915), nos. I–LXXIV, pp. 3–58, illustrate the German, Hungarian, and Italian preoccupation with the Turkish war during the half dozen or more years preceding 1479. In the summer of 1478 the Turks had ravaged Styria and Carinthia, after which the estates of Carniola had addressed a sharp remonstrance and rebuke to Frederick III, exhorting him to rouse himself from his sloth and slumber and protect his people from the infidels' depredation, on which see the old but useful monograph of Karl Haselbach, *Die Türkennoth im XV. Jahrhundert*, Vienna, 1864, pp. 46–47, and append., pp. IX–XV, who publishes the text of the estates' remonstrance. In 1479 legatine missions were sent to Germany, Hungary, Bohemia, and Poland to preach the crusade *contra Turchum* (Arch. Segr. Vaticano, Reg. Vat. 680, fols. 151 ff., 167 ff., by mod. stamped enumeration). On 30 November, 1482, Sixtus IV lamented the vast range and destructiveness of the Turkish invasions which reached into Austria and adjacent territories. Mehmed II was believed to be preparing for further attacks upon Styria, the province of Salzburg, Gorizia, and neighboring areas. Sixtus had resolved to renew his efforts against the Turks in order to achieve in eastern Europe some measure of the success which had been scored in their expulsion from Otranto the preceding year [see below, Chapter 12] (Reg. Vat. 548, fols. 273^r–278^v).

[54] Babinger, *Maometto*, p. 638.

writer who says this believes it not unlikely that Teodoro Spandugnino's statement that Mehmed II caused the deaths of 873,000 people is actually not far off the mark, "because as an annual average they would amount to about 29,000 victims for the man who made the world tremble: nor does this figure take into account the terrible harvest reaped by the black death as a result of the maelstrom of war during so many years of the Conqueror's reign over his people, so that vast areas of the countries struck by the plague were depopulated and perished. . . ."[55] On many a road there was greater peace than hitherto because there were neither travelers nor banditti left, but it is easy for the westerner to paint too grim a picture. Actually the Turkish conquest united a wide area of Orthodoxy in the Balkans under the patriarch of Constantinople, whose exposure to Moslem intolerance, political oppression, and financial extortion was probably little harder to bear than the earlier effects of Latin domination. And now at least there was less of the rancor generated by theological controversy with Rome.

Recent studies of the economic history of the Levant for the two centuries following the Turkish occupation of Constantinople have modified earlier accounts of economic stagnation. The passing years brought a revival of commerce to the Balkans under the so-called *pax ottomanica*, for Moslem law and the Ottoman state generally favored the merchant class. Artisans and shopkeepers, however, were caught in the straitjacket of a rigid guild system, which the East knew quite as well as the West. The Ottomans seem also to have taken over what remained of the Byzantine, Serbian, and other tax systems, and skillfully adapted them to their own use *in situ*, so to speak, which made life easier for the conservative peasants, who knew what to expect from year to year.[56] The generally short supply of specie in circulation, the exactions of the state in coin of good quality, and the tendency of the military élite to hoard gold, made barter a frequent method for the exchange of smaller quantities of goods. The Ottoman peace now made possible a considerable increase in the population, in Greece as elsewhere, after more than two centuries of constant warfare.

The economic recovery of the Balkans came well after the reign of Mehmed the Conqueror, but he did help start the process. In certain regions along the Danube and the Black Sea, Turkish merchants or their agents sold Persian silks, Italian woolens, Indian spices and dyes, and Anatolian mohair and cotton cloth; Turkish and especially Greek merchants became a familiar sight in Ancona, Florence, and Venice; and agents of Italian firms were usually on hand in the silk marts of Brusa (the Turkish Bursa). The western hinterland of the Black Sea supplied Istanbul with grain, meat, wool, hides, and other products, but the area was gradually closed to Italian shipping. According to Inalcik, "In 1490, of 157 merchants entering Caffa by sea, 16 were Greeks, 4 Italians, 2 Armenians, 3 Jews, 1 Russian, and 1 Moldavian; the remaining 130 were Muslim. The Muslim rarely penetrated inland from these ports; the goods were transported into Poland, the Crimean Khanate, the Desht-i Kipchak, and Russia by local merchants or by Armenians, Jews, and Greeks (mainly Ottoman subjects)."[57]

As time went on, Turks, Jews, and Greeks made fortunes in farming the taxes and the

[55] *Ibid.*, p. 633. As Angiolello has said of Mehmed II, his cruelties were "without number" (*Hist. turchesca*, ed. Ursu, pp. 121–23): ". . . delle sue crudeltà, le quali dirò che sono infinite. . . ."

[56] Speros Vryonis, Jr., "The Byzantine Legacy and Ottoman Forms," *Dumbarton Oaks Papers*, XXIII–XXIV (1969–70), 276–78.

[57] Halil Inalcik, "Capital Formation in the Ottoman Empire," *Journal of Economic History*, XXIX (1969), 112, and concerning the increasing volume of trade from the reign of Mehmed II on, see Inalcik, "Bursa and the Commerce of the Levant," *Journal of the Economic and Social History of the Orient*, III (Leiden, 1960), 131–47. At this point we may observe that economic and demographic data can be compiled in large detail from the surviving Ottoman records, because officials wanted to know the facts, and no one worried about the cost of paper. See, for example, the sixteenth-century statistical data culled by Bernard Lewis from 21 cadastral registers in the Ottoman archives in Istanbul for the four sanjaks of western Palestine—Safad, Nablus, Gaza, and Jerusalem, with a population of about 300,000 persons, from whom the Ottoman government drew about 6,330,000 aspers or about 800,000 gold pieces in revenue. The Palestinian sanjaks lay in the eyālet (or vilāyet) of Damascus, which was apparently well governed (Lewis, "Studies in the Ottoman Archives," *Bulletin of the School of Oriental and African Studies* [Univ. of London], XVI [1954], 469–501). Similar studies of sanjaks in the Balkans and Greece would be most valuable.

On 31 December, 1544, the Venetian Senate, reacting against the proposed publication of a papal bull excommunicating those who bought alum from the Turks and sold them "alcune robbe delle qual si possono servir in guerra contra Christiani" (as Venice did), noted that Turkish goods constantly entered the states of the Church, and that there was a Turkish colony in the papal city of Ancona! (Arch. di Stato di Venezia, Sen. Secreta, Reg. 63, fols. 204^r–205^r [224^r–225^r]). The Holy See had acquired Ancona in 1532, on which *cf.* below, Chapter 13, note 50.

customs duties. Money-changers and jewelers, textile manufacturers and brokers amassed sometimes huge sums, but the richest members of Ottoman society were high-ranking members of the military class, of whom there were many in the capital city of Istanbul and the high commandery at Adrianople (the Turkish Edirne), where military stores were assembled for the frequent campaigns into central Europe, and whence various goods, especially textiles, were also shipped throughout the Balkans. Harness, saddles, boots, shoes, and other leather goods were made in Adrianople. Large amounts of woolen cloth were woven at Thessalonica, especially for the janissaries. Iron was produced at Sofia, used extensively in Istanbul, and transported into various parts of the Levant from both Istanbul and Adrianople. It was a valuable commodity, the raw material of armament. Numerous papal bulls and briefs forbade Christians to sell iron to the Moslems, which of course they regularly did, for there are always high profits in contraband.

From the later fifteenth century to the eighteenth, the Turks were international traders and bankers. Pashas, beys, and sipahis invested heavily in commercial enterprises, and loaned money at interest to Balkan villagers to help them pay their poll taxes. Even the imams (Moslem "priests" or prayer-leaders) engaged in this lucrative business; the interest rates tended to rise with the inflation of the late sixteenth century (eventually to 25 per cent); and villagers in wide areas of the Ottoman empire were caught by usury in a morass from which they could never pull out. Pious foundations (in Turkish *evkāf*) invested their funds in toll bridges, flour-mills, vineyards, hostels, shops, saddleries, bathhouses, bakeries, tanneries, and the like, and were sometimes set up as family foundations, whose income was to support the founder's descendants.[58] Among Moslems as well as Christians there were many who believed that charity began at home.

The mechanics of buying and selling on credit were highly developed in the Ottoman empire. The great merchants pursued international commerce with a considerable degree of economic sophistication, following the exchange rates in the chief money markets of Europe as well as of the Levant. But Moslem laws and the customs of inheritance broke up a rich man's fortune at his death, into bequests for his various wives, the often numerous members of his family, and the pious foundations, to which Moslem society attached such large importance. The foundations were the only fictitious persons recognized by Moslem law; each generation of entrepreneurs had to start from the beginning. The century-long existence of the Medici bank was a European phenomenon. Such firms did not exist in the Ottoman empire.[59]

After the sack of Rome in 1527 the Italians took an increasingly gloomy view of life while the inhabitants of the erstwhile Byzantine empire enjoyed a large measure of internal peace under the Ottomans. For the Greeks, however, the fall of their "God-guarded" city on the Bosporus marked the end of an era, without the clear-cut beginning of another. Everything seemed left in limbo. The masses of the people in Greece and the Balkans were hardly well off, separated from their conquerors by the threefold barriers of language, religion, and tradition. An objective assessment of the efficiency of the Ottoman government, however, must await the publication of many more documents from the state archives in Istanbul (the *Basvekalet Arsivi*). Western historians have tended to regard the officers of the Porte as corrupt, for gifts or "bribery," expectation of *bakhshish*, was a way of life, but we actually know little of the judicial and administrative history of the Ottoman empire in the great period of the fifteenth and sixteenth centuries.

From the end of the fourteenth century the Turkish tribute in boys, the *devshirme*, levied on both towns and the countryside, was a source of anxiety to the parents of young sons (and of anguish when the *devshirme* fell on their household). The tribute in boys was widely exacted in the Balkans and, later on, in the surviving Christian communities of Anatolia.[60] During and after the time of Mehmed II the

[58] On the pious foundations and various religious endowments (called *waqf*, pl. *auqāf*, in Arabic, and *vakîf*, pl. *evkāf*, in Turkish), see H. A. R. Gibb and Harold Bowen, *Islamic Society and the West*, I-2 (London, 1957, repr. 1965), 165–78.

[59] Inalcik, "Capital Formation in the Ottoman Empire," *Journ. Econ. Hist.*, XXIX, 97–140.

[60] There is a brief sketch of the *devshirme*, with bibliography, by V. L. Ménage in the *Encycl. of Islām*, II (1965), 210–13; see also Speros Vryonis, Jr., "Isidore Glabas and the Turkish *Devshirme*," *Speculum*, XXX (1956), 433–43, and especially "Seljuk Gulams and Ottoman Devshirmes," *Der Islam*, XLI (1965), 224–52.

levy might be taken every five years or so, usually from among boys between the ages of about twelve and eighteen (or even older), who were removed to Istanbul, converted to Islam, taught Turkish, and eventually trained for military service in the janissaries' corps. Sometimes they were put to work on the land in Anatolia while they learned Turkish. Some of the brighter recruits were trained in the administrative offices of the state, whence after 1453 came the vizirs, provincial governors, generals, and high officials of the Porte.[61]

The gradual appearance of wealthy Greek merchants does not lighten very much the somber colors of the picture. There are always those whom chance, family connections, and their own enterprise will make exceptions to any general rule of misfortune, but in any event the wealth, power, and prestige of the Phanariotes came late, reaching (it is true) extraordinary heights in the eighteenth century when they began to dream of reviving old Byzantium.[62] In the meantime Mehmed the Conqueror carried on his relentless war against Christendom for almost thirty years after the fall of Constantinople, finally engaging in the spectacular ventures at Rhodes and Otranto. Continental Greece and the Morea were added to the Ottoman empire, the Balkans were entirely subdued, and terrible assaults launched upon Wallachia (Vlachia) and Hungary; Croatia, Carniola, and Carinthia; Styria and Austria. If the Greeks and certain of the Balkan peoples suffered the most, the Italians also sustained severe losses. It was the Turks who caused the decline of Italian commerce, often attributed to the voyages of Columbus and the opening up of the new Atlantic trade routes. In fact the discovery of these new routes was partly the consequence of the hardships which Italian commerce now faced in the Levant. The Venetians had fought the Turks almost single-handedly for some sixteen years, and at times it seemed as though more than six centuries of Venetian trade in eastern waters might be drawing to a close. A weakened Venice emerged from the war of 1463–1479, which was followed a generation later by the attacks upon her of her western neighbors in the League of Cambrai. In the mid-1470's the Turks captured the Genoese colonies of Caffa in the Crimea and Tana on the Sea of Azov, thus bringing to an end the long history of Genoese enterprise in the Black Sea.

The Black Sea became a Turkish lake, largely closed to Italian merchantmen. During the Conqueror's reign trade declined on the Danube, which with the Sava had formed a great highway between the Adriatic and the Black Sea from the earliest days of Roman colonization and the establishment of the legions in ancient Dacia. Despite numerous interruptions in its use, this highway had served to connect Italy and central Europe with the Black Sea through most of the middle ages. The

---

[61] *Cf.* Babinger, *Maometto*, pp. 639–41, and especially Gibb and Bowen, *Islamic Society and the West*, I-1 (1950, repr. 1963), 43, 56–66, 107 ff., 145, 179 ff., 314 ff., 356. The *devshirme* system was abandoned about the middle of the seventeenth century (*ibid.*, I-1, 180–81), although there were a few later levies (Ménage, *Encycl. of Islām*, II [1965], 212b). Incidentally, Gibb and Bowen, I-1, 113, state that the designation "Sublime Porte" refers to the official residence of the grand vizir, a huge building, which also contained the administrative offices of state (except that of finance), after 1654, when Sultan Mehmed IV conferred the building upon the then grand vizir, Dervish Mehmed Pasha, but their implication that "Sublime Porte" is thus incorrectly applied to the Turkish government before the mid-seventeenth century is inaccurate. The Venetians had used the expression for generations before the accession of Mehmed IV.

Almost at random I cull from my notes the term *Eccelsa Porta* in Venetian documents of March, 1543 (Sen. Secreta, Reg. 63, fols. 2^{r} [22^{r}], 3^{r} [23^{r}], 4^{v} [24^{v}], 7^{r} [27^{r}], *et passim*), and more to the point is the contemporary Italian translation of a letter from Sultan Suleiman to the Doge Francesco Donà, referring to "la fidel et sincera amicitia vostra antiqua con *la Sublime Porta nostra*," in the Arch. di Stato di Venezia, Documenti turchi, in a volume now labeled "A. Depeschen. No. 2: Verschiedenen Gesandten zu Konstantinopel" (the title being added during the time of the Austrian possession of the Venetian archives). We may find "Sublime Porte" in the official text of a letter dated 4 June, 1552, from the Venetian Senate to Sultan Suleiman (Sen. Secreta, Reg. 68, fol. 32^{v} [52^{v}]) as well as in documents dated 19 November and 22 December, 1567, and in numerous other documents of the same period in the Docc. turchi, volume labeled "No. II: Lettere diverse del Signor Turco, bassa, et altri, 1530 fin 1569:" ". . . alla presentia del magnifico et honorato Chubat Zaus della Sublime Porta;" "l'humile servo Cubat Chiaus della Sublime Porta. . . ." Indeed, the expression "Sublime Porte" appears in Venetian documents from early in the sixteenth century (Sen. Secreta, Reg. 50, fol. 149^{r} [161^{r}], doc. dated 13 June, 1525): "et questa operatione de . . . [le] nostre galie fu etiam alhora explicata *alla Sublime Porta della Celsitudine vostra*, et fu commendata. . . ."

[62] See in general the valuable study by Traian Stoianovich, "The Conquering Balkan Orthodox Merchant," *Journal of Economic History*, XX (1960), 234–313, with an extensive bibliography, to which may be added Ioakeim Martinianou, Ἡ Μοσχόπολις, Thessaloniki, 1957, on Greek, Graeco-Vlach, and Albanian merchants in Italy, Austria, and the Balkans. Moschopolis is the present-day (largely abandoned) Voskopojë, about twenty miles northwest of Korçë.

lines of trade and travel had of course been broken often, by Slavs and Avars, Bulgars, Magyars, and Germans, Pechenegs (Patzinaks), Uzes, Cumans (Polovtzi), and others. However, from the seventh century or so the volume of commerce had tended to increase, and the Byzantines could afford to purchase peace in the Balkans by paying tribute when necessary, for they usually got their money back again, owing to the favorable balance of trade they enjoyed with the more primitive peoples on their northern borders. The late Henri Pirenne maintained a well-known thesis to the effect that the Arabs closed the western Mediterranean from the late seventh century, causing the true end of antiquity and the beginning of the middle ages; that Frankish Gaul was largely debarred from trade with Italy and the East, and reverted to a purely agrarian economy; and that gold was abandoned for silver monometalism, markets were localized, and the towns disappeared. While Pirenne's critics have claimed that he disregarded many historical facts inconsistent with his theory, and paid insufficient attention to the chronology of known events from the seventh century to the tenth, his friend and colleague, Alexandre Eck, has applied some of his ideas to the history of south Russia in the eleventh and twelfth centuries. Eck has seen much the same debarment of south Russia from the trade routes which led to Byzantium, the lower Danube, the Crimea, and even the West as a consequence of the incursions of the Cumans, who are said to have made about fifty invasions of south Russia between 1055 and 1210. The once prosperous centers of trade were ruined by these invasions, and transformed into merely local markets: "ils se disloquaient, en se localisant." In the thirteenth century, according to Eck, the invasions of the Tatars completed the process, and south Russian society reverted to a purely agrarian economy.[63]

But Turkish hegemony over the Black Sea and the enterprise of Balkan merchants (as well as the decline of the Tatars) helped bring Russia back into the orbit of Mediterranean trade,[64] and as the economic pace quickened in the Balkans at the turn of the sixteenth century, landowners (as well as adventurous merchants) began to prosper again. In Rumelia and Bulgaria, Serbia and Bosnia, Wallachia and Hungary, great landed estates were being formed; serfdom was much increased; and large sums were made in grain growing and stock raising, especially by members of the Ottoman military class.[65]

---

[63] Eck, *Le Moyen-âge russe* (with a preface by Henri Pirenne), pp. 24–27, 29–32. Russian trade with the East by way of the Caspian had already been largely ruined in the ninth century by the coming of the Pechenegs, and disappeared entirely after the Mongolian invasion of Persia and Khorasan in the eleventh (*ibid.*, pp. 24–25). The Tatars destroyed the towns and civilization of eastern and central Russia, "making into a desert all the region of Kiev" (*ibid.*, pp. 25–26, 322 ff., 332 ff.). After the Turkish conquest of Caffa in 1475 the Tatars in the Crimea recognized the overlordship of Sultan Mehmed II (Mustafa A. Mehmed, "La Politique ottomane à l'égard de la Moldavie et du khanat de Crimée vers la fin du règne du sultan Mehmed II 'le Conquérant,'" *Revue roumaine d'histoire*, XIII-3 [1974], 509–33, esp. pp. 523 ff.). As for the Pirenne thesis, the complexity of the sources, and the need for a judicious interpretation of the evidence, note the learned article of Eliyahu Ashtor, "Quelques Observations d'un orientaliste sur la thèse de Pirenne," *Journal of the Economic and Social History of the Orient*, XIII-2 (1970), 166–94. Ashtor has made a brilliant defense of the Pirenne thesis in recent articles: "Che cosa sapevano i geografi arabi dell' Europa occidentale?" in the *Rivista storica italiana*, LXXXI (1969), 453–79; "Nouvelles Reflexions sur la thèse de Pirenne," *Schweizerische Zeitschrift für Geschichte*, XX (1970), 601–7; and "Aperçus sur les Radhanites," *ibid.*, XXVII (1977), 245–75.

[64] In the sixteenth century Russian trade increased dramatically. It was carried on chiefly with the English and Dutch, who often came by the White Sea. Eck, *Le Moyen-âge russe*, pp. 348–65, gives an informative account of this trade, but believes that the Turks hindered Russian economic expansion to the south (*ibid.*, pp. 352, 356), which is doubtless true, but a fair abundance of Russian furs and other products reached the Mediterranean through middlemen in Istanbul.

[65] The economic and social history of Ottoman domination in Bulgaria and Serbia, Wallachia, Transylvania, and Moldavia, Macedonia and Greece (as well as in Hungary and even Bohemia) cannot be properly written without large employment of the extant Turkish sources. Aside from the rich archival materials in Turkey (and Egypt), thousands of Turkish documents and various relevant literary works exist in manuscript in the Central Historical State Archives and the Cyril and Methodius National Library in Sofia and elsewhere although, to be sure, there are relatively few extant documents concerning the Balkans earlier than the sixteenth century.

Much progress has been made in weighing the social and cultural impact of the Turks upon the Balkan peoples, but formidable tasks still lie ahead, as emphasized by J. Kabrda, "Les Problèmes de l'étude de l'histoire de la Bulgarie à l'époque de la domination turque," *Byzantinoslavica*, XV (1954), 173–208, and note the same author's "Les Anciens Registres turcs des cadis de Sofia et de Vidin et leur importance pour l'histoire de la Bulgarie," *Archiv Orientální*, XIX (Prague, 1951), 329–92, and "Les Sources turques relatives à l'histoire de la domination ottomane en Slovaquie," *ibid.*, XXIV (1956), 568–80. On the untapped riches of the Ottoman archives in Istanbul, the most important of all for the European provinces of the empire, see the notice by Bernard Lewis, "The Ottoman Archives," *Archives*, IV

When the Turks closed the Black Sea to Italian shipping, the Porte gradually organized the resources of the region for the benefit of the state. Wallachians and Moldavians, Jews and Armenians, Turks and Greeks, and not only those in Istanbul, were able to take over the trade which had formerly been in Venetian and Genoese hands.[66] In his widely read biography of Mehmed II, the late Franz Babinger has emphasized a familiar theme, to which we have already alluded:

It can be maintained without exaggeration that even the discovery of the new maritime routes across the Atlantic with the profound changes which they produced in the economy of the West must be viewed in relation to the Ottomans' territorial expansion into the area of the Black Sea. The voyages of exploration to the New World were supposed to find another connection with India and the interior of Asia, because the ways followed up to that time were henceforth completely blocked by the Moslem states, and the long-range elimination of this barrier could no longer be hoped for.[67]

If the reader finds nothing novel in this, he will understand that these facts could be just as clear to those who lived in the late fifteenth century. The economic significance of Mehmed II's conquests was well understood by the Venetians, who had begun in the war of 1463–1479 more than two centuries of determined effort against the Ottoman empire to prevent the dissolution of the Republic's entire commercial establishment in the Levant, for when the banner of the winged lion no longer floated over the fortresses in the Morea, the Aegean islands, and Crete, Venice could herself sink to the level of any other state in Italy. She had, to be sure, already extended her sway to include Friuli in the north (in 1420) and Bergamo in the west (1441), reaching the Adda as her boundary with the Milanese duchy, while she pressed south against Ferrara to Ravenna and Cervia.[68] Thus she protected

---

(1960), 226–30. The periodical literature is most conveniently located in J. D. Pearson, *Index Islamicus (1906–1955)*, Cambridge, England: Heffer, 1958, repr. 1961, esp. pp. 568–88, with the *Supplements*, 1962, pp. 178–85, and *ibid.*, 1967, pp. 191–92. The Turks "cut off from their past" the Serbs and (even more) the Bulgarians, and A. Vaillant has sketched the linguistic consequences in a brief essay on "Les Langues slaves méridionales et la conquête turque," *Byzantinoslavica*, XIV (1953), 123–29. The Greek past was far too strong for obliteration.

[66] In central and eastern Europe from the mid-fifteenth century, as everywhere and at all times, political and economic affairs went hand in hand. The rulers of Hungary and Poland debased their coinage (an inflationary measure) to pay their troops as the Poles carried on war with the Teutonic Knights (in 1453–1466), and at one time or another the Hungarians took the field against the Turks, the Czechs, and the Germans. Polish and Hungarian merchants, with their debased coinage, exported the inflation of their homelands into Wallachia and Moldavia, where the voivodes responded in a *guerre monétaire* by devaluing their own coinage and prohibiting the export of gold and silver beyond the borders of the Rumanian principalities. The voivodes also restricted foreign commerce to certain designated marts or "staples."

After Wallachia and Moldavia had fallen under Turkish suzerainty, however, the voivodes usually kept their coinage in alignment with that of the Porte, and as tribute-paying subjects of the sultan their merchants had free access to the markets at Adrianople, Istanbul, and Bursa (Brusa). Since for a time the Turks exercised less economic than political domination, the Rumanians (if we may so call them), continuing their mercantilist restrictions on foreign coinage and commerce, enjoyed a notable prosperity until the Turks bore down on them in the later sixteenth century. During their good period the Wallachian and Moldavian traders tended to displace the Genoese in the Ottoman markets. See especially Matei Cazacu, "L'Impact ottoman sur les pays roumains et ses incidences monétaires (1452–1504)," *Revue roumaine d'histoire*, XII-1 (1973), 159–92, and *cf.* the general survey by Carl M. Kortepeter, "Ottoman Imperial Policy and the Economy of the Black Sea Region in the Sixteenth Century," *Journal of the American Oriental Society*, LXXXVI-2 (1966), 86–113, esp. pp. 96 ff.

[67] Babinger, *Maometto*, p. 511, a topic of perennial discussion, on which *cf.* A. H. Lybyer, "The Ottoman Turks and the Routes of Oriental Trade," *English Historical Review*, XXX (1915), 577–88, and the older works there cited. Although the Turks were more interested in conquest, they had no antipathy to trade, and (until the eighteenth century) they indulged in it freely. The object of Ottoman military and naval enterprise was, however, the control of land and its products, yielding lucrative taxes, in the Balkans and throughout the eastern Mediterranean, including Egypt after 1517. The Ottomans sought ascendancy over land masses, and used their galleys like the janissaries, to hold them together in taxable, administrable districts (*eyālets* divided into *sanjaks*). The chief objective of the maritime states of the West was to maintain trading stations, whence they might reap wealth from commerce.

While the Venetians had largely to concentrate their efforts in the eastern Mediterranean, where the Turks met them in direct and dire confrontation, the Portuguese could circumnavigate Africa, enter the Red Sea and the Persian Gulf, and press on to gather some of the wealth of the Indies. The Portuguese encountered the Turks only on the southern (Arabian) periphery of the Ottoman empire (after 1517), and these encounters were not such as either to exhaust the Portuguese or to divert them from their commercial goals, on which see in general Andrew C. Hess, "The Evolution of the Ottoman Seaborne Empire in the Age of the Oceanic Discoveries," *American Historical Review*, LXXV (1970), 1892–1919, with much recent bibliography. The Venetians were caught in the Mediterranean by the commitments incurred from the time of the Fourth Crusade on, as well as by their geographical location.

[68] Kretschmayr, *Gesch. v. Venedig*, II (1920, repr. 1964), 265–69, 334, 347–48, 353–54.

the gateways to her European trade on land, as she was trying to do in the Levant on the sea; her conquests on *terra ferma* were very costly, but they were also very lucrative. It was the same *d'oltre mare*, where the profits were high, if she could only maintain her position. It was probably not pride alone, as Toynbee seems to think,[69] that kept the Venetians in the long struggle against the Turks. As Galeazzo Maria Sforza, duke of Milan, had reminded the Venetian diplomat Giovanni Gonela in October, 1467, "Dubius est eventus belli."[70] Venice might win at sea as well as lose on land (or vice versa), but she could not hold her own against the Turks by withdrawing from the contest. If she spent millions on the Turkish wars, she also made millions in the East.

By the year 1478 Lorenzo de' Medici's unwavering opposition to Sixtus IV's temporal ambitions had produced a state of dangerous hostility between the Florentine Signoria and the Holy See. The pope's nephew, Girolamo Riario, the lord of Imola, and the old Florentine family of the Pazzi joined forces to effect the overthrow of the Medici, which would in their opinion free papal hands to build up the states of the Church and restore liberty to the republic on the Arno. On Sunday, 26 April, 1478, during the celebration of high mass in the Duomo in Florence, the so-called conspiracy of the Pazzi sought to achieve these purposes by the murder of Lorenzo de' Medici and his brother Giuliano, grandsons of the great Cosimo. Giuliano fell beneath the blows of Francesco de' Pazzi and Bernardo Bandini de' Baroncelli. Lorenzo was only slightly wounded, however, and escaped behind the bronze door of the Old Sacristy, which the humanist Angelo Poliziano promptly locked behind him. The conspirators also failed in their efforts to seize the Palazzo Vecchio and arouse the people to their support by the cry of freedom. Almost all the guilty were slain in the hours and days that followed, and Lorenzo availed himself of the excitement to put various of his other enemies out of the way also. But Bernardo Bandini, who had been the first to strike down Giuliano, escaped on a Neapolitan galley to Istanbul, where he had friends and relatives (a Carlo de' Baroncelli served as Florentine consul at Pera from 1472 to 1476). His subsequent extradition forms an interesting chapter in the history of Florentine relations with the Ottoman court. Lorenzo de' Medici emerged from the dastardly attempt upon his life before the altar of S. Reparata more firmly in control of the state than ever. In vain did Sixtus IV impose the ban of major excommunication upon him (on 1 June) and the interdict upon the outraged citizens and other subjects of Florence (on 22 June).[71] In July the principals in the great contest, which attracted the attention of all

[69] A. J. Toynbee, *Study of History*, IV (London, 1951), 274–89, has an interesting excursus on the latter-day history of Venice to the effect that she tried to maintain S. Mark's imperial estate in the East when she could no longer afford to do so, needlessly expending great numbers of lives and quantities of treasure "in a sphere where the policy was ruinous from every material standpoint" (p. 279). When Pieter Geyl in criticism of these pages in Toynbee asks (*Debates with Historians*, Groningen and The Hague, 1955, p. 113), "Was there really a large percentage of the Venetian aristocracy that bled in the Turkish wars?" I think the sources enable us to answer him in the affirmative. We may be unwilling, nevertheless, to accept Toynbee's assertion that it was as with ancient "Athens' fatal aberration of idolizing her own dead self" (p. 274) that Venice poured her resources into the long and unsuccessful War of Candia (1645–1669), and thereafter joined Pope Innocent XI's Holy League against the Turks (1684–1699), struggling always to recreate the past "in her infatuation with the dead self of her medieval Levantine glory" (p. 281). I think that Toynbee's thesis is at best a half-truth, born rather of rationalization than a study of the documents. It is obviously easier for a historian to speculate on the decline of Venetian fortunes, when he knows they declined, than it was for the Senate and Council of Ten to formulate policy by trying to weigh the risks of an enterprise against the rewards of success. *Chi non s'arrischia non guadagna*. If the first of the two wars to which Toynbee refers did not prevent the loss of Crete, the second regained the Morea for some time (and both dealt severe blows to Turkish power and prestige). Venetian policy, even that of Vettore Capello (see, above, pp. 283–85), was almost always dictated by practical considerations, which explains the survival of the Republic as an independent state until 1797.

[70] Malipiero, *Annali veneti*, ad ann. 1467, in *Arch. stor. italiano*, VII-1 (1843), 218.

[71] Arch. Segr. Vaticano, Arm. XXXI, tom. 62, fols. 164^r–170^v, by mod. stamped enumeration, "datum Rome apud Sanctum Petrum, anno incarnationis dominice, MCCCC-LXXVIII, Kal. Iunii, pontificatus nostri anno septimo," the condemnation of Lorenzo and his associates, and, *ibid.*, fols. 170^v–173^r, "datum . . . decimo Kalendas Iulii . . . ," the imposition of the interdict on all Florentine territories. Various other anti-Florentine bulls followed in the course of the next fourteen months (*ibid.*, fols. 173^v–183^v, 210^r–214^r, 216^v–217^r). All who took service under the Florentines, accepted remuneration from them, or rendered them the slightest assistance were declared subject to the same ecclesiastical penalties. Actually Florence, Fiesole, and Pistoia had been placed under immediate interdict on 1 June, 1478, by the bull excommunicating Lorenzo (*ibid.*, fol. 169^v). Carlo de'Baroncelli was appointed Florentine *consul Levantis* in Pera on 3 September, 1472 (G. Müller, *Documenti sulle relazioni delle città toscane coll'oriente cristiano e coi Turchi*, Florence, 1879, pt. I, no. 172, pp. 216–17, and *cf.* no. 175). Carlo returned to Florence in 1476 (*ibid.*, no. 182, p. 221).

Europe, had recourse to the so-called "Tuscan war."[72]

From consideration of a large issue we may descend for a moment to a small one, and follow briefly the fortunes of Bernardo Bandini de' Baroncelli, who after his escape to Istanbul was arrested by Mehmed II, probably at the beginning of May, 1479. On 18 June, a secretary of the Signoria wrote Lorenzo Carducci, the Florentine consul in Pera:

> By letters of Bernardo Peruzzi we have learned with great pleasure how that most glorious prince [Mehmed] has seized Bernardo Bandini, most heinous parricide and traitor to his country, and declares himself willing to do with him whatever we may want—a decision certainly in keeping with the love and great favor he has always shown toward our Republic and our people [*natione*] as well as with the justice of his most serene Majesty. . . . [And] although as a result of the innumerable benefits done by his most glorious Majesty in the past for the Republic and our people, we owe him the greatest indebtedness and are the most faithful and obedient sons of his Majesty, nevertheless because of this last benefit it would be impossible to describe the extent to which our obligation to his most serene Majesty has grown. . . .[73]

The historian of Italy may find it sad to note that through the years when Venice fought, however unwillingly, for the Christian cause in Greece and the Aegean, the Florentines had been receiving such favors from the Porte as to make them the sultan's "most faithful and obedient sons," but obviously the internecine rivalries in the peninsula had for centuries made such developments part of the expected course of events.

On 5 July, 1479, and again on the tenth the Signoria sent letters to the consul and the Florentine merchants in Pera, having finally received the consul's letter (dated 8 May) containing the same news that Bernardo Peruzzi had sent from Istanbul "of the arrest there of Bernardo Bandini, impious parricide and rebel against us." The consul was informed that Antonio de' Medici was being sent to the Porte as a special envoy. He was expected to be "on the road at the latest within eight days, for the journey by land." The sultan had said that he would hold the assassin until the middle of August, and so haste was necessary for the Signoria to arrange for his return to Florence. Nothing in the world seemed of higher importance, the consul was informed, than the punishment of Bandini, and that official must see to it that the culprit was kept alive, and must render every assistance to Antonio de' Medici, the envoy, upon his arrival in Istanbul. Full instructions were issued to Antonio, who was to acquaint himself fully with the ceremonies attending the reception of ambassadors at the Porte and, when granted an audience, to explain "il caso nostro de dì 26 di aprile dello anno passato," i.e., to describe to the sultan the murder of Giuliano, the attempt on Lorenzo's life, and the political significance of these events in the affairs of Florence. Antonio's instructions are dated 11 July. He left for Istanbul on the fourteenth. His mission was successful, and he arrived back in Florence on 24 December, bringing the miserable Bandini with him. On the twenty-ninth Bandini was hanged from the windows of the Bargello. Leonardo da Vinci sketched his dangling body (the drawing is now in the Musée Bonnat in Bayonne). The Signoria sent the sultan an official letter of thanks on 11 May, 1480, together with excuses for the failure of Florentine ships to make the voyage to Istanbul for some time: conditions in Italy had rendered the voyage impossible without the gravest danger to men and ships and goods.[74]

In the meantime King Ferrante of Naples had entered the "Tuscan war" on the papal side, hoping to acquire Siena, which was itself supporting the pope. Lorenzo de' Medici's appeals for aid were favorably received in Venice,

[72] *Diarium parmense*, ad ann. 1478, in *RISS*, XXII (Milan, 1733), cols. 277–79 and ff.; *cf*. Sanudo, *Vite de'duchi*, *ibid*., col. 1207; Raynaldus, *Ann. eccl*., ad ann. 1478, nos. 1–33, vol. XIX (1693), pp. 270–77; Pastor, *Hist. Popes*, IV, 300–20; append., nos. 57–58, pp. 512–15, and *Gesch. d. Päpste*, II, 532–47; append., nos. 123–24, pp. 785–87; and see especially Francesca Morandini, "Il Conflitto fra Lorenzo il Magnifico e Sisto IV dopo la congiura de' Pazzi," *Arch. stor. italiano*, CVII (1950), 113–54, which is based upon the correspondence of Lorenzo with Girolamo Morelli, the Florentine ambassador to Milan.

[73] Müller, *Documenti*, pt. I, no. 189, pp. 225–26.

[74] Müller, *Documenti*, pt. I, no. 189, pp. 226–28, and *cf*. p. 501; no. 191, pp. 230–31; the contemporary annalist of Parma tells the story briefly, confusing Bandini with "Franciscus de Bardis" (*Diarium parmense*, in *RISS*, XXII, col. 329CD). See in general Franz Babinger, "Lorenzo de' Medici e la corte ottomana," *Arch. stor. italiano*, CXXI (1963), 305–61, esp. pp. 316–17, and *Maometto*, pp. 572–75. In the Archivio di Stato di Firenze, Dieci di Balia: Carteggi, Responsive, Reg. 25 (old classification: Cl. X, disting. 4, no. 25), fol. 73 (renumbered fol. 78), I find Antonio de' Medici's report to the Signori Dieci with respect to Bernardo Bandini, dated 12 November, 1479. An annotation on the reverse of the letter indicates that it was received in Florence on 16 December.

Milan, Ferrara, and France. For the preceding half-dozen years Louis XI had been threatening the pope with the restoration of the Pragmatic Sanction (which under royal protection asserted the liberties of the Gallican Church) and with the alleged necessity of summoning an oecumenical council for ecclesiastical reform. The Venetians could be counted on to support any action against Ferrante. Fearful of the coalition being formed against him, Sixtus IV relaxed the bans against Lorenzo and the Florentines on 4 April, 1479, and declared a temporary restoration of peace. Believing the pope's gesture to be an effort to placate the French, who were pro-Florentine, his opponents refused his tentative proposals for peace, and on 27 May sent him through the Venetian ambassador to the Holy See an ultimatum that, if he did not conclude a final peace within eight days (thus giving him insufficient time to consult Naples and Siena), they would recall their envoys from the Curia. Sixtus IV had no alternative to refusal. The ambassadors of the Italian states in the coalition left Rome in June. But if the futility of Lorenzo's hope of assistance from France was made manifest by the fall of 1479, the pope's expectations of Ferrante were soon shown to be equally illusory. In December Lorenzo made his famous visit to Naples, appealing in person for peace, and Ferrante, who was as infirm as faithless, abandoned his understanding with the pope, who now lacked the means of attaining victory. The war dragged on in desultory fashion until November, 1480, when a Florentine embassy to Rome made peace with the pope, who finally removed the ecclesiastical bans on 3 December, 1480.[75] Shortly thereafter Baccio Pontelli began work on the church of S. Maria della Pace, which still stands as a memorial to Sixtus's peace with the Florentines.

Lorenzo de' Medici's pact with Ferrante of Naples, which was confirmed in March, 1480, had not immediately released Florence from the hardships and constraint of war. Pope Sixtus's distrust of Ferrante now strongly inclined him toward the Venetians, from whom Lorenzo still hoped for support. A shift occurred in diplomatic relations in the peninsula. The Holy See and Venice faced the triple alliance of Naples, Florence, and Milan. The change was not as great as one might think, however, for Venice and Naples were still on opposing sides. When Sixtus joined the Venetians, he made the claim of every statesman entering an alliance with hostile intent. He was doing it all for peace.[76] Ferrante's bold son Alfonso, the duke of Calabria, entered Siena toward the end of June, and in August Sixtus's nephew Girolamo Riario added the county of Forli to his possession of Imola.[77] Riario

---

[75] Pastor, *Hist. Popes*, IV, 320–30, with append., nos. 59–63, pp. 515–18, and *Gesch. d. Päpste*, II, 547–57, with append., nos. 125–29, pp. 787–89; *Diarium parmense*, ad ann. 1479–1480, in *RISS*, XXII, cols. 302E–303A, 304 ff., 328–29 ff., 335E; Sanudo, *Vite de'duchi*, *ibid.*, cols. 1209–11. The French view of Italian affairs, with some mention of the Gran Turco's relation thereto, was summarized by the Florentine ambassador to Paris, Guidantonio, in a letter to the Signori Dieci from Paris on 6 August, 1479 (Arch. di Stato di Firenze: Dieci di Balia: Carteggi, Responsive, Reg. 25, fol. 123, renum. 131, and *cf.* fols. 135, 139, 170).

[76] In a brief dated 20 May, 1480, addressed to the Marquis Federico Gonzaga, Sixtus IV stated, "Cupientes ut omnium Italie potentatuum generalis aliqua unio subsequatur, ad quam omnia consilia nostra semper rettulimus, pro communi reipublice Christiane utilitate inivimus nuper quandam cum dominio Venetorum intelligentiam. . . . Que quidem intelligentia sine cuiusque offensione est, solum ad defensionem status Sancte Romane Ecclesie instituta, ea quidem spe ut reliqui quoque ad eandem accessuri sint quibus honorabilem ingrediendi locum reliquimus et ad eundem finem diebus superioribus pacem inter reliquos Italie potentatus Neapoli factam ratificavimus . . ." (Arch. di Stato di Mantova, Arch. Gonzaga, Busta 834).

On 16 April, 1480, a twenty-five years' mutual assistance pact had been arranged between the Venetian Doge Giovanni Mocenigo and his successors and Pope Sixtus and his successors "for the preservation and tranquillity of all Italy" (Arch. Segr. Vaticano, A.A., Arm. I–XVIII, no. 1443, fols. 100^v–102^v). On the same day Sixtus had written the doge that Giovanni della Rovere, count of Sinigaglia (Senigallia), duke of Sora, and prefect of Rome, and Girolamo Riario, papal vicar of Imola, "secundum carnem nepotes [nostri]," would always be faithful to Venice, which had extended its protection to them (Pasolini, *Caterina Sforza*, III [1893], doc. no. 142, pp. 70–71). On 1 May Riario promised fealty to the Venetians, who took him under their wing "statumque meum tam presentem quam quem me in Italia adipisci quoquo modo contigeret in futurum" (*ibid.*, III, no. 143, p. 71). The documents are preserved in the Venetian Commemoriali, Reg. 16, fols. 161–62.

[77] Pasolini, *Caterina Sforza*, I, 104–5. Girolamo Riario also aspired to possession of Pesaro, from which he wanted to oust Costanzo Sforza, whose Milanese relatives were prepared to defend him. On 17 May, 1480, an envoy of the anxious Costanzo appeared before the Venetian Senate; "gratulatus est de federe inito cum summo pontifice;" sought some assurance of Venetian protection against Riario; and was informed that the Senate would bear his interests in mind, but that the Republic was under no obligation to Pesaro (Arch. di Stato di Venezia, Sen. Secreta, Reg. 29, fols. 101^v–102^r [111^v–112^r]). For a while the Neapolitans played with the idea of encouraging Riario to aim at Faenza rather than Pesaro, but Lorenzo did not want Riario so close to Florence. There was much intrigue at Naples, and even more at Milan. Federigo da Montefeltro, duke of

nurtured an abiding disappointment that the conspiracy of the Pazzi had not succeeded in killing Lorenzo; the pope still hoped to oust the Medici from Florence in one way or another. Now, however, Mehmed II rendered Lorenzo a much greater service than the extradition of Bandini. He also relieved the Venetians of the necessity of taking more vigorous and more costly measures against the Neapolitans. In late July, 1480, the Turks landed in force at Otranto, in the heel of the Italian boot.

Having made peace with Sultan Mehmed in January, 1479, the Venetians intended to stay at peace with him. In April a Turkish envoy, Lutfi Beg, appeared before the Doge Giovanni Mocenigo and the Collegio. He brought letters from Mehmed, and explained the latter's "comandamenti" to the Signoria, requesting confirmation of the peace "made between your Highness and us," as the Senate wrote the sultan on 4 May, "through negotiation with our most faithful secretary, Giovanni Dario." The Senate confirmed all the articles of the pact which Dario had made with the Porte, and did so "with a glad heart," swearing to abide by every detail of the agreement. A bailie would be sent immediately to Istanbul. He had already been chosen. He would attend to whatever was necessary for the "observantia dei capitoli" from the standpoint of Venice, and the Senate begged the sultan to instruct "all his sanjakbeyis and subashis" in Turkish territories bordering upon those of the Republic not to make unwarranted demands upon Venetian officials. They should all live together as good neighbors "ala bona amicicia reintegrata fra nuy."[78]

Battista Gritti would serve as the Republic's bailie to Istanbul. The motion was now made in the Senate, however, and carried by seventy votes to two, with four neutral votes (*non sinceri*), to send an *honorabilis orator* to the Porte. Refusal to accept the post would entail a fine of five hundred ducats. Benedetto Trevisan was elected, and agreed to go. As ambassador, he was to receive two hundred ducats a month salary for the first four months in office and thereafter one hundred ducats. He would be allowed to take with him a notary (who might have one servant), a chaplain, ten male servitors (*domicelli*), and a cook, all "at the expense of our Signoria," and he was authorized to spend five ducats a day for the maintenance of his whole household.[79]

On 21 May the Senate voted that Trevisan must embark upon his new responsibilities with all possible speed.[80] His commission, dated 12 June, prescribes his route in full detail. He was not to spend more than two days in any one place. The voyage to Istanbul was to take him first to Spalato, next to Cattaro, thence into the area of Antivari, thereafter to Dulcigno, Durazzo, Corfu, Lepanto, Modon, Coron, and Nauplia, and so to the shores of the Bosporus, where he would present his letters of credence *iuxta consuetudinem* and distribute to the pashas the gifts he was bringing with him (the value of which had been determined by the Collegio). All along the way Trevisan was to inquire minutely into the pre-war boundaries between Venetian and Turkish territories as well as into the recent activities of Turkish subashis and *flamburi*. He must look into the various problems relating to the export and import of merchandise and salt, which had caused difficulties in the past. Trevisan was to learn all he could about such matters, so that he might see to the proper resolution of all differences between the sultan and the Signoria, and thus guarantee the continuance of the hard-won peace.

Like every ambassador, Venetian or otherwise, he was to keep his eyes and ears open to learn whatever he could which might have a bearing upon the commerce or the foreign policy of his government. The Senate now wished, however, particularly to know "whether envoys of King Ferrante as well as of the king

---

Urbino, was said to be about to attack Pesaro on Pope Sixtus's behalf, and in June, 1480, the Venetian Senate sent Zaccaria Barbaro as their ambassador to Rome with instructions to urge the pope to give up any plans he had for war.

Such was the diplomatic confusion in Italy, however, that the Senate informed Barbaro that they found it difficult to understand some of the contradictions of policy that the Italian princes seemed to be pursuing (Sen. Secreta, Reg. 29, fol. 108^v [118^v]), on which see in general Edoardo Piva, "L'Opposizione diplomatica di Venezia alle mire di Sisto IV su Pesaro e ai tentativi di una crociata contro i Turchi, 1480–1481," *Nuovo Archivio veneto*, new series, anno II (1902), tom. V, pt. 1, pp. 49–104 (cited hereafter as Piva, I); *ibid.*, pt. 2, pp. 422–66 (Piva, II); and *ibid.*, anno III (1903), tom. VI, pt. 1, pp. 132–72 (Piva, III).

[78] Arch. di Stato di Venezia, Sen. Secreta, Reg. 29, fols. 14^v–15^r [24^v–25^r], doc. dated 4 May, 1479. The letter was, as usual, approved by the Senate, and sent in the doge's name.

[79] Sen. Secreta, Reg. 29, fol. 15^r [25^r], resolution of the Senate also dated 4 May, 1479.

[80] *Ibid.*, fol. 16^v [26^v].

of Hungary are or have been there [in Istanbul], and whether they have reached any sort of peace or are trying to do so, and you will work in opposition to their machinations, which will all be motivated by ill-will toward us and to our disadvantage, so that their perfidy may be understood. . . ." It had been reported in Venice that the lord of Andros, Crusino II Sommaripa, had been captured by the Turks, with a large number of other persons *et . . . cum omni supelectile*. Trevisan must find out whether this was true or not. If it was true, he must determine whether Crusino's capture had happened before or after the conclusion of the peace. But even if it had taken place before the *pax conclusa*, Trevisan was to do his utmost to secure the release of all the captives.[81]

For months and years every Venetian effort was to be directed toward peace with the Turks. The instructions which on 3 June, 1480, the Senate gave Zaccaria Barbaro, their new ambassador to the Curia Romana, directed him to work for peace in Italy and to avoid involvement in the general league being planned (or at least discussed) against the Turks.[82] The Senate regarded the enmity of Ferrante, Lorenzo de' Medici, and the Milanese as quite enough for Venice and the Holy See to contend with, for (as Barbaro was reminded) Ferrante was a rogue, thoroughly untrustworthy, ready to make and break promises as the fancy seized him, and fearful of the alliance which Sixtus had recently made with the Republic. The Turks were holding a great naval armament in readiness at Valona. They might descend upon Italy at a moment's notice if they saw the Italian states at armed odds with one another. In fact, some months before this (on 23 August, 1479), during the Tuscan war, the Senate had politely declined the proposal of Gedük Ahmed Pasha, the conqueror of Caffa (in 1475) and now commander in the district (*sanjak*) of Valona, to attack the pope and the king of Naples, both of whom he declared to be the bitterest enemies of the Signoria. Ahmed Pasha's envoy to Venice had stated that his master was ready to attack either with or without Venetian assistance.[83] Obviously

[81] *Ibid.*, fols. 18^{v}–21^{v} [28^{v}–31^{v}], from Trevisan's commission, dated 12 June, 1479, and in general note fols. 30^{v}–31^{v}, 32, 34^{v}–35^{r}, 67^{r}–68^{r}, 80, 82, 86^{r}, 90 ff. [40^{v}–41^{r}, 42, etc.]. Conditions remained tense along the Veneto-Turkish front (fols. 149^{v} ff. [159^{v} ff.], and, *ibid.*, Reg. 30, fols. 11 ff. [21 ff.]).

[82] Sen. Secreta, Reg. 29, fol. 109^{r} [119^{r}]: ". . . Altera pars importantissima est de liga generali que tentatur, et in hoc non erimus ita diffusi quoniam materia non exigit et quoniam sufficienter opinionem nostram summo pontifici declaravimus . . . ," on which see Piva, I, 71–72 ff., 90 ff., who incorrectly dates Barbaro's instructions 4 June (*ibid.*, I, 66 ff.). Barbaro had previously been appointed Venetian envoy to the duke of Ferrara in October, 1479 (Sen. Secreta, Reg. 29, fols. 48^{v}–49^{r} [58^{v}–59^{r}]).

[83] Sen. Secreta, Reg. 29, fol. 32^{r} [42^{r}]: "Quod oratori Achmat basse, qui ex Avalona huc venit et ea exposuit que huic consilio per serenissimum dominum ducem relata fuerunt de optima dispositione illustrissimi domini Turci et suprascripti basse ad conservationem pacis . . . et tandem de voluntate eiusdem basse offendendi vel una nobiscum vel sine nobis modo id requiratur tam pontificem quam regem Ferdinandum, quos ambos affirmabat esse hostes acerrimos nostri dominii . . . respondeatur in hunc modum . . . ," the reply being in effect that, with all respect to the pasha, whom the Venetians loved and esteemed (as they did the sultan, with whom they enjoyed a peace which they appreciated more with each passing day), the contestants in the Tuscan war had inflicted no injuries upon the citizens of their opponents in their respective territories. Venetian merchants had suffered no losses either in the papal states or in the Neapolitan kingdom. *Cf.* Piva, I, 72–73, who would exonerate the Venetians of the charge that in various ways they encouraged the Turks to launch an attack upon southern Italy.

Piva's point of view was challenged by Felice Fossati, "Alcuni Dubbi sul contegno di Venezia durante la ricuperazione d'Otranto (1480–1481)," *Nuovo Archivio veneto*, new ser., XII (1906), 5–35, and *cf.* the same writer's article "Dal 25 luglio 1480 al 16 aprile 1481: l'opera di Milano," *Arch. stor. lombardo*, 4th ser., XII (1909), 137–203. Fossati believes that Venice saw in the Turkish invasion a means of clipping Ferrante's wings, forcing him to give up the Florentine territory which the duke of Calabria had occupied during the Tuscan war (Milan was also insisting upon this), and putting a stop to the further aggrandizement of the Aragonese dynasty in Italy. But since the Turks held Valona, their permanent establishment at Otranto would have bottled up the Venetians in the Adriatic, and would have soon destroyed the commercial empire of the Republic, as Alessio Bombaci, "Venezia e l'impresa turca di Otranto," *Rivista storica italiana*, LXVI (1954), 159–203, has correctly emphasized. Very likely Venice was satisfied with what eventually happened: the Turks put a stop to the Aragonese advance, and they failed to secure a lasting foothold in Italy. Bombaci, *op. cit.*, pp. 196–97, gives a faulty transcription of the Venetian text of 23 August, 1479. See his valuable article on "Nuovi Firmani greci di Maometto II," *Byzantinische Zeitschrift*, XLVII (1954), nos. VIII–IX, pp. 311–14, providing the texts of two letters in Greek dated 17 February, 1480, from Mehmed II to the Doge Giovanni Mocenigo, requesting Venetian assistance for Ahmed Pasha, who was being sent on an important maritime mission (πρὸς τινὰς τόπους παραθαλασσίους), clearly the projected attack upon Otranto (see Bombaci, "Venezia e l'impresa turca," pp. 178–79), and justifying Ahmed Pasha's retention of five *castra* in southern Albania (or northern Epirus), which had been seized from Venice during the late war (and were being properly held according to Mehmed's interpretation of the terms of January, 1479). Mehmed states that the Venetian subjects captured in these places had already been sold into slavery, and their property confiscated and put on the block.

the Turks had been seriously considering an invasion of the kingdom of Naples for at least a year before their landing at Otranto. Nevertheless, no decisive plans could be made until the beginning of January, 1480, when Ahmed Pasha went to Istanbul and Mehmed II gave his consent to the enterprise.[84]

Sultan Mehmed's expedition had thus been a good while in the making. The Venetians had taken no step to dissuade him by dilating on its obvious costs and likely difficulties. They must have known what was in the offing toward the end of March, 1480, when Mehmed's letter of 27 February reached Venice, requesting assistance for Ahmed Pasha in his forthcoming maritime venture.[85] If they did not in fact encourage the sultan to attack southern Italy, they certainly kept his secret. Mehmed was a fearsome, unpredictable person. The forces he was gathering against the Neapolitan kingdom could always be used against the Republic's possessions in Greece. Venice wanted to maintain the peace that had cost her so much, protect her Greek and Adriatic stations, and continue her profitable trade with the Ottoman empire, for the privilege of which she was paying ten thousand ducats a year. One could never be sure that Mehmed might not denounce the peace on some pretext or other. Venetian eyes were constantly scanning the eastern shore of the Adriatic, where towns and fortresses belonging to the Serenissima frequently suffered from unexpected and unwarranted Turkish attacks.[86]

The atmosphere was heavy with uneasiness. During the late summer of 1479 Leonardo III Tocco, titular despot of Arta, duke of Leucadia (S. Maura), and count palatine of Cephalonia and Zante, had fled for his life before a Turkish armada which sailed from Valona to his island base of S. Maura. As the Turkish commander sailed through the channel of Corfu, he encountered the Venetian captain-general of the sea "with some of our galleys," says a Venetian dispatch of 7 September, 1479, "and he was saluted and honored by our aforesaid captain, as he passed by on his way to the lord Leonardo's state, and he went first to S. Maura, which he found abandoned by the aforesaid lord, and garrisoning [the place] with Turks, he then continued on to Cephalonia, took the island, then the fortress, pillaging everything. He burned and destroyed the castello, leaving the whole island deserted. . . ." Being at peace with the Gran Turco, the Venetian galleys stood by, and watched the utter desolation of the Tocchi heritage, while the Republic began pressing a claim at the Porte for possession of the island of Zante.[87]

Leonardo sought refuge in Naples, where he was well received by King Ferrante, whose niece Francesca Marzano he had married two years before, and where his descendants lived in prosperity until the later nineteenth century. According to the diarist Jacopo Gherardi da Volterra, Leonardo appeared in Rome on 29 February, 1480, with his brothers Giovanni and Antonio and his son Carlo to seek a pension from Sixtus IV. He was met at the Porta [S. Giovanni] Lateranense by the *famiglie* of the cardinals, and taken to a house which had been prepared for him between the Via Pellicciaria and the Botteghe Oscure (near the present Piazza del Gesù). Sixtus received him two days after his arrival, commiserated with him over his misfortune, gave him one thousand ducats, promised him two thousand a year, and expressed the hope of giving him still more "if God would grant us surcease from [these] wars."[88]

Later on, after the Turkish invasion of Otranto, Niccolò Sadoleto, the Ferrarese ambassador to Naples, wrote Duke Ercole I d'Este about the mission which he was undertaking (in April, 1481) to Ahmed Pasha at Valona on behalf of the Neapolitans to try to arrange an exchange of prisoners. Protesting Ferrante's love and esteem for both the Signor Gran Turco and Ahmed Pasha, Sadoleto expressed

---

[84] Bombaci, "Venezia e l'impresa turca," p. 172.

[85] *Cf.* Bombaci, "Nuovi Firmani greci," doc. no. VIII, pp. 311–12, and "Venezia e l'impresa turca," pp. 178–79.

[86] *Cf.* Sen. Secreta, Reg. 29, fols. 71^{v} [81^{v}], 77^{v} [87^{v}], letters dated 11 February, 1480 (Ven. style 1479) and 23 November, 1479 (the latter document being inserted in the register with the note *posita hic quia non data in tempore*, which explains the order in which they were copied). Both texts are letters to Battista Gritti, the Venetian bailie in Istanbul.

[87] Sen. Secreta, Reg. 29, fols. 34^{v}–35^{r} [44^{v}–45^{r}], on which note Alessio Bombaci, "Venezia e l'impresa turca di Otranto," *Rivista storica italiana*, LXVI (1954), 163–65. On the Tocchi, see the genealogical tables in Chas. Hopf, *Chroniques gréco-romanes*, Berlin, 1873, repr. Brussels, 1966, pp. 530–31. Hopf's tables are often inaccurate, and always to be used with caution. Mehmed's son and successor Bayazid II ceded Zante (for a tribute in cash) to the Venetians in a firman of 22 April, 1484.

[88] Jacopo Gherardi da Volterra, *Diarium romanum*, ad ann. 1480, in *RISS*, XXIII-3 (1904), 12, and note also Stefano Magno, *Annali veneti*, ad ann. 1479, in Hopf, *Chron. gréco-romanes*, p. 208, and at length in Sathas, *Docs. inédits*, VI (1885), 215.

the king's astonishment at the invasion of Otranto. Mehmed had given Ferrante the fullest assurances of peace and friendship in an exchange of embassies, and had even written him a letter in which he had "sworn by his own head that he wanted a fair peace and friendship with his Majesty, and that his Majesty must remain convinced that he would never come to do him harm." Ferrante had believed that no ruler on earth kept his word more faithfully than the Gran Turco. The Otrantine attack had been a complete surprise (which was not true, as Sadoleto was well aware).[89] Ferrante had known all about the size of the Turkish armada at Valona, Sadoleto informed Ahmed Pasha, but he had made no provision against it, "perche non mai se poté dare ad intendere che la fosse preparata a li danni suoi." It had never occurred to him that the armada would be used for a hostile landing on Neapolitan territory, but even so (according to Sadoleto) Ferrante regretted the loss he had sustained at Otranto less than he grieved over the impairment of the affection and good will which had obtained between him and the Gran Signore. In replying to Sadoleto's urbane expressions of injured innocence, Ahmed Pasha acknowledged "that it was true that his Gran Signore had written the lord king that letter and had loved him as a good brother, but that his Majesty had dealt with him neither as a brother nor even as a friend, [for] he had always received his enemies . . . , and that this had been the cause of this war."[90]

Among the most prominent of these refugees was, of course, Leonardo Tocco, although Ferrante had befriended a good many others. Ahmed Pasha also informed Sadoleto that, if Ferrante wanted peace with the Gran Signore, he must give up to him the state which the late Giovanni Antonio del Balzo Orsini, prince of Taranto, had possessed in southern Italy, "which does not belong to the lord king, and which it is not right that his Majesty should have occupied as he did." When Sadoleto protested the full justice, popular approval, and papal confirmation of Ferrante's taking over the Tarentine inheritance, Ahmed Pasha flatly declared that the king had poisoned the prince of Taranto, after which their conversation continued in sustained and (to Sadoleto) rather frightening disagreement.[91]

Embassies were exchanged between Venice and Istanbul, and the statesmen of the lagoon were soon accused of encouraging the Turks to attack Apulia and Sicily. Ahmed Pasha seems to have egged the sultan on, representing the Venetians as favorably disposed to assist the Turkish effort.[92] At first, however, the Venetians were not actually sure whether the Turkish armada at Valona was going to be used against Rhodes or Apulia or even against Venetian territory. On 21 March, 1480, a senatorial resolution had been passed, providing that five thousand ducats be sent to Vettore Soranzo, captain-general of the sea, to fortify strategic locations against the Turks as he thought best. Except for the usual consignment of funds to the Venetian officials at Corfu, no money had been sent to the Venetian stations on the eastern Adriatic or in Greece since peace had been made with the Porte.[93]

---

[89] On 14 May, 1480, Sadoleto had himself written Duke Ercole of Ferrara from Naples that Ferrante "sta molto in suspecto del Turco, il quale se dice ha XX m. persone a la Valona per voltare verso Puglia" (see the text in the collection of documents published by C. Foucard, "Fonti di storia napoletana nell'Archivio di Stato in Modena: Otranto nel 1480 e nel 1481," *Archivio storico per le province napoletane*, VI [1881], 80). The Ferrarese ambassador to Venice, Alberto Cortese, had written Ercole on the preceding 27 March that the Turk was preparing a huge armada for an attack upon Apulia or Sicily (*ibid.*, p. 128). Foucard's work was intended to commemorate the fourth centenary of the Turkish occupation of Otranto.

[90] Sadoleto's (undated) letter to Ercole d'Este is published in Piva, III, 158–62, and see, *ibid.*, I, 77–78.

[91] Piva, I, 160 ff. Although Sadoleto would have had Ahmed Pasha believe that he knew nothing of the Turkish insistence upon securing the prince of Taranto's possessions, he had already written Ercole d'Este from Naples some eight months before (on 24 August, 1480) that the Turks "have sent to inform the archbishop of Brindisi . . . and all the council of the province that the Gran Turco wants all the prince of Taranto used to hold, for it does not belong to the king . . ." (Foucard, "Fonti," *Arch. stor. nap.*, VI, 93). A fragment of Ahmed Pasha's letter to Francesco de Arenis, archbishop of Brindisi, is still extant (*ibid.*, p. 156). It is dated 18 August.

[92] Piva, I, 74–78, and especially Bombaci, "Venezia e l'impresa turca," pp. 179–80.

[93] Sen. Secreta, Reg. 29, fol. 83^v [93^v], doc. dated 21 March, 1480: "Nullum est efficatius remedium atque provisio magis salutaris ad faciendum quod Turcus nobis pacem servet quam munitio et fortificatio terrarum et locorum nostrorum Orientis, proinde hac tempestate huic rei . . . omni studio, opera et solicitudine est incumbendum. Et quoniam post factam predictam pacem ad hunc diem nihil pecuniarum missum fuit in Orientem supradicta de causa preterquam ad locum nostrum Corphoy, vadit pars quod ex primis denariis qui exigentur ex decima numero XL m. mittantur ducati quinque mille ad capitaneum nostrum generalem maris cum ordine et mandato ut illos dispenset de tempore in tempus in fortificationibus terrarum et

The Turks seemed to be putting so many irons into the fire that the Venetian Senate doubtless expected them to keep the peace. News of eastern affairs was always awaited with anxiety. Dispatches flowed into the Senate with daily regularity, and the responses were usually quick and always cautious. On 2 July (1480) the Senate wrote the captain-general Soranzo that they had just received four letters from him, of which the last was dated at Corfu on 24 June, as well as a report from one Marco de Mello. From these dispatches they had learned not only of the departure of the sultan's fleet from Istanbul, but also of its division into two parts, the larger making for Rhodes and the remainder heading for the Adriatic (*deque adventu residui in Culphum*). Soranzo was to keep his forces together in the Adriatic, but to keep out of the Turks' way; if they should attack any Venetian possessions, however, he was to defend them. But if the Turkish armada continued on to Apulia, Soranzo was to remain in the Adriatic or drop anchor at Corfu, as seemed best to him.[94]

As the days passed, the tension increased. The petty ambitions of Girolamo Riario and the deep-rooted enmity of the Venetians toward Ferrante of Naples made talk of an anti-Turkish league a tragic farce. On 25 July, 1480, Naples, Milan, Florence, and Ferrara renewed their alliance for twenty-five years, a counterpoise to the pact between Sixtus and Venice. In the meantime scouts had been watching the southern reaches of the Adriatic, while the Curia Romana was trying to collect levies to assist the beleaguered Knights of S. John on the distant island of Rhodes. On 27 July Sixtus addressed an almost hysterical brief to the Italian princes. He had summoned envoys to Rome, he said, to take the necessary steps for the defense of Rhodes. However, the envoys had expressed the fear that war was going to break out in Italy, and they wanted reassurance on this score from the pope, who wrote the princes:

> We are certainly not the ones, as we told [the envoys], who intend to disrupt the Italian peace, which through the whole span of our pontificate we have always tried to preserve with our every effort, precaution, and vigilance, especially in these times in which this vast danger assails us, so that we think of nothing else than how the Italian states may with a union of purpose resist the terrible power of the Turks. . . . [Now] we have the enemy before our very eyes. He has already been sighted, poised to strike at the province of Apulia with a large fleet. If he should seize Ragusa or Rhodes (which God forbid!), nothing would be left of our safety. . . . Hear our paternal voice, consider the common peril, and judge for yourself how great is the need to quicken our pace. . . . We have been the first to do what we could. . . . We cannot act alone, [and] all men will acquit us of blame if amid so clear a disaster our paternal appeals go unheeded![95]

On 28 July (1480), three days after the renewal of the league of Naples, one day after the pope's frantic brief to the princes, the Turks landed on the eastern shore of the Salentine peninsula. They disembarked near Otranto, less than fifty miles from the Albanian coast, where they had been assembled under Ahmed Pasha at Valona. Europe was shocked, Italy terrified, and one wondered what lay in store for the future. Was this merely an expedition against Ferrante of Naples? The sultan hated the Aragonese, the ally of Scanderbeg. Or was it the prelude to a full-scale invasion of Italy? Mehmed is said to have thought of himself as a world conqueror like Alexander or Caesar. Contemporaries were hardly better equipped than we are to provide the answers, and they had less time to contemplate the questions. As Sadoleto wrote the duke of Ferrara on 1 August,

> This morning four horsemen have come [to Naples], riding at breakneck speed from Apulia and the region of Otranto. They have gone to find the lord king at Aversa, where he went yesterday evening, and they have brought him the news of how the Turks have landed at Otranto with 150 sail, and have made three assaults upon the castle. The news is all over Naples. I have no certain information, however, except that the lord king has in fact returned post-haste from Aversa within the hour. . . .

Shortly afterwards, Sadoleto could add in a postscript to the letter that the news of the Turkish landing was certainly true: "the number of ships is uncertain, but the armada is

---

locorum supradictorum iuxta necessitatem et importantiam illorum. . . ." Vettore Soranzo was then captain-general of the sea (*ibid.*, fol. 85^{v} [95^{v}]), and the Venetians had become very apprehensive about their possessions on the eastern Adriatic and in Greece (fols. 90^{r}–92^{v} [100^{r}–102^{v}]).

[94] Sen. Secreta, Reg. 29, fol. 115 [125]; Piva, I, 96–97.

[95] A copy of this brief, dated 27 July, 1480, sent to the Marquis Federico Gonzaga of Mantua, may be found in the Arch. di Stato di Mantova, Arch. Gonzaga, Busta 834. The same text was widely distributed—*idem aliis scribimus*.

so great that it is believed to contain all the vessels that were at Rhodes!"[96]

While the pope was scheming to acquire Pesaro for his nephew and to drive the Medici from Florence, and while the king of Naples was seeking to acquire Siena and to find some way of assailing the Venetians, the Turk had struck. On the night of 2 August the king wrote his son, Alfonso of Calabria, summoning him home from Siena with his troops; then he wrote to the pope "in optima forma," enmity being put aside in the common danger. Sadoleto believed that he would soon ask all the members of the league of Naples to help him. The Turks were already reported to have taken three villages, namely Cutrofiano, with 300 houses (*fochi*) and a fine castle, and Sogliano and Risigliano, the one with 80 houses and the other with about one hundred. There were thought to be about 18,000 Turks; the number of horses was unknown; they were said to have many vessels, 18 long galleys and more than 120 other ships, not counting transports (*palandarie*). Then a horseman arrived from Taranto, "who says that there are more than 350 vessels, and that the Turks have attacked the castle of Otranto and ranged as far as Lecce, burning villages, taking prisoners, and killing little children as though they were dogs. . . . For this evening I have nothing else to report except that [the king's] secretary says that this business arises from the Signoria of Venice."[97]

Rumors flew thick and fast as to both the size of the Turkish armada and the extent of its success. Ahmed Pasha may have had something over 70 ships, but fewer than 10,000 men; as time passed the estimates of Turkish strength became less fanciful. But to invade the Terra d'Otranto, while the siege of Rhodes was still under way (from 23 May to 18 August, 1480), was a fearful display of Turkish power.[98]

As appeals for aid went out to the Italian states and the European monarchs, Sadoleto was told that Ferrante had no money, which he did not believe, but the ambassador from Lucca assured him it was true. Ferrante owed from 80,000 to 100,000 ducats, and was looking everywhere for money. He wanted his allies, especially Milan, to assist him beyond their stated obligations, because (as his secretary said) your interests are involved when your neighbor's house is on fire.[99] On the morning of 14

---

[96] Foucard, "Fonti," *Arch. stor. nap.*, VI, 81, and "Relazione della presa di Otranto scritta dal commissario del duca di Bari, al duca stesso, Ludovico Sforza," *ibid.*, pp. 162–63, which puts the Turkish force at 150 vessels and about 10,000 men, "tra li quali erano molti Christiani renegati de ogni natione . . . ," and dates the appearance of the Turkish armada off the Salentine coast to the morning of 29 July. On the Christian loss and recovery of Otranto, see Vincenzo Saletta, "Il Sacco di Otranto (11 agosto 1480)," *Studi meridionali*, V (1972), 209–47, with full bibliography. Note also, among numerous works on the subject, P. Palumbo, "Gli Aragonesi alla guerra d'Otranto (da documenti sincroni)," *Rivista storica salentina*, III (1907), 357–78; S. Panareo, "In Terra d'Otranto dopo l'invasione turchesca del 1480," *ibid.*, VIII (1913), 35–56; P. Egidi, "La Politica del regno di Napoli negli ultimi mesi dell'anno 1480," *Arch. stor. per le province napoletane*, XXXV (1910), 697–773, with nine documents; M. Viora, "Angelo Carletti da Chivasso e la crociata contro i Turchi del 1480–81," *Studi Francescani*, new ser., XI (XXII, 1925), 319–40, with five documents; and *cf.* A. Antonaci, *Hydruntum (Otranto)*, Galatina, 1954, pp. 159–67, and *Otranto: Testi e monumenti*, Galatina, 1955.

[97] Sadoleto to Ercole d'Este, 2 August, 1480, in *Arch. stor. nap.*, VI, 82–83. When a false report reached Venice on the evening of 7 August that the Turks had taken Otranto, the ambassador of the Estensi, Cortese, wrote Duke Ercole that, if it had been allowed, some of the citizens (*brigata*!) would have lighted fires and rung bells to celebrate the news, although there were others who were by no means pleased with the prospect of Turkish success (*ibid.*, p. 132).

[98] An undated letter from Naples, of which the contents were transmitted on 24 August from Florence to Ferrara, reports the Turkish armada at Otranto as containing 15,000 persons and 400 horses. There were said to be 132 vessels in all, 22 light galleys, 35 transports, and the rest *fuste* and other small boats (*Arch. stor. nap.*, VI, 122). On 26 June the rector and council of Ragusa had written Ferrante that the Turkish armada consisted of 70 vessels, including 17 galleys, 32 transports, and 20 fuste. It was apparently going to join another fleet, of which the size is not given. The Ragusei did not know the purpose or destination of either fleet (*ibid.*, p. 152). See in general Raynaldus, *Ann. eccl.*, ad ann. 1480, nos. 1–16, vol. XIX (1693), pp. 286–89, on the siege of Rhodes; nos. 1, 17–32, *ibid.*, pp. 286, 289–92, on the fall of Otranto; *Diarium parmense*, in *RISS*, XXII (Milan, 1733), cols. 336–37, 343–48, 349, 352C, 357–58; Sanudo, *Vite de'duchi*, *ibid.*, cols. 1211–13; Navagero, *Storia veneziana*, in *RISS*, XXIII (1733), cols. 1165–66; Pastor, *Hist. Popes*, IV, 332 ff., and (with the omission of an anti-Venetian passage) *Gesch. d. Päpste*, II, 559 ff.; Babinger, *Maometto*, pp. 565–68, 588–93.

[99] Sadoleto to Ercole d'Este, 3 August, 1480, in *Arch. stor. nap.*, VI, 84, 83. The pope sent Ferrante 10,000 ducats (*ibid.*, pp. 89, 90–91, 111, 142, 155), and the Milanese undertook to provide the same sum (pp. 90, 116). Typical of the papal appeals for aid addressed to the princes is the brief of 5 August sent to the Marquis Federico Gonzaga (Arch. di Stato di Mantova, Arch. Gonzaga, Busta 834): The Turks had landed at Otranto with a large fleet, were laying siege to the city, and were devastating everything "flama ferroque . . . ita ut nisi celeri occurratur remedio dubitandum sit ne in cetera loca Italie penetrent. . . . Quamobrem considerata vicina et imminenti calamitate non est aliqua ex parte cunctandum, sed celerrime ne ulterius serpat subveniendum. Te ergo, dilecte fili, per misericordiam Dei nostri obtestamur ut taxam illam qua superioribus diebus taxatus fuisti, huc sine mora mittas. . . ."

August the terrible news reached Naples that Otranto had fallen (on the eleventh). Ferrante summoned Sadoleto and the Milanese and Florentine ambassadors, and dilated on the gravity of the situation: "chiaro si può vedere la destructione de Italia." He was sending an envoy to Rome to beseech the pope to persuade Venice to join with the Neapolitan allies in defense against the Turks. Sadoleto proposed, however, that all the allied states send envoys directly to Venice; maybe Venice would decline to help, but then at least they would know "in how many feet of water" they were standing. There was general agreement that this was a good idea.[100]

In the meantime, however, on 9 August, the Venetian Senate had ordered the commander of a squadron on its way to Corfu (to join the captain-general's armada) to avoid the Turkish fleet, but if (*quod Deus avertat!*) he should encounter the Turks on his way, he should give them a wide berth, *facendoli pero cum bombarde et altri segni la debita salutatione et honori*, without deviating from his course.[101] On the same day the Senate renewed the instructions to Barbaro to avoid even discussion of a general league against the Turks.[102] The Neapolitan appeal had thus been rejected even before it was made. Only for her own survival or that of her Levantine possessions, would Venice go to war with the Turks again.

Recalled from Tuscany by his frantic father, Duke Alfonso hurried south from Siena in early August, but no help had reached the small garrison at Otranto, when it fell to a Turkish assault after a two weeks' siege. The city was sacked. The older inhabitants were killed, the younger reduced to slavery; Stefano Pendinelli, the aged archbishop of Otranto, was slain with all his priests. The churches were destroyed or converted into stables and quarters for troops. The nearby monastery of S. Nicola di Casole suffered severely (we shall return to its fame and its plight in Chapter 12). Sacred relics were thrown to the dogs as so many bones. Virgins were raped on the altars. No cruelty was forgotten, no impiety overlooked; every noble had his head cut off and stuck upon a lance. Jacopo da Volterra, who gives us this graphic account, feared that the Turkish conflagration might well consume all Italy and the rest of Europe.[103] The "eight hundred martyrs" of Otranto became a legend which is still cherished in their city.

Although Archbishop Stefano had urged everyone to fight and die for the faith, Ferrante remarked that he would have done better to spend the 18,000 ducats he was hoarding, to repair the walls and to provide for the garrison at Otranto.[104] He spoke very much to the point. The Turks had established a beachhead in the Salentine peninsula, from which they might well expand their operations. And as far as anyone in Italy knew, by this time they might also have taken the island of Rhodes.

---

[100] Sadoleto to Ercole d'Este, 14 August, in *Arch. stor. nap.*, VI, 85–88; Piva, II, 431–33. Envoys of the so-called "league of Naples" did go to Venice in early October, but their efforts to persuade the Senate to take a stand against the Turks were entirely unavailing (Piva, II, 448–49). Battista Bendedei, the ambassador of the Estensi in Rome, informed Ercole on 12 August that Otranto had fallen the day before, and that a consistory was immediately ordered to consider what should be done (*Arch. stor. nap.*, VI, 111). It is hard to see how even bad news could have traveled so quickly unless semaphores were employed or Bendedei's letter is misdated. Letters from Lecce dated on the thirteenth were read to the pope on the nineteenth "confirmando la perdita de Idronto" (*ibid.*, p. 113), which was known in Venice by the fourteenth (pp. 132–33).

[101] Sen. Secreta, Reg. 29, fol. 123 [133]. The vote was 133 in favor of the order, with only two members of the Senate opposed to it and none casting neutral ballots (*non sinceri*).

[102] *Ibid.*, Reg. 29, fols. 123^v–124^r [133^v–134^r]. The vote was 160 *de parte*, with one neutral ballot, and none *de non*.

[103] *Diarium romanum*, ad ann. 1480, in *RISS*, XXIII-3 (1904), 22–23, which gives 11 August as the date of the Turkish capture of Otranto. *Cf.* Foucard, pp. 88–89, on the bloodshed attending the event. Alfonso left Siena on 7 August (Piva, II, 429), and of course the Florentines were glad to see him go. On the eighteenth Sadoleto wrote from Naples that the Turks had killed almost everyone except the children whom they had sent off to Valona and Istanbul (*Arch. stor. nap.*, VI, 89–90). Ferrante's secretary said that only seventeen men and a few women had saved their lives at Otranto by paying ransom (*ibid.*, p. 92). Stefano Pendinelli had been archbishop for some thirty years by the time of the Turkish invasion (Eubel, *Hierarchia*, II, 166); his end is described in some detail in the "Relazione della presa di Otranto," *Arch. stor. nap.*, VI, 166, which says he died of fright.

[104] Sadoleto to Ercole d'Este, 20 August, in *Arch. stor. nap.*, VI, 92.

11. PIERRE D'AUBUSSON AND THE FIRST SIEGE OF RHODES (1480)

EVER SINCE the fall of Constantinople more or less grave incidents had involved the Knights Hospitallers of Rhodes in hostilities with the Ottoman Turks, the Egyptians, and even the Venetians. Despite the aura of chivalry which later historians of the Order have cast over the Knights, the fact is that piracy and the slave trade were among the chief sources of their income. While they fought off the attacks of Turkish pirates, they preyed on Moslem merchantmen—and on Christian vessels carrying Moslem traders. From the time of the election of Pierre d'Aubusson, prior of Auvergne, as grand master of the Hospital (on 17 June, 1476),[1] the Knights had expected each spring to learn that a fleet and a siege army had left the Bosporus to undertake the reduction of their island.

When Venice finally made peace with the Turk (in January, 1479), it was felt to be only a matter of months before the attack would come. For three years d'Aubusson had repaired and added to the walls and fortifications of the city. Today there are still about one hundred and fifty escutcheons of the grand masters mounted on the ramparts of Rhodes; of these almost one-third bear the arms of d'Aubusson, *d'or à la croix ancrée de gueules*, showing something of the extent of his work in refortifying the city. Although most of d'Aubusson's escutcheons postdate the famous siege of 1480 and the earthquake of 1481, a good number date from the first three years of his grand magistracy. D'Aubusson also built up a large store of food supplies and munitions, recruited mercenaries, and called upon the Knights in Europe to come to the defense of their Aegean stronghold,[2] and he made the inevitable appeal to Rome and to the princes of Europe. For the siege of

---

[1] Royal Malta Library, Valletta, also called the Malta Public Library (and hereafter Malta Library), Archives of the Order at Malta (abbr. AOM), Reg. 75 [*Liber Conciliorum, 1473–1478*], fols. 114ᵛ–117ʳ: "Die XVII mensis Iunii lune intitulata MCCCCLXXVI ab incarnatione de mandato reverendi domini locumtenentis magisterii . . . in aurora pulsata est campana assemblee publice et circa horam quintam diei dicta assemblea congregata fuit in ecclesia Sancti Iohannis Collaci Rhodi in qua interfuerunt omnes et singuli fratres tunc Rhodi existentes qui fuerunt in numero CCLVIII . . ." [distributed according to the eight *langues* as follows:]

1.	Provence	38	5.	England	14
2.	Auvergne	36	6.	Germany	16
3.	France	36	7.	Castile and Portugal	16
4.	Italy	37	8.	Aragon and Catalonia	65

"[Et elegerunt . . .] ad magistrum Hospitalis Sancti Johannis Hierosolimitani . . . reverendissimum dominum Fratrem Petrum Daubusson, priorem Alvernie, tamquam dignum, ydoneum et sufficientem. . . . Intonarunt 'Te deum laudamus' campaneque pulsate sunt et organa musicam resonarunt. Ipse quoque reverendissimus dominus magister illic presens a circumstantibus apprehensus est et humeris hominum est delatus ad altare maius super quo stetit et illic stabilimenta observare iuravit ac bonas consuetudines Religionis . . ." (fol. 117ʳ). There is a brief sketch of the organization, offices, sources of income, administrative and legal procedures of the Hospitallers during the fourteenth and fifteenth centuries in B. Waldstein-Wartenberg, *Rechtsgeschichte des Malteserordens*, Vienna and Munich, 1969, pp. 91–138.

[2] Guillaume Caoursin, *Gulielmi Caorsici* [*sic*] *Rhodiorum vicecancellarii obsidionis Rhodiae urbis descriptio* [Rome: Silber, *ca.* 1480–81, the text to which reference is made in this chapter], unnumbered fol. 2 (= signature A2). The copy of this work in the Gennadius Library at Athens contains 18 unnum. fols., with 26 lines per page, whence I assume from J.-Chas. Brunet, *Manuel du libraire*, I (repr. Berlin, 1922), col. 1556, that it is the edition of Euchar. Silber, published at Rome shortly after the siege (to which Brunet assigns the date "vers 1475"!); and *cf.* J. G. T. Graesse, *Trésor de livres rares et précieux*, II (repr. Berlin, 1922), 40, who sets the date of Caoursin's tract "vers 1478" (thus being, I suppose, more accurate by three years than Brunet). The *Obsidio Rhodia* is the first item given in the full edition of Caoursin's works (Ulm, 1496), "impressum Ylme per Ioannem Reger: anno Domini, etc., MCCCCXCVI, die XXIIII Octobris." On the escutcheons of the grand masters, still extant in the walls and towers, see the remarkable work of the French architect Albert Gabriel, *La Cité de Rhodes*, 2 vols., Paris, 1921–23, I, 93–104, 109–10. Although it has nothing to do with either the grand masters' escutcheons or Pierre d'Aubusson, I would note here that the intriguing inscription PALI·THARO, depicted with the hourglass in more than one context at Rhodes (*cf. Clara Rhodos*, V-2 [Rhodes, 1932], 48), does not in my opinion mean "I take courage again" (πάλι θαρρῶ), as is commonly stated, but rather "I shall flow again" (πάλι θὰ ῥῶ).

About two weeks after his election as grand master, Pierre d'Aubusson on 2 July, 1476, took up before a council of the Knights the question of refortifying Rhodes (Malta Library, AOM, Reg. 75, fol. 118ᵛ [fol. 126ᵛ by modern enumeration]): "Die II Iullii 1476 fuit congregatum consilium ordinarium coram quo proposuit reverendissimus dominus magister, dominus Frater Petrus Daubusson, imminentem necessitatem agendi et accelerandi reparationes et edificationes murorum castelli Rhodi . . . ," published in Gabriel, *La Cité de Rhodes*, I, 147–48, and *cf.* vol. II, pp. 228–29, doc. of 18 December, 1476 (AOM, Reg. 75, fol. 137ʳ).

Rhodes of 1480 we have two quite contemporary literary sources—Guillaume Caoursin, vicechancellor of the Hospital, and one Mary Dupuis, probably a soldier (despite the name) of Auvergne, of whom nothing seems to be known except that he arrived in Rhodes shortly after the withdrawal of the Turks.[3] Such was the terror and confusion within the walls during the siege that public acts were not drafted.[4]

While awaiting some response from the West, the Hospitallers set in order their castle on the island of Cos and that at Halicarnassus (Bodrum), ten miles away on the mainland. On the island of Rhodes itself the strong coastal castles of Pheraclus (Feraclo), Lindus, and Monolithus were put in readiness to meet an attack. The castle on Mount Phileremus (Fileremo), with its delightful church of the Virgin, was left to the Turks as being too hard to defend. The diplomats were also busy, as usual before a great contest of arms. At a meeting of the "ordinary council" on 14 April, 1479, a warning was sounded against the Turkish preparations going on in Istanbul "contra Rodum et loca religionis,"[5] but in the late summer of 1479 Pierre d'Aubusson solemnly agreed to a truce with the Turks through the mediation of Sultan Mehmed's second son, Jem Sultan. The Turks needed more time to prepare their fleet and army; the grand master wanted more time for the European priories to send their due contingents of knights. D'Aubusson had already made peace with Ka'itbey, the Mamluk soldan of Egypt, who had no desire to see the Osmanlis established in Rhodes,[6] and had secured a thirty-

---

[3] For editions and translations of Caoursin's *Obsidio Rhodia*, see Brunet, *Manuel*, I, cols. 1556–57, and Graesse, *Trésor de livres rares*, II, 40. Among the translations is a mediocre one by John Kay, poet laureate of Edward IV of England, *The dylectable newesse and tithynges of the glorious victorye of the Rhodyans agaynest the Turkes*, Westminster: W. Caxton, *ca.* 1490. On Caoursin's career, note G. S. Picenardi (see below, note 19), *Itinéraire d'un chevalier de Saint-Jean de Jérusalem*, Lille, 1900, pp. 129–30. For Mary Dupuis, *La Defense de Rhodes contre les Turcs en 1480*, Lyon, *ca.* 1480–81, see Brunet, *Manuel*, II (1922), cols. 900–1, and Graesse, *Trésor*, *Suppl.* (vol. VII), repr. Berlin, 1922, p. 264. Mary Dupuis's original text appears to be lost, but the work is preserved in the Abbé René d'Aubert de Vertot, *Histoire des Chevaliers Hospitaliers de S. Jean de Jérusalem*, etc., II (Paris, 1726), 598–616. Mary Dupuis describes himself and his purpose thus (*op. cit.*, p. 598): ". . . je Mary Dupuis gros et rude de sens et de entendement je veuille parler et descripre au plus brief que je pourray et au plus pres de la verite selon que je peu voir a lueil. . . ." This I think he has done, using the first printed text of Caoursin as well as information which he acquired first-hand in Rhodes soon after the termination of the siege. There are notes from Caoursin in a late hand in the Bibl. Apost. Vaticana, Cod. lat. 11,813 (formerly Arm. III, tom. 226), fols. 81–89, but they seem to be of no value.

[4] *Cf.* Sebastiano Paoli [Pauli], *Codice diplomatico del sacro militare ordine Gerosolimitano*, II (Lucca, 1737), "Al lettore," *ad fin.*, quoting Caoursin's assertion to this effect. Confirmation of this fact may be found in an interesting note in the *Libri Conciliorum* of the Convent of Rhodes, in the AOM, Reg. 76, fol. 35: "Quia civitas Rhodi obsidebatur per Turcos et summo conatu oppugnabatur, in tanta rerum perturbacione ac formidine peracta, in scriptis non sunt redacta, sed habita victoria historia est edita per Guillelmum Caoursin, Rhodiorum vicecancellarium, que per orbem impressorum arte est divulgata quapropter in hoc spacio [two-thirds of the folio is blank, 'hoc spacium' being used for this notice] nil est registratum: Ita est Gcaoursin Rhodiorum vicecancellarius." Under the rubric "Partes Citramarinae" in AOM, Reg. 387, *Libri Bullarum* [1479–1480/81], fols. 159 ff., nothing is registered between 19 May and 3 October, 1480, and under the rubric "Salviconductus et diverse scripture," *ibid.*, fols. 198 ff., no safe-conducts are recorded as having been issued between 16 May and 5 September, 1480 (fol. 211). The document of 19 May, 1480, was a commission addressed to a German named Johann Berger of Nordlingen, "considerantes igitur vestram in rebus bellicis experienciam presertim circa tormentorum seu machinarum vulgo nuncupatorum bombardarum et culvinarum usum . . ." (AOM, Reg. 387, fol. 163^{r}). The entry of 3 October contains a copy of a brief of Sixtus IV, "datum Rome apud Sanctum Petrum sub annulo piscatoris die XXVII Augusti MCCCCLXXVIIII, pontificatus nostri anno nono," lifting the restrictions on commerce with the infidels of Syria and Egypt because of the Knights' and the Rhodians' dire need of foodstuffs, timber, pitch, etc., although they were not themselves to supply arms to the Syrians and Egyptians (*ibid.*, fol. 163^{v}). This brief was also entered in the current *Liber Conciliorum* on 7 October, 1480 (AOM, Reg. 76, fol. 22).

The last Christian ship being issued a safe-conduct to enter Rhodes before the siege began, received it on 12 February, 1480 (AOM, Reg. 387, fols. 208^{r}–209^{r}): "magnifico ac nobili viro d. Ludovico Peyxo, navis onerarie capitaneo . . . ," "datum Rhodi in nostro conventu die XII mensis Februarii, anno ab incarnatione domini MCCCCLXXVIIII," i.e., 1480, since according to this style the year began on 25 March. The last non-Christian merchants to receive a safe-conduct to enter Rhodes did so on 10 March, 1480 (*ibid.*, fol. 209^{v}), and the last Christian merchant, a Rhodian, to receive one is recorded under the date 22 March (fol. 210^{r}). The first Christian ship to get a safe-conduct to enter Rhodes after the siege received it on 12 October, 1480 (*ibid.*, fol. 213^{r}). I first acquired these and a number of other important references to the Archives of the Order in Malta from my generous friend Professor Lionel Butler, who observes that safe-conducts might cover more than one visit to Rhodes if an additional entry or entries into port could be made within the period specified. The data with which Professor Butler furnished me made my few weeks in the Archives at Malta more valuable than an equal number of months might otherwise have been.

[5] Malta Library, AOM, Reg. 76, fol. 11^{v}.

[6] Niccolò Sadoleto, ambassador of the Estensi in Naples, wrote Duke Ercole I of Ferrara later (on 22 September,

one years' truce from Abū-'Amr 'Uthmān, the ruler of Tunisia, with an agreement for the export of thirty thousand measures of wheat without the payment of duty or any other restriction. At the chapter general which opened on 29 October, 1478, d'Aubusson had already described to the assembled knights the terrible danger which they faced. They had affirmed their determination to oppose the Turk to the end, and had voted the grand master special financial and military powers to help meet the coming crisis.[7]

Mehmed II had been gathering his land forces in the area of Scutari, across the Bosporus from Istanbul, whence they moved gradually southward through Brusa (Bursa), Pergamum, and Magnesia to winter quarters on the bay of Marmaris (Physkos, Fisco). At the beginning of December, 1479, the Turkish admiral Mesīh Pasha, a member of the erstwhile imperial family of the Palaeologi,[8] sailed with the first ships of a fleet that is said finally to have numbered one hundred and sixty sail. He made a half-hearted effort to establish a beachhead

---

1480) "chel Soldano ha mandato ad confortare el grande Maistro de Rhodi, promettendoli ogni soccorso et alturio contra el Turcho," for which text see C. Foucard, "Fonti di storia napoletana nell'Archivio di Stato in Modena: Otranto nel 1480 e nel 1481," *Archivio storico per le province napoletane*, VI (1881), 99.

[7] Giacomo Bosio, *Dell'Istoria della sacra religione et illustrissima militia di San Giovanni Gierosolimitano*, II (Rome, 1594), bks. x–xi, pp. 292–319, explores in some detail Pierre d'Aubusson's manifold activities on behalf of Rhodes and the "Religione" during the three years preceding the siege. I have not had access to the second edition of Bosio's second volume (he calls it *parte seconda*), Rome, 1629. Note Caoursin, *Obsidio*, unnum. fol. 3ᵛ (=sign. A3), on putting the castles in readiness to meet an attack, the *castellum Langonis* being that of Cos, the *castellum S. Petri* that of Halicarnassus; for their present condition see A. Maiuri, in *Clara Rhodos*, I (Rhodes, 1928), 173–81; and for Cos, *cf.* also G. Gerola, *I Monumenti medioevali delle tredici Sporadi*, Bergamo, 1914–15, pp. 216 ff. On the treaties with Egypt and Tunisia, *cf.* the Jesuit Fr. Dom. Bouhours, *Histoire de P. d'Aubusson-la-Feuillade, grandmaître de Rhodes*, 4th ed., Paris, 1806, pp. 64–66 (previously published at Paris, 1676, 1677; The Hague, 1739; and in slightly abridged English translation, as *The Life of the Renowned Peter D'Aubusson, Grand Master of Rhodes*, London, 1679, *cf.* pp. 92–94); on the grand master's truce with the Turks, *ibid.*, pp. 70–76, 80–81 (Engl. trans., pp. 100–11, 116–18); and on the chapter general which opened on 29 October, 1478 (not 1479), *cf.*, *ibid.*, pp. 77–78 (Engl. trans., pp. 111–14).

Full records of the chapter general of 1478 are fortunately preserved in a register in the Malta Library, AOM, No. 283 [*Sacra Capitula Generalia: 1466, 1471, 1475, 1478*], fols. 155–89. They may also be found in a late, rather unreliable copy, AOM, Reg. 315, pp. 489–562. After a papal prorogation of some months, the chapter general opened on 29 October (AOM, Reg. 283, fol. 156ᵛ): "In nomine domini nostri Jesu Christi amen. Die XXVIIII mensis Octobris Jovis intitulata non feriata anno MCCCCLXXVIII ab incarnatione cepit sollemnis celebratio capituli generalis sacri Ordinis Sancti Johannis Hierosolimitani in quo quidem capitulo incorporati sunt qui sequuntur per quorum suffragia ordinata et deliberata sunt acta capitularia" [there follow more than sixty names, the first being that of the Grand Master d'Aubusson: another name rather conspicuous in the proceedings which lay ahead is that of "Guillelmus Caoursin Rhodi vicecancellarius et secretarius, liberalium artium doctor (parisiensis)" (fols. 158ʳ, 161ᵛ, *et alibi*)].

The chapter general provided for a searching examination of personnel, a reorganization of practice, and the care of the Order's property, galleys, and defenses on Rhodes. The Turks are seldom mentioned in the successive sessions of the chapter, because the members were necessarily concerned with the internal affairs of the Order, but in d'Aubusson's two long bulls of 17 November (1478) special provision was made "pro defensione civitatis Rhodi, castellorum, insularum et locorum que dictus Ordo tenet in Oriente contra potentiam inimici fidei que in dies augetur, quorum quidem fratrum soldee solventur in panno condecenti exceptis illis qui debent habere solutionem in pecuniis numeratis secundum quod deliberatum fuit in generali capitulo anni MCCCCLXXV sicut reverendi domini baiulivi conventuales fratres anglici et aliqui officiales etiam ad satisfaciendum tabulis et soldeis anni proxime preteriti, preterea pro armatura unius galee per totum annum et duarum galearum pro quatuor mensibus quolibet anno ad defendendum populum et agricolas ab assiduis Turcorum insultibus . . . " (AOM, Reg. 283, fol. 185ʳ). ". . . Ordo noster grandioribus sarcinis ob Turcorum invasiones agrorumque vastationes et depopulationes oppressus et in Oriente ob fidei catholice hostis in nostram urbem Rhodiam et castella insulasque nostras assiduos apparatus et instructas classes expende [*sic*] admodum grandes valuerunt quo populum catholicum nostre fidei commissum a pernicioso tirannidis iugo tutaremur, cupientes igitur omni cogitatu erarii nostri conditionem atque qualitatem detegere, vulneri quoque pestifero pro virili parte mederi, decrevimus cum diligentia et accuratissima inquisitione debita ipsius thesauri redditus vero calculo intelligere et computo intellecto etiam expensis ordinariis et extraordinariis ad nostri status manutentionem recognitis rebus ingruentibus et necessariis mutua deliberatione providere statuimus . . ." (AOM, Reg. 283, fol. 187ʳ).

[8] Caoursin, *Obsidio*, fols. 1ᵛ–2ʳ (=A1–2): "[Turcus] quendam bassam graeculum ex nobili Paliologorum familia natum ad nephandum facinus allexit." *Cf.* Bouhours, *Pierre d'Aubusson* (1806), pp. 83–84, on "le bacha Misach Paléologue." I do not know what relation Mesīh Pasha was in fact to the imperial family. Cecil Torr, *Rhodes in Modern Times*, Cambridge, 1887, p. 17, thinks he was the "son of the last despot of the Morea and nephew of the last emperor of Constantinople," which seems unlikely, but note Averkios Th. Papadopulos, *Versuch einer Genealogie der Palaiologen, 1259–1453*, Munich, 1933, repr. Amsterdam, 1962, no. 101, p. 68. On the career of Mesīh Pasha, see N. Beldiceanu and I. Beldiceanu-Steinherr, "Un Paléologue inconnu de la région de Serres," *Byzantion*, XLI (1971), 13, note 2.

near the castle of Phanes (Fane) on the northern coast of Rhodes, and failed also in an eight days' attempt to capture the Hospitallers' northerly island of Telos.[9] He then sailed on to the harbor of Marmaris. Meanwhile in Rhodes the grand master proceeded with his preparations for the forthcoming Turkish assault, pulling down two churches outside the walls, one of them being the church of S. Anthony to the north of the city, lest they provide shelter for the Turks when they arrived. Fruit trees were cut down, and the wood was brought into the city; the barley, oats, and wheat were cut, and stored in the city granaries.[10] After 29 April (1480) no ships were allowed to leave the harbor of Rhodes; final precautions were taken for the defense of the inhabitants and of certain strongholds.[11]

Eight nations were charged with the defense of the eight sectors of the city walls and harbor installations (France, Germany, Auvergne, "Spain" [Aragon], England, Provence, Italy, and Castile), as we shall note again in connection with the siege of 1522, for the Hospitallers were organized and voted by "tongues" or nations, more or less after the fashion of the later medieval church councils, universities, and certain other international corporations. The Hospitallers commonly referred to the eight nations which comprised their order as the "languages," as in the record of the ordinance (written in French) of the Grand Master Pedro Ramón Zacosta, which in 1465 assigned to each language its sector for defense of the walls and fortifications. Until the time of Zacosta there had been only seven languages, but in 1462 he had divided that of "Spain" into two languages, one of which included the Aragonese and Catalans, the other the Castilians and Portuguese. Zacosta's regulation, preserved in the *Libri Conciliorum* of the Archives of the Order at Malta under the date of 3 February, 1465, established "la partition des postes et de la muralle de Rode par les VIII langues," and there appears to have been no significant reassignment of posts between that date and the Turkish siege of 1480.[12]

Despite the years of preparation for the coming crisis, the Grand Master d'Aubusson placed his chief dependence upon divine assistance, and sent for the image of the Virgin from her church on Mount Phileremus (which could not be held against the Turks). The Italians have reconstructed the church and monastery of Phileremus, a beautiful ensemble of buildings just beside the excavated foundations of an ancient temple of Athena, the Christian Virgin having displaced her pagan counterpart. When the Turks occupied Rhodes in 1523, this image of the Virgin was taken to Malta, where it remained until the end of the eighteenth century; despoiled of its jeweled setting by Napoleon Bonaparte, it was taken to Russia in 1799, when Czar Paul I became grand

[9] Bosio, II (1594), bk. x, pp. 318–19; Bouhours, *Pierre d'Aubusson* (1806), pp. 85–86; Franz Babinger, *Maometto il Conquistatore*, Turin, 1957, pp. 565–68.

[10] Bosio, II (1594), bk. x, p. 320; Gabriel, *La Cité de Rhodes*, II (1923), 211; Bouhours, *Pierre d'Aubusson* (1806), p. 87. The church or oratory of S. Anthony probably stood more or less on the site of the present Turkish mosque of Murad Reis, the admiral of Suleiman the Magnificent in the siege of 1522. Murad Reis died in Rhodes where his well-kept tomb, near the mosque that bears his name, is still a shrine for local Moslems and an object of great interest to tourists. The garden of S. Anthony is now the Turkish cemetery, the only one the Italians left in their reconstruction of the city of Rhodes.

[11] Malta Library, AOM, Reg. 76, fol. 33r: "Die XXVIIII Aprilis MCCCCLXXX: Consideratis novis que habentur de classe Turcorum que est preparata contra Rhodum fuit deliberatum quod naves et navigia que sunt in portu retineantur. . . ." Two weeks later a conciliar decision was recorded to see to the defense of the population and of various places: "Le XIII de May MCCCCLXXX. Entendue la preparacion que faict le Turc ennemy de la foy tant par mer comme par terre . . . contre la cite de Rhodes, chasteaulx et places de la religion, . . . le maistre et son reverend concil vigilans solicites de mieux de la conservacion . . . du peuple et habitans christiens le lisle de Rhodes et aultres ysles circumiacentes pour esviter la captivite dudit ennemy . . ." (*ibid.*, fol. 34r). "Item est deliberé pour garde et defenze des places de Lindo, Ferraclou et Monolito que les habitans des chastellanies desdits chasteaulx se doyent en iceulx . . . ainssy que a Castelnou e Cicaptania soyent deputes alcuns de defenze fino a nombre de X ou environ pour place" (fol. 34r).

[12] The text of Zacosta's ordinance may be found in Gabriel, *La Cité de Rhodes*, I (1921), 143–44, from the Malta Library, AOM, Reg. 73, fols. 145r ff., in the *Libri Conciliorum, 1459–1466*; and *cf.* Gabriel, I, 19–29; S. Pauli, *Codice diplomatico*, II (1737), no. 119, pp. 140–41; Bosio, II (1594), bk. VIII, p. 221. The two "Spanish" languages are distinguished as: "l'une des langues despaigne appellee arragon qui contient les castellanie damposte, priores de cathalongne et navarre" and "l'aultre langue des langues despaigne nommee castille qui contient les priores de castille et de portugale" (AOM, Reg. 73, fols. 145v, 146r). At Rhodes, as long as the Knights were there, French was the chief language of administration and high society. In 1462–1463, at the time of Zacosta's reorganization of the personnel of the Order, Rhodes had seemed to be in especial danger (*cf.* S. Ljubić, *Listine*, X [Zagreb, 1891], 232, Venetian document dated 15 January, 1463, Ven. style 1462). Zacosta's tombstone is now in the Vatican Grottoes.

master of the Hospitallers.[13] Knowing nothing perhaps of the Virgin's displacement of Athena on Mount Phileremus, the seventeenth-century biographer of Pierre d'Aubusson, the Jesuit Fr. Bouhours, remarks: "Ce que l'image fatale de Minerve étoit au peuple de Troye, celle de la Vierge le fut au peuple de Rhodes; il crut que le salut de la ville en dépendoit, et qu'il n'auroit rien à craindre tandis qu'elle seroit au milieu d'eux."[14] The image of the Virgin was carried in a solemn ceremony around the walls, and for d'Aubusson's time at least she kept the city of Rhodes under her protection.

When spring came, Rhodes had need of protection. Although a large Turkish fleet was soon to be deployed in the Adriatic for the attack upon Otranto which was to shake all Italy, another great fleet left the straits of Gallipoli in the first days of May. The fact was soon known in Rhodes, where the grand master was enlisting whatever trained gunners and other mercenaries he could find. On 19 May (1480), for example, a commission was issued to Johann Berger of Nordlingen, an experienced cannoneer, who was enrolled for life in the service of the Order at a stipend of eighty florins a year in cash and another twenty in cloth as well as double the "daily pittance" of a knight conventual. He was to receive his payments from "our common treasury at Rhodes."[15]

It must have been about this very day that the watchman in the look-out on the hill of S. Stefano, which rises from the shore just to the west of the walled city, gave the alarm that the Turkish fleet had arrived in Rhodian waters under full sail. The Order required Johann Berger's skill. The excited people flocked to the walls and other heights to watch the ships sail past Sandy Point (Saburra) to the harbor of Marmaris, where they joined the detachment which had arrived the previous December. The Turkish forces were embarked rapidly, being carried to the northern shore of Rhodes, where they landed on 23 May, 1480. Both Caoursin and Dupuis estimate there were about a "hundred sail" in the Turkish fleet;[16] other sources set the size of Mesīh Pasha's fleet at from 84 to 130 sail.[17] It was later reported in Rome, however,

[13] Bosio, II (1594), bk. xi, pp. 320, 325; G. S. Picenardi, *Itinéraire d'un chevalier de Saint-Jean* (1900), pp. 216–17, 228–29. Cristoforo de'Buondelmonti (fl. 1420), *Liber insularum Archipelagi*, ed. Ludwig von Sinner, Leipzig and Berlin, 1824, p. 74, noted that "ad quintum milliare prope civitatem [Rhodianam] in monte Filermus est oppidum et domina omnium gratiarum saepe visitata adoratur a multis." The Virgin of Phileremus was the *domina omnium gratiarum*, the Madonna di Tutte le Grazie, whose church and monastery the Italians rebuilt during their occupation of Rhodes (1912–1943).

[14] Bouhours, *Pierre d'Aubusson* (1806), p. 88.

[15] Malta Library, AOM, Reg. 387, fol. 163^{r} (doc. already noted above, in note 4): "Considerantes igitur vestram in rebus bellicis experienciam presertim circa tormentorum seu machinarum vulgo nuncupatorum bombardarum et culvinarum usum artemque propriam, . . . his causis impulsi vos prefatum Iohannem vita vestra durante in nostri ordinis obsequiis ad usum rerum bellicarum et artilleriarum suscipimus et retinemus cum annuis gagiis et stipendiis infrascriptis, videlicet octoginta sive LXXX florenorum Rhodi currencium . . . et alios viginti sive XX florenorum in panno ex[s]olvendorum, etiam cum cothidiaria duplici fratrum pictancia, que omnia quolibet anno omni cessante contradictione a nostro communi thesauro Rhodi habere, sumere, et recipere realiter et cum effectu debeatis. . . . Datum Rhodi in nostro conventu die XVIIII Maii, anno ab incarnatione MCCCCLXXX."

[16] Caoursin, *Obsidio*, fols. 3^{v}–4^{r} (=A3–4): ". . . appulit itaque ea classis velorumque centum decimo Kal. Junii anno incarnationis verbi divini MCCCCLXXX militeque in terram exposito. . . ." Mary Dupuis, in Vertot, *Hist.*, II (1726), 599–600: "est assavoir que le vingt et troysesme jour de May . . . arriverent au tour de ladicte ville cent voelles ou environ, c'est assavoir galeres, fustes, pallendrees, gapperies," etc. In general Bosio, II (1594), bk. xi, pp. 320–21, follows Caoursin, and *cf.* Bouhours (1806), p. 89.

[17] On 3 June (1480) one Gabriele Pisitillo wrote his brother from Rhodes: "Avisovi come, ali XXII de magio, arivoe larmata del Turcho quà, in canale de Rhodi, et adì XXIII messe scalla ala terra, ala rocha de San Stefano, vicino ala terra, quanto poteva agiungere lartigliaria ala terra, et messe XV. m. persone, dove ce haveno obsidiata la terra intorno intorno; et poi, laltro dì, parte dela dicta armata, la quale è in tuto 84 velle, fra galee grosse et fuste, et parce vedere che sono 50 galee sotile; siche, l'altro dì, come è dicto, andareno circa 30 velle alo Fescho [Marmaris], porto de terra ferma de Turchi, et vicino qua a XVIII miglia, a levare altre 4. m. persone, le qual sono là . . ." (C. Foucard, "Fonti," *Archivio storico per le province napoletane*, VI [1881], 135). Niccolò Sadoleto, the ambassador of the Estensi in Naples, wrote Duke Ercole I of Ferrara on 1 July: "Io credo che V[ostra] Exc[ellenza] habie inteso, per la via de Venexia, come ad Herodi [Rodi] è l'armata del Turco, cum cento trenta velle et cum 14 bombarde grosse, et che octantamilia turchi sono smontati nel isola, et como quindixe galee grosse de le sue, et trenta palandarie, et molte altre galee sottile sono nel golfo ala Valona . . ." [for the coming attack on Otranto] (*ibid.*, VI, 80).

At first the Venetians were concerned as Mehmed II's naval armament was being deployed both in the Adriatic and in Rhodian waters (Arch. di Stato di Venezia, Sen. Secreta, Reg. 29, fol. 115 [125], doc. dated 2 July, 1480). The Senate was afraid lest the movement of part of the Turkish fleet "in Culphum" (i.e., into the Adriatic) might mean an attack upon Venetian-held territory, which in view of their recent peace (of January, 1479) with the Porte seemed unlikely. The Senate soon had further news, however: "Preterea quoniam post scriptas presentes nostras [the letter, *ibid.*, is addressed to Vettore Soranzo, captain-that Pierre d'Aubusson wrote King Ferrante of Naples on 28 May that the Turkish fleet totaled one hundred and sixty sail, and that about seventy thousand men had been landed to lay siege to the city of Rhodes.[18]

The Turks promptly occupied the hill of S. Stefano, the acropolis of the ancient city of Rhodes, as the center of their encampment, as they were to do again in the fatal siege of 1522. Part of the fleet returned to the Anatolian mainland to collect more troops at Marmaris. After a few preliminary assaults to test the defenses of the walls, the Turks concentrated their attacks upon Fort S. Nicholas, with its staunch tower, which had been erected twenty-five years before by the Grand Master Pedro Ramón Zacosta. This tower, or rather its successor, still stands at the end of the ancient mole extending into the sea northward from the city walls. The mole is the long upright of an L, of which the lower portion is formed by the eastward prolongation of the northern range of city walls along a shorter mole which terminated in the handsome square Tower of Naillac. The latter tower, built shortly after 1400, loomed up about one hundred and fifty feet above the harbors of Rhodes. Part of it fell during an earthquake in April, 1863, and the rest of it was later cleared away as a menace, but it is well known from the contemporary and modern drawings.[19]

---

general of the sea] sumus advisati ex quibusdam litteris particularibus unum existentem super illo grippo qui venit ex Rhodo retulisse quod illa classis turcicha retinuit in canale Rhodi tres naves nostras onustas gottonis [cotton] que ex partibus Syrie huc revertebantur, de cuius rei veritate vos antehac certior factus esse debetis. . . ." Actually the Venetians were not much exercised by the news from the East (*cf.*, *ibid.*, fols. 117^{v}, 120^{v}–121^{r}, 123–25 [127^{v}, 130^{v}–131^{r}, 133–35]), but (with reference to the text just quoted) they would be distressed by Turkish interference with their export of Syrian cotton which, after spices, was the chief staple of their Levantine commerce at this time, on which see Eliyahu Ashtor, "The Venetian Cotton Trade in Syria in the Later Middle Ages," *Studi Medievali*, 3rd ser., XVII-2 (1976), 675–715, esp. pp. 689 ff.

[18] So Battista Bendedei, ambassador of the Estensi to the Holy See, wrote the duke of Ferrara from Rome on 29 June (1480): "Ecce che intesii: li giunge uno cavallaro, volando da Napoli, cum una lettera regia a lui [i.e., Anello Arcamono, King Ferrante's ambassador to the Holy See] et una al Papa aperta, una perchè la potesse legere, et un altra, inclusa in la sua, del gran Maestro de Rhode a sua Maestà, data in ipsa insula ali XXVIII del passato. . . . . . cum ciò sii chel Turcho è a campo, cioè li soi, ala cità sua, cum circa septanta millia persone, et è lì cum CLX velle, fornito de victualia, artegliaria, macchine, et altri instrumenti bellici da expugnare cità . . ." (C. Foucard, "Fonti," *Arch. stor. nap.*, VI [1881], 103). The Neapolitans were urgently beseeching the pope's help for Rhodes. A dispatch from Florence dated 3 July, 1480, stated that the Signori Otto "dicevano dela armata era a Rode del Turcho, et che ci era adviso como li era a campo, cum 160 vele, tra galee et palandete, et eragi 60 milia turchi . . ." (from the ambassador Antonio da Montecatino to his government in Ferrara, *ibid.*, p. 118). Sadoleto reported to Ferrara that the Turkish land forces contained eighty thousand men (see the preceding note), which was the figure often given in later accounts of the siege (*cf.* H. Pantaleon, *Militaris ordinis Johannitarum, Rhodiorum aut Melitensium equitum . . . historia nova*, Basel, 1581, p. 131).

The encyclical letter of Pierre d'Aubusson to members of the Order, "datum Rhodi in nostro conventu die XXVIII mensis Maii, anno ab incarnato Christo Jesu domino nostro MCCCC octogesimo" [28 May, 1480], may be found in the Malta Library, AOM, Reg. 387, fols. 16^{v}–17^{v}. It bears the heading "Mandatum quum Turchorum armata Rhodum applicuit" (*Sent when the Turkish armada reached Rhodes*), and carried an eleventh-hour appeal to the Knights everywhere to join in defense of "hec urbs antiqua priscorum monimentis celebrata" (Reg. cit. fol. 17^{r}), with the assurance of the ultimate triumph of the besieged over the insane fury of the Turk. I do not give much of the text since the letter appears in Pauli, *Codice diplomatico*, II, no. 125, pp. 148–49 (and *cf.* Bosio, II [1594], bk. xi, pp. 322–23). As usual, however, Pauli's text leaves much to be desired, inaccurately stating that the Turkish fleet numbered "about 109 sail:" the date 15 June is given for the initial attack although the letter itself is dated 28 May! E. F. Mizzi, ed., *Le Guerre di Rodi*, Turin, 1934, pp. 17 ff., cites this document from the AOM, "Liber Bullarum, 1470–1480, vol. IV, p. 16," misdating it 18 May. He seems to be referring to Reg. 387, which covers only the years 1479–1480, and is so described on the front cover of the contemporary binding. (I also see no evidence of this register's ever having been vol. IV of any series.)

The beginning of d'Aubusson's encyclical reads, "Frater Petrus Daubusson, etc., et nos conventus, etc., universis et singulis prioribus, preceptoribus et fratribus Ordinis nostri ubilibet constitutis ad quos nostre presentes littere pervenerint, salutem in eo qui est omnis vera salus: Quod in Rhodios Turcorum tyrannus iam pridem machinatus est, perficere conatur. Concepit olim fidei inimicus in nos et Ordinem nostrum inexorabile odium quod pro fide Christi sibi resistimus. Augetur quoque eius insanus furor quod annos quatuor et viginti quo Constantinopolis expugnata est nulla dicionis nostre porcione subacta sue tyrannidi vires opponimus et censum petitum recusavimus. Itaque nuper ingenti classe velorum CLX vel circiter parata contractisque undique copiis ex provinciis Rhodo vicinis quas ex continenti terraque firma devexit traicitque in insulam nostram, Rhodiorum agros ac urbem nostram potenti manu X Kal. Iunii aggressus est, obsedit et circumdat. Comportavit ad urbem nostram oppugnandam tormentorum, machinarum, bombardarum lignearumque turrium ingeniorumque bello aptorum grandem numerum suntque in castro in nos collocatis hostes circiter LXX^{m} qui nos assiduis insultibus petunt, invadunt, obpugnant . . ." (Reg. 387, fol. 16^{v}). A note following the encyclical states that "facta sunt alia mandata septem in simili forma, etc." (fol. 17^{v}).

[19] The picturesque Tower of Naillac, with its bartizan turrets rising from the four corners of the overhanging battlements, is shown in a woodcut view of the entrance to the main harbor of Rhodes (called from the early seventeenth century the Port of Commerce) in the first

If the Turks could occupy Fort S. Nicholas and mount cannon at the end of the promontory, they could rake the main (east) harbor of Rhodes, later called the Port of Commerce, and prevent the entry of Christian ships with reinforcements of men and materials of war within the Rhodian lines of defense. Well supplied with artillery, as at Constantinople twenty-seven years before, the Turks set up a battery of three huge brass cannon near the site of S. Anthony's church to the north of the city, and shot across the narrow Mandraki, the later Port of Galleys, at Fort S. Nicholas, a distance of two hundred yards from the mainland.[20] The Turks could not themselves enter the main (east) harbor, which was blocked off by a chain carried on baulks from the Tower of Naillac to the Tower of the Windmills, so called because it stood at the end of a picturesque procession

edition of Breydenbach's *Peregrinationes in Terram Sanctam*, Mainz, 11 Feb. 1486, reproduced in Hugh Wm. Davies, *Bernhard von Breydenbach and his Journey to the Holy Land, 1483–4*, London, 1911, pl. 21. This view, from the northwest looking toward the southeast, shows the heavy chain which the Hospitallers stretched across the entrance to the harbor in times of emergency. (The chain went from the Tower of Naillac on the west to the opposing Tower of the Windmills on the east.) The woodcut was made from a drawing done by Erhard Reuwich of Utrecht in 1483, and "clearly indicates the damage done by the Turks in 1480" (Davies, *op. cit.*, pp. XXIII–XXIV). The Tower of S. Nicholas is shown in two other woodcuts in Davies, plate 22 coming from the first edition of Breydenbach (Mainz, 1486) and plate 23 from the third edition (by Peter Drach, Speyer, 24 Nov. 1502), Drach's block being a close copy of Reuwich's, according to Davies, p. XXIII. A view from somewhat the same angle as the Breydenbach-Reuwich woodcut of the entrance to the harbor (Davies, pl. 21) may be found in the splendid lithograph of Eugène Flandin, *L'Orient*, 2: *Rhodes* (Paris, 1853 [1858]), pl. 1, showing the majestic Tower of Naillac on the right; *cf*. pl. 5 with Fort S. Nicholas on the left and the Tower of Naillac in the center; pl. 6 is a fine view of the Tower of Naillac (called here the "Tour St. Michel"); and pl. 9 shows Fort S. Nicholas as it was in 1844 when Flandin drew his memorials of Rhodes. (The imprint on the title page of the copy of Flandin in the Gennadeion bears the date 1853, but his preface refers to the explosion which destroyed the Hospitallers' church of S. John in 1856, and is dated 1858.)

An excellent view of the Tower of Naillac is also given in Albert Berg, *Die Insel Rhodus*, Brunswick, 1862, pt. 1, pl. 1, opp. p. 4, looking toward the Tower of the Windmills; pl. 32 illustrates very well how the long mole extending northward links Fort S. Nicholas to the city of Rhodes; pl. 33 shows the eastward extension of the walls from the northeast corner of the city to the Tower of Naillac; and pt. 2, pl. 38, opp. p. 18, gives a good view of the Naillac on the left and S. Nicholas on the right with ships in the Mandraki (later called the Port of Galleys), the shallow northern harbor of Rhodes. The mole of S. Nicholas, which separates the Mandraki from the main harbor, is thus described by Caoursin, *Obsidio*, fol. 5ʳ (=A5): "Est enim molis ipsa trecentorum circiter passuum in mare protensa miro artificio ab antiquis manufacta, quae suo progressu portum triremibus ["galleys"] aptum a parte occidentis efficit." Caoursin believed the ancient Colossus of Rhodes had stood on the site of Fort S. Nicholas, as do certain modern writers, such as the Baron F. de Belabre (*Rhodes of the Knights*, Oxford, 1908, pp. 23–25) and Albert Gabriel ("Le Colosse de Rhodes," *Bull. corr. hellénique*, LVI [1932], 330–59). This was in fact the medieval tradition, and is also repeated by the Capuan pilgrim Niccolò da Martoni at the close of the fourteenth century (*Revue de l'Orient latin*, III [1895], 585) as well as by Jacobus Fontanus (historian of the siege of 1522), *De bello Rhodio libri tres*, Rome, 1524, I, unnumbered folio 23ʳ (=Fiii). Notice that in the expression "portus triremibus aptus" Caoursin comes very close to the name Port of Galleys.

A good deal of historical detail concerning the Knights at Rhodes is given in G. S. Picenardi (a grand prior of the order), *Itinéraire d'un chevalier de Saint-Jean de Jérusalem dans l'île de Rhodes*, Lille, 1900, whom F. de Belabre subjects to much criticism in his own far from impeccable book on *Rhodes of the Knights*. Giulio Jacopi, *Rodi*, Bergamo, 1933, reproduces a number of views from Rottiers, Flandin, Berg, and other sources, and gives some excellent modern photographs of most of the gates, towers, and other sites which figure prominently in the sieges of 1480 and 1522, and similar material may be found in the popular work of Raymond Matton, *Rhodes*, Collection de l'Institut Français d'Athènes, no. 62, 2nd ed., Athens, 1954. *Cf*. also Giuseppe Gerola, *I Monumenti medioevali delle tredici Sporadi*, Bergamo, 1914–15, and the studies of A. Maiuri, G. Jacopi, and P. Lojacono, in *Clara Rhodos*, Istituto storico-archeologico di Rodi, 10 vols., 1928–41, vols. I (1928), 129–81; V-2 (1932), 36–58; and VIII (1936), 245–362. The best topographical study of Rhodes, with plans of the city as it was in 1480 and 1522, is that by Albert Gabriel, *La Cité de Rhodes, MCCCX-MDXXII*, 2 vols., Paris, 1921–23, on whom I have chiefly depended for such data. Gabriel publishes most illuminating photographs, and his "essai de restitution" at the end of vol. II provides a marvelous view of the whole city, with all its walls and towers, as it would have looked if one could have flown above it about the year 1500.

Of value for a study of the Hospitaller monuments of Rhodes is the work of B.E.A. Rottiers, *Description des monumens de Rhodes*, 2 vols., Brussels, 1828. The first volume is a memoir of Rottiers's sojourn in Rhodes from January to April, 1826, with a description of the various monuments sketched for him by his companion, the Flemish artist J. P. Witdoeck, who worked with limited talent under very difficult circumstances. The second volume is an album (in small folio) of Witdoeck's sketches, which are as generally deficient in detail as Rottiers's historical and topographical commentary is lacking in accuracy. The *Monumens de Rhodes* was nevertheless helpful to the Italians in their reconstruction of the palace of the grand masters and the conventual church of S. John, both destroyed in the explosion of November, 1856, as noted below (in Volume III). More generally useful is the better work of Eugène Flandin, *L'Orient*, 2: *Rhodes* (1858), pls. 10, 22–26, which lacks however any view of the interior of S. John's, to which it was apparently very difficult to gain access under the Turks, who had converted it into a mosque.

[20] Bosio, II (1594), bk. XI, p. 321.

of windmills on the mole that flanked the east side of the harbor. Even without the chain the Turks would have got caught in the Knights' crossfire from the two towers. The chain could be opened, however, and supply ships glide into the harbor before the westerly winds, which usually fought for the defenders of Rhodes.

The grand master later informed the Emperor Frederick III that Fort S. Nicholas was almost demolished by the impact of three hundred stone cannon-balls,[21] to the savage rejoicing of the Turks. A thousand men working day and night, however, constructed defenses along the whole length of the mole, digging a ditch and throwing a timbered rampart around the badly battered tower of the fort. A group of resolute men was placed in the fort, and the southern (landward) end of the mole was also heavily defended, for here the water was shallow. If the Turks could effect a lodgment on the mole, they would cut off the fort from the city, and probably soon take it. They would also threaten the harbor. But of course it would be exceedingly difficult to hold the mole (unless the fort was taken quickly). The Hospitallers mounted cannon on the northern walls of the city, whence they raked with shot the Turkish battery at S. Anthony's and could direct a protecting fire along the mole. Before daylight one morning some Turkish galleys suddenly rounded Sandy Point and immediately bore down on Fort S. Nicholas, landing an attacking force. The Turks were repulsed, suffering about seven hundred casualties, as deserters informed the Hospitallers. They promptly resumed their cannonading of the fort, however, and after some days made another attempt to take it. They had built a floating bridge long enough to reach from the shore near S. Anthony's across the Mandraki to the fort at the end of the mole. Planning to haul this across the water by a cable running through the ring of an anchor which some bold Turks had embedded in the rocks by the base of the fort, they discovered as they began the second attack that their anchor had been dislodged, and so the bridge had to be towed and pushed across by small boats. This time Mesīh Pasha had prepared thirty galleys for the attack, as well as heavy transports (*parendariae*) to carry stones and cannon within close range of the fort. Landing craft had also been built to carry men across to establish a beachhead on the mole. The second attack was launched, as the grand master informed the emperor, at midnight on 19 June.[22]

The Hospitallers had been well aware of what

---

[21] Caoursin, *Obsidio*, fol. 5^v (=A5), also informs us that the round tower at Fort S. Nicholas almost disintegrated under the bombardment of three hundred shots, especially the exposed west side, but notes that the inner core of rubble and mortar stood up much better than the large tailored facing stones: ". . . iactuque trecentorum lapidum spericorum dirruit eam praesertim partem [turris] quae occidentem spectat. Ruina quidem turrim munit licet enim suo pondere ictuumque vehementia saxa ingentia ex quibus aedificata erat laberentur, tamen materia calce harena et lapillis immixtis confecta adeo demoliri non potuit quin turris potior pars staret ex quo facilis ascensus hosti negatur." This is a good text for the modern classical archaeologist to consider as he draws erroneous cultural conclusions from the contrast between the well-cut ancient blocks of a re-used foundation and the rubble-and-mortar superstructure of some "Frankish tower." Of course medieval builders did much damage to ancient monuments, from which they liked to quarry well-cut stones. The Hospitallers, for example, made extensive use of Hellenistic materials in their castle of Lango (Cos), and incorporated the last remains of the Mausoleum of Halicarnassus in their castle of S. Peter at Bodrum.

On 3 July (1480) the ambassador of the Estensi in Florence wrote home to Ferrara that it was reported the Tower of S. Nicholas had been struck by about "120 colpi de bombarde" up to 4 June (Foucard, "Fonti," *Arch. stor. nap.*, VI, 118). These shots were being heard throughout Europe.

[22] Caoursin, *Obsidio*, fol. 10^r (=A 10), also states that Mesīh Pasha's second attack on Fort S. Nicholas took place on 19 June (*tertio decimo Kal. Iulii*), while Mary Dupuis dates the *first* attack on the fort on "le neufviesme jour du moys de Juing environ deux heures devant le jour" (*Relation du siège de Rhodes*, ed. Abbé de Vertot, *Hist. des Chevaliers Hospitaliers*, II [1726], 603). Mary Dupuis does not specify the date of the second attack, which he merely says began "ung jour apres minuyt" and ended at ten o'clock the following morning (*ibid.*, pp. 607–8). In between the two attacks on Fort S. Nicholas, both Mary and Caoursin place Turkish cannonading and an assault upon the Jewish quarter (for which see Caoursin, *Obsidio*, fols. 6^v–8^v [=A6–8], and Mary Dupuis, in Vertot, II, 605–7). Bosio, II (1594), bk. XI, pp. 324–25, 327–30, follows Caoursin in his description of the two attacks.

In his letter to Frederick III, Pierre d'Aubusson deals with the two attacks upon the fort in sequence; presumably Caoursin, as vice-chancellor of the Order, composed the grand master's letter, with which his own account corresponds very closely despite the rather different order in which he presents the facts. There are a few discrepancies between d'Aubusson's letter and Caoursin's *Obsidio*, which seem to indicate deficiencies in Pauli's text of the letter. In a letter to Pope Sixtus IV, dated at Rhodes on 15 September (1480) and misdated 18 November by J. P. de Ludewig, *Reliquiae manuscriptorum omnis aevi diplomatum ac monumentorum ineditorum adhuc*, V (Frankfurt and Leipzig, 1723), 290 ff., the second attack is incorrectly dated "XIII die Iulii," by an obvious error for the thirteenth day before the Calends of July (19 June).

was in the offing. They had spared neither effort nor expense to meet the challenge, believing like the Turks that Rhodes would probably stand or fall with the retention or the loss of S. Nicholas. The Turks assailed the fort on the three sides exposed to the sea, and successfully landed a number of men on the mole. The floating bridge was struck by Christian cannon fire and broken up, plunging into the water the Turks who were trying to press across it. Four galleys and some transports were sunk; other ships were set on fire, and forced to withdraw from the engagement. As the morning came on, the Christian gunners could aim with greater accuracy. It was soon apparent that again the Turks had failed to take the fort; they called a halt to all their operations about 10:00 A.M. They had lost many of their commanders, and (deserters later reported) had suffered 2,500 casualties.[23] Mesīh Pasha decided Fort S. Nicholas could not be taken. The grand master and his knights rendered thanks in a special ceremony "a Dieu et a Nostre Dame de Philerme et a Monseigneur saint Jehan Baptiste, de la grace que Dieu leur faisoit de obtenir victoire a lencontre de leurs ennemis."[24]

Mesīh Pasha did not, of course, confine his attacks to Fort S. Nicholas. Shortly after the first attack upon the fort, he moved eight of his sixteen largest cannon to the southeast of the city, opposite the bulwarks of Provence and Italy, behind which lay the Rhodian Jewish quarter (Juifrie, Giudecha).[25] The sources all emphasize the severity of the Turkish cannonade, sustained day and night, which could be heard as far away as the island of Cos to the northwest and at Chasteau Rouge on the coast of Asia Minor, each of which places Mary Dupuis puts "a cent mille de Rhodes." Mortars bombarded the town, and the stone balls fell by the hundreds in an indiscriminate profusion which drove non-combatants into caves and cellars and within the lee of the walls. Lighted arrows were shot, and fire-balls catapulted, upon the roof tops, but the Hospitallers organized brigades which extinguished fires as soon as they started. The Turks tried to mine the approaches to the fosses and walls, but they proved far less adept at mining than was to be the case in the siege of 1522. They tried to fill the foss with stones, earth, and other débris; parts of the curtain wall itself fell into the foss under the heavy impact of the cannon fire. The Hospitallers made a tunnel beneath their walls, and under the cover of night tried to bring into the city the stones which the Turks were throwing into the foss. The Turks soon noticed that the work they did by day was being undone by night, however, and they hastened their plans for a general assault. Behind the walls Pierre d'Aubusson had already decided to throw up another rampart, for which houses had been torn down. A ditch was dug in front of the new rampart. Everyone had joined in the work, carrying stones, earth, and mortar on his shoulders, and donating gold, silver, and other valuables to help pay the costs.[26] The co-operation of Greek and Latin was wonderful. The many little churches in the city were constantly full as men, women, and children confessed their sins, expecting to die almost from day to day and hour to hour, and offered unending prayers heavenward that their lives and the city might be saved "de la main des faulx chiens Turcs."[27]

A number of Christian renegades in the Turkish camp were admitted into the city during the course of the siege, as repentant sinners anxious to make amends for their past treacheries. Among them was a Master George of Saxony,

---

[23] Pierre d'Aubusson's letter to Frederick III, dated at Rhodes on 13 September, 1480, is given in Seb. Pauli, *Codice diplomatico*, II, no. 126, pp. 149–53 (reprinted in John Taaffe, *History of the . . . Order of St. John of Jerusalem*, IV [London, 1852], pp. cxv–cxxiii), and *cf.* Caoursin, *Obsidio*, fols. 4r–6v (=A4–6), for the first attack upon Fort S. Nicholas, and fols. 9r–11r (=A9–B1), for the second attack; Mary Dupuis, *Relation*, in Vertot, II, 601, 603–4, 607–8 (but see the preceding note). D'Aubusson's letter to Frederick III (of 13 September, 1480) is given in German translation in the popular Turkish history of Johann Adelphi, *Die Türckisch Chronica*, Strassburg, 1513, unnum. fols. 23r–26r (=Dv-Eii), and the Latin text of his letter of 15 September is given, as we have noted, by J. P. de Ludewig, *Reliquiae*, V (1723), 290–99, with numerous errors of transcription.

[24] Mary Dupuis, *Relation*, in Vertot, II (1726), 608–9.

[25] On 15 July (1480) Alberto Cortese, ambassador of the Estensi in Venice, wrote the duke of Ferrara that news had reached the Rialto "como a Rhodi pur fanno gran danno i Turchi, et dì et nocte bombardano da tre lochi, da la Zodecha [the Giudecca], da Sam Nicolò et dala Porta, et fanno male asai cum quelli mortali, et hanno buttato una gran quantità de muro per terra, da quello canto dela Zudecha" (Foucard, "Fonti," *Arch. stor. nap.*, VI, 131). *Cf.* a dispatch dated at Candia on 21 June concerning the assaults on the Giudecca (*ibid.*, pp. 137–38).

[26] Caoursin, *Obsidio*, fols. 6v–8v (A6–8), 11r (B1), followed by Bosio, II (1594), bk. XI, pp. 325–26; and *cf.* Pierre d'Aubusson's letter of 15 September to Sixtus IV, in J. P. de Ludewig, *Reliquiae*, V (1723), 294–95.

[27] Mary Dupuis, in Vertot, II (1726), 606.

a cannon founder and expert bombardier, who had once lived in Rhodes, and then moved with his wife and family to Istanbul, where the pay was better and the opportunities to employ his talents much more numerous. George's personality made a great impression upon Caoursin, who knew him; suspected of treachery at the height of the Turkish pressure upon the Italian bulwark, George was put to death. Another of these refugees from Mesīh Pasha's camp was alleged to have come into the city with the express purpose of poisoning the grand master, who had a stone tied around his neck and had him thrown into the sea. D'Aubusson suspected all those who deserted the crescent to join him in those weeks of peril, *tant Turcs que Chrestiens*, of whom there were said to be about sixty, and after the siege he had them put on board a ship and sent to Rome, where inquisitors might decide who had been sincere and who had plotted mischief.[28]

It took some time for the plight of Rhodes to become known in the West. By the beginning of July (1480) representatives of Pierre d'Aubusson had arrived in Rome, bringing news of the siege and appealing for aid. Processions were organized throughout the city converging on S. Maria del Popolo, where Pope Sixtus IV heard mass, and prayers were said *contra Turcum*. Assistance to Rhodes became the subject of earnest discussion. Plans were made to arm four large ships and send them right away to Rhodes with men, provisions, and artillery. The need was known to be for men and munitions, for it was said in Rome (rightly or wrongly) that there were bread and wine enough for two years in Rhodes. But money was always a problem at the Curia Romana. Even if the ships could be found promptly, the estimate of costs amounted to 34,000 ducats for a period of three months. No ships were to be got from Venice, always inimical to the Hospitallers, nor from the Genoese, who feared to deflect the sultan's interest from Rhodes to their own island of Chios. King Ferrante of Naples, very well disposed toward the Knights, could supply some immediate help and was eager to do so. Considering the size of the Turkish armada, however, eight large ships (*nave grosse*) and forty to fifty galleys would probably be needed not only for the defense of Rhodes but to obtain a decisive victory over the Turks. Some galleys could be located quickly; there were six in the harbor at Rhodes. As for money, Sixtus IV could provide 10,000 ducats immediately, and Ferrante a like sum, but 34,000 ducats were needed, and 20,000 simply would not suffice. In the meantime Sixtus IV would have two large ships put in order, and so would Ferrante. They would be sent to Rhodes with all speed.

On 5 July the pope informed the resident ambassadors that he had not wanted war in Italy (the so-called "Tuscan war"). If he had entered the conflict, the reasons impelling him to do so were obvious. Now Rhodes was imperiled; he was most anxious quickly to send help. He had already appealed to the princes beyond the Alps, and had ordered the preparation of ships. Eight large ships and forty galleys would be necessary, he told the ambassadors, whom he urged most strongly to write their governments to assume their shares of the costs. He asked the ambassadors to go to the house of Cardinal Guillaume d'Estouteville, his chamberlain (*camerlengo*), before 5:00 P.M. (*ale XX hore*) that afternoon. The count of Imola, Girolamo Riario, would be there too. The costs of the eight ships and forty galleys would then be reckoned for a period of three months. A tax would have to be imposed to raise the amount needed. To help Rhodes the pope would make peace in Italy; the diplomats warmly applauded his decision. They all agreed to write immediately to their lords and governments with the express hope that proper responses would be forthcoming to meet this emergency. Gathering at d'Estouteville's house at the appointed time (on 5 July), they found Riario present; naval experts now informed them that the expenses of the projected fleet would amount to 60,000 ducats for three months. The estimate being subsequently increased to 64,000, a tax was assessed, in which process the ambassadors were not invited to participate, and a set sum was assigned to each state.[29]

---

[28] Mary Dupuis, in Vertot, II, 606–7, and on Master George, see Caoursin, *Obsidio*, fols. 2ᵛ–3ʳ (A2–3), 4ᵛ–5ʳ (A4–5), 12ᵛ–13ʳ (B2–3), and Mary Dupuis, in Vertot, II, 601–2, 609–10. *Cf.* Bosio, II (1594), bk. XI, pp. 321–22, 326, 332–33.

[29] See the dispatches of Battista Bendedei from Rome to Duke Ercole I of Ferrara, dated 2–12 July (1480), in Foucard, "Fonti," *Arch. stor. nap.*, VI, 104–9. According to Antonio da Montecatino's dispatch from Florence to Ferrara on 7 July (*ibid.*, VI, 118): ". . . et che [Rodi] è fornito de pane et vino per dui anni." During the reign of Sixtus IV the annual gross income of the Holy See was apparently close to 280,000 ducats, for which see Clemens Bauer,

It was decided that the pope's two galleys would be armed in Genoa. Ferrante could make provision for his own two at Naples. The pope was expanding his plans for a major expedition against the Turks when the Ottoman landings in Apulia threw the Italian peninsula into a feverish excitement. Rhodes was not forgotten, but it lacked the geographical proximity of Otranto.[30] In the meantime the Rhodian tax (*tassa per defesa de Rodi*) had been assessed and assigned as follows: the pope, 10,000 ducats; the king of Naples, 20,000; the duke of Milan, 15,000; the signoria of Florence, 8,000; the duke of Ferrara, 4,000; the signoria of Siena, 4,000; the marquis of Mantua, 1,000; the marquis of Montferrat, 1,000; the signoria of Lucca, 1,000; and the duke of Savoy, 3,000. The total came to 67,000 ducats.[31] Venice was not included in the assessments. The Republic would take no step, to help relieve either Rhodes or Otranto, which the Turks might interpret as an act of hostility. Sixtus hoped, however, that when the Venetians saw the other Italian powers assembling their resources for a crusade, they would abrogate their treaty of January, 1479, with the Porte, and join in the Christian enterprise.[32]

Conditions in Italy naturally helped to determine Venetian policy in the Levant. As we have noted in the preceding chapter, the Venetians and King Ferrante of Naples were enemies. He felt strongly drawn toward the embattled Knights at Rhodes. They did not. They had also had their fill of war with the Turk for a while, and had observed in Pius II's time with how little efficacy an Italian league was likely to be formed against the Turk. After the Turkish landing at Otranto it was reported from Naples, to Ferrante's indignation, "that it appears the Venetian ambassador had said at Rome that all Italy should be obliged to the Turk because if he had not presented the king with [this] obstacle, his Majesty would be the lord of Siena, and he was trying to make himself the king of Italy."[33] We shall note in the next chapter Ferrante's self-righteous defense against this charge, and confine our attention here to the troubled affairs of Rhodes.

From about the middle of June (1480) the Turks had been digging in around the bastion of Italy, slowly pushing toward the ramparts in covered trenches. They were also building up earthworks close to the foss, which was gradually getting filled up, so that an ascent to the top of the ramparts was becoming feasible. Owing to the complete rebuilding of the Italian (southeastern) sector in later years, especially by

---

"Studi per la storia delle finanze papali durante il pontificato di Sisto IV," *Archivio della R. Società romana di storia patria*, L (1927), 319–400, esp. pp. 343–44, who publishes what may be a somewhat theoretical papal "budget" or ledger for the year 1480–1481 (*ibid*., pp. 349 ff.), and note Peter Partner, "The 'Budget' of the Roman Church in the Renaissance Period," in E. F. Jacob, ed., *Italian Renaissance Studies*, London, 1960, pp. 256–78, esp. pp. 260–64, 269, who estimates Sixtus IV's annual income at about 290,000 ducats. The alum mines at Tolfa were yielding about 50,000 ducats in 1480–1481. Sixtus's expenses were high.

The aged Cardinal d'Estouteville was named *camerarius* (*camerlengo*) on 12 August, 1477; he died on 22 January, 1483, and was succeeded in the office by Raffaele Riario [Sansoni], the cardinal of S. Giorgio (Pastor, *Gesch. d. Päpste*, II [repr. 1955], 633 note 5, 679; *cf*., *ibid*., III-1 [repr. 1955], 207, and Eubel, *Hierarchia catholica*, II [1914, repr. 1960], pp. 8, 18, and nos. 472–73, p. 46).

[30] Bendedei to Ferrara, 24 July and 5 August, in *Arch. stor. nap*., VI, 109–111.

[31] Antonio da Montecatino, from Florence, to Ferrara, 7–14 July (1480), in *Arch. stor. nap*., VI, 118–20. On 9 July, 1480, Sixtus IV wrote the Marquis Federico Gonzaga, "Ex litteris Rhodianorum cognovimus civitatem et insulam Rhodi a Turchis obsideri remque in periculo esse. Itaque ad subveniendum illis licet hactenus non defuerimus oportunam nunc classem cum auxilio Christianorum principum et potentatuum parandam statuimus ex quo spes datur nedum Rhodianos liberatum sed Turchos ipsos profligatum iri. Et cum causa hec communis sit, debet ab omnibus confoveri. Igitur ad presentem expeditionem taxatio uniuscuiusque facta est secundum quam contribuere debeat. . . . Et nos primi taxam nostram iam persolvimus. Taxa autem tua mille ducatorum est . . . ," but half the Mantuan levy of 1,000 ducats was to come from ecclesiastical tithes, leaving the marquis to pay a *taxa* of 500 (Arch. di Stato di Mantova, Arch. Gonzaga, Busta 834). The same brief was sent to Duke Ercole I d'Este, setting the Ferrarese *taxa* at 4,000 ducats (Arch. di Stato di Modena, Canc. ducale, Cart. di principi esteri, Busta 1293/A, no. 132, dated 9 July, 1480). Although by this brief of 9 July, Sixtus claimed he had "already paid" his *taxa* of 10,000 ducats, on 24 July he made available (an additional?) 2,000 ducats, and the College of Cardinals 5,000, "pro expeditione subsidii Rhodi contra Turcos" (Arch. Segr. Vaticano, Introitus et Exitus, Reg. 500, fols. 20^r, 48^v, and *cf*. fols. 49^r, 53^v, and Reg. 501, fols. 49^v, 50^r). The Turks were about to strike at Apulia also, and a papal brief of 27 July has a rather desperate tone (Arch. Gonzaga, Busta 834).

[32] Bendedei to Ferrara, 24 July, in *Arch. stor. nap*., VI, 110.

[33] Niccolò Sadoleto from Naples to the duke of Ferrara, 20 August (1480), in *Arch. stor. nap*., VI, 91. Since February, 1478, Siena had been allied with Ferrante and Sixtus IV against Lorenzo de' Medici, who had the support of Venice and Milan (see the preceding chapter, and *cf*. Pastor, *Hist. Popes*, IV, 297–99, and *Gesch. d. Päpste*, II [repr. 1955], 529–30).

the Grand Master Fabrizio del Carretto in 1515–1517, it is no longer possible to envisage with much accuracy either the details of the Turkish offensive or the Christians' countermoves.[34] The Hospitallers had some sailors and builders construct a large catapult or mortar of some kind, which they dubbed the "Tribute," and with which they shot heavy stones at the enemy, crushing many of them and inflicting some damage on the earthworks. It was hard going hour after hour. The Knights accumulated casks of pitch, sulphur, gunpowder, and other inflammables on the grand master's hastily improvised inner wall, which was faced with timber, branches, and wattlework to absorb the impact of the cannonballs. The Turks now shot letters over the walls into the city, offering the Greek natives and Latin residents their lives as well as full possession of their property and other privileges in return for an immediate surrender; if they persisted in their opposition, however, all those who were taken alive were going to be impaled, for which purpose (it was said) eight thousand stakes had already been prepared.[35]

Thirty-seven or -eight days were thus spent (19 June–26 July) in the unremitting toil of defense and offense.[36] But now the time for the great assault had come. Caoursin informs us that before the attack the Turks *suo more* invoked divine aid, washed their persons in purificatory rites, and got ready their sacks for plunder and ropes for captives. On the day before the attack, all night, and even at dawn on that memorable day, the eight great cannon pounded the walls and bulwarks. They almost reduced the fortifications to a smouldering mass of ruins, firing three hundred shots "in such a little while." The assault began Friday morning, 28 July, when a mortar fired the call to action. The Turks could scramble to the tops of the ramparts up an incline of rubble and débris more easily than the defenders could climb the twenty feet by ladders on the inside.[37] Turkish standards

[34] Bosio, II (1594), bk. XI, pp. 330–31; A. Gabriel, *La Cité de Rhodes*, I (1921), 53–57.

[35] Caoursin, *Obsidio*, fols. 12, 13 (=B2, 3); Mary Dupuis, in Vertot, II (1726), 610. According to the latter, Mesīh Pasha prepared only four hundred stakes for impaling his captives (*ibid.*, p. 612), perhaps reserving this treatment for the Knights, of whom there were probably about three hundred in Rhodes during the siege. Bosio, II (1594), bks. XI–XII, pp. 331–36, follows Caoursin.

[36] We may best note here a few of the more important differences between d'Aubusson's account of the siege and Caoursin's *Obsidio*. According to d'Aubusson, ". . . in his operibus XXXVIII diebus consumptis, quo in tempore 3,500 vel circiter ingentium saxorum in moenia et urbem iacti sunt" (Pauli, *Codice diplomatico*, II, 151–52), but Caoursin, *Obsidio*, fol. 14^v (=B4), says, ". . . secundum igitur alterumque proelium ad turrim molis divi Nicolai commissum diebus septem et triginta exactis." In any event the period must be 19 June to 26 July, which if counted inclusively is thirty-eight days, otherwise thirty-seven, as Torr, *Rhodes in Modern Times* (1887), pp. 20–21, realizes, but he places the coming battle of the Rhodian ramparts on 27 July, following Mary Dupuis, in Vertot, II (1726), 612. Bosio, II (1594), bk. XII, p. 337, also places the attack on 27 July. The correct date is probably 28 July, as Caoursin, *Obsidio*, fol. 13^v (=B3), gives it, *quinto chalendas Augusti*. D'Aubusson, who knew the date of the battle, informs Frederick III that it took place on 26 July, *VII Kalen. Augusti* (according to the text in Pauli, II, 152). The German translation of d'Aubusson's letter in J. Adelphi, *Türckisch Chronica* (1513), unnum. fol. 25 (=Eii), gives the date as "am XXV. tag des monats Julii." Obviously the texts have gone awry. However, in d'Aubusson's letter of 15 September to Sixtus IV, in J. P. de Ludewig, *Reliquiae*, V (1723), 296, the date is given as 28 July, *Vto die Augusti* being an error of transcription for *quinto Kal. Augusti*, as given by Caoursin.

The Augustinian Giacomo de Curti, in E. F. Mizzi, *Le Guerre di Rodi* (1934), p. 84, dates the last great encounter on the walls 27 July, but I think little reliance can be placed on his text. Nevertheless, some twenty years later (on 15 December, 1502), d'Aubusson wrote Pope Alexander VI that the battle had occurred on the twenty-seventh (*VI Kal. Aug.*) [AOM, Reg. 394, fols. 237^v–238^v, ref. from L. Butler], which could be a lapse of memory or a slip of the pen, but which seems to make absolute certainty as to the date a difficult matter. Both d'Aubusson and Caoursin date the beginning of the battle (in sentences which are almost word for word the same!) from the Turkish mortar signal, *ad signum iactus mortarii quod pridem eo in loco constituerunt*. Since Caoursin undoubtedly composed d'Aubusson's letter, which so closely resembles his own much longer *Obsidio*, obviously an error has entered Pauli's text, which founders also on the number of Turks who took part in the final assault: d'Aubusson is made to state that "affirmarunt profugae MMMM. Turcorum invasioni adesse" (Pauli, II, 152), while Caoursin, *Obsidio*, fol. 16^v (=B6), says that "affirmant perfugae quadraginta milia Turcorum invasioni adesse." Whatever the actual number of Turks involved in the attack, there cannot be any doubt that 40,000 is textually the proper figure (*cf.* Bosio, II [1594], bk. XII, p. 338).

[37] Caoursin, *Obsidio*, fols. 13^v–14^r (=B3–4), 17^r (=B7): "Erat namque muri altitudo ad intra fere pedum XX." Mary Dupuis, in Vertot, II (1726), 612–13. *Cf.* Bosio, II (1594), bk. XII, pp. 336–37, who places the attack on 27 July, presumably because Pierre d'Aubusson soon set aside the day of S. Pantaleon (27 July) as a memorial day of victory (*ibid.*, p. 344), and that victory was to be long remembered. Some five years later Pope Innocent VIII by the bull *Redemptor noster*, dated 31 May, 1485, made S. Pantaleon's day a solemn feast day forever in thanksgiving for the Rhodian victory over the Turks (Malta Library, MS. 142, F. [=vol. VI], pp. 669–73): "Auctoritate apostolica presentium tenore statuimus et ordinamus quod de cetero perpetuis futuris temporibus dies festivitatis eiusdem S. Pantaleonis qua habita fuit victoria predicta

were planted on the walls in more than one place, even on the Tower of Italy. Above the din of hand-to-hand battle rose the Hospitallers' signal of alarm. The defenders promptly launched flanking attacks from the right and left upon the threatened areas, and drove their assailants from the tops of the walls and ramparts. According to Mary Dupuis, d'Aubusson climbed up with a body of Knights into the thickest part of the fray, to prevent the Turks' descending the wall into the town. During the contest about three hundred Turks were thrown the twenty feet from the summit into the *vicus Judaeorum* below, where they were quickly dispatched to a man. About 2,500 Turks, "beautifully armed," had climbed the walls in the first assault, being quickly followed by a "huge multitude." It was later affirmed that 40,000 Turks had participated in the great assault.[38]

The battle of the Rhodian ramparts lasted for two hours, fortune wavering in the balance, *modo ad nostros modo ad Turcos victoria inclinante*, but when the Christians began to get the upper hand, they were able most effectively to press their advantage. Being repulsed, many of the Turks took fright. They pushed back upon their oncoming fellows, even striking at one another as panic seized them. The Hospitallers now took the offensive, and killed many Turks as they retreated, capturing the gold- and silver-decked Ottoman imperial standard, which was borne into the city over the ruin of the walls amid Christian cries of joy and triumph. D'Aubusson and Caoursin say (their accounts here are identical) that 3,500 Turks perished in Mesīh Pasha's final failure to take the city. According in fact to refugees who were on hand when Mesīh Pasha had a count made of his troops, the Turkish losses during the whole siege were

---

[de Turcis hostibus] in dictis insula et civitate aliisque terris et locis temporali dominio dicto Hospitali subiectis, et in quibus magister et conventus prefati tam in Oriente quam in Occidente merum habeant imperium, debeat ab omnibus et singulis utriusque sexus personis, incolis civitatis, insule et locorum eorundem, cessando ab omni opere ad instar aliarum solemnium festivitatum solemnizari et custodiri [p. 670] . . . Datum Rome apud Sanctum Petrum anno incarnationis dominice 1485, pridie Kal. Iunii, pontificatus nostri anno primo" (*Ex Libro Conciliorum Ordinis Hierosolimitani Cancellariae ab anno 1478 ad 1488*, fol. 211).

[38] Caoursin, *Obsidio*, fols. 15^r (=B5), 16^v–17^r (=B6–7); Mary Dupuis, in Vertot, II (1726), 613; d'Aubusson, in Ludewig, *Reliquiae*, V, 297–98. The sources indicate that d'Aubusson was seriously wounded while fighting on the walls. In 1522, at the time of the second siege, d'Aubusson's body richly dressed in the robes of a cardinal (he received the red hat in 1489) was exposed to public veneration, with his arms and other trophies of the great events of 1480, including the red velvet tunic with the white cross (which he wore over his armor on 28 July) "stained with his blood and that of the enemy" (Picenardi, *Itinéraire* [1900], p. 78, and *cf.* pp. 103–4). *Cf.* Bosio, II (1594), bk. XII, pp. 337–38.

On 7 August, 1480, a certain William, who was of noble birth, was accepted into the Order by a decision of the Council because of the heroism he had displayed in the fighting in the Jewish quarter either on 28 July or on an earlier occasion (Malta Library, AOM, Reg. 76, fol. 35^v): "Die VII Augusti MCCCCLXXX. Considerato quod Guillermus vir nobilis laudabiliter se gessit in obsidione Rhodi contra Turcos et presertim in dicta et bello confecto ad muros Judeorum ubi strenue pugnavit, per reverendissimum dominum magistrum et reverendum consilium fuit deliberatum [the scribe has inadvertently written *deliberavit*] quod recipiatur in fratrem militem religionis et de gracia speciali sibi conceditur passagium." On 8 November, 1480, Antonio Palapanno, who had lost his right hand in battle as he helped defend the wall in the Giudecca, was granted an annual pension for life of forty florins in cloth and thirty-six *modia* of grain. Obviously not a member of the Order, Palapanno may have been a resident of Rhodes (AOM, Reg. 76, fols. 41^v–42^r): "Die eodem [i.e., die VIII Novembris, MCCCCLXXX] considerato quod Anthonius Palapanno in die aggressionis Turcorum ad muros Iudeorum viriliter pugnavit et tutatus est murum in quo casu pugne perdidit manum dexteram, ideo ad subveniendum sue vite et sustentacionem suam fuit deliberatum quod vita sua durante exspectando maius commodum habeat a thesauro soldeam fratris militis quadraginta florenorum Rhodi currencium in panno et XXXVI modia granerii frumenti quolibet anno."

On 27 June, 1481, the Grand Master d'Aubusson praised Bernardino Reyes, Olivier de Morat, and the "magnificent and noble" Baltazar de Liechtenstain (*sic*) for the valor they showed in fighting in the Giudecca: "Frater Petrus [Daubusson Dei gratia sacre domus Hospitalis Sancti Iohannis Hierosolimitani magister humilis ac pauperum Iesu Christi custos:] Nobili viro Bernardino de Regibus salutem: Obsequia fidei catholice prestita nequaquam reticenda sunt, sed verbo et scripto predicanda. . . . Itaque optima racione inducti universis presentes litteras inspecturis notum facimus te in obsidione turcensi que Rhodum anno elapso crudelibus armis oppugnavit optimi comilitonis facinus egregium perpetrasse et ad muros Iudeorum in truculentissima aggressione magno animo hostibus obivisse egregieque manum conseruisse" (AOM, Reg. 388, fol. 201^r). Also, *ibid.*, "Spectabili viro Oliverio de Morat salutem, etc. Obsequia, etc., ut in precedenti." Again, with the same date, the grand master recognized that ". . . magnificus ac nobilis vir Baltazar de Liechtenstain miles nonnullorum sue nationis comilitonum capitanei officio fungens egregia quidem perpetratus sit facinora: Ipse quoque fidus commitatus commilitonibus in acerrima Turcorum aggressione ad Hebrorum menia se turcis strenue ac fortiter, nostri germani vestigia sequens, obiverit magnoque animo cum hoste manum conseruit et fortiter pugnavit pluraque clarissimo eius ingenio excogitavit que Rhodie urbis tuitioni conducerent . . ." (*ibid.*, fols. 201–201^v—by a scribal error of numbering there is no fol. 202 in this register). Baltazar had apparently fought beside d'Aubusson's nephew, the sieur de Monteil, who was killed at Rhodes.

reckoned at 9,000 killed and 15,000 wounded. These refugees also said that the Turks had been terrified by a miraculous vision which had caused their disastrous retreat in the last engagement: At the very height of the conflict on the walls d'Aubusson had ordered a standard to be raised depicting the crucified Christ between the Virgin Mary and S. John the Baptist, together with the Hospitallers' own standards,[39] whereupon the enemy had suddenly seen a wonderful golden cross in the heavens, and the Virgin (or at least a virgin) had appeared, clad in glowing white and armed with a shield and spear. In this vision there was also a man clothed in vile raiment, S. John himself, who was accompanied by a splendid retinue coming to aid the city. Such was the manner of the Christian victory; Caoursin says it descended from heaven. While the Rhodians were burning heaps of Turkish bodies to avoid the plague, the Turks were dismantling their tents and hauling their cannon to the shore. Before Mesīh Pasha re-embarked his men and equipment, he laid waste to such gardens, vineyards, and fields as had so far escaped, and he rounded up all the sheep he could.

At this point the two ships sent by King Ferrante of Naples arrived one afternoon at Rhodes, where they were met by adverse winds and Turkish fire, which struck the mast of one ship. The injured ship, however, easily made the harbor when the wind shifted toward the west, but the other had to spend the night in a heavy swell. The next day the wind died down. As the second ship tried to enter the harbor, it was pursued by twenty Turkish galleys. Its crew fought off all attacks manfully for three hours; the Turkish admiral was killed; and the king's ship finally made the port under full sail. The Neapolitans brought the joyful news that aid would soon be on its way to beleaguered Rhodes (but of course they knew nothing of the Turkish attack upon Otranto). At Ferrante's behest the Council of the Order on 17 August granted an exemption from customs' duties on eight hundred casks of wine which had come on one of the ships from Naples, since the shipment had been originally consigned to a western port, and its destination altered to Rhodes when the ship was diverted to assist the Hospitallers against the Turkish fleet.[40]

Letters from Pope Sixtus IV were publicly read, assuring the Rhodians that the Ottoman fleet would be assailed and the Turks tracked to their very lairs. Caoursin says that there was high praise for the pope in Rhodes. The rumor of a Christian armament is said also to have reached the Turks and to have hastened their departure, their last contingents leaving Rhodes on 18 August for Marmaris, whence both the fleet and the army returned to Istanbul. Mesīh Pasha was promptly stripped of his high honors and emoluments by the angry Sultan Mehmed, but rose again to some measure of imperial favor during the reign of his son Bayazid II. In the meantime the Christian victory at Rhodes filled all Europe with rejoicing. The vice-chancellor of the Hospital, Caoursin, immediately wrote his famous account of the siege "for praise of God, exaltation of the Christian religion, and the glory of the knights of Rhodes."[41] On 29 November (1480)

---

[39] Caoursin, *Obsidio*, fol. 17r (=B7), is rather ambiguous in his description of the raising of the standards, but Mary Dupuis, in Vertot, II (1726), 613, states that "Monseigneur le Maistre feist desploier une bandiere en laquelle estoit en peinture le crucefix estandu en l'arbre de la croix, nostre Dame dung couste et saint Jehan Baptiste d'aultre couste," etc., showing that there was only one such banner, as Torr, *Rhodes in Modern Times*, p. 78, noted, but he got the information not from Caoursin, whom he cites, but from Mary Dupuis, to whom he makes no reference. The banner has the importance of initiating the much-heralded and long-believed miracle, which Caoursin (fols. 17r–17v) and Mary Dupuis (Vertot, II, 615) describe in almost the same terms. Following Caoursin, Bosio, II (1594), bk. XII, p. 339, describes "gli stendardi." Giacomo de Curti, in Mizzi, *Le Guerre di Rodi*, p. 85, speaks of a single banner. On 5 September, 1480, it was reported in Ragusa that Turkish casualties at Rhodes included more than 17,000 killed (Foucard, "Fonti," *Arch. stor. nap.*, VI, 143).

[40] Malta Library, AOM, Reg. 76, fol. 35v: "Die XVII Augusti MCCCCLXXX. Habitis et intellectis litteris serenissimi domini regis Ferdinandi super immunitate gabelle et commerciorum VIIIc vegetum vini que nomine mercatorum venerunt super navi subsidiaria quam misit sua Majestas Rhodum: Considerato quod sua Majestas favit religioni et quod dicta navis venit in subsidium que erat naulizata pro occidente et mutavit partitum intuitu classis, fuit deliberatum quod dicte vegetes VIIIc sint immunes iuribus gabelle et commerciorum."

[41] Caoursin, *Obsidio*, fols. 17–18 (=B7–8), reckons the siege of Rhodes as having lasted eighty-nine days (fol. 18v, last fol. in the tract). Mary Dupuis, in Vertot, II (1726), 614, says that in the Turkish attempt to storm the walls, the defenders lost forty men killed, including fifteen Knights, with more than five hundred wounded. Mary (*ibid.*, pp. 615–16), in describing the entry of Ferrante's ships into the harbor of Rhodes, says that the second ship (attacked by the Turkish galleys) was three days in making port. It may be observed that before the Turkish attack upon Otranto had become a certainty, King Ferrante and the Neapolitan royal council on 1 July, 1480, had talked of sending to

King Louis XI of France, always much attached to the Hospitallers, happily informed the people of Angers that the siege of Rhodes had been raised, and ten to twelve thousand Turks had been killed: there were to be sermons and solemn processions, bells were to ring, and God's praises to be sung in the churches to celebrate the victory.[42]

---

the assistance of Rhodes "quatro nave grosse et XXVI galee," which were to be financed by the king, the Neapolitan baronage, the clergy, and the Hospitallers in the kingdom, while it was assumed that the pope would pay his share (Foucard, "Fonti," *Arch. stor. nap.*, VI, 81). A dispatch of the Estense ambassador to the duke of Ferrara, dated 20 August (1480), notes that Ferrante had indeed sent two ships to Rhodes (*ibid.*, p. 91). *Cf.* Bosio, II (1594), bk. XII, pp. 339–40, following Caoursin as always.

According to the great Turkish polyhistor Hajji Khalīfa (Kātib Chelebi), when the janissaries and other Turkish troops were scaling the Rhodian ramparts (on 28 July) bent on the kill and thirsting for plunder, "Messih Pasha, unwilling that the riches of a fortified place like Rhodes should fall a prey to the soldiery, gave orders that as the treasury of the place belonged exclusively to the Sultan, no one should dare to touch it: as soon as this unwelcome intelligence was spread among the soldiers, those on the outside would proceed no farther, whilst those in the interior remained motionless; and the enemy, having made a violent rush from one quarter, put to the sword all they met" (Jas. Mitchell, trans., *History of the Maritime Wars of the Turks, translated from the Turkish of Haji Khalifeh*, London, Oriental Translation Fund, 1831, p. 18). On Hajji Khalīfa (1609–1657), see F. Babinger, *Geschichtsschreiber d. Osmanen u. ihre Werke*, Leipzig, 1927, pp. 195–203. By this master stroke of avarice Mesīh Pasha is thus represented as having outmaneuvered success and achieved defeat, which seems most unlikely, although Babinger, *Maometto* (1957), pp. 592–93, accepts it. On the siege, *cf.* also G. M. Angiolello, *Hist. turchesca*, ed. I. Ursu, Bucharest, 1909, pp. 112–14, and Raynaldus, *Ann. eccl.*, ad ann. 1480, nos. 1–16, vol. XIX (1693), pp. 286–89.

The date of the Turkish withdrawal from Rhodes (18 August, 1480) is fixed by the archival record of the conciliar decisions of the Order (AOM, Reg. 76, fol. 35v): "Die XVIIII Augusti MCCCCLXXX. Considerato quod classis Turcorum *heri* recessit itura Constantinopolim, viso quod venerunt due naves subsidiarie ex Neapoli cum soldatis, ideo ad alleviandum religionem et diminuendum expensas fuit deliberatum quod naves domini Ludovici Peixo et aliorum stipendiatorum et etiam stipendiati pro tuicione molis licentientur et relaxentur. Item fuit deliberatum quod considerato quod dicta classis adhuc est propinqua, soldati qui venerunt super dictis navibus subsidiariis deputentur ad custodiam molis. Item fuit deliberatum quod armentur ille naves que restant et debeant navigare ad visum classis ad prohibendum ne classis tangat Langonem et insulas religionis." The Turkish fleet having withdrawn "yesterday" and two ships having arrived from Naples with mercenaries, the Council decided to license the departure of the vessels of Ludovicus Peixo and the other *stipendiati* (which had been pressed into service) and to dismiss the soldiers employed to guard Fort S. Nicholas during the siege. This action would reduce expenses since the mercenaries from Naples would now provide a garrison for the fort. Finally, it was decided to arm the ships remaining at Rhodes, so that they might follow the Turkish fleet and try to prevent its attacking Cos (Lango) and other islands belonging to S. John.

[42] Joseph Valsen and Étienne Charavay, eds., *Lettres de Louis XI*, Soc. de l'Hist. de France, VIII (1903), no. 1548, pp. 318–19, cited by Clarence D. Rouillard, *The Turk in French History*, Paris, 1938, pp. 26–27. The king writes that the defenders of Rhodes had numbered only "V mille et Vc gens de fait." When the smoke of battle had cleared, the grand master issued bulls of commendation, to which the black wax seal of his office was appended, to certain persons who had distinguished themselves during the siege, as to one Johannes de Fieru (*cf.* Malta Library, AOM, Reg. 387, fol. 212v): "Fr. Petrus Daubusson, etc. Universis presentes litteras inspecturis. Notum facimus qualiter zelo fidei ductus et impulsus nobilis vir Iohannes de Fieru presencium exhibitor transfretavit in orientem, audita Rhodiorum obsidione a Turcis fidei catholice inimicis facta, ubi cum nonnullis navibus Ianuensium in subvencionem ordinis nostri per S[anctissimum] D[ominum] N[ostrum] missis applicuit cum sancto proposito et catholica mente [ad] urbem contra hostes Cristi tutandum. Nunc autem cum soluta sit obsidio, ad lares proprios remeare proponit, principem suum visurus eidemque obsequuturus et eius negotia tractaturus. Que cum ita sint, ipsius intuitu fidei summopere commendamus. Est enim vir laude et commendatione dignus qui tot maria et terrores in subvencionem fidei peragravit de quo testimonium quod verum est perhibemus in cuius rei testimonium bulla nostra magistralis in cera nigra presentibus est impressa. Datum Rhodi in nostro conventu die VII Octobris MCCCCLXXX." On 23 October, 1480, Caoursin's brother Sidrianus also received a bull of commendation, to which "bulla nostra magistralis plumbea presentibus est appensa . . ." (*ibid.*, fol. 212v).

One Antonio de Brancato of Syracuse, skipper of a caravelle, *qui contra immanes Turcos egregium semper complevit facinus*, received the right to fly the Hospitallers' banner (*vexillum armorum nostrorum*) on his vessel (AOM, Reg. 388, fol. 184v, entry dated 4 February, 1481). On 9 June, 1481, a magistral bull of commendation with the black seal was issued to one Pierre de Beaumez: "Itaque notum facimus qualiter spectatus vir nobis dilectus Petrus de Beaumez [in] Gallia bellgica natus in obsidione Turcorum que anno preterito Rhodiam urbem oppugnavit tanquam catholice fidei commilito egregiam navavit operam eaque virili parte exequutus est que tuitioni urbis congruerunt . . ." (*ibid.*, fol. 203r). We have already observed (above, note 38) that full recognition was given Bernardino Reyes, Olivier de Morat, and Baltazar de Liechtenstain for their displays of heroism in encounters with the Turks in the Jewish quarter.

A Genoese noble named Branca Doria received on 2 August, 1481, the right to fly on any ship he owned the banner of the grand master's own family and was made a *domesticus familiaris* of the magistral household, "dignum quidem duximus vestram personam quodam specialis gracie favore prosequi . . . vos in domesticum familiarem excipientes ascribentesque vexilla armorum nostrorum qua domus ex qua nati sumus utitur in quocumque navigio vobis spectante et pertinente . . ." (AOM, Reg. 388, fols. 205v–206r). On 20 June, 1482, one Sebastian Bosch, skipper of a balinger (*balinerii patronus*),

Three days after the Turkish withdrawal, while horsemen were still picking their way through rubble in the streets, the Grand Master d'Aubusson and the members of the Council assembled to consider the business of the hour. They decided that the prior of Capua should be sent to Italy to inform Pope Sixtus and King Ferrante of the victory over the Turks and to request further aid, "for it is of course assumed that the enemy proposes to come back." The Council also decided to send out a brigantine to observe the movements of the Turkish fleet and determine whether it was in fact really withdrawing from Rhodian waters.[43] Two days later (on 23 August, 1480) the Council disposed of two related problems by agreeing to send the Turks who had been captured at Pheraclus (Feraclo) to Europe for sale in the slave marts, and also to send deserters from the Turkish camp westward for judgment as to the sincerity of their purpose in abandoning the crescent for the cross.[44] We have already noted the suspicion with which the grand master had greeted those who sought refuge, real or feigned, within the walls of Rhodes during the siege.

Before the siege began the grand master had ordered the demolition of the church of S. Anthony, pleasantly set amid gardens to the north of the city, lest its stone walls afford protection to Turkish gunners who would inevitably choose it as the site from which to aim their bombards at Fort S. Nicholas. On 11 September, 1480, the Council resolved in a ballot vote to complete the destruction of S. Anthony, because its location presented an enduring peril to Fort S. Nicholas, upon which the safety of Rhodes depended. A side chapel would be spared for services for the dead. It could easily be demolished whenever another siege appeared imminent. There would be no diminution, however, in the number of masses commonly said in S. Anthony's, for some could be celebrated in the chapel, and the rest in other churches designated for the purpose. If and when the Hospitallers someday faced a more assured and tranquil future, S. Anthony's would be restored and rebuilt "lest the memory of those who died should perish with them."[45]

By the beginning of October, 1480, the Knights were finally certain that the Turkish fleet had entirely vacated Rhodian waters and their islands were safe. The Council therefore agreed to allow the departure of Ferrante's ships and mercenaries.[46] To retain them in the service of the Order would be expensive, and much money was obviously going to be required for the reconstruction of the battered defenses of the city and for the replacement of some of the houses which had been destroyed during the siege. On 8 November an Aragonese knight, Ramón Fluvià (*de Fluviari*), was given permission to bring into the harbor and put in dry-dock a Turkish *fusta* which he had captured, and which the Order would presumably arm and employ in its own service. On the

tanquam fidei verus commilito et athleta in obsidione Turcorum que Rhodiam urbem nostram oppugnavit, in his que urbis tuicionem concernunt optimam navastis operam, received for life the right to fly the Hospitallers' banner, *videlicet signum vere crucis albe in campo rubri coloris* (*ibid.*, fol. 210^r), but under the white cross on a red field he was not to inflict injury either on Christians or on friends of the Order.

[43] Malta Library, AOM, Reg. 76, fol. 35^v: "Die XXI Augusti MCCCCLXXX. Fuerunt electi oratores ad S.D.N. et Ec. d. regis Ferdinandi reverendus d. prior Capue et preceptor Daliage ad manifestandum victoriam habitam de Turcis et tractandum de succursu pro vere considerato quod inimicus proponit venire. / Fuit deliberatum quod mittatur bringantinus [*sic*] ad sciendum de armata si recessit vel non."

[44] AOM, Reg. 76, fol. 36^r: "Die eodem [i.e., die XXIII Augusti MCCCCLXXX] fuit deliberatum quod sclavi turci capti in Ferraclou vendantur pro partibus occiduis eo quod non vadant in Turchiam. / Die eodem fuit deliberatum quod perfuge mittantur ad partes occiduas [et] de illis de quibus habetur suspicio provideatur."

[45] AOM, Reg. 76, fol. 37: "Die XI Septembris MCCCCLXXX. Quia per experienciam habitam in obsidione Turcorum que nuper Rhodi vigebat compertum est quod ecclesia Sancti Anthonii affert maximum damnum Sancti Nicolai . . . , et deliberatum [fuit] per reverendissimum dominum magistrum et reverendum consilium cum scrutinio balotarum consulendo indempnitati eiusdem turris et civitatis quod dicta ecclesia diruatur in totum excepta capella que est in latere respiciente castellum Rhodi que remaneat ad facienda servicia solita pro defunctis et alia ita tamen quod adveniente certitudine classis instaurata pro obsidione Rhodiorum illa capella illico diruatur pro communi utilitate religionis et conservacione Rhodi cum reservacione quod misse solite illic celebrari non diminuantur, ymo cantentur et celebrentur in ecclesiis deputatis ac dicta capella etiam si religio pro futuro devenerit ad pacifficam et tranquiliorem statum quod dicta ecclesia Sancti Anthonii denuo edificetur et restauretur ad celebrandum et ad ordinacionem divini cultus ne intereat defunctorum memoria."

[46] AOM, Reg. 76, fol. 38^r: "Die II Octobris MCCCCLXXX. Per reverendissimum dominum magistrum et reverendum consilium ordinarium considerato quod classis Turcorum recessit ex terminis Religionis et quod res sunt in pacaciori statu, ad evitandas expensas fuit deliberatum quod licencientur dicte naves subsidiarie regis Ferdinandi et soldati qui venerunt super dictis navibus."

same day the Council enrolled one Lupo Pignera, a noble from Galicia, as a knight conventual in recognition of his efforts to defend Rhodes during the siege.[47] One Cosma Centurione, who had completed the term for which he had hired out his ship to the Order, wanted a license to leave the island; on 14 November the grand master and the Council granted his request since there was no longer any pressing need to retain him. Thus more money was saved, but the times were fraught with peril, and so one hundred or one hundred and fifty of the men who had come to Rhodes with the prior of Rome were to be kept in service at a monthly stipend of three gold ducats each.[48]

The Hospitallers had various kinds of recognition and assistance to render those who had distinguished themselves during the terrible summer of 1480. The noble Jean de Bigny, described as "viscount" of Rhodes but not a member of the Order, who with great and diligent effort had raised a force at his own expense and fought against the enemy, had lost all his property on the island, and so on 18 May, 1481, the Order granted him an annual pension and twice the daily food allotment of a knight conventual.[49] On 12 July, 1481, the grand master wrote an interesting letter of commendation for a Dominican priest who had administered the sacraments, during the whole period of the siege, to the hardpressed defenders of the tower and mole of S. Nicholas. The brave friar had suffered from the damp cold of night and acquired a nervous affliction from the prolonged ordeal (*ob algorem maris nocturnum mala validitudine nervorumque contractione affecta*). He was now leaving Rhodes, presumably going west, to seek the recovery of his health at certain spas (*balnea*). The grand master besought those to whom the friar might present his letter to receive with favor one who had endured such hardship for the faith, and whose example might tempt others to a like performance.[50]

On 14 July, 1482, the grand master asked Queen Isabella of Castile to pardon one Fernando de Vergonde, a noble of Galicia, who was among those convicted of crime whom the queen apparently had allowed to go free, provided they would go to Rhodes and help defend the city against the Turks. Vergonde had come to the island on one of the ships (*balinerii*) of Pedro Pignera, also a *gallego*, with letters from Isabella explaining his situation. The grand master now requested that Vergonde's strenuous performance at the siege constitute the expiation of his crime, and letters were written *in simili forma* on the same date for two other nobles and eighteen non-nobles, suggesting that the Knights of the "Langues d'Espaigne" had indeed had a motley crew of adventurers fighting with them on the Rhodian battlements.[51]

When on Friday, 28 July, 1480, Mesīh Pasha's troops were launching their final assault upon the southern walls and bulwarks of Rhodes, the Ottoman fleet was casting anchor off the Apulian coast, preparatory to the attack upon the Terra d'Otranto. Sultan Mehmed II had reached the pinnacle—and now the end—of his career. It was just a year after the first shots were fired upon Fort S. Nicholas from Mesīh Pasha's battery in the gardens of S. Anthony's church that the news reached Rhodes of Mehmed's death. The great second expedition against the Knights, which (it was assumed) he was preparing, would now come to nothing. On 31 May, 1481, Caoursin, vice-chancellor and public orator of the Hospital, delivered an oration *De morte Magni Thurci* before an assembly of the Knights, in which he gave expression to a savage joy:

> If a pen could describe the pleasure in my heart [*mens*], and speech explain the happiness in my soul [*cor*], today has certainly provided the occasion . . . , for lo! not without God's love and the divine judgment, to which all things are subject, the festering wound of Christendom has been healed, the consuming fire put out . . . , and we behold the dispatch of the fiercest enemy of orthodoxy. Satan, whose minion he was, has rejoiced at the coming of his lost companion, and the denizens of hell have greeted his advent with great applause—if we can conceive of any joy among them. The grim

[47] AOM, Reg. 76, fols. 41ᵛ–42ʳ.

[48] AOM, Reg. 76, fol. 42: "Die XIIII Novembris MCCCCLXXX. Per reverendissimum dominum magistrum et reverendum consilium fuit licenciata navis Cosme Centuriori que complevit suum terminum et requisivit patronus licenciam considerato quod de presenti non est vigens causa ut retineatur. / Insuper fuit deliberatum quod pro ingruencia temporum retineantur ad stipendia thesauri ad racionem ducatorum auri de Rhodo III pro mense centum vel centum quinquaginta homines de his qui venerunt cum reverendo d. priore urbis capitaneo apostolico."

[49] AOM, Reg. 76, fols. 51ʳ–51ᵛ. De Bigny is said to have been a resident of Rhodes for twenty-six years.

[50] AOM, Reg. 388, fol. 205ʳ.

[51] AOM, Reg. 388, fol. 211ᵛ.

abode of eternal confusion is the just due of the unspeakable tyrant who has destroyed the souls of so many children whom he compelled to abjure the faith, and thus blinded they have descended into hell. [He had caused virgins and matrons to be defiled, slaughtered young men and old, profaned sacred relics, polluted churches and monasteries, destroyed, oppressed, and seized kingdoms, principalities, and cities, including imperial Constantinople, which he took for himself and made the scene of unbelievable crimes.]

Caoursin could hardly find the words, which he trembled and blushed to use in the grand master's presence, to describe this second Lucifer, this second Mohammed, this second Antichrist. *Horrescit quidem animus, haeret lingua palato*. Mehmed II's passing had been attended by the most extraordinary manifestations of Earth's own abhorrence of his heinous crimes:

For about the time of his departure from life frequent earthquakes occurred in Asia, Rhodes, and the islands roundabout, especially two of the most marked severity, which were so great and terrible that they laid low many castles, strongholds, and palaces. Even the sea rose more than ten feet and flooded the shores, and straightway rolling back into the deep it sank as many feet as it had risen, and finally flowed back to its accustomed level. So abundant in fact was the exhalation [of his corpse], and so great the explosion [*velocitas*] confined within the caverns of the earth, that seven times it sent through the earth its violent shocks and caused a sudden outflow of the sea. The phenomenon is worth recording, and something the Rhodians have never seen before. Although it is explicable by physical principles, nevertheless it usually portends some great event.[52]

[52] Caoursin's *Oratio in senatu Rhodiorum de morte Magni Thurci habita pridie Kalendas Iunias MCCCCLXXXI* may be found in the full edition of his works published by Johann Reger at Ulm on 24 October, 1496, which also contains Caoursin's tract *De terremotus labe qua Rhodii affecti sunt*, in which he dates the two worst shocks on 18 March, *quindecimo Kalendas Aprilis*, and 3 May, *quinto nonas Maii*, and associates the latter with Mehmed's death, *sicut in congratulatione de excessu Magni Thurci nuper edita annotavimus*. *Cf.* Bosio, II (1594), bk. XII, pp. 349–50. Whatever the explanation for the *exalationis copia atque velocitas intra terre cavernas conclusa*, which caused the earthquake of 3 May, Mehmed II was buried above ground, and still lies, apparently undisturbed, in an eighteenth-century tomb (*türbe*) in the garden of the Fatih Jamii in Istanbul.

The earthquake is the subject of two unpublished briefs of Sixtus IV dated 1 June, 1482 (Biblioteca Nazionale Centrale, Florence, Bibl. Magliabecchiana, MS. II–III 256, fols. 268^v–269^r): "Nuper, ut accepimus, insula Rhodi adeo terremotibus quassata est ut, nisi de aliquo presidio succurratur, cogantur illius incole eam omnino deserere, quod magnum Christiane reipublice detrimentum afferre posset cum semper unicum fidei adversus perfidos Turcos propugnaculum fuerit . . . ," and so financial provision had to be made to repair the damage done. *Cf.*, *ibid.*, fols. 282^r ff., for various similar briefs.

Mehmed II's death was known in Venice by 29 May (Sen. Secreta, Reg. 30, fols. 16^v–17^r [26^v–27^r], and note fols. 19^r [29^r], 23^v–24^r [33^v–34^r], 24^v ff. [34^v ff.], relating to the succession of Bayazid II).

12. SIXTUS IV AND THE RECOVERY OF OTRANTO (1480–1484)

After the fall of Otranto, Pope Sixtus IV is said to have contemplated flight to Avignon,[1] but he quickly saw that the Terra d'Otranto had now become the first line of Christian defense against Sultan Mehmed's vast ambition. Exasperated with Ferrante for his recent desertion of the papal cause, Sixtus had to help him; still incensed with Lorenzo de' Medici, he was obliged to come to terms with him also. If fear prevailed in Rome and Naples, however, it seems not to have extended to the Arno, where a medal was designed in 1480, on Lorenzo's order, by the Florentine sculptor Bertoldo di Giovanni, commemorating Mehmed's triumphs as the "emperor of Asia, Trebizond, and Magna Graecia" (*Maumhet Asie ac Trapesunzis Magneque Gretie Imperat*[*or*]). Although the last area of Mehmed's sovereignty was rather ambiguously described, it could nevertheless mean southern Italy. There was talk at the time that as ruler of Constantinople Mehmed had a right to this old Byzantine territory.[2]

In a bull issued in the late summer of 1480 Sixtus IV declared that all Europe now knew that Rhodes was under unrelenting assault, and that Otranto had been taken by the fierce hordes of Islam. The aged archbishop of Otranto had been slaughtered with his canons and clergy almost at the cathedral altar. The city had been sacked, and the surrounding areas plundered as far as Brindisi. The size of the Turkish army and the extent of the Turkish victory grew day by day (*eorumque exercitum et victoriam in dies continuo augeri*). Many Hospitallers and Rhodians had perished, the walls of the island fortress had almost been leveled, and the Christian defenders were caught in a siege of unparalleled ferocity. (The news of the Turkish withdrawal from Rhodes had not yet reached the Curia Romana.) Unless the Italian states united now to send aid overseas, no one could doubt that victory would attend Islamic efforts.

> How perilous it has become for all Christians, and especially the Italian powers, to hesitate in the assumption of arms against the Turks and how destructive to delay any longer, everyone can see . . . , and so if the faithful, and especially the Italians, want to keep their lands, homes, wives, children, liberty, and the very faith in which we are baptized and reborn, let them believe us that they must now take up arms and go to war!

They were not to despair of divine clemency, but rather to reprove their own negligence, for their sins had delayed the mercy of heaven. Sixtus therefore called upon the faithful to convert fraternal strife into love, take up sword and buckler, gird their weakness with strength, and beat down the arrogance of those, "who place not their faith in God but in their own savagery." The Christian hope must be in God, whose voice rose above the din of battle, and who had cast the chariot of Pharaoh beneath the sea.

Sixtus stated in the bull that he had sent no small sum of money to the Grand Master d'Aubusson, granted a plenary indulgence to those who would help defend Rhodes, and dispatched a large grain ship which by some miracle had reached the island three days before the Turkish landing. As soon as he had heard of the siege, moreover, Sixtus had sent from Genoa two great shiploads of men and arms, and issued an appeal to the emperor, the Christian kings, and all the faithful to assist Rhodes and expel the Turks from Apulia. Finally he had sent Cardinal Gabriele Rangone to Naples with all the money he could raise to help King Ferrante repel the Turkish attacks and assail the enemy by land and sea. Papal

---

[1] Sigismondo de' Conti, *Le Storie de' suoi tempi*, 2 vols., Rome, 1883, I, 107–9; Pastor, *Hist. Popes*, IV, 334, and *Gesch. d. Päpste*, II (repr. 1955), 560–61; Piva, III, 465 (for the last reference, see above, Chapter 10, note 77). On the papal secretary and historian Sigismondo, whose work we have cited in an earlier chapter, see Ignazio Ciampi, "Dei Libri *Historiarum sui temporis* di Sigismondo de'Conti da Foligno," *Archivio storico italiano*, 4th ser., I (1878), 71–89.

[2] Sir Geo. Hill, "Medals of Turkish Sultans," *Numismatic Chronicle*, 5th ser., VI (London, 1926), 290; Emil Jacobs, "Die Mehemmed-Medaille des Bertoldo," *Jahrbuch der preussischen Kunstsammlungen*, XLVII (Berlin, 1927), 1–17, esp. p. 14; Franz Babinger, *Maometto il Conquistatore* (1957), pp. 576–79 (opp. p. 569 the medal is reproduced), 615, 747–48. *Cf.* A. Navagero, *Storia veneziana*, in *RISS*, XXIII (Milan, 1733), col. 1165D: "Il qual Signore come Imperadore di Costantinopoli pretendendo la città di Brindisi, quella di Taranto, e d'Otranto, di ragione di quell'Imperio. . . ." Navagero, *loc. cit.*, writing about twenty years after the event, also states that the Venetian government asked the Porte to attack Ferrante, on which, however, see A. Bombaci, "Venezia e l'impresa turca di Otranto," *Riv. storica italiana*, LXVI (1954), 173 ff., and *cf.* above, Chapter 10, note 83.

efforts would not cease until the siege of Rhodes was raised and the Turks had been driven from the Italian peninsula.[3]

Although Sixtus was sounding the alarm, Lorenzo de' Medici was actually relieved by the withdrawal of his Neapolitan allies from Siena. As we have already noted, the Venetian ambassador to Rome, Zaccaria Barbaro, was quoted (in Naples) as saying that the Italians should in fact be grateful to the Turk, because if he had not stopped Ferrante, "his Majesty would be the lord of Siena, and he was trying to make himself king of Italy." Ferrante claimed that Barbaro was wrong to say such a thing, because his desire had always been and still was to see peace in Italy and a general league open to all the Italian states. This should have been clear to everyone, and especially to the pope. He had wanted to join the Venetians in their war against the Turks; he had been willing to risk all his revenues in the war, retaining only enough for his own expenses. No one had listened to him, however, and at that time he had not been attacked by the Turk. He recalled that he had sent a subsidy to the Venetians under assault at Negroponte, risked his ships and galleys for the benefit of the Venetians, and just sent two ships to aid the Hospitallers at Rhodes.[4] But even when Ferrante told the truth, he told it untruly, for he neglected to mention that the two ships he had sent to Rhodes had flown the banner of S. Mark, as the Venetian Senate informed their ambassador in Istanbul when they sent a special envoy to the Porte to explain Ferrante's intolerable deception.[5]

The Turkish landing at Otranto had frightened Sixtus IV almost as much as if it had taken place at Ostia. The ally of Venice, he was also the supreme pontiff, with a special obligation to defend Christendom against the infidel invader. He added his own voice to the chorus of appeals being directed at the Venetians, who would not alter their policy of strict neutrality. They deplored the fall of Otranto, as they instructed Zaccaria Barbaro to tell the pope, but for "seventeen successive years" they had fought the Turk almost alone, with an unbelievable cost in men and money. They had done their part for the faith, freedom, fortunes, and safety of Europe. It had been exhausting. They could do no more.[6] Two weeks after this

---

[3] For the text of the bull, see Raynaldus, *Ann. eccl.*, ad ann. 1480, nos. 20–24, vol. XIX (1693), pp. 289–91. Gabriele Rangone was appointed *legatus de latere* to Naples in a secret consistory of 18 August, 1480 (the very day of the Turkish withdrawal from Rhodes), as appears from the Acta Consistorialia, in Arch. Segreto Vaticano, Arm. XXXI, tom. 52, fol. 94^r, by modern stamped enumeration: "Die Veneris XVIII^a mensis Augusti anno a nativitate Domini MCCCCLXXX . . . in consistorio secreto, ut moris est, reverendissimus in Christo pater et dominus, dominus Ga[briel] tituli Sanctorum Sergii et Bachi presbyter cardinalis Agriensis [Erlau, Eger in Hungary] nuncupatus, fuit creatus legatus de latere contra nephandissimos Theucros in civitatem et regnum Neapolitanum et fuit sibi per Collegium concessum ex gratia ut participaret de comunibus et minutis servitiis, etc., ut ceteri reverendissimi domini cardinales non obstante eius absentia." (An abbreviated and rather casual transcription of this text is given in Eubel, *Hierarchia catholica*, II [1914, repr. 1960], no. 433, p. 43). Rangone left Rome for Naples on 23 August (*ibid.*), and took with him the ten thousand ducats which Sixtus IV had raised to assist Ferrante (C. Foucard, "Fonti di storia napoletana . . . ," *Arch. stor. nap.*, VI [1881], 90–91, 142). Sixtus had previously intended to send Corrado de'Marcellini, bishop of Terracina, on the Neapolitan legation, but changed his mind immediately (*ibid.*, pp. 89, 90–91, 154–55).

[4] Sadoleto to Ercole d'Este, 20 August, 1480, in *Arch. stor. nap.*, VI, 91. *Cf.*, above, p. 356b.

[5] Sen. Secreta, Reg. 29, fol. 124^r [134^r], doc. dated 14 August, 1480.

[6] Sen. Secreta, Reg. 29, fols. 126^v–127^r [136^v–137^r], a letter of the Senate to Zaccaria Barbaro in Rome, dated 22 August, 1480: ". . . Volumus . . . vobisque mandamus ut cum summo pontifice esse debeatis et verbis humilibus, gravibus et reverentibus indoleatis casum Idronti[Otranto]. . . . [But Barbaro was to remind the pope:] nos post subactum et eversum regnum Bossine ad bellum cum Turco lacessitos ab eo devenisse, quod pro status nostri defensione pro fide, pro libertate, pro fortunis et salute universali annos XVII continuos incredibili magnitudine impensarum, cede, et strage ingentis numeri nobilium civium stipendiariorum et omnifariam hominum subditorum nostrorum pertinacissime sustinuimus . . . ."

Despite the frantic appeals Venice had made to the Christian princes, no one had come to her aid in that long, terrible, and unequal struggle with the Turk. She had fought alone in Friuli and Dalmatia, Albania and the Morea, "et in cunctis maritimis oris et insulis nostris." The war had drained her resources. This time Venice simply could not—and would not—enter the fray against the all-powerful Turk (Sen. Secreta, Reg. 29, fols. cited above). This letter seems to have been voted into effect *de parte* 114, *de non* 44, *non sinceri* 10, although the text lacks the upright cross in the left margin which would indicate that it was actually sent.

Should the situation arise, however, as the Senate wrote Barbaro on 10 October (1480), "quo Turchus cum classe provintiam Marchie [the region of Ancona] et statum Ecclesie adoriretur, vos respondete neminem posse aut debere de animo nostro dubitare quin ille idem sit qui fuerit et in nostris maioribus et in nobis erga rem christianam et erga statum Ecclesie . . ." (Sen. Secreta, Reg. 29, fol. 135^v [145^v]). Such rhetorical statements carried little weight in Rome, where rhetoric was a stock in trade, and in fact on 28 October the Senate again instructed Barbaro (as noted below, in the text) to take no part in meetings, reply to the papal entreaty, the Senate received an envoy from Duke Maximilian of Burgundy (in early September, 1480); he had come to urge the Serenissima to take up the cudgels against the Turks in these dire days of Christian need. The Senate informed him that, during the long years of their terrible war with the Turks, they had had abundant opportunity to observe the faith, constancy, and kindly feelings of the Italian powers toward Venice. The virtuous sons of S. Mark had been ill repaid in those frightful years for their exemplary conduct toward their fellow Italians. If the Venetians entered the war against the Turks, they would only be taking another's war upon themselves (*nil aliud in effectu esset quam sumere alienum bellum*), removing the flames from a neighbor's house to throw them on their own. They would end up bearing by themselves the awful brunt of Turkish hatred and attack on land and sea (and certainly they were most vulnerable to attack along the eastern Adriatic, in Corfu, and in Greece). Not only had they learned from past experience how much they could expect from their allies, but the present word from Naples was that Ferrante was hardly venturing into the field, and his alleged allies were not assisting him.[7]

In briefs of 22 September, 1480, Sixtus had requested that all the Christian princes send envoys to Rome by 1 November with full and sufficient powers to commit their principals to adequate contributions toward the defense of the peninsula. King Louis XI gave every indication of lending his powerful support to the allied effort to expel the Turks, as could be seen from the copies of letters from the king and the papal legate in France which Sixtus enclosed with the briefs he sent out convoking the assembly of envoys.[8] The Sforza dukes in Milan in a reply to the papal brief expressed full willingness to co-operate (on 5 October, 1480), but stated that peace must be established in Italy before Louis XI would help, "for we confess that we cannot see how we may expect foreign aid if we make light of our troubles at home." When the Milanese envoys in Rome reported that the papal summons seemed to have evoked no enthusiasm of response, the dukes replied on 27 October that they feared the patient might well die before the physician's arrival.[9] The patient was obviously Ferrante of Naples, and the suspicion obtained in some quarters that the Venetians would not be overcome with grief if in fact he did die.

To the annoyance of the Venetian government the envoys of the league of Naples gathered on the lagoon at the beginning of October, 1480. They had nothing to say of the Turkish peril which had not been said many times before.[10] When Ferrante's envoy presented the request "del trar de questa nostra cita et de li altri luogi nostri arme et munitione per

---

discussions, and negotiations relating to the campaign being organized against the Turks (*ibid.*, fol. 137^v [147^v]).

The Venetian stance inevitably evoked calumny as well as criticism. The Republic was accused of assisting the Turkish invasion of the Italian peninsula (Sen. Secreta, Reg. 29, fol. 140^v [150^v]). The Turkish presence, however, made the Venetians uncomfortable, and they were much relieved as the invaders began to falter and finally lost Otranto after Mehmed II's death (*cf.*, *ibid.*, Reg. 30 [1481–1482], fols. 2^v, 3^v ff., 16^v–17^r, 19, 20^v, 32^v–33^r [12^v, 13^v ff., etc.]).

[7] Sen. Secreta, Reg. 29, fols. 130^r–131^r [140^r–141^r]: ". . . In bello dum mansimus omnium truculentissimo et periculosissimo experti plurifariam sumus fidem, constantiam et benivolentiam in nos potentatuum Italie cum quibus ut semper studiose quesivimus non solum in pace sed etiam in benivolentia, charitate et officio vivere . . ." (fol. 131^r [141^r]). See also Piva, II, 446, who quotes part of this document.

[8] *Cf.* the text of the brief sent to the Marquis Federico Gonzaga in the Arch. di Stato di Mantova, Arch. Gonzaga, Busta 834: "Evocavimus omnes Christianorum principum oratores ut ad Kalendas Novembres proxime futuras apud nos sint cum plenis et sufficientibus mandatis ad consulendum et contribuendum in tam manifesta reipublice Christiane calamitate ea que pro communi salute oportuna videbuntur. . . . [Federico is urged to send *statuto tempore* his envoys to the congress.] Et ut ad hoc sanctissimum opus carissimi in Christo filii nostri Ludovici Francorum regis animum et optimam dispositionem intelligas, mittimus ad nobilitatem tuam his inclusum litterarum tam eius quam legati nostri quem ad constituendam in Galliis pacem transmisimus exemplum ut voluntas tua ad publicam salutem bene constituta ex hoc etiam ad rem ipsam complectendam alacrius insurgat et accendatur." At this time Genoa and Florence were on the brink of war, each lodging complaints against the other at the Curia; Sixtus was trying to preserve peace between them (*ibid.*, brief dated 28 September, 1480).

[9] Felice Fossati, "Milano e una fallita alleanza contro i Turchi," *Archivio storico lombardo*, 3rd ser., XVI (1901), 52–53. Lodovico il Moro, duke of Bari, was already conducting the affairs of Milan on behalf of his young nephew Gian Galeazzo, duke of Milan, whose mother and titular regent, Bona of Savoy, neglected state business, carried on with her young lover Antonio Tassino, and soon left Milan for the court of her brother-in-law, Louis XI of France.

[10] *Cf.* Sen. Secreta, Reg. 29, fol. 133^r [143^r], doc. dated 4 October: "Quod oratoribus Regis [Ferdinandi] et sociorum responderi in hunc modum debeat: . . . Tuto quello che ne hano dicto del pericolo de Italia et de universa re Christiana e verissimo et antiveduto et cognoscuto da nui gia molto tempo . . . ."

diffexa de le terre et paixe suo," the Senate had to refuse: Venice had exhausted her own supplies in the long war against the Porte.[11] And when the proposal was put forth in the Senate that, owing to the importance of the matters in hand, the departure of the Neapolitan and other envoys should be postponed "for some days," it was decided that the time had passed for suggesting a longer stay in Venice. The envoys were in fact remaining "with no other hope and purpose than that in oblique and indirect fashion they may thwart our intentions [and achieve] what they cannot accomplish in the right way." The Senate had made clear upon their arrival, more than three weeks before, that the Republic was glad to receive them and to hold discussions with them. But the Senate had given final answers to their requests, and surely it was clear that the continuance of their stay in Venice was unnecessary.[12]

At the same time the Senate wrote Barbaro in Rome that they were moved to repeat the instructions they had given him "more than once," that he should absent himself from all meetings, discussions, and negotiations relating to an expedition against the Turks, for the envoys of the Christian powers would soon be assembling in Rome in response to the summons which the pope had issued for 1 November. In Venice it was easy to envisage, Barbaro was told, the magnificent speeches that would be made, and the brilliant schemes proposed, which would (as in the past) be more like flights of fancy than anything approaching reality.[13] Actually Sixtus's anti-Turkish congress did not begin until toward the end of November,[14] and the discussions were no less spectacular than the Senate assumed they were going to be.

If Sixtus has much to answer for before the bar of history, it is not because of his lack of effort against the Turks. Very likely he could have done more. He was certainly distracted from the crusade by his constant desire to satisfy the inordinate ambition of his unworthy nephew Girolamo Riario. But he did embark immediately on plans to build a papal fleet at Genoa and Ancona; appealed to England, Germany, and France for assistance against the Turkish invaders; and imposed heavy taxes and tithes upon the papal states. Nothing could be expected from England and Germany, however, and although Louis XI made grandiose offers, he attached impossible conditions to them. The Italian states were highly suspicious of one another, and with good reason. On 5 November, 1480, to be sure, the dukes in Milan emphasized in a dispatch to their envoys in Rome that aid from the north (*li subsidii ultramontani*) would doubtless be long in coming, and that a united Italy should employ its own strength against the Turks before the danger got worse. On the same day the dukes subscribed *manu nostra*, and had their seals added, to a formal instrument granting their envoys full, free, and ample powers to commit them to the crusade, "because we are prepared to strive beyond our strength for the common safety and to defeat in war the barbarous, butcherly, and savage Turks."[15]

Even in the private instructions the dukes gave their envoys leaving Milan, they began with the statement, "We do not believe that for many centuries a more grave and perilous thing has befallen not only Italy but all Christendom than this . . . invasion of Calabria by the Turk, both because of the inestimable power and great cruelty of the enemy and because of the utter shame it brings to our religion and the Christian way of life. . . ." While commending Sixtus for summoning the princes and the Christian powers to find the means of striking back at the "dog Turk," and in no wise indicating that they would not do their duty, the dukes also informed their envoys that "you are at no time to agree to any promise and obligation to contribute to, and concur with, any expense unless you first advise us and have then received a reply from us." Before undertaking anything they wanted to know "quid, quomodo, et quando," and of course what the other princes and powers were going to do, "and with them to

[11] *Ibid.*, fols. 135^{v}–136^{r} [145^{v}–146^{r}], dated 23 October.

[12] *Ibid.*, fol. 137^{r} [147^{r}], dated 28 October.

[13] *Ibid.*, fol. 137^{v} [147^{v}], letter of the Senate to Barbaro, dated 28 October: ". . . Ex superiori materia in alteris contenta litteris et ex ista etiam movemur ad replicandum id quod alias vobis plusquam semel imposuisse meminimus ut scilicet abstineatis a congressibus, sermonibus et practicis expeditionis contra Turchum: venturi enim sunt oratores potentiarum vocati pro Kalendis Novembris proximis et videre videmur quod multa dicentur et proponentur magnifica et speciosa similia et conformia magis preteritis imaginationibus quam alicui vero aut necessario effectui. . . ."

[14] Piva, II, 453–54.

[15] Fossati, "Milano e una fallita alleanza," *Arch. stor. lombardo*, XVI, 55–56, and doc. I, pp. 73–75.

proceed in unison, and insofar as we can, we shall not fail in our duty as Catholic princes with respect to the said expedition." On their way to Rome the envoys were to consult Giovanni Bentivoglio in Bologna and Lorenzo de' Medici in Florence, who were undoubtedly giving their own envoys much the same instructions.[16]

It is hard to believe that Sixtus would have been in the least surprised if he could have read the Milanese envoys' private instructions. He knew that the Holy See and Naples would have to set a good example for the other Italian states. In a consistory held on 15 December, 1480, he undertook to arm and maintain twenty-five galleys. Ferrante was to provide forty. On the twentieth, Cardinal Giovanni Battista Savelli was sent on a hurried legation to Genoa. He was to settle the civil strife between the Campofregosi and Adorni and to prepare the papal galleys for service against the Turks when spring came, "or rather to prevent them," says Jacopo Gherardi da Volterra, "from assailing Italy with a greater effort and a larger fleet than they did last summer."[17]

The pope and cardinals together agreed to contribute 150,000 ducats to the Christian defense. Two-thirds of this sum would go to equip the twenty-five galleys for which the papacy was paying; the remaining 50,000 would be sent to Matthias Corvinus, who could be expected to divert Turkish attention from southern Italy to central Europe. The pope was also recruiting a force of three thousand infantry "ad expellendos Hydrunto hostes." The ambassadors, who had finally come to Rome in response to the papal summons, believed that a fleet of a hundred galleys should be prepared for action against the Turks, and that 200,000 ducats should be sent to Corvinus each year of the Christian offensive. Since the pope and the cardinals were assuming such heavy financial obligations (allegedly beyond their capacity to do so), the Italian states and the great powers must also assume their share of the burden. Briefs to this effect were sent to all the princes, who were informed of the assessments which the Curia Romana was levying on them for the crusade.[18] Europe was to be bound together for three years in an anti-Turk league. Besides his forty galleys for the Christian fleet, Ferrante was to send Corvinus 100,000 ducats. Milan was to contribute 30,000 to the cause, and Florence 20,000; Genoa, five galleys; Ferrara and Siena, each four; Bologna, two; Lucca, Mantua, and Montferrat, each one. The assessments in galleys may not seem very high, but it is well to recall that it cost 4,000 ducats to fit out and arm a single galley for six months' service.[19]

France had long been regarded as the

[16] Fossati, *op. cit.*, pp. 56–57, and doc. II, pp. 75–78, dated at Milan on 5 November, 1480.

[17] Jacopo da Volterra, *Diarium romanum*, ad ann. 1480, in *RISS*, XXIII-3 (1904), 29, 30; Sigismondo de'Conti, I, 110; Acta Consistorialia, in Eubel, II (1914, repr. 1960), nos. 437–38, p. 43.

[18] The brief sent to the Marquis Federico Gonzaga of Mantua is dated 4 January, 1481, and is still preserved in the Arch. di Stato di Mantova, Arch. Gonzaga, Busta 834: ". . . singulos de consilio venerabilium fratrum nostrorum Sancte Romane Ecclesie cardinalium pro eorum facultatibus taxavimus, a nobis et a cardinalibus ipsis incipientes, qui taxam centum et quinquaginta millium ducatorum nobis ipsis assumpsimus ut ceteros hoc exemplo subsidii quod sane est supra vires nostras et fratrum ipsorum ad prompte et liberaliter pro rata sua contribuendum invitaremus. . . . Eorum autem centum millia parandis et armandis viginti quinque triremibus, quinquaginta vero carissimo in Christo filio nostro Mathie Hungarie regi illustri ad bellum adversus Turcos ipsos per continentem gerendum destinamus. Ea enim fuit omnium [oratorum] sententia ut classis centum triremium instruatur, regi vero illi ducenta millia ducatorum singulis annis durante expeditione subministrentur. . . ." *Cf.* Pastor, *Hist. Popes*, IV, 337–38, and (with improved text) *Gesch. d. Päpste*, II (repr. 1955), 563–64.

[19] *Cf.* the brief of 4 January to Federico Gonzaga, cited in the preceding note: ". . . Tibi et dilecto filio nobili viro Guillelmo marchioni Montisferrati simul et coniunctim taxa unam triremem comparandi et armandi, prout ad eum pariter scribimus, assignata est, que certe inconveniens et immoderata censeri non potest. . . . [If Federico had the means to arm a galley, it should be ready to join the papal fleet the following March; otherwise he should send the necessary funds to the cardinal legate Savelli in Genoa, where galleys were being readied.] Exigit enim unaqueque triremis in conficienda et armanda pro semestri summam quattuor millium ducatorum . . . [The extreme peril made haste absolutely necessary.] Iam enim magnus Turcorum numerus Valonam applicuit qui nihil aliud expectant nisi oportunitatem traiiciendi. . . ."

The numbers of galleys to be provided seem to vary somewhat in the sources, but in general see Raynaldus, *Ann. eccl.*, ad ann. 1481, no. 13, vol. XIX (1693), pp. 297–98; Fossati, *op. cit.*, p. 66, and docs. III, V, pp. 80, 84, 86; and note G. Grasso, "Documenti riguardanti la costituzione di una lega contro il Turco nel 1481," in the *Giornale ligustico di archeologia, storia e belle arti*, VI (1879), 328. Grasso's work (*ibid.*, pp. 321–494) is a collection of 123 documents relating to Genoese concern with Turkish affairs, for the most part in 1481, and especially with the occupation of Otranto. It is a *diplomatarium* in itself, and is hereafter cited as Grassi, "Documenti." Genoa was assessed, as indicated above, five galleys (*ibid.*, nos. I, V, pp. 343, 344, *et alibi*). On Savelli's legation to Genoa, see, *ibid.*, doc. XII, pp. 345–50, dated 24 March, 1481.

crusading nation par excellence, but in the opinion of the Curia Romana, King Louis XI had not followed in the footsteps of his royal forebears, and had fallen below the level of his father, "who was most obedient to the Apostolic See." Louis had held papal authority in contempt, passed laws against ecclesiastical freedom, treated the clergy harshly, and introduced some irreverent novelty every day into the French Church. Contrary to all precedent, according to the Curia, he had decreed that all ecclesiastical cases *in prima instantia* should be settled within the confines of the kingdom and not in the Curia, and that citations of first instance emanating from auditors of the Rota were of no moment in France. He had prohibited apostolic notaries from issuing certain legal instruments in his kingdom "so that none may take effect except by his command, and so in these matters he makes himself superior to the Roman pontiff . . . ." Unmindful of his own salvation, Louis had forbidden his subjects to receive benefices from the Curia, but had himself made appointments to such livings in the French Church. The indignant officials of the Curia found the list of his transgressions almost unbelievable. He had prohibited ecclesiastics from going to Rome without his permission, reformed churches and monasteries (and disposed of their revenues as he saw fit), imprisoned and punished clerics, and ignominiously thrust them into latrines, taxed and tallaged them, and even stated publicly that the incomes [*fructus*] being derived from churches should be taken from the clergy and distributed among the laity. Of all these offenses was he guilty, *haec omnia et alia multa*.[20] These were pretty much the stock charges to be leveled against recalitrant kings. The French had heard them before.

The policies of Louis XI, however, were merely part of the increasing secularism of his time. As Pope Pius II had found, Europe was not enthusiastic about crusades. Learned clerics might prepare rhetorical, even eloquent, memoranda on the impelling urgency of a united opposition to the westward movement of the Turks. But the kings of France and England were now pursuing increasingly national policies, and the Hapsburgs, who would soon feel the harsh impact of the Turkish advance, were struggling feebly with the *Hauspolitik* they had inherited from the past. The Italian states had diverse interests and different traditions, which had long engendered strife and suspicion. It would be no easy task to reconcile Venice and Naples, but now the Turk was in Italy, and something had to be done.

Sixtus IV had already sent his able nephew Giuliano della Rovere, cardinal priest of S. Pietro in Vincoli, as his legate to France.[21] Giuliano was directed to appeal to Louis XI for aid against the Turks, and to summon him *ad sui presentiam* to Rome with the other Christian princes or their ambassadors on 1 November (1480). Louis had understood from the pope's summons "that, alas, things were getting worse." But the shortness of time and many other reasons, which (he said) he had already explained, had prevented his sending envoys to the Curia. Now, however, on 20 December he was finally able to send two envoys, Jean de Chassaignes, president of the court of the parlement of Bordeaux, and Jean Darse, a royal chamberlain, soldier, and lord of S. Loup, "and they will inform your Holiness of what we think in this matter and of what we want." Louis asked the pope "to deign to hear them and to put faith in their words, not otherwise than in ourself."[22]

Louis's envoys entered Rome on 8 March (1481) by the Porta S. Pietro, and on the fourteenth they were received by the pope and the cardinals in a secret consistory. Jacopo Gherardi da Volterra knew that they offered 300,000 ducats in support of the league being formed against the Turks. He believed that Louis proposed collecting 200,000 from the

[20] Arch. Segr. Vaticano, Miscellanea, Arm. II, Reg. 20 (Politicorum Varia, tom. XX), fols. 46^{v}–49^{r}, but for the actual facts, see the learned study of Paul Ourliac, "Le Concordat de 1472: Étude sur les rapports de Louis XI et de Sixte IV," *Revue historique de droit français et étranger*, 4th ser., XXI (1942), 174–223, and XXII (1943), 117–54. Ourliac's article has been translated into English by G. F. Martin in P. S. Lewis, ed., *The Recovery of France in the Fifteenth Century*, London, 1971, pp. 102–84, 370–93.

[21] Giuliano was created *legatus de latere in Franciam* on 28 April, and left Rome for France on 9 June, 1480 (Acta Consistorialia, in Eubel, II [1914, repr. 1960], nos. 423, 426, p. 43). He had already served in this capacity from February to October, 1476 (*ibid.*, nos. 351, 355, pp. 39, 40). See P. Ourliac, "Le Concordat de 1472," *Revue historique de droit français et étranger*, 4th ser., XXII (1943), 118 ff.

[22] Arch. Segr. Vaticano, Miscell., Arm. II, Reg. 20, fol. 46^{r}, by mod. stamped enumeration, "scriptum apud Plessiacum de Parco prope Turonis die vigesima Decembris [1480]."

French clergy and 100,000 from the laity, but when he made the entries in his diary, he did not yet know what conditions Louis was attaching to the subsidies.[23] The French envoys brought to the Curia the instructions and proposals dated the preceding 20 December. In replying to the recurrent ecclesiastical exhortations to do his part in resisting the fierce Turkish encroachments upon Christendom, Louis stated that he was as anxious to do so as he was for the salvation of his soul, "and that it seemed to him according to what he had seen of war that an effective resistance could not be achieved at a lesser cost than 100,000 gold ducats [*scuta*] a month, and for his share he offered to give 200,000 ducats in any [one] year."[24]

In fact if the pope would grant him a general *facultas taxandi* to levy imposts upon all ecclesiastics who held benefices in France, both regular and secular clergy, "he would add another 100,000 ducats." Louis believed that Italy could easily provide 40,000 ducats for defense against the Turks; Germany, 200,000; "all the Spains," another 200,000; "and the king of England, who is so powerful and has such rich benefices, 100,000 ducats." Louis had also been informed "that the Venetians are willing to declare themselves against the Turks, provided they are assured that all Italy is going to join in and not leave them in the lurch." The French envoys were authorized to commit their sovereign, *una cum aliis Italiae*, to his pledge of 300,000 ducats (with a free rein to tax the clergy!) and to making payment at the same time and on the same terms as the Italians, Germans, Spanish, and English furnished their proper shares. Insofar as the other kings and peoples (*nationes*), however, were unwilling to support the crusade to the extent of the sums "of which mention is made above," the envoys were to reduce the French offer of support accordingly, "prefati oratores deducent similiter de dicta summa quam rex offert dare. . . ." Louis also required the assurance of peace along his eastern frontiers, "and in making the aforesaid offer he does not discount the fact that he must be safe from the king of England through the duration of the war [against the Turks] and for one year thereafter . . . ." Of course Louis realized, he said, that the king of England was a good brother to him "and as good a friend as he had in the world" (*et amicum quantum haberet in mundo*), but the pope could well understand the responsibility which rested upon a king to provide for the security of his realm.[25]

It was all very much as the Venetian Senate had written Barbaro the preceding October. Magnificent speeches would be made, brilliant schemes proposed, but nothing would come of them. Nevertheless, the "general league" seemed to be getting off to a good start, for the Neapolitan fleet had just scored a victory over the Turkish naval forces at Otranto.[26] Hopes were running high. A crusade was proclaimed, and on 8 April, 1481, the pope addressed the bull *Cogimur iubente altissimo* to all the European princes, summoning them to arms against the Turks.[27]

---

[23] *Diarium romanum*, ad ann. 1481, in *RISS*, XXIII-3 (1904), 39, 40; Fossati, "Milano e una fallita alleanza," *Arch. stor. lombardo*, XVI, 59 ff. Two days before the French envoys arrived in Rome, Peter Schott, canon of Strassburg, classical scholar, and friend of Johann Burchard (Burckard), later papal master of ceremonies, says in a letter written at Bologna (on 6 March, 1481) that he had just visited the Eternal City in order to see it before its conceivable capture by the Turks, . . . *ut si a Thurcis sit capienda prius eam viderim* (Chas. Schmidt, *Histoire littéraire de l'Alsace à la fin du XVe et au commencement du XVIe siècle*, 2 vols., Paris, 1879, II, 10, and note 22, cited by Louis Thuasne, ed., *Johannis Burchardi Argentinensis . . . Diarium sive rerum urbanarum commentarii* [*1483–1506*], 3 vols, Paris, 1883–85, I, pp. III–IV).

[24] Arch. Segr. Vaticano, Miscell., Arm. II, Reg. 20, fol. 44^r.

[25] *Ibid.*, fols. 44^v–45^v. *Cf.* Pastor, *Gesch. d. Päpste*, II, 565–66, and the somewhat confused account in Piva, I, 82–85, and III, 137–38. Zaccaria Barbaro sent full reports to Venice, as one might expect, of the developments in Rome during March (Arch. di Stato di Venezia, Sen. Secreta, Reg. 30, fol. 6 [16]). Giuliano della Rovere had been received at Vendôme on 24 August, 1480, by Louis XI, who had first outlined his plans for financing the crusade on that occasion, as described in a letter which Giuliano wrote the pope later the same day (for the text see Ourliac, in the *Revue historique de droit français et étranger*, 4th ser., XXII, 153–54).

[26] Sen. Secreta, Reg. 30, fol. 2^v [12^v], doc. dated 12 March, 1481.

[27] There is a beautifully written copy of this bull in the handsome volume of *Sixti IV Bull. diver., An. I ad X*, in the Arch. Segr. Vaticano, Arm. XXXI, tom. 62, fols. 246^v–252^r, by mod. stamped enumeration, "datum Rome apud Sanctum Petrum, anno etc. MCCCCLXXX primo, sexto Idus Aprilis, pontificatus nostri anno decimo:" "Cogimur iubente altissimo ac urgente rei publice Christiane grandi necessitate universos Christianos principes Christianos ac omnes Christifideles requirere eisque mandare vice Dei, cuius locum quamquam immeriti tenemus in terris, ut a vigentibus inter eos bellis et guerris omnino cessent, et pro illius honore et salute Christiane religioni[s] in maximo periculo constitute adversum impiam Turcorum gentem arma sumant. . . ." The siege of Rhodes and the occupation of Otranto had, of course, made a profound impression on the pope and the Curia, and it was believed that worse was to come "cum

On 3 May, 1481, Mehmed II the Conqueror died suddenly in Asia Minor, and despite an attempt to put his younger son Jem Sultan on the throne, he was succeeded by his elder son Bayazid II, who had long been at odds with his father. The news of Mehmed's death was known in Venice by 29 May, from letters dated on the fourth and sixth of the month from the Republic's ambassador and the bailie in Istanbul.[28] Rumors of his death had reached Rome about the same time. When the fact was confirmed by the Venetians (on 2 June), cannon were fired, church bells rung, and bonfires lighted throughout the city. That evening Pope Sixtus IV gave thanks for deliverance at the vesper service in the church of S. Maria del Popolo, which he had himself rebuilt, and where the cardinals and the resident ambassadors now joined him in the solemn expression of their jubilation.[29] Celebrations of Mehmed's death were organized throughout Italy. On 4 June Sixtus wrote the Marquis Federico of Mantua, the Florentines, and others that God had opened up the way to safety, "showing us a light from on high to free us forever from that peril which for years past has struck the Christian commonwealth with so many calamities . . . ." Here was the great opportunity, according to the pope, to avenge the blows and recoup the losses of the past, before the Turks could put their affairs in order, and the sons resume the barbarities of the father. "We have our fleet ready in Genoa; thirty galleys and four ships splendidly equipped will soon be at the Tiber docks; at Ancona also we are arming others; and they will all be joined in good course with the royal fleet [of Naples]."[30] The terms of the pope's appeal make clear his realization that the Italians' crusading fervor would subside with the passing of Mehmed's dominant figure from the eastern scene, and he was quite right; within a few days the Bolognese wished to retract their pledge of a subsidy, for "with the Turkish tyrant's death necessity presses us no more."[31] The papal commissioners in Mantua had already reported to Rome that the Marquis Federico was holding back funds collected for the crusade, a fact which Sixtus professed not to believe.[32]

The papal fleet under Cardinal Paolo di Campofregoso joined forces with those of King Ferrante in the siege of Otranto, which they reoccupied when the Turks surrendered on 10 September, 1481,[33] and again all Italy set about

---

autem nuper intellexerimus eosdem Turcos maximam classem parare et omnibus curis omissis ad insule predicte, Italie et Pannonie ac Haustrie occupationem et fidei Catholice omnimodam conculcationem omnes suos divertisse cogitatus . . ." (*ibid.*, fol. 248^{v}). Sixtus imposed a three years' peace on Christendom, beginning with 1 June (1481), to permit the organization of a crusade, lest western Europe go the way of Constantinople and the Morea, Serbia and Bosnia, and the empire of Trebizond, whose rulers (and peoples) had all come to grief: "aliorum exempla nos docent" (fols. 249^{v}–250^{r}).

There is an abridged and inaccurate transcription of this bull (also made from Arm. XXXI, tom. 62, fols. 244^{v} and ff., by original enumeration) in Raynaldus, *Ann. eccl.*, ad ann. 1481, nos. 19, 20–23, vol. XIX (1693), pp. 298–99, and ed. Bar-le-Duc, vol. XXX (1887), pp. 6–7, on which see Pastor, *Hist. Popes*, IV, 340–41, and note, and *Gesch. d. Päpste*, II (repr. 1955), 566, and note, who says there is a complete copy of the bull in the Archivio di Stato, Milan, but makes no reference to the archival copy in the Vatican. In a brief of 4 May, 1481, Sixtus wrote the Marquis Federico Gonzaga of Mantua, ". . . Cum perfidissimus et vigilantissimus hostis apparatum maximum adversus Italiam, Germaniam et Rhodum indefesso studio, ut ex pluribus locis compertum habemus, instruat, triennales inter omnes Christianos principes et potentatus indutias indiximus: ad defensionem Catholice fidei paterna caritate omnes hortati sumus" (Arch. di Stato di Mantova, Arch. Gonzaga, Busta 834). There is an original text of the bull *Cogimur iubente altissimo*, with the cord and lead seal torn away, in the Arch. di Stato di Modena, Can. ducale, Cart. di principi esteri, Busta 1293A/8, no. 136.

[28] Sen. Secreta, Reg. 30, fols. 16^{v}–17^{r} [26^{v}–27^{r}].

[29] Jacopo da Volterra, *Diarium romanum*, ad ann. 1481, in *RISS*, XXIII-3 (1904), 53–54, with the notes of the editor, Enrico Carusi. Despite the terror which Mehmed II had caused through the years in Italy, a minor Vicentine humanist, Giovanni Stefano (who called himself Quinto Emiliano Cimbriaco), wrote a sort of lament for his death in the form of an epitaph in irregular elegiac stanzas, on which see Franz Babinger, "Eine lateinische Totenklage auf Mehmed II," in *Studi orientalistici in onore di Giorgio Levi Della Vida*, I (Rome, 1956), 15–31, reprinted in Babinger's *Aufsätze und Abhandlungen zur Geschichte Südosteuropas und der Levante*, 2 vols., Munich, 1962–66, II, 151–61.

[30] Arch. di Stato di Mantova, Arch. Gonzaga, Busta 834, brief dated 4 June, 1481; G. Müller, *Documenti*, pt. I, no. 195, p. 233; *cf.* Navagero, *Storia veneziana*, in *RISS*, XXIII, cols. 1166E–1168. Sixtus IV was keenly aware of the opportunity which Mehmed's death offered the Christians for a *reconquista* in the Levant (Raynaldus, *Ann. eccl.*, ad ann. 1481, nos. 1–13, vol. XIX [1693], pp. 295–98). Marino Sanudo, *Diarii*, IV (Venice, 1880), cols. 324–28, preserves a chronological list of the chief events (largely victories) in Ottoman history as they affected Venice from 1451 to 1502, which shows at a glance the extent of Mehmed's military successes against Christendom.

[31] Pastor, *Hist. Popes*, IV, 342, note, and *Gesch. d. Päpste*, II (repr. 1955), 567, note.

[32] Arch. di Stato di Mantova, Arch. Gonzaga, Busta 834, brief dated 16 July, 1481.

[33] Jacopo da Volterra, *Diarium romanum*, ad ann. 1481, *RISS*, XXIII-3, 69, gives the text of Ferrante's letter to Sixtus, dated 11 September, announcing that "receptum

rejoicing. Pope Sixtus IV had intended from the beginning of the expedition that, after retaking Otranto, his fleet should proceed with the Neapolitans and with a Portuguese fleet of twenty-one ships under the indolent Garsias Meneses, bishop of Evora, across the Adriatic straits to the coastal fortress of Valona, which was also to be captured from the Turks, an enterprise in which the Albanians would presumably be happy to participate, but the pope's plans were soon to be frustrated by the appearance of the plague at Otranto, the intractability of his sailors, and the general contrariness of Cardinal Campofregoso.[34]

In the meantime, however, Sixtus entertained wider ambitions still, confident that Mehmed's death was the first chance in more than two generations for an effective movement against

---

est Hidruntum decimo mensis huius die. . . ." Ten days later the Venetians expressed their great pleasure in the news (Arch. di Stato di Venezia, Sen. Secreta, Reg. 30, fols. 32ᵛ–33ʳ [42ᵛ–43ʳ]). For the later fifteenth-century Neapolitan chronicle of one Ferraiolo, to be found in the Pierpont Morgan Library, MS. 801, which contains at fols. 80ʳ ff. a series of six full-page drawings in color of the army of Duke Alfonso of Calabria on the march to relieve Otranto, see Riccardo Filangieri, ed., *Una Cronica napoletana figurata del Quattrocento*, Naples, 1956, sec. 14, pp. 35–48. These drawings are well done, and noteworthy as contemporary illustrations of costumes, arms, and artillery, trappings of horses, tents, wagons, etc. Ferraiolo gives a rather detailed account of the campaign, mentioning the chief Neapolitan participants; the value of this work is enhanced by Filangieri's historical commentary.

The appointment of Cardinal Campofregoso as legate of the papal fleet was known in Genoa before 25 February, 1481, "de che qui se fa solemnità grande" (Grasso, "Documenti," no. VIII, p. 344). The Genoese were conspicuous in the fleet (*ibid.*, nos. IX, X, XII, XV, XXXII, XXXIX, XLII, LI), and when their galleys returned home, they received from the pope a brief, "per quod vestra Beatitudo que a nostris in bello Idrontino gesta sunt et probat et extollit" (doc. CXV, p. 485, dated 10 November, 1481). They hoped that the death of Mehmed II and a signal defeat of the Turks would help assure the safety of the *mahonesi* of Chios and assist their government to regain some of the lost Genoese possessions in the Levant, especially Caffa (docs. XVI, XIX, XX, XXI, XXVII, XXVIIbis, XLV, L, LV, LXIX, XCIX, CXIII, CXXII–CXXIII).

[34] See the valuable collection of Sixtus IV's letters *De Curia annus undecimus 1481* in the Biblioteca Nazionale Centrale di Firenze, Bibl. Magliabecchiana, MS. II–III 256. On 27 August, 1481, Sixtus wrote Campofregoso from Rome, ". . . Ex Po[r]tugallia viginti adsunt caravelle et navis una oneraria quas in dies apud Sanctum Paulum expectamus quarum prefectus est venerabilis frater Garsias episcopus Elborensis. Cum primum eas ibi viderimus, iubebimus statim ad te proficisci sub signis nostris et imperio tuo navigaturas: hortamur ut benigne et prefectum ipsum et commilitones omnes suscipias. Sunt enim, ut audivimus, egregie et viris et armis instructe . . ." (*ibid.*, fol. 2ʳ). *Cf.*, *ibid.*, fols. 6ᵛ, 13ʳ, 14ᵛ–15ʳ, 19ᵛ, 20 ff., 24ʳ, 25ʳ, 27ᵛ–28ʳ, 36ᵛ ff., 40, 49ᵛ–50ʳ, 54ʳ.

On 7 September Sixtus informed King Ferrante that "proficiscitur Hydruntum classis quam ex Portugallia accersivimus. . . . Speramus illam magno usui Hydruntine expugnationi futuram . . ." (fol. 15ᵛ). Endless difficulties were being encountered in Campofregoso's fleet, including the plague and an alleged inability to pay the crews, as noted in Sixtus's letter to the cardinal dated at Rome on 10 September, the very day of the Turkish surrender at Otranto: "Accepimus litteras tuas datas primo huius mensis quibus plures causas propter quas patroni triremium velle[nt] discedere enumeras et inter alia narras quattuor triremes peste iam infectas esse et de quinta dubitari, sed quod potissimum est, queruntur patroni de non soluto stipendio . . ." [although Sixtus insisted that Campofregoso would soon receive the needed funds] (fols. 22ʳ–23ʳ, and *cf.* fols. 25ᵛ–26ʳ). The Portuguese fleet had made no move toward Otranto by 14 September, as indicated by Sixtus's letter of that date from Bracciano to the papal vice-chamberlain in Rome: "Accepimus litteras tuas quibus intelleximus ea que in urbe acta sunt: imprimis illud vehementer admiramur quod caravelle Portugallenses nondum discesserint . . ." (fol. 31ᵛ, and *cf.* fol. 32ᵛ, revealing suspicion of Garsias Meneses' intentions).

When Garsias heard of the recovery of Otranto from the Turks, he wanted to regard his mission as over, but not so the pope: "Episcopo Elborensi: Venerabilis frater, salutem etc. Intelleximus fraternitatem tuam audita Hydrunti recuperatione nolle ulterius progredi, sed statuisse istic morari. Miramur vehementer et te animadvertere credimus non esse ob hanc expugnationem omnia executa que tibi commissa sunt. . . . Volumus ac tibi pro quanto gratiam nostram caram habes et indignationem cupis evitare strictissime precipiendo mandamus quatinus acceptis presentibus statim discedas et cum cetera classe nostra que ad Vallonam invadendam progreditur te coniungas ut aliquid dignum Christiana religione et honore tuo regeque illo [Alfonso V of Portugal had died on 28 August, 1481] ac tanta classe gerere possis. [Datum Braciani die XV Septembris 1481, anno undecimo.]" (fol. 33).

The manuscript from which these entries are taken is clearly the original archival copybook of Leonardo Grifo, Sixtus IV's *secretarius intimus et domesticus* (on whom see W. von Hofmann, *Forschungen zur Geschichte der kurialen Behörden*, II [Rome, 1914], 123), and must have been removed at some time or other from the Vatican Archives. Grifo was born in Milan in 1437; he became bishop of Gubbio in 1473 and archbishop of Benevento in 1482 (Eubel, *Hierarchia*, II [1914, repr. 1960], 151, 104). A prominent figure at the Curia Romana, he appears often in the ceremonial diary of Johann Burchard (Enrico Celani, ed., *Johannis Burckardi Liber notarum ab anno MCCCCLXXXIII usque ad annum MDVI*, in *RISS*, XXXII, pt. 1 [Città di Castello and Bologna, 1907–42], vol. I, pp. 20, 22 [as archbishop of Benevento], 72, 97, 109–10 [esp. note 4]). Grifo died in the Vatican Palace on 24 November, 1485 (*ibid.*, pp. 127–28); he was buried in S. Maria del Popolo, his obsequies being held on 15 December (p. 133 with note 3). There is no longer any trace of his burial place (behind the high altar), but in 1677 a commemorative plaque was set up to his memory in the church of S. Carlo al Corso, the national church of the Lombards (the first plaque on the right as one enters by the corridor opening upon the Vicolo del Grottino).

the Turks. On 15 September, 1481, he wrote the bishop of Evora, from Bracciano, an Orsini stronghold north of Rome, directing him to help Andreas Palaeologus cross the short stretch of the Ionian Sea to the Morea so that Andreas could begin the reconquest of his father's despotate, lost to Mehmed twenty years before.[35]

Three days later, on 18 September, Sixtus addressed letters to the emperor, the kings of France, England, Hungary, and Spain, and most of the other important rulers in Europe, informing them of the recapture of Otranto, "which we have been waiting for with all our heart, and which has been most pleasing to us—today we have learned it from our people!" His letter was not only eloquent, it was eminently sensible: "This is the time of deliverance, of glory, of victory, such as we shall never be able to regain if it is neglected now. With a little effort the war can now be brought to a successful conclusion which later on can be done only at the greatest cost and with the greatest injuries to ourselves. . . ."[36] In a letter of congratulation to Cardinal Campofregoso, written the same day, Sixtus said that the undertaking, which had begun so auspiciously, must be carried through with all endeavor. Italy must be freed forever from the Turkish danger. He had urged all the Christian princes to take up the cause, and Campofregoso was now to continue the offensive, inflicting all the damage he could on the Turks, "lest we prove unequal to the chance which heaven has offered us."[37]

Pope Sixtus's exhortations were in vain, however, and Cardinal Campofregoso sailed for Civitavecchia, where he arrived at the beginning of October.[38] There had been dissension in the Christian army at Otranto, and plague aboard the papal ships. Campofregoso assured Sixtus that an expedition such as he had envisaged was impossible. In any event Italy was no longer in imminent danger. Although, to be sure, Otranto lay in ruins, the Turks had been expelled from their beachhead on the peninsula.

Time has passed slowly in Otranto, where the memory of the events of 1480–1481 remains to this day as vivid as if the Turks had come and gone but a brief while ago. At the edge of the town, on the hill of Minerva, the church of S. Francesco di Paola is entirely dedicated to the memory of those events. As one enters the gateway to the stairs leading up to the church, modern inscriptions on pilasters to the left and right recall that "ottocento Otrantini s'immolarono in olocausto a Dio." The inscriptions pay rhetorical tribute to the troops of Alfonso of Calabria, who recovered the city in September, 1481: ". . . Voi generosi che pugnando nel 1480[!] fugaste dai lidi ausoni le orde musul-

[35] Bibl. Naz. Centrale, Florence, Bibl. Magliab., MS. II–III 256, fol. 34ʳ: "Episcopo Elborensi: Venerabilis frater salutem etc. Commendavimus alias fraternitati tue dilectum filium nobilem virum Andream Paleologum despotem Romeorum qui nunc ad te proficiscitur. Quare hortamur te ut, postquam Dei benignitate Hydruntina civitas recuperata est, cures et studeas illum in Peloponessum cum caravellis transvehere ut patriam ac dominium suum a Turcis occupatum recuperare possit. Erit hoc tibi gloriosum et plenum laudis et genus elemosine existimabitur affecisse hunc tanto beneficio. Datum Braciani die XV Septembris 1481, anno undecimo." *Cf.* Pastor, *Hist. Popes*, IV, 346, note, and *Gesch. d. Päpste*, II (repr. 1955), 570, note 3. The bishop of Evora (Elbora), whose name Pastor omits, is identified as Garsias Meneses in the papal briefs as well as in Eubel, *Hierarchia*, II (1914, repr. 1960), 149; in P. B. Gams, *Series episcoporum*, Regensburg, 1873, p. 99; and in Raynaldus, *Ann. eccl.*, ad ann. 1481, no. 39, vol. XIX (1693), p. 305. There are a number of *schede* from 1469 to 1484 relating to Garsias in the *Schedario Garampi* in the Arch. Segr. Vaticano (*Schedario Garampi*, vol. 46: *Vescovi*, no. 16: Indice 490, fols. 74ʳ–74ᵛ, by mod. stamped enumeration).

[36] Bibl. Nat. Centr., Florence, Bibl. Magliab., MS. II–III 256, fols. 52ᵛ–53ᵛ. The copy of this brief, dated 19 September, which was sent to the marquis of Mantua, is still preserved in the Arch. di Stato di Mantova, Arch. Gonzaga, Busta 834: ". . . Nam ad reliquos omnes idem scribimus, ecce nunc tempus salutis, tempus glorie, tempus victorie, quod si negligetur, nullum tale umquam recuperare poterimus: parvo negocio bellum nunc confici potest quod non sine maximo dispendio maximis calamitatibus nostris (quod Deus advertat) postea conficietur si cunctabundi expectare voluerimus donec efferus hostis se colligat, vires recuperet, et adversus nos muniatur. Nos et libenter hactenus fecimus supra quam vires nostre ferre potuerunt. . . ." Part of the text is given in Pastor, *Hist. Popes*, IV, append., no. 64, p. 518, and *Gesch. d. Päpste*, II, append., no. 130, p. 789. Copies of the brief went to the Florentines, Lucchesi, and Sienese, but not to the Venetians. Numerous entries in the *Diarium parmense*, ad ann. 1480–1481, in *RISS*, XXII (Milan, 1733), cols. 347–79, describe the Turkish occupation of Otranto in detail and with some inaccuracy, the chronicler apparently being in much doubt as to how and when the Christian forces recovered the city. *Cf.* Iorga, *Gesch. d. osman. Reiches*, II (Gotha, 1909), 192–93; P. P. Argenti, *Occupation of Chios*, I (Cambridge, 1958), 239–44.

[37] Bibl. Magliab., MS. II–III 256, fol. 38: "Legato classis: . . . Accepimus litteras Circumspectionis tue datas ad XI diem presentis quibus certiores nos facis de receptione Hydrunti et aliis que istic subsecuta sunt . . . ," and for the important portion of the text, see Pastor, *Hist. Popes*, IV, append., no. 65, p. 519, and *Gesch. d. Päpste*, II, append., no. 131, p. 790, and in general note Raynaldus, *Ann. eccl.*, ad ann. 1481, nos. 14, 25, 27–34, vol. XIX (1693), pp. 298, 300, 301–4.

[38] Bibl. Magliab., MS. II–III 256, fols. 59ʳ ff.

mane." Midway on the stairs another inscription (on the right) marks the spot where the eight hundred martyrs of Otranto are said to have died for the faith. This inscription calls attention also to the small column that stands opposite (on the left as one ascends the stairs), set up in honor of the Turkish executioner who, marveling at the spectacle of Christian heroism, himself embraced the faith. According to tradition, he suffered martyrdom along with his erstwhile victims. ". . . Passagiero, chiunque tu sei, plaudi alla fortezza dei nostri martiri e ai trionfi della cristiana religione."

An inscription on the façade of the church of S. Francesco records the construction by Alfonso of Calabria of a shrine to the martyrs of Otranto and, *vetustate pene collapsum*, its replacement in 1614 by the present church, rebuilt on a grander scale and endowed with a larger revenue by Gianfrancesco Arnesanno of Lecce and his wife Marcia Lucia. Inside the church, on the walls to the left and right, are inscribed the names of those known or believed to have perished in the Turkish seizure of the city in August, 1480, and in the struggle for its recovery thirteen months later. Among the former one reads the name of the Turkish executioner "Berlabei," whose dramatic conversion has become part of the local legend.

In the small public square under the Torre Alfonsina, on the south side of the harbor of Otranto, a monument was erected (in 1922) "agli eroi e ai martiri otrantini del MCDLXXX." Bronze reliefs of the strife and slaughter fill the east and west sides of the monument. Here and there throughout old Otranto Turkish cannon balls stand outside the doorways, at the tops of stairs, and in the backyard gardens. Now Christianized, like Berlabei himself, these stone cannon balls have been conspicuous pieces of Otrantine décor for five hundred years.

When the Turks burst into the cathedral basilica of Otranto on the morning of 11 August, and are said to have slain the archbishop Stefano Pendinelli and his priests at the high altar, they began the dilapidation of the magnificent mosaic floor (laid in 1164–1166 and restored in 1875), one of the best-known and most beautiful in Italy. To the right of the high altar the Otrantini have built the "chapel of the martyrs." The walls are lined with tall cabinets containing the bones of some five hundred and sixty of the eight hundred martyrs, Alfonso of Calabria having removed to Naples the remains of most of the others.

On the shore road about two kilometers, just over a mile, to the south of Otranto one may still find the extensive remains of the once-famous Basilian monastery of S. Nicola di Casole. They stand amid broad fields on high ground, with a beautiful view of the surrounding countryside. Today, however, the site is occupied by a *masseria*, an ill-kept farmstead, with a disorder of hay and hens, manure, sheep, and dogs. Once it was the home of the abbot or "igoumen" Nectarius (1219/20–1235), who had borne the secular name Nicola. Twice in times of religious crisis Nicola-Nectarius had served as Greek interpreter to cardinal legates—to Benedict of S. Susanna (in 1205–1207) and to Pelagius (in 1214–1215), as they vainly sought to effect the union of the churches after the Fourth Crusade.

The monastery and the rich library at Casole had been the center and often the scene of the Otrantine poets in the halcyon days of Frederick II Hohenstaufen, and one of them at least, John Grassus, had probably joined him more than once at the distant hunting lodge of Castel del Monte. Among these Italo-Greek poets we must include Nicola-Nectarius himself, the seventh abbot of Casole, who served the papacy again in 1223–1225 as a go-between with imperial Nicaea. He was the good friend of the illustrious George Bardanes, Athenian diplomat and metropolitan of Corfu. The poet John Grassus "Idruntinus" (of Otranto) was also a friend of Bardanes; John was a fiery Ghibelline and an imperial notary; he was also the onetime student and long-time friend of the abbot Nectarius. John Grassus's son Nicola wrote little poems in iambic tetrastichs to Christ, the Virgin, and the saints. Another poet of the "school of Otranto" was George the Chartophylax, archivist of the church of nearby Gallipoli, a rough-and-ready fellow who sprawled at the foot of Mount Parnassus, and wrote poems robust enough to please himself if not, perhaps, his fellows.

Rich memories still clung to the hallowed precincts of S. Nicola di Casole when the Turks attacked the monastery, set fire to the roofs, and brought them tumbling to the ground, as the terrified monks fled for their lives. We know the names of some twenty abbots of Casole, from the foundation of the monastery in 1098–1099 to the year 1469, but the name and the fate of the poor abbot of 1480 still elude us. With the destruction of the monastery the silver age of Otranto had come to an end. The southland of Salento, however, had been declining long before the intrusion of the Turks had broken the soft tranquillity of life set amid the olive groves and vineyards. There was no recovery for the monastery at Casole. Through the early sixteenth century, at least, an abbot and some monks still inhabited S. Nicola, cluttered with the debris of Turkish destruction. Attempts were made at preservation and even reconstruction, for the monastery had an income from properties scattered throughout the heel of Italy. Indeed, S. Nicola had been for more than two centuries the richest Basilian monastery in the peninsula. But by the beginning of the seventeenth century the monastery was deserted, although we should note that in 1665 two chaplains were celebrating mass every day in the spacious church for the spiritual well-being of the few rustics who lived in the area roundabout. The church was abandoned in the eighteenth century; by the beginning of the nineteenth it was closed, because it had become structurally unsafe. Now little remains of the church but one arched wall of the apse with clusters of columns on each side. The nave of the church has become a stoneyard, with building blocks piled up against the arched wall and strewn about in profusion, a sad memorial to the Turkish occupation of what had been an important place.

Sixtus IV's resolve to take the offensive against the Turks was soon diverted. On 27 May, 1482, to be sure, he thanked the Ragusei for sending him word of the "apparatus quos contra Christianos Turcorum tirannus facit et quid moliatur," and urged them to keep him informed in the future, assuring them that he would always do everything he could to meet the Turkish peril in the quickest possible fashion.[39] But his attention already lay elsewhere. Sixtus was in fact caught up in another Italian war which he owed to the intrigues of his nephew, Girolamo Riario, who had contracted an alliance with Venice against King Ferrante of Naples. Riario had expressed the desire to visit Venice and confer with the Signoria as early as July, 1481.[40] He came on 9 September, and "one received him like an emperor."[41]

The Venetians wanted to destroy the Estense duchy of Ferrara, for ever since the hard-headed Ercole d'Este had ascended the Ferrarese throne (in August, 1471), he had been trying to loosen the commercial shackles with which the tradesmen on the lagoon had bound his state. Venice maintained a *vicedominus* in Ferrara to see to the observance of various pacts which tied Ercole's hand to the disadvantage of his subjects. Strengthened by his marriage with Eleonora, the daughter of Ferrante, and by bonds of increasing friendship with Lorenzo de' Medici and with the Sforza of Milan, Ercole looked the other way when his merchants broke the conventions by which the Venetians sought to curb their freedom to trade. Ferrarese officials disregarded the exemptions from tolls and the like, which the Republic had secured in earlier years, expropriated Venetian property, and generally infuriated the Senate by their allegedly high-handed procedures.[42]

Nothing loath to repay Ferrante for deserting him in the Tuscan war, Pope Sixtus went along with Riario, who had designs on Faenza and above all desired to overthrow Ferrante and the Aragonese regime in Naples. Venice was to receive Ferrara for her assistance. In mid-April Ferrante invaded the papal states,[43] and some two weeks later Venice declared war on Ercole d'Este. To offset the alliance of the papacy and Venice, Naples and Ferrara found support in Florence and Milan, Mantua and Urbino.

---

[39] Bibl. Magliab., MS. II–III 256, fol. 259^v.

[40] Arch. di Stato di Venezia, Sen. Secreta, Reg. 30, fol. 26^v [36^v].

[41] Pastor, *Gesch. d. Päpste*, II (repr. 1955), 574–75. On 23 October, 1481, the Venetian Senate wrote Roberto Malatesta, lord of Rimini and captain-general of the Republic's land forces, "Habemus, sicuti Excellentie vestre non est ignotum, sub nostra protectione illustrissimum dominum comitem Hieronimum de Riario et statum suum" (Sen. Secreta, Reg. 30, fol. 37^r [47^r], and *cf.* fols. 41^v–42^r, 49^v, 55^v–56^r, 57^v, 59^v and ff.). Riario wanted Faenza, which was agreeable to Venice (fol. 44^r [54^r]).

[42] Sen. Secreta, Reg. 29, fols. 142^v [152^v], dated 25 November, 1480, on the complaints of the Venetian *vicedominus* in Ferrara; 148^v–149^r [158^v–159^r], 22 December, on the "multe innovationes . . . contra iurisdictiones et pacta nostra;" and 152^v–153^r [162^v–163^r], 31 December, on the Senate's willingness to receive a Ferrarese envoy to review the disagreements which Venice regarded as "nè litigiose nè dubiose," after which relations between Venice and Ferrara deteriorated rapidly (*ibid.*, Reg. 30, fols. 28, 31^v–32^r, 33^r, 41–44, 46–47^r and ff. [fols. 38, etc.]). Alberto Cortese, the Ferrarese ambassador resident in Venice, gave up his mission at the beginning of February, 1482 (Reg. 30, fol. 52^r [62^r]). The Venetian documents are full of actions to be taken against Ercole d'Este.

[43] Bibl. Magliab., MS. II–III 256, fol. 217, papal brief of 18 April, 1482, to Ferrante, expressing surprise at the incursion of Neapolitan troops and demanding their withdrawal. On the same day Sixtus wrote to Ercole d'Este of Ferrara, urging him to maintain peace with Venice, *sicuti maiores tui fecerunt*, and informing him that the Turks were preparing another fleet with which to attack Italy (*ibid.*, fols. 217^v–218^r). War would be disastrous to them all, Sixtus wrote, while at the same time numerous briefs show him taking various defensive and offensive actions in preparation for the war which (he said) must be avoided. Note the long brief to the Beneventans in this context (fols. 277^v–278^v, dated at Rome on 12 June, 1482).

Ferrante's son Alfonso, the duke of Calabria, carried the war to the very walls of Rome through the late spring and early summer,[44] and the Campagna was pillaged by a Turkish cavalry force which Alfonso had recruited after the surrender of the sultan's army at Otranto.[45]

When in late July, however, Roberto Malatesta, son of the impious Sigismondo, arrived in Rome in charge of the papal and Venetian troops, Alfonso retreated southward beyond Velletri into the Pontine Marches, going toward the Tyrrhenian coast in the direction of Anzio and Nettuno. He took his stand at Campomorto, a lonely crossroads about eight miles from Anzio. Here Roberto Malatesta defeated Alfonso on 21 August, 1482, and sent him scurrying farther south to Terracina and the protection of the Neapolitan fleet.[46] But Roberto died of the fever a few weeks later; the papal party was soon as hard pressed as before; and Sixtus IV, becoming suspicious of the Venetians, agreed to a peace with Naples, Florence, and Milan on 12 December, 1482. By the terms of the treaty, in which the Venetians might be included if they wished, the independence of the duchy of Ferrara was guaranteed, but the Venetians rejected the terms and gave vent to their anger against Sixtus for his abandonment of the alliance which his own nephew had contrived.[47]

The persistence of the Venetians against the duchy of Ferrara brought into being a league against them; its members included the papacy, Naples, Ferrara, Florence, and Milan; and Sixtus now plunged into still another war with his customary zeal, imposing an interdict upon Venice in May, 1483.[48] But after more

[44] Sen. Secreta, Reg. 30, fol. 96^v [106^v], a letter of the Venetian Senate dated 22 June, 1482, addressed to the Conservators of the city of Rome: "Frequentibus litteris oratoris nostri in urbe agentis facti sumus certiores quanta fide, constantia, et animi magnitudine illustrium maiorum vestrorum vestigia sequentes neglectis iacturis et damnis vobis illatis pro deffensione iustissime cause summi pontificis adversus ducis Calabrie insidias usi fueritis. . . ."

[45] See the general account in Pastor, *Hist. Popes*, IV, 348–57, and *Gesch. d. Päpste*, II (repr. 1955), 572–79. Incidentally, Pastor's account of the attempts of Andreas Zamometić, titular archbishop of Granea, to organize a schismatic council in Basel at this time (IV, 358–63) has been entirely rewritten in the last edition of the *Gesch. d. Päpste*, II, 579–85. The final revision of the German text of this work is much more reliable than the English translation.

[46] Bibl. Magliab., MS. II–III 256, fols. 269^v–270^r, 289^r, and 369^r, the last reference being to a papal brief dated 22 August, addressed to the Genoese, announcing the victory at Campomorto. On 24 August Sixtus sent a brief of fulsome praise to Malatesta (fol. 370). A full account of Campomorto may be found in Pastor, *Gesch. d. Päpste*, II (repr. 1955), 586–92. The pope had appealed for aid from Venice toward the end of June (Sen. Secreta, Reg. 30, fols. 99^v–100^r ff. [109^v–110^r ff.]). The Signoria was naturally delighted with Malatesta's victory (*ibid.*, fols. 111^r ff.). Incidentally, the papal bull legitimizing Roberto and Malatesta, sons of Sigismondo, may be found in Reg. Vat. 393, fol. 174, dated in Nicholas V's fourth pontifical year, i.e., 31 August, 1450.

[47] From mid-November, 1482, papal relations with Venice became very strained. The Senate expressed astonishment at the political change of climate in Rome in view of "la filial nostra devotione, constantia, fede, veneratione, observantia, syncerita, et integerrima volunta et promptissima dispositione verso lei [la sua Beatitudine]" (Sen. Secreta, Reg. 30, fols. 141^v–143^r [151^v–153^r], doc. dated 23 November), after which the senatorial records show that the dissipation of amity between Venice and the Holy See was rapid. On 27 December the Senate recalled Francesco Diedo, who had replaced Barbaro as the Venetian ambassador in Rome, since he could no longer retain his post "absque maxima et expressa ignominia nostra et aperto dedecore nostri status" (*ibid.*, fol. 154^v [164^v]), and on 7 January, 1483, they wrote Sixtus with some bitterness, "Accepimus breve Sanctitatis vestre ea qua decuit . . . reverentia et devotione: intelleximus ex eo causas que eam videntur impulisse ad phedus nostrum deserendum et insinuandum sese paci federique communium hostium nostrorum. Hortatur preterea nos paterno affectu et compluribus verbis humanissimis ad pacem cum ceteris Italie potentatibus ineundum abstinendumque deinceps ab Ferrariensi bello" (*ibid.*, Reg. 30, fol. 157^v [167^v]).

Diedo had, however, already made the Venetian position abundantly clear in Rome. The pope's desertion would have been a great blow to Venice if her Senate and citizens did not entertain the hope that God himself, the supreme judge of human affairs, would in the end attest to the justice of the Republic's cause. The pope had appealed to Venice, which had provided a fleet of some eighty galleys and transports, to help him against his enemies. Malatesta was the Venetian commander; it was he who won the "victoria nobilissima" near Nettuno. As for Ercole d'Este, from the time he became duke of Ferrara he had dared "quod unquam nullus suorum progenitorum ausus est, iura nostra ferrariensia infringere, cives venetos vexare, extinguere nostrum magistratum, in venetos denique fines atque adeo in ducatum ipsum irrumpere" [i.e., into the Veneto proper], etc., etc. (*ibid.*, fols. 157^v ff.). This intolerable state of affairs had gone on for years. Venice would not make peace with Ercole, etc. The letter of the Senate closed with the ironic reflection that "we cannot but hope for the fortunate outcome of that war, to which the authority of the supreme and most holy pontiff [Sixtus himself] has persuaded, impelled, and aroused us!" (fol. 158^v).

[48] Sixtus IV launched his long bull *Ad bonorum tutellam* in condemnation of the Venetians on 23 May, 1483 (Arch. Segr. Vaticano, Reg. Vat. 549 [*Sixti IV Secret., tom. IV*], fols. 245^r–259^r, "datum Rome apud Sanctum Petrum, anno, etc., MCCCCLXXX tertio, decimo Kal. Iunii, pontificatus nostri anno duodecimo"). On 15 July (1483) he rejected a Venetian remonstrance against this gross misuse of his spiritual authority (*ibid.*, fols. 259^v–264^v, the bull bearing the signature of Giovanbattista Poggio, son of the humanist

than a year of the most desultory co-operation with the papacy Lodovico Maria Sforza "il Moro," then governor of Milan, saw small profit in the continuance of the war. He merely wanted the Venetians held in check, not defeated, and as a result of his withdrawal from the contest the Venetians were able to secure very favorable terms in the peace of Bagnolo (on 7 August, 1484), which finally put an end to the renownless war. Sixtus IV knew self-interest when he saw it. He condemned il Moro's faithless indifference to the Holy See, and his last political act was to reject the provisions of Bagnolo.[49]

Tidings from central Europe had, in the meantime, added much to the worries of the Curia Romana. Sixtus had sent his good friend and faithful servitor Bartolommeo de' Maraschi, bishop of Città di Castello (1474–1487), into the troubled area, and the latter's reports of October, 1483, from Bohemia and Hungary showed central Europe to be breaking down into chaos: ". . . Rapinae, stupra, incendia, plurimae atque horrendae caedes committuntur, iugulantur sacerdotes ut quod non habent aurum ex[s]olvant. . . ." King Matthias Corvinus of Hungary kept up constant attacks on the domains of the doddering Emperor Frederick III, who had lost to his vigorous opponent many castles and towns in Carinthia, Carniola, Styria, and Austria. Frederick was just creeping along from day to day with his usual stolid ineptitude, "et quotidie serpit serenissimus vero imperator, adhuc dormitat," He was believed, however, to be planning some great move since he obviously could not tolerate the loss of so many important lands. Bishop Bartolommeo had arrived in Buda on 16 October, 1483. Corvinus received him the following day. He tried to persuade Corvinus, in the pope's name, "to desist from war upon the emperor," reminding him that he was the emperor's adopted son, and that it did not become a son thus to strive against his father.

Nothing made Sultan Bayazid II happier than this war as he planned even greater evils for Christendom than his father had perpetrated. Bayazid now had Mehmed II's abundant gold, and was more popular with the Turkish soldiery than "his severe, faithless, and cruel father;" he knew that the Hungarians were worn out, lacked money, and had suffered a large loss of life. To all this, Corvinus replied that he had in fact always desired peace with Frederick, but got nothing but war from him as he egged on his son Maximilian or the king of Poland or others to attack him while he was engaged with the Turk. Corvinus spoke with indignation and dilated on the injuries he had suffered at Hapsburg hands. Bartolommeo tried to soothe him, reminding him that Frederick also claimed various wrongs had been done him, to which the sharp intelligence and fluent tongue of Corvinus had a ready rejoinder. The great Hungarian's personality made a profound impression upon the Italian bishop: "Beatissime pater, rex Ungariae Mars ipse est, nihil nisi bellum cogitans!" Corvinus's heavy artillery, *tormenta* and *bombardae*, was tremendous; Bartolommeo saw a stone cannonball weighing 1,500 pounds. Everywhere at Buda the evidence suggested that Corvinus was preparing to enlarge his efforts against Frederick rather than make peace with him.

"I thought the king had been impoverished by his daily warfare," Bartolommeo wrote the pope, "which had also been suggested to me in [König]grätz, and in rehearsing the reasons which should make for peace, I gave not the least emphasis to this one. Hence, I gather, it came about that on the twentieth [of October] a certain friend invited me to see the king's palace. . . ." The wealth of the wardrobe astonished him, with its precious garments loaded with gold, jewels, and pearls; there were great tapestries on the walls and any number of gold and silver vessels "worked with a wondrous art." Bartolommeo saw one lampstand of such weight as to be worth 3,500 ducats, which he described with all the admiration of the Renaissance ecclesiastic who loved to be surrounded by beauty and by opulence. He saw crosses, marvelous altar adornments, five hundred large silver plates, three hundred golden goblets, and other such ware, *preciosissima, exquisita vasa*, "and I saw a hall so furnished that I do not think the glory of Solomon could have surpassed it!" Bartolommeo does not mention Corvinus's library of beautiful manuscripts. Whatever hardships Corvinus and his famous father John Hunyadi had found on the field of battle, obviously personal poverty was not among them.

Poggio Bracciolini). The pope also entered an alliance with the Sienese on 14 August (1483), *ibid.*, fols. 268^r–271^r, 276^r–278^r, by mod. stamped enumeration.

[49] Jacopo da Volterra, *Diarium romanum*, ad ann. 1484, in *RISS*, XXIII-3 (1904), 136.

Bartolommeo de' Maraschi did not allow himself to be overwhelmed by the magnificence of Matthias Corvinus's private life, however, and when he was next admitted to the royal presence, he continued to preach peace. Corvinus was reasonable and amiable, but got somewhat angry when he thought of the injustices done him in the past. No one was more aware than he of the Turk's power and preparations (to which Bartolommeo gave unneeded emphasis); he wanted peace with the Christian powers, but heartily resented the Hapsburg aggressions, "and when he spoke of the Venetians, he accused them of perfidy, and not to himself alone but to all the kings of Hungary." Corvinus flourished documents to make his points, and requested Bartolommeo to send copies of them to the pope and the cardinals. He sounded a trifle paranoid as he excoriated the treachery of his opponents, but he also sounded honest and did not lack a sense of humor. He said he knew his cause was just; so did the princes of Germany. When Bartolommeo asked with a smile whether the current war with the emperor was redounding much to his glory,

> since a lion was fighting with a mouse, for the moment he was caught by the phrase, so I continued, praying that he might choose kindliness, piety, and religion to overcome the plots, deceits, and injuries of which he spoke, to turn his arms against the Turks, by which means he might make his name more famous and respected, and the way would finally open up into heaven, where he might enjoy not a fleeting and meaningless reputation, but true and eternal glory with Christ. . . .

According to Bartolommeo, the Hungarians themselves did not want the war, neither did the queen, and the search for peace simply had to go on "until an end might be put to this malady from which we could see the Christian commonwealth would waste away: [the king] replied that he would do his part, and gave me his hand with the greatest courtesy, and told his prelates to take me home."

Their conversations were resumed on the following day, exploring the road to peace in central Europe. Bartolommeo dined with Corvinus, the queen, the voivode Stephen of Transylvania, and John de Pruisz, the bishop of Grosswardein (Nagyvárad), "a favorite of the king and queen and most respectful of your Holiness." He attended other court functions, and preached peace with Frederick at the king on every possible occasion. They talked of a diet which might be assembled to settle the Austro-Hungarian war; Corvinus thought the Venetians little better than the Turks; and of course the Germans bore arms against one another with no less enthusiasm than against the Turks. So their conversations went on and on. Bartolommeo's long letter to Sixtus IV closes with a report which the voivode Stephen of Transylvania gave him of the persistent, ominous movement of Turks up the Danube.[50]

Another letter of Bishop Bartolommeo to the pope, dated at Buda on 24 October, 1483, relates to discussions he had had with Corvinus concerning Jem Sultan, "who is held by the knights of Rhodes." Corvinus had been dreaming of plans to use Jem against his brother Bayazid II, who is now said to have been universally disliked in the Ottoman empire. Some of the leading pashas had already secretly conspired with Jem to kill Bayazid on the battlefield, but the plan had failed, owing to Jem's own precipitate action and the retreat of his troops at the critical juncture. A renegade pasha, who had got out of a Turkish prison, was then in Buda, encouraging Corvinus and Peter de Varda, archbishop of Kalocza (*Colocensis*) in Hungary, in the hope that treachery at the Porte might still lay Bayazid low. Corvinus proposed to send the pasha to Rome, and asked Bartolommeo to let a member of his household accompany the Turk

[50] Arch. Segr. Vaticano, Miscellanea, Arm. II, Reg. 20 (Politicorum Varia, tom. XX), fols. 51^r–58^v. Bartolommeo de'Maraschi was deeply involved in the financial affairs of the Holy See from the summer of 1473 on (Arm. XXXI, tom. 62, fols. 71^r–72^r, papal bull dated 30 September, 1473). In June, 1480, he passed from the office of receiver (*depositarius*) in the Camera Apostolica (Introitus et Exitus, Reg. 500, fols. 2^r, 31^v, and Reg. 501, fols. 3^r, 32^v) to that of *generalis thesaurarius* (Intr. et Ex., Reg. 502, fols. 20^r, 26^v, 73^r, *et alibi*). He is described as "treasurer-general" in the credential letter which Sixtus IV addressed to Corvinus on 8 June, 1483 (*Monumenta Vaticana historiam regni Hungariae illustrantia*, 1st ser., VI [Budapest, 1891]= *Mathiae Corvini Hungariae regis epistolae ad Romanos pontifices datae et ab eis acceptae*, no. CLIX, p. 206). Corvinus alludes to Bartolommeo's mission to Buda in a letter to Sixtus dated 6 November, 1483, informing the Curia Romana of the incursions of Turkish bands into Croatia, Carniola, and Styria, and their dramatic defeat by the ban of Croatia on 29 October (*ibid.*, no. CLXVI, pp. 210–12). For other references to Bartolommeo's mission, *cf.*, *ibid.*, nos. CLXVIII, CLXX, pp. 214, 217. His name appears constantly in the registers of Introitus et Exitus. On the warfare, deplored by Bartolommeo, which Corvinus was waging against Frederick III, see Gyula Rázsó, *Die Feldzüge des Königs Matthias Corvinus in Niederösterreich, 1477–1490*, Vienna, 1973, esp. pp. 15 ff. (Militärhistorische Schriftenreihe herausgegeben vom Heeresgeschichtlichen Museum, Heft 24).

to the papal court, to which request of course Bartolommeo acceded, and promptly wrote his Holiness, "whom I ask in the king's name to admit the Turkish pasha into his presence." The pasha should also be allowed to see Jem, of whose person Corvinus wished to secure possession to employ as a figurehead against the sultan. Bartolommeo makes it quite clear that Corvinus was anxious to add as much of the erstwhile Byzantine empire to his own domains as possible, and closes his letter with another expression of his admiration for the militant monarch, on whose broad shoulders the future of central Europe then seemed to be resting.[51]

For some years the Turkish danger would be rather less than Bartolommeo de' Maraschi seems to have thought. At any rate a divided Italy had shaken off the Turkish invaders in almost miraculous fashion. As Moses and the Israelites had escaped from servitude in Egypt, and Pharaoh and the pursuing host had been swallowed up in the onrushing waters of the Red Sea (Exodus, 14), so Sultan Mehmed II was now dead, and so had the Turkish hosts been stopped at Rhodes and overcome at Otranto. While the city and the Curia were still contemplating with wonderment these Christian victories, a painter was at work in the spring of 1482 on scaffolding set up against the south wall of the new *capella maior palatii*, the recently finished Sistine Chapel. He was in fact at work on the Mosaic theme suggested by the bull which Sixtus IV had promulgated in the late summer of 1480. The archenemy of the faith had finally died in defeat, his forces repulsed by God, *qui currum Pharaonis deiecit in mare*.[52]

The Sistine fresco of the drowning of Pharaoh and the Egyptians may be seen at two levels of representation. It both tells the story of Exodus, and commemorates the Turkish defeat. Toward the left of the picture, just behind Moses' left shoulder, stands the bearded figure of Cardinal Bessarion, holding the silver-gilt reliquary containing the revered head of S. Andrew, in a pose which thousands had seen in April, 1462, at the reception of the relic into the Vatican. Bessarion had died a decade before this fresco was painted, but he still remained the symbol of the anti-Turkish crusade. His presence in the picture clearly suggests that the oriental forces being smitten by the engulfing waves are in fact the Osmanlis, who had crossed the seas to attack Rhodes and Otranto, and over whom the Grand Master d'Aubusson and Cardinal Campofregoso had achieved the victories which the fresco thus served to recall.[53] In 1481 Andrea Guaccialotti struck a dated medal with a portrait of Sixtus IV on the obverse, and on the reverse the figure of

---

[51] Arch. Segr. Vaticano, Miscell., Arm. II, Reg. 20, fols. 50^r–51^r: ". . . Quod si rex Ungariae illum detentum [a Rhodiensibus Turcum] habeat, tribus regnis illico potietur quae Christiana fuerunt."

[52] *Cf.* the text of the bull in Raynaldus, *Ann. eccl.*, ad ann. 1480, no. 23, vol. XIX (1693), p. 290b.

[53] *Cf.* Pastor, *Gesch. d. Päpste*, II (repr. 1955), 698–700, with notes, material not in the English translation. This is an interpretation of the "Passaggio del Mar Rosso" apparently unknown to L. D. Ettlinger, *The Sistine Chapel before Michelangelo: Religious Imagery and Papal Primacy*, Oxford, 1965. Contrary to Ettlinger's belief, the Sistina was not in fact the place where "the conclaves were meant to be held" (p. 10), and so was never intended "to provide a proper setting for conclaves" (p. 119). The cardinals and *conclavistae* ate and slept in the Sistina when it became the chapel major (replacing the earlier *capella maior* on the same site), but every one of the twelve "conclaves" (*scrutinia*) from 1455 to 1534 was held in the Chapel of S. Niccolò da Bari, the *capella parva S. Nicolai*, which lay just across the *aula prima* (later Sala Regia) from the *capella maior*, as the Sistina in its turn was called. (Ettlinger, p. 10, is also mistaken in identifying "Fra Angelico's chapel" with that of "S. Nicolai.") As the number of cardinals increased under Paul III, the *capella parva* of S. Niccolò became too small for papal elections; it had also become the *cappella vecchia*. As Sixtus IV had replaced the old *capella maior* with the Sistina, so Paul III demolished the Chapel of S. Niccolò in 1538, and built the present Paolina to take over its functions. The site of the old chapel of S. Niccolò is now filled by the stairway which descends from the Sala Regia to the Cortile del Maresciallo (*cf.* Franz Ehrle and Hermann Egger, *Der Vaticanische Palast* . . . [1935], pp. 103–38, and C. L. Frommel, "Antonio da Sangallos Cappella Paolina . . . ," *Zeitschrift für Kunstgeschichte*, XXVII [1964], 1–42, to which previous reference has been made above, in Chapter 9, note 1).

The identity of the painter or painters of the drowning of Pharaoh and his six hundred chariots in the Red Sea has been the subject of doubt and dispute for many years (*cf.* Fritz Knapp, *Piero di Cosimo*, Halle a. S., 1899, pp. 21–22, and Mina Bacci, *Piero di Cosimo*, Milan, 1966, pp. 128–29 and pl. 64). Vasari says that Cosimo Rosselli painted the scene, and Ettlinger, *op. cit.*, thinks he is right; modern scholars have "attributed" it to Piero di Cosimo, Fra Diamante, Benedetto Ghirlandaio, Biagio d'Antonio, and others. Ernst Steinmann, *Botticelli*, trans. C. Dodgson, London, 1901, p. 55, believed that the fresco represented the papal victory over the Neapolitan forces at Campomorto, where Turkish *akinjis* fought in the army of Alfonso of Calabria. This interpretation, which has received a rather general acceptance (*cf.* Paul Schubring, *The Sistine Chapel*, Rome, 1910, pp. 15–16, 59), is rightly rejected by Ettlinger. Christian opponents, i.e., Ferrante and his son Alfonso, would hardly be represented as orientals when they had just joined with the pope in aiding d'Aubusson and had shared with Campofregoso the victory over the Turks at Otranto.

Constantia holding a tall staff, her left elbow resting on a column, with galleys and crouching Turks, arms, and banners at her feet.[54]

Pope Sixtus IV had had ample time to handle this medal to his full satisfaction and to contemplate the Sistine painting before he died on Thursday, 12 August, 1484.[55] The unending feud between the Orsini and the Colonnesi, which had raged with especial virulence through the recent wars, threatened for a while to destroy wide areas in Rome. The Colonnesi hated the della Rovere. Girolamo Riario hastened back to the city (from a siege of Paliano); his enterprising wife Caterina seized the Castle of S. Angelo; and their allies, the Orsini, barricaded themselves against attack across the river in the Castle of Monte Giordano in the ancient Campus Martius. After Sixtus's death the Roman populace turned against the Rovere-Riario faction. The Colonnesi were acclaimed. Sixtus, builder of the Sistine Chapel, refounder of the Vatican Library and Archives, patron of the arts and literature, beautifier of Rome and of almost thirty other cities in Italy, has been harshly dealt with by many historians, who have given unwarranted credence to the unsavory strictures made on his life by the contemporary diarist Stefano Infessura.[56] But even a generous judgment of his career will not absolve him of grave misdemeanor. Although he had a clear vision of the Turkish problem, and was indeed anxious to resolve it by a great offensive against the Porte, Sixtus was a confirmed and unblushing nepotist, who willfully confused the well-being of the Church with the aggrandizement of his many nephews. He had appointed most of the cardinals who elected his unworthy successors Innocent VIII and Alexander VI.

[54] Roberto Weiss, *The Medals of Pope Sixtus IV (1471–1484)*, Rome, 1961, pp. 21–22, with refs., and nos. 29, 33. Guaccialotti used the same reverse in a medal struck shortly afterwards for Alfonso, duke of Calabria.

[55] Acta Consistorialia, in Eubel, *Hierarchia*, II (1914, repr. 1960), 47; S. Infessura, *Diaria rerum romanarum*, ad ann. 1484, ed. Oreste Tommasini, Rome, 1890, p. 155; Jacopo da Volterra, *Diarium romanum*, in *RISS*, XXIII-3 (1904), 135–37; Pastor, *Gesch. d. Päpste*, II (repr. 1955), 604–6.

[56] *Diaria*, pp. 155–61, on which, however, see Pastor, *Hist. Popes*, IV, 416–71, and *Gesch. d. Päpste*, II (repr. 1955), 640–710, who gives Sixtus more praise than he probably deserved; *cf.* Egmont Lee, *Sixtus IV and Men of Letters*, unpubl. diss., Univ. of Wisconsin, Madison, 1970, and José Ruysschaert, "Sixte IV, fondateur de la Bibliothèque Vaticane (15 juin 1475)," *Archivum historiae pontificiae*, VII (1969), 513–24, with the text of the bull establishing the papal library. On the main events of the last four years of Sixtus IV's pontificate, from the Turkish expeditions against Otranto and Rhodes in the summer of 1480 until his death, see Pastor, *Gesch. d. Päpste*, II, 558–606; and *cf.* Navagero, *Storia veneziana*, in *RISS*, XXIII, cols. 1166–91; Sanudo, *Vite de'duchi*, *ibid.*, XXII, cols. 1214–34; Raynaldus, *Ann. eccl.*, ad ann. 1480–1484, vol. XIX (1693), pp. 286 ff., a full account, with numerous documents and quotations from contemporary sources. Thirty months after Sixtus's death Innocent VIII made provision for the restoration of the well-known Basilian church and monastery of S. Nicola di Casole, which had been partly destroyed by the Turks at the time of their occupation of Otranto (Reg. Vat. 719, fols. 296r–297r, "datum Rome apud Sanctum Petrum, anno etc., MCCCCLXXXsexto [O. S.], Idibus Februarii, pont. nostri anno tertio," i.e., 13 February, 1487).

13. INNOCENT VIII, JEM SULTAN, AND THE CRUSADE (1484–1490)

When Mehmed II the Conqueror died on 3 May, 1481, he had only two surviving sons. The elder was Bayazid [II], then governor of distant Amasya, who occupied Istanbul on 20 May, and took over control of the government. Bayazid's accession to the throne was much facilitated by the support of the janissaries, who frustrated the efforts of the grand vizir Karamānī Muḥammad on behalf of the late sultan's younger and favorite son, Prince Jem (Cem), the governor of Caramania (Karaman). Karamānī Muḥammad had tried to conceal the Conqueror's death long enough for Jem Sultan to reach the capital, but his plan had miscarried, and he had lost his life in a revolt of the janissaries, who carried his head through the streets of Istanbul. Their slogan was Sultan Bayazid and double pay. Bayazid rewarded their loyalty by a special gift of money, which subsequently became an expensive custom at the accession of each new sultan.[1]

In the meantime Jem Sultan was in revolt. The extraordinary turn which his fortunes took from this time was to make him a legendary figure in eastern as well as in western literature. Jem was born in Adrianople on 22 December, 1459. His mother, to whom he was very devoted, is said to have been a Slavic princess.[2] Like most Ottoman princes, he acquired an early experience of government and military command. He was also given to athletics, and enjoyed literary composition. In December, 1474, he had succeeded his brother Mustafa as governor of Caramania, establishing himself with his staff at Konya. He had been responsible for the Turkish negotiations with Pierre d'Aubusson, grand master of the Hospitallers, before the island of Rhodes was subjected to the extraordinary siege of 1480, which we have described above, in Chapter 11. Now Jem seized Bursa (Brusa) as his center of opposition. He proposed a division of the empire: he would retain Asia, and Bayazid would rule European Turkey. The sultan would not hear of it, however, and after eighteen days Jem had to give up Bursa as the imperial army bore down upon him. On 20 June (1481) Jem was badly defeated near Yeni-Shehir, and his small army was scattered. He barely managed to escape to his erstwhile capital of Konya, and thence on 28–29 June into the mountain fastnesses of Cilicia with his mother, his harem, his daughters, and his son Murad, who later resided at Rhodes.

Jem Sultan's career as a ruler was over. By way of Tarsus, Adana, Aleppo, Damascus, where he spent seven weeks, and Jerusalem he made his way to Cairo, where in late September, 1481, he was courteously received by the Burjī Mamluk "Soldan" Ka'itbey (1468–1495). From Egypt, Jem made the pilgrimage to Mecca, the only prince of his house to do so. He returned to Cairo on 20 February, 1482, trying once more to arrange some division of the Ottoman empire with the victorious Bayazid, who would go no farther than promise him a pension.

[1] J. W. Zinkeisen, *Gesch. d. osman. Reiches in Europa*, II (Gotha, 1854), 473 ff.; Louis Thuasne, *Djem-Sultan, fils de Mohammed II, frère de Bayezid II, 1459–1495*, Paris, 1892, pp. 26 ff.; Giacomo Bosio, *Militia di San Giovanni Gierosolimitano*, II (Rome, 1594), bk. XII, pp. 354 ff; Fr. Babinger, "Die Chronik des Qaramānī Meḥmed-Pascha, eine neuerschlossene osmanische Geschichtsquelle," *Mitteilungen zur osmanischen Geschichte*, II (1923–26), 242–47, reprinted in his *Aufsätze und Abhandlungen zur Geschichte Südosteuropas und der Levante*, 2 vols., Munich, 1962–66, II, 1–5. Guillaume Caoursin, vice-chancellor of the Knights of S. John of Jerusalem and historian of the siege of Rhodes in 1480, has left a first-hand account *De casu regis Zyzymy*, one of nine tracts published in his *Obsidionis Rhodie urbis descriptio*, Ulm, 1496. Extensive extracts from Caoursin's work on Jem Sultan (usually called Zizim by westerners) are given in L. Thuasne, ed., *Johannis Burchardi Argentinensis, capelle pontificie sacrorum rituum magistri, Diarium sive rerum urbanarum commentarii (1483–1506)*, 3 vols., Paris, 1883–85, I, append., no. 34, pp. 528–46. There are brief accounts of Jem's career by J. H. Mordtmann, in the *Encyclopaedia of Islām*, I (Leyden and London, 1908), 1034–35, and by Halil Inalcik, *ibid.*, new ed., II (1965), 529–31; on Bayazid II, note Cl. Huart, *ibid.*, I (1908), 685, and V. J. Parry, new ed., I (1960), 1119–21, with bibliography; as well as Jos. von Hammer-Purgstall, *Gesch. d. osman. Reiches*, II (1828, repr. 1963), 250 ff. Documents relating to Jem and some of his own letters (from the Archives in the Topkapi Palace in Istanbul) have been published in facsimile by I. H. Ertaylan, *Sultan Cem*, Istanbul, 1951. There is an extensive bibliography relating to Jem (and his portraits) in Semavi Eyice, "Sultan Cem'in Portreleri Hakkinda," in the Turkish *Belleten*, XXXVII (Ankara, 1973), 1–49.

[2] Sigismondo de' Conti (da Foligno), *Le Storie de' suoi tempi dal 1475 al 1510*, 2 vols., Rome, 1883, II, 4. Although Thuasne believed that Jem Sultan's mother was "issue d'une race royale de Serbie," Franz Babinger did not (*Spätmittelalterliche fränkische Briefschaften aus dem grossherrlichen Seraj zu Stambul*, Munich, 1963, pp. 32–33, note 108, and

Finding support in Anatolia, Jem decided again to take his chances on the roulette of war, and quickly gathering his forces at Aleppo in April and early May (1482), he proceeded to Adana, where reinforcements were to join him. His chief ally was the Karaman-oghlu Kasim Beg, the "Gran Caramano," whom westerners knew as the king of Cilicia, and who was anxious to recover the lands and sovereignty which the Conqueror had taken from his father.[3] Although Jem's army took Ereghli and Ankara, it could not take well-defended Konya. As Bayazid marched against him in mid-June, Jem was obliged again to take flight into the rugged highlands of Cilicia. Although he was now hard-pressed on all sides, without resources or any conceivable hope of success, Jem's fierce pride led him to refuse Bayazid's offer of a handsome pension if he would take up a peaceful abode in Jerusalem, which lay safely within the range of the Egyptian soldan's power. Jem soon found it necessary to let his forces go, and embarked at ancient Corycus on the coast of Lesser Armenia (Goṛigos, Turkish Korgos) for the island of Rhodes, where he arrived on 29 July (1482). He had received from the grand master the fullest assurances as to his safety before making the extraordinary decision to seek aid from the Christian *giaour*.[4] The Hospitallers had made elaborate preparations for his coming.

A holiday spirit pervaded the fortress town of Rhodes as the Knights and townsmen looked forward to the arrival of Jem Sultan. The Grand Master d'Aubusson had ordered a wooden pontoon constructed at the shore where Jem was to disembark. It was covered with cloths of gold and silk. The townspeople crowded down to the shore to watch Jem's landing, and lined the flower-strewn streets through which he would have to pass. Many of them climbed to the rooftops of their houses. Beautiful maidens and their mothers watched from windows decked out with fine hangings. Officials of the Order, knights, and pages rode richly caparisoned horses in a procession which went from the grand master's palace down to the shore. They went in pairs through the narrow streets. The grand master rode alone on a magnificent mount; resplendent in gold embroidery, he was a striking figure. He halted opposite the church of S. Sebastiano, to await Jem in the Piazza.

When the galley bearing Jem Sultan docked, and he stepped onto the pontoon, he was received by lords of the Grand Cross with all honors befitting a prince of highest station. Cannon were fired from emplacements on the walls and towers. Jem was given a "most beautiful horse;" all the more important members of his retinue were also mounted; and the company started forward slowly to the sound of trumpets, drums, and other instruments. The sadness of the scene struck the watching crowds; they burst into applause at the sight of the Ottoman prince. When Jem had reached the church of S. Sebastiano, he found the grand master quietly waiting for him amid the chivalric splendor of mounted knights and floating pennants. Jem put his forefinger to his mouth three times as though to request silence, for "such is the custom of Turkish princes when they exchange solemn salutations." Jem and d'Aubusson extended their hands one to the other,

---

p. 45, note 139 [Südosteuropäische Arbeiten, no. 61]).

[3] Bosio, *Militia di San Giovanni*, II (1594), bk. XII, pp. 357–58; Thuasne, *Djem-Sultan*, pp. 40–53; Inalcik, "Djem Sultan," *Encyclopaedia of Islām*, II (1965), 529.

[4] Bosio, *Militia di San Giovanni*, II (1594), bks. XII–XIII, pp. 360–66. Jem Sultan's ambassadors had arrived in Rhodes on 10 July (1482); negotiations had proceeded swiftly thereafter to expedite Jem's coming to Rhodes. According to the safe-conduct which the Grand Master d'Aubusson sent Jem, the latter could leave the island whenever he chose (V. Lamansky, *Secrets d'état de Venise*, St. Petersburg, 1884, repr. New York, 1968, pp. 261–62). *Cf.* D. Malipiero, *Annali veneti*, in *Archivio storico italiano*, VII, pt. 1 (1843), 133–34; Thuasne, *Djem-Sultan*, pp. 53–64. The date of Jem's entry into Rhodes is fixed by an archival text in the Malta Library, Archives of the Order at Malta (abbr. AOM), Reg. 76, fol. 94^v: "Ingressus illustrissimi domini Zyzymi Soldani in Rhodum: Die XXVIIII Iullii MCCCCLXXXII quo intravit Rhodum illustrissimus d. Zyzymuy Soldanus, frater Magni Turci qui nunc imperat, filius vero quondam Turci. . . ." His arrival at Rhodes was known in Venice before 13 September, when the Senate forbade all Venetian rectors and naval officers to grant Jem asylum or render him the slightest assistance (Sen. Secreta, Reg. 30, fols. 118^v–119^r [128^v–129^r]).

In a letter dated 27 August (1482) Bayazid II wrote the Signoria of Venice that he had defeated Jem, "unde necessariamente el montò sopra uno navilio picolo cum trenta compagni et andato a Rodi, el resto di suo homeni tuti sono dissipadi per tuto et smariti," adding (to upset the Venetians) the unlikely statement: "Al presente veramente intendemo che li Rodiensi voleno armar certi suo navilii et mandar quello cum tuto el suo apparato ala Morea over de li ale parte de Italia per comover ancor qualche tumulto et conturbatio." Bayazid also stated that he was assuming Venice wished to preserve "the good and sincere and faithful peace and friendship which we have between us," to which the Senate returned an effusive answer on 29 September, affirming the peace and congratulating Bayazid on his "degna et glorioxa victoria conseguita contra el fradello cum la fuga" (Sen. Secreta, Reg. 30, fols. 123^v–124^r [133^v–134^r]).

and each spoke words of greeting. Then the whole cavalcade moved forward, riding in pairs again. An interpreter rode with Jem and d'Aubusson. It took but a little while to reach the Auberge de France, on the Street of the Knights, which had been sumptuously prepared for Jem and his suite. The grand master suggested that his guest would wish to rest from the hardships of his voyage. Despite his obesity, Jem dismounted with agility, as Turkish attendants rendered ceremonial assistance on either side, went up the stairs of the Auberge, and retired into his rooms, much gratified (according to Caoursin and Bosio) with the friendliness, courtesy, and magnificence of the reception and hospitality being accorded him by the Knights of S. John.[5]

The wheel of fortune was spinning marvelously for the Knights. Within two years they had seen their position change from a desperate siege which might have proved their undoing to a position almost of arbiter of Ottoman destiny. So it seemed, at least, even to Sultan Bayazid, with whom the Hospitallers were soon in communication. On 17 August, 1482, Pierre d'Aubusson and the council of the Order decided to send Jem Sultan to Europe, apparently at his own request.[6] Ten days later they were ready to send ambassadors to the Porte. The text of the *pax antiqua* of the Grand Master Jean de Lastic was reviewed, and note was taken of the issues to be dealt with in Istanbul. The Hospital did not intend henceforth to pay tribute, give annual gifts, or send an embassy to the Porte every year.[7]

By action of the council on 31 August (1482) the decision was confirmed to send Jem Sultan to France, to seek aid of Louis XI to regain his paternal inheritance. From France he wanted to go to Hungary or to some other country from which he might attempt, with western help, to lead an expedition against his brother. Pierre d'Aubusson, therefore, ordered the preparation of the *navis thesauri oneraria* to convey Jem to France, and appointed certain members of the Order to accompany him and attend to the expenses involved. The arrangements were explained to Jem by interpreters "skilled in Latin and in Turkish," and being satisfied, he confirmed the Hospitallers' plans *signo turchico solito*. He had already promised that, if by divine (and western) aid he should ever sit upon his father's throne and secure his *dicio paterna*, he and his descendants would maintain a "perpetual peace" on land and sea with the grand master of the Hospital and with his successors. He guaranteed freedom of trade to Rhodian citizens and merchants, who would be allowed to export foodstuffs from his dominions without payment of a *gabella commercii* or any other exaction. The Hospitallers would be permitted in any or every year to remove from Turkey three hundred Christians, doubtless slaves, to settle them in islands belonging to the Order. Jem promised the grand master and the Order 150,000 ducats in repayment of the expenses they were undergoing for him and his retinue. He swore to turn over to them all the islands which his father had taken from the Christians, giving the grand master and the Order the right to make any disposition of them that they might wish. And again, when the interpreters had explained the

---

[5] Bosio, II (1594), bk. XIII, pp. 366–67. Bosio says that Jem Sultan arrived in Rhodes on 24 July. His account follows closely that of Caoursin, in Thuasne, *Burchardi diarium*, I, 534. The correct date of Jem's entry into Rhodes is 29 July (see the preceding note, and *cf.* Lamansky, *Secrets d'état de Venise*, pp. 262–63, doc. dated 4 August, 1482, and Thuasne, *Djem-Sultan*, pp. 65–67, esp. note 2).

[6] Malta Library, AOM, Reg. 76, fols. 95^{v}–96^{r}: ". . . Illustrissimus et serenissimus dominus Zyzymy Soldanus . . . instanter postulavit et petiit libertatem recedendi de Rhodo et eundi ad partes occiduas quo opportunum fuerit ad securitatem sue persone et exequutionem suorum agendorum, implorando super his favorem et presidium Religionis, visis necessitatibus in quibus est constitutus, quo audito fuit deliberatum per reverendissimum d. magistrum et reverendum consilium ordinarium multis bonis respectibus et urgentibus de causis quod dictus illustrissimus dominus Zyzymy Soldanus conducatur ad partes occiduas, et quod navis thesauri oneraria preparetur ad ipsum conducendum, fueruntque deputati et ordinati qui eum conducant et omnia hec exequantur" [there follow three names, of which one is the grand master's nephew Guy de Blanchefort, the deputies being bound to execute their mission "ad conservacionem persone dicti domini Zyzymi pro indemnitate honoreque Religionis predicte"].

[7] AOM, Reg. 76, fol. 97^{v}: "Pro pace cum Magno Turco: Die XXVII mensis Augusti, MCCCCLXXXII. . . . Fuit per reverendissimum d. magistrum et reverendum consilium deliberatum quod tractetur de pace et concludatur cum Magno Turco qui nunc imperat. . . . Et pro exequutione predictorum fuerunt electi ambaxiatores. . . . In presentia reverendissimi domini magistri et reverendi consilii lecta per vice-cancellarium minuta instructionum ac articulorum pacis fiende fuit, etiam lecta pax antiqua facta tempore Magistri Johannis de Lastic et aliorum ad noticiam rerum agendarum: Demum multis colloquiis habitis fuit deliberatum quod dicta pax tractetur et concludatur modo et forma quo ordinatum est per duas minutas, reiecto omni tributo ac annuo munere et annua ambaxiata quibus oratores nullo pacto possint assentire. . . ." On the negotiations for peace between d'Aubusson and Bayazid II, see, *ibid.*, fols. 100^{r}–104^{r} and ff.

articles of the agreement to Jem, he had confirmed them *signo turchico solito*.[8] The Hospitallers had employed Jem's residence among them to good advantage.

Jem Sultan and his thirty attendants remained at Rhodes only five weeks. On 1 September (1482) they were on board the Grande Nef du Trésor, under the command of Guy de Blanchefort, nephew of the grand master, bound for France or rather Savoy. On the day preceding Jem's departure the grand master gave him a banquet which is said to have pleased him greatly, the variety of foods and magnificence of the service astonishing him.[9]

In the meantime the Grand Master Pierre d'Aubusson was already treating with the Conqueror's more successful son. Immediately after Jem Sultan's arrival in Rhodes, d'Aubusson had notified Pope Sixtus IV as well as the kings and chief princes of Europe of the pawn which fate had placed in Hospitaller hands. Now d'Aubusson negotiated a "true peace," for which the pope granted permission, with Sultan Bayazid, under which the Rhodians were to enjoy freedom of trade in all parts of the Ottoman empire, paying only the customary tolls and duties. Furthermore, Bayazid bound himself to pay every year on 1 August 35,000 Venetian ducats for the honorable maintenance and custody of his brother Jem. Since the Knights' revenues had suffered some diminution in consequence of the great siege of 1480, Bayazid "of his own accord" agreed to pay every year (also on 1 August) another 10,000 Venetian ducats into the hands of the grand master at Rhodes. This peace bears the date 7 December (1482). The understanding was that Jem was to be kept "quiet and pacific . . . , so that no war would be waged against Bayazid on his account."[10]

Never before and never again could the Christians secure quite the same diplomatic advantage over the Porte as that afforded them by the acquisition of Jem Sultan's person. On 3 January, 1483, the Grand Master d'Aubusson wrote the pope that the peace with Bayazid did honor to the Christian Order, and gained a badly needed respite for the Hospital's subjects in the Levant. It assured the safety of the castle of S. Peter (Bodrum), at ancient Halicarnassus, which had long served and would now serve even more as a refuge for Christians who could escape from slavery in Turkish Asia Minor. D'Aubusson spoke also of the advantages accruing to Rhodes from the reciprocal-trade agreements made with the Porte. Bayazid had been forced into this treaty "because of his brother, who is in our power." But d'Aubusson and the Convent at Rhodes would nevertheless remain on guard and continue the refortification of their city, already the world's strongest fortress, as though war existed between the Hospitallers and the Turks. The peace would introduce no somnolence into the Order's concern for its self-preservation. Possession of Jem imposed a wonderful restraint on Bayazid, who had recently put to death Ahmed Pasha, the captor of Otranto, on suspicion of treason, "and . . . some of the leading kadis and subashis of the city of Constantinople have been strangled," all because of their assumed partiality for Jem. D'Aubusson would keep the Curia informed of further developments.[11]

---

[8] AOM, Reg. 76, fols. 98^r–99^v. The conciliar decision to send Jem Sultan to France is dated 31 August, 1482 (*ibid.*, fol. 98^r); the articles of agreement between him and the Order are dated the twenty-second (fols. 98^v–99^v). On the latter date Jem also gave the grand master full powers of attorney to deal on his behalf with Bayazid II, on the grounds that he wished to compose his differences with the latter and live peacefully with him in the common enjoyment of their inheritance: "Sperat namque eius [i.e., d'Aubusson's] tractatu, consilio, et prudentia cum suo germano serenissimo domino Yldrymy Soldano res posse componi et concordiam iniri qua quiete vivant et paterna dicione concordi mente gaudeant" (fols. 99^v–100^r). Jem also ratified this document *signo turchico solito*, which might be useful to the Order's ambassadors to the Porte.

[9] Bosio, II (1594), bk. XIII, pp. 370, 373–75; Zinkeisen, *Gesch. d. osman. Reiches*, II, 481; Thuasne, *Djem-Sultan*, pp. 76–77, 80–81. According to Caoursin, in Thuasne, *Burchardi diarium*, I, 536, and Bosio, *op. cit.*, p. 375, Jem Sultan left Rhodes on 1 September, after thirty-eight days on the island.

[10] Bosio, II (1594), bk. XIII, pp. 370–72, 376–80, and *cf.* Felix Fabri, *Evagatorium*, III (1849), 290, on the 45,000 ducats paid by the sultan to the Knights (in the Bibliothek des literarischen Vereins in Stuttgart). Fabri follows Breydenbach. Caoursin, in Thuasne, *Burchardi diarium*, I, 544, says simply that Bayazid undertook to pay 45,000 gold pieces a year for Jem Sultan's maintenance, and Pierre d'Aubusson would take care "ne dissidii materia oriatur." On 30 August, 1482, d'Aubusson wrote Pope Sixtus IV that Jem was being sent to France (Bosio, II, 375–76); Sixtus replied in approving terms in a letter dated at Rome on 9 November (Raynaldus, *Ann. eccl.*, ad ann. 1482, no. 36, vol. XIX [1693], p. 313a). See in general Thuasne, *Djem-Sultan*, pp. 81–87. Texts of the treaty of 7 December, 1482, and some attendant documents, in both Latin and Greek, are given by Sebastiano Pauli, *Codice diplomatico del sacro militare ordine Gerosolimitano*, II (Lucca, 1737), no. XXIX, pp. 419–30.

[11] Pauli, *Codice diplomatico*, II, no. XXX, pp. 430–31, where the Latin text of d'Aubusson's letter to Sixtus IV is dated 3 January, 1483; Bosio, II (1594), bk. XIII, pp. 381–82, with the same letter dated 4 January. D'Aubusson wrote again to the pope on 17 May, 1483

In the meantime Jem Sultan had been landed safely at Villefranche in the territory of Duke Charles I of Savoy on 15 October, 1482. He was taken the next day to Nice, "where there were many beautiful women," says Jem's biographer Sa'd-ad-Dīn, "and a number of very pleasant gardens."[12] After four months at Nice, Jem was transferred to Chambéry, capital of Savoy, and thence apparently to Les Échelles on the Guiers (and not to Rumilly), a commandery of the Hospitallers, where he arrived on 20 February, 1483. On 27 June he was removed to Le Pouët in Dauphiné. By this time the Knights had abandoned most of the pretense of hospitality; poor Jem was merely a prisoner, and he knew it well. He was kept for about two months at Le Pouët, and then was removed to the castles of Rochechinard and Sassenage, spending another two months in each place. It was at this time that Jem appears to have fallen in love with Philippine-Hélène, the beautiful daughter of Jacques, baron of Sassenage. About February, 1484, Jem was removed from Dauphiné to the region of the upper Creuse. More than a little doubt remains as to the details of his itinerary. Louis XI of France, who had died at the end of August, 1483, had shown no interest in supporting Jem's ambition to replace his brother Bayazid on the throne in Istanbul, whatever the concessions Jem might be prepared to promise the Christians.[13] Matthias Corvinus was the only possible crusader in Europe, by geographical necessity, for his was the misfortune to have the Turks as neighbors.

Jem Sultan was lodged for a brief while at Bourganeuf (Creuse, arr. de Guéret), an important Hospitaller commandery, center of the Langue d'Auvergne, homeland of the Grand Master d'Aubusson, but the Knights soon removed him to the castle of Monteil-le-Vicomte, which belonged to the grand master's brother Antoine d'Aubusson, one of the heroes of the siege of Rhodes. Always fearful lest Jem should establish some rapport with his servitors or his surroundings, the Knights moved him often. After two months at Monteil, they took him to Morterolles (probably in May, 1484), their commandery in the diocese of Limoges. In July, 1484, they transferred him to Boislamy, in the area of the Creuse; the castle belonged to Antoine de Blanchefort, the brother of Jem's keeper Guy. Here Jem remained for two years contemplating the past and living on hopes for the future.[14] His days were intolerably tedious, and his nights filled with dreams of escape.

(according to Pauli, II, no. xxxi, pp. 431–32) or 26 May (according to Bosio, II, 385–86), on which *cf.* Thuasne, *Djem-Sultan*, pp. 104–5. Ahmed Pasha had initially supported Bayazid, who owed much to him (Caoursin, in Thuasne, *Burchardi diarium*, I, 529–30, 540, 542). Late in the year 1483 Cardinal Rodrigo Borgia, vice-chancellor of the Church, became protector of the Hospitallers (Bosio, II, 386–87). The French Cardinal Jean de la Balue was protector of the Order, however, when the first accord was reached in February, 1486, for the surrender of Jem Sultan to the papacy (Lamansky, *Secrets d'état de Venise*, pp. 263–69; Thuasne, *Djem-Sultan*, pp. 138 ff.). Borgia and de la Balue hated each other, and on one occasion an exchange of insults between them scandalized the Curia (*ibid.*, p. 143). Lamansky, *op. cit.*, pp. 201 ff., publishes a series of documents relating to Jem from the Venetian Archives.

Concerning the negotiations for peace between the Hospitallers and Bayazid II in the late summer and fall of 1482, see AOM, Reg. 76, fols. 100ʳ–103ʳ, containing the "instructione alli religiosi cavallieri frari Guidone de Monte, Arnaldo comendator de Condat, et Leonardo Prato, nostri oratori verso lo gran signore lo serenissimo re Bayazit Soldano," with the marginal note "pro componenda pace cum Turco." In addition to the proposed articles of peace the emissaries received the customary *memoriale secretum* (*ibid.*, fols. 102ʳ–103ʳ). For archival copies of letters exchanged between Ahmed Pasha (9 July, 1482) and d'Aubusson (2 September, 1482) and for other relevant documents, see, *ibid.*, fols. 103ʳ–104ʳ and ff.

[12] Sa'd-ad-Dīn, "Aventures du prince Gem" (traduites du turc de Saad-eddin-effendi par M. Garcin de Tassy), in *Journal asiatique*, IX (1826, repr. 1965), 157, and *cf.* Thuasne, *Djem-Sultan*, pp. 98–99.

[13] Thuasne, *Djem-Sultan*, pp. 98–99, 106–10, 115–16. On 26 August, 1483, Paolo da Colle, a Florentine merchant who had had a long association with the Porte (and was an agent of Lorenzo de'Medici), wrote Bayazid II from Florence of a visit he had paid to Jem Sultan in France. Paolo had accompanied a Turkish envoy who had hoped for an audience with Louis XI; the envoy's mission was to see Jem or at least to learn "se era vivo o morto o con che signore habitava" (Babinger, *Spätmittelalterliche fränkische Briefschaften*, pp. 21–42, with the text of Paolo's letter, *ibid.*, pp. 31–36).

[14] Thuasne, *Djem-Sultan*, pp. 121–23, 146, whose chronology is inaccurate (see below, note 15). The Venetians tried to follow all developments respecting Jem Sultan (Lamansky, *Secrets d'état*, pp. 209 ff.), and curried favor with the Porte by informing Sultan Bayazid of his brother's movements. When, for example, Antonio Ferro was to leave for Istanbul as envoy and vice-bailie, his commission included the following instructions: "Si fueris interogatus de fratre domini Turci [and the pashas were certain to make the inquiry], respondebis quod postquam iam antea ille fuit mutatus de loco ad locum et positus in illa arce sita in regno Francie, prout tunc notificavimus Excellentie domini Turci per medium fidellissimi nostri Ioannis Dario, nil ulterius intelligere potuimus nisi quod adhuc in ipsa arce ille reperitur ubi diligenter custoditur. Et si quid aliud de illo intellexissemus pro officio benivolentie nostre libenter eidem Excellentie notificavissemus" (Sen. Secreta, Reg. 33, fol. 49ʳ [59ʳ], doc. dated 31 December, 1486, and *cf.*, *ibid.*, fols. 65ʳ [75ʳ], 95 [105], 104 [114], 151ʳ [161ʳ], 161ʳ [172ʳ], and Reg. 34, fols. 4ᵛ [16ᵛ], 11ᵛ [23ᵛ], 15ᵛ [27ᵛ], 26ᵛ [38ᵛ], 187ᵛ [198ᵛ]).

About July, 1486, Jem Sultan was returned to the castle of Bourganeuf, where a tower, still known as *La Tour Zizim*, had been built in 1484 especially for his residence. The tower was equipped with special kitchens, Turkish baths, and quarters for his Moslem attendants as well as his Hospitaller guards. Every precaution had been taken to make escape impossible, for Jem was the object of endless intrigues on the part of various princes, and was himself inclined to meditate flight on all possible occasions.[15] At long last, after difficult negotiations between the French court and the Curia Romana, arrangements were made for the pope to take custody of Jem. On or about 10 November, 1488, Jem finally left Bourganeuf on his historic journey to Rome. On 5 December he embarked at Lyon to sail, *molto adagio*, down the Rhone to Avignon, his progress likely to be halted at any moment if the continuing negotiations should take a turn for the worse. But the Hospitallers, in whose charge he remained, fearing (quite rightly) that some impediment might arise to delay Jem's departure from France, suddenly began to travel more rapidly. On 11 February (1489) Jem and his guardians arrived at Toulon, where the Grande Nef du Trésor and two large galleys of the Order were riding at anchor. They had to wait ten days for favorable winds, but finally sailed from Toulon on 21 February, headed for the Italian coast and Rome. Contrary to his every expectation, Jem Sultan had spent almost seven years in Savoy and France.[16]

In their own time the Knights Hospitaller were charged with violating the safe-conduct and pledges they had given Jem Sultan. The French element was predominant in the Hospital, however, and their disposition of Jem would inevitably depend upon the decision of the French king. Certainly the Knights prevented Jem from going to Hungary or even establishing direct contact with Matthias Corvinus, who in 1486–1487 had entertained plans in collusion with Duke Ercole d'Este of Ferrara for the flight or release of Jem from his French abode, so that he might march with a Hungarian army to drive his brother from the Ottoman throne.[17] Through much of the

[15] *Cf.* Thuasne, *Djem-Sultan*, pp. 157–63. Jem Sultan was also kept under such surveillance as Turkish spies found possible. They would presumably have killed or even captured him if the opportunity had ever presented itself. See the excellent article by V. L. Ménage, "The Mission of an Ottoman Secret Agent in France in 1486," *Journal of the Royal Asiatic Society*, London, 1965, pp. 112–32. The agent in question was a Turkish-born seaman named Barak Re'is. His account of the mission on which he was sent makes it clear that Jem was already lodged in the Grosse Tour at Bourganeuf by October or November, 1486. Ménage has corrected Thuasne's chronology of Jem's various places of residence in France.

[16] Thuasne, *Djem-Sultan*, pp. 213, 215, 222–23. Jem had first arrived in Savoy at Villefranche on *15 October*, 1482. By a slip of the pen, Thuasne, *op. cit.*, p. 222, writes that "le 21 février, [Djem] quittait la France où il était demeuré plus de sept années (15 février 1482 = 21 février 1489)."

The Curia's own working copy of the French release of Jem Sultan may be found in the *Liber rubeus diversorum memorabilium*, in the Arch. Segr. Vaticano, A. A., Arm. I-XVIII, 1443, fols. 116^{v}–118^{r}. On 10 April, 1488, Charles VIII gave permission for Jem to be turned over to the pope. Jem was to be taken "into the March of Ancona or into some other place in Italy in the lands of the Church" (from a copy of the royal letter in French, *ibid.*, fol. 118^{r}). The instrument granting the pope custody of Jem is dated 4 July, 1488:

"Promissio regis Francie super relaxatione Zizimini Sultani Turchi existentis in Francia pro Religione Rhodianorum: In Dei nomine amen. Anno a nativitate eiusdem millesimo CCCCLXXXVIII, indictione sexta, pontificatus sanctissimi in Christo patris et domini nostri, domini Innocentii divina providentia papae VIII anno quarto, die vero quarta mensis Iulii. Cum reverendus pater, dominus Petrus Dambusson, magister Hospitalis Sancti Johannis Ierosolimitani et venerabiles viri Conventus Rodi hospitalis eiusdem dudum Ziziminum Sultanum, Turchorum tiranni germanum, captivum tenerent pro illius tutiori custodia eum ad partes gallicanas et loca temporalis dominii serenissimi principis domini Caroli, Francorum regis Christianissimi, traduci fecerint et in illis ex tunc diligenter custodiri ac postmodum sanctissimus dominus noster et magister ac conventus prefati ex certis rationabilibus causis firmiter credentes et arbitrantes Reipublice Christiane et fidei catholice plurimum expedire quod idem Ziziminus ad loca temporalis dominii Romane Ecclesie et presertim provinciam Marchie Anchonitane traduceretur et custodiretur in illis que propinquiora sunt locis Christianorum que tirannus ille dudum occupavit et occupat . . . [fol. 116^{v}].

"Et . . . idem sanctissimus dominus noster de dictorum reverendissimorum dominorum Cardinalium consilio et consensu promisit prefatis oratoribus [the envoys' names are deleted] et michi notario ut publice persone pro prefato serenissimo rege stipulantibus et recipientibus quod idem Ziziminus non tradetur in manibus et posse alicuius eiusdem regis odiosi et malivoli vel inimici aut alicuius alterius quam ipsius s.d.n. iuxta conventa inter suam Sanctitatem, magistrum, et conventum prefatos. . . . Que omnia sanctissimus dominus noster et oratores prefati sibi invicem dictis nominibus promiserunt attendere et observare bona fide et non contrafacere vel venire aliqua ratione vel causa sub pena mille librarum auri per partem que non adimpleret incurrenda et alteri parti applicanda. Quam penam una pars alteri et altera alteri dare et solvere promisit totiens quotiens fuerit contrafactum et pena commissa soluta vel non omnia et singula firma perdurent . . ." [fol. 117^{rv}].

[17] Thuasne, *Djem-Sultan*, pp. 146 ff., 165–70. The commission given by the Venetian Senate to the venerable diplomat Giovanni Dario on 7 April, 1487 (Sen. Secreta, Reg. 33, fols. 64^{v}–65^{r} [74^{v}–75^{r}], given in Lamansky,

year 1487 Corvinus had continued his efforts to secure Jem's release. The Venetians had maintained a persistent opposition, however, and urged the pope to prevail upon the French king to have him sent to Rome. In the meantime the Venetian envoy at the court of Charles VIII did everything he could to frustrate the efforts of an elaborate Hungarian embassy which tried (in vain) to get Jem sent to Buda. It has often been said that the Hospitallers had no desire to lose the 45,000 ducats which the sultan was supposed to pay annually for his brother's custody. But the historian of the Order, Bosio, claims that Jem was supported in the grand manner befitting his princely station. Guarding him was also expensive. The Hospital had to bear the costs of numerous embassies to various courts on business relating to his custody or the possible employment of his presence on a crusade.[18]

The diplomatic correspondence of the later 1480's shows repeated attempts being made to get possession of Jem Sultan by Matthias Corvinus and his father-in-law Ferrante of Naples,[19] Ferdinand of Aragon, the Mamluk Soldan Ka'itbey of Egypt, and Pope Sixtus IV's successor Innocent VIII. Eastern and western sources alike indicate that Jem had himself expected to go to Hungary, whence with the aid of Corvinus he might invade Rumelia. At long last, as we have seen, Charles VIII of France had agreed to release Jem to Pope Innocent, to whose troubled reign and futile efforts to deal with the "eastern question" we shall come shortly. Jem's plight was to serve as a main theme in the propaganda being directed toward the East, for Innocent was planning a crusade. Jem arrived at Civitavecchia on the Italian coast on 6 March (1489). He entered Rome about 3–4:00 P.M. on 13 March.[20] Pierre d'Aubusson had already received his reward. A few days before, on the ninth, he had been created a cardinal in secret consistory,[21] obviously not because he had saved Rhodes for Christendom, but because he had surrendered Jem to the papacy. Jem's coming was a great event. According to Sigismondo de' Conti, there had long been a prophecy widespread throughout Christendom that the ruler (*princeps*) of the Turks would come to Rome before the year 1484, "and he would reside in the Vatican." Jem's arrival in the city and lodgment at the Vatican fulfilled the prophecy in most auspicious fashion, to the joy of the populace at Rome and elsewhere.[22]

Secrets d'état, p. 214), notes that Sultan Bayazid thought about his brother Jem continually and was always seeking information about him. The commission makes it very clear that supplying such information was one means employed by Venetian diplomats to ingratiate themselves with the sultan.

[18] Bosio, II (1594), bk. XIII, pp. 384 ff.; Steph. Katona, *Historia critica regum Hungariae*, XVI, 517–20, cited by Zinkeisen, *Gesch. d. osman. Reiches*, II, 482–83; W. Fraknói, *Mathias Corvinus, König von Ungarn (1458–1490)*, Freiburg im Breisgau, 1891, pp. 220–21; and *cf.* Raynaldus, *Ann. eccl.*, ad ann. 1482, no. 36, vol. XIX (1693), p. 313a. Relations were very close between Ercole d'Este of Ferrara and Matthias Corvinus, who tried in 1485 to have Ercole's young son Ippolito (the later cardinal) made archbishop of Gran (Raynaldus, ad ann. 1486, no. 37, vol. XIX, p. 372a). Matthias Corvinus won his contest with the pope over appointment to the archbishopric of Gran, and in 1487 Ippolito went to Hungary and was installed in the ecclesiastical primacy of the country (Fraknói, *Mathias Corvinus*, pp. 286–90). On the machinations of Venice in 1487, see Thuasne, *Djem-Sultan*, pp. 152 ff., 164–71, and the documents in Lamansky, *Secrets d'état*, pp. 213–24; on the Venetian desire to see Jem Sultan handed over to the pope rather than to Corvinus, see esp. Sen. Secreta, Reg. 33, fol. 105^v [115^v], doc. dated 15 September, 1487, and *cf.* fols. 109^v [119^v], 150^v [160^v], and note Reg. 34, fol. 11^v [23^v], dated 10 May, 1489.

[19] Corvinus never abated his efforts to get Jem Sultan sent to Hungary (Thuasne, *Djem-Sultan*, pp. 198–99, 200, 220–21, 237, 250, 255 ff., and see the documents cited in the preceding note in Lamansky's *Secrets d'état*). Ferrante was no less active in attempting to get possession of Jem, and above all was anxious to keep him from going to Rome (*cf.* Lamansky, *op. cit.*, p. 227). Corvinus had married Ferrante's daughter Beatrice, who later helped frustrate Corvinus's efforts to have his illegitimate son John succeed him as king of Hungary.

[20] Burchard, *Diarium*, ed. Thuasne, I, 336, and ed. Celani, I, 254 (see below, note 92); A. de Boüard, "Lettres de Rome de Bartolomeo de Bracciano à Virginio Orsini (1489–1494)," *Mélanges d'archéologie et d'histoire*, XXXIII (1913), no. I, pp. 273–74.

[21] Innocent VIII created Pierre d'Aubusson a cardinal in the secret consistory of 9 March, 1489, along with four others (Burchard, *Diarium*, ed. Thuasne, I, 332–33, and ed. Celani, I, 251–52). At the same time Innocent created another three cardinals *in petto*, including Lorenzo de'Medici's son Giovanni, afterwards Pope Leo X (*ibid.*, ed. Thuasne, I, 333, note 2; 526–27; 544–45, 548). Note also Stefano Infessura, *Diaria rerum romanarum*, ed. Oreste Tommasini, *Diario della città di Roma di St. Infessura scribasenato*, Rome, 1890, pp. 238–40 (Fonti per la storia d'Italia, no. 5); Bosio, II (1594), bk. XIV, p. 411; Raynaldus, *Ann. eccl.*, ad ann. 1489, no. 22, vol. XIX (1693), p. 397a. In the consistory of 9 March the pope had also been obliged to give the red hat to André d'Épinay, archbishop first of Bordeaux and later of Lyon, brother of the French ambassador to the Holy See, and close relative of the Admiral de Graville, virtual ruler of France at that time (Thuasne, *Djem-Sultan*, pp. 187–98, 201, 213–14, 215, 226–27, 236). D'Épinay's promotion, no less than that of d'Aubusson, was part of the agreement under which the French court released Jem to Rome.

[22] Sigismondo de' Conti, I (1883), 325; Infessura, *Diaria*, ed. Tommasini, p. 254.

For centuries as certainly as day had followed night the demise of one pope had been followed by the election of another. The era was past, however, of such long vacancies on the throne as had preceded the election of Innocent IV and Gregory X, Celestine V and John XXII. In 1484 everyone knew that Sixtus IV would soon have a successor. On 26 August twenty-five cardinals assembled for the conclave in the Vatican palace, where cells had been prepared for them in the newly built Sistine Chapel. The cells were assigned by lot; the cardinals were to eat and sleep in them. As usual each cardinal was allowed two attendants (*conclavistae*), who would serve him and share the general confinement until the election of a new pope. Two of the august members of the conclave were ill, and so were each allowed three attendants. Early on the morning of the twenty-seventh the Venetian Cardinal Marco Barbo and some of his confrères celebrated mass in the Chapel of S. Niccolò da Bari, just across the hall (the later Sala Regia) from the Sistina, and after certain other ceremonies all the cardinals withdrew to the so-called *aula tertia* (now the east wing of the Sala Ducale), where they continued the discussions which they had been holding concerning the election "capitulations." They made various financial provisions for themselves, and all but one of them subscribed to a series of *capitula*, which were to be promulgated in three bulls within the first three days following the coronation in the likely event any one of them should be elected pope.[23]

These articles, to which twenty-four cardinals agreed, provided that the new pope should expend, if necessary, all the revenues from the alum mines at Tolfa, the "Cruciata," for the defense of Christendom against the Turks. If the revenues did not amount to the sum of 50,000 ducats, the pope was to make available other funds to bring the total up to such a figure. Included in this, however, was to be a sum not exceeding 8,000 ducats for the support of refugee nobles who had fled the Turks. The income from the alum mines was thus to be reserved, as it was supposed to be, for the Crusade. When the European powers were finally prepared to launch a real offensive against the Turks, the Church was to contribute 100,000 ducats from the alum revenues, as well as from the imposition of tithes, the sale of indulgences, and other suitable sources of revenue. The cardinals held themselves in readiness to contribute 20,000 ducats to further the progress of such a "general expedition." The new pope was also to reform the Curia Romana *in capite et membris* three months after his coronation, and was to convoke as soon as possible a general council "according to the form of the ancient councils, in a safe and convenient place."

The purpose of this council would be to preach the crusade, and to effect the reform of the entire Church with respect to the faith and the moral life of the secular and regular clergy, the military orders, the princes, and the cities and towns (*communitates*). The pope was not to create anyone a cardinal unless he was over thirty and a doctor of theology or the canon or civil law, "or at least as far as the sons and nephews of rulers are concerned, is of sufficient literacy." In an effort to limit nepotism the cardinals required that the pope not add more than one (properly qualified) relative to the Sacred College, which was never under any circumstances again to exceed twenty-four in number. The pope was not to alienate church lands, rights, or properties by enfeoffment or otherwise; he was not to make war or entangling alliances with any king, duke, prince, lord, or city without the express consent of two-thirds of the cardinals. Since the bulls to be promulgated announcing these and other such commitments by the new pope were to "have the force of a decretal and perpetual law," the members of the College on this occasion (as they had often done in similar "capitulations" in times past) envisaged the government of the Church as an elective constitutional monarchy.[24] Even the most hope-

[23] The original texts of the election *capitula* of August, 1484, with the signatures of the twenty-four cardinals (all in their own handwriting), may be found in the Bibl. Apost. Vaticana, Cod. lat. 12,518, formerly in the Arch. Segr. Vaticano, Miscellanea, Arm. XV, tom. 109, fols. 12^r–17^r, 21^r and ff., and *cf.* fols. 32^r ff., 36^r ff., copies made from the signed originals. Cardinal Pietro Foscari refused to sign the so-called capitulations, as we are informed by the ceremonial diarist Johann Burchard, *Diarium*, ed. Thuasne, I, 32–33, and ed. E. Celani, I, 30, on which work see the following note.

[24] Burchard, *Diarium*, ed. Thuasne, I, 23–54: ". . . habentes vim decretalis et constitutionis perpetue inviolabiliter observande . . ." (p. 47), and ed. Celani, I, 23–43, 39; Raynaldus, *Ann. eccl.*, ad ann. 1484, nos. 28–39, vol. XIX (1693), pp. 337b–339b; Pastor, *Hist. Popes*, V, 232 ff., and *cf.* pp. 354–55, and *Gesch. d. Päpste*, III-1 (repr. 1955), 209 ff., and

cf. p. 320. When Burchard became master of ceremonies of the "pope's chapel" in January (1484), there were thirty-two cardinals (*Diarium*, ed. Thuasne, I, 3–4, but see also Celani's edition of Burchard, I, 4–6, with note on p. 4). In describing the conclave of 1484, Infessura, *Diaria*, ad ann. 1484, ed. Tommasini, pp. 169–70, says, ". . . Cardinales omnes, nemine discrepante, intraverunt conclave in cappella maiori [the Sistina] palatii Sancti Petri, et fuerunt numero XXV, et tres alii cardinales fuerunt absentes," and all the sources agree that twenty-five cardinals were in the conclave (*cf.* the Acta Consistorialia, in Arch. Segr. Vaticano, Arm. XXXI, tom. 52, fol. 102^r, by mod. stamped enumeration, where their names are given). As for the question of reform, Innocent VIII did finally give serious thought to improving the administration of justice in the Curia and especially in the city of Rome, as shown by the long and interesting bull *Consulta diualia sequentes*, in Reg. Vat. 692, fols. 168^r–174^r, "datum Rome apud Sanctum Petrum, anno etc. MCCCCLXXXVII [blank space left for the day and month was never filled in], pontificatus nostri anno quarto," i.e., after 12 September, 1487, the anniversary of Innocent's coronation.

Page references to Thuasne's edition of Burchard are given in the better edition of Enrico Celani, *Johannis Burckardi Liber notarum ab anno MCCCCLXXXIII usque ad annum MDVI*, in the new Muratori, *RISS*, XXXII, pt. 1, 2 vols., Città di Castello, 1907–10, 1911–42 (index still unfinished). Since Burchard is a most valuable source for a span of more than twenty years, something should be said concerning him and the two major editions of his work.

Even a rather casual perusal of the *Bibliografia dell'Archivio Vaticano*, 4 vols., Città del Vaticano, 1962–66, will make clear that more than a score of Vatican registers contain important documents relating to the rather checkered career of Johann Burchard (or Burckard). He was born about 1450 at Hasslach in the diocese of Strassburg, and (contrary to statements of Thuasne and Gnoli) it is quite certain that he never took the doctorate in law, and did not in fact use the title. At an early age he became one of the secretaries of Johann Wegeraufft, canon of S. Thomas of Strassburg and vicar-general of the prince bishop. With more enterprise, alas, than honesty Burchard surreptitiously prepared dispensations from the publication of marriage bans, all duly sealed and with blank spaces left to receive names and dates, intending to sell them for his own profit. He also stole a sword of some apparent value, and removed a florin from a pouch kept in a room in the vicar's house. When he fell under suspicion, and his own bedroom was searched, his thefts were discovered, and so were the letters of dispensation. He lost his position in the vicar's household. In October, 1467, he went to Rome (Bibl. Apost. Vaticana, Cod. lat. 12,343, fol. 123^r by mod. stamped enumeration), where there was a large German community.

Having obtained an expectancy to a benefice in the diocese of Strassburg by a *motu proprio* of Paul II, Burchard was appointed to a living in the church of S. Eligius when it became vacant. As usually happened with expectancies, his appointment was contested, but he won his case before the Rota. This decision was rejected in Strassburg, however, because of the censures which he had incurred for his previous misconduct, *censure et pene . . . inhabilitatis et infamie macula*, which would normally render him ineligible for ecclesiastical office. Thus on 2 April, 1473, he confessed his illegal preparation of the letters of dispensation, to obtain confirmation of his appointment (Arch. Segr. Vaticano, Reg. Suppl. 695 [formerly 688], fols. 157^v–158^r), but still made no acknowledgment of his thefts, which required a fuller confession two years later (*ibid.*, Reg. Suppl. 717 [710], fols. 159^r–160^r, dated 10 April, 1475, ed. J. Lesellier, "Les Méfaits du cérémoniaire Jean Burckard," *Mélanges d'archéologie et d'histoire*, XLIV [1927], 32–34, and *cf.* Reg. Suppl. 719 [712], fols. 144^v–145^r, by mod. stamped enumeration).

For a brief while Burchard occupied a lowly place in the crowd of eighty familiars and retainers in the service of Cardinal Marco Barbo, who (as Lesellier observes) was then living in the still unfinished Palazzo Venezia. Burchard had managed to attract Barbo's attention and win his favor, and other expectancies in Strassburg followed, as indicated by various bulls of Sixtus IV cited by Lesellier, *op. cit.*, pp. 14 ff., and especially by Pio Paschini, "A proposito di Giovanni Burckardo, ceremoniere pontificio," *Archivio della R. Società romana di storia patria*, LI (1928), 33–59. Lesellier is probably a bit too hard on Burchard for the misdemeanors of his youth, but like Paschini he affirms the factual reliability of the *Liber notarum* or *Diarium*, which is certainly the opinion I have derived from reading the entire work.

Burchard soon left the Palazzo Venezia, entering the service of Cardinal Giovanni Arcimboldo and next that of Tommaso Vincenzi, bishop of Pesaro and treasurer-general, with whom he lived for a short time at the Vatican, where doubtless his eyes were further opened to the rich possibilities which curial politics presented to an ambitious young man. As time passed, he acquired at least one Italian benefice, an appointment as a papal abbreviator before 15 July, 1478 (*cf.* Reg. Lateran. 786, fol. 216), and further expectancies, small pensions, and canonries in Germany. He became an apostolic protonotary on 2 February, 1481 (Reg. Vat. 658, fol. 124 by mod. stamped enumeration), and served on occasion as an advocate in ecclesiastical courts.

With the aid of Agostino Patrizzi (Patrizi), who was tiring of his service as master of papal ceremonies, Burchard was named his successor by a bull of investiture dated 29 November, 1483 (Reg. Vat. 659, fols. 137^v–138^v), *dilecto filio Johanni Burckardo, canonico ecclesie Sancti Thomae Argentinensis, capelle nostre cerimoniarum clerico. . . .* The office cost him, all told, the tidy sum of 450 ducats, as he informs us himself. Burchard actually took over the responsibilities of the office on 26 January, 1484. Whatever his deficiencies, Burchard loved the liturgy. His *Liber notarum* (or *Diarium*) was intended as a sort of formulary or guide for his complicated duties as master of ceremonies, but it also includes many notes of events occurring in the city and the Curia Romana. There may be some truth in Lesellier's belief that Burchard pillaged the (presumably small) archive of the papal chapel for material on the "science of ceremonies" (*Mél. d'arch. et d'hist.*, XLIV, 27–31), just as the charge is probably true that he refused to share either his knowledge or his collection of ceremonial books with his colleagues, especially with his successor Paride Grassi, who hated him and charged that he practiced the fine art of master of ceremonies "ex diversis libris occultissimis occultissime" (Thuasne, III, 427, note 2; Lesellier, *op. cit.*, p. 30).

Burchard certainly employed the years in Rome to constant financial advantage. Lesellier and Paschini list numerous bulls granting favors or appointments to Burchard, but do not attempt to note them all. Thus on 8 June, 1486, Burchard, *qui etiam capelle nostre clericus ceremoniarum existit*, received a benefice in the church of S. Andreas in Worms (Reg. Vat. 719, fols. 265^v–267^r, in connection with which *cf.* the bull of the same date, *ibid.*, fols. 340ᵛ–342ᵛ, granting a certain Amandus Wolff Eckeboltzbem a benefice in the same church of S. Andreas). A bull of 11 April, 1491, recalls Burchard's involvement in a contest, which required papal intervention, with one Johann Pfeiffer (*Pfifer*, *Phyfer*) and a certain Johann Meyer over a *prepositura et canonicatus* of a church in the diocese of Basel. Pfeiffer and Meyer claimed the right to exclude Burchard by producing an alleged letter of special reservation granted by Sixtus IV. Burchard's opponents were also opposed to each other, and Innocent VIII settled the dispute in favor of the *ceremoniere*: ". . . nosque cessionem ipsam duxerimus admictendam . . . dicto Iohanni Burchardo, qui etiam continuus commensalis noster et capelle nostre clericus cerimoniarum existit, premissorum obsequiorum et meritorum suorum intuitu gratiam specialem facere volentes ipsumque Iohannem Burchardum a quibuscumque excommunicationis, suspensionis et interdicti aliisque ecclesiasticis sententiis, censuris et penis a iure vel ab homine quavis occasione vel causa latis si quibus quomodolibet innodatus existit . . . absolventes et absolutum fore censentes, motu proprio," etc., etc. (Reg. Vat. 754, fols. 64ᵛ–68ʳ, "datum Rome apud Sanctum Petrum, anno etc. MCCCCLXXXXI, tertio Idus Aprilis, pont. nostri anno septimo"). Burchard succeeded in wheedling grants from Alexander VI, although the latter was not very fond of him (Mario Menotti, ed., *Documenti inediti sulla famiglia e la corte di Alessandro VI*, Rome, 1917, nos. 299–301, pp. 226–28, docs. dated in 1495, 1497, and 1501).

In 1503, after having acquired a number of lucrative benefices and various honors, Burchard was appointed bishop of Orte and Civita Castellana. He died on 16 May, 1506, in his handsome Gothic house (still preserved, but much altered, at no. 44, Via del Sudario, in Rome), and was buried the next day in S. Maria del Popolo. On Burchard's life, see especially the articles of Lesellier and Paschini, cited above, and *cf.* Thuasne, ed., *Burchardi diarium*, III, pp. II ff., and Celani, ed., *Liber notarum*, I (=*RISS*, vol. XXXII, pt. 1 [1907–10]), pp. XII ff. The insufficiency of the MSS. employed by Thuasne makes his edition of Burchard's text less desirable for use than that of Celani, but Thuasne's notes and the documents published in his appendices help preserve the value of his volumes, of which indeed Celani has made much use.

A fascicule of twenty-seven folia of Burchard's original (autograph) MS. survives (formerly in Arch. Segr. Vaticano, Miscell., Arm. XII, tom. 13, now in Bibl. Apost. Vaticana, Cod. lat. 12,265), written in so crabbed a hand that Burchard's successor as master of ceremonies, Paride Grassi, said that he must have had the devil for his copyist. Although Grassi hated Burchard, his strictures on the latter's handwriting are not unjust; Celani, I, opp. p. XVI, reproduces fol. 8ʳ from this MS., and this is not one of the worst pages. The MS. fragment of the original diary begins on 12 August, 1503, and ends in May, 1506. I examined it in July, 1966, and in April, 1972. The diary proper stops with 27 April, 1506, after which Burchard's secretary Michael Sander added the notices concerning Burchard's death and burial (16–17 May) and a few other notices coming down to 31 May, 1506 (Cod. Vat. lat. 12,265, fol. 27ᵛ). The twenty-seven folia of Burchard's original diary were once bound at the end of Cod. Vat. lat. 4,739, which contains the diary of Paride Grassi, who himself bears witness to the fact they are in Burchard's hand (*ibid.*, fol. IVᵛ): "In fine totius huius voluminis in quinterno alligata erant scripta de manu propria Jo. Burchardi comagistri et collige mei." *Cf.*, *ibid.*, fol. 235ᵛ, another annotation by Grassi. See in general G. Constant, "Deux Manuscrits de Burchard," *Mélanges d'archéologie et d'histoire*, XXII (1902), 209–10 and ff., and especially Franz Wasner's general discussion in "Eine unbekannte Handschrift des Diarium Burckardi," *Historisches Jahrbuch*, LXXXIII (1964), 300–31. Although an important addition to Burchardiana, no part of Wasner's new MS. of portions of the *Diarium* (Bibl. Nazionale, Naples, VI G 23) is in Burchard's own hand, but the MS. does date from the end of the fifteenth and/or early years of the sixteenth century.

Another copy of the diary in the Vaticana, Cod. lat. 5,632, consisting of 257 fols. and covering the period from 2 December, 1492, to the end of 1496, was certainly prepared under Burchard's own supervision (Celani, I, pp. XVIII–XXIII). It was later owned by Paride Grassi (d. 1528), who made numerous notes and comments in the margins. Burchard kept his extraordinary diary for his own use, although after his time the *cerimonieri* were required to keep a record of "omnia que in dies aguntur in officio." Two MSS. in Munich (Latt. 135, 137), prepared for Onophrius Panvinius about 1562–1564, are also valuable for the establishment of the parts of Burchard's text missing from Codd. Vatt. latt. 12,265 and 5,632. Despite Celani's rather devastating criticism of Thuasne's edition, I have generally supplied references to the latter as well as to Celani's better text. G. B. Picotti believes that Vatican Cod. lat. 5,632 as well as 12,265 is probably in Burchard's hand, which is quite possible, for after all Burchard began his career as a secretary to the vicar-general of Strassburg, and could presumably write legibly when he chose to do so. In fact a comparison of various letter formations in the generally legible Vat. lat. 5,632 (hardly the work of a calligrapher) with the small, crabbed, but not entirely illegible hand of Vat. lat. 12,265 suggests that Picotti is correct. See Picotti's article, "Nuovi Studi e documenti intorno a papa Alessandro VI," *Rivista di storia della Chiesa in Italia*, V (Rome, 1951), 173–80, for a discussion of the historical value of the diary, which he believes should be used with at least some caution when we come to the Borgias since it is fairly apparent that Burchard disliked the Borgias.

Many events relating to the history of the papacy during the Renaissance as well as the contemporary texts can be understood only with some knowledge of the Vatican palace, in which connection the reader should consult some such plan as that given by Celani in his edition of Burchard's diary (*Liber notarum*, I, opp. p. 9). Unfortunately Celani's plan, which has been copied and adapted more than once, is inaccurate. It fails to show the old Chapel of S. Niccolò da Bari across the *aula magna sive prima* (the present Sala Regia) from the Sistina. The Chapel of S. Niccolò, also known as the Cappella del SS. Sacramento, was demolished in 1538 when the space it had occupied was used for the descent of the (present) stairway to the Cortile del Maresciallo. Also the Cappella Paolina (named after Paul III, who built it), shown by Celani as existing "ai tempi di Innocenzo VIII," was not constructed until after the removal of the Chapel of S. Niccolò, which it replaced as the papal electoral chamber.

The errors in Pastor's *Geschichte der Päpste* to the contrary, every pope from Calixtus III to Paul III (from 1455 to 1534) was elected in the Chapel of S. Niccolò da Bari, *capella parva sancti Nicolai*, not to be confused (as historians have usually done) with the tiny chapel on the floor above, *parva capella superior* [*Nicolai papae V*], named after Nicholas V, who had Fra Angelico decorate it with the still extant frescoes. The name Nicholas has obviously helped cause confusion. See above, Chapter 9, note 1.

ful cardinal could sign his name below the articles, however, because he knew (as Innocent VI had ruled when elected pope under similar circumstances) that it was unlawful to delimit the authority of the supreme pontiff.

The conclave of 1484 was marked by intense electioneering. The papal master of ceremonies, Johann Burchard, took part in the proceedings, and has preserved an extraordinarily full account of them in his *Diarium*, including the names of all the cardinals' attendants and the food served during the conclave. As usual the voting took place in the Chapel of S. Niccolò da Bari, which no longer exists. The vice-chancellor Rodrigo Borgia, the most prominent of the cardinals supporting the peace of Bagnolo, entered the chapel as pope, at least in his own opinion. He was to leave it still a cardinal. Cardinal Marco Barbo got eleven votes on the first scrutiny, taken on the morning of 28 August. Thereupon the energetic Cardinal Giuliano della Rovere worked all day and all night on behalf of his friend, the affable Genoese Giovanni Battista Cibo, cardinal of S. Cecilia and bishop of Molfetta, who signed the petitions of certain cardinals that night as he knelt in his cell. Cardinal Francesco Piccolomini of Siena, amused at the turn of events, observed: "This is going in reverse: the pope is signing on his knees, and we, who present our requests, remain standing!" By the morning of the twenty-ninth, however, Cibo had seventeen to nineteen votes, which ensured his election. The cardinal of Siena, as ranking deacon, made the announcement from the window in the sacristy behind the chapel altar: "I announce to you tidings of great joy. We have a pope! The most reverend lord cardinal of Molfetta has been elected Supreme Pontiff, and he has chosen the name Innocent VIII." The crowd shouted its approval in the courtyard below. Bells rang in the Vatican palace and S. Peter's basilica, and fusiliers of the palace guard shot their guns in celebration of the new pope's elevation.[25]

Giuliano della Rovere had been responsible for Cibo's elevation as bishop, as cardinal, and now as pope. The predominance of his influence was felt even before the coronation, which took place outside S. Peter's on 12 September. The next day Bonfrancesco Arlotti, the Ferrarese ambassador to the Holy See, wrote of Giuliano: "While he could do little or nothing with his uncle [Sixtus IV], he can put through anything with the new pope."[26] Two weeks before this, on 29 August, the astute Guidantonio Vespucci, the Florentine ambassador, wrote Lorenzo de' Medici that Innocent VIII had a most kindly disposition, was rather lacking in "letteratura" but not entirely ignorant, and was the creature of Giuliano della Rovere, the cardinal of S. Pietro in Vincoli, who had got him made a cardinal: So see that a good letter gets off to S. Pietro in Vincoli—he

---

[25] Burchard, *Diarium*, ed. Thuasne, I, 55–63, and ed. Celani, I, 43–48. See also the documents in the appendix to Thuasne, I, nos. 10, 12, pp. 503 ff., especially on the efforts of Cardinal Rodrigo Borgia, papal vice-chancellor, to win votes before the conclave, and, *ibid.*, nos. 16–18, 20–28, pp. 510 ff., letters to Lorenzo de'Medici from Guidantonio Vespucci, Florentine ambassador to the Holy See, dated 24–30 August, 1484; Infessura, *Diaria*, ed. Tommasini, pp. 169–73; Raynaldus, *Ann. eccl.*, ad ann. 1484, nos. 40, 45, vol. XIX (1693), pp. 339b–341a. By a bull dated 12 September, 1484, Innocent notified Francesco Gonzaga, marquis of Mantua, of his election on 29 August (Arch. di Stato di Mantova, Arch. Gonzaga, Busta 834, and *cf.* Busta 85, B. XXXIII, no. 13, fols. 128–31). The contemporary diarists note the circumstances attending the death of Sixtus IV and the election of Innocent VIII: Sigismondo de'Conti, I, 207–12; *Il Diario romano di Gaspare Pontani, già riferito al "Notaio del Nantiporto" [1481–1492]*, ed. Diomede Toni, in *RISS*, III, pt. 2 (1908), pp. 37–42. Toni has shown that this diary, cited by older historians under the title "Notaio del Nantiporto," is actually the work of the Roman notary Gaspare Pontani, *notarius de regione Pontis*, who lived from about 1449 to about 1524 (*ibid.*, pp. XLVI–LV). On the physical arrangements for the conclave which elected Innocent VIII and the similar arrangements for those which elected his successors, see Franz Ehrle and Hermann Egger, *Die Conclavepläne: Beiträge zu ihrer Entwicklungsgeschichte*, Città del Vaticano, 1933 (Studi e documenti per la storia del Palazzo Apostolico Vaticano, fasc. V).

The death of Sixtus IV, with whom the Venetians had had constant difficulty, was greeted with satisfaction on the lagoon, where Innocent VIII's election was known by 7 September (Sen. Secreta, Reg. 32, fol. 89^r), but the Senate could show little more enthusiasm for Innocent, who was taking his own good time about removing the interdict which Sixtus had placed upon their city (*ibid.*, fols. 93^v–94^r, 121 ff.). Innocent lifted the interdict on 28 February, 1485 (fol. 135^v). The Venetian embassy of obedience, consisting of Aloisio Bragadin, Pietro Diedo, Bernardo Bembo, and Antonio Loredan, finally received its commission to go to Rome on 9 May, 1485 (fols. 146^r–147^v).

On the remarkable oration of obedience delivered by the Portuguese humanist Vasco Fernandes at the Curia Romana on 9 December, 1485, and its importance in the history of geographical exploration, see Francis M. Rogers, *The Obedience of a King of Portugal*, Minneapolis, 1958, and Geo Pistarino, "I Portoghesi verso l'Asia del Prete Gianni," *Studi medievali*, 3rd ser., II (Spoleto, 1961), 75–137, with a rich bibliography.

[26] Pastor, *Gesch. d. Päpste*, III-1 (repr. 1955), 217, citing a letter dated 13 September, 1484.

is pope and more than pope, *et lui è Papa et plusquam Papa*![27] After the election, on 29 August, when the cardinals had left the Vatican for their own homes, "certain ones sad, but others rejoicing," the cardinal of S. Pietro in Vincoli "remained in the palace with the pope."[28] The following December the pope made the cardinal's brother, Giovanni della Rovere, who was then prefect of Rome, the captain-general of the Church, and received from him the oath of fealty "in due and accustomed form."[29]

Among the various embassies sent to Rome to render obedience to the new pope, that of the Knights of S. John of Jerusalem most forcibly brought the eastern question before the Curia Romana. Innocent VIII had informed the Grand Master d'Aubusson of his predecessor's death and his own elevation, as Bosio informs us, in a "breve amorevolissimo," which was dispatched from Rome on 12 September (1484) and arrived in Rhodes on 18 October. Rather unnecessarily, but according to epistolary convention, the new pope urged upon d'Aubusson an unremitting vigilance in defense of the Catholic faith. The vice-chancellor of the Order, Guillaume Caoursin, was chosen as spokesman of the embassy, which sailed by galley from Rhodes to Ancona in forty days, and made its solemn entry into Rome on 23 January, 1485, by the gate of S. Maria del Popolo, being met by the papal *famiglia* and guard, various bishops and prelates, the households of the cardinals, and the resident ambassadors of the European princes. The papal master of ceremonies, Johann Burchard, was inclined to think that too much ceremony had attended their entry into the city, for the pope and the cardinals did not commonly send their *famiglie* to mark the arrival of prelates since they were "mere subjects" of the Roman Church. Exceptions were made of the archbishops of Mainz, Trier, and Cologne, for they were electors of the Holy Roman Empire.[30] At any rate, a few days after their reception at the Porta del Popolo, the pope received them at the Vatican palace in the Sala del Pappagallo. Innocent was attended by the cardinals, after the fashion of a secret consistory, but on this occasion the doors of the hall were left standing open. According to Bosio, the ambassadors were present as well as numerous bishops, prelates, and other members of the Curia, who had gathered to witness the ceremony and to hear the vice-chancellor's formal address before the throne.[31]

In the grand master's name Caoursin made an unctuous expression of obedience to Innocent, "eighth pope of this name, true, sole, and undoubted vicar of our own Lord Jesus Christ, successor of S. Peter the Apostle, and pastor of the Catholic and universal Church." When the good news of Innocent's election had been learned at Rhodes, the Knights, citizens, and other inhabitants of the island had rejoiced: "The Rhodians hope, most blessed father, to see the Turkish tyranny extinguished under your most fortunate pontificate!" Suggesting a mystic connection between Innocent, eighth of the name, and the eight-pointed cross of the Hospital of S. John, Caoursin recalled various Turkish audacities and the recent siege with some rather forced classical allusions. He made much of the siege and the heroism of d'Aubusson, and well he might; he spoke of one of the great events and one of the brave men of the century. In concluding, Caoursin bespoke the pope's help and protection for the Knights. Paride Grassi notes that he spoke "most elegantly," and Bosio has incorporated the oration in his history of

---

[27] Burchard, *Diarium*, ed. Thuasne, I, append., no. 27, p. 518, and on the character and family of Innocent VIII, *cf.* another letter of 29 August from Vespucci to Lorenzo, *ibid.*, no. 26, p. 517. As master of ceremonies Burchard had much of the responsibility for the elaborate preparations before the coronation on 12 September (see, *ibid.*, I, 75–89, and for the coronation itself, I, 90 ff., and ed. Celani, I, 58–70, 71 ff.).

[28] Burchard, *Diarium*, ed. Thuasne, I, 71, and ed. Celani, I, 54, lines 11–13.

[29] Burchard, *Diarium*, ed. Thuasne, I, 124, and ed. Celani, I, 95; Pontani, *Diario*, ed. Toni, in *RISS*, III-2, p. 45; *cf.* Pastor, *Gesch. d. Päpste*, III-1 (repr. 1955), 217, 332–33.

[30] Burchard, *Diarium*, ed. Thuasne, I, 136–37, and ed. Celani, I, 106.

[31] Burchard, *Diarium*, ed. Thuasne, I, 137, and ed. Celani, I, 106–7. Burchard was not present, and describes the ceremony inaccurately according to Paride Grassi, who says that he was an eyewitness, *tunc interfui et vidi* (Thuasne, I, 137, note 1). According to Paride, the ceremony took place "hora XX" (about 1:30 P.M. in late January). Besides the pope, to whom the Knights' embassy rendered obedience, the cardinals were on hand "and other prelates and the household [*familia*] of the pope." Burchard dates the Knights' formal expression of obedience to Innocent VIII on 26 January, and Paride does not challenge his date. Bosio says that it took place five days after their entry into Rome, i.e., on the twenty-seventh, if one counts inclusively, or on the twenty-eighth.

the Order.[32] The Knights had been assured of a cordial welcome at the Curia, and Caoursin's turgid rhetoric received close attention and rapt appreciation, for the pope was much worried at this time about an increasing build-up of Turkish forces across the southern Adriatic at Valona.[33]

Innocent replied briefly but graciously to Caoursin's discourse, accepting the Hospitallers' obedience and praising the exploits of d'Aubusson and the Order. He said they were worthy of every honor, and deserved well of the Holy See. A few days later Caoursin and his fellow envoys were received by the pope in private audience to discuss the affairs of the Order. They gave the pope gifts, including a vase full of pure balsam, for which he thanked them. He granted the Order certain spiritual privileges commemorated in a letter dated 28 April (1485). To Caoursin he also awarded the rank of a count palatine and apostolic secretary. The envoys returned several times to discuss their business with the pope, who expressed the strong desire to have Jem Sultan transferred to some fortress in the patrimony, where he might still be kept in the Hospitallers' custody. Caoursin and his confrères said, however, they had no authority to deal with this problem, and the pope asked them to take the matter up with d'Aubusson when they returned to Rhodes. Much honor was shown them during their stay in Rome. At the feast of the Purification of the Virgin they carried the pope's *baldachino*, together with the ambassadors of Naples, Milan, and Florence. They also received letters from King Ferrante, asking them to pass through Naples on their way back to Rhodes, for he had business of the greatest importance to talk over with them. One of the Hospitallers' envoys apparently went sightseeing in Venice. Caoursin and the Turcopolier of the Order went on to Naples, where they learned that Ferrante, like the pope, wanted to secure possession of Jem. They gave him the same answer they had given Innocent, and he also agreed to address himself to d'Aubusson.[34] The sojourn in Rome was an experience

[32] Burchard, *Diarium*, ed. Thuasne, I, 137, note; Bosio, *Militia di San Giovanni*, II (1594), bk. XIV, pp. 398–400; Caoursin, *Obsidionis Rhodie urbis descriptio*, Ulm, 1496, signn. hiii ff.; Thuasne, *Djem-Sultan* (1892), pp. 130–31.

[33] On 21 November, 1484, Innocent VIII had informed King Matthias Corvinus of Hungary: "Et qui Rhodiani scribunt se a Turcho litteras recepisse quibus expresse affirmat se iturum in expeditionem, non tamen ad eorum damna, et carissimus in Christo filius noster Fer[dinandus], Rex Sicilie, de illius apparatu qui fit apud Avlonam [Valona] significat, atque idem Ragusei affirmant . . ." (Arch. Segr. Vaticano, Arm. XXXIX, tom. 18, fol. 69^v, by mod. stamped enumeration). The fear was that Turkish preparations at Valona betokened an attack upon Italy, as Ferrante had warned the pope. *Cf.* Innocent's letter to Ferrante of the same date (*ibid.*, fol. 70): "Fecit prudenter Maiestas tua gratumque nobis fuit quod de his omnibus que nuper ab immanissimo Turchorum tiranno parari [*sic*] apud Valonam et alibi Italiam sensit. . . ." The pope says that he has written to the Italian states and especially to Matthias Corvinus of Hungary, urging them to respond to the emergency and the peril which Christendom faced in the light of this disheartening news. Italy must be defended. *Cf.*, *ibid.*, fols. 73–74, a letter to d'Aubusson, dated 30 November (1484), and fol. 74, the pope's letter *Ad potentatus Italie et ad omnes principes Christianos*, dated 21 November, sent to twenty-nine kings, princes, and states. I pass over other notices in this register to the same general effect. Particular efforts were made at this time to collect the *pecuniae subsidii et cruciatae*. There were many false alarms relating to possible Turkish attacks upon Italy. This was not one, and we shall presently note attacks upon the Anconitan littoral.

While the pope was exercised about the assumed activity of the Turks, the Venetian Senate received an envoy from Sultan Bayazid, who had been offended by the conduct of one Piero Vitturi, the rector of Nauplia. Such was the Senate's desire to maintain their *bona pace et amicitia* (and their commercial position in the Ottoman empire) that they claimed to have removed Vitturi from office and to have imprisoned him until they could determine the extent to which he had exceeded their instructions (Sen. Secreta, Reg. 32, fols. 103^v–104^v, 111, letters dated 2 and 29 November, 1484, to the sultan and to Giovanni Dario, the Republic's secretary in Istanbul).

[34] Bosio, *Militia di San Giovanni*, II (1594), bk. XIV, pp. 400–1; Thuasne, *Djem-Sultan*, pp. 131, 133. In a letter to the Grand Master d'Aubusson, dated at Rome on 22 April, 1485, the pope expressed his appreciation of the Hospitallers' embassy of obedience and of Caoursin's "elegant address" (Raynaldus, *Ann. eccl.*, ad ann. 1485, no. 7, vol. XIX [1693], p. 350b). The high-minded d'Aubusson was anxious, however, to secure some fitting reward for his services. He had proposed that his brother Guiscard, undistinguished bishop of Carcassonne, should be made a cardinal in the next creation. On 28 April (1485) the pope wrote d'Aubusson of the paternal affection he entertained for both him and his brother; he said he would do what he could when the opportunity arose, provided proper attention were paid to his wishes respecting Jem Sultan (Thuasne, *op. cit.*, p. 132, note 2, gives the papal brief). Guiscard d'Aubusson never became a cardinal.

On 22 April, 1485, Innocent VIII wrote (as noted above) to the Grand Master d'Aubusson and the Knights (Arch. Segr. Vaticano, Arm. XXXIX, tom. 18, fol. 160, by mod. stamped enumeration): "Dilecti filii, salutem, etc. Venerunt ad nos dilecti filii Ioannes Quendal Turcupollerius, procurator generalis et locumtenens, ac Edeardus de Camedino, preceptor Langonis, et Guillelmus Caoursin vicecancellarius Religionis Hierosolymitane, oratores vestri ad Sedem Apostolicam destinati qui plenam et debitam eidem sedi obedientiam vestro et Religionis nomine prestiterunt which Caoursin and his fellow envoys could recall with pleasure when they had gone back to the beautiful island of Rhodes, far from the intrigues and preferments of the Curia Romana.

Amid all the tiring ceremonies which claimed Innocent VIII's attention from week to week (and which Burchard describes with loving attention to every detail), the Curia began to make the most far-reaching plans for the crusade. Through the eight years of Innocent's reign, however, these plans were to be frustrated by events in the turbulent kingdom of Naples, where the revolt of the barons against King Ferrante and his son Alfonso of Calabria, *la congiura dei baroni*, was to involve the Curia in perilous fashion and divert papal resources from the eastern question.[35] When the barons' war broke out, in the early summer of 1485, it was allegedly feared that one side or the other might well appeal to the Turks for assistance.[36] However that may be, Innocent followed Giuliano della Rovere's anti-Aragonese policy, which was in tune with his own hostility to Ferrante.[37] On the other hand, Lodovico il Moro lent Ferrante the weight of the Milanese duchy. Lorenzo de' Medici also rejected the pope's overtures, and supported Naples against the papacy. In this respect Lorenzo was only maintaining Cosimo's old policy of the triple alliance which had long bound Florence, Milan, and Naples together.[38] Hungary also sided with Naples, for Matthias Corvinus had married a daughter of Ferrante. Matthias in fact maintained peace with the Turks in order to pursue his anti-papal policy, and the Turks are said to have undertaken to prevent the Venetians from rendering effective aid to the pope.[39] Although Innocent had removed Sixtus IV's ban from Venice in February, 1485, the Senate had no intention of putting troops into the field to support the pope, but did finally relinquish the services of the condottiere Roberto di Sanseverino,[40] who entered Rome on 10 November (1485) by the gate of S. Maria del Popolo, being met by various members of the papal and cardinals' households and

---

multaque et accurate et eleganter rettulerunt de singulari vestra erga sacrosanctum hoc Romanum solium et sedentem in eo devotione et fide. Quod et si novum non fuit utpote qui cognoscimus bonum zelum et sinceritatem animi vestri iucundissimum tamen extitit tale quid de vobis audire. Enarrarunt preterea oratores ipsi eleganti tersaque oratione egregia facinora insignis vestre Religionis precipue vero recentem victoriam de Turcis habitam et oportunum remedium ad cohibendos ipsorum Turcorum conatus qui classem in Appulos pridem extrusisse feruntur. Hec quidem ut laude digna sunt ita omnibus placuerunt vobisque plurimum commendationis et glorie attulerunt. Nos vero ante alios mirifice sumus oblectati et propterea nostra erga vos dilectio propensior quodammodo est effecta. Reliquum est hortari vos ut pro innata virtute animi et precipua in orthodoxam fidem affectione velitis quod digne ceptum est viriliter prosequi et rem publicam Christianam hoc est Dei et Creatoris nostri causam toto animo, toto studio et toto favore amplecti cum de nulla alia re gloriosius sit benemereri. Nos autem et prefatam sedem semper vobis benignos propitiosque in omnibus que cum Deo poterimus sentietis. Datum Rome, etc. die XXII Aprilis 1485, anno primo." The papal brief of 28 April answering d'Aubusson's request that his brother Guiscard be made a cardinal may be found, *ibid.*, fol. 161, together with two other letters to d'Aubusson, dated 28–29 April.

35 A large number of the rebellious barons were put to death. On the so-called "congiura dei baroni," and their defeat and execution by Ferrante, see the contemporary account of the chronicler Ferraiolo, in the Pierpont Morgan Library MS. 801, published by Riccardo Filangieri, *Una Cronaca napoletana figurata del Quattrocento* (1956), secs. 16–36, pp. 48–74, where Filangieri's notes provide addenda and guidance to the chronicler's often inaccurate description of events. As in Ferraiolo's account of the Turks in Otranto, however, his numerous full-page illustrations of the fall of the barons are instructive, showing that a number of the rebels perished on a guillotine (very like the instrument of the French Revolution) which was set up beside the Castel Nuovo. *Cf.* Raynaldus, *Ann. eccl.*, ad ann. 1484, nos. 47–48, 60, vol. XIX (1693), pp. 341, 343b, and ad ann. 1485, nos. 38–39, p. 358, and see Camillo Porzio (fl. 1565), *La Congiura de' baroni del regno di Napoli contro al re Ferdinando I*, Naples, 1769; Jos. Calmette, "La Politique espagnole dans l'affaire des barons napolitains (1485–1492)," *Revue historique*, CX (XXXVII, 1912), 225–46, with eight documents; Giuseppe Paladino, "Un Episodio della congiura dei baroni: La Pace di Miglionico (1485)," *Archivio storico per le province napoletane*, XLIII (n.s., IV, 1918), 44–73, 215–52; and Paladino, "Per la Storia della congiura dei baroni: Documenti inediti dell'Archivio Estense (1485–1487)," *ibid.*, XLIV (n.s., V, 1919), 336–67; XLV (n.s., VI, 1920), 128–51, 325–51; XLVI (n.s., VII, 1921), 221–65; and XLVIII (n.s., IX, 1923), 219–90, a collection of 164 documents.

36 Sigismondo de' Conti, I, 229; Raynaldus, *Ann. eccl.*, ad ann. 1486, nos. 3–4, 25, vol. XIX (1693), pp. 366b, 369b.

37 Roberto Palmarocchi, *La Politica italiana di Lorenzo de'Medici: Firenze nella guerra contro Innocenzo VIII*, Florence, 1933, *passim*, and on the alleged fear of Turkish intervention in Italian affairs, *ibid.*, pp. 5, 33–34, 51.

38 *Cf.* A. Desjardins (and G. Canestrini), *Négociations diplomatiques de la France avec la Toscane*, I (Paris, 1859), 205 ff. (Documents inédits sur l'histoire de France, XL).

39 *Cf.* Raynaldus, *Ann. eccl.*, ad ann. 1486, nos. 25–31, vol. XIX (1693), pp. 369b–371a; Fraknói, *Mathias Corvinus* (1891), pp. 227–28; and Thuasne, *Djem-Sultan*, pp. 118–19.

40 Arch. di Stato di Venezia, Sen. Secreta, Reg. 32, fols. 162r–164v, 167r–168r, 173v–181r, and note esp. fols. 166v, 177v–178r, docs. dated 26 August and 7 October, 1485.

by the envoys of the various powers. The imperial envoy brought him within the gate in the name of the emperor, advocate of the Church. Roberto was thereafter conducted to the papal palace where he was received in the rooms of the Camera Apostolica, the usual place for the reception of princes.[41]

On 30 November Roberto di Sanseverino took the oath of fealty as Gonfaloniere of the Church, swearing "that henceforth from this hour I will be loyal and obedient to the Blessed Peter, to the Holy Roman Church, and to you, my lord Pope Innocent VIII, and to your successors canonically entering office." It was an impressive ceremony (for which Roberto had arrived a trifle late), not so elaborate as it might have been, however, for the Roman clergy had doubtless not yet recovered from the prolonged obsequies which had followed the death of the young Cardinal Giovanni d'Aragona (on 17 October, 1485), who had apparently succumbed to the plague in Rome while on a mission for his father, King Ferrante.[42] In the procession which followed his investiture as gonfaloniere, Roberto rode between Cardinal Rodrigo Borgia, papal vice-chancellor and governor of Rome, and Giovanni della Rovere, prefect of the city and captain-general of the Church.[43] He took the field against the Neapolitan forces on 28 December.[44]

Pope Innocent VIII had some support against Ferrante, especially from his compatriots, the Genoese, who began preparations for a fleet. Cardinal Giuliano della Rovere went to Genoa to encourage them. The barons' war lasted a full year or more, with most of the successes going to the Neapolitan forces under Alfonso of Calabria. In the winter of 1485–1486, however, Sanseverino did break up an investment of Rome by the troops of Alfonso and the Orsini, although the following May Alfonso defeated him at Montorio and again advanced upon Rome, while Florentine agents tried to lure the chief cities in the papal states from their allegiance to Innocent. Cardinal della Rovere was the backbone of the opposition to Ferrante. On his advice Innocent appealed to Charles VIII of France and Duke René of Lorraine, thus reviving the Angevin claim to Naples and Sicily. It was a dangerous game. Violent differences of opinion were expressed in the consistory as to the wisdom of this move, which Ferdinand and Isabella of the Spains watched with natural apprehension. They urged Innocent to make peace. It was to transport René to Naples that the Genoese were building their fleet.[45] The war went so

---

[41] Burchard, *Diarium*, ed. Thuasne, I, 158, and ed. Celani, I, 124–25; Infessura, *Diaria*, ed. Tommasini (1890), pp. 186, 188; Sigismondo de' Conti, I, 239, 241. Sanseverino came without his army, which arrived on 24 December (Sigismondo, I, 242). A papal brief dated 10 November and addressed to the inhabitants of L'Aquila reads (in full): "Hodie hora XXII [about 3:00 P.M.] ingressus est urbem dilectus filius nobilis vir Robertus de Sanctoseverino cum quo de rebus omnibus colloquemur et deliberationem capiemus. Postea statim certiores reddemini de iis que inter nos concludentur" (Arch. Segr. Vaticano, Arm. XXXIX, tom. 19, fol. 56[v]). This volume of papal briefs, needless to add, contains many letters relating to Roberto di Sanseverino, as does the Venetian Sen. Secreta, Reg. 32. See in general Ernesto Pontieri, "La Politica di Venezia di fronte alla congiura dei baroni napoletani e al conflitto tra Innocenzo VIII e Ferrante I d'Aragona (1485–1492)," in his studies *Per la Storia del regno di Ferrante I d'Aragona, re di Napoli*, 2nd ed., Naples, 1969, pp. 445–525; *idem*, "L'Atteggiamento di Venezia nel conflitto tra Papa Innocenzo VIII e Ferrante I d'Aragona . . . ," *Archivio storico per le province napoletane*, 3rd ser., II (LXXXI, 1962–63), 197–324, and V-VI (LXXXIV–LXXXV, 1966–68), 175–309; and *idem*, "La 'Guerra dei baroni' napoletani e di Papa Innocenzo VIII contro Ferrante d'Aragona in dispacci della diplomazia fiorentina," *ibid.*, IX (LXXXVIII, 1970–71), 197–347; X (LXXXIX, 1971–72), 117–77; XI (XC, 1972–73), 197–254; XII (XCI, 1973–74), 211–45; and a continuation of this article is promised. In these two lengthy studies Pontieri has published some 384 documents from the Archivi di Stato in Venice and Florence.

[42] *Cf.* Pastor, *Gesch. d. Päpste*, III-1 (repr. 1955), 225–27. Infessura, *Diaria*, ed. Tommasini, pp. 186–87, gives Giovanni d'Aragona's death incorrectly as 19 October, and alleges without foundation that he was poisoned (see Pastor, III-1, 226).

[43] Burchard, *Diarium*, ed. Thuasne, I, 164–65, and ed. Celani, I, 128–30; Pontani, *Diario*, ed. Toni, in *RISS*, III-2, p. 51; Raynaldus, *Ann. eccl.*, ad ann. 1485, nos. 40–43, vol. XIX (1693), pp. 358b–359a; Pastor, *Gesch. d. Päpste*, III-1 (repr. 1955), 227–28, and vol. III-2 (repr. 1956), append., nos. 4–5, pp. 1047–48, docs. dated 12 and 30 October, 1485.

[44] Infessura, *Diaria*, ed. Tommasini, p. 193; Pontani, *Diario*, ed. Toni, in *RISS*, III-2, p. 54; Raynaldus, *Ann. eccl.*, ad ann. 1485, no. 42, vol. XIX (1693), p. 359a; and *cf.* Burchard, *Diarium*, ed. Thuasne, I, 173–74, and ed. Celani, I, 136. Incidentally, Thomas Palaeologus's son Andreas, who was known at the Curia Romana as the *imperator Constantinopolitanus*, was present in the Sistine Chapel on the feast of the Purification of the Virgin (2 February, 1486) when the pope blessed the candles, and Domenico della Rovere, cardinal of S. Clemente, celebrated mass. The pope had wanted to give Andreas an ordinary candle (*de cera communi*), although the cardinals had just received candles of white wax, "sed ille dicens albam sibi deberi, ut cardinali, albam habuit!" (*ibid.*, ed. Celani, I, 137, lines 4–6). Andreas cut a pathetic figure in Rome.

[45] Infessura gives a full account of the war in his *Diaria*, ed. Tommasini, under the years 1485 and 1486; *cf.* Raynaldus, *Ann. eccl.*, ad ann. 1485, nos. 42, 44, vol. XIX

badly for Innocent, however, that he was soon ready to listen to the Spanish appeals for peace. An accord was finally reached in Rome on 11 August, 1486; the humanist Giovanni Gioviano Pontano represented Ferrante. (Charles VIII of France had promised the pope financial and military aid, but there seemed little likelihood of its arrival in a form that would do him any good.) A month later the formal treaty was announced (on 12 September). Ferrante, fearful of the French, had proved conciliatory, acknowledging his kingdom to be a papal fief, promising to pay the old feudal levy (*census*) and the arrears due, and agreeing to grant an amnesty to the rebellious barons upon their recognition of his authority.[46]

King Ferrante was a practical man. He saw no reason for excessive haggling over conditions he had no intention of observing. The town of L'Aquila, which had been a bone of bloody contention early in the barons' war, was supposed to make its own choice between papal or Neapolitan suzerainty, according to the treaty of 11 August (1486). In September, however, Ferrante treacherously occupied the city, and the pro-papal archdeacon Vespasiano de' Gaglioffi, the bishop's brother, was killed in the tumult.[47] Ferrante never allowed promises to impede policy. The rebellious barons paid a considerable price for the weakness of their papal ally. The entente between Ferrante and Matthias Corvinus, as well as the persistent threat of Turkish attack upon Italian shores, finally drew Venice into a pact with the papacy. On 1 February, 1487, the pact was announced in Rome with trumpets resounding through the ancient streets. It was to last for twenty-five years, "and thereafter for as long as it shall please the [contracting] parties."[48]

The apparent end of the war with Naples and the papal-Venetian pact raised the hopes of the Curia Romana, but the political economy of Italy was chaotic. The institutional means were lacking to achieve peace in the peninsula, where every prince was trying to despoil his neighbors, and every state sought its own immediate advantage with little regard for the consequences. The papacy was caught up in the vortex as fully as any other Italian power, unfit to lead the crusade and hardly able to preach it. In April, 1486, the condottiere Boccolino Guzzoni seized the papal town of Osimo, a few miles south of Ancona. He was soon in correspondence with the Turks, whom he proposed to admit into the March. Innocent's insufficient forces could not dislodge him, but Lorenzo de' Medici bought him off in the summer of 1487 as a gesture of friendliness to the baffled pontiff, whose policies

(1693), p. 359a, and ad ann. 1486, nos. 1–2, 12, pp. 366, 368a; H. F. Delaborde, *L'Expédition de Charles VIII en Italie*, Paris, 1888, pp. 176 ff.; Pastor, *Hist. Popes*, V, 249–65, and *Gesch. d. Päpste*, III-1 (repr. 1955), 223–35. The war was the main topic of conversation in Rome, as shown by the entries in Pontani's diary. On 12 February, 1486, Innocent VIII denounced Ferrante as "discordiarum sator bellique Italici nutritor" (Arch. Segr. Vaticano, Arm. XXXIX, tom. 19, fol. 191ʳ). Among the various briefs relating to Cardinal della Rovere's mission to Genoa, I would note chiefly that of 20 May (1486) appointing Raffaello Grimaldi as commander (*patronus*) of two of the best galleys in the Genoese fleet being prepared for the papal service (*ibid.*, fols. 385ᵛ–386ʳ). Another brief to della Rovere was intended to make sure that Grimaldi received his appointment even if all assignments of galleys had already been made (*ibid.*, fol. 386).

The pope's troubles in Italy were unfortunately not offset by security on the eastern fronts. On 5 July, 1486, he issued a plenary indulgence for service against the Turks and Tatars (Arm. XXXII, tom. 21, fols. 83ᵛ–90ʳ, by mod. stamped enumeration; Reg. Vat. 715, fols. 8ʳ–17ʳ, a detailed crusading indulgence granting the full remission of sins under certain specified conditions). Although Venice was in close diplomatic contact with the Porte at this time (Sen. Secreta, Reg. 33, fols. 26ʳ [36ʳ] and 32ᵛ [42ᵛ], docs. dated 28 July and 9 September, 1486), the Senate was soon strengthening the Venetian fleet for fear of a large Turkish armada which was reported as ready to sail (*ibid.*, fol. 47ʳ [57ʳ]).

[46] Burchard, *Diarium*, ed. Thuasne, I, 207, 208, and 209–10, and ed. Celani, I, 157, 158 (with refs. in note 5), and 159, on the return of Giuliano della Rovere from Genoa; Infessura, *Diaria*, ed. Tommasini, pp. 201–3, 205, 214–15, 219, 220; Pontani, *Diario*, ed. Toni, in *RISS*, III-2, pp. 63–64; Raynaldus, *Ann. eccl.*, ad ann. 1486, nos. 1, 7–17, vol. XIX (1693), pp. 366, 367–68; Delaborde, *Expédition de Charles VIII*, pp. 184–85; Pastor, *Gesch. d. Päpste*, III-1 (repr. 1955), 231–35, and vol. III-2 (repr. 1956), append., no. 7, p. 1048, doc. dated 11 August, 1486.

[47] Burchard, *Diarium*, ed. Thuasne, I, 217, and ed. Celani, I, 165; Infessura, *Diaria*, ed. Tommasini, pp. 209–10, esp. pp. 220, 225–6, 232; Pontani, *Diario*, ed. Toni, in *RISS*, III-2, pp. 64–65; Raynaldus, *Ann. eccl.*, ad ann. 1486, nos. 18–23, vol. XIX (1693), p. 369; Delaborde, *Expédition de Charles VIII*, pp. 202 ff. There are numerous references to the affairs of L'Aquila in the briefs of Innocent VIII.

[48] Burchard, *Diarium*, ed. Thuasne, I, 237, and ed. Celani, I, 180; Infessura, *Diaria*, ed. Tommasini, pp. 221–22; Pontani, *Diario*, ed. Toni, in *RISS*, III-2, p. 65; Raynaldus, *Ann. eccl.*, ad ann. 1487, no. 1, vol. XIX (1693), p. 380b; and *cf.* Arch. Segr. Vaticano, Miscell., Arm. II, tom. 56, fols. 141ʳ–145ᵛ, instructions to a papal envoy on his way to Florence and Milan, dated 4 September, 1487. On the fate of the rebellious barons, note the brief, *ibid.*, fols. 517ʳ–520ᵛ, dated 16 September, 1487: ". . . Demum fere omnes ipsius regni proceres iussu regio capti, detenti, et ut rei lese majestatis carceribus mancipati fuere" (fol. 518ᵛ).

the ambitious Florentine was now aspiring to dominate.[49] Sixtus IV had been right. Failure to proceed vigorously against the Turk after Mehmed II's death had caused the loss of all opportunity to do so. Christians in Greece and the Balkans were entering the long night of Turkish domination, able to do little for themselves against a military power which held them in sorry subjection.

The passing months and the papal-Venetian accord did nothing to abate Matthias Corvinus's ambition to fish in the troubled waters of Italy. Early in the year 1487 Ancona rejected the pope's suzerainty in secret negotiations with Corvinus, and in April of the following year raised the Hungarian banner atop the tower of the town hall and fixed it to the masts of ships, signalizing the Anconitans' acceptance of Corvinus's protection.[50] Corvinus was anxious

[49] Sanudo, *Vite de'duchi*, in *RISS*, XXII, col. 1241; Raynaldus, *Ann. eccl.*, ad ann. 1486, nos. 30–32, vol. XIX (1693), p. 371, and ad ann. 1487, nos. 6–7, p. 381, on Boccolino, who asked for a force of 10,000 Turks with which he would subject all Piceno to Bayazid II, and thereafter all Italy could easily be taken. *Cf.* Dom. Malipiero, *Annali veneti*, ad ann. 1487, in *Arch. storico italiano*, VII, pt. 1 (1843), 137; Filippo Ugolini, *Storia dei conti e duchi d'Urbino*, 2 vols., Florence, 1859, II, 49–57, esp. p. 56, for Boccolino's dealings with the Turks; Moritz Brosch, *Papst Julius II. und die Gründung des Kirchenstaates*, Gotha, 1878, pp. 40–42, 309–10; Carlo Cipolla, *Storia delle signorie italiane dal 1313 al 1530*, 2 vols., Milan, 1881–82, II, 640–42; Sigismondo de' Conti, *Storie de' suoi tempi*, I, 272 ff., 310; and G. Cecconi, *Vita e fatti di Boccolino Guzzoni da Osimo*, Osimo, 1889, pp. 50 ff., 74 ff., cited by Pastor, *Gesch. d. Päpste*, III-1 (repr. 1955), 233, 237.

Boccolino Guzzoni's activities in Osimo, where he obviously had the support of many of the inhabitants, naturally earned the especial attention and castigation of the pope, who devoted numerous briefs to the subject (Arch. Segr. Vaticano, Arm. XXXIX, tom. 19, fols. 340^v, 355^v–356^r, 357^v–358^r, 360, 372^v, 373, 393, 395–96, 426^v, 511^v, 512, and 513^r, docs. dated in the spring and early summer of 1486). On 13 March, 1487, the pope informed the Grand Master Pierre d'Aubusson of Boccolino's appeal to the Turks (Bosio, *Militia di S. Giovanni Gierosolimitano*, II [1594], bk. XIV, p. 405). Boccolino finally made peace with the Church in July, 1487. The pope was to pay him 7,000 ducats, according to the news Infessura received, and Boccolino was to sell his movable goods in Osimo and withdraw from the city (*Diaria*, ed. Tommasini, p. 227). *Cf.* Enrico Carusi, ed., *Dispacci e lettere di Giacomo Gherardi, nunzio pontificio a Firenze e Milano* [1487–1490], Rome, 1909, pp. 287–88, doc. dated 3 March, 1489 (Studi e testi, no. 21). References to Boccolino abound in the Vatican registers. For a description of his alleged atrocities, perfidies, and treacherous dealings with the Turks, see Innocent VIII's bull of 1 May, 1492, inc. *Detestanda iniquorum perversitas*, in Reg. Vat. 693, fols. 199^r–203^r, by mod. stamped enumeration, "datum Rome apud Sanctum Petrum, anno etc. MCCCCLXXXX secundo, Kal. Maii, pont. nostri anno octavo," and on his dealings with the Turks, note esp., *ibid.*, fols. 200 ff., and Miscellanea, Arm. II, tom. 56, fols. 403^v ff., by mod. stamped enumeration. Nevertheless, the memory of the adventurous Boccolino still remains fresh in the charming town of Osimo, where the main piazza is named after him.

[50] Fraknói, *Mathias Corvinus*, p. 229, and *cf.* pp. 254–55, 262–63. As early as 23 April, 1486, Innocent VIII wrote the governor of the March of Ancona (Arch. Segr. Vaticano, Arm. XXXIX, tom. 19, fol. 327): "Ex quodam magne fidei viro e partibus Segnie nuper accepimus Regem Hungarie aliquas copias suas navibus versus Anconam transmittere decrevisse, non tam ut Regi Neapolitano auxilium ferat quam ut terris nostris damnum aliquod inferat." *Cf.*, *ibid.*, fols. 338^r, 340, 353^r. The pope had received his information about Corvinus's designs upon Ancona from Count Angelo de' Frangipani (or Frangipane, Frankopan), as appears from a brief dated 29 April (*ibid.*, fol. 341^r).

In a letter dated at Vienna on 10 May, 1488, Corvinus wrote the pope in tones of injured innocence of the devotion he had nurtured for the Holy See from the time of his boyhood and of the considerable services he had rendered against Turks, heretics, and schismatics through these many years. Indeed, he had recently offered to assist his Holiness in suppressing the revolt of the citizens of Osimo (which would have put him conveniently on the Adriatic coast, next door to Ancona). As for Ancona, however, he was quite guiltless of seducing its citizens from their papal allegiance (Arch. Segr. Vaticano, A. A., Arm. I–XVIII, 1443, fols. 113^r–115^r): ". . . Anchonitanos igitur non credat Sanctitas vestra ab ea [Sancta Sede] rebellasse et ad me defecisse, neque suspicetur me illos oblatione vexilli mei aut aliter ab eiusdem obedientia et devotione avocare voluisse. Subditos enim Ecclesie et Sanctitatis vestre in officio potius continere quam ab ipsius obedientia abstrahere semper studui, nec ipsi tanquam peculiari domino aut perpetuo protectori michi adhesere, sed ut sub meo nomine liberiores ac tutiores in mari essent et eis illud a Turchorum rabie, cum quibus inpresentiarum pacem habeo et in qua etiam ipsos Anchonitanos inclusi, tranquillum redderetur: ad quandam mecum intelligentiam condescenderunt et vexillum tandem petierunt ut illo ad salutem commodumque privatum ac terrorem hostis immanissimi uterentur . . ." (fol. 114^r). In other words Hungarian suzerainty over Ancona was merely a device to protect Anconitan commerce from Turkish depredation at sea. Innocent VIII should not take this arrangement too seriously. Corvinus's entire letter is given in a poor transcription in *Mathiae Corvini Hungariae regis epistolae ad romanos pontifices datae et ab eis acceptae*, Budapest, 1891, no. CLXXXIV, pp. 234–37 (Monumenta Vaticana Hungariae, 1st ser., vol. VI). It has also been published by Theiner.

Ancona was finally and forcibly annexed to the papal states by the legate of the March in September, 1532, during a period of singular prosperity in the city's history, by which time it had become (along with Venice and Ragusa) a leading center for the distribution of textiles, hides, dyes, spices, and foodstuffs. See Peter Earle, "The Commercial Development of Ancona, 1479–1551," *The Economic History Review*, 2nd ser., XXII (1969), 28–44, who sees Ancona in this connection "as a true frontier between Islam and Christendom" (p. 40). There was a Turkish colony in Ancona, and the port throve for some time under the tolerant policies of the Holy See. See above, Chapter 10, note 57.

to secure possession of Jem Sultan, whose person would supply a weapon to employ against the Porte more valuable to Hungary than any fortress on the eastern front. As a matter of fact, Jem had wanted to go into Hungary at the time he sought refuge in Rhodes,[51] believing that Corvinus, who was allegedly planning an expedition against Sultan Bayazid, was the only ruler in Europe likely and able to try to set him upon his father's throne. At that time Venice, at peace with the Turk after the long war which was concluded in January, 1479, was loath to see the East again set on fire on Jem's behalf.[52] In the meantime Corvinus was quite content to see the Italian powers at armed odds with one another. His attitude encouraged Ferrante in his shortsighted hostility to the Holy See, manifested by studied insults to the pope and unwarranted intrusions into ecclesiastical affairs.[53] At length, on 11 September, 1489, Ferrante was declared in a public consistory to have lost by forfeiture the kingdom of Naples, a papal fief, which now reverted (it was said) by escheat to the Holy See. Ferrante's intransigence was in no way abated, however, and he seized upon every diplomatic opportunity to show his scorn for the pope, who cut a sorry enough figure as he looked in vain for aid from Milan or Florence or Venice. Innocent talked of departing from Italy if the Italians continued to leave him exposed now to Ferrante's brazen insolence and next to his armed aggression.[54]

Avignon was still of course a papal city (as it remained until 1791), and it was only there that Innocent VIII, if he was really serious, could have thought of going. French relations with the papacy were especially close at this time, for Charles VIII required certain dispensations for his precipitate marriage to Anne of Brittany, who had been betrothed a year before to Maximilian of Hapsburg, king of the Romans.[55] By now it was abundantly clear to Innocent, however, that neither Lorenzo de' Medici nor Lodovico Sforza would ever assist him against Naples. If he would have peace, he would have to make it.

The failure to achieve peace in the peninsula had prevented Innocent VIII from having the satisfaction of seeing a crusade launched against the Turks. From the first months of his pontificate disquieting news of Turkish activities was reported at the Curia. Bayazid was said to be preparing a great fleet for an attack upon Italy. On 21 November, 1484, Innocent had addressed a letter to the Italian states and all the European princes, informing them that information just received from Ferrante of Naples, from the grand master of Rhodes, and from other sources made clear the extent of the Turkish threat, especially to Italy. Time was pressing. The defense of Christendom should be the concern of all the princes (the letter was sent to twenty-nine states), and the pope requested that envoys be sent to him with full and sufficient powers to pledge

[51] Sa'd-ad-Dīn, "Aventures du prince Gem," *Journal asiatique*, IX (1826, repr. 1965), 165, indicating Jem Sultan's desire to go from Rhodes to Rumelia. Sa'd-ad-Dīn's story that, later on, Innocent VIII urged Jem to go to Hungary, and that he declined, wishing only to rejoin his mother and children in Egypt, seems unlikely (*ibid.*, p. 166). On Corvinus's effort to get possession of Jem's person, note the Venetian Senate's letter of 10 September, 1487, to their secretary Giovanni Dario, who was to transmit the information to the Porte (Sen. Secreta, Reg. 33, fol. 104 [114]).

[52] Fraknói, *Mathias Corvinus*, pp. 216–19, 220; Bosio, *Militia di San Giovanni*, II (1594), bk. XIV, pp. 406–8; and see above, notes 14, 17–18.

[53] *Cf.* Raynaldus, *Ann. eccl.*, ad ann. 1487, nos. 9–12, and ad ann. 1489, nos. 5–9, vol. XIX (1693), pp. 381b–383a, 393b–394a; Lamansky, *Secrets d'état* (1884, repr. 1968), pp. 227–29. Innocent VIII expressed himself at some length on the trials and treacheries he had suffered at the hands of Ferrante, in the instructions issued to a papal envoy on his way to Venice on 22 March, 1489, in Arch. Segr. Vaticano, Miscell., Arm. II, tom. 56, fols. 507^r–516^r, by mod. stamped enumeration, inaccurately dated by the copyist "XXII Marcii, 1494 [!], pontificatus nostri anno V:" Innocent VIII's fifth year extends from 12 September, 1488, to 11 Sept. 1489.

[54] Burchard, *Diarium*, ed. Thuasne, I, 335 ff. (on the arrival of Jem Sultan in Rome, 13 March, 1489, on which see below, p. 407), 346, 364, 390, 410–11, and ed. Celani, 252 ff., 261, 275, 294–95, 309; Infessura, *Diaria*, ed. Tommasini, ad ann. 1489, pp. 245, 249–50. Innocent VIII's contemplating the abandonment of Italy is reported in a dispatch of the Florentine ambassador to the Holy See, Pierfilippo Pandolfini, dated 28 July, 1490, given in A. Fabronius, *Laurentii Medicis Magnifici vita*, 2 vols., Pisa, 1784, II, 353–58, on which *cf.* A. von Reumont, *Lorenzo de' Medici il Magnifico*, 2nd ed., 2 vols., Leipzig, 1883, II, 377–78, cited by Pastor, *Gesch. d. Päpste*, III-1 (repr. 1955), 246–50.

[55] *Cf.* Burchard, *Diarium*, ed. Thuasne, I, 436, and ed. Celani, I, 331, with note; Raynaldus, *Ann. eccl.*, ad ann. 1491, nos. 15–16, vol. XIX (1693), p. 405b. Maximilian and Anne of Brittany had been married by proxy on 19 December, 1490; Charles VIII married her on 6 December, 1491, and Louis XII on 8 January, 1499. She died at Blois on 9 January, 1514.

the assistance of their principals.[56] On the same day Innocent wrote King Matthias Corvinus of Hungary, urging him to make peace with the Emperor Frederick III, and turn his victorious arms against the Turks.[57]

If the danger seemed great—and the Ragusei affirmed that it was—so was the opportunity. Matthias Corvinus, despite his private war with the aging emperor, seemed to think himself strong enough to take on Sultan Bayazid, especially since the latter was not too firmly seated on the throne which his brother Jem Sultan had contested with him. In 1483 Corvinus had equipped an army of 70,000 men (it was said),[58] and had tried to persuade the relevant powers to let Jem join him in Hungary. Aggressive warfare was, however, the tradition of the Ottoman sultanate. Bayazid could best preserve his position and provide for his future by conquest. Turkish troops invaded imperial territory, but Matthias Gereb, the ban of Croatia, scored an impressive victory over them, encouraging to Corvinus and most irritating to Bayazid. Toward the end of 1483 the sultan had sent envoys to Corvinus, offering a truce on terms advantageous to Hungary; after some negotiation Corvinus accepted the terms, and a five years' truce was arranged. Corvinus reminded the European princes that the defense of Christendom was a responsibility which they shared in common (a constant papal refrain), and since they had neglected to meet their obligation, he had to look to the well-being of his own kingdom.[59]

In the summer of 1484 Sultan Bayazid invaded Moldavia with the aid of the Tatars of Crimea. He captured two most important fortress towns on the Black Sea, Kilia (Kiliya) and Akkerman (now Belgorod Dnestrovskiy), just south of Odessa. Christian efforts to recover these towns were to prove unavailing. When Corvinus protested this aggression, Bayazid replied that Moldavia was not included in the terms of the truce. Actually Hungarians and Turks had little reason for trusting each other, and Bayazid had, presumably, no intention of abiding by the terms of the truce. A Turkish force of some 7,000 raiders burst into the area around Temesvar (the modern Timişoara, in western Rumania), where on 13 September, 1484, Paul Kinizsi met and destroyed them in battle. Quite understandably Corvinus turned his thoughts again to the crusade. Of all the recipients of the pope's letter of 21 November, to which we have just alluded, he had the greatest need to ponder its contents.[60]

On 30 November (1484) Innocent VIII wrote the Grand Master Pierre d'Aubusson, acknowledging receipt of the news he had sent concerning the successes of the Turks in Mol-

[56] Arch. Segr. Vaticano, Arm. XXXIX, tom. 18, fol. 74, by mod. stamped enumeration (this letter has been noted above in a different context); a copy of the original, addressed to Francesco Gonzaga, marquis of Mantua, may be found in the Arch. di Stato di Mantova, Arch. Gonzaga, Busta 834 (and note, *ibid.*, the briefs dated 14 December, 1484, and 7 March, 1487, the latter being partially destroyed by dampness); Raynaldus, *Ann. eccl.*, ad ann. 1484, nos. 60–61, vol. XIX (1693), pp. 343b–344a; Pastor, *Gesch. d. Päpste*, III-1 (repr. 1955), 256–57. Innocent VIII's interest in the crusade is well attested by the "Bullae diversorum annorum pontificatus felicis recordationis d. Innocentii papae VIII," in Reg. Vat. 771, the first folio of which begins with a verbal attack upon the Turks, "hii nephandissimi hostes fidei Catholice."

[57] Arch. Segr. Vaticano, Arm. XXXIX, tom. 18, fols. 68^v–70^r; Raynaldus, *Ann. eccl.*, ad ann. 1484, nos. 62–63, vol. XIX (1693), p. 344.

[58] See in general the reports to the Holy See from the papal nuncio in Buda, during the autumn of 1483, in Arch. Segr. Vaticano, Miscell., Arm. II, tom. 56, fols. 347^v–358^r, by mod. stamped enumeration. In the nuncio's opinion Matthias Corvinus is very much the hero of the unfolding drama: ". . . Beatissime pater, rex Hungarie Mars ipse est, nihil nisi bellum cogitans et sine sermone faciens . . ." (fol. 350^v). His military preparations were gigantic (*quo vere obstupui*). Corvinus's personality was no less impressive: ". . . Hunc regem si Sanctitas vestra videret quanta gravitate, prudentia, suavitate, et quodam lepore dicendi polleat, diceret inter primarios Italos habendum et latine lingue incubuisse. . . . Rex intrepidus est . . ." (fol. 357^r). Despite a good deal of classical and biblical rhetoric, these reports contain much information concerning Carinthia, Carniola, Styria, Austria, Poland, and above all Hungary. The nuncio in question was Bartolommeo de' Maraschi, on whom see above, Chapter 12, pp. 377–79.

[59] Fraknói, *Mathias Corvinus*, pp. 219–20; Thuasne, *Djem-Sultan*, p. 127.

[60] Raynaldus, *Ann. eccl.*, ad ann. 1484, nos. 64–65, vol. XIX (1693), pp. 344b–345a, and ad ann. 1486, no. 61, *ibid.*, p. 378b; Bosio, *Militia di San Giovanni*, II (1594), bk. XIV, p. 403; Fraknói, *Mathias Corvinus*, p. 220; Cl. Huart, in *Encyclopaedia of Islām*, I (1908), 685; Thuasne, *Djem-Sultan*, pp. 126–27, from Hammer. On the readiness of Stephen, the voivode of Transylvania, and Paul Kinizsi, *aliud belli fulmen*, to meet any Turkish attack, *cf.* the report to the Holy See, in Arch. Segr. Vaticano, Miscell., Arm. II, tom. 56, fols. 357^v–358^r, by mod. stamped enumeration, and on Bayazid II's conquest of Kilia and Akkerman, see Nicoară Beldiceanu, "La Campagne ottomane de 1484: Ses préparatifs militaires et sa chronologie," in the *Revue des études roumaines*, V–VI (Paris, 1960), 67–77, reprinted in his *Le Monde ottoman des Balkans (1402–1566): Institutions, société, économie*, London: Variorum, 1976.

davia and the increase in their naval armament, sad facts confirmed also by intelligence received from Naples. With the usual denunciation of the rabid Turk, Innocent informed d'Aubusson of the contents of his encyclical of 21 November; expressed his hope that the princes would respond "like men to so sacred an undertaking;" assured the grand master of his own papal dedication to the noble cause of protecting Christians; and finally warned him to be on guard against whatever snares or enticements the serpent might extend to Rhodes from neighboring Istanbul.[61] One can imagine how much the defender of Rhodes required such admonitions from the onetime bishop of Molfetta.

Innocent also reminded Ferdinand of Aragon, ruler of Sicily, that his island domain might well be the next object of the Turkish cupidity for conquest. For years Hungary had been dealt almost annual blows. One might hope that the time would come when the daring arrogance of the enemy would be repressed by a *publicum bellum* which the Christian world would initiate against him. The Turk had taken Asia and Greece while Christians were at odds with one another. Now he was turning his attention toward Italy and Sicily. Day and night Innocent thought of nothing else, he said, and he warned Ferdinand that Italy and Sicily were quite unprepared to withstand any large-scale attack.[62]

Clerks in the papal chancery must have long remembered that late November of 1484 when the *terror Turcicus* filled the new pope's mind. Letters were being sent to all corners of Christendom, recounting the danger, appealing for peace and unity, and requesting the dispatch of envoys to Rome with powers of decision and commitment. Among the various letters written (or at least dated) on the twenty-first of the month, was one to Ferrante of Naples on the defensibility of Italy if only the proper measures were taken.[63]

The Curia had been using such means as it had to avert the apparent peril. Pierre d'Aubusson had already been requested to warn Sultan Bayazid that a Christian federation would return Jem Sultan *vi et armis* to rule in the Ottoman empire if Bayazid made war on any Christian prince. The departure of the Turkish fleet from the Dardanelles into Mediterranean waters, it was said, would be regarded as an act of aggression and a violation of the pact between the Porte and the Knights of Rhodes. Bayazid had then professed his peaceful intentions, and had even presented d'Aubusson with one of the chief relics which Mehmed the Conqueror had taken from the treasury of Hagia Sophia, the right arm of John the Baptist, which had once baptized Christ in the river Jordan.[64] However appealing this diplomatic traffic in relics might be to the contemporary mind, most officials of the Curia knew perfectly well that Istanbul was no weaker and Rhodes no stronger for the grand master's acquisition of one of several right arms of John the Baptist, even though an investigation revealed that the Knights had got the true and authentic relic.

It was not the desiccated muscle of S. John's right arm but money which supplied the sinews of war. On 2 February, 1485, Innocent VIII wrote Ferrante of Naples again concerning the Turkish question. A fleet of sixty galleys and twenty transports was needed merely for the defense of Italy, according to the pope, who noted that for any offensive action a much larger naval force would be required. It would cost 500 ducats (*aurei*) a month to maintain each galley, and 1,000 ducats a month to maintain each transport, which would amount to 200,000 ducats for a period of four months, presumably as long as Italy would require a protective fleet against Turkish attack in any one year. But to this we must add, his Holiness continued, 1,000 ducats a galley to rotate the hulls of twenty galleys, since only forty would be kept in service at any one time, bringing the cost up to 220,000 ducats. Following a formula devised in another connection, the pope proposed to pay 40,000 ducats, and believed that the king of Naples and the duke of Milan should each pay 75,000. The Florentines should be assessed for 30,000. Ferrante would learn further details from the papal envoy to Naples.[65]

[61] Arch. Segr. Vaticano, Arm. XXXIX, tom. 18, fols. 73^r–74^r, and *cf.* Raynaldus, *Ann. eccl.*, ad ann. 1484, no. 66, vol. XIX (1693), p. 345a.

[62] Arm. XXXIX, tom. 18, fols. 75^r–76^r; Raynaldus, *Ann. eccl.*, ad ann. 1484, nos. 67–68, vol. XIX (1693), pp. 345–346a, also dated at Rome on 21 November, 1484.

[63] Arm. XXXIX, tom. 18, fol. 70; Raynaldus, *Ann. eccl.*, ad ann. 1484, no. 71, vol. XIX (1693), p. 346b.

[64] Bosio, II (1594), bk. XIII, pp. 387–91; Raynaldus, *Ann. eccl.*, ad ann. 1484, nos. 72–73, vol. XIX (1693), pp. 346b–347a; Zinkeisen, *Gesch. d. osman. Reiches*, II (1854), 483.

[65] Arm. XXXIX, tom. 18, fols. 112^r–113^r, by mod. stamped enumeration; Raynaldus, *Ann. eccl.*, ad ann. 1485, no. 3, vol. XIX (1693), p. 349b.

Raynaldus supplies the further details from Innocent's unpublished briefs. Duke Ercole d'Este of Ferrara was assessed for 8,000 ducats, as were the Sienese; the marquises of Mantua and Montferrat, 6,000 and 2,000 respectively; the Lucchesi, 2,000, and the despot of Piombino, 1,000. Since efforts would be made to collect funds from other sources, the total sum being sought was well in excess of the amount which Innocent had considered necessary for the fleet. One could hardly expect every state to pay its assessment. The Florentines, for example, claimed they could not pay at all. The war with Genoa had cost them too much, which led Innocent to warn them of the greater dangers which lay ahead (in a letter of 23 February, 1485), while he pointed out the inevitable advantages of a just peace.[66]

The pope sought Milanese intervention to help resolve the war between Florence and Genoa in order that the Italian states might join forces to defend the peninsula against the Turks. Lorenzo de' Medici's father, Piero, had purchased Sarzana, which commanded the coastal road from Liguria into Tuscany, from the Genoese almost twenty years before (in 1468). The Genoese had taken advantage of Florentine difficulties about a dozen years later, however, in the war that followed the Pazzi conspiracy, and had repossessed Sarzana. In 1484 the Florentines took Pietrasanta, fifteen miles to the south of Sarzana. An agreement was made whereby the Florentines would retain Pietrasanta, and the Genoese, Sarzana, but the terms of the agreement not being kept, the war soon broke out again (the Florentines finally regained Sarzana in 1487).[67] Turks or no Turks, peace was a rare commodity in Italy.

Innocent VIII again appealed to Ferdinand of Aragon to send a strong fleet to Sicily, where Turkish landings were feared. While urging other princes to protect their domains, the pope followed his own advice. In the early months of 1485 he directed Cardinal Battista Orsini, legate of the March, to look to the defenses of Ancona and the southward coasts of Piceno.[68] One Stefano Corso was sent a brief of commendation dated 25 May, 1486, for his vigilance in protecting Fano and neighboring areas against Turkish raids.[69] Turkish *fuste* were often sighted on the Adriatic in the spring of 1486. On 12 June Innocent ordered that coast guards be organized along the shore of the March to alert the inhabitants against sur-

---

[66] Raynaldus, *Ann. eccl.*, ad ann. 1485, no. 4, vol. XIX (1693), p. 350a; Pastor, *Gesch. d. Päpste*, III-1 (repr. 1955), 257. Raynaldus, no. 3, gives the Florentine assessment as 30,000 florins, and in no. 4 as 36,000. In a letter of 23 February (1485) to the duke of Milan the pope estimates the total cost of the crusading fleet at 300,000 ducats (Arm. XXXIX, tom. 18, fols. 129^v–130^v). The letter of the same date to the Florentines may be found, *ibid.*, fols. 130^v–131^v. On 6 March the pope wrote Ercole d'Este of Ferrara that "ex diversis locis quotidie huc rumores et certi quidem nuntii afferuntur de ingenti apparatu quem Turcus toto conatu facit ut Italiam invadat, et nisi celeriter et in tempore occurratur, facile unusquisque potest existimare rem Italicam in aperto discrimine versari . . ." (*ibid.*, fol. 139, where a note in the register gives the assessments, as noted in the text, for Siena, Mantua, Lucca, Montferrat, and Piombino). The lord of Piombino was Jacopo d'Appiano, an immoral character, to whom Innocent administered chastisement on 4 June, 1485 (*ibid.*, fol. 183), and who was later dispossessed by Cesare Borgia.

[67] On the capture of Pietrasanta and Sarzana, *cf.* Luca Landucci, *Diario fiorentino*, ed. Iodoco del Badia, Florence, 1883, pp. 49, 56, trans. Alice de Rosen Jervis, London, 1927, pp. 40–41, 43; *Diario ferrarese*, in *RISS*, XXIV, pt. 7 (1933), p. 119; Delaborde, *Expédition de Charles VIII* (1888), pp. 190–91, 194. The pope's appeal to the duke of Milan (of 23 February, 1485) is cited in the preceding note from Arm. XXXIX, tom. 18, fols. 129^v–130^v. *Cf.*, *ibid.*, tom. 18, fols. 159^v–160^r, a letter to the Florentines dated 26 April, 1485, and, *ibid.*, tom. 19, fols. 196–197^r, letters dated 15 February, 1486, insisting that, when peace was made between the Genoese and Florentines, the latter should return the castle of Sarzanello to the Genoese. Sarzana surrendered to the Florentines after a siege of forty days on 22 June, 1487 (Sigismondo de'Conti, I [1883], 281; Infessura, *Diaria*, ed. Tommasini [1890], p. 226, where the city is called *Ceresana*; Pontani, *Diario*, ed. Toni, in *RISS*, III-2 [1908], p. 67). On the affair of Sarzana and the complicated relations of Florence and Genoa, see Roberto Palmarocchi, *La Politica italiana di Lorenzo de'Medici: Firenze nella guerra contro Innocenzo VIII*, Florence, 1933, *passim*, esp. pp. 11–12, 15–22, 55 ff., 80–81, 114–16, 194 ff., 210 ff.

[68] Arm. XXXIX, tom. 18, fols. 102^v–103, 106, 108^v, 110, 112–114^v, 129^v–130, 139, 147^v–148^r, 156; Adolf Gottlob, *Aus der Camera Apostolica des 15. Jahrhunderts*, Innsbruck, 1889, pp. 126–27; Raynaldus, *Ann. eccl.*, ad ann. 1485, no. 5, vol. XIX (1693), p. 350a; Pastor, *Gesch. d. Päpste*, III-1 (repr. 1955), 220–21, 257. On the failure of the Florentines to live up to the terms of peace with Genoa (in April, 1486), *cf.* Infessura, *Diaria*, ed. Tommasini, pp. 199, 222, and Raynaldus, ad ann. 1486, no. 34, p. 371b, and ad ann. 1487, no. 8, p. 381b.

[69] Arm. XXXIX, tom. 19, fol. 401^v: "Intelleximus ex plurimorum verbis ac litteris diligentiam tuam in custodienda civitate nostra Fani aliisque circumvicinis locis et in repellendis Turcis qui regionem istam infestabant: laudamus summopere prudentiam et diligentiam tuam hortamurque ut in bono proposito et laudabili incepto perseveres in diesque maiorem huiusmodi custodie ad quam missus es [Corso was a papal constable] curam atque industriam adhibeas. . . ." He was promised financial reward for his services.

prise landings and thus to make possible concerted counterattacks upon the enemy.[70]

Although Bayazid II dealt with his enemies no more honestly than they with him, the Turkish fuste operating off the Adriatic coast probably belonged to corsairs, whose raids were a matter of private enterprise, and not undertaken by order of the Porte. In an imperial firman of early July, 1486, Bayazid acknowledged the receipt in Istanbul of a letter from the Venetian Signoria protesting that corsairs, obviously on the Adriatic, had robbed and sunk certain Venetian vessels. Bayazid made clear his disapproval of such depredation, and recognized the Republic's right to punish pirates, as agreed upon in the "capitulations" which existed between the two states. He also stated that he had ordered the sanjakbeyi and kadis of Albania to look into the whole business, punish the culprits, make good the losses, and report back to the Porte. The Signoria was even invited to send an agent of their own to conduct an investigation.[71] Bayazid did not want a renewal of the war with Venice, not with Jem Sultan in Christian hands, but the Turks were apparently not sparing what little remained of the so-called Genoese empire in the Levant.

The Genoese colony at Chios appealed to the pope for protection against frequent harassment by the Turks. Innocent replied that all his slender resources were being employed in the defense of Italy, but he would send help to Chios when he could.[72] In the meantime he requested the Grand Master d'Aubusson, who (as we know) had a non-aggression pact with Bayazid, to take the Genoese colony under his protection.[73] The fact that Innocent's father had been born on the island of Rhodes,[74] was conceivably an additional reason for his concern for the colonists who lived in the midst of a Turkish sea. In any event he claimed to be doing all he could to organize a grand offensive against the Porte. During this period Bayazid never seemed to be far distant from Innocent's thoughts. To Ferdinand and Isabella, *reges Hispaniarum*, he wrote on 8 February, 1486, to continue their war against the Moors and, when they had been overcome (*debellati*), to turn their arms against the Turk and achieve a like victory over that "truculent enemy."[75] When Casimir IV of Poland asked for a crusading bull, the pope ordered that it be sent to him. Casimir had also requested the right to retain three-fourths of the amounts collected, remitting only one-fourth to the Holy See. Permission was promptly granted for this, although Innocent reminded him that it had always been customary to send a third of such collections to the Camera Apostolica, where there was a pressing need for money for operations against the Turks.[76]

In December, 1486, Innocent dispatched the French ecclesiastic Raymond Peraudi (Pérault)

[70] Arm. XXXIX, tom. 19, fol. 427r, by mod. stamped enumeration, postscript to a letter addressed to the governor of the March: "Post scripta intelleximus ex ultimis litteris tuis preter alia nonnullas Turcorum fustas in isto Mari Hadriatico apparuisse, quare operam dabis ut omnes terre et loca marittima intenta sint studiosissime ad circumspectandum undique si quod Turchorum navigium se ostendat quod cum perspexerint quisque vicinis suis signo aliquo id manifestet ut omnes in tempore una convenire possint ad subveniendum ubi opus erit." *Cf.* Raynaldus, *Ann. eccl.*, ad ann. 1486, no. 31, vol. XIX (1693), p. 371a, where the text has been rather carelessly transcribed, and Pastor, *Gesch. d. Päpste*, III-1 (repr. 1955), 257.

[71] Arch. di Stato di Venezia, Documenti turchi, Busta 6, doc. dated I dec. Reğeb 891 (3–12 July, 1486), cited in the "Regesti Bombaci," Busta 20.

[72] Arm. XXXIX, tom. 18, fols. 161v–162r; Raynaldus, *Ann. eccl.*, ad ann. 1485, nos. 5–6, vol. XIX (1693), p. 350. The Genoese on Chios had written the pope on 11 March (1485); his reply is dated 29 April.

[73] *Cf.* Bosio, *Militia di San Giovanni*, II (1594), bk. XIV, pp. 404–5, who shows, however, that the Genoese of Chios were also appealing directly to d'Aubusson. Pauli, *Codice diplomatico*, II (1737), nos. XXXVI ff., pp. 435 ff.; Thuasne, *Djem-Sultan*, pp. 141–42. The Knights of Rhodes were themselves not immune from the Turkish danger, and on 11 December, 1486, Innocent VIII was preparing to take such steps as he could "pro defensione civitatis et insule predictarum" (Reg. Vat. 692, fol. 97, and *cf.* the bull of 15 July, 1488, *ibid.*, fols. 215 ff.).

[74] *Cf.* Jacques Heers, *Gênes au XVe siècle*, Paris, 1961, p. 422.

[75] Arm. XXXIX, tom. 19, fol. 182, by mod. stamped enumeration.

[76] Arm. XXXIX, tom. 19, fol. 476r, by mod. stamped enumeration: "Carissime in Christo fili noster, salutem etc. Expediri mandavimus bullam cruciate quam petiisti et licet moris sit semperque fieri consueverit ut tertia pars proventuum ex similibus concessionibus cruciate percipiendorum ad cameram apostolicam perveniant, tamen contemplatione Maiestatis tue cuius catholicam mentem et optimam dispositionem erga nos et S.R.E. magni facimus et gratissimam habemus de quarta tantum parte contenti fuimus ut cognoscas nos tibi plurimum tribuere et que pro te possumus libenter facere. Hortamur Maiestatem tuam [ut] velit ordinare et efficere ut quarta huiusmodi pars et portio proventuum et reddituum omnium ex ipsa cruciata colligendorum et percipiendorum ad eandem cameram apostolicam omnino perveniat sicuti te pro tua religione et equitate facturum speramus. Datum Rome, etc. die XII Iulii 1486, anno secundo." *Cf.*, *ibid.*, fols. 476v, 526.

to the Emperor Frederick III to discuss the possibility of German participation in the crusade. At the same time the Spanish theologian, Gratian of Villanova, procurator-general of the Carmelites, was sent to the court of Maximilian in the Netherlands. Although Frederick thought he had some cause for complaint against the pope, he gave a surprisingly favorable reception to the project for a crusade. Gratian of Villanova was back in Rome by April (1487) to report on Maximilian's approval. For Peraudi this was the beginning of a distinguished diplomatic career which was to extend over almost twenty years, until his death in 1505. Later years were to find him nuncio or legate in Germany, France, and Italy. He was to receive the bishopric of Gurk in 1491 and the red hat in 1493. Trithemius has left a glowing tribute to Peraudi's zeal for justice and contempt for worldly goods. Encouraged by Peraudi's letters and Gratian's report, Innocent stated on 20 April (1487) that he was devoting all the revenues of the Roman Church to the crusade, retaining barely enough to support the papal household, and declared that the cardinals were giving of their own accord far more than a tithe of their incomes to the same noble cause.[77] On 13 November (1487) Innocent promulgated the bull *Universo pene orbi*, in which he dilated upon the seriousness of the Turkish threat to Germany and Italy, affirming his determination to leave no stone unturned to arouse Christendom to offensive action. He announced the emperor's readiness to go on the crusade with the other kings and princes, and imposed a year's tithe upon all imperial churches and churchmen. Peraudi and Gratian of Villanova were named collectors-general of the tithe in the imperial domains, with all the customary faculties and rights pertaining to their function.[78]

Gratian of Villanova was again to try to induce the emperor, the German electors and princes, and especially Maximilian to prepare for war against the Turks. His instructions, dated 12 April, 1487, emphasized the great danger which Europe was facing. The princes must be awakened from their slumber. Events were to prove that the danger was not as great as the pope believed it to be. Whenever the princes were awakened from their slumber, however, they were likely to go to war with one another. Maximilian was deeply involved in Flanders and had serious differences with France. Frederick III had to carry on the war with Matthias Corvinus, and was then trying to raise forces in Germany to win back Austria from the victorious Corvinus.[79] Innocent continued his apparently futile efforts to bring about concord among the Christian princes. He sent an embassy to Charles VIII of France, and warned him in several letters to compose his quarrels with Maximilian, pointing out how much better it would be to shed Turkish than Christian blood. Charles did not reply.

---

[77] Raynaldus, *Ann. eccl.*, ad ann. 1487, no. 4, vol. XIX (1693), p. 381a; *cf.* A. Ciaconius, *Vitae et res gestae pontificum romanorum*, ed. A. Oldoinus, III (1677), col. 172. The pope also noted that the Emperor Frederick could not embark on a crusade without the co-operation of the other kings and princes. He repeated the pledge to devote all the revenues of the Roman Church to the crusade, "vix tenui parte pro nostre familie sustentatione retenta," in the bull *Universo pene orbi* of the following 13 November (1487), in Reg. Vat. 692, fol. 122^v (see the following note). On 6 March, 1487, an apostolic bull had been issued of *adhortatio contra Turcum* (Arm. XXXII, tom. 21, fols. 97^v–98^v, by mod. stamped enumeration).

[78] Adolf Gottlob, "Der Legat Raimund Peraudi," *Historisches Jahrbuch*, VI (Munich, 1885), 438–39, 450, a critique of the monograph by Johann Schneider, *Die kirchliche und politische Wirksamkeit des Legaten Raimund Peraudi (1486–1505)*, Halle, 1882. Gottlob, *loc. cit.*, dates the bull *Universo pene orbi* 20 May, 1487, and Pastor, *Hist. Popes*, V, 291, misdates it 27 May, 1486, altered to 20 April, 1487, in the *Gesch. d. Päpste*, III-1 (repr. 1955), 258. The bull may be found in Reg. Vat. 692, fols. 121^v–124^v, "datum Rome apud Sanctum Petrum, anno etc. MCCCCLXXXVII, Idus Novembris, anno quarto," which makes clear its promulgation on 13 November, 1487. The bull contains an eloquent condemnation of that "son of iniquity and alumnus of perdition, Buccolino Gazonio [Boccolino Guzzoni]," a willing ally of the Turks. Lionello Chieregato and Antonio Florez were named collectors of the tithe in French territory (*ibid.*, fols. 123^v, 125, 146–62, 216 ff.). A plenary indulgence for service against the Turks had been granted by the bull *Catholice fidei* on 5 July, 1486 (Arm. XXXII, tom. 21, fols. 83^v–90^r, by mod. stamped enumeration), followed by a plea for action against the Turks on 6 March, 1487 (*ibid.*, fols. 97^v–98^v). About seven years later Gratian of Villanova was sent by Alexander VI on an embassy to the French court (arriving at Tours on 13 January, 1494), but despite his reputation for diplomatic adroitness he handled his mission badly (Delaborde, *Expédition de Charles VIII en Italie*, pp. 296, 307–9).

[79] *Instructiones a S.D.N. ad serenissimum Romanorum regem date Magistro Gratiano de Villanova . . .* , in Arch. Segr. Vaticano, Miscell., Arm. II, tom. 56, fols. 132^v–136^v, dated 12 April, 1487 (in a seventeenth-century MS. copy). *Cf.* Gottlob, *Histor. Jahrbuch*, VI, 450–51; Raynaldus, *Ann. eccl.*, ad ann. 1487, no. 5, vol. XIX (1693), p. 381b. Some years later, on 27 February, 1492, Gratian of Villanova was granted a pension by the pope for his services, "datum Rome apud Sanctum Petrum, anno etc. MCCCCLXXXX primo [O.S.], quarto Kal. Martii, pont. nostri anno octavo" (Reg. Vat. 693, fols. 63^v–67^r).

Conditions in the Netherlands went from bad to worse. The rebellious burghers of Bruges took Maximilian prisoner in early February, 1488; held in confinement for more than three months, he sent envoys to the pope, asking for his assistance.[80] Frederick prepared for military action, and requested ecclesiastical sanctions against the defiant Flemings. Not long afterwards Archbishop Hermann of Cologne laid Ghent, Bruges, and Ypres under the interdict.[81] As for the pope, he kept crying peace, and there was no peace.

On 4 May, 1488, the crusading tithe was imposed upon all officials of the Curia Romana without exception, including the cardinals.[82] The crusading imposition was a failure in Germany. A year before (on 26 June, 1487), Berthold von Henneberg, archbishop of Mainz (1484–1504), and the electors of Saxony and Brandenburg had appealed to Innocent for exemption from the tithe to be paid in the empire, pleading that the German Church had been ravaged by war and impoverished by extortion. For centuries the German Church had been, to be sure, in the hands of noble families, whose younger sons like vampires had been living on the blood and booty of their disheartened flocks. Johannes Trithemius, abbot of the Benedictine monastery of Sponheim, says that the clergy held meetings to protest the tithe in various places throughout the empire, and finally had recourse to the old device of appealing from the pope ill-informed to a pope well-informed.[83] Innocent had to abandon all hope of seeing the tithe collected from the Germans, who as usual would not willingly pay their allotted share of the costs for an expedition against the Turks. After all, they had a first line of defense in the Hungarians, whom they disliked. But what of France, traditional home of crusaders?

In November, 1487, Innocent sent Lionello Chieregato of Vicenza, then bishop of Traù (Trogir in Dalmatia), and the papal protonotary Antonio Florez as nuncios to Paris, where on Sunday, 20 January (1488), Chieregato delivered an eloquent discourse before Charles VIII and members of his court. He held up before their eyes the model of their crusading ancestors and contrasted their own failure to respond to the dire needs of the Church and of their Christian neighbors in Italy who lived in constant fear of a Turkish invasion. The news soon came, however, of the Flemings' imprisonment of Maximilian and thereafter of the interdict laid upon their chief cities, against which Charles protested on the grounds that Flanders was a French fief, and that the Flemings were quite justified in their opposition to Hapsburg pretensions.[84] The anti-Roman faction at

[80] In a letter dated at Innsbruck on 12 March, 1488, Frederick indignantly informed Innocent of his son Maximilian's imprisonment by the rebellious citizens of Bruges (A.A., Arm. I–XVIII, 1443, fols. 108^v–109^v by mod. stamped enumeration): ". . . ipsi Brugenses nescitur quo spiritu ducti contra apostoli doctrinam iurisiurandi religionem fidelitatem prestitam ac omnes vires equi et equitatis rationem violentas manus in ipsum serenissimum filium nostrum [Maximilianum] iniecerunt ex suoque regali palatio ad quandam privatam domum iuxta sui furoris libitum deduxerunt et ibidem ipsum in contemptum sacratissime regalis unctionis misere et ignominiose tractant. . . ." Frederick informed the pope that his Holiness was bound to favor anointed kings above others and favor even an inferior person of any sort above the rabble, "contra huiusmodi populi nephandos." He also wrote to the College of Cardinals (*ibid.*, fol. 110).

[81] Gottlob, *Histor. Jahrbuch*, VI, 451–52; Heinrich Ulmann, *Kaiser Maximilian I.*, 2 vols., Stuttgart, 1884–93, I, 19 ff.; Raynaldus, *Ann. eccl.*, ad ann. 1488, nos. 1–2, vol. XIX (1693), p. 387b.

[82] Arch. Segr. Vaticano, Reg. Vat. 692, fols. 206^r–207^r, "datum Rome apud Sanctum Petrum, anno etc. MCCCCLXXXVIII, quarto Nonas Maii, pont. nostri anno quarto," misdated 6 May (1488) by Gottlob, *op. cit.*, p. 444. But the collection of all tithes was a source of never ending frustration to the Curia Romana (Reg. Vat. 692, fols. 22–24, 34^v ff., 39 ff., 43 ff., etc., 110, 174 ff., 177 ff., etc., 235 ff., *et alibi*).

[83] Joann. Trithemius, *Annales Hirsaugienses*, II (S. Gall, 1690), 529, cited by Pastor, *Gesch. d. Päpste*, III-1 (repr. 1955), 260. On the difficulties of Gratian of Villanova and other collectors and sub-collectors of the crusading tithe, *cf.* Innocent's bull of 16 March, 1488, "datum Rome apud Sanctum Petrum, anno etc. MCCCCLXXXVIII, decimoseptimo Kal. Aprilis, [pont. nostri] anno quarto," in Reg. Vat. 692, fols. 226^r–228^r.

[84] Thuasne, *Djem-Sultan*, pp. 173 ff., 179–94, 211–13; Pastor, *Gesch. d. Päpste*, III-1 (repr. 1955), 260–62; Pio Paschini, *Leonello Chieregato, nunzio d'Innocenzo VIII e di Alessandro VI*, Rome, 1935, pp. 54 ff. (Lateranum, new ser. I-3). On 3 November (1488) Pope Innocent lifted the interdict as part of his bargain with the king of France to secure the person of Jem Sultan. On the mission of Chieregato and Florez to Paris, see Reg. Vat. 692, fols. 120^r–121^v, 123^v, 125, 146–162, and Reg. Vat. 693, fols. 132^r–140^r, by mod. stamped enumeration. Innocent VIII granted Florez a pension on 12 September, 1484 (Reg. Vat. 700, fols. 27^r–29^r, and Reg. Vat. 720, fols. 285^v–287^r). *Cf.* also Reg. Vat. 700, fols. 31^v ff., 57^r ff., 148^v ff. I have made no effort to record the papal favors bestowed on Florez, but he received others on 10 December, 1486 (Reg. Vat. 719, fols. 74^r–75^v, 98^r–99^v) and on 13 November, 1490 (Reg. Vat. 751, fols. 223^r–224^r, by mod. stamped enumeration, and *cf.* Reg. Vat. 752, fol. 162, dated 14 November, 1490).

the French court, defenders of the old Pragmatic Sanction of Bourges, was delighted with the turn of events.

Raymond Peraudi now went to France, where it was hoped he might effect some measure of peace between Charles VIII and Maximilian. From France Peraudi returned to Germany to attend the Reichstag which opened on 6 July, 1489, at Frankfurt on the Main. He bore with him a papal brief dated 12 April and addressed to all the Christian princes, in which Innocent re-emphasized the imminence of the Turkish peril, and warned of the terrible increase of Turkish power. He urged the princes to send envoys to Rome immediately with sufficient authority to commit their principals to a plan for the crusade. There must be peace in Europe. Innocent said that not only was he willing to pledge all the resources of the Holy See to the crusade but, if it seemed necessary, he would himself take part in the expedition. He informed the Germans that he had written in the same vein to the other European princes, and hoped that they too would hearken to the admonition and prayers of their father in Rome.[85] Peraudi had a gift for negotiation. To ready speech and a warm manner, he added the gentle, courteous persistence of the born diplomat. Within ten days he had helped bring about peace between Maximilian and the French envoys at the Reichstag.

On 21 July (1489) Peraudi wrote the pope that about 10:00 P.M. the preceding evening "peace had been concluded and stipulated by oath, at his own hands as the apostolic nuncio, by Maximilian, most serene king of the Romans, and by the envoys of the French king, to be observed in perpetuity between the aforesaid kings." The articles of peace, Peraudi wrote, would be forwarded to Rome as soon as possible. Peraudi's letters arrived on Thursday, 30 July, and just before the midday meal were

[85] The brief of 12 April, 1489, which Peraudi took to the Reichstag seems both interesting and important enough to warrant some quotation and analysis (Arch. Segr. Vaticano, Miscell., Arm. II, tom. 56, fols. 371^v–374^v, by mod. stamped enumeration): *Copia brevis Domini Innocentii ad Principes et Potentatus Christianos super causa expeditionis contra Turcum*: "Quanto studio et labore contenderint sancte memorie predecessores nostri Romani pontifices ut Christiani pontifices [*sic* for principes] et populi depositis odiis atque inimicitiis et simultatibus mutuis contra immanissimum Turcorum tyrannum perpetuum Christiane reipublice hostem in unum convenirent: non solum nostre religionis hominibus verum etiam barbaris atque infidelibus nationibus satis exploratum est. . . ."

The brief reviews the crusading efforts of Calixtus III and Pius II, and notes that ". . . quotidie everso funditus Bosnie regno ac universo [*sic*] Peloponeso in miserrimam servitutem redacta crudelissimi tyranni vires contra nos invalescerent. . . ." Paul II and Sixtus IV had done their part, but the peril was all the greater after the fall of Negropontè in 1470 (*crudelissime per eosdem infideles Calcide Euboica occupata*). Rhodes had been besieged, and Otranto occupied; only divine clemency had prevented the cruel calamity from further extension into Italy. Innocent VIII intended to follow in the footsteps of his predecessors: ". . . huic rei potissimum animum adiecimus crebrisque literis et nunciis principes Christianos omnes in hanc ipsam expeditionem permovere atque impellere curavimus: Quod eo impensius tunc fecimus cum hostis idem Turcus Italie inhians in Picenum missis triremibus predabundus sepius impetum fecisset quedam mediterranea loca expugnare conatus subditis etiam nostris ad defectionem solicitatis." Experience had shown only too clearly that there were Italians in Piceno willing to assist the Gran Turco for profit.

Innocent had given his days and nights to devising a means of striking back at the enemy when God presented him and Christendom with an undreamed-of opportunity in Jem Sultan, possession of whose person Innocent had been anxious to secure: "Hec de fratrum nostrorum S.R.E. cardinalium consilio ad tuam Maiestatem scribere necessarium omnino esse existimavimus:" Their Majesties, all of them, must realize that this heaven-sent opportunity should not be lost. Either existing ambassadors or special envoys should be empowered to deal—at the Curia Romana—with the question of the crusade. Quickness of decision was necessary (*cum res ipsa dilationem non patiatur*).

Peace in Europe was the prime requisite for the crusade, and Innocent offered his services to help allay whatever discords might impede an expedition against the Turks. Jem's presence gave the Christians peculiar hopes of success: "Interea dum in hac expectatione oratorum erimus hunc ipsum Zizimum honorifice et maiori cum authoritate ac securitate in palatio nostro apostolico observari iussimus quo promptius ipse acrioreque in fratrem studio arma movere possit." Innocent was writing the other princes (in the same vein as in the brief which Peraudi had received): "Scribimus enim hoc eodem tempore in eandem sententiam de huiusmodi negocio ceteris principibus et potentatibus Christianis quos non dubitamus pro sua religiosa et catholica mente presentique rerum necessitati opitulante domino audituros paternas exhortationes et admonitiones nostras."

An original of this brief of 12 April, 1489, addressed to Francesco Gonzaga, marquis of Mantua, is preserved in the Arch. di Stato di Mantova, Arch. Gonzaga, Busta 834. It may also be found in the Arch. Segr. Vaticano, Miscell., Arm. II, tom. 2, fols. 524^r–529^v, by mod. stamped enumeration, as well as in Arm. XLIV, tom. 18, fols. 16 ff. In the latter volume the text has become almost illegible, owing to the corrosive effect of the ink upon the paper. *Cf.* Gottlob, *Histor. Jahrbuch*, VI, 452; Heinrich Ulmann, *Kaiser Maximilian I.*, 2 vols., Stuttgart, 1884–91, I, 68 ff.; Pastor, *Hist. Popes*, V, 295–96, and (with fuller notes) *Gesch. d. Päpste*, III-1 (repr. 1955), 262–64. Commissioners of the crusade were also appointed for England (Reg. Vat. 692, fol. 223^r).

given to the pope, who directed that a request to assemble at 4:30 P.M. [*pro hora XX*] be sent to all the cardinals then in Rome as well as to the ambassadors of the empire, France, the Spains, Hungary, and certain of the Italian states. After a brief conference with the cardinals, the pope had the ambassadors admitted to his presence. Having made their genuflections before the pope and the cardinals sitting in the usual circle, the ambassadors heard the pope's announcement of the peace, concerning which they might inform their principals immediately. His Holiness declined, however, to furnish them with copies of Peraudi's letters. That evening at the Vatican and the nearby Castle of S. Angelo, before the houses of some of the cardinals and even of curial officials, bonfires were lighted as a sign of rejoicing.[86]

In the meantime Innocent VIII had sent a third envoy to France, Baldassare da Spino, to work with Chieregato and Florez. Baldassare brought new proposals to Charles VIII for the settlement of certain ecclesiastical problems and for the surrender of Jem Sultan to the Holy See. It must have been Baldassare, as Paschini has said, who wrote Innocent on 17 February, 1488, that he had arrived in Paris that afternoon, and that he had found Chieregato and Florez on the Rue S. Jacques, where they were lodged at the inn of the Two Angels. He has left us an engaging account of his arrival in the city and of his first encounter with the nuncios at the inn.[87]

Their mission took some time, but Chieregato and Florez finally achieved a diplomatic stroke of no mean proportions, having won Charles VIII's consent for Jem Sultan's dispatch to Rome. The Grand Master Pierre d'Aubusson had been ready to surrender him to the pope for some time. If the papacy exacted a price for its favors, it always had to pay in turn. As we have seen, d'Aubusson was made a cardinal (on 9 March, 1489), exciting news for the Hospitallers. The pope sent the red hat to Rhodes, where d'Aubusson received it in a solemn ceremony in the Church of S. John the Baptist in the Collachium, across the piazza from the palace of the grand masters, on 29 June, the feast of SS. Peter and Paul.[88] Other concessions had to be made to Charles VIII. The Hospitallers were to continue their guard of Jem. The pope was to receive the 45,000 ducats a year being paid by the sultan for Jem's maintenance, but in the event the pope should turn Jem over to any other power without Charles VIII's consent, he was to be subject to a penalty of 1,000 pounds of gold, the commitment being guaranteed by a public contract authorized by the Sacred College.[89]

---

[86] Burchard, *Diarium*, ed. Thuasne, I, 362, and ed. Celani, I, 273–74; Schneider, *Raimund Peraudi* (1882), pp. 14 ff.; Gottlob, *Hist. Jahrbuch*, VI, 452–53; H. Ulmann, *Kaiser Maximilian I.*, I, 70.

[87] Léon G. Pélissier, ed., "Catalogue des documents de la Collection Podocataro à la Biblioteca Marciana à Venise," *Centralblatt für Bibliothekswesen*, XVIII (1901), no. 29 [Cod. 178, 92], pp. 595–96: ". . . Demum ex Lugduno [Lyon] veniens versus Parisius, obviavi cuidam cabalario qui michi interroganti respondit reverendos dominos, oratores vestrae Sanctitatis esse Parisius, in vico Sancti Jacobi, in hospicio Duorum Angelorum. . . . Et divino auxilio XIII huius mensis, hora secunda post meridiem, Parisius applicui curavique quaerere ubi esset idem vicus, ad quem me contuli, et inspecto insigni ubi depicti erant duo angeli, in illud ingressus sum. . . . Visitavi eos. . . . Et post prandium ad eos redii, exhibui breve vestrae Sanctitatis, et communicavi instructiones quas eis dimisi. Interrogavi quid fecissent. Responderunt se fuisse honorificentissime exceptos et benignissime auditos, ac res esse in bonis terminis, sed adhuc non esse aliquid conclusum. . . ." Paschini (see the following note) has misdated this letter 1489 by a typographical error.

[88] Bosio, II (1594), bk. XIV, p. 411, and *cf.* Sa'd-ad-Dīn, in *Journal asiatique*, IX (1826, repr. 1965), 161–62, 164. On the prolonged negotiations of Chieregato and Florez at the French court, see Thuasne, *Djem-Sultan*, pp. 196–97, 200–23, 292. Little purpose would be served by a detailed investigation of Innocent VIII's long efforts to secure possession of Jem Sultan's person. As early as 7 December, 1485, Innocent had written the duke of Bourbon concerning the "negotium fratris Turci," emphasizing that for the common safety of all Christians Jem should not be allowed to pass into any but the pope's own hands: "Nam si in nostra fuerit potestate, modum et viam adinveni[e]mus quibus illo tamquam instrumento ad res magnas pro religione christiana et Dei laude gerendas uti possimus" (Arch. Segr. Vaticano, Arm. XXXIX, tom. 19, fol. 85, by mod. stamped enumeration). *Cf.*, *ibid.*, fol. 85^v, to the same effect. For a late stage of Innocent's negotiations with Charles VIII to assume custody of Jem, see the *Instructiones pro fratre Balthasare* [*de Spino*], given to a French envoy on 12 July, 1488 (for transmission to Baldassare da Spino in Paris, where he had gone to join Chieregato and Florez), in the Miscellanea, Arm. II, tom. 56, fols. 115^v ff., 121^v–123^v, and *cf.* fols 131^r–132^v, by mod. stamped enumeration, and on the activities of Baldassare, who seems to have made two trips to France, *cf.* A. A., Arm. I–XVIII, 1443, fols. 116^v, 118^r, and note Paschini, *Leonello Chieregato* (1935), pp. 60–61, 70–71 ff.

[89] Both Zinkeisen, *Gesch. d. osman. Reiches*, II, 485, and Pastor, *Gesch. d. Päpste*, III-1 (repr. 1955), 265, put the penalty to which the Holy See exposed itself at 10,000 ducats; Caoursin, in Thuasne, *Burchardi diarium*, I, 544, says "ad penam decem milia librarum auri cui sit Romana ecclesia obnoxia," and *cf.* Petrus Beneficiatus, *ibid.*, I, append., no. 36, p. 548; Bosio, II (1594), bk. XIV, p. 411, "sotto pena di dieci mila libre d'oro." The correct sum was apparently 1,000 pounds (see, above, note 16, *ad fin.*).

As might be expected, Ferrante of Naples had done everything he could to frustrate the pope and the Venetians. The latter had been urging Jem Sultan's transfer to Rome, lest somehow their enemy Matthias Corvinus should get hold of him. Ferrante had offered the grand master large sums of money, undoubtedly on Corvinus's behalf, to have Jem sent to Naples, and had even contemplated his abduction as he was being transferred from France to Rome.[90] But, as we have already noted, Jem's transfer was safely effected from Provence to Rome, despite a stormy voyage. He entered the city during the afternoon of 13 March, 1489, through the Porta Portese in Trastevere, being met by the *famiglie* of the pope and various cardinals as well as by certain groups of lay dignitaries. High ecclesiastics doffed their birettas, and the Turk inclined his turbaned head. The papal master of ceremonies, Burchard, participated in the proceedings, and has left a detailed account of them.

After protracted greetings, Jem Sultan rode between the pope's son Franceschetto Cibo and the grand master's nephew Guy de Blanchefort, prior of Auvergne, who had been his chief guardian for years. Outside the city gate an Egyptian envoy, sent by the Soldan Ka'itbey to discuss what should be done with Jem,[91] had greeted the Ottoman prince with an oriental obsequiousness fascinating to Burchard, who was a great authority on court etiquette. The ceremonies of reception got off to a rather awkward start when Blanchefort had some dispute as to protocol with Emilio Parisiano d'Ascoli, the Senator of Rome, as well as with the ambassadors of Naples, Venice, and some others who had very close ties with the pope. The prior refused to yield his place of honor to any of them. The Senator of Rome finally rode ahead, but the ambassadors had to fall back. Burchard rode beside Jem's interpreter. From the Porta Portese the long procession crossed the river by the ancient bridges of the Isola Tiberina, and veered sharply left, traversing the Piazza Giudea and Campo dei Fiori on the way to the Vatican palace. Huge crowds had gathered to see Jem. No one of the thousands who saw him on this occasion and on others could forget that here was the very son of the Conqueror of Constantinople, who had filled the western world with terror for almost thirty years.

On the following day, Saturday, 14 March (1489), at a public consistory which began early in the morning Innocent VIII bestowed red hats upon the new cardinals who were present. After this Jem Sultan made his anxiously awaited entry into the consistory. With Franceschetto Cibo and Blanchefort on either side, and with sergeants-at-arms preceding and fourteen of his own servitors following him, Jem entered the consistory and appeared before the pope. Although the expectation had been that Jem would render obeisance to the pope in the Turkish fashion by touching the floor and kissing his hand, he refused to do so. He also refused to genuflect before the pope; in fact he barely inclined his turbaned head. Then he mounted the steps to the throne, embraced his Holiness, and lightly kissed his right shoulder, remaining covered throughout this unconventional salutation. Standing before the pope, he stated through his interpreter that he was glad to be in Rome, and in a few courteous phrases said that he would explain other things in private. Innocent answered that his Excellency (*nobilitas sua*) had been brought to Rome for his own advantage; he was to entertain no doubts on that score, but to live happily; everything had been arranged to come to a good conclusion. Jem said that he trusted so, thanked the pope, and then stepped back. He embraced the cardinals one by one as they stood in their customary circle. Next his Turkish attendants approached the papal throne. Each one, genuflecting and touching the floor with his right

---

[90] Fraknói, *Mathias Corvinus*, p. 221, who cites *MHH*, *Acta extera*, IV (Budapest, 1878), 6, a letter dated 10 February, 1489, of the Venetian government to Domenico Trevisan, their envoy in Rome (also in Lamansky, *Secrets d'état de Venise* [1884, repr. 1968], pp. 227–28), and note the letter to Trevisan dated 18 March, 1489, in Lamansky, pp. 228–29. *Cf.* Bosio, II (1594), bks. XIII–XIV, pp. 382–83, 401, and especially Thuasne, *Djem-Sultan*, pp. 216–23, 225–26, and Arch. Segr. Vaticano, Miscell., Arm. II, tom. 56, fols. 189r ff., by mod. stamped enumeration.

[91] It was reported at the Hungarian court that the Egyptian envoy had offered Innocent VIII 200,000 ducats for possession of Jem Sultan's person, and that the pope was willing to accept it. Innocent allegedly sent an emissary to Rhodes on the pretext of attending to certain Hospitaller affairs, "sed inde mutatis vestibus ibit ad soldanum pro compositione istius pecunie et aliarum rerum." Ka'itbey and Jem would then make war on the sultan, "sed dominus sanctissimus deberet cogitare quod soldanus et ille Turchus [Jem] ambo sunt infideles et si isti fiant magni, erunt maximi inimici fidei nostre, et si vincet iste Turchus qui nunc est captus, . . . non habebimus duriorem inimicum quam istum magnum Turchum?" (Miscell., Arm. II, tom. 56, fols. 187v–188r, by mod. stamped enumeration). A victorious Jem might be a more dangerous enemy than Bayazid.

hand, made the obeisance of osculation. Jem then returned to his rooms in the palace.[92]

Raymond Peraudi had been no less successful in Germany, as we have seen, than Chieregato and Florez in France. He preached and peddled the indulgence for the crusade, and now he helped Bishop Angelo of Orte, papal nuncio at the Hungarian court, to effect the long-desired truce between old Frederick III and Matthias Corvinus.[93] Angelo's mission was not an easy one. Anxious to have Jem Sultan sent to Hungary, where he wanted to go, Corvinus feared that Innocent VIII's plans for the expedition against the Turks included putting Jem aboard a Venetian fleet. Corvinus told the nuncio that he simply did not believe the Venetians were interested in a war against the Turks. They wanted to pursue their own ambitions. A Turkish envoy had been in Buda for some time. Now that he had left for home (as Angelo wrote the pope) Corvinus apparently planned to send a Hungarian envoy to Istanbul: "Puto, pater beatissime, quod Maiestas sua inter spem et metum naviget et pedem unum in duobus calceis inhabere velit!" If the pope put Jem aboard a Venetian fleet, however, Corvinus would immediately come to terms with the sultan (*illico cum Turco federa faciat*), "and I cannot convince his Majesty that not only the counsel of the Venetian Signoria is to be sought, but that his Majesty's own counsel and that of the rest of the Christian princes must be considered." Angelo assured Corvinus that the pope would not make an unseemly decision.[94]

"I tell you, my lord legate," replied Corvinus, "the pope can do nothing with the Turk [Jem Sultan] except what the king of France decides. He received [Jem] with this understanding. The whole matter rests in the hands of [Cardinal Jean] de la Balue. He manages everything, although the king of France was perfectly willing that [Jem] should come into my hands."

Corvinus obviously entertained no small animus against Jean de la Balue, cardinal of Angers (d. 1491), who had been involved in the negotiations which led to the Hospitallers' turning Jem Sultan over to the pope.[95] De la Balue had in fact taken custody of Jem at Civitavecchia (on 10 March, 1489), whither Guy de Blanchefort had brought him. The cardinal had then accompanied Jem to Rome, where they arrived on the thirteenth. Bishop Angelo tried to soothe the irate Corvinus:

> Most serene king, these details are unknown to me. . . . I think our lord [the pope] has the free disposition of the Turk [Jem], but his Holiness wants to hear the desires [*vota*] of the Christian princes in order the better and more wisely to consider the declaration of war, and may your Majesty deign to recall that our lord [the pope] strongly urges you not to put so much faith in informers [*delatores*], who always want to cause trouble.

"You may not believe, my lord legate, the things I say. They do not come from the person you are thinking of. I have my information from elsewhere and from a good source." Corvinus then showed the nuncio two letters from the Egyptian soldan, written in Arabic and Turkish, and gently pressed by the nuncio as to what the letters said, Corvinus seemed

---

[92] Burchard, *Diarium*, ed. Thuasne, I, 336–42, and ed. Celani, I, 254–58; Caoursin, in Thuasne, I, append., no. 34, pp. 545–46; Matteo Bosso, *Epistolae*, Mantua, 1498, no. 30, also in Thuasne, I, append., no. 33, pp. 527–28; Petrus Beneficiatus, in Phil. Bonanni, *Numismata pontificum romanorum*, I (Rome, 1699), 108–9, in Thuasne, I, append., no. 36, pp. 547–49; Sigismondo de'Conti, I (1883), 325–26; Bosio, II (1594), bk. XIV, pp. 411–12, based on Caoursin. According to Caoursin and Bosio, Jem Sultan kissed the papal foot, although very reluctantly, but this assertion is expressly belied by the eyewitness report of Burchard. *Cf.* Infessura, *Diaria*, ed. Tommasini (1890), pp. 241–42; Raynaldus, *Ann. eccl.*, ad ann. 1489, nos. 1–4, vol. XIX (1693), p. 393; Thuasne, *Djem-Sultan*, pp. 227–33, and append., nos. 11–12, pp. 422–25, two letters of Jacopo Botta, bishop of Tortona, to the duke of Milan, dated 14 March, 1489; Pontani, *Diario*, ed. Toni, in *RISS*, III-2 (1908), p. 69; Sa'd-ad-Dīn, in *Journal asiatique*, IX (1826, repr. 1965), 164–66; Pastor, *Gesch. d. Päpste*, III-1 (repr. 1955), 265–66. The contemporary accounts of Jem Sultan's reception in Rome vary considerably in detail.

[93] For Bishop Angelo of Orte's Hungarian mission, *cf.* the documents collected in Arch. Segr. Vaticano, Miscell., Arm. II, tom. 56, fols. 153r–202v, by mod. stamped enumeration. The bull, dated 1 September, 1488, nominating Angelo as nuncio "cum plena potestate legati de latere . . . ad nonnulla Germaniae, Hungariae, Poloniae, et Bohemiae . . . regna" is given in Raynaldus, *Ann. eccl.*, ad ann. 1488, no. 11, vol. XIX (1693), pp. 399b–400a.

[94] Miscell., Arm. II, tom. 56, fols. 183r, 184, and *cf.* fols. 189v–191.

[95] *Cf.* V. Lamansky, *Secrets d'état de Venise* (1884, repr. 1968), pp. 263–69, doc. dated 20 February, 1487 (O.S. 1486), de la Balue being the "Cardinalis Andegavensis" in the text. *Cf.* B. Buser, *Die Beziehungen der Mediceer zu Frankreich während der Jahre 1434–1494* . . . , Leipzig, 1879, pp. 260 ff., 270–71, and esp. Henri Forgeot, *Jean Balue, cardinal d'Angers (1421?–1491)*, Paris, 1895, pp. 142–47 (Bibliothèque de l'École des hautes études, fasc. 106).

to have second thoughts and changed the subject, *velut obaudiens alio sermonem divertit*.[96]

There were more problems in Hungary, however, than those to be found at the court. Conditions in the eastern lands that bordered on Turkey were unsettled. Hungarian bishops sought the nuncio's advice about the treatment "of wives whose husbands or of husbands whose wives were slaves [*servi*] of the Turkish enemy." Concubinage was often the consequence of connubial separation. The question was whether the sacraments could be given to those who persisted in such concubinage. Husbands or wives might be held indefinitely by the Turks. Since their spouses were no more successful in practicing sexual continence than in securing the release of their absent partners, "if the sacraments should be denied to them, they threaten that they will migrate to the Turks, and, as your Holiness knows, going over to the Turks is easy for Hungarians and Slavs."[97] The nuncio believed that such cases should be referred to Rome for settlement.

Matthias Corvinus had fared well during these latter years. As a result of his third war with Frederick III, he had occupied Vienna in June, 1485, making it his capital, and had thereafter overrun Styria, Carinthia, and Carniola. A truce had been arranged, however, as we have noted, between Frederick and Corvinus (on 19 February, 1490). It was to last until 8 September, but less than two months after its negotiation Corvinus died (on 6 April, 1490). Frederick's son Maximilian was soon hastening eastward to regain Vienna and the rest of the Hapsburg domains.[98]

For almost seven years Jem Sultan had been a captive of the Hospitallers in France. His imprisonment at the Vatican would last almost as long. Through all the years he spent in Rome, however, no less than through those he had spent in Auvergne, Jem never ceased personally to excite the liveliest curiosity. Nor did his political importance diminish, as we shall have ample occasion to note, for he remained the major figure around whom any crusade could be organized with the ostensible purpose of driving the "usurper" Bayazid II from Istanbul and from Europe. Although Jem was considerably younger than his brother, he claimed to be the Conqueror's true heir inasmuch as Bayazid had been born before their father's accession to the throne.[99] Those who held him in their power liked to regard him as the Grand Turk.

According to Caoursin, Jem Sultan was twenty-eight years old at the time of his flight, and so would have been thirty-five when he came to Rome in 1489. Sigismondo de' Conti in fact gives his age as thirty-five, but Matteo Bosso thought he was about forty. Jem's corpulence made him look older than he was. When he arrived in Rome, he was actually twenty-nine, having been born on 22 December, 1459. Tall and strong in appearance, Jem gave an impression of cruelty, and was easily moved to anger. Caoursin says that Jem had a small mouth, large lips, and blue eyes (*oculis . . . ceruleis*) with heavy eyebrows, aquiline nose, dark complexion, and a thin, well-trimmed beard. Obesity made him ungainly in gait. The painter Mantegna, who used to see him at the Vatican, thought he walked like an elephant. Nevertheless, he preserved the agility of youth, and was said to be an expert horseman. His voice was shrill, especially when aroused, but he was usually taciturn. He loved to eat, and stoked food as though his stomach were a furnace, says Caoursin, who observes that Jem ate and drank "more avidly than becomes a prince." Mantegna states that he had five meals a day, and slept a while after each. Caoursin says that Jem avoided wine unless it was flavored with aromatic spices, but Mantegna states that he was addicted to Bacchus. He was especially fond of fruit and of water heavily sugared; he ate some bread and a good deal of meat. He perspired freely, but bathed frequently, liked to swim,

[96] Miscell., Arm. II, tom. 56, fols. 184^v, 185^r. Bishop Angelo of Orte's letter was written to Innocent VIII in June, 1489. On Jem Sultan and Cardinal de la Balue, see Burchard, *Diarium*, ed. Thuasne, I, 335–36, and ed. Celani, I, 252–54, with notes.

[97] Miscell., Arm. II, tom. 56, fol. 185: ". . . et ut novit Sanctitas vestra facilis Hungaris et Sclavis ad Turchos est transitio."

[98] Raynaldus, *Ann. eccl.*, ad ann. 1490, nos. 10–14, vol. XIX (1693), pp. 399–400, and ad ann. 1491, nos. 11–12, pp. 404b–405a, from Bonfinius; Schneider, *Raimund Peraudi*, pp. 14–19; Gottlob, *Histor. Jahrbuch*, VI, 453; Ulmann, *Kaiser Maximilian I.*, I, 85 ff.; Fraknói, *Mathias Corvinus* (1891), pp. 265–66, 270; Gyula Rázsó, *Die Feldzüge des Königs Matthias Corvinus in Niederösterreich, 1477–1490* (1973), pp. 16–23 (a brochure of 36 pp. published by the Heeresgeschichtliches Museum in Vienna, on which *cf.*, above, Chapter 12, note 50).

[99] So Caoursin, in Thuasne, *Burchardi diarium*, I, 535, represents Jem Sultan as arguing to the Grand Master d'Aubusson at the time of the flight to Rhodes.

and had no compunction about doing so naked. He enjoyed sumptuous dress. According to Caoursin, Jem was a rigorous Moslem, refusing to tolerate drunkenness among any of his followers. He found it hard to stay in one place, and would even sleep now in one room, now in another, and sometimes on the terrace. He was well educated, with an excellent knowledge of Turkish and Persian. He enjoyed poetry. His mother, says Caoursin, was a Serbian princess. Despite his obesity and the fact that he was a homeless exile, Jem managed a grave and regal dignity. Although at first the Curia Romana thought of housing Jem at Spoleto or Orvieto, the decision was finally made to keep him at the Vatican.[100] Bayazid was believed to be constantly plotting against his life. The lordly son of a great father, Jem Sultan lived like a prince. According to Sigismondo de' Conti, it cost the papacy 15,000 ducats a year to maintain him.[101] The pope was not complaining. He had great plans for Jem.

In western eyes the succession in the Ottoman state had more than once appeared a precarious affair. It seems hard to believe that Jem Sultan's chances of displacing his brother were more than the illusion which made his exile bearable (and he was melancholy enough), but inevitably Jem had a following among all the politically articulate groups which were disaffected under Bayazid's rule. As time passed, long after Jem's death, this disaffection made possible the *coup d'état* of Bayazid's son Selim, who dethroned his father and set aside his brother Ahmed (in 1512). These events lay more than twenty years in the future. In the meantime Bayazid was having trouble in the East, and was not well prepared to withstand large-scale attacks from the West. He was at war with the Egyptian Soldan Ka'itbey, whose army had defeated the Turks in 1486. Bayazid had then lost Adana and Tarsus. Although these places were recovered two years later, they were lost again when the Egyptians scored another victory over the Turks in mid-August, 1488, in a bloody battle fought between the mountains of Amanus and the gulf of Issus.

On 28 May (1488) the Hospitallers and townsfolk of Rhodes had watched an Ottoman fleet sail past their island, headed for the coasts of Syria, where ten of the galleys were later lost in a storm. On the return voyage the Turks sailed past Rhodes again on 8 September. They fired a long salvo of artillery in greeting to the Rhodian garrison, which responded with shots from the many cannon mounted in the defense towers along the walls. The Turkish commander sent his cousin ashore with a note conveying "mille saluti" (the note was written in Italian) and some valuable gifts in a courtesy call on the grand master, who gave the Turks an urbane reception. The fleet continued on its way to Istanbul. The Hospitallers had naturally watched the great but indecisive struggle between Turkey and Egypt with much interest. On 4 September the grand master wrote the pope that Jem Sultan was the cause of the war between the eastern powers, both of which had sent embassies to Rhodes. Ka'itbey worked hard for a western alliance both before and after his victory, and was most anxious to have Jem sent to Egypt.[102]

---

[100] On 13 August, 1489, the Venetian Senate wrote Onfreo Giustinian, bailie in Istanbul, to inform the sultan that his brother Jem was then being housed "in el proprio palazo de la Sanctità del Papa allozato in certi albergi belli, commodi, et honorifici, separati dala habitation dela dicta Sanctità, custodito molto bene da bon numero de persone notabile et de degne conditione, dove el vive honoratamente et cum bon contento pigliandose quotidianamente di piaceri delectevoli de diverse sorte come se convien a signori et reducendose ale fiate a solazo nel zardino del dicto palazo tuta volta sempre ben et seguramente accompagnato cum assai honore . . ." (Sen. Secreta, Reg. 34, fol. 26^{v} [38^{v}], and *cf.* fols. 42^{r} [54^{r}], 51^{v} [63^{v}], 58^{v} [70^{v}]).

[101] Caoursin, in Thuasne, *Burchardi diarium*, I, append., no. 34, pp. 537–38, from whom Bosio, II (1594), bk. XIII, pp. 373–74, derives his description of Jem Sultan (at the time of the flight to Rhodes). Also Matteo Bosso, in Thuasne, I, append., no. 33, pp. 527–28; Sigismondo de'Conti, I, 328, who says that Jem's quarters in the Vatican palace were adorned with gold and silver and looked out on a vineyard and pleasant gardens. Mantegna's description of Jem comes in a letter of 15 June, 1489, to Marquis Francesco Gonzaga of Mantua (G. Bottari, ed., *Raccolta di lettere sulla pittura*, etc., VIII [Milan, 1825], 23–25, cited by Thuasne, *Djem-Sultan*, pp. 245–46, and Pastor, *Gesch. d. Päpste*, III-1 [repr. 1955], 266–68). Mantegna was then working in the Belvedere. In comparing Mantegna's description of Jem with that drawn by Caoursin, one must remember that about eight years had elapsed from Jem's landing at Rhodes to the time that Mantegna saw him at the Vatican. James Dennistoun, *Memoirs of the Dukes of Urbino*, ed. Edward Hutton, II (London and New York, 1909), 297–98, gives Mantegna's description of Jem, which he regards as amusing "but obviously caricatured."

[102] Bosio, II (1594), bk. XIV, pp. 403–11. According to the reports received by the Hospitallers, the Turks suffered 30,000 casualties, and the Mamluks, 8,000. *Cf.* Raynaldus, *Ann. eccl.*, ad ann. 1488, no. 9, vol. XIX (1693), p. 389; Thuasne, *Djem-Sultan*, pp. 198–200, 254–55; Delaborde, *Expédition de Charles VIII* (1888), p. 201; Huart, in *Encyclopaedia of Islām*, I (1908), 685b. On 4 September, 1488,

Such was the background to Innocent VIII's plans for a crusade through the year 1489. The preceding year part of the fleet which Sultan Bayazid had prepared for an attack upon Syria, during the great Turkish campaign against the Mamluks, had actually been diverted to an attack upon Malta, which had led Ferdinand of Aragon himself to get a fleet ready for the island's defense. It was feared the sultan might try to establish a Turkish haven in Malta, whence he might attack Sicily and Italy.[103] Bayazid's non-aggression pact with the Hospitallers was obviously of limited utility, and of course the papacy was the archenemy of the Porte. Papal documents usually characterized Islam and the Turks in the most insulting terms. We have already seen that an Egyptian envoy had been one of the first to greet Jem Sultan as he was entering Rome. Although this worthy was hardly more willing than Jem to kiss the papal foot,[104] he urged Innocent to declare war on Bayazid.

Bosio says that much was made of the Egyptian envoy at the Curia Romana, and the pope sent a nuncio to Ka'itbey. Bayazid was worried. Promptly sending an envoy of his own to Rhodes, he protested to the grand master that the transfer of his brother Jem Sultan from France to the Curia was a breach of the pact between the Porte and the Order. The hostile intent of the papacy was obvious, the envoy indicated, from the presence of the Egyptian embassy in Rome. Knowing the disunion among the Christian princes, and how little prospect there really was of a crusade, the grand master sent the sultan various reassurances, noting that the pope had no forces of his own, and depended on the princes. The king of France was very powerful; in his hands Jem might be dangerous to Bayazid. The way for Bayazid to have peace, which he said he wanted, was to keep the Turkish armada from venturing into the Mediterranean, for the dispatch of galleys from Gallipoli was the surest way to unite the Christian princes.[105]

The pope kept searching for a way to unite the Christian princes, and (as d'Aubusson had acknowledged to Bayazid) it was no easy matter. It was an age of cloak-and-dagger intrigue. The poisoner lurked in the shadows. On 7 May, 1490, one Cristoforo Castracano, also called Macrino, onetime lord of Castel Leone in the district of Fano in the March of Ancona, was condemned to death for seeking to poison the fountain in the courtyard of the Belvedere, whence water was drawn both for the pope's table and for Jem Sultan's. Two years before, papal forces had expelled Macrino from his fief, which was given to another. Infessura reports the rumor current at the time (*ut fertur*) that Macrino had in desperation repaired to the Gran Turco in Istanbul, where he was well received and four times granted an imperial audience. Bayazid allegedly gave him large sums of money, two garments of gold brocade, and a diamond worth 400 ducats. He is said also to have promised Macrino the city of Negroponte and the command of two hundred armed galleys, as well as providing various other inducements,

> that the said Macrino should betake himself to Rome and throw a certain poison, which he took from Constantinople in a small ampule, into the fountain just outside the Porta Viridaria, hard by the papal palace, for from this fountain the chief occupants of the palace received their water, especially our most holy lord [the pope] and the Turk, second son of the Grand Turk [Mehmed II] and brother of the aforesaid sultan of Constantinople. . . .

---

the Grand Master d'Aubusson sent a report of the Egyptian victory to the pope (Pauli, *Codice diplomatico*, II [1737], no. XLVII, pp. 446–47, apparently composed by Caoursin): Bosio incorporates the substance of this report in his account.

[103] Raynaldus, *Ann. eccl.*, ad ann. 1488, no. 9, vol. XIX, p. 389a.

[104] Infessura, *Diaria*, ed. Tommasini, p. 242. About fifteen months earlier, on 20 December, 1487, the Florentine government had directed its consul in Pera to inform Sultan Bayazid—lest he give the fact a sinister explanation—that an Egyptian envoy had come to Florence to negotiate a new agreement concerning Florentine trade in Egypt and Syria. The envoy had brought with him a giraffe and a lion as gifts to the Florentines. The giraffe excited a good deal of curiosity. From Florence the envoy was going to Naples, and thence back to Egypt. See Giuseppe Müller, ed., *Relazioni delle città toscane coll'Oriente cristiano e coi Turchi*, Florence, 1879, pt. I, no. CCIII, p. 237; Thuasne, *Djem-Sultan*, pp. 174–75, with refs. to numerous sources; Luca Landucci, *Diario fiorentino*, ed. Iodoco del Badia, Florence, 1883, pp. 52–53, trans. A. de Rosen Jervis, London, 1927, p. 44.

[105] Bosio, II (1594), bk. XIV, pp. 413–14; Raynaldus, *Ann. eccl.*, ad ann. 1489, no. 4, vol. XIX (1693), p. 393b, and ad ann. 1490, no. 1, p. 397b. The French were said at this time to be especially mindful of their role in defending Rhodes against the Turks, to desire an effective league with the Italian states to combat the Turks, and to be offering prayers, organizing processions, etc., "quia Turchus inimicus fidei facit magnos conatus et apparatus ad usurpandam Christianitatem" (Arch. Segr. Vaticano, Miscell., Arm. II, tom. 56, fols. 220^r, 226^r, 226^v–227^r, by mod. stamped enumeration, *et alibi*).

The poison had the virtue of killing in five days, not sooner.

The indiscreet Macrino had been apprehended in Venice before he even got to Rome, where he was sent to receive justice at the pope's hands. Securing possession of Macrino appears to have been one of Innocent VIII's major preoccupations during December, 1489. Macrino confessed his guilt. He claimed, however, that the sultan had recruited many men to perform the task in which he had failed, "so that the pope and the others could hardly escape." Macrino stated that there were others involved in his own conspiracy, whose names Infessura did not know, but among whom was said to have been the Dominican friar who had poisoned Matthias Corvinus of Hungary on the Wednesday of Holy Week. (But 6 April, 1490, fell on a Tuesday, and Corvinus was not poisoned.) Macrino was tortured and executed. His body was drawn and quartered, and (to encourage other would-be assassins) the four parts were hung at different gates of the city. For four or five days after Macrino's cruel death, according to Infessura, Rome and its environs were enveloped in dark clouds and swept by torrential rains. There were those who attributed the phenomena to the wrath of Christ, for Macrino had been dealt with contrary to the example He had set of mercy, restraint, and humility.[106]

Although Infessura informs us that nothing commendable happened in Rome during May and June, 1489—the city was merely the scene of the most scandalous robberies, homicides, and acts of sacrilege[107]—Innocent VIII had issued a brief on 8 May, summoning representatives of the European powers to meet in Rome to make plans for the crusade against the Turks.[108] Other briefs were dispatched in early December, setting the following 25 March (1490) as the opening day for the congress. One of them, for example, dated 7 December (1489) was sent to Raymond Peraudi for forwarding to King Casimir IV of Poland, urging him to send plenipotentiaries to the congress to give counsel on the Turkish problem and to help prepare for the crusade. Peraudi himself wrote the Polish king from Linz on 20 January, 1490, sending his letter along with the papal brief. He informed Casimir that Pope Innocent, from the first day of his pontificate to that very hour, had thought of nothing but how he might defend Christendom against the Turks. Now the possession of Jem Sultan offered an extraordinary opportunity. Jem had promised that, if he acquired his father's throne through the Christians' help, he would withdraw the Turks from Europe and even relinquish Constantinople. Innocent had therefore sent legates, Peraudi told the king, to all the European courts to get them to stop fighting with one another and to unite their peoples in the common cause of the crusade. Peraudi said that he had himself gone to France and then to Germany; the result had been the establishment of peace between Charles VIII and Maximilian. There was peace in Brittany, Flanders, England, and Brabant. Now he was working at a peace between the Emperor Frederick III and Matthias Corvinus of Hungary. He did not doubt that they would soon compose their differences. In closing, he implored Casimir as a good Catholic and pious king to heed the pope's request. In a postscript to his letter on the same day, Peraudi added that he had just had an audience with the Emperor Frederick and Maximilian. They wanted the congress postponed until the middle of April. Peraudi stated that the pope would be asked to open the congress at the beginning of May, and he hoped that Casimir would see to it that his envoys were in Rome on time.[109]

---

[106] Infessura, *Diaria*, ed. Tommasini, pp. 254–56; Lamansky, *Secrets d'état*, pp. 230–32; Sigismondo de' Conti, II (1883), 39; Thuasne, *Djem-Sultan*, pp. 261–63, 268–70, and append., no. 14, pp. 428–29, a letter of Michelozzi to Lorenzo de' Medici, dated at Rome on 16 February, 1490; and Pastor, *Gesch. d. Päpste*, III-1 (repr. 1955), 268–69. Macrino, also called Magrino, was a cousin of Boccolino, and had been implicated in the seizure of Osimo. He had confessed his criminal intentions in Venice and sought pardon of the papal legate; it seems not unlikely that his repentance was sincere, and that he need not have been put to death. For Innocent VIII's account of Macrino's treachery, see the brief of 3 February, 1490, to Francesco Gonzaga, in the Arch. di Stato di Mantova, Arch. Gonzaga, Busta 834, and the bull *Detestanda iniquorum perversitas* of 1 May, 1492, in the Arch. Segr. Vaticano, Reg. Vat. 693, fol. 201^{v}, by mod. stamped enumeration.

[107] Infessura, *Diaria*, ed. Tommasini, pp. 242–45.

[108] Johann Schneider, "Der Türkenzugscongress in Rom (3. Juni bis 30. Juli 1490)," in the *Programm des städtischen Realgymnasiums zu Gumbinnen* (1893), p. 4, cited by Pastor, *Gesch. d. Päpste*, III-1 (repr. 1955), 269, and *cf.* Thuasne, *Djem-Sultan*, pp. 254–55.

[109] Arch. Segr. Vaticano, Arm. XXXII, tom. 21, fols. 107^{v}–108^{v}, 109^{r} [cited above], by mod. stamped enumeration; Gottlob, in *Histor. Jahrbuch*, VI (1885), 453–54; and *cf.* Pastor, *Gesch. d. Päpste*, III-1 (repr. 1955), 269–70. Rather than a general crusade, Casimir had preferred that the

As the month of March, 1490, advanced, Innocent VIII made a point of announcing that he had written the princes months before, warning them that the Ottoman sultan was preparing a fleet, and urging them to send their envoys to Rome before the Annunciation of the Blessed Virgin (25 March) to deal with the task of setting in motion an expedition "contra Turcum." He hoped that the execution of crusading plans could be easily provided for "by means of the Turk [Jem Sultan]," says Burchard, "who dwells with his Holiness, true heir of his late father [Mehmed II], much beloved by his subjects, and the bitter enemy of his brother who now rules the Turkish empire. . . ."[110] When 25 March came, after the celebration of a solemn mass of the Holy Spirit in the Sistine Chapel, Pietro Mansi of Vicenza, the young bishop of Cesena, preached an eloquent sermon before the pope, the cardinals, and the envoys of the Christian powers.

Pietro spoke of the pope's sleepless nights spent in anxious worry over the Turkish menace and of his finally successful efforts to secure peace in Italy. He remarked upon the papal summons to the Christian princes to meet in a great expedition against the Turks, and mentioned the large number of ambassadors who had come to Rome for the congress. God had bestowed great power upon the princes in order that they might employ it to rescue vast numbers of Christians from the crushing servitude under which they were living in the lands conquered by the Turks. Every Christian must do what he could; otherwise he was no Christian; if he could make some contribution to the crusade, his very salvation depended on it. Was it not better for a man to use the seven or eight decades of his life (at the most) striving for the well-being of Christendom, for Christ and eternal life, than to waste them in pleasure and self-indulgence leading to everlasting damnation and the unquenchable fires of hell? Pietro recalled the glorious days of the First Crusade, when about 300,000 men (he said) took the cross at Urban II's appeal, and Godfrey of Bouillon with his brother Baldwin of Boulogne, Hugh le Maisné of France, and Bohemond performed their heroic exploits in winning counties, a principality, and a kingdom in the Holy Land. He spoke also of the leaders and achievements of the later crusades, "quae omnia numerare dies non sufficeret." To another such expedition and to a like glory Innocent VIII was now summoning all who would aspire to the demonstration of their faith and the attainment of life eternal.

Lavishing a wealth of classical and biblical allusions upon his text, Pietro reviewed the widespread conquests which the Moslems had made over the centuries during the periods of their greatest strength. But now their forces were no longer invincible; badly shaken by the defeats the Egyptians had inflicted on them, the Turks seemed to have lost all their warlike prowess. Jem Sultan, whose person the pope had acquired at great expense, was the rightful ruler of the Turks, who loved him and desired his return. It was Jem whom his usurping brother feared like the plague. Jem was to accompany the coming crusade, "non quidem ut vobis proficiat, sed ut rem suam agat." From the Ottoman brothers' hatred of each other the Christians might derive great benefits. Delay was perilous, however, for the Moslems—Turks, Egyptians, and others—might compose their differences. Then they would again be laying waste to Christian lands, burning cities, profaning churches, destroying families, violating women, enslaving multitudes, and committing other enormities which Pietro shuddered to mention or to contemplate. If this should happen, Pietro told his auditors, their generation would be marked with everlasting infamy.

Ending with an appeal to the Hungarians and Germans, French and Italians, the Poles, English, and Scots, he lamented their civil wars, and urged them to mount the highways of faith and fame: "Remember what your ancestors did! Rewin yourselves that holy city of Jerusalem, the sacred sepulcher of our Savior. . . . Leave to posterity deeds worthy of all praise and imitation! . . ."[111] After the papal

papacy subsidize Polish efforts against the Turks (*ibid.*, p. 269, note 1). The date for the congress was set "circa finem Marcii proxime futuri ad festum Annunciationis beate Marie Virginis" (from Innocent's bull, *tom. cit.*, fol. 107^{v}), i.e., 25 March, 1490. Note also E. Carusi, *Dispacci e lettere di Giacomo Gherardi* . . . [1487–1490], p. 401, and *cf.* p. 403.

[110] Burchard, *Diarium*, ed. Thuasne, I, 399–400, and ed. Celani, I, 300. On the pope's efforts to protect Jem Sultan against would-be assassins (of whom there were allegedly several besides Macrino) and on his efforts to maintain Jem's prestige, *cf.* Thuasne, *Djem-Sultan*, pp. 243 ff.

[111] Pietro Mansi's sermon of 25 March, 1490, is given in the appendix to Sigismondo de'Conti, II, 413–23; Burchard, *Diarium*, ed. Thuasne, I, 400, and ed. Celani, I, 300–1; Thuasne, *Djem-Sultan*, p. 266. Mansi died in 1504 at fifty years of age; his sepulchral monument is still preserved in the church of Aracoeli.

benediction, Pietro Mansi announced a seven years' indulgence for the crusade. His sermon had been eloquent but unrealistic, more likely to win the applause of curial officials than of the lay envoys to the congress.

The congress was well attended by representatives of the major powers, but the Venetians had sent no envoy to Rome to participate in its deliberations, anxious to keep their hard-won peace with the Porte and to preserve "la pace et el quieto et felicità de la sua Signoria."[112] At an assembly of the cardinals and envoys held in the apostolic palace on 3 June, Innocent VIII reviewed the measures he had tried to take in the past to promote the crusade. He emphasized the effort and funds he had expended to get custody of Jem Sultan, who was always regarded as the key to Sultan Bayazid's defeat. The tide, in Levantine affairs, had come in, and the Christian powers must not allow their chance of success to recede with the next change of circumstance. The envoys must plan the size, character, and places of recruitment of the military and naval forces. They must study all problems relating to the supreme and subordinate commands; the probable costs of the expedition and the best sources of money to meet them; the time to start, and the likely duration of, operations both by land and by sea; and they must study all other questions of supply and armament, strategy, and the apportionment of expenses among the various states involved. Thought should also be given to the desirability of the pope's imposing a peace or truce *auctoritate apostolica*, following the precedent of Sixtus IV, upon the Christian princes to make practicable a joint expedition against the Turks. Innocent was prepared to go on this expedition himself. He wanted all the princes to read the history of the crusades and note the glorious deeds performed by their ancestors, so that they might emulate in their time the heroic exploits of earlier generations.[113] This was an old exhortation; Europe had been hearing it for years. Only the papal custody of a sultan's brother was new.

After due deliberation and debate the envoys replied in writing to the papal instructions and appeal. First of all, they expressed their gratitude and satisfaction that the pope was anxious to launch a crusade, and that he had succeeded in gaining custody of Jem Sultan, of whose utility to the enterprise everyone was convinced, and of whose person, the envoys said, the most careful guard should be maintained against the intrigues of Bayazid. The envoys believed that three great forces (*exercitus*) would be needed, two land armies and a sufficient fleet. Of these the Holy See and the Italian states should supply one; the Germans, Hungarians, Bohemians, and Poles, the second; and the French, Spanish, Portuguese, Navarrese, Scots, and English should provide the third. As for the high command, the German envoys maintained that if the aged Frederick III or his son Maximilian, king of the Romans, should take part in the expedition, one or

[112] From a dispatch of the Senate to the Venetian bailie in Istanbul, dated 11 March, 1490, in Thuasne, *Djem-Sultan*, p. 265, note 2, and to be found in Sen. Secreta, Reg. 34, fol. 58 [70].

[113] *Considerationes generales concepte supra* [*sic*] *introducenda materia expeditionis decernende contra Turcum*, in Arch. Segr. Vaticano, Miscell., Arm. II, tom. 56, fols. 374^v–376^r, by mod. stamped enumeration: ". . . Optat et hortatur principes et potentatus Christianos ut unusquisque legat annales antiquos et que gloriose gesta sunt per eorum progenitores ad illorum imitationem se componant." The text of the "general considerations" may also be found in the Miscell., Arm. II, tom. 29, fols. 47^r–59, and, *ibid.*, Arm. II, tom. 20 (Politicorum Varia, XX), fols. 106^v–118^v, and it occurs, with numerous errors of the copyist, in the Bibl. Apost. Vaticana, Cod. lat. 13,451 (a late seventeenth-century MS.). Note in general the course of events and discussions outlined in Raynaldus, *Ann. eccl.*, ad ann. 1488, nos. 9–11; ad ann. 1489, nos. 1–4; ad ann. 1490, nos. 1–9; and ad ann. 1491, nos. 13–14, vol. XXX (1887), pp. 147–49, 154–55, 162–64, and 174–75.

On 12 June, 1490, Innocent VIII issued the crusading bull *Salvatoris et domini nostri*, which sought for "omnia nobis possibilia remedia ad resistendum infidelibus omnibus et presertim nephandissimis Turchis" (Reg. Vat. 693, fols. 164^v–167^v by mod. stamped enumeration, "datum Rome apud Sanctum Petrum, anno etc. MCCCCLXXXX, pridie Idus Iunii, pont. nostri anno sexto"). The bull makes clear that the surest means of preparation against the Turks was the collection of ample funds, in which activity the faithful Gratian of Villanova was apparently doing his best. *Cf.*, *ibid.*, fols. 169^r–170^v, the bull *Turcos crucis* of 17 July, 1490, imposing the crusading tithe in France and Burgundy, "datum Rome . . . . , anno etc. MCCCCLXXXX, sextodecimo Kal. Augusti, [pont. nostri] anno sexto." *Cf.* J. Schneider, "Der Türkenzugscongress in Rom (3. Juni bis 30. Juli 1490)," in the *Programm des städtischen Realgymnasiums zu Gumbinnen* (1893), pp. 5–6, cited by Pastor, *Gesch. d. Päpste*, III-1 (repr. 1955), 270–71; Sigismondo de' Conti, II, append., pp. 424–25. Seventeen years later (in a letter of 9 July, 1507) Pope Julius II recalled the futility of this congress to Henry VII of England (Jas. Gairdner, ed., *Letters and Papers . . . of Richard III and Henry VII*, II [London, 1863], no. XXXI, pp. 172–73).

the other should be chosen generalissimo. But the other envoys preferred that, once the recruiting had been done, the princes should elect the "captain-general," with the advice and consent of the pope, although each of the three armies should have its own elected commander.

It was also felt that, if conceivably possible, the pope himself should accompany the expedition for a number of reasons, among them to settle "differences and discords if (which God forbid) some should arise in the expeditionary force." Each nation should support its own army, taxing both clergy and laity for the required funds, concerning which matter they said further discussion would be necessary. Provision would have to be made for replacements, especially if some disaster should overtake more than a third of any given army. The envoys were of the opinion that the expedition should last three years. The most binding oaths must be exacted of the proper persons that all the armies would set out against the Turk in the same month and even, if possible, on the same day. The targets for attack should be planned in secret communications among the princes, in consultation with the pope. At the outset it seemed likely, however, that the Germans and their allies should go through Hungary and Wallachia to make their attack upon the Turks. The pope would have to secure them a safe transit through Christian territories. The fleet would assail the Turks in the Morea, Negroponte, and the islands. The French and Spanish, with a contingent of the Italians, should lay waste the general region of Albania.

The army of the "German nation" might gather at Vienna; the other forces at Ancona, Brindisi, or even Messina in Sicily. His Holiness was reminded of other details to be attended to—safe-conducts to be procured for the advance and return of the armies; pledges to be exacted of all troops to inflict no damage on persons or properties in the areas through which they passed; and the levying of taxes to support the enterprise (*gabelle et impositiones, passagia, pedagia, aliaque onera*). The need for food and other supplies must be anticipated at all major points along the lines of march. Much study would have to be given to the division and government of whatever territories might be won from the Turks. The Moslem states in Africa would have to be prevented from attacking the southern reaches of Europe while the Christian forces were engaged in the East. Peace in Europe, the envoys concluded, was the indispensable prelude to the crusade.[114]

On 26 July (1490) Innocent VIII commended the envoys for their diligent study of the problems requiring solution before the crusade could get under way. He emphasized again the great value of Jem Sultan's accompanying the expedition, and cautioned against the evil and perilous consequences of delay. Every day "new men" were coming to the fore among the Turks who had never seen Jem, did not know him, and entertained no affection for him. Matthias Corvinus had already warned the Curia of this fact when he was seeking custody of Jem. Jem was mortal. He could die in the merest moment (*minimo momento*). The longer he was absent from Turkey, the less ardent he was to go back, and as the hope of his return diminished among his own people, there was a corresponding decline in his reputation. His Holiness was in general agreement with the envoys on the necessity of recruiting three armies, dealing effectively with the manifold questions of finance and logistics, getting sufficient arms and cannon, enlisting competent navigators and seamen, and so on. Basing his opinion on previous estimates for the crusade, Innocent thought that 15,000 helmeted knights, for each of whom "we should reckon five horses,"[115] together with 80,000 footsoldiers would suffice.

---

[114] *Deliberationes et advisamenta oratorum ultramontanorum super generalibus considerationibus S.D.N. de expeditione contra Turcos iuxta ea que pro nunc potuerunt cogitare*, in Arch. Segr. Vaticano, Miscell., Arm. II, tom. 56, fols. 376ʳ–379ʳ, by mod. stamped enumeration; *cf.* Bibl. Apost. Vaticana, Cod. lat. 13,451, fols. 14ᵛ–17ᵛ; and see Sigismondo de' Conti, II, append., pp. 426–28. Sigismondo's own account (*ibid.*, pp. 1–3) is merely a summary of the memorandum which the envoys presented to Innocent VIII. *Cf.* Thuasne, *Djem-Sultan*, pp. 266–68, and Pastor, *Gesch. d. Päpste*, III-1 (repr. 1955), 271–72.

[115] *Responsa S.D.N. domini Innocentii PP. VIII ad capitula dictorum oratorum ultramontanorum super materia expeditionis contra Turcos, die lune 26 Iulii 1490*, in the Miscellanea, Arm. II, tom. 56, esp. fols. 380ʳ–381ᵛ, by mod. stamped enumeration (and *cf.* Sigismondo de' Conti, II, append., p. 431): ". . . videretur aliquibus huic sancte expeditioni sufficere posse quindecim millia armigerorum, quos alio vocabulo elmettos vocamus, ut pro quolibet armigero seu elmetto computemus quinque equos . . ." (slightly different text in Miscell., Arm. II, tom. 20, fol. 111ᵛ). Sigismondo, II, 3, says that Innocent proposed 20,000 men-at-arms and 100,000 foot. The text of the *Responsa* appears also in the Miscellanea, Arm. II, tom. 29, fols. 61ʳ–86ᵛ, and Cod. Vat. lat. 13,451, fols. 18ʳ–25ᵛ. There are variations of wording in the several copies.

The princes must decide, however, both upon how many men were necessary and how many they could maintain. As for the generalissimo (*imperator*) or captain-general of the host, the pope said that the emperor or the king of the Romans, since they were the defenders of the Church, should take the supreme command if either one went on the crusade. After the fashion of his revered predecessors, Innocent would do everything he could to promote the great enterprise, and he would himself go into the Levant if the affairs of the Church and the papal states allowed him to do so. The princes should levy the lay assessments on their people; the pope would see to taxing the clergy for the sacred war, which he thought would last five years rather than three. The first campaign should begin next year, for one could hope that the victorious soldan of Egypt (*Babilonia*) would thus be encouraged also to attack the Turks. Innocent replied in detail to every article in the envoys' memorandum—the targets of attack, places of assembly, safe-conducts, financial imposts, food and supplies, guarding and governing conquered territories, restraint of the Moslem states in Africa, and the preservation of peace in Europe. But he lamented the envoys' failure to come to Rome with full powers to commit their principals. They had referred too much "ad approbationem principum vestrorum." His Holiness had requested and vehemently desired that the envoys come to the congress "cum mandatis plenis consulendi et tractandi ac deliberandi:" "Therefore we exhort you . . . and by the passion of our Redeemer . . . , whose cause is at stake, we enjoin upon you, if by the authority of your commissions you cannot now proceed further, that either at your return or by letters you so incite your princes to undertake and carry through this sacred expedition that they do not allow this advantage of time and Jem to be lost. . . ."[116]

Once more papal plans for a crusade were failing. Matthias Corvinus had died before the crusading congress was fully assembled in Rome. During his early years Corvinus had had to suppress uprisings in Hungary, but when he had a free hand, he had turned his attention toward Bosnia and the West. He had fought with the Germans, Czechs, and Poles far more than with the Turks. In the early spring of 1490 he was not yet fifty, at the height of his success. He had had experience of land warfare with the Turks, and no one had stood to gain as much as he by a Christian victory over the Ottoman regime in the Balkans. He had built up a standing army supported by a broadly based taxation. He might have used Jem Sultan to advantage. He might have embarked upon an anti-Turkish offensive. His failure to secure possession of Jem's person, however, had strained Hungarian relations with the Holy See, and had increased his bitterness toward Venice, which boded ill for Innocent's crusading hopes. But now Corvinus was dead; the strongest figure in eastern Europe was gone. With the accession of the feeble Ladislas II of Bohemia to the Hungarian throne, the rapacious and self-seeking Magyar nobles took control of the kingdom. Hungary descended into a feudal morass. Taxes were no longer collected, the standing army melted away, the towns dwindled, and the peasantry was oppressed. The bulwark protecting central Europe against the Turks was broken.

---

[116] *Responsa Innocentii VIII*, in Miscell., Arm. II, tom. 56, fols. 379r–388r, by mod. stamped enumeration, and *cf.* Sigismondo de' Conti, II, 3–4, and append., pp.429–36. Since the fall of Constantinople the Turks had enlarged their territories, increased their power and financial resources, and improved their weaponry and their skill in navigation, but Innocent believed that the years had diminished the Christians' striking force (*Responsa*, in Miscell., Arm. II, tom. 56, fol. 381r): "Ita tamen ut etiam rebus antiquis accedat in consideratione imperii Constantinopolitani, totius Grecie ac tot regnorum et provinciarum occupatio facta per Turcum, cuius potentia non solum dominiis sed etiam armis, pecuniis ac novis machinarum et instrumentorum bellicorum formidabilibus inventionibus ac peritia navigandi et classis maritime robore mirabiliter ex patrum et avorum nostrorum memoria aucta, Christianorum autem viribus et occasione gerendi belli longo intervallo diminuta: Que consideratio forte maiores copias exposceret quam antea. . . ."

The difficulties of organizing a crusade at this time seemed insuperable, however, for as Innocent lamented in a bull of 24 July, 1490, parts of Bohemia and central Europe were still being wracked "propter guerras, incursiones et alias varias calamitates, quibus partes ille per hereticos et alios infideles iam pluribus et pluribus annis—proh dolor!—oppresse fuerunt" (Reg. Vat. 748, fol. 86r, by mod. stamped enumeration, "datum Rome apud Sanctum Petrum, anno etc. MCCCC nonagesimo, nono Kal. Augusti, pontificatus nostri anno sexto").

14. INNOCENT VIII AND ALEXANDER VI, CHARLES VIII AND FERRANTE I (1490–1494)

IN THE FIFTEENTH CENTURY the *respublica Christiana* was a religious and cultural concept in no way inconsistent with a growing national self-consciousness. Politically, the idea of Christendom marked communicants of the Latin Church off from non-Christians, most notably from the Moslems. Greek Orthodoxy, almost like Judaism, was no longer a military or political factor of large importance, and Europe was not yet concerned with either India or the Americas. From the time of Martin Luther, early in the following century, to which we shall come in the next volume, the *respublica Christiana* became divided into two or more religious camps, often at war with one another, but even so the concept of Christendom set off Catholic and Lutheran, Calvinist and Anglican from the Moslem inhabitants of the Ottoman empire, of Mamluk Egypt, Syria, and Palestine, and of Safavid Persia (Iran). On the whole, the Christians were religiously less tolerant than the Moslems. While all these competing groups or peoples were hostile to one another, fear of the Ottoman Turks was making Venetian and even papal embassies welcome in Cairo and at the court of the shah of Persia.

It is not surprising, however, that Ka'itbey, the soldan of Egypt, should have been much irritated by the determined war of Ferdinand and Isabella against the Moors in Spain. He threatened reprisals against Christians in Beirut, Damascus, and Alexandria, Jerusalem and Bethlehem, where Christian merchants and pilgrims were always to be found. To the soldan's protest Ferdinand replied that the cities and lands held by the Moslems in the Spains had belonged to his forebears (*maiores*), and that he was fighting a just war for the recovery of his possessions. He reminded Ka'itbey that there were many Moslems in Spain on whom vengeance would be taken for any harm that might come to Christians in Egypt and Syria.[1] For a while it looked as though the crusade might be losing its chief potential ally in the East, for Ka'itbey was as hostile to the Ottomans as the Christians were.

Anxious months passed at the Curia Romana. As usual important events on the ecclesiastical calendar were solemnly celebrated under the watchful eyes of Johann Burchard, the master of ceremonies. The envoys of the Italian states and foreign powers brought Pope Innocent no commitments from their principals as to armed participation in the great expedition against the Turks, but they continued their customary disputes about place and precedence at all papal functions. In late May and early June (1490) their altercations became intolerable, and more than once the pope had to intervene to effect a settlement. Finally, on 4 June, his Holiness informed Burchard that he had decided to re-enact a provision of Pius II "in which it is stated that envoys are to be accounted 'lobbyists' after six months, not envoys."[2] With reduced privileges and rights of entry, various persons would presumably be less of a nuisance at the Curia. Shortly afterwards, however, Burchard left for his home in the diocese of Strassburg, and a most unfortunate gap of fourteen months appears at this point in his diary.[3]

---

[1] Sigismondo de' Conti (da Foligno), *Le Storie de' suoi tempi dal 1475 al 1510*, 2 vols., Rome, 1883, I, 363; Louis Thuasne, *Djem-Sultan, fils de Mohammed II, frère de Bayezid II, 1459–1495*, Paris, 1892, pp. 270–72. On 21 March, 1490, Innocent VIII had consigned the golden rose to the Spanish ambassador to the Holy See to be presented to Isabella (Johann Burchard [Burckard], *Diarium . . . [1483–1506]*, ed. L. Thuasne, I [Paris, 1883], 399, and *Liber notarum . . .* , ed. E. Celani, I [1907–10], 300).

A public mass was celebrated in the Sistine Chapel on 29 April for the repose of Matthias Corvinus's soul (*ibid.*, ed. Celani, I, 305). Despite the bad feeling between the Curia and Corvinus, until the hour of the latter's death papal attention had been fastened upon him "pro defensione fidelium . . . ab oppressionibus immanium Turchorum . . ." (Arch. Segr. Vaticano, Reg. Vat. 745, fol. 5, "datum Rome apud Sanctum Petrum, anno etc. MCCCCLXXXX, tertio Kal. Aprilis, pontificatus nostri anno sexto," i.e., 30 March, 1490).

[2] Burchard, *Diarium*, ed. Thuasne, I, 413, and ed. Celani, I, 311, lines 20–21: ". . . qua continetur quod oratores post sex menses censeantur procuratores, non oratores" (Celani's text).

[3] Burchard was granted a leave of four months by the pope, to extend from 29 June to 1 November, 1490, but for some reason all MSS. of his diary seem to have the same gap, lacking entries after 9 June, 1490, and before 8 August, 1491 (*cf.* Thuasne, *Burchardi diarium*, I, 415, note 1, and vol. III, pp. XVII–XIX, and see below, note 15).

The cares of state and the disappointments were weighing heavily on Innocent VIII. In August, 1490, he was ill, and the Venetian government became fearful lest vigilance should in any way be relaxed in furnishing the fullest protection to Jem Sultan, against whose life there was believed to be no end of plotting.[4] On 27 September a tumult broke out in Rome, according to Infessura, and all the apothecaries closed their shops. Workers in the fields and vineyards fled to their homes. Citizens and foreigners took to arms, "because it was everywhere declared for certain that Pope Innocent was dead." Rumor had it that his son Franceschetto Cibo had tried to seize the papal treasury, but had been prevented from doing so by the cardinals. Cibo had then tried, it was said, to get possession of Jem Sultan in order to turn him over to the Florentines or the king of Naples. The next morning, on the twenty-eighth, the cardinals went to the Vatican palace, where the pope lay gravely ill. They made an inventory of papal belongings "although a good part of them had been taken and shipped to Florence by the said Franceschetto." What was found, was put in the custody of Cardinal Savelli, who remained in the palace for some time while the uncertainty persisted.[5]

While Innocent lay ill, rumors multiplied. It was said that 800,000 ducats were found in a chest (in the palace) and another 300,000 in a chest in the Castel S. Angelo. But the pope recovered, and told those who were keeping the vigil in his chamber that he hoped to see the death of the cardinals who had been hoping for his own.[6] On 20 November the pope withdrew from Rome for ten days' rest and a visit to Ostia and Porto. On the feast of S. Andrew, 30 November, however, an Ottoman envoy, Mustafa Beg, made his formal entry into Rome, being met by members of the *famiglie* of the pope and cardinals, various ambassadors accredited to the Holy See, and great crowds of curious Romans. Mustafa Beg had landed at Ancona on a Hospitaller galley, Guy de Blanchefort, the prior of Auvergne, traveling with him. The next day the pope received him in a formal audience attended by the cardinals, ambassadors, and officials of the Curia.

Mustafa Beg bore a letter from Sultan Bayazid II, greatest king of kings and emperor of two continents . . . , to the supreme father and lord of all Christians, Innocent by divine providence supreme pontiff of the Roman Church. . . . The letter was written in Greek and dated at Istanbul on 17 or 20 May, 1490. An interpreter translated the letter aloud into Latin. The sultan had learned, according to the letter, from the Grand Master Pierre d'Aubusson that Jem Sultan had been conveyed to Rome, "a fact in which we take great pleasure." Indeed Bayazid hoped that Jem might be maintained at the Curia on the same terms as the grand master had undertaken his custody some years before, "according to a convention of peace entered into between us, which has been kept by both sides up to now, and has been the cause of our friendship." To secure papal approval of the conditions of Jem's pension "we have sent our faithful slave, the Kapudan Pasha Mustafa, with one of the officials of the cardinal [grand]master in order that we may be assured by him that you also have confirmed this agreement, so that our friendship may increase: whatever therefore our envoy, the most faithful slave Mustafa, shall say in the presence of your Magnificence, receive as though they were our own words."[7]

Mustafa Beg wished of course to be certain that Jem Sultan was still alive. In the event that

[4] V. Lamansky, *Secrets d'état de Venise*, St. Petersburg, 1884, repr. New York, 1968, pp. 234–36, letter of the Consiglio dei Dieci to Ermolao Barbaro, Venetian envoy in Rome, dated 20 August, 1490.

[5] Stefano Infessura, *Diaria rerum romanarum*, ed. Oreste Tommasini, Rome, 1890, p. 260; Thuasne, *Djem-Sultan*, pp. 272–75; and *cf.* A. de Boüard, "Lettres de Rome de Bartolomeo de Bracciano à Virginio Orsini (1489–1494)," *Mélanges d'archéologie et d'histoire*, XXXIII (1913), nos. XVI–XVII, pp. 293–95, letters dated 9 August and 15 October, 1490.

[6] Infessura, *Diaria*, ed. Tommasini, pp. 260–61.

[7] Sigismondo de' Conti, II, 23–24, whose text of the letter I have followed; other versions are given in Steph. Baluze, *Miscellanea*, ed. J. D. Mansi, 4 vols., Lucca, 1761, I, 517, and in Pastor, *Gesch. d. Päpste*, III-1 (repr. 1955), 275, note, with refs., from a contemporary Latin translation in the Milanese Archives in the series on "Turchia." The text also appears in Hartmann Schedel and Angiolello as well as in various MS. collections (*cf.* Pastor, *loc. cit.*) The date of the sultan's letter is variously given as 17, 20, and 28 May, 1490.

Guy de Blanchefort and Mustafa Beg had sailed from Rhodes on 4 August, 1490 (Giacomo Bosio, *Militia di San Giovanni Gierosolimitano*, vol. II [Rome, 1594], bk. XIV, p. 415). On 23 September the Consiglio dei Dieci instructed the Venetian envoy in Rome, Ermolao Barbaro, to warn the pope against the coming of Mustafa Beg, the purpose of whose embassy was "ut praticet, operetur et agat, quantum in eo sit, contra vitam suprascripti Zen" (Lamansky, *Secrets d'état*, p. 236), i.e., against the life of Jem Sultan.

he was, Bayazid was most anxious that he be well guarded. The envoy explained his master's intention of abiding by the agreement with the grand master, the terms of which were now reviewed. The pope expressed himself as pleased with the sultan's attitude; he said that he would seek counsel of the cardinals, and would give his answer in a later audience. Before withdrawing, Mustafa Beg presented the pope with rich gifts from the sultan—textiles worked in gold, tapestries, and furs of sable, vair, and ermine.[8] A week later, on 8 December, the pope summoned Mustafa Beg again to the palace, where he found only the cardinals and Franceschetto Cibo present to hear his words. Now he asked the envoy how much the sultan had paid the Grand Master d'Aubusson up to that time. From Mustafa's response the pope is said to have realized that d'Aubusson had been misrepresenting the facts. Mustafa Beg was then dismissed with the statement that he would have the pope's answer in a few days, so as not to delay his return to Istanbul.[9]

Mustafa Beg is said to have brought 120,000 ducats, three years' pension for Jem Sultan. He promised the pope payment henceforth of 40,000 ducats a year for Jem's maintenance, but insisted that, before turning over any money, he was under orders from the sultan to see Jem with his own eyes. Despite the Hospitallers' objections, Mustafa Beg was permitted to request an audience of the Ottoman prince, who agreed to receive him, but only in an imperial setting. Jem's lodgings on an upper floor of the Vatican palace were quickly decked out in tapestries and cloths of gold and silk. A special throne was prepared for him and covered with rich adornments. Jem received his brother's envoy, as Infessura says, *more regali et in maiestate sua*. He was seated on his elaborate throne, cross-legged in the Turkish fashion, with the officers of his own household on either side and two papal nephews in attendance. Before Mustafa Beg was admitted into the presence, however, one of Jem's officers met him at the entrance to the hall, and dusted him off from head to foot with a piece of linen cloth "just as if he had been covered with flour or dust," according to Infessura, and then required the envoy to kiss the cloth. After this, Mustafa Beg was allowed to advance, prostrating himself three times as he approached the throne. The third time he remained on his knees, his head lowered in silence. At a gesture from Jem, Mustafa was directed to speak only in answer to questions. Jem then asked him in Turkish whether he had any letters. Mustafa immediately produced one, closed and sealed. To the astonishment of the western observers, he then licked it on all sides with his tongue. Two members of Jem's household examined the *clausura et sigillum*. When they were satisfied that the letter had not been tampered with, Mustafa himself opened the letter and broke the seal. Again he licked the letter inside and outside, doubtless to illustrate its harmless character. Now Jem's two Turkish attendants took the letter and read it into Jem's ear. No one learned, apparently, what Sultan Bayazid wrote to his brother. When the letter had been read, Mustafa moved his hand toward the presents which the sultan had sent, some pieces of brocaded cloth and some jewels (*ornamenta*). Jem now motioned to Mustafa Beg to withdraw, and "when all those present had been dismissed, [the Turks] had a good deal to say among themselves, which our people neither heard nor understood." As so often in Infessura's diary, great events were accompanied by strange natural phenomena. Never had the atmosphere been so stormy as it now became; there followed rain, snow, hail, and heavy winds with severe cold and blinding darkness.[10]

[8] Thuasne, *Djem-Sultan*, pp. 277–78, from the report of the Florentine ambassador Pierfilippo Pandolfini to the Otto di Pratica, dated 4 December, 1490.

[9] Thuasne, *Djem-Sultan*, p. 278, from a report of Pandolfini to Lorenzo de' Medici, dated 8 December, 1490.

[10] Infessura, *Diaria*, ed. Tommasini, pp. 262–64. Sigismondo de' Conti, II, 24, says Bayazid's letter to Jem Sultan stated that the latter would have acted more wisely if he had trusted his brother rather than aliens, but that in any event Bayazid could not but be concerned "as a brother for a brother's safety." *Cf.* Raynaldus, *Ann. eccl.*, ad ann. 1490, no. 2, vol. XIX (1693), p. 397b, and Thuasne, *Djem-Sultan*, pp. 279–80. That the cost to the sultan of maintaining Jem in papal custody was in fact 40,000 ducats a year cannot be called into question (Arch. Segr. Vaticano, Miscell., Arm. II, tom. 56, fol. 308^r, from a papal brief of 18 January, 1491): "Et subito princeps [Turcorum] mittet Rhagusium vel ad aliquem locum Maris Adriatici ducatos quadraginta milia auri venetos omni periculo et impensa sua donec fuerint repositi in aliquo navigio maritimo nostro nomine ac deinde singulis annis in predictis locis ac predicto modo alia ducatorum quadraginta milia similium auri venetorum persolvi faciet cum effectu. Annusque incipere intelligatur a Kalendis Decembris preteriti [i.e., from 1 December, 1490], et sic de Decembri in Decembrem, prout incipit ex forma capitulorum inter ipsum [Bayazid] et cardinalem magnum magistrum Rhodi. . . ." The brief furnishes further details as to the method of payment. The sum had previously been set at 45,000 ducats a year (see above, Chapter 13, note 10).

The opportunity to question Mustafa Beg had revealed to the pope that Pierre d'Aubusson had been less than candid in dealing with the Holy See. Mustafa stated that the sultan had paid d'Aubusson considerably more than the sums stipulated in the written agreements which existed between them. The prior of Auvergne alleged, however, that there were no such written agreements, merely verbal ones. The pope regarded this as a manifest prevarication, and demanded a copy of the text of the convention between the Hospital and the Porte. When the pope questioned Mustafa in another meeting at which the cardinals were present, the envoy denied that his master had ever requested that Jem Sultan should be guarded by Hospitallers, as the latter had always claimed, interjecting themselves vociferously into all discussions concerning Jem. The Florentine ambassador Pierfilippo Pandolfini wrote Lorenzo de' Medici on 23 December (1490) that the pope was holding the Hospitallers up to opprobrium for this unwarranted deception. Mustafa Beg required an answer to take back to Istanbul, but the pope was unwilling to commit himself until he was more fully informed about the entente between the sultan and d'Aubusson. "He hoped thus to gain time," says Thuasne, "and to secure in the meantime a decision favorable to the crusade."[11]

The failure of Johann Burchard's diary during this period makes it more difficult for us to step behind the scenes in the Vatican palace. On 3 January, 1491, Pope Innocent summoned the cardinals and the diplomatic corps to an audience to inform them of his intended reply to the Turkish envoy Mustafa Beg. In a preliminary session the pope noted that the envoy's initial pronouncements, which the Hospitallers had translated, were to the effect that the sultan was willing to live at peace with all the Christian princes. Subsequently, however, Mustafa Beg had insisted that his first statements represented merely his own point of view. His commission from the sultan provided only that, if Jem Sultan was kept well guarded in papal custody, the sultan was ready to keep peace with Rhodes and with Rome. In view of such different declarations, the pope said that he had now decided to dismiss the Turkish envoy and give him the answer he sought, which had been prepared with the advice of the cardinals. He directed his secretary, Girolamo Balbano, to read the text of the answer in order that the ambassadors who were present might inform their principals both of the contents of the document and of the circumstances which produced it. Innocent denounced the Hospitallers and Mustafa Beg for their lack of probity and plain dealing, and then directed that both they and he be admitted to the audience chamber.

Turning first to Mustafa Beg, the pope declared that his Magnificence had come before him with a letter from his master, Sultan Bayazid, and had led him to understand, in accordance with the translation which the Hospitallers had furnished of his remarks, that if Jem Sultan were well guarded at Rome, the sultan would refrain from attacking any Christian prince. The pope's own nephew, Niccolò Cibo, archbishop of Arles, who knew Turkish, now acted as interpreter. Innocent asked Mustafa whether the facts, as just stated, were really in accord with the commission the sultan had given him. The Turk replied that he had never said his master was prepared to grant peace to all Christian princes, but only to the grand master of Rhodes, the pope, and the Venetians. He had certainly not intended, he said, that any other meaning be ascribed to his words.

Innocent then addressed himself to the Hospitallers, chiding them for their active concealment of the facts. They answered that, when they had left Rhodes (on 4 August, 1490), they had understood Mustafa Beg's mission was to offer peace to all the Christian princes. They could not now account, they said, for this disavowal of that intention. They assured the pope of the grand master's sincerity and of their own in every aspect of the present affair; they were sure that his Holiness would render a proper decision with respect to the purpose of Mustafa Beg's embassy. At this point Innocent informed the Turkish envoy that he could depart when he wished; the answer to the sultan, already prepared, would be read to him, and he would presently receive the text. The arch-

---

[11] Thuasne, *Djem-Sultan*, pp. 280–81, from letters of Pandolfini to the Otto di Pratica and Lorenzo de' Medici, dated 11 and 23 December, 1490. The pope wrote d'Aubusson in remonstrance against his lack of candor in dealing with the Holy See (I find nothing in Bosio, bk. XIV, concerning this matter). D'Aubusson had also accepted 20,000 ducats from Ka'itbey to equip vessels to take Jem Sultan to Egypt (Sa'd-ad-Dīn, "Aventures du Prince Gem," in *Journal asiatique*, IX [1826, repr. 1965], 153, 167). Guy de Blanchefort, the grand master's nephew, was now obliged to restore 5,000 ducats of the sum (Thuasne, *op. cit.*, p. 281).

bishop of Arles then translated it into Turkish for Mustafa Beg, who withdrew immediately thereafter.[12]

Innocent's letter to Bayazid is dated 3 January, 1491,[13] the same day as the memorable audience at which he gave vent to his exasperation. The pope wrote the sultan of the hospitable reception

[12] Thuasne, *Djem-Sultan*, pp. 282–83, summarizing a letter from Pandolfini to the Otto di Pratica, dated 3 January, 1490 (from the Incarnation, i.e., 1491), cited from Arch. di Stato di Firenze, Classe X, dist. 5, no. 28, fol. 99 (Cl. X, d. 5, no. 28, containing a number of Pandolfini's letters). Thuasne of course cites Florentine documents according to the old classification in the Archives, under which system Classe X contained correspondence, divided into eight *distinzioni*: 1–2, of the Signoria; 3–4, of the Dieci di Balia; 5–6, of the Otto di Pratica; and 7–8, of the Signoria of Pisa. There is an account of the pope's address to the ambassadors in A. de Boüard, "Lettres de Rome de Bartolomeo de Bracciano . . . ," *Mélanges d'archéologie et d'histoire*, XXXIII (1913), no. XXIII, pp. 300–1, dated 3 January, 1491.

Niccolò Cibo's knowledge of Turkish is interesting, and passes with little comment in the pages of Thuasne. Cibo is said by Burchard, *Diarium*, ed. Thuasne, I, 481, and *cf.* p. 486, and II, 202 ff., 208–9, with append., no. 8, pp. 621–22, and ed. Celani, I, 363–64, and *cf.* pp. 367, 547 ff., 551–54, to have been a cousin (*consobrinus*) of the Genoese Giorgio Bocciardi (Busardus, Buzardus, Bucciardus), an apostolic scribe, who also knew Turkish, and served the Turkish envoy as an interpreter in May, 1492, when Sultan Bayazid II sent, as we shall observe, the reputed Holy Lance as a gift to the papacy. In his account of Jem Sultan, Caoursin refers to "episcopus Nicolaus Cibo ex familia Busardorum ad pontificis gentem accitus" (in Thuasne, *Burchardi diarium*, I, append., no. 34, p. 545, and *cf.* p. 548). Niccolò appears often in the briefs of Innocent VIII: "Nicolaus Bucciardus, noster secundum carnem affinis" (Arch. Segr. Vaticano, Arm. XXXIX, tom. 19, fols. 31^r, 33^v). He was the pope's nephew (*ibid.*, fols. 41^v, 42^r, 54^r).

In a letter dated at Rome on 16 January, 1492 (i.e., 1493), after Innocent VIII's death, the Florentine ambassador Filippo Valori reported to the Otto di Pratica on an embassy which Giorgio Bocciardi had just made to Istanbul to try to collect the 40,000 ducats' pension for Jem Sultan, which Bayazid was refusing to pay. Valori identified Bocciardi as the brother of Niccolò Cibo ". . . Giorgio Bocciardo Genovese fratello dello Arciveschovo di Arli . . ." (Thuasne, II, append., no. 8, p. 622). Although Archbishop Niccolò bore the name Cibo, he was a Bocciardi, one of four brothers who served the papacy under Alexander VI as well as Innocent VIII in diplomatic relations with the Porte. The others were, besides Giorgio, Ambrogio and Tommaso. They were, as noted, nephews of Innocent VIII (*cf.* Thuasne, *Djem-Sultan*, p. 320, note 2).

[13] The text of the letter is given in Sigismondo de' Conti, II, 25–26, with no indication of the day of issuance, "datum Rome apud Sanctum Petrum anno Incarnationis dominice MCCCCLXXXX" (i.e., 1491), but Pastor, *Gesch. d. Päpste*, III-1 (repr. 1955), 276, note 1, supplies the date from a contemporary copy in the State Archives at Milan: "1490 tertio nonas Ianuarii, anno septimo."

An important brief dated 18 January, 1491, containing instructions for a papal nuncio going to Istanbul, recounts the pope's experience with Mustafa Beg (Arch. Segr. Vaticano, Miscell., Arm. II, tom. 56, fols. 306^r–310^r, "datum Rome apud Sanctum Petrum sub annulo piscatoris die XVIII Ianuarii, pontificatus nostri anno septimo" [1491]): "Dilecte fili, salutem et apostolicam benedictionem: Venit ad nos superioribus diebus orator potentissimi principis Turcorum, qui in sacro consistorio nostro assistentibus nobiscum venerabilibus fratribus nostris S. R. E. cardinalibus, in presentia oratorum principum atque potentatuum Christianorum admissus et publice auditus est. Et una cum oratoribus Rhodiis presentatis litteris principis sui credentialibus, per interpretem Rhodium proposuit inter alia mentis sui principis esse, dare quietem Christianis fratre suo Zizimo Sultano in manibus nostris remanente postulavitque capitula et conventiones initas inter dilectum filium nostrum cardinalem magnum magistrum Rhodi et se per nos ratas haberi et approbari.

"Visum fuit pro gravitate tante rei ut consultius ageremus, ea omnia prius communicare omnibus principibus Christianis, eo maxime quia dum consulimus . . . dictus orator quietem, quam Christianis obtulerat, declaravit se non ad omnes Christianos sed ad particulares referre exclusis aliquibus, quod nobis intulit necessitatem profundioris considerationis. . . . Unde iterato eum ad consistorium nostrum evocavimus ubi restrictione dicte quietis per eum declarate in presentia dictorum cardinalium et oratorum publice eis respondimus et breve quod ei plumbatum dedimus ad principem suum deferendum legi fecimus, cuius et tibi copiam damus. Hortati fuimus oratorem ipsum [ut] moneret principem ipsum [ut] abstineret a damnis et infestationibus Christianorum utque eos quietos dimitteret per universum orbem, in quo orator ipse pollicitus est se operam daturum et nos bene sperare hortatus est. Nos interim consilia principum et potentatuum Christianorum intelligemus cum quibus in toto negotio melius decernere poterimus. . . ." There follow instructions to the nuncio being sent to Istanbul and details relating to the sultan's annual payment of 40,000 ducats for his brother's maintenance at the Vatican (quoted above, note 10). But the pope had other desires, as he informed his nuncio:

"Magno desiderio affectamus habere plura corpora sanctorum que in illis partibus sunt necnon tunicam inconsutibilem domini nostri Iesu Christi ac ferrum lancee, spongiam et cannem que fuerunt in mysterio passionis et ideo nostro nomine instantissime requires ut ad singularem nostram consolationem velit ipse potentissimus princeps de his omnibus aut saltem potiori parte complacere. Curabis omnia predicta ea celeritate qua poteris expedire et statim per proprium tabellarium nobis que gesta erunt notificare ut si qua provisio facienda fuerit, fieri possit in tempore. Religio Hierosolimitana est membrum huius Sancte Sedis et nobis subiecta. Eam ut nostram valde diligimus et civitatem Rhodiam salvam esse cupimus." The pope did not forget certain of his Genoese relatives who were having trouble in Istanbul: "Curabis etiam apud predictum principem ut bona quorundam civium nobilium Ianuensium qui etiam nobis sanguine coniuncti sunt sub certo pretextu fraudationis gabellarum per eum occupata restituantur." He also interceded on behalf of a Florentine whose family had been dispossessed by Bayazid's father Mehmed II.

he had given his envoy Mustafa Beg in consistory before the cardinals. The envoy's words, "which we believe have come from your own heart," betokened peace. Since the sultan's written proposals and the envoy's spoken messages were matters of great moment, however, and concerned all Christians, the pope believed they must be shared with the Christian princes. The pope had wanted the ambassadors of the Christian states to be present when Mustafa Beg was heard, so that they might report to their home governments and seek advice. When fortified with such advice the pope would be in a better position to answer, but lest Mustafa Beg be unduly inconvenienced by prolonged delay, the pope was sending him back to Istanbul, whither eventually Innocent's answer would follow him. In the meantime Mustafa Beg had had the opportunity to see Jem Sultan safe and sound and "honorably treated" in the papal palace.

The intention of the letter was obviously to gain time and to cause the sultan some concern but no offense. The activities of the princes could furnish little hope that they might join together in a crusade. Charles VIII of France was engaged in a struggle with Brittany, while from time to time Henry VII of England gave some assistance to Duchess Anne. Profiting from Matthias Corvinus's death, Maximilian of Hapsburg had recovered Vienna in August (1490) and thereafter even invaded Hungary. Maximilian and Charles VIII were soon at violent odds again. Papal preachments of peace had small effect. Ferrante of Naples always bore watching, and was still being troublesome. Ferdinand and Isabella were preoccupied with the last stages of the Spanish *reconquista*, soon to reach its dramatic ending. French relations with the Curia Romana were rather strained; Gallicanism and the collection of tithes were almost perennial problems. The French wanted recognition of Charles's rights in Brittany and reassurance that the pope would not surrender Jem Sultan to any other prince or state without their permission. On 11 November, 1491, a French embassy arrived in Rome to deal with some of these questions, and early the following month the news arrived of Charles VIII's marriage with Anne of Brittany, which increased the pope's difficulties. Innocent withheld action on Charles's request for certain dispensations to secure canonical propriety for his marriage with Anne, so as not to offend Maximilian. He also withheld condemnation of the marriage, so as not to offend Charles.[14] At the same time the alliance of Lodovico il Moro with France increased the disquietude of the Curia. It also effected a marked improvement in Ferrante's attitude toward the pope.

For some weeks there had been an atmosphere of high excitement and expectation at the Curia Romana. Granada had fallen on 2 January, 1492, and the massive silver standard of the cross, which Sixtus IV had sent to Ferdinand the Catholic, was mounted on the Alhambra. The news reached Rome about one o'clock in the morning of 1 February, and set off the most fervent celebrations. Almost eight centuries of Islamic history in the Iberian peninsula came to an end. Castile and Aragon-Catalonia were already united, at least after a fashion. A new Spain was ready to play a far larger role than hitherto in the affairs of Europe and the Mediterranean, and we need not speak here of the *conquistadores* who ventured into the western hemisphere after 1492. The treacherous Ferrante of Naples, fearful of his Catholic cousin's success, had secretly aided the Moors in their final struggle. Ferdinand was to remember the fact. Less than a decade later the house of Aragon in Naples was to get short shrift when by the terms of the treaty of Granada (in November, 1500) Ferdinand divided the kingdom of Naples with Louis XII of France. Then all Italy was to worry, but now was a time of rejoicing. In the meantime Ferrante could see no further profit in the petty harassment of the pope, especially after Corvinus's death, and he was prepared for at least the partial fulfillment of the terms of the papal-Neapolitan treaty of 11 August, 1486. Undoubtedly Charles VIII's alli-

[14] Burchard, *Diarium*, ed. Thuasne, I, 430, 436, and ed. Celani, I, 324–26, 331, describes the entrance of the French embassy into Rome on 11 November, 1491, and notes the arrival on 5 December of the news "ipsum regem Francie contraxisse matrimonium et illud carnali copula confirmasse cum illustrissima domina Anna regina Romanorum et Britannie ducissa, que prius ante annum vel circa matrimonium per verba de presenti cum invictissimo Maximiliano Romanorum rege contraxerat, quod fuerat etiam in facie Ecclesie solemnizatum" (Celani's text). The marriage astonished and scandalized Europe. *Cf.* Sigismondo de' Conti, II, 20–23. Charles had been affianced to Maximilian's daughter Margaret, which tie the pope dissolved (says Sigismondo) "because she had not yet attained the twelfth year of her age." *Cf.* H. F. Delaborde, *L'Expédition de Charles VIII en Italie*, Paris, 1888, pp. 215 ff., 231, 254 ff.; H. Ulmann, *Kaiser Maximilian I.*, I (Stuttgart, 1884), 137 ff.

ance with Lodovico il Moro and the increasing French interest in the pope's Neapolitan problem disposed Ferrante to meet the Curia half way. Giovanni Gioviano Pontano, who had negotiated the treaty of 1486 (and whom the pope respected), returned to Rome in November, 1491, and "on 27 January [1492] in secret consistory . . . peace was concluded between our most holy lord, the pope, and the most illustrious Ferrante, king of Naples."[15] Conspicuous in the background of these negotiations was the corpulent figure of Jem Sultan. Ferrante was eager to have him brought to Naples. Jem remained to the day of his death the object of endless machinations.

On Saturday evening, 4 February (1492), the great bell on the Capitolium sounded its full peal in celebration of the fall of Granada. The Vatican and Castel S. Angelo were illuminated with torches and bonfires, as were many houses in the Borgo and palaces throughout Rome. The next day, Sunday, a great procession of the city clergy including the pope and the cardinals made its way from the apostolic palace "ad ecclesiam sancti Jacobi de Gallicia, hospitalis Hispanorum nuncupati," as Johann Burchard describes the church of S. Giacomo degli Spagnoli in the Piazza Navona.[16] Even a steady rain did not extinguish the joy of the occasion. Burchard was distressed, however, because the pope insisted upon wearing a white rather than a red *capuccinus*, and the cardinals apparently fell into line in the wrong place. At the church itself there was some disagreement between Burchard and Agostino Patrizzi, the bishop of Pienza, as to whether the sermon should come at the end of the mass or after the gospel. But when the bulk of the clergy reached the church, they made

[15] Burchard, *Diarium*, ed. Thuasne, I, 442, and ed. Celani, I, 335, lines 14–15; Raynaldus, *Ann.eccl.*, ad ann. 1492, no. 10, vol. XIX (1693), p. 409b, dates the peace incorrectly as 28 January. Pastor, *Hist. Popes*, V, 284, 315, dates it first on 29 January, and thereafter on the twenty-second; in the last German edition, *Gesch. d. Päpste*, III-1 (repr. 1955), 253, 278, he dates it correctly on 27 January, and thereafter retains his old error of the twenty-second. Consistency is, alas, as hard to maintain as accuracy. *Cf.* Thuasne, *Djem-Sultan*, pp. 289–93, and A. de Boüard, "Lettres de Rome . . . ," *Mélanges d'archéologie et d'histoire*, XXXIII, no. XL, pp. 318–19, where Pontano's arrival in Rome is dated the morning of 4 November (1491).

The course of Ferrante's relations with Innocent VIII, Giuliano della Rovere, and Ascanio Sforza may be traced in the correspondence published by Francesco Trinchera, *Codice aragonese*, II, pt. 1 (Naples, 1868), pp. 1–4, 9, 10–12, 14–19, 21–22, 37–38, 40–42, letters dated from 2 October, 1491, to 25 February, 1492. On 2 March, after Giovanni Pontano's return to Naples, Ferrante wrote Innocent a letter of fulsome thanks for the pope's expressions of amity toward him and all the royal house of Aragon in Naples, for the restoration of peace between the Holy See and his kingdom, and for the contract of marriage made between the young prince Luigi d'Aragona, marquis of Gerace, and Innocent's "niece" Battistina di Usemari (*ibid.*, II-1, pp. 43–44). Actually Battistina was Innocent's granddaughter (*ibid.*, II-1, pp. 53–54). The marriage took place on 3 June (1492), as we shall see later.

At this point it should perhaps be noted again that Innocent VIII granted Johann Burchard a leave from his duties as papal master of ceremonies (to return to his home in Germany) from 29 June to 1 November, 1490, but his *Diarium* contains no entries between 9 June, 1490, and 8 August, 1491. The date June, 1491, in the page heading of Thuasne's edition (I, 414) is an error for June, 1490. *Cf.* Celani, I, pp. xxv, 312. The diplomatic correspondence helps to make up for the lack of information with which Burchard would have provided us.

[16] On the rather sad fortunes of the old church of S. Giacomo degli Spagnoli, where the royal arms of Castile and León may still be seen on the tympanum over the portal, see P. Romano and P. Partini, *Piazza Navona nella storia e nell'arte*, Rome, n.d., pp. 32–38. The Piazza Navona was the scene of many fêtes and spectacles (*ibid.*, pp. 139 ff.). The site of Domitian's Stadium, it was named from Campus Agonis, Agonalis, Platea Agonis, etc. (*Nagone*, *Naona*, *Navona*). *Cf.* the brief monograph of Luigi de Gregori, *Piazza Navona prima d'Innocenzo X*, Rome, n.d. [1926?] (Quaderni di Studi romani, no. I).

Innocent VIII had aided Ferdinand and Isabella's efforts against Granada by various grants of indulgence in the bull *Orthodoxe fidei* of 9 October, 1489, "universis Christi fidelibus . . . Saracenos dicti regni Granate in auxilium regis et regine predictorum et tam sancte expeditionis personaliter militantibus seu alias militantes suis expensis mittentibus . . ." (Arch. Segr. Vaticano, Reg. Vat. 743, fols. 39^v–43^r, by mod. stamped enumeration). The same spiritual benefits were extended to all who might aid the Spanish enterprise against Islam in the West, from soldiers and shipwrights to physicians and apothecaries (*ibid.*, fol. 40^r). *Cf.*, *ibid.*, fols. 281^r–282^v, another bull of the same date on behalf of Ferdinand and Isabella, "veluti intrepidi Christi pugiles et athlete manu potenti et fortissimo brachio infideles Sarracenos regni Granate cum validissimo exercitu continuo debellando hactenus pertulerunt et perferre non cessant . . . ," in return for which services rendered and expenses incurred Innocent had renewed the indulgences granted by Sixtus IV "in subsidium sancte cruciate" (fol. 281^r): "Nos igitur qui summo opere affectamus ut regnum Granate predictum ad iugum Christiane religionis quam citius reducatur et ad hoc omnibus modis quibus possumus auxilia eisdem regi et regine semotis quibusvis obstaculis prebere curamus . . ." (fol. 281^v). Almost three years before, on 18 January, 1487, Innocent in a favorable response to the Catholic Kings' request for a crusading subsidy had encouraged them to an unflagging continuance of their offensive against the Moors of Granada (Reg. Vat. 719, fol. 71). On the assistance rendered by Sixtus IV and Innocent VIII in this connection, see José Goñi Gaztambide, "La Santa Sede y la reconquista del reino de Granada (1479–1492)," *Hispania sacra*, IV (1951), 43–80, with eight documents.

so much noise that the pope intervened, and the sermon was postponed until the end of the mass. After the sermon the *Te Deum* was sung, and the pope said the *Pater noster*; he gave the assembled people his solemn benediction, and plenary indulgences were pronounced. The service was over. His Holiness removed his pluvial and miter, donned the offending white humerale, and the procession went back to the palace. Beyond the bridge, by the Castel S. Angelo, the pope granted the cardinals permission to return to their homes.[17]

After the day's repast Cardinal Rodrigo Borgia, vice-chancellor of the Church, staged a bullfight in an arena built in the courtyard of his palace and the adjoining street, presumably the first bullfight ever seen in Rome. Five bulls were slain, and several men wounded and killed. The Spanish envoys built a miniature castle with a tower in the middle of the Piazza Navona and another by the church of S. Giacomo in order to stage a dramatic representation of the siege and taking of Granada. The spectacle was scheduled for Sunday, the twelfth, but owing to the persistent rain, it had to be postponed until the nineteenth of the month, also a Sunday, when it was preceded by a solemn mass in S. Giacomo and a procession of the Spanish clergy. Another bullfight was held, this time in the Piazza Navona. Four bulls were slain, a horse was lost, but there were no human casualties. Several Spanish prelates made gifts of bulls for other public exhibitions; others made gifts of bread and wine through all one day to such of the populace as wanted them. Raffaele Riario, the cardinal of S. Giorgio, staged a joust in the Piazza Navona. The prize was to be a silver casque (*galea*) worth about two hundred ducats for the most skillful wielder of the lance. The contest lasted many days, says Burchard, and finally on Friday, 2 March, a certain Mascoletto, a constable of the governor of Rome, was adjudged the winner, to the abundant complaints of the Colonnesi.[18] The last great scene in this festival of Spanish triumph depicted Ferdinand and Isabella in a high carriage drawn by four white horses. The victorious sovereigns held a palm of gold, says Sigismondo de' Conti, and at their feet the Moorish king, Abū-'Abd-Allāh, was drawn in chains. The trappings of the tableau were gorgeous—with helmets, bows, breastplates, spears, and shields suspended on wooden frames—"such as are shown in the trophies of the ancients and on the monuments of the Caesars."[19]

The carriage of Ferdinand and Isabella was preceded by footsoldiers with gleaming arms and followed by knights in full panoply. One wonders what thoughts passed through the mind of Jem Sultan as he witnessed certain parts, at least, of these festivities. Sigismondo de' Conti explains the general rejoicing by the fact that Christian ears had heard nothing but sad and terrifying news of Moslem exploits for some forty years. Now came a great Christian victory. Did not the capture of Granada in the West offset the loss of Constantinople in the East? Europe hailed as warmly as Rome the new star on the crusading firmament. There were some who assumed that Ferdinand would move next against the Moslem states in North Africa, but of course the Neapolitan kingdom was to prove a far stronger attraction.

The French had never abated their interest in Naples. As Lodovico il Moro, managing badly with the Neapolitans, found an ally in Charles VIII, the latter protested against the pope's intention to invest Ferrante [II], called Ferrantino, son of Duke Alfonso of Calabria and grandson of Ferrante I, with the right of succession to the southern kingdom.[20] The elder

[17] Burchard, *Diarium*, ed. Thuasne, I, 444–47, and ed. Celani, I, 336–38, whose text I follow; Sigismondo de'Conti, I, 374–75; Gaspare Pontani, *Il Diario romano . . . (1481–1492)*, ed. Diomede Toni, in *RISS*, III, pt. 2 (1908), p. 70; Thuasne, *Djem-Sultan*, p. 294, who by a slip of the pen refers to the church of "Saint-Jean de Galice;" Pastor, *Gesch. d. Päpste*, III–1 (repr. 1955), 277–78. Sigismondo, I, 375, indicates that the news of the fall of Granada came on 31 January. Pastor, III–1, 278, note 1, cites a letter of Gianandrea Boccaccio, bishop of Modena, dated at Rome on 1 February to the effect that "in questa nocte passata circa le sette hore giunse la nova vera et certa de la intrata del Re de Spagna in Granata. . . ." Infessura, *Diaria*, ed. Tommasini (1890), pp. 269–70, also gives 1 February as the date. Ferdinand and Isabella entered the castle of Granada on 7 January (Burchard, *Diarium*, I, 446, with Thuasne's notes, and *ibid.*, append., no. 38, pp. 554–55; Bernardo del Roi's letter from Granada dated 7 January, 1492, in *Lettere di principi*, Venice, 1575, II, fol. 3; and *cf.* D. Malipiero, *Annali veneti*, in *Archivio storico italiano*, VII, pt. 1 [1843], 312). The Spanish occupation of Granada is recounted in dozens of contemporary texts. It was regarded, as Pastor says, "als ein Ersatz für den Verlust Konstantinopels."

[18] Burchard, *Diarium*, ed. Thuasne, I, 447, and ed. Celani, I, 338; Pontani, *Diario*, ed. Toni, in *RISS*, III–2, p. 70; Trinchera, *Codice aragonese*, II–1, p. 45.

[19] Sigismondo de' Conti, I, 374; Thuasne, *Djem-Sultan*, pp. 295–96.

[20] *Cf.* Trinchera, *Codice aragonese*, II–1, pp. 115–17, letter of King Ferrante dated 12 June, 1492, to Giovanni Battista Coppola, Neapolitan ambassador to the French court.

Ferrante was now pretending to entertain a great concern for the Turkish problem. Sultan Bayazid was well aware of some potential danger in the new liaison between Rome and Naples. As long as Jem Sultan remained in Christian hands Bayazid always felt uneasy.

On 25 September, 1491, the Venetian government had directed its ambassador in Rome, Dr. Girolamo Donato (Donà), to warn the pope that it was widely rumored in the Levant that the sultan was trying to bribe certain members of the papal court to assassinate Jem Sultan "by poison or by any other means."[21] After Ferrante's reconciliation with the Holy See, he had tried hard to get possession of Jem. The pope had refused his request, however, being loath to lose the 40,000 ducats' pension and fearing to go back on his pledge to Charles VIII. On 27 February, 1492, the Venetians instructed Donato to convey to his Holiness their "great and reverent thanks" for informing them of Ferrante's new attempt to secure Jem's person. Donato was also to congratulate the pope upon his steadfastness. The Church had a wonderful warranty in Jem, "on whose life and safety, as we have often said before, depend most surely the peace, quiet, and tranquillity of the entire Christian commonwealth."[22]

A year or more before, while the Ottoman envoy Mustafa Beg was still in Rome, Ka'itbey, the soldan of Egypt, was said to have offered the pope 40,000 ducats for the safe return of Jem Sultan to Cairo. Ka'itbey also promised permanent Christian dominion over Jerusalem and its environs; full freedom of Christians to go to and from the Holy Land without tribute or payment of any kind; and the cession of all lands formerly Christian, even including Constantinople, when Ka'itbey and Jem should succeed in conquering the city from Bayazid.[23] Even if the pope did not believe it, the offer, if actually made, was extraordinary. But now, in the spring of 1492, another envoy of the Gran Turco was coming to Rome by way of Ancona, bringing with him as a gift to the papacy the iron head of the lance with which Longinus had pierced Christ's side at the Crucifixion. The envoy also brought a protest to the pope against the Grand Master d'Aubusson's allowing constant asylum to the corsairs infesting Turkish waters. It was thought, too, that the envoy was probably bringing the 40,000 ducats for Jem's maintenance for the year 1492. The Venetian government informed the pope that Bayazid was preparing a fleet of about sixty sail, of which twenty-five were galleys. At first the Venetians had assumed that this armament was going to be directed against the pirates but, considering its size, Ragusa seemed a more likely objective.[24]

Warnings of the Turkish peril carried different estimates of the extent of Bayazid's preparations. On 7 May (1492) the Venetian Senate received from the Savi the text of a letter to be transmitted, if approved, to Girolamo Donato, who had been the Signoria's ambassador to Rome for the past year. Donato was to seek an audience with the pope, according to this letter, and inform him that the sultan was assembling a powerful army at Adrianople as well as a fleet of more than "eighty sail, including thirty galleys" at certain naval stations. As usual with the Turks, they were keeping their plans secret. There were those who believed, however, that the army was intended for a siege of Belgrade and the fleet for an attack upon Ragusa. The Ottoman fleet, larger than all previous estimates, had been on the point of leaving Gallipoli on 4 April, which was the date of the Senate's last communication from Istanbul. Since peace had recently been made and confirmed between the Turkish sultan and the soldan of Egypt, the forces of Bayazid, who was becoming bolder and more arrogant all the time, could only have a Christian objec-

[21] Lamansky, *Secrets d'état* (1884, repr. 1968), pp. 238–39. The alleged plotters against Jem Sultan's life are said to have been a Genoese named Giovanni Battista Gentile, a certain Evangelista, and a Dominican named Leonardo, identified in letters of the Consiglio dei Dieci to their ambassador in Rome, dated 30 April and 3 June, 1490, and 12 December, 1491 (Lamansky, pp. 232–34, 241–43). Girolamo Donato (Donà) had been elected the Venetian ambassador to the Holy See on 11 March, 1491 (Arch. di Stato di Venezia, Sen. Secreta, Reg. 34, fol. 86^r [98^r]); his commission, issued in the name of the Doge Agostino Barbarigo, is dated 27 April (*ibid.*, fols. 90^v–92^r [102^v–104^r]).

[22] Lamansky, *op. cit.*, pp. 244–45.

[23] Infessura, *Diaria*, ed. Tommasini, p. 262, relating to events recorded under December, 1490. On 14 June, 1491, the Neapolitan ambassador in Rome announced that the Turks had made a landing in Sicily with sixteen galleys and fourteen large *fuste* (A. de Boüard, "Lettres de Rome . . . ," *Mélanges d'archéologie et d'histoire*, XXXIII, no. XXXIX, p. 317).

[24] Thuasne, *Djem-Sultan*, pp. 296–97. On 27 March, 1492, Ferrante of Naples directed Giacomo Pontano, his ambassador to the Holy See and a relative of the humanist Giovanni Gioviano, to warn the pope "deli preparatorii del Turcho" (Trinchera, *Codice aragonese*, II–1, p. 60, and *cf.* pp. 73, 79–80, 92, 94, 96, 98, 99, 101 ff.).

tive. Although Venice was also at peace with the Turk, and in fact expected him to abide by the peace, the Senate was taking steps "pro bona securitate locorum et navigiorum nostrorum." The Senate wished, alas, as the letter goes on to say, that it had been possible to ask Donato to convey happier news (*delectabiliora*) to his Holiness. Even so, Innocent was reminded that he had in his own hands "that instrument which is most suited to restraining the appetite and ambition of the said Turk." The *instrumentum* was Bayazid's brother Jem Sultan, whose presence in Rome, as previously his custody by the Hospitallers, had served for some years to moderate Bayazid's "appetite and ambition." In his infallible wisdom his Holiness would certainly know how to employ the fortunate possession of Jem's person both for the furtherance of his own affairs and for the universal well-being of the Christian flock.[25]

On 19 May (1492) Ferrante of Naples informed his secretary Giovanni Pontano, who was sent back to Rome, that reports from Corfu and Venice revealed that a Turkish armada had put to sea, and that the sultan was making great preparations also to put an army into the field. Ferrante was readying his own naval forces and marshaling men-at-arms. Pontano was to let the pope know of these developments and to send the news to Milan, Florence, Ferrara, France, Castile, and Hungary. Since the pope was the head of Christendom, Ferrante felt that a special responsibility rested upon his shoulders for the common safety, and in Jem Sultan his Holiness had an instrument of exceptional utility to employ against the Porte.[26]

Innocent VIII responded to the appeal from Naples. Christian negligence and slothfulness had done nothing to check Turkish aggression, as he wrote Francesco Gonzaga, marquis of Mantua, in a brief dated 14 July (1492). King Ferrante, *qui et ipse periculo propinquior est*, had informed the Curia that Sultan Bayazid, with a great land army recruited from both his Asian and European territories, had moved toward Hungary and was going to descend upon Epirus. He had sent strong forces ahead, and was planning himself to follow them. He had summoned his fleet from the Dardanelles. One said that it was expected to go to Acroceraunia and Corfu, where it was to join a smaller fleet already drawn up in those waters. Report also had it that an incredible number of cannon were being sent toward the threatened areas. Ferrante's long shoreline was exposed to attack although he had placed strong garrisons in various parts of his domain. His means were not equal to a prolonged campaign. "His perils are our perils. The common enemy can enter our homes through his doorway, for if any corner of his dominion were to be occupied, it would open the way to the destruction of other Christians." The March of Ancona was exposed to attack and expensive to protect. Once more, therefore, Innocent turned to all the princes and powers of Europe, among whom Francesco Gonzaga found himself. They must ponder the dangers to which their faith and lands were exposed. They must consult with—and give aid to—the Holy See to forfend disaster. *Si quod possumus omnes coniunctis animis ac viribus efficere voluerimus, iuvabit deus causam suam simulque securitati et glorie nostre prospiciet.*[27]

Sometimes it seemed as though papal, Venetian, Neapolitan, and Turkish foreign policy had come to depend upon what became of Jem Sultan. Toward the end of the summer the Venetian Senate said so in so many words, in a letter to their ambassador in Naples.[28] When the awkward question was raised of who could use Jem in a campaign against his brother, it was difficult to find a satisfactory answer. Corvinus might have done so, but he was dead. The Venetians wanted to avoid war with the Porte. Neither Innocent nor Ferrante had the re-

---

[25] Sen. Secreta, Reg. 34, fol. 118^v [129^v], and *cf.* fols. 123^v ff., [134^v ff.]. The letter was not sent in the form summarized above, but in a shorter, more jejune text.

[26] Trinchera, *Codice aragonese*, II–1, p. 106–108, letter dated in Castel Nuovo on 19 May, 1492, and *cf.* a letter of 29 June to Pontano, *ibid.*, II–1, pp. 125–27, also pp. 129, 130–31. Ferrante apparently chose to remain excited over the prospect of a Turkish invasion of Italy after the Venetians had decided there was no likelihood of any such direct attack (*ibid.*, II–1, p. 134).

[27] Arch. di Stato di Mantova, Arch. Gonzaga, Busta 834, brief dated 14 July, 1492.

[28] Sen. Secreta, Reg. 34, fol. 130^v [141^v], dated 10 September, 1492: "Et interim ad rem nostram pertinet et omnium pariter Christianorum hortari Beatitudinem pontificiam [by this time, of course, Alexander VI was pope] ad habendam vigilantissimam custodiam persone Gien Sultani, unde salus pendet ac quies Christiane religionis, cuius sua Sanctitas est caput et pastor." The fact that this letter also was never sent, does not much diminish its value as evidence of the importance which the Venetians attached to Jem Sultan as a negotiable "instrument" in dealing with Bayazid, "come se convien ala bona pace ch'è tra nui et el Signor Turco," as the Senate wrote the Venetian count of Sebenico, "et alo amor che sapete li portamo!" (doc. dated 23 August, 1492, *ibid.*, fol. 129^r [140^r]).

sources to embark on a so-called crusade. Although the alarm which was sounded in May, 1492, proved *un peu fort*, no one could be sure when or where or whether the Turk would strike. Except for the usual hassles along the Dalmatian border and except for the corsairs who followed in the wake of the Turkish fleet, Venetian citizens and subjects had little to fear that summer either on the mainland or in the Archipelago. And the Turks made no attacks upon either Belgrade or Ragusa.[29]

The news that the iron head of the Holy Lance was on its way to Rome seems to have caused as much commotion in the Curia as the Venetian report that Bayazid was building a fleet. On 4 May (1492) eight cardinals, including Borgia and Giuliano della Rovere, had met in the Camera del Pappagallo of the Vatican palace to discuss the ceremonies which should accompany the reception of the relic. Some were of the opinion that the lance-head should be received with all the solemnity and veneration which had been accorded the head of S. Andrew when it was brought to Rome in Pius II's time. Others urged caution, however, pointing out that allegedly authentic heads of the Holy Lance were preserved in Nuremberg and in other cities such as Paris, "where in the king's chapel a similar lance-head is preserved." Still others could cite a "certain very old chronicle" to the effect that the lance-head had in fact remained at Constantinople, where it was an object of public veneration "usque ad hec tempora." Indeed there were a good many witnesses still living who had seen the lance-head in Constantinople before the Turks captured the city in 1453. The Venetians were said once to have offered 70,000 ducats for the relic, but the sultan would not relinquish it to them. Some of the cardinals or others who were consulted considered the possibility that Bayazid, the chief enemy of Christendom, might well be making his gift rather "in derisum et derisionem quam aliter." Having pondered these and other such questions, the eight cardinals put the matter up to the pope. Although most of the cardinal-priests were of the opinion that his Holiness should receive the lance-head from the Turkish envoy without solemnity, pending a proper investigation of the claims for authenticity of the relics in Nuremberg and the Sainte-Chapelle in Paris, Innocent VIII decided otherwise, and sent his nephew Niccolò Cibo, the Turkish-speaking archbishop of Arles, together with Luca Borsano, bishop of Foligno, to Ancona to receive the lance-head and bear it in formal procession on the way back to Rome.[30]

Cibo and Borsano left Rome on 7 May (1492). Aldello Piccolomini, a canon of Siena, "my colleague," says Burchard, "in the office of ceremonies," went with them to take charge of the general procession and such ceremonies as should prove necessary along the way. On the twenty-fourth Cardinal Giuliano della Rovere of Ostia left Rome with Cardinal George Costa of Lisbon, appointed legates *de latere*, to meet the oncoming procession at Narni. In the meantime the Curia had learned of the departure of young Ferrante [II], prince of Capua, from Naples to Rome. The pope had sent his son Franceschetto Cibo to meet Ferrante at the southern confines of the territories of the Church.[31] On 27 May Ferrante entered Rome by the Porta Asinaria, being welcomed by the cardinals of Benevento and Siena. Infessura says that he came "with 900 knights and 260 mules loaded with boxes and things." The pope received Ferrante in the Camera del Pappagallo, with the cardinals seated in a circle around him *more consistoriali*. The prince of Capua commended his grandfather, King Ferrante, and his father, Alfonso of Calabria, as well as himself to the pope in a short, set speech, to which Innocent replied with equal brevity. After greeting the cardinals, beginning with Borgia, with the *oris osculum*, the prince was seated after the cardinal of Siena. The members of his entourage could then approach the papal throne. Thereafter the Neapolitans were soon allowed to return to their rooms.[32] During Ferrante's stay in Rome,

---

[29] *Cf.* Sen. Secreta, Reg. 34, fols. 123^r–124^v [134^r–135^v], 128^v–129^r [139^v–140^r], 132^r [143^r], and 135^r [146^r], docs. dated from 2 July to 15 October, 1492.

[30] Burchard, *Diarium*, ed. Thuasne, I, 473–75, and ed. Celani, I, 356–58, with notes; Infessura, *Diaria*, ed. Tommasini, p. 274.

[31] Burchard, *Diarium*, ed. Thuasne, I, 475–76, and ed. Celani, I, 358–59.

[32] Burchard, *Diarium*, ed. Thuasne, I, 477–79, and ed. Celani, I, 360–62; Pontani, *Diario*, ed. Toni, in *RISS*, III-2, p. 71; Trinchera, *Codice aragonese*, II-1, pp. 115–17. The Porta Asinaria was closed about 1572; it opened into the Via Appia Nuova, and was also called the Porta Lateranensis (*cf.* Burchard, *Diarium*, ed. Thuasne, I, 489, and ed. Celani, I, 369, lines 24–25). It was replaced by the Porta S. Giovanni in 1575 (L. Cassannelli, G. Delfini, and D. Fonti, *Le Mura di Roma*, Rome, 1974, p. 182).

he was invited by Cardinal Ascanio [Sforza] to a dinner which lasted from the twentieth to the fifth hour of the night [from 5:00 P.M. to about 2:00 A.M.], at which there were so many and such magnificent displays and sumptuous things that it would be impossible to detail them here. . . . It is enough to say that if the king of France or another such were coming, more could not have been done. Nothing is being clearly stated as to the reason for his coming.[33]

The reason, however, was clearly understood in Paris and Milan.

On 29 May the Turkish envoy entered Rome by the Porta del Popolo, having been met after some confusion by Niccolò Orsini, count of Pitigliano, Franceschetto Cibo, and various Roman nobles. He had only five servants with him. Giorgio Bocciardi, brother of the archbishop of Arles, had come with him to serve as interpreter. The envoy rode into the city between Orsini and Franceschetto, followed by the ambassadors of Poland, Venice, Milan, Florence, and Siena. The cavalcade proceeded from the Porta del Popolo along the (present) Via del Corso to the church of S. Maria in Via Lata, after which it turned right for some distance and passed through the Campo dei Fiori, thence northwestward to the Piazza S. Pietro, and on to the house of one Bartolommeo Montani, one-time papal chamberlain, which had been prepared as the envoy's residence during his stay in Rome. Upon arrival the envoy thanked the company for attending him, and they all withdrew,[34] presumably eager to seek news of the progress of Cardinals della Rovere and Costa, whom the pope had sent to Narni to convey the iron head of the Holy Lance to Rome.

Johann Burchard had made elaborate plans for the reception of the relic. The cardinals of Ostia and Lisbon had apparently reached Rome shortly after the arrival of the Turkish envoy. Despite the hot weather and the threat of rain, of which there had been much lately, the sickly Innocent VIII went himself in the early-morning hours of 31 May (1492) to the church of S. Maria del Popolo, where just outside the city gate the two cardinals awaited him, with the lance-head in a crystalline tabernacle. It was Ascension day. The pope had entered the church long enough for a prayer to be said before the altar, and for donning a rich pluvial and precious miter. Then he followed the long line of officials, prelates, and cardinals out of the church into the piazza; the *baldacchino* was abandoned because of the pressure of the crowd outside. Some forty or more paces beyond the Porta del Popolo, stood Giuliano della Rovere and his confrère of Lisbon.

As Innocent approached, they advanced to meet him. Cardinal Giuliano held out to the pope the crystalline tabernacle containing the lance-head. Innocent removed his miter before accepting it, "et illud osculatus est reverenter." It was hard now to organize the procession for the return to S. Peter's. A great crowd filled the area around the gate and before the church of S. Maria del Popolo. It took the papal chamberlain more than an hour to get the procession started. The city clergy were as excited and tumultuous as the members of the Roman guilds and confraternities. Guildsmen refused to follow the clergy, and even debated among themselves over the order of precedence. At length a cardinal commanded them to proceed or withdraw under penalty. They proceeded, and the clergy followed; Burchard has scrupulously recorded the clerical order of procession. Neapolitan nobles in the suite of the young prince of Capua helped carry the papal *baldacchino*. Despite the difficulty in beginning, the procession now moved easily. The way had all been cleaned up and hung with banners, says Burchard, from the Palazzo Martelli to S. Peter's basilica. Under the portico of the basilica the procession was disbanded. The tired pope, obviously ill, gave the crowd his benediction, while Rodrigo Borgia held the tabernacle containing the lance-head. Plenary indulgences were granted those who had witnessed the reception of the precious relic.

The Turkish envoy, whom Burchard calls "Chasimpuerg," now approached the pope, and delivered letters to him. With Giorgio Bocciardi acting as interpreter, he explained that Sultan Bayazid had sent the lance-head to Rome. The envoy then requested permission to see Jem Sultan. The pope replied that he would see the letters later, and then give his response; he gave them to Niccolò Cibo, the archbishop of Arles, for safe-keeping. The letters were not opened and read at the time of their presentation to the pope, because it was said that the

---

[33] Infessura, *Diaria*, ed. Tommasini, pp. 273–74.

[34] Burchard, *Diarium*, ed. Thuasne, I, 481–82, and ed. Celani, I, 363–64. Montani's name appears in different forms in different MSS. of Burchard. On Giorgio and Niccolò Bocciardi (Bucciardo), note the sketches by Roberto Zapperi, in the *Dizionario biografico degli italiani*, XIV (1972), 769–73.

envoy had brought the 40,000 ducats' pension for Jem, and they would thus contain mention of the fact. (The envoy had not, however, brought the money, which Bayazid would soon refuse to pay.) Innocent retired into the palace, while the cardinals entered S. Peter's. The cardinal of S. Clemente celebrated a public mass which Ferrante of Capua dutifully attended. The presence of the young prince raised various problems of ecclesiastical protocol, which the indefatigable Burchard was quite equal to solving.[35]

Sigismondo de' Conti has preserved the text of Sultan Bayazid's letter to the pope, which merely states that he was sending to Rome the lance-head which had pierced the side of the great Prophet Jesus Christ. The sultan asked that his envoy be permitted to see Jem Sultan and quickly bring back to Istanbul reassuring news of the pope's own good health.[36] There was no mention of money although undoubtedly the envoy was questioned as to his master's intentions in this respect.

On Sunday, 3 June (1492), the pope's granddaughter Battistina was married to Luigi of Aragon, marquis of Gerace and uncle of the prince of Capua. The ceremony took place in the Vatican palace, "in prima camera post aulam pontificum, supra hortum," sumptuously prepared for the occasion. The wedding was performed by Archbishop Giovanni de' Sacchi of Ragusa in the presence of the pope; the cardinals of S. Pietro in Vincoli, Benevento, and S. Anastasia; the prince of Capua; the pope's daughter Theodorina, mother of the bride; Peretta, sister of the bride; Franceschetto Cibo and his wife Maddalena, daughter of Lorenzo il Magnifico; Alfonso Piccolomini, duke of Amalfi; "and many other barons [and] nobles to the number of forty or thereabout." The humanist and statesman Giovanni Gioviano Pontano, first secretary of the king of Naples, was also present, and assisted Luigi in the ceremony, the full details of which are supplied by Burchard.[37]

On the following day, the fourth, there was a secret consistory at which Ferrante, the prince of Capua, was invested with the kingdom of Naples, *regnum Sicilie*, to take effect after the deaths of his father Alfonso of Calabria and his grandfather King Ferrante. Two days later the prince of Capua departed for Naples, accompanied by the cardinals of Siena and Benevento beyond the Porta Asinaria. He left just after noon, dined at Grottaferrata, and spent the night at Marino.[38] Young Ferrante's investiture had been necessitated by the papal declaration in public consistory (in November, 1489) that the house of Aragon had been dispossessed, and that the kingdom of Naples had reverted by forfeiture to the Holy See.

The ailing pontiff received the Ottoman envoy in a farewell audience on 14 June, directing him to warn Sultan Bayazid that if he broke his pledge of peace, the Christians would employ Jem Sultan against him. No attack against Hungary would be tolerated. Bayazid continued to build up his forces, however, as the Venetians warned King Ferrante,[39] and Innocent VIII's activities would soon be over. His secretary, Sigismondo de' Conti, writes that the reception of the Holy Lance "was almost Innocent's last act." His reign had been full of war and the fear of war, so that he had not dared even to fulfill his vow to visit the shrine of S. Maria

[35] Burchard, *Diarium*, ed. Thuasne, I, 482–87, and ed. Celani, I, 364–68; Sigismondo de' Conti, II, 28–29, who says that Innocent VIII had been suffering for some months with a urinary disorder and a persistent fever (*qui menses aliquot dissuria et febre ethica laborarat*); Infessura, *Diaria*, ed. Tommasini, p. 274, where the editor cites a description of the lance-head, from a letter of the Florentine ambassador Filippo Valori to the Otto di Pratica, summarized in Thuasne, *Djem-Sultan*, pp. 300–1; Pastor, *Gesch. d. Päpste*, III-1 (repr. 1955), 278–79, with refs. Valori, of whom there will be further mention, was born in 1456, and died at the age of thirty-eight on a diplomatic mission to Naples. He was a Platonic scholar and friend of Lorenzo de' Medici, Poliziano, and Marsilio Ficino. Something of a protégé of Matthias Corvinus, Valori taught Plato in Hungary for some time.

[36] Sigismondo de' Conti, I, 27–28; also in Baluze, *Miscellanea*, ed. Mansi, I (1761), 651. The Latin version of the sultan's letter identifies the Turkish envoy as "Zaus Cassiminus."

[37] Burchard, *Diarium*, ed. Thuasne, I, 487–88, and ed. Celani, I, 368–69. On 2 March, 1492, King Ferrante wrote a letter of thanks to the pope upon the completion of the marriage contract (Trinchera, *Codice aragonese*, II, pt. 1 [1868], 43–44).

[38] Burchard, *Diarium*, ed. Thuasne, I, 488–89, and ed. Celani, I, 369–70; Sigismondo de' Conti, II, 34; Raynaldus, *Ann. eccl.*, ad ann. 1492, nos. 10–13, vol. XIX (1693), pp. 408–10. There is a break in Burchard's diary from Thursday, 14 June, to the first Sunday of Advent, 2 December, 1492, during which time Innocent VIII died, and Rodrigo Borgia was elected Pope Alexander VI (*cf.* Celani, I, 371, note 1).

[39] Thuasne, *Djem-Sultan*, p. 302. In late June and July, 1492, Ferrante of Naples expected a Turkish attack upon Italy (Trinchera, *Codice aragonese*, II–1, pp. 125–27, 129, 130–31, 134).

di Loreto. In fact he had rarely been able to set foot outside the city walls, and then only to go to Ostia with a heavy guard or to his villa at Magliana, on the Via Portese six miles from Rome.[40]

Innocent had been ill for about two years. His secretary informs us that he suffered from a quartan fever and a urinary disorder, although the skill of his aged physician Giacomo di San Genesio succeeded in holding the worst effects of his ailments in abeyance for some time. After Giacomo's death, the pope's new physicians proved unequal to the problem.[41] From the early spring of 1492 Innocent's decline became very marked. On 8 April Lorenzo de' Medici had died, "il primo cittadino d'Italia." His passing removed from the political scene the chief advocate of maintaining peace in the peninsula as the best way to obviate the ever-threatening French intervention in Italian affairs. Innocent's son Franceschetto was married, as we know, to Lorenzo's daughter Maddalena. The pope felt Lorenzo's death keenly, but his sense of loss was caused more by political than by personal considerations. As the pope got worse from day to day, the cardinals returned to Rome despite the heat of mid-July. The last days of Innocent VIII are recorded in detail in the dispatches which the Florentine ambassador, Filippo Valori, sent to the Otto di Pratica.[42]

Valori reports that the cardinals all came to the palace on 17 July (1492). They carried off the holy lance-head, which was in the pope's room, to return it to the treasury of S. Peter's.[43] They also granted their permission for the pope to distribute 48,000 ducats among his relatives. From 18 to 21 July Innocent was badly off, showed a slight improvement, and then suffered a serious relapse; his physicians gave him up for dead, and stopped giving him medicine. On the morning of the twentieth the cardinals assembled and took measures to maintain the government during the pope's illness and in the expected event of his death. Niccolò Orsini, count of Pitigliano, was assigned one hundred archers to police the streets and two hundred infantry to guard the gates and bridges in the city.[44] That was on 20 July. On the twenty-third Orsini's infantry force was raised to four hundred, and another hundred men were recruited as a special guard for Jem Sultan.[45]

As the pope grew worse, tension mounted in the Curia and in the city. Valori informed his principals in Florence that on 24 July a congregation of cardinals delegated all the authority of the Sacred College to Raffaele Riario, the Camerlengo. The recruitment of infantry was raised to eight hundred to guard the Borgo, the Vatican, and other parts of the city. Besides this, the energetic abbot of S. Denis, Jean de Bilhères-Lagraulas, who was Charles VIII's ambassador to the Holy See, was made governor of Rome with a force of four hundred men. The count of Pitigliano was assigned the protection of the Borgo and the Vatican; now he had at least eight hundred infantry at his command, and measures had been taken to meet any emergency that might arise within some two miles of the city. On the morning of the twenty-fifth the Vatican and several other places were fortified. Artillery was placed in strategic positions. Jem Sultan was moved into the apartment above the Sistine Chapel, "a very strong place," writes Valori, "where he will be

[40] Sigismondo de' Conti, II, 29.

[41] Sigismondo de' Conti, II, 36; Pastor, *Gesch. d. Päpste*, III-1 (repr. 1955), 280–81, with refs.

[42] Thuasne, *Burchardi diarium*, I, append., nos. 44–52, pp. 567–75, from Arch. di Stato di Firenze, Lettere agli Otto di Pratica (Classe X, dist. 6, filza 8, by the old classification), letters dated at Rome from 15 to 26 July, 1492. The "Eight" were a special committee which dealt with foreign and military affairs in Florence. Innocent sent Niccolò Cibo, archbishop of Arles, to Florence "ad condolerse de la morte de Lorenzo" (A. de Boüard, "Lettres de Rome . . . ," *Mélanges d'archéologie et d'histoire*, XXXIII, no. XLIV, pp. 322–23). Lorenzo de' Medici had certainly not been alone in the desire to maintain peace and the balance of power in Italy. The Venetians had been equally interested, although for different reasons. *Cf.* Ernesto Pontieri, "La 'Guerra dei baroni' . . . in dispacci della diplomazia fiorentina," *Arch. stor. per le province napoletane*, 3rd ser., IX (LXXXVIII, 1970–71), esp. pp. 199–200 (*cf.* above, Chapter 13, note 41).

[43] Thuasne, *Burchardi diarium*, I, append., no. 46, p. 569, and *cf.* Sigismondo de' Conti, II, 37, and Thuasne, *Djem-Sultan*, p. 303.

[44] Thuasne, *Burchardi diarium*, I, append., no. 48, p. 570, dispatch of 20 July; *cf.* Trinchera, *Codice aragonese*, II-1, pp. 140, 142–43. Innocent VIII's *gravis egritudo* was known in Venice by 20 July, when the Senate sent the Sacred College an appropriate expression of regret. The news had come in a letter dated 16 July from Andrea Capello, Girolamo Donato's colleague in the Venetian embassy at Rome (Sen. Secreta, Reg. 34, fols. 124v–125r [135v–136r]). Capello had been elected to share the Roman mission with Donato on 7 February, 1492 (*ibid.*, fol. 110r [122r], Ven. style 1491).

[45] Thuasne, *Burchardi diarium*, I, append., no. 50, p. 571, dispatch of 23 July. On 15 July there was a rumor in Ferrara that Sultan Bayazid had put 800 sail to sea for an invasion of Italy "et più de cento milia persone a la guera" (*Diario ferrarese*, in *RISS*, XXIV, pt. 7 [1933], p. 127).

as secure as he would be in the Castel S. Angelo." That morning the pope had received extreme unction. His physicians had said that he would not live until midnight. Negotiations were going on among the cardinals with a view to the forthcoming conclave.[46]

The pope's physicians were not mistaken. Innocent VIII's condition was hopeless. He died on the night of 25–26 July, 1492. The Sacred College assembled in the Vatican palace. As usual after a pope's death, the cardinals whom he had created accompanied his body to S. Peter's. The castellan of S. Angelo swore fealty to the College, another usual procedure *in obitu pontificis*. The resident Italian ambassadors offered the College the support and resources of their states if they should be needed, a courteous but not very significant gesture. The cardinals seemed singularly united. The city was in arms, but there was no tumult; the Orsini and Colonnesi were as peaceful as the rest of the local barons. Some of them had pledged their support to the city government to maintain order. The period of mourning with its attendant ceremonies was to begin on Saturday, the twenty-eighth, and would last for nine days. The conclave would begin on the tenth day (6 August). The city remained surprisingly quiet. Behind the scenes negotiations were going on among the cardinals. As the conclave began, Valori informed the Otto di Pratica in Florence that Cardinals Oliviero Carafa of Naples and George Costa of Lisbon, both highly thought of, seemed the most likely candidates for the triple tiara.[47]

Innocent VIII was buried on 5 August in old S. Peter's, near the great altar of the Virgin, opposite the tomb of Paul II, "whom he tried to imitate as a good and laudable pontiff."[48] He had not been too good a pope; perhaps he had not chosen a high enough model to imitate. According to Sigismondo de' Conti, on the day before his death Innocent had summoned the cardinals to the palace and, although his voice was very weak, expressed at some length the regret that he had been unequal to the burden they had placed upon him. He asked their pardon, and urged them in a spirit of concord to elect a better pope than he had been.[49] It remained to be seen whether they would do so.

A corrupt College could not produce a high-minded conclave. Innocent VIII might hope for a successor better than he, but the prospects of electing a worthy pope were not good, considering the worldliness of such cardinals as Ascanio Sforza, Rodrigo Borgia, Giuliano and the other della Roveres, Raffaele Riario, Giangia-

---

[46] Thuasne, *Burchardi diarium*, I, append., no. 51, pp. 572–73, dispatch of 25 July. According to Infessura, *Diaria*, ed. Tommasini, p. 274, the cardinals removed Jem Sultan to the Castel S. Angelo during the second week in July, which in view of Valori's statement is apparently untrue. Although Infessura is usually well informed, it is clear that he always remained an outsider to events in the Vatican. *Cf.* Sa'd-ad-Dīn, in *Journal asiatique*, IX (1826, repr. 1965), 168, who says that Jem was kept for twenty days in a "place of security." It was for Jean de Bilhères[-Lagraulas], abbot of S. Denis, that Michelangelo some years later carved the Pietà now in S. Peter's (*cf.* Sigismondo de'Conti, II, 94, note 2, and Pastor, *Gesch. d. Päpste*, III–1 [repr. 1955], 339). On his appointment as governor of Rome, see Sigismondo, II, 51, and on his name, see below, Chapter 16, note 100.

[47] Thuasne, *Burchardi diarium*, I, 491, note, and append., nos. 52–56, pp. 573–78, dispatches of 26 July to 6 August, and on Innocent VIII's funeral, *cf. ibid.*, no. 57, pp. 578–80; Infessura, *Diaria*, ed. Tommasini, pp. 275–79; Trinchera, *Codice aragonese*, II–1, p. 144. By a slip of the pen, Thuasne, *Djem-Sultan*, p. 303, says that Innocent VIII died "dans la nuit du 25 au 26 août." See G. B. Picotti, *La Giovinezza di Leone X*, Milan, 1927, pp. 404 ff. The Sacred College immediately informed the rulers of the Italian and other states of the pope's death (Arch. di Stato di Mantova, Arch. Gonzaga, Busta 834, letter dated 26 July, 1492).

[48] Sigismondo de' Conti, II, 37. On 30 January, 1498, Innocent VIII's body was transferred to the bronze tomb prepared by Antonio Pollaiuolo (Burchard, *Diarium*, ed. L. Thuasne, II [1884], 431–32, and ed. E. Celani, II [1911–42], 72, in the new Muratori, *RISS*, XXXII, pt. 1). This is one of the few monuments restored to the new S. Peter's from the old. It may still be seen against one of the pillars on the left aisle of the nave, but is set much higher up than the artist intended. According to the present epitaph, the tomb was transferred to the new basilica in 1621 by Alberigo Cibo Malaspina, prince of Massa. *Cf.* Thuasne, *Burchardi diarium*, I, 492; Pastor, *Gesch. d. Päpste*, III–1 (repr. 1955), 282–83, with refs.; and Renzo U. Montini, *Le Tombe dei Papi*, Rome, 1957, pp. 297–301. Innocent's epitaph also recalls Bayazid II's gift of the Holy Lance to the papacy, *lancea quae Christi hausit latus a Baiazete Turcarum tyranno dono missa*. The tomb itself is said to have cost 4,000 ducats (Eugène Müntz, *Les Arts à la cour des papes Innocent VIII, Alexandre VI, Pie III [1484–1503]*, Paris, 1898, pp. 89–90).

[49] *Cf.* Sigismondo de' Conti, II, 36, who dates Innocent's address to the cardinals to "the day before he died," but Pastor, *Gesch. d. Päpste*, III–1 (repr. 1955), 282, note 3, suggests it may have taken place on 17 July when Valori reports that "sua Santità usò molte tenere et buone parole" in commending the Church to the cardinals (Thuasne, *Burchardi diarium*, I, append., no. 46, p. 569). Nevertheless, on that occasion he proceeded to ask them for their consent to his distribution of 48,000 ducats among members of his family. Maybe he had reformed "pridie quam exspiraret."

como Sclafenati, Lorenzo Cibo, Antoniotto Pallavicini, Maffeo Gherardo, Federigo di Sanseverino, and Battista Orsini. During an interregnum the Cardinal Camerlengo ruled the city and states of the Church. In this position Riario showed himself competent.

On 6 August, 1492, twenty-three cardinals entered the conclave, which was held in the chapel of S. Niccolò da Bari in the Vatican Palace. The cynicism with which most of them went about their business is astonishing. The atmosphere in the conclave was tense, owing to the hostility between Milan and Naples, which threatened to plunge Italy into war. Innocent VIII had been as necessary for the preservation of peace as Lorenzo de' Medici, and now both were dead. Ascanio Sforza represented the interests of his brother Lodovico il Moro. King Ferrante was, therefore, supporting Giuliano della Rovere, Ascanio's bitterest enemy and most distinguished opponent. We have much information concerning the conclave, including the three scrutinies of 8–10 August, but once again there is a gap in the ceremonial diary of Johann Burchard (who was present at the conclave), extending from 14 June to 2 December, 1492. In the early morning hours of 11 August announcement was made of the election of Cardinal Rodrigo Borgia as Pope Alexander VI. It was Pastor's considered judgment that the election, although indisputably valid, had been obtained by simony and intrigue, "durch masslose simonistische Umtriebe erzielt."[50]

Some historical issues seem destined to unending controversy. One of them is whether Alexander VI's election was really simoniacal. The problem is in fact more complex than Pastor seems to have realized. Years ago Picotti expressed some technical reservations as to Rodrigo Borgia's being literally guilty of simony, "non potendo essere simonia, quando il prezzo non determina la volontà di chi lo riceve, ma tutt'al più lo rafforza nella deliberazione già presa."[51] That is, there is a difference between a bribe and a reward. Picotti believed that Ascanio entered the conclave with the intention of making Borgia the pope, to protect Milanese interests and to frustrate his archenemy Giuliano della Rovere. He doubtless knew what his reward would be by prior arrangement with Borgia, but his activities in the conclave were not primarily motivated by the expectation of that reward. The three scrutinies of 8–10 August are preserved in a unique copy in a Vatican manuscript.[52] Analysis and interpretation of them

---

[50] Pastor, *Gesch. d. Päpste*, III–1 (repr. 1955), 341–48, and vol. III–2 (repr. 1956), append., nos. 10–20, pp. 1049–56, and *Hist. Popes*, V, 377–86, and append., nos. 8–18, pp. 532–42, all documents but the first being dated in August, 1492; Thuasne, *Burchardi diarium*, I, append., no. 57, pp. 579–80, and vol. II, pp. 1–4 (from Infessura), esp. Thuasne's notes, and append., nos. 1–3, pp. 607–12; Infessura, *Diaria*, ed. Tommasini, pp. 279, 280–82; Sigismondo de'Conti, II, 51–54; Raynaldus, *Ann. eccl.*, ad ann. 1492, nos. 24–26, vol. XIX (1693), pp. 412b–413b. Rodrigo Borgia had been made cardinal-deacon of S. Niccolò in Carcere by his uncle Calixtus III in the creation of 17 September, 1456 (Eubel, *Hierarchia*, II [1914, repr. 1960], 12).

Borgia's election was known in Venice by 19 August, as shown by the Senate's letter to Andrea Capello, the Republic's ambassador in Rome (Sen. Secreta, Reg. 34, fols. 127^v–128^r [138^v–139^r]): "Quod plurimis rationibus futurum existimabamus et procul dubio expectabamus id vestre littere priores diei XI hora VIIII nobis reddite die insequenti hora XVI et item alie subsequentes quarum postreme sunt diei XIIII instantis significarunt ad illud scilicet suppremum pontificatus fastigium reverendissimum dominum vicecancellarium fuisse provectum, expectabamus diximus quoniam animo nostro voluntatibus nobis ratas excelentissimas et prope divinas virtutes et dotes quibus ipsum insignitum et ornatum conspiciebamus videbatur a divina providentia talem pastorem gregi dominico et Sacrosancte Romane Ecclesie vicarium suum fuisse delectum et proordinatum, gavisi profecto sumus cum universo senatu nostro ex intimis cordis nostri et gaudii ac consolationis nostre signa edidimus et hic et in universa ditione nostra qualia magnitudini gaudii nostri congrua arbitrati sumus. . . ."

[51] G. B. Picotti, *La Giovinezza di Leone X*, Milan, 1927, pp. 406–35, 445–60 (quotation on p. 427); *cf.* Picotti, "Giovanni de'Medici nel conclave per l'elezione di Alessandro VI," *Archivio della R. Società romana di storia patria*, XLIV (1921), 87–168, with thirteen documents, and esp. pp. 124 ff. (with the same quotation appearing on p. 126).

[52] Bibl. Apost. Vaticana, Cod. lat. 12,518, formerly in the Arch. Segr. Vaticano, Miscell., Arm. XV, tom. 109, fols. 43^v–48^v, published by Vinzenz Schweitzer, "Zur Wahl Alexanders VI.," in *Historisches Jahrbuch*, XXX (1909), 809–14; Ferdinando La Torre, *Del Conclave di Alessandro VI, papa Borgia*, Florence and Rome, 1933, pp. 89–92; and G. B. Picotti, "Nuovi Studi e documenti intorno a papa Alessandro VI," *Rivista di storia della Chiesa in Italia*, V (1951), 243–47. I examined the three scrutinies of 8–10 August in the Vaticana in July, 1966, and found (needless to add) that Picotti's edition and commentary are excellent.

Cardinals Domenico della Rovere, Ascanio Sforza, Antoniotto Pallavicini, Giovanni Battista Zeno, Oliviero Carafa, and Giangiacomo Sclafenati voted for Rodrigo Borgia on all three scrutinies. Giovanni de' Conti voted for him on the second and third. Battista Orsini voted for him on the first scrutiny only, Raffaele Riario on the second, and Francesco Todeschini Piccolomini on the third (Cod. Vat. lat. 12,518, fols. 43^v–44^r, 45^v–46^r, 47^v–48^r, and *cf.* Picotti, "Nuovi Studi," p. 245). The reverse of the third scrutiny bears the note (MS. cit., fol. 48^v): "Tertium scrutinium X Augusti 1492, die festivitatis Sancti Laurentii." Borgia was still not elected.

would be baffling except for a good deal of other evidence, because even the third scrutiny gives no promise of Borgia's election before sunset on 10 August.[53] Not infrequently in a conclave each cardinal voted for two or three candidates. Sometimes such votes were gestures of courtesy; sometimes, on the early scrutinies, they were designed to mislead one's opponents. After the third scrutiny, however, at about 7:00 P.M. on 10 August, 1492, Ascanio Sforza wrote a note from the conclave itself to his brother Lodovico il Moro that the cardinals had decided to elect the vice-chancellor Rodrigo Borgia as pope "tomorrow morning."[54] And, indeed, the following morning, the eleventh, the last scrutiny was held. There was already some fear of a French expedition against Naples, and the vice-chancellor was apparently regarded as standing for a strong and independent papacy. He now received all the votes except his own, which he gave to Carafa.[55]

At the strategic moment in the conclave Ascanio, who had no chance of being elected himself, had directed his partisans to designate Rodrigo Borgia as their candidate, and they had done so. Their votes, together with those of Borgia's own supporters, had gained the electoral victory for which Ascanio thanked God in his letter to il Moro. The Senator of Rome, Ambrogio Mirabilia, wrote to Bartolommeo Calco, the ducal secretary in Milan, that Ascanio "è stato causa luy solo de farlo papa."[56] When the contest had been decided, all the cardinals joined the chorus of assent, even Giuliano della Rovere, who disliked Borgia as much as he did Ascanio. The papal secretary and chronicler Sigismondo de' Conti says that the election was unanimous,[57] and during the second half of August the Sacred College informed all Europe of the final harmony of opinion which obtained in the conclave.[58] Nevertheless, the Venetian envoy in Milan voiced the dissatisfaction of others besides his countrymen when he informed his confrère from Ferrara "that by simony and a thousand villanies and indecencies the papacy has been sold, which is a disgraceful and detestable business," and that when France and Spain understood the enormity of the new pope's transgression, they would withhold their obedience from him.[59] It might be that Ascanio bore a larger guilt of simony in the election of August, 1492, than did his friend Rodrigo Borgia, but apparently the Venetian envoy in Milan was not adequately sensitive to the canonical distinction between a bribe and a reward when it came to papal elections. The more Picotti himself studied the conclave of 1492, however, the more he moved toward the opinion of simony. He has himself observed that it is probably no accident that no accounts of papal income and expenditure exist in the registers of *Introitus et Exitus* for August '92—the books seem to have been tampered with—and that fictitious debts were apparently invented as

[53] *Cf.* Pastor, *Gesch. d. Päpste*, III–2 (repr. 1956), append., no. 12, p. 1052, a dispatch of Filippo Valori (whom Pastor misnames "Bartolomeo") to the Otto di Pratica in Florence, dated 10 August, 1492, at about 11:00 A.M. (*hora decima quinta*): ". . . si è inteso come [e signori cardinali] hanno facto due squittini mercoledì et giovedì mattina et stamani hanno facto il terzo, et benchè sia difficil cosa intenderne il vero, pure si ritrahe che tra loro sono in discordia non pichola. . . ."

[54] Picotti, "Nuovi Studi," doc. no. III, p. 247.

[55] Thuasne, *Burchardi diarium*, II, append., no. 2, pp. 610–11, dispatch of Valori to the Otto di Pratica, dated at Rome on 12 August, 1492, at about 5:00 P.M. (*hora vicesima prima*). Pastor, *Gesch. d. Päpste*, III–1 (repr. 1955), 347, note 1, cites the Acta consistorialia, fol. 1ᵛ, to the effect that the election was announced "de mane circa horam undecimam" (about 7:00 A.M.), which accords with the belief of the notary Pietro Merili that the election took place "summo mane ante ortum solis" (Fabio Gori, ed., *Archivio storico, artistico . . . di Roma*, IV [Rome and Spoleto, 1883], 242, also cited by Pastor). *Cf.* Picotti, "Nuovi Studi," p. 205.

[56] Pastor, *Gesch. d. Päpste*, III–2 (repr. 1956), append., no. 13, p. 1053, letter dated at Rome on 13 August, 1492.

[57] Sigismondo de' Conti, II, 54; J. Schnitzer, "Zur Wahl Alexanders VI.," *Zeitschr. für Kirchengeschichte*, XXXIV (1913), 375; and *cf.* Pastor, *Gesch. d. Päpste*, III–1 (repr. 1955), 346, note 4, and p. 349, note 1.

[58] *Cf.* the letter of 28 August to Francesco Gonzaga of Mantua, to whom the cardinals wrote that, owing to Innocent VIII's removal *septimo Kalendas Augusti ex hac erumnosa ad feliciorem vitam*, they had proceeded in the conclave to elect his successor, ". . . atque illic spiritus sancti inspiratione afflati ad electionem summi pontificis procedentes, post aliquas consultationes non solum unanimi omnium voto concordiaque sed nemine discrepante reverendissimum patrem dominum Rodericum tunc episcopum Portuensem Sancte Romane Ecclesie vicecancellarium, nunc Alexandrum VI nuncupatum, omni laude cumulatissimum et longa experientia probatissimum communi consensu et unanimi voto concordiaque Romane Ecclesie dignissimum pastorem ac pontificem elegimus . . ." (Arch. di Stato di Mantova, Arch. Gonzaga, Busta 834). This letter received a wide distribution (note Pastor, *Gesch. d. Päpste*, III–1, 346, note 4, quotation from the *Kerkhistorisch Archief*, III [Amsterdam, 1862], 65–67, and Picotti, "Nuovi Studi," p. 205 and note 161).

[59] Pastor, *Gesch. d. Päpste*, III–1, 356, and III–2, append., no. 16, p. 1054, letter of the Ferrarese envoy Giacomo Trotti to Duke Ercole d'Este, dated at Milan on 28 August, 1492. *Cf.* Picotti, "Nuovi Studi," p. 199.

owing to Cardinals Campofregoso, Domenico della Rovere, Sanseverino, and Orsini for payment by the Apostolic Camera.[60]

Giuliano della Rovere wa regarded as pro-French although, as we have seen, he was also favored by King Ferrante of Naples. Giuliano's prominence throughout Innocent VIII's reign had prejudiced many of his colleagues against him. His *animo terribile* had alienated the upright Cardinal Francesco Todeschini Piccolomini quite as much as had the licentiousness of Rodrigo Borgia. Nevertheless, Giuliano's time would come. The election of August, 1492, came as an equal surprise to the Curia Romana and to Europe. Borgia had not appeared to have much support, but Gianandrea Boccaccio, bishop of Modena and Ferrarese envoy to the Holy See, had reminded Duchess Eleonora in a dispatch of 4 August that his immense wealth made him a strong contender for the papacy. He could dispose of the lucrative vice-chancellorship, *ch'è uno altro papato*, and the towns of Civita Castellana and Nepi, the fortress of Soriano, an abbey at L'Aquila worth 1,000 ducats, another such at Albano, and two larger ones in the kingdom of Naples, the bishopric of Porto with revenues of 1,200, the abbey of Subiaco with twenty-two villages (*castelli*) bringing in 2,000, as well as allegedly sixteen excellent bishoprics in Spain, including that of Valencia worth 16,000, Cartagena worth 7,000, and Majorca worth 6,000, not to speak of various rich abbeys and other benefices.[61] Boccaccio does not mention Borgia's great palace in Rome, now the Palazzo Sforza-Cesarini on the Corso Vittorio Emmanuele, located near the house then owned by Vannozza de' Catanei on the Piazza Branca, midway between the bridge of S. Angelo and the Campo dei Fiori.[62] Vannozza had been Borgia's mistress. She was the mother of four of his children, including the famous Lucrezia and the infamous Cesare. Borgia had been quite willing to give his palace, whether by way of reward or of remuneration, to Ascanio Sforza, who was entirely responsible for his election.

On 12 August, the day after the election, the Florentine ambassador Filippo Valori wrote the Otto di Pratica: "The manner in which this election was held your lordships will hear from Ser Niccolò Michelozzi, who will leave here in a few days—for good reasons it is well not to write it, and in any event many details cannot be stated so well by letter as by word of mouth." To Ascanio Sforza, Rodrigo promised—and gave—the vice-chancellorship and the Palazzo Borgia, the fortress of Nepi, the Hungarian bishopric of Erlau (Eger) with its annual revenue of 10,000 ducats, "et molte altre cose." Cardinal Battista Orsini was to receive the Rocca Soriano and the town of Monticelli, the Anconitan legation, "and the church of Cartagena in Spain which yields 5,000 ducats a year." Cardinal Giovanni Colonna got the abbey of Subiaco with a score of villages producing 3,000 ducats or more a year, "of which abbey and its lands the pope is making the house of Colonna *padroni* in perpetuity." To Giovanni Battista Savelli were promised Civita Castellana, the bishopric of Majorca, and other favors. Raffaele Riario was given Spanish benefices worth 4,000 ducats, and was promised that the house which Ascanio Sforza had been occupying on the Piazza Navona would be restored to the children of the late Count Girolamo. Sanseverino received Rodrigo Borgia's house in Milan as well as other things. Antoniotto Pallavicini was granted the bishopric of Pamplona, and Giovanni Michiel that of Porto. Sclafenati and Domenico della Rovere were also paid the price of their votes. Borgia's elevation to the throne was popular neither in the city nor in the Curia, but

---

[60] Picotti, "Nuovi Studi," p. 200, note 135. Nevertheless F. La Torre, *Del Conclave di Alessandro VI*, pp. 43 ff., 79 ff., 124–25, believes that the election of the Borgia pope was not the consequence of simony, and is followed in this view by G. Soranzo, *Studi intorno a papa Alessandro VI (Borgia)*, Milan, 1950 (Pubblicazioni dell'Univ. catt. del S. Cuore, n. s., XXXIV), who has generally attempted some vindication of both Alexander and his pontificate.

[61] Pastor, *Gesch. d. Päpste*, III-2 (repr. 1956), append., no. 11, pp. 1050–51. Eleonora was the wife of Ercole d'Este, duke of Ferrara; she was the daughter of King Ferrante of Naples (and the sister of Beatrice, who had married Matthias Corvinus of Hungary). *Cf. Diario ferrarese*, in *RISS*, XXIV, pt. 7 (1933), p. 126. Cardinal Ardicino della Porta fell sick of the "quartan fever" on 3 September, 1492, and was beset with *multiplicia accidentia* thereafter; he died on the following 4 February (Burchard, *Diarium*, ed. Thuasne, II, 36–39, and ed. Celani, I, 394–96). If the members of the conclave could have foreseen his early demise, they might have elected him. His five months' illness would have given the rivals for the tiara more time to marshal their forces, although Borgia's wealth would have made it hard to outbid him.

[62] The Palazzo Sforza-Cesarini lies between the Corso Vittorio Emmanuele (with the entrance at no. 282) and the Via dei Banchi Vecchi (formerly the Via di S. Lucia), with an unused entrance at no. 118 on the latter street. The palace has been much altered since the days of Rodrigo Borgia's occupancy.

everyone felt the necessity to praise it and express contentment.[63]

Infessura repeats the current gossip that, even before the conclave began, Rodrigo Borgia had sent four mules loaded with silver to Ascanio Sforza's palace on the grounds that it would be safer there than in his own, all said to be part of the price for Ascanio's vote. But Infessura also says five cardinals refused to sell their votes—Carafa, Piccolomini, Costa, Battista Zeno, and of course Giuliano della Rovere. There were a few more. Girolamo Basso della Rovere, Lorenzo Cibo, and the young Giovanni de' Medici had no intention of selling theirs, at least not to Rodrigo Borgia. Nevertheless, when the aged Maffeo Gherardo, cardinal patriarch of Venice, yielded to the solicitations of Borgia's supporters to give him the last vote he needed, Christ's vicar had been elected, and the conclave was over. The Venetians were disgusted by the thought of Borgia's being pope. On 28 August the envoy of the Serenissima at Milan told his Ferrarese colleague, as we have noted, that the purchase of the papacy was a "cosa ignominiosa et detestabile," and that he fully expected France and Spain to withhold their obedience when they realized the shocking extent of Borgia's simony.[64] Not everyone, however, was so unhappy. The new pope was generally regarded as energetic, intelligent, affable, handsome, well informed, and very efficient. On Sunday, 26 August, despite the dust and heat the coronation of Pope Alexander VI was celebrated, as the Mantuan ambassador to Rome wrote his master, "with more pomp and with more fanfare than any pope has ever been crowned in our time."[65]

Alexander VI began his reign well enough with an attempt to impose law and order in Rome, where (if we can believe Infessura) more than two hundred and twenty murders had been committed between the onset of Innocent VIII's last illness and his own enthronement. He maintained a strict economy in his household, of which the costs are said to have amounted to a mere seven hundred ducats a month. Alexander rarely yielded to the enticements of fine cooking—although Infessura relates that he had a full wine cellar in the tower at Porto when he ceded it to Cardinal Michiel—and the gourmets in the Sacred College were not anxious to be invited for dinner in the apostolic palace. Alexander assured the Italian envoys that he was eager to preserve peace in the peninsula in order to deal properly with the everlasting problem of the Turks. Here his uncle Calixtus III had outlined the course for him to follow.[66]

On the island of Rhodes in the meantime Cardinal Grand Master Pierre d'Aubusson wrote a papal secretary that he and the Hospitallers "were moved with no small pleasure" to learn of the election of Alexander VI, who had been cardinal protector of their Order, and by whose wisdom and high-mindedness one might hope to see the East freed from Turkish tyranny: "Alexander the Great once conquered the East, and reduced it to a single state [*monarchia*]: Tradition recalls no few Alexanders,

---

[63] Thuasne, *Burchardi diarium*, II, append., no. 2, pp. 610–11, dispatch of Valori dated 12 August, 1492. *Cf.* Infessura, *Diaria*, ed. Tommasini, p. 281, who was not well informed, and Pastor, *Gesch. d. Päpste*, III–1 (repr. 1955), 344–47, with refs., and III–2 (repr. 1956), append., nos. 13–16, 20, pp. 1053–54, 1056. In October, 1484, Ascanio Sforza had written his brother Lodovico il Moro a delighted description of the sumptuousness of Borgia's palace (*ibid.*, no. 2, p. 1046). Alexander VI soon changed his mind about ceding Civita Castellana to Savelli and Monticelli to Orsini (Thuasne, II, append., no. 5, p. 614; Pastor, III–2, append., no. 20, p. 1056). Valori gives the income from the abbey (*badia*) of Subiaco and twenty *terre* as 3,000 ducats "or better;" Gianandrea Boccaccio estimates the income from Subiaco and twenty-two *castelli* as 2,000 ducats.

[64] Infessura, *Diaria*, ed. Tommasini, pp. 281–82; Pastor, *Gesch. d. Päpste*, III–1, 346–47, 356, and III–2, append., no. 16, p. 1054, letter of Giacomo Trotti to Ercole d'Este, dated 28 August, 1492.

[65] Pastor, *Gesch. d. Päpste*, III–2 (repr. 1956), append., no. 20, p. 1056, dispatch of Floramonte Brognolo to Francesco Gonzaga, marquis of Mantua, dated at Rome on 31 August, 1492. The streets were draped with hangings and adorned with triumphal arches for the two-mile route of the papal procession. The celebration was concluded about 10:00 P.M. (*la sera circa due ore di notte*) when the pope returned to the Vatican accompanied by the cardinals. The whole court was "dead tired" (*morte di straccha*). Thuasne, *Burchardi diarium*, II, append., no. 7, pp. 615–21, reprints Bernardino Corio's account of the festivities accompanying Alexander VI's coronation (from Corio's history of Milan, 1st ed., 1503), and *cf.* in general Michael Mallett, *The Borgias*, London, 1969, pp. 112–21.

[66] Infessura, *Diaria*, ed. Tommasini, pp. 282–83, and *cf.* p. 281 for the *cella vinaria plena vino* at Porto; Pastor, *Gesch. d. Päpste*, III–1 (repr. 1955), 359. If the pope's household expenses were really 700 ducats a month, Jem Sultan's *personal* provision of 300 ducats a month (Thuasne, *Djem-Sultan*, append., no. 16, p. 431) does not appear quite as niggardly as Thuasne, *ibid.*, p. 306, implies. It would seem quite unnecessary to observe that the 40,000 ducats a year paid by the Porte for Jem's maintenance was tribute and hardly a true "pension:" as long as Jem got food enough to eat himself to death, Sultan Bayazid was hardly concerned with his brother's well-being or enjoyment of life.

who have shone with illustrious deeds." No less was being expected of the new Alexander.[67]

During Innocent's final illness and the novena of mourning which followed his death, preparations for the conclave and the maintenance of order in the city had occupied the harassed dignitaries moving in and out of the Vatican. Jem Sultan had been confined, as we have noted, to the rooms over the Sistine Chapel; now he was returned to the more attractive quarters of his own apartments. This more rigid surveillance had lasted about three weeks, however, and had much increased his restiveness. On 13 October, 1492, the Venetian Consiglio dei Dieci warned Andrea Capello, envoy of the Republic to the Holy See, to advise Alexander that Jem was "male contentus de loco et statu, in quibus de presenti reperitur." Jem was believed to have found the method and the means of flight; all he lacked was a place whither he might flee with hopes of improving his fortune.[68] Two days later the Venetian government instructed Capello to urge patience upon Jem through an intermediary and not to risk by any consideration of flight the good will of the pope, the king of France, and the Hospitallers. The Venetians, whose envoy in Milan two months earlier had seemed to prefer ecclesiastical schism to general recognition of Alexander VI, now referred to the latter as the "universal pastor and father of the Christian commonwealth." Jem must be made to understand that attempted flight would destroy his own glorious hopes for the future as well as expose his person to the most manifest peril. He must be content to wait for "el tempo della propria gloria sua," not so far distant now, and place confidence in the affection and esteem which the virtuous Venetians entertained for him and for his cause.[69] Alexander responded to the Venetians' concern by having Jem transferred from the Vatican to the Castel S. Angelo where, it was apparently stated, he would be safer from the persistent efforts to poison him.[70] The Venetians knew whereof they spoke, for Jem had been in contact with them through a secret agent, requesting the dispatch of a galley or *fusta* which might pick him up on the Tiber.[71] After ten years' captivity poor Jem realized only too well that his "time of glory" was never coming.

Although Alexander VI insisted to the Italian envoys every day that he wanted peace in the peninsula, and aspired "to be a good father to all," the Florentine envoy Filippo Valori was quite aware that his Holiness was constantly intriguing for an alliance of the Vatican with Milan and Venice. By the exclusion of King Ferrante of Naples, to whom both Alexander and Lodovico il Moro were opposed, such an alliance would upset the balance of power in Italy so long fostered by Cosimo de' Medici and (with one disastrous departure) by Lorenzo il Magnifico. Valori informed the Otto di Pratica on 16 January, 1493, that he had learned from a cardinal in a position to know that the Venetians were anxious to keep the peace and not to alter conditions in Italy. They wanted no part of an alliance with the pope, "because they did not have much faith in the enterprises of priests" (*per non havere molta fede nelle imprese de preti*). Also the cardinal in question had told Valori that the Venetian bailie in Istanbul had been expelled by Sultan Bayazid "when some of his letters in cipher were intercepted" by the Turks, and that now the Republic was sending Domenico Trevisan, onetime envoy to the Holy See, on an embassy to the Bosporus. In the meantime, as Valori states, the Genoese Giorgio Bocciardi (Busardo), brother of Niccolò Bocciardi-Cibo, archbishop of Arles, had returned from a mission to Istanbul, whither the pope had sent him to try to persuade the sultan to pay Jem Sultan's "provision" of 40,000 ducats. Bocciardi reported that Bayazid refused to pay the pension any more, and that he was in fact preparing to build ships for a renewal of his naval armament.[72] Italian envoys, currying favor at the

[67] Lamansky, *Secrets d'état* (1884, repr. 1968), p. 289, letter dated at Rhodes on 10 November, 1492. It was written to Luigi Podocataro, bishop of Capaccio, a secretary of Alexander VI.

[68] Lamansky, *Secrets d'état*, pp. 246–47, and *cf.* Thuasne, *Djem-Sultan*, pp. 305–6, where the letter (written and sent in the doge's name) is misdated 13 December.

[69] Lamansky, *Secrets d'état*, pp. 248–49, letter dated 15 October, 1492, and see, *ibid.*, pp. 252–53, letter dated 12 December.

[70] Thuasne, *Djem-Sultan*, p. 306.

[71] Lamansky, *Secrets d'état*, pp. 251–52, letter of the Consiglio dei Dieci to Andrea Capello, dated 21 November, 1492.

[72] Thuasne, *Burchardi diarium*, II, append., no. 8, pp. 621–22, letter dated at Rome, 16 January, 1492 (i.e., 1493). Shortly afterwards Alexander denied to Valori that he was trying to negotiate any alliances, claiming that he wished to remain free and without obligation to anyone, being interested solely in seeing a just peace preserved in Italy (*ibid.*, no. 9, pp. 623–24, letter of Valori to the Otto di Pratica, dated at Rome 20 January, 1493). *Cf.* Thuasne, *Djem-Sultan*, pp. 308–9. Trevisan's embassy to Istanbul

Porte, undoubtedly kept Bayazid's advisers well informed. There had been many small wars in Italy since the peace of Lodi, but on the whole the concert of Italy had endured. Now it was being broken. If the fact was of some interest to the sultan, who perceived that it was not necessary to pay Jem's pension, it was even more interesting to the king of France, who soon saw a golden opportunity to assert his old claim to the kingdom of Naples.

Since the internal affairs of Italy always had a most important bearing on the so-called Turkish question (as the sultan knew), we must cast at least a passing glance at them. The facts are well known. An ever-wider cleavage was growing between Alexander VI and Ferrante of Naples as well as between the latter and Lodovico il Moro. We may deal first with the contest between Naples and Milan. Here Lodovico was trying to defraud his young nephew Giangaleazzo Sforza, for whom he had served as regent since 1479, of the ducal authority in Milan. The rather feeble Giangaleazzo, however, now of age to rule, was married to Isabella, a granddaughter of Ferrante, to whom she addressed indignant appeals for help against Lodovico's usurpation of her husband's position. Since Lodovico presumably intended the deposition of the young duke, obviously no peaceful resolution could be found of the conflict between him and Ferrante.[73] Alexander VI was also growling at Ferrante, with an important bone of contention between them, which was incidentally drawing Florence to the side of Naples.

When Innocent VIII died, his son Franceschetto Cibo left Rome for Florence. He had married Lorenzo's daughter Maddalena, and now looked to the Medici for protection. Remembering Girolamo Riario's troubles after the death of Sixtus IV, Franceschetto sold his lordships of Cerveteri (in Etruria) and Anguillara (about fifteen miles northwest of Rome), together with Monterano, Viano, and other lands and castles in the Campagna to Gentile Virginio Orsini for 45,000 gold ducats. The transaction took place on 3 September, 1492, in the palace (and in the presence) of Cardinal Giuliano della Rovere, near the church of S. Agnese fuori le mura. Orsini was the chief commander of the Neapolitan forces; both Lorenzo il Magnifico and his son Piero had married daughters of the Orsini family. Della Rovere had known and approved of the projected sale since Franceschetto had first revealed his intentions. Passing mention of it had been made to Alexander VI, who had not forbidden it, assuming that nothing would come of the proposal, for the transfer of these properties on Roman territory would require both his sanction and that of the Sacred College. The sale was in fact negotiated, however, and Virginio eventually occupied the towns, to the pope's indignation. Alexander complained of the transaction in a consistory, upbraiding della Rovere for encouraging Virginio, who was an archenemy of the Holy See. When his friends later spoke to the same effect, Giuliano used to tell them that it was better for Virginio to get the towns than have them go to the Sforzeschi.

Ferrante of Naples had also fostered Virginio Orsini's ambition to acquire the two towns. Considering the large sum required for their purchase, it seemed likely that Piero de' Medici and possibly Ferrante had helped him raise the money. Alexander VI found the situation intolerable, for Virginio and the Roman baronage were a menace to the papacy. Cardinals Giuliano della Rovere and Ascanio Sforza used inevitably to clash in the consistory. About the end of the year 1492 Giuliano withdrew from Rome to the castle which Baccio Pontelli had built for him (in 1483–1486), near the modern station of Ostia Antica. Despite all Alexander's assurances of his safety, della Rovere refused to return to Rome.[74] The affair

accomplished nothing, for the sultan decided "che no staghi più bailo in quella città" (Malipiero, *Annali veneti*, in *Arch. stor. italiano*, VII, pt. 1 [1843], 142). Ferrante of Naples took note of the sultan's refusal to pay the pope 40,000 ducats in a letter of 22 February, 1493, to the Neapolitan ambassador in Rome (Trinchera, *Codice aragonese*, II–1 [1868], p. 300, and *cf.* p. 323). There had been apprehension for some time in southern Italy that the Turkish fleet might make an attack upon the vulnerable coastline from Monopoli to Gagliano (*ibid.*, III [Naples, 1874], pp. 56, 323).

[73] *Cf.* Malipiero, *Annali veneti*, in *Arch. stor. italiano*, VII–1, 319. Duke Giangaleazzo Sforza died on 15 October, 1494, *morto da flusso*, "and it was the common belief that his uncle Lodovico had caused his death by poison" (*ibid.*, p. 320). On the nineteenth Lodovico entered Milan "clad in ducal garb." *Cf.* Burchard, *Diarium*, ed. Thuasne, II, 193, and ed. Celani, I, 539–40, and in general H.-F. Delaborde, *L'Expédition de Charles VIII en Italie*, Paris, 1888, pp. 217–18 ff., 259–60, 424 ff. Up to this time Lodovico had borne the title duke of Bari.

[74] Thuasne, *Burchardi diarium*, II, append., nos. 8–14, 16–19, pp. 621–36, letters of Filippo Valori to the Otto di Pratica in Florence, dated at Rome from 16 January to 28 February, 1493; Sigismondo de'Conti, II (1883), 54–57, 94; Infessura, *Diaria*, ed. Tommasini, pp. 283–84; Trinchera, *Codice aragonese*, II–1, pp. 252–53, 291, 307 ff., 335–36,

of Anguillara was more than one of the petty tempests always blowing over the Roman Campagna. Indeed, the Venetians were fearful lest the dispute it was causing should provide the Turks with the "occasio et opportunitas" to plan an invasion of Italy.[75]

There were other causes of dissension between Alexander VI and Ferrante of Naples, one of which was attracting much attention at this time. Ladislas, king of Hungary and Bohemia, was trying to secure the annulment of his marriage to Beatrice, widow of Matthias Corvinus and the daughter of Ferrante. The question of the necessary dispensations was discussed on 8 January, 1493, in the pope's presence at a long consistory, which lasted from one o'clock in the afternoon until about eight in the evening.[76] In late February Cardinals Carafa and Piccolomini remonstrated on Beatrice's behalf with the pope, who said he wanted still more time to think about the problem, although he left them with "buona speranza" that he would satisfy Ferrante's petition.[77] At the end of the month Alexander left the Florentine envoy Valori under the impression that briefs would be sent to Hungary settling the issue in the queen's favor.[78] The matter dragged on for years, however, until well after Ferrante's death Alexander VI finally annulled the marriage of Beatrice to Ladislas (on 3 April, 1500), and imposed perpetual silence on her.[79]

While the question of the Hungarian annulment was exercising the minds of various members of the Curia, the pope received a letter from King Ladislas dated 1 March (1493), in which the latter announced "that he had won a great and singular victory over the Turks, who had invaded the kingdom of Hungary, and that he had killed and laid low about 15,000 men, and brought back from the encounter no small booty."[80] If this was good news for all Italy, more ominous news came from France, making the Venetians more inclined to listen to the pope's overtures for an alliance and much

337, 339–40, 348, 349–50, 354, 358–59, 369–71; F. Guicciardini, *Storia d'Italia*, ed. C. Botta, I (Paris, 1837), bk. I, chap. 1, p. 82; Pastor, *Gesch. d. Päpste*, III–1 (repr. 1955), 368–70. Giuliano della Rovere had not yet left Rome at Christmas of 1492 (Burchard, *Diarium*, ed. Thuasne, II, 26, 29–30, and ed. Celani, I, 387, 389–90). Innocent VIII had purchased Cerveteri from Bartolommeo della Rovere in 1487 for Franceschetto Cibo. After the death of Domenico d'Anguillara, Innocent had also bestowed upon his son the castle of Anguillara, so called from a lake of that name (Sigismondo, II, 54, 94). According to Ferrante of Naples, in a letter dated 7 June, 1493, and written to his envoy to Spain, Cerveteri and Anguillara had already been promised to Virginio Orsini during Innocent's lifetime in the event of Franceschetto's relinquishing them (Trinchera, *op. cit.*, II–2 [Naples, 1870], pp. 43–44). Ferrante also said that Orsini's acquisition of these places was achieved "in Fiorenza per mezo de Piero de' Medici," which presumably means that Piero supplied most of the money. At any rate Ferrante denied that he had supplied it. On the whole affair, see Ernesto Pontieri, "Uno Scontro tra Alessandro VI e Ferrante d'Aragona: La Questione di Anguillara e di Cerveteri," in his collected studies *Per la Storia del regno di Ferrante I d'Aragona, re di Napoli*, Naples, 1969, pp. 527–90, with nine documents, and *cf.* Giovanni Soranzo, *Il Tempo di Alessandro VI Papa e di Fra Girolamo Savonarola*, Milan, 1960, pp. 56–58.

[75] Thuasne, *Djem-Sultan*, p. 309.

[76] Burchard, *Diarium*, ed. Thuasne, II, 33, and ed. Celani, I, 392: "hora vigesima . . . ab ea usque ad tertiam horam noctis. . . ." There is a break at this point in the MSS. of Burchard. *Cf.* Raynaldus, *Ann. eccl.*, ad ann. 1492, no. 30, vol. XIX (1693), p. 414b, and the dispatches of Piero Alamanni from Naples to Piero de' Medici in Florence (A. Desjardins [and G. Canestrini], *Négociations diplomatiques de la France avec la Toscane*, I [Paris, 1859], 435 ff.).

[77] Thuasne, *Burchardi diarium*, II, append., no. 18, p. 633, a letter of Valori to the Otto di Pratica, dated at Rome on 23 February, 1492 (i.e., 1493).

[78] *Ibid.*, II, append., no. 19, p. 636, letter of Valori to the Otto di Pratica, dated at Rome on 28 February, 1493, and *cf.*, *ibid.*, II, nos. 20, 21, pp. 637, 640. Already on 29 January (1493) Ferrante had accused Alexander VI of having a brief prepared "in contrario contra l'ordine preso in consistorio," in a letter to Antonio Gennaro, Neapolitan envoy to Lodovico il Moro (Trinchera, *Codice aragonese*, II–1, p. 260). King Ladislas claimed to have married Beatrice with unwillingness and reservations "per havere lo regno;" and although he stated that his marriage to her had never been consummated, he insisted that she was sterile (*ibid.*, II–1, pp. 241–43, 336–37, and *cf.* pp. 261–62, 264–66, 271–72, 275, 278–79 *et alibi*). Ferdinand and Isabella of Spain were affirming the justice of Beatrice's cause (*ibid.*, pp. 295, 302, 315, 334). At length on 22 March (1493) Ferrante informed Andrea Carafa, his agent in Hungary, that the pope had sent briefs favorable to Beatrice (*ibid.*, pp. 333–34), but the affair was not settled (*ibid.*, II–2, pp. 72–73).

[79] Burchard, *Diarium*, ed. Thuasne, III, 31–32, and ed. Celani, II, 212; Raynaldus, *Ann. eccl.*, ad ann. 1492, no. 30, vol. XIX (1693), p. 414b. Raynaldus cites Burchard's diary to the effect that the annulment took place in a secret consistory *feria sexta, tertia mensis Aprilis*, but although 3 April fell on a Friday only twice in the reign of Alexander VI, in the years 1495 and 1500, Raynaldus places the text among his entries for 1492!

[80] Burchard, *Diarium*, ed. Thuasne, II, 63, and ed. Celani, I, 415. From the beginning of the year there had been consistent reports in Italy of extensive Turkish preparations (Trinchera, *Codice aragonese*, II–1, pp. 278, 285, 287, 290, 314, 320, 328–29). On 29 March, 1493, however, Ferrante of Naples sent Sultan Bayazid a gift of some gerfalcons with

increasing the affability of Ferrante's gestures toward his Holiness. There was even some discussion of a marriage between a natural daughter of Ferrante and the pope's son, Cesare Borgia, who had recently been made archbishop of Valencia, but had no intention of remaining a priest. The pope returned soft answers to Ferrante's various messages, and the king was emboldened to request that Jem Sultan be sent to Naples, where he would know how to use the chief pawn in the power politics of the Levant to the fullest benefit of Christendom. Ferrante even boasted that, owing to the friendliness and understanding which now existed between Alexander VI and him, the pope had relinquished to him "tota custodia et gubernatio domini Zen Sultani." When Ferrante sent word of this alleged development directly to Istanbul, the Porte dispatched an agent to Venice, the clearing-house of European political information, to find out whether the report was true. On 1 April, 1493, the Consiglio dei Dieci instructed their secretary to inform the agent that Jem was in Rome, more carefully guarded than ever, and that actually the pope and the king of Naples were quite at odds, because the king was holding a certain castle (Anguillara) through the instrumentality of one of his barons, "et questo è certissimo."[81] On 10 April the Council of Ten wrote Andrea Capello, their ambassador to the Holy See, in response to a letter he had sent them on the third with the interesting information that the eunuch Ali Pasha had sent one of his relatives as an envoy to Rome, making certain proposals to the pope, "which will be to the convenience and satisfaction of his Holiness and to the great benefit of Christendom." The Turkish envoy had gone to Apulia to get two of his sons whom he would bring back to Rome to leave as hostages with the pope as evidence of the sincerity of his master's offers. Upon the envoy's return the pope wished Capello to talk directly with him, so that he might inform the Venetian government at first hand of the issues involved. Capello was instructed to thank the pope heartily for his consideration in this matter and to commend his willingness to hear all those who came to him from the Porte, but Capello was himself to avoid dealing directly with the envoy if he really returned to the Curia with his sons as hostages. Capello was, however, to urge the pope to keep Venice informed of everything the envoy had to say.[82]

At the same time the Ten wrote Capello that an adventurer of evil reputation named Lactantio Benzio, who claimed to be a nephew of Cardinal Piccolomini and a member of Ascanio Sforza's household, had gone to Istanbul in September, 1492. From there he was supposed to go to Rome. The Ten had directed their captains and officials overseas to arrest Benzio, but so far they had not learned whether they had been able to do so. Capello was to learn with all

---

a most affectionate letter (*ibid.*, II-1, p. 341); Ferrante had received a gift of two dogs from the Turks (*ibid.*, p. 342). Malipiero, *Annali veneti*, in *Arch. stor. italiano*, VII-1, 145, reports under the year 1494 that the Hungarians had cut to pieces 10,000 Turks on the Danube, "where they had gone on a raiding party."

[81] Lamansky, *Secrets d'état*, pp. 253–54; *cf.* Thuasne, *Djem-Sultan*, p. 310; and see Trinchera, *Codice aragonese*, II-1, pp. 323, 338.

[82] Lamansky, *Secrets d'état*, pp. 254–55. Sultan Bayazid was strengthening his Italian connections whenever and wherever he could at this time. Having recently begun a correspondence with [Gian] Francesco Gonzaga, the marquis of Mantua (1484–1519), who sent him cuirasses, mules, and other gifts in return for permission to export Arab horses (for the famous stud farm in the fields of the Tè, outside the walls of Mantua), Bayazid sent Francesco the following greeting:

"Sultan Payazit Kan, Dei gratia magnus imperator Asie et Grecie, etc., illustrissimo et magnifico domino Francisco de Gonzaga, marchioni Mantue, salutem ac honoris et glorie felicia incrementa. Al presente mandamo lo nostro schiavo Casim volendo perseverare lo bono amore et amicicia che è fra nui, laquale è a nui molto grata, et volendo in ella perseverare desyderamo de intendere de la vostra bona sanitade et etiam per notificarvi el simile essere de nui, et per questo mandamo el predicto Casim, alquale havereti da prestare fede a quello vi referira. Ex Constantinopoli die XII Aprilis, 1493" (Arch. di Stato di Mantova, Arch. Gonzaga, Busta 86, leather-bound volume marked B. XXXIII, no. 17, fol. 43^v).

On 24 July, 1493, Francesco replied to Bayazid, *ibid.*, fol. 44, thanking him for earlier expressions of his friendship, "et anche del dono che . . . me ha facto de cossi nobili et electi cavalli. . . . Et benchè mi reputasse havere facto supremo aquisto essendo pervenuto el nome et desyderio mio ad noticia de la Maestà vostra in modo che per tutta Italia si diceva quella amarmi et havermi nel numero de li suoi chari et che ad me paresse de ciò potermi assai contentare. . . . Mantue XXIIII Julii 1493: El vostro schiavo et servitore Francisco marchese de Mantua manu propria." Francesco, the sultan's slave and servitor, was at this time commander of the Venetian land forces. On Mantuan relations with the Porte in Francesco's time, see Hans Joachim Kissling, *Sultan Bâjezîd's II. Beziehungen zu Markgraf Francesco II. von Gonzaga*, Munich, 1965, who publishes the texts of various letters from the Gonzaga Archives, some of which had already been printed by P. Ferrato, *Il Marchesato di Mantova e l'impero ottomano alla fine del secolo XV*, Mantua, 1876.

secrecy whether Benzio had got to Rome. Inquiry must be made with the greatest discretion whether he was to be found in the household of either Piccolomini or Sforza. The man was obviously up to no good. If possible, the pope should have him arrested, and his papers seized. Torture might be needed to ascertain his reason for going to the Porte. Capello was to try to learn whether Benzio had ever served in the household of either cardinal and, if so, whether he was really the nephew of Piccolomini. In any event his Holiness must be persuaded never to reveal the source of this warning concerning Benzio.[83]

By now cordial relations existed between Alexander VI and the Venetian government. On 9 April (1493) the Venetians instructed Andrea Capello to ask the pope to include specific mention of Jem Sultan among the articles of the proposed alliance between the Holy See and the Serenissima.[84] By the terms of the treaty the Signoria agreed to furnish the pope with two hundred men-at-arms if he were attacked (by Virginio Orsini); if he were the aggressor, however, Venice was not bound to assist him. On the other hand, if the Turks attacked the Venetians, the pope agreed to turn Jem Sultan over to them to make such use of him as they could.[85] On 23 April, two days before the scheduled announcement of the pact in Venice, Rome, and Milan, the Senate informed Charles VIII of France that this new triple alliance had been formed for the preservation of peace and tranquillity in all Italy. Ferrara, Mantua, and Siena were included as allies of the big three. A special instrument in the treaty carefully guaranteed that the peace and friendship between France and Venice would not and could not be infringed or trespassed upon in any way by any obligations which the Venetians assumed under the treaty.[86]

The alliance of the pope, the doge of Venice, and the duke of Milan was celebrated on Thursday, 25 April (1493), the feast of S. Mark the Evangelist. A special service was held in Rome in the church of S. Marco, whither the pope went on horseback. Because of the number of chamberlains present, complains Burchard, the pope and cardinals were uncomfortably crowded in the choir. The pope granted plenary indulgences "as a sign of joy for so great a pact." Bartolommeo Flores, bishop of Sutri and Nepi, preached a simple sermon, apologizing for the brevity of his remarks because he had not had even a day's warning that he was to give the sermon. He read the articles of the treaty. Prayers for peace were said with a new confidence that those who trusted in the Almighty need "fear the arms of no hostility."[87] Alexander VI was not placing his trust solely in the Almighty, however, for two weeks later Ferrante of Naples informed his envoy in Spain that there were more soldiers than priests in Rome.[88] The following June (1493) Alexander's daughter Lucrezia was married at the Vatican to Giovanni Sforza, a cousin of Lodovico il Moro and Cardinal Ascanio, thus adding a dynastic connection to the triple alliance.

As for poor Jem Sultan, he was coming to fear nothing so much as tedium. He found that time

---

[83] Lamansky, *Secrets d'état*, pp. 255–56, doc. dated 10 April; Thuasne, *Djem-Sultan*, p. 311.

[84] Thuasne, *Djem-Sultan*, p. 312.

[85] Malipiero, *Annali veneti*, in *Arch. stor. italiano*, VII–1, p. 142, who dates the Venetian alliance with Alexander VI on 16 April, 1493.

[86] Thuasne, *Djem-Sultan*, p. 312, and append., no. 17, pp. 432–33. On 23 April the Venetian government also sent Ferrante of Naples an official notification of the pact, and informed the ambassadors of the foreign powers. Despite the secrecy of the negotiations Ferrante had a pretty good idea of what was going on, as is shown by his letter of 22 April (1493) to Luigi Paladini, his envoy to the Holy See (Trinchera, *Codice aragonese*, II–1, pp. 371–75): Paladini was to remind the pope that at the time of the latter's accession to the throne "all Italy was at peace, and there was not a man who spoke of arms;" political disturbances could be quickly created, but it took time to put them down. Without direct allusion either to Milan or to Venice, Ferrante stated that what Italy needed was "una lega generale per removere li altri da suspecti." Two days later Ferrante knew all about the triple alliance, as is clear from a letter of the twenty-fourth to Antonio Gennaro, Neapolitan envoy to Milan (*ibid.*, II–1, pp. 376–81). By 30 April Ferrante was seeking to effect the distribution of his military forces to meet every likely eventuality (*ibid.*, pp. 382–84). *Cf.* in general Ferrante's subsequent denunciation of Alexander VI to the court of Spain, through the Neapolitan ambassador to Ferdinand and Isabella (*ibid.*, II–2 [Naples, 1870], pp. 42 ff., letter dated 7 June, 1493).

[87] Burchard, *Diarium*, ed. Thuasne, II, 66–68, and ed. Celani, I, 417–18; Infessura, *Diaria*, ed. Tommasini, pp. 284–85; Sigismondo de' Conti, II, 58–59; Sanudo, *Vite de'duchi*, in *RISS*, XXII (1733), cols. 1250–51; and the dispatches of 24–26 April, 1493, from Giacomo Trotti, envoy of the Estensi in Milan, to the duke of Ferrara, published by Cesare Foucard, in *Arch. stor. per le province napoletane*, IV (1879), 773–77; Pastor, *Gesch. d. Päpste*, III–1 (repr. 1955), 371; Pontieri, *Per la Storia del regno di Ferrante I d'Aragona* (1969), pp. 540–42.

[88] Trinchera, *Codice aragonese*, II–2, p. 46, letter dated 7 June, 1493, to Antonio d'Alessandro: ". . . Et Roma e tutta piena de soldati più che de preiti. . . ."

passed with the same futility in Rome as it had in France. On occasion he would join a papal cavalcade, and he seems to have struck up a sort of friendship with the pope's son Juan, the duke of Gandia.[89] One of Jem's most interesting public appearances took place on a Sunday afternoon, 5 May (1493), when he accompanied the court on a long excursion through Rome. A cross was conspicuous in the mounted procession. Jem rode between Count Niccolò Orsini of Pitigliano and Juan de Borja (Borgia), duke of Gandia. The latter wore a turban, and was dressed *alla turchescha*, perhaps out of courtesy to Jem. The pope came next, *precedente cruce*, followed by five cardinals and a number of attendants. Burchard's diary and a letter of the Florentine ambassador Valori fix their itinerary through Trastevere and over the bridge of S. Maria, now known as the Ponte Rotto, along the (present) Via dei Cerchi to the church of S. Gregorio Magno, where they turned left, passing SS. Giovanni e Paolo on the Caelian, until they reached the Coliseum. A right turn then took them to the basilica of S. Giovanni in Laterano, where they dismounted. The practical pope, who had to pay the bills, examined the roof. Jem and Juan went into the church together to see the tomb of Martin V, who still lies there undisturbed, and various other sights of interest to the tourist of every century. Mounting their horses again, they rode northward to S. Maria Maggiore, thence westward to SS. Apostoli and S. Marcello, along the (present) Via del Corso to the Piazza S. Maria del Popolo, "and from here turning to the left along the road by the river," says Burchard, "past the house of the cardinal of Parma, by the bridge of S. Angelo, they returned to the apostolic palace."[90] The Roman weather can be lovely in May.

Every week bad news came to Venice, where on 3 June, 1493, it was reported that Turkish corsairs had captured two Venetian vessels in the waters off Modon. Another had been seized off the nearby island of Cerigo. Venetian galleys were sent to the troubled area, and Domenico Trevisan, who had just returned from Istanbul, was sent back to lodge a protest at the Porte. Geronimo Contarini, commander of two galleys patrolling the Barbary coast, recovered the captured vessels on 10 August after a running battle with the corsairs in the harbor of Tripoli, which was damaged in the engagement. On 20 June the Venetian government received the news that Count Bernardino de' Frangipani (Frankopan), having failed to recover the castles which Matthias Corvinus had taken from him in Croatia, had gone over to the Turks, who had sent some five thousand men to Segna (the modern Senj). They built a fort at S. George, five miles from Segna, ten miles from the islands of Veglia (Krk) and Arbe (Rab). "If they should get Segna," writes the annalist Malipiero, "there would be grave danger of losing all the Quarnero." In November (1493) Maximilian, king of the Romans, sent an embassy to the Venetians urging them to join him in a united action against the Turks, to which he received the answer that when the Christian princes moved against the Turks, the Signoria would move with them. Maximilian was reminded that the Venetians hardly ever had fewer than forty galleys in service to restrain Turkish depredation at sea.[91] And so it went. Letters were

---

[89] *Cf.* Burchard, *Diarium*, ed. Thuasne, II, 48–49, and ed. Celani, I, 404–5, entry relating to 4 March, 1493, and *Djem-Sultan*, p. 313. On the duke of Gandia and the family circle of the Borgias, *cf.* J. Sanchis y Sivera, *Algunos Documentos y cartas privadas que pertenecieron al segundo Duque de Gandía don Juan de Borja: Notas para la historia de Alejandro VI*, Valencia, 1919, letters and documents preserved in the Archivo de la Catedral de Valencia.

[90] Burchard, *Diarium*, ed. Thuasne, II, 68–69, and ed. Celani, I, 418–19, who gives the text of the relevant portion of Valori's letter to the Otto di Pratica in Florence, dated 7 May, 1493, which also appears in Thuasne, *Djem-Sultan*, pp. 313–14, note 4. Thuasne misdates the excursion through Rome 15 May. Sclafenati was the "cardinal of Parma." His house was on the north end of the present Piazza Lancelotti (just off the Via dei Coronari), at the "Via dell' Arco di Parma." The Ponte S. Maria was partly carried away by a flood in 1598; never being repaired, it became known as the Ponte Rotto; it was the ancient Pons Aemilius (S. B. Platner, *Topography and Monuments of Ancient Rome*, Boston, 1911, p. 79; F. Castagnoli, C. Cecchelli, G. Giovannoni, and M. Zocca, *Topografia e urbanistica di Roma*, Bologna, 1958, pp. 200–1, and *cf.* pp. 247–48, 406–7; and Giuseppe Lugli, *Itinerario di Roma antica*, Milan, 1970, p. 92). There are slight differences in the description of the excursion as given by Burchard and Valori.

[91] Malipiero, *Annali veneti*, in *Arch. stor. italiano*, VII–1, pp. 142–44; *cf.* Trinchera, *Codice aragonese*, II–2, p. 99. On Venetian concern over Veglia, *cf.* Thuasne, *Djem-Sultan*, p. 317. During the summer of 1493 Turkish raids into Dalmatia, especially the region of Sebenico (Šibenik) and Traù (Trogir), were followed immediately by further depredation in northern Croatia (Arch. di Stato di Venezia, Sen. Secreta, Reg. 34, fols. 169^v [180^v], 181^v [192^v], 186^v ff. [197^v ff.], 202^r [213^r]), to the extent that the Venetian Senate wrote their envoys at the court of Maximilian I, king of the Romans, "timuimus ne victoriam secuti versus Goritiam et exinde in patriam [i.e., into Friuli] descenderent

written, embassies sent. Turkish armies marched into Austria and Transylvania; corsairs attacked various places in the Mediterranean. The Turkish thrusts, however, were no longer on the grand scale they had been during the lifetime of Mehmed the Conqueror. Only the objects of their attacks were much distressed. Maximilian, Ladislas, and the Venetians had the most to fear. Alexander VI was more interested in Italian politics than the crusade, but as always the two problems went together. If Charles VIII of France could be persuaded to follow the path and emulate the glory of his crusading ancestors, the threatened French expedition against Naples would be averted, and the papacy itself spared who could tell what disaster. The French were arming. It would be well to deflect their arms against the Turks.

According to Infessura, rumor had it that on 11 June, 1493, a Turkish envoy brought Alexander VI 90,000 ducats' tribute for the maintenance and restraint of Jem Sultan, which sum was to provide for two years' "pension" and to supply Jem with 10,000 ducats, because the latter "wished to be supported at his own expense." Infessura says that the envoy was received in Rome with great honor, "and all marveled that the Grand Turk should have sent tribute to the pope and the Church of God."[92] The Florentine ambassador Valori mentions merely some presents of small value which the Turkish envoy brought Alexander with Sultan Bayazid's congratulations upon his accession to the papal throne. Very likely Alexander received no money at all from Istanbul on this occasion. As Bayazid's envoy prepared to return home, he received a papal letter dated 22 June to take back to his master. The pope thanked the sultan for the satisfaction he had expressed in his elevation to the papacy, and asked him to refrain from all attacks upon Christians as the best evidence of the amity he claimed to entertain for the Holy See: "sic enim mutua inter nos benivolentia servabitur." The Turkish envoy had seen Jem, talked with him, and could therefore report the extent of his well-being.[93] Although some good might come of exchanging such diplomatic courtesies, and they did help keep open the channels of communication, naturally neither side took them very seriously. We shall soon see Alexander VI urging the Christian princes to embark on the crusade.

The Italians had learned to live with the fear of a French invasion, but now the menace was clearly increasing. Thoughtful men realized that the French were a far greater danger to Italy than were the Turks. Ferrante's policy with respect to the papacy was always swinging back and forth like a pendulum. No arrangement that he made ever lasted very long, but now he wanted to settle the affair of Anguillara. Charles VIII was known to be sending an embassy to Rome to ask Alexander VI for the investiture of the kingdom of Naples.[94] Ferdinand the Catholic, who regarded the affairs of Naples as pertaining to the Crown of Aragon, watched the French maneuvers with apprehension. In the midsummer of 1493, while a Spanish embassy was in Rome, Ferrante hastened to make peace with the pope, who agreed to absolve Virginio Orsini and cede to him Cerveteri and Anguillara as hereditary papal fiefs for the payment of 35,000 ducats. On 24 July Virginio and Cardinal Giuliano della Rovere came to Rome. They dined with the pope, and peace seemed to be restored. The guards were removed from the city gates. It would remain to be seen how long the reconciliation would last.[95]

---

subditisque et rebus nostris aliquod detrimentum afferrent" (*ibid.*, fol. 202ʳ [213ʳ]). *Cf.* Sen. Secreta, Reg. 35, fols. 2ᵛ [14ᵛ], 11ᵛ–12ʳ [23ᵛ–24ʳ], lamenting the *combustio domorum* at Traù and Sebenico.

[92] Infessura, *Diaria*, ed. Tommasini, pp. 285–86. Thuasne, *Djem-Sultan*, pp. 314–15, erroneously states that Sultan Bayazid was alleged to have sent 150,000 ducats to Rome. His statement is based upon the faulty text of Infessura which he reproduced in his edition of the *Burchardi diarium*, II, 78.

[93] Thuasne, *Djem-Sultan*, p. 315, and append., no. 18, pp. 433–34.

[94] Trinchera, *Codice aragonese*, II–2, pp. 145–46, letter of Ferrante of Naples, dated at Capua on 13 July, 1493, to Antonio d'Alessandro, Neapolitan ambassador in Spain, and *cf.*, *ibid.*, pp. 164–65. On the French embassy, headed by Perron de Baschi, see Delaborde, *Expédition de Charles VIII* (1888), pp. 281–83, summarizing a letter of 13 August from Cardinal Ascanio Sforza to his brother Lodovico il Moro, in the Arch. di Stato di Milano, Potenze estere: Roma. The pope was noncommittal. He deliberately led Perron to believe, however, that he favored the French invasion. Like Piero de'Medici, Alexander was still operating with the hope that the invasion would not take place.

[95] Infessura, *Diaria*, ed. Tommasini, p. 292; Trinchera, *Codice aragonese*, II–2, pp. 183–96. Trinchera has published numerous documents illustrating Ferrante of Naples's official attempts to reconcile Alexander VI and Virginio Orsini (*cf.*, *ibid.*, I–1, pp. 316–17, 319, 330, 348, 349–50, 353, 358, 365–68, 380–81, and I–2, pp. 5, 7–16, 20–25, 31–37, 38–48, 54–55, 56, 60–61, 88–95, 113 and ff.). Ferrante always insisted that he neither had prior knowledge of, nor gave financial assistance to, Virginio's

A Florentine witness who participated in the transactions between the pope and the representatives of Virginio on 16 August (1493) sent a full report of what was said and done, to the Otto di Pratica on the seventeenth. The question of Anguillara was settled. A marriage contract was read, providing for the union of Alexander's young son Gioffredo (Geffrè) with a natural daughter of Duke Alfonso of Calabria, heir to the Neapolitan throne. The young lady's dowry was to be the principality of Squillace and the county of Cariati, with a guaranteed income of 10,000 ducats a year, which sum the pope undertook to match, thus giving Gioffredo and his bride 20,000 a year. The pope also agreed to give the bride, Madonna Sancia (Xances), 10,000 ducats' worth of jewelry. After many other stipulations and statements of obligation the marriage was performed by proxy, with the witticisms and laughter that such ceremonies sometimes produced. Then the pope spoke at length of the great friendship he had always entertained for Ferrante. Cardinal Carafa and the Spanish ambassador, who had witnessed the proceedings, commended Alexander on the happy end of hostilities with Virginio and King Ferrante, "saying that certainly inasmuch as his Holiness was now at peace and on terms of friendship with both the neighboring barons and potentates, it could be said that he was more pope than he had been hitherto."[96]

That was not, however, the view now held in Milan and Venice. The pope had apparently sought an alliance with them chiefly to put pressure upon Ferrante and Virginio Orsini. Having achieved his purpose, he seemed to be adopting a pro-Aragonese policy, apparently leaving the Sforzeschi out in the cold. The Venetians could take care of themselves. Lodovico il Moro would have no recourse but to throw himself into the arms of his French ally. Then one would see how productive of peace Alexander's efforts would be; in any event his friendship with Ferrante would not last long. For some time Piero de' Medici and the Otto di Pratica had kept Florence in step with Naples, especially during the long course of the affair of Anguillara. When Virginio and Cardinal Giuliano made their peace with the pope, and it looked as though the young Don Gioffredo would in fact marry Donna Sancia, Piero de' Medici suddenly but quite understandably manifested a desire to reach an accord with the pope.[97] From the diplomatic correspondence of the period one can, with the wisdom of hindsight, already perceive the alignment of the powers which Charles VIII was to face when he invaded Italy the following year.[98]

For some time the Italian courts had been seeking news of Alexander VI's intentions with respect to the Sacred College, which contained several members whose independence was little to the pope's liking. Before his elevation, *sede vacante*, Alexander had accepted with other members of the conclave the usual articles of capitulation according to which (among other restraints) the cardinal who was elected pope should not increase the size of the Sacred College without the full consent of its members.[99]

---

purchase of Anguillara and Cerveteri. He was probably lying. Vicious opponent as Ferrante was, however, Alexander VI was little better; Ferrante's complaints of papal machinations were not without justification (*ibid.*, II–2, pp. 42 ff.).

[96] Thuasne, *Burchardi diarium*, II, append., no. 22, pp. 641–44, report of Antonio Guidotti di Colle to the Otto di Pratica, dated at Rome on 17 August, 1493. *Cf.* Infessura, *Diaria*, ed. Tommasini, p. 292; Trinchera, *Codice aragonese*, II–1, pp. 320–23, 325–26, 331–33, 338, 343–47, 348, 351–52, 355–62 and ff., 373, and II–2, pp. 135–38, 141–43, 161–64, 166–69, 190 ff.; Pastor, *Gesch. d. Päpste*, III–1, 373–76. Despite the successful negotiation of the marriage contract between Gioffredo and Sancia, Ferrante still found Alexander VI very difficult to deal with (Trinchera, II–2, pp. 211–12, 378–79, 381 ff.). The actual marriage of the young couple did not take place until 7 May, 1494 (Burchard, *Diarium*, ed. Thuasne, II, 151–53, and *cf.* pp. 160–61, and ed. Celani, I, 504–5, and *cf.* pp. 511–12, with notes, for Gioffredo's investiture with the principality of Squillace).

[97] Trinchera, *Codice aragonese*, II–2, pp. 172–73, letter of Ferrante to his son Federigo, prince of Altamura, Neapolitan plenipotentiary in Rome, dated at Capua on 25 July, 1493, and *cf.* pp. 174, 245–50, 271–72.

[98] *Cf.* Desjardins (and Canestrini), *Négociations diplomatiques*, I (1859), 250 ff., 285 ff., 379 ff. The political background is rapidly sketched in Nino Valeri, *L'Italia nell'età dei principati dal 1343 al 1516*, Verona, 1949, pp. 624–32, 725 ff. (Storia d'Italia, V), and in Luigi Simeoni, *Le Signorie*, 2 vols., Milan, 1950, II, 711 ff., and the military history of the 1490's in Piero Pieri, *Il Rinascimento e la crisi militare italiana*, Turin, 1952, pp. 320 ff.

[99] In the consistory of 31 August, 1492, Alexander VI had made his nephew Juan de Borja (Borgia), archbishop of Monreale, the cardinal priest of S. Susanna (Raynaldus, *Ann. eccl.*, ad ann. 1492, no. 28, vol. XIX [1693], p. 414a, where the date should read *pridie Kal. Septembris*; *cf.* Eubel, *Hierarchia*, II [1914, repr. 1960], 21, 65, and Pastor, *Gesch. d. Päpste*, III–1 [repr. 1955], 360–61, and III–2 [repr. 1956], append., no. 18, p. 1055). Seventeen cardinals subscribed to Juan's nomination to the cardinalate. On 19 February, 1496, Alexander made another

On 20 September, 1493, however, Alexander created twelve cardinals, some of whom were to figure prominently in later years.

Infessura says that only seven cardinals consented to this wholesale creation, which alienated Giuliano della Rovere, Carafa, Costa, Campofregoso, Conti, and Piccolomini. It pleased the Sforzeschi, for it might help restore Cardinal Ascanio's influence in the Curia. The requests of various important princes were attended to in these promotions except that no representative of Naples was named recipient of a red hat. Sigismondo de' Conti remarks on the significance of the omission. The pope, who was always motivated by self-interest, was again estranged from Ferrante despite the recent efforts at reconciliation and the marriage by proxy of Gioffredo Borgia to Donna Sancia. The cardinals created on 20 September were: Raymond Peraudi, bishop of Gurk in Carinthia; Jean de Bilhères, abbot of S. Denis and bishop of Lombez; Bernardino Lopez de Carvajal, bishop of Cartagena; John Morton, archbishop of Canterbury; Frederick Casimir, administrator of Cracow and son of the king of Poland; Domenico Grimani, patriarch of Aquileia, a theologian and son of the Doge Antonio Grimani; Bernardino Lunati of Pavia, an apostolic protonotary, supporter of the Sforzeschi; Alessandro Farnese, an important curial official, bishop of Montefiascone and Corneto, brother of the pope's mistress Giulia, and later Paul III; Giuliano Cesarini, a Roman, bishop of Ascoli; Ippolito d'Este, then fifteen years old, son of Duke Ercole of Ferrara, already archbishop of Gran (Esztergom) in Hungary; Giovanni Antonio Sangiorgio of Piacenza, a jurisconsult, bishop of Alessandria; and, as the twelfth, the pope's son Cesare Borgia, archbishop of Valencia, a young man, says Sigismondo de' Conti, "sed spei magnae et indolis optimae."[100] This extensive creation of cardinals, although it alienated some powerful figures in the College, especially Giuliano della Rovere, greatly strengthened the pope's hand in the consistory.

After the apparent loss of Segna (Senj) to the Turks, Alexander VI wrote to the Catholic princes on 2 October, 1493, appealing to them for *consilia et auxilia . . . in tanto Italie et Christiane religionis periculo*. While stating that for his part he would leave nothing undone to protect the Italian shores, he wrote that "this business brooks of no delay, but requires immediate preparation." He wanted Giangaleazzo Sforza and Lodovico il Moro, the dukes in Milan, to inform him within two weeks of what contribution they proposed to make to the common cause.[101] On the nineteenth the Florentine agent Antonio Guidotti di Colle wrote the Otto di Pratica from Rome that the pope had decided to send an envoy to Istanbul to make clear to the sultan that the continuance of Turkish attacks upon Christians in Croatia and elsewhere could only result in Jem Sultan's being turned over to the European princes to serve as the spearhead of a crusade greater and stronger than the Ottoman forces could resist. Guidotti also wrote that the pope planned to remind the princes of the perilous condition

---

relative, his grandnephew, also named Juan de Borja, cardinal deacon of S. Maria in Via lata (Eubel, II, 23, 67). Until the death of the latter Juan in January, 1500, they are sometimes confused. The former (and elder) Juan was the son of Alexander's sister Juana de Borja-Lanzol, who was herself the grandmother of the younger Juan (see the biographical sketches of both Juans, by G. De Caro, in the *Dizionario biografico degli italiani*, XII [1970], pp. 713–17, and on the grants made to both Juans note Mario Menotti, ed., *Documenti inediti sulla famiglia e la corte di Alessandro VI*, Rome, 1917, nos. 130, 164–82, 451, pp. 98, 150–58, 308, *et alibi*, where there seems, however, to be some confusion between the two).

[100] Sigismondo de' Conti, II (1883), 61; Infessura, *Diaria*, ed. Tommasini, p. 293; Raynaldus, *Ann. eccl.*, ad ann. 1493, nos. 33–34, vol. XIX (1693), p. 425a; A. Ciaconius, *Vitae et res gestae pont. roman.*, ed. A. Oldoinus, III (1677), cols. 167–82; Pastor, *Gesch. d. Päpste*, III-1 (repr. 1955), 377–80, with notes, and III-2 (repr. 1956), append., nos. 22–24, pp. 1057–58; and see Eubel, *Hierarchia*, II (1914, repr. 1960), 22–23. Ferrante of Naples had been watching the pope's efforts to persuade the cardinals to accept numerous new creations since the preceding June, understanding well enough that no Neapolitan subject would be given the red hat (Trinchera, *Codice aragonese*, II-2, pp. 85, 147, 149–50, 241–44). Guillaume Briçonnet, a rich bourgeois of Touraine, who had become the bishop of S. Malo and was one of Charles VIII's chief counsellors, was also bitterly disappointed in his failure to get a hat, which added to the ample suspicions of the pope already entertained by the French king (Delaborde, *Expédition de Charles VIII*, pp. 284, 294–95).

[101] Jos. Chmel, "Briefe und Actenstücke zur Geschichte der Herzoge von Mailand von 1452 bis 1513," *Notizenblatt: Beilage zum Archiv für Kunde österreichischer Geschichtsquellen*, VI (1856), 421–22, text of the brief dated 2 October, 1493: "Tertius nunc agitur mensis, ex quo intelleximus novos in Corvatia [Croatia] Turcorum motus eorumque dominum ad civitatem Segnie opprimendam inhiare, capta occasione, ex discidiis dilectorum filiorum nobilium de Fregepanibus [the Frankopans], quos sibi variis pollicitationibus conciliare et ad stipendia sua conducere studuit. . . ." I have found copies of this brief in the Arch. di Stato di Mantova, Arch. Gonzaga, Busta 834, and in the Arch. di Stato di Modena, Cancelleria marchionale poi ducale Estense, Estero: Carteggio di principi e signorie, Italia, Roma, Busta 1295/10, no. 10. *Cf.* Soranzo, *Il Tempo di Alessandro VI Papa*, pp. 69–70 and note 28.

of Christian affairs "and to urge them on to an expedition against the Turk, showing how great a victory may be expected by means of the Turk's brother, who is here." The Venetians were always pressing the pope to threaten the sultan that Jem would really be sent with such an expedition. When Alexander decided to send two of the brothers Bocciardi to Istanbul, the Venetian government was anxious they should go by the quickest route, but of course the Signoria would not allow them to go in a state galley. The statesmen of the Republic were unwilling to compromise ever so slightly their constant protestations of neutrality so long as they could preserve peace with the Porte. Actually the papal envoys did not leave Rome until June, 1494. Giorgio Bocciardi remained in Istanbul until late that September.[102] By that time, however, momentous events were occurring in Italy. The papacy faced in the French invaders a more frightening foe than the Turks. When Bocciardi came back to Italy in November (1494), he met with greater surprises than he had experienced in Istanbul. We shall return to him shortly.

On 7 October, 1493, Ferrante of Naples had written Luigi Paladini, his ambassador in Rome, with reference to the papal brief urging the Christian princes to unite against the Turks. Paladini was to inform the pope that Italy had need of union against the ultramontanes as well as against the Turks. But Alexander VI actually held the key to the Porte in Jem Sultan, whom the sultan feared so much; since his Holiness was on good terms with all the princes, and was as much revered as any pontiff who had occupied the throne for a long time, he could proceed boldly. Men and munitions should go immediately into Croatia. Alexander should not do as so many popes had done in the past—begin with fine words and eloquent briefs, and then let every effort be dissipated in the wind, so that the Turks got stronger every day. A papal envoy should be sent to Istanbul to protest against this depredation in Croatia and to threaten the sultan with a summons of the European princes to arms and the employment of Jem to redress Christian grievances. Alexander should take a firm stand, "because the Turks are of such a nature that when you run away from them, they don't stop pursuing you, but when you face them, they come to a halt!" Hungary required internal stability such as would follow from King Ladislas's just acknowledgment of Beatrice as his wife. A union of the barons and prelates of Hungary was necessary for the kingdom to oppose the Turks. Ferrante said he was as much concerned for the public good in this matter as for the proper recognition of his unhappy daughter.[103] Alexander's attention had already turned northward, toward Hungary.

Orso Orsini, bishop of Teano, had been sent as legate *a latere* to Ladislas of Hungary and Bohemia, and to John Albert, king of Poland. His object was to secure the return to Catholic orthodoxy of the heretical communities in Bohemia and to help the two kings compose their differences as a prelude to their participation in the crusade. John Albert made peace with the Turks, but Orsini published in Hungary and Bohemia the papal bull *Orthodoxe fidei* (of 18 October, 1493), providing plenary indulgence to all Christians who would serve Ladislas in the *sancta expeditio* for six months or die in harness before the expiration of this period. The indulgence was also to be granted to individuals and religious houses furnishing mercenaries to the projected enterprise. Religious houses would have to put one armed man in the field for every ten of their members. The mercenaries would themselves receive the indulgence if they were poor. The full remission of sins was also granted, after the customary confession and absolution, to all who contributed to the crusade by their various skills and labors—physicians, apothecaries (*aromatarii*), surgeons, cobblers, cooks, butchers, workers in iron and wood, wheelwrights (*carpentarii*), experts in mechanics, and artificers of all kinds, as well as dealers in medicines, foodstuffs, and other necessities of war, preachers of the crusade, women who tended the sick in the camps, and certain others whose efforts would advance the sacred cause on the eastern fronts. All other indulgences were to be suspended for one year in Hungary.[104]

---

[102] Thuasne, *Djem-Sultan*, pp. 314 and note 3, 316 and note 1, 317–20. A later copy of Alexander VI's *Instructiones . . . date Georgio Buzzardo nuntio ituro ad Baiazzettum Turcarum imperatorem, anno 1494*, may be found in Arch. Segr. Vaticano, Fondo Pio, Reg. 124 (previously 222), fols. 9ᵛ–12ʳ, by mod. stamped enumeration, and another in the Bibl. Apost. Vaticana, Cod. lat. 13,451, fols. 76ʳ–78ᵛ.

[103] Trinchera, *Codice aragonese*, II–2, pp. 262–64, and *cf.* p. 269.

[104] Arch. Segr. Vaticano, Reg. Vat. 779, fols. 39ᵛ–49ʳ, "datum Rome apud Sanctum Petrum, 1493, XV Kal. Novembris, pontificatus [nostri] anno secundo." The list of *artifices et operarii ac mercatores* occurs on fol. 42ʳ.

In the meantime Ferrante had written his ambassador in Venice (on 12 October, 1493) that the blow which the Turks had dealt the Christians in Croatia must give everyone cause to think. Naples and Venice stood as the gateways to Europe. The Turks were trying to seize all Dalmatia. They had reached the Adriatic. If the princes and especially the pope would do their duty, the Turks would have to withdraw even from Greece. Ferrante recalled Venetian efforts over a long period to preserve peace in Italy (with which of course he had always sympathized). Now, however, every day made clearer the French intention to descend into Italy and to attack the kingdom of Naples. Surely the Venetians must realize as well as anyone "that the movement of the French into Italy against us cannot be accomplished without disturbing the peace [*reposo*] of the Italian states." The conquest of other states would inevitably follow that of Naples, "for the French are insolent and bad neighbors and on other occasions have done Italy evil turns." Whenever the French enjoyed peace at home, their thoughts always turned to the mischief they could do in Italy. The Venetians must reflect on the danger which lay ahead—the Turks at the very gates and the French within the peninsula, *cioè li Turchi ad le porte et Francesi dentro Italia*! The Signoria had already aided the Neapolitans against a previous French invasion. It had been a matter of enlightened self-interest, and the harassed Ferrante hoped that the Republic would see the light again.[105]

For years Ferrante had contributed as much as any ruler of his time to the political unrest in Italy. In these days of need he found it difficult to secure allies with whom to meet the expected invasion of the French. In vain did he plead, in letter after letter, for a union of the Italian states to meet the approaching danger from Charles VIII and the likelihood of the Turks' profiting from the turmoil into which the peninsula would obviously be plunged.[106] On 25 October (1493) Ferrante informed Alexander VI that he was sending an agent to Rome within three days with 6,000 ducats as a "subvention for Segna," assuring the pope that not only in this but in all other matters he placed his resources at the pope's disposal.[107] Despite every gesture he could make, however, to win the approval and support of the pope, Ferrante found that Alexander remained hostile to him and to the interests of Naples. The betrothal of Donna Sancia to Gioffredo Borgia seemed to have accomplished nothing. Catalans both and *Arcades ambo*, Ferrante and Rodrigo Borgia knew well they could not trust each other.

Conferences had been held in Rome to provide for the defense of Christendom against the Turks. Venice had been secretly represented at these discussions, and the Republic was to be taxed 25,000 ducats as her share of the costs. While protesting that nothing should be done to compromise the Turco-Venetian peace until a general expedition of the European princes should actually be ready to set out against the Turks, the statesmen on the lagoon were willing to provide 32,000 ducats for use against the enemy in Croatia.[108] All thought of a crusade, however, was but the pursuit of a chimera as long as Charles VIII was determined upon the conquest of Naples. The Emperor Frederick III had died in late August, 1493, and his son Maximilian had succeeded him, full of ambitious plans for offensive action against the Turks. Burchard records the arrival in Rome on 11 January, 1494, of Marquard Breisacher, *doctor et miles*, on an embassy from Maximilian to the pope. Maximilian had been trying to dissuade Charles from his projected Neapolitan adventure. Amicable relations had existed for some time between Maximilian and Ferrante. A letter of 8 January emphasizes that Maximilian was trying to draw Lodovico il Moro from his dangerous connection with the French king.[109] Breisacher could be sure of a sympa-

---

[105] Trinchera, *Codice aragonese*, II–2, pp. 273–75. On the measures taken by Ferrante for the defense of Naples against the French, see Delaborde, *Expédition de Charles VIII*, pp. 297 ff.

[106] *Cf.* Trinchera, *Codice aragonese*, II–2, pp. 275–79, 322–31, 332, 334, 344–46, 348–56, 371–75, 378–79, 381–83, 390–401, 404, 406–409, 411–14, 418–19, 421–31, and *cf.* pp. 294–95, 360–61, 385, 434–35.

[107] Trinchera, *Codice aragonese*, II–2, pp. 291–92, 314. We have already had occasion to note the close connection of Albania with Naples in the time of Ferrante's father Alfonso V; the interest in Albanian affairs had continued, and Ferrante seems to have had a genuine concern for the problem presented by "li Turchi in Corvatia" [Croatia]. *Cf.*, *ibid.*, II–2, pp. 292–93, 298, 435.

[108] Thuasne, *Djem-Sultan*, pp. 320–21.

[109] Trinchera, *Codice aragonese*, II–2, p. 408, letter dated at Naples on 8 January, 1494, to the treasurer of Spain. The crusade against the Turk remained Maximilian's major ambition and the basis of his foreign policy (Ulmann, *Kaiser Maximilian I.*, I [1884], 204 ff.). Marquard Breisacher appears in various documents during the long reign of Maximilian's father Frederick III (Jos. Chmel, *Regesta chronologico-diplomatica Friderici IV. Romanorum regis* [*im-*

thetic hearing in Rome, for it was axiomatic that the pope should prefer Charles to go crusading on some eastern front in co-operation with Maximilian than to enter Italy with the intention of conquering Naples. But in the midst of the discussions the news reached Rome on 27 January, 1494, that Ferrante had died in Naples on the twenty-fifth. His son Alfonso had succeeded him.[110] The death of the old king and the accession of a new one were a sign and a summons to Charles to continue with his plans for the invasion of Italy. Whatever right to the crown Ferrante had had *de facto*, after some thirty-five years of rule, lapsed with his death, and Charles was determined that Alfonso should not long remain on the shaky throne.

---

peratoris III.], Vienna, 1838, repr. Hildesheim, 1962, nos. 318, 1625, 2779–80, 7678, 8093, 8467, 8657, and 8786, dating from the year 1441 to 1492!).

[110] Burchard, *Diarium*, ed. Thuasne, II (1883), 86–89, and ed. Celani, I, 456–58. Ferrante's last letter, composed by Giovanni Pontano, is dated at Naples on 24 January (Trinchera, *Codice aragonese*, II–2, p. 440). *Cf.* Infessura, *Diaria*, ed. Tommasini, pp. 294, 295; Desjardins (and Canestrini), *Négociations diplomatiques*, I, 277; *Diario ferrarese*, in *RISS*, XXIV, pt. 7 (1933), p. 134; Delaborde, *Expédition de Charles VIII*, pp. 303, 304–5. Charles VIII claimed that his "recovery" of Naples was the necessary first step in the French crusade against the Turks and the reconquest of the Holy Land, while the prophecies of one Jehan Michel apparently circulated in France as an echo of those of Savonarola, exhorting the king to reform the Church and effect "la récupération de Jérusalem à lui destinée" (J. de la Pilorgerie, *Campagne et bulletins de la grande armée d'Italie commandée par Charles VIII* [*1494–1495*], Nantes and Paris, 1866, pp. 43–50, 431–33).

15. ALEXANDER VI AND CHARLES VIII, THE FRENCH EXPEDITION INTO ITALY (1494–1495)

COSIMO DE' MEDICI'S old policy of the triple alliance of Florence, Milan, and Naples had not been easy to maintain. His grandson Lorenzo had turned to Venice in November, 1474, leaving Naples in the lurch, when he needed assistance to frustrate Sixtus IV's effort to extend papal dominion in the Romagna. Four years later, after the Pazzi conspiracy, as we have seen, Lorenzo had found himself at war with both the papacy and Naples (in 1478–1480). Although Lorenzo had learned his lesson from that experience and reverted to the alliance with Milan and Naples, he had still found no rose-strewn path to peace. Sixtus IV, always nurturing the Romagnole ambition, had next made a pact with the Venetians to partition the duchy of Ferrara (in 1482), causing another war in Italy when the triple alliance intervened to prevent the spoliation of the Estensi. This struggle had no sooner been concluded than Sixtus's successor Innocent VIII was embroiled in his contest with Ferrante of Naples. For his remaining years Lorenzo had tried to reconcile the Holy See and Naples without getting drawn into the conflict himself.

Every time the Italian states had had recourse to arms, some envoy or other had been sent to the French court to discuss the Angevin claim to Naples, the Orléanist claim to Milan, or the general desirability of the French establishing peace in Italy to make possible a crusade against the Turks. Charles VII and Louis XI had had too many problems to undertake the grand adventure south of the Alps. Continued success against England and Burgundy, however, with some advance in prosperity and with the achievement of domestic tranquillity in France, presented Charles VIII with an opportunity (or at least a temptation) such as his predecessors had not known since the old days of Charles of Anjou.

Upon receiving the news of Ferrante's death, Charles VIII had promptly sent two special envoys to Rome to request the pope not to invest Alfonso [II] with the kingdom of Naples. Should the pope intend to proceed with the investiture, the envoys were to tell him that Charles would appeal from his decision to that of a general council. Under the circumstances this was rather a crude threat. While the French problem was thus assuming alarming proportions, an envoy arrived in Rome on 4 February (1494) from the soldan of Egypt. He was accompanied to his lodging by members of Jem Sultan's household as well as by papal retainers. A month later a Rhodian embassy of obedience arrived in Rome, sent by the Grand Master d'Aubusson, another reminder that western affairs should not be allowed to distract the pope from those of the East.[1]

The French threat placed Alexander VI in a most awkward position. As a conciliatory gesture he decreed on 9 March that the golden rose should be sent to Charles.[2] But on the twentieth of the month his Holiness answered the French king in a long brief. He rejoiced that Charles was ready to undertake the defense of Christians against the Turks, whose un-

---

[1] Johann Burchard [Burckard], *Diarium . . . (1483–1506)*, ed. Louis Thuasne, 3 vols., Paris, 1883–85, II, 89, 91–92, and ed. Enrico Celani under the title *Liber notarum*, 2 vols., in the new Muratori, *RISS*, XXXII, pt. 1, Città di Castello and Bologna, 1907–42, I, 458, 459–60. Upon the arrival of the Rhodian embassy a dispute arose as to whether the Knights' envoys should be accorded a formal reception by the papal and cardinals' households. Burchard contended that a formal reception should not be accorded subjects of the Church and religious. A representative of the Order said that the envoys of the Knights had been so received in the time of Sixtus IV and Innocent VIII. Burchard replied that in Sixtus's reign ceremonies were badly handled, and that he had himself subsequently informed Innocent as to the proper procedure. When the matter came up for discussion before Alexander VI, he overruled Burchard: ". . . respondit pontifex me nihil scire." The Rhodian envoys were given a formal reception into Rome. Burchard was right, however, and the pope wrong, as we may gather from Paride Grassi's reflections on the correct etiquette to be observed in assigning the Knights and their grand master to their proper place in the hierarchical order (Thuasne, II, 94–95, note).

[2] Burchard, *Diarium*, ed. Thuasne, II, 93, and ed. Celani, I, 461, lines 7–14; H. F. Delaborde, *L'Expédition de Charles VIII en Italie*, Paris, 1888, p. 308. Alexander was seeking to dissuade Charles from the Neapolitan venture, "perche li Turchi sonno al presente per invadere la Italia" (A. de Boüard, "Lettres de Rome de Bartolomeo de Bracciano à Virginio Orsini [1489–1494]," *Mélanges d'archéologie et d'histoire*, XXXIII [1913], no. XLIX, pp. 329–30, dated 16 February, 1494).

heard-of slaughter of Christ's faithful had been causing him the cruelest anguish day and night. He was confident that a union of the great princes, inflamed with an ardor to match Charles's own, would arise against the enemies of the faith. The pope was now requesting the princes to send to Rome plenipotentiaries to commit their principals to the necessary steps to organize the crusade. He was astonished, however, by the king's statement that he must assert his claim to the kingdom of Naples before embarking on the crusade. A French expedition against Naples would place all Italy in unspeakable peril. Would the Turks *tamquam ludorum spectatores* quietly await the issue of a war between Charles and Alfonso? Might not the rulers of both Turkey and Egypt, learning of Charles's great military preparations, fear for themselves and become reconciled? But Christianity had hoped for so much from their enmity!

> We are therefore again compelled to urge and pray your Serenity to give up this war against Naples, for the common defense of Christendom; and turn with us to the expedition we have planned which without question this war would obstruct completely. Let your Majesty consider how you are at odds with yourself, for while you say that you are arming against the infidels, you are undertaking a war with Naples. . . .

Charles had alleged that possession of Naples would give him the point of departure for the crusade, which the pope flatly branded as a shallow pretense. He did not urge Charles to abandon whatever right he might have to Naples, but to seek his due by the *via justitie*. Alexander offered his own services as arbitrator. As for Alfonso, his investiture would not prejudice Charles's claims if they were just. Innocent VIII had invested Alfonso's father Ferrante with the unanimous assent of the consistory. Alexander could not properly withhold the same investiture from Alfonso, who like his father before him actually possessed the kingdom and had been designated as Ferrante's heir: "We cannot defraud him of possession of his right nor can we abandon justice in his case." It was an eloquent text, composed (we may assume) largely by Luigi Podocataro, whose signature it bears.[3] Alexander had finally made his decision after months of temporizing.

The envoys of the Knights of Rhodes, when making their obeisance to the pope on 10 March, had urged the crusade upon him, claiming that the time was opportune at long last to employ Jem Sultan against his brother in Istanbul.[4] But the time was far from opportune, at least in the West. On 14 March a Neapolitan embassy, headed by Don Luigi of Aragon, marquis of Gerace, and Archbishop Alessandro Carafa of Naples, arrived in Rome to render King Alfonso's obedience to the pope and to negotiate various details relating to the young Gioffredo Borgia's marriage to Donna Sancia. They were met by the usual members of the papal and cardinals' households. Don Luigi stayed at the Orsini palace on Monte Giordano; Alessandro Carafa lodged with his brother, Cardinal Oliviero. As the weeks passed, they participated in the ceremonial pageants that made up the most conspicuous part of life at the Curia Romana, and Burchard had more than one occasion to shake his head over the poor form upon which Alexander VI often insisted in ceremonies. At last, after much delay, on Friday, 18 April, a secret consistory authorized the investiture of Alfonso II as king of Naples. The pope's nephew Juan Borgia-Lanzol, cardinal of S. Susanna, was named *legatus de latere* to go to Naples to perform the actual rites of investiture and coronation. Some of the cardinals protested. The pope, however, had made up his mind. Burchard was sent ahead to Naples to arrange for the coronation. Before his departure from Rome he drew twenty-five gold ducats from the bank of the heirs of Ambrogio Spanocchi, which were charged to the Neapolitan royal account managed by Spanocchi et Compagnia. The crusty and opinionated master of ceremonies much enjoyed the experience, which he has reported fully in his diary.

Burchard arrived in Naples on 24 April with an elaborate schedule for the coronation, and had soon adapted the details of the schedule to the gates, streets, and churches of the city as

---

[3] L. Thuasne, *Djem-Sultan, fils de Mohammed II, frère de Bayezid II, 1459–1495*, Paris, 1892, append., no. 20, pp. 437–40, and *cf.* no. 21, pp. 440–41; Pastor, *Gesch. d. Päpste*, III-1 (repr. 1955), 381–84, and III-2 (repr. 1956), append., no. 26, pp. 1058–59; Abel Desjardins (and Giuseppe Canestrini), *Négociations diplomatiques de la France avec la Toscane*, I (Paris, 1859), 280, 287; D. Malipiero, *Annali veneti*, in *Arch. stor. italiano*, VII, pt. 1 (1843), 320; Delaborde, *Expédition de Charles VIII*, pp. 306–7, 308–9.

[4] Burchard, *Diarium*, ed. Thuasne, II, 93–94, and note, and ed. Celani, I, 461.

well as to the customs and personnel of the court. The coronation of Alfonso II took place on 8 May in the presence of a great throng of Neapolitan nobles and clergy, court officials, visiting dignitaries, and ambassadors of the foreign powers, including an envoy from the Porte with a retinue of a dozen Turkish attendants. There were the inevitable errors of protocol, the despair of Burchard's well-ordered life, as when by inadvertence the bishop of Tropea, whom Burchard had carefully instructed, allowed Alfonso to remain seated throughout the recitation of the *Credo*. The ambassadors were as usual dissatisfied with the places assigned to them, and were so importunate that poor Burchard had to oust some prelates from their bench to provide for them. Owing to Burchard's thoughtfulness, however, the Turkish ambassador was able to withdraw from the ceremonies after the actual coronation, when the legate was beginning to say mass, for the master of ceremonies knew that it would be neither appropriate to the occasion nor agreeable to the Turk if he had to witness the elevation of the host.[5]

Immediately after his coronation, over which Cardinal Juan Borgia had presided, Alfonso II had made the pope's son Juan—already the duke of Gandia—prince of Tricarico and count of Chiaromonte, Lauria, and Carinola, "because of his singular merits," and had then made another papal bastard, Gioffredo, because of his possession of similar merits, prince of Squillace and count of Cariati.[6] The Catalans had indeed got together. The French were furious. Charles VIII declared that he would withdraw his obedience from Alexander VI. Cardinals who supported the pope were going to lose their French benefices, which would be given to Cardinal Ascanio Sforza, brother of il Moro, the ally of France. For obvious reasons Ascanio was anxious to leave Rome, but in early April the pope had refused him permission to do so. On the twenty-third of the month, however, at about midnight (*ad 4 hore de nocte*), Cardinal Giuliano della Rovere had sailed in a well-armed brigantine with twenty men aboard from his stronghold at Ostia, which he left in the hands of a garrison with sufficient provisions to last for two years. Giuliano went first to Genoa, thence to Avignon, and on 1 June appeared in Charles VIII's headquarters at Lyon. Giuliano's fortress at the mouth of the Tiber did not hold out very long against the forces of Niccolò Orsini and the Neapolitans, whom the pope summoned to his aid. Giuliano's friend and ally Fabrizio Colonna, apparently regarding the situation as hopeless, helped negotiate the surrender of Ostia in return for a papal promise to be left alone at Grottaferrata. Alexander VI was in possession of "arx nostra Ostiensis" by 24 May (1494). And now Giuliano seemed to be as much at war with the pope as Charles VIII was with the king of Naples.[7]

---

[5] Burchard, *Diarium*, ed. Thuasne, II, 97, 107–62, and ed. Celani, I, 463–64, 470–513; Stefano Infessura, *Diaria rerum romanarum*, ed. Oreste Tommasini, Rome, 1890, pp. 295–96; Sigismondo de' Conti (da Foligno), *Le Storie de' suoi tempi dal 1475 al 1510*, II (Rome, 1883), 62, who says that Alfonso promised the pope regular payment of the feudal tribute for Naples, and that he also secured the submission of Virginio Orsini to the Holy See. *Cf.* Raynaldus, *Ann. eccl.*, ad ann. 1494, nos. 3–14, vol. XIX (1693), pp. 427–431a. The Milanese ambassador to Naples, Antonio Stanga, described Cardinal Juan Borgia's arrival in Naples and the coronation of Alfonso II in letters to Lodovico il Moro dated 5 and 8 May, 1494 (Pietro Magistretti, "Lutto e feste della corte di Napoli: Relazione diplomatica dell'ambasciatore milanese al duca di Bari," *Archivio storico lombardo*, VI [Milan, 1879], 712–15).

[6] Burchard, *Diarium*, ed. Thuasne, II, 160–61, and ed. Celani, I, 511–12, with notes. Gioffredo Borgia had been intended originally for the Church, and is described as *Gaufridus de Borgia, clericus Romanus, notarius noster . . . in septimo tue etatis anno constitutus* and as *canonicus Valentinus, notarius noster . . . in octavo tue etatis anno constitutus* in four grants procured on his behalf from Innocent VIII by Cardinal Rodrigo in September, 1489 (Arch. Segr. Vaticano, Reg. Vat. 771, fols. 122r, 123r, 123v, 126r, 127r), being referred to in the fourth of these documents, a letter addressed to Cardinal Rodrigo, as *dictus Gaufridus, natus tuus* (*ibid.*, fol. 127v, doc. dated 18 September, 1489). Gioffredo was certainly the son of Vannozza de' Catanei, Rodrigo Borgia's mistress, but was he the son of Rodrigo?

On 6 August, 1493, as Alexander VI, Rodrigo legitimatized Gioffredo, and acknowledged paternity (*cf.* the bull in Pastor, *Gesch. d. Päpste*, III-2 [repr. 1956], append., no. 21, p. 1057). According to two letters, however, of Giovanni Lucido Cattanei (a relative of Vannozza?), dated 30 June and 21 August, 1499, Alexander regarded Gioffredo's birth as the consequence of Vannozza's indiscretion with her husband or with an unknown lover, and indeed Cattanei asserts in the latter dispatch that the pope had told him "che quell'ultimo [Don Gilfredo, filiolo reputato del Papa] non era so filio. . . !" (see Alessandro Luzio, "Isabella d'Este e i Borgia," *Archivio storico lombardo*, 5th ser., XLI [1914], 508–10, and, *ibid.*, XLII [1915], 428, 431, the latter refs. being to Cattanei's dispatches to the Gonzagas in Mantua). Cattanei was a native of Mantua, an apostolic protonotary resident in Rome from 1487 to his death in 1505.

[7] Sigismondo de' Conti, II, 62–63; Malipiero, *Annali veneti*, in *Arch. stor. italiano*, VII-1, 318–19; Pastor, *Gesch. d. Päpste*, III-1 (repr. 1955), 384–86, and III-2 (repr. 1956), append., nos. 27–29, pp. 1059–60; Delaborde, *Expédition*

In the meantime a Turkish envoy had come to Venice, apparently full of smiles and pleasantries, bringing a letter or letters from Sultan Bayazid II, assuring the Signoria of the latter's devotion to the Republic. Bayazid intended to make good the losses which Venetian merchants had suffered at the hands of Turkish corsairs. Indeed, his Ottoman Excellency seemed eager to maintain the "bona pace" which existed between Venice and the Porte.[8] While the Venetians were thus on friendly terms with the Turks, Maximilian, king of the Romans, had been evolving elaborate plans for the crusade, which the march of events was rendering nugatory. On 19 April (1494) he had sent detailed instructions to Marquard Breisacher, his envoy to the Holy See. Breisacher was to inform the pope "that we shall meet the king of France personally in Burgundy about the end of this month, and we hope to prevail upon him to make peace with the king of Naples, lest their discord should obstruct us all in our crusade [*expeditio*] against the Turk." The king of the Romans, who said that his armies did not easily tolerate the heat of a Balkan summer, stated his intention with the aid of God, the Holy See, and the Christian princes personally to take the field against the Turks in the coming autumn. Very shortly he would be sending troops into Croatia, which was subjected to daily raids by the Turks, who were carrying off much booty. Unfortunately the king of Poland had made a truce with the Turks; it was expected that the king of Hungary would follow suit. The Hungarians had little faith either in their own strength or in receiving assistance from their fellow Christians, and believing that their only safety lay in negotiating a peace with the Turks, they were all inclined to do so. The imperial envoy was to ask his Holiness to write immediately to the king of Hungary to persuade him not to make such a peace, which the Turks would not in any event observe honorably, for if the opportunity arose, peace or no peace, they would attack the Hungarians or Germans, the subjects of the Church or of Naples, the Venetians or the Knights of Rhodes, or any Christian people at all. Maximilian sent Breisacher a detailed blueprint for a two years' war to be waged against the Porte by the soldan of Egypt and the Christian princes.[9] But some three weeks after the final text of Breisacher's instructions had been prepared, Cardinal Juan Borgia had crowned Alfonso II king of Naples in the name of Pope Alexander VI. A now embittered Charles VIII was preparing to descend into Italy to drive Alfonso from the throne and to hold Alexander accountable for his simoniacal dealings with the house of Aragon.

When it came to simony and self-seeking, Alexander had a lot to answer for, and doubtless the full measure of his failings both as pope and

---

de Charles VIII, pp. 346–48. Francesco della Casa, Florentine envoy to the French court (now at Lyon), informed Piero de' Medici on 13 March, 1494, that French preparations for the invasion of Italy were almost complete (Desjardins, I, 282–84). On the arrival in France and the reception of Giuliano della Rovere at Lyon, see Desjardins, I, 297, 299, 303, 307, esp. pp. 310, 313, 392. It was believed in France that the invasion might have to be postponed if Ostia passed into papal hands (undated dispatch to Piero de' Medici, *ibid.*, I, 388).

[8] Arch. di Stato di Venezia, Sen. Secreta, Reg. 35, fol. 2^v [14^v by mod. enumeration], dated 1 April, 1494: "Domino Turco: Per la venuta al conspecto nostro del egregio homo et honorato orator de la Excellentia vostra, Cassaim Zaus, habiamo ricevuto lettere di quella piene de amore et charita et declaratione de la bona valitudine de vostra Excellentia, il che ne è stato de grande contento et apiacer. Habiamo etiam inteso per quelle la perseverante mente et dispositione sua a la conservatione de la bona pace nostra, la qual cossa . . . ne sia etiam sta dechiarita per el fidelissimo et da nui ben amato secretario nostro Aluvise [*sic*] Sagundino, noviter retornato da la Porta de la Excellentia vostra. . . ." Bayazid had informed Sagundino of his annoyance (*molesto*) that Turkish corsairs or at least subjects of the Porte had been preying on Venetian shipping.

The sultan was also said to be annoyed at "le incursion et robarie facte sopra territorii nostri de Sibinico [Šibenik] et Trau [Trogir] per le zente sue, et maxime per Suliman Bassa, al presente sanzacho de Graina. . . ." The Senate sought restitution for the losses which the piracy had caused Venetian citizens and subjects, and decided to send Sagundino back to Istanbul with the Turkish envoy to seek repayment for the damages in question and to request the removal of the troublesome Suleiman Beg from the Republic's borders in Dalmatia. Although it would appear that Venetian subjects had not been blameless, Suleiman Beg agreed to make restitution and to mend his ways in the future, and Sagundino was instructed that his government would be content "ut preterita cuncta recedant et sopita remaneant" (*cf.* Sen. Secreta, Reg. 35, fols. 11^v–12^r [23^v–24^r]). There were the usual rumors that spring of a Turkish armada's sailing into the Aegean (*ibid.*, fol. 8^r [20^r]).

[9] Thuasne, *Djem-Sultan*, pp. 324–25, who summarizes rather carelessly Maximilian's *instructio* to Breisacher, which he has himself published, *ibid.*, append., no. 22, pp. 441–45. There is a seventeenth-century MS. copy of this material in the Arch. Segr. Vaticano, Miscellanea, Arm. II, tom. 56, fols. 147^r ff. In early June (1494) Charles VIII did go into Burgundy (Desjardins, I, 399–400, 403, 404–5), but the proposed personal interview with Maximilian did not take place (Delaborde, *Expédition de Charles VIII*, pp. 340, 349–53). *Cf.* H. Ulmann, *Kaiser Maximilian I.*, I (Stuttgart, 1884), 232–33, 269 ff.

as a man was energetically recounted to Charles VIII by Cardinal della Rovere, who claimed that a general council was necessary to proceed against the pope and to reform the Curia. Gallicanism was always strong in France. The pope had also to fear renewal of the Pragmatic Sanction, which would effect the virtual independence of the French Church from Rome. The Florentine agents Guidantonio Vespucci and Piero Capponi wrote Piero de' Medici from Lyon on 6 June, 1494, that della Rovere was planning to seek the support of Maximilian as well as of Charles VIII for the summoning of a general council "per tribulare il Papa." They believed, however, that the pope, "who is by nature despicable and conscious of his own crime, could easily be returned to decency because of his apprehension of developments in this quarter." It would be very desirable, they thought, to reconcile della Rovere and the pope, which could be done if the cardinal might be assured of just treatment.[10]

Two days later Vespucci and Capponi wrote Piero that the French were making extraordinary maritime preparations. Every provision, therefore, should be made for the defense of Pisa and the Florentine littoral. The French were bringing with them a most extensive artillery, mobile cannon of no great size but of unusual striking power. They were putting 1,500 horse in the field and enrolling ten or twelve thousand Gascon, Swiss, and Italian mercenaries. Their descent into Italy was well planned. Charles VIII was going into Burgundy not with any expectation of reaching an accord with Maximilian but for the security of the border lands. Charles insisted that he was going in person into Italy. There were some who doubted it. He was so persistent, however, in the statement of his intention that it was much to be feared he would do so. Although the French were having financial difficulties, the pope should be warned that they had effective connections in Rome.[11] On 14 June Vespucci and Capponi wrote the Otto di Pratica that King Charles had now gone into Burgundy. He was expected back in Lyon soon, and after another four or five days in Lyon it was said that he would leave for Asti, where his forces would assemble. Thence he would go to Genoa. According to their information, Charles was putting 22,000 men in the field, of whom seven or eight hundred would be *uomini d'arme*. There were still many in Lyon who did not believe that Charles would leave the kingdom. Cardinal della Rovere had gone into Burgundy with the king.[12]

By now the Medici bank in Lyon was concluding its business, and was closed. Vespucci and Capponi informed Piero on 19 June that "vostri del banco" had departed the preceding day.[13] With fewer resources than his father and far greater problems to face, Piero now must ponder what his policy would be when the French began their southward march on Italian soil.[14]

Sultan Bayazid and his vizirs watched developments in Italy with interest and apprehension. Charles VIII had constantly insisted that his expedition was but the prelude to a crusade,

[10] Desjardins, I, 399–400.

[11] Desjardins, I, 400–4, letter dated at Lyon on 8 June, 1494. The plague was bad in Provence and Languedoc; by 14 June it had reached Lyon (*ibid.*, I, 406). The French minister Guillaume Briçonnet, bishop of S. Malo, had raised an initial war fund of 600,000 ducats, and another 800,000 were expected from taxation in addition to ordinary revenues (Delaborde, *Expédition de Charles VIII*, pp. 290, 297, 327–28, and *cf.* pp. 429–30).

[12] Desjardins, I, 404–5. There were good reasons for thinking that the expedition would not cross the Alps into Italy, considering the number of great feudatories and royal counsellors who were dragging their heels (Delaborde, *Expédition de Charles VIII*, pp. 328 ff., 343 ff.).

[13] Desjardins, I, 408, and *cf.* pp. 313 ff. Delaborde, *Expédition de Charles VIII*, p. 181, has emphasized the importance of the Medici bank in Lyon as "une sorte de bureau de renseignements politiques sur les affaires de France." According to Philippe de Commines, Capponi was inimical to Piero de' Medici, and had actually advised the expulsion of the Florentines from France (*Mémoires*, bk. VII, chap. 7, ed. B. de Mandrot, 2 vols., Paris, 1901–3, II, 143). This was the end of the Medici bank in Lyon, which closed its doors for good after August, 1497 (Raymond de Roover, *The Rise and Decline of the Medici Bank, 1397–1494*, New York, 1966, pp. 310–11). *Cf.* B. Buser, *Die Beziehungen der Mediceer zu Frankreich während der Jahre 1434–1494* . . . , Leipzig, 1879, pp. 331–32. As Carlo Barbiano, Lodovico il Moro's envoy in France, wrote from Lyon on 3 July, 1494, the Medici bank would suffer grave losses, "perchè havendo a pagare et ricevere in questo reame grande summa de dinari, sarano astrecti pagare el debito senza dilatione et li crediti non porrano ritrare senza grandissima difficultà" (*ibid.*, p. 550). Barbiano goes on to say that the Medici agents had moved from Lyon to Chambéry in Savoy. If Lodovico wished to cause them still greater losses, Barbiano would ask Charles VIII to request Duchess Blanche of Savoy to expel them "per darli magior perdita."

[14] On 2 February, 1494, Charles VIII had demanded that Piero de'Medici put a stop to his vacillation and generally pro-Neapolitan policy, and supply the French with three hundred lances, one hundred infantry, and six galleys when they should arrive in Italy (Desjardins, I, 362). *Cf.* Delaborde, *Expédition de Charles VIII*, pp. 277 ff., 353–56, 387.

and that Naples was to be his *point de départ* for the Levant.[15] On 26 April, 1494, the Grand Master Pierre d'Aubusson had written Alexander VI that the sultan desired the frequent exchange of embassies between Istanbul and Rhodes, and that he was apparently willing to make reparation for certain damage done by his subjects to the goods and persons of Rhodians. D'Aubusson was, however, informed that the sultan was preparing a land army, presumably to send against the Hungarians. He was also getting some galleys ready for employment against the pirates who infested the Turkish coastlands. The grand master cautioned the pope that the astute Mustafa Beg, onetime envoy of the Porte to Innocent VIII, was then staying near Durazzo and was thought to be hatching some plot against Jem Sultan, for whose protection especial care and vigilance were needed.[16]

Bayazid doubtless dreamed of some misfortune overtaking his brother, and would have happily risked the ire of Rome to bring about his death. In the face of the French expedition, however, a desire for friendly relations with the Porte was quite as marked at the Curia Romana as in Naples. On 12 May, 1494, Alexander VI wrote Bayazid that he had been glad to learn of the strong friendship which now existed between the sultan and King Alfonso. Good relations between the two sovereigns were particularly gratifying to the pope since his beloved son Alfonso was bound to him by family ties as well as by the paternal benevolence he felt for him. The pope had taken Alfonso and his kingdom under the protection of the Holy See, and besought for him the same consideration that the sultan would show the pope. His Holiness would do as much for the preservation of Naples as of Rome.[17] Bayazid's apparent friendliness produced no illusions in the West. Everyone, especially the Venetians, knew that the Turk bore watching.

Despite the "good peace" which Bayazid and the Venetians said they wanted to preserve —particularly in view of the threat of a French invasion of Italy, which was supposed to be the beginning of a crusade—Niccolò da Ca Pesaro, the Republic's captain of the Gulf, was maintaining a vigilant patrol in the Aegean. Niccolò's six galleys just happened to be in the harbor of Naxos when on 1 July, 1494, Giovanni III Crispo, duke of the Archipelago, died. Giovanni left a mistress and two illegitimate children, according to Stefano Magno, a son named Francesco then eleven years of age and a daughter of seven. Niccolò and the galley commanders (*sopracomiti*) buried the dead duke, whose tyrannical rule the Naxiotes had heartily resented. Although there was some division among them, most of the islanders now expressed a strong preference for an end to the rule of the Crispi and for the submission of the Archipelago to Venice. Niccolò appointed one Francesco Morosini as governor of Naxos, and sent members of his staff to occupy the late duke's other islands of Santorin, Nio, Syra, and Melos. On 31 July an envoy of the Naxiotes arrived in Venice to plead the islanders' case, and on 20 August their bishop put into the lagoon "with ambassadors of the people to swear fealty to the Signoria and to ask for privileges."[18]

The facts seem to have been presented somewhat differently in Venice, where the matter came before the Senate on 12 September (1494). Duke Giovanni's son Francesco is said to have been thirteen, his sister eight, and their mother the duke's "coniunx."[19] In any event it was proposed that the Senate elect a Venetian noble to administer "ius et iusticia" as governor of Naxos, with appeal from his decisions to be made to the colonial government of nearby

[15] *Cf.* Desjardins, I, 273, 362, 377; Giacomo Bosio, *Militia di San Giovanni Gierosolimitano*, II (1594), bk. xv, p. 423; Delaborde, *Expédition de Charles VIII*, pp. 295, 304, 305, 313–14, 335, 364, 373.

[16] V. Lamansky, *Secrets d'état de Venise*, S. Petersburg, 1884, repr. New York, 1968, p. 290.

[17] Thuasne, *Djem-Sultan*, p. 326, where a corrupt text is given of the pope's letter, "datum Rome XII Maii 1494;" *cf.* Pastor, *Gesch. d. Päpste*, III-1 (repr. 1955), 388 and note 1.

[18] Stefano Magno, *Annali veneti*, in C. N. Sathas, ed., *Documents inédits relatifs à l'histoire de la Grèce au moyen âge*, 9 vols., Paris, 1880–90, repr. Athens, 1972, VI, 241, and *cf.* Hopf, *Chron. gréco-romanes* (1873, repr. 1966), pp. 209, 482, who follows a text of Magno which makes Giovanni Crispo's daughter three years old. On Niccolò da Ca Pesaro and Francesco Morosini, *cf.* Arch. di Stato di Venezia, Sen. Secreta, Reg. 35, fol. 37^r [49^r].

[19] Sen. Secreta, Reg. 35, fol. 26^r [38^r], doc. dated 12 September, 1494: "Cum nuper ex hac vita migraverit illustrissimus quondam dominus Joannes Crispo, dux Egeopelagi, recommendatus noster, qui sequens vestigia patris, avi et maiorum suorum semper fidelissimus et in omnibus obsequentissimus fuit dominio nostro et reliquerit coniugem cum uno filio aetatis annorum XIII et una filia annorum octo, convenit officio status nostri, qui semper consuevit esse benignus erga eius fidelissimos et benemeritos, attenta tenera aetate ipsorum pupillorum et importantia illarum insularum dare modum et formam quod ille ducatus bene gubernetur et conservetur sub umbra nostra. . . ."

Crete or to distant Venice. The island was to be governed as in Duke Giovanni's lifetime; the governor was to collect the customary revenues, from which his salary would be paid as well as the salaries of those who were to be appointed to guard the fortresses on the various islands. Although this proposal was defeated for some reason on the twelfth, it was easily passed on the sixteenth when its proponents resubmitted it. The islands of the Archipelago, especially Naxos and Melos, were said to be of "incredibilis importantia" tò the Republic, whose galleys, transports, and other vessels were constantly obliged to seek the shelter of their harbors on their annual runs to the East. The Senate estimated the population of all the islands comprising the duchy of Naxos or the Archipelago at more than 25,000 persons. Their envoys (*nuntii*) had just emphasized their dire need for protection, obviously against the Turks and Turkish corsairs. The Senate seemed almost ready to take over the historic duchy, then almost three centuries old, and to accept the envoys and inhabitants of the islands "as our dearest and most faithful subjects." Duke Giovanni's "wife" and children might come to Venice (according to another motion), where the Senate would make "appropriate and honorable provision for them." This motion also had rough going on 12 September, and indeed it appears not to have passed on the sixteenth.[20]

In accordance with the first motion, which was passed on 16 September, Pietro Contarini received his commission as *gubernator Nixiae* on 30 October (1494), with detailed instructions, from the Doge Agostino Barbarigo. Contarini was to take the then available "galley of Romania" from Venice to Modon, where he was to board another galley "which we have ordered to be given to you, so that therewith you may betake yourself to Naxos." His appointment was for two years. The Senate allotted him five hundred ducats a year for expenses of all kinds, meaning presumably for his salary. The money was to come from the *introitus et redditus* of Naxos and the other islands. He was absolutely forbidden to engage in trade of any sort. Above all, he must do nothing in any way "to contravene the good peace and friendship which we have with the lord Turk."[21] Within five years, however, Venice was again to be at war with the lord Turk, and in October, 1500, the Senate restored the duchy of the Archipelago to Duke Giovanni's son Francesco, who in time became a madman and a murderer. For one reason or another the duchy of the Archipelago always remained a source of disquiet or vexation.

In the meantime an Italian league was being formed with the hope of stopping the French advance. Alexander VI and Alfonso II of Naples were joined in their opposition to French ambition by Florence, Siena, Bologna, Pesaro, Urbino, and Imola. Bayazid had sent an envoy to Naples to condole with Alfonso for Ferrante's death and to offer the new king aid both by land and by sea against the French, "saying that he did not want them in Italy." In August (1494) the news reached Venice that Alfonso had himself sent an embassy to Istanbul to ask aid of the Turks and to suggest that Bayazid attack Chios to divert the Genoese from their cooperation with the French. Malipiero reports the rumor that Alfonso offered the sultan Brindisi and Otranto, which he apparently preferred to see surrendered to the Turks than to the long-standing enemies of his house. By this time, however, Bayazid understood more fully the striking power of the French juggernaut, and he replied that he did not wish to become embroiled in Christian affairs, since he was at peace with all the princes. If he were attacked, however, he would take vengeance.

A Turkish envoy arrived in Venice on 21 November (1494). He was formally received on the twenty-seventh, and recommended Alfonso II to the Signoria. Some days before his arrival an extraordinary event had occurred near Ancona. The envoy informed the Venetian government, with vast indignation, that another Turkish emissary, Kasim Beg, on his way to Rome had been stopped by the lord of Sinigaglia (Senigallia)—Giovanni della Rovere, prefect of Rome and Cardinal Giuliano's brother—who had relieved the emissary of the 40,000 ducats he was taking to the pope as pension or provision for Jem Sultan. The Venetian Senate already knew of the almost incredible incident,[22] as indeed all Italy did within the next

[20] Sen. Secreta, Reg. 35, fol. cit., and fol. 26^{v} [38^{v}].

[21] Sen. Secreta, Reg. 35, fols. 37^{r}–38^{r} [49^{r}–50^{r}], doc. dated 30 October, 1494, and *cf.* Magno, *Annali veneti*, in Sathas, *Docs. inédits*, VI, 241–42.

[22] The Venetians were shocked at the news "quae Cossaymbei [elsewhere Chassumbey], orator domini Turci ad summum pontificem, ex Anchona scripsit ad nos de aggressu sibi facto per gentes domini prefecti super territorio anchonitano dum Romam versus iter arripuisset, a quibus

few days.[23] Malipiero says that, when the sultan learned of what had happened, he ordered another 40,000 ducats to be sent to Rome. The Turkish envoy assured the Signoria of his master's good will. Malipiero also describes the memorable occasion on which the French ambassador—it was Philippe de Commines himself—was leaving the Collegio and met the Turk: Commines wanted to return to the hall of the Collegio to learn what Bayazid's envoy had to say. He was told that diplomatic protocol did not allow the representative of one prince to be present when an audience was granted to the envoy of another. Commines withdrew in some perturbation, waiting anxiously until the Turkish envoy had withdrawn from the audience chamber.[24]

Some weeks later (on 14 January, 1495) Francesco II Gonzaga, marquis of Mantua, wrote his good friend and faithful correspondent, Sultan Bayazid, of how the latter's envoy (*Casim Bei*) had been set upon by the Prefect Giovanni della Rovere with more than two hundred and fifty horse about ten miles from Ancona. Kasim Beg had fortunately escaped with his life by taking shelter in a neighboring castle, where he had raised the drawbridges, after which the prefect had departed. The following day the Anconitans themselves, in obvious fear of Turkish reprisals, rescued Kasim Beg with a force of more than two hundred horse, and took him to Ancona "cum la vesta sola che havea in dosso, 'che tutto el resto el prefecto li havea levato." Francesco sent Kasim Beg prompt assistance, and received him in his palace at Mantua because of the love he bore the sultan. Now he was sending him safely back to Istanbul, having tried unsuccessfully to recover "el dono che portava Cassimbei," as Bayazid could see from the prefect's own letter (sent in response to Francesco's protest against the attack) which Kasim was taking back to Istanbul. Francesco assured Bayazid that Kasim had served the Porte faithfully in every respect, and had done everything possible to fulfill the mission with which he had been entrusted.[25]

The account in Francesco Gonzaga's letter and in Malipiero's *Annali veneti* can be filled in from other sources. We have already noted that in early June, 1494, Alexander VI had sent the Turkish-speaking Genoese, Giorgio Bocciardi (Busardi), on an embassy to Istanbul to ask the sultan to send his brother's pension to Rome, where funds were needed to buttress the papal and Neapolitan defense against the French.[26] Although Sultan Bayazid had previously refused to send any more money to the pope, he now saw reason to do so in view of Charles VIII's crusading plans. In Istanbul Bocciardi had stated, in accordance with the pope's instructions, that Charles wanted to get possession of Jem Sultan, so that after the conquest of Naples he might use him as a figurehead in a French attack upon the Ottoman empire. Bocciardi had also asked the sultan to bring pressure upon the Venetians to get them to give up their neutrality and join the anti-French league. In November Bocciardi had landed at Ancona with the Turkish envoy who was bringing Jem's pension to Rome, and (as stated by Francesco Gonzaga) their party was set upon about ten miles from Ancona by Giovanni della Rovere. The Turkish envoy gave up the money but managed to escape. Bocciardi was seized and confined at Sinigaglia. Not only did della Rovere get the

quidem gentibus et munera tum ad summum pontificem suprascriptum tum ad illustrissimum dominum marchionem Mantuae destinata a domino Turco vestesque ipsius oratoris rapte fuere . . ." (Sen. Secreta, Reg. 35, fols. 45ᵛ–46ʳ [57ᵛ–58ʳ], from the text of a commission [dated 20 November, 1494] submitted to the Senate for Alvise Sagundino, whom some senators wanted to send to Giovanni della Rovere to protest this unwarranted aggression against a Turkish envoy). According to this commission, which was not accepted by the Senate, Sagundino was to demand that della Rovere make immediate restitution to the Turkish envoy of everything he had seized. The Senate did, however, lodge a complaint with della Rovere.

[23] Giovanni della Rovere's exploit was known in Rome as early as 18 November (Paolo Negri, "Le Missioni di Pandolfo Collenuccio a papa Alessandro VI [1494–1498]," *Archivio della R. Società romana di storia patria*, XXXIII [1910], doc. no. XIV, pp. 425–26).

[24] Malipiero, *Annali veneti*, in *Arch. stor. italiano*, VII-1 (1843), 320, 323, 327, 144–45; Marino Sanudo, *La Spedizione di Carlo VIII in Italia*, ed. Rinaldo Fulin, in *Archivio veneto*, Suppl., 1873–82, pp. 124–25; Thuasne, *Djem-Sultan*, p. 332; Delaborde, *Expédition de Charles VIII*, pp. 372–74. Venice made a great impression on Commines, who has left a famous description of the city, its inhabitants, wealth, monasteries, rich buildings, diplomatic customs, and the like (*Mémoires*, bk. VII, chap. 18, ed. B. de Mandrot, II, 206 ff.).

[25] Arch. di Stato di Mantova, Arch. Gonzaga, Busta 86, leather-bound volume marked B. XXXIII, no. 17, fol. 47, letter dated at Mantua on 14 January, 1495, and signed "El vostro schiavo et servitore Francisco [Gonzaga], marchese de Mantua, de manu propria." See in general H. J. Kissling, *Sultan Bâyezîd's II. Beziehungen zu Markgraf Francesco II. von Gonzaga*, Munich, 1965, pp. 39–46.

[26] V. V. Makušev, *Monumenta historica slavorum meridionalium*, II (Belgrade, 1882), pp. 202–3, a letter dated at Rome in June, 1494, written by an unknown to Lodovico il Moro in Milan. *Cf.* above, Chapter 14, note 102.

40,000 ducats for Jem's pension, but he also secured a number of documents which Alexander VI's enemies promptly published as being most damning to the vicar of Christ.[27]

Johann Burchard, papal master of ceremonies, gives the texts of these documents, including a copy of the pope's verbal instructions to Bocciardi, which the latter was obviously obliged to prepare at Sinigaglia. Bocciardi's commission begins with the injunction that

> you will signify [to the sultan] in our name that the king of France is pushing on toward Rome with the greatest land and sea forces, supported by the Milanese, Bretons, Portuguese, Normans, and others in order to wrest from us Jem Sultan, the brother of his Highness, and to seize the kingdom of Naples and oust King Alfonso to whom we are bound by the closest ties of blood and friendship, and whom we must defend since he is our feudatory and pays us every year the required impost (*census*). . . .

The French king intended to send Jem with a fleet into Turkey, and himself to cross over into Greece to attack the sultan's lands. The pope was having to expend large sums for the defense of Rome and the Curia. Therefore he brought up again the question of Jem's pension (*subsidium*), placing his hope in the friendship which he and the sultan entertained for each other. Bocciardi was to urge Bayazid to send 40,000 Venetian gold ducats to Rome as soon as possible as payment for the present year, which would end on the last of November (1494).

Since the king of France was far more powerful than the pope, the latter needed the assistance of the Venetians, who were rendering Rome no aid at all, and indeed were maintaining the closest relations with the enemy. Charles VIII's success in Italy would entail his seizure of Jem. Then the French would embark on a crusade in which they would be assisted by the Spaniards, English, Maximilian and the Hungarians, the Poles, and the Bohemians. Stressing again the "good and true friendship" which existed between the pope and the sultan, Bocciardi was to exhort the Turk to send an envoy to the Doge Agostino Barbarigo of Venice, asking him to aid the papacy and Naples and cautioning him about the consequences of the French securing Jem's person. If the Venetians dragged their heels, the Turkish envoy was to threaten them with his master's extreme displeasure.

Alluding to the efforts of the soldan of Egypt, Bayazid's formidable rival in the East, to have Jem Sultan sent to Cairo, the pope virtuously assured Bayazid that he would keep the promises he had made, and that he intended "accrescere et meliorare nostram bonam amicitiam." Alexander asked his good friend in Istanbul not to harass Hungary, Croatia, Segna, or other Christian territories "for some time." His Holiness would see to it that the Hungarian king did not molest Turkish subjects. If the sultan should decide to attack the Christian states, however, Alexander would be forced to reconsider the situation. Great preparations were being made [by the French] for an offensive against the Porte. (Since a French crusade would mean *ipso facto* the success of Charles VIII's Neapolitan venture, the pope was in the odd position of hoping that in this context at least there would be no crusade.) Bocciardi had received two papal briefs to submit to the sultan, one requesting the payment of the 40,000 ducats and the other comprising his letter of credence. Once possessed of the money Bocciardi was to return directly to Ancona by a safe ship, immediately inform the pope of his arrival, and there await further instructions.[28]

If these protestations of the pope's friendship for the sultan were not enough to distress the faithful from whom money had so often been collected to organize expeditions against the archenemy of Christendom, there was more to come. All the Italian states were quite willing at this time to enter into friendly relations with

---

[27] Pastor, *Gesch. d. Päpste*, III-1 (repr. 1955), 388–90, note 2; Delaborde, *Expédition de Charles VIII*, pp. 479–80; Thuasne, *Djem-Sultan*, pp. 334–35.

[28] Burchard, *Diarium*, ed. Thuasne, II (1884), 202–6, and ed. Celani, I [in *RISS*, XXXII, pt. 1, fasc. 6, 1910], 547–50. Burchard's text comes from a copy of Bocciardi's own deposition, in which he stated (under duress) that he received his commission verbally from the pope in July, 1494, although the papal brief of accreditation to the Porte is dated in June, as given in Sanudo's *Spedizione di Carlo VIII in Italia*, ed. R. Fulin, pp. 42–46. In fact we have a contemporary witness to the effect that "al principio del mese presente [June, 1494] la Santità del Nostro Signore [Alexander VI] mandò Giorgio Bogiardo, fratello dell'arcivescovo de Arles, al Turco per haver li quaranta milia ducati . . ." (Makušev, II, 202, cited above in note 26). The copy of Bocciardi's deposition which Burchard incorporated in his *Diarium* was transcribed by one Filippo de' Patriarchi, a notary of Forli, "ex originali ex Senogallia" (Celani's text, I, 550, line 26), and is dated at Florence on 25 November, 1494. On that date Cardinal della Rovere was himself in Florence with Charles VIII (Delaborde, *Expédition de Charles VIII*, p. 480). We have noted above the (later) copies of the pope's instructions to Bocciardi in the Arch. Segr. Vaticano, Fondo Pio, Reg. 124 (previously 222), fols. 9^v–12^r, by mod. stamped enumeration, and in the Bibl. Apost. Vaticana, Cod. lat. 13,451, fols. 76^r–78^v.

the Turks. The unusual aspect of Giorgio Bocciardi's mission was the papal appeal to the Porte for assistance against the "most Christian" king of France. Della Rovere, however, had acquired other documents from the Turkish envoy's dispatch case, among them four letters dated at Istanbul on 15 and 18 September, 1494, and addressed to Alexander VI, expressing the sultan's delight in the pope's friendship, praising Bocciardi's zeal in the execution of his mission, and requesting a cardinal's hat for Bocciardi's brother, Niccolò Cibo, archbishop of Arles![29] There seems to be little reason to doubt the genuineness of these letters.

In a fifth letter, however, dated 15 September, the authenticity of which has been assailed and defended by various scholars,[30] Bayazid proposed that Alexander VI have Jem Sultan put to death, which would be "useful to your Excellency, most conducive of peace, and most gratifying to me." It would in fact be well, as quickly as possible, "to have the said Jem removed from the narrow confinement of this world and transfer his soul to another existence where he will enjoy a finer peace." If Alexander would contrive this beneficent service, and send Jem's body to Turkey, the sultan promised him 300,000 ducats, "so that your Excellency can buy with these funds dominions for your children." Indeed the sultan was willing to pay before the actual delivery of Jem's corpse, and assured the pope of his everlasting friendship as well as safety for Christians on both land and sea.[31]

Was this letter forged or tampered with by the enemies of Alexander VI? Was the notary Filippo de' Patriarchi, who certified that his copy of this letter was made from the sultan's original written in Italian, a hireling of the della Rovere party? It must be remembered that at the time these letters were transcribed Charles VIII was in Florence, as we shall see, and Cardinal Giuliano was with him. A few years later Raymond Peraudi (Pérault), the cardinal of Gurk, who was much at odds with the pope, confidentially informed the Florentine notary Alessandro Bracci that he had seen briefs sent by the pope to the Gran Turco and the latter's replies thereto as well as a copy of certain articles and a convention that were exchanged between them: "Besides [the cardinal] knew that the Turk had offered [Alexander VI] 200,000 ducats if he would have his brother put to death. . . ." Peraudi spoke of the horror with which the Curia under Alexander VI

---

[29] Burchard, *Diarium*, ed. Thuasne, II, 206–8, and ed. Celani, I, 550–53. These letters were translated from Greek into Latin by the "eruditus vir [Ioannes] Lascarus, natione grecus" for the notary Filippo de' Patriarchi, who subscribed the texts. The fourth letter of the sultan to the pope, recommending Niccolò Cibo's promotion to the cardinalate, is erroneously dated "XVIII decembris" in Thuasne, II, 208. Janus Lascaris had just published his edition of the anthology of Maximus Planudes in Florence (Thuasne, *Djem-Sultan*, p. 338). Three of these letters exist in a MS. copy in the Arch. Segr. Vaticano, Fondo Pio, Reg. 124 (formerly 222), fols. 12^r–14^r.

The Latin poet Michael Marullus Tarchaniotes (Tarcagnota), a native of Constantinople, aided Lascaris in the translation. On Marullus, see the note in Celani's edition of Burchard, I, 553. Marullus's wife Alessandra Scala was the object of Poliziano's vindictive passion (*cf.* Börje Knös, *Un Ambassadeur de l'hellénisme, Janus Lascaris, et la tradition gréco-byzantine dans l'humanisme français*, Uppsala, 1945, pp. 67 ff., and Sergio Bertelli, "Machiavelli and Soderini," *Renaissance Quarterly*, XXVIII [1975], 3–4). Knös, *op. cit.*, p. 74, following the inferior text of Burchard given in Heinrich Heidenheimer, "Die Korrespondenz Sultan Bajazet's II. mit Papst Alexander VI.," *Zeitschrift für Kirchengeschichte*, V (1882), 532–33, believes that the "suprascriptae quaternae litterae erant scriptae *sermone Turcico* . . . ," and that Janus Lascaris, "versé aussi dans le turc," translated them from Turkish, which is not true. While Thuasne's text (II, 208) does not give the language in which the letters were written, Celani, I, 552, gives *sermone greco*, which was certainly the case. Relying on poor texts of Burchard, Knös, p. 74, also (like Heidenheimer) fails to realize that "un certain Marcelle de Constantinople" is actually the poet Marullus, with whom he has just been concerned (pp. 68 ff.). While generally readable, Knös's monograph contains some unfortunate historical errors.

[30] Pastor, *Gesch. d. Päpste*, III–1 (repr. 1955), 388–90, note 2; Thuasne, *Djem-Sultan*, pp. 338–39; Celani, I, 547–48, note 5; Wm. H. Woodward, *Cesare Borgia*, London, 1913, pp. 72–73; and *cf.* the refs. to Pfeffermann and Kissling in the following note.

[31] Burchard, *Diarium*, ed. Thuasne, II, 209–10, and ed. Celani, I, 553–54. The text in Burchard concludes with Filippo de'Patriarchi's notarial subscription dated at Florence in the Franciscan convent of S. Croce on 25 November, 1494. The original is said to have been written in Latin letters in the Italian language "on an oblong sheet of paper, in the Turkish fashion, which had at the head the seal of the Grand Turk in gold, at the foot in black." Sanudo, *Spedizione*, ed. R. Fulin, pp. 46–47, gives the text in Italian, dated 12 September; it also appears in Angiolello and the *Lettere di principi*, II, fol. 3, cited by Thuasne; and *cf.* A. Ciaconius, *Vitae et res gestae pont. roman.*, ed. A. Oldoinus, III (1677), col. 163, a Latin version dated 12 September, 1494; Malipiero, *Annali veneti*, in *Arch. stor. italiano*, VII–1, 146; Thuasne, *Djem-Sultan*, pp. 339–40; Hans Pfeffermann, *Die Zusammenarbeit d. Renaissancepäpste mit den Türken*, Winterthur, 1946, pp. 109–11; Kissling, *Sultan Bâjezîd's II. Beziehungen zu Markgraf Francesco II. von Gonzaga*, pp. 42–43. The (fifth) letter of 15 September, correctly dated, is also preserved in a late copy in the Arch. Segr. Vaticano, Fondo Pio, Reg. 124 (formerly 222), fols. 14^r–15^r; four of these five letters are given in another late MS. in the Bibl. Apost. Vaticana, Cod. lat. 13,451, fols. 79^r–82^r, including the letter in question.

inspired him, "nor did he want to go there unless God reformed His Church, speaking to this effect with religious emotion and as a Catholic prelate."[32]

Whether Sultan Bayazid's fifth letter is genuine or not, Alexander VI certainly never received any part of the alleged bribe to put Jem Sultan out of the way, nor is there any evidence that he ever considered moving Jem "from the narrow confinement of this world." We know from a dispatch of Filippo Valori dated at Terracina on 9 October (1494) that, owing to a plot of the Colonnesi against both Jem and the pope, the latter had the Turkish prince transferred to the Castel S. Angelo and placed under a heavy guard.[33] Two of the pope's own nephews, Francisco and Galcerán Borgia, were made Jem's special guardians; Francisco was a papal chamberlain, Galcerán a Hospitaller. Although before his election to the papacy Alexander VI had been cardinal protector of the Hospital of S. John, he may have doubted the loyalty of the predominantly French Order in view of Charles VIII's invasion of Italy. Be that as it may, he dismissed from Rome the Knights who comprised Jem's guard, sending them back to the island of Rhodes with a brief dated 25 October (1494) addressed to the Grand Master d'Aubusson. The pope wrote that since the grand master had informed him, a fact also confirmed from other sources, of the many plots being hatched against Jem Sultan, brother of the Gran Turco, it had seemed best some days before to place Jem in the security of the Castello, and so it was no longer necessary to retain in Rome the Knights who had been guarding him. Commending the integrity and loyalty of the Knights he was dismissing, the pope named six Frenchmen, three Italians, and one Spaniard.[34] Although there are so many momentous issues depicted in the documents of this period that Jem tends to get crowded off the scene, he still remained an important political pawn, and two months later was to be one of the chief subjects for contention between the pope and the king of France.

Cardinal Ascanio Sforza, vice-chancellor of the Church and the virtual elector of Rodrigo Borgia to the papacy, had already moved out of the apostolic palace and withdrawn from Rome on 28 June (1494), having all his property taken from the palace. He got away to the castle at Frascati in the lands of the Colonnesi. According to Thuasne's text of the *Diarium*, Burchard professed not to know the reason for Ascanio's departure. Alexander VI himself left Rome on 12 July for Vicovaro, where he met Alfonso of Naples on the fourteenth, and the two conferred for hours on the strategy they would follow in opposing Charles VIII. Alfonso was accompanied by a number of Turks, some of whom performed acrobatic feats of arms for the pope and cardinals. The pope returned to Rome on the

---

[32] Thuasne, *Burchardi diarium*, II, append., no. 27, pp. 668–69, Alessandro Bracci to the Florentine Dieci di Balia, dated at Perugia on 8 April, 1497. *Cf.* Delaborde, *Expédition de Charles VIII*, pp. 477–79; Adolf Gottlob, "Der Legat Raimund Peraudi," *Historisches Jahrbuch*, VI (1885), 456–57; Thuasne, *Djem-Sultan*, p. 339.

The startling episode of Sinigaglia long rankled in Alexander VI's usually untroubled mind. After the death of Charles VIII and Louis XII's accession to the French throne (in the spring of 1498), Alexander sent nuncios to France to convey to the new king the usual expressions of grief at the passing of his predecessor. The pope assured Louis of his strong desire to promote the crusade and expressed the ardent hope that Louis would lead an expedition against the Turks (Arch. Segr. Vaticano, Miscell., Arm. II, tom. 56, fols. 311^r–314^v), at the same time as he denounced Giovanni della Rovere to the king:

"Si mentionem fecerit [and his Majesty was likely to mention it!], significabitis Majestati sue quod prefectus [Giovanni] non solum publicam rapinam in terris nostris contra nuntios nostros, quos in carcere inclusit, et contra legatum Turchorum principis commisit, illi quadraginta millia florenorum auri pro expensis fratris, quem apud nos magna cum impensa custodiri faciebamus, et alias pecuniarum et bonorum magni valoris quantitates auferendo. Verum etiam gentes nostras et Bartholomeum Serram, illarum ductorem et sanguine nobis coniunctum, per terras nostras iter facientes, invadendo, spoliando, et captivos detinendo, se in rebellionem manifestam erexit. . . ."

Giovanni della Rovere was also trying to blacken the pope's reputation *falsis machinationibus . . . contra nos fingens quod cum Turcis sentiremus*. He had been excommunicated and deprived of the prefecture, his dignities, and various fiefs: Louis XII is asked to show such a rebel no favor (*ibid.*, fol. 314). This text, like several others, makes it clear that Giovanni seized 40,000 florins (or ducats) from the Turkish envoy Kasim Beg, not 80,000 as a "doppeltes Jahrgeld für Dschem-Sultân," as stated by Kissling, *Sultan Bâjezîd's II. Beziehungen zu Markgraf Francesco II. von Gonzaga*, pp. 40, 42.

[33] Desjardins, I, 459–60, dispatch of 9 October, 1494, to Piero de'Medici: Valori, now Florentine envoy to Alfonso of Naples, was with the king in his headquarters at Terracina. *Cf.* Thuasne, *Djem-Sultan*, p. 330, and Sa'd-ad-Dīn, "Aventures du prince Gem," in *Journal asiatique*, IX (1826, repr. 1965), 170–71, on the confinement of Jem Sultan in Castel S. Angelo.

[34] Bosio, *Militia di San Giovanni Gierosolimitano*, II (1594), bk. XIV, p. 421. Jem Sultan, long accustomed to his French Hospitaller guards, was sorry to see them go, and also wrote a letter of appreciation of their services to d'Aubusson (*ibid.*, pp. 421–22). However, the Catalan pope retained one member of Jem's customary guard, a Catalan named Antonio de Santo Martino (*cf.* Thuasne, *Djem-Sultan*, pp. 330–31, note 5, relating to payment to Antonio for *custodia* of the Turk, dated 16 February, 1495).

seventeenth.[35] According to the plans they had evolved, Alfonso was to hold Tagliacozzo against the French advance, and Virginio Orsini, who was said to have been made a viceroy of the kingdom, would take his stand in the Roman Campagna to oppose the Colonnesi. Alfonso's son Ferrante [II], or Ferrantino as he was called, now the duke of Calabria, had been named the chief commander of the Neapolitan army; with the bulk of the royal and papal forces, and such aid as Piero de' Medici finally contributed, Ferrantino was to proceed northward into the Romagna, whence he might invade Lombardy if the necessity or opportunity arose. The king's brother, Federigo of Aragon, was named *capitano generale* of the fleet, which was to attack the Genoese. Alfonso of Naples had made generous financial dispositions for the more important members of his family, reduced certain of the tax burdens weighing upon his people, distributed presents and money to various feudatories of the realm, and even, it was said, paid the merchants all that his father had owed them.[36]

While the pope and the king of Naples were planning, their opponents were acting. On 18 September (1494) some of Fabrizio Colonna's troops took over Cardinal Giuliano della Rovere's castle at Ostia, having received help from within the walls. The papal castellan was expelled. The standards of Charles VIII, of Cardinal Giuliano, and of Fabrizio himself were raised over the citadel. On the following day the loss of Ostia was discussed in a nine-hour consistory, but Burchard did not learn what happened therein.[37] On 6–7 October Alexander VI commanded by a public proclamation issued in Italian that all Romans and other subjects of the Church, both lay and ecclesiastical, who were then in the pay or the service of the Colonnesi, the Savelli, or Girolamo Tuttavilla, should within six days of the publication of the proclamation withdraw from such pay or service with all their equipment, arms, and horses. They were personally to appear in Rome, ecclesiastics before Giovanni de' Sacchi, archbishop of Ragusa, then governor of the city, and laymen before the lieutenant of the captain of the guard at the apostolic palace "under penalty of rebellion and confiscation of all their goods, movable and immovable, and the demolition of their houses and loss of their benefices and offices." The Colonnesi, Savelli, and their supporters were given six days to restore the Rocca d'Ostia to the pope and appear in Rome and render proper obeisance. Those who obeyed the terms of the proclamation would receive employment and stipends suitable to their station. The ban was posted at the portal of S. Peter's, in the Camera Apostolica, on the Campidoglio, and in the Campo dei Fiori.[38] Needless to say, the Colonnesi did not return Ostia, and their control of the mouth of the Tiber rendered the provisioning of Rome both difficult and expensive.

On 31 October Cardinal Cesare Borgia went at his father's command to Marino, near Frascati, where Ascanio Sforza was staying under the protection of the Colonnesi. Ascanio had asked the pope for a safe-conduct to come to Rome to discuss matters of such importance that he could not commit them to any agent. He said that he would be coming as the friend

---

[35] Burchard, *Diarium*, ed. Thuasne, II, 180–85, and ed. Celani, I, 529–33; Giovanni Soranzo, *Il Tempo di Alessandro VI Papa e di Fra Girolamo Savonarola*, Milan, 1960, pp. 96–97.

[36] Sanudo, *Spedizione*, ed. R. Fulin, pp. 50 ff.; Commines, *Mémoires*, bk. VII, chap. 6, ed. B. de Mandrot, II, 135 ff.; Thuasne, *Burchardi diarium*, II, append., no. 23, pp. 644–45; Delaborde, *Expédition de Charles VIII*, pp. 369–70, 376, 384, 387; Bosio, II (1594), bk. XIV, p. 420; Desjardins, I, 467 ff., 478 ff.; Pastor, *Gesch. d. Päpste*, III-1 (repr. 1955), 390; and Nicola Barone, "Notizie storiche," *Arch. stor. per le province napoletane*, XIV (1889), 180–81 and ff. Although Alfonso and his advisers recognized the importance of occupying Genoa if possible (Desjardins, I, 449), the Neapolitan fleet under Federigo arrived in Genoese waters too late to make an attempt on the city, which Swiss and Lombard troops had already occupied on behalf of the French. In fact the duke of Orléans had arrived in Genoa at the same time as Federigo's fleet (Delaborde, *op. cit.*, p. 384). Alfonso, however, had not underestimated the difficulty of the enterprise and anticipated failure without substantial Florentine and papal aid (Desjardins, I, 463, 465–66, *et alibi*).

[37] Burchard, *Diarium*, ed. Thuasne, II, 186, and ed. Celani, I, 534; Sigismondo de' Conti, *Storie*, II (1883), 65–66; Paolo Negri, "Missioni di Pandolfo Collenuccio . . . ," *Arch. della R. Società romana di storia patria*, XXXIII (1910), doc. no. III, pp. 401–2, a letter of 19 September, 1494, from P. Collenuccio, the Ferrarese envoy in Rome, to Duke Ercole d'Este: ". . . la nova de la perdita de Ostia, qual li dede [i.e., to Alexander VI] tanta turbatione che più non si po' dire. . . ."

[38] Burchard, *Diarium*, ed. Thuasne, II, 189–92, and ed. Celani, I, 536–38, gives the text of the ban, which was posted "die lune VI et martis VII mensis octobris 1494." Girolamo Tuttavilla was the natural son of the late French cardinal Guillaume d'Estouteville. On 13 October both his house in Rome and that of Prospero Colonna were razed because of their failure to appear before the lieutenant of the guard (*ibid.*, I, 539). The Colonnesi, Savelli, and Tuttavilla had been in the employ of Charles VIII for some time (Delaborde, *Expédition de Charles VIII*, pp. 366–67, 419–20). Tuttavilla's career is well known (see Celani, I, 536–37, note 4).

and loyal servitor of his Holiness to tell him things that would please him. Alexander VI consented to hear him, and Cesare went to Marino, where he was to remain as a hostage until Ascanio's safety should be assured. Ascanio entered Rome on 2 November at the third hour of the night (about 8:00 P.M.). He went directly to the Vatican. Alexander had already informed the Neapolitan envoys, however, that if Ascanio had good intentions, he would hear him, but if he tried to turn him against his alliance with King Alfonso, he would dismiss him immediately. Alexander said that he would rather die than abandon Alfonso.[39]

Antonio Guidotti di Colle wrote the Otto di Pratica on the third that Ascanio was closeted with the pope for five hours (Burchard says three), which obviously gave them ample time to explore all the differences which existed between the Borgias and the Sforzeschi. Ascanio urged Alexander to remain neutral in the war to guarantee the safety of his children and the well-being of the Church, for Charles VIII in his determination to pursue his conquest of Naples "potrebbe volgere le forze sue contro lo Stato di questa Santa Sede et fare infiniti damni." Since his Holiness could not possibly resist the striking force of the French, it would be far better to yield to Charles than to oppose him "con certeza della perdita et ruina di tucto questo Stato." To all this Alexander returned a public answer (on 3 November), in the presence of the cardinals, that he had undertaken the just defense of Alfonso as his vassal for the papal fief of Naples, and that he would lose the miter, the States of the Church, and even his life before he would fail in his defense of Alfonso. As for the power of the French king, whom he could not withstand, "he hoped that God would help him." Ascanio himself then said that he had come to Rome to do his duty as a cardinal. Since the Stato Ecclesiastico was in dire peril, it had seemed best to share with his Holiness his thoughts for the safety of the Church, "just as the Florentines have done, who seeing that they could not resist the power of the king of France have taken the side of his Majesty." Although the pope did not choose to accept this advice and token of Ascanio's friendship, he had done his duty as a good cardinal and servitor of his Holiness. When Ascanio had said this, the pope left the hall with all the cardinals and entered the chapel. Ascanio then left the Vatican for Ostia, where the French fleet had already arrived.[40] It looked as though Charles VIII would soon be in Rome.

The Florentines' abandonment of the anti-French league and the recent antics of Piero de'Medici, to which Cardinal Ascanio alluded on 3 November, must have caused Alexander VI grave misgivings. Well might he hope "che Dio lo aiuterebbe," as the Florentine envoy Guidotti wrote his government. The French invasion of Italy was initiating the modern era of the national state in the most dramatic fashion. France, Spain, and England with their vast military and financial resources would henceforth dominate the smaller political units which survived in Italy and Germany from the later middle ages. The three great national monarchies became notably richer and more powerful than the states of eastern Europe. It was these latter, however, which were continually exposed to the experience as well as the threat of Turkish attack. Spanish unity was more apparent than real, since the Castilians and Catalans remained quite distinct peoples. But the Siglo de Oro was beginning; Catalan pride was being submerged in Castilian prestige; and through much of the sixteenth century Spain would dominate Europe.

The English were too far from the eastern fronts to be crusaders. In another generation or two, as we shall see, the French would actually make a sort of alliance with the Turks to forge a counterweight against the excessive power of the Hapsburgs in Spain and Germany. This would

[39] Burchard, *Diarium*, ed. Thuasne, II, 194, and especially the Florentine envoy Antonio Guidotti's dispatch of 2 November (1494) to the Otto di Pratica (*ibid.*, II, 194–95, note), and ed. Celani, I, 540, with the same dispatch, *ibid.*, I, 540–41, note 3; Sigismondo de' Conti, II, 83.

[40] Thuasne, *Burchardi diarium*, II, append., no. 24, pp. 646–47, dispatch of Antonio Guidotti to the Otto di Pratica, dated at Rome on 3 November, 1494. Guidotti also notes that some people believed the pope had to stand by Alfonso, because his son Juan was in Spain and Gioffredo was in Naples. Others thought that he would give in, and presently make an accord with the French. *Cf.* Delaborde, *Expédition de Charles VIII*, pp. 477–78. Pandolfo Collenuccio, the Ferrarese envoy in Rome, informed Ercole d'Este of Ascanio's meeting with the pope: "Li ragionamenti fra loro furono longhissimi e grandi . . . ," in the course of which "el papa se offere andar lui in persona e con tucto il potere de la Chiesa col christianissimo re contra el Turcho" (Negri, "Missioni di P. Collenuccio . . . ," *Arch. della R. Società romana di storia patria*, XXXIII, doc. no. XI, pp. 415–16, dated 7 November, 1494). Charles VIII, however, was going to Naples before "el passare in Grecia," which did not satisfy the pope.

raise havoc with Venetian interests in the Aegean, where the Turks would occupy various islands. With the rise of the national states the international position of the papacy seemed to be endangered and was certainly complicated. Charles VIII's invasion in 1494 began the long period of Franco-Spanish rivalry for the domination of Italy. The papacy would have to make peace with the victor, and the victor would have to assume the leadership of the crusade. Time would assign this role to the Spanish, as we know, but in the meantime Charles VIII was claiming it for France.

The French expedition began the ruination of Italy. Nevertheless, the woes which now descended upon the peninsula were the consequences of the Italians' own blindness. If the fact is clear to the modern historian, it was also clear to contemporaries. Gianandrea Boccaccio, envoy of the Estensi to the Holy See, says as much in a dispatch of 22 January, 1495, but he believed that if the Italian leaders would awaken from their slumbers and allow prudence and good counsel to prevail, the French would not win out in the end "unless for the punishment of our sins."[41]

Charles VIII had crossed the Alps over the picturesque pass of Mount Genèvre on 2 September, 1494, with a land army (it is said) of about 31,500 men. Another 10,400 or thereabouts were being transported by the sea route. He was at Turin on the fifth, and four days later reached Asti, where his advance was delayed by a light encounter with smallpox. He left Asti on 6 October. Contrary to many expectations and against the advice of most of his counsellors, he had really begun the descent into Italy.[42] The Italians were almost mesmerized as they watched his marching columns, burnished helmets flashing in the autumnal sun. Before he had left France, Charles had sent Guy de Blanchefort, prior of Auvergne, to the Grand Master d'Aubusson with letters requesting him to come to Rome to confer with him about the projected French crusade against the Turks. Now from Lodovico il Moro's model farm at Vigevano, near Milan, Charles wrote d'Aubusson again, telling him of his arrival in Italy and assuring him of his royal resolution to proceed against the Turks for the extension of the Catholic faith, the recovery of the Holy Land, and the liberation of those thousands of unhappy souls who lived under the harsh servitude of the barbarian infidels. Charles repeated his earlier request that d'Aubusson should come to Rome, for he would have need of the grand master's knowledge of the Turks and their affairs.[43]

Raymond Peraudi, the cardinal of Gurk, was passionately devoted to the crusade. Although no friend of Alexander VI, who had made him a cardinal, he was opposed to the French war against Naples as likely to be a fatal diversion of Charles VIII's announced plans to attack the Turks. Apparently without the knowledge of the French king, Peraudi had been taking steps to gain him a formal claim to the throne of Byzantium. While French troops were pouring into Liguria and Lombardy, Peraudi thought that he had found a way of moving them on into the East. If there were flaws in Charles's title to the kingdom of Naples, Peraudi had prepared the means of his securing an official and legitimate claim to the old empire of the Palaeologi. Andreas Palaeologus had visited the

---

[41] From a dispatch of 22 January, 1495, published by Cesare Foucard, "Proposta di pubblicazione di carteggio diplomatico" [degli Estensi], *Arch. stor. per le province napoletane*, IV (1879), 753, 795. Foucard was director of the Arch. di Stato di Modena, rich repository of the archives of the Estense dukes of Ferrara. A fascinating picture of conditions in Rome and at the Curia is provided by the dispatches of another Ferrarese envoy—P. Collenuccio—in Paolo Negri, "Le Missioni di Pandolfo Collenuccio a papa Alessandro VI . . . ," *Arch. della R. Società romana di storia patria*, XXXIII (1910), 333–439, with nineteen dispatches from 12 September, 1494, to 25 December, 1498 (*ibid.*, pp. 387 ff.), all addressed to Duke Ercole I.

[42] Thuasne, *Djem-Sultan*, pp. 327–28; Pastor, *Gesch. d. Päpste*, III-1 (repr. 1955), 391–92. On the number of men recruited for the French land and naval forces, see esp. Delaborde, *Expédition de Charles VIII*, pp. 324–27, who has described all aspects of the French invasion in great detail, pp. 395 ff.; *cf.* also Pastor, III-1, 393 ff., and Carlo Cipolla, *Storia delle signorie italiane dal 1313 al 1530*, 2 vols. in 1, Milan, 1881, II, esp. pp. 701–41. Sigismondo de'Conti, II, 86, says that the French army numbered about 40,000 men. Commines traces the course of Charles VIII's Italian expedition in some detail in his *Mémoires*. On the state of mind in France at this time, see in general Augustin Renaudet, *Préréforme et humanisme à Paris pendant les premières guerres d'Italie (1494–1517)*, 2nd ed., Paris, 1953 (Bibliothèque Elzévirienne), and on the intellectual unrest of the years following 1494, *ibid.*, pp. 205 ff.; on the strengths and maneuvers of the opposing forces in Italy, *cf.* Piero Pieri, *Il Rinascimento e la crisi militare italiana*, Turin, 1952, pp. 324 ff.

[43] Bosio, II (1594), bk. xv, p. 423. On Charles VIII's desire to draw the Grand Master d'Aubusson to Rome for consultation concerning "les affaires de la Turquie," *cf.* Thuasne, *Djem-Sultan*, pp. 328, 329.

French court in the fall of 1491. His presence at Laval and Tours must have excited some curiosity. On 31 October Charles had paid the expenses of the journey to France of "nostre cher et bon amy Andreas Paléologue, prince de Constantinoble, seigneur de la Moree . . . pour aucuns grans affaires touchans le bien de nous et de nostre royaume. . . ."[44] Having received 143 livres and fifteen sous shortly after his arrival at the court, Andreas was given another 350 livres by royal order on 16 December (1491) as he prepared "to return to Rome to our Holy Father, the Pope."[45] For years Andreas had been a familiar figure in Rome, where he had taken part in papal ceremonies as the *dispotus Moree olim imperator constantinopolitanus*.[46] Andreas had contrived to make the always sorry spectacle of a monarch in exile even more pathetic. He married a Roman prostitute named Caterina, and lived on a papal pension, with the occasional sale of honorific titles and other privileges to those whose gullibility and social pride brought them, money in hand, to his doorstep.[47] It seems rather safe to assume that Andreas had gone to France to sell the imperial title to Charles VIII, whose fascination with the romances of chivalry and whose ambition to emulate the great deeds of Charlemagne and Charles of Anjou were well known to all habitués of the Italian courts.

Knowing full well the purpose of Andreas Palaeologus's visit to France in 1491, the cardinal of Gurk now secured from Andreas, without previously seeking Charles VIII's consent, the conditional abdication to the king of France of all the Palaeologian rights to the empires of Constantinople and Trebizond as well as to the despotate of Serbia in exchange for an annual pension of 4,300 gold ducats, of which 2,000 were to be paid at the time of ratification. Andreas was also to receive the command of one hundred lances, to be maintained at the king's expense and for his service as well as a grant of lands, either in Italy or elsewhere, sufficient to produce an annual revenue of about 5,000 ducats. The king was to employ his land and naval forces to recover the despotate of the Morea for Andreas, whose feudal payment (*pro perpetuo censu*) for the restoration of his family's erstwhile Greek dominion was to be one white saddle horse (*unus gradarius albus*). The king would also make every effort, and use all his influence, to have renewed the papal pension of 1,800 ducats once granted to Andreas by Sixtus IV *de pecuniis Cruciatae*, which obviously had not been paid for some years.[48]

Andreas's act of cession was to be considered valid unless Charles VIII formally rejected it before the coming feast of All Saints (1 November, 1495). The document was prepared on 6 November, 1494, by the pontifical and imperial notary Francesco de Schracten of Florence, now a Roman citizen, and subscribed by Camillo Beninbene, Roman citizen and notary, doctor of civil and canon law. It was witnessed by five ecclesiastics in the church of S. Pietro in Montorio, on the height of Monteverde, after celebration of a mass of the Holy Spirit by the cardinal of Gurk, "both the lord cardinal and the lord despot standing between those two

---

[44] Sp. P. Lampros, Παλαιολόγεια καὶ Πελοποννησιακά, IV (Athens, 1930), 301–2, 302–3, documents dated at Laval on 31 October, 1491, and *cf.* Delaborde, *Expédition de Charles VIII*, p. 226. Andreas received "la somme de sept vings trois livres quinze solz tournois" (143 l. and 15 s. tournois). He had presented Charles with a white falcon (*autour blanc*), presumably a female peregrine (Thuasne, *Burchardi diarium*, II, append., no. 26, p. 667). Lampros, *op. cit.*, IV, 297 ff., publishes several documents relating to Andreas. B. de Mandrot, ed., *Mémoires de Philippe de Commynes*, II, 203, note 3, repeats the errors of Delaborde, *op. cit.*, pp. 226, 404, to the effect that Andreas had been summoned to Tours from Constantinople (!), and was later promised the "retrocession" of Serbia (!).

[45] Lampros, *Pal. kaì Pel.*, IV, 303–4, doc. dated at Montils-lès-Tours on 16 December, 1491.

[46] Burchard, *Diarium*, ed. Thuasne, I, 238, 272, 281, 297, and II, 65, 104, the last reference being to the celebration of Easter (30 March), 1494, and ed. Celani, I, 180–81, 207, 215, 227, 416 ("tispotus"), 468. Subsequently, on 31 December, 1497, Andreas had occasion to complain to the pope at a vespers service that his usual place, immediately after the cardinals, had been given to a visiting duke (Celani, II, 67, lines 31–36). *Cf., ibid.*, II, 153, 162: Andreas's sad appearance in the passages of Burchard and a number of other contemporary texts constitute, as it were, the last chapter in the long history of Byzantium.

[47] *Cf.* Lampros, *Pal. kaì Pel.*, IV, 297–98, 305–6. If we may compare the social position of Andreas's customers, as represented by the first grant (13 April, 1483) in contrast to the second (12 May, 22 July, 1493), it would appear that both the quality of his clientele and the size of his fees declined as the years passed. The first grant, giving the Manrique family the right to use the arms and insignia of the Palaeologi, to create counts palatine, to bestow knighthoods, and to legitimatize bastards, was first published by W. Regel, "Chrysobull of the Emperor Andreas Palaeologus of 13 April, 1483" [in Russian], *Vizantiiskii Vremennik*, I (1894), 151–58.

[48] The grant of a papal pension to Andreas Palaeologus *super introitibus alumerie* (from the alum revenues, devoted to the "crusade"), "datum Rome apud Sanctum Petrum anno, etc., MCCCCLXXIIII pridie nonas Iulii, pont. nostri anno tercio" (6 July, 1474), may be found in Arch. Segr. Vaticano, Reg. Vat. 563, fols. 122^r–123^r.

most sacred columns, on the spot where the Blessed Peter, Prince of the Apostles, received the crown of sacred martyrdom."[49] From the terrace of the church of S. Pietro in Montorio, the cardinal of Gurk and Andreas commanded one of the finest views of Rome.

It was a Rome with much scurrying back and forth as Alexander VI was taking precautions against the possible appearance of the French army. If Charles VIII did not yet know of Andreas Palaeologus's act of imperial cession, the pope undoubtedly did, for after all Raymond Peraudi was a cardinal and Andreas a papal retainer. The plan fitted in, however, very well with the pope's most sanguine hopes. The deed of cession made no reference to Charles's projected invasion of Naples, but was based on the happy assumption that the French army was to be employed for the common defense of Christendom and for an attack upon the Ottoman sultan, that "cruelest enemy of Christians."[50] If the Emperor Maximilian should protest to the pope that an imperial rival was thus being conjured up, his Holiness could always observe that Andreas's act contained no statement of papal sanction, and that the cardinal of Gurk had acted improperly on his own initiative.[51] Later on, Charles did accept the conditions of Andreas's very doubtful sacrifice, but he did not allow himself to be distracted from the Neapolitan enterprise. After he had vindicated his rights to the southern kingdom by force of arms, then he would go eastward. While still at Asti, he had considered affixing to his surcoat the hallowed cross of Jerusalem, emblem of the crusader.[52]

---

[49] Étienne de Foncemagne, "Sur quelques Circonstances du voyage de Charles VIII en Italie . . . ," in *Mémoires de littérature, tirés des registres de l'Académie Royale des Inscriptions et Belles-Lettres*, XVII (Paris, 1751), esp. pp. 558–78, the Latin text of Andreas's act of cession being given on pp. 572–77. This document was extracted from the notarial register of Camillo Beninbene (notary in Rome from 1467 to 1505) in the Archivio Collegiale di Campidoglio (it was to be found on fol. 839 in Beninbene's register where a copy was put in its place). This depredation of the Archives of the Campidoglio was accomplished by order of Pope Benedict XIV on 9 October, 1740, at the request of Paul Hippolyte de Beauvilliers, duke of S. Aignan, French ambassador to the Holy See. The document was presented to Louis XV as a curiosity, and was placed in the Bibliothèque du Roi. Foncemagne secured a copy of it. C. de Cherrier, *Histoire de Charles VIII*, 2 vols., Paris, 1870, I, 443–44, 491–92, gives a brief summary of the document, but mistakenly says that Charles was to re-establish Andreas in the despotate of Serbia rather than the Morea. Delaborde, *Expédition de Charles VIII*, pp. 403–4, who cited Foncemagne but read Cherrier, makes the same mistake.

Since the requirements of Andreas's cession were never put into effect, it was obviously invalid, and in his will dated 7 April, 1502, Andreas bequeathed his imperial rights to Ferdinand and Isabella of Spain. *Cf.* Gerónimo Zurita, *Anales de Aragón*, V: *Historia del Rey Don Hernando el Católico*, Saragossa, 1670, bk. I, chap. 40, fol. 50^{v}; bk. IV, chap. 39, fols. 109^{v}–110^{v}. On Camillo Beninbene (Beneimbene), see Pastor, *Gesch. d. Päpste*, III–1 (repr. 1955), 631. He also appears about a dozen times in Johann Burchard's *Diarium* (see the index to E. Celani's edition, in the new Muratori, *RISS*, XXXII, pt. 1, fascc. 12–13 [Bologna, 1940] = vol. II, p. 552), and heads the list of "sollicitatores literarum apostolicarum" given by Burchard in May, 1497 (ed. Thuasne, II, 373, and ed. Celani, II, 29). Beninbene was a well-known figure in Rome and a friend of the Borgias.

One of Andreas Palaeologus's successors as despot of the Morea raised grave problems of protocol in 1518, when he invited Pope Leo X to become *compater* and ten cardinals personally to attend the baptism of his son Giovanni Martino Leonardo in the church of S. Marco in Rome (see Paride Grassi, *Diarium Curiae Romanae*, ed. Christ. G. Hoffmann, *Nova scriptorum ac monumentorum . . . collectio*, I [Leipzig, 1731], 418–20). This despot may have been Constantinus Comnenus, who served as *capitaneus urbis* and was descended "from the princes of Macedonia" (*ibid.*, I, 478). In Cod. Vat. lat. 5,250, fol. 176^{v}, I find a notice of the following epitaph "in ecclesia XII Apostolorum:"

D.O.M.
Lucretiae Andreae Paleologi filiae
Jacobi Raynaldi uxori
Jacobus iunior filius
matri cariss.
non sine lachrymis pos.
Vix. an. XLVIIII, m. VII, d. XII.
Obiit IIII no. Sept. MCCCCLXXXVII

If Lucretia "Palaeologina" died on 2 September, 1487, and had lived forty-nine years, seven months, and twelve days, she was born on 21–22 January, 1438. Whoever her father was, he was not the Despot Andreas, who was born on 17 January, 1453 (Geo. Sphrantzes, *Chron. minus*, in *PG* 156, 1060D, and ed. V. Grecu, *Georgios Sphrantzes: Memorii [1401–1477], in anexă Pseudo-Phrantzes . . .*, Bucharest, 1966, p. 96, lines 7–9; Pseudo-Sphrantzes, III, 3 [Bonn, p. 236, lines 8–13; ed. Grecu, p. 380, lines 25–28]).

[50] Foncemagne, *op. cit.*, pp. 572–73. Incidentally Foncemagne knew, in the middle of the eighteenth century, a good deal about the French MSS. of Burchard's *Diarium* (*ibid.*, pp. 597–606).

[51] Maximilian liked to dream about being emperor in the East as well as in the West (*cf.* H. Ulmann, *Kaiser Maximilian I.*, I [1884], 205, 268, 272).

[52] *Cf.* Delaborde, *Expédition de Charles VIII*, pp. 404, 406. Popular rumor cast both the king of France and the Emperor Maximilian as crusaders who were going "a conquistare Jerusalem a la Sancta Madre Giesia" (*Diario ferrarese*, in *RISS*, XXIV, pt. 7 [1933], p. 136). Maximilian was an unlikely crusader, and Antonio Marongiu, "Carlo VIII e la sua crociata (come problema storiografico)," in Luigi de Rosa, ed., *Ricerche storiche ed economiche in memoria di Corrado Barbagallo*, II (Naples, 1970), 237–58, has no doubt that Charles's crusading declarations were merely propaganda, and that he never seriously intended to embark upon an eastern expedition.

Since Charles VIII was supported by a powerful fleet as he advanced into Italy, Sultan Bayazid looked to his own naval forces, so that he might be able to put to sea one hundred and twenty sail in due time. The defenses of the Dardanelles were strengthened, and artillery mounted in a series of shore batteries. Three thousand janissaries were sent to Gallipoli, and the sultan dispatched one of his sons to Negroponte and another to Mytilene, always fearful lest Charles should cross over into Greece with Jem Sultan and raise the country to revolt against him. If, however, there was concern in Istanbul, there was consternation in Naples, where Alfonso published in the piazza a "pace perpetua con Turchi."[53]

Although the death of King Ferrante had given Charles VIII additional reasons for the French expedition, it had caused Lodovico il Moro to hesitate. Given to vacillation and easily moved to terror, Lodovico had been posing sometimes as the savior of Italy and again as the partisan of the French. No one trusted him. Piero Alamanni, Florentine envoy to Milan, had written Piero de' Medici from Vigevano on 8 April (1494), "This man is a Proteus." Having done more than anyone else to entice Charles VIII into Italy, Lodovico now feared the consequences of a French occupation of Naples. He did not desire, he had written his brother Ascanio on 18 March, the ruin of Alfonso of Naples, *allo quale ho bon risguardo*. On one occasion he informed the Florentines that it was he who had dissuaded Charles VIII from seizing the goods and money of their fellow citizens in France, and on another he implied that Charles had offered him Tuscany. He told the Florentines that the French expedition would be a formidable affair, while he assured the Neapolitans that it would eventually amount to little or nothing. Voluble ally of the French, he could state that he was anxious to help Alfonso.[54]

Alexander VI's determined alliance with Alfonso had frightened Lodovico into returning to the full measure of his French devotion. The French were poor financiers, however, and some of the king's chief ministers were unreliable. Great pressure was from time to time brought to bear upon Lodovico to make loans to the crown beyond his willingness and possibly his capacity to do so.[55] The French expedition had hardly got under way before Lodovico began to pay the price of his treachery and shortsightedness. If the day came when he would himself need allies to protect himself from French aggression, he might well wonder where or whether he could find them. The Venetians were determined to maintain their neutrality, constantly expressing doubt (whatever they really thought) that the French king would actually embark upon a full-scale invasion of the peninsula. Even after the expedition had begun, the Venetians saw no reason to alter their position. In an interesting report sent from Venice by the Florentine envoy Paolantonio Soderini to Piero de' Medici on 12 September, 1494, we read that the statesmen of the lagoon had no confidence in the members of the anti-French league, especially Alexander VI. They were afraid that, if by intervention they drew the war in their direction, they would be left "in the lurch" (*nella pesta*). The Emperor Maximilian was hostile to them, and the Turks always needed watching. Nevertheless, they insisted that Charles was coming with too few troops for any such enterprise as the conquest of Naples. In their opinion he was only on an excursion "to see Italy," *ma più tosto per vedere Italia*![56] On 11 October Piero replied to Soderini

---

[53] Malipiero, *Annali veneti*, in *Arch. stor. italiano*, VII-1 (1843), 145. According to a dispatch of Filippo Valori to Piero de'Medici, dated at Terracina on 20 October, 1494, the sultan threatened to attack the Venetians if they did not declare their support for Alfonso and the pope (Desjardins, I [1859], 477). As the French expedition progressed, Bayazid added to his naval armament (Sanudo, *Spedizione*, ed. R. Fulin, p. 158). There is a brief conspectus of Ottoman naval activities during Bayazid's reign in Hans Joachim Kissling, "Betrachtungen über die Flottenpolitik Sultan Bâjezîds II. (1481–1512)," *Saeculum*, XX (Munich, 1969), 35–43, and see also Hans-Albrecht von Burski, *Kemāl Re'īs: Ein Beitrag zur Geschichte der türkischen Flotte*, diss. Bonn, 1928.

[54] Delaborde, *Expédition de Charles VIII*, pp. 337–40; *cf.* Buser, *Die Beziehungen der Mediceer zu Frankreich*, pp. 327–30, 545–46. The tortuous rationale behind Lodovico il Moro's double-dealing is explained in the letter which he wrote Ascanio from Vigevano on 18 March, 1494, which Delaborde, p. 338, translates from the text in the Milanese Archives. Charles VIII did contemplate placing Tuscany under the rule of Lodovico in early April, 1494 (*ibid.*, p. 354). On Lodovico's treachery toward Charles VIII, *cf.* Delaborde, pp. 530 ff., in reading whose work one is aware of a measure of French nationalism which occasionally colors some of his judgments.

[55] Delaborde, *Expédition de Charles VIII*, pp. 344–45, 378–82, 412, 438, 502.

[56] Desjardins, I, 512, and see in general Arturo Segre, "Lodovico Sforza, detto il Moro, e la Repubblica di

that the Venetians were grossly misled if they believed that any Italian state could go it alone in the face of the French peril.[57]

We cannot be concerned with details of the French campaign, but the plans discussed by Alexander VI and Alfonso at Vicovaro in mid-July were never put into full effect. The sanguine expectations and thereafter the increasing discomfiture of the Italian allies can be traced in detail in the numerous gossipy letters which Bernardo Dovizi da Bibbiena, the secretary of Piero de' Medici, wrote the latter from the papal-Neapolitan camp between 2 September and 25 October, 1494. Frivolity and entertainment seem to have cost the allied leadership as much time as trying to devise means of meeting the French invasion.[58] Finally, however, the rapid advance of the French in late October caused the duke of Calabria to retreat to the Florentine stronghold of Castrocaro, near Forli, and when Piero de' Medici unexpectedly made his peace with Charles VIII, the Neapolitan troops abandoned the Romagna and withdrew toward Rome. The French moved into Tuscany. The Otto di Pratica were terrified, and insisted that Piero de' Medici yield to Charles VIII. On 26 October, remembering the great Lorenzo's famous trip to Naples fifteen years before, Piero suddenly left Florence for the French camp. Arriving at Empoli he wrote the Signoria on the same day that he was offering his person to the French king as the best way to assuage the anger or hatred he felt for Florence.[59] From Pisa he wrote Bibbiena the next day that he had been abandoned by all, friends and foes alike, without sufficient reputation, money, or credit to carry on war. He had always been loyal to Alfonso of Naples and done his best to stand by him throughout these tragic days. Unable to serve Alfonso by force of arms, he would serve him at least "with the desperation which leads me to place myself in the power of the king of France without condition or hope of any consideration. . . ."[60]

From Pisa, Piero de' Medici went to Pietrasanta, where he waited for the safe-conduct which he had requested of Charles. The French had reached positions south of Sarzana, which with its citadel of Sarzanello was under siege. Their army was overrunning the countryside. Pietrasanta and Pisa were in danger. On 29 October Piero wrote Bibbiena that the French camp was between Pietrasanta and Sarzana. Ortonovo and Nicola had surrendered; the fortress of Castelnuovo was under assault. Assistance should be sent to Castelnuovo as well as to Pietrasanta and Pisa. Although he had already decided to surrender these places to the French, it was important that they hold out until he could bargain with Charles, "for I am losing my labor and perhaps throwing away my life if I try to give away what has been taken away from me by force."[61] But the Signoria had given Piero no authority to surrender or alienate these towns; he hoped of course thus to win Charles's support, and so maintain himself at the head of the Florentine state. After a delay of twenty-four hours, Piero's safe-conduct arrived. On 30 October he was taken to the king, who was then at S. Stefano. The next day an accord was arranged between the king and Piero: Sarzana and Sarzanello, Librafratta, Pietrasanta, Pisa, and Livorno were to be turned over to the French for the full extent of the Neapolitan campaign as guarantee of a loan of 200,000 ducats. Although the entire cession was illegal, for Piero had no right to commit the Florentines to the acceptance of these conditions, the towns in question opened their gates to the French.[62]

Venezia dall'autunno 1494 alla primavera 1495," *Archivio storico lombardo*, 3rd ser., XVIII (anno XXIX, 1902), 249–317, esp. pp. 261 ff., 287 ff.; XX (ann. XXX), 33–109, 368–443, with an appendix of four documents. In mid-February, 1495, Lodovico il Moro told Sebastiano Badoer, the Venetian ambassador in Milan, that he had loaned the French king 180,000 (or 182,000) ducats (*ibid.*, pp. 82, 101).

[57] Desjardins, I, 523.

[58] G. L. Moncallero, "Documenti inediti sulla guerra di Romagna del 1494," *Rinascimento*, IV (1953), 233–61; V (1954), 45–79; and VI (1955), 3–74, and *cf.* Pier Desiderio Pasolini, *Caterina Sforza*, 3 vols., Rome, 1893, I, 338 ff., and III, esp. docs. 524–60, pp. 207–25.

[59] Desjardins, I, 587, and *cf.* Bibbiena's letters as published by Moncallero, in *Rinascimento*, VI, 68–73. On Charles VIII's progress in Italy after crossing the Alps, note A. Segre, "Lodovico Sforza, detto il Moro . . . ," *Arch. stor. lombardo*, XVIII (ann. XXIX), 279 ff.

[60] Desjardins, I, 589. Charles was said to be at Pontremoli at this time.

[61] Desjardins, I, 591, and *cf.* Sen. Secreta, Reg. 35, fols. 33 [45] ff.

[62] Delaborde, *Expédition de Charles VIII*, pp. 430–36; Cipolla, *Le Signorie italiane dal 1313 al 1530*, II, 704. Lodovico il Moro had vainly hoped to be granted Pisa, Sarzana, and Pietrasanta (Delaborde, pp. 430, 438, 449); *cf. Diario ferrarese*, in *RISS*, XXIV-7, p. 137, and Negri, "Missioni di P. Collenuccio . . . ," *Arch. della R. Società romana di storia patria*, XXXIII, doc. no. x, pp. 412–13, dated 7 November, 1494.

Piero returned to Florence on 8 November. He had confections, bread, and wine distributed to the worried populace in a sad effort to gain sympathy and support. Ugly rumors about him were circulating in the city. When the next morning he went to the Palazzo Vecchio, he found himself debarred from entering. An uprising soon followed. The familiar cry *Popolo e libertà*! filled the air; few were found to rally to the opposing Medici cry of *Palle*! All classes and factions within the city appeared to be united against Piero; generally pro-French, they had long been dissatisfied with his Aragonese alliance. Perhaps Charles VIII's persistent announcement that after the conquest of Naples he would attack the Turks may have added to the French appeal. Now, on 9 November, Piero fled from the city through the Porta San Gallo, then held for him by his brother Giuliano and Paolo Orsini. The young Cardinal Giovanni also fled. Sixty years of Medici rule on the banks of the Arno had come to an abrupt and inglorious conclusion.

After six days at Sarzana, Charles VIII went on to Massa and Pietrasanta. On 8 November he entered Lucca, where he received a Sienese embassy. He had already refused to see Alexander VI's legate, Cardinal Piccolomini, who had conferred at length with Cardinal Giovanni de' Medici at Florence in late October. The latter had tried to explain to Piccolomini, a partisan of the Neapolitans, the Medici's change of heart, *ostendens quantum periculi sibi et familie imminebat*. Piccolomini had in fact found the Florentines determinedly pro-French. He had gone on to Lucca, uncertain of Charles's next move. He was still there, waiting hopefully for a chance to see the king, when he was peremptorily informed (as he wrote the pope from Fucecchio on 8 November) that "since his royal Majesty declined to admit me [to his presence], I was to leave Lucca lest my being there should hinder his entrance into the city, which was scheduled to take place before 9:00 P.M. [*intra quartam horam*]. . . ." Piccolomini protested, but left Lucca "within the space of an hour, for everything was ready for me to take to the road."[63] And take to the road he did. His "legation" had been a dismal failure. He had been a poor choice. Although Charles VIII doubtless respected him as a cardinal (and he was an upright man), it is not surprising that he declined to receive as papal legate an advocate of the Neapolitans, the nephew of Pius II, who had once been the enemy of his father and the protector of the Aragonese. Piccolomini departed for Siena.[64]

Pandolfo Collenuccio, who put in a daily appearance in the pope's antechamber at the Vatican, informed the duke of Ferrara that the Roman populace and "with few exceptions" even the members of the Curia were awaiting Charles VIII's arrival in Rome "with complete devotion." There was almost a famine in the city. The king's coming would bring (they believed) an abundance of food, for the sea lanes were open. At Valona on the Adriatic coast, however, four thousand Turkish horse were said to be ready to board transports which had been prepared for them. They would undoubtedly come to the aid of the royal family of Naples. Ferdinand of Aragon was holding out hope of Spanish assistance. As for the pope, Collenuccio wrote, he was given more to words than to action, and seemed to do the opposite to what he said. He would yield to the king of France.[65]

---

[63] Joseph Calmette, "La Légation du cardinal de Sienne auprès de Charles VIII (1494)," *Mélanges d'archéologie et d'histoire*, XXII (1902), 361–77, publishes eight letters from Cardinal Piccolomini to Alexander VI, dated from 29 October to 4 December, 1494. Calmette believes that the reference to Charles's "ingressus in hanc urbem, qui intra quartam horam futurus erat" (*ibid.*, ep. v, p. 371), means that Piccolomini was thus told "à quitter Lucques dans un délai de quatre heures" (p. 363), which I think would have been written *intra quattuor horas* (and would have been worded differently). In December the fourth hour was about 9:00 P.M., before which time Charles would enter Lucca. On the fall of Piero de' Medici, the activities of Savonarola, and the end of the Medicean regime in Florence, see Nicolai Rubinstein, "Politics and Constitution in Florence at the End of the Fifteenth Century," in E. F. Jacob, ed., *Italian Renaissance Studies*, London, 1960, pp. 148–83, and *cf.* Rubinstein, *The Government of Florence under the Medici (1434 to 1494)*, Oxford, 1966, pp. 232–35.

[64] Delaborde, *Expédition de Charles VIII*, pp. 443–47; Pastor, *Gesch. d. Päpste*, III-1 (repr. 1955), 397; Cipolla, *Le Signorie italiane*, II, 704–5; Thuasne, *Djem-Sultan* (1892), pp. 332–33; Cherrier, *Hist. de Charles VIII*, II, 12; Malipiero, *Annali veneti*, in *Arch. stor. italiano*, VII-1, 323; Sigismondo de' Conti, *Storie*, II (1883), 71–72; Sanudo, *Spedizione*, ed. R. Fulin, p. 110; J. de la Pilorgerie, ed., *Campagne et bulletins de la grande armée d'Italie commandée par Charles VIII (1494–1495)*, Nantes and Paris, 1866, pp. 84–90; Negri, "Missioni di P. Collenuccio . . . ," *Arch. della R. Società romana di storia patria*, XXXIII, doc. no. XII, pp. 419–20. On Piccolomini's career, see the careful study of Alfred A. Strnad, "Francesco Todeschini-Piccolomini, Politik und Mäzenatentum im Quattrocento," *Römische historische Mitteilungen*, VIII–IX (1964–66), 101–425, and on his mission to Charles VIII, *ibid.*, pp. 373–79.

[65] Negri, "Missioni di P. Collenuccio . . . ," doc. no. XIII, pp. 421–22, dated 13 November, 1494, and *cf.* no. XIV.

On 9 November, the day of Piero de' Medici's expulsion from Florence, Charles VIII entered Pisa, where French troops had been awaiting him for a week, and was lodged in a house belonging to the Medici. He received a Florentine embassy and Fra Girolamo Savonarola, whose prophecies of the descent into Italy of an avenging reformer of the Church had seemed to foretell the fact of his own invasion. Savonarola hailed him as a minister of divine justice, and begged his clemency for the Florentines. The king recognized their long-standing friendship with the French, but said he would soon be in Florence, where he would set the terms of an accord with them. The Pisans took the opportunity to petition Charles for their own freedom (*libertà*). Commines observes that the king, *qui n'entendoit que ce mot valoit*, had no right to bestow liberty on the Pisans, for the city did not belong to him, but he gave his amiable assent to whatever it was they were requesting. Announcement of the new *libertà* was made from the windows of the Opera del Duomo, where the king had dined, to the crowd assembled below.

The enraptured Pisans immediately spread through the city destroying the visible signs of Florentine domination, toppling the Florentine lion, the *Marzocco*, from its column by the Ponte Vecchio, dragging it through the mud, and throwing it into the Arno. Later on, they issued coins bearing images of the Virgin and Child on the obverse with the legend *Virgo Pisas Protege*, and on the reverse the lilies of France surmounted by the royal crown with the legend *Karolus Rex Pisanorum Li* [*berator*]. Charles had presumably not meant to remove the Pisans from Florentine sovereignty. Such an act would probably have been in violation of the agreement he had made with Piero de' Medici at S. Stefano, but he did little to gainsay the joyous interpretation which the Pisans placed upon the dinnertime gesture he had made at the Opera del Duomo.[66]

The liberation of Pisa was as great a blow to the Florentines as the subjection of their own city. And subject it was, for during the late afternoon of 17 November Charles VIII rode into Florence through the Porta San Frediano with his handsomely accoutered troops. He was given a splendid reception, but the fear that Piero de' Medici might be allowed to return soon turned most of the inhabitants against the French. Negotiations were conducted in a charged atmosphere, with sharp bargaining on both sides. At length on 25 November a treaty was signed "in the house of the heirs of Lorenzo de' Medici of Florence," in which the Florentines received detailed assurances of having Pisa retroceded to them after the Neapolitan enterprise. They were obliged, however, to promise that henceforth their regime would be less onerous than it had been in the past. Sarzana and the castle of Sarzanello as well as Pietrasanta were also to remain in the king's hands "durante sua dicta impresia," but after the Neapolitan campaign he would restore them to the Florentines. Livorno was to be returned at the same time. (Except for Livorno, as is well known, the Florentines encountered prolonged difficulties in recovering these towns, and the Pisans defended their freedom for fifteen years until in June, 1509, one Niccolò Machiavelli effected their surrender.) Charles VIII promised to defend the Florentines forever and to oblige the Genoese to make peace with them. He guaranteed the full freedom of their persons and goods in all their commercial activities throughout his dominions, "both those already acquired and those to be acquired," including Naples. Florentine ships were to be regarded as French, and the Florentines were to enjoy all the privileges and immunities of the French. In return for these and other concessions, the Florentines "of their own generosity" were to give the king 120,000 gold florins to help him regain his kingdom of Naples, an enterprise which they regarded as conducive to the common good of the peninsula. They also agreed to remove the price from Piero de' Medici's head, and exempted his brothers Giovanni and Giuliano from the vengeance of the state.[67] There is no mention

[66] Delaborde, *Expédition de Charles VIII*, pp. 447–51, and *cf.* Commines, *Mémoires*, bk. VII, chap. 9, ed. B. de Mandrot, II, 157 ff.; Vittorio Fanucci, "Le Relazioni tra Pisa e Carlo VIII," *Annali della R. Scuola normale superiore di Pisa*, X (=XVI, 1894), 1–83, with thirteen documents.

[67] The treaty was published by Gino Capponi, "Capitoli fatti dalla città di Firenze col re Carlo VIII, a dì 25 di novembre del 1494," *Arch. stor. italiano*, I (1842), 362–75, and reprinted by Thuasne, *Burchardi diarium*, II, append., no. 25, pp. 647–56; Burchard, *ibid.*, II, 195–96, and ed. Celani, I, 541–52, knew the terms of the treaty, but thought the king was to receive 130,000 florins; Malipiero, *Annali veneti*, in *Arch. stor. italiano*, VII–1 (1843), 324–25; Desjardins, I, 601–6; Sanudo, *Spedizione*, ed. R. Fulin, pp. 133–37; Delaborde, *Expédition de Charles VIII*, pp. 470–77; Pastor, *Hist. Popes*, V, 439, where by a slip Charles VIII's indemnity is given as 12,000 florins, but the amount is given correctly as 120,000 in *Gesch. d. Päpste*, III–1 (repr. 1955), 398.

of Charles's projected crusade, to which the Florentines made no commitment.

Three days before, however, on 22 November (1494), Charles VIII had issued a crusading manifesto, which was published in Latin and French to secure it as wide circulation as possible. Emphasizing in rhetorical language the *horrendissima facinora* of the Turks ever since the fall of Constantinople, the king pledged anew his zeal for the faith and his determination to recover the Holy Land. He stated that his forebears had received twenty-four investitures of the kingdom of Naples although Pius II, anxious to raise his own family from plebeian to princely status, had unjustly taken the kingdom from the French and bestowed it on a "certain Ferrante of Aragon." But now Charles would recover Naples, which belonged to him *iure hereditatis*, and its possession would enable him to attack the perfidious Turks by way of Valona and other convenient places. This was the prime purpose of his expedition. He intended no harm to Rome or the States of the Church. His mission required that he traverse territories belonging to the Church in order to get to Rome. Therefore, he was requesting the pope, the college of cardinals, and all their officials and subjects to allow him free passage and the right to purchase food, just as they had done for his Aragonese enemies, adversaries of his *sacrum propositum* to go on the crusade. If such passage were denied, he would force his way through, seizing food by whatever means he could, and the responsibility would lie with those who tried to impede his pious and sacred purpose.[68]

Alexander VI was at a loss where to turn. On 24 November he summoned Rudolf of Anhalt, who was then in Rome, and denounced to him the *insolentia* of the king of France, who was not only seeking to make himself master of Italian cities and territories which belonged to the Holy Roman Empire, but was even seeking to usurp the name and title of the Empire itself. Burchard reports the audience at which he acted as interpreter. His Holiness would never consent, however, to the French usurpations. He would rather have his throat slit. He urged Rudolf to appeal to Maximilian, king of the Romans, as sole advocate of the Sancta Romana Ecclesia, to provide for the needs and honor of the Church and indeed of all Italy, "which responsibility the aforesaid prince humbly undertook."[69] Such appeals were not without their effect. By the beginning of December (1494) a league was already being discussed which should include Spain, Venice, Naples, and Milan.[70] The French were proving successful beyond anyone's anticipation.

In the meantime Charles VIII had learned from the Venetians of the deployment of Turkish troops in the areas of Durazzo and Valona as well as of the departure of three envoys from Istanbul to confer with the pope, the king of Naples, and the Venetian government. The Venetians told Charles that the exigencies of the times made it impossible for them to give him a loan of fifty thousand ducats, as he had requested. On 27 November a Turkish envoy did appear before the Signoria, as we have noted, to urge the government to send aid to the pope and the king of Naples. The Venetians replied that such was the friendship which existed between them and the French that they could do no more than urge peace upon the combatants.[71] Charles had not come so far, however, merely to make peace, at least not with Alfonso of Naples.

On 28 November Charles left Florence for Siena, where he arrived on Tuesday, 2 December, and was well received. To the Sienese he showed generosity as well as courtesy. Now it was hard to avoid Cardinal Piccolomini, who was archbishop of the city; perhaps Charles received him in that capacity, but Piccolomini addressed him in the pope's name. Having listened to the cardinal's necessarily brief

[68] The Latin text of Charles VIII's manifesto of 22 November, 1494, is given in Burchard, *Diarium*, ed. Thuasne, II, 196–98, and ed. Celani, I, 542–43; Malipiero, *Annali veneti*, in *Arch. stor. italiano*, VII-1, 325–27; Sigismondo de'Conti, II, 73–76; and *cf.* J. de la Pilorgerie, *Campagne et bulletins* (1866), pp. 101–3; Delaborde, *Expédition de Charles VIII*, pp. 480–81; Thuasne, *Djem-Sultan*, p. 333; Pastor, *Gesch. d. Päpste*, III-1 (repr. 1955), 398–99. It is possible that the pious emphasis given to the crusade in the manifesto was inspired by the knowledge that Alexander VI was dealing with Sultan Bayazid, as shown by the letters which Giovanni della Rovere had just seized from the papal agent Giorgio Bocciardi, although Thuasne, *Djem-Sultan*, p. 340, declines to make this connection.

[69] Burchard, *Diarium*, ed. Thuasne, II, 198–99, and ed. Celani, I, 543–44.

[70] Delaborde, *Expédition de Charles VIII*, p. 438.

[71] Sanudo, *Spedizione*, ed. R. Fulin, pp. 124–25; S. Romanin, *Storia documentata di Venezia*, V (Venice, 1856), 50; Delaborde, *Expédition*, pp. 481–82. Sa'd-ad-Dīn, "Aventures du prince Gem," *Journal asiatique*, IX (1826, repr. 1965), 170, states that Charles VIII made his expedition into Italy chiefly to free Jem Sultan from the pope, but also notes that Charles planned to attack the Turks.

allocution, with its expected references to the Turkish peril and to the benign intentions of the Holy See, Charles replied that if he found a good father in the pope, the pope would find a good son in him. Then he departed (on 4 December) in a heavy rainstorm.[72] In the meantime French troops were headed south toward Rome, meeting no resistance along the way and even capturing the pope's mistress Giulia Farnese on the road from Montefiascone to Rome. Detained a few days at Viterbo, Giulia was sent to Rome with a French escort of four hundred men.[73] Alexander VI had much to think about.

On 2 December Cardinal Ascanio Sforza, vice-chancellor of the Church and brother of Lodovico il Moro, returned to Rome at the pope's invitation. Collenuccio says that he came with one squadron of *stradioti* and another of crossbowmen, all well mounted, together with some twenty grooms dressed in black. Ascanio offered Alexander VI the protection of Milan and Venice if Charles VIII did him any violence, but they would not of course come to the assistance of Naples. The vice-chancellor was prepared to go to Charles to try to persuade him to accept passage through the lands of the Church without coming to Rome. The price he asked, however, was the complete domination of the papacy by the Sforzeschi, including Alexander's promise not to name a single cardinal without the prior approval of Lodovico and Ascanio. The pope made more reasonable counter-proposals, but no decisions were reached. On 9 December Ascanio went to the Vatican palace, presumably to take leave of the pope, along with Cardinals Federigo di Sanseverino and Bernardino Lunati, both supporters of the Sforzeschi and Ascanio's representatives in the recent conferences with the pope. Prospero Colonna and Girolamo Tuttavilla went with him. That evening they were detained in the palace. The next morning there was a secret consistory at which the three cardinals were present. The pope spoke in high praise of Ascanio, who had the wit to reply in kind, placing all his resources at the service of the Church, his Holiness, and the Sacred College. When the consistory had finished, however, Ascanio and Sanseverino were conducted to upper rooms in the palace, over the papal apartment, where they were kept in well-guarded confinement. Colonna and Tuttavilla were removed to the Castel S. Angelo. Lunati was dispatched to Ostia to attempt the recovery, for the pope, of the fortress from the Colonnesi.[74]

The reason for the pope's courage was doubtless to be found in the arrival of Ferrantino, duke of Calabria, at the head of the Aragonese army on 10 December. After a leisurely lunch in the vineyard of Cardinal Orsini, near the church of S. Susanna, Ferrantino rode in the early afternoon to the apostolic palace, where day after day the envoys of Charles VIII had been requesting letters patent *pro passu et victualibus*. Now they were repeating their request on the tenth, but as Ferrantino's troops were entering Rome, Alexander refused the king of France both the safe passage and the

---

[72] Calmette, "La Légation du cardinal de Sienne," *Mélanges d'archéologie et d'histoire*, XXII, ep. VIII, pp. 375–77: ". . . Salutavi Majestatem suam Sanctitatis vestre nomine . . . ," as Piccolomini wrote the pope on the same day (4 December). Elena Vecchi-Pinto, "La Missione del Card. Francesco Piccolomini legato pontificio presso Carlo VIII," *Arch. della R. Deputazione romana di storia patria*, LXVIII (new ser., XI, 1945), 97–110, publishes an *Oratio ad regem Francorum*, undoubtedly the address which Piccolomini intended to make to Charles VIII at Lucca (on 8 or 9 November), but was never given the opportunity. He lays great stress upon the Turkish danger (*ibid.*, pp. 106 ff.): "Quam vicini sint Italiae littoribus Turci non ignorat regia tua Celsitudo. Ex Aulona [Valona], ex Scutari, ex Epyro una nocte Brundusium, Idrontum [Otranto], Tarentum navigatur."

[73] Sanudo, *Spedizione*, ed. R. Fulin, pp. 144–48; Commines, *Mémoires*, bk. VII, chap. 11, ed. B. de Mandrot, II, 167–68; Delaborde, *Expédition*, pp. 489–90, 494; Pastor, *Gesch. d. Päpste*, III–1 (repr. 1955), 401–2, and III–2 (repr. 1956), append., no. 30, pp. 1060–61, a dispatch of Giorgio Brognolo, Mantuan envoy in Rome, dated 29 November, 1494; Negri, "Missioni di P. Collenuccio . . . ," *Arch. della R. Società romana di storia patria*, XXXIII, doc. no. XVI, p. 432: "Una optima novella c'è per alcuno, che madama Iulia se è ricuperata, . . . et è venuta in Roma, e dicesi che domenica de nocte [30 November, 1494] allogiò in palazzo."

[74] Burchard, *Diarium*, ed. Thuasne, II, 200, and ed. Celani, I, 545; Negri, "Missioni di P. Collenuccio . . . ," *Arch. della R. Società romana di storia patria*, XXXIII, docs. nos. XVII–XVIII, pp. 432–35, letters dated 3 and 8 December, before Ascanio's detention; Delaborde, *Expédition*, pp. 495–99, where on p. 498 the date 29 December is an error for 9 December. Lodovico il Moro was furious at the arrest of Ascanio, who was released on 25 December (*cf.* Thuasne's note 2 in Burchard, *loc. cit.*, and Sanudo, *Spedizione*, ed. R. Fulin, pp. 149–52; Romanin, *Venezia*, V, 56–59; Delaborde, pp. 499–501; and Segre, "Lodovico Sforza . . . ," *Arch. stor. lombardo*, XVIII [ann. XXIX, 1902], 302–17). Lunati did not succeed in persuading Fabrizio Colonna to give up the fortress of Ostia to a papal force. Woodward, *Cesare Borgia*, p. 74, thinks Tuttavilla, whom he calls Jerôme d'Estouteville, was a cardinal.

right to purchase food for which the latter had made public petition in the manifesto issued on 22 November in Florence.[75]

During the early evening of 16 December the pope summoned members of the German colony in Rome to an audience at which he assailed the *infestatio et insolentia* of the French king, "who was occupying lands of the Church and was coming to lay siege to the city." He wanted the Germans to take their stand in the city, not outside it. The next day two German innkeepers, a half-dozen shoemakers, a merchant, a barber, a surgeon, and a tailor conferred on the pope's request, but asked Burchard, who seems to have been spokesman for the German colony, to explain to the pope that they were all subject to the heads of the city regions, whose orders they had to obey in an emergency. They could not operate on their own, and so they could not follow the pope's wishes (apparently by placing themselves at his disposal). Burchard relayed their answer to the pope instead of trying to deliver it directly.[76] Alexander's effort to organize the Germans (and the Spaniards) into special detachments for the defense of Rome shows that he was very doubtful about the ability of the Neapolitan army to stand up to the French, concerning whose prowess fantastic stories were beginning to spread throughout Italy.

Hour by hour, day by day the danger was getting closer. On 4 December Charles VIII left Siena, as we have seen, and was soon in papal territory. He entered Viterbo on the tenth. The weather was fine now, and in any event the French were accustomed to a worse climate. By the nineteenth Charles had reached Bracciano without having yet drawn his sword. He directed a legatine mission from the Curia to tell the pope to release Ascanio Sforza and to inform his Holiness that he expected to celebrate Christmas in Rome. French troops had already taken a number of *castelli* along the roads to Rome, built wooden bridges over the Tiber, and by the nineteenth they had even reached Rome, challenging the duke of Calabria to come out and do battle with them.[77]

Sanudo's chronology of events corresponds with that of Burchard, who reports that French troopers made incursions over Monte Mario as far as S. Lazaro and the fields around the Castel S. Angelo on 19, 21, 22, and 23 December. They tried to sail up the Tiber from Ostia, but the wind was too strong. A break was made through the gate of S. Paolo on the south side of the city, where fires were set and other damage done. Some people said Raymond Peraudi, the cardinal of Gurk, was responsible for this. He had rendered the French great service by winning over the inhabitants of Acquapendente and other papal territories to an acceptance of Charles VIII, whom he praised to the skies, telling the peasants that the French would pay in full for every hen, every egg, they took en route. On 23 December Peraudi also addressed an open letter to the German prelates, curial officials, and others of the German community in Rome, telling them that he had done his best to effect an understanding between the pope and the king of France. His failure had not been the fault of the king, who demanded nothing more than to be the devoted son of the pope and the Holy See—the reason for the failure must be *propter peccata nostra et demerita*. Peraudi informed the Germans that no one would be injured when the French entered Rome unless he were found bearing arms against the king. He assured them of Charles's good will, offering them his own house as a place of refuge should tumult accompany the French entry into the city. "Farewell, my dearest children," he concluded, "and pray God for my purpose, which is universal peace among Christians and universal war against the Turks!"[78]

The Colonnesi at Ostia prevented supplies from going up the Tiber, while their raids to the very walls of Rome had made it difficult at times to bring food into the city from the countryside. Nevertheless, the Castel S. Angelo was stocked with provisions enough to carry it through a lengthy siege. Ferrantino urged Alexander VI to excommunicate Charles VIII and retire with the Curia into the kingdom

---

[75] Burchard, *Diarium*, ed. Thuasne, II, 200, and ed. Celani, I, 545, whose text I follow; Sanudo, *Spedizione*, ed. R. Fulin, pp. 149–50; Pastor, *Gesch. d. Päpste*, III-1 (repr. 1955), 402–3; Thuasne, *Djem-Sultan*, pp. 340–41.

[76] Burchard, *Diarium*, ed. Thuasne, II, 201–2, and ed. Celani, I, 546–47. The pope also appealed to the Spaniards in Rome to form a special corps for the defense of the city.

[77] Sanudo, *Spedizione*, ed. R. Fulin, p. 154.

[78] Burchard, *Diarium*, ed. Thuasne, II, 211–13, and ed. Celani, I, 555–56, Peraudi's letter being dated "ex Formello, hac die XXIII Decembris." *Cf.* Sigismondo de' Conti, II, 84–85. In one context or another there was constant reference to Charles's projected "sancta expeditione contra infideles" (Segre, "Lodovico Sforza . . . ," *Arch. stor. lombardo,* XVIII [ann. XXIX, 1902], 314–15). Alfonso II had appealed to the sultan for aid (*ibid.*, XX [ann. XXX, 1903], 34–35), which was said to be on its way.

of Naples while there was still time. Alfonso II had offered the pope a pension of fifty thousand ducats of gold, the fortress of Gaeta, and ten thousand ducats for Jem Sultan's maintenance. He had also guaranteed (how could he do otherwise?) not to reach a separate accord with Charles. Quite understandably, Alexander feared that he might lose the papacy with Rome. He had been pushed to the brink of disaster; a false step now, and he might be lost. No doubt the emperor and the king of Spain were aroused by this time. Even the Venetians might be prepared to come to his assistance. They were all far away, however, and the king of France was almost at the city gates.[79]

No one in Rome ever forgot that Christmas day of 1494. Alexander VI began by sending his nephew Juan Borgia, cardinal of Monreale, who was supposed to say mass in the Sistine Chapel, to the French king. Charles was making his headquarters at the Orsini stronghold of Bracciano. Before entering the chapel, the pope summoned all the cardinals to the Camera del Pappagallo. There he made a brief statement of the necessity which drove him to submit to Charles's insistence upon entering Rome. Donning then the proper vestments, he went into the Sistina, where a solemn mass was celebrated. There was no sermon. Again in the Camera del Pappagallo, where he took off his vestments, he summoned Ferrantino, duke of Calabria, to him and spoke to him privately in the presence of all the cardinals, who were standing around them. Ferrantino then kissed the pope's foot and hand, received from him the *oris osculum*, and withdrew, accompanied by Cardinals Carafa, Ascanio Sforza, and Cesare Borgia. Mounting horses, they rode toward the gate of S. Lorenzo, but when Ascanio reached his palace, he took leave of them. Carafa and Cesare rode on either side of Ferrantino to S. Lorenzo, where he thanked them, joined his troops, and made for Tivoli and then on to Terracina. He withdrew from Rome under a French safe-conduct of assurance that he and his troops would not be attacked. Juan Borgia was on his way to Bracciano. Ferrantino's withdrawal from the city was marked by the release, it will have been noted, of Ascanio Sforza from his detention in the Vatican.[80]

On Friday, 26 December, the feast of S. Stephen the Protomartyr, mass was celebrated in the pope's presence in the Sistine Chapel. Three French envoys were present, Pierre de Gié, viscount of Rohan and marshal of France; Jean de Ganay, president of the Parlement de Paris; and Étienne de Vesc, sénéchal of Beaucaire. Burchard, the master of ceremonies, had assigned them to places near the papal throne, above the Senator of Rome, but the numerous members of their retinue unceremoniously occupied whatever benches seemed convenient, including a number always reserved for prelates. The conscientious Burchard, to whom curial etiquette and protocol seemed to be almost the totality of existence, was all for removing them and putting them in proper places. But the pope, who sometimes lost patience with Burchard's humorless fulfillment of his functions, motioned the master of ceremonies to him, and angrily said to him, "You're making me lose my mind: let the French take any places they please!" Burchard asked the pope not to be distressed; knowing his wish in the matter, he would not say another word to the French about seating.[81]

The French envoys encountered some difficulty in reaching an accord with Alexander VI.

---

[79] *Cf.* Sanudo, *Spedizione*, ed. R. Fulin, pp. 148–49; Delaborde, *Expédition de Charles VIII*, pp. 504–5; Pastor, *Gesch. d. Päpste*, III–1 (repr. 1955), 405; Thuasne, *Djem-Sultan*, pp. 342–43. The *capitula foederis* between Alexander VI and Ferrantino on behalf of his father, providing for the pope's refuge in the kingdom of Naples with a pension of 50,000 ducats, may be found in A. Theiner, *Codex diplomaticus dominii temporalis Sanctae Sedis*, III (Rome, 1862, repr. Frankfurt am Main, 1964), no. 426, pp. 510–11, doc. dated at Rome on 25 December, 1495 [1494]. The pope approved, but never signed, the various articles of the treaty.

[80] Burchard, *Diarium*, ed. Thuasne, II, 214–15, with append., no. 26, pp. 656–57, and ed. Celani, I, 556–57; *Diario ferrarese*, in *RISS*, XXIV–7 (1933), p. 136; J. de la Pilorgerie, *Campagne et bulletins*, p. 145; Delaborde, *Expédition*, p. 505; Thuasne, *Djem-Sultan*, p. 344; Pastor, *Gesch. d. Päpste*, III–1 (repr. 1955), 405–6. Sanudo, *Spedizione*, ed. R. Fulin, p. 161, says that the pope took the occasion of Ferrantino's leave-taking to invest him with the duchy of Calabria as a final gesture of friendship for the house of Aragon. Despite the fact that Ferrantino and Cardinal Ascanio were on opposing sides, the latter was his uncle and, one may gather from Sanudo, *loc. cit.*, not personally inimical to him, hence the cardinal's accompanying him at his departure from the Curia. Ascanio had in fact been released at the request of Ferrantino's father Alfonso II. Terracina was actually ecclesiastical territory at this time, but had been occupied by Alfonso of Naples by agreement with the pope.

[81] Burchard, *Diarium*, ed. Thuasne, II, 215, and ed. Celani, I, 557–58; on Marshal de Gié, note U. Chevalier, *Répertoire des sources historiques du moyen âge: Bio-bibliographie*, 2nd ed., 2 vols., Paris, 1905–7, repr. New York, 1960, II, cols. 4052–53, which is the source of Celani, *loc. cit.*, note 4.

The formalities attending Charles VIII's entry into Rome did not much concern the pope. By and large they could be left to Burchard to arrange. Charles demanded the unconditional surrender of Jem Sultan, however, while the pope was unwilling to give up his custody until the king was actually ready to embark on his crusade. Charles also insisted that the pope authorize his occupation of the fortress towns of Soriano, Velletri, Civitavecchia, Narni, and even Terracina, which the pope declined to do. It was said that he demanded the Castel S. Angelo also. Charles cut short the Italian tendency to negotiate ad infinitum by stating that, after he arrived in Rome, he would deal directly with the pope, to whom he sent solemn assurances that he would do him neither spiritual nor temporal injury. The king fixed 1 January (1495) as the day of his entry into Rome.[82] The pope had no alternative but to acquiesce.

Early on the morning of 31 December, Burchard rode out of Rome by order of the pope with some curial and civic officials to instruct the king on the "order of his reception according to ceremonial." After some time they met up with Cardinals Giuliano della Rovere, Raymond Peraudi, and Giovanni Battista Savelli, whom Burchard saluted on horseback, *non descendendo*, and a little way behind these came Charles VIII himself. Burchard and his companions made their obeisance to the king on horseback also "because of the mud and the rainy season and the swiftness of the king's march." The master of ceremonies explained to his Majesty his purpose in riding out to meet him, but Charles said that he wished to move on to Rome without delay and without ceremony. An official of the city government offered the hospitality of the *populus Romanus*, to which Charles gave a curt response. After the royal entourage had got started again, however, Charles summoned Burchard to him, and questioned him at length concerning ceremonies, the pope's status, the position of Cardinal Cesare Borgia, and so many other things that the master of ceremonies was hard put to it to supply the answers.

Presently the Venetian ambassadors arrived to make their salutations to the king, and after them Cardinal Ascanio Sforza riding on a mule. Ascanio fell into line on the king's left, apparently occupying his attention to the exclusion of Burchard. They went over the Milvian bridge, past the shrine of S. Andrew. The road was muddy, filled with large pools of water. The royal company entered the city by the Porta del Popolo and made its way along the (modern) Via del Corso to the Palazzo Venezia, then the Palazzo S. Marco, where the king was to have his lodgings. Once within the city their progress was lighted by fires or torches at almost every house. There were cries of Francia, Francia! Colonna, Colonna! Vincula, Vincula! It was already dark, about seven o'clock in the evening or a little later. At the palace Ascanio took his leave of Charles without dismounting from his mule. Giuliano della Rovere also went his way without accompanying the king into the palace. Before Charles's entrance into the city the keys to all the gates had been given to Marshal de Gié, more a gesture of courtesy than a precaution for safety.

In the meantime Alexander VI had shut himself up in the Vatican with his Spanish guard. His military forces, a thousand light horse and some infantry, were stationed in the Borgo. If necessary, the pope could reach the Castello by the secret passageway running along the upper part of the wall which still reaches from the Vatican palace almost to the great fortress. Charles VIII had entered Rome a day earlier than his announced intention, because he had learned of the favorable conjunction of the planets on 31 December.[83] Time would tell how lucky his stars would be as his Italian expedition was moving ever closer to its Neapolitan goal.

All through the last night of the year 1494 the gates of Rome remained open as French soldiers marched into the city. On the first day of the new year five thousand Swiss entered in perfect array. Houses were demolished around the

[82] Sanudo, *Spedizione*, ed. R. Fulin, p. 162; Delaborde, *Expédition*, pp. 505–6; Thuasne, *Djem-Sultan*, pp. 344–45, and *Burchardi diarium*, II, append., no. 26, pp. 658–59.

[83] Burchard, *Diarium*, ed. Thuasne, II, 216–17, with append., no. 26, pp. 656 ff., and ed. Celani, I, 558–59, whose text differs slightly from that of Thuasne; Sigismondo de'Conti, II, 85–87; Sanudo, *Spedizione*, ed. R. Fulin, pp. 162–64, who speaks of the *opinione astrologica*, which induced Charles VIII to enter Rome on the last rather than the first day of the year. The modern Via del Corso was then the Via Lata, the name being retained by the church of S. Maria in Via Lata (on the Corso). *Cf.* Delaborde, *Expédition*, pp. 507–8; Thuasne, *Djem-Sultan*, pp. 344–45; Pastor, *Hist. Popes*, V, 450–52, and *Gesch. d. Päpste*, III–1 (repr. 1955), 407–9. In the English translation of Pastor, V, 454, erroneous reference is made to the "underground passage to the Castle of S. Angelo," but actually Pastor, *Gesch. d. Päpste*, III–1, 410, speaks of "der bedeckte Gang in die Engelsburg," which is quite another matter.

Palazzo S. Marco to clear an area for artillery. Although the French are said to have been fairly well behaved,[84] the Germans and the Swiss did some plundering. Gallows were erected in the Campo dei Fiori and the Piazza Giudea, symbols of royal authority. Rome was ruled from the Palazzo S. Marco, not the Vatican.[85] Cardinals and condottieri, envoys of the Italian states, Roman nobles, curious sightseers, and even Piero de' Medici appeared in the piazza outside the palace. Most of them had requests, few of which were granted. As the cardinals paid their expected calls on the king, he showed them none of the courtesies in which Burchard had instructed him on the road to Rome.[86] The city was filled with rumors and ominous signs. Part of the upper wall of the Castel S. Angelo collapsed on the night of 10 January (1495), killing three guards.[87]

In the meantime the Venetians were reading other signs and portents. Astonished though they were at the extent of Charles's success, they were also being held partly responsible for this incredible invasion—for this fall of Rome to the barbarians—for it could never have happened but for their timid neutrality. Already, however, the Signoria was quietly recruiting horse and foot, offering contracts to condottieri, and increasing the striking force of the fleet on the Adriatic. Already it was being widely assumed that now the Republic would bide her time until she could strike at the French. Amid all the wagging tongues and nodding heads in the Venetian Senate there were a good many who realized that the French invasion betokened the beginning of a new, perhaps a darker era, in the history of the Italian peninsula.[88]

In a vague way Charles VIII was also aware that he was putting historians in his debt for a long time to come—even in retrospect his expedition remains one of the more notable undertakings of a century that began in turmoil and was now ending in turmoil. Considering the seclusion of his childhood and the poverty of his education, Charles showed a singular sense of propriety and self-discipline during these months in Italy. An outlandish little "monkey of a man," he began to look like a king. Cardinal Cesare Borgia negotiated with him on the pope's behalf; a royal commission waited on the pope in the Vatican. Charles proposed three conditions for an accord with the pope: Cesare Borgia himself should accompany the French to Naples as papal legate (and of course as a hostage); charge of the Castel S. Angelo should be committed to a French garrison; and Jem Sultan should be released into French custody. The pope's initial response to all these demands was negative: legates were chosen in consistory; the Castello was inalienable from the Holy See, the common property as it were of Christendom; and it was not yet the proper time to turn Jem over to the king. The pope, who was subject to fainting spells, alternated between firmness and fear. A consistory supported his decisions with respect to the royal demands, and Charles was informed that he must settle for free passage through papal territories. The king's answer was that he would send his barons to apprise the pope of his intentions. On 6 or 7 January Alexander VI left the Vatican to go by the roofed corridor or "covered gallery" concealed within the wall to the Castel S. Angelo. The French talked of moving cannon to the Castello. The rebellious cardinals again urged the pope's deposition, but Charles was not prepared for such extremes.[89]

---

[84] Burchard, *Diarium*, ed. Thuasne, II, 218, and ed. Celani, I, 560, finds much to be desired in the conduct of the French, but his house was one of the residences chosen to accommodate them, although he managed to evict his unwelcome guests (*ibid.*, Thuasne, II, 219; Celani, I, 561–62). The house of Vannozza de' Catanei, the mother of Cesare Borgia, was also plundered (Thuasne, II, 220; Celani, I, 562). *Cf.* Delaborde, *Expédition*, pp. 508–9. For the entry of the 5,000 Swiss, see Sanudo, *Spedizione*, ed. R. Fulin, p. 166, who says that more than 30,000 persons entered Rome with Charles VIII.

[85] Burchard, *Diarium*, ed. Thuasne, II, 235–36, and ed. Celani, I, 573.

[86] Burchard, *Diarium*, ed. Thuasne, II, 218, and ed. Celani, I, 560, who says that the French were making a pigsty of everything in the Palazzo S. Marco. Sanudo, *Spedizione*, ed. R. Fulin, pp. 166–67, also notes the small honor paid the cardinals by the French: he gives a list of the full membership of the Sacred College in 1494–1495 (pp. 168–69).

[87] Burchard, *Diarium*, ed. Thuasne, II, 220, and ed. Celani, I, 564; Sanudo, *Spedizione*, ed. R. Fulin, p. 171; *cf. Diario ferrarese*, in *RISS*, XXIV-7 (1933), p. 136.

[88] *Cf.* Segre, "Lodovico Sforza . . . ," *Arch. stor. lombardo*, 3rd ser., XX (ann. XXX, 1903), 40–46 and ff., 84 ff.

[89] Sanudo, *Spedizione*, ed. R. Fulin, pp. 167, 170–71; Burchard, *Diarium*, ed. Thuasne, II, 220, and ed. Celani, I, 564, on the pope's removal to Castel S. Angelo; Malipiero, *Annali veneti*, in *Arch. stor. italiano*, VII-1 (1843), 329–30; J. de la Pilorgerie, *Campagne et bulletins*, pp. 147–48; Delaborde, *Expédition*, pp. 511–15; Pastor, *Gesch. d. Päpste*, III-1 (repr. 1955), 409–11, and III-2 (repr. 1956), append., nos. 31–33, pp. 1061–62. Besides Civitavecchia and Ostia, various towns in the March of Ancona and the Patrimonium S. Petri received French garrisons.

Awaiting the resumption of negotiations, Charles started some of his forces along the road to Naples. It was wise to reject any idea of deposing Alexander VI. The complication of a schism would not advance either the conquest of Naples or his plans for the crusade. It would magnify the difficulties which his Italian success was bound to create in Germany and Spain. The Venetians had become apprehensive, and Lodovico il Moro was not a man to trust when the going became rough. Charles was already suspicious of Lodovico, and quite justifiably so. Considering, moreover, that the Castel S. Angelo was of little value to him since he could not expect indefinitely to occupy Rome, Charles gave way on his demand for custody of S. Angelo, but he insisted on the Neapolitan investiture, the legatine appointment of Cesare Borgia, the surrender of Civitavecchia, and the acquisition of Jem Sultan, whose presence would attest the royal sincerity as a crusader. These proposals were made and accepted on 11 January (and signed on the fifteenth). The pope agreed to release Jem to the king for six months in return for the immediate payment of twenty thousand ducats and certain guarantees for his return at the expiration of that period. Burchard says that the pope also agreed to crown Charles king of Naples without prejudice to the rights of any other claimant, and promised not to harass or proceed against the rebellious members of the Sacred College, della Rovere, Peraudi, Savelli, and Colonna. Despite the objections of della Rovere and Peraudi (whose interests, however, were protected), the accord with the pope was made, and on 12 or 13 January, for the first time, Charles VIII left the Palazzo S. Marco to go sight-seeing among the majestic ruins of Rome, and to visit some of the world's best-known churches.[90]

On the morning of 16 January Charles VIII rode to the basilica of S. Peter, where he heard mass celebrated by one of his chaplains in the chapel of S. Petronilla. Thereafter he mounted the stairs to the Vatican palace to some recently built rooms which had been prepared for him and where he dined. In the early afternoon, shortly after one o'clock, the pope was borne along the gallery from Castel S. Angelo to the palace,[91] the king and the cardinals advancing to meet him "up to about the end of the second private garden," from which one ascended to the gallery. When the pope reached the garden, the cardinals approached him first. Charles then came forward to a respectful distance. The pope pretended not to see his first two genuflections. When Charles drew nearer to make still a third, however, the pope removed his biretta (*biretum*), and stepped forward to greet him, restraining him from the third obeisance and kissing him, so that the king kissed neither the papal foot nor hand. They were both bareheaded. The pope was unwilling to replace his biretta until the king replaced his hat. They covered their heads at the same time. Charles immediately asked the pope to make a cardinal of his councillor Guillaume Briçonnet, bourgeois bishop of S. Malo. The request was granted on the spot. The pope directed Burchard to find the necessary robe and hat. Cesare Borgia supplied the *cappa cardinalaris* (time was to show how willingly he could give it up!), and a red hat was fetched from the room of the cardinal of S. Anastasia.

Moving on to the Camera del Pappagallo, the pope mounted the consistorial throne. The king sat almost in the midst of the cardinals. Alex-

---

[90] Burchard, *Diarium*, ed. Thuasne, II, 220–21, and ed. Celani, I, 564–65; J. de la Pilorgerie, ed., *Campagne et bulletins de la grande armée d'Italie commandée par Charles VIII (1494–1495)*, Nantes and Paris, 1866, pp. 134–43; Sanudo, *Spedizione*, ed. R. Fulin, p. 184; Sigismondo de'Conti, II, 91–92; *Diario ferrarese*, in *RISS*, XXIV-7 (1933), pp. 136–37; Delaborde, *Expédition*, pp. 516–17; Thuasne, *Djem-Sultan*, pp. 348–49; Pastor, *Gesch. d. Päpste*, III-1 (repr. 1955), 412–14. The accord between Alexander VI and Charles VIII was not formally signed until 15 January, 1495 (for the French text see Thuasne's edition of Burchard's *Diarium*, II, append., no. 26, pp. 661–66; the French text is also given in Giuseppe Molini, *Documenti di storia italiana*, I [Florence, 1836], 22–28). The accord left Ascanio Sforza out in the cold, although Giuliano della Rovere retained the fortress at Ostia, the Avignonese legation, and all his benefices and property (Segre, "Lodovico Sforza . . . ," *Arch. stor. lombardo*, 3rd ser., XX [ann. XXX, 1903], 52–57, 61 ff.).

[91] Although Delaborde, *Expédition de Charles VIII*, p. 518, says that on 16 January Alexander VI returned to the Vatican from the Castel S. Angelo "par la galerie couverte" (for a picture of which see Emilio Lavagnino, *Le Château Saint-Ange*, Rome, 1950, fig. 7), Burchard, *Diarium*, ed. Thuasne, II, 221–22, and ed. Celani, I, 565, states that he returned by the "deambulatorium sive curritorium discoopertum," which suggests that he used the upper passage between the crenellations (for which see Lavagnino, *op. cit.*, fig. 5). During the first days of Charles VIII's presence in Rome, the pope frequently went back and forth between the Vatican and the Castello "per la via coperta," according to a dispatch of the Mantuan envoy Giorgio Brognolo, dated 4 January, 1495 (Pastor, *Gesch. d. Päpste*, III-2 [repr. 1956], append., no. 31, p. 1061), for then he obviously desired the greater safety and secrecy of the interior corridor.

ander VI said that he had recently received the votes of all the cardinals to raise the bishop of S. Malo to the cardinalate, and now his Majesty especially requested it. The members of the Sacred College signified their assent. Briçonnet, kneeling before the pope in Cesare Borgia's cappa, was pronounced a cardinal according to the *Caeremoniale romanum*—"Authoritate Omnipotentis Dei," etc.—and confirmed in his rights to the church of S. Malo and all the monasteries and benefices which he had previously obtained *in titulum et commendam*. Briçonnet then kissed the foot and hand of the pope, who raised him up and received him *ad oris osculum*. He knelt again, and the pope placed the red hat on his head with the appropriate words required by the *Caeremoniale*. After he had thanked both the pontiff and the king, Briçonnet was given the "kiss of peace" by each cardinal.[92] He had satisfied the ambition of many years. At long last he was a prince of the Church.[93] After the ceremony Alexander VI said that he would accompany the king to the apartment prepared for him, but Charles would not accept so great an honor, and so the cardinals went with the king to his chamber, traversing various interesting halls and new rooms to do so. Briçonnet was probably all eyes. Whether as a consequence of papal courtesy or of French caution, the king's Scottish guards were posted at all the doors leading to the royal apartment.[94]

On Sunday, 18 January, Charles VIII paid a visit to the pope's apartment, where there was about three hours' bickering over the guarantees which the king was to furnish for the safe return of Jem Sultan within six months. Charles was to restore Jem to the pope when he left Italy to return to France, and was to protect papal territory in the event Sultan Bayazid should make an attack upon the March of Ancona or elsewhere. The French princes, barons, and prelates of the royal company were to pledge 500,000 ducats as surety for Jem "payables pour une fois à nostre dit saint père et à la chambre apostolique." Jem's annual pension of 40,000 ducats was to be paid (if the funds were forthcoming from Bayazid while his brother was in French custody) to the pope, "comme il est acoustumé."[95] Alexander VI tried to provide for every contingency, but certainly he did not expect to receive Jem's pension or tribute, as it was sometimes called, once he had turned Jem over to the king of France.

In the meantime the "first hall" or *sala regia* in the Vatican palace had been prepared for a public consistory at which Charles VIII would be formally received by the pope and make his obeisance, as a dutiful son, to the Holy Father. The king's visit to the pope's apartment on Sunday, the eighteenth, had interrupted a discussion which the pope was having with Burchard concerning the protocol to be followed at the ceremony which was to take place the following day. By this time the gracious exchange of courtesies was wearing a little thin, and Charles deliberately delayed his reception until he had heard mass and had breakfast. Finally he went to the hall of the consistory, where Jean de Ganay,

---

[92] Burchard, *Diarium*, ed. Thuasne, II, 221–23, and ed. Celani, I, 565–66; Sanudo, *Spedizione*, ed. R. Fulin, pp. 185–86; J. de la Pilorgerie, *Campagne et bulletins*, pp. 153–54; Foucard, in *Arch. stor. per le province napoletane*, IV (1879), 791–92, dispatch of the Estense envoy Gianandrea Boccaccio, bishop of Modena, to the duke of Ferrara, dated 16 January, 1495. Briçonnet's creation as cardinal was, to say the least, unusual. Agostino Patrizzi and Burchard himself had defined the proper procedures in the *Caeremoniale romanum* (of 1488), published by Cristoforo Marcello, *Rituum ecclesiasticorum sive sacrarum caerimoniarum SS. Romanae Ecclesiae libri tres non ante impressi*, Venice, 1516, repr. Ridgewood, N. J., 1965, fols. xxxix ff., where the formula *Auctoritate Dei Patris omnipotentis* [*sic*], etc., occurs on fol. xxxix^v. Briçonnet became archbishop of Rheims in August, 1497 (Eubel, *Hierarchia*, II [1914, repr. 1960], 23, 223), and received the abbey of S. Germain-des-Prés four years later. He had taken orders after his wife's death (*cf.*, above, Chapter 14, note 100). His son, also named Guillaume Briçonnet, became in his turn bishop of Lodève and Meaux, and succeeded his father as abbot of S. Germain (Michel Veissière, "Guillaume Briçonnet, abbé rénovateur de Saint-Germain-des-Prés [1507–1534]," *Revue d'histoire de l'église de France*, LX [1974], 65–84).

[93] *Cf.* Delaborde, *Expédition de Charles VIII*, pp. 284, 294, 330, 519.

[94] Burchard, *Diarium*, ed. Thuasne, II, 224, and ed. Celani, I, 566–67.

[95] Burchard, *Diarium*, ed. Thuasne, II, 226, and ed. Celani, I, 567–68; see the *Articles entre nostre saint père le pape et le roy très chrestien accordez*, in Thuasne, II, append., no. 26, p. 662, treaty dated 15 January, 1495, on which *cf. Djem-Sultan*, pp. 351–52. Alexander VI granted the rebellious cardinals and their allies among the Colonnesi, Savelli, and Vitelli a general amnesty, but Giovanni della Rovere, the prefect of Rome, was to give the pope the 40,000 ducats taken from the Turkish envoy and Bocciardi near Sinigaglia (Thuasne, II, append., no. 26, pp. 663–64). As a guarantee that Charles VIII and the French *noblesse* would meet their pledges with respect to Jem Sultan, the pope wanted to retain thirty to forty French seigneurs and prelates as hostages while the President de Ganay wanted to limit the number, according to Burchard, "to ten persons only" (*Diarium*, ed. Thuasne, II, 226, and ed. Celani, I, 568), all of which seems quite contrary to the agreements of 1488 by which the French surrendered Jem to Innocent VIII. No agreement was reached as to the number of French hostages to be left at the Curia Romana.

president of the Parlement de Paris, served as his spokesman. Charles did a modified form of obeisance to the pope (on 19 January) requesting, through Ganay, the confirmation of all past privileges granted to the French royal family by past pontiffs, the investiture of the kingdom of Naples, and the abrogation of any commitment the French might have made the previous day as to giving the pope pledges or hostages (*fidejussores*) for the return of Jem Sultan to the Holy See. Alexander granted the first request, for it seemed adequately ambiguous, but stated that the second must be fully discussed in consistory, for the interests of a third party were prejudicially involved. Nevertheless, the pope said that, to the fullest extent he could, he would try to please the king. As for Jem, Alexander was certain that a satisfactory agreement would be worked out (and what else could he say?). After Charles had made his rather restrained statement of obeisance to the Holy Father, Alexander concluded the ceremony with a few appropriate words. The bad manners of the French caused the cardinals some discomfiture, but the pope and the king withdrew with no untoward incident.[96]

The disaffected cardinals were not to be reconciled to the pope, whom they distrusted. Giuliano della Rovere's hostility to Alexander VI was well known. He could hardly be expected to return to the consistory, nursing as he did an implacable hatred for the pope. Raymond Peraudi seemed at first to be prepared for a reconciliation, but on 22 January in the presence of Cardinals Giambattista Orsini and Raffaele Riario, Peraudi charged Alexander with simony, sins of the flesh, and maintaining intelligence with the Gran Turco. He called the pope a *magnus simulator et verus deceptor*.[97] The papal ties with Istanbul seemed to Peraudi to be even more reprehensible than Alexander's immorality and double-dealing.

A dangerous disquiet pervaded Rome as long as the French army remained within the walls. The Catalan mercenaries employed to guard the Castel S. Angelo had a good deal of trouble with the Swiss.[98] Charles VIII and the pope consulted frequently during this period, being closeted together on one occasion for four hours. Alexander VI was still trying to get the king to abandon his campaign against Alfonso, and accept the latter as his vassal (*tributario*) for the south Italian kingdom. Charles persisted in plans for the conquest; it was enough, he said, for the Aragonese to have enjoyed their usurpation since 1442. Charles said that he planned a general council of all Christendom, especially of the Italian powers, from whom he intended to ask aid for his overseas crusade and the destruction of Turkish power. By this time the Neapolitan kingdom was in hopeless confusion. No one obeyed Alfonso, says Sanudo, and cries of Francia! Francia! were frequently heard in the streets of rebellious cities, especially in Anzio.[99] It was difficult to look as far ahead as the French crusade, although the conquest of Naples now seemed to be a foregone conclusion.

On the evening of 27 January Jem Sultan was turned over to Charles VIII, according to the agreement which had been reached with the pope about two weeks before.[100] There were false rumors that the pope had invested Charles with the kingdom of Naples. Sanudo says that Alexander VI, when trying to dissuade the king from his southward march, had offered to crown him emperor of Constantinople, but Charles had replied that he preferred first to conquer the eastern empire, "et poi haver el titolo d'imperator."[101] The appearance of friendship

---

[96] Burchard, *Diarium*, ed. Thuasne, II, 226–30, and ed. Celani, I, 568–70; Sanudo, *Spedizione*, ed. R. Fulin, p. 186; J. de la Pilorgerie, *Campagne et bulletins*, p. 156.

[97] Burchard, *Diarium*, ed. Thuasne, II, 233, and ed. Celani, I, 572, who had not witnessed the scene himself; *cf.* Thuasne, *Djem-Sultan*, p. 354.

[98] Burchard, *Diarium*, ed. Thuasne, II, 233, and ed. Celani, I, 572. Conditions had been miserable in Rome for weeks, since in fact well before the king's entry into the city (*cf.* Negri, "Missioni di P. Collenuccio . . . ," *Arch. della R. Società romana di storia patria*, XXXIII, doc. no. XVIII, pp. 434–35, dated 8 December, 1494).

[99] Sanudo, *Spedizione*, ed. R. Fulin, p. 188.

[100] Burchard, *Diarium*, ed. Thuasne, II, 235, and ed. Celani, I, 573; Sanudo, *Spedizione*, ed. R. Fulin, pp. 190, 192, who assigns the surrender of Jem Sultan to the French on 26 January, and believes incidentally that if Jem had secured the Ottoman throne, ". . . tutta la christianità, ymo tutto el mondo, di questo haria sentito afflitione." *Cf.* Thuasne, *Djem-Sultan*, pp. 355–56.

[101] Sanudo, *Spedizione*, ed. R. Fulin, p. 188. Charles VIII was erroneously claimed to have coined money with the legend *Carolus Imperator*. Such alleged imperial intentions had evoked the ire of the Germans (Malipiero, *Annali veneti*, in *Arch. stor. italiano*, VII-1 [1843], 329). Delaborde, *Expédition*, p. 405, reproduces an insipid portrait of Charles VIII bearing the imperial insignia, from the Collection Gaignières of the Bibliothèque Nationale. The Ferrarese envoy to the court of Naples, Sigismondo Cantelmo, wrote Duke Ercole that Charles had been invested with the Neapolitan kingdom and created emperor of Constantinople, "to which title the despot has ceded him all his rights for a pension of 5,000 ducats a year" (Cesare Foucard, *Carteggio diplomatico*, Naples, 1879, p. 46), which like much of the ambassadors' information was largely wrong. *Cf.* also

between the pope and the king deluded some envoys and other observers for a while. Alexander was an old hand at deception, and played the diplomatic game well. Except for a cardinal's hat, custody of Jem Sultan, and papal consent to Cesare Borgia's legatine mission with the French army, all Charles received was the public concession of a bull granting him free passage through the States of the Church. He did not receive the Neapolitan investiture. Charles was anxious to be gone from Rome, where he had spent time enough. His soldiers had suffered appreciably from the current lack of food. In Rome the poor were always hungry, and the presence of an army of some thirty thousand men with a defective commissariat had produced a near famine in the city. Even before the entry of the French there had been a serious shortage of food, which the Romans had found difficult to cope with—"especially the priests," Sanudo noted, "accustomed to every delicacy, they could hardly bear the great scarcity."[102] Lack of firewood had added to the discomfort of the French army. The soldiers cut down trees in the gardens, and burned interior beams and the window frames of houses to keep warm. The southward march to Naples seemed to present another bleak prospect, for the Aragonese had devastated much of the territory through which the French would have to march, destroying the harvests and burning fodder as well as food, filling up the wells and cutting the aqueducts. All houses, convents, and other shelters had been burned to the ground along the three roads leading southward from the Roman Campagna. There had been a good deal of snow in the highlands.[103]

The French also had grounds for encouragement. The towns of Narni and Terni, Tagliacozzo and L'Aquila had been seized or had surrendered, and soon all the Abruzzesi were proclaiming their French sympathies. During the forenoon of 28 January Charles VIII and his staff took leave of Alexander VI, who was attended by thirteen cardinals, including Cesare Borgia, who was to accompany the king as papal legate. After the farewells and benedictions, the royal entourage set off, the king on horseback and Cesare Borgia riding a mule, for the town of Marino, which belonged to the Colonnesi. Cardinals Giuliano della Rovere, Savelli, and Colonna went with them, and that evening Raymond Peraudi, cardinal of Gurk, also departed for Marino. Jem Sultan had already left to join the king on the southward march.[104]

That same evening, 28 January (1495), according to Burchard, the pope was informed that King Alfonso II had withdrawn from Naples with a vast treasure in four galleys, on his way to Sicily and possibly headed for Spain. The following evening the news arrived that Ferrantino, duke of Calabria, had taken over the kingdom as his father's successor, and that by Alfonso's order he was betrothed to his aunt Isabella [actually Joanna] of Aragon. He had made the ceremonial ride through Naples as king, and had received the oaths of fealty from his vassals. Various barons and nobles imprisoned by his grandfather and father had been released, but those known to have been in communication with the French were executed.[105] Alfonso had abdicated on 22 January, although the queen mother and Ferrantino had implored him on bended knees not to do so, for his departure would mean the certain loss of the kingdom. He told the queen mother that his own sins had brought this vast misfortune on his house. Years before he had taken a vow to become a monk. Now he wanted to enter the monastery at Mazara in southwestern Sicily,

---

Foucard, in *Arch. stor. per le province napoletane*, IV (1879), 794, dispatch of 22 January, 1495. The author of the *Diario ferrarese*, in *RISS*, XXIV–7 (1933), p. 145, notes that in March, 1495, the news reached Ferrara that Charles had adopted the titles *Ierusalem Rex, urbis Constantinopolitane et Trebisonde Imperator maximus et dominus dominantium. . . .* Charles's Byzantine ambitions were well known (Commines, *Mémoires*, bk. VII, chap. 7, ed. B. de Mandrot, II, 144). *Cf.* Delaborde, *op. cit.*, pp. 522, 533, and Pastor, *Gesch. d. Päpste*, III–1 (repr. 1955), 415.

[102] Sanudo, *Spedizione*, ed. R. Fulin, p. 148.

[103] Sanudo, *Spedizione*, ed. R. Fulin, pp. 172–73, 184, 190; Delaborde, *Expédition*, pp. 523–24. The weather had been very good, but Commines, *Mémoires*, bk. VII, chap. 9, ed. B. de Mandrot, II, 152, mentions the heavy snow which the French had previously encountered in Tuscany.

[104] Burchard, *Diarium*, ed. Thuasne, II, 236, and ed. Celani, I, 573–74, whose account of Charles VIII's departure differs in various details from that found in Sanudo, *Spedizione*, ed. R. Fulin, pp. 195–96; *cf.* Sa'd-ad-Dīn, in *Journal asiatique*, IX (1826, repr. 1965), 172, who despite his flights of fancy and imaginary conversations has an accurate knowledge of Jem Sultan's career and gives a generally sound chronology of events.

[105] Burchard, *Diarium*, ed. Thuasne, II, 237, and ed. Celani, I, 574. Ferrante II did in fact marry his aunt, the sixteen-year-old Joanna [IV] of Aragon, on 28 February, 1496. She was the daughter of Ferrante I and the latter's second wife, Joanna III. On these two "sad queens of Naples," see Adele Scandone, "Le Tristi Reyne di Napoli, Giovanna III e Giovanna IV d'Aragona," *Archivio storico per le province napoletane*, n.s., XIV (LIII, 1928–29), 114–55, esp. pp. 151–55, and XV (LIV, 1929), 151–205.

where the queen mother had lands. He would live there quietly. Maybe Ferrantino would have better luck than he. It was enough to have reigned a year with the anguish and affliction that he had known. With a dozen monks Alfonso had taken up residence in the Castel dell'Uovo, built on the seashore, whence he could leave when he chose. He had got together his jewels, his most beautiful tapestries, and his library, "ch'era di le belle cosse de Italia," says Sanudo, one of the best collections of the time, beautifully written manuscripts, with painted miniatures, bound by great craftsmen, in good part undoubtedly the famous library of his grandfather, Alfonso the Magnanimous. According to Sanudo, it required five galleys, a *fusta*, and two transports to carry the king's attendants, furniture and household goods, great quantities of foodstuffs, various kinds of wine, and so on. Before sailing, Alfonso addressed an encyclical to his subjects, declaring that his son had now succeeded him as king. He besought their loyal support.[106] Although the course of Alfonso's flight was soon well known, Commines relates that some people said "qu'il alloit au Turc,"[107] for his relations with Istanbul had been close ever since the French expedition had been in the offing.

Alfonso, however, was giving little thought to the Turks at this time, and his more powerful contemporaries were giving no more. Ferdinand the Catholic and the Emperor Maximilian were watching the progress of French arms in Italy with an astonishment exceeded only by their disappointment. The brilliance and the apparent prosperity of Italian social life had blinded most Europeans (and most Italians) to the likely consequences of centuries of political disunion and internecine warfare, vendettas and local hostilities, cultural differences and antipathies, and the constant dissipation of resources in extravagant display. In Italy the field of warfare had become a great chessboard on which condottieri and princelings moved their mercenaries like pawns from one position to another, although their battles were far more bloody than some historians have asserted.

The era of the city states was past, and the Italians were feeling for the first time the full impact of the new nation state, capable of putting tens of thousands of men under arms. And the mystique of kingship, always a little baffling to the Italians, somehow engendered an extraordinary loyalty to the sovereign even when he was such a puny, odd-looking figure as Charles VIII. The Italians had become afraid, and the astute Ferdinand the Catholic set himself to capitalize on their fears. Lodovico il Moro, who was actually hostile to the French and understandably apprehensive about the presence of his rival Louis of Orléans in nearby Asti, had drawn closer to the Venetians, who in their turn feared the hostility of the Emperor Maximilian as well as the possible movement of the French into the Veneto. Il Moro had also approached the Florentines and even Alexander VI, who had some reason to hold him and his brother Ascanio accountable for the French invasion of Italy. The treacherous duke of Milan was looking for an ally if he could find one, and of course the French king, who had entered the peninsula largely at his invitation, wielded the power against which he felt the need of an ally.

The Emperor Maximilian had once dreamed of conquering Venice while his French partner in the exploitation of Italy conquered Naples. As usual he had not got beyond dreaming, however, and Charles VIII was about to enter Naples. Both Lodovico il Moro and Ferdinand the Catholic were now trying to reawaken his enmity toward Charles, who was said to be

[106] Sanudo, *Spedizione*, ed. R. Fulin, pp. 193–94, who dates Alfonso II's abdication and departure on 21–22 January (1495), in which he is followed by Delaborde, p. 540: this is the correct date for the abdication (Giovan Vincenzo Fusco, *Intorno alle Zecche ed alle monete battute nel reame di Napoli da Carlo VIII di Francia*, Naples, 1846, pp. 118–19, letter dated in the Castel Nuovo on 22 January, in which Alfonso informs Luigi di Capua, count of Altavilla, of his abdication). The public decree of Alfonso's renunciation of the throne was dated 23 January; he was still in the Castel dell'Uovo on the twenty-seventh (Fusco, *op. cit.*, p. 129). He is said to have left Naples on 3 February (Scipione Volpicella, ed., *Diurnali di Giacomo Gallo e tre scritture pubbliche dell'anno 1495*, Naples, 1846, p. 8). *Cf.* Commines, *Mémoires*, bk. VII, chap. 14, ed. B. de Mandrot, II, 184–85; Sigismondo de' Conti, II, 104; *Diario ferrarese*, in *RISS*, XXIV-7 (1933), pp. 138–39; Segre, "Lodovico Sforza . . . ," *Arch. stor. lombardo*, 3rd ser., XX (ann. XXX, 1903), 67–68. Alfonso II died in Mazara on 18 November, 1495, still professing a great piety, but also eyeing the possibility of return to power. It is said that in his coffers were found some 200,000 ducats, which were turned over to Ferrantino (*cf.* Thuasne, *Djem-Sultan*, p. 357, note 4, with refs.). He was buried in Messina. The queen mother of Naples was Joanna, sister of Ferdinand the Catholic; she had married Ferrante I in 1476 (after the death of his wife Isabella di Chiaramonte). On the library, which Sanudo regarded as "one of the finest things in Italy," see Tammaro de Marinis, *La Biblioteca napoletana dei re d'Aragona*, 4 vols., Milan, 1947–52, esp. I, 97 ff., 195–204, on the dispersal of the books after Alfonso II's death.

[107] Commines, *Mémoires*, bk. VII, chap. 14, ed. B. de Mandrot, II, 184, and *cf.* J. de la Pilorgerie, *Campagne et bulletins*, p. 453.

aspiring to the imperial honors of Byzantium. Nevertheless, Maximilian remained much attached to the crusade. His French adviser Peraudi was always urging him to maintain his entente with Charles VIII, who might still embark on the crusade if an alliance of his western enemies were not formed to deflect him from that lofty ambition, the ideal of Peraudi's own life. And now, in January, 1495, an imperial embassy in Venice tried to reach an agreement with the Signoria to allow the unimpeded passage of Maximilian and an army during the coming Easter season, so that Maximilian, king of Romans, might proceed to Rome for the imperial coronation and even, if necessary, to drive the French from Italy. Maximilian assured the Venetians that he would never reach an accord with Charles VIII against the Serenissima, which had previously been one of his main diplomatic objectives.[108]

Very likely the influence of Ferdinand the Catholic had been the decisive force in Maximilian's change of policy. Ferdinand was trying to arrange an anti-French league to include both Maximilian and Henry VII of England, no easy task since the two were at odds. At least the Venetians were interested, and Maximilian had been persuaded to abate his hostility toward them. Ferdinand (and Isabella of course) had sent envoys to Italy who arrived in Rome shortly after Charles VIII had left for Marino. They caught up with him along the way, presenting their letters of credence to him on horseback. They told him bluntly that he must abandon his march to Naples or the king and queen of Spain would declare war on him, threatening that Ferdinand would begin hostilities immediately. Charles calmly told the envoys to follow him to Marino and thence to Velletri, where he would give them his answer. There were Spanish envoys everywhere at this time—in Rome, Venice, and Naples, Portugal, England, and Germany. Maximilian was at Worms in January. The Spanish ambassador to Venice was a close friend of Marino Sanudo, who learned much from him of Ferdinand's diplomatic efforts to halt the southward drive of the French.[109]

Charles VIII spent the night of 28 January at Marino and arrived the next day at Velletri. Here and at Valmontone he received the Spanish envoys again, adeptly parrying their complaints. As for Naples, he said it belonged to him. The envoys replied that the kingdom had been acquired *per forza* by Ferdinand's uncle Don Alfonso (the Magnanimous); if the claims of Alfonso II and Ferrantino were to be set aside, obviously those of Ferdinand himself came to the fore. The envoys said, however, that if Charles believed he had a right to Naples, a just adjudication of the conflicting claims was always possible. But by whom? By the pope, they said, *come capo di la Christianità*. Charles was having none of Alexander VI's judgments.[110] Indeed, he believed that he had already seen more than enough evidence of Alexander VI's treachery.

Charles VIII had directed Cesare Borgia to precede him into Velletri while he consulted with his advisers and got ready to go hunting. Cesare used the opportunity well. He was hardly lodged in the municipal palace before he began putting into effect his intention of escaping from the clutches of the French. Sanudo says that Cesare knew the commander of the local garrison. Ascanio Landi, the contemporary historian of Velletri, states that Cesare was aided by (among others) one Pietro Sorio Borgia, presumably a relative, who conducted him outside the walls by certain secret exits while French soldiers guarded the gates and fortifications. Charles learned of Cesare's flight in the early afternoon of his second day at Velletri; believing that various inhabitants of the town had been privy to the event, he ordered that Velletri should be sacked and burned the following morning. Cardinal Giuliano della Rovere, however, who was bishop of Ostia and Velletri, interceded for the terrified officials and inhabitants, and Charles rescinded the orders and spared the town.[111] Cesare had fled disguised as a groom or lackey. He was believed to have gone to Spoleto, but Burchard

---

[108] Ulmann, *Kaiser Maximilian I.*, I (1884), 271–79; Delaborde, *Expédition*, pp. 527–35, 538–39; and *cf.* Sanudo, *Spedizione*, ed. R. Fulin, pp. 201–2.

[109] Sanudo, *Spedizione*, ed. R. Fulin, pp. 196, 198 ff.

[110] Sanudo, *Spedizione*, ed. R. Fulin, pp. 204–5: Charles VIII said that he would recognize only the verdict of the Parlement de Paris on the justice of his claim to Naples. *Cf.* Gerónimo Zurita, *Anales de Aragón*, V: *Historia del Rey Don Hernando* (Saragossa, 1670), fols. 54–55^r; Delaborde, *Expédition*, pp. 542–43, 544–45; Thuasne, *Djem-Sultan*, pp. 358–59, and append. no. 23, pp. 447–48, a dispatch of the Florentine envoys from Velletri on 31 January, 1495; Pastor, *Gesch. d. Päpste*, III-1 (repr. 1955), 416.

[111] Sanudo, *Spedizione*, ed. R. Fulin, pp. 197–98; Sigismondo de' Conti, II, 101–2, and Ascanio Landi, *Memorie storiche di Velletri*, cited by the editors of Sigismondo, II, 143, note 2; Thuasne, *Djem-Sultan*, p. 359, and append., no. 23, p. 447.

reports his sleeping in Rome on the night of 30 January, in the house of Antonio Florez, auditor of the Rota and onetime nuncio to France. Alexander VI professed complete ignorance of Cesare's intention to flee and of his whereabouts, although he carefully refrained from promising Charles that he would require his son to return to the legatine mission which he had so unceremoniously abandoned. Furthermore, no cardinal was sent to accompany the French army in Cesare's place.[112]

The pope was not easy to deal with, and a return to Rome was not practicable, for the French army was moving on toward Naples. When Charles VIII learned of Cesare's flight, he observed that the Italians were a pack of rogues, and the Holy Father the worst of all.[113] He had even more reason to think so when the French detachment sent to take possession of Civitavecchia in accordance with the signed agreement of 15 January was refused admission by the papal castellan. Civitavecchia soon surrendered, however, as did Terracina, whence an Aragonese garrison was withdrawn.[114] In the meantime Charles had left Velletri for Valmontone, where he dismissed the Spanish envoys with the statement, as we have seen, of his determination to see the Neapolitan enterprise through to its just conclusion. On 5 February he left Valmontone for Castel Ferentino, and then on to Veroli; on the ninth he took by storm the castle town atop Monte S. Giovanni, whose governor had cruelly abused two French trumpeters sent to demand the surrender of the castle. All the inhabitants of Monte S. Giovanni were slain except children and a few women. The massacre served as an example, says Sanudo, to other *castelli*, and had a deadly effect on the already demoralized forces of the Neapolitans.[115]

In Naples all had been lost, including honor. Ferrantino's position was hopeless. Almost two weeks before, on 27 January (1495), he had written to his resourceful agent Camillo Pandone, then in Istanbul, to urge Sultan Bayazid to fulfill the promises of armed assistance he had made to Alfonso II. The French advanced like a torrent, and they had Jem Sultan with them, showing clearly that Charles VIII's ambition would soon extend from the Neapolitan Regno to Turkey.[116] (But poor Jem would not much longer be a pawn in western hands.) Letters reaching Venice from merchants in Istanbul (dated 19 January) bore witness to the sultan's fear of Charles VIII. The Turks were preparing extensive naval and land armaments, and had added to the fortifications of the Dardanelles, Negroponte, and Valona. Anxious to conciliate the Venetians, the sultan was said to be ready to allow the return to Istanbul of the Republic's bailie, expelled some time before. In Istanbul, Pandone, *secretario dil re Alphonso*, had appealed for aid, and the sultan had assured him that it would come in due time, *potentissimo a soccorrerlo*. Pandone held the Genoese up to opprobrium as allies of the French. Bayazid stated that he would revoke their commercial licenses (*trate*), and that they should trade no more in his dominions. He also said that he would send an expedition against Chios, which would diminish the enthusiasm of the Genoese for the king of France. Other reports sent to Venice from the bailie and captain of Corfu were to the same effect, *che Turchi erano in grandissima paura dil Re de Franza*: the Turks lived in the greatest fear of Charles VIII, and were loath to inhabit coastal sites, much preferring to dwell inland.[117]

Of Sultan Bayazid's willingness to aid Ferrantino there could be no doubt, but he preferred to employ his resources in defense of Turkish territory, and fearful as the prospect

---

[112] Burchard, *Diarium*, ed. Thuasne, II, 238, with notes, and ed. Celani, I, 575; Sanudo, *Spedizione*, ed. R. Fulin, p. 208; Delaborde, *Expédition*, pp. 543–44.

[113] Sanudo, *Spedizione*, ed. R. Fulin, p. 197: "Malvas Lombard, et lo primiero lo Santo Pare!"

[114] Sanudo, *Spedizione*, ed. R. Fulin, pp. 197–98; Thuasne, *Djem-Sultan*, pp. 360–61, and append., no. 23, p. 446.

[115] Sanudo, *Spedizione*, ed. R. Fulin, pp. 208–9; Sigismondo de'Conti, II, 103; J. de la Pilorgerie, *Campagne et bulletins*, pp. 176–77, 449, 451; Delaborde, *Expédition*, pp. 547–49; Thuasne, *Djem-Sultan*, pp. 361–62.

[116] Giovan Vincenzo Fusco, *Intorno alle Zecche ed alle monete battute nel reame di Napoli da Carlo VIII di Francia*, Naples, 1846, pp. 132–33, cited by Delaborde, *Expédition*, p. 541, and Thuasne, *Djem-Sultan*, p. 358. Ferrante's letter was composed by Giovanni Pontano. Pandone was informed that "con Re de Francza vene lo cardinale de Valencia [Cesare Borgia], figlio del Papa, et lo fratello del Gran Signore [Bayazid II], e dato impotere de Re de Francza che lo tenera in una fortecza guardato da sua gente finchè habbia obtenuta questa impresa, et poi andera contro el Gran Signore. . . . Datum Neapoli XXVII Januarii MCCCCLXXXXV. Rex Ferdinandus. . . ."

[117] Sanudo, *Spedizione*, ed. R. Fulin, pp. 221–22; *cf.* Malipiero, *Annali veneti*, in *Arch. stor. italiano*, VII-1 (1843), 146–47; Burchard, *Diarium*, ed. Thuasne, II, 242, and ed. Celani, I, 577, on the Turkish fear of Charles VIII; and note the essay of Paul Durrieu, "Valona, base d'une expédition française contre les Turcs projetée par le roi Charles VIII (1494–1495)," *Comptes rendus de l'Académie des Inscriptions et Belles-Lettres*, 1915, pp. 181–90.

might be of a French invasion of the Morea with Jem Sultan in the king's train, it had not happened yet. Meanwhile the Christians were at war with one another. The crusade-preaching papacy was paralyzed. From the sultan's standpoint things could be worse. Besides, there was no time to help Ferrantino.

The French were carrying all before them. On the night of 11–12 February (1495) it was reported that the Neapolitan forces, forty squadrons of cavalry and four thousand infantry, had withdrawn from San Germano, key to the kingdom of Naples, and were falling back on Capua. On the fourteenth Charles VIII entered San Germano, hailed in triumph by the inhabitants. Sanudo says that children dressed in white and carrying olive branches sang the *Te Deum* and repeated the verse *Benedictus qui venit in nomine Domini*. The Venetian ambassadors offered Charles the Republic's congratulations at this auspicious entry into the kingdom of Naples. Sanudo notes that the French wasted no time sleeping. They occupied one place after another without drawing their swords: "but I'll say one thing, that poor King Ferrantino had Frenchmen to the right and left of him and face-to-face!" Giovanni della Rovere, titular prefect of Rome, took over the Abruzzi, and the Colonnesi accompanied the French who seized the Terra di Lavoro. In San Germano, Charles issued an edict permitting the return of those banished by the Aragonese and restoring to all, of both high and low estate, whatever properties their families had possessed "in the time of Queen Joanna." He also proclaimed a perpetual exemption for the inhabitants of San Germano of the 1,500 ducats which they had paid as an annual tax to the Crown of Naples. The bandy-legged little conqueror was the very spirit of generosity, granting the remission of other obligations, and in San Germano as well as in other places he abolished various corvées (*angarie*) and scattered privileges of immunity.[118]

Still allegedly planning a crusade against the Turk, Charles VIII employed Martino Albari, the Albanian archbishop of Durazzo, as well as the regent Constantine Arianiti of Montferrat, whose name recalls his Albanian ancestry. (Constantine claimed Macedonia and Thessaly.) These worthies were to stir up rebellion along the coast from Valona to Istanbul, for as the French army advanced into the Regno, it was getting closer to Turkey. Commines observes in his *Mémoires* that from Otranto to Valona was only about sixty miles, and any merchant would tell you that from Valona to Istanbul was a journey of but eighteen days. There was hardly a good stronghold along the way, which passed through lands inhabited by Albanians, Slavs, and Greeks, none of whom was enamored of the Turk.[119] But the archbishop of Durazzo was more given to talk than to action, according to Commines, and his plans for raising thirty thousand Albanians to revolt against the Porte had no further result than to cause trouble for those who responded to his machinations.

While the archbishop tarried in Venice, his plans were cut short by the sudden death of Jem Sultan on 25 February. The news was known in Venice on 4 March, and two days later the Council of Ten dispatched an envoy to Istanbul to take the glad tidings to Sultan Bayazid and to disclaim all responsibility for the uprisings in Albania. On the seventh the Venetians arrested the archbishop of Durazzo. With Jem dead, they did not believe there was going to be a crusade, and obviously they did not wish to embroil themselves with the Gran Turco.[120]

As the southward march of the French became a promenade of victory, and one place after another surrendered to them, Ferrantino and the Aragonese royal family fled to the island of

[118] Sanudo, *Spedizione*, ed. R. Fulin, pp. 215–16. San Germano, scene of the well-known peace of 23 July, 1230, between Frederick II and Pope Gregory IX, is now called Cassino. The town (largely destroyed in 1944), like the abbey which looms above it, has been entirely rebuilt.

[119] Commines, *Mémoires*, bk. VII, chap. 17, ed. B. de Mandrot, II, 202–5; Lamansky, *Secrets d'état de Venise*, pp. 292–93. On Constantine Arianiti, see Fr. Babinger, *Das Ende der Arianiten*, Munich, 1960, pp. 36 ff., esp. pp. 43–45, who gives the name of the Albanian archbishop of Durazzo as Albari (*ibid.*, p. 43). He appears as Firmani in Eubel, II, 148, and as Albari in Sanudo.

[120] Malipiero, *Annali veneti*, in *Arch. stor. italiano*, VII-1 (1843), 146; Thuasne, *Djem-Sultan*, pp. 362–64, 366, 376, and append., no. 25, pp. 451–52; Sigismondo de'Conti, II, 111–12; Sanudo, *Spedizione*, ed. R. Fulin, pp. 254–55; Lamansky, *Secrets d'état*, pp. 294–95. According to Malipiero, *loc. cit.*, "A'4 de marzo, se hebbe aviso della morte de Gen Sultan per via de Catharo" [Cattaro, Kotor]! The news of Jem Sultan's death was indeed known in Venice on 4 March, but it came directly from the Republic's envoys accredited to Charles VIII: "Acceptis hodie litteris oratorum nostrorum apud Christianissimam Maiestatem diei XXV mensis preteriti ex Neapoli facti sumus certiores illo mane dominum Giemsultanum fratrem domini Turci ex quodam descensu reumatis diem clausisse supremum" (Sen. Secreta, Reg. 35, fol. 70^r [82^r], doc. dated 4 March, 1495).

Ischia.[121] Charles VIII entered Naples in triumph on 22 February (1495).[122] On Wednesday, the twenty-fifth, as we have just noted, Jem Sultan died in Naples in the Castel Capuano: "His death was a very great loss to the king of France as to all Italy," says Sanudo, "and especially to the pope, for it deprived him of the 40,000 ducats of gold which he received every year from his brother [the sultan] by reason of having custody of him."[123] The French accused Alexander VI of having poisoned Jem. Sanudo knew of the charge, and declared it false out of hand. Jem may well have succumbed to pneumonia. Charles VIII was much distressed by this unexpected development. He did not, however, immediately give up his often announced intention of attacking the Turks. Raymond Peraudi did not abate his efforts to make Charles persevere in these plans, although everyone knew that Jem's death was an irremediable loss. For more than a dozen years all discussion of the crusade had revolved around the part that Jem would play in a European expedition against Sultan Bayazid.

The French expedition into Italy had been a startling success. Charles VIII had conquered the kingdom of Naples almost without striking a blow. Sigismondo de' Conti pauses in his narrative to observe, "I have no doubt but what these events will seem to posterity not like facts, but fiction." He also notes that, after the death of Jem Sultan, Charles "seemed to have abandoned all thought of a war against the Turks."[124] Charles knew that a league of the great powers was being formed against him; at first he took the prospect lightly, or at least his followers appear to have done so. Burchard dryly relates a report reaching Rome to the effect that on 15 March "the Castel dell'Uovo in Naples was surrendered to the king of France, and his people performed before the king in sportive and derisive fashion, *more gallico*, tragedies or comedies representing the pope, the king of the Romans, the Spanish sovereigns, the doge of Venice, and the duke of Milan entering into their league and confederation."[125] If the performances were entertaining, they may also have been instructive, for such a league was indeed being formed by precisely the august personages whom Burchard mentions.[126]

---

[121] Sanudo, *Spedizione*, ed. R. Fulin, pp. 229, 234, and *cf.* Burchard, *Diarium*, ed. Thuasne, II, 241, and ed. Celani, I, 576–77; Commines, *Mémoires*, bk. VII, chap. 16, ed. B. de Mandrot, II, 194; Delaborde, *Expédition de Charles VIII*, p. 559.

[122] Sanudo, *Spedizione*, ed. R. Fulin, pp. 230–35; Burchard, *Diarium*, ed. Thuasne, II, 242, and ed. Celani, I, 577; *Diario ferrarese*, in *RISS*, XXIV-7 (1933), pp. 141–42; J. de la Pilorgerie, *Campagne et bulletins*, pp. 192–203; Delaborde, *Expédition*, pp. 552–56; P. Pélicier, ed., *Lettres de Charles VIII, roi de France*, 5 vols., Paris, 1898–1905, IV, 176; Segre, "Lodovico Sforza . . . ," *Arch. stor. lombardo*, 3rd ser., XX (ann. XXX, 1903), 74–77.

[123] Sanudo, *Spedizione*, ed. R. Fulin, pp. 243–44; Burchard, *Diarium*, ed. Thuasne, II, 242, with Thuasne's note as to whether or not Jem Sultan was poisoned [which seems unlikely], and especially his *Djem-Sultan*, pp. 364–75. *Cf.* Commines, *Mémoires*, bk. VII, chap. 17, ed. B. de Mandrot, II, 202; Malipiero, *Annali veneti*, in *Arch. stor. italiano*, VII-1 (1843), 145; Sigismondo de' Conti, II, 111–12, who notes that many people thought Alexander VI had poisoned Jem; and Segre, "Lodovico Sforza . . . ," *Arch. stor. lombardo*, 3rd ser., XX (ann. XXX, 1903), 375–76. Both Paolo Giovio and Guicciardini allege that Alexander had poisoned Jem, and of course the charge was to be irresponsibly repeated by various later historians. Sa'd-ad-Dīn, "Aventures du prince Gem," *Journal asiatique*, IX (1826, repr. 1965), 172–73, also holds the pope responsible for the death of Jem, whose body (he says) was sent to Istanbul and buried at Adrianople (*ibid.*, p. 174). Pastor, *Gesch. d. Päpste*, III-1 (repr. 1955), 419, had no doubt that Jem died of natural causes. Jem ate too much, drank too much, and was generally debauched. As Giorgio Brognolo, the Mantuan envoy in Rome, wrote Francesco Gonzaga on 3 March (1495), ". . . credo di sua morte, benche molti dicano che li sia stato dato da bevere: queste hè vero che l'era disordenatissimo de ogni cosa" (quoted by Pastor), i.e., Jem was most intemperate in everything. Pfeffermann, who holds no brief for the popes, does not believe that Jem was poisoned (*Die Zusammenarbeit der Renaissancepäpste mit den Türken* [1946], p. 114), although Kissling, *Sultan Bâjezîd's II. Beziehungen zu Markgraf Francesco II. von Gonzaga* (1965), esp. pp. 35–36, 43, seems to think on very slender evidence that Gonzaga was probably involved in a Turkish plot to murder Jem, and that the pope was a party to the "Zusammenspiel." Contrary to the statement in the French translation of Sa'd-ad-Dīn, Jem was buried in Brusa (Bursa), near the grave of his grandfather Murad II (Kissling, *op. cit.*, p. 49).

[124] Sigismondo de' Conti, II, 109, 111.

[125] Burchard, *Diarium*, ed. Thuasne, II, 246, whose text is clearly defective, and ed. Celani, I, 580, whom I follow.

[126] Segre, "Lodovico Sforza . . . ," *Arch. stor. lombardo*, 3rd ser., XX (ann. XXX, 1903), 89–107, 370 ff.

16. THE FRENCH IN NAPLES, THE LEAGUE OF VENICE, AND PAPAL PROBLEMS (1495–1498)

ALTHOUGH King Charles VIII's entry into Naples did not mean the immediate end of hostilities, the Castel Nuovo was surrendered by the Aragonese commanders on 7 March, 1495. A week or more later the French entered the Castel dell'Uovo, the last of the Neapolitan fortresses to hold out. Gaeta was given up on the twenty-fifth or the twenty-seventh. Taranto, Otranto, Gallipoli, and other distant towns sent envoys to negotiate the terms of their surrender. But the fleur-de-lys did not appear over every fortress; the faithful Camillo Pandone held Brindisi for Ferrante II. The Neapolitans, however, were said to have welcomed Charles as a liberator. On 28 March the king wrote the duke of Bourbon that he had brought his new subjects relief from a mass of charges and special exactions totaling some 260,000 ducats a year.[1]

By 5 March Charles had already confirmed the articles of petition (*capitoli*) which the representatives of Naples had presented to him at Poggio Reale, guaranteeing the privileges and properties of the clergy, baronage, and people. He approved the continued bondage of all slaves, *tanto bianchi como nigri*, domestic slavery being still a common institution in Italy. Although feudal lands were restored to the families which had held them "al tempo di la rayna Zuanna," as Sanudo says, a general amnesty was granted to those who had served the ill-fated house of Aragon. Charles planned to reform the administration of justice by the importation of French jurists and magistrates. Reform was undoubtedly necessary, even though this was not the way to achieve it. Charles granted so many of the requests made to him that a Neapolitan who returned to France with him is alleged to have observed that it was a good thing his Majesty was not a woman since he had never learned how to say no.[2] The French commanders were, to be sure,

---

[1] Marin[o] Sanudo, *La Spedizione di Carlo VIII in Italia*, ed. R. Fulin, Venice, 1873, pp. 258, 262, 265–66, 291–92; J. de la Pilorgerie, *Campagne et bulletins de la grande armée d'Italie commandée par Charles VIII (1494–1495)*, Nantes and Paris, 1866, pp. 207–9, 213–14, 221; Burchard, *Diarium*, ed. Thuasne, II, 245, 246, 247–48, and *Liber notarum* (same as preceding, in *RISS*, XXXII, pt. 1), ed. E. Celani, I (1907–10), 579, 580–81; Malipiero, *Annali veneti*, in *Arch. stor. italiano*, VII-1 (1843), 344; H.-F. Delaborde, *L'Expédition de Charles VIII en Italie*, Paris, 1888, pp. 560–66, 570. Camillo Pandone was soon killed in a skirmish at Misagne, about eight miles from Brindisi (Sanudo, *op. cit.*, p. 316).

Pierre II, duke of Bourbon (1488–1503), was the husband of Louis XI's daughter Anne, and regent of France during Charles VIII's absence from the kingdom. His daughter Suzanne later married (in 1505) Charles, also de Bourbon, count of Montpensier, son of Gilbert and Chiara Gonzaga. Gilbert de Montpensier played a prominent part in the French invasion of Italy, dying at Pozzuoli on 11 November, 1496; his more famous son, Charles, constable of France (from 1515), was to lose his life at the sack of Rome in 1527 (Benvenuto Cellini, as is well known, claimed to have fired the shot which killed him). On the date of Gilbert's death, *cf.* Burchard, *Diarium*, ed. Thuasne, II, 339, and ed. Celani, I, 648.

Charles VIII's expedition was, throughout its entire course, complicated by the family relationships of those on both sides of the contest. Thus Chiara Gonzaga, the wife of Charles's commander Montpensier, was the sister of [Gian] Francesco Gonzaga, marquis of Mantua and husband of Isabella d'Este. The latter was the sister of Beatrice d'Este, the young wife of Lodovico il Moro. The d'Este sisters were nieces of Alfonso II of Naples, their mother Eleonora's brother. Francesco Gonzaga had been in the employ of the Venetians for the past four years. His brothers-in-law, Montpensier and il Moro, were pulling at him from different directions, but Gonzaga preferred to serve the Venetians rather than the French. On 23 February (1495) his *condotta* as commander of the Republic's land forces was renewed, at the considerable sum of 44,000 ducats a year for five years, although the Signoria withheld the title of captain-general or "governor-general" from him for some time (Arturo Segre, "Lodovico Sforza, detto il Moro, e la Repubblica di Venezia dall'autunno 1494 alla primavera 1495," *Archivio storico lombardo*, 3rd ser., XX [XXX, 1903], 379–84). Gonzaga would command the Venetian troops, as we shall see shortly, when the forces of the anti-French league sought to cripple or destroy Charles VIII's army at Fornovo, as most of the French were trying to withdraw from the peninsula in early July, 1495.

[2] Sanudo, *Spedizione*, ed. R. Fulin, pp. 260–61; J. de la Pilorgerie, p. 215; Delaborde, pp. 566–68; A.-M. de Boislisle, "Notice . . . sur Étienne de Vesc," *Annuaire-Bulletin de la Société de l'histoire de France*, Paris, 1881, pp. 275 ff., on the French administration of Naples; and Michele Rizzio (Ris), in Boislisle, *Étienne de Vesc, sénéchal de Beaucaire*, Paris, 1884 [reprint of the preceding with additions], p. 260: "Nichil umquam profecto petentibus [rex] negavit, ita quod semel joci causa, secum ayebam valde michi suspectam fuisse ipsius pudiciciam, si feminam esse contigisset, ex benigna consuetudine sua quibuscumque petentibus an-

awarded fiefs, and Alexander VI's son Gioffredo, who had fled to Ischia, lost the principality of Squillace to Philippe de Bresse. Lodovico il Moro was regranted the duchy of Bari (whence he had drawn his ducal title until he had acquired that of Milan) as well as the county of Rossano, both of which the Aragonese had confiscated. The French had not yet occupied Bari, however, and il Moro was kept in continual fear by the nearby presence at Asti of Louis d'Orléans, who was quite prepared to claim Bari as well as Milan.[3] Charles rewarded the della Rovere and the Colonnesi with rich grants, retaining for himself only Naples and a dozen other places (*terre*).[4]

The humanist Giovanni Gioviano Pontano, who had served the Aragonese for years with loyalty and distinction, did not join the flight to Ischia, and soon received preferment from the king. As in the old days of Charles of Anjou, French barons were placed in the chief offices of state. Seduced by the easiness of victory, the mildness of the climate, the abundance of spoils, and the enjoyment of *la dolce vita*, the French succumbed to idleness and gambling, sparkling wines and debauchery. They began dressing in silk rather than wool. Discipline was relaxed. The citizen's daughter was no safer than the merchant's goods, as the French respected neither persons nor property.[5] Prostitutes did a thriving business. Syphilis suddenly achieved historical recognition as the *morbo gallico* or *mal de Naples*.

As the Neapolitans got to know the French, their initial enthusiasm for them vanished. Delaborde charges Sanudo with slandering his countrymen.[6] It is possible, but armies of "liberation" have not been noted for the delicacy with which they have treated those whom they have freed from the "tyranny" of other regimes. On 6 March Charles had informed the citizens of Naples that he had not been brought to their city by any base desire for gain "nè per usurpar cosa alcuna, ma per beneficio et augumento universal, *per liberar questo regno de tyrannide!* . . ."[7] The history of our own times has made it quite clear that most peoples do not like to be occupied by their "liberators." There was a reaction against the French, probably intensified by rumors of a grand alliance being formed against them. Certainly to remain long in Naples they needed more money and more troops than they had.

Charles VIII's presence was required in France, but when would he return and by what route? Piero de' Medici wanted him to go back by way of Florence and in the process to restore Medici rule over the city. The della Rovere wished him to include Rome on his homeward march in order to effect the deposition of Alexander VI. Others advocated a return by way of Milan or Genoa or by sea to the Bouches-du-Rhône. But Raymond Peraudi, the cardinal of Gurk, did his best to persuade Charles to undertake an expedition against the Turks. Peraudi sent letters to Venice which were read in the Senate, requesting the government to direct the Republic's envoys in Naples to urge Charles "to such an enterprise against the infidels." Sanudo informs us that Peraudi was now badly off financially. Alexander VI was unwilling to allow him the annual grant of 1,000 ducats customarily made to all cardinals from the Camera Apostolica, "because he did not reside in Rome." The Venetians had no intention of encouraging Charles to go on the crusade, as Sanudo frankly acknowledges, "because of the good peace we had with the Signor Turco."[8]

The Venetians in fact did not want Charles in Turkey any more than they wanted him in Italy. Their envoys in Naples had written the home government, shortly after the French entry into the city, of a rumor in the king's camp to the effect that Charles wanted to return to France as soon as he had secured the kingdom "et poi seguir el suo voler contra infedeli."[9] Charles continued to talk about an attack upon the Turks, and refused to allow the transfer of Jem Sultan's body to Istanbul, where the absolute certainty of Jem's death

nuendi." (Boislisle, *ibid.*, p. 258, quite rightly comments on the deficiency of Rizzio's Latinity.) In mid-April, 1505, Michele Rizzio (also Riccio) was a member of the French embassy of obedience sent by Louis XII to Pope Julius II (P. Villari, ed., *Dispacci di Antonio Giustinian*, III [Florence, 1876], 485, and Burchard, *Diarium*, ed. Thuasne, III, 385, and ed. Celani, II, 477–78). Michele had a distinguished career in France. He died in Paris in 1515 (Celani, II, 477, note 5). *Cf.* Sanudo, *Diarii*, VI, 156.

[3] Sanudo, *Spedizione*, ed. R. Fulin, pp. 246, 249. Gioffredo had accompanied Ferrante II to Naples (*ibid.*, p. 234). On the French occupation of Bari, *cf.*, *ibid.*, p. 332.

[4] Sanudo, *Spedizione*, ed. R. Fulin, p. 261.

[5] Sanudo, *op. cit.*, pp. 236–41, 250, 267, 291, 340, and esp. pp. 344–45; Sigismondo de' Conti, II, 112–13.

[6] Delaborde, *Expédition de Charles VIII* (1888), p. 575.

[7] Sanudo, *Spedizione*, ed. R. Fulin, p. 248.

[8] Sanudo, *Spedizione*, ed. R. Fulin, pp. 265, 267.

[9] Sanudo, *op cit.*, p. 231.

would strengthen Sultan Bayazid's position. Bayazid was reported to be preparing a great armada of some two hundred sail. Delighted by the news of his brother's death, he had accorded a Venetian envoy a most cordial reception, speaking happily of the "bona paxe" between the Porte and the Signoria. When some of the pashas asked why the Venetians were also building up a large armada and recruiting *stradioti*, the envoy remarked that when one's neighbor's house is on fire, it is well to have a supply of water on hand.[10]

The Neapolitan house was on fire, and the conflagration threatened to spread. Charles VIII had issued orders that all naval caulkers and joiners in the southern kingdom should come to Naples, "because he wanted to have trees cut down and to prepare other things in order to build a very large fleet," says Sanudo, who also notes that the Genoese were preparing ten galleys for the French king. When the Venetian envoys in Naples informed Charles of the Turkish fleet in the making, he replied laconically that he would be ready for any eventuality. By now Charles had come to distrust the intentions of the Venetians, and rarely granted their envoys an audience.[11]

If there were political fires aglow in Italy, they were lighting a gloomy sky. There was so much rain in Venice in March, 1495, that it seemed more like the advent of winter than summer. On the twenty-seventh it snowed. Foreign relations reflected the weather. Diplomats discussed the anti-French league in quiet corners; Alexander VI was very fearful of announcing his adherence to it. The king of France was too close at hand, and Rome would probably be his first objective if the pope came out against him. The Curia Romana was said to be considering a possible flight to Ancona. Alexander was loath to leave Rome, however, and asked the Venetians and Lodovico il Moro for five hundred light horse and a thousand infantry for the greater protection of the city "and especially of his own person." He thought it best not to leave the city, because too many cardinals would not have followed him; the temptation to declare his deposition and elect another in his stead would probably have been too great for them to resist. Indeed Sanudo states that they wanted nothing better than such an opportunity.[12] Alexander now added to the fortifications of S. Angelo. The ditches surrounding the castle were excavated, and "mosaics, pieces of porphyry and serpentine, ancient coins and other beautiful things" were uncovered by the diggers. The Tiber was diverted into the ditches, and made to flow around the castle. The pope and Ascanio Sforza, vice-chancellor of the Church, were reconciled. The latter returned to Rome in March, telling the pope that they should "let bygones be bygones: let us start over again" (*recedant vetera, nova sint omnia*). Venetian diplomats had helped to bring them together. Thereafter Ascanio was often closeted with the pope, and discussed with him their current problems, "especially the league which was being devised at Venice, which was much desired by his brother, the duke of Milan, for fear lest he should lose his state."[13]

In Venice in the meantime the French ambassador Philippe de Commines, the sire d'Argenton, was generally aware of what was transpiring as he witnessed the arrival of envoys sent by Maximilian, Ferdinand of Aragon, and Lodovico il Moro, but he could learn no details of the projected alliance. The envoys' secretaries, who could come and go easily, began the discussions secretly and at night, says Commines, for the Venetians and the duke of Milan could risk no public exposure of their machinations until they could be certain of the final conclusion of the anti-French league. The Milanese envoys, professing ignorance of what was going on, had the effrontery to ask Commines whether he could tell them the purpose of the Spanish and German embassies. When Commines remonstrated with the Signoria concerning the rumors he had heard with respect to the league, the doge told him that he ought not to believe what was being said about town:

[10] Sanudo, *op. cit.*, pp. 348–50, and *cf.* pp. 351, 360.

[11] Sanudo, *op. cit.*, p. 259.

[12] Sanudo, *op. cit.*, pp. 276–77, and *cf.* pp. 326–27. There were always those who like Savonarola and Pietro Dolfin, general of the Camaldolesi, might have seen in the deposition of Alexander VI the first great act of that reform which the Frateschi expected of Charles VIII (*cf.* G. Soranzo, *Il Tempo di Alessandro VI Papa e di Fra Girolamo Savonarola*, Milan, 1960, pp. 18–30 and ff.). Dolfin, however, soon came to believe that Savonarola was going too far in his attacks upon the pope and the Curia.

[13] Sanudo, *op. cit.*, pp. 256–57, 337; Burchard, *Diarium*, ed. Thuasne, II, 244, and ed. Celani (in *RISS*, XXXII-1), I, 578; Sen. Secreta, Reg. 35, fols. 72^v–73^r [84^v–85^r by modern enumeration], letter of the Senate to the Venetian envoy in Milan, dated 11 March, 1495.

there was freedom of speech in Venice, and anyone could say what he wished. The Republic, Commines was informed, had never contemplated a league against the king of France. The Venetians wanted a league formed between the king of France and the kings of Spain and Germany, together with the Italian states, "and that it should be directed against the Turk." They complained to Commines, however, of the way in which Charles VIII continued to hold papal and Florentine possessions, particularly Pisa, for had not Charles often stated that all he wanted in Italy was the Neapolitan kingdom and a basis for operations against Turkey? Yet at that hour he seemed to be anxious to seize whatever he could in Italy and to be making no demands upon the Turk at all. The Venetians also noted the threat which the duke of Orléans and his followers in nearby Asti posed for Lodovico il Moro and the Milanese. But they promised Commines they would take no diplomatic or other action until he could communicate with Charles VIII and receive a reply concerning French intentions. "De tout advertiz le Roy," says Commines, "et euz mesgre responce."[14]

On his way back to Naples from a mission to Florence in search of funds, Guillaume Briçonnet, the new cardinal of S. Malo, stopped off at Rome to confer with Alexander VI. Like everyone else engaged in Italian politics at a high level, Briçonnet knew that the anti-French league was being discussed by those who feared the consequences of Charles VIII's astonishing success. But Briçonnet learned nothing from Alexander.[15] Less than three weeks after Briçonnet's departure for Naples, François de Bourbon, the count of S. Pol, came to Rome on a formal embassy from Charles to request again the Neapolitan investiture and coronation. S. Pol arrived on 28 March. He claimed that the king was ready to go on the much-heralded crusade against Sultan Bayazid, and requested the pope to exhort the Italian powers to assist his expedition. Charles asked that a cardinal be sent to Naples to place the crown upon his head, as had been promised. Otherwise he might find it necessary to receive the crown in Rome. (Charles had already indicated that he would like to spend Holy Week in Rome, where he wanted to celebrate Easter.) S. Pol had let it be known that, although the king was well aware of the negotiations in progress at Venice, he was certain his Holiness would do nothing detrimental to the king's interests.

The pope replied that his response would have to be determined after a consistory. According to Sanudo, he immediately sought Venetian and Milanese advice as to what that response should be. S. Pol was so insistent upon an answer that the pope summoned a consistory on the twenty-ninth. The pro-French cardinals were in favor of acceding to the king's requests, but there was some objection to the investiture and coronation, since Ferrante II was still within the boundaries of the Neapolitan realm. Everyone, including the pope, professed joy in the king's victory, and praised his announced intention of going on the crusade: "et zerca a l'andar contra infedeli," the pope told S. Pol, "metteremo ogni nostra forza." As for the investiture and the coronation, the pope needed to know more precisely the terms upon which the king made his request. There were of course various political problems as well as facts of canon law to be considered. The pope was well disposed toward his Majesty. S. Pol might write to the king, and say that the pope would oblige him. There was no need, however, of his coming to Rome and indeed, if he did, he might not find the Curia in the city. Alexander acknowledged that he was being urged to join a league being formed by the chief powers in Christendom, *da li primi potenti dil mondo*, and again requested that the body of Jem Sultan be sent to him.[16]

During these weeks Rome was marked by disorders. The vagaries of papal policy were reflected in the streets and public squares. On 1 April (1495) some Swiss mercenaries on their

[14] Commines, *Mémoires*, bk. VII, chap. 19, ed. B. de Mandrot, II, 215–20. Full details of Commines' mission to Venice in 1494–1495 may be found in Kervyn de Lettenhove, *Lettres et négociations de Philippe de Commines*, II (Brussels, 1868), 104 ff., esp. pp. 162 ff. (Académie Royale de Belgique).

[15] Sanudo, *Spedizione*, ed. R. Fulin, pp. 257, 262–63; Burchard, *Diarium*, ed. Thuasne, II, 244, and ed. Celani, I, 578. On 15 March (1495) Briçonnet, having just returned to Naples from Florence and Rome, informed the Venetian envoy Paolo [Domenico?] Trevisan that he knew of the league being formed in Venice, and that "mons. di Arzenton [Commines] etiam ha scritto al Roy ch'è una fama in Rialto di questa liga" (Sanudo, *Spedizione*, ed. R. Fulin, pp. 262–63). Of course Trevisan denied all knowledge of it. Sanudo has described Commines' audience with the Venetian Signoria (*ibid.*, p. 271).

[16] Sanudo, *Spedizione*, ed. R. Fulin, pp. 263, 277–79; Burchard, *Diarium*, ed. Thuasne, II, 248, and ed. Celani, I, 581; and *cf.* Segre, "Lodovico Sforza . . . ," *Arch. stor. lombardo*, 3rd ser., XX (XXX, 1903), 401–3, 406.

way home were attacked by the pope's Spanish guard. About sixteen of them were killed, a woman also. Numerous Swiss were robbed of their possessions, allegedly by order of Cesare Borgia, who was now showing himself openly in the city, obviously contemptuous of French opinion. Rumor had it that Cesare was retaliating against the Swiss because, when Charles VIII was in Rome, some of the mercenaries had seized 800 ducats and various other valuables belonging to his mother Vannozza.[17] Despite the unrest and the anti-French sentiment in the Curia Romana, the count of S. Pol was probably not entirely prepared for what followed. On 29 March, however, the day after his arrival in Rome, he had watched the pope bless the golden rose which, it was announced, was being sent to the doge of Venice.[18] He realized that such a public demonstration of the pope's attachment to the Republic boded ill for the king of France.

Alexander VI had no further need to dissemble or to spare the sensibilities of the French envoy. The formal instrument of a "Holy League" was signed in Venice on 31 March in the chamber of the ailing doge, Agostino Barbarigo. The envoys of the high contracting parties had worked until the second hour of the night (about 9:00 P.M.) to give the final touches to the text and to supervise the preparation of five official copies of the document: "Von diesem Mächtebund," says Gregorovius, "datiert die Geschichte des neuen Europa."[19] Formation of the league was announced in Rome on Saturday, 4 April, "pro communi Christianorum beneficio et cura ac totius Italie quiete."[20] It was supposed to last for twenty-five years, and included five major "Italian" powers—the pope, the duke of Milan, and the doge of Venice, as well as Maximilian, king of the Romans, who possessed certain historic rights in the peninsula, and Ferdinand and Isabella, who exercised sovereignty over Sicily and Sardinia. The objectives of the league were said to be the preservation of peace in Italy, the success of the faith, the guarantee of papal and imperial rights, and the protection of the contracting parties against aggressors, including those then holding states in the peninsula. Each member of the league was to furnish 8,000 horse and 4,000 foot in the event of need although the pope was to furnish a contingent only half as large as his confederates on whose behalf he would employ his spiritual weapons. Money or ships might be substituted for troops. Other powers would be admitted into the league on the same terms. Maximilian was to be allowed free passage to Rome for his coronation, the Venetians and Milanese agreeing to furnish him "going and coming" with an escort of four hundred men-at-arms, which meant in fact a cavalcade of 3,200 horse.[21]

Meanwhile, on 1 April, the doge had summoned Commines, who was lodged on the Isola S. Giorgio Maggiore. The doge informed him of the league, protesting the greatest good will toward Charles VIII. Even as the doge spoke, the bells of S. Marco pealed "in segno de grande alegreza." Sanudo says that Commines was astonished at the news, but stated that he had for some time suspected what was going on, although he had never really believed that such

[17] Burchard, *Diarium*, ed. Thuasne, II, 248–49, and ed. Celani, I, 582; *cf.* Sanudo, *Spedizione*, ed. R. Fulin, p. 292.

[18] Burchard, *Diarium*, ed. Thuasne, II, 248, and ed. Celani, I, 581; Sanudo, *Spedizione*, ed. R. Fulin, pp. 279–82; Malipiero, *Annali veneti*, in *Arch. stor. italiano*, VII-1 (1843), 334–36. Occasionally events are given slightly different dates in Sanudo and Burchard: for facts relating to the papal court I usually follow the latter, who was an eyewitness and participant in most of the events he describes.

[19] F. Gregorovius, *Gesch. d. Stadt Rom im Mittelalter*, 2nd ed., VII (Stuttgart, 1873), 378, trans. Annie Hamilton, from 4th ed., VII, pt. 1 (London, 1900), 395. The Venetian archival text of the "articles of the league" (*capitula ligae*), dated 28 March, 1495, may be found in the Sen. Secreta, Reg. 35, fols. 77^v–79^r [89^v–91^r]. The Senate rejoiced in the union of papacy and empire, *coniunctis duobus gladiis*, against the ambition of the French king (*ibid.*, fols. 81^v–82^r [93^v–94^r]).

[20] Burchard, *Diarium*, ed. Thuasne, II, 250, and ed. Celani, I, 583; *cf.* Sanudo, *Spedizione*, ed. R. Fulin, p. 288.

[21] Sanudo, *Spedizione*, ed. R. Fulin, pp. 256, 257–58, 270–71, 277, and esp. pp. 283–88; J. Christ. Lünig, *Codex Italiae diplomaticus*, I (Frankfurt and Leipzig, 1725), pt. 1, sect. 1, no. XXIV, cols. 111–18; Malipiero, *Annali veneti*, in *Arch. stor. italiano*, VII-1 (1843), 333–34, 336–37; Predelli, *Regesti dei Commemoriali*, VI (Venice, 1903), bk. XVIII, no. 4, pp. 6–8; H. Ulmann, *Kaiser Maximilian I.*, I, 282–85; Delaborde, *Expédition de Charles VIII*, pp. 590–91; Pastor, *Hist. Popes*, V, 465–67, and *Gesch. d. Päpste*, III-1 (repr. 1955), 420–21. Beginning on 1 May (1495) Venice took into her employ as a condottiere the pope's son Juan Borgia, duke of Gandia, who however "colle sue milizie potrà stanziare negli stati papali ed ubbidirà con esse al papa . . ." (Predelli, *Commemoriali*, VI [1903], bk. XVIII, no. 10, pp. 8–9). Venice engaged various other condottieri at this time (*ibid.*, VI, bk. XVIII, nos. 13, 15, 18, 19). No end of diplomatic dexterity had been necessary to put together the league, on the formation of which note Segre, "Lodovico Sforza . . . ," *Arch. stor. lombardo*, 3rd ser., XX (XXX, 1903), 374–78, 384–85, 388–97, 399 ff.

an alliance would actually be formed. When Commines alluded to the hazards that would now beset the king's homeward march, the doge replied that, if he returned as a friend, he would encounter no trouble. If he returned as an enemy, the alliance would be invoked against him: "But write the king," he was urged, "that by joining this league we have had no desire to break the friendship we have with his Majesty. Nay, we wish to be good friends, and this league has been formed for the preservation of our states. . . ."[22] Commines has himself reported his appearance before the Signoria, and says that the doge told him the league had three purposes: 1) the defense of Christianity against the Turk; 2) the protection of Italy; and 3) "la preservation de leurs estatz."[23] This was the old refrain.

Charles VIII was informed of the league by Domenico Trevisan and Antonio Loredan, Venetian envoys in Naples, during the late morning of 5 April (1495). They told the king that the league had been formed "per conservation di stadi," because they understood that the Turk was preparing a great armada. Charles was almost beside himself with indignation: "So they have formed a league because the Turk is equipping a fleet!" he cried: "Great fear they have of the Turks!" He assailed the Venetians' participation in the league as disgraceful, and reminded the envoys that he could cut off their trade with Flanders if he wished. Cardinal Giuliano della Rovere tried in vain to calm him. Charles would not be calmed: He had given Perpignan and Elna to the king of Spain; he could halt Maximilian in his tracks with a single letter; he excoriated the pope and the duke of Milan, uttering furious threats against the latter. He had been invited by other kings, he said, to join a league; he had never wanted to do so; now he would look to himself, and not inform Venice of his decisions. Charles was standing by a window as Trevisan and Loredan withdrew. He hardly turned to them as they departed, hurrying off to their lodgings to send home a request that they might be allowed to return to Venice.[24]

News of the league was simultaneously published with the most elaborate festivities at Venice, Milan, and Rome on Palm Sunday, 12 April (1495).[25] The French had reason for distress but certainly not despair. Whoever had Lodovico il Moro for a friend obviously required no enemy. Maximilian was also a shaky

---

[22] Sanudo, *Spedizione*, ed. R. Fulin, p. 285. Sanudo dwells on Commines' extreme dejection (*ibid.*, pp. 285–86), observing that he was particularly bitter against Lodovico il Moro, charging the latter with treachery, for "if it had not been for him, the king would not have gone into Italy" (p. 286).

[23] Commines, *Mémoires*, bk. VII, chap. 20, ed. B. de Mandrot, II, 224, and *cf.* Kervyn de Lettenhove, *Lettres et négociations*, II, 176 ff. On 7 April, Alexander VI sent the following brief relating to the purposes of the league to Duke Ercole I d'Este of Ferrara (Arch. di Stato di Modena, Cancelleria marchionale poi ducale Estense, Estero: Carteggio di principi e signorie, Italia, Roma, Busta 1295/10, no. 22):

". . . Quoniam rerum nostrarum successibus nobilitatem tuam . . . plurimum letari non dubitamus, ideo tibi pro tua consolatione significamus pro communi Christianorum quiete nostraque ac totius Italie tranquilitate nuper initam et conclusam fuisse ligam et confederationem inter nos et carissimos in Christo filios nostros Maximilianum Romanorum ac Ferdinandum Hispanie reges et Helisabet reginam illustres necnon nobiles viros Augustinum Barbadico inclytumque Venetorum dominium ac Ludovicum Sfortiam Anglum Mediolani duces pro qua gratias acturi omnipotenti Deo bonorum omnium largitori ac totius consolationis et pacis auctori in proxima die dominica celebritatis palmarum dictam ligam et fedus in ecclesia Sancti Petri principis Apostolorum solemniter in Dei nomine publicari faciemus. Que res cum ad communem letitiam et publicum commodum pertineat, hortamur et requirimus nobilitatem tuam ut dicta die factis processionibus et reliquis in huiusmodi publica letitia servari solitis idem fedus in locis tuo dominio subiectis publice intimari et proclamari ignesque et omnia letitie solita signa fieri mandes ut solemnis illa dies agatur et ad omnes federis tam salutaris gaudium perveniat. Datum Rome apud Sanctum Petrum sub annulo piscatoris die VII Aprilis MCCCCLXXXXV, pontificatus nostri anno tertio. L. Podocatharus."

[24] Sanudo, *Spedizione*, ed. R. Fulin, pp. 294–95; Delaborde, pp. 595–96; G. Soranzo, *Il Tempo di Alessandro VI Papa*, pp. 280–81. In May, 1495, the galleys were not sent to Flanders because of Charles's threat (Sanudo, *op. cit.*, p. 330).

[25] Sanudo, *Spedizione*, ed. R. Fulin, pp. 299–306; Malipiero, *Annali veneti*, in *Arch. stor. italiano*, VII-1 (1843), 337; Burchard, *Diarium*, ed. Thuasne, II, 251–52, and ed. Celani, I, 583–84; *cf. Diario ferrarese*, in *RISS*, XXIV-7, pp. 146, 147; Kervyn de Lettenhove, *Lettres et négociations*, II, 179 ff.; Cipolla, *Signorie italiane* (1881), II, 720–21.

After the celebration of a public mass in S. Peter's on Palm Sunday, the sermon was delivered by Lionello Chieregato, now bishop of Concordia, extolling the formation of the league and preaching the necessity of the crusade. Chieregato's sermon is given in an appendix to Sigismondo de' Conti, II, 439–44. Chieregato had also given the sermon of 2 February, 1487, before Pope Innocent VIII and the Sacred College, commemorating the previous alliance of the Holy See with Venice (Sigismondo, I, app., pp. 423–27). On 28 July, 1492, he had delivered the funeral oration on Innocent VIII in S. Peter's. See Pio Paschini, *Leonello Chieregato, nunzio d'Innocenzo VIII e di Alessandro VI*, Rome, 1935, pp. 49–52, 89, 94 (Lateranum, new ser., I-3).

Here we must note that from 12 April to 10 December, 1495, there is a most unfortunate gap of eight months in Burchard's *Diarium* (*cf.* E. Celani, ed., *Liber notarum* [in *RISS*, XXXII, pt 1], I, pref., p. xxv).

ally, as Charles had suggested to the Venetian envoys. Although as king of the Romans he wanted to receive the imperial coronation at the pope's hands, he was no lover of the Venetians, and had proposed to Charles an alliance against them the year before. A settlement of the Burgundian dispute in Maximilian's favor would presumably bring him to the French side in a hurry. Considering the peril to which the Turks constantly exposed the Hapsburg lands in central Europe, Maximilian was dedicated to the crusade, of which French propagandists had made so much during the whole course of Charles's expedition. The Venetians prepared for war, "non volendo però romper alcuna lianza al Re de Franza." Charles and his advisers had the same point of view. Until they had withdrawn safely north of the Alps, they could see no good reason for manifesting their hostility toward Venice. When on 1 May the Venetian envoys left Naples, Charles very courteously furnished them with an armed escort of a hundred horse because the roads were unsafe.[26]

Charles VIII planned his return march by way of Rome with 8,000 horse and 4,000 foot, leaving in Naples and the southern kingdom 5,000 French horse and 4,000 foot as well as 4,000 Italian infantry, which had been recently recruited for his service. The date for his departure was tentatively set as 10 May; he expected to be in Rome on the twentieth; and thereafter he would go on to Florence and Pisa. He made an accord with the Genoese, promising them (according to Sanudo) possession of the French-held towns which had formerly belonged to Florence.

Since the announcement of the league Alexander VI had known nothing but anxiety, despite the constant assurances of the Venetian and Spanish ambassadors. On 4 May he summoned a consistory to consider *quid faciendum*. The question was whether to await the French king's coming to Rome or to seek safety by removal elsewhere. A delegation of some three hundred citizens, led by the *caporioni* or chief officials of the thirteen regions, was admitted to the papal palace. They pledged their fidelity to Alexander, to whom they offered hostages, but they said they needed arms and bread. Both the Curia and the citizens were heartened by the news that the Venetians were sending 10,000 horse and 2,000 *stradioti* for the pope's protection. Rome remained in a turmoil, however, and the citizens got along badly with the Spaniards. Robberies and murders were of daily occurrence. Sensible men did not go about the city at night.[27]

On 17 May Domenico Trevisan and Antonio Loredan returned to Venice from their mission to the French king in Naples. They reported to the Senate that Charles lacked men as well as money. He had no more than 12,000 horse and 8,000 foot, not counting about 3,000 Italian horse and some other infantry whom he would have to leave in the Regno. The Neapolitans were utterly weary of French insolence. Charles was now anxious to be gone, having loaded upon his galleys and other ships a "bona parte di le cosse dil castello . . . per mandar in Franza," including the bronze gates of the Castel Nuovo and the bronze statue of Alfonso the Magnanimous. He was much aroused against the Venetians. Trevisan and Loredan had remained in their house from the time the league was announced until they went to the king to ask his permission to leave Naples. Although he gave it readily, his councillors told them to inform the Signoria that it must maintain its alliance with the king, "and that he would not have come into Italy if he had not had the alliance [with Venice]." Nevertheless, the Venetians were now preparing to inflict as great losses as they could upon their erstwhile friend as he tried to return to France.[28]

Although the French kept up the pretense of planning a crusade,[29] Sigismondo de' Conti is certainly right in emphasizing that after Jem Sultan's death, Charles VIII seemed to have given up all thought of actually embarking on an expedition against the Turks.[30] Abandoned by Milan and facing the sudden hostility of Venice, Charles lacked even the means to hold

[26] Sanudo, *Spedizione*, pp. 322 ff.; Delaborde, pp. 596–97. Minor acts of hostility to the French were soon evinced by members of the league of Venice (Predelli, *Regesti dei Commemoriali*, VI [1903], bk. XVIII, nos. 22, 23, 24, 30).

[27] Sanudo, *Spedizione*, ed. R. Fulin, pp. 325–28, 336–37. On 7 May, 1495, the Senate wrote the Venetian captain-general of the sea "chel re de Franza par habi in animo cum zente darme et exercito partirsi da Napoli et venir verso Roma per offender et inferir violentia ala Santità del Pontefice" (Sen. Secreta, Reg. 35, fol. 99r [110r]).

[28] Sanudo, *Spedizione*, pp. 314, 340–41; Malipiero, *Annali veneti*, in *Arch. stor. italiano*, VII-1 (1843), 339–40.

[29] *Cf.* Delaborde, pp. 598–99.

[30] Sigismondo de' Conti, II, 112: "Navium, quibus in Epirum traiiceretur, facultatem nullam habebat, et Zizimus, in quo maxima spes frangendi Turcorum vires sita fuerat, morte ut supra demonstravimus [*ibid.*, p. 111, and see above, p. 482] erat subtractus."

Naples. Although Pastor finds it "incomprehensible" that he should have wasted precious time trying to induce the pope to grant him the investiture of the kingdom,[31] the fact is that he wished to commemorate his conquest by as many political symbols as possible. If the pope would not formally invest him with the kingdom, he would attend to his own coronation which, if it suffered the serious defect of papal noncompliance, would at least signalize the historic fact of conquest.

Charles was crowned king of Naples on 12 May.[32] Without the consent of the pope, long recognized as suzerain of the southern kingdom, the brilliant ceremony had no meaning but what force of arms could give to it. A French embassy promised the pope regular payment of the annual *census* of 50,000 ducats and even to pay arrears of another 100,000 which Ferrante and Alfonso had owed the Church. The envoys, Cardinal de Bilhères, Philippe de Bresse, and François de Luxembourg, also informed the pope that the king wanted to come to Rome "as a good son of Holy Church," to talk with his Holiness—outside the city if need be—"and that . . . they should reach some conclusions about the expedition against the Turks." Always seeking to gain time, Alexander summoned a consistory on 22 May, and then informed the three envoys that he would send his own agents to the king, but that he needed more information and time to render his judgment concerning the investiture. Eventually he would give the king his answer in writing.[33]

Knowing that the pope would not grant him the coveted investiture until the "Greek calends," Charles VIII was concerned about the operations of a Spanish squadron in Sicilian waters and fearful of a possible union of Venetian and Milanese troops in northern Italy. On 20 May (1495) he finally left Naples, to which he never returned. Gilbert de Bourbon, count of Montpensier, an energetic jouster but a lethargic administrator, remained in the city as the king's viceroy with some 7,000 horse and 5,000 foot under his command. About one-third of this army of occupation was Italian. Charles began his northward march with about 12,600 men, of whom almost all were ultramontanes.[34] In a consistory of 25 May the frightened pontiff decided to leave Rome. On the morning of the twenty-seventh he departed for Orvieto, leaving the Genoese Antoniotto Pallavicini, cardinal of S. Anastasia, as his *locotenente*. The officials of the Curia remained in the city, while twenty cardinals accompanied his Holiness into the Tuscan hills. When the pope realized how many Venetian horse (Sanudo says about 10,000) were apparently deployed for action in the areas through which he was traveling, he said: "We are worse than women, and if we had known that so many valiant men were at hand, we should not have left Rome." The Venetian ambassador, who had however urged the pope to withdraw from the city, was pleased by this recognition of the Republic's determination to fulfill its responsibilities under the league: "Beatissime Pater, I have always told your Holiness the truth." The pope replied, "You are our dearest friend," and asked the delighted envoy to ride beside him. The papal entourage arrived in Orvieto on Saturday, 30 May. Despite the presence of numerous troops around the city, Alexander still felt unsafe, and now considered going on to Perugia.[35]

---

[31] Pastor, *Gesch. d. Päpste*, III-1 (repr. 1955), 422, and *cf. Hist. Popes*, V, 468. On 8 May (1495) Guillaume Briçonnet, cardinal of S. Malo, came to Rome from Naples, "et alozò in palazo dil Papa" (Sanudo, *Spedizione*, ed. R. Fulin, p. 337); he requested the investiture of Naples for Charles *sine praejudicio tercii*, which Alexander VI refused *pro nunc* (*ibid.*, pp. 338–39, and *cf.* pp. 343, 347).

[32] Notar Giacomo, *Cronica di Napoli*, ed. Paolo Garzilli, Naples, 1845, pp. 190–91; Delaborde, pp. 602–3. The French also celebrated their conquests with jousts and tournaments, which lasted from 23 April to 1 May (Sanudo, *Spedizione*, ed. R. Fulin, pp. 314–15; Delaborde, pp. 600–2).

[33] Sanudo, *Spedizione*, ed. R. Fulin, pp. 343, 347. Cardinal de Bilhères, de Bresse, and François de Luxembourg arrived in Rome on 19 May (*ibid.*, p. 343). On Cardinal de Bilhères, see below, note 100.

[34] J. de la Pilorgerie, *Campagne et bulletins* (1866), pp. 279, 281; Commines, *Mémoires*, bk. VIII, chap. 1, ed. B. de Mandrot, II, 230 ff.; Sanudo, *Spedizione*, ed. R. Fulin, pp. 356, 606; Sigismondo de' Conti, II, 113; Delaborde, pp. 605–7.

[35] Sanudo, *Spedizione*, ed. R. Fulin, pp. 356–58. On the appointment of Cardinal Pallavicini as legate in Rome during the pope's absence, see Raynaldus, *Ann. eccl.*, ad ann. 1495, nos. 20–21, vol. XIX (1693), pp. 443–44, where the bull of nomination should be dated "octavo Kal. Iunii" (25 May, 1495). *Cf.* A. Ciaconius, *Vitae et res gestae pont. roman.*, ed. A. Oldoinus, III (1677), col. 130A. (Pastor, *Hist. Popes*, V, 470–71, and note, was wrong in stating that the English Cardinal John Morton was appointed legate in Rome on this occasion, but the error is corrected in the last German edition, *Gesch. d. Päpste*, vol. III, pt. 1 [1924, repr. 1955], pp. 424–25). *Cf.* Malipiero, *Annali veneti*, in *Arch. stor. italiano*, VII-1 (1843), 342, 344; *Diario ferrarese*, in *RISS*, XXIV-7, p. 152; Sen. Secreta, Reg. 35, fols. 110v–111v [120v–121v], letters of the Venetian Senate dated 1–4 June, 1495.

Cardinal Antoniotto Pallavicini is buried in S. Maria del

Great events seemed to be in the making. Letters from Naples dated 24 May, which arrived in Venice on the thirty-first, confirmed Charles VIII's departure, "et che Napoli restò molto povero et quasi ruinato, et li cittadini mal contenti." The French had apparently reached the end of their success. Troops of Ferrante II had already landed in Calabria and retaken Reggio, where some two hundred French were killed. The people of Taranto also wanted to surrender, although the local baronage feared Ferrante's vengeance for their desertion of his cause. He granted them a public pardon; he could always deal with them later. The French were now withdrawing from Calabria, in flight toward Naples. The Aragonese reconquest of the southland had begun.[36]

In the harbor at Brindisi was a Turkish *fusta*, which had brought an envoy of Sultan Bayazid to offer Ferrante II eighteen thousand troops then at Valona, whose services were said not yet to be needed. Adversity pursued the French. Venetian naval forces might have acquired all Apulia at this time, in Sanudo's opinion, if their commander had been given leave to undertake such an extensive operation.[37]

In the meantime the vagaries of Christian politics were raising questions in Istanbul, where it was only too clear that the Venetian league had entirely frustrated Charles VIII's alleged intention of using Naples as his point of departure for a crusade. The secretary of the Venetian embassy at the Porte informed his government by letters dated 12 May (1495) that the pashas had been asking him how it had come about (*come va queste cosse*?) that Lodovico il Moro had invited King Charles into Italy and now joined the league against him. The Venetians, who could have prevented his coming, had calmly watched him prosper, and now organized the league against him. The pope had declared his friendship for the king of Naples, and then granted Charles an uncontested passage through papal territory. The king of Spain had promised his good faith and peace, for which he had received two counties (Perpignan and Elna), and now added his weight to those opposing the king of France. The Emperor Maximilian, also a newly found friend of Charles VIII, was pursuing the same dubious policy as Ferdinand of Aragon. *Come va queste cosse*? The Venetian secretary gave the pashas the stock answer: the allies were only seeking the "conservatione di stadi loro." The Turks had of course anticipated the reply before they asked the question. Their purpose was obviously to illustrate the unreliability of the Christian states, even in dealing with one another. The secretary's report of 12 May shows, however, that Bayazid was still not absolutely sure of Jem Sultan's death.[38]

On the unreliability of his erstwhile friends Charles VIII could have told the sultan a good deal. Charles arrived in Rome on 1 June (1495), accompanied by Cardinals Giuliano della Rovere, Jean de Bilhères, and Paolo di Campofregoso of Genoa. The legate Pallavicini placed the Vatican palace at his disposal, observing that his Holiness had departed to insure the king's every comfort and convenience. Charles declined the invitation and, after a prayer of thanksgiving before the high altar in S. Peter's, was lodged in Cardinal Domenico della Rovere's sumptuous palace in the Borgo. (Domenico was with the pope in Orvieto.) In accordance with his earlier promises Charles removed the garrisons from Terracina and Civitavecchia (and he needed the troops), but the French garrison was left at Ostia, undoubtedly at Giuliano della Rovere's request. Since most of the pope's Spanish guard had gone with him to Orvieto, and Charles had kept most of the Swiss out of the city, the Romans suffered much less from this second occupation than had been feared. On Wednesday, 3 June, Charles attended an early-morning mass in S. Peter's, took his leave of Pallavicini on the steps before the church, and resumed his northward march to Baccano, where he spent the night.[39] Hoping to confer with the pope, Charles had sent Perron de

---

Popolo, in the first chapel on the left as one enters the church; the inscription on his sarcophagus reads, "Antoniotus Card. S. Praxedis, mortem prae oculis semper habens, vivens sibi pos[uit] an. MDI." He died on 10 September, 1507.

[36] Sanudo, *Spedizione*, ed. R. Fulin, pp. 361–62, 372, 377, 415–16 and ff., 430–31, 440, 460–61, 501 and ff.; Malipiero, *Annali veneti*, in *Arch. stor. italiano*, VII-1 (1843), 352; *Diario ferrarese*, in *RISS*, XXIV-7, pp. 153–54, a pro-French source.

[37] Sanudo, *Spedizione*, p. 373.

[38] Sanudo, *Spedizione*, p. 374. The Venetian secretary in Istanbul was Alvise Sagundino, on whose presence in Venice, see Segre, "Lodovico Sforza . . . ," *Arch. stor. lombardo*, 3rd ser., XX (XXX, 1903), 378–79. Sagundino knew the Turks well, and had in fact just gone back to Istanbul (Segre, *loc. cit.*), after having been "noviter retornato da la Porta" on 1 April, 1494 (Arch. di Stato di Venezia, Sen. Secreta, Reg. 35, fol. 2^v [14^v]).

[39] Sanudo, *Spedizione*, pp. 365–66; Malipiero, *Annali veneti*, in *Arch. stor. italiano*, VII-1 (1843), 345, a letter of Francesco Guidiccioni, dated at Rome on 8 June, 1495; Sigismondo de' Conti, II, 114.

Baschi on an embassy to Orvieto, but the day after Perron's arrival his Holiness set out for Perugia (on 5 June), intending to keep a safe distance from the French.[40]

On 13 June (1495) Charles entered Siena, where Commines awaited him with such information as he had been able to acquire concerning Venetian intentions. During his four days in Siena Charles gave his approval to a plan to seize Genoa from a pro-Milanese faction headed by the brothers Agostino and Giovanni Adorno, who were prepared to aid the French only so long as Lodovico il Moro directed them to do so. In view of il Moro's changed attitude toward the French, the Adorni were now leading the Genoese into the Venetian camp. Cardinal Campofregoso (or Fregoso) had been three times doge of Genoa. He was eager for an opportunity to turn the tables on the Adorni; to Charles, Genoa was a necessary link in the long line of communications from France to Naples. Charles's need and Campofregoso's ambition were both frustrated, however, and the Adorni were not dislodged from power until Charles's successor seized Milan a few years later.[41] The Florentines, almost desperate in their anxiety to regain Pisa and the various fortresses which Piero de' Medici had surrendered to the French, had already sent envoys to Charles. In return for the prompt restoration of these places the Florentines pledged themselves not to enter the anti-French league and to add 70,000 ducats to the 30,000 still owing on the loan they had made him the preceding November. They would also furnish him with a condotta of three hundred men-at-arms and two thousand foot under the command of Francesco Secco. Commines thought that the king ought to accept the offer, retaining only Livorno (Leghorn) until the French army had reached Asti. But a contrary opinion prevailed.[42] In any event Charles would certainly have retained Sarzana, Sarzanello, and Pietrasanta as a lure to the Genoese populace, whose co-operation he wanted at this critical juncture of French affairs.

Charles VIII left Siena on 17 June, appointing his cousin, the young count de Ligny, as captain-general of the city. On the eighteenth he was at Poggibonsi, where he received Savonarola and listened respectfully to the friar's solemn warnings of his royal responsibility to reform the Church. The next day Charles was at Castelfiorentino. By this time it was generally known that a state of war existed between the French and the members of the league. Some ten days before (on 8 June) advance units of the French army had sacked the papal town of Toscanella. The Venetians had more than once informed Commines that, if Charles withdrew from Italy as a friend, he would be treated as such. Since the sack of Toscanella had apparently taken place in violation of Charles's orders for a peaceable advance, it might have been argued that there were extenuating circumstances.[43] There had been numerous other incidents, however, and the Venetians had for some time regarded an open break with the French as inevitable. On 5 June Francesco Gonzaga, marquis of Mantua and husband of Isabella d'Este, had been appointed "governor-general" (*governador zeneral*) of the Venetian forces,[44] which were now prepared to attack the French when a favorable opportunity presented itself.

The opportunity was not long in coming. Following the Val d'Elsa to the Arno, Charles entered Pisa (on 20 June), where he remained for three days, subjected by the Pisans to constant importunities to guarantee their freedom against the Florentines.[45] From Pisa Charles went to Lucca, where he spent the twenty-fourth, and then pushed on to Pietrasanta and Sarzana. The king's councillors were now uncertain what route should be taken northward.

---

[40] Sanudo, *Spedizione*, p. 367, and *cf.* pp. 401–3; Malipiero, *Annali*, p. 342.

[41] Cardinal Campofregoso died in Rome on 22 April, 1498, not living quite long enough to witness the fall of the Adorni (Ciaconius, *Vitae et res gestae pont. roman.*, ed. Oldoinus, III [1677], cols. 77–78, and note Philip P. Argenti, *The Occupation of Chios by the Genoese*, I [Cambridge, 1958], 260, 263–64, 273–74). *Cf.* Sigismondo de'Conti, II, 115; Sanudo, *Spedizione*, pp. 375–76, 396–97, 400, 413, 429–30, 436, 441, 461–62, 466, and 510–11; Delaborde, pp. 613–16, 626–27, 657–58.

[42] Commines, *Mémoires*, bk. VIII, chap. 2, ed. B. de Mandrot, II, 240; Sanudo, *Spedizione*, pp. 387, 393–94, 462–63; Kervyn de Lettenhove, *Lettres et négociations de Philippe de Commines*, II (1868), 206 ff., 213–14.

[43] Sanudo, *Spedizione*, pp. 386, 403, 426–27; Commines, *Mémoires*, bk. VIII, chaps. 2–3, ed. B. de Mandrot, II, 241–43. The duke of Orléans' seizure of Novara from Lodovico il Moro (before 13 June) had also reduced the chances of Charles's being able to withdraw from Italy in peace (Sen. Secreta, Reg. 35, fols. 121^v, 122^v–123^r, 136 [131^v, 132^v–133^r, 146]).

[44] Sen. Secreta, Reg. 35, fol. 113^r [123^r], and *cf.* Sanudo, *Spedizione*, p. 370.

[45] Commines, *Mém.*, VIII, 4, ed. B. de Mandrot, II, 244–45; Sanudo, *Spedizione*, p. 421; J. de la Pilorgerie, pp. 303–4; Delaborde, *Expédition de Charles VIII*, pp. 620–21.

Commines states that at Sarzana for the first time he heard it said that the French would have to fight a battle with the allies.[46] When it was decided to go down the mountainous Taro valley, the army advanced to Pontremoli, where the king stayed from 29 June to 2 July. Savonarola's prophecy that God would conduct the king to safety seemed to be coming true. Pontremoli was an important stronghold; the Italian allies should have occupied it with a large force.[47] Charles's ill-disciplined Swiss sacked the town, which belonged to the duke of Milan,[48] lending additional credence to the charge of cruelty which the Italians were now generally making against the French. The rugged descent of the Taro valley led to Fornovo (*Forum Novum*), on the right bank of the river,[49] near which the Italian allies were concentrating most of their forces.

The Swiss mercenaries labored over the mountain passes with the French artillery which Charles VIII had wisely refused to abandon despite the advice of some of his councillors. From the heights looking into the river valley Commines says the French could see the Italian host, which he estimated at about 35,000 men, of whom four-fifths were in Venetian pay.[50] The Venetians had told Commines that together with the duke of Milan they could put 40,000 men into the field. They had not been exaggerating. On the whole the quality of their troops was high. Agents of the Republic had recruited numerous *stradioti* from the Morea and Albania. Commines has described the stradioti, whose muster he had watched on the Lido at Venice. They dressed like Turks, he tells us, except that they did not wear turbans. They were a hardy lot, and could sleep outdoors at any season of the year. They rode Turkish horses. Brave in combat, they took no prisoners, but cut off the heads of their captives. Years before, Mehmed the Conqueror had paid them a ducat a head, and (says Commines) "the Venetians did likewise." The stradioti, allegedly unaccustomed to artillery, were shy of cannon fire, before which they would retreat.[51] Sanudo's account makes clear that there were also numerous stradioti in the Milanese and Bolognese contingents of the allied army.

The stradioti were the first to strike a blow at the French. On 1 July the allied commander Francesco Gonzaga had set up his camp at Giarola, between Fornovo and Parma. French advance units were soon in Fornovo; the stradioti scored two minor successes against them. Gonzaga was elated by this apparently auspicious beginning.[52] He undoubtedly trusted too much in the numerical superiority of his forces, but like all condottieri who served the Serenissima he was hampered in his preliminary planning and movements by too detailed instructions from Venice. His opponent, Charles VIII, spent the night of 3 July at Cassio, and was at Terenzo on the evening of the fourth. The next day the French army was descending in battle order upon Fornovo, efforts having failed to negotiate a peaceful passage northward. Owing to the diversion of forces to Genoa, the French did not number more than ten or twelve thousand men, tired, hungry, and slowed down by a long baggage train. But they had managed to keep much of their artillery.

On Monday morning, 6 July, *envyron sept*

---

[46] Commines, VIII, 5, ed. B. de Mandrot, II, 248–49.

[47] Commines, VIII, 6, ed. B. de Mandrot, II, 250–51.

[48] Commines, VIII, 6, ed. B. de Mandrot, II, 251–52; Sanudo, *Spedizione*, pp. 436–37; J. de la Pilorgerie, pp. 315–16.

[49] Sanudo, *Spedizione*, pp. 422–23. Commines, VIII, 7, ed. B. de Mandrot, II, 256–57, notes that Fornovo is at the foot of the mountain (actually high hills) at the beginning of a plain: he says that the avarice of the Italians, who much outnumbered the French, was so great that they awaited their enemy in the plain, lest the French should be able to escape into the mountains (with the rich Neapolitan booty they were believed to be carrying), and then fall back upon Pisa, Pietrasanta, and Sarzana. The environs of Fornovo are illustrated by a map appended to B. de Mandrot's edition of Commines' *Mémoires*, vol. II (1903). Concerning the charge of French cruelty, we may note that on 15 June, 1495, the Venetian Senate had written Alexander VI, "Visum nobis fuit atrocissimum et abominabile facinus patratum a Gallis in illis terris ecclesie, in quibus depredatis tantam stragem hominum crudelissime fecerunt . . ." (Sen. Secreta, Reg. 35, fol. 123^v [133^v]). Later, on 22 July, the Senate was to write the Venetian envoy at the Curia, "Quis enim non novit caedes, rapinas, strages, violentias, et inauditas Gallorum crudelitates, potissimum in terris et locis ecclesie perpetratas . . ." (*ibid.*, fol. 143^r [153^r]).

[50] Commines, VIII, 8, ed. B. de Mandrot, II, 261, and *cf.* the report of Gilbert Pointet in J. de la Pilorgerie, *Campagne et bulletins* (1866), pp. 351 ff., which sets the size of the Italian forces at 36,000 to about 40,000 men. Sanudo, *Spedizione*, pp. 393, 422, says there were more than 30,000 men in the Venetian army alone, on which *cf.* Malipiero, *Annali veneti*, in *Arch. stor. italiano*, VII-1 (1843), 349–51, 354, 357.

[51] Commines, VIII, 7, ed. B. de Mandrot, II, 257–58. Sanudo, *Spedizione*, pp. 319, 329, had observed Commines on the Lido "a veder la mostra di stratioti."

[52] Alessandro Luzio and Rodolfo Renier, "Francesco Gonzaga alla battaglia di Fornovo (1495) secondo i documenti mantovani," *Arch. stor. italiano*, 5th ser., VI (Florence, 1890), 212–16, 231 ff.

heures, Charles VIII mounted his handsome black horse, a gift of the duke of Savoy, and summoned Commines to him. Lacking the build and stance of a warrior, Charles surprised Commines that morning: he looked splendid and spoke bravely and wisely. Then Commines recalled Savonarola's words that God would take the king by the hand and guide him along the road to safety and to honor. Commines had for some time advised the king's councillors to try to negotiate rather than fight their way out of the difficulty in which they found themselves, and now the king had summoned him "to talk if these people want to talk." If a free passage were still negotiable, Briçonnet and Gié were to take part in the discussions. Commines answered the king: "Sire, I will do it willingly, but I have never seen two such great armies so close to each other go their ways without fighting!"[53]

Although the time was past for talking, Briçonnet and Commines dictated letters to the Venetian provveditori in Gonzaga's camp, stressing the king's peaceful intents and urging them to come to a parley. The French army crossed the Taro to the left bank (by a ford which remained passable to the village of Bernini) despite the rocks and heavy rains. It was a wise move. Gonzaga's strongly fortified position at Giarola, on the right bank of the Taro (near the road to Parma), became irrelevant. Rather than wait for an attack upon their well-prepared defenses, the Italians would now have to take the initiative across the rocky terrain of the river. In the area of Fornovo the Taro can be forded farther downstream opposite Felegara and, more easily, at Oppiano. By whatever fords the Italians undertook to cross the river to attack the French, a relentless rain increased the difficulties of their offensive with each passing hour. But attack they did in a murderous mêlée, riding and wading through water up to their midriffs. For a brief while it looked as though Gonzaga's assurance of victory would be justified. The heavy rains were diminishing the effectiveness of the French artillery. At a critical point in the battle, when persistent attack would probably have overwhelmed the French, Gonzaga's light horse and infantry left the Italian knights and men-at-arms the task of crushing the enemy, and headed for the baggage train (which they had been encouraged to believe contained the spoils of Naples), as it moved slowly along the hillsides above the combatants on the left bank of the Taro.

The stradioti, placed on the nearby hilltop of Montebago and instructed to delay their attack until the French lines should begin to crumble, could not abide the thought of missing a share of the plunder. They swept down from their eminence upon the baggage train. When loaded with booty, Italian, Greek, and Albanian alike thought only of getting back across the river to the encampment at Giarola. By an almost incredible turn of fortune, the Italians were themselves in disorganized retreat, racing for the fords over the river or taking their chances by plunging into the swiftly moving waters. The French gave chase all along the embattled bank. Varlets and grooms, sutlers and cooks finished off Italian men-at-arms, thrown from their horses amid the rocks and unable to secure a footing in the current. Of the thousands of Italians who withdrew from the scene of battle, some made their way to Parma, others to Reggio d'Emilia. The French might have converted the Italian defeat into a disaster if they had pursued them across the river.[54] But they were

[53] Commines, *Mém.*, VIII, 10, ed. B. de Mandrot, II, 267–68.

[54] Commines describes in detail the battle of Fornovo, in which he participated (*Mémoires*, bk. VIII, chaps. 9–12, ed. B. de Mandrot, II, 261–85, where the editor has collected and commented on various other sources in his notes). Malipiero has incorporated in his *Annali veneti*, in *Arch. stor. italiano*, VII-1 (1843), 356–63, four letters by Venetian officials who witnessed the battle, one of whom stated that "havemo habudo senza dubio gloriosa vittoria!" The official Venetian reaction, expressed on 8 July, was one of "singular piacer et iucundita de animo" for the outcome at Fornovo, in which Gonzaga had won "immortal gloria . . . per tuto el mondo" (Sen. Secreta, Reg. 35, fols. 134^v [144^v] ff.). Both sides claimed victory, and the first (unofficial) news to reach Venice was that of a great "rota delle genti Francesi," which had even included the capture of Charles VIII! (Malipiero, *op. cit.*, p. 355). Sigismondo de'Conti, II, 116–26, gives a full account of the battle, as do Paolo Giovio, *Hist. sui temporis*, II, in *Opera quotquot extant omnia*, Basel, 1578, pp. 64–76, and of course Marino Sanudo, *Spedizione*, ed. R. Fulin, esp. pp. 446–56, 464–66, 473–82, 535–37. *Cf.* A. Desjardins, *Négociations diplomatiques de la France avec la Toscane*, I (1859), 624–27; J. de la Pilorgerie, pp. 321–61, esp. the letter of Gilbert Pointet dated at Asti on 15 July; *Diario ferrarese*, in *RISS*, XXIV-7, pp. 159–60. There is a well-written (but unduly pro-French) account of events at Fornovo in Delaborde, *Expédition de Charles VIII*, pp. 634–47, but see esp. A. Luzio and R. Renier, "Francesco Gonzaga alla battaglia di Fornovo," *Arch. stor. italiano*, 5th ser., VI (1890), 205–46, with numerous documents, and some interesting observations on the sources (pp. 218–19). In July the Taro should have been easy to cross at almost any point, but the heavy rains had produced strong currents which were rendered even more treacherous by alternate stretches of sand and rock.

tired, and the way to Asti lay open. Although neither side had succeeded in destroying the other, the French had won. However, when the French pushed on to Asti in a haste that resembled flight, the Italians could well believe themselves the victors. The French treasure had been looted, and Gonzaga, who was not yet thirty, gained a great reputation as a brave and resourceful soldier. Mantegna painted his Virgin of Victory, now in the Louvre, to celebrate Gonzaga's alleged success on the banks of the Taro. Gonzaga was able to say that he had freed Italy and redeemed the honor of his countrymen.[55] On 24 July the Venetian government promoted him from "governor" to captain-general of all the forces of the Republic,[56] and poets of the day extolled his performance at Fornovo with a patriotic verve such as had rarely been felt in Italy since the time of Petrarch.

Some days after the battle of Fornovo the Ferrarese diarist recorded in his chronicle that the news had come to Ferrara of how the Venetians had been celebrating the rout of their own forces. According to him, they wanted to make their subjects believe that the Republic's effort against the king of France had been successful, their usual practice being to greet losses and bad news with bonfires, bells, and festivals.[57] The diarist shared the pro-French or rather anti-Venetian sentiments of his master, Duke Ercole d'Este. Fornovo had been reported at Venice as a victory, and was officially so regarded.[58] After further attempts on Commines' part to parley with the allied Italian command,[59] the French army went by way of Borgo S. Donnino and Fiorenzuola, over the Trebbia above Piacenza and past Castel S. Giovanni and Tortona, through the Lombard plain on a seven days' march of eighty miles to the safety of Asti, where they arrived on 15 July.[60] On the sixth, however, the very day of the battle of Fornovo, Ferrante II had appeared in the harbor of Naples aboard ship in a Spanish fleet, "volendo ritornar nel Regno." On the following day he entered the city and lodged in the Castel Capuano although the French still held the Castel Nuovo, the Castel dell'Uovo, and a number of other strongholds in the city. At the same time the Aragonese banners were raised in Capua, Aversa, and elsewhere. The French conquest was being rapidly undone.[61]

In mid-July the Genoese, rejecting the appeal of Cardinals della Rovere and Campofregoso, captured the French fleet carrying some of the spoils from Naples. Thus the famous bronze doors of the Castel Nuovo, said to have cost 20,000 ducats, were recovered,[62] for the Genoese later returned them to Ferrante, who restored them to their sockets, where they may still be seen (now bearing, however, the marks inflicted by Gonsalvo de Cordova's gunners during the siege of Naples in 1503).[63] On 17 July (1495) Charles VIII left Asti, and divided his time for the next two months between Chieri and Turin.

Charles now found an apparent ally in the Florentines, however, to whom by an agreement reached at Turin on 26 August he restored Pisa and Livorno. He also granted them Sarzana, Sarzanello, and Pietrasanta, with the proviso that if the Genoese accepted French suzerainty within two years, the Florentines were to surrender these places "into the king's hands that he may give them to the Genoese,

---

[55] *Cf.* Gonzaga's letters of 12 and 16 July, 1495, to Cardinal Ippolito d'Este and Elisabetta of Urbino, in Luzio and Renier, *Arch. stor. italiano*, VI (1890), 223–4, and note 1. On Mantegna's Madonna della Vittoria, *cf.*, *ibid.*, pp. 226–27. The small church in which the painting once hung has been secularized, but may still be found in present-day Mantua at the corner of the Via Madonna della Vittoria and the Via Domenico Fernelli. When I last saw it (in 1970), it housed a workshop. Facing the Via Fernelli, a side portal is framed by a fine ogival arch. The painting, which celebrated the alleged Italian victory over the French in 1495, was lost to Napoleon's troops in January, 1797, during another French invasion, on which see Alessandro Luzio, "La'Madonna della Vittoria'del Mantegna," *Emporium*, X (July–Dec., 1899), 358–74, with several unpublished documents.

[56] Sen. Secreta, Reg. 35, fol. 144r [154r]; Malipiero, *Annali veneti*, in *Arch. stor. italiano*, VII-1 (1843), 372; Sanudo, *Spedizione*, p. 527.

[57] *Diario ferrarese*, in *RISS*, XXIV, pt. 7 (Bologna, 1933), p. 161.

[58] *Cf.* Predelli, *Regesti dei Commemoriali*, VI (1903), bk. XVIII, no. 32, p. 13.

[59] *Cf.* Sen. Secreta, Reg. 35, fols. 136v, 142v, 143v [146v, 152v, 153v], where of course Commines is referred to as "Monsignor de Argenton."

[60] Commines, *Mém.*, VIII, 13–14, ed. B. de Mandrot, II, 287–98, with notes; Sanudo, *Spedizione*, pp. 487–89, 506–8; *Diario ferrarese*, in *RISS*, XXIV-7, p. 161; Desjardins, I, 626; Delaborde, *Expédition de Charles VIII*, pp. 652–57.

[61] Sanudo, *Spedizione*, pp. 501–3, 517 ff., 530 ff., 572 ff.; Malipiero, *Annali veneti*, in *Arch. stor. italiano*, VII-1 (1843), 367, 372; Sigismondo de' Conti, II, 130; Sen. Secreta, Reg. 35, fol. 141r [151r].

[62] *Cf.* Sanudo, *Spedizione*, p. 510: ". . . le porte enee di Castelnuovo di Napoli, le qual costono ducati 20 milia, *ut dicitur*. . . ."

[63] Delaborde, *Expédition de Charles VIII*, pp. 657–58.

and in compensation he promises to give the Florentines other lands closer to their own and to bring about friendship between Genoa and Florence." Otherwise after two years Florence might retain the towns with their fortresses. The Florentines were bound to pay the king, within twenty-four days, 30,000 ducats still owing from the convention of November, 1494. They were also to grant the Pisans a general amnesty, loan the king another 70,000 ducats for the period of one year, and furnish him with two hundred and fifty men-at-arms "per soccorso delle genti francesi [che] sono nel regno di Napoli."[64]

In the meantime Alexander VI had returned to Rome on 27 June with twenty-one cardinals, enthusiastically welcomed by the populace.[65] He soon forbade the Florentines to join any alliance with Charles VIII, whom he had already threatened with excommunication on 5 August. Detailing the offenses committed by the French in Italy, the pope reminded Charles of the grievous loss which the Christian cause had suffered in the death of Jem Sultan, *qui manibus tuis periit*, and charged the French with worse conduct than that exhibited by the Goths in their invasion. He commanded the king and his followers to lay down their arms and promote peace in Christendom.[66] On 21 August Alexander sent the doge of Venice a laudatory brief: the Venetians had won immortal fame by their heroic liberation of Italy from French oppression.[67] On the same day Charles VIII wrote the pope from Chieri that he was directing the castellan of Ostia to refrain from interfering with shipments of food up the Tiber, of which the pope had complained. He observed that the French victory at Fornovo had been the work of God,

> who knows well that our intention was to proceed against the Turks for the increase and exaltation of the faith and Holy Church, had it not been for the machinations and evil spirits which have impeded us to these very days. . . . We have been ill content with the shedding of blood. Here nothing less has been reported than that there have been bonfires of joy in Rome, [with some people] believing that we were dead or taken a prisoner to Milan or Venice.

The king had also been informed that the pope and some of the cardinals were sending men and money to help Ferrante II in Naples. His Holiness would do well to contemplate the advantages of neutrality. Charles wrote that he intended to preserve his kingdom of Naples and so to increase his strength as entirely to frustrate the evil intentions of his enemies. If bloodshed lay ahead, Charles regretted it "with all his heart:" he would rather turn his arms against the Turks.[68] Such communications had no effect upon the pope, who on 8 September wrote the Florentines of the restraints he had imposed upon the king of France, called upon them to rescind their pact of 26 August, and reminded them of the necessity of Christian union "because of the danger of a Turkish attack upon us" (*ob Turcarum in Christianos invasionis periculum*). If the Florentines persisted in their alliance with the French, however, his Holiness warned them they would incur the penalties of excommunication and an interdict to be laid upon all their territories.[69]

However boldly Charles VIII might proclaim his intention to reconquer Naples, his presence was badly needed in France, which was now threatened by a double attack from Germany and Spain. Thousands of Swiss mercenaries were recruited in the cantons with the aid of Florentine money and other inducements. On 9 October (1495) the worried Lodovico il Moro accepted a treaty of peace with Charles, largely negotiated by Commines, who loved secret parleys. Lodovico recognized French suzerainty over the Milanese fief of Genoa, and promised to allow free passage to limited numbers of French troops through Milanese territories to help Charles preserve his hold on Naples. If Venice did not subscribe to the treaty, Lodovico was to furnish five hundred men-at-arms for service with the French against the Serenissima. Novara was to be restored to Lodovico in return for

[64] Desjardins, *Négociations*, I, 626–32; Sanudo, *Spedizione*, pp. 582, 584. The Florentines did not receive Sarzana, Sarzanello, and Pietrasanta, owing to the French commandant's violation of the king's pledge (Commines, VIII, 21, ed. B. de Mandrot, II, 343–45, and *cf.* Sen. Secreta, Reg. 35, fols. 158^{v}, 171^{r} [168^{v}, 181^{r}]).

[65] Sanudo, *Spedizione*, p. 439; Malipiero, *Annali veneti*, in *Arch. stor. italiano*, VII-1 (1843), 352.

[66] Malipiero, *Annali veneti*, in *Arch. stor. italiano*, VII-1 (1843), 383–89; Sigismondo de' Conti, II, 131–41; Sanudo, *Spedizione*, pp. 546–47.

[67] Malipiero, *op. cit.*, pp. 391–93.

[68] Letter, "data a Quier die 21 Augusti 1495," in Sanudo, *Spedizione*, pp. 579–81. On the rumor of the king's death, dangerous for the French cause in Naples, *cf.* Commines, *Mém.*, VIII, 15, ed. B. de Mandrot, II, 303–4.

[69] Papal brief, "datum Romae sub annulo piscatoris die octavo Septembris 1495," in Sanudo, *Spedizione*, pp. 584–86.

an indemnity of 50,000 ducats to Louis d'Orléans, who had held the city since June.[70] Charles agreed not to support Louis's claim to the Milanese duchy. Throughout almost three weeks of negotiations the Venetians had wanted to preserve the league and have the Neapolitan question adjudicated by the pope, the emperor, and the king of Spain. (Small chance Charles VIII would have had with that trio of judges!) The Venetians were willing to accept French suzerainty over Naples, which Ferrante II might recognize by an annual payment. (But of course Alexander VI was suzerain of the Neapolitan kingdom, and for generations the annual *census* had been paid to the pope.) The Venetians were allowed two months to accept the terms of the treaty. Although the allies had claimed that the league of Venice was not specifically directed against the French king, everyone knew that its purpose had been his expulsion from Italy. Lodovico's desertion of his allies was a shattering blow to the league. The Spanish ambassador was disgusted; in Venice Lodovico was castigated as a traitor. He advanced various sophistical arguments in his own defense, asserting that he was going to Venice personally to vindicate his honor.[71]

After vainly trying to arrange an interview with Lodovico il Moro, Charles VIII began his return to Lyon on 15 October. Before his departure, however, he sent Commines back to Venice to secure the withdrawal of the Republic's forces from the kingdom of Naples (and especially from Monopoli, on the Adriatic coast, which the Venetians had seized from the French) as well as to guarantee that Ferrante II should not be recognized as a member of the league. Going by way of Milan, Commines arrived in Venice on the evening of 4 November, accompanied by a retinue of ten persons. The Signoria had directed various patricians to meet him, but few came, the others pleading the lateness of the hour.[72]

Commines was lodged on the Salizzada S. Moisè, in the house of Matteo Barozzi, just west of the Piazza S. Marco. He was received by the Signoria on the morning of the seventh. The old doge, Agostino Barbarigo, observed, "My lord, you have lost weight!" Commines replied, "Most serene prince, the trials of war have done it, and besides, when I was here before, it was your lordships' hospitality which maintained my good appearance." He then explained that his royal master wished to be at peace with the Venetians; however, he wanted them to send no further aid to Ferrante II, for the French intended to reconquer the kingdom of Naples. Commines had to wait two weeks for his answer, during which time he took note of three days of general processions, almsgiving, and public sermons whereby the Venetians sought divine aid in making the right decisions. He was impressed by the apparent general piety, "and in truth [Venice] seems to me the most reverent city that I have ever seen in ecclesiastical matters. . . ." The churches were well adorned and equipped, "and in this respect I regard [the Venetians] as quite equal to the Romans, and I believe that the grandeur of their

---

[70] Sanudo, *Spedizione*, p. 621, and not 500,000 ducats, as stated by Delaborde, *Expédition de Charles VIII*, p. 670. *Cf.* Sigismondo de' Conti, II, 142, and Kervyn de Lettenhove, *Lettres et négociations*, II, 227–31.

[71] Commines, *Mém.*, VIII, 16–18, ed. B. de Mandrot, II, 314–29; Sanudo, *Spedizione*, pp. 608–27; Malipiero, *Annali veneti*, in *Arch. stor. italiano*, VII-1 (1843), 395–97. One of the articles of 28–31 March, 1495, establishing the league for the preservation of the *status quo* in Italy, was to the following effect: ". . . Si forte occurreret, quod Deus avertat, quod ad bellum deveniretur, non possit quovis modo fieri pax nisi cum scientia sociorum et cum reservatione et sine praejudicio presentis confoederationis et ligae" (Sen. Secreta, Reg. 35, fol. 78^v [90^v], article no. VII; Lünig, *Codex Italiae diplomaticus*, I, pt. 1, sect. 1, no. XXIV, col. 113). The intent of the statement was quite clear: if war occurred, peace should be made only with the common consent of the allies. But the critical phrase employed was *scientia sociorum*, as Lodovico il Moro informed the Spanish ambassador, not *consensu sociorum*: "Et mostrato ditto capitulo el Duca a l'ambassador, disse: el dice *saputa*, non dice *consultatione*: lo ho za scritto a la Majestà dil Re vostro . . ." (Sanudo, *op. cit.*, pp. 608–9). Such were the difficulties of dealing with Lodovico il Moro.

[72] Commines had been very active and in constant touch with the Senate before coming to Venice (Sen. Secreta, Reg. 35, fols. 169^v, 170^v, 171^v–172^r, 173^r, 174^r, 174^v–175^r and ff. [179^v, etc.], docs. dated September, 1495, and fols. 191^v [201^v] ff., 195^v–196^r [205^v–206^r], dated 2–8 November, giving the time of Commines' arrival and reception by the Senate "heri mane" [of the seventh]); Kervyn de Lettenhove, *Lettres et négociations de Philippe de Commines*, II (1868), 234 ff., and III (1874), 98–99; Commines, *Mém.*, VIII, 19, ed. B. de Mandrot, II, 332; Sanudo, *Spedizione*, p. 651. Charles VIII arrived back in Lyon on 7 November, 1495, taking up residence in the archiepiscopal palace near the church of S. Jean, remaining until 9 February, 1496. He presented to the churches of Lyon the pieces of artillery he had captured in Italy in order to have bells made of them. Sigismondo de'Conti, II, 142, says of Charles "in regnum suum septimo Idus Novembris [the seventh] sese recepit," which the editors, *loc. cit.*, incorrectly translate "il dodici di novembre!" On the Venetian retention of Monopoli, note Sen. Secreta, Reg. 35, fol. 147^r [157^r]; Reg. 36, fol. 70^r [82^r]; and Reg. 38, fols. 174 [183], 200^v [209^v].

Signoria proceeds therefrom. . . ." As the days passed the Venetians hoped to learn that the Aragonese forces had captured the Neapolitan fortresses then under siege. On 17 November Commines was invited to hear the Signoria's answer, "qui fut de refux de toutes mes demandes," to the effect that the Venetians had no war with the king of France: what they had done, was merely to aid their ally, the duke of Milan, whom the king had wanted to destroy. Privately the doge renewed to Commines the old offers that with the pope's permission Ferrante should do homage to Charles VIII for the southern kingdom and pay Charles an annual *cens* of 50,000 ducats, which sum the Venetians themselves would advance. As surety for such a loan to Ferrante, they would retain the ports they then held in Apulia such as Monopoli, Brindisi, Otranto, Trani, and some others.

According to Commines, the doge assured him that Don Ferrante would grant Charles some place in Apulia (presumably Taranto which the French still held) as his point of departure for the expedition against the Turks, "dont le Roy avoit fort parlé quant il entra en Ytalie, disant que à ceste fin faisoit ceste entreprinse. . . ." Commines describes the doge's alleged proposals as a grievous display of hypocrisy, "for it was a lie, and one cannot hide his thoughts from God." The doge had not finished. He assured Commines that if the French king went on the crusade, all Italy would contribute to his effort, the king of the Romans would fight at his side, and Venice would herself supply one hundred galleys and five thousand horse.[73] Publicly the doge stated that, having apprised the members of the league of the purpose of Commines' mission, the Venetian government would have to await the advice of the several allies. Immediately after his conference with the doge, Commines left Venice to go by way of Milan over the Alps to Chambéry and thence to Lyon, where he arrived on 12 December to make his report to the king.[74] Charles VIII's expedition was over, a memorable chapter in both French and Italian history. Although Charles dreamed and spoke constantly of his intention to retake the kingdom of Naples from Ferrante, he never returned to Italy. The Aragonese reoccupied the Castel Nuovo on 8 December, 1495, and the Castel dell'Uovo on 17 February following. Ferrante died on 6 October (1496), and his uncle Federigo, prince of Altamura, succeeded him as king of Naples.[75] As the months dragged on, the French were obliged to surrender one place after another, but it was not until 18–20 January, 1497, that they gave up Taranto to the officers of the new king who, however, from the day of his coronation was harassed by the disaffection of certain of his magnates.

As though the difficulties of the French invasion had not been harassment enough for Alexander VI, natural forces added the terrible inundation of Rome on 4–6 December, 1495. The Tiber overflowed its banks to reach the disastrous levels still recorded by an inscription on the façade of S. Maria sopra Minerva and by markers still exhibited in the Castel S. Angelo.[76] At least there was no alarming news

[73] Sen. Secreta, Reg. 35, fol. 198^v [208^v], dated 17 November, 1495; Commines, *Mém.*, VIII, 19, ed. B. de Mandrot, II, 333–34, with notes; Kervyn de Lettenhove, *Lettres et négociations*, II, 234–37; Delaborde, pp. 672–73. On 5 November the Venetian Senate had decided to send troops and 10,000 ducats to assist Ferrante in Naples (Sen. Secreta, Reg. 35, fol. 194^r [204^r]; Sanudo, *Spedizione*, p. 652). Ferrante ceded Venice the Apulian ports on 21 January, 1496, to secure the continued assistance of the Venetians (Malipiero, *Annali veneti*, in *Arch. stor. italiano*, VII-1 [1843], 418–22, and Marino Sanudo, *I Diarii*, vol. I, ed. F. Stefani, Venice, 1879, cols. 12–15). *Cf.* Predelli, *Regesti dei Commemoriali*, VI (1903), bk. XVIII, nos. 38–39, pp. 16–17. On what remained to the French of their conquest of southern Italy in April, 1496, *cf.* Sanudo, *Diarii*, I, cols. 132–33.

[74] Commines, *Mém.*, VIII, 19–20, ed. B. de Mandrot, II, 334–39; Sanudo, *Spedizione*, p. 656; Malipiero, *Annali veneti*, in *Arch. stor. italiano*, VII-1 (1843), 403, 406; Kervyn de Lettenhove, *Lettres et négociations*, II, 239–40, and III, 100–101. Sigismondo de'Conti, II, 151 ff., devotes the first half of the twelfth book of his *Historiae sui temporis* to the Aragonese *reconquista* of the Neapolitan kingdom.

[75] Sanudo, *Diarii*, I, cols. 344–56; Burchard, *Diarium*, ed. Thuasne, II, 335, and ed. Celani, I, 645. In July, 1496, Charles VIII was gathering a fleet "pour le fait de nostre royaulté de Naples" (J. de la Pilorgerie, *Campagne et bulletins*, pp. 473–74, and *cf.* Predelli, *Regesti dei Commemoriali*, VI, bk. XVIII, nos. 78–79, p. 25).

[76] *Cf.* the interesting letters sent from Rome by two Venetians on 4 and 8 December, 1495, in Malipiero, *Annali veneti*, in *Arch. stor. italiano*, VII-1 (1843), 409–15, summarized in Pastor, *Gesch. d. Päpste*, III-1 (repr. 1955), 429–32, with refs. to other sources; Burchard, *Diarium*, ed. Thuasne, II, 252–58, and ed. Celani, I, 584–88, esp. the note on p. 585; *cf.* Sigismondo de' Conti, II, 271, of slight value; *Diario ferrarese*, in *RISS*, XXIV-7, p. 166, which observes that the Tiber flood reached eighteen cubits, "più che mai facesse;" Luca Landucci, *Diario fiorentino*, ed. I. del Badia, Florence, 1883, p. 120, trans. Alice de Rosen Jervis, London and New York, 1927, p. 98; A. Ciaconius, *Vitae et res gestae pont. roman.*, ed. A. Oldoinus, III (1677), col. 164D. The "idrometro" on the south face of the church of S. Rocco also records the height of the flood of December, 1495.

from the East, and no cause to worry about the Turks, whom the pope had come to look upon almost as allies during the French invasion. When the Venetian secretary Alvise Sagundino had returned from Istanbul, he brought the reassuring information that although Sultan Bayazid II had an income of 2,400,000 ducats, he spent all his money maintaining separate courts for his six or seven sons and eight sons-in-law. He reported that the Conqueror had left Bayazid a vast treasure, but that he was a peaceful man, whom his pashas had to urge to make war.[77] Although it is easy to find in contemporary texts the usual statements of the Turkish menace, there was little fear of the crescent in the West at this time, "car le Turc qui regne est de petite valeur."[78]

It was just as well. Alexander VI was too much preoccupied with re-establishing his own position to worry about the Turks. According to Sanudo, he spent 80,000 florins on the fortifications of the Castel S. Angelo. He was short of funds and was deriving no income from France, but remained firm in his alliance with the league of Venice,[79] for the great fear was always that Charles VIII was going to come back.[80] Beginning with the year 1496 the extraordinary *Diarii* of Marino Sanudo inform us in almost incredible detail concerning the affairs of all Italy and indeed of most of Europe. We learn of the dispatch of Turkish envoys to Naples, Milan, and Venice, and the activities of Turkish corsairs from the Archipelago to the western Mediterranean. From the diplomatic correspondence collected by the indefatigable Sanudo we know of Charles VIII's preparations (or lack of them) for his return to Italy; the Venetians' recruitment of stradioti at their various stations in the Morea; the futile expedition of Maximilian I into northern Italy; the desire of the citizens of French-held Taranto to surrender to Venice—or to the Turk;[81] the return home of two Venetian citizens of the Zorzi family who had been enslaved as boys when the Turks took Negroponte twenty-six years before (in 1470);[82] and, as almost always, the Turkish raids and Christian counter-attacks on the Hungarian front.[83]

Alexander VI's unsuccessful war against his old enemies, the Orsini, in which he managed only to secure his hold over the castle towns of Anguillara and Cerveteri, did not add to papal prestige.[84] He had tried to expropriate some of

[77] Sanudo, *Diarii*, I, 397–400, gives somewhat conflicting details, and dates Sagundino's report to the Venetian Senate on 2 December, 1496, also noting "che ancora dubita [el Signor turcho] di Giem sultam suo fradello, et voria el suo corpo volentiera." *Cf.* Malipiero, *Annali veneti*, in *Arch. stor. italiano*, VII-1 (1843), 147, who dates Sagundino's report [the same one?] to his return from an earlier mission on 9 November, 1495. Malipiero gives Bayazid's income as 2,200,000 ducats, and says he had six sons and seven sons-in-law, "cadaun de i quali tien corte separada."

Sagundino was given a commission for one of his several embassies to Istanbul on 30 May, 1496 (Sen. Secreta, Reg. 36, fols. 27ᵛ–28ʳ [39ᵛ–40ʳ by mod. enumeration]), and was soon on his way back to Istanbul (*ibid.*, fols. 99ʳ ff. [111ʳ ff.]). He knew the Turks well, having served on previous missions to the Porte (Sen. Secreta, Reg. 35, fols. 2ᵛ [14ᵛ by mod. enumeration], 8ʳ, 11ᵛ–12ʳ, dated April to June, 1494, and *cf.* above, note 38).

[78] Commines, *Mémoires*, bk. VII, chap. 5, ed. B. de Mandrot, II, 127, and *cf.* chap. 17, pp. 201–2.

[79] Sanudo, *Diarii*, I, 6.

[80] *Cf.* the pope's brief of 4 September, 1496, to the doge of Venice, in Sanudo, *Diarii*, I, 295–99. The French still held Ostia (*ibid.*, col. 297).

[81] Sanudo, *Diarii*, I, 367, 376–79, 380, 382–83, 400, 410–11, 420–21, 441–42, 447, 454, etc. Three-fourths of the population of Taranto were said to be Slavs, Albanians, and Greeks, the rest native Tarentines or Aragonese (*ibid.*, I, 377). The Venetians regarded "la inclinatione [che] monstrano haver Tarentini de darse a Turchi" as "pernitiosissima et supramodum detestanda," as the Senate wrote their provveditore in Monopoli on 1 October, 1496 (Sen. Secreta, Reg. 36, fol. 70ʳ [82ʳ]). The Senate was willing, however, to receive the Tarentine envoys who were expected to come to the lagoon to offer their city to the Republic (*ibid.*, fol. 77ʳ [89ʳ]), and did in fact receive them with "summa benivolentia et amicitia," but put off their offer to submit to Venetian rule with a rather vague answer. The Senate finally suggested that the Tarentines seek reconciliation with the king of Naples, which appeared to render the envoys desperate. The whole affair caused prolonged and apparently excited discussion among members of the Senate "ob incomparabilem magnitudinem potentie Turcorum incredibilemque facilitatem medio Tarenti invadendi et occupandi totam Italiam, a quo succederent non solum infinita mala et incommoda, sed etiam certissimus interitus reipublice Christiane!" (fols. 81ʳ–83ᵛ, 86ᵛ–89ᵛ, 91ʳ–95ʳ [93ʳ ff.], with quoted text on fol. 83ᵛ). Everyone recalled the Turkish occupation of Otranto in 1480–1481. The problem which the Senate faced, disappeared in January, 1497, however, when the Aragonese acquired Taranto (Sanudo, *Diarii*, I, 498–99), to the obvious dismay of many a Tarentine.

[82] Sanudo, *Diarii*, I, 379.

[83] *Ibid.*, I, 199, 295. The Hungarians and Poles made a truce with the Porte in January, 1497 (*ibid.*, I, 552, and *cf.* col. 800), but in April, 1498, the report reached Venice of a league formed against the Turks by the Poles, Hungarians, Bohemians, and Russians (*ibid.*, I, 950).

[84] Sigismondo de' Conti, II, 165–72; Malipiero, *Annali veneti*, in *Arch. stor. italiano*, VII-1 (1843), 484–85; Sanudo, *Diarii*, I, 447, 472, 478, 483–84, 506–7, 547; Burchard, *Diarium*, ed. Thuasne, II, 355, and ed. Celani, II (1911–42, unfinished), 15 [=*RISS*, XXXII, pt. 1]; Guicciardini, *Storia d'Italia*, III, 5, ed. G. Rosini, I (Paris, 1837), 446–51. Peace was made between the pope and the Orsini on 5 February, 1497.

their chief possessions in order to give them to his favorite son, Juan Borgia, duke of Gandia. On 9 March (1497), however, the Spanish captain Don Gonsalvo Fernando of Cordova succeeded in forcing the French to surrender Cardinal Giuliano della Rovere's fortress at Ostia, which made the shipment of food up the Tiber both less expensive and less hazardous.[85] The pope had deprived Giuliano of his benefices "come nemicho di la sedia apostolicha," says Sanudo, without the consent and despite the opposition of the College of Cardinals. His brother Giovanni della Rovere, from whom the pope was still trying to collect the 40,000 ducats taken from the Turkish envoy,[86] was deprived of his title of prefect of Rome.[87]

As evening began to fall on Wednesday, 14 June (1497), the pope's son Juan Borgia, second duke of Gandia and captain-general of the military forces of the Holy See, who on the seventh had added to his titles and possessions the newly created duchy of Benevento and the cities of Terracina and Pontecorvo,[88] left a dinner for family and friends given by his mother Vannozza de' Catanei in her vineyard near the church of S. Pietro in Vincoli.[89] The dinner had probably been given in honor of his brother Cesare, who was soon leaving for Naples. Suddenly bidding Cesare goodbye when they had reached their father's former palace [the present Palazzo Sforza-Cesarini on the Corso Vittorio Emmanuele], Juan departed with a masked man (*facie velata*), who had been calling on him almost daily at the apostolic palace for the past month. Cesare watched Juan disappear into the gathering dusk. Obviously he intended to keep some sort of assignation (*alibi solatii causa*), presumably a clandestine love affair. That was the last time Juan was seen alive by either family or friends. His failure to return during the course of the following day, Thursday the fifteenth, spread consternation throughout the Vatican palace. Burchard says the pope was "omnino contristatus ac totis visceribus commotus," overwhelmed with worry and sick at heart.

---

[85] Sanudo, *Diarii*, I, 465–66, 507, 522, 527–28, 539, 547, 555–56, 561, 569–70; *Diario ferrarese*, in *RISS*, XXIV-7, p. 171; Burchard, *Diarium*, ed. Thuasne, II, 358–59, and ed. Celani, II, 18–19. Don Gonsalvo resented the figurehead command of the pope's son Juan Borgia, the duke of Gandia, to whom precedence was accorded in court ceremonies (Burchard, *Diarium*, ed. Thuasne, II, 360, and ed. Celani, II, 19). The fortress at Ostia remains in an excellent state of preservation. On the composition of the army of Don Gonsalvo [Gonzalo Fernández de Córdoba], see Paul Stewart, "The *Santa Hermandad* and the First Italian Campaign of Gonzalo de Córdoba, 1495–1498," *Renaissance Quarterly*, XXVIII (1975), 29–37.

[86] Sanudo, I, 450, report of January, 1497; Malipiero, *Annali veneti*, in *Arch. stor. italiano*, VII-1 (1843), 488.

[87] Sanudo, I, 555, reports from Rome received in Venice on 14 March, 1497. In 1474 Giovanni della Rovere (d. 1501), lord of Sinigaglia (Senigallia), had married Giovanna (d. 1514), sister of Guidobaldo da Montefeltro, duke of Urbino, the last of his line. Their son Francesco Maria della Rovere (born in 1490) was regarded as the heir to the duchy of Urbino, toward which the Borgias were directing their covetous attention. A vassal of the Church, Guidobaldo commanded the papal forces in the war against the Orsini, but he was hardly a committed partisan of the Borgias. Eventually Francesco Maria succeeded Guidobaldo as duke of Urbino (in April, 1508). *Cf.* Jas. Dennistoun, *Memoirs of the Dukes of Urbino*, ed. Edw. Hutton, II (London and New York, 1909), 282–83, 291–300, 313 ff.

[88] Burchard, *Diarium*, ed. Thuasne, II, 386–87, and ed. Celani, II, 41; Sanudo, *Diarii*, I, 650b.

[89] It may not be irrelevant to observe that Vannozza de'Catanei's funeral inscription, which Pastor believed to be lost (*Gesch. d. Päpste*, III-1 [repr. 1955], 327, note 1), was found toward the end of 1947 during certain work of restoration being carried out in the basilica of S. Marco in Rome. Her burial stone had been used, face down, as a paving block, probably from the middle of the seventeenth century. The bronze filler had been gouged out of the lettering, which was somewhat defaced in the process. The stone has now been cleansed of the adherent mortar, and set up on the right wall of the portico of S. Marco.

Vannozza was buried (in 1518) in S. Maria del Popolo, but her monument (like scores of others) was removed in the reconstruction of the latter church. Her children are listed in the order of their birth, as usual in such inscriptions, and the text makes clear that Cesare was the eldest. Her funerary inscription had been published in Vincenzo Forcella, *Iscrizioni delle chiese e d'altri edificii di Roma dal secolo XI fino ai giorni nostri*, 14 vols., 1869–84, I, no. 1276, p. 335, from a copy made in 1576. It has been reprinted, with corrections, by Antonio Ferrua, "Ritrovamento dell'epitaffio di Vannozza Cattaneo," *Archivio della Società romana di storia patria*, LXXI (1948), 139–41: "D.O.M. / Vannotiae Cathaneae, Caesare Valentiae, / Ioanne Gandiae, Iafredo Scyllatii et / Lucretia Ferrariae ducibus filiis nobili, / probitate insigni, relligione eximia, / pari et aetate et prudentia, optime / de xenodochio Lateranensi meritae, / Hyeronimus Picus fideicomm. procurator / ex testamento posuit: / Vixit annos LXXVI, menses IIII, dies XIII. / Obiit anno MDXVIII, XXVI Novembris."

On Vannozza, note Celani, I, 562–64, note 2. She was rich, and in her later years a benefactress of churches in Rome and a patroness of artists, on which see P. Fedele, "I Gioielli di Vannozza ed un'opera del Caradosso," *ibid.*, XXVIII (1905), 451–71, with eight documents. Mario Menotti has published 470 documents relating to the family, friends, and retainers of Alexander VI in *Documenti inediti sulla famiglia e la corte di Alessandro VI*, Rome, 1917; these documents are largely concerned with grants of revenue and benefices, marriages, investitures, etc., and payments for Cesare Borgia's soldiery (from March, 1500). Those having to do with Vannozza, *ibid.*, nos. 12–24, pp. 9–18, are conspicuous in Menotti's collection, and include Vannozza's will dated 15 January, 1517 (no. 23).

Investigation revealed that a certain Giorgio Schiavone (*Georgius Sclavus*), a lumber merchant with a yard on the Tiber near the Church and Hospital of S. Girolamo degli Schiavoni (hard by the street which ran from the bridge of S. Angelo directly to the church of S. Maria del Popolo),[90] had seen a man mounted on a white horse, and four servitors who addressed him as *signore*, throw a body into the river about 2:00 A.M. (*circa horam quintam*) on Thursday. Giorgio was keeping watch on board a little boat tied up along the river bank, lest anyone steal part of a recent shipment of lumber. He stated that, after two of the footmen had emerged from an alley and looked up and down the waterfront without seeing anyone, they had withdrawn, and the other two appeared and surveyed the gloomy scene in the same way. There was still no one in sight. Then the horseman appeared with a body dangling behind him, slung over the rear of his horse and steadied by the first two footmen, who walked on either side of their gruesome charge. At the river's edge the horseman turned his mount around, tail to the water; the two footmen flung the corpse as far out as they could. The horseman asked whether the body had sunk, and they answered, "Signor si!" Then he asked what that black thing was floating down there; they replied it was the dead man's cloak, and one of them sank it by throwing stones at it. Now the three of them joined the other two footmen who had been keeping watch. Their job done, they all disappeared into the night.

When the papal authorities asked Giorgio Schiavone why he had not reported such a heinous crime to the governor of the city, he said that in his time he had seen a hundred bodies thrown into the Tiber at the same spot. No account had ever been taken of them. He had therefore attached no particular importance to this one. The next step was to recover the body. Burchard was given to understand that some three hundred fishermen and divers were assembled for the purpose with their nets and grappling hooks. Before the hour of vespers on Friday the sixteenth Juan Borgia, duke of Gandia, was fished out of the Tiber, his throat slit and his body bearing eight other wounds. Obviously the motive for his murder had not been robbery. He was completely and expensively dressed; his gloves were still tucked under his belt; his purse contained thirty ducats. His body was taken to the Castel S. Angelo, where under the watchful eyes of Burchard's colleague, Bernardino Gutterii, it was washed, clad in military garments, and prepared for burial. That Friday evening, about 9:00 P.M., Juan Borgia's body was carried from S. Angelo to the church of S. Maria del Popolo, preceded by one hundred and twenty torches and all the prelates of the palace *cum magno fletu et ululatu*. He seemed less dead than asleep when he was interred in the church, "where he remains to this day."[91]

"When the pope understood," says Burchard,

[90] *Cf.* Burchard, *Diarium*, ed. Celani, II, 42–43, and note 3: ". . . juxta seu prope hospitale sancti Hieronymi Sclavorum nuncupatum, in via qua de ponte sancti Angeli recta via itur ad ecclesiam beate Marie de Populo. . . ." The Hospital no longer exists, but did so into quite modern times. The Church once attached thereto is now called the Ven. Chiesa di S. Girolamo dei Croati (or degli Illirici); it was entirely rebuilt by Sixtus V in 1588, and is located at the east end of the modern Ponte Cavour.

[91] Burchard, *Diarium*, ed. Thuasne, II, 387–90, with append., no. 28, pp. 669–70, and ed. Celani, II, 42–44, with notes of Thuasne and Celani; Sanudo, *Diarii*, I, 651–52, 653–55, 657–58, the last entry being a letter dated 16 June, 1497, from Ugolino Matteo in Rome to Niccolò Paniglino of Udine, then apparently in Venice, which agrees closely with Burchard's account of the duke of Gandia's murder. Malipiero, *Annali veneti*, in *Arch. stor. italiano*, VII-1 (1843), 489–91, gives a letter sent from Rome on 17 June, also in Sanudo, I, 658–60, where the text is better, and see, *ibid.*, I, 660–63, copies of letters sent by the pope on 19 June informing the duke of Milan and the doge of Venice of Gandia's death, together with the doge's consolatory answer of the twenty-ninth. I have found a copy of the letter of 19 June to Duke Lodovico Sforza of Milan in the Arch. di Stato di Modena, Cancelleria Estense, Estero, Carteggio di principi, Roma, Busta 1295 / 10, no. 29. Note in general the *Diario ferrarese*, in *RISS*, XXIV-7, p. 200; Alois Knöpfler, "Der Tod d. Herzogs von Gandia," *Theologische Quartalschrift*, LIX (Tübingen, 1877), 438–76; A. Luzio and R. Renier, "Relazione inedita sulla morte del duca di Gandia," *Archivio della R. Società romana di storia patria*, XI (1888), 296–303, a letter dated at Rome on 16 June (1497) to the Marquis Francesco Gonzaga by the Mantuan envoy Gian Carlo Scalona, whose account corresponds more or less to that of Burchard; Pastor, *Hist. Popes*, V, 493–96 ff., with several minor errors, and append., nos. 36–40, pp. 552–58, and *Gesch. d. Päpste*, III-1 (repr. 1955), 443–45 ff., and III-2 (repr. 1956), append., nos. 38–42, pp. 1064–68. The news of Gandia's murder was generally known in Florence by 19 June (Luca Landucci, *Diario fiorentino*, ed. del Badia [1883], p. 153, trans. Alice de Rosen Jervis [1927], p. 123).

The Italians commonly began the first hour just after sunset (from after 5:00 P.M. to after 9:00 P.M., depending on the season), but the practice varied, and reports of time are often careless and (with reference to the same event) inconsistent with one another. In mid-June Burchard is properly beginning the first hour just after 9:00 P.M. in the three specific references to time in his description of the death and burial of Juan Borgia (in Celani's edition, vol. II, p. 42, line 19; p. 43, l. 19; and p. 44, l. 8), and in the text above I have so indicated the hours of the day and night, on which see B. M. Lersch, *Einleitung in die Chronologie*, I (Freiburg im Breisgau, 1899), 8–9.

"that the duke had been killed and thrown like dung into the river, he was quite overcome, and in grief and bitterness of heart he shut himself up in his chamber and wept terribly. . . . He neither ate nor drank from the evening of Wednesday the fourteenth to the following Saturday, nor from Thursday morning to the following Sunday did he get even an hour's sleep. . . ."[92] Ascanio Sforza wrote his brother Lodovico il Moro on 19 June that the pope had just said in consistory that he could only view his son's murder as a divine punishment for his own failings, and that now his thoughts were turning to the improvement of his own way of life and to the reform of the Church, for which latter purpose he had immediately appointed a commission of six cardinals.[93]

Neither the murderer of the duke of Gandia nor the reason for his violence was ever discovered. Certainly, as the Florentine ambassador Alessandro Bracci wrote the Dieci di Balia the day after the body was discovered, whoever was responsible "has certainly handled the affair well, has had his wits about him and much courage, and in any event it is recognized that he has shown a masterly touch. . . ."[94] Diligent rumor fastened the guilt on a number of persons—the Orsini and the Sanseverineschi; Cardinal Ascanio Sforza and Duke Guidobaldo of Urbino; Giovanni Sforza, lord of Pesaro, whose marriage to Lucrezia Borgia the pope was determined to annul; and even Gioffredo Borgia, prince of Squillace, Gandia's brother, the accusation against whom the pope himself summarily dismissed in the consistory of 19 June.[95] We may agree with Enrico Celani that we shall probably never learn with certainty who was really guilty; some document may still be found in one archive or another, "ma esso non sarà mai tale da precisare il vero assassino."[96] Those who struck the nine blows that felled Gandia were presumably not the true assassins. The Orsini may have been responsible for the deed, but for weeks to come (according to the Venetian envoy Niccolò Michiel) popular opinion in Rome attributed it to Ascanio Sforza, who removed himself from the city to Frascati, Grottaferrata, and Genazzano, where he found the atmosphere healthier (and not alone because of the persistent plague in Rome).[97] Information reaching Venice in December (1497), however, was to the effect that the pope was determined upon the ruin of the Orsini, "e questo perchè li Orsini certo havia fato amazar suo fiol ducha di Gandia."[98] Later on, when Cesare Borgia was earning the almost universal reprobation of Italy, he was widely believed to have begun his secular career with fratricide.[99] Some months after Gandia's death

[92] Burchard, *Diarium*, ed. Thuasne, II, 390–91, and ed. Celani, II, 44. Burchard's diary stops here, to be resumed on 7 August. Gregorovius, *Storia della città di Roma*, VII, 474, believed that Burchard found it advisable to discontinue his chronicle of events at the papal court for some time after Gandia's death; but Celani, *loc. cit.*, note 3, doubts this, observing that most lacunae in the diary come during the summer months when presumably Burchard employed the customary summer vacation to attend to his own affairs.

[93] Pastor, *Hist. Popes*, V, 500 ff., 512 ff., and append., nos. 37–38, 40, pp. 552–54, 557, and *Gesch. d. Päpste*, III-1 (repr. 1955), 448 ff., 457 ff., and III-2 (repr. 1956), append., nos. 39–40, 42, pp. 1064–66, 1067–68. Since Ascanio Sforza did not attend the consistory, his letter of 19 June (Pastor, III-2, append., no. 39, pp. 1064–65) is presumably a less certain account of the consistory than the report dated the twentieth of the Venetian ambassador, who was present (Sanudo, *Diarii*, I, 653–54), in which the pope is alleged to have said that "if we had seven papacies, we would give them all to restore the duke's life," which would seem to indicate that Alexander VI, even in the midst of his announced dedication to reform, was likely to put the interests of the Borgias before those of the Church. But at least through June and July, 1497, the pope's reform program produced a spate of documents, on which note M. Tangl, *Die päpstlichen Kanzleiordnungen*, Innsbruck, 1894, repr. 1959, pp. 386–421.

[94] Thuasne, ed., *Burchardi diarium*, II, append., no. 28, p. 670, letter dated at Rome on 17 June (1497).

[95] Sanudo, *Diarii*, I, 653. The pope also disclaimed belief in Giovanni Sforza's guilt.

[96] Celani, in his edition of Burchard's diary, *Johannis Burckardi liber notarum*, II (1911–42, unfinished), p. 44, note 2 [in *RISS*, XXXII, pt. 1].

[97] Sanudo, *Diarii*, I, 686, 689, 695, 698, 710, 737, 843. As late as June, 1498, a Venetian report was received to the effect that the pope had found out who had murdered the duke of Gandia, and that Cardinal Ascanio was implicated (*ibid.*, I, 994), which seems however most unlikely (Pastor, *Gesch. d. Päpste*, III-1 [repr. 1955], 451–52).

[98] Sanudo, *Diarii*, I, 827, 883, and *cf.* Pastor, *Gesch. d. Päpste*, III-1 (repr. 1955), 452–54, and Knöpfler, in *Theologische Quartalschrift*, LIX, 467–69, who believes that the Orsini together with Ascanio Sforza were responsible for the crime.

[99] Pastor, *Gesch. d. Päpste*, III-1, 454–58, and *cf.* Luzio and Renier, in *Arch. della R. Società rom. di storia patria*, XI, 296–99, and Knöpfler, in *Theologische Quartalschrift*, LIX, 456–61, 470–76, who first demolished Gregorovius's quite unwarranted attribution of the murder of Gandia to Cesare. Apparently the first reference to Cesare as the probable murderer of his brother comes on 22 February, 1498, when Giovanni Alberto della Pigna wrote Duke Ercole d'Este from Venice, "Di nuovo ho inteso che de la morte del duca di Gandia fu causa il cardinale suo fratello . . . e detto avviso di detta morte l'ho da buonissimo luogo" (Maria Bellonci, *Lucrezia Borgia* [1939, repr. 1969], pp. 112, 505–6, and *cf.* Woodward, *Cesare Borgia*, pp. 118–19). Later

Cardinal Jean de Bilhères, the abbot of S. Denis and French ambassador in Rome, commissioned Michelangelo to do the extraordinary Pietà now in S. Peter's, in the first chapel on the right as one enters the church. Almost from the time when Michelangelo's work was first exhibited, there have been those who have seen Gandia's features and his beard in those of the dead Christ and (still more) his mother Vannozza's features in those of the Virgin.[100]

The pope's reform commission of six cardinals, two auditors of the Rota, and their various assistants held regular morning sessions in the Vatican. A reform bull was drafted in the midsummer of 1497, regulating papal elections, condemning simony and nepotism, and forbidding the alienation of church lands under the guise of vicariates. According to the bull, no cardinal should hold more than one bishopric or receive an annual income of more than 6,000 ducats from all his benefices. Members of the Sacred College should also limit their households to eighty attendants, their stables to thirty mounts, and their funeral expenses to 1,500 florins. They should not go about the city at night without lanterns or attend jousts, carnivals, comedies, or other frivolous entertainments. Abuses were to be eradicated from the papal chancery, the penitentiary, and various other offices of the Curia.[101] Despite the sincerity of most members of the reform commission, time soon made it clear that, if the Curia was conceivably corrigible, the pope was not, and the ambitions which he had entertained for the incompetent duke of Gandia seemed likely to be shifted to the far sturdier shoulders of Cardinal Cesare Borgia.

On 22 July (1497) Cesare left Rome with a retinue of three hundred horse on the most important—and the last important—function that he was to perform as a member of the Sacred College. He was going as *legatus de latere* to Naples, "in which kingdom," Venetian intelligence stated, "conditions were more disturbed than they had ever been." Alexander VI had selected him to crown Federigo as king of Naples. The ceremony was to take place in Capua. When Cesare arrived there, his cavalcade was said to number seven hundred, "which would give great expense to the king, who is very poor." Federigo had summoned all his barons to Capua to attend the coronation. Some of the more powerful personages in the kingdom failed to appear. In mid-August Federigo received at Cesare's hands the crown, scepter, and orb, and thereafter distributed some titles and knighthoods. The Venetian envoy noted that there were few jewels in the crown.[102] The last and perhaps the most upright of the Aragonese kings of Naples was beginning his brief reign.[103]

After the coronation the king and the cardinal-legate returned to Naples with the chief members

---

on, Sigismondo de'Conti, Machiavelli, Guicciardini, and the Venetian ambassador Paolo Capello all fixed responsibility for Gandia's death on Cesare. Paolo Capello was elected ambassador to the Holy See on 15 May, 1499 (Sen. Secreta, Reg. 37, fols. 92^{v}–93^{r} [106^{v}–107^{r}]), by which time the gossips had been busy for more than a year. Capello's predecessor in the Venetian embassy in Rome had been the discreet Girolamo Donato, elected on 4 October, 1497 (*ibid.*, Reg. 36, fol. 166^{r} [178^{r}]). There is no doubt that Cesare ordered the strangulation of Duke Alfonso of Bisceglie, Lucrezia's second husband, on 18 August, 1500, after which he was widely believed to have been guilty of his brother's assassination. Thus in May, 1504, Cesare's henchman Micheletto, while a prisoner in the Torre de Nona in Rome, was "interrogato della morte de assai persone, dei quali quei de più conto sono el duca de Gandia . . . ," etc. (Pasquale Villari, ed., *Dispacci di Antonio Giustinian*, III [Florence, 1876], 129).

[100] Mario Menotti, "Vannozza Cattanei e i Borgia," *Nuova Antologia di lettere, scienze ed arti*, 6th ser., CLXXXVI (=CCLXX, Rome, 1916), 470–86, esp. p. 478. Commonly and erroneously called Jean Villiers de la Groslaye [or Grolaie], the cardinal's name was actually Bilhères-Lagraulas; see Chas. Samaran, *Jean de Bilhères-Lagraulas, cardinal de Saint-Denis, un diplomate français sous Louis XI et Charles VIII*, Paris, 1921, p. 13, note 2, and on his relations with Michelangelo, *ibid.*, pp. 78–80. Jean de Bilhères died in Rome on 6 August, 1499 (Burchard, *Diarium*, ed. Thuasne, II, 549–52, and ed. Celani, II, 156–57).

[101] Pastor, *Gesch. d. Päpste*, III-1 (repr. 1955), 458–62, and III-2 (repr. 1956), append., no. 43, pp. 1068–72; Christ. G. Hoffmann, *Nova scriptorum ac monumentorum . . . collectio*, I (Leipzig, 1731), 520–22, who also gives excerpts from proposed reforms of the College under Martin V, Sixtus IV, and Julius III, as well as from the Councils of Basel and the Lateran; Sanudo, *Diarii*, I, 653–54, 655, a letter of Ugolino Matteo dated at Rome on 8 July, 1497, also *ibid.*, col. 844; *cf.* Malipiero, *Annali veneti*, in *Arch. stor. italiano*, VII-1 (1843), 494.

[102] Sanudo, *Diarii*, I, 694–95, 698, 709–10, 713, 719–21; J. C. Lünig, *Codex Italiae diplomaticus*, II (Frankfurt and Leipzig, 1726), pt. 2, sect. 2, doc. no. 133, cols. 1309–12, papal brief to Federigo informing him of Cardinal Cesare's legatine mission to perform the coronation (misdated 9 June, 1498).

[103] With reference to the famine in Naples in September, 1497, Sanudo notes "that the king, Don Federigo, especially favored the people, for which reason the barons hated him" (*Diarii*, I, 793), and the impoverished Federigo soon had to take the field against the rebellious barons (*ibid.*, I, 796). *Cf.* Burchard, *Diarium*, ed. Thuasne, II, 408, and ed. Celani, II, 55.

of the court and the diplomatic corps. The stark avarice of Borgia demands was such that the Florentine envoy Alessandro Bracci had written on 19 July (1497): "It would not be astonishing if the poor king had recourse to the Turk in his despair, were it only to free himself from these annoyances."[104] Cesare arrived back in Rome on the night of 5 September, lodging at the monastery of S. Maria Nova, his titular church, where the cardinals rode out to meet him the following morning. Although in the public consistory which followed, the pope altered customary proceedings slightly to do especial honor to Cesare (as Burchard supposed), neither father nor son spoke a word to each other.[105] What private communications may have passed between them while Cesare was in Naples, it is impossible to say, but by mid-September it was understood in Venice that the pope wanted Cesare to give up the red hat and his ecclesiastical benefices. His father was planning to establish a state for him in Italy, it was said, and to make him gonfalonier of the Church. Rumor had it that he wanted to marry Cesare to Ferrante II's widow, a niece of the king of Spain, and that he was requesting King Federigo to invest him with the principality of Taranto as a dowry.[106] Some days later additional information was entered by Sanudo in his *Diarii* to the effect that Cesare, who had about 35,000 ducats a year revenue from his benefices and was the second richest cardinal in the College, wanted to resign his position and embark on a military career (*or per esser cupido di exercitarsi in cosse bellice*). His father was granting him the dispensation to marry. Furthermore, the scandalized Sanudo goes on to note that Alexander VI was even planning to dissolve his younger son Gioffredo's marriage to Sancia of Aragon, princess of Squillace, on the grounds that it was still unconsummated, in order to marry her to Cesare, who had already made her his mistress anyhow. Although Sanudo appears not to believe all this gossip, he says it was current in Rome. King Federigo was thought willing to make Cesare prince of Taranto; the pope was going to make him captain of the Church. Don Gioffredo, who was thus supposed to be losing his wife, was to be made a cardinal and receive Cesare's benefices and income! At any rate Lucrezia's marriage to Giovanni Sforza of Pesaro was being dispensed. It was certainly a fact in Sanudo's opinion "che questo papa fa cosse excessive et intollerabile!"[107] On that score at least there could be no doubt.

Sanudo received his information concerning Alexander VI and Cesare Borgia from the Venetian envoy to the Holy See, Niccolò Michiel, who had received it from Cardinal Costa of Lisbon.[108] Burchard had noted the coolness which developed between Costa and Cesare upon the latter's return from Naples. Although Costa had gone out *more solito* to the monastery of S. Maria Nova, he arrived rather late, did not enter the monastery, failed to dismount from his mule when Cesare appeared, and did not speak to him at all.[109] One of the more upright members of the College, George Costa was not impartial where Cesare Borgia was concerned. But resignation from the College was Cesare's idea, not his father's. When in early December (1497) Giangiacomo Sclafenati, the cardinal of Parma, died in Rome, Alexander VI gave all his benefices to Cesare. Sanudo records their value as 12,000 ducats a year, "uno bel presente de beneficii. . . ."[110] Whether the pope was trying to dissuade Cesare from returning to lay life by heaping ecclesiastical wealth upon him or was thus holding Sclafenati's benefices in abeyance for subsequent disposal, is not clear. Pastor cites a letter of 24 December from Cardinal Ascanio Sforza to Lodovico il Moro in which Cesare was said daily to be increasing his efforts to leave the College, while the pope was anxious, if Cesare's resignation had to be, that it take place under the guise of the best pretext possible and with a minimum of scandal.[111]

Alexander VI had troubles enough without the Turk. On the day of the duke of Gandia's disappearance (14 June, 1497) a priest who slept above the chapel in S. Peter's, a practice

---

[104] P. Villari, *Niccolò Machiavelli*, trans. Linda Villari, I (New York, 1898), 195; Pastor, *Hist. Popes*, V, 519, and *Gesch. d. Päpste*, III-1 (repr. 1955), 462–63; and *cf.* Sanudo, *Diarii*, I, 758.

[105] Burchard, *Diarium*, ed. Thuasne, II, 402–4, and ed. Celani, II, 51–52.

[106] Sanudo, *Diarii*, I, 787.

[107] Sanudo, *Diarii*, I, 792–93. (Sanudo is summarizing a diplomatic dispatch from Rome, presumably from the Venetian ambassador Niccolò Michiel; sometimes it is hard to distinguish Sanudo's impressions from those of the writer of the initial report.)

[108] *Cf.* Sanudo, *Diarii*, I, 795.

[109] Burchard, *Diarium*, ed. Thuasne, II, 403, and ed. Celani, II, 52.

[110] Sanudo, *Diarii*, I, 832.

[111] Pastor, *Hist. Popes*, V, 520, and *Gesch. d. Päpste*, III-1 (repr. 1955), 463, quotation from a letter in cipher, dated at Rome on 24 December, 1497, in the Milanese State Archives. *Cf.* Sanudo, *Diarii*, I, 863, 871, which latter notice lists the titles which Cesare allegedly proposed for himself.

properly forbidden, had seen mysterious torches carried by the unseen legion of Lucifer.[112] Six months later on the night of 16 December an unearthly, terrifying voice filled the Vatican, frightening the pope and the residents of the palace half to death, and many knowing persons identified the phenomenon as Gandia's ghost.[113] Extraordinary events seemed of almost weekly occurrence. Late in the night of 14 September the pope suddenly ordered the arrest of his first secretary Bartolommeo Flores (Florido), archbishop of Cosenza, and had him imprisoned in the Castel S. Angelo for issuing a vast number of fraudulent bulls and briefs, some of an extraordinarily daring nature, as well as bestowing benefices and expectations without papal knowledge or consent, grants of exemption from the jurisdiction of ordinaries, and the like: Burchard notes that Flores was believed to have issued about 3,000 false briefs, a scandal likely to shake the ecclesiastical structure of Europe to its foundations. Deprived of his archbishopric, and stripped of "all honor, dignity, order, and benefices," after trial by a commission, Flores was lowered by a rope into the terrible cell known as the *Sammarocco* or *Sammalo*, of which Benvenuto Cellini later had a brief experience, in the Castel S. Angelo. In the Sammarocco, Flores could live as long as bread, water, and oil for a lamp, a breviary, the Bible, and the epistles of S. Peter might sustain him.[114] Flores had offered no defense; his confession was said to have been gained by trickery. His fate was such that even the stolid Burchard was moved to compassion.

Flores was lowered to his destiny on the evening of 28 October. The next morning, Sunday the twenty-ninth, lightning struck the powder magazine in the great upper tower of the Castel S. Angelo, destroyed the marble figure of the angel, and ruined the battlements of the fortress, scattering stones into the Borgo and across the Tiber. Fifteen persons were injured. Malipiero says the effects of the lightning penetrated even to the papal antechamber. The Florentine apothecary Luca Landucci heard the news in Florence on 3 November. The thunderbolt had struck the angel, which fell among the munitions, setting them on fire and hurling wood and stones, crossbows and armor across the river: "it was a frightful thing!"[115] It was also, as Sanudo noted, a portent of something to come.

Alexander VI had no need of further troubles, but they were in the offing. To the flood of the Tiber, the murder of the duke of Gandia, the adverse reaction to the cynical annulment of Lucrezia Borgia's marriage, Cesare's determination to quit the College, the scandal of Flores' forgeries and falsifications, and the obvious portents that left all Italy discussing Alexander's ill-starred reign, must be added the Curia's struggle with the courageous and astute Fra Girolamo Savonarola, prior of the Dominican convent of S. Marco in Florence. Savonarola's prophetic utterances were a constant source of embarrassment and irritation to Rome. Although in his long experience of Italian affairs the wily pope had watched reformers come and go, this time he feared that the burning sincerity of Savonarola's sermons was converting Florence into a city of saints hostile to his papacy. Since the expulsion of the Medici from Florence (in November, 1494), the friar had been the dominant political as well as religious influence on the banks of the Arno. He had helped keep the Florentines loyal to the French alliance, to the vast annoyance of the pope and the Venetians. Again and again he had proclaimed Charles VIII as God's emissary to reform the Church and remove the notorious rascalities of the Curia. The persistent attachment of Florence to France gave added incentive to Charles VIII's announced intention of returning to Italy. The Florentines were quite certain that he was coming back.[116] Of course a long tradition bound the city of the red lily to the royal fleur-de-lys. Florentine bankers and merchants had made fortunes in France, which was still the major market for Florentine manufactures and the (now sadly diminished) woolen industry.

While the pope, whose own career was more of a scandal than that of Flores, celebrated

---

[112] Sanudo, *Diarii*, I, 656–57.

[113] *Ibid.*, I, 842, 879.

[114] Burchard, *Diarium*, ed. Thuasne, II, 405–6, 408–11, and ed. Celani, II, 54, 55–58; Sanudo, I, 787; *cf.* E. Lavagnino, *Le Château Saint-Ange*, Rome, 1950, p. 8. Although the report that Flores had issued 3,000 false briefs is a patent exaggeration, I know of no reason to assume that the charge against him was trumped up by the Borgias to seize his property (Villari, *Machiavelli*, Engl. trans., I, 195–96). Flores died in the Castel S. Angelo on 23 July, 1498 (Burchard, ed. Thuasne, II, 490, and ed. Celani, II, 114).

[115] Burchard, *Diarium*, ed. Thuasne, II, 411–12, and ed. Celani, II, 58; Sanudo, *Diarii*, I, 814, 815; Malipiero, *Annali veneti*, in *Arch. stor. italiano*, VII-1 (1843), 497; Luca Landucci, *Diario fiorentino*, ed. Iodoco del Badia, Florence, 1883, p. 159, trans. Alice de Rosen Jervis (1927), p. 127.

[116] *Cf.* Sanudo, *Diarii*, I, 491–92.

mass in the Sistina, Flores was dying in the Sammarocco. Savonarola was untiring in his excoriation of priestly vice and corruption. On 7 November, 1496, a papal brief had rescinded the independence of S. Marco, and ordered all persons concerned (including Savonarola) under pain of excommunication to unite the convent to the recently created Tusco-Roman congregation, to whose vicar the friar would be subject. Actually the brief was addressed to sixteen convents, of which S. Marco was but one. Savonarola was not mentioned in it, but it was obvious against whom it was directed.[117] Savonarola defied the brief as he had earlier ones; he continued his passionate parade of prophecy, inspired by texts from the Old Testament. He had long been comparing Rome to Babylon and denouncing the pope who, he was quoted as saying, was worse than a Turk while (be this as it may) the sultan was reported to have had some of Savonarola's sermons translated into Turkish in order to read them himself.[118] The inevitable time came on 13 May, 1497, when a papal brief was issued to the Florentines excommunicating "a certain Fra Girolamo Savonarola" and forbidding all association with him under pain of the same excommunication. The brief was translated into Italian, and printed to secure it a wide circulation. Ironically enough, it bore the signature of Bartolommeo Flores, the pope's first secretary—but this was not a forged brief![119]

Landucci informs us that Savonarola's excommunication was officially published in Florence in five different churches on the morning of 18 June. He heard it read himself in S. Spirito.[120] Although every major development which affected the papacy during this era had its relevance to the Curia's attitude toward the Turk and the crusade, there are obviously limits to the extent to which we may pursue interests as peripheral as that of Savonarola's defiance of Alexander VI. At the end of February, 1498, however, Savonarola made a notable assault upon the corruption of the clergy and Rome: "Write to Rome that the friar who is in Florence, together with his followers, is ready to fight against you as against the Turks and pagans! . . ."[121]

As the friar contemplated a universal appeal for a general council, the Curia planned to arrest the Florentine merchants in Rome and to seize their goods to force the vacillating Signoria to send that "son of iniquity" to Rome for trial. Tension had been running high in Florence for months when Savonarola's devoted follower Fra Domenico da Pescia accepted the challenge of a rival Franciscan preacher, Francesco di Puglia, to test the validity of the friar's doctrine and contentions through the ordeal by fire, which after much bickering on both sides was finally set for 7 April. Savonarola's enemies in the Signoria skillfully exploited the situation. Although the contending Dominicans and Minorites assembled in the Piazza dei Signori for the ordeal, to which the excited populace had been looking forward as the spectacle of the century, the fire was never lighted. The Minorites delayed the proceedings by one trivial objection

[117] The Latin text may be found in the *Bullarium Ordinis FF. Praedicatorum*, ed. Thos. Ripoll, IV (Rome, 1732), 124–25, and see esp. Roberto Ridolfi, *Vita di Girolamo Savonarola*, I (Rome, 1952), 269–71.

[118] P. Villari, *Girolamo Savonarola*, I (new ed., Florence, 1930), 445, 462, and trans. Linda Villari, London, 1897, pp. 423, 439; Pastor, *Hist. Popes*, VI, 13–16, and *Gesch. d. Päpste*, III-1 (repr. 1955), 477–80.

[119] Sanudo, *Diarii*, I, 632–33. Sanudo says that he reproduces the Italian translation circulating in Florence in printed form (*ibid.*, I, 633–34). P. Villari, *Girolamo Savonarola*, II (new ed., Florence, 1930), append., no. 5, gives the Latin text, previously published by Del Lungo, which had been addressed to the friars of the Badia (pp. XXXIX–XL). *Cf.* Pastor, *Hist. Popes*, VI, 20–21, and *Gesch. d. Päpste*, III-1 (repr. 1955), 484–85, and esp. Ridolfi, *Savonarola*, I, 296 ff.

[120] Landucci, *Diario fiorentino*, ed. del Badia (1883), pp. 152–53, with note; trans. Alice de Rosen Jervis (1927), pp. 122–23. The bearer of the numerous copies of the brief of excommunication was one Giovanvittorio da Camerino, who had been banished by the Eight, and lingered long in Siena, fearful of entering Florence; Giovanvittorio, an enemy of Savonarola, was in fact refused a safe-conduct when he requested one, and he improperly gave the briefs to someone else to deliver to their addressees. Only five churches of Orders opposed to Savonarola accepted delivery of the documents (Ridolfi, *Savonarola*, I, 297–301, and II, 188–89, notes).

[121] Ridolfi, *Savonarola*, I (1952), 334, from the sermons on Exodus; *cf.* Pastor, *Hist. Popes*, VI, 26–28, and *Gesch. d. Päpste*, III-1 (repr. 1955), 490–92. On the other hand Alexander VI said on the same day that "even Turks would not endure such insubordination against lawful authority" (*ibid.*, VI, 29, and III-1, 493). Savonarola had stated in May, 1496, that ". . . tu non troverai che la Chiesa fusse mai in peggiore che oggi . . . , io ti mostrerò che la non fu mai in peggiore termine che oggi," while the following February he was expecting soon to witness "el flagello della Italia, la renovazione della Chiesa, *la conversione delli turchi*." He set store by the divine conversion of the Turks, and seems not to have been much interested in the crusade. And we may note *en passant* that Savonarola never called Alexander VI the Antichrist, although his followers later did so (Romeo De Maio, "Savonarola, Alessandro VI e il mito dell'Anticristo," *Rivista storica italiana*, LXXXII [1970], 533–59, and *cf.* below, Chapter 17, note 144).

after another (presumably by prearrangement with the Signoria), and the Dominicans were hardly less stubborn. Time passed. The crowd grew restless and suspicious. Finally a heavy rain came. Both sides withdrew from the piazza. Back in S. Marco, Savonarola claimed a victory, but the Florentines had expected a dramatic miracle of some kind, such as a true saint and prophet should—somehow—have contrived to give them. Their profound disappointment, abetted always by agents of the Signoria, now produced an extraordinary reaction against Savonarola. The following evening, the gloomy Sunday of Florentine history, a howling mob attacked the convent of S. Marco. Savonarola and Domenico da Pescia were arrested and taken to the Palazzo, where their comrade Fra Silvestro was brought next morning. Savonarola was confined in the "alberghettino," the tower cell where Cosimo de' Medici had been imprisoned in September, 1433. Subjected to repeated tortures, his confessions "edited," he was tried twice before a secular commission, and then tried a third time before two ecclesiastical commissioners sent by the pope from Rome to see that injustice was done. He was tortured again, and adjudged to be a heretic and a schismatic. On 23 May (1498) Savonarola was hanged with the friars Domenico and Silvestro, and their bodies were burned in an elaborate auto-da-fé in the Piazza dei Signori, where a memorial set into the pavement still attests the ignominy of that day.[122] The execution of Savonarola, however, appeared to have solved one of the pope's major problems at a time when his attention was being drawn most forcibly toward France.

The allies of the Holy League were now at odds with one another. A truce was negotiated at Lyon on 25 February, 1497, suspending hostilities between France and the Spanish kingdoms from 25 April to 1 November.[123] There was much anxiety at Venice, but Charles VIII had finally, reluctantly, agreed to include Italy in the truce.[124] It appeared that Ferdinand and Isabella might be prepared to join with Charles in a division of the Neapolitan kingdom and certain other parts of Italy.[125] Maximilian was again evincing his hostility toward the Venetians. Unless he had his own interests to serve, Alexander VI was always an undependable ally and, as we shall see, he was becoming disenchanted with the upright Federigo of Naples. The prospects looked good for Charles VIII's success in another expedition into Italy when on 7 April, 1498, he died suddenly at the château of Amboise. The duke of Orléans became Louis XII of France. Months before this (in the preceding August) Marino Sanudo had recorded in his diaries that he had seen a large gold ducat, worth two ordinary ducats, which Louis had already struck bearing the significant legend, "Louis of Orléans, duke of Milan and Asti."[126] This was the shape of things to come.

---

[122] Ridolfi, *Savonarola*, I (1952), 347–85, 392–407, with notes in vol. II; Pastor, *Hist. Popes*, VI, 40–51, and *Gesch. d. Päpste*, III-1 (repr. 1955), 503–14; Sanudo, *Diarii*, I, 900, 920, 930–32, 935, 940, 942, 946–47, 951–52, 955, 968–69, 987–88, 995; Sigismondo de' Conti, II, 193–95; Luca Landucci, *Diario fiorentino*, ed. del Badia, pp. 162–79, and Engl. trans., pp. 130–44; Burchard, *Diarium*, ed. Thuasne, II, 444–54, 461–73, and ed. Celani, II, 81–86, 92–99; various texts and documents published in A. Gherardi, *Nuovi Documenti e studi intorno a Girolamo Savonarola*, 2nd ed., Florence, 1887; the extensive appendices to P. Villari, *Storia di Girolamo Savonarola*, 2 vols., new ed., Florence, 1930; and Jos. Schnitzer, *Quellen u. Forschungen zur Geschichte Savonarolas*, 4 vols., Munich and Leipzig, 1902–10.

The clash between Savonarola and Alexander VI continues to let loose a stream of books. Besides such popular works as those of Michael de la Bedoyere (New York, 1958), Pierre van Paassen (New York, 1960), Christian Loubet (Paris, 1967), and Giacinto M. Scaltriti (Turin, 1970), we have the long, stalwart work of Jos. Schnitzer, *Savonarola, ein Kulturbild aus der Zeit der Renaissance*, 2 vols., Munich, 1924; the four detailed studies of Giovanni Soranzo in *Il Tempo di Alessandro VI Papa e di Fra Girolamo Savonarola*, Milan, 1960; and the learned monograph of Romeo De Maio, *Savonarola e la Curia Romana*, Rome, 1969, in which Cardinal Oliviero Carafa, protector of the Dominican Order, figures almost as prominently as Savonarola.

[123] Sanudo, *Diarii*, I, 550, 585–90, and *cf.* Predelli, *Regesti dei Commemoriali*, VI (1903), bk. XVIII, no. 105, p. 30.

[124] Sanudo, *Diarii*, I, 788. This truce was of some importance in the career of Savonarola in Florence, whose defiance of the corrupt Curia constituted one of the larger problems of Alexander VI's papacy (*cf.* Ridolfi, *Vita di Girolamo Savonarola*, I, 281, 318–19).

[125] Sanudo, *Diarii*, I, 711, 712–13, 866–68.

[126] Sanudo, *Diarii*, I, 713. The coin was shown to Sanudo by Marco Lipomani (Lippomani), Venetian envoy to Milan. As for the death of Charles VIII, we may note that Commines, *Mémoires*, VIII, 25, ed. B. de Mandrot, II, 380–81, says that while passing under a gate at the château of Amboise, the king struck his forehead and died nine hours later. Commines says that he was not himself present in Amboise at the time, and his account seems unlikely in view of the contemporary reports of Charles's death given in Sanudo, I, 935–39. Burchard, *Diarium*, ed. Thuasne, II, 457, and ed. Celani, II, 88, states that "Carolus VIII, rex Francorum, apoplexia vita functus est . . . ," which seems to have been the fact. *Cf.* Malipiero, *Annali veneti*, in *Arch. stor. italiano*, VII-1 (1843), 500.

17. THE DIPLOMATIC REVOLUTION: FRANCE AND SPAIN, THE PAPACY AND VENICE (1498–1503)

MOST STUDENTS of history probably share the view that makes the last decade of the fifteenth century the beginning of the modern era. The first voyage of Columbus opened up the new world; Savonarola was the last great medieval preacher; and the expedition of Charles VIII initiated the contest between France and Spain for the control of Italy. To the thoughtful observer there was a peculiar correspondence of one enemy to another in the three major groupings of the powers with which we shall be primarily concerned from this point on. In eastern Europe the loosely knit empires of the Turks and the Germans faced each other along the harassed Hungarian frontier. The small but rich Italian states, of which Venice and the papacy were for various reasons the most important, had for centuries been fighting futile wars among themselves, often appealing to outsiders, especially the Germans and the French, for aid against one another. That tendency, which had continued to the close of the fifteenth century, was now fraught with new perils.

France, Spain, and England were to fight among themselves in the generations that lay ahead. Warfare demands of its participants a large measure of equality and likeness; otherwise the stronger power simply imposes its will on the weaker, and the more advanced on the more primitive. France, Spain, and England were much alike, nationally organized monarchies, whose kings could control their revenues, armies, and administrations to a larger extent than any heads of states since Hellenistic and Roman times. It was an age given to political speculation, and contemporaries were well aware of all these factors.

The anti-Turkish tradition was by and large too strong for the Italians to have recourse to the Turks for assistance against their enemies, although they sometimes did so, as when Boccolino Guzzoni turned to Istanbul for aid against the pope, and the Aragonese of Naples for aid against the French. But the Italians always had (they thought) better allies in Christendom, and for a while they tried to exploit for their own advantage the great resources of the French or Spanish. Almost like the Guelfs and Ghibellines appealing to popes and emperors in earlier generations, certain states now professed a French or Spanish allegiance, which was determined by the leader of the state. Florence was pro-French, and Naples pro-Spanish. Milan was at first pro-French, as we have seen, and then pro-Spanish,[1] as Lodovico il Moro determined. The papacy was pro-Spanish, and then became pro-French, as Alexander VI was soon to determine. The Venetians looked out for themselves, and the Ferrarese feared them. The lesser states yielded to political necessity to survive in time of crisis, pursuing policies of expediency in order to live from day to day. Principles were for the philosophers who could afford them. The historical sources are almost too numerous. The archives preserve miles of documentary evidence.

The extraordinary extensiveness of Sanudo's *Diarii*, for example, would make possible the accounting of events throughout this period in such detail as to satisfy any historian, even one whose passion for completeness might exceed his common sense. Statements of fact and rumor, letters, memoranda, private reports, official documents, and texts of treaties keep us informed of developments in Venice and Rome, Milan, Mantua, and Ferrara, Naples, Florence, Pisa, Genoa, and Montferrat, as well as in France, Spain, and Germany, and on the eastern front. No Venetian could overlook the affairs of the Levant. Sanudo keeps careful record of news from Istanbul and Alexandria.[2] More than once Sultan Bayazid II is said not to be a man of action. We are informed that Florence, Mantua, and Ferrara sent missions to Istanbul, giving presents to the sultan, and trying to damage the Turkish opinion of Venice.[3] When Jacopo Contarini, the Venetian envoy to Spain

[1] *Cf.* Sanudo, *Diarii*, I, 1099. In late August, 1498, Ferdinand of Aragon assured the Milanese ambassador that he would aid Lodovico il Moro in the event he were attacked (although aggression against Milan could only come from Louis XII of France, with whom Ferdinand had for some time been discussing the blessings of peace).

[2] Sanudo, *Diarii*, I, 83–84, 136–37, 295, 323–24, 387, 552, 624–25, 634–40, 643–45, 678–80, 691 ff., 702–4, 707–8, 726 ff., 739–41, etc., 809, 823, 846 ff.

[3] *Ibid.*, I, 846.

and previously to Portugal, returned home on 9 June, 1498, he was most restrained in his praise of Ferdinand and Isabella, who in his opinion had joined the league only to defend themselves with Venetian money against France. Contarini believed in fact "che spagnoli sono più di parole cha de fati."[4] Even shrewd Venetians were obviously capable of egregious mistakes.

Sanudo's diaries recount many events which, however petty they now seem to us, were much discussed on the Rialto in his day. On 16 February (1497), for example, the news reached Venice that on the preceding 7 January a ship, commanded by one Piero Brocheta and belonging to Alvise Contarini, was wrecked on the island of Sapienza, just off the coast of Modon. The ship was loaded with about 20,000 ducats' worth of wool from Saloniki. Since it had sunk only to half-mast, there were hopes of salvage. A few sacks of wool and the ship's rigging and tackling had been recovered, but in any event both insurers and shareholders (*asegura-dori et parcioneveli*) had clearly suffered great loss.[5]

Despite the supposedly good relations existing between the Serenissima and the Porte, Venetians and Turks could easily find themselves at odds and soon in hostile encounter almost anywhere in Levantine waters.[6] But generally there was peace, and the sultan was even said to desire a formal accord with Maximilian, king of the Romans.[7] Of course such an Ottoman peace with Maximilian might not be the best thing for Venice.

The Venetians would soon be casting anxious eyes toward the East. Just now, however, they were giving their main attention to Lodovico il Moro, with whom they disagreed over the affairs of Pisa. When their envoys offered Louis XII the congratulations of the Republic upon his accession to the throne, they also indicated that if his Majesty entertained any desire for an alliance with them, he would find his wishes quite in accord with their own.[8] When Louis notified the pope of his accession, three apostolic nuncios were sent to France on 4 June to console him for the death of his predecessor and to congratulate him upon the honor which had come to him.[9]

According to the written instructions which Alexander VI gave to his nuncios, they were to inform Louis that his Holiness had hoped ever since his election as pontiff to see the organization of a crusade against the Turks, "perpetual enemies of our faith." He had wished, as much as God would allow him, in this respect to imitate the noble examples set by his uncle Calixtus III and by Pius II, but unfortunately the times had been adverse to such an undertaking, and many obstacles had been put in his way. Louis's ascent to the throne of France renewed the hopes of his Holiness and those of the entire Christian commonwealth that with his Majesty's aid it might be possible to embark upon the expedition. The peace must be kept in Italy; the pope hoped to be able to resolve any controversies that might arise; and it was his earnest desire that all the Italian powers should support the crusade. Louis's ancestors, in whose footsteps he would be following, had employed almost all the resources of France in the common cause of Christendom. They had often protected the popes from assault and oppression. An expedition against Sultan Bayazid II would bring the new king immortal glory. As for Louis's claim to the Neapolitan kingdom, the pope now offered, as he had offered Charles VIII, to weigh the justice of that claim with full impartiality. He reminded Louis, however, that for well nigh fifty years the dukes of Orléans as well as the kings of France had left the Milanese duchy in the hands of the Sforza family, and the Sforzeschi claimed that they had been legally invested with the duchy by the emperor. There is a prophetic touch in the instructions:

> But if his Majesty decides to reject our counsel and invade the duchy, let him carefully consider that so great an effort of war will bring to both the Italian and French nations the destruction of cities, slaughter of peoples, and loss of souls, and that [his Majesty] will receive more of calamity and infamy than honor and glory from such renewal of the tumults of war![10]

[4] *Ibid.*, I, 987.

[5] *Ibid.*, I, 514. It was presumably another Piero Brocheta who was captain of a grain ship sailing from Sicily when it was seized by a French corsair in March, 1497 (*ibid.*, I, 571).

[6] *Ibid.*, I, 728–32, a letter dated at Candia on 10 July, 1497, and *cf.* cols. 739, 744, 757, 1071–73.

[7] *Ibid.*, I, 736.

[8] *Ibid.*, I, 1011–12, and *cf.* in general Camillo Manfroni, *Storia della marina italiana*, Rome, 1897, pp. 212 ff.

[9] Burchard, *Diarium*, ed. Thuasne, II, 474–75, and ed. Celani, II, 100–1.

[10] Thuasne, ed., *Burchardi diarium*, II, append., no. 31, pp. 673–76. The pope also exhorts Louis XII not to favor or protect Giovanni della Rovere, *prefectus Urbis*, who had

Actually, however, Alexander VI had become more interested in the aggrandizement of his son Cesare Borgia than in the well-being of either Italy or France. In the summer of 1497 Cesare had decided to resign from the Sacred College, as we have seen, and the Borgias were soon hoping to acquire the kingdom of Naples by means of matrimonial alliances. On 21 July, 1498, Lucrezia was married to the young Alfonso, duke of Bisceglie and Quadrata, natural son of Alfonso II.[11] But Alexander VI failed to secure Cesare's marriage to Carlotta of Naples, the daughter of King Federigo, who wrote the Gran Capitano Gonsalvo de Cordova on 24 July, 1498, that the pope's motives and evil designs upon the kingdom of Naples were notorious, as were his insatiability and depraved desires—the more he had, the more he wanted—and now he sought "with the greatest insistence . . . marriage between our legitimate daughter and the cardinal of Valencia, a thing as extraordinary and unbecoming as could ever have been imagined, and contrary to all reason. . . ." Federigo stated he would prefer to lose his kingdom, his children, and life itself rather than to give his consent.[12]

On 17 August (1498) a secret consistory unanimously granted the request of Cesare Borgia, cardinal of Valencia, "to return to the world and contract marriage,"[13] or as Sanudo puts it, "et farsi soldato et maridarsi."[14] On the same day Burchard records the arrival in Rome of the French envoy Louis de Villeneuve, baron of Trans, who had come "to conduct the reverend lord cardinal of Valencia into the kingdom of France." Annoyed with the king of Naples and worried about the apparent accord just reached between the warring families of Colonna and Orsini, Alexander VI had been entering into close negotiations with Louis XII. Sigismondo de' Conti says that Cesare "burned with a great desire to see France," and on 28 September the pope wrote the French king with his own hand that "we are sending your Majesty our heart, namely our beloved son the duke of Valentinois, than whom we hold nothing more dear. . . ."[15] From this brief it is clear that the French duchy of Valentinois had been formally promised or already granted to Cesare although the actual investiture was performed later. By an odd chance the cardinal of Valencia (*card. Valentinus*) had become the duke of Valentinois (*dux Valentinensis*); poets and seers could play with the correspondence of names (*nomen et omen*); for the present Cesare's projected journey to France seemed the augury of a great career. Although he withdrew from Rome quietly and without pomp on the morning of 1 October,[16] a fortune had been spent on his entourage. His clothes were of silk and velvet, glittering with gold and precious stones. Many of his horses were shod with silver, their saddle-cloths stitched with pearls. Sanudo notes that Cesare was said to have spent 100,000 ducats on such accoutrements. Boarding a French galley at Civitavecchia on 3 October, he landed at Marseille on the nineteenth. In Avignon he was received by Cardinal Giuliano della Rovere, who was now quite reconciled with the pope, and had received back his fortress at Ostia. Passing through Lyon (on 25 October), Cesare arrived on 19 December (1498) at Chinon, where Louis XII was then residing. His entrance into the town was of unparalleled magnificence; the king received him in the dining hall of the castle; Cardinal della Rovere was with the king. Cesare brought

---

committed public rapine in papal territories by robbing the Turkish envoy of 40,000 gold florins, etc. (see above, Chapter 15, note 32). The magnitude of the sum seemed as offensive to the pope as the violence of the act. *Cf.* Sigismondo de'Conti, II, 200; Pastor, *Hist. Popes*, VI, 56, and *Gesch. d. Päpste*, III-1 (repr. 1955), 519–520.

[11] Burchard, *Diarium*, ed. Thuasne, II, 493–94, and ed. Celani, II, 116; Sanudo, *Diarii*, I, 1030, 1042; Pastor, *Gesch. d. Päpste*, III-1 (repr. 1955), 521–22, and III-2 (repr. 1956), append., nos. 44–46, pp. 1072–73.

[12] Giuseppe Canestrini, *Documenti per servire alla storia della milizia italiana* (in *Archivio storico italiano*, XV, Florence, 1851), pp. 235–36. Federigo also dwells on the "effrenata cupidità e rapacità de'Veneziani" (*ibid.*, p. 233), whom he regards as fit allies for a degenerate pope. Alexander VI was said to draw 50,000 ducats a year from the kingdom of Naples (*ibid.*, p. 235, and Sanudo, *Diarii*, II, 1102).

[13] Burchard, *Diarium*, ed. Thuasne, II, 492–93, and ed. Celani, II, 115–16.

[14] Sanudo, *Diarii*, I, 1054, and *cf.* Sigismondo de' Conti, II, 201.

[15] Giuseppe Molini, *Documenti di storia italiana*, I (Florence, 1836), 28–29, "datum Rome apud Sanctum Petrum die XXVIII Septembris;" Sigismondo de'Conti, II, 200; Pastor, *Hist. Popes*, VI, 60–61, and *Gesch. d. Päpste*, III-1 (repr. 1955), 523–24. The pope received back Cesare's annual revenues of some 32,000 ducats; Cardinal Juan Borgia "the Younger" was given the coveted archbishopric of Valencia (Sanudo, *Diarii*, II, 67, 1269). This Cardinal Juan Borgia is not to be confused with his uncle of the same name, who was archbishop of Monreale in Sicily; the younger Juan, good friend and contemporary of Cesare, died in January, 1500 (*cf.* above, Chapter 14, note 99, and Wm. H. Woodward, *Cesare Borgia*, London, 1913, append., no. II, pp. 385–86, with some errors in dating).

[16] Burchard, *Diarium*, ed. Thuasne, II, 495–96, and ed. Celani, II, 118.

Louis the dissolution of his union with Jeanne de France to make possible the king's marriage to Anne, the duchess of Brittany, his predecessor's widow, as well as the red hat for Georges d'Amboise, archbishop of Rouen. With gifts like these Cesare could be assured of a royal welcome.[17]

The Venetian ambassador in Rome reported to his government in a dispatch dated 10 December that there had been an altercation the previous day in the consistory between the pope and Cardinal Ascanio Sforza. The latter charged that Cesare's going into France would prove to be "la ruina de Italia," to which his Holiness promptly replied that it was Ascanio's brother il Moro who had invited the French into the peninsula.[18]

Since the Venetians were firm in their opposition to Milan and were seeking an alliance with France, the pope's new pro-French policy seemed likely to assure Louis XII's hegemony in Italy, which was a distasteful prospect to Ferdinand of Aragon, who had his own designs upon Naples. On more than one occasion during the winter of 1498–1499 the Spanish and Portuguese envoys upbraided Alexander VI for simony, lectured him on the need for reform, and threatened him with a church council. Alexander found scant comfort in Louis's bland assurance that there was no cause for alarm, because the French had an understanding with Spain. Papal policy seemed especially mistaken when, after the alienation of Ferdinand, it became clear that Cardinal della Rovere could not induce Carlotta of Naples (who resided in France) to accept Cesare Borgia for her husband. This was why Cesare had gone to France, however, and Spanish ire had been evoked in vain as the Neapolitan princess humiliated the Borgias by the firm dignity of her refusal.[19] She said she would not marry Cesare without her father's consent, which was not likely to be forthcoming. In vain did the pope protest that the king of France had promised Cesare the daughter of King Federigo.[20]

On 12 March the Venetian ambassador in Rome wrote that the pope had finally been advised that the negotiations for Carlotta's hand "è andà in fumo," and that if Cesare had not been in France, the pope would be making an accord with the duke of Milan.[21] Two months before (on 19 January) the envoy had written the home government that the pope was saying he wanted "to pacify Italy in order to attend to Turkish affairs."[22] When everything was going badly in the Curia, one usually talked about the Turks. The body of Jem Sultan had been returned to Istanbul early in the year 1499.[23] The complete assurance of his brother's death may have helped to induce Bayazid II to resume hostilities against the West. Disquieting news reached Venice from time to time concerning Turkish activities or demands.[24]

---

[17] *Cf.* Sanudo, *Diarii*, I, 1059, 1091, 1095, esp. cols. 1110–11, and II, 11, 15, 25, 39, 67, 83, 102, 112, 157–58, 158–59, 163, 175, 186, 199, etc., 317–18, 320–22, 765, etc., 827. The reconciliation of Alexander VI and Cardinal della Rovere had been a long process (*ibid.*, I, 695, 700–1, 738, 833, 924, 1091). As for Cardinal della Rovere's fortress at Ostia, the Spanish commander Gonsalvo de Cordova had taken it from the French castellan "Minaldus de Guerra" (Menaut d'Aguerre) in early March, 1497, "bombardis et machinis," as described by Burchard, *Diarium*, ed. Thuasne, II, 358–59, and ed. Celani, II, 18–19. Menaut, who was brought into the pope's presence, was dealt with in surly fashion by his Holiness, and (as reported by Burchard) doubtless owed his life and freedom to the fact that Gonsalvo had taken him "under his protection." About eighteen months later (on 26 August, 1498) Menaut accused the pope of employing against the garrison at Ostia "poisons en eawe artificielles, en autre maniere de veinin et en feu ardant et fumee empoisonnant," on which see Gilbert Ouy, "Le Pape Alexandre VI a-t-il employé les armes chimiques?" *Recueil de travaux offert à M. Clovis Brunel* . . . , II (Paris, 1955), 321–24 (Mémoires et documents publiés par la Société de l'École des chartes, XII).

[18] Sanudo, *Diarii*, II, 217: ". . . et il papa disse: 'Sapete ben, monsignore, chi è stato causa,' etc."

[19] Sanudo, *Diarii*, II, 279–80, 343, 349–50, esp. cols. 385, 412–13; Burchard, *Diarium*, ed. Thuasne, II, 506–7, and ed. Celani, II, 124, on the pope's reception of the Spanish envoys (23 January, 1499); Zurita, *Anales*, V (1670), fols. 159^v–161^r; Pastor, *Hist. Popes*, VI, 62–66, and *Gesch. d. Päpste*, III-1 (repr. 1955), 525–28.

[20] Sanudo, *Diarii*, II, 434–35, 448.

[21] *Ibid.*, II, 530–31.

[22] *Ibid.*, II, 364.

[23] *Ibid.*, II, 430, 436, 596, 610, 1172.

[24] *Ibid.*, II, 289–94, 336, 419–27, 760, 781 ff., 790 ff., 822–23, 833, 839 ff. Although pirates and the plague made travel in the Levant hazardous for individuals toward the end of the fifteenth century, two Florentine ecclesiastics (among others) undertook a journey to the Holy Land during the reign of Bayazid II, leaving home in late July, 1497, and returning in mid-November, 1498. They sent more than twenty letters home, preparing them in duplicate in an effort to make sure of their reaching their destination. They sailed from Pesaro (on 1 September) for Ragusa, whence they traveled overland to Adrianople (Edirne) and Istanbul. Thereafter they went to Brusa (Bursa), Cyzicus, Troy, Lesbos, Pergamum, Phocaea, Chios, Patmos, Halicarnassus, Rhodes, Cyprus, and the Holy Land, where they spent two weeks, and returned to Florence by way of Cyprus, Modon, and Venice. The details of their journey are extraordinarily interesting. See Eve Borsook, "The Travels of Bernardo Michelozzi and Bonsignore Bonsignori

Turkish affairs were not foremost in the pope's thoughts, however, when on 24 May a letter was read in consistory from Louis XII, written in the latter's own hand, announcing the marriage of Cesare Borgia on 10 May to the French princess Charlotte d'Albret, who also wrote *sua manu* a letter of filial devotion to his Holiness, expressing the pleasure she took in obeying the wishes of the king and her father in marrying Cesare and hoping to come soon to Rome "ad osculandum pedes sue Beatitudinis. . . ."[25] His Holiness immediately became full of praise for the Venetians (now the allies of Louis XII), worried about their fortunes in the Levant, and recalled how they had stood alone "anni 19 in guera col Turcho," thus adding two or three years to one of the greatest trials in Venetian history. Now the pope wanted to join with the French and the Venetians; looked forward to the expulsion of Lodovico il Moro from Milan; and placed his hope in France and Venice that his son Cesare "might have some place in Italy."[26]

Eight months before this, in September, 1498, the Venetians had been informed that Alexander VI along with the king of Naples, the duke of Milan, and the Florentines had sent envoys to Istanbul complaining that the Venetians wanted to attract Louis XII into Italy. Since there was no representative of the Republic then in Istanbul, "except for merchants and the like," Andrea Zanchani was chosen Venetian envoy to the Gran Turco for four months with a salary of one hundred ducats a month and an allowance of five ducats a day for "expenses of the mouth." Although Zanchani was to protest against Turkish piracy in the Aegean and lawless incursions into Venetian-held Sebenico, Traù, and Spalato, the purpose of his embassy was to keep the Turk in his usual peaceful frame of mind.[27]

Certainly Lodovico il Moro's suspicions of Venice were quite justified. Sanudo summarizes letters dated at Blois on 29 October and 3 November (1498) received from the Republic's envoys to Louis XII. An agreement had been reached in principle between the envoys and the king's councillors, but solutions were required to certain problems. Louis wanted the Signoria to assure him 1,500 men-at-arms and 4,000 infantry, preferably Swiss. He also wanted the grand master of Rhodes and the Florentines included in the pact, and was eager to secure control of Pisa, so that the Florentines would not render any assistance to the duke of Milan. Finally, he requested 100,000 ducats to pay 6,000 Swiss mercenaries for a period of six months, or rather he wished the Venetians to meet the paymasters' demands for the period. If the campaign (*impresa*) exceeded six months, Louis would himself pay the additional sums in-

---

in the Levant (1497–98)," *Journal of the Warburg and Courtauld Institutes*, XXXVI (1973), 145–97, with the texts of seventeen letters. Travel had been easier when Felix Fabri made his two pilgrimages to the Holy Land (in 1480 and 1483).

[25] Pastor, *Gesch. d. Päpste*, III-1 (repr. 1955), 530, note, and *cf.* Burchard, *Diarium*, ed. Thuasne, II, 532, and ed. Celani, II, 142; Sanudo, *Diarii*, II, 759–60. Part of the price of Charlotte d'Albret's hand was a red hat for her brother Amanieu. On Cesare Borgia's marriage as well as the tortuous path by which Alexander VI withdrew from his entente with Milan and Naples to enter an alliance with France, see the detailed study of Léon G. Pélissier, "Sopra alcuni documenti relativi all'alleanza tra Alessandro VI e Luigi XII (1498–1499)," *Archivio della R. Società romana di storia patria*, XVII (1894), 303–73, and XVIII (1895), 99–215, with numerous hitherto unpublished documents.

[26] Sanudo, *Diarii*, II, 776, esp. cols. 798–99: ". . . sichè el papa è diventato tutto francese." *Cf.*, *ibid.*, II, 812–13, 826–27, 832–33, 923, 958. As time passed, the pope kept accusing Lodovico il Moro of inciting Sultan Bayazid II against the Venetians, to whom the pope soon sent Cardinal Juan Borgia (Sen. Secreta, Reg. 37, fols. 110^v–111^r [124^v–125^r], doc. dated 19 August, 1499) to enlist the Republic's support for Cesare's territorial ambitions in Italy (*ibid.*, fols. 125^r ff. [139^r ff.], docs. dated 19–23 September). The Senate gave the Borgias continued assurance of their co-operation (fols. 133^r [147^r], 152 [166], 153^r [167^r], 155^v–156^v [169^v–170^v]), but at the end of November (1499) Venetian forces occupied Faenza to prevent its falling into Cesare's hands (fols. 157^v–158^r [171^v–172^r]). The Venetians would not interfere with Cesare's occupation of Imola, Forlì, and Pesaro (fol. 156^v), but drew the line at Faenza, Urbino, and Rimini (fols. 160, 162^r, 163^r, 166^r, 175, 176^r [174 ff.]). In mid-December Lucrezia Borgia's erstwhile husband, Giovanni Sforza, lord of Pesaro, appealed for aid to the Venetian Senate "non sine singultibus et lachrymis;" he was told, however, that the Venetians were the pope's "devotissimi filii," and the Republic's ambassador to Rome was instructed to inform the pope of Giovanni's secret trip to Rome, in disguise and with only two servants (fols. 161^v–162^r [175^v–176^r]). Later on, Cesare occupied Urbino.

[27] Sanudo, *Diarii*, I, 1090, 1095–96, and II, 101, 164, 362, 459, 530, 598 ff., 677, 684, 791, 842, 856, *et alibi*; Pietro Bembo, *Historiae venetae libri XII*, Venice, 1551, bk. IV, fol. 60. Zanchani was elected envoy to the Porte on 15 September, 1498 (Sen. Secreta, Reg. 37, fol. 45^r [59^r]), but had still not left Venice two months later (*ibid.*, fol. 58^v [72^v], dated 15 November). His commission is dated 20 November (fols. 60^r–63^r [74^r–77^r]), and contains an interesting, brief sketch of the foreign policies of France, Florence, and Milan (fol. 61^r [75^r]). The Senate had, as usual, been keeping an eye on the Turkish fleet (fols. 2^v–3^r, 31^r, 71^r [16^v ff.], docs. dated in 1498).

volved. Details were discussed of the projected division of Lodovico il Moro's territories between the Venetians and the king of France.[28]

As Alexander VI became estranged from King Federigo of Naples and il Moro, he kept in constant touch with the Venetian ambassador in Rome, anxiously watching Cesare's progress in France. In the meantime, on All Saints (1 November, 1498), he had appeared in church with an armed guard for fear, it was said, of il Moro, Cardinal Ascanio Sforza, and King Federigo.[29] When the pope became firmly committed to the French alliance, after the announcement of Cesare's marriage to Charlotte d'Albret, Ascanio Sforza once more found the atmosphere of Rome singularly unhealthful. One Sunday morning (14 July, 1499), pretending that he was going hunting, he left Rome by the gate of the Castel S. Angelo without securing papal permission for his departure.[30] Fleeing first to the Colonnesi, Ascanio later boarded a Neapolitan ship for Genoa, and then joined his brother in Milan. The lines were being drawn for a new French invasion of Italy, this time with Milan as its objective. A diplomatic revolution had taken place. Now Venice and the papacy would support the king of France. Lodovico il Moro would naturally oppose him, and so of course would King Federigo. Naples, however, was too far from Lombardy and the king too poor for Lodovico to expect much help from that quarter.

The Turk had figured prominently in French propaganda during the expedition of Charles VIII. It seemed likely that he would do so again as Louis XII tried his luck on the roulette of war. News of Turkish preparations was disturbing the minds and upsetting the plans of the Venetians.[31] To be sure, Federigo of Naples wrote Alexander VI, urging him to promote peace among the Christian princes in order that they might meet the Turkish danger with the strength of union, but a Venetian dispatch from Milan (dated 17 July, 1499) stated that Lodovico il Moro had just sent "Don Fernando, son of the despot of the Morea, nephew of the lord Constantine [Arianiti, governor of Montferrat], to the Turk with five horses. . . ."[32] Two days later the pope informed the Venetian ambassador in Rome that il Moro was responsible for the Gran Turco's restlessness, because he was sending money to Istanbul.[33] It was even reported that plans had been made for the Turks

---

[28] Sanudo, *Diarii*, II, 112, and *cf.* cols. 336, 343–44, 348, 453 ff., 522–26. The Franco-Venetian treaty (of 9 February, 1499) was confirmed at Blois on 15 April, 1499 (Predelli, *Regesti dei Commemoriali*, VI [1903], bk. XVIII, nos. 149–50, pp. 39–40). See A. Lizier, "Il Cambiamento di fronte della politica veneziana alla morte di Carlo VIII . . . ," *Ateneo veneto*, CXX (1936), 20 ff. On 20 February the Senate wrote Andrea Zanchani of the "vera intelligentia et lianza" which had been reached on the ninth with Louis XII (Sen. Secreta, Reg. 37, fol. 77^{v} [91^{v}]).

[29] Sanudo, *Diarii*, II, 102, 113.

[30] Burchard, *Diarium*, ed. Thuasne, II, 546, and ed. Celani, II, 154. Even Lucrezia's husband Alfonso of Aragon fled to Naples "absque licentia, scitu et voluntate pontificis" (*ibid.*, ed. Thuasne, II, 548, and ed. Celani, II, 155). *Cf.* Sanudo, *Diarii*, II, 933, 959, 1017. Obviously Luca Landucci's information that Cardinal Ascanio had passed through Florence *sconosciuto* on 13 July was inaccurate (I. del Badia, ed., *Diario fiorentino dal 1450 al 1516*, Florence, 1883, p. 197).

Cesare Borgia was now beginning his remarkable career of conquest. Alexander VI was busy collecting munitions for him, in which connection note the pope's letter of 11 December, 1499, to Francesco Gonzaga, the marquis of Mantua: "Dilecte fili, salutem et apostolicam benedictionem: Intelligentes ex litteris dilectorum filiorum Cardinalis de Borgia et ducis Valentinensis [Cesare] in castris, que ad presens ad Imolam posita sunt, pulverem pro bombardis et aliis machinis bellicis defecisse, cum nos hinc de illo providere non possimus, hortamur nobilitatem tuam pro ea fiducia quam in ea locavimus ut istinc pulverem in maiore quam poteris quantitate pro expeditione suscepta Imolam ad prefatum ducem quam primum mittere velis. Pro quo litteris tuis certiores effecti libenter pretium persolvemus nobisque preterea rem gratam facies. Datum Rome apud Sanctum Petrum sub annulo piscatoris die XI Decembris MCCCCLXXXXVIIII, pontificatus nostri anno octavo" (Arch. di Stato di Mantova, Arch. Gonzaga, Busta 834, brief expedited by the papal secretary [later Cardinal] Adriano Castellesi).

[31] *Cf.* Sen. Secreta, Reg. 37, fol. 73 [87], docs. dated 15 January, 1499 (Ven. style 1498); fols. 82^{r}, 83^{r} [96 f.], docs. dated 26 March; and fols. 88 ff. [102 ff.], 91^{v}, 94, 96^{v} ff., docs. dated up to 27–29 June.

[32] Sanudo, *Diarii*, II, 938. Constantine Arianiti was the uncle of the late marquise of Montferrat and the guardian of her two young sons, heirs of the Monferratine possessions. Constantine had been a close friend of Commines, who had wanted to see him made "king of Macedonia" in the time of Charles VIII (Kervyn de Lettenhove, *Lettres et négociations*, II, 225). He belonged to the family of the Arianiti-Comneni, whose genealogy is given (probably inaccurately) by Hopf, *Chroniques gréco-romanes*, geneal. tables, p. 535. Constantine later became the envoy of Maximilian of Hapsburg in Rome, and figures rather prominently in the correspondence of the Venetian envoy to the Holy See, Antonio Giustinian, who often calls him "Costantino Cominato" (P. Villari, ed., *Dispacci di Antonio Giustinian*, 3 vols., Florence, 1876, vols. II–III, and *cf.* vol. III, p. 350, note 1). *Cf.* Celani's edition of Burchard, II, 445, note 2; Sen. Secreta, Reg. 38, fol. 146 [155]; and Franz Babinger, *Das Ende der Arianiten*, Munich, 1960, pp. 37–48.

[33] Sanudo, *Diarii*, II, 958, and *cf.* col. 970.

to go through the Tyrol to Como in order to aid the harassed duke of Milan.[34] In July, 1499, a Turkish envoy was said to be on his way to Milan to demand the 200,000 ducats which il Moro had promised the sultan for attacking Venice,[35] and il Moro was quoted in a dispatch from Turin as having said that "the Turk will reach Venice as soon as the French do Milan!"[36]

The years 1499–1500 were full of rumors and even the expectation of Turkish incursions into Italy. The Florentine apothecary Luca Landucci noted in his diary the reports of Turkish depredation of the country around Zara and the capture of Corfu. He also says that the king of Naples was alleged to have informed the pope that, if the latter did not help prevent any attempt by Louis XII to invade the Regno, he would call upon the Turks for assistance. Landucci believed the Turks would have come into Italy if the French expedition had not in fact been directed against Milan rather than Naples. On 19 October (1499) Landucci picked up the information from Venice that the Turks had raided to within twenty miles of the city. News on the Rialto was ominous. The Turks had burned seventeen villages, taken 8,000 prisoners, and killed a like number of others. Refugees were flooding into the areas close to Venice, and the government had arrested for dereliction of duty its commissioners and military commanders in the afflicted regions. Under the twenty-fifth of the month Landucci recorded the rumor that 20,000 Turks had arrived at Valona, and some were even said to have passed into Apulia. A few months later (on 15 February, 1500) "it was said also that the Turkish ambassador had come to Naples, and that the king had received him with great honours and jousting."[37] Again, on 27 February, Landucci wrote in his diary that he had heard the Turkish ambassador had gone to Rome to request a safe-conduct of the pope "for the Turks to go to Milan against the king of France: but it was not granted."[38]

If the Turks could not reach the king of France, they could at least get at his allies, the Venetians. After the famous Turco-Venetian peace had been made in 1479, the lion banner of S. Mark still flew from the battlements of Lepanto in continental Greece and from those of Coron, Modon, and Navarino, Nauplia, Monemvasia, and a few other places in the Morea. The Venetians continued to hold some of the Ionian islands, especially Corfu, the northern Sporades, Tenos, Mykonos, and the great island of Crete. Cyprus was also a Venetian possession. Obviously the evangelist still had a large stake in the Levant. The Venetians had excluded from the peace of 1479 their erstwhile friend Leonardo III Tocco, duke of Leucadia and so-called despot of Arta, who had exercised for some thirty years a prosperous dominion over the islands of Leucadia (S. Maura) and Ithaca, Cephalonia and Zante. Of his family's old claims to the despotate of Epirus (Ianina), acquired by marriage and by conquest, all that had remained to Leonardo on the mainland was the fortress of Vonitza, near the ancient Actium, on the Gulf of Arta (Ambracia). Mehmed the Conqueror had lost little time in proceeding against the Tocchi, who were driven from Vonitza and from their beautiful islands. In the late summer (of 1479) Leonardo had fled for his life before a Turkish armada which had sailed from Valona to his island base at Leucadia.[39]

Leonardo found refuge in Naples, where he was well received by King Ferrante, who gave him a pension of 500 florins (as we have seen)

---

[34] *Ibid.*, II, 1018.

[35] *Ibid.*, II, 910, 911, 912, 915.

[36] *Ibid.*, II, 933: ". . . el Turcho sarà a Veniexia che francesi in Milan." On 19 July Lodovico il Moro denied to the Venetian ambassador the charges being made against him with respect to the Turks, but he acknowledged he had sent an envoy to Istanbul, and reminded the ambassador of the "potentia informidabile" of the Turk (*ibid.*, II, 1004, 1032–33). In early August the Milanese ambassador to the Holy See defended il Moro against the papal and Venetian charges that he had incited the Turks against the Republic (II, 1088, and *cf.* cols. 1089–90). Federigo of Naples, also apprehensive of Louis XII's coming Italian expedition, negotiated a peace with the Porte dated 17 July (II, 1020–23).

[37] I. del Badia, ed., *Diario fiorentino dal 1450 al 1516*, Florence, 1883, pp. 197, 201, 203, 206, trans. Alice de Rosen Jervis (1927), pp. 158, 161, 163, 165; *cf.* Burchard, *Diarium*, ed. Thuasne, II, 578, and ed. Celani, II, 176. Parts of Friuli were a shambles in 1499–1500 as a result of Turkish raids, on which see Antonio de Pellegrini, "Danni recati dai Turchi nel 1499 ai villaggi di San Martino e San Leonardo nel territorio di Aviano," *Memorie storiche forogiuliesi*, VIII (1912), 193–96, and Pellegrini, *Le Incursioni turchesche in Friuli ed i castelli di Porcia e di Brugnera, Note e documenti (1470–1499)*, Udine, 1911, on which note P. S. Leicht, in the *Memorie storiche forogiuliesi*, VII (1911), 271–73.

[38] Del Badia, ed., *Diario*, p. 207; Engl. trans., p. 166. *Cf.* also Landucci's entries for 9 May and 5 September (1500), the latter being the report of the Turkish capture of Modon; 19 June and 13 July (1501); 10 March (1502); as well as 28 May and 28 October (1509).

[39] Arch. di Stato di Venezia, Sen. Secreta, Reg. 29, fols. 34^v–35^r [44^v–45^r].

and bestowed upon him the lands of Briatico and Calimera in Calabria. In 1480 he appeared in Rome (like the Palaeologi before him), where Sixtus IV gave him an annual pension of 1,000 ducats and promised him 2,000, as still attested by one of the frescoes of the Corsia Sistina in the Ospedale di S. Spirito in Rome. Although Venice soon acquired Zante (1482) and eventually Cephalonia (1500),[40] Turkish rule persisted, with a single brief interlude (1502–1503), for more than two centuries in S. Maura. Such had been the price paid by Leonardo Tocco and his family for preferring an alliance with Ferrante of Naples to one with the Venetians. Experience had shown the Tocchi, however, that Venice could not protect them from the Turks. The Neapolitans proved even less effective allies, being soon caught up in the French invasion of their own realm.

The sage statesmen of the Serenissima had relied too long on Sultan Bayazid's reputation for pacificity. They should have known that the Turks, like all conquerors, would allow no end to conquest but their own defeat, that ambition outstrips success itself. After years of neglect, Venice suddenly took a great interest in the fortified town of Lepanto (Naupactus), her last important possession on the Greek mainland. One Giovanni (Zuan) Viaro, rector and provveditore of the place, died in late October, 1498, of his exertions to set the Lepantine defenses in order.[41] It was too late.

The news arrived in Venice at the beginning of the following year (1499) that the Gran Turco had ordered the *flambulari* of Trikkala and the Morea "venir a la expedition di Lepanto." The Turkish land forces were to be aided by a large fleet.[42] Then reports came pouring in. Some said the Turk was preparing to march against the Albanians; others found his objective in Rhodes or Syria, Corfu or Apulia. The bailie of Corfu repaired the walls of the nearby fortress of Butrinto, the better to defend his island charge. Fears were entertained for "l'isola nostra di Cypro."[43] Conditions in Lepanto had long been scandalous although Viaro had repaired the walls and dug out the foss. Efforts were now being made to protect the *poveri* against the *potenti* by the administration of summary justice, but in a matter of months it was hard to right the wrongs of thirty years. Supplies had been mismanaged. There were four important castles in the district of Lepanto—Galata, Peritorio, Uromario, and Neocastro. A survey of 18 November, 1498, revealed their walls to be in sad disrepair, munitions lacking, cisterns broken, garrisons under strength and poorly paid. Indeed the garrison of Uromario consisted of one old woman, and the Venetian inspector found the gates open when he visited the castello! Properly maintained, however, Uromario would be hard to take because of its hilltop location and the single approach to its walls. Recommendations were made to restore

[40] Navagero, *Storia veneziana*, in *RISS*, XXIII, 1180–81. Venice seized Cephalonia also in 1482–1483, shortly after her occupation of Zante, but was soon obliged to surrender it to the Porte, which also exacted an annual tribute of 500 ducats for Zante (*ibid.*, 1189AB). This tribute is often mentioned by Sanudo in his *Diarii* (e.g., II, 611, 612, and *cf.* Miklosich and Müller, *Acta et diplomata*, III, 332–33; Stefano Magno, in Sathas, *Docs. inédits*, VI, 234, and *ibid.*, I, 315–16; Predelli, *Regesti dei Commemoriali*, V [1901], bk. XVI, no. 205, p. 248, and *ibid.*, bk. XVII, no. 169, p. 317).

The Venetians had succeeded, more or less, in getting the Turks to recognize their right to Zante and Cephalonia after more than three years' effort (*cf.* Sen. Secreta, Reg. 30, fols. 8v–9r, 11 [18v–19r, 21], docs. dated 29 April and 7 May, 1481; Reg. 31, fol. 121v, dated 5 January, 1484 [Ven. style 1483]; and Reg. 32, fol. 50, dated 14 June, 1484). The Republic's astute secretary, Giovanni Dario, who had concluded the peace of January, 1479, with Mehmed II's pashas, had inevitably been drawn into the negotiations.

Dario was resident in Istanbul, and vigilant in the interests of his government throughout most of the years 1484–1486 (Sen. Secreta, Reg. 31, fols. 125, 128r, 132, 136v–137r; Reg. 32, fols. 25, 50, 92, 104, 111, 132, 141, 147v–149r, 156v–157r, 168, 194, 196r–197r; and Reg. 33, fols. 11 [21], 12v [22v], 14r [24r], 23v–24r [33v–34r], 26r [36r], docs. dated from January, 1484, to July, 1486).

When Bayazid II dismissed Dario, the Venetian Senate was distressed, for his performance at the Porte had been remarkable even by the exacting standards of Venetian diplomacy. When it became known that Dario's return to Istanbul would be welcome, the Senate gladly sent him back on the first appropriate galley (Sen. Secreta, Reg. 33, fol. 61 [71], doc. dated 27 March, 1487). The commission for his return to the Porte is dated 7 April (1487); he was to sail on the *Loredana*, and preserve the Republic's "good peace" with the Turks (*ibid.*, fols. 64v–65r [74v–75r]). He had arrived in Istanbul by 25 May, and was well received at the Ottoman court (fol. 95 [105], and *cf.* fols. 103 ff. [113 ff.]). On Dario's career, see Fr. Babinger, *Johannes Darius (1414–1494), Sachwalter Venedigs im Morgenland, und sein griechischer Umkreis*, Munich, 1961, to which reference has already been made.

After the death of Leonardo III the title despot of Arta was inherited by his son Carlo III, who served as captain of the Sacred College in Rome at the time of Alexander VI's death (Burchard, *Diarium*, ed. Thuasne, III, 244, and ed. Celani, II, 355). For the genealogy of the Tocchi, *cf.* the rather inaccurate tables of Hopf, *Chron. gréco-romanes*, p. 530, and for their later history, Wm. Miller, *Latins in the Levant*, pp. 488–89.

[41] Sanudo, *Diarii*, II, 165, letter from Lepanto, dated 1 November, 1498.

[42] *Ibid.*, II, 289–90, 554.

[43] *Ibid.*, II, 290–91, and *cf.* cols. 382, 554, 597 ff., 610–12, 677, 790.

the defenses of the castles and to man them properly, and everything necessary could be done (according to the inspector) from two years' local revenues.[44]

Every report from Istanbul bore witness to the Gran Turco's extensive naval preparations. The numbers and kinds of ships were usually specified; much of this information was probably fairly accurate. The naval objective was not so clear, and rumor continued to identify it as Syria or Rhodes, Apulia or Corfu, but as time passed, Napoli di Romania (Nauplia) was added to the list.[45] On 2 March, 1499, the Venetian envoy to the Porte, Andrea Zanchani, wrote the home government that the Turkish armada would be in action by May; to the usual speculation about Rhodes, Apulia, and Syria, he added the observation that some people now thought the Turks would sail against "our places in the Morea, . . . Modon, Coron, Nauplia, and Lepanto."[46] Without knowing it, Zanchani was getting pretty close to the facts. When on 10 May he returned to Venice from Istanbul, Zanchani reported in such detail as he could on the great Turkish naval armament, which he now expected to set sail in May or June. He did not know where it was going, but he did not believe it was the sultan's intention to attack any of the Republic's possessions. Zanchani thought it quite likely that Rhodes would be the objective, because it was being said in Istanbul that the king of France was helping to arm Rhodes. The envoy presented a letter written in Greek from Sultan Bayazid, which was read in the Senate. Bayazid expressed pleasure in the doge's good health, commended Zanchani for the competent discharge of his assignment to the Porte, and confirmed the "good peace" (*bona paxe*) which obtained between the Republic and the Porte.[47]

Although Pierre d'Aubusson, the grand master of Rhodes, wrote the Doge Agostino Barbarigo on 5 April, 1499, that everyone held the opinion that the Turkish expedition would be directed against the Knights Hospitaller, he informed the doge that no faith could be put in the infidel: the Knights would be ready, and could hope again to enjoy their "old course of victory."[48] D'Aubusson knew of the hospitable reception Zanchani had received in Istanbul. He was sure that the latter would have no difficulty fulfilling his commission, but he prayed God might grant the Christians that union of strength and concord of spirit which could produce a great victory over the Moslem. The letter has an odd sound, as though the doge were expected to read between the lines. The Venetians could see no point, however, in reading between the lines of d'Aubusson's letter. They had too many other letters to read, most of which repeated the common assumption that the Turkish armada was going to attack Rhodes. After all, Venice had been at peace with the Porte since most members of the Senate were young men. Bayazid had just confirmed the *bona paxe* which old Giovanni Dario had negotiated twenty years before.

At a consistory held in Rome on Monday, 10 June (1499), Alexander VI had a letter from d'Aubusson read to the cardinals. It was dated at Rhodes on 30 April. The grand master wrote he had been informed "that the Turk himself was getting ready a huge fleet of about three hundred sail to lay siege to the city of Rhodes, where he was expected to arrive for certain sometime in May: [d'Aubusson] suspected that the siege would be a long one, because the Turk was coming in person to the nearby province of Lycia, where vast preparations were being made of all things essential to

---

[44] Sanudo, *Diarii*, II, 292–94. On 22 May, 1498, the Venetian government suspended the operation of a "council of thirty" (doubtless composed of *potenti*) as an illegal and unheard-of body conducting the affairs of Lepanto, obviously as a consequence of the failure of the home government to attend to the affairs of the colony (Lamansky, *Secrets d'état de Venise*, p. 593, note 1). For some reason the gulf of Lepanto seemed to a Venetian official "fuora dil mondo" (Sanudo, II, 292), which had made it possible for local worthies to "grow fat" at the expense of the surrounding peasantry and others. Special care was being taken to garrison Modon and supply it with adequate provisions (Sathas, *Docs. inédits*, I, 317). In response to a petition from the leaders of the Lepantine community, the Venetian Senate had made some rather inexpensive provisions on 23 July, 1485, for both the defense and the economy of "quella fidelissima comunità nostra" (Sathas, V, 7–12, doc. dated 31 July).

[45] Sanudo, *Diarii*, II, 597. On the eight kinds of vessels most commonly used by the Turks from the fourteenth century to the seventeenth, see Svat Soucek, "Certain Types of Ships in Ottoman-Turkish Terminology," *Turcica*, VII (1975), 233–49.

[46] Sanudo, *Diarii*, II, 598–99, and *cf.* col. 612. It was widely believed, however, that Rhodes was to be the destination of the armada (*ibid.*, II, 626, 666, 710, 712, 716, 757, 794, etc.).

[47] Sen. Secreta, Reg. 37, fol. 94 [108], doc. dated 16 May, 1499; Sanudo, *Diarii*, II, 695–96, 702. Sanudo gives an Italian translation of the sultan's letter, which is dated 15 March. *Cf.*, *ibid.*, II, 980 ff. Zanchani had left Istanbul on 18 March.

[48] Sanudo, *Diarii*, II, 666.

a siege." D'Aubusson had therefore warned the religious of his Order to come as soon as possible to the assistance of Rhodes, and now he humbly begged his Holiness, as universal pastor of the Church, to grant the Hospitallers *auxilium et favor* as well as the other concessions which crusaders received for service "against the perfidious Moslems." When the letter had been read, Alexander announced that he would indeed assist the threatened Hospitallers—if any members of the Order in Italy had not yet paid their arrears (*arrelagia*) and the annate for the current year 1499, they were to do so, but thereafter they should pay nothing more for the next three years. Four days later Alexander observed in the consistory that the Turk might already have placed Rhodes under siege. Cardinal Francesco Todeschini-Piccolomini (later Pius III) outlined the proposals being made to assist the Hospitallers: funds would be collected, and the pope would send briefs to all the princes appealing for their help. This was what everyone in the Curia had assumed would be done. Alexander also wanted to know more precisely, however, what measures the Holy See had taken to help frustrate the great Turkish siege of Rhodes in Sixtus IV's time.[49]

The Turks had concealed their plans exceedingly well, yet inevitably the suspicion grew into certainty that they intended an attack upon either Lepanto or the Moreote possessions of the Republic.[50] By 21 July (1499) it seemed pretty clear to a Venetian naval commander at Modon that the Turkish objective was in fact Lepanto.[51] Two large *fuste* and a brigantine of the Turkish fleet raided the island of Aegina, carrying off seven men and three hundred *capi di animali*. The Turks burned a number of houses, after which the poor islanders were visited by a fusta of the *flambulario* of Negroponte, which seized two more men and another seventeen animals. The main body of the fleet entered the Gulf of Coron, where it did considerable damage to Venetian property and installations. The Venetian captain-general of the sea, Antonio Grimani, prepared careful plans for a possible attack upon the Turks, but timidly refrained from making the attack.[52] His indecision caused confusion in the Venetian fleet. During the first week in August it became abundantly clear that the Turkish fleet was headed for Lepanto, not Corfu,[53] and it must have been equally clear to those on the spot that Grimani was miscast in the role of admiral. The Curia Romana was informed of developments. With bared head and on bended knees the pope said special prayers that "God should give victory to the Signoria."[54] The Turks burned five churches in the area between Coron and Modon. A Venetian provveditore found three heads along the road, one of a priest.[55] Sanudo is full of details. The costs of what had become a war between the Republic and the Porte mounted with each passing hour. The Venetian rectors of *terra ferma* were busy collecting the subsidies which the Senate had demanded (on 11 July, 1499) from Padua, Vicenza, Verona, Brescia, Bergamo, Crema, Ravenna, Treviso, Asolo, Udine, Cividale, Bassano, and other mainland possessions of Venice, "laqual defende el nome Christiano da la perfidia de infideli."[56]

---

[49] Arch. Segr. Vaticano, Acta Vicecancellarii, Reg. 1 (from the Archivum Consistoriale), fols. 60, 63–64, and *cf.* fols. 68ᵛ, 70ʳ.

[50] Sanudo, *Diarii*, II, 740, 757, 840, 857, 867, 873, 918, 919, 920, 978, 979 ff., 1004–6, etc., 1065–66, 1073–74. The Curia Romana still believed, as of 4 July (1499), that the Turkish armada would sail for Rhodes (*ibid.*, II, 912), but on 1 August a papal bull imposing a double tithe on the Venetian clergy lamented the Turkish assault upon the Republic's territories (Predelli, *Regesti dei Commemoriali*, VI [1903], bk. XVIII, no. 157, p. 41).

[51] Sanudo, *Diarii*, II, 1054. Despite the Venetian peace with the sultan, "confirmata solennemente per lui cum il nobel homo Andrea Zanchani orator nostro," by 27–29 June, 1499, the Senate had become grievously aware that the Turks' "grandi apparati . . . maritimi et terrestri" had in fact been prepared "in molte parte contra de nuy et per terra et per mar" (Sen. Secreta, Reg. 37, fols. 97ᵛ, 98ʳ [111ᵛ f.], and *cf.* fols. 100 ff.).

[52] Sanudo, *Diarii*, II, 1122–26, and *cf.* cols. 1241 ff.; Malipiero, *Annali veneti*, in *Arch. stor. italiano*, VII-1 (1843), 174–75, who participated as a provveditore in the events he describes; P. Bembo, *Hist. veneta* (1551), bk. v, fols. 65 ff. Antonio Grimani had become *capitaneus generalis maris* in mid-April, 1499 (Sen. Secreta, Reg. 37, fol. 86ʳ [100ʳ]); his commission is dated 30 April (*ibid.*, fols. 88ʳ–90ʳ [102ʳ ff.]). Grimani was an imposing personality. He was thought to be the man to meet what might prove to be a serious emergency: "The reason, as you know, for your election and your mission has been the report and widespread knowledge of the powerful fleet of the Turks . . ." (*ibid.*, fol. 88ᵛ [102ᵛ]). He was to follow every move of the Turks, and his reports were to be sent in the cipher then being used by the Venetian mission in Istanbul. If the Turks attacked Rhodes, he was to take no action, but was "manfully" to defend all the overseas possessions of the Republic, including the islands of the duchy of Naxos (fol. 90ʳ).

[53] Sanudo, *Diarii*, II, 1126–29, 1141 ff.

[54] *Ibid.*, II, 1134–35.

[55] *Ibid.*, II, 1154.

[56] Sen. Secreta, Reg. 37, fol. 104ʳ [118ʳ], where the "subsidii Christiani" being levied on the cities and towns of *terra ferma* amount to 56,100 ducats.

The Venetians were not getting much for their money. Grimani failed to prevent the Turkish fleet from entering the Gulf of Corinth. Letters from Lepanto dated 14 August (1499) brought to Venice the sad news that the Turks were encamped around the city although the battle had not yet begun.[57] A French fleet of twenty-two sail, composed largely of Hospitaller ships, arrived in mid-August in the waters off Zante with the intention of assisting the harried Venetian admiral.[58] On 21 August, however, the besieged in Lepanto learned that 1,500 janissaries had arrived the previous morning to support the efforts of the Turkish naval commanders.[59] While we need not be concerned with minor episodes in the Veneto-Turkish struggle,[60] we must note that the French captain was no more anxious for a decisive engagement with the Turkish fleet than was Grimani, and on 29 August (1499) Lepanto was surrendered to the Turks. [61] It was a severe blow to Venetian prestige; immediately the incompetent Grimani was "in grandissimo odio a tuta la terra."[62] By a vote of the Senate on 14 September he was removed from his post, and on the following day Melchior Trevisan was elected captain-general of the sea.[63] Trevisan's commission contains the notice that Alexander VI had just granted a *plenaria indulgentia de colpa et de pena* as well as all the benefits of the coming jubilee (for the year 1500) to those who were serving and had served in the Venetian armada.[64] As for Grimani, after a desultory trial in Venice he was banished to the island of Cherso (Cres) in the Quarnero (on 12 June, 1500). A distinguished name nonetheless counted for much on the lagoon. Twenty-one years later (on 6 June, 1521) Antonio Grimani was elected doge of Venice.[65] In the meantime the Venetians

---

[57] Sanudo, *Diarii*, II, 1230–35, 1287.

[58] *Ibid.*, II, 1237 ff., 1253, 1291, where the *armada francese* is given as twenty-two sail. Malipiero, *Annali veneti*, p. 177, says the French fleet consisted of "16 nave, 3 galie, 2 fuste, e un bergantin."

[59] Sanudo, *Diarii*, II, 1240.

[60] *Cf.*, *ibid.*, II, 1257–59, 1290–92, 1322–23, 1325–26, 1332. Malipiero, *Annali veneti*, pp. 176–77, describes the personal heroism of the Venetian captains Alban d'Armer and Andrea Loredan, and criticizes the admiral Grimani as "homo de poco cuor." Actually the Turkish fleet, although Grimani reported that it amounted to 260 vessels, contained many *navilii picoli*, and was clearly a much weaker armament than the Venetian fleet with a total of 88 *legni da battaglia* (*cf.* in general L. Fincati, "La Deplorabile Battaglia navale del Zonchio [1499]," in *Rivista marittima*, XVI [Rome, Feb. 1883], esp. pp. 187–201). Zonchio was not modern Navarino, located to the south of the island of Sphacteria, but Navarino Vecchio to the north; the well-preserved Venetian castle just above the modern town of Navarino did not of course exist in the fifteenth and sixteenth centuries. In the so-called "battle of Zonchio" the Venetians lost a few ships and eight hundred men; it was chiefly remarkable for the ineptitude of Grimani and the subsequent loss of Lepanto. Fincati's views concerning Grimani's handling of his command have a special interest since he was a well-known tactician and rear admiral in the Italian navy. Probably the years of peace with the Turks had lessened the effectiveness of most Venetian commanders, who Manfroni says had become "più amanti del loro avere che dell'onore" (*Storia della marina italiana*, Rome, 1897, pp. 216–17). Such leadership would obviously help demoralize the common seamen. Manfroni also believes that Fincati was unjustified in heaping all the blame for the loss of Negroponte in 1470 upon the shoulders of Niccolò da Canale, offering this criticism of Fincati's work: "In una parola il suo lavoro ha intenti regionali, e per iscolpare i marinai veneti, getta la colpa d'ogni loro sconfitta sull'infelice loro condottiero" (Manfroni, *op. cit.*, p. 71, note 3).

[61] Sanudo, *Diarii*, II, 1339–40, and vol. III (1880), ed. R. Fulin, cols. 11 ff.; Malipiero, *Annali veneti*, pp. 178–80; Hajji Khalifeh, *History of the Maritime Wars of the Turks*, trans. James Mitchell, London, 1831, pp. 19–21. As late as 3 September, 1499, as the (still uninformed) Senate wrote Grimani, the Venetians were hoping for victory (Sen. Secreta, Reg. 37, fol. 115^{v} [129^{v}]), but by Grimani's own letters of 25, 27, and 29 August, received in Venice on the morning of 13 September, the loss of Lepanto became known, to the Senate's immense distress (*ibid.*, fols. 119^{r} ff. [133^{r} ff.]). Lepanto had been under Venetian domination for ninety-five years, having been acquired in 1404 (*Chronicon venetum*, in *RISS*, XXIV [Milan, 1738], cols. 113–14).

On the fall of Lepanto, note also Hans-Albrecht von Burski, *Kemāl Re'īs: Ein Beitrag zur Geschichte der türkischen Flotte*, diss. Bonn, 1928, pp. 40 ff.; Georges Vajda, "Un Bulletin de victoire de Bajazet II," *Journal asiatique*, CCXXXVI (Paris, 1948), 91–92, where the date 27 August (1499) is given for the occupation of the fortress; and G. S. Ploumides, "'Έγγραφα γιὰ τὴ Βενετοκρατουμένη Ναύπακτο," in the 'Επετηρὶς 'Εταιρείας Βυζαντινῶν Σπουδῶν, XXXIX–XL (1972–73), 500–1.

[62] Sanudo, *Diarii*, II, 1335; Malipiero, pp. 181–82; Burchard, *Diarium*, ed. Thuasne, II, 570, and ed. Celani, II, 170.

[63] Sen. Secreta, Reg. 37, fols. 121^{v}–122^{r} [135^{v}–136^{r}]. Trevisan's commission, dated 26 September, 1499, is preserved, *ibid.*, fols. 128^{v}–131^{r} [142^{v} ff.]. As usual, the election took place in the Maggior Consiglio.

[64] *Ibid.*, fol. 129 [143]. Trevisan was given a copy of the bull.

[65] Sanudo, *Diarii*, III, 5, 46–47, 49, 58–59, 100, 102–3, 143–44, 172–75, etc., and esp. cols. 387–90, 393–94. See in general S. Romanin, *Storia documentata di Venezia*, V (1856), 134–44; L. Fincati, in *Rivista marittima*, XVI (1883), 204–13; C. Manfroni, *Storia della marina italiana* (1897), pp. 214–22; Wm. Miller, *Latins in the Levant* (1908), pp. 492–94; H. Kretschmayr, *Gesch. von Venedig*, II (1920, repr. 1964), 409–11. Antonio Grimani was imprisoned before 10 November, 1499 (Sen. Secreta, Reg. 37, fol. 153^{v} [167^{v}]); he was granted an "absolution di l'exilio" in June, 1509 (Sanudo, *Diarii*, VIII, 412–13, and *cf.* col. 502).

had to carry on the badly managed war with Turkey.

Some months after the Turkish acquisition of Lepanto, Sultan Bayazid II is alleged to have stated that up to then the Venetians had been wed to the sea, but henceforth it belonged to him. Louis XII told the Republic's envoy that, while the Venetians were wise in their deliberations and possessed of great riches, they lacked courage in warfare (*tanto timor haveti di la morte*), whereas the French undertook the trials of war with the determination to win or die. The burden of defeat was not lightened by humiliation, and how often in the years to come would visitors to Venice who witnessed the state festival of the Sensa, in which the doge married the sea, mutter under their breath the mocking lines of Joachim du Bellay:[66]

Mais ce que lon doit le meilleur estimer,
C'est quand ces vieux coquz vont espouser la mer,
Dont ilz sont les maris et le Turc l'adultere.

As the Senate wrote the Venetian representatives then at the court of Louis XII, "With the seizure of Lepanto, the fearsome enemy now wants to occupy the rest of the Peloponnesus and all the Levant, where the greatest alarm prevails. On the other front a huge Turkish force of more than twenty thousand horse has at this very hour invaded Istria and Cividale [Forum Julium], as you will perceive from the summaries of dispatches which we are sending you." Venice had become the "shield and bulwark" of Christendom, and although she would do her best, she could not bear so great a burden by herself. The Senate had been much comforted by the assurance of French help, but speed was necessary. In the meantime heartfelt approval was given to Cardinal d'Amboise's idea that Louis XII should write Bayazid II "that he should desist from his offensive against us." Louis had already named an envoy to Ladislas II, king of Hungary and Bohemia; Alexander VI was also about to send a nuncio to Hungary. The Hungarians could help to relieve the pressure on Venice, "and we too have taken steps to send our representative [to Hungary] to this effect." Maximilian I, the king of the Romans, was also in a position to help, and an appeal must be addressed to him. "A universal crusade was once declared against the infidels in the time of Pope Urban II," the Senate stated, "and there followed therefrom the greatest benefits to Christendom." At that time 300,000 or more Christians set out on expeditions against the common enemy; just as many or even more could now be organized to strike at the Turks.[67] One such letter must take the place of several which could easily be cited to illustrate the terrible concern which gripped the Senate after the Venetian loss of Lepanto.

The Turks now built the twin forts of "Rumelia" and the "Morea," the ruins of which still guard the strait of Lepanto, the narrow gateway to the Corinthian gulf. While in Venice the unfortunate admiral Antonio Grimani was languishing in prison, comforted and defended by his loyal sons (of whom one was Cardinal Domenico), the diplomats were busy. Maximilian confirmed his peace with Venice, and "offered to proceed against the Turks;" on 18–19 November (1499) Russian envoys arrived in the city "per far ligha contra i Turchi." The Russians had instructions also to go to Rome and into France

[66] J. du Bellay, *Les Regrets*, no. CXXXIII, ed. Pierre Grimal, Bibl. de Cluny, vol. 50, Paris, 1948, p. 181; Kretschmayr, *Gesch. von Venedig*, II, 411–12, 463. For Louis XII's statement to the Venetian ambassador Antonio Loredan, see Malipiero, *Annali veneti*, in *Arch. stor. italiano*, VII-1 (1843), 183, and Sanudo, *Diarii*, III, 11: "Vui, venitiani, seti sapienti in le vostre deliberation, habondanti de richeze, et poveri de animo e virilità in le vostre guerre: tanto timor haveti di la morte! E nui tolemo le imprese di guerra con animo de morir o vencer."

[67] Sen. Secreta, Reg. 37, fol. 132 [146], dated 28 September, 1499, and on the Venetian mission to Hungary, *ibid.*, fols. 135 [149], 146^v [160^v], 164 [178], 174 [188], 181^r–182^v [195^r–196^v], *et alibi*. Ladislas II of Hungary and Bohemia had, however, already renewed his treaty of peace with Bayazid (on 1 May, 1498), on which see V. Ćorović, "Der Friedensvertrag zwischen dem Sultan Bayazid II. und dem König Ladislaus II.," *Zeitschrift der Deutschen Morgenländischen Gesellschaft*, XC (new ser., XV, Leipzig, 1936), 52–59. War with Turkey was doubtless beyond the resources of Venice (G. Priuli, *Diarii*, II, 14, in *RISS*, new ed., vol. XXIV, pt. 3). Louis XII later sent two heralds to Istanbul. They passed through Venice toward the end of July, 1500, on their return to France, but the Senate could take no satisfaction in their report. The Turks were up to their old tricks, "fallacie et versutie," the Senate wrote the Venetian ambassador to the French court, "dicendo et dimonstrando una cossa in parolle et facendone cum effecti unaltra per poter mandar ad executione el suo cativo pensiero contra de nuy et contra tuta la Christianita" (Sen. Secreta, Reg. 38, fols. 51^v ff. [61^v ff.], dated 31 July, 1500). The Senate was also very critical of the Grand Master Pierre d'Aubusson. Two Turkish envoys were accompanying the heralds to France; they came without safe-conducts: "Nuy habiamo allozati questi ambassatori Turchi commodamente, ma ben non li lassamo parlar ad alcuno" (*ibid.*, fol. 52^r). The Turkish envoys accomplished nothing at the French court (fols. 57^v ff. [67^v ff.]).

in further pursuit of the same objective. The Venetians sent Alvise Manenti, secretary of the Council of Ten, to Istanbul to undertake negotiations for the re-establishment of peace and the restitution of Lepanto. He was to proceed with extreme caution, because there was talk in the European chanceries of a general league against the Turks.[68] Malipiero has incorporated in his *Annali* a long report which Manenti sent the Signoria concerning the course and eventual failure of his difficult mission. He arrived at Castel Tornese on 20 December and at Patras on the twenty-second, accompanied by a cavalry force of the Turkish commander Ali Pasha, who received him very courteously on the twenty-third, professing a great love for Venice and for peace. Ali Pasha said that the "young Turks" (*i giovani*) at the Porte were all for war; they had diverted the expedition from Rhodes to Lepanto. "He said that the Signoria knew that the bad offices of the duke of Milan, and of other evil Christians, have been the cause of this war, and God has punished him, and made him lose his state,"[69] of which we shall have more to say in its proper context.

With endless protestations of his friendship for Venice and his dedication to peace, "because those who do not want peace are evil men," Ali Pasha furnished Manenti with the opportunity to buy horses, although he "bought them at great expense." He also gave Manenti his secretary as an escort to Adrianople, doubtless as a means of checking up on his activities and the progress of his mission. On 27 December Manenti was at Lepanto. He arrived at Adrianople on 17 February (1500), having seen constant evidence of Turkish military and naval preparations for the coming season. On 22 February he was received at the Turkish court (the sultan was at Adrianople). After presenting his letters of credence and paying his hosts the usual compliments, Manenti spoke of Venetian love for the Signor Turco and the Republic's long-continued good faith toward the Porte. During all Jem Sultan's later years, from his residence in Cairo to his imprisonment in Rome, Venice "had never tried to make a move against his Excellency, and had always wanted friendship and peace with him more than with any other ruler in the world." Manenti requested the return of Lepanto, which as a commercial center under Venetian administration would be more profitable to the sultan than if he kept possession of it in his own hands. He blamed the war on Lodovico il Moro, whom God had punished with the loss of Milan, and appealed to the pashas "that they might support my just request, which means peace for the lords and peoples who live through two thousand miles of territory."

One of the pashas answered him that Venice was to blame for the war, because subjects of the Republic in Albania and the Morea were continually guilty of thefts and homicides to the serious injury of subjects of the Porte, "and we have written to the Signoria to punish them, but it has never done so." The Venetians had not appreciated the boon of years of peace with the Porte, although relying on that peace they had been able to defeat their enemies, acquire Cyprus, lands in Apulia, and Cremona and other places in Lombardy. The other pashas agreed with the speaker. They were astonished that Manenti could ask for the return of Lepanto. No one who valued his life would dare suggest it to the sultan, who had "decided to have the sea as his boundary with the Signoria." As for Lodovico il Moro, he had had no influence upon the sultan's decision to attack the Signoria's possessions, "but rather the reasons which have been stated." Manenti protested gently, choosing his words, that his government knew nothing of the alleged homicides and thefts. . . . The Turks had little more to say: "Ambassador, we have heard you freely, and have told you the sultan's intentions. Tomorrow we shall tell him all that you have said, and on Monday we shall give you his answer." Manenti then returned to his lodgings.

On Monday, 24 February, Manenti was summoned again to the Porte. The spokesman for the pashas said that the sultan was still determined to make the sea the dividing line between Turkish and Venetian territories. The pashas declared, however, they had all urged the sultan to make peace with Venice, "which they all know to have been a good and faithful

---

[68] *Cf.* Sanudo, *Diarii*, III, 41, 86, 118, 125, 127, 132, 162, 171; P. Bembo, *Hist. veneta* (1551), bk. v, fols. 71ᵛ–72ᵛ. Manenti's instructions may be found in the Sen. Secreta, Reg. 37, fols. 148ʳ–150ʳ [162ʳ–164ʳ]; they included an investigation of the charges against Antonio Grimani (*ibid.*, fol. 182ʳ [196ʳ]).

[69] Malipiero, *Annali veneti*, in *Arch. stor. italiano*, VII-1 (1843), 188–89, 191. On Manenti's meeting with Ali Pasha ("Halli Bassa"), note Sen. Secreta, Reg. 38, fols. 4ʳ [14ʳ], 15ʳ [25ʳ]. Sanudo, *Diarii*, III, 61, notes the appearance of two Russian envoys before the Venetian Signoria on 1 December, 1499, and *cf.*, *ibid.*, cols. 54–55, 66: they were expected in Rome on 26 December (col. 135), and note col. 136, and Romanin, V, 144.

friend of their lord, in the time of Jem Sultan as at other times. . . ." The price of peace would be the cession to the Porte of the fortress towns of Nauplia, Modon, Coron, and Monemvasia, as well as an annual gift to the sultan of 10,000 ducats, "as was given to his father." The Turks would send an envoy (*schiavo*) to Venice with Manenti to bring back the Signoria's reply. If the Venetians wished to make peace on these terms, they should send an ambassador to the Porte. "If not, God would work his will, and [they said] that we were to leave immediately, for the matter did not brook any delay."

Manenti replied that these were heavy demands. Venice would not be able to accept them. He would never have believed that any such request could be made. The pashas said there was no point in further discussion. On 26 February Manenti received a brocaded gown as a gift from the sultan, and on the following day called on the leading pasha for a further brief exchange of views and to bid him goodbye. The Turk was as intractable as previously: "I think that he had been informed by the Florentines, our good friends. . . ." The sultan would begin his campaign in April, and it was public knowledge that he had sworn to proceed against Nauplia, Modon, Coron, and Monemvasia. Manenti picked up various pieces of rumor and information in Adrianople: The king of France was actually not well disposed toward Venice; an envoy of Maximilian and Lodovico il Moro had arrived in Turkey; the sultan had sent a military mission into Hungary "to keep that king at peace with him;" and so on. "The first pasha is planning the attack [*impresa*] upon the Morea; the second, upon Cyprus; the third, the island of Sicily; the fourth, the kingdom of Naples; the fifth, Friuli, and he is asking for men, and he promises to go all the way into Lombardy."[70]

Manenti was probably not far wrong in his assumption that the Serenissima's *buoni amici*, the Florentines, were informing and even advising the sultan. Several documents attest the close and amicable relations then being cultivated between the cities on the Arno and the Bosporus. In February, 1499, the Florentines were preparing to send Geri Risaliti as a special envoy to Istanbul "renovare la antiqua amicitia," to seek confirmation of the privileges and immunities granted to them in the past, and to thank his Ottoman majesty for the good treatment always hitherto accorded Florentines. He was to petition for full continuance of the trading rights which the Florentines had enjoyed in Turkish territory "now for many years." Risaliti's commission abounds in praise of Bayazid's father, Mehmed the Conqueror, "principe di immortal memoria." The Florentine government wanted the free and secure passage of goods and merchants through the sultan's dominions, and reminding Risaliti that quarrelsome Florentines had often brought "infamia a tucta la natione nostra," the government wanted him to unite the members of the Tuscan colony in Istanbul in tighter bonds of amity to one another. Since oddly enough the Florentine archives contained no copy of the "articles, privileges, and immunities," the confirmation of which Risaliti was to request, he was to have a copy made in Istanbul, written in a good hand on paper of good quality, "authenticated according to the custom of the country in two languages [*nell' una lingua et l'altra*], or at least in Greek," which he was to bring back with him upon his return to Florence. Risaliti set out for Istanbul on 9 May (1499) as Bayazid was beginning the Lepantine campaign.[71] A year later, as Bayazid was embarking on another career of conquest, the Florentine Signoria sent him heartfelt thanks for his gracious reception of Risaliti and his favorable consideration of their requests.[72]

By the beginning of April, 1500, Alvise Manenti was back in Venice, where he made his report to the Senate.[73] The Turkish preparations which he had noted on the long journey

[70] Malipiero, *Annali veneti*, in *Arch. stor. italiano*, VII-1 (1843), 193–96; Romanin, V, 144–49; and on Manenti's return to Venice in the spring of the year 1500, see Sanudo, *Diarii*, III, 171, 179–81, with a summary of Manenti's report; *cf.*, *ibid.*, cols. 188, 190–91, 192–93, 194, 197, and Manfroni, *Marina italiana*, p. 222. During February, 1500, one day after another brought news of the "maximi apparatus domini Turci et terra et mari ad invasionem Christianorum" (Sen. Secreta, Reg. 37, fol. 187 [200], 189^v–190^r ff. [202^v ff.]): the Turks were now using Lepanto as a base of operations as well as other places within easy reach of the Italian coast, and the Venetians were moved to a new burst of activity.

[71] Giuseppe Müller, ed., *Documenti sulle relazioni delle città toscane coll' Oriente*, Florence, 1879, pt. 1, no. CCIX, pp. 242–44, and *cf.* docs. CCVI–CCVIII, CCX, CCXIII ff.

[72] Müller, *Documenti*, pt. 1, no. CCXII, pp. 245–46, docs. dated at Florence, 23–27 May, 1500.

[73] Sen. Secreta, Reg. 38, fols. 14 ff. [24 ff.]. Published reports to the Senate of envoys to Istanbul, including that of Alvise Manenti on 9 April, 1500 (Sanudo, *Diarii*, III, 179–81), are listed in Francesca Antonibon, *Le Relazioni a stampa di ambasciatori veneti*, Padua, 1939, pp. 28 ff.

from Lepanto to Adrianople had not been without obvious purpose. From May the rumors and reports of the sultan's advance began;[74] Bayazid himself was leading a large army into the Morea. At this critical juncture the Venetian captain-general of the sea, Melchior (or Marchio) Trevisan, fell ill, and on 28 July (1500) Benedetto Pesaro was appointed his successor.[75] The Venetians made great efforts to send men and provisions to Corfu, Modon, Coron, and Nauplia. Modon proved to be the sultan's objective, one of the "eyes of the Republic." On 17 August (1500) Don Gonsalvo Fernando de Cordova, the "grand captain," offered the Spanish fleet to the Venetians "in socorso de Modon et altri luochi nostri de Levante."[76] But after a six weeks' siege the janissaries had made a lucky assault upon the battered walls of the famous seaport, capturing Modon on 9 August (1500), just as supplies and reinforcements were coming into the harbor.[77] Navarino and even Coron now surrendered. From this terrible disaster Venetian power in the Morea found recovery impossible.

[74] *Cf.* Sanudo, *Diarii*, III, 333.

[75] Sen. Secreta, Reg. 38, fols. 50^r–51^v [60^r–61^v], "commissio . . . Ser Benedicti de Cha de Pesaro," the Ca de Pesaro possibly being the Palazzo Pesaro-Fortuny on the Campo S. Benedetto.

[76] Sen. Secreta, Reg. 38, fols. 60^v–61^v [70^v–71^v], letters dated 2 September, 1500, to Gonsalvo, to the Venetian captain-general of the sea, and to the Venetian ambassador in Rome.

[77] Sanudo, *Diarii*, III, 419, 485, 488, 502, 526–27, 574, 599–600, 602, 610 ff.; 620 ff., 637, 640, and esp. cols. 688–94, 717–19, etc., 824 ff.; Hajji Khalifeh, *Maritime Wars of the Turks*, trans. Jas. Mitchell, London, 1831, pp. 21–22. On 5 September (1500) official letters were authorized by the Venetian Senate to be sent to the pope and the cardinals, the king of the Romans, the king of France, the sovereigns of Spain, and the kings of Hungary, Poland, England, Portugal, and Naples, as well as the duke of Burgundy and the Electors of the Empire, to inform them all of the calamitous loss of Modon (Sen. Secreta, Reg. 38, fols. 63^v ff. [73^v ff.], and Sanudo, III, 750–52).

The Senate wrote Alexander VI that they had always stated to an unbelieving Europe that Venice was not strong enough to carry the Turkish burden by herself. Now the bulwark had been broken: "Expugnatum est Mothonum, viris omnibus illis fortissimis ad unum trucidatis praeter eos dumtaxat qui sese ac suos ut a foedissima hostium servitute subtraherent cum uxoribus et liberis in propriis domibus sponte concremarunt! Lachrymabile horrendumque spectaculum!" (Sen. Secreta, Reg. 38, fol. 63^v). The Venetians claimed that Bayazid II had led 150,000 men into the Morea (*ibid.*, fol. 64^r). The fall of Modon was known in Rome by 10–11 September (Burchard, *Diarium*, ed. Thuasne, III, 75, with note, and ed. Celani, II, 242). *Cf.* Manfroni, *Marina italiana*, pp. 224–28, and Jos. von Hammer-Purgstall, *Gesch. d. osman. Reiches*, II (repr. 1963), 316 ff. For Bayazid II's official description of the Moreote campaigns of 1499–1500, see Georges Vajda, "Un Bulletin de victoire de Bajazet II" [dated 8 November, 1500], *Journal asiatique*, CCXXXVI (1948), 87–102, which places the conquest of Modon on 11 August (1500) and the capitulation of Coron seven days later.

Having received "diebus hiis" the news of the Turkish occupation of Modon, Alessio Celidonio, then bishop of Gallipoli in southern Italy, a suffragan see of Otranto (Eubel, *Hierarchia*, II [1914, repr. 1960], 157), addressed three anti-Turkish tracts called *sermones* to Oliviero Carafa, cardinal of Naples, between 15 October and 1 November, 1500. The tracts are entitled *De ratione belli in Turcos ineundi*, *De bello in Turcos apparando*, and *De bello cum Turcis gerendo*; the contents are summarized, with illustrative quotations, in N. Iorga, ed., *Notes et extraits pour servir à l'histoire des croisades au XVe siècle*, V (Bucharest, 1915), no. CCCLXIII, pp. 313–30, and are discussed in H.-J. Kissling, "Militärisch-Politische Problematiken zur Türkenfrage im 15. Jahrhundert," *Bohemia: Jahrbuch des Collegium Carolinum*, V (Munich, 1964), 117–21, 126–27, 133–36.

Celidonio, who was born in Sparta, lamented the loss of the Morea, *meum natale solum*. He thought that he saw the beginning of the end, "atque utinam falsus sim vates!" (Iorga, *Notes et extraits*, V, 314). The Christians had brought some of the tragedy upon themselves by their own discord and divisiveness, while the Turks had shown a unity of leadership and possessed an abundance of resources lacking in the West. Moral reform must be the first step toward effective defense against the Turks. The clergy must do its part. Clerics with an annual income of more than 200 ducats (*aurei*) should give one third of their revenues for the war against the Turks, and so should the cardinals, if their income exceeded 2,000 ducats a year. The pope should make a like contribution, and should summon a "conventus Christianorum omnium" to meet in some town in the lower Alpine regions.

At this congress the unity of Christendom should be proclaimed, a papal call to arms issued. This crusading congress must not be called a council, however, "quandoquidem . . . nomen quoque ipsum quibusdam nostrorum suspectum esse video" (*ibid.*, V, 318). Celidonio had proposals for the economical feeding and housing of the delegates to the congress, which should be divided into "nations" (as at Constance in 1414–1418) to avoid the usual quarrels.

The congress should declare the existence of a new Christian alliance, and itself vote for another war against the Turks, who were to be assailed both by land and by sea. The commander-in-chief of the crusading forces should possess the qualities of a Cicero, "Marcus Tullius, au[c]tor eminentissimus!" (V, 320). We may leave the interested reader to pursue Celidonio's proposed routes for his two or three crusading armies and for his fleet, which (especially the latter) must be prepared for five years' service (V, 320–22). Displaying an unecclesiastical interest in arms and armor, Celidonio was full of tactical advice for the deployment of troops in the field as well as for the naval maneuvers which the crusading high command should follow. He acknowledged that his advice was not based upon experience (and nothing is more obvious), "sed ex aliqua rerum cognitione." Envoys should be sent, he said, to Uzun Ḥasan's eldest son and the soldan of Egypt and other eastern enemies of the Turks to enlist their aid. He recalled the crushing defeat of Sultan Bayazid I by Timur the Lame (at Ankara in 1402), "victum a se devinctumque catenis argenteis ac ferreis cancellis inclusum secum ducens" (V, 328). This brief summary may do less than justice to

The Republic now held in the Morea only the castle of Monemvasia and those at Nauplia, together with the latter town's dependencies at Kastri and Thermisi on the mainland opposite the barren island of Hydra. The Turkish war went on. In the years 1500–1501 there were few weddings in Venice; commerce lagged, and employment fell; banks failed; and they were fortunate who knew whence tomorrow's bread would come.[78] With the aid of the Spanish fleet under Gonsalvo de Cordova, the Venetian captain-general Benedetto Pesaro besieged and took the castle of S. George, the capital and commanding position on the island of Cephalonia (on 24 December, 1500),[79] and after Gonsalvo's return to Sicily the captain-general, assisted by thirteen papal galleys (under the command of his cousin Jacopo Pesaro), captured S. Maura (on 30 August, 1502). Benedetto's tomb in the church of the Frari in Venice still recalls these exploits. We shall return to them later. The Venetians would have to surrender S. Maura to the Turks, however, when peace was finally agreed to by the sultan in Istanbul on 13–19 December, 1502, and confirmed by the doge in Venice on 20 May, 1503.[80] Among various other provisions guaranteeing the resumption of free trade and the mutual return of prisoners and runaway slaves, the Venetians would agree to continue paying the annual tribute of five hundred ducats for Zante.[81] These years were long remembered on

---

Celidonio's views, but I doubt that they merit more space than I have given them. *Cf.* Franz Babinger, "Alessio Celidonio (+1517) und seine Türkendenkschrift," in *Beiträge zur Südosteuropa-Forschung*, Munich, 1966, pp. 326–30.

[78] Hajji Khalifeh, *Maritime Wars*, pp. 22–23, on the surrender of Navarino and Coron; Coron fell on 16 August, 1500 (Sanudo, *Diarii*, III, 770–74), and Navarino about the same time. *Cf.* Sen. Secreta, Reg. 38, fol. 72^{r} [82^{r}]; Romanin, V, 150–51 ff.; Manfroni, *Marina italiana*, pp. 229–30; Wm. Miller, *Latins in the Levant*, pp. 496–98; Kretschmayr, *Gesch. von Venedig*, II, 412–14. On the plight of the Lippomani bank in May, 1500, *cf.* Sanudo, *Diarii*, III, 356, *et alibi*.

[79] Sen. Secreta, Reg. 38, fols. 87^{v} [97^{v}], 97^{r} [107^{r}]; P. Bembo, *Hist. veneta* (1551), bk. v, fols. 75^{v}–77^{v}; Sanudo, *Diarii*, III, 1340 ff.; Manfroni, *Marina italiana*, pp. 231–32. Pesaro also recovered Navarino ("Zonchio") at the beginning of December, 1500 (Sen. Secreta, Reg. 38, fol. 92, letters to Pesaro dated 27–28 December, replying to his of the third to the sixth of the month).

[80] On 24 December, 1502, Bayazid II wrote the Doge Leonardo Loredan and the Signoria that he had presented the Venetian ambassador in Istanbul with the proposed treaty of peace, and had himself sworn in the ambassador's presence to observe its terms. In the meantime Bayazid was sending to Venice his "slave" Ali, to whom the doge and Signoria were to give a copy of the treaty in full agreement with the one which the Venetian ambassador had received. Bayazid allowed sixty days for Ali's return to the Bosporus, during which time he would observe the peace. The doge was to swear on the four gospels to abide by the treaty (Arch. di Stato di Venezia, Documenti turchi, Busta 3, doc. dated at Istanbul 24 jumādī II 908).

The sultan wrote the doge and Signoria again on 5 August, 1503, that the slave Ali, who had taken the treaty to Venice with the Venetian ambassador, had returned to Istanbul with Messer Andrea Gritti, who had duly reported that the doge had accepted the text and sworn to its observance. The doge had also accepted the necessity of settling the claims being made by the Porte as a result of the Venetian seizure of certain Turkish goods or property on the island of S. Maura (*ibid.*, Busta 3, doc. dated at Istanbul II dec. safer 909). Andrea Gritti remained in Istanbul as the Republic's new ambassador. He was beginning a distinguished career which would lead to his election as doge twenty years later. He had been in Istanbul (as a merchant) when the war broke out between the Porte and Venice. Being imprisoned during the summer of 1499 (Malipiero, *Annali veneti*, in *Arch. storico italiano*, VII-1 [1843], 172–73), he had been freed in January, 1502, on which see James C. Davis, "Shipping and Spying in the Early Career of a Venetian Doge, 1496–1502," *Studi veneziani*, XVI (1974), 97–108.

[81] Sen. Secreta, Reg. 39, fols. 62^{r}–64^{r} [74^{r}–76^{r}], docs. dated 23 January, 1503, when the news of Bayazid's willingness to make peace had reached Venice. On 4 May Andrea Gritti was elected ambassador to the Porte to see to the necessary last formalities of the peace (*ibid.*, fols. 81^{v}–82^{r} [93^{v}–94^{r}]). Gritti's commission, dated 16 May (fols. 84^{v}–87^{r}), specifies that "per la forma di capituli de la pace nuy siamo tenuti ad doe cosse essentiale, l'una è la restitutione de S. Maura [together with the Turkish prisoners, cannon, and munitions], l'altra de restituir i homeni et robe che furono prese a Napoli de Romania . . ." (fol. 85^{r} [97^{r}]). On 20 May the doge swore to abide by the terms of the peace in the presence of the Turkish envoy (fols. 89^{r}–91^{r}). The Venetian *regimina* throughout the Levant and the Adriatic were notified of the final arrangements for peace in letters dated 23 May, 1503—Corfu, Crete, Cyprus, Zante, and Cephalonia; Nauplia, Monemvasia, and Aegina; Tenos, Skyros, Skiathos, and Skopelos; Zara, Spalato, Sebenico, Traù, Lesina, Curzola, and other fortress towns on the Dalmatian coast (fol. 93^{r} [105^{r}]). Hostilities were supposed to cease on 14 December, 1502, and the fact that they did not was the cause of some later difficulty (*cf.*, *ibid.*, Reg. 40, fol. 42^{r} [56^{r}]). Note in general Sanudo, *Diarii*, IV, 667–68, 751–52, and V, 22, 26–27, 32, 41–48; Predelli, *Regesti dei Commemoriali*, VI, bk. XIX, nos. 9–12, pp. 65–66, docs. dated 14 December, 1502, and 20 May, 1503.

As for Pope Alexander VI during this period, we should note that on 17 September, 1500, five weeks or more after the fall of Modon, he addressed a brief to Gonsalvo de Cordova directing him to join his fleet to that of the Venetians for action against the Turks (Sanudo, III, 824–26). The pope had been trying for some time to get Gonsalvo to move into eastern waters (*ibid.*, III, 577, 589–90, 752–54); on the papal fleet of thirteen galleys which aided Benedetto Pesaro to take S. Maura, note Sigismondo de' Conti, II, 278–79, on which see below, p. 533. *Cf.* Predelli, *Commemoriali*, VI, bk. XVIII, nos. 216 and 220; Romanin, V, 151–54, with a brief summary of the treaty of 1502–3; Zinkeisen, II, 537–38, 540–43; Pastor, *Hist. Popes*, VI, 100–1, and *Gesch. d. Päpste*, III-1 (repr.

the lagoon as marking the first great decline in the failing strength of the Republic.

During this time of troubles for Venice Alexander VI had not been entirely inactive on behalf of Christian interests in the Levant. In the early autumn of 1499 he had asked the European princes to send envoys to a congress which was to meet in Rome the following March to initiate a crusade. But there were many who thought that the self-seeking pope could be trusted only to advance the interests of the house of Borgia. There was little response to his summons, which was repeated in early February, 1500. A brief dated the third of the month and addressed, among others, to the Florentines warned of the recent Turkish devastations (in the Morea and in Hungary) and the capture of Lepanto as well as of the preparations which the Turks were making both on land and at sea to renew the war in the spring. The pope was sure that the princes would respond *pro rei magnitudine que omnes tangit*, and claimed to have received a number of zealous responses. He asked that Florentine envoys be sent to Rome with full and sufficient mandate "for the conclusion and provision of everything required for this so sacred and necessary expedition."[82]

On 24 February (1500) a Turkish envoy rode through the streets of Rome to the apostolic palace for an audience with the pope. He was accompanied by the Venetian ambassador. The curious Johann Burchard, master of ceremonies, knew that something was afoot, but apparently acquired no information about the Turk's mission. Raymond Peraudi, the cardinal of Gurk, believing that the envoy's presence in Rome betokened an effort on the sultan's part to avert the preaching of a crusade, suddenly left his legatine mission in Perugia and hastened back to the Curia. He arrived in Rome on 6 March, "without the pope's permission, as I have understood," says Burchard.[83] On the eleventh the pope held a secret consistory to which he summoned all the ambassadors of the Christian powers. There came to the consistory the representatives of Maximilian, Louis XII, Henry VII of England, Federigo of Naples, and Ferdinand of Aragon, as well as those of Venice, Savoy, and Florence. The pope spoke of the danger which threatened Christendom, and said that in October, 1499, he had written all the kings and princes of Europe requesting them to send envoys with instructions "ad consulendum et providendum necessitati Christiane." When no one had replied, he had issued his warning again. Burchard understood that someone stated at the consistory that peace and concord would have to be established among the princes before the Turkish problem could be properly dealt with. The pope had high praise for the Venetians, who were holding the Turks at bay, and for the Spanish government, but was disappointed with the German, French, and Neapolitan response to his appeal.[84]

1955), 559–60; Manfroni, *Marina italiana*, pp. 239, 242; Wm. Miller, *Latins in the Levant*, pp. 498–500. See in general Gaetano Cogo, "La Guerra di Venezia contro i Turchi (1499–1501)," *Nuovo Archivio veneto*, XVIII (1899), 5–76, 348–421, and *ibid.*, XIX (1900), 97–138, with documents, and *L'Ultima Invasione de' Turchi in Italia in relazione alla politica europea dell'estremo Quattrocento*, Genoa, 1901; also the dissertation of Hans-Albrecht von Burski, *Kemāl Re'īs: Ein Beitrag zur Geschichte der türkischen Flotte*, Bonn, 1928. Eight letters, all original, dating from December, 1500, to September, 1502, written by the Venetian admiral Benedetto Pesaro to the doge and heads (*capi*) of the Council of Ten may be found in the Arch. di Stato di Venezia, Capi del Consiglio dei Dieci: Lettere di rettori e di altre cariche, Busta 301. Several of Pesaro's letters are dated February, 1500 [i.e., 1501] "ex triremi nostra in portu Corfoy." They relate to movements of the fleet, supplies, and the like.

[82] Müller, *Documenti*, pt. 1, no. CCXI, p. 245, brief dated at Rome on 3 February, 1500. Similar briefs were sent to Francesco Gonzaga, marquis of Mantua (Pastor, *Gesch. d. Päpste*, III-1 [repr. 1955], 549, note 5), to Ercole d'Este, duke of Ferrara (see below, note 84), and to other princes and states. These texts state that envoys of the recipients were to convene in Rome on 1 March. Alexander VI issued various bulls and briefs on behalf of Venice during 1499–1500 (Predelli, *Regesti dei Commemoriali*, VI [1903], bk. XVIII, nos. 157, 159, 165–68). There is a copy of the bull issued in the autumn of 1499 (this one to Grand Duke Alexander of Lithuania), seeking envoys "ita ut pleno sufficienti mandato ad providendum, concludendum, contribuendumque in hanc sanctam expeditionem proximis Kalendis Martii in hac alma urbe cum aliis principum oratoribus coram nobis conveniant," in Arch. Segr. Vaticano, Arm. XXXII, tom. 21, fols. 124^v–126^r, by mod. stamped enumeration, "datum Rome M. quad. 99." The copyist's title of this bull, *Exortatio contra Turcos post acceptum Modon et Coron*, is wrong since the Turks did not take Modon and Coron until August, 1500.

[83] Burchard, *Diarium*, ed. Thuasne, III, 16, 23, 39, and ed. Celani, II, 202, 206, 216; J. Schneider, *Die kirchliche u. politische Wirksamkeit d. Legaten Raimund Peraudi (1486–1505)*, Halle, 1882, pp. 53–54, cited by Pastor, *Gesch. d. Päpste*, III-1 (repr. 1955), 550, note 1.

[84] Burchard, *Diarium*, ed. Thuasne, III, 24, and ed. Celani, II, 207; Zurita, *Anales*, V (1670), fol. 175; Raynaldus, *Ann. eccl.*, ad ann. 1500, nos. 5–6, vol. XIX (1693), p. 487. Sanudo, *Diarii*, III, 342, summarizes a report from the Venetian ambassador in Rome of a consistory held on 16 May in which the crusade was discussed at length. Burchard records no such consistory in his diary. On 3 February,

Shortly before the secret consistory of 11 March (1500) Alexander VI had asked Stefano Taleazzi, titular archbishop of Patras and bishop of Venetian Torcello, to prepare in writing what would today be called working papers for an expedition against the Turks. Taleazzi wrote three crusading tracts, but it is not clear that they were of much value to the Curia Romana. In the first tract, called *Summarium de considerationibus pro expeditione contra Turcos*, he explored briefly twenty-three "considerations" relating to the crusade, but the work is so general as to have been of little more than hortatory value to anyone who read it, and sufficiently misleading as to suggest that the Turks had munitions and armament enough for an army of 300,000 warriors. Taleazzi's survey of contemporary politics and hostilities reveals, however, knowledge as well as some serious thought about the problems of individual states, but the rhetorical assertion that the crusade required a decade of peace in Europe as well as the union of the faithful was unlikely to prove helpful to the pope and his advisers. Indeed, the whole tract reminds us of that kind of anti-Turkish literary exercise to which Erasmus alludes with a laugh in his introduction to the *Praise of Folly*.[85]

Taleazzi's second tract, called a *Declaratio generalis*, begins with a somewhat erroneous historical sketch of the crusades, and then seeks to assess the military strength of the Ottoman empire. The sultan's manpower is divided into four classes: 1) 60,000 holders of small fiefs or timars, *quo[s] sua lingua "Timatos" vocant, nos autem armigeros*, who some years before (says Taleazzi) had been ordered to arm themselves like western archers; 2) 80,000 irregular horse or akinjis, *quos "Acanzeos" vocant equestres*, who like the timariots were said to serve without pay; 3) 10,000 to 15,000 janissaries, who were well known as the sultan's élite infantry; and 4) 40,000 to 50,000 mariners, *quos ["Asapos"] nos ferentarios, vulgo vastatores vel cernedas vocamus*,[86] who were maintained in a state of readiness at the expense of the provinces (or vilayets). The Turks were said to have killed as many as 40,000 Christians during the past two years. When the Christian offensive was launched, booty would of course be taken, and Taleazzi was of the opinion that "all things captured must be kept in the hands of the Apostolic See, . . . to be divided later." Much money would be necessary to support the Christian host. A thirtieth should be imposed upon the laity, two tithes upon the "exhausted" Italian clergy, and a third upon the ultramontane clergy, "especially in churches which have good revenues." But no one was to be forced; everyone was to be the object of benign persuasion. "I have wanted hastily to make note of these few things today," Taleazzi concludes, "despite some physical indisposition, in order to satisfy the anxiety I feel in my heart and to meet the wishes of your Holiness, to whom I humbly commend myself."[87]

1500, Alexander had rehearsed the Turkish peril, as we have noted above (e.g., in the brief of that date to Duke Ercole d'Este of Ferrara), "nobilitatem tuam hortantes atque quo possumus studio et diligentia requirentes ut ad id temporis [i.e., Kalendis Martiis] pro conclusione ac provisione rerum omnium huic tam sancte ac necessarie expeditioni necessariarum tuos quoque oratores cum pleno ac sufficienti mandato ad nos mittere velis" (Arch. di Stato di Modena, Cancelleria Estense, Estero: Carteggio di principi, Roma, Busta 1295/10, no. 51). A serious start on plans for a crusade was now made at the consistory of 11 March.

[85] See the valuable study of Bernardino Feliciangeli, "Le Proposte per la guerra contro i Turchi presentate da Stefano Taleazzi, vescovo di Torcello, a Papa Alessandro VI," *Archivio della R. Società romana di storia patria*, XL (Rome, 1917), 5–63, with the previously unpublished text of Taleazzi's first tract (*op. cit.*, pp. 42–50), which was written between February and April of the year 1500. Taleazzi later delivered the sermon *contra Turcos* at the tenth session of the Fifth Lateran Council on 4 May, 1515.

[86] I have here identified the *asapi* as "mariners" on the basis of such texts as the following: On 20 June, 1517, Leonardo Bembo, the Venetian bailie in Istanbul, wrote his government that the Turks were building ships, apparently for an attack upon Christian territories, "et ordenato mandino per la Turchia e Grecia a far scriver asappi et homeni da remo, che sono signali a tempo nuovo sia per far grossissima armata, la qual armata sarà a danno de' Christiani" (Sanudo, *Diarii*, XXIV, 506). A letter written on 13 March, 1518, in the name of Cardinal Giulio de'Medici, states that the Turks "haveano scripto 60 mila asapi, cioè gente da remo, de quali due terzi erano turchi et il resto cristiani" (Cesare Guasti, ed., "I Manoscritti Torrigiani donati al R. Archivio Centrale di Stato di Firenze," *Archivio storico italiano*, 3rd ser., XXI [1875], 231). Tommaso Contarini, who succeeded Leonardo Bembo as bailie in Istanbul, reported on 2 June, 1520, "el Signor [Turcho] aver licentià li asapi di la Grecia, resta solum 12 milia, sichè è da pensar non habbi a ussir grossa armada . . ." (Sanudo, XXIX, 13–14). A similar letter from Ragusa relates "come el Signor Turco avea dato universal licentia a tutte le gente da remo et da fatti . . ." (*ibid.*, XXIX, 14, and *cf.* col. 15, "che 'l Signor fece dar licentia a tutti li asapi et homeni da remo").

[87] Feliciangeli, "Le Proposte per la guerra contro i Turchi," pp. 50–53, gives the text.

Taleazzi's third lucubration is called a *Declaratio magis particularis*, and he thus refers to its contents:

Since . . . I have said enough about the power of the Turk, let us now come first to the army we need for such an attack [upon him]. Secondly, [let us speak] of the funds necessary for maintaining the army each year for ten years at least—otherwise it would be better to stop planning than to attempt so great a venture for one or two years. Thirdly, we shall consider the means of raising money, and fourthly of carrying on the war, both by whom and in what way [our objectives] may be better and more easily [achieved].

Taleazzi then provides a rather haphazard list of the personnel and matériel which he regarded as essential to the crusade: ten cannoneers each to be paid 8 to 10 ducats a month, ten physicians at 10 ducats, twenty surgeons at 7 ducats, apothecaries, sappers, artisans, blacksmiths, bakers, tailors, and saddlers, as well as a hundred women for washing clothes; also of course heavy and lighter artillery, ammunition, transport, weapons, tools, baskets, draught horses, grain, meat, wine, hay, fodder, and so on. He had in mind an army of more than 50,000 men, costing hundreds of thousands of ducats, and believed that his army could best get into Turkey through Albania since the Adriatic could be crossed from Brindisi, Otranto, Bari, or Ancona. An approach by land through Croatia and Serbia was also practicable. A large fleet of galleys, transports, and other ships was a necessary adjunct to the land forces which Taleazzi had in mind.

Although Taleazzi's tracts smell more of the library lamp than of the camp fire, the sincerity of his effort and his devotion to the crusading ideal are quite apparent. His honesty is also refreshing:

For getting the crusade under way and maintaining it . . . , I should think—considering the bad opinion which other nations have of us because of funds hitherto collected in vain and diverted to other uses—that your Holiness might concede the tithes and offerings to be collected. . . . In this way the princes, towns, and people could be sure of the true purpose and good intention of the Apostolic See, and more willingly approach all tasks, and we ourselves should be freed of work as well as of suspicion.

Taleazzi closed his third tract with the hope that the data he had collected and his reflections might possibly be of some use to the pope, and with the acknowledgment of a suspicion of his own, *suspitio quod nihil fiet*, the suspicion that nothing was really going to be done to launch the crusade.[88]

News was always anxiously awaited from Hungary, for the great fear was that the Hungarians might agree to an accord with the sultan, who had sent an envoy to Buda. The Venetian envoys to the Hungarian court were told that it would be a good idea if King Maximilian would join Louis XII against the Turks. The Hungarian barons, they were also told, were quite willing to fight, but the prelates preferred peace, because they were likely to end up paying a disproportionately large share of the costs of war.[89] The Venetian Senate worked hard to enlist the aid of John Albert, king of Poland, as well as that of his brother, Ladislas II of Hungary and Bohemia, seeking to conclude with them a "confederation and league" against the unspeakable Turks.[90] The response of Ladislas was encouraging, for he promptly announced that he would make no new truce (*induciae*) or reach any other entente (*intelligentia*) with the Turks that did not include Venice, and "this we have certainly been most grateful to hear!"[91]

The fall of Lepanto had dramatized the Turkish peril. Even Henry VII of England appeared much concerned, and on 7 April, 1500, he wrote Louis XII at length concerning the great Turkish naval preparations which Louis had informed him were going to be employed very shortly against Italy, "which would cause the greatest terror to all Christendom. . . ." Henry agreed heartily with his "dearest and most beloved brother and cousin" on the necessity of beating back the Turkish armada, but England was so far from the sultan's naval objectives that the king and his council saw no practicable way to help repulse the Turk, as they would certainly like to do.[92] Alexander VI

---

88 Feliciangeli, "Proposte per la guerra," pp. 53–63.

89 Sanudo, *Diarii*, III, 287–88, and *cf*. cols. 316–17, 356–57. Vettore Soranzo and Sebastiano Giustinian received their commissions and instructions as the Republic's envoys to Buda on 10–12 March, 1500 (Sen. Secreta, Reg. 38, fols. 2^v–6^r [12^v–16^r]). On Hungary, note in general, *ibid*., fols. 54 ff. [64 ff.], 75^v ff., 88^v ff., 102^r ff. [112^r ff.], 129^v ff., and Reg. 39, fols. 22^r ff. [34^r ff].

90 Sen. Secreta, Reg. 38, fols. 2^v, 5^v–6^r [12^v, 15^v–16^r].

91 Sen. Secreta, Reg. 38, fols. 6^r–8^r [16^r–18^r], 11^v [21^v], a letter of 12 March, 1500, to Alvise Manenti, who was likewise to make no truce with the Turks that did not include the kings of both Hungary and Poland.

92 Sanudo, *Diarii*, III, 298–300, an Italian version of Henry VII's letter to Louis XII, "scrita in la cità nostra de Londra, el septimo zorno de aprile, l'ano 1500, avanti pasqua."

would be in the line of fire, however, if the Turks really planned to attack Italy as they had done twenty years before. In early May (1500) he proposed in the consistory the imposition of the crusading tithe upon the clergy of France, Germany, Hungary, and elsewhere for use against the Turk. The cardinals were to be included, "e lui papa vol esser il primo." The cardinals were not enthusiastic about paying the tithe, but the pope insisted. He also wanted to send a cardinal-legate into Hungary, to unite the Italian powers, and to do whatever else would make possible the expedition against the Turks.[93]

Alexander had already imposed a levy of one twentieth upon the property of the Jews (on 4 February, 1500) as well as a tithe upon the income of the clergy, both assessments to be paid for three years.[94] On 1 June Alexander issued the crusading bull *Quamvis ad amplianda*, in which the Turks were assailed with the usual abusive epithets, "perfidissimi Turce, Christi nominis hostes, christianum sanguinem sitientes." Both this year and the year before, powerful Turkish forces had been invading Venetian possessions (in Greece), devastating cities and towns, carrying off thousands into servitude, laying waste wide areas with fire and sword, desecrating churches, and seeking day and night to subvert the law of Christ and subject all Christians to the hideous sect of Islam. Now the Turks had a stronger fleet and a larger army (says the pope), and they planned to seize all the strategic coastal points and Christian ports leading to the states of the Church "ac presertim ad hanc almam Urbem nostram in qua Petri sedes est locata."

If Rome fell, which God forbid, the Turks did not doubt that they could acquire world dominion. They were elated by their successes, and saw the Christian princes at odds with one another, intent upon their private interests, neglecting the common good. It was no wonder that the Turks had been able to inflict irreparable losses upon Christians in Germany, Hungary, Poland, Croatia, and other eastern territories. (King Maximilian's subjects had suffered even more than those of Venice.) The pope would himself accompany the Christian princes on the crusade and shed his own blood if necessary (or so at least the bull stated), and the cardinals would willingly go too because of their pious devotion to the faith. The tithe was demanded of all ecclesiastical revenues, everywhere and of every possible description, to help finance the crusade against the Turks. Those who failed to pay their tithe exposed themselves to excommunication and deprivation of their churches, benefices, and offices. The cardinals were also to pay the tithe, which would last for three years. Copies of the bull of 1 June were to be read in all churches on Sundays or other feast days, and the bull was to be expounded in the vernacular whenever necessary to make its contents clear to all.[95]

Alexander VI also wrote Louis XII of France that his Majesty knew well the papal efforts of recent and earlier years to promote the crusade. Turkish strength had been increasing daily; so had Turkish audacity, encouraged by Christian negligence. The preceding summer Lepanto had fallen, and Germany had been harried. The one remedy for Turkish madness was the union of the princes under the aegis of Rome. The pope had tried in vain to assemble on 1 March a congress of representatives of the powers "with sufficient mandate and full authority to act, transact, and conclude." But

[93] Sanudo, *Diarii*, III, 309, 327, 342–43, 352, 354–55, 378–79. On French objections to paying the crusading tithe, see Augustin Renaudet, *Préréforme et humanisme à Paris* (1953), pp. 316–19. Alexander was then granting the Venetians the right to collect two tithes a year (Sen. Secreta, Reg. 38, fol. 96[r] [106[r]]).

[94] Burchard, *Diarium*, ed. Thuasne, III, 46, and ed. Celani, II, 220: the levies were posted on the doors of the chancery.

[95] Burchard, *Diarium*, ed. Thuasne, III, 46–53, and ed. Celani, II, 220–24; Raynaldus, *Ann. eccl.*, ad ann. 1500, nos. 7–8, vol. XIX (1693), pp. 487–88. Another bull, also dated 1 June, 1500, imposed the twentieth upon the Jews (Burchard, *op. cit.*, ed. Thuasne, III, 53–56, and ed. Celani, II, 224–26; Raynaldus, ad ann. 1500, no. 9, vol. XIX, pp. 488–89). On 21 June, 1500, a jubilee was declared for Hungary and Poland "pro sancta expeditione contra Turcos" (Arch. Segr. Vaticano, Arm. XXXII, tom. 21, fols. 131[v]–134[v], "undecimo Kal. Julii, p[ontificatus nostri anno] octavo").

On 22 May, 1500 (*XI Kal. Iunii, pont. nostri anno octavo*), if in fact the date is not the same as the preceding, the kings of Poland and Hungary were granted a portion of the tithe to be levied *super spiritualibus* by the bull *Universo pene orbi* [meant to recall Innocent VIII's crusading bull with the same incipit, dated 13 November, 1487] (Arch. Segr. Vaticano, Arm. XXXII, tom. 21, fols. 135[r]–137[v], "datum Rome, anno M. quingentesimo, XI Kal. Iunii, pont. nostri [anno] octavo"). Alexander's bull recalls the tragedies attending the fall of Lepanto the year before. Now the Turks were preparing a fleet and a land army to assail Hungary and Poland, for the sultan had not yet spilled Christian blood enough to satisfy him. The Turkish peril is the major theme running through the Venetian Senatus Secreta, Reg. 38, a bulky volume.

not all the powers had sent representatives, and those who came had lacked the authority to commit their principals. In the meantime Turkish envoys had been pressing King Ladislas of Hungary to renew his peace with the Porte. Ladislas would prefer war, however, provided he were supplied with the necessary funds and with dependable allies. The Hungarians were the "bulwark of Christendom" (*antemurale Christianitatis*). Now the pope had recourse to the king of France, who had become an Italian prince with his conquest of Milan. The Turkish peril must be met with speed; otherwise "Italy will be done for" (*de Italia actum erit*). The eyes of Europe were turned toward Louis. The pope was looking to him also. The Spanish sovereigns were zealous for the faith, anxious about their island of Sicily, and ready to take action. The Spanish fleet might be joined to that of Venice, whose power was well known. If Louis would now aid the Hungarians, the other princes would hearken to the call and follow his example. Louis could employ the tithe for the crusade. The pope, the cardinals, all the officials of the Curia, and all the clergy everywhere in Europe would pay the tithe. They would give in fact not only their incomes but their very lives, if the need presented itself, for the safety of their fellow Christians.[96]

When it came to paying the crusading tithe, one may doubt that Alexander VI really "wanted to be the first," but he was serious about the cardinals' paying the tenth part of their incomes for the purpose of outfitting a fleet. The papal master of ceremonies, Burchard, has preserved a list of cardinals with an indication of the income of each (as prepared in the fall of 1500 and published early in 1501). The chief importance of Burchard's list, which contains forty-five names, lies in the information it furnishes concerning the annual incomes of almost all members of the Sacred College. The amounts are given in ducats:

	Income	Tithe
1. Oliviero Carafa [on whom see Ciaconius-Oldoinus, II, cols. 1097–1105].	10,000	1,000
2. Giuliano della Rovere [later Pope Julius II].	20,000	2,000
3. Giovanni Battista Zeno [died 8 May, 1501, on whom see Ciaconius-Oldoinus, II, 1112–13, and III, 208].	15,000	1,500
4. Giovanni Michiel [died 10–11 April, 1503, *ibid.*, II, 1113–14, and III, 209, but see Pastor, *Gesch. d. Päpste*, III-1 [repr. 1955], 585, for the date].	12,000	1,200
5. George Costa [Ciac.-Old., III, 55–56].	7,000	700
6. Girolamo Basso della Rovere [*ibid.*, III, 64].	11,000	1,100
7. Domenico della Rovere [died 22 April, 1501, *ibid.*, III, 76–77, 208].	10,000	1,000
8. Lorenzo Cibo [died 21 December, 1503, *ibid.*, III, 124–26].	10,000	1,000

[96] Sanudo, *Diarii*, III, 435–38, brief undated, but entered by Sanudo under June, 1500. In a brief to Cardinal Ippolito d'Este, dated 13 February, 1501, Alexander began with the sad reflection "quo in articulo res Christiana versetur et quibus quantisque periculis ab imanissimo Turcorum domino nunc urgeatur, que adeo innotescunt ut nulla opus sit eorum commemoratione vel repetitione . . . ," and came to the tithe which the cardinals were to pay, ". . . etiam de ipsorum fratrum consilio et unanimi consensu per omnes cardinales tam absentes quam presentes decimam omnium beneficiorum et officiorum suorum imposuimus, quam ipsi non modo promptissimo et liberali animo unanimiter persolvendam sed ultro etiam maiorem longe summam decimam excedentem susceperunt, quod nihil esse putarent indignius quam in hac tanta Christianitatis necessitate atque discrimine se cardinales solos immunes esse."

Because of the amplitude of their wealth and honors Alexander knew that the cardinals were anxious to make payments as befitted their status ". . . ut carissimo in Christo filio nostro Wadislao Hungarie et Boemie regi illustri bellum Turcis potenter terrestri et valido exercitu illaturo XL m. aureorum persolvantur classisque Sancte Romane Ecclesie nomine instructa cum cardinale legato preficiendo primo statim vere mittatur si nos contingeret, non veniente Francorum Christianissimo [rege] vel Hispaniarum rege illustri, sicut speramus et optamus, cum ea personaliter non proficisci." A commission of three cardinals was to receive the tithes of their fellows in the Sacred College; the funds were to be used solely for the crusade, than which nothing was closer to the pope's heart. If only the princes and especially the illustrious king of the Spains would respond to the need of Christendom, "non veremur quin brevi res Christiana in bonum statum restituatur. Datum Rome apud Sanctum Petrum sub annulo piscatoris die XIII Februarii MCCCCCI, pont. nostri anno nono" (Arch. di Stato di Modena, Cancelleria Estense, Estero: Carteggio di principi, Busta 1295/10, no. 58).

	Income	Tithe
9. Antoniotto Pallavicini [*ibid.*, III, 129–31].	10,000	1,000
10. Juan Borgia "the Elder" [died 1 August 1503, *ibid.*, III, 167, 210].	10,000	1,000
11. Giovanni Battista Orsini [died 22 February, 1503, *ibid.*, III, 85–86; Burchard, ed. Celani, II, 351].	10,000	1,000
12. Giovanni Antonio di Sangiorgio [Ciac.-Old., III, 168].	8,000	800
13. Bernardino Carvajal [*ibid.*, III, 170–71].	10,000	1,000
14. Raymond Peraudi [*ibid.*, III, 172–73].	3,000	300
15. Juan de Castro [*ibid.*, III, 185–86].	2,000	200
16. Juan Lopez [died 5 August, 1501, *ibid.*, III, 186, 208].	10,000	1,000
17. Domenico Grimani [*ibid.*, III, 180–81].	7,000	700
18. Giacomo Serra [*ibid.*, III, 192].	2,000	200
19. Pietro Isvalies [*ibid.*, III, 195].	2,000	200
20. Francisco Borgia [*ibid.*, III, 196].	3,000	300
21. Juan Vera [*ibid.*, III, 196].	3,000	300
22. Luigi Podocataro [a Cypriote Greek from Nicosia, died 25 August, 1504, *ibid.*, III, 197].	2,000	200
23. Antonio Trivulzio [in Celani's edition of Burchard *Cumanus* stands for *Comensis*, cardinal of Como; Ciac.-Old., III, 197–98].	6,000	600
24. Giovanni Battista Ferrari [died 20 July, 1502, *ibid.*, III, 199, 208].	3,000	300
25. Francesco Piccolomini [later Pope Pius III, died 18 October, 1503].	9,000	900
26. Raffaele Riario Sansoni [*ibid.*, III, 70–76].	18,000	1,800
27. Giovanni Colonna [*ibid.*, III, 80].	3,000	300
28. Ascanio Maria Sforza [vice-chancellor of the Church, brother of Lodovico il Moro, *ibid.*, III, 86–88].	30,000	3,000
29. Giovanni de' Medici [later Pope Leo X].	6,000	600
30. Federigo di Sanseverino [*ibid.*, III, 142–44].	13,000	1,300
31. Ippolito d'Este [*ibid.*, III, 176–78].	14,000	1,400
32. Giuliano Cesarini [*ibid.*, III, 179].	2,000	200
33. Alessandro Farnese [later Pope Paul III].	2,000	200
34. Lodovico Borgia-Lanzol [nephew of Cardinal Juan, *ibid.*, III, 191–92].	10,000	1,000
35. Marco Cornaro (Corner), *qui nullos habet redditus* (says Burchard) [Ciac. -Old., III, 200].	nihil	nihil
36. Guillaume Briçonnet [*ibid.*, III, 182–83].	12,000	1,200
37. Philippe de Luxembourg [*ibid.*, III, 184–85].	9,000	900
38. Georges d'Amboise [cardinal archbishop of Rouen, *ibid.*, III, 187–90].	9,000	900
39. Amanieu d'Albret [brother-in-law of Cesare Borgia, *ibid.*, III, 191].	2,000	200
40. Luis Juan de Milà [cousin of Alexander VI, *ibid.*, II, 989–90].	8,000	800
41. Diego Hurtado de Mendoza [died 24 October, 1502, *ibid.*, III, 190, 208].	14,000	1,400
42. Luigi d'Aragona [*ibid.*, III, 187].	2,000	200

	Income	Tithe
43. Pierre d'Aubusson [grand master of the Hospital of S. John of Jerusalem, died 3 July, 1503, *ibid.*, III, 134–40, 209].		
44. Frederick Casimir [son of the king of Poland, cardinal-deacon of S. Lucia in Septemsoliis, died 19 March, 1503, *ibid.*, III, 178–79, 208].	Hi qui in bello existunt, nihil solvunt.	
45. Thomas Bakócs [cardinal archbishop of Gran, *ibid.*, III, 192–95].[97]		
	349,000	34,900

A tax levied upon all officials of the Curia Romana, upon certain municipal officials, and upon fourteen hospitals in the city was intended to produce 12,442 ducats.[98] Venetian dispatches from Rome appear to attest Alexander VI's serious intention to support both the Republic and the kingdom of Hungary against the Turks. In a three-hour consistory held on 13 July (1500) the cardinals proposed giving the Hungarians a subsidy of 25,000 ducats; the pope wanted to make it 40,000, and no action was taken.[99]

On 12 September the Florentine envoy to the Holy See, Francesco Capello, wrote the Signoria that "yesterday morning the sad news came of the loss of Modon . . . ," although the fact had already been learned from unofficial sources.

---

[97] For this list see Burchard, *Diarium*, ed. Thuasne, III, 56–57, and ed. Celani, II, 226–27. In Thuasne's edition the twenty-third name, *Cumanus* (=*Comensis*, i.e., Antonio Trivulzio), is omitted; it is also omitted in Raynaldus, *Ann. eccl.*, ad ann. 1500, no. 9, vol. XIX (1693), p. 489, and in Pastor, *Hist. Popes*, VI, 91–92. Pastor, VI, 93, note, observes that A. Gottlob, "Der Legat Raimund Peraudi," *Hist. Jahrbuch*, VI (1885), 444–45, says that the cardinals were bound to pay an annual total of 34,900 ducats for the years 1501, 1502, and 1503 to help support the war against the Turks: In the English translation of his great work Pastor, VI, 92, got a total of only 34,300 ducats, as a consequence of omitting Trivulzio's tithe of 600 ducats. Unfortunately in the last German edition, *Gesch. d. Päpste*, III, pt. 1 (1924, repr. 1955), 551–53, although he cites Celani's edition of Burchard, he obviously has not used it very carefully. He still believes "dass die Kardinäle als Türkenzehnten im ganzen 34,300 Dukaten zu zahlen haben: die Steuer der römischen Beamten und Spitäler wird auf 11,076 Dukaten angesetzt, was als Gesamtsumme 45,376 Dukaten ergibt." All three figures are inaccurate; the correct sums (I believe) appear above in the text.

At this point we must note that Celani's edition of Burchard's text assigns Raffaele Riario Sansoni (no. 26 in the list) only 8,000 ducats' income (instead of 18,000) and so only 800 ducats' tithe (instead of 1,800). Celani's edition also assigns Briçonnet (no. 36 in the list) only 7,000 ducats' income (instead of 12,000) and so only 700 ducats' tithe (instead of 1,200). These reductions for Sansoni (1,000) and Briçonnet (500) would lower the total of the cardinals' tithe by 1,500 ducats. But since Gottlob, *Aus der Camera Apostolica* (1889), pp. 65–66, had already shown that forty-one cardinals were to pay a total of 34,900 ducats, Celani's text is apparently inferior here to that of Thuasne (except that Celani restores the cardinal *Cumanus* or *Comensis*): four of the cardinals listed above paid no tithe. On 4 February, 1501, the bull (dated on the first of the month) imposing the tithe for three years was "published" by being affixed to the doors of the papal chancery (Burchard, ed. Thuasne, III, 113–16, and ed. Celani, II, 266–68). For the convenience of the interested reader references are given to the lives of the cardinals concerned in A. Ciaconius, *Vitae et res gestae pont. roman.*, ed. A. Oldoinus, vols. II–III, Rome, 1677. I have noted the dates of death (as given by Eubel) of those cardinals who died during the three-year period that payment of the crusading tithe was to be in effect. Twelve of the cardinals in this list of forty-five were created on 28 September, 1500 (Burchard, *Diarium*, ed. Thuasne, III, 76–78, and ed. Celani, II, 242–43). Trivulzio was one of the twelve (Sanudo, III, 881). Burchard gives the sums the new cardinals were alleged to have paid for the red hats. The number of Spaniards and Catalans in the list of cardinals is notable. Of forty-four cardinals created during the reign of Alexander VI, sixteen were natives of the Iberian peninsula (Pastor, *Gesch. d. Päpste*, III-1 [repr. 1955], 633, and E. Müntz, *Les Arts à la cour des papes*, Paris, 1898, p. 144, note 1). For the dates of creation of the older members of the Sacred College appearing in the assessment list, together with a miscellany of other relevant data, see Conrad Eubel, *Hierarchia catholica*, II (1914, repr. 1960), esp. pp. 12 ff.

The family relationships of the Borgia cardinals, not easy to keep straight, may be checked in Wm. H. Woodward, *Cesare Borgia*, London, 1913, append., no. II, pp. 383 ff., where unfortunately occasional errors of dates occur. The tithes imposed on the cardinals (e.g., Giuliano della Rovere) may not accurately reflect their incomes, but may well have had the "criterio di colpire gli avversari o i tepidi amici dei Borgia" (G. B. Picotti, *La Politica italiana sotto il pontificato di Giulio II*, Pisa, 1947–48, p. 109). On the evil reputation in financial matters of Cardinal Giovanni Battista Ferrari, the confidant of Alexander VI, *cf.* M. Tangl, *Die päpstlichen Kanzleiordnungen*, Innsbruck, 1894, repr. 1959, pp. 388–89.

[98] *Cf.* Burchard, *Diarium*, ed. Thuasne, III, 57–60, and ed. Celani, II, 227–30, where the latter text appears to be much better (numerous officials and the charges against them being omitted in Thuasne's edition). Pastor, *Hist. Popes*, VI, 92, and *Gesch. d. Päpste*, III-1, 551, reckons the levy upon the curial officials and hospitals as 11,076 ducats, but again (although he cites Celani) he used only Thuasne's deficient text.

[99] Sanudo, *Diarii*, III, 521.

The Venetian ambassadors went immediately to the Vatican palace, where they read in consistory letters confirming what had hitherto been a rumor. The pope and the cardinals were profoundly disturbed. On the twelfth the Sacred College was again assembled, and although Capello understood that no definite steps were taken for action against the Turks, it seemed quite clear that the pope and cardinals would make suitable provision for the common good of Christendom as well as for Venice. The pope wanted Gonsalvo de Cordova's fleet, which was then in Sicily, to join the Venetian armada (as we have seen), and spoke of sending legates to appeal for help in France and Germany. Alexander complained, however, to the Venetian envoys that the Republic had not assisted Cesare Borgia in his designs upon Rimini and Faenza, to which they replied that the Venetians were now ready "et abracciare il Ducha Valentinense et tenerlo per loro buon figluolo et darli soldo con optime et convenienti conditioni." The papal answer was that the time had passed for fine words. Action was needed on Cesare's behalf.[100] However much he might be concerned about the Turkish successes in Greece, obviously the pope intended to take as much advantage as he could of the Venetians' dire predicament to advance the fortunes of his son Cesare, who was then embarking upon the conquest of the Romagna.

On 5 October (1500) three legates *a latere* were chosen in consistory. Raymond Peraudi, "qual à gran praticha, è caldo a queste cosse dil turco," was to be sent into Germany, Denmark, and the northern kingdoms. Juan Vera, the newly created cardinal of Salerno, was supposed to go to France, Scotland, England, and Spain; Pietro Isvalies, who had also received the red hat in the recent creation of cardinals (on 28 September), was being sent to Hungary, Bohemia, and Poland.[101] If we

[100] Thuasne, *Burchardi diarium*, III, 76, note, gives the text of most of Francesco Capello's letter of 12 September, 1500, to the Florentine government. *Cf.* the summary of the Venetian ambassadors' own accounts, dated 11–12 September, of their dealings with the pope and cardinals in Sanudo, *Diarii*, III, 788–89. Although the pope told one of the Venetian ambassadors, Marino Giorgio (Zorzi), that "desiderava morir per la fede," Giorgio reported that his Holiness seemed to be more interested in Cesare Borgia's conquest of the Romagna (*ibid.*, III, 856).

Sanudo's diaries are a whole private *archivio di stato*, a vast reservoir of information, from which the historian may easily derive an excessive documentation to illustrate facts or points of view which no one is likely to dispute, but in the present context we may quote the Venetian ambassador's statement of 2 December (1500), "Chome il papa solum à a cuor l'impresa di Romagna, e dil turcho si cura pocho, licet dicha voler andarvi im persona" [i.e., to go personally on the crusade] (*ibid.*, III, 1166). I think the ambassador's statement is probably not far from the truth although Pastor, *Gesch. d. Päpste*, III-1 (repr. 1955), 554, 560–61, refuses to accept the fact. The ambassador had already made the same statement on 28 September (Sanudo, III, 879).

[101] Sanudo, *Diarii*, III, 892–93, and *cf.* cols. 1171, 1174. Apparently neither Louis XII of France nor the Spanish sovereigns wished to receive a papal legate to promote the crusade (*ibid.*, III, 1166). *Cf.* Sen. Secreta, Reg. 38, fol. 82^{v} [92^{v}], 87^{r}, and Predelli, *Regesti dei Commemoriali*, VI, bk. XVIII, no. 169, pp. 43–44, dated 20 January, 1501, relating to Cardinal Isvalies in Hungary, and see, *ibid.*, no. 177, p. 47, bull dated 22 March, 1501.

Peraudi's instructions may be found in Arch. Segr. Vaticano, Miscellanea, Arm. II, tom. 56, fols. 331 ff., by mod. stamped enumeration: "Instructiones dilecto filio nostro Ray. tituli Sancte Marie Nove presbytero cardinali ad . . . Maximilianum, Romanorum regem illustrissimum, electores, principes S.R.I. et nationem germanicam legato nostro: Cum res impiissimorum Turchorum sicut omnibus palam est cum aperto totius Christianitatis periculo in dies fortius invalescant, cogitamus quod semper hactenus fecimus remedia oportuna adhibere et quod potissimum iudicamus catholicorum principum animos ad eam rem movere ut presto sint ne propter temporis intervalla penitudo moram sequatur neve posterior diligentia priorem negligentiam emendare possit. . . ." From his earliest days in the papacy Alexander had been anxious (according to the document) to free the Christian world *ab infanda Turchorum scabie et rabie*, but he had made little progress because of the dissension in Europe, the princes' cool response, and his own sins (*et peccatis etiam nostris causantibus*). Turkish success had been fostered by Christian negligence and disunion. Now Lepanto, Modon, and Coron had fallen, "magnaque edita clade ferocius in Christianos assurgit [tirannus ille Turchorum] et per tota illa littoralia loca liber debacchatur nulli sexui, nulli aetati, nulli ordini parcendo et sacra omnia profanando et polluendo, fitque victoria quotidie insolentior et ad interiora iam Italie penetrare omni conatu meditatur, cuius furori nisi oportuno tempore obviam eatur obsessam immo oppressam Italiam brevi sentiemus . . ." (fol. 332^{r}). "Sciat [Majestas sua] quoque pecunias illas omnes [i.e., decimas, cruciatam, et jubileum in locis et dominiis Majestatis sue et tota Germania], que inde proventure sunt, etiam ad nos et ecclesiam spectantes, in predictum fidei opus et non in alium usum, integre et sine aliqua diminutione converti debere . . ." (fol. 334^{r}).

Maximilian, the princes, and the German electors were to appoint the custodians of the crusading funds to be collected; these custodians were to keep the money until it could be used for the expedition against the Turks, "[illa expeditio] in Thurcos, in qua dies noctesque versamur, ac studia et curas omnes nostras convertimus . . ." (fol. cit.). ". . . Et affirmes deliberationem nostram omnimodam per quam decrevimus cum sacro collegio nostro ad hanc sanctam expeditionem non solum nostras et Ecclesie facultates omnes verbo et opere prestare sed personam etiam nostram tanquam hostiam Deo placentem omnino offerre . . ." (fol. 334^{v}). Alexander VI's plan for two land armies must follow one of these legates, let it be Peraudi, whose task was especially difficult, for the Germans were notoriously indifferent to the crusade and always ready to accuse the Curia Romana of collecting money under false pretenses. The Turkish menace was an old theme in Germany. It had just been discussed, and men and money requested, at the Reichstag of Freiburg in 1498 and at that of Augsburg in 1500. Peraudi left Rome on his legatine mission on 26 October (1500) to announce the jubilee and crusading indulgences to a people who would prove almost as inhospitable as their winter. He carried with him the crusading bull *Domini et salvatoris* (dated 5 October, 1500). Although King Maximilian placed various obstacles in his path, Peraudi was able to set forth the purpose of his mission before the imperial government at Nuremberg in the late summer of 1501. It was agreed that one-third of the proceeds from the sale of indulgences should go to Peraudi to cover the costs of collection; the other two thirds were to be kept in Germany and to be spent only for the war against the Turks. The pope had, however, already renounced all claim to share in the proceeds of these indulgences, and ordered that all the funds collected were to be employed in Germany.[102] It would be hard to say how much was realized from the sale of indulgences in Germany, but in October, 1502, Peraudi's vice-legate, Bishop Tommaso Malombra of Curzola, informed the Venetian government that some 300,000 Rhenish gulden had probably been collected. The Venetian ambassador Zaccaria Contarini, who left Germany toward the end of the year 1502, estimated the sum at about 400,000 gulden.[103]

These figures seem excessively high, but obviously the sale of the jubilee indulgences was not unsuccessful in Germany. The tithe was also collected from the English clergy. Henry VII is said to have contributed £4,000, notwithstanding his unwillingness to furnish either ships or soldiers for the crusade. In France the clergy were more conspicuous for their complaints than for their contributions. On 30 May (1501), however, a triple alliance was announced in Rome of the pope, the king of Hungary, and the Venetian Signoria; it was celebrated by ringing the large bell on the Capitolium and by lighting the customary bonfires throughout the city.[104] The pope had already pledged a subvention of 40,000 ducats a year to assist the Hungarians to make war on the Turks; the

---

and a fleet was rather similar to that discussed at the Curia in the early summer of 1490 (fols. 335 ff.). ". . . Nos ex introitibus nostris tam temporalibus quam spiritualibus, qui omnes non ascendunt ad summam ducentorum millium ducatorum, quotannis quadraginta millia ducatorum dare obtulimus, aliis etiam principibus in hoc contribuentibus . . ." (fol. 337ʳ). ". . . Nam si pro desiderio nostro expeditio generalis per omnes principes Christianos peccatis nostris facientibus fieri non possit, nos tamen et Majestas sua si voluerit, ut optamus, etiam rex Christianissimus ac Hungarie et Polonie reges illustrissimi, et dominium Venetorum omnes contra Thurcos consociati dictam exequutionem auxiliante Domino suscipiemus" (fol. 338ʳ). My MS. source (Arm. II, tom. 56), being of the seventeenth century, has altered *more classico* the spelling of the original text (*Sanctae Mariae Novae presbyter* for *Sancte Marie Nove presbyter*, etc.), which I have restored.

Pietro Isvalies's instructions for the legation to Hungary, Bohemia, and Poland, dated 18 November, 1500, may also be found in the Miscellanea, Arm. II, tom. 56, fols. 469ᵛ–486ʳ, by mod. stamped enumeration. They take much the same form, *mutatis mutandis*, as those issued to Peraudi.

[102] From N. Paulus, *Gesch. d. Ablasses im Mittelalter*, III (Paderborn, 1923), 215–16 and ff., and *cf.* A. Gottlob, "Der Legat Raimund Peraudi," *Hist. Jahrbuch*, VI, 459–60. Peraudi's troubles with Maximilian had been foreseen: "Il re di romani non lo acepterà per esser francese" (Sanudo, *Diarii*, III, 939, and *cf.* cols. 1175, 1231–32); he left for Germany on Monday, 26 October, 1500 (*ibid.*, III, 977). There is a brief account of Peraudi's mission in Pastor, *Gesch. d. Päpste*, III-1 (repr. 1955), 554–56, 612–13, and a full account in Heinrich Ulmann, *Kaiser Maximilian I.*, II (Stuttgart, 1891), 40–94. Peace was announced in the fall of 1501, a *perpetua pax*, between Maximilian and Louis XII; the former was to take the cross, and Louis was to protect the Hapsburg dominions (Burchard, *Diarium*, ed. Thuasne, III, 165–66, and ed. Celani, II, 302; also Sanudo, *Diarii*, IV, 152–56). Peraudi returned from his German legation in October, 1504 (Burchard, ed. Thuasne, III, 367–68, and ed. Celani, II, 461).

[103] Sanudo, *Diarii*, IV, 369, 374, 696: ". . . 300 milia fiorini di Rens . . ." (*ibid.*, col. 374)—". . . zercha fiorini 400 milia . . ." (*ibid.*, col. 696). Tommaso Malombra remains the most important personage in the history of the church of Curzola (Korčula), where his handsome sarcophagus is affixed to the south wall of the cathedral. Despite the names now inscribed on the (reused) sarcophagus, it is Malombra's funeral monument; his recumbent figure lies atop the sarcophagus, his thin face being done from a death mask, of which there is a later copy in the adjoining episcopal museum.

[104] Burchard, *Diarium*, ed. Thuasne, III, 141, and ed. Celani, II, 285–86; Sanudo, *Diarii*, IV., ed. N. Barozzi (Venice, 1880), cols. 41–42. The purpose of the alliance was "ad offension et destrution et extermination del perfido turcho et del stato suo, et a conservation et defesa de la christiana religion e de li comuni stadi, contra esso turcho." *Cf.* Manfroni, *Marina italiana*, p. 235. Fifteen months later there was talk of forming a new league which should include the king of France (Sen. Secreta, Reg. 39, fol. 30ʳ [42ʳ], dated 2 September, 1502).

Venetians agreed to furnish 100,000 ducats and press the war against the Turks at sea.[105] The Hungarians under the desultory King Ladislas II accomplished even less than the Venetians, who (as we have seen) seized the island of S. Maura despite stubborn Turkish resistance. In this exploit Alexander VI had a hand.

In the spring of the year 1502 Alexander added thirteen galleys to the Venetian fleet in eastern waters.[106] Of these, five galleys had been armed in Venice, six in Apulia, and two in Ancona. Sigismondo de' Conti says that the papal galleys were equipped by means of money left by Giovanbattista Zeno, late cardinal of S. Maria in Portico, a nephew of Paul II. At his death in Padua (on 8 May, 1501) Zeno had bequeathed the sum of 60,000 ducats to the Venetian Senate to help prosecute the war against the Turks.[107] Cardinals' testaments were largely subject to the papal will, but Alexander requested that Zeno's legacy be employed to outfit the thirteen galleys which were placed under the command of Jacopo Pesaro, bishop of Paphos and a cousin of Benedetto Pesaro, captain-general of the Venetian fleet. Bishop Jacopo joined Benedetto on the island of Cerigo, whence the two Pesari launched their successful attack upon S. Maura (Leucadia), which fell to the Christian assaults on 30 August (1502).[108] We have already noted that according to the terms of the Turco-Venetian peace of 1502–1503 the Republic was obliged to return the island of S. Maura to the Porte. The Venetians needed peace; their finances were almost exhausted; their trade had suffered badly. Since the Hungarians could not carry on war with the Turks without the Venetian subsidy, on 22 February, 1503, King Ladislas accepted a seven years' truce with the Porte.[109] Five months later (on 1 August) Benedetto Pesaro was relieved of his command as captain-general "per la grave et periculosa egritudine de febre et fluxo."[110] He died soon after.[111] The Turks had won their war

[105] Sanudo, *Diarii*, III, 1536–38, 1606; Predelli, *Regesti dei Commemoriali*, VI, bk. XVIII, nos. 172, pp. 44–45, and 176–77, pp. 45–47; Romanin, V, 151; Zinkeisen, II, 514–15; Kretschmayr, II, 414. The alliance was concluded in Buda on 13 May, 1501. The Venetians paid their 100,000 ducats (Sen. Secreta, Reg. 38, fol. 168v [177v]).

[106] In August, 1501, Alexander had planned to arm ten galleys "per conto dela cruciata" (Sen. Secreta, Reg. 38, fol. 158v [167v]). For months reports had been reaching Venice of huge Turkish preparations for a great offensive against Christendom (*ibid.*, fols. 168v [177v], 173v [182v], 194r [203r]).

[107] Sen. Secreta, Reg. 38, fols. 152r–153r [161r–162r], letters of the Senate dated 23 July, 1501, to the Venetian ambassador in Rome, seeking Alexander VI's validation of the legacy, and note, *ibid.*, fol. 159r [168r], and fols. 167v–168r [176v–177r], 178v–179r [187v–188r]. Often living beyond their means (and falling into debt) to maintain their exalted social position, few cardinals resident at the Curia left estates as large as that of Zeno (*cf.* in general D. S. Chambers, "The Economic Predicament of Renaissance Cardinals," *Studies in Medieval and Renaissance History*, III [Lincoln, 1966], 289–313).

[108] The news of the taking of S. Maura reached Venice on the morning of 16 September, as the Senate was preparing to send an envoy to Istanbul "in la materia de tractar la pace cum el Signor Turco, che veramente ne è molto a cor" (Sen. Secreta, Reg. 39, fols. 37v–38r [49v–50r]). The sources include Sigismondo de'Conti, II, 278–79; Sanudo, *Diarii*, IV, 19, 45, 46, 63 ff., 79–82, 307, 308, 313–17 and ff., 340, the last refs. relating to the capture of S. Maura; Burchard, *Diarium*, ed. Thuasne, III, 135–36, and ed. Celani, II, 282–83; Raynaldus, *Ann. eccl.*, ad ann. 1502, nos. 19–21, vol. XIX (1693), p. 537; Zinkeisen, II, 541; Guglielmotti, III, 30–48; Pastor, *Gesch. d. Päpste*, III-1 (repr. 1955), 559–60; Manfroni, *Marina italiana*, p. 239. The Turco-Venetian war made life in the Aegean Archipelago extremely dangerous during the autumn of 1502 (Sanudo, *Diarii*, IV, 401 ff.).

On Cardinal Giovanbattista Zeno, note Eubel, *Hierarchia catholica*, II (1914, repr. 1960), 15, 55b, where his death is dated 7 May (after the Acta consistorialia), and esp. Giovanni Soranzo, "Giovanni Battista Zeno, nipote di Paolo II, cardinale di S. Maria in Portico (1468–1501)," in *Rivista di storia della Chiesa in Italia*, XVI (Rome, 1962), 249–74, where the date of his death is given as 8 May in accordance with the text of his sepulchral monument (*op. cit.*, pp. 270, 273), which is in the "Zen Chapel" of S. Mark's, entered to the right of the atrium, in the southwest corner of the basilica. A papal brief dated the very day of Zeno's death, and addressed to Duke Ercole d'Este of Ferrara, had reserved all the cardinal's goods, money, jewels, and gold and silver plate for the apostolic treasury "pro hac sancta expeditione contra perfidos Turcos." The pope revoked whatever "testandi et disponendi facultas" either he himself or his predecessors might have granted Zeno, word of whose death in Modena had just been (incorrectly) reported to the Curia (Arch. di Stato di Modena, Cancelleria Estense, Estero: Carteggio di principi, Roma, 1295/10, no. 60, dated 8 May, 1501).

[109] Sanudo, *Diarii*, IV, 879–84, doc. dated 22 February, 1503 (Ven. style 1502), and V, 26–27, 32, 41 ff., 84; Lamansky, *Secrets de'état de Venise*, pp. 330–36; Zinkeisen, II, 517–18. The Venetian surrender of S. Maura involved endless details and petty problems (Sen. Secreta, Reg. 39, fols. 154r ff. [166r ff.], and Reg. 40, fols. 2r ff. [16r ff.], 8v [22v], 9r [23r], 15v [29v], 36 [50], 58v–59r [73v–74r]).

[110] Sen. Secreta, Reg. 39, fol. 99r [111r].

[111] Benedetto Pesaro's tomb may still be seen over the entrance to the sacristy of S. Maria Gloriosa dei Frari in Venice. His funeral inscription celebrates the capture of Leucadia (S. Maura) and Cephalonia, and recalls that *pace composita* he died in 1503 on the island of Corfu. His cousin Jacopo, "qui Turcas bello, se ipsum pace vincebat," is also buried in the Frari. His sarcophagus is on the wall

with Venice, taking advantage of the realignment of aggressions and hostilities in Europe and especially in Italy.

Hardly a decade before (in 1494–1495) Alexander VI had appealed to Sultan Bayazid II for aid against the king of France. Of late he had been appealing to the king of France for aid against the sultan. The Venetians had been opposed to the king of France, with whom they were now in alliance. Lodovico il Moro had invited Charles VIII into Italy, and now Charles's successor had driven him from Milan. A diplomatic revolution had occurred although, actually, events had followed a logical course. Lodovico il Moro had alienated the Venetians, whose cupidity had been stimulated by the possibility of sharing with Louis XII some of the spoils of Milan. Alexander's animus had been aroused against Federigo of Naples, and his ambitions for his son Cesare had driven him into the French camp. The success of Louis XII in Italy had excited the jealousy of Ferdinand of Aragon, who was casting his own covetous eyes upon the rich peninsula. When Ferdinand had learned of the death of Charles VIII, he had piously informed the Venetian ambassador that "God helps the good!"[112] God is also reputed to help those who help themselves, among whom Ferdinand himself could certainly be counted.

In the late summer of 1499 Louis XII's army had overrun the Milanese duchy, easily vindicating the old claims of his house. Lodovico il Moro fled from Milan at the end of August to take refuge with Maximilian in Germany. Before his departure he warned the Venetian envoy: "You, my lords of Venice, send me the king of France as a luncheon guest. I assure you that you will have him at dinner!" The news of Lodovico's flight was known in Rome by 4 September.[113] Louis XII entered Milan on 6 October, being received with the most elaborate civic ceremonies.[114] He withdrew from the city on 7 November to return to France.[115]

In a rapid reversal of French fortunes, however, Lodovico re-entered Milan on 5 February, 1500, "con gran jubilo," supported by Swiss and German mercenaries.[116] Lodovico made prompt overtures to the Venetians, trying to lure them from the French side: he informed the Signoria that the Gran Turco was his friend and, if the statesmen of the Republic so wished, he was willing to employ his good offices "a pacifichar le cosse," referring presumably to the expected Turkish offensive in the Morea.[117] The Venetians were not favorably disposed toward friends of the Turk at this time, however, and no one on the lagoon took very seriously Lodovico's influence at the Porte. Besides, the Venetians had had quite recent experience of the Turkish regard for a formal peace as well as of the quality of Lodovico's friendship. Concentrating his forces in the region of Novara, Lodovico met the long-expected French counterattack on

---

to the left as one enters the south doorway of the church. Jacopo died in his eighties on 24 March, 1547 (. . . *vixit annos Platonicos*, according to his epitaph). In 1519 he commissioned Titian's famous painting, the Madonna di Ca Pesaro (unveiled in December, 1526), which was placed to the left of his tomb, above the Pesaro Altar. On a red banner in the painting the Borgia arms are depicted, as on an earlier altarpiece (now in the Antwerp Museum) which Titian did for Jacopo shortly after the Pesari took Leucadia from the Turks, on which *cf.* Pastor, *Gesch. d. Päpste*, III-1 (repr. 1955), 559–60; Erwin Panofsky, *Problems in Titian*, New York, 1969, pp. 178–79, with figs. 16, 185–86; and Philipp Fehl, "Saints, Donors and Columns in Titian's *Pesaro Madonna*," in *Renaissance Papers 1974* (1975), pp. 75–85, with refs.

[112] Sanudo, *Diarii*, I, 970, on 21 April, 1498.

[113] Burchard, *Diarium*, ed. Thuasne, II, 562–63, and ed. Celani, II, 165, with notes; Senarega, *De rebus genuensibus*, *RISS*, XXIV, 567; Wm. H. Woodward, *Cesare Borgia*, London, 1913, pp. 146–47; Piero Pieri, *Il Rinascimento e la crisi militare italiana*, Turin, 1952, pp. 377 ff. The facts are too well known for extensive annotation.

[114] Sanudo, *Diarii*, III, 23–26; Burchard, *Diarium*, ed. Thuasne, II, 564–68, and ed. Celani, II, 166–69; Jean d'Auton, *Chroniques*, ed. Maulde la Clavière, I, 92 ff. (see the following note).

[115] Burchard, *Diarium*, ed. Thuasne, II, 575, and ed. Celani, II, 174. The French cleric Jean d'Auton (1466–1528), *Chroniques de Louis XII*, ed. René de Maulde la Clavière, 4 vols., Paris, 1889–95 (publ. by the Société de l'histoire de France), describes in detail the French conquest of Milan. Maulde la Clavière also gives a number of valuable documents in a series of *pièces annexes* appended to his first three volumes, including some letters from Ascanio Sforza to Lodovico il Moro in April and May, 1499 (I, 324 ff., 334), as well as a number from Cesare Guasco, Milanese envoy in Rome, to il Moro, one of which (dated 15 July, 1499) is full of the charge being made by the pope "ch' el Duca de Milano habij provocato el Turcho contra Venetiani" (I, 339–47). Maulde la Clavière also publishes two or three discourses by the Greek humanist John (Janus) Lascaris, who served as a French publicist during the Milanese war (I, 359–78).

[116] Sanudo, *Diarii*, III, 103, 105–6, 107–8, 110–12, 116, 123, 132–33, etc.; Jean d'Auton, *Chron.*, ed. Maulde la Clavière, I, 177 ff.

[117] Sanudo, *Diarii*, III, 120. According to Sigismondo de'Conti, II, 272–73, about this time 6,000 Turks entered Italy through the Julian Alps, devastating and burning villages as far as the river Livenza.

10 April. He was defeated and captured. Sanudo had followed his adventures with great care. After midnight on 11–12 April a courier reached Venice bringing word of the battle of Novara; admitted into the doge's presence, he stated, "Bone nuove! El signor Lodovicho è stà preso da francesi. . . ." On the morning of the twelfth, says Sanudo, all the Veneto was full of the good news.[118]

Lodovico was later imprisoned in the castles of Lys-S.-Georges in Berry and Loches in Touraine. His brother, Cardinal Ascanio, fled from Milan during the night of the tenth, falling into the hands of the Venetians,[119] who turned him over to the king of France.[120] Ascanio was imprisoned at Bourges, and (if we may glance ahead) only gained his freedom on 3 January, 1502, at the behest of Cardinal Georges d'Amboise, with whom he returned to Rome on 10 September, 1503, to enter the conclave which elected Pius III (on 22 September). Ascanio died in Rome toward the end of May, 1505. He was buried in the church of S. Maria del Popolo, where his sepulchral monument by Andrea Sansovino has evoked the admiration of the art historian as well as of the tourist.[121]

---

[118] Sanudo, *Diarii*, III, 145, 147, 149–50, 154 ff., 163 ff., 170–71, 175–76, 187 ff., 207, 213, and esp. cols. 214 ff. for the news of 10 April, and *cf.* cols. 225–226, etc., 265, 269; Jean d'Auton, *Chron.*, ed. Maulde la Clavière, I, 242–61; Sen. Secreta, Reg. 38, fol. 20 [30], docs. dated 13 April, 1500. On the French establishment in Milan, see Léon G. Pélissier, *Documents pour l'histoire de la domination française dans le Milanais (1499–1513)*, Toulouse, 1891 (Bibliothèque méridionale, 2nd ser., vol. I), and Pélissier, *Documents relatifs au règne de Louis XII et à sa politique en Italie*, Montpellier, 1912 (Notes italiennes d'histoire de France, fasc. XXXV), the latter volume giving documents of the period 1499–1501. The best general account of the French victory over Lodovico Sforza and of Louis XII's occupation of Milan is also by Pélissier, *Louis XII et Ludovic Sforza*, 2 vols., Paris, 1896 (Bibliothèque des Écoles françaises d'Athènes et de Rome, fascs. 75–76), which deals in large detail with all the diplomatic and military maneuvers as well as with the involvement of the Venetians, Ferrarese, Mantuans, Germans, Swiss and others in the events which culminated in Louis's finally securing the full submission of the Milanese duchy to his authority.

[119] Sen. Secreta, Reg. 38, fols. 20^v–21^r [30^v–31^r], dated 14 April, 1500; Sanudo, *Diarii*, III, 219, 223–24, 225, 227–30, 232 ff., 250.

[120] Sen. Secreta, Reg. 38, fols. 25^v, 33 [35^v ff.]; Sanudo, *Diarii*, III, 259–60, 265, 280, 284, 285–86, etc.; Burchard, *Diarium*, ed. Thuasne, III, 41, 46, and ed. Celani, II, 218, 220; Jean d'Auton, *Chron.*, ed. Maulde la Clavière, I, 262–67. Alexander VI was of course pleased by the capture of the Sforzeschi (Sanudo, III, 254–55). In early June (1501) he appropriated much of Ascanio's movable property, including twelve famous silver gilt statues of the Apostles (Burchard, *op. cit.*, ed. Thuasne, III, 141, and ed. Celani, II, 286): Ascanio's treasures had been secreted in a monastery; apparently Alexander had just learned their whereabouts. On the imprisonment of il Moro and Ascanio in France, see Jean d'Auton, *op. cit.*, I, 278–84.

When Alexander first learned of Ascanio's capture by the Venetians, he dispatched Angelo Leonini, bishop of Tivoli, to the Signoria in an effort to have Ascanio sent to Rome (Arch. Segr. Vaticano, Miscellanea, Arm. II, tom. 56, fols. 341 ff., by mod. stamped enumeration): ". . . Itaque quantum potes [from the instructions addressed to the bishop of Tivoli on 4 May, 1500] commodatioribus verbis instabis ut prefatum cardinalem libere ut debent nobis restituant eo modo ut ad nos tuto perveniat in quo non solum nostro ipsiusque collegii desiderio satisfacient, sed etiam iusticie, debito, honori, et rebus suis bene consulent. Quos certificare poteris quod ipse Ascanius nullibi quietius quam apud nos manere poterit . . ." (fol. 342^r). ". . . Et eos ad hanc liberationem inducendos poteris adducere inconvenientia que occurrerunt ex detentione cardinalium et ut antiquiora omittantur sciunt quod tota patria Austrie fuit supposita ecclesiastico interdicto propter detentionem bone memorie Cardinalis Sancti Petri ad Vincula detenti a Sigismundo archiduce Austrie qui liberato dicto cardinale absolutionem tamen obtinere non potuit nisi prius clare memorie Federicus Tertius Imperator eius frater coram legato apostolico veniam suppliciter flexis genibus petiisset . . ." (fol. 343). The reference is to Cardinal Nicholas of Cusa's difficulties with Sigismund of the Tyrol (see above, Chapter 7, note 54).

Alexander gave two other instances of the results of secular authorities' detaining cardinals, including Cardinal Riario's detention by Lorenzo de' Medici after the Pazzi conspiracy in 1478 (but it seems rather unlikely that he would have laid the Republic under the interdict if the Signoria had ventured to keep Ascanio under arrest). If the Venetians stated that they wanted to refer the matter to the French king, the bishop of Tivoli was to reply "quod nos qui etiam ipsi regi afficimur, nichil petimus in damnum vel iniuriam sue Majestatis, sed repetimus quod nostrum est et quod ad nos et non aliquem alium pertinet" (fol. 344^r). If the Venetians persisted in their refusal to surrender Ascanio, however, Alexander acknowledged that the situation would be awkward: ". . . Scis quod id nobis molestissimum foret et quod versaremur in magnis angustiis, quia effugere vellemus quantum possibile esset publicationem dictarum censurarum et penarum. . . ." But if on the way the bishop of Tivoli learned that Ascanio had fled to the French or had been promised or surrendered to them, he was to stop in his tracks, and wait for further instructions from Rome (fol. 345^r). Before 30 May the bishop of Tivoli knew that the Venetians had effected "la consignation del Cardinale Ascanio in mano de la Christianissima Maestà" (Sen. Secreta, Reg. 38, fol. 33^r [43^r]).

[121] Sanudo, *Diarii*, IV, 234, notes the release of Cardinal Ascanio Sforza in an entry of late February, 1502 (Ven. style 1501), and says that he was then "in gratia dil re," and on Ascanio's coming to Rome with d'Amboise, *cf.*, *ibid.*, V, 72, 76, 81, 82; Burchard, *Diarium*, ed. Thuasne, III, 268–78, and ed. Celani, II, 373–87, on the election of Pius III. Ascanio was joyfully received by the Romans upon his return to the city (Burchard, *op. cit.*, ed. Thuasne, III, 262–63, and ed. Celani, II, 368–69). *Cf.* Sanudo, V, 81, 82. After the election of his old enemy Giuliano della Rovere as pope, Ascanio lived quietly in Rome, but

For the Italians the future looked dark indeed during the last few years of Alexander VI's reign. The advancement of the Borgias under the banner of the fleur-de-lys was hardly consistent with the well-being of either Italy or the papacy, for Ferdinand of Aragon would inevitably contest French hegemony in the peninsula. The major development in Italian politics at this time was certainly the French conquest of Milan. The Venetians and Hungarians needed the crusade to relieve the Turkish pressures to which they were exposed with the advent of the campaigning season each spring. Later on, the popes saw in the crusade a means of diverting the French (and Spanish) from the Italian scene. Although Alexander VI was more of a politician than a statesman, his interest in the crusade probably had the same objective. But now he was chiefly concerned to use the presence of the French in northern Italy to help establish his son Cesare Borgia in a new duchy in the Romagna, while Cesare's ambition encompassed the extension of his power to Urbino and Tuscany, the March of Ancona, Camerino, and elsewhere. It was said of Cesare that "habet diabolum in corpore,"[122] and this was a mild description of his character.

Louis XII regarded his initial successes as the prelude to the conquest of Naples and possibly of the entire peninsula. He had the mind of a merchant, however, which is why he understood the Venetians, and as he recalled his predecessor's retreat in the summer of 1495, he felt obliged to count the probable costs of a Neapolitan campaign. His Milanese success had excited the envy and hostility not only of Ferdinand of Aragon, but also of Maximilian of Hapsburg and even Henry VII of England,[123] who could not watch with complete equanimity the aggrandizement of his near neighbor across the Channel. Nor would Ferdinand see King Federigo of Naples ousted without a struggle; but Ferdinand's own avarice was well known, and Louis was of the opinion that half a loaf was better than none.[124] When he proposed to Ferdinand that they divide the kingdom of Naples between them, he received a guarded consent. By the treaty of Granada, in November, 1500, the high contracting parties finally agreed that the French should take the northern, and the Spanish the southern, half of the kingdom.[125]

The interests of the great powers always determined the course of crusading history. In April, 1501, the Venetian Senate tried to persuade Louis XII not to undertake a campaign of conquest in Italy. They explained to a French envoy who had brought a "secret communication" to the lagoon that the Spanish and Portuguese fleets were soon going to effect a rendezvous in Sicilian waters. The Venetian and French fleets were supposed to join them in the "sanctissima expeditione contra el Turcho." Louis would thus be choosing an inopportune time to embark upon the "Neapolitan enterprise." Once more the Venetians would probably be left to meet the Turk by themselves. The Hungarians were facing total ruin, and might have to reconsider their rejection of peace with Bayazid. A French campaign in Italy would also diminish Maximilian's apparent readiness to participate in the crusade. Having no alternative, the Senate stated that, as always, Venice would defer to the wisdom and good will of his most Christian Majesty.[126] The winds of speculation were blowing in all directions.

In May, 1501, it was reported in Venice that Federigo, *per mezo di reali di Spagna*, was offering to give Louis 300,000 ducats and to pay an annual tribute of 100,000 to be left at peace in the southern kingdom.[127] A month later the Venetian envoy to France wrote from Lyon that Louis had declared he was sending the French fleet against the Turks, for like most kings of

---

without losing his interest in politics (*cf.* P. Villari, ed., *Dispacci di Antonio Giustinian*, II [Florence, 1876], 400–1, 411–13, and III, 14–15, 46, 53, 165, 167–68, 194–95, 226–27, 242, 265, 291–92, 293, 331, etc.; Sanudo, *Diarii*, VI, 84, 171, 176, notice of Ascanio's death in May, 1505, on which see Sen. Secreta, Reg. 40, fols. 104^v–105 [119^v–120]).

122 Sanudo, *Diarii*, IV, 439.

123 *Cf.* Sanudo, *Diarii*, III, 36.

124 By early September, 1499, Federigo of Naples knew that the French conquest of Milan meant his own undoing (Sanudo, *Diarii*, II, 1313).

125 The treaty of 11 November, 1500, is given in J. Dumont, *Corps diplomatique*, III, pt. 2 (1726), pp. 445–47, and see in general Carlo Cipolla, *Le Signorie italiane dal 1313 al 1530*, 2 vols., Milan, 1881, II, 771 ff.; Luigi Simeoni, *Le Signorie*, 2 vols., Milan, 1950, II, 758 ff.; and Tommaso Pedio, *Gli Spagnoli alla conquista dell'Italia*, 3rd ed., Reggio Calabria, 1974, pp. 48 ff.

126 Sen. Secreta, Reg. 38, fols. 127^v–128^r [136^v–137^r], dated 17 April, 1501, and *cf.*, *ibid.*, fol. 160^r [169^r]. The Hungarians agreed to a seven years' truce with the Turks on 22 February, 1503, as stated above, p. 533.

127 Sanudo, *Diarii*, IV, 38.

France, Louis professed allegiance to the crusade. He also wanted the assistance or at least the neutrality of Venice. The French army was said to be strong enough to conquer Naples without naval support, and "more than a year ago he had reached an accord with the king of Spain, with whom he has divided the kingdom [of Naples] in half. . . ."[128] The rights of Federigo were thus cavalierly set aside. French and Spanish commanders were instructed to take over their sovereigns' respective shares of his erstwhile dominion. Federigo eventually sought refuge in France, where his daughter had been educated.[129] Louis and Ferdinand were soon to discover, however, that it is not easy to divide a kingdom with an ally. It is simpler to conquer it for oneself.

The division of Naples had of course involved the pope, who was suzerain of the kingdom. Alexander VI was quite ready to participate in the spoliation of Federigo's realm, which he confirmed in a long bull dated 25 June, 1501. The document charges Federigo with breaking his oath of fealty to the pope, receiving and aiding rebels against the Holy See, violating the freedom of the Church, and "what is worse and more abominable and quite unworthy of a Christian prince," maintaining intelligence with the Turkish sultan, with whom he had frequently exchanged embassies in an effort to encourage a Turkish invasion of Christian territories, even Italy. The pope sanctioned the division of the realm in the interests of peace and the crusade. The cities of Naples and Gaeta, the Terra di Lavoro, and the province of the Abruzzi were to go to Louis with the title king of Naples and Jerusalem; the territories of Calabria and Apulia were to go to Ferdinand and Isabella with the titles duke and duchess of Calabria and Apulia. (As a papal preserve Benevento was excluded from the division.) Both the French and Spanish sovereigns, and their heirs after them, were to swear fealty and do homage according to a prescribed text which would guarantee the continued suzerainty of the papacy over southern Italy. In the event that any one of the sovereigns or their successors should be elected king of the Romans, the Regno or the two duchies would revert to the Holy See, unless the emperor-elect were expressly granted a papal mandate to hold his hereditary share of the southland. No woman inheritor could marry a king of the Romans. Both the French and Spanish holders and inheritors of the divided realm were to pay each year to the Holy See a census of 4,000 ounces of gold on the feast of S. Peter the Apostle (29 June). Every three years they were each to give the pope a good white palfrey "in recognition of his true dominion of their kingdom and duchies." Together they were to pay, when they had finally taken over their new possessions, 50,000 marks sterling for their investitures, the amount to be divided equally by the two sides. They were not to seek or hold office in lands under papal jurisdiction, including the Romagna, and ecclesiastical rights of all kinds were protected by detailed stipulations. The bull was subscribed by the pope and eighteen cardinals.[130]

Alexander VI had joined the Franco-Spanish league. On Tuesday morning, 29 June (1501), on the feast of SS. Peter and Paul, the Roman clergy streamed from their churches and monasteries in procession headed for the basilica of S. Peter, where in the papal presence Girolamo Porcari, bishop of Andria, announced the adherence of the Holy See to Louis XII's entente with Ferdinand of Aragon. The day before, from a loggia of the Castel S. Angelo, the pope had watched a French force of twelve thousand foot and two thousand horse, with thirty-six cannon following behind them, march over the Tiber on their way to Naples.[131] Burchard indicates that no statement was made of the articles of the league, but they were known to many persons. Doubtless more than one observer in the basilica on that June day, as the Venetians were losing out to the Turks in the Morea, had cause to wonder at a pope joining two royal thieves in the partition of southern Italy—to keep peace in Christendom, he said, and to promote the crusade!

---

[128] Sanudo, *Diarii*, IV, 52, and *cf.* col. 65; Raynaldus, *Ann. eccl.*, ad ann. 1501, no. 50, vol. XIX (1693), p. 519; Sen. Secreta, Reg. 38, fols. 136ᵛ–137ʳ [145ᵛ–146ʳ], 138ᵛ–139ʳ.

[129] *Cf.* Sanudo, *Diarii*, IV, 146, 175, 176–77, 190–91, 234.

[130] The bull is given in Raynaldus, *Ann. eccl.*, ad ann. 1501, nos. 53–72, vol. XIX (1693), pp. 520–27. *Cf.* Guicciardini, *Storia d' Italia*, V, 3, ed. Florence, Salani, 1963, I, 479.

[131] Burchard, *Diarium*, ed. Thuasne, III, 148–50, and ed. Celani, II, 290–91; Sanudo, *Diarii*, IV, 61–62; Jean d'Auton, *Chroniques*, ed. Maulde la Clavière, II, 35–37. (The dispatch in Sanudo, *loc. cit.*, dated 29 June, gives different figures for the size of the French force on its way to Naples.) *Cf.* Sanudo, IV, 82. Jean d'Auton, *op. cit.*, II, 32–33, indicates that French and Spanish soldiers fought in the streets of Rome over the Neapolitan question.

At the beginning of July, Cesare Borgia's troops left Rome to aid the French in their occupation of the Neapolitan kingdom. He followed them some time later, and during the night of 26 July the news was brought to the pope of Cesare's capture of the important city of Capua. Seized by the treachery of one of the inhabitants (whom Cesare promptly killed), the city was sacked. It was related in Rome that some six thousand persons, including priests and monks, women and children, lost their lives in the senseless carnage. The Curia Romana had already learned of the French occupation of Aversa, Nola, and numerous other places. In the meantime the standards of Aragon were being raised throughout Calabria and Apulia, where the soldiers of Gonsalvo de Cordova were hastening to take over the two duchies in accordance with the terms of the papal bull of 25 June.[132] The French commander Stuart d'Aubigny entered Naples on 4 August and occupied all the castles by an agreement with the defeated King Federigo, who was allowed to withdraw to Ischia, where he might reside undisturbed for six months to see whether he could solicit aid from any source, conceivably the Turks. If no such aid was forthcoming within this period, Federigo was to surrender Ischia also to d'Aubigny.[133] This was the end of royal power for Federigo, and as he relinquished the broken reins of government, he must have recalled his brother Alfonso II's own abdication seven years before and recalled also his despairing description of rule in Naples as a burden too heavy to bear.

The French seemed to be doing very well. On 27 August, in consideration of Louis XII's devotion to the faith and to the Church, and since he was already taking steps which should lead to an expedition against the Turks (*tuque etiam in presentiarum contra ipsos perfidos Turcos facere coepisti*), the pope remitted completely the census of 4,000 ounces of gold as well as the entire sum of 25,000 marks for the right of investiture. Alexander still wanted Louis and his heirs, however, henceforth to pay the feudal fee of one good white palfrey for the kingdom of Naples.[134] It was a small charge.

Before the French and Spanish turned their arms in force against the Turk, they were to go to war with each other. The French and the Hospitallers had rendered some naval aid to the Venetians before the fall of Lepanto in August, 1499, as we have seen, and a Spanish fleet under Gonsalvo de Cordova had assisted the Venetian admiral Benedetto Pesaro in his attack upon Turkish-held Cephalonia in December, 1500. But it all seemed to no avail. Durazzo fell, and

---

[132] Burchard, *Diarium*, ed. Thuasne, III, 151, 152–53, whose text says that about four thousand were killed in Capua, and ed. Celani, II, 292, 293; Jean d'Auton, *Chron.*, ed. Maulde la Clavière, II, 61–62, who says that the streets ran with blood; Sanudo, *Diarii*, IV, 76–78, gives a summary of *avvisi* from Rome dated 27 July; Guicciardini, V, 5, ed. Florence, Salani, 1963, I, 492–93.

[133] Burchard, *Diarium*, ed. Thuasne, III, 154–55, with refs., and ed. Celani, II, 295; *Cronica di Napoli di Notar Giacomo*, ed. Paolo Garzilli, Naples, 1845, p. 242; Jean d'Auton, ed. Maulde la Clavière, II, 70–75, with the docs. in the notes; Sen. Secreta, Reg. 38, fol. 164^r [173^r].

[134] Raynaldus, *Ann. eccl.*, ad ann. 1501, no. 75, vol. XIX (1693), p. 528. Louis XII describes his extensive plans and preparations against the Turks in the commission issued at this time to Philippe de Clèves et la Marck, lord of Ravenstein, governor of Genoa and admiral of the (French) kingdom of Naples, given in Jean d'Auton, *Chron.*, ed. Maulde la Clavière, II, 78–83, note. Actually the French merely planned a naval parade in eastern waters to justify collection of the crusading tithe in France: Alexander VI also had allegedly collected 60,000 *livres* in France to arm twenty galleys in Venice, but clearly did not use the money, if he got it, for that purpose (*ibid.*, II, 83–84, note).

Ravenstein did lead a French expedition to the East, launching an unsuccessful attack upon Mytilene at the end of October, 1501, which Jean d'Auton, *op. cit.*, II, 149–93, describes in great detail, attributing the failure of the French to the inadequacy of their Venetian allies. There are various references to Ravenstein in Sen. Secreta, Reg. 38. He had a very difficult return voyage (d'Auton, II, 195 ff.). The progress of the French armada can also be followed in Sanudo, from Genoa to Mytilene and back to the West again (*Diarii*, IV, 71, 113, 145–46, 148–49, 180–81, 205–6, 207–8, 211, 231), where Venetian dispatches claim that the Christians failed to take the island "per manchar di piere e polvere" (col. 180), which is possible, and "per pusilanimità de'francesi" (col. 207), which seems less likely. On 4 December, 1501, the Venetian Senate had rather prematurely informed their envoy in Spain of Ravenstein's "gloriosa victoria de la insula de Metellino" (Sen. Secreta, Reg. 38, fol. 181^r [190^r]), but by the following 21 January they knew better (*ibid.*, fol. 194^r [203^r], and *cf.* fol. 200^r [209^r]).

At Trent on 13 October, 1501, Cardinal Georges d'Amboise negotiated an "inviolate and perpetual union and confederation" with Maximilian, king of the Romans, with the provision "quod Christianissimus Francorum rex secundum totam suam potentiam juvet serenissimum Romanorum regem, futurum imperatorem, contra perfidissimos Turcas Christianae religionis rabidos hostes, si et in quantum reliqui Christiani reges et principes aut major eorum pars suam Caesaream majestatem etiam juverint. Et hoc proximis tribus annis facere teneatur" (J. C. Lünig, *Codex Italiae diplomaticus*, I [1725], pt. 1, sect. 1, no. xxv, col. 118). An article also provided for the release of Ascanio Sforza and the restoration of his offices and benefices (col. 119). An interpretation of certain articles in the treaty was added at Blois on 13 December, 1501 (cols. 120–24).

the Turks appeared to be invincible,[135] as the pope lamented in a bull of 23 October, 1501,[136] and yet he had done little to halt the Turkish advance in the ten years of his papacy.[137] Now he was to have no opportunity to do so.

It had been easier for the French and Spanish to divide the kingdom of Naples by verbal and written agreements than to arrange the boundary lines with final specificity.[138] The issues could not be resolved by diplomacy; Louis XII and Ferdinand of Aragon soon had recourse to war. Efforts to arrange a peace failed. On 12 May, 1503, Antonio Giustinian informed the Venetian government that Gonsalvo de Cordova had warned Alexander VI not to assist the French, whose situation in the Neapolitan kingdom was going from bad to worse, and two days later he wrote that the Spaniards were not likely to make peace since they were preparing for war with the certainty of victory.[139]

On 16 May Giustinian reported that affairs had reached a desperate pass. It was said that Capua, Aversa, and Cerignola had been lost. On the eighteenth he learned that Louis XII, indignant at the continued Spanish success, was preparing to strike back. He was sending 1,800 lances into the field, and was negotiating for the hire of 10,000 Swiss and Gascon mercenaries. The next morning the news reached Rome that from Monday (the fifteenth) the Spaniards had been rushing artillery to Naples, and on Wednesday Gonsalvo de Cordova had himself entered the city. To make a good impression on the Neapolitans, Gonsalvo had lowered the price of wheat from fifteen to five *carlini* a measure. Spanish cannon had been mounted before the Castel Nuovo, defended by no more than five or six hundred French infantry, and Spanish troops were being sent to oppose the French forces located north of the Garigliano. The old Cardinal Oliviero Carafa, from whom Giustinian was getting information, was much distressed, for in Gonsalvo's success he saw the ruin of his own family. The Carafeschi had been unduly pro-French.[140] Gonsalvo was said to have 20,000 men in the southern kingdom, which would make the French reconquest very difficult, as Giustinian reminded the pope. Alexander VI, although disturbed by the enterprise of the Spaniards, had lost his affection for the French. He was looking out solely for his own advantage.[141]

Thus it went from day to day and from week to week. The pope had little faith any longer in French arms, and was seeking ways to ally himself with the Spanish, "perchè li vede potenti, e dubita delle cose sue per la unione che hanno cum Colonnesi." He feared the Colonnesi, as did the rest of the Roman baronage. Actually it made little difference to Alexander VI whether the French or Spanish ruled in Naples.

---

[135] *Cf.* Sen. Secreta, Reg. 38, fol. 168ʳ [177ʳ].

[136] Raynaldus, *Ann. eccl.*, ad ann. 1501, no. 78, vol. XIX (1693), pp. 528–29. In the first audience which Alexander VI granted the newly appointed Venetian envoy to Rome, Antonio Giustinian, on 4 June, 1502, he complained of the projected peace between the Republic and the Turk: "subiunse però, sorridendo, che non credeva, per esser *sacrilegium et nefandum* . . ." (Pasquale Villari, ed., *Dispacci di Antonio Giustinian, ambasciatore veneto in Roma dal 1502 al 1505*, 3 vols., Florence, 1876, I, 15). With this audience begins the long series of Giustinian's detailed dispatches to the Venetian Senate and the Consiglio dei Dieci; his commission, issued on 21 May, 1502, may be found in the Sen. Secreta, Reg. 39, fols. 9ʳ–10ʳ [21ʳ–22ʳ]. Alexander, *sorridendo*, probably knew that the Turco-Venetian peace was more than likely (*cf.* Villari, *Dispacci*, I, 28–29, 58); on 7 June the Senate denied it (Sen. Secreta, Reg. 39, fol. 14 [26]), but was soon trying almost desperately to end hostilities with the Turks (*ibid.*, fols. 32ᵛ ff. [44ᵛ ff.]). On the relations of the papacy with Venice at this time, *cf.* Roberto Cessi, ed., *Dispacci degli ambasciatori veneziani alla corte di Roma presso Giulio II*, Venice, 1932, pref., pp. VII ff. (R. Deputazione di storia patria per le Venezie).

[137] The pope was, however, always ready enough to make promises and issue anti-Turkish briefs (*cf.* Villari, *Dispacci di A. Giustinian*, I, 20, 24, 26, 28, 43, 48–49, 68). In early September, 1502, Alexander VI was much annoyed with the Venetians for allegedly making the Turkish peace, "della qual sempre parla quando li manca che dir, perchè la ghe dispiace quanto dir se possa . . ." (*ibid.*, I, 105): Giustinian adds that the pope wanted nothing so little as that Venice should be free of the burden of war with Turkey (*cf.*, *ibid.*, I, 178–79, a dispatch of 27 October, 1502). On 8 December the envoy notified the pope that peace had in effect been made (*ibid.*, I, 250 ff., 263 ff., 507 ff.). It is interesting to note that, according to Giustinian, the pope was planning in October to give the son of the despot of the Morea, "che è persona de poco valor," command of a troop of two hundred light horse "for public effect" (*ibid.*, I, 164).

[138] Jean d'Auton, *Chroniques*, ed. R. de Maulde la Clavière, II (Paris, 1891), 249–56 and ff.; Sanudo, *Diarii*, IV, 160, 335, 359, 370, 371, 421 ff., 441, 477–78, etc., 526–30, etc. There were frequent armed encounters between the French and Spanish all through the summer of 1502. *Cf.* Villari, ed., *Dispacci di Antonio Giustinian*, I, 40–41, 103–4, 118–19, 154.

[139] Villari, *Dispacci*, II, 14, 15.

[140] Villari, *Dispacci*, II, 15–17. On 16 June Giustinian reported that Gonsalvo had taken the Castel Nuovo in Naples (*ibid.*, II, 39–40); on the twenty-seventh he wrote that the Spaniards were bombarding the Castel dell'Uovo (*ibid.*, II, 52), which they took on 11 July (II, 68).

[141] Villari, *Dispacci*, II, 18, 45–46.

He merely wanted to protect Cesare Borgia in the Romagna.[142] The crusade was largely forgotten during the anxiety and turmoil of this period.

The Franco-Spanish war for the Neapolitan kingdom had not reached its final issue, however, when the reign of Alexander VI came rather abruptly to an end. Feeling ill on Saturday, 12 August (1503), Alexander was believed to have the *febris tertiana*, in the treatment of which some fourteen ounces of blood were drawn from his aged veins on the fifteenth. On Thursday, the seventeenth, he was given medicine, but was obviously fighting a losing battle. Early in the morning of the eighteenth he made his confession, and mass was said in his presence. At the hour of vespers he received extreme unction and died. He was laid in state in the Sala delle Arti liberali (in the Borgia Apartment), which adjoins the room in which he died.[143] Cesare Borgia, who was also sick, sent Micheletto Corella (who had murdered the leaders of the Orsini faction about eight months before, at Sinigaglia and Castel della Pieve) with some cutthroats to secure all doors leading to the pope's apartment and take possession of the papal treasure, some of which they overlooked. The palace doors were opened shortly before 7:00 P.M., and the pope's death announced. According to the diarist Burchard, Cesare did not visit his father during the latter's last illness, nor did the dying pope once mention either Cesare or Lucrezia Borgia.

On the morning of 19 August the bloated, blackened body of Alexander VI was unceremoniously buried, to the jeers and blasphemies of the workmen, in a corner (to the left of the altar) of the chapel of S. Maria delle Febbri, adjoining S. Peter's. On the twenty-second, at the fourth meeting of the Sacred College in the church of S. Maria sopra Minerva, a chastened Cesare Borgia was said to be ready to swear fealty to the College, and (subject to his doing so) was reappointed captain of Holy Church "usque ad electionem futuri pontificis." The cardinals then decided to hold the conclave in the Castel S. Angelo.[144] On 3 September, however, they decided to assemble in the Sistina, for the Vatican chapel of S. Niccolò da Bari was the usual place for the cardinals to elect a pope.[145]

---

[142] *Cf.* Villari, *Dispacci*, II, 21–23, 24 ff., and Piero Pieri, "La Guerra franco-spagnuola nel Mezzogiorno (1502–1503)," *Archivio storico per le province napoletane*, new ser., LXXII (ann. XXXIII, 1952), 21–69.

[143] *Cf.* Burchard, *Diarium*, ed. Thuasne, III, 239, and ed. Celani, II, 352: ". . . et posuerunt eum in alia camera ante salam in qua mortuus est, super unam lecticam, super panno setonino cremisino et tapete pulchro" (text from Celani).

[144] Burchard, *Diarium*, ed. Thuasne, III, 238–46, and ed. Celani, II, 351–57. *Cf.* Sigismondo de' Conti, II, 267 ff.; Thuasne, *op. cit.*, III, append., nos. 14–15, pp. 447–50; Villari, *Dispacci*, II, 107–39, daily reports of Antonio Giustinian to the Venetian government; Raynaldus, *Ann. eccl.*, ad ann. 1503, nos. 10–12, vol. XIX (1693), pp. 540–41; Pastor, *Hist. Popes*, VI, 132–37, and append., nos. 9–11, pp. 617–19, and *Gesch. d. Päpste*, III-1 (repr. 1955), 588–94, with refs., and III-2 (repr. 1956), append., nos. 53–55, pp. 1076–78. The incredible sight of the pope's corpse, *el più brutto, monstruoso et orrendo corpo di morto che si vedesse mai, senza alcuna forma nè figura de omo*, as Giustinian described it (Villari, *Dispacci*, II, 124–25), helped link the deceased with the devil, and played its part in the later legend of the papal Faust, leading in some quarters to the identification of Alexander VI with the Antichrist (Romeo De Maio, "Savonarola, Alessandro VI e il mito dell'Anticristo," *Rivista storica italiana*, LXXXII [1970], 545–52).

The story that both Alexander VI and his son Cesare were poisoned at a dinner in the villa of Cardinal Adriano Castellesi da Corneto (on 5 or 6 August) has been widely believed almost from the time of their deaths. The legend has been very persistent (note J. Schnitzer, *Der Tod Alexanders VI.*, Munich, 1929, and *cf.* P. M. Baumgarten, "Um den Tod Alexanders VI.," *Historisches Jahrbuch*, L [1930], 109–13), but Pastor has shown how unlikely it is, and Pio Paschini, "Adriano Castellesi, cardinale di S. Grisogono," in *Tre Illustri Prelati del Rinascimento*, Rome, 1957, pp. 61–62, also rejects it. On 23 August the Venetian Senate addressed a formal letter of condolence to the Sacred College (Sen. Secreta, Reg. 39, fols. 102^{v}–103^{r} [114^{v}–115^{r}]).

Although Cesare Borgia eventually complied with the various demands of the College, the cardinals wanted him out of Rome. After protracted negotiations he withdrew from the city on 2 September (Burchard, *Diarium*, ed. Thuasne, III, 248–56, and ed. Celani, II, 358–64; Villari, *Dispacci*, II, 167–72). The first of the nine days of Alexander VI's obsequies was observed on 4 September. Cardinal Giuliano della Rovere arrived in Rome on the same day. On Alexander's death and the subsequent plight of Cesare, *cf.* Sanudo, *Diarii*, V, ed. F. Stefani (Venice, 1881), cols. 65–66 and ff., 73–75, 76–78, 80–82, 83–84, and Sigismondo de' Conti, II, 289–90. Both the Borgia popes, Calixtus III and Alexander, are now buried in the church of S. Maria di Monserrato in Rome. Their modest sarcophagus, the work of F. Moratilla in 1881, is attached to the wall of the first chapel on the right as one enters by the front portal. The late King Alfonso XIII of Spain is buried below them in the same chapel.

[145] Burchard, *Diarium*, ed. Thuasne, III, 257, and ed. Celani, II, 364; Sanudo, *Diarii*, V, 86. According to Burchard, *loc. cit.*, ed. Celani, ". . . Decretum fuit et de eorum mandato [i.e., of the fifteen cardinals who had gathered on 3 September in Oliviero Carafa's palace] post prandium intimatum . . . quod ordinaretur conclave in capella maiori palatii [the Sistina] apud Sanctum Petrum loco solito et quod fierent XXXVIII camere . . ." [i.e.,

Probably no pope's death has ever been less lamented. Alexander VI's reign had been full of warfare, which he feared, and intrigue, which he loved. As cardinal and pope, for almost fifty years, he had performed his ecclesiastical duties according to the religious etiquette of the Curia Romana. His orthodoxy was that of one indifferent to theology. Not all his efforts had been directed toward evil. He had given some support to the monastic orders, resisted lay encroachments upon ecclesiastical properties, and imposed the first censorship upon the German press (by the bull *Inter multiplices* dated 1 June, 1501).[146] In 1493 he had drawn lines of demarcation dividing the new worlds of West Africa, America, and the East Indies into zones for conquest and colonization by the Portuguese and Spanish,[147] though his lines were superseded in 1494 by those established in the treaty of Tordesillas.

Alexander had extended little patronage to the humanists and added few books to the Vatican Library, for he much preferred to use his resources to enrich his family and promote the political ambitions of his son Cesare. He built far less than his immediate predecessors although he did some important building. On 5 May, 1499, for example, Alexander paid a visit, accompanied by a dozen cardinals and a large armed guard, to the construction site of the University of Rome, "ubi papa vidit structuram novi studii et mandavit in pluribus locis stratas ampliari. . . ."[148] Work on the University continued until the end of the pope's reign (the building was later reconstructed by Alexander VII, a Chigi). Despite the diversion of his money into spectacles and into Cesare's military enterprises, the Borgia pope found the means to restore S. Niccolò in Carcere (his titular church as a cardinal) and SS. Apostoli. He completed the new roof on S. Maria Maggiore, which his uncle Calixtus III had begun, and reconstructed the apse of S. John Lateran. He strengthened the ancient circuit of the Aurelian Wall around Rome, and added to the fortifications of Subiaco, Tivoli, Civitella, Civita Castellana, Nepi, Osimo, and Civitavecchia. In the Vatican palace he built the Torre Borgia, and commissioned Pinturicchio to decorate the so-called Appartamento Borgia (in an area of the palace which Nicholas V had entirely rebuilt). Here he lived during his last years. Alexander also restored the thirteenth-century passageways along the wall extending from the Vatican to the Castel S. Angelo. The Castel as it appears today is largely his work. He was also responsible for laying out the old Via Alessandrina, now the Borgo Nuovo.[149]

Some famous buildings went up in Alexander's reign. Before his elevation to the papacy he had built the handsome palace now known under the name Sforza-Cesarini, which he gave to Ascanio Sforza (together with the vice-chancellorship and various other considerations) for the latter's support in the conclave which made him pope. Cardinal Raffaele Riario built as his palace the well-known Cancellaria, and Cardinal Guillaume Briçonnet built the church of S. Trinità dei Monti on the Pincio. The German envoy Matthias Lang laid the cornerstone of the church of the German hospice, S. Maria dell'Anima, on 11 April, 1500, at which time the papal diarist Johann Burchard was still doubtless the *prefectus fabricae* as he had been the year before. Buildings in Renaissance Rome are always interesting. Burchard mentions many that are still well known to us. In March, 1500, Burchard finished the construction of his own house, now in the Via del Sudario (no. 44), a small palace of pure German Gothic, certainly designed by a northern architect. This house once had a beautiful semicircular stairway (probably like that of the Frauenhaus at Strassburg), handsome ribbed

---

cells for the cardinals and the *conclavistae*]. But as always during this period the actual voting would take place in the *parva capella* (*cf.* ed. Celani, II, 172, line 40), the Chapel of S. Niccolò da Bari, on which see Franz Ehrle and Hermann Egger, *Der Vaticanische Palast in seiner Entwicklung bis zur Mitte des XV. Jahrhunderts*, Città del Vaticano, 1935, pp. 103–9, 123 ff. While the voting proceeded in the Chapel of S. Niccolò, the *conclavistae* were locked up in the Sistina (*op. cit.*, p. 105).

146 Raynaldus, *Ann. eccl.*, ad ann. 1501, no. 36, vol. XIX (1693), pp. 514–15; Heinrich Reusch, *Der Index der verbotenen Bücher*, 2 vols., Bonn, 1883–85, I, 54–55, with a German translation of the important parts of the bull; Pastor, *Hist. Popes*, VI, 154–56, and *Gesch. d. Päpste*, III-1 (repr. 1955), 614–15.

147 Pastor, *Hist. Popes*, VI, 159–64, and *Gesch. d. Päpste*, III-1 (repr. 1955), 619–23.

148 Burchard, *Diarium*, ed. Thuasne, II, 530, and ed. Celani, II, 140; Pastor, *Gesch. d. Päpste*, III-1 (repr. 1955), 624.

149 *Cf.* Pastor, *Hist. Popes*, VI, 165–81, and esp. *Gesch. d. Päpste*, III-1 (repr. 1955), 635–56, where the first edition (the text of the English translation) is largely rewritten and much improved. The bibliography is extensive, and need not concern us here, but mention should perhaps be made of Eugène Müntz's well-known book *Les Arts à la cour des papes Innocent VIII, Alexandre VI, Pie III (1484–1503)*, Paris, 1898, pp. 144 ff., where numerous archival and other texts are given.

vaulting, an impressive loggia, and a pleasant courtyard. Unfortunately the exterior of the house has been rebuilt, but the interior still reveals the Gothic construction which Vasari deplored as barbaric. On one side Burchard's view encompassed the sumptuous gardens of Giuliano Cesarini, cardinal bishop of Ascoli Piceno, who was much annoyed when in 1491 Burchard acquired the land with a dilapidated house from the famous monastery of Farfa. Today the Torre Argentina derives its name from the location of Burchard's house, and recalls its builder's native city of Strassburg (*Argentina*).[150]

It was perhaps to be expected that the notable figures of Alexander VI's reign should make a great impression upon posterity. Although every tourist who reads his guidebook knows that Alexander gave the Castel S. Angelo very much the form it still retains, there are numerous more subtle, more tenuous memorials of this period to be found by the antiquarian, reminders of the past quite unknown to the modern Roman who scurries about his business. Who that daily traverses the old Via dell'Arco di Parma (R. V), which leads into the decaying Piazza Lancellotti (near the Via de' Coronari), associates the name with Giangiacomo Sclafenati, the cardinal of Parma, whom we have had more than one occasion to note in this volume? The nearby Piazza Nicosia recalls Aldobrandino Orsini, archbishop of Nicosia in Cyprus, whose appointment to office in 1502 Burchard records in his diary.[151] In the same area the Via d'Ascanio (R. IV), which runs from the Via della Scrofa to the little Piazza di Firenze, preserves the memory of Cardinal Sforza, and gives us the location of his gardens. The statue of "Pasquino" still stands at a corner of Piazza Navona, near the spot where Cardinal Oliviero Carafa had it set up, by a wall of his own house. The *statua magistri Pasquino nuncupata* is also referred to by Burchard,[152] and we shall have cause to mention it in the next volume.

If in 1492 the conclave had elected the worst of the cardinals in Alexander VI, few were entirely aware of the fact. Many of the cardinals were much like him. Alexander had, to be sure, lacked the delicacy to add hypocrisy to his other failings. They were a robust lot, those cardinals, and some of them would leave worthier heirs to drink their Caecuban wine.

[150] On Burchard's house, see E. Celani's edition of the *Diarium* (which, after Burchard, he calls the *Liber notarum*), II, 347–50, note, and esp. D. Gnoli, "La Torre Argentina in Roma," in *Nuova Antologia di lettere, scienze ed arti*, vol. 135 (May–June, 1908), pp. 596–605.

Strassburg was known first as *Argentoratum* and later as *Argentina*. The "modern" name Strateburgus occurs first in the sixth century (Celani, II, 336, note). Burchard was actually a native of Hasslach, near Strassburg (see above, Chapter 13, note 24). A stemma found in the house at no. 44, Via del Sudario, corresponds to Burchard's seal. *Cf.* Friedrich Noack, *Das Deutschtum in Rom seit dem Ausgang des Mittelalters*, 2 vols., Berlin and Leipzig, 1927, I, 12, who gives the house its old number (45).

[151] Burchard, *Diarium*, ed. Thuasne, III, 224, and ed. Celani, II, 339.

[152] Burchard, *Diarium*, ed. Thuasne, III, 157, and ed. Celani, II, 296. The statue of Pasquino now stands at the corner of the Palazzo Braschi.

INDEX

No names of modern scholars (and no references to their works) are included in this index

VENECIE